Lecture Notes in Artificial Intelligence 10334

Subseries of Lecture Notes in Computer Science

More information about this series at http://www.springer.com/series/1244

Francisco Javier Martínez de Pisón · Rubén Urraca
Héctor Quintián · Emilio Corchado (Eds.)

Hybrid Artificial Intelligent Systems

12th International Conference, HAIS 2017
La Rioja, Spain, June 21–23, 2017
Proceedings

Springer

Editors
Francisco Javier Martínez de Pisón
University of La Rioja
Logroño, La Rioja
Spain

Rubén Urraca
University of La Rioja
Logroño, La Rioja
Spain

Héctor Quintián
University of A Coruña
Ferrol, A Coruña
Spain

Emilio Corchado
University of Salamanca
Salamanca
Spain

ISSN 0302-9743 ISSN 1611-3349 (electronic)
Lecture Notes in Artificial Intelligence
ISBN 978-3-319-59649-5 ISBN 978-3-319-59650-1 (eBook)
DOI 10.1007/978-3-319-59650-1

Library of Congress Control Number: 2017942982

LNCS Sublibrary: SL7 – Artificial Intelligence

Printed on acid-free paper

This Springer imprint is published by Springer Nature
The registered company is Springer International Publishing AG
The registered company address is: Gewerbestrasse 11, 6330 Cham, Switzerland

Preface

This volume of *Lecture Notes in Artificial Intelligence* (LNAI) includes the papers presented at HAIS 2017 held in the beautiful city of Logroño (La Rioja), Spain, in June 2017.

The International Conference on Hybrid Artificial Intelligence Systems (HAIS), has become a unique, established, and broad interdisciplinary forum for researchers and practitioners who are involved in developing and applying symbolic and sub-symbolic techniques aimed at the construction of highly robust and reliable problem-solving techniques and bringing the most relevant achievements in this field.

Hybridization of intelligent techniques, coming from different computational intelligence areas, has become popular because of the growing awareness that such combinations frequently perform better than the individual techniques, such as neurocomputing, fuzzy systems, rough sets, evolutionary algorithms, agents and multiagent systems, etc.

Practical experience has indicated that hybrid intelligence techniques might be helpful for solving some of the challenging real-world problems. In a hybrid intelligence system, a synergistic combination of multiple techniques is used to build an efficient solution to deal with a particular problem. This is, thus, the setting of the HAIS conference series, and its increasing success is the proof of the vitality of this exciting field.

HAIS 2017, the 12th event in the series, received more than 130 technical submissions. After a rigorous peer-review process, the international Program Committee selected 60 papers, which are published in these proceedings.

The selection of papers was extremely rigorous in order to maintain the high quality of the conference and we would like to thank the Program Committee for their hard work in the reviewing process. This process is very important to the creation of a conference of high standard and the HAIS conference would not exist without their help.

The large number of submissions is certainly not only testimony to the vitality and attractiveness of the field but an indicator of the interest in the HAIS conferences themselves.

HAIS 2017 enjoyed outstanding keynote speeches by distinguished guest speakers: Prof. Bartosz Krawczyk, assistant professor in the Department of Computer Science, Virginia Commonwealth University, USA, and Dr. Dario Izzo, scientific coordinator of the Advanced Concepts Team in the European Space Agency.

HAIS 2017 has teamed up with *Neurocomputing* (Elsevier) and the *Logic Journal of the IGPL* (Oxford journals) for a suite of special issues including selected papers from HAIS 2017.

Particular thanks go to the main sponsors of the conference, Startup OLE, COESI, the Office of Innovation, Labour, Industry and Comerce of the Goverment of La Rioja, the Office of Culture and Tourism of the Goverment of La Rioja, the University of

La Rioja, the Foundation of the University of La Rioja, the University of Salamanca, and the International Federation for Computational Logic, who jointly contributed in an active and constructive manner to the success of this initiative.

We would like to thank Alfred Hofmann and Anna Kramer from Springer for their help and collaboration during this demanding publication project.

June 2017

Francisco Javier Martínez de Pisón
Rubén Urraca
Héctor Quintián
Emilio Corchado

Organization

General Chair

Emilio Corchado	University of Salamanca, Spain

Local Chairs

Francisco Javier Martínez de Pisón Ascacibar	University of La Rioja, Spain
Rubén Urraca Valle	University of La Rioja, Spain
Eliseo Vergara González	University of La Rioja, Spain

Honorary Committee

José Ignacio Ceniceros González	President of the Goverment of La Rioja
Julio Rubio García	Chancellor of the University of La Rioja
Leonor González Menorca	Counselor of Economy and Innovation of the Government of La Rioja
Concepción Gamarra Ruiz-Clavijo	Mayoress of Logroño City
Julio Antonio Herreros Martín	General Director of Innovation, Labour, Industry and Comerce of the Goverment of La Rioja
Eduardo Rodríguez Osés	General Director of Culture and Tourism of the Goverment of La Rioja

International Advisory Committee

Ajith Abraham	Machine Intelligence Research Labs, Europe
Antonio Bahamonde	University of Oviedo, Spain
Andre de Carvalho	University of São Paulo, Brazil
Sung-Bae Cho	Yonsei University, Korea
Juan M. Corchado	University of Salamanca, Spain
José R. Dorronsoro	Autonomous University of Madrid, Spain
Michael Gabbay	Kings College London, UK
Ali A. Ghorbani	UNB, Canada
Mark A. Girolami	University of Glasgow, UK
Manuel Graña	University of País Vasco, Spain
Petro Gopych	Universal Power Systems USA-Ukraine LLC, Ukraine
Jon G. Hall	The Open University, UK
Francisco Herrera	University of Granada, Spain
César Hervás-Martínez	University of Córdoba, Spain

Tom Heskes	Radboud University Nijmegen, The Netherlands
Dusan Husek	Academy of Sciences of the Czech Republic, Czech Republic
Lakhmi Jain	University of South Australia, Australia
Samuel Kaski	Helsinki University of Technology, Finland
Daniel A. Keim	University Konstanz, Germany
Marios Polycarpou	University of Cyprus, Cyprus
Witold Pedrycz	University of Alberta, Canada
Xin Yao	University of Birmingham, UK
Hujun Yin	University of Manchester, UK
Michał Woźniak	Wroclaw University of Technology, Poland
Aditya Ghose	University of Wollongong, Australia
Ashraf Saad	Armstrong Atlantic State University, USA
Fanny Klett	German Workforce Advanced Distributed Learning Partnership Laboratory, Germany
Paulo Novais	Universidade do Minho, Portugal
Rajkumar Roy	The EPSRC Centre for Innovative Manufacturing in Through-life Engineering Services, UK
Amy Neustein	Linguistic Technology Systems, USA
Jaydip Sen	Innovation Lab, Tata Consultancy Services Ltd., India

Program Committee

Emilio Corchado	University of Salamanca, Spain (PC Chair)
Francisco Javier Martínez de Pisón Ascacibar	University of La Rioja, Spain (PC Chair)
Abdel-Badeeh Salem	Ain Shams University, Egypt
Adolfo R. De Soto	University of León, Spain
Alberto Cano	Virginia Commonwealth University, USA
Alfredo Cuzzocrea	ICAR-CNR and University of Calabria, Italy
Alicia Troncoso	Pablo de Olavide University, Spain
Álvaro Herrero	University of Burgos, Spain
Amelia Zafra Gómez	University of Córdoba, Spain
Ana M. Bernardos	Polytechnic University of Madrid, Spain
Ana Madureira	Instituto Superior de Engenharia do Porto, Portugal
Anca Andreica	Babes-Bolyai University, Romania
Andreea Vescan	Babes-Bolyai University, Romania
Ángel Arroyo	University of Burgos, Spain
Antonio D. Masegosa	University of Deusto/IKERBASQUE, Spain
Antonio Dourado	University of Coimbra, Portugal
Antonio Morales-Esteban	University of Seville, Spain
Arkadiusz Kowalski	Wrocław University of Technology, Poland
Barna Laszlo Iantovics	Petru Maior University of Tg. Mures, Romania
Bogdan Trawinski	Wroclaw University of Science and Technology, Poland
Bruno Baruque	University of Burgos, Spain

Camelia Pintea	Technical University of Cluj-Napoca, North University Center at Baia Mare, Romania
Carlos Carrascosa	GTI-IA DSIC Universidad Politecnica de Valencia, Spain
Carlos Pereira	ISEC, Portugal
Cezary Grabowik	Silesian Technical University, Poland
Damian Krenczyk	Silesian University of Technology, Poland
Dario Landa-Silva	The University of Nottingham, UK
David Iclanzan	Sapientia, Hungarian Science University of Transylvania, Romania
Diego P. Ruiz	University of Granada, Spain
Dragan Simic	University of Novi Sad, Serbia
Eiji Uchino	Yamaguchi University, Japan
Eneko Osaba	University of Deusto, Spain
Enrique Onieva	University of Deusto, Spain
Esteban Jove Pérez	University of A Coruña, Spain
Eva Volna	Univerzity of Ostrava, Czech Republic
Fabrício Olivetti De França	Universidade Federal do ABC, Brazil
Fawad Hassan	Pakistan Institute of Engineering and Applied Sciences, Pakistan
Federico Divina	Pablo de Olavide University, Spain
Fermin Segovia	University of Granada, Spain
Fidel Aznar	University of Alicante, Spain
Francisco Javier Martínez de Pisón Ascacíbar	University of La Rioja, Spain
Francisco Martínez-Álvarez	Pablo de Olavide University, Spain
George Papakostas	EMT Institute of Technology, Greece
Georgios Dounias	University of the Aegean, Greece
Giancarlo Mauri	University of Milano-Bicocca, Italy
Giorgio Fumera	University of Cagliari, Italy
Gloria Cerasela Crisan	Vasile Alecsandri University of Bacau, Romania
Gonzalo A. Aranda-Corral	University of Huelva, Spain
Gualberto Asencio-Cortés	Pablo de Olavide University, Spain
Guiomar Corral	La Salle University, Spain
Héctor Quintián	University of A Coruña, Spain
Henrietta Toman	University of Debrecen, Hungary
Ignacio Turias	University of Cádiz, Spain
Ioannis Hatzilygeroudis	University of Patras, Greece
Irene Diaz	University of Oviedo, Spain
Isabel Barbancho	University of Málaga, Spain
Iskander Sánchez-Rola	University of Deusto, Spain
J.M. Luna	University of Córdoba, Spain
Javier Bajo	Polytechnic University of Madrid, Spain
Javier De Lope	Polytechnic University of Madrid, Spain
Jorge García-Gutiérrez	University of Seville, Spain
Jorge Reyes	NT2 Labs, Chile

José Alfredo Ferreira Costa	Federal University, UFRN, Brazil
José Dorronsoro	Universidad Autonoma de Madrid, Spain
José García-Rodriguez	University of Alicante, Spain
José Luis Calvo-Rolle	University of A Coruña, Spain
José Luis Casteleiro-Roca	University of A Coruña, Spain
José Luis Verdegay	University of Granada, Spain
José M. Molina	Carlos III University of Madrid, Spain
José Manuel Lopez-Guede	Basque Country University, Spain
José María Armingol	Carlos III University of Madrid, Spain
José Ramón Villar	University of Oviedo, Spain
Jose-Ramón Cano De Amo	University of Jaén, Spain
Juan Humberto Sossa Azuela	National Polytechnic Institute, Mexico
Juan J. Flores	Universidad Michoacana de San Nicolas de Hidalgo, Mexico
Juan Pavón	Complutense University of Madrid, Spain
Julio Ponce	Universidad Autónoma de Aguascalientes, Mexico
Khawaja Asim	PIEAS, Pakistan
Krzysztof Kalinowski	Silesian University of Technology, Poland
Lauro Snidaro	University of Udine, Italy
Lenka Lhotska	Czech Technical University in Prague, Czech Republic
Leocadio G. Casado	University of Almeria, Spain
Luis Alfonso Fernández Serantes	FH Joanneum, University of Applied Sciences, Austria
M. Chadli	University of Picardie Jules Verne, France
Manuel Graña	University of the Basque Country, Spain
Maria Guijarro	Complutense University of Madrid, Spain
María Martínez Ballesteros	University of Seville, Spain
Mario Koeppen	Kyushu Institute of Technology, Japan
Miroslav Bursa	Czech Technical University in Prague, Czech Republic
Oscar Fontenla-Romero	University of A Coruña, Spain
Ozgur Koray Sahingoz	Turkish Air Force Academy, Turkey
Paula M. Castro	University of A Coruña, Spain
Paulo Novais	University of Minho, Portugal
Pavel Brandstetter	VSB-Technical University of Ostrava, Czech Republic
Pedro López	University of Deusto, Spain
Peter Rockett	University of Sheffield, UK
Ramon Rizo	University of Alicante, Spain
Ricardo Del Olmo	University of Burgos, Spain
Ricardo Leon Talavera Llames	Pablo de Olavide University, Spain
Robert Burduk	Wroclaw University of Technology, Poland
Rodolfo Zunino	University of Genoa, Italy
Roman Senkerik	TBU in Zlin, Czech Republic
Rubén Fuentes-Fernández	Complutense University of Madrid, Spain
Rubén Urraca Valle	University of La Rioja, Spain

Sean Holden	University of Cambridge, UK
Sebastián Ventura	University of Córdoba, Spain
Stella Heras	Polytechnic University of Valencia, Spain
Theodore Pachidis	Kavala Institute of Technology, Greece
Urszula Stanczyk	Silesian University of Technology, Poland
Wiesław Chmielnicki	Jagiellonian University, Poland
Yannis Marinakis	Technical University of Crete, Greece
Zuzana Kominkova Oplatkova	Tomas Bata University in Zlin, Czech Republic

Organizing Committee

Francisco Javier Martínez de Pisón	University of La Rioja, Spain
Rubén Urraca Valle	University of La Rioja, Spain
Eliseo Vergara González	University of La Rioja, Spain
Alpha Verónica Pernía Espinoza	University of La Rioja, Spain
Juan Félix San Juan Díaz	University of La Rioja, Spain
Angel Luis Rubio García	University of La Rioja, Spain
César Domínguez Pérez	University of La Rioja, Spain
Fernando Antoñanzas Torres	University of La Rioja, Spain
Javier Antoñanzas Torres	University of La Rioja, Spain
Javier Ferreiro Cabello	University of La Rioja, Spain
Esteban Fraile García	University of La Rioja, Spain
Iván Luis Pérez Barrón	University of La Rioja, Spain
Emilio Corchado	University of Salamanca, Spain
Héctor Quintián	University of A Coruña, Spain

Contents

Data Mining, Knowledge Discovery and Big Data

Bio-inspired Models and Evolutionary Computation

Learning Algorithms

Visual Analysis & Advanced Data Processing Techniques

Hybrid Intelligent Applications

Data Mining, Knowledge Discovery and Big Data

Word Embedding Based Event Detection on Social Media

Ali Mert Ertugrul[1], Burak Velioglu[2], and Pinar Karagoz[2](✉)

[1] Informatics Institute, METU, 06800 Ankara, Turkey
alimert@metu.edu.tr
[2] Computer Engineering Department, METU, 06800 Ankara, Turkey
{velioglu,karagoz}@ceng.metu.edu.tr

Abstract. Event detection from social media messages is conventionally based on clustering the message contents. The most basic approach is representing messages in terms of term vectors that are constructed through traditional natural language processing (NLP) methods and then assigning weights to terms generally based on frequency. In this study, we use neural feature extraction approach and explore the performance of event detection under the use of word embeddings. Using a corpus of a set of tweets, message terms are embedded to continuous space. Message contents that are represented as vectors of word embedding are grouped by using hierarchical clustering. The technique is applied on a set of Twitter messages posted in Turkish. Experimental results show that automatically extracted features detect the contextual similarities between tweets better than traditional feature extraction with term frequency - inverse document frequency (TF-IDF) based term vectors.

Keywords: Event detection · Neural feature extraction · Word embedding · Neural probabilistic language models

1 Introduction

Social media has become a basic tool for communication among the Internet users. Micro-blogging platforms enable users to broadcast digital contents including texts, images and videos. Twitter is currently the most popular micro-blogging platform in which people can share their experiences and ideas. Although the twitter messages, tweets, are limited to 140 characters, they constitute an important source of information. Additionally, the propagation of the short information is easier and faster.

Tweets are the time-stamped information and Twitter can be considered as an up-to-date source of event related messages [1]. Individuals who are taking part in or watching an event tend to share a number of event-relevant messages and communicate with each other to exchange opinions about that event [2]. Therefore, it is expected that when an important event, such as a disaster, political election and football game, occurs, the number of the tweets related to

F.J. Martínez de Pisón et al. (Eds.): HAIS 2017, LNAI 10334, pp. 3–14, 2017.
DOI: 10.1007/978-3-319-59650-1_1

that event considerably increases. Consequently, analysis and extraction of event related information from social media resources enable individuals to obtain important knowledge faster and easier.

Event detection can be described as a clustering process of the similar indicators. In our case, tweets are used as indicators. Yet, clustering the semantically similar tweets is not a straightforward task for the researchers. The conventional approach is to construct term vectors representing tweets and calculating the similarity between term vectors. There are several ways to assign weights to terms, yet the mostly used weight assignment schema is using TF-IDF of the tweet terms.

In this study, our purpose is to detect events from Twitter using word-embedding based representation of tweets. To this aim, we represent each word of each tweet as a continuous vector utilizing the word2vec model [3]. Each tweet is represented in terms of vector representations of its words. Next, we cluster the tweet representations with hierarchical clustering methods.

The technique is applied on a set of collected tweets in Turkish. In addition to difficulties due to informal language, working on a morphologically complex and agglutinative language poses challenges in traditional NLP tasks. Events detected under word-embedding based representation is compared against TF-IDF based term vector representation. Experimental analysis show that word embedding based clustering improves event detection performance.

The contributions of this work can be summarized as follows: Word embeddings are used for event detection on micro-blogging platform, which uses short message length and generally involves informal use of language. The technique is applied on Turkish, which is an agglutinative and morphologically complex language. The technique is experimentally analyzed on a collected set of tweets including four different events, where two of them are unexpected events such as a terrorist attack, and two other events are scheduled events such as a celebration. Hence, the performance can be analyzed according to the nature of the event.

This paper is organized as follows. In Sect. 2, related work is summarized. In Sect. 3, proposed method is described. In Sect. 4, experiments on the performance of the proposed method are presented. The paper is concluded with an overview in Sect. 5.

2 Related Work

In the literature, there exists a number of studies related to event detection and retrieval from social media data, especially Twitter. These studies can be classified into three categories according to their detection approaches, namely supervised, unsupervised and hybrid [4]. Among the studies employing supervised approach, Popescu et al. extract the features including part-of-speech tags, regular expressions and relative positional information, then uses gradient boosted decision trees to identify controversial and noncontroversial events [5]. Similarly, Sakaki et al. detect domain specific events like earthquake, which are manually labeled, using SVM classifier [6]. There also exists studies for event extraction from social media platforms using other types of supervised approaches like random forest and logistic regression [7,8]. Supervised approaches are mostly used for specified event detection. However, labeling tweet messages by annotators is time consuming and requires intensive work load.

Unsupervised approaches for event detection and retrieval are generally based on cluster analysis. Some studies employ incremental clustering algorithm based on a similarity threshold to form clusters [9,10]. These studies consider the features containing number of tweets, users and term vectors while clustering. Likewise, Ozdikis et al. apply agglomerative clustering technique to detect events in Turkish, using words with and without semantic expansions as tweet vectors [11,12]. Parikh et al. propose an event detection method by exploring textual and temporal components of the tweets so that events are detected using hierarchical clustering technique [13]. Additionally, several studies employ graph-based clustering for the detection of new events including detection techniques; hierarchical divisive clustering [14], community detection [15], and wavelet analysis and graph partitioning [16].

In addition to these approaches, there are also studies combining both supervised and unsupervised approaches for event detection. Becker et al. use both online clustering and SVM classifier to distinguish the messages belonging to real world events and non-event messages [17]. Moreover, Hua et al. [18] employ semi-supervised approach to detect targeted events like crimes and civil unrests.

The studies in the literature related to event detection and retrieval can also be analyzed in terms of the features they employ. Apart from utilization of hand crafted features, word embedding techniques are used as a feature extraction process for many problems in NLP literature. Tan et al. [19] make a lexical comparison between Twitter and Wikipedia corpora by pursuing a linear relation between obtained word embeddings. To extract Adverse Drug Reactions (ADR), Lin et al. [20] feed the vectors obtained by word2vec algorithm into conditional random fields. To learn a sentiment-specific word embeddings, Tang et al. [21] proposed their own word embedding algorithm and compare their results with classical word2vec algorithm. Besides these studies, Fang et al. [22] utilize word embedding technique to evaluate the coherence of topics from Twitter data.

Number of the studies related to event detection learn features from the sentences instead of using hand crafted features. Among them, Nguyen et al. use Convolutional Neural Network (CNN) to detect events [23]. In [24], Nguyen et al. use deep neural networks to both identify informative tweets and classify them into classes in an online fashion to detect crisis from tweets. As far as we know, neural feature extraction of the words for event detection on Turkish has not been applied before. However, there are studies in which learning continuous vector representations of words is used to develop a Named Entity Recognition (NER) system for Turkish [25,26].

3 Proposed Method

In this work, we propose an event detection approach based on clustering continuous vector representations obtained by word embedding. We use an agglomerative clustering technique with time constraint.

3.1 Data Collection

In order to access Twitter data, Twitter provides two general APIs namely REST API[1] and Streaming API[2]. We use REST API to create a corpus. Using this dataset, we aimed to learn continuous representation of the tokens (words) in tweets by using word embedding technique. We gathered nearly 2.1M tweets for the corpus during three days. On the other hand, we use Streaming API to collect messages posted between April 23rd, 2016 and May 10th, 2016, which is used for event detection. For event detection, more than 1 M tweets have been collected within 18 days. During the collection of data for both datasets, only Turkish tweets are selected.

3.2 Data Preprocessing

We start with removing the tweets including *"I'm at"* text since they are the Foursquare[3] related ones showing the check-in activities of users. We remove the words whose length is less than 2 characters (except numbers), hashtags, mentions, links and *"RT"* keyword. We also remove a number of emoticons. In order to detect and remove various types of emoticons, we use the java library *com.vdurmont*[4]. Furthermore, we omit a number of punctuation marks including (- + . ; ? ! % * / : ; [ ] { } =). We also filter out the stop words from the tweets using the list of Turkish stop words provided by *Lucene*[5].

After basic removal and parse operations, we fix misspelled words and obtain word stems. To this aim, we use *Zemberek API*[6], which is a general purpose natural language processing library and toolset designed for Turkish language. Turkish is an agglutinative language. We perform stemming on all words of all tweets we collect (both corpus dataset and event detection dataset) and then separate them into form of word stem, derivational affixes and inflectional suffixes using Zemberek API. Inflectional suffixes do not change the meaning of the words, yet they diversify the words. Due to this reason, we extract stems of the words by omitting inflectional suffixes. As a result of preprocessing step, the test dataset has 881 K tweets.

[1] https://dev.twitter.com/rest/public.
[2] https://dev.twitter.com/streaming/public.
[3] https://foursquare.com/.
[4] https://github.com/vdurmont/emoji-java.
[5] http://lucene.apache.org/.
[6] https://github.com/ahmetaa/zemberek-nlp.

3.3 Word Embedding

In this study, continuous vector representation of each word is obtained by word2vec algorithm [3], which is one of the Neural Probabilistic Language Model (NPLM)-based models. This representation can be obtained by either predicting the word itself using its neighbor words or predicting neighbor words using only corresponding word. NPLM models can be trained using maximum likelihood (ML) principle. Note that, in this study representations are obtained by estimating the neighbor words using the word itself, since it is much faster than the other approach [3].

Note that optimizing the model using maximum likelihood would take $O(|V|)$ time, since maximizing the cost function with ML principle iterates over all words included in the vocabulary. So, rather than maximizing the log-likelihood over all words, lately developed word2vec model is trained utilizing negative sampling. In this approach, objective is optimized by maximizing the probability of words and contexts being in the corpus, and minimizing sampled others which are not in the context. Real words are represented by w and imaginary target words are represented by w^*. Then, the cost function can be defined as,

$$J_{NEG} = logQ_\theta(D = 1|w, h) + k\mathbf{E}[logQ_\theta(D = 0|w^*, h)], \tag{1}$$

where $Q_\theta(D = 1|w, h)$ is the logistic regression calculated in terms of the learned embedding vectors θ. h represents the matrix of embedded representations.

Each preprocessed tweet is represented as a vector using the skip-gram model [3]. Due to character limitation of Twitter, window size is used as 2. After eliminating the tweets with less than 5 words, word vectors are created by training word2vec algorithm with 1.5 million tweets. The length of the continuous vectors are selected as 150 and the number of negative words is selected as 10, empirically. That means, neighbor words are estimated with the center word projected into 150 dimensions and neighbor words are mixed randomly ten times. The five nearest neighbor words of five sample words are given in the Table 1.

Table 1. Sample words and their five nearest words. Skip-gram is trained with 1.5 M tweets

Word	Nearest 5 words
maç match	{hakem, Galatasaray, gol, seyircisiz, Beşiktaş} {referee, Galatasaray, goal, without spectators, Besiktas}
terör terror	{azdıran, bölücü, örgüt, menfez, terörist} {arouser, separatist, organization, culvert, terrorist}
bomba bomb	{roketatar, araçlı, patlat, bombala, patlama} {bazooka, with vehicle, explode, bombing, explosion}
Beşiktaş Besiktas	{şampiyon, Galatasaray, namağlup, Fenerbahçe, taraftar} {champion, Galatasaray, unbeaten, Fenerbahce, supporter}
bayram festival	{gün, işçi, kutlu, nisan, emekçi} {day, worker, blessed, April, laborer}

In order to obtain vector representation of a tweet, vector representations of its all words are summed. Note that, summation vector is divided by the length of tweet to handle tweets with varying lengths.

3.4 Clustering Algorithm

We follow a special type of agglomerative clustering technique based on time constraint for event detection. Basically, vector representation of each tweet is individually evaluated considering its time-stamp and similarity to active clusters. Then, it is included into the matching cluster or a new cluster is created for the corresponding tweet.

In order to add a tweet into an existing cluster, the following two conditions should be satisfied. Firstly, the difference between time-stamp of the latest tweet in the cluster and the tweet to be clustered should be less than or equal to the parameter $\boldsymbol{T_{max}}$. If this condition is satisfied for the given cluster, then it is called active cluster. In our experiments, this parameter is set to 3 and 6 h. Secondly, the similarity between the vector of an active cluster and the vector representation of the tweet to be clustered should be greater than or equal to $\boldsymbol{S_{min}}$. A cluster vector corresponds to cluster centroid which is the arithmetic mean of the vector representations of the tweets in that cluster. In the experiments, cosine similarity measure is used and the parameter S_{min} is set to 0.60, 0.65, 0.70 and 0.75. If there exists clusters satisfying these two conditions for a given tweet, the one with the maximum similarity value is chosen and the tweet is put into that cluster. On the other hand, a new cluster is created for the corresponding tweet unless there exists a cluster satisfying the conditions. The pseudo code of the clustering algorithm we employ is given in Algorithm 1.

Algorithm 1. Clustering Algorithm

for $t \in Tweets$ **do**
  $is\_assigned \leftarrow$ **false**
  $active\_clusters \leftarrow getActiveClusters(t.getTime(), T_{max})$
  if $active\_clusters \neq \emptyset$ **then**
    $optimum\_cluster \leftarrow findMaxSimilarCluster(t, active\_clusters)$
    if $similarity(t, optimum\_cluster) \geq S_{min}$ **then**
      $optimum\_cluster.add(t)$
      $optimum\_cluster.calculateNewCentroid()$
      $is\_assigned \leftarrow$ **true**
    end if
  end if
  if not $is\_assigned$ **then**
    $new\_cluster \leftarrow createNewCluster(t)$
    $all\_clusters.add(new\_cluster)$
  end if
end for

4 Experiments and Results

During the 18-day test data collection period between April 23rd, 2016 and May 10th, 2016, we focused on four events to analyze, where two of them are unexpected events and two other events are scheduled events as celebrations. The unexpected events are the suicide bomb attack in Bursa and gun attack to a Turkish journalist in Istanbul. On the other hand, the scheduled events are anniversaries of national sovereignty and children's day and labor day. The information about the events are presented in Table 2.

In order to identify the event clusters for each event, we firstly specify representative query words. We ask ten Turkish participants to determine the words to represent corresponding events. Based on their answers, we finalize the query sentences. For example, the query sentence for E_1 is "Bursa canlı bomba saldırı (Bursa suicide bomb attack)" as given in Table 2. For each event, we obtain word2vec representation of the query sentence and calculate the similarity between this representation and cluster vectors. Finally, if the similarity between the query sentence representation and the cluster vectors are larger than the threshold, which is specified for the clustering process, corresponding clusters are called event clusters.

In order to compare performance of word2vec representation, we obtain TF-IDF [27] based vectors for each tweet, perform clustering by using these term vectors, as the baseline. IDF weight for each word is calculated using only corpus dataset. Note that, TF-IDF based vectors are obtained after the same preprocessing step. There exist 59214 unique words included in the corpus dataset. Then, normalized TF score for each word of each test tweet is calculated. The TF weight of a word that occurs in a tweet is simply proportional to the word frequency. To represent each tweet as a feature vector, bag-of-words representation is used. In other words, each tweet is represented as a feature vector where features correspond to words in the corpus. For each word in the tweet, TF-IDF

Table 2. Description of the events

	Id	Event type	Event time	Query
Suicide bomb attack in Bursa	E_1	Unexpected	27.04.2016 17:30	Bursa canlı bomba saldırı (Bursa suicide bomb attack)
Armed attack to journalist	E_2	Unexpected	06.05.2016 17:25	[Ad, soyad] saldırı ([Name, surname] attack)
National sovereignty and children's day	E_3	Scheduled	23.04.2016 All day	23 nisan çocuk bayramı (April 23 child festival)
Labor day	E_4	Scheduled	01.05.2016 All day	1 mayıs işçi bayramı (May 1 labor day)

Table 3. Information related to clusters obtained using word2vec

		3 H				6 H			
		0.60	0.65	0.70	0.75	0.60	0.65	0.70	0.75
Number of event clusters	E_1	8	6	5	3	9	6	5	4
	E_2	26	16	11	5	37	19	16	7
	E_3	3	3	1	1	3	3	2	1
	E_4	8	7	6	3	10	9	6	5
Number of Tweets in the best cluster	E_1	323	619	393	407	492	332	343	423
	E_2	943	749	586	462	902	823	615	590
	E_3	1229	889	679	545	1552	784	727	581
	E_4	1169	1075	778	676	1297	949	915	505
Avg. size of event clusters	E_1	1220,8	963.2	444.8	274	1143.89	898.33	509	338.5
	E_2	1573.46	1641.31	324.36	864.2	1235.11	1398.37	320	513.43
	E_3	1339.7	775.67	679	545	1347	850.33	420.5	581
	E_4	768.5	662.25	578.67	624.67	579.3	583.89	585.5	374.8

scores are computed and assigned to corresponding element of feature vector. The remaining entries of the feature vector are 0. Using this representation, each tweet is represented by 59214 dimensional feature vector. In our implementation, each feature vector is stored sparsely as hash map to overcome memory problem.

We perform clustering experiments using word2vec and TF-IDF representations of the tweets as term vectors with the following parameters; $S_{min} \in [0.60, 0.65, 0.70, 0.75]$ and $T_{max} \in [3, 6]$ hours. During the experiments, for each event we analyze the number of event clusters, number of tweets in the best event cluster and average size of the event clusters obtained using word2vec (see Table 3) and TF-IDF (see Table 4) representations. *Best* event cluster refers to the cluster whose cluster vector is the most similar to the query sentence representation for a given event. Experiments show that the number of event clusters obtained using word embedding are less than the ones obtained by TF-IDF regardless of the parameters and event. Also, the number of the tweets in the best event cluster and average size of event clusters obtained by word embedding are extremely larger than those obtained by TF-IDF. These results reflect that, employing word embedding leads to better clusters compared to TF-IDF.

In addition to measures given in Tables 3 and 4, we compute precision scores of the best event clusters to evaluate the success and quality of clustering based on word embedding. The tweets in the best event clusters are labeled by two annotators and the precision scores are given in Table 5. The results show that the precision of the scheduled events, E_3 and E_4, increases with an increase in the parameter S_{min}, regardless of the parameter T_{max}. We also observe that the number of tweets in the best event clusters decrease as the parameter S_{min} increases. This can be inferred in such a way that people are more likely to share structured tweets for the scheduled events such as celebrations. On the other hand, it is observed that the unexpected events E_1 and E_2 exhibit a different pattern compared the scheduled events E_3 and E_4. When $T_{max} = 3$ h, the precision values of the best event clusters reach its peak value at $S_{min} = 0.65$. However, the precision values are maximum at $S_{min} = 0.70$ when $T_{max} = 6$ h.

Table 4. Information related to clusters obtained using TF-IDF

		3 H				6 H			
		0.60	0.65	0.70	0.75	0.60	0.65	0.70	0.75
Number of event clusters	E_1	9	8	3	1	9	8	2	1
	E_2	65	37	32	15	56	37	26	15
	E_3	9	8	5	4	8	8	5	3
	E_4	39	26	15	10	34	17	12	6
Number of Tweets in the best cluster	E_1	3	3	6	4	3	7	6	4
	E_2	4	4	3	2	4	4	2	3
	E_3	1	1	1	1	4	1	1	1
	E_4	1	1	1	2	1	1	1	2
Avg. size of event clusters	E_1	5	4	1.83	4	5.22	4	5	4
	E_2	2.28	1.81	1.97	1.93	2.2	3.35	1.65	2.53
	E_3	2.22	2	1.6	1.6	2.5	2	1.6	2.67
	E_4	2.15	1.88	2.8	1.7	2	1.76	3	1.67

In other words, unlike in scheduled events, we cannot observe a monotonically increasing pattern with an increase in the parameter S_{min}. We observe that, after a similarity threshold (0.65 for 3 h and 0.70 for 6 h), the precision value decreases for unexpected events. We can infer that, tweets related to unexpected events are less likely to be structured as in scheduled events and less similar tweets are shared for these events.

Table 5. Precision scores of the best event clusters obtained using word2vec, with respect to the parameters T_{max} and S_{min}

	3 H				6 H			
	0.60	0.65	0.70	0.75	0.60	0.65	0.70	0.75
E_1	62.54	**83.52**	79.39	79.61	76.42	81.33	**90.08**	84.63
E_2	85.04	**86.92**	84.13	84.20	85.03	86.03	**88.78**	83.73
E_3	50.04	76.38	82.03	**91.74**	50.19	88.78	94.49	**94.84**
E_4	89.48	82.83	93.18	**95.71**	80.26	90.94	94.86	**95.84**

Note that, precision values of the best event clusters obtained using TF-IDF are 100% for all events and conditions. The reason for this is that, event clusters contain only a few tweets which are highly similar to query sentences. Due to the large amount of data, it is time-consuming to annotate all event related tweets and calculate recall values. However, it is clear that, since event clusters consist of only a few tweets, they miss a large amount of event related tweets. It results in very low recall values obtained using TF-IDF compared to word embedding.

In order to analyze temporal information of the tweets belonging to the best event clusters, we plot the figures revealing the number of tweets shared within

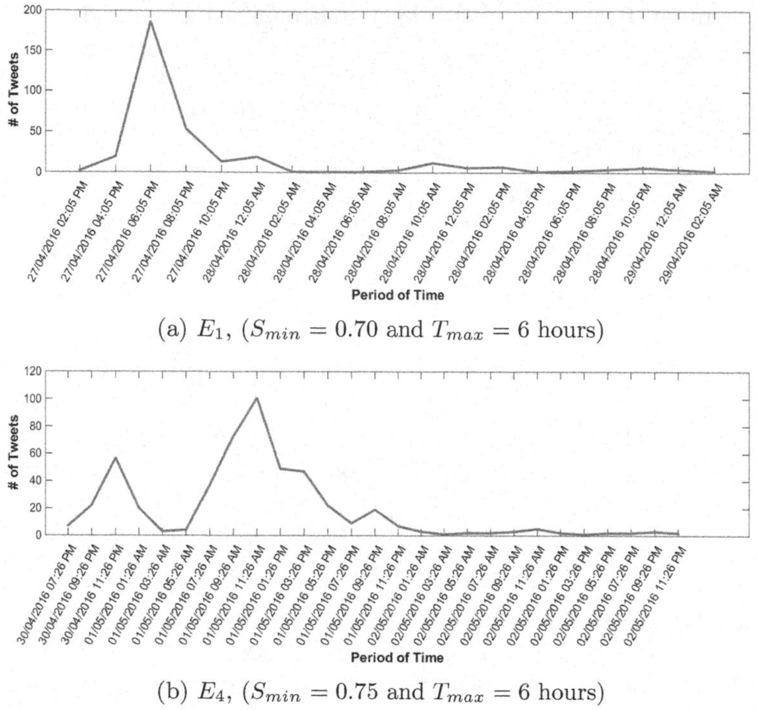

(a) E_1, ($S_{min} = 0.70$ and $T_{max} = 6$ hours)

(b) E_4, ($S_{min} = 0.75$ and $T_{max} = 6$ hours)

Fig. 1. The number of tweets shared within the periods of 2 h for each of the best event clusters obtained by the corresponding parameters S_{min} and T_{max}

the periods of 2 h. Due to space limitation, we do not present the figures for E_2 and E_3 since their behaviors are similar to E_1 and E_4, respectively These best event clusters are the ones having the highest precision values where $T_{max} = 6$ h. We compare the original event times given in Table 2 with the corresponding times of number of shared tweets in Fig. 1. We observe that the tweets related scheduled events are shared during the all-day and even the beginning of the following day. We also observe that tweets related to scheduled event E_2 are posted starting from the last hours of the previous day. The number of the shared tweets for the same event are minimum between two peaks since people are most likely to sleep in that interval (03:26 AM – 07:26 AM). Moreover, the unexpected events E_3 and E_4 gets their peak values just after the corresponding original event times.

5 Conclusion

In this study, we explore the effectiveness of word-embedding based representation of tweets to detect events from Twitter. In that regard, the words of the tweets are represented as a continuous vector employing the *word2vec* model. We analyze the proposed method on a set of collected tweets in Turkish, which contains four events, in comparison to the TF-IDF based vector representations of tweets. The results reflect that utilizing word2vec features improves the performance on event detection on Twitter although it includes mostly short-length and informal data.

As a future work, we are planning to compare the performance of different continuous vector representations of words techniques such as GloVe [28] in event detection in Turkish. Additionally, we will analyze the effect of employing embedding techniques at different granularity namely *sentence2vec* and *doc2vec* [29], which are extensions of word2vec algorithm, for the event detection on micro-blogging platforms.

References

1. Goodchild, M.F.: Citizens as sensors: the world of volunteered geography. GeoJournal **69**(4), 211–221 (2007)
2. Abdelhaq, H., Sengstock, C., Gertz, M.: EvenTweet: online localized event detection from twitter. Proc. VLDB Endowment **6**(12), 1326–1329 (2013)
3. Mikolov, T., Sutskever, I., Chen, K., Corrado, G.S., Dean, J.: Distributed representations of words and phrases and their compositionality. In: Advances in Neural Information Processing Systems, pp. 3111–3119 (2013)
4. Atefeh, F., Khreich, W.: A survey of techniques for event detection in Twitter. Comput. Intell. **31**(1), 132–164 (2015)
5. Popescu, A-M., Pennacchiotti, M., Paranjpe, D.: Extracting events and event descriptions from Twitter. In: Proceedings of the 20th International Conference Companion on World Wide Web, pp. 105–106 (2011)
6. Sakaki, T., Okazaki, M., Matsuo, Y.: Earthquake shakes Twitter users: real-time event detection by social sensors. In: Proceedings of the 19th International Conference on World Wide Web, pp. 851–860 (2010)
7. Kallus, N.: Predicting crowd behavior with big public data. In: Proceedings of the 23rd International Conference on World Wide Web, pp. 625–630 (2014)
8. Reschke, K., Jankowiak, M., Surdeanu, M., Manning, C.D., Jurafsky, D.: Event extraction using distant supervision. In: LREC, pp. 4527–4531 (2014)
9. Phuvipadawat, S., Murata, T.: Breaking news detection and tracking in Twitter. In: 2010 IEEE/WIC/ACM International Conference on Web Intelligence and Intelligent Agent Technology (WI-IAT), vol. 3, pp. 120–123 (2010)
10. Petrović, S., Osborne, M., Lavrenko, V.: Streaming first story detection with application to Twitter. In: Human Language Technologies: The 2010 Annual Conference of the North American Chapter of the Association for Computational Linguistics, pp. 181–189 (2010)
11. Ozdikis, O., Senkul, P., Oguztuzun, H.: Semantic expansion of Tweet contents for enhanced event detection in Twitter. In: 2012 IEEE/ACM International Conference on Advances in Social Networks Analysis and Mining (ASONAM), pp. 20–24 (2012)
12. Ozdikis, O., Senkul, P., Oguztuzun, H.: Context based semantic relations in Tweets. In: Can, F., Özyer, T., Polat, F. (eds.) State of the Art Applications of Social Network Analysis. Lecture Notes in Social Networks, pp. 35–52. Springer, Switzerland (2014)
13. Parikh, R., Karlapalem, K.: ET: events from Tweets. In: Proceedings of the 22nd International Conference on World Wide Web, pp. 613–620 (2013)

14. Long, R., Wang, H., Chen, Y., Jin, O., Yu, Y.: Towards effective event detection, tracking and summarization on microblog data. In: Wang, H., Li, S., Oyama, S., Hu, X., Qian, T. (eds.) WAIM 2011. LNCS, vol. 6897, pp. 652–663. Springer, Heidelberg (2011). doi:10.1007/978-3-642-23535-1_55
15. Sayyadi, H., Hurst, M., Maykov, A.: Event detection and tracking in social streams. In: ICWSM (2009)
16. Weng, J., Lee, B-S.: Event detection in Twitter. In: ICWSM, vol. 11, pp. 401–408 (2011)
17. Becker, H., Naaman, M., Gravano, L.: Beyond trending topics: real-world event identification on Twitter. In: ICWSM, vol. 11, pp. 438–441 (2011)
18. Hua, T., Chen, F., Zhao, L., Lu, C-T., Ramakrishnan, N.: STED: semi-supervised targeted-interest event detection in Twitter. In: Proceedings of the 19th ACM SIGKDD International Conference on Knowledge Discovery and Data Mining, pp. 1466–1469 (2013)
19. Tan, L., Zhang, H., Clarke, C.L.A., Smucker, M.D.: Lexical comparison between Wikipedia and Twitter corpora by using word embeddings. In: Short Papers, vol. 2, p. 657 (2015)
20. Lin, W-S., Dai, H-J., Jonnagaddala, J., Chang, N-W., Jue, T.R., Iqbal, U., Shao, J.Y-H., Chiang, I-J., Li, Y-C.: Utilizing different word representation methods for twitter data in adverse drug reactions extraction. In: 2015 Conference on Technologies and Applications of Artificial Intelligence (TAAI), pp. 260–265 (2015)
21. Tang, D., Wei, F., Yang, N., Zhou, M., Liu, T., Qin, B.: Learning sentiment-specific word embedding for Twitter sentiment classification. In: ACL, no. 1, pp. 1555–1565 (2014)
22. Fang, A., Macdonald, C., Ounis, I., Habel, P.: Using word embedding to evaluate the coherence of topics from Twitter data. In: Proceedings of SIGIR (2016)
23. Nguyen, T.H., Grishman, R.: Event detection and domain adaptation with convolutional neural networks. In: Proceedings of the 53rd Annual Meeting of the Association for Computational Linguistics and the 7th International Joint Conference on Natural Language Processing, vol. 2, pp. 365–371 (2015)
24. Nguyen, D.T., Joty, S., Imran, M., Sajjad, H., Mitra, P.: Applications of online deep learning for crisis response using social media information. arXiv preprint arXiv:1610.01030 (2016)
25. Demir, H., Özgür, A.: Improving named entity recognition for morphologically rich languages using word embeddings. In: 2014 13th International Conference on Machine Learning and Applications (ICMLA), pp. 117–122 (2014)
26. Onal, K.D., Karagoz, P.: Named entity recognition from scratch on social media. In: ECML-PKDD, MUSE Workshop (2015)
27. Luhn, H.P.: A statistical approach to mechanized encoding and searching of literary information. IBM J. Res. Dev. **1**(4), 309–317 (1957)
28. Pennington, J., Socher, R., Manning, C.D.: Glove: global vectors for word representation. In: Empirical Methods in Natural Language Processing (EMNLP), pp. 1532–1543 (2014)
29. Le, Q.V., Mikolov, T.: Distributed representations of sentences and documents. In: ICML, vol. 14, pp. 1188–1196 (2014)

Sentiment Analysis on TripAdvisor: Are There Inconsistencies in User Reviews?

Ana Valdivia[1(✉)], M. Victoria Luzón[2], and Francisco Herrera[1]

[1] Department of Computer Science and Artificial Intelligence, University of Granada, 18071 Granada, Spain
avaldivia@ugr.es, herrera@decsai.ugr.es
[2] Department of Software Engineering, University of Granada, 18071 Granada, Spain
luzon@ugr.es

Abstract. The number of online reviews has grown exponentially over the last years. As a result, several Sentiment Analysis Methods (SAMs) have been developed in order to extract automatically sentiments from text. In this work, we study polarity coherencies between reviewers and SAMs. To do so, we compare the polarity of the document evaluated by the user and the aggregated sentence polarity evaluated by three SAMs. The main contribution of this work is to show the flimsiness of user ratings as a generalization of the overall review sentiment.

Keywords: Sentiment Analysis · Opinion mining · Online reviews

1 Introduction

The concept of Sentiment Analysis (SA), also referred as Opinion Mining, has experienced an important growth through the last few years [15]. This topic has been established as a new Natural Language Processing (NLP) research branch which processes automatically written opinions so as to extract insights and knowledge. Moreover, the proliferation of the Web 2.0 and social networks has led to a huge amount of online recorded text. Users are free to express their opinions about products, places and experiences. This has implied a high development of SAMs for sentiment extraction ([21,22]).

TripAdvisor[1] is one of the most popular travel social network websites [12]. This Web 2.0 contains millions of written and ranked reviews about restaurants, hotels and attractions from a large number of travelers over the world. Tourists are able to plan their trip checking information, ranking list and experiences from others. In this website, users write opinions of 100 character minimum and rank them with 1 to 5 score (1 is representing a *Terrible* assessment and 5 an *Excellent* assessment). TripAdvisor has therefore become a rich source of data for SA research and applications.

[1] https://www.tripadvisor.com.

F.J. Martínez de Pisón et al. (Eds.): HAIS 2017, LNAI 10334, pp. 15–25, 2017.
DOI: 10.1007/978-3-319-59650-1_2

The purpose of this work is to study the robustness of the user's polarity comparing with three SAM polarities. For doing so, we analyze TripAdvisor reviews from three popular monuments in Spain: the Alhambra, the Sagrada Família and the Mezquita de Córdoba. We define the *User's Polarity* as the user rating. We then define the *SAMs' Polarities* by computing the sentiment on each sentence applying the corresponding method (*Syuzhet* [13], *Bing* [10] and *CoreNLP* [17]). In order to obtain an overall polarity, we aggregate sentence polarities by majority vote. Finally, we correlate the polarities.

The results show that there exists a latent inconsistency between the *User's Polarity* and the *SAMs' Polarities.* There is around 50% of correlation between positive sentiments.

The rest of this work is organized as follows: in Sect. 2 we describe the theory of SA thus far, including an introduction to the SA problem (Sect. 2.1) and the presentation of the three SAM that we select for this study (Sect. 2.2). After that, in (Sect. 3) we explain the developed methodology for our purpose. In there, we explain TripAdvisor structure (Sect. 3.1), how we scrap the web (Sect. 3.2) and the experiments layout (Sect. 3.3). Section 4 includes the analysis of results. We firstly explain the structure of datasets (Sect. 4.1) and then we present the numerical report (Sect. 4.2). Lastly, we present the conclusions and suggest future research lines in Sect. 5.

2 Sentiment Analysis

In this section we define the main concepts related to SA. In Sect. 2.1 we introduce the SA problem. Section 2.2 briefly describes the three sentiment tools used in this work.

2.1 The Sentiment Analysis Problem

Liu defines SA in [15] as the field of study that analyzes people's opinions toward products, services, organizations, individuals, events, issues, or topics in written text. SA is widely known as Opinion Mining, but recently has been popularized with the first bigram.

Liu organizes this problem proposing that an *opinion* can be mathematically defined as a 5-tuple $(e_i, a_{ij}, s_{ijkl}, h_k, t_l)$ where: e_i is the i-th opinion *entity*, i.e., the product, service, place, person, company or event which the opinion is addressed to; a_{ij} is the j-th *attribute*, a property related to the entity e_i; s_{ijkl} is the *sentiment* of the opinion towards an attribute a_{ij} of entity e_i by the opinion holder h_k at time t_l; h_k is the k-th *opinion holder* or the reviewer and t_l is l-th *time* when the opinion was emitted. Over this problem, the *sentiment* can be identified in different ways: polarity {positive, neutral, negative}, numerical rating {1, 2, ..., 5} or emotions {anger, disgust, fear, happiness, sadness, surprise}.

One other fact that makes this problem complex is that there exists several types of opinions [14]. *Regular opinions* express a sentiment about an aspect of an entity. On the other hand, *comparative opinions* compare two or more entities. *Subjective opinions* express a personal feeling or belief and thus are more likely to present sentiments. On the other side, *objective sentence* present factual information.

There exists three different levels of analysis to this problem. The first one is the *document level* and extracts the sentiment of the whole opinion. This is considered to be the simplest task. The next level is the *sentence level* which extracts a sentiment in each sentence of the text. Finally, the *aspect level* is the fine-grained level. This is the most challenging analysis because it extracts the sentiment related to its target (an entity or aspect's entity). Due to this fact, Aspect Based Sentiment Analysis (ABSA) has been widely studied over the literature. For example, Hu and Liu propose in [11] a methodology to extract product features from reviews. ABSA task has been repeatedly proposed in the International Workshop of Semantic Evaluation [19].

Because of the complexity of the SA, different task with different targets are related to this problem. The authors describe in [22] a total of 6 task:

1. **Sentiment Classification**: This is the most known task. The aim of Sentiment Classification is to develop models capable of detecting sentiment in texts. The first step is to collect text or reviews to set our analysis. After that, the sentiment is detected. It can be computed by the reviewer or computed with SAMs. Then, features are selected to train the classification model. In this step, text mining techniques are commonly used to extract the most significant features. Finally, machine learning or lexicon-based techniques can be used to address this problem [18].
2. **Subjectivity Classification**: This task is related to Sentiment Classification in the sense that the objective is to classify subjective and objective opinions. The purpose is to filter subjective sentences because they are more opinionated and thus can improve classification models.
3. **Opinion Summarization**: Also known as aspect based summary or feature based summary. It consists in developing techniques to sum up large amounts of reviews from people. The summarization should focus on entities or aspects and their sentiment and should be quantitative.
4. **Opinion Retrieval**: This is a retrieval process, which requires documents to be retrieved and ranked according to their relevance.
5. **Sarcasm and Irony**: This task is aimed to detect opinions with sarcastic or ironic expressions. As in Subjectivity Classification, the target is to delete these opinions from the SA process.
6. **Others**: Due to the fact that SA is a growing branch of knowledge, over recent years many new tasks have been appearing. Spam detection is one of the most popular.

2.2 Sentiment Analysis Methods (SAMs)

We define SAMs as those tools that are able to evaluate sentiments in text. There exists three main types of SAMs:

(a) Lexicon Dictionary Based Method: It mainly consists in creating a sentiment lexicon, i.e., words carrying a sentiment orientation. These methods can create the dictionary from initial seed words, corpus words (related to a specific domain) or combining the two. Frequently, the dictionary is fed with synonyms and antonyms.
(b) Machine Learning Based Method: It develops statistical models with classifier algorithms. These methods can be divided into super and unsupervised. The main difference is that the first group uses labeled opinions to build the model. One of the most important step in these methods is the feature extraction for representing the classes to be predicted.
(c) Hybrid Based Method: They combine both Lexicon Dictionary and Machine Learning approaches.

Thus, we define three examples of SAM methods based in the aforementioned:

1. Syuzhet: Syuzhet is a Lexicon Dictionary Based Method developed in the Nebraska Literary Lab under the direction of Matthew L. Jockers . Its dictionary is created from a collection of 165,000 human coded terms taken from corpus of contemporary novels [13]. Syzhet reports three polarity levels: {*negative*, *neutral*, *positive*}.
2. Bing: It is a Lexicon Dictionary Based Method developed by Hu and Liu at University of Illinois [10]. This dictionary contains around 6,800 words classified in positive or negative terms. In this case, the output of Bing is a numerical scale: {–1, 0, 1} representing {*negative*, *neutral*, *positive*}.
3. CoreNLP: CoreNLP is a Machine Learning Based Method created by the Stanford NLP Group. It is defined as an integrated toolkit capable of executing different NLP tasks [17]. One of these tasks is related to SA: they developed a deep learning algorithm, Recursive Neural Tensor Network (RNTN), which outperforms old methods in different metrics. This algorithm extracts sentences sentiment representing a phrase through word vectors and parse trees. Unlike Lexicon Dictionary Based Methods this algorithm is capable of capturing sentiment changes detecting scope negations and contrastive conjunctions like *but* (see attached Fig. 1). Finally, the output of this algorithm is a numerical scale: {0, 1, 2, 3, 4}. We set the polarities {0, 1} as *negative*, {2} as *neutral* and {3, 4} as *positive* to work with the same polarity levels.

3 Methodology

In this section we describe the setup of our experiments. The first part, Sect. 3.1, is focused on introducing TripAdvisor as our data source. In Sect. 3.2, we explain how we get the data from websites. Finally, an outline of the experiments is given in Sect. 3.3.

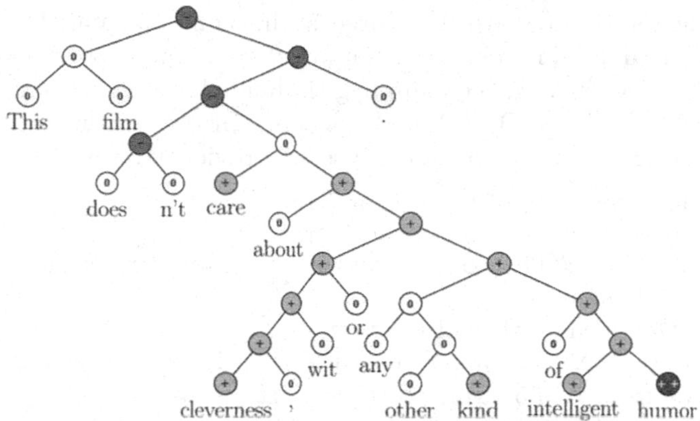

Fig. 1. Example of RNTN extracted from [23]. The algorithm predicts five sentiments, from very negative ({0}) to very positive ({4}). As it is shown in the example, the algorithm captures the negation which shifts the polarity of the whole sentence.

3.1 TripAdvisor

According to Wikipedia[2], TripAdvisor is an American travel website company, founded in 2000, providing reviews from travelers experiences about accommodations, restaurants and attractions.

TripAdvisor is considered one of the first web 2.0 adopter: its information and advice index is constructed from the accumulated opinions of million of tourists. For this reason, this website has made up the largest travel community, reaching 340 million unique monthly visitors reporting more than 350 million online reviews and opinions[3].

Due to these facts, this website has become a rich source for SA. Examples of works analyzing hotels reviews are [1,4–7,16,20,24]. Restaurant reviews are analyzed in [7,9,27].

However, one of the major concerns of user-generated content is the credibility of the opinions. Awaring of it, TripAdvisor has thought up several measures in order to avoid spam and fictitious reviews like allowing the use of commercial email addresses or posting warnings about the zero tolerance for fake opinions. Regarding to this, it has been carried out several studies for analyzing credibility and truthfulness of this website ([3,8,12,26]).

3.2 Web Scraping

We first describe the structure of TripAdvisor monuments websites to explain how do we scrap the data from the web.

---

[2] https://en.wikipedia.org/wiki/TripAdvisor.
[3] Source: TripAdvisor log files, Q1 2016.

All monuments websites are structured in the same way. On the top, it displays the total number of reviews, written in different languages, and a *Popularity Index ranking*. After that, the main page is divided in five sections: Overview, Tours & Tickets, Reviews, Q & A and Location. In the review section we find all the opinions written by TripAdvisor users. A review is formed by:

User Name: The name of the user in TripAdvisor.
User Location: The location of the user.
User Information: The total number of reviews, attraction reviews and helpful votes of the user.
Review Title: A main title of the text.
User Rating: The visit valuation of the user. It is expressed as a discrete number scale from 1 to 5 (from *Terrible* to *Excellent*).
Review Date: The reviewing time.
Review: The text of the opinion.

Finally, we develop a code in R software with `rvest` package which allow us to extract the TripAdvisor reviews from HTML and XML codes [25].

3.3 Experimental Setup

The aim of this work is to study the consistency of TripAdvisor's user ratings. To do so, we define *User's Polarity* from User Rating previously defined. We set the polarity as follows: from 1 to 2 is negative, 3 is neutral and from 4 to 5 is positive. Note that this is a document-level polarity.

The second step is to define *SAM Polarities*. We split in sentences each review and apply both *Syuzhet* and *Bing* methods with the `syuzhet` R package [13] and CoreNLP with the `coreNLP` R package [2].

In order to obtain a document-level polarity, we aggregate sentences scores by majority vote. In a tied event, the final result is neutrality.

Final step is to perform a quantitative analysis of the four polarities and study the correlation between them.

4 Experiment Results

In this section we insightfully describe the quantitative analysis of our experiments. A description of datasets is given in Sect. 4.1. After that, we discuss the results reporting some numbers and plots in Sect. 4.2.

4.1 The Data Sets

We base our experiments on TripAdvisor reviews of three monuments in Spain: the Alhambra, the Sagrada Família and the Mezquita de Córdoba. We base our study only in English reviews due to the fact that SAMs are mainly developed for this language. We create three data sets with reviews from July 2012 until June 2016. As it is shown in Table 1, we collect a total of 45,303 reviews. The monument of Barcelona holds a large amount of reviews during the selected period, 76.29 % of the total. Surprisingly, reviews of the Alhambra are in average larger than other reviews.

Table 1. Summary of text properties of the three data sets.

	Reviews	Words	Sentences	Word avg.	Sentence avg.
Alhambra	7,218	676,398	35,867	93.72	4.97
Sagrada Família	34,559	2,220,719	136,181	64.26	3.94
Mezquita de Córdoba	3,526	217,640	13,083	61.72	3.70

4.2 Analysis of Results

To begin with, Table 2 presents the polarity distribution of *User's Polarity* and the three *SAMs' Polarities*. The positive polarity predominates over the *User's Polarity* which means that TripAdvisor users are usually satisfied with their visit to these monuments. However, the three SAMs seem to detect more neutrality and negativity in the same reviews.

Table 2. Distribution of sentiments of monuments reviews.

User's polarity	Positive	Neutral	Negative
Alhambra	6,781	293	143
Sagrada Família	32,664	1,443	451
Mezquita de Córdoba	3,454	55	17
Syuzhet's polarity	Positive	Neutral	Negative
Alhambra	5,423	911	883
Sagrada Família	25,379	4,805	4,374
Mezquita de Córdoba	2,704	466	356
Bing's polarity	Positive	Neutral	Negative
Alhambra	3,310	1,252	2,655
Sagrada Família	16,541	6,644	11,373
Mezquita de Córdoba	1,918	642	966
CoreNLP's polarity	Positive	Neutral	Negative
Alhambra	3,154	1,143	2,920
Sagrada Família	17,561	6,007	10,990
Mezquita de Córdoba	1,992	577	957

Table 3 shows match rates between *User's Polarity* (columns) and *Syuzhet, Bing* and *CoreNLP Polarities* (rows). The shares represent the average of the three monuments due to the fact that the percentages are very similar (see Table 4).

As can be hinted from the table, the analysis of the data revealed a clear disparity between polarities. *Syuzhet* shows a high correlation in the positive opinions, 76% of matching, while Bing and CoreNLP get around 50%. However,

Table 3. Correlation arrays between *User Rating* (rows) and SAMs (columns) sentiments. The numbers are the average of the three monuments

Syuzhet sentiment	Positive	Neutral	Negative
Positive	0.76	0.13	0.11
Neutral	0.60	0.18	0.22
Negative	0.42	0.23	0.35
Bing sentiment	Positive	Neutral	Negative
Positive	0.50	0.18	0.31
Neutral	0.35	0.18	0.48
Negative	0.09	0.14	0.77
CoreNLP sentiment	Positive	Neutral	Negative
Positive	0.52	0.16	0.32
Neutral	0.17	0.17	0.66
Negative	0.09	0.26	0.84

Table 4. Standard deviation of *User Rating* (rows) and SAMs (columns) sentiments. This table clearly shows that sentiments are equally distributed over the three monuments

Syuzhet sentiment	Positive	Neutral	Negative
Positive	0.02	0.01	0.01
Neutral	0.02	0.03	0.04
Negative	0.07	0.07	0.06
Bing sentiment	Positive	Neutral	Negative
Positive	0.04	0.01	0.04
Neutral	0.08	0.07	0.14
Negative	0.10	0.07	0.12
CoreNLP sentiment	Positive	Neutral	Negative
Positive	0.06	0.01	0.06
Neutral	0.03	0.06	0.08
Negative	0.05	0.30	0.09

this correlation decreases in the neutral and negative opinions where it detects a 35% of total negative reviews. Although *Bing* and *CoreNLP* show a low rate of detection in positive reviews, the match share on negative reviews is 77% and 84%, respectively. In neutral user's reviews distributions are more scattered. This has sense because when the sentiment is neutral is more frequent to write both equally, positive and negative sentences. However, the tendency is the same as before: *Syuzhet* tends to detect more positivity and *Bing* and *CoreNLP* more negativity.

One more fact is that although *Syuzhet* and *Bing* are both Lexicon Dictionary Based, their behavior analyzing sentiments is different.

5 Conclusions and Future Work

In this study we develop an empirical experiment for studying the consistency of user-based polarities. We download TripAdvisor reviews from three Spanish monuments. After that, we define the *User's Polarity* as the polarity given by the reviewer and the *SAMs' Polarities* as the most recurrent polarity of sentences in the review evaluated by three different SAMs. After obtaining the four polarity labels, we analyze its correlation.

Our analytic experiments show that there exists a low correlation between sentiment labels depending on the SAM. This led us to conclude that there exists disparity between polarities. Users may tend to write negative sentences on positive reviews, and vice versa. Therefore, we should recommend not to analyze reviews with the overall sentiment due to the polarity disparity in sentences. Additionally, *SAMs' Polarities* may wrongly assessed polarity in sentences due to the fact that they are not 100% precise. A study of the SAM's sentence labelling should be carried out in order to extend this work.

We suggest considering a classification method taking into account the sentiment extracted by SAMs. Moreover, we suggest to develop an opinion summarization methodology taking into account sentence sentiment instead of the overall sentiment. In this sense, more detailed insights can be discovered.

Acknowledgments. We thank the anonymous reviewers for their constructive feedback. This research has been supported by FEDER and the Spanish National Research Project TIN2014-57251-P.

References

1. Aciar, S.: Mining context information from consumers reviews. In: Proceedings of Workshop on Context-Aware Recommender System, vol. 201. ACM (2010)
2. Arnold, T., Tilton, L.: R packages. In: Arnold, T., Tilton, L. (eds.) Humanities Data in R. Quantitative Methods in the Humanities and Social Sciences, pp. 179–182. Springer, Heidelberg (2015)
3. Ayeh, J.K., Au, N., Law, R.: Do we believe in tripadvisor? examining credibility perceptions and online travelers attitude toward using user-generated content. J. Travel Res. **52**(4), 437–452 (2013)
4. Baccianella, S., Esuli, A., Sebastiani, F.: Multi-facet rating of product reviews. In: Boughanem, M., Berrut, C., Mothe, J., Soule-Dupuy, C. (eds.) ECIR 2009. LNCS, vol. 5478, pp. 461–472. Springer, Heidelberg (2009). doi:10.1007/978-3-642-00958-7_41
5. Banić, L., Mihanović, A., Brakus, M.: Using big data and sentiment analysis in product evaluation. In: 2013 36th International Convention on Information & Communication Technology Electronics & Microelectronics (MIPRO), pp. 1149–1154. IEEE (2013)

6. Duan, W., Cao, Q., Yu, Y., Levy, S.: Mining online user-generated content: using sentiment analysis technique to study hotel service quality. In: 2013 46th Hawaii International Conference on System Sciences (HICSS), pp. 3119–3128. IEEE (2013)
7. ElSahar, H., El-Beltagy, S.R.: Building large arabic multi-domain Resources for sentiment analysis. In: Gelbukh, A. (ed.) CICLing 2015. LNCS, vol. 9042, pp. 23–34. Springer, Cham (2015). doi:10.1007/978-3-319-18117-2_2
8. Filieri, R., Alguezaui, S., McLeay, F.: Why do travelers trust tripadvisor? antecedents of trust towards consumer-generated media and its influence on recommendation adoption and word of mouth. Tourism Manag. **51**, 174–185 (2015)
9. García, A., Gaines, S., Linaza, M.T., et al.: A lexicon based sentiment analysis retrieval system for tourism domain. Expert Syst. Appl. Int. J. **39**(10), 9166–9180 (2012)
10. Hu, M., Liu, B.: Mining and summarizing customer reviews. In: Proceedings of the Tenth ACM SIGKDD International Conference on Knowledge Discovery and Data Mining, pp. 168–177. ACM (2004)
11. Hu, M., Liu, B.: Mining opinion features in customer reviews. In: AAAI, vol. **4**, 755–760 (2004)
12. Jeacle, I., Carter, C.: In tripadvisor we trust: rankings, calculative regimes and abstract systems. Acc. Organ. Soc. **36**(4), 293–309 (2011)
13. Jockers, M.: Package syuzhet (2016)
14. Liu, B.: Sentiment analysis and subjectivity. In: Indurkhya, N., Damerau, F.J. (eds.) Handbook of Natural Language Processing, 2nd edn., pp. 627–666. Chapman and Hall/CRC, Boca Raton (2010)
15. Liu, B.: Sentiment Analysis: Mining Opinions, Sentiments, and Emotions. Cambridge University Press, New York (2015)
16. Lu, B., Ott, M., Cardie, C., Tsou, B.K.: Multi-aspect sentiment analysis with topic models. In: 2011 IEEE 11th International Conference on Data Mining Workshops (ICDMW), pp. 81–88. IEEE (2011)
17. Manning, C.D., Surdeanu, M., Bauer, J., Finkel, J.R., Bethard, S., McClosky, D.: The stanford coreNLP natural language processing toolkit. In: ACL (System Demonstrations), pp. 55–60 (2014)
18. Medhat, W., Hassan, A., Korashy, H.: Sentiment analysis algorithms and applications: a survey. Ain Shams Eng. J. **5**(4), 1093–1113 (2014)
19. Pontiki, M., Galanis, D., Papageorgiou, H., Androutsopoulos, I., Manandhar, S., Al-Smadi, M., Al-Ayyoub, M., Zhao, Y., Qin, B.: Orphée de clercq, véronique hoste, marianna apidianaki, xavier tannier, natalia loukachevitch, evgeny kotelnikov, nuria bel, salud marıa jiménez-zafra, and gülsen eryigit. semeval-2016 task 5: Aspect based sentiment analysis. In: Proceedings of the 10th International Workshop on Semantic Evaluation, SemEval, vol. 16 (2016)
20. Popescu, A.M., Etzioni, O.: Extracting product features and opinions from reviews. In: Kao, A., Poteet, S.R. (eds.) Natural Language Processing and Text Mining, pp. 9–28. Springer, London (2007)
21. Ribeiro, F.N., Araújo, M., Gonçalves, P., Benevenuto, F., Gonçalves, M.A.: Sentibench-a benchmark comparison of state-of-the-practice sentiment analysis methods. arXiv preprint arXiv:1512.01818 (2015)
22. Serrano-Guerrero, J., Olivas, J.A., Romero, F.P., Herrera-Viedma, E.: Sentiment analysis: a review and comparative analysis of web services. Inf. Sci. **311**, 18–38 (2015)
23. Socher, R., Perelygin, A., Wu, J.Y., Chuang, J., Manning, C.D., Ng, A.Y., Potts, C., et al.: Recursive deep models for semantic compositionality over a sentiment

treebank. In: Proceedings of the Conference on Empirical Methods in Natural Language Processing (EMNLP), vol. 1631, p. 1642. Citeseer (2013)
24. Titov, I., McDonald, R.T.: A joint model of text and aspect ratings for sentiment summarization. In: ACL, vol. 8, pp. 308–316. Citeseer (2008)
25. Wickham, H.: rvest: Easily harvest (scrape) web pages. R package version 0.2. http://CRAN.R-project.org/package=rvest (2015)
26. Yoo, K.H., Lee, Y., Gretzel, U., Fesenmaier, D.R.: Trust in travel-related consumer generated media. In: Höpken, W., Gretzel, U., Law, R. (eds.) Information and Communication Technologies in Tourism, pp. 49–59. Springer, Vienna (2009)
27. Zhang, H.Y., Ji, P., Wang, J., Chen, X.: A novel decision support model for satisfactory restaurants utilizing social information: a case study of tripadvisor.com. Tourism Manag. **59**, 281–297 (2017)

Sentiment Classification from Multi-class Imbalanced Twitter Data Using Binarization

Bartosz Krawczyk(✉), Bridget T. McInnes, and Alberto Cano

Department of Computer Science, Virginia Commonwealth University, Richmond, VA 23284, USA
{bkrawczyk,btmcinnes,acano}@vcu.edu

Abstract. Twitter became one of the most dynamically developing areas of social media. Due to concise nature of messages, rapid publication and high outreach, people share more and more of their opinions, thoughts and commentaries using this medium. Sentiment analysis is a specific subsection of natural language processing that concentrates on automatically categorizing opinions and attitudes expressed in a given portion of textual information. This requires dedicated machine learning solutions that are able to handle various difficulties embedded in the nature of data. In this paper, we present an efficient framework for automatic sentiment analysis from high-dimensional and sparse datasets that suffer from multi-class imbalance. We propose to approach it by applying a one-vs-one binary decomposition and reducing the dimensionality of each pairwise class set using Multiple Correspondence Analysis. Then we apply preprocessing to alleviate the skewed distributions in reduced number of dimensions. After that, on each pair of classes we train a binary classifier and combined them using a weighted multi-class reconstruction that promotes minority classes. The proposal is evaluated on a large Twitter dataset and obtained results are in favor of the proposed solution.

Keywords: Machine learning · Text mining · Sentiment analysis · Imbalanced learning · Multi-class imbalance

1 Introduction

Twitter is a widely used microblogging environment which serves as a medium to share opinions on various events and products. Because of this, analyzing twitter would allow us to gain valuable insight into modern social dynamics, public opinion on ongoing local and global events, as well as discover patterns in human behavior. Sentiment analysis is the task of computationally categorizing opinions expressed in a piece of text in order to determine if the authors attitude towards a particular topic is positive, negative, or neutral. Sentiment analysis has been a research topic since the late 1970s although with the recent rise of social media there has been a resurgence of interest in this area [8], with Twitter being popular due the variety of topics discussed [7]. However, mining the content of

F.J. Martínez de Pisón et al. (Eds.): HAIS 2017, LNAI 10334, pp. 26–37, 2017.
DOI: 10.1007/978-3-319-59650-1_3

Twitter messages is a challenging task due to a multitude of reasons including the shortness of the posted content, the informal and unstructured nature of the language used, the speed at which tweets arrive, and the imbalanced distribution of sentiments within the tweets. This makes learning any meaningful classifier difficult and additionally hinders performance of popular preprocessing solutions.

Despite of more than two decades of developments, learning from imbalanced data is still to be counted among vital contemporary challenges in machine learning [2]. Due to skewed distributions, a classifier being trained tends to get biased towards the more frequent class, while at the same time the less frequent one is usually the more important one [9]. Hence, the primary challenge lies in using dedicated preprocessing or training methods that are able to alleviate this disadvantage. We aim at creating such a learning system that is able to offer improved predictive power on the minority class, while not sacrificing its performance on the majority one. In case of multi-class imbalance, this becomes even more difficult as relationships among classes are no longer clearly defined. Classes are characterized by much more complex distributions. A given class may be at the same time minority compared to some, majority to others, and even in a relative balanced with remaining ones. This makes such a learning scenario much more difficult, as it is easy to gain on some of the classes, while simultaneously loosing on others. Therefore, we need an in-depth understanding of the nature of learning difficulty in order to properly address it. So far only few works deal explicitly with this type of class imbalance, offering preprocessing [10], decomposition [4], single classifier [6] and ensemble approaches [11].

In this paper, we propose a novel system for tackling multi-class imbalanced Twitter sentiment data, characterized by a high-dimensional, skewed feature space, and the scale to which tweets are created. On average 6,000 tweets are tweeted on Twitter every second which is approximately 350,000 tweets sent per minute, 500 million tweets per day and 200 billion tweets per year. Traditional approaches that utilize computationally expensive techniques to represent tweets for machine learning are not feasible. In order to address these challenges, we propose to combine a binarization scheme (multi-class decomposition) with pairwise dimensionality reduction and data preprocessing using lexical feature information extracted from the tweets. We use a one-vs-one multi-class decomposition that generates pairwise dichotomies [12]. Then, for each class pair independently, we apply Multiple Correspondence Analysis in order to project the sparse feature space into less dimensional one. Then we apply preprocessing methods for balancing class distributions and train local binary classifiers. Finally, we apply a weighted aggregation of two-class outputs into a multi-class decision, modifying the importance of classifiers based on the type of classes they were trained on. This allows us to conduct efficient sentiment analysis from such challenging collection of Twitter instances.

2 Proposed Classification System

In this section, we will describe the proposed framework for sentiment classification from multi-class imbalanced and sparse high-dimensional data in detail.

2.1 General Overview

In order to efficiently handle multi-class imbalanced data one needs to choose one of two approaches: using decomposition into two-class problems or using ad-hoc multi-class solutions. While the former ones may oversimplify the problem by transforming it to a number of dichotomies, the latter ones will suffer significantly from sparse high-dimensional feature space, as they are not designed to operate under such conditions. While some feature space transformations may be applied to both binary and multi-class data, their complexity increases with the number of classes. Additionally, due to the specific nature of the multi-class imbalanced problems, each class may be better analyzed in their own new decision spaces. Therefore, using binarization allows for applying various feature space transformation for each pair of classes in hope for better capturing their unique properties. We decided to go with this approach and utilize one-vs-one (OVO) decomposition. It transforms a M-class problem into $M(M-1)/2$ pairwise subproblems. Another popular solution is one-vs-all, which outputs lower number of base classifiers, yet at the same time creates additional artificial imbalance (as $M-1$ classes are aggregated into one). Thus, it is not recommended to use it for multi-class imbalanced problems. After applying OVO, we reduce our dataset into a collection of classical binary imbalanced problem.

Before applying any preprocessing and classification algorithms, we need to tackle the sparse high-dimensional feature representation, as it may harmfully impact these methods. For this, we propose to use Multiple Correspondence Analysis (MCA) [5]. It is a feature transformation method designed for categorical data that allows to create liner combination of features in order to reduce the input dimensionality. By applying it independently to each of binary subproblems, we are able to obtain varying new feature spaces and select the most suitable number of new dimensions (principal components) that will allow to capture local characteristic of these classes. Then, on lower-dimensional feature spaces we may apply selected data preprocessing methods to alleviate binary skewed distributions and train classifiers on balanced data.

Finally, in order to classify new instances, we apply a classifier combination scheme to reconstruct multi-class decision from binary outputs. We propose a modified weighted voting approach, where classifier weights correspond to the difficulty of classes they were trained on. In following subsections, we will describe components of our framework in details.

2.2 Feature Space Reduction with Multiple Correspondence Analysis

Let us assume that we have n instances described by d categorical features and that j-th feature d_j can take q_j different values. This allows to create an indicator matrix $\mathbf{G}_j$ in form of $n \times q_j$. By concatenating all indicator matrices over all features we obtain a matrix $\mathbf{G}$. Furthermore, $\mathbf{G}$ is divided by a grand total of instances and features in order to obtain the correspondence matrix $\mathbf{F} = \frac{1}{nd}\mathbf{G}$, with assumption that $\mathbf{1}_n^T\mathbf{F}\mathbf{1}_q$, where $\mathbf{1}_i$ is $i \times 1$ vector of ones. Vectors $\mathbf{r} = \mathbf{F}\mathbf{1}_q$

and $\mathbf{c} = \mathbf{F}^T\mathbf{1}_n$ are respectively row and column marginals, in form of vectors of their masses. We may define now diagonal matrices as $\mathbf{D_r} = \text{diag}(\mathbf{r})$ and $\mathbf{D_c} = \text{diag}(\mathbf{c})$.

MCA can be defined as an application of weighted Principal Component Analysis (PCA) on centered matrix $\mathbf{D_r}^{-\frac{1}{2}}\left(\mathbf{F} - \mathbf{r}\mathbf{c}^T\right)$, with distances between profiles calculated using chi-squared metric from $\mathbf{D_c}^{-1}$. This allows to calculate n row principal coordinates (projected coordinates of row profiles). Let us denote as $\mathbf{X}$ a $n \times k$ matrix of row principal coordinates that is defined as:

$$\mathbf{X} = \mathbf{D_r}^{-\frac{1}{2}}\tilde{\mathbf{F}}\mathbf{V}, \tag{1}$$

where

$$\tilde{\mathbf{F}} - \mathbf{D_r}^{-\frac{1}{2}}\left(\mathbf{F} - \mathbf{r}\mathbf{c}^T\right)\mathbf{D_c}^{-\frac{1}{2}}, \tag{2}$$

and $\mathbf{V}$ is a $q \times k$ matrix of k largest eigenvalues $\lambda_1, \cdots, \lambda_k$ of the matrix $\tilde{\mathbf{F}}'\tilde{\mathbf{F}}$.

Identical approach can be applied to column profiles. We may define a $q \times k$ matrix $\mathbf{Y}$ of columns principal coordinates as:

$$\mathbf{Y} = \mathbf{D_c}^{-\frac{1}{2}}\tilde{\mathbf{F}}^T\mathbf{U}, \tag{3}$$

where $\mathbf{U}$ is a $n \times k$ matrix of k largest eigenvalues $\lambda_1, \cdots, \lambda_k$ of the matrix $\tilde{\mathbf{F}}\tilde{\mathbf{F}}^T$.

MCA is a highly effective feature extraction and dimensionality reduction technique for datasets with categorical features. Therefore, it is a suitable choice for our high-dimensional and sparse Twitter binary features. We propose to transform them using MCA, select a suitable number of principal components for each binary subtask and train classifiers with them as new features on respective class instances.

2.3 Balancing the Skewed Distributions

High-dimensional feature spaces pose significant challenges for any preprocessing method for imbalanced data. The popular Synthetic Minority Oversampling Technique (SMOTE) algorithm is especially vulnerable to such difficulty [1]. It uses a neighborhood of each minority class instance to determine the placement of a new artificial object. However, in high-dimensional spaces the definition of distance loses meaning. Therefore, SMOTE tends to introduce new instances in semi-random fashion, not actually contributing to empowering the minority class. The proposed MCA-based projection into spaces of lower dimensionality should be beneficial to this algorithm, allowing for a more meaningful artificial data injection.

Two other popular preprocessing methods for imbalanced data are random undersampling and random oversampling [4]. These methods at first seem to be more robust to high-dimensional feature spaces, as they either remove or multiply original instances without a need for any distance calculations. This is partially true, as usually we need to deal with scenarios where not only number of features is very high, but also number of instances is lower than number of features. This leads to situations, in which despite manipulating minority or majority class distribution, we still cannot achieve an efficient balance. This happens due to the fact that it is extremely difficult to capture actual class structure in sparse high-dimensions and even such operations may lead to adding/removing instances in incorrect regions of the decision space. Thus those two algorithms may also contribute from proposed MCA-based low-dimensional projections.

2.4 Weighted Classifier Combination

After applying OVO decomposition, reducing the dimensionality of the feature space, applying preprocessing and training binary classifiers, we need to use the proposed system for classifying new instances. For this, we require a method that is able to combine binary outputs of base classifiers and reconstruct from them the original multi-class decision. There are many approaches proposed for OVO case and in this paper we apply weighted voting solution that can be expressed as follows:

$$Class(x) = \arg \max_{i=1,\cdots,M} \sum_{1 \leq j \neq i \leq M} w_i w_j s_{ij}(x), \tag{4}$$

where

$$s_{ij}(x) = \max \left\{ F_{\Psi}(x,i), F_{\Psi}(x,j) \right\}, \tag{5}$$

where $F_{\hat{\Psi}}(x,i)$ is a continuous output (support function) of a binary classifier for i-th class ($F_{\hat{\Psi}}(x,i) \in [0,1]$), while w_i and w_j are weights assigned i-th and j-th classes respectively ($w_i \wedge w_j \in [0,1]$). The higher the weight, the bigger the importance of given classifier in the multi-class reconstruction phase.

In standard solutions, each pair of classes has assigned its own weight. In our proposal, we assign separate weights to each individual class. Therefore, a weight for a binary classifier is calculated from weights associated to classes that are used in this pairwise subtask. This allows us to more efficiently model the varying importance of classes in multi-class imbalanced data. In general, we advise to create a descending weight hierarchy. Here, majority classes have assigned lowest weights, while minority classes have the highest ones. In case of multi-majority or multi-minority, weights should be assigned by sorting classes regarding to their size in the training set. This will allow for a *aposteriori* increase of skew robustness that will enhance the preprocessing balancing done at each binary subtask level.

3 Feature Extraction

Prior to learning, the tweets are converted into a feature vector, where each feature represents some property of the tweet that is considered to be relevant to determining its sentiment. Given the complexity of human language and the uniqueness of tweets there is an undefinite number of features that could be used. Typically these features consist of information that can be easily identified in the tweet such as the part-of-speech information, the presence of certain key words or acronyms, emoticons and various semantic properties. The difficulty with using many of these features is that they can be computationally expensive to obtain considering the rate of tweets that need to be processed. For this task, we evaluate using domain-independent linguistic features which can be easily and quickly extracted from the tweet. We explore two approaches.

Unigrams: Lemmas of unigrams which appear more frequently than a predefined threshold in the entire corpus. We lower case all words and exclude those in a list of stopwords. We empirically set the threshold to 2.

Salient bigrams: Salient bigrams within the tweets that have a high goodness of fit statistic. Goodness of fit statistics are computed using various co-occurrence and individual frequency counts of a bigram. Table 1 shows a contingency table for the bigram X and Y where $\overline{X}$ and $\overline{Y}$ to indicates any word except X or Y respectively and $*$ indicates any single word. The cell n_{11} is the joint frequency of the bigram; n_{12} is the frequency in which X occurs in the first position but Y does not occur in the second position; n_{21} is the frequency in which Y occurs in the second position of the bigram but X does not occur in the first position; and n_{22} is the frequency in which neither X nor Y occur in their respective positions. The cells, n_{1p}, n_{p1}, n_{2p} and n_{p2} represent the marginal totals which are the number of times a word does not occur in the first or second position of the bigram. The cell n_{pp} is the total number of bigrams found in the corpus.

Table 1. A bigram contingency table.

	Y	Y	Totals
X	$n_{11} = XY$	$n_{12} = X\overline{Y}$	$n_{1p} = X*$
$\overline{X}$	$n_{21} = \overline{X}Y$	$n_{22} = \overline{XY}$	$n_{2p} = \overline{X}*$
Totals	$n_{p1} = *Y$	$n_{p2} = *\overline{Y}$	$n_{pp} = **$

We use the goodness-of-fit statistic, the Log-Likelihood Ratio (G^2) [3] with a cutoff of 6.635. G^2 measures the divergence of how often you observe a pair of words occurring (n_{ij}) versus how often you would expect them to occur by chance (m_{ij}) providing an automated way to identify key terms within the text:

$$m_{ij} = \frac{n_{i+} * n_{+j}}{n_{++}}. \tag{6}$$

Given the expected values, G^2 is formally defined as:

$$G^2 = 2 * \sum_{i}^{j} n_{ij} * log(n_{ij}/m_{ij}). \tag{7}$$

4 Experimental Study

This experimental study was designed in order to answer the following research questions:

- Do the lexical features provide enough information for the machine learning algorithms to achieve good sentiment classification?
- Does MCA allow for low-dimensional embedding that will improve the performance of classifiers on sparse and high-dimensional data?
- Should we select a fixed number of principal components for all of classes, or select them individually for each binary subtask?
- Which preprocessing and classification algorithms will benefit the most from the combination of OVO decomposition and MCA dimensionality reduction?

Following subsections present in detail the used Twitter dataset, experimental set-up, as well as obtained results and their discussion.

4.1 Dataset

We use the SemEval2016 Message Polarity Classification dataset [7]. This dataset consists of 26 630 tweets that were labeled as either a positive, negative, or neutral sentiment. Table 2 shows the class distributions of the dataset, the average number of features, and the average number of features per tweet.

Table 2. Semeval 2016 message polarity classification dataset.

# of Tweets	Labels			Average # Features	Average # Features/Tweet
	Positive	Negative	Neutral		
26 630	10 153 (38%)	4 094 (15%)	12 383 (47%)	606 762	9.46

4.2 Set-Up

Below, we present the detailed set-up for the experimental study:

- We examine the effectiveness of four popular classifiers in Twitter sentiment classification: k-nearest neighbors, Naïve Bayes, Random Forest, and Support Vector Machine. Their details, along with examined parameters are given in Table 3.
- Parameters of each classifier were optimized using internal 3-fold cross validation on the training set with the usage of grid search procedure over all possible combinations.
- We examine three popular preprocessing methods for imbalanced data: random undersampling, random oversampling and SMOTE (with $k = 5$ neighbors generating artificial instances). For each of these methods, we use three sampling ratios $s \in \{0.5, 1.0, 1.5\}$. This informs how many instances are generated or discarded during respective preprocessing. For example, an oversampling with $s = 1.0$ will generate such a number of minority instances for this class to be equal to 100% of majority one, while undersampling with $s = 1.5$ will reduce the size of the majority class to exactly 50% of the minority one.

- MCA extracts number of principal components equal to the number of features. Then, for each examined method and each binary subset of classes independently, we select $p \in \{25, 50, \cdots, 500\}$ first principal components to be used as new features.
- We deal with three classes: majority (positive), intermediate (neutral) and minority (negative). We propose to set their weights to $w_{maj} = 0.1$, $w_{int} = 0.2$ and $w_{min} = 0.4$ in order to reflect their varying imbalance ratio in the considered problem.
- For training and testing, we use 10-fold cross validation with pairwise F-test combined over all of the folds for statistical analysis of multiple algorithms over a single dataset. We assume significance level $\alpha = 0.05$.
- We evaluate the performance of examined methods using multi-class G-measure, expressed as: $mGM = \sqrt[M]{\coprod_{i=1}^{M} precision_i \cdot recall_i}$, where G-measure on i-th class we calculate as $GM_i = \sqrt{precision_i \cdot recall_i}$.

Table 3. Used classifiers and their parameters.

Acronym	Name	Parameters
k-NN	k-nearest neighbors	$k \in \{1, 3, 5, 7\}$
		Distance = Euclidean
NB	Naïve Bayes	–
RF	Random Forest	Ensemble size $\in \{20, 40, \cdots, 200\}$
		Kernel = linear
SVM	Support Vector Machine	C $\in \{0.01, 0.05, \cdots, 1.0\}$
		Training procedure = SMO

4.3 Results and Discussion

The obtained results with the respect to mGM metric are depicted in Fig. 1, average number of principal components as features used by each binary subtask is presented in Fig. 2, while Table 4 presents the outcomes of 10-fold CV F-test.

Table 4. Results from pairwise combined 10-fold CV F-test among the best performing combinations of classification and preprocessing algorithms.

Hypothesis	p-value	Hypothesis	p-value
$\text{SVM}_{ov1.5}$ vs $k\text{-NN}_{ov1.5}$	0.0000	$\text{RF}_{ov1.5}$ vs $k\text{-NN}_{ov1.5}$	0.0098
$\text{SVM}_{ov1.5}$ vs $\text{NB}_{ov1.5}$	0.0000	$\text{RF}_{ov1.5}$ vs $\text{NB}_{ov1.5}$	0.0072
$\text{SVM}_{ov1.5}$ vs $\text{RF}_{ov1.5}$	0.0317	$k\text{-NN}_{ov1.5}$ vs $\text{NB}_{ov1.5}$	0.6404

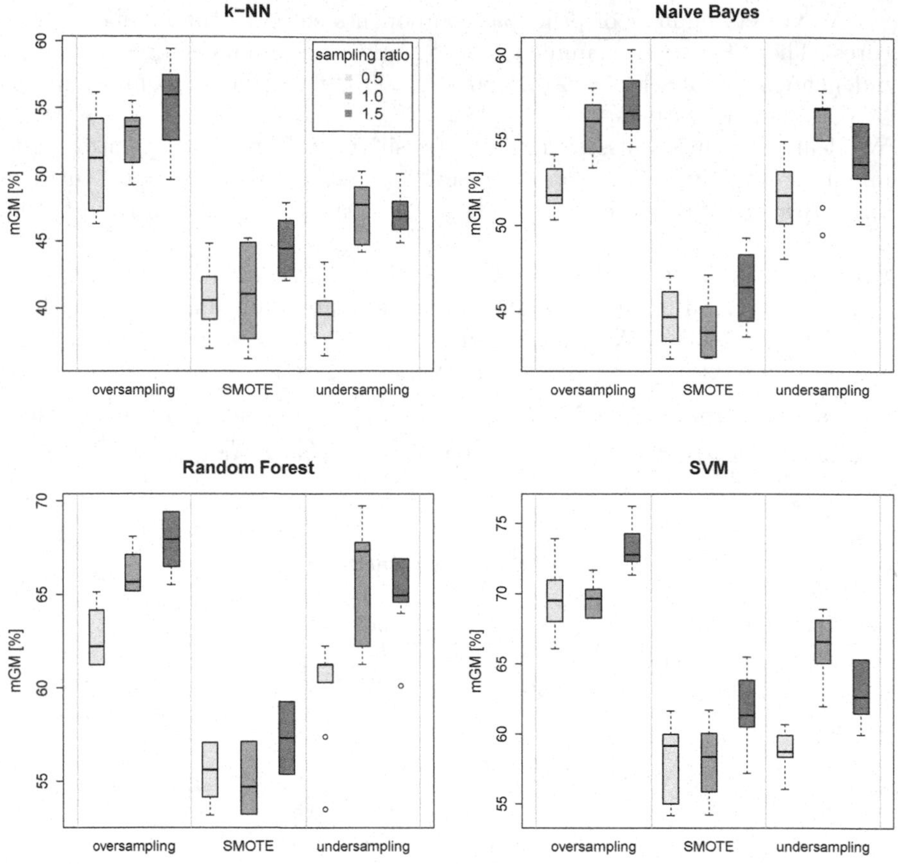

Fig. 1. Obtained performance of examined classifiers with the respect to mGM metric and used preprocessing algorithm.

Let us now analyze the obtained results. Firstly, we will take a closer look on the performance of analyzed preprocessing methods. We have examined in total 9 different combinations (three algorithms with three different sampling ratios for each). When looking at Fig. 1, one may clearly see that random oversampling with $s = 1.5$ returned best performance for all of used classification algorithms. These results can be contributed to two factors. Oversampling does not discard any of instances, thus alleviating the risk of removing valuable objects that may be important for forming classification boundaries. Even after MCA dimensionality reduction, oversampling is a safer choice as it not leads to empty regions in the decision space (that could appear after removing to many majority class instances). Additionally, by using high sampling factor, we boost the presence of minority class in each binary subtask and make its instances more numerous than the original majority class. Although one could expect that this would lead to a significant drop of accuracy on the majority class, this actually does not

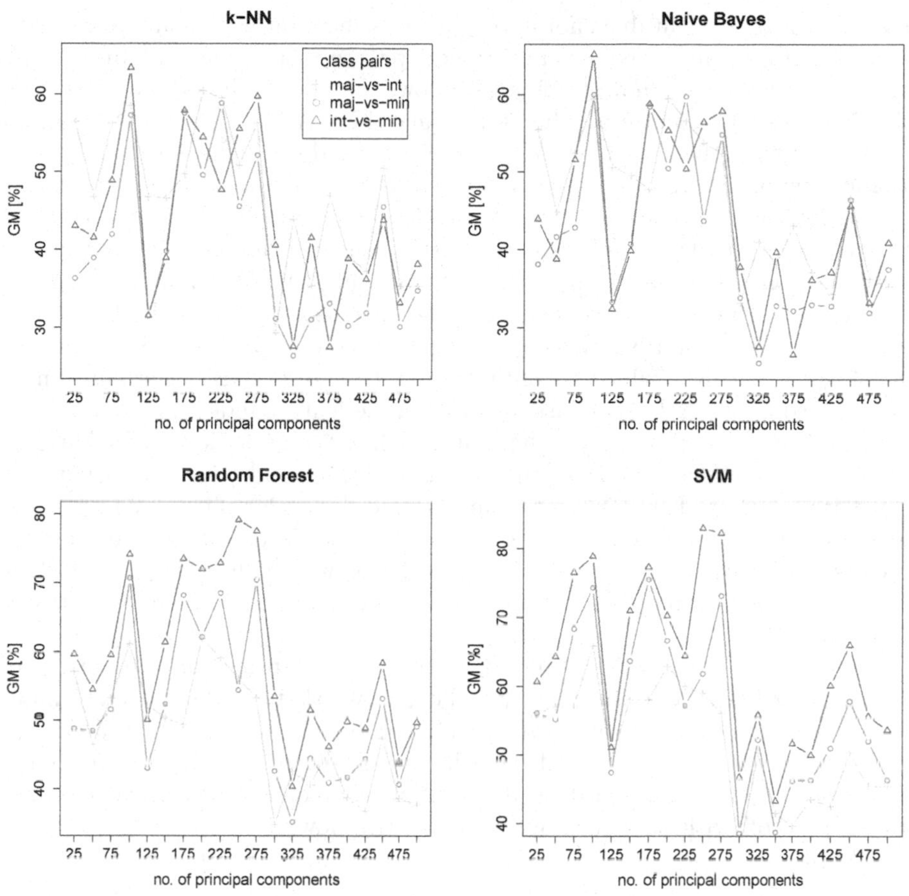

Fig. 2. Average number of principal components used by each pair of classes and their relation to respective G-measures obtained with examined classifiers.

happen as in our dataset the majority class is well-enough represented. Therefore, oversampling with high factor is the best choice for analyzed Twitter data. One can see that undersampling is also able to perform reasonably well for NB and RF classifiers, but returns much weaker results for k-NN and SVM. In case of undersampling factor $s = 1.0$ offers the best performance, as it equally balances both classes. SMOTE is not able to deliver satisfactory performance for any of examined classifiers. This shows that the dimensionality of the feature space is still too high even after applying MCA, or the new features are too convoluted (as they are linear combinations of original sparse features) for SMOTE to inject new instances properly.

Out of four examined classifiers, SVM returns the best results. This can be contributed to the fact that it is a natively binary classifier, thus is naturally suitable for OVO decomposition. Furthermore, the used linear kernel has proven itself to be a suitable choice for NLP classification. SVMs are able to efficiently learn from high-dimensional spaces, yet are more likely to found better kernel representations when starting from lower number of dimensions and work well with convoluted features. Therefore usage of MCA dimensionality reduction worked well with this classifier. RFs are widely used for high-dimensional data classification and performed almost as well as SVMs. F-test shows that there exist statistically significant differences between RF and SVM, on the favor of the latter one. We may hypothesize that RF when selecting only a subset of features loses some information encoded in sequential principal components. SVM uses the entire feature space and this may be the reason behind its better performance. Both k-NN and NB deliver unsatisfactory performance and are inferior to both SVM and RF (which is confirmed by the F-test). NB performance may be explained by its underlying assumption on the feature independence. We use outputs of MCA for training, which are in fact linear combinations of all features. Therefore, this strongly violates the NB assumptions and thus may negatively impact its accuracy. For k-NN even the reduced dimensionality may be too big and thus it is unable to efficiently estimate the neighborhood (or the underlying density of each class). It is similar situation as with SMOTE approach. It is interesting to notice that there are no statistically significant differences between k-NN and NB.

Finally, Fig. 2 shows that using different number of principal components in each class lead to better local results. This shows that selecting a fixed number of new features for all of classes would not be able to capture well enough the characteristics of each created classification dichotomy. Therefore, additional computational effort for selecting different number of features in each binary subtask pays off with improved overall predictive power.

5 Conclusions and Future Works

In this paper, we presented a novel framework for Twitter sentiment classification from multi-class imbalanced data described by a sparse and high-dimensional feature space. The proposed classification framework consisted of five main steps: (i) using OVO decomposition to create subclass dichotomies from the multi-class data; (ii) applying MCA dimensionality reduction technique (suitable for categorical features) in each binary subtask independently; (iii) local selection of the number of principal components for each pairwise problem; (iv) applying binary preprocessing to alleviate class skewness and train classifiers on each dichotomy; and (v) apply class-weighted voting to provide multi-class decision from binary outputs for each new instance.

Experimental study, conducted on large Twitter dataset, proved the usefulness of the proposed approach. Best results were obtained for combination of random oversampling with sampling ratio = 1.5 and SVMs using linear kernel.

This preliminary study encourages us to further develop new methods for multi-class imbalanced Twitter sentiment classification. In our future works, we plan to investigate different feature extraction methods (in order to obtain more informative features), adjust type and ratio of preprocessing in each skewed binary subtask independently according to local characteristics, and examine the potential of using active and semi-supervised methods for using only a small subset of labeled instances.

References

1. Blagus, R., Lusa, L.: SMOTE for high-dimensional class-imbalanced data. BMC Bioinform. **14**, 106 (2013)
2. Branco, P., Torgo, L., Ribeiro, R.P.: A survey of predictive modeling on imbalanced domains. ACM Comput. Surv. **49**(2), 31:1–31:50 (2016)
3. Dunning, T.: Accurate methods for the statistics of surprise and coincidence. Comput. Linguist. **19**(1), 61–74 (1993)
4. Fernández, A., López, V., Galar, M., del Jesús, M.J., Herrera, F.: Analysing the classification of imbalanced data-sets with multiple classes: binarization techniques and ad-hoc approaches. Knowl. Based Syst. **42**, 97–110 (2013)
5. Greenacre, M.J., Blasius, J.: Multiple Correspondence Analysis and Related Methods. Chapman & Hall/CRC, London (2006)
6. Hoens, T.R., Qian, Q., Chawla, N.V., Zhou, Z.-H.: Building decision trees for the multi-class imbalance problem. In: Tan, P.-N., Chawla, S., Ho, C.K., Bailey, J. (eds.) PAKDD 2012. LNCS (LNAI), vol. 7301, pp. 122–134. Springer, Heidelberg (2012). doi:10.1007/978-3-642-30217-6_11
7. Nakov, P., Ritter, A., Rosenthal, S., Stoyanov, V., Sebastiani, F.: SemEval-2016 task 4: sentiment analysis in Twitter. In: Proceedings of the 10th International Workshop on Semantic Evaluation, SemEval 2016. Association for Computational Linguistics, San Diego, California, June 2016
8. Pang, B., Lee, L., et al.: Opinion mining and sentiment analysis. Found. Trends® Inf. Retrieval **2**(1–2), 1–135 (2008)
9. Porwik, P., Doroz, R., Orczyk, T.: The k-nn classifier and self-adaptive hotelling data reduction technique in handwritten signatures recognition. Pattern Anal. Appl. **18**(4), 983–1001 (2015)
10. Sáez, J.A., Krawczyk, B., Wozniak, M.: Analyzing the oversampling of different classes and types of examples in multi-class imbalanced datasets. Pattern Recogn. **57**, 164–178 (2016)
11. Wang, S., Yao, X.: Multiclass imbalance problems: analysis and potential solutions. IEEE Trans. Syst. Man Cybern. Part B **42**(4), 1119–1130 (2012)
12. Woźniak, M., Graña, M., Corchado, E.: A survey of multiple classifier systems as hybrid systems. Inf. Fusion **16**, 3–17 (2014)

An Ontology for Generalized Disease Incidence Detection on Twitter

Mark Abraham Magumba(✉) and Peter Nabende

Department of Information Systems,
College of Computing and Information Sciences, Makerere University,
P.O. Box 7062 Kampala, Uganda
magumbamark@hotmail.com, peter.nabende@gmail.com

Abstract. In this paper, we present an ontology of disease related concepts that is designated for detection of disease incidence in tweets. Unlike previous key word based systems and topic modeling approaches, our ontological approach allows us to apply more stringent criteria for determining which messages are relevant such as spatial and temporal characteristics whilst giving a stronger guarantee that the resulting models will perform well on new data that may be lexically divergent. We achieve this by training supervised learners on concepts rather than individual words. Effectively, we map every possible word to a fixed length lexicon thereby eliminating lexical divergence between training data and new data. For training we use a dataset containing mentions of influenza, common cold and Listeria and use the learned models to classify datasets containing mentions of an arbitrary selection of other diseases. We show that our ontological approach results in models whose performance is not only good but also stable on lexically divergent data versus a word-level lookup unigram, bag of words baseline approach. We also show that word vectors can be learned directly from our concepts to achieve even better results.

Keywords: Epidemiology · Twitter · Sentiment analysis · Text classification · Concept ontology · Data mining · Knowledge engineering

1 Introduction

In this paper, we propose an ontological approach for deriving features for classification models that can generally detect disease incidence in tweets and possibly other unstructured data sources. Methods based on twitter surveillance typically count the volume of messages about a given disease topic as an indicator of actual disease activity via keywords such as the disease name [1–3]. Generally speaking some positive correlation is assumed between the volume of messages and disease activity at a given time. However, in many cases this assumption is too weak as the volume of disease related messages can be influenced by panic and other factors as noted by [4]. Therefore it is important to incorporate the semantic orientation of tweets to discriminate between relevant and irrelevant mentions on a certain target word as in many cases many messages about a given disease may actually mention it in a non-incidence related context or one that is spatio-temporally irrelevant. For instance, "I remember when the

F.J. Martínez de Pisón et al. (Eds.): HAIS 2017, LNAI 10334, pp. 38–51, 2017.
DOI: 10.1007/978-3-319-59650-1_4

Challenger went down, I was home sick with the flu!" is an actual reference to an incidence of the flu but the Challenger disaster occurred in 1986 therefore it would be incorrect to count this mention for an outbreak in 2016.

In our approach we employ an ontology of concepts to overcome the problems of Natural Language Processing (NLP) on Twitter, particularly those associated with its high lexical diversity which results over-fitted models that perform poorly on new data in spite of the fact that state of the art NLP techniques can achieve arbitrary high performance on retrospective data; but where there is such a high lexical diversity there is very little confidence that models that perform well in training will give robust performance when applied to an online application where new data is generated on the fly.

1.1 Related Work

The use of online unstructured data sources for disease surveillance constitutes a very active area of research. The general approach involves the use of a list of keywords to filter a stream of documents. For some systems like BioCaster [5] these key terms have been arranged into ontologies. Ontologies are used for explicit knowledge representations for inference support. In the domain of medicine and epidemiology, several ontologies have been created such as International Health Terminology Standards Organization's SNOMED-CT (Systematic Nomenclature of Medicine – Clinical terms), the Syndromic Surveillance Ontology (SSO) [6], the Dictionary of Epidemiology [7], the OBO (Open Biomedical Ontology) ontologies [8] such as the disease ontology [9] for diseases and the Epidemiology Ontology (EPO) [10]. These ontologies have been developed with different foci and audiences in mind. For the most part the goal is to arrive at a standardized domain terminology for instance SNOWMED-CT is an attempt to harmonize divergent terminology for equivalent medical concepts.

In terms of approach and rationale the most similar work to ours is the BioCaster ontology [5]. Our approach differs from these efforts in two significant ways. Firstly we have developed it specifically for twitter where it is expected that the input text is a lot more messy and sparser than technically oriented texts such as biomedical communications [11] and medical studies and systematic reviews [12] that have been the focus of previous work or even RSS feeds for news articles as employed by the BioCaster system. Secondly, we consequently exclude any technical terms such as names or strains of specific pathogens and even names of specific diseases for instance the BioCaster method has partially defined word lists which include terms such as "human ehrlichiosis" and "enzootic bovine leukosis". In our approach we solely concentrate on the basic linguistics of communicating illness. In this respect at the ontology level our work is in the same spirit as the proposed but unimplemented Medical Wordnet project [13].

2 Materials and Methods

We employ two key intuitions; firstly that for the purpose of classifying messages as relevant or not some words are more important than others. Secondly, that words themselves are representative of some higher mental concepts and that in the bounds of a given topic of discourse there is a fairly small number of concepts but a possibly infinite number of words and ways to express them. So, what we have attempted is to identify these higher concepts that communicate illness and train classifiers on them rather than words to achieve low performance variance across lexically divergent data sets.

Figure 1 below is a visualization of the word frequency in three data sets containing tweets that mention a selection of diseases. The frequency of words is encoded as their font size and this visualization shows the 100 most frequent words per data set. In producing this visualization we also removed certain elements like URLs and stop words in addition to the names of the actual diseases. So, the figure is actually a visualization of the context of disease mentions by name for these diseases.

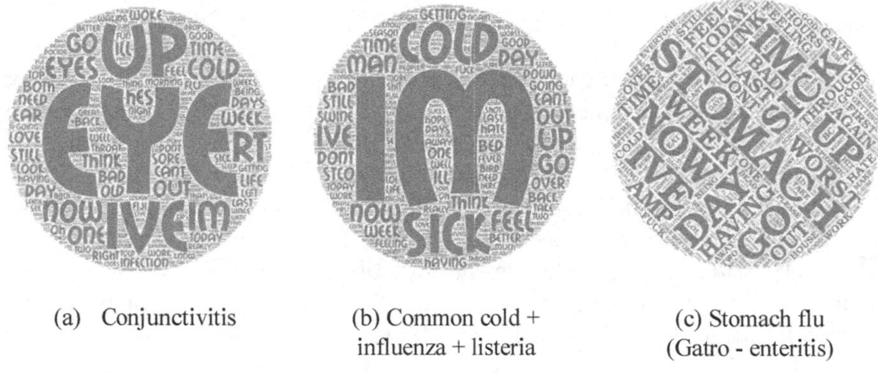

(a) Conjunctivitis

(b) Common cold + influenza + listeria

(c) Stomach flu (Gatro - enteritis)

Fig. 1. Word clouds generated from data sets

From the preceding figure it is quite clear that these words can easily be grouped into categories. For instance "eye" is prominent in the conjunctivitis dataset as is "stomach" in gastroenteritis dataset and with some domain knowledge we can easily infer that these symbolize the sites of infection for the corresponding diseases. Therefore, from this knowledge we can create a category for anatomical references. Furthermore, even though we do not encounter the word "leg", as humans we can easily predict that it too is a member of this category and hence extend the category. Furthermore, even though the term "cell nucleus" refers to a part of the body it is way too technical and specific to expect it to occur in casual twitter posts with significant regularity therefore it is our opinion that we can safely ignore it and simply register it as a noun. In creating the ontology this is exactly what we do. In deriving concepts for the ontology we simply repeat this process several times until we obtain a set of concepts that we think are representative of the domain.

2.1 An Ontology for Disease Incidence Detection on Twitter

These higher concepts can be organized into an ontology to detail how they relate with each other. These concepts are of two broad categories, those that directly describe disease incidence such as references to disease causing organisms such as bacteria and general linguistic terminology like words that imply negation and references to temporality such as words like "now" and "then" and descriptions of space and time. As depicted in Fig. 2, at the top of the hierarchy everything is conceptualized as an object, there are two types of objects that is, real objects and abstract objects. Real objects refer to tangible things and abstract objects refer to concepts like time, negation and events. Real objects are either Living or inanimate.

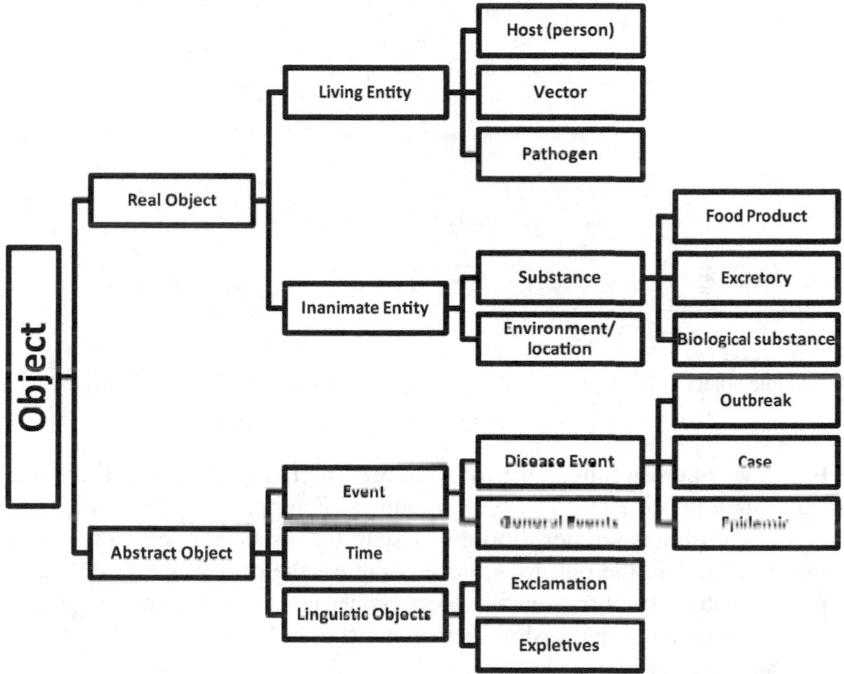

Fig. 2. Partial class hierarchy for human disease language concept ontology

Living things comprise all the key biological actors such as hosts (the organism that suffers disease which in this case is a person), pathogens (disease causing organisms) and vectors (disease spreading organisms). Inanimate objects are of two major classes namely environments and substances.

There are three types of concepts namely relationships and properties and actions. Relationships describe interactions between concept classes in the object hierarchy and correspond to OWL (Web Ontology Language) object properties whereas properties describe object and relationship attributes and correspond to OWL data properties. Actions describe object behavior for certain objects like people where a typical action is to exercise and can be thought of as data properties for which the range and domain are the same.

The concept hierarchy allows for additional semantics including sub classing and inheritance. Figure 3 depicts a partial decomposition of the People conceptual object, inheritance means that all definitions made in the top level object are inherited by the child classes in this case care provider, patient and government. In addition there is support for some polymorphic behavior meaning that even though inheritance allows for one time definition of shared behavior in the hierarchy, it is not necessarily implemented uniformly. For instance all objects have a "Magnitude" property that allows for quantification but this is invoked differently depending on the object for instance it could be a discrete quantity or quantification by degree.

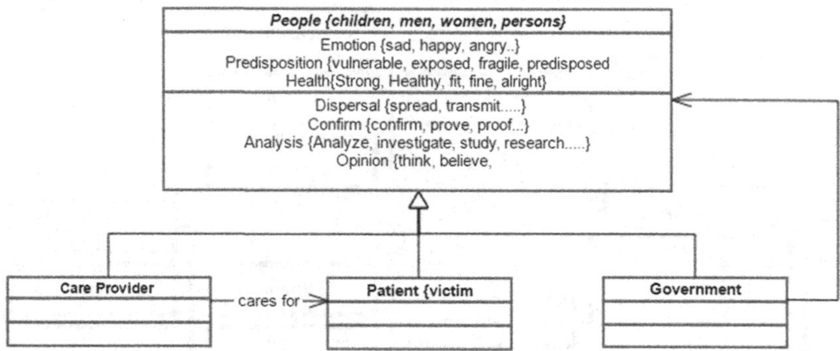

Fig. 3. People object sub hierarchy with corresponding concept dictionaries indicated in curly braces

In Fig. 3 we have employed a UML like representation as opposed to the more technically appropriate RDF schema diagram for compactness of notation. In our case the class attributes are descriptions of state for instance a person may exhibit emotional state and in the ontology these comprise the data properties. The UML class methods may be interpreted as object properties for which the range and the domain is the same and relationships between different UML classes directly correspond to object properties.

Concept Dictionaries

Finally, for each conceptual object be it a relationship, object or action there is a corresponding concept dictionary. In Fig. 3 these are indicated in curly brackets. The full ontology along with a description is publically available in OWL/XML format at our Github repository[1]. The concept dictionary is simply a list of words related to the concept. Roughly speaking the members of a given concept dictionary are related by three relationships namely synonymy, hyponymy/hypernymy and meronymy. Synonymy refers to semantically equivalent words such as "skin" and "dermis", hypernymy is refers to increasing generalization for instance "location" is a hypernym of "house", hyponymy is the inverse of hypernymy as in "house" would be a hyponym of "location". Generally speaking immediate hyponyms and hypernyms are grouped together with concept synonyms. Meronyms are similarly grouped together. Meronymy implies a part of relationship for instance "arm" is a meronym of "body".

[1] https://github.com/MarkMagumba/Twitter-Disease-incidence-Description-Language-Ontology.

However, in many cases we have applied some subjective judgments like expectations on the expected frequency of words belonging to a given concept to bundle words on some other thematic criteria. As an example there is a treatment concept which bundles together any treatment related word such as treatment nouns like *stethoscope, syringe and medicine* and treatment verbs like *treat, therapy.* The result is a fairly coarse grained classification.

Semantic Ambiguity
In some cases there is semantic ambiguity for instance the word "fall" can imply a kind of motion as in "I am falling down" and also getting sick for instance "I am falling sick". It would be inaccurate to bundle it with other motion verbs like "jump" as that would be to tell the learner that they always imply similar connotations. Particularly in the case of polysemy, words may present different meanings meaning they can legitimately belong to multiple concepts, in this situation the most semantically accurate approach is to create special single word concepts.

2.2 Feature Extraction

We transform each tweet into a vector of features as follows. Firstly, we flatten out our ontology into a list of its constituent concepts. As stated in Sect. 2.1 each concept is associated with a group of words or tokens referred to as the concept dictionary. Each concept is effectively a list of words and the full ontology is basically a list of lists. In this sense it is a heavily redacted English dictionary containing only words we consider to be of epidemiological relevance. To obtain the feature vector we simply tokenize each tweet and for each token we do a dictionary look up in our flattened ontology.

If the token exists in the ontology, we simply replace it with the concept in which it occurs. As an example the sentence "I have never had the flu" is encoded as "SELF_REF HAVE FREQUENCY HAVE OOV OOV". SELF_REF refers to "Self references" which is the concept class for terms that persons use to refer to themselves such as "I", "We" and "Us" used as an indicators of speaking in the first person, "HAVE" is the concept class for "have" or "had" which is a special concept class since the verb "to have" is conceptually ambiguous as it can legitimately indicate two senses that is falling sick or possession. The "FREQUENCY" terms refers to a reference to frequency concept which denotes temporal periodicity.

The "OOV" terms at the end of the CNF representation stands for "Out of Vocabulary". To arrive at the concept representation we merely perform a simple list lookup; for each token we iterate through all concepts to see if it exists in any concept's dictionary. If it does, then that concept's label is returned, otherwise the "OOV" flag is returned. The current version of our ontology has 136 concepts corresponding to 1531 tokens versus a vocabulary of about 59,000 tokens for our full corpus (or several billion words in English). Needless to say, most words are out of vocabulary. Rather than completely ignore these, we introduce a two-step categorization as described in the next section.

Part of Speech Enriched Padding

Instead of completely ignoring out of vocabulary tokens we replace them with their part of speech tag therefore our previous example, "I have never had the flu" becomes "SELF_REF HAVE FREQUENCY HAVE DT NN". For Part of Speech tagging we employ the Penn treebank [14] part of speech tags in addition to some special tags for twitter specific phenomena such as "RT" for re-tweet, "USR" for users denoted by tokens beginning with "@", HT for "hash tag" denoted by tokens beginning with "#" and "URL" for http universal resource locators denoted by tokens beginning with "http". Figure 4 below depicts the transformations for the message "I have never had the flu!"

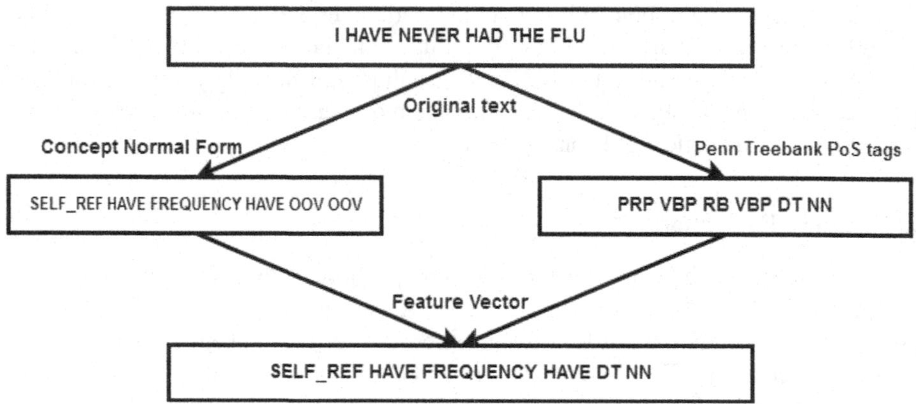

Fig. 4. Deriving feature vector from CNF and POS tags

The value of this step is that we can potentially acquire more information from the data for instance even though we have defined concepts to specifically deal with temporality, the Penn treebank tag set differentiates between past and present tense verb forms which given enough data may augment the resulting models' temporal awareness. Also a result of the huge lexical diversity of twitter in some cases it is more useful to cluster terms using their part of speech information. Furthermore, state of the art part of speech tagging is at least 80% accurate on twitter data for models trained on generic publicly available corpora like the Wall Street Journal data set and even more with further tuning [15]. This means that even though many terms will be out of vocabulary regardless of the comprehensiveness of any reference dictionary, given the fact that people make up words and there is a lot of misspellings on twitter, we are still able to determine any word's grammatical category with a fair amount of certainty. For part of speech tagging we employ the GATE[2] twitie-tagger application [15, 16] which is a variant of the log linear maximum entropy Stanford Part of Speech Tagger [17, 18] trained on twitter data.

In summary the features for the learner are generated as follows. For each tweet, the method replaces each word with the concept under which it is listed. If the word does not appear in any of the concept dictionaries, then it is "out of vocabulary" in which case it is replaced by its Penn treebank part of speech tag. The concepts plus part of

[2] General architecture for text engineering.

speech tags for out of vocabulary words are what we feed into the learners as features. Also for the remainder of this paper this is what we shall actually mean when we refer to the CNF representation.

3 The Twitter Disease Incidence Detection Pipeline

The following is a description of the pipeline for generic disease incidence detection on Twitter using our ontological approach. Figure 5 below summarizes the steps.

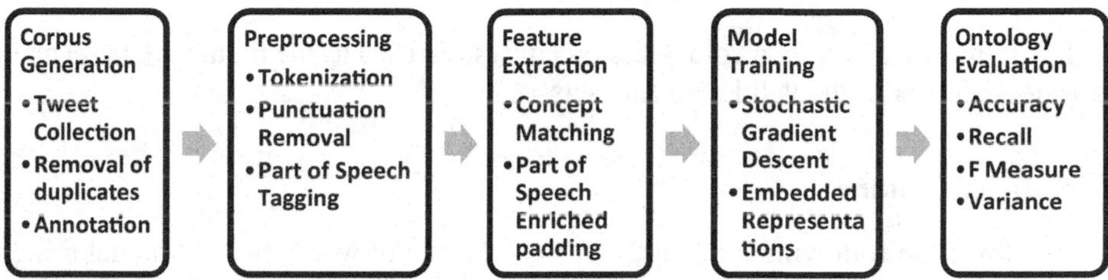

Fig. 5. The disease incidence detection pipeline

3.1 Corpus Generation

The first step is the creation of the corpus. We obtain tweets from a basic twitter account using some specific keywords via a python script through Twitter's Streaming API. The tweets we download are those that are marked as public, this is the default security level and they are only marked private if expressly indicated by users. Next we partition the tweets into training and testing data sets. We created data sets for four diseases namely influenza + common cold + Listeria, stomach flu (gastro enteritis), norovirus, conjunctivitis 1 and conjunctivitis 2. There are two conjunctivitis data sets because for some tweets it is referred to as "pink eye" (conjunctivitis 2). We used the flu data set for training because it had a higher volume of tweets and was most likely to be representative.

At this phase we eliminated duplicates as much as possible by removing any tweets with the "RT" tag (retweets) and manually reading through the tweets as many tweets were practically the same even though they did not have this tag differing only in minor details like the URLs they contained. At the annotation phase we simply label each tweet as either positive or negative, where a positive tweet is a reference to an actual case of disease in the required time window which is basically the present time or the recent past to a period of a few weeks where we expect a disease to roughly be in its communicable period. The data is summarized in Table 1 below.

Table 1. Summary of experimental data

Data Set	Number of tweets	Split	
		Positive	Negative
Influenza + common cold + Listeria	13004	0.57	0.43
Conjunctivitis 1	656	0.55	0.45
Conjunctivitis 2 (pink eye)	721	0.63	0.37
Norovirus	1288	0.51	0.49
Gastroenteritis (Stomach flu)	646	0.84	0.16

The influenza + common cold + Listeria data set is used as the training data set and the other data sets as the validation data sets.

3.2 Model Training

We employed the following methods, first we did a bag of words (BOW) model using our original, untransformed dataset with a Stochastic Gradient Descent (SGD) classifier to obtain a baseline, then we extracted features using the procedure in Sect. 2.2 and created a unigram bag of words model, a unigram + bigram model and a Doc2Vec + Logistic Regression classifier. For the bag of words models we used the SGD classifier with the same parameter settings.

Using Distributed Word Embedding for text classification is a two-step process, first word vectors must be learned for each word in the vocabulary which is an unsupervised step then these vectors can be fed into a supervised learning method. The Doc2Vec algorithm is an extension of word2Vec first described by Tomas Mikolov [19]. The word2vec algorithm takes a collection of documents and returns a vector (word embedding) for each word. The similarity between two words can be calculated from the cosine distance between their word embedding. Generally vectors of words that are close in meaning are also close in value. It has also been shown that word2vec is also capable of preserving non trivial semantic relationships between words for instance the vector for "Brother" – "Man" + "Woman" produce a result that is close to "Sister". Word2vec may employ one of two architectures, either skip gram or continuous bag of words (CBOW). Doc2Vec extends word2vec to entire documents [20]. Roughly speaking, there are two ways in which this can be achieved. That is by computing the average of context word vectors or the concatenation of context vectors. In our case we use the former approach.

There are several parameters that need to be tuned to obtain good word vectors but some of the more important ones include the vector dimensionality, the window and whether or not to use negative sampling and the number of noise words to be drawn. The window specifies how many context words to use. The corresponding architectures to CBOW and skip gram in Doc2Vec are distributed memory and distributed bag of words.

3.3 Doc2Vec Tuning

Doc2Vec is an unsupervised method and the quality of vectors is heavily reliant on model hyper parameters set at the beginning of training. The Doc2Vec algorithm generates both word vectors and document vectors. In our optimization procedure we employ the word vectors as indicators of how good the model since as opposed to document vectors because their implication in terms of human language is unambiguous. In a good model we expect the vectors of words that are semantically similar to be closer in value than those that are semantically divergent. If we are unsatisfied with the results, we update the model hyper parameters discussed in Sect. 3.2 until we obtain satisfactory results. This is a manual procedure and we simply use trial and error guided by a few general rules. In particular, the quality of vectors generally improves with the number of dimensions, training epochs and window size up to some point.

For Doc2Vec we use the gensim package [21] which provides a most_similar() method that returns the most similar words to a given word in the vocabulary by word vector. As already discussed, in a good model these are close in meaning to the queried word. In our situation there is one additional subtlety which is the fact that our vocabulary comprises concepts not words. Furthermore, this is complicated by the fact that the concepts abstract several words which in some cases like the "treatment" concept may not even be in the same grammatical category implying that they most definitely have different distributional characteristics. In this situation we have to give some thought to how to interpret vectors obtained for concepts in our vocabulary.

To do this we leverage the fact that as a result of part of speech enriched padding discussed in Sect. 2.2, the final representation is a combination of concepts and part of speech tags for out of vocabulary words, we can instead use the part of speech tags where the semantics are more straightforward. For instance we expect noun categories to be closer to themselves than adjectives, that is, in a good model we would expect that the closest "concepts" to the NN (Noun, Singular) tag are NNS (Noun Plural) and NNP (Proper Noun Singular) tags.

In our best model, we verify that indeed noun categories cluster together as the most similar concepts to NN are indeed NNS and NNP. We obtained our best results with 200 dimensions, with negative sampling with 8 noise words, a context window of 5, and with 20 epochs with distributed memory architecture. For Doc2Vec we employ our full corpus with the labels removed for the unsupervised portion. For the supervised learning portion we employ a logistic regression classifier. All code is written in python and we use the Scikit-learn package [22] for all machine learning tasks besides the Doc2Vec algorithm.

4 Evaluation

For a tweet to be relevant it must refer to an ongoing or recent (not exceeding a maximum time span of a few weeks) disease event and its location must be determinable and must not be aggregated beyond a users' geographical country. All other references are deemed irrelevant. To test our ontology we compare results obtained on the baseline against those obtained with our ontology concept features. We use the unigram bag of words

SGD model as the baseline. We opt for precision, recall and f-measure as the performance metrics. For results on the training data set we used 10 fold cross validation.

In replacing each word with its corresponding concept in the ontology two problematic situations may arise in terms of attempting to use this representation to distinguish between messages on some criteria. Firstly, the representation may be so general that it fails to preserve enough information to distinguish between relevant and irrelevant messages. Take for instance if we replaced each word with its part of speech tag this would most likely make it very difficult to distinguish between relevant and irrelevant messages as their representations would nearly be identical. This would lead to stable but poor performance. Secondly, it is possible that the representation is incomplete, in other words we end up with an ontology that only partially specifies the domain leading to unstable performance that varies according to how closely classification models correspond with test data in terms of lexical composition.

The optimal ontology is complete and has the right concept granularity. We expect that if we replaced individual words with their corresponding concepts in such an ontology, we would obtain classification models whose performance approaches that of the unigram baseline model on the training data set and is probably better on the test data set since it eliminates the effects of over fitting by abstracting individual words with ontology concepts. As a result of this we expect these models to have more stable performance in terms of having a smaller performance variance between different data sets.

4.1 Results and Discussion

To measure the model performance we employ un-weighted average performance as the overall performance across all datasets. To measure the reliability of the model on new data, we employ the performance variance as a measure of the impact of lexical differences between the data sets. A small variance means the classifier's performance on different data sets is similar and that our concept model is sufficiently general. The results are summarized in Table 2. The unigram word level lookup bag of words SGD baseline model and the unigram CNF SGD model are a like-for-like comparison as we do not change any model parameter apart from replacing words with their CNF representations. As the results show, this change alone increases the overall classifier performance by F1-score from 0.6133 to 0.714 and reduces the performance variance by F1-score by nearly 700%.

The increase in overall performance is mainly a result of improved performance on the norovirus data set for which performance with the baseline model by F1-score is 0.0016 and 0.5929 for the unigram CNF SGD model. A large performance bump is also obtained from a substantial increase in overall recall performance from 60.35% in the baseline model to 82.67% on the unigram CNF SGD model. Given a choice between high recall and high precision, we would prefer high recall as it is our thinking that it is better to miss some actual cases of a disease than to misclassify irrelevant messages as reports of disease incidence.

Table 2. Performance of ontology based models on different datasets versus word level lookup unigram bag of words baseline model

Method	Metric	Influenza + Common Listeria	Conjuctivitis	Conjuncti vitis 2 (Pink eye)	Norovirus	Stomach flu	Overall performance	Variance
Unigram BOW (Baseline)	F1 Score	0.8435	0.6746	0.6607	0.0016	0.8860	0.6133	0.1269
	Precision	0.8144	0.8120	0.7020	0.0075	0.8370	0.6346	0.1256
	Recall	0.8747	0.5770	0.6240	0.0009	0.9410	0.6035	0.1379
Unigram BOW + CNF	F1 Score	0.7278	0.7592	0.5946	0.5929	0.8954	0.7140	0.0160
	Precision	0.7387	0.6599	0.4265	0.5679	0.8713	0.6529	0.0284
	Recall	0.7173	0.8937	0.9814	0.6203	0.9209	0.8267	0.0230
Unigrams Bigrams + CNF	F1 Score	0.8130	0.7375	0.6270	0.5288	0.8766	0.7166	0.0197
	Precision	0.7890	0.6813	0.4702	0.6247	0.8976	0.6926	0.0264
	Recall	0.8385	0.8038	0.9405	0.4584	0.8566	0.7796	0.0348
Doc2Vec + Logistic regression + CNF	F1 Score	0.7043	0.8940	0.8489	0.9344	0.9049	0.8573	0.0083
	Precision	0.6977	0.9068	0.8194	1.0000	0.9330	0.8714	0.0136
	Recall	0.7111	0.8815	0.8806	0.8768	0.8784	0.8457	0.0057

At this point we can actually stop as these results empirically show that our representation approaches our stated objectives for the ontology in terms of completeness and optimal concept granularity. The additional experiments with the N-gram CNF and the Doc2Vec CNF models are attempts to further improve the overall performance as these methods normally lead to improved performance in message classification tasks with word level lookup models. We find there is little benefit in using concept N-grams beyond the unigram + Bigram CNF model whose performance is only slightly better than the unigram only model. However, the most remarkable results by far are produced when we use the CNF Doc2Vec + logistic regression model. As shown in Table 2, it is the strongest approach both in terms of maximizing overall classification performance and minimizing performance variance across data sets with an overall performance of 0.857 by F1-score versus 0.6133 on the baseline model and more than 1400% reduction in model performance variance.

Generally speaking, using the CNF representation leads to weaker performance on the training data (the flu + common cold + listeria data set). This is a penalty we pay for using a more general representation as the high performance on the training data set in the baseline unigram word level lookup model partly emanates from the classifier learning spurious relationships for instance we find that the word "game" is a strong positive predictor whereas its plural "games" is a strong negative predictor.

This is because of phrases like "I am going to have to bring my flu game" which refers to indulging in sports whilst sick with the flu in homage to a legendary display by Micheal Jordan when he led the Chicago Bulls to victory against Utah Jazz in the 1997 NBA final whilst stricken with the flu. "Flu games" on the other hand, is a reference to a brand of sporting footwear in homage to the same feat. In general terms such an inference is obviously invalid and is necessary overlooked by the CNF representation.

5 Conclusion and Future Work

For the best performing model we employ a distributional approach to arrive at the vectors for use in the classification task. However, if indeed the ontology sufficiently specifies the concepts required to communicate illness then we can justifiably arrive at these vectors via some topological approach such as graph concept similarity measures. We expect this to be a more reliable approach than a distributional measure which generates different vectors for different corpora and is incapable of generating vectors for concepts not encountered in training even when they may be defined in the ontology. Therefore, this approach largely ignores the internal structure of the ontology but is a necessary first step in demonstrating that it reasonably models the relevant domain concepts. In addition the method is incapable of returning the actual diseases mentioned in the discourse since we deliberately exclude them in our concept representations. We will shortly be investigating methods to automatically extract the disease/ailment names in addition to developing methodologies that exploit the ontology's topological structure to derive concept vectors for input to message classification models.

In conclusion, the results offer an indirect, empirical proof of concept for our initial intuitions as stated in Sect. 2 as in the ontology we have defined a group of core concepts and in part of speech enriched padding we generalize over all other words using their part of speech information. In essence we approximate the minimal amount of information required to make a decision about the classification of a given message within the context of disease incidence detection.

References

1. Lee, K., Agrawal, A., Choudary, A.: Real time disease surveillance using twitter data: case study flu and cancer. In: ACM, Chicago, Illinois, USA, pp. 1474–1477 (2013)
2. Google Inc, https://www.google.org/flutrends/about/
3. Paul, M.J., Dredze, M.: Discovering health topics in social media using topic models. PLoS ONE **9**, 8 (2014)
4. Lampos, V., Cristianini, N.: Tracking the flu pandemic by monitoring the social web, pp. 411–416. IEEE, Naregno, Elba island, Italy (2010)
5. Collier, N., Doan, S., Kawazoe, A., Goodwin, R.M., Conway, M., Tateno, Y., et al.: Biocaster: detecting public health rumors with a web-based text mining system. Bioinform. **24**(24), 2940–2941 (2008)
6. Okhmatovskaia, A., Chapman, W., Collier, N., Espino, J., Buckeridge, D.L.: SSO: The Syndromic Surveillance Ontology https://www.bioontology.org/sites/default/files/SSO.pdf
7. Porta, M.: A Dictionary of Epidemiology. Oxford University Press, New York (2008)
8. Smith, B., Ashburner, M., Rosse, C., Bard, J., Bug, W., et al.: The OBO foundry: coordinated evolution of ontologies to support biomedical data integration. Nat. Biotech. **25**, 1251–1255 (2007)
9. Osborne, J.D., Flatow, J., Holko, M., Lin, S.M., Kibbe, W.A., Zhue, L., et al.: Annotating the human genome with disease ontology. BMC Genom. **10**, 1 (2009)
10. Pesquira, C., Ferreira, J.D., Couto, M.F., Silva, M.J.: The epidemiology ontology: an ontology for semantic annotation of epidemiological resources. J. Biomed. Semant. **5**, 4 (2014)

11. Clark, T., Ciccarese, P.N., Goble, C.A.: Micropublications: a semantic model for claims, evidence, arguments and annotations in biomedical communications. J. Biomed. Semant. **5**(1), 1–33 (2014)
12. Elliott, J., Mavergames, C., Becker, L., Meerpohl, J., Thomas, J., Gruen, R., Tovey, D.: Achieving high quality and efficient systematic review through technological innovation. BMJ Rapid Response (2013) http://www.bmj.com/content/346/bmj.f139/rr/625503
13. Smith, B., Fellbaum, C.: Medical Wordnet: A New Methodology for the Construction and Validation of Information Resources for Consumer Health, p. 371. ACM, Geneva (2004)
14. Taylor, A., Marcus, M., Santorini, B.: The Penn Treebank: An Overview. In: Abeille, A. (ed.) Treebanks. Building and Using Parsed Corpora, pp. 5–22. Springer, Netherlands (2003)
15. Derczynski, L., Ritter, A., Clark, S., Bontcheva, K.: Twitter part-of-speech tagging for all: overcoming sparse and noisy data. In: ACL, Hisar, Bulgaria, pp. 198–206 (2013)
16. Cunningham, H., Maynard, D., Bontcheva, K., Tablan, V.: Gate: an architecture for development of robust HLT applications. In: ACL, Philadelphia, USA, pp. 168–175 (2002)
17. Toutanova, K., Manning, C.D.: Enriching the knowledge sources used in a maximum entropy part-of-speech tagger. In: ACL, Hong Kong, pp. 63–70 (2000)
18. Toutanova, K., Klein, D., Manning, C.D., Singer, Y.: Feature-rich part-of-speech tagging with a cyclic dependency network. In: ACM, Edmonton, Canada, pp. 252–259 (2003)
19. Mikolov, T., Chen, K., Corrado, G., Dean, J.: Efficient Estimation Of Word Representations In Vector Space. Google Curran Associates Inc., Arizona, USA (2013)
20. Le, Q., Mikolov, T.: Distributed representations of sentences and documents. In: JMLR Workshop and Conference Proceedings, Beijing, China, pp. 1188–1196 (2014)
21. Rehurek, R., Sojka, P.: Software Framework for Topic Modeling with Large Corpora, pp. 46–50. University of Malta Valetta, Malta (2010)
22. Pedregrosa, F., Varoquaux, G., Gramfort, A., Michel, V., Thirion, B., Grisel, O., et al.: Scikit-learn: machine learning in python. J. Mach. Learn. **12**, 2825–2830 (2011)

Hybrid Methodology Based on Bayesian Optimization and GA-PARSIMONY for Searching Parsimony Models by Combining Hyperparameter Optimization and Feature Selection

Francisco Javier Martinez-de-Pison(✉), Ruben Gonzalez-Sendino, Alvaro Aldama, Javier Ferreiro, and Esteban Fraile

EDMANS Group, University of La Rioja, Logroño, Spain
edmans@dim.unirioja.es
http://www.mineriadatos.com

Abstract. This paper presents a hybrid methodology that combines Bayesian Optimization (BO) with a constrained version of the GA-PARSIMONY method to obtain parsimonious models. The proposal is designed to reduce the computational efforts associated to the use of GA-PARSIMONY alone. The method is initialized with BO to obtain favorable initial model parameters. With these parameters, a constrained GA-PARSIMONY is implemented to generate accurate parsimonious models using feature reduction, data transformation and parsimonious model selection. Finally, a second BO is run again with the selected features. Experiments with Extreme Gradient Boosting Machines (XGBoost) and six UCI databases demonstrate that the hybrid methodology obtains analogous models than the GA-PARSIMONY but with a significant reduction on the execution time in five of the six datasets.

Keywords: GA-PARSIMONY · Bayesian optimization · Hyperparameter optimization · Parsimony models · Genetic algorithms

1 Introduction

Hyperparameter optimization (HO) is extremely important for finding accurate models. Also, feature selection (FS) is useful for seeking the less complex models among solutions with similar accuracy. These parsimonious models are more robust against perturbations or noise, easier to maintain, and besides, they mitigate the effects of the curse of dimensionality.

In the last years, there is an increasing interest in reducing the human efforts in HO and FS because these tasks are time-consuming and quite tedious. Besides, newest learning methods such as deep learning or gradient boosting machines have up to a dozen of tuning parameters (hyper-parameters), which hinder the use of traditional optimization methods like grid or random search. Therefore,

F.J. Martínez de Pisón et al. (Eds.): HAIS 2017, LNAI 10334, pp. 52–62, 2017.
DOI: 10.1007/978-3-319-59650-1_5

companies are demanding new methodologies to automatize these processes, because they prefer to invest their efforts in other critical KDD tasks like data transformation or feature engineering that are harder to automatize [13].

Among the different existing methods to tackle this issue, soft computing (SC) seems to be an effective approach to reduce computational costs [4,7,22,33]. In this context, there is an increasing number of studies reporting SC strategies that combine FS and HO applied to multiple fields [5,8,9,14,15,24,31,32]. New libraries are emerging to perform HO with Bayesian Optimization (BO) like *Hyperopt* [2] in Python, or *mlr* [3] and *rBayesianOptimization* in R. Besides, there exists other tools that are focused on the optimization of more KDD stages such as algorithm selection (AS), data transformation (DT), dimensional reduction (DR), model selection (MS) or feature construction (FC). For example, the *SUMO-Toolbox* [12] from MATLAB adopts different plugins for each of the different KDD stages. They can be optimized with other 'meta' plugins available in the toolbox. Also, the *Auto-WEKA* [29] from *Weka* suite combines MS and HO. Finally, TPOT [17] is a Python library that automatically optimizes machine learning pipelines using genetic programming. These pipelines consist on several KDD tasks as FS, DT, FC or MS among others.

In this context, we proposed the GA-PARSIMONY [23], a Genetic Algorithm (GA) methodology whose main objective is to obtain accurate parsimonious models. It optimizes HO, DT, and FS with a new model selection process based on a double criteria that considers accuracy and complexity in two steps. However, although this methodology has successfully been applied in several practical fields [1,10,30], it might be too computationally expensive when implemented with large and high dimensional databases. Hence, the main objective of this work is to present a new hybrid methodology that combines BO with the GA-PARSIMONY to obtain similar models than GA-PARSIMONY alone but with a reduced computational effort.

The rest of the paper is organized as follows: Sect. 2 presents a brief description of BO, GA-PARSIMONY and the hybrid method. Section 3 describes the experiments performed with the three methods to obtain parsimonious XGBoost models in six UCI datasets. In Sect. 4 analysis of the experiment results are shown. Finally, Sect. 5 presents the conclusions and suggestions for further research.

2 Materials and Methods

2.1 Extreme Gradient Boosting Machines

Nowadays, *eXtreme Gradient Boosting* (XGBoost) [6] is one of the most popular machine learning methods. This powerful method is based on gradient boosting machines (GBM) [11]. GBM use a gradient-descent based algorithm that optimizes a differentiable loss function to create a boosting ensemble of weak prediction models. The main idea is to construct each new additive base-learner to be maximally correlated with the negative gradient of the loss function of the ensemble. However, XGBoost with tree-based learners is computationally more efficient and scalable than GBM. Thus, it incorporates more regularization strategies to reduce over-fitting and control model complexity, such us the limitation of the minimum loss reduction at each tree partition, the sum of instances weight per leaf or the depth of each tree. Also, it incorporates Lasso (L1) and Ridge (L2) penalties, similar to other machine learning methods. Moreover, it integrates "random subspaces" and "random subsampling" parameters to shrink the variance.

However, the high number of model parameters increases the computational efforts of the tuning process. Besides, despite tree-based ensemble methods having good performance with high-dimensional data, the inclusion of irrelevant or noisy features can degrade the accuracy of these models [18]. Therefore, there is an increasing interest in developing new SC methods to efficiently optimize HO and FS and obtain models with good generalization capabilities.

2.2 Bayesian Optimization

Since 2007, *Bayesian optimization* (BO) has become one interesting alternative among other HO classical alternatives like random search or grid search [21]. BO uses Bayesian models based on *Gaussian processes* (GP) to formalize the relationship between model's error/accuracy, y_n, with its parameters by means a sequential design strategy. According to GP, any finite set of N points, where $\{\mathbf{x}_n \in \emptyset\}_{n=1}^{N}$, induces a multivariate Gaussian distribution on $\Re^n$. Then, GP defines a powerful prior distribution on functions $f : \emptyset \rightarrow \Re$ where the nth model performance is obtained from $f(\mathbf{x}_n)$ and the marginals and conditionals are calculated by the marginalization properties of the Gaussian distribution. These properties are determined by a predefined mean function $m\colon \chi \rightarrow \Re$ and a positive-definitive kernel or covariance function $k\colon \chi \times \chi \rightarrow \Re$.

From a practical point of view [27], BO starts with the evaluation of a small number N of models with a random set of parameters $\mathbf{x}_n$ where $y_n \sim \mathcal{N}(f(\mathbf{x}_n, v))$ is the nth measured model performance and v is the variance of functions' noise. Thus, considering that $f(\mathbf{x})$ is obtained from a Gaussian process prior and with the precomputed experiments, a posterior over function $a(\mathbf{x})$ is induced. This function, denoted acquisition function, depends on the model through its predictive mean function $\mu(\mathbf{x}; \{\mathbf{x}_n, y_n\}, \theta)$ and predictive variance function $\sigma^2(\mathbf{x}; \{\mathbf{x}_n, y_n\}, \theta)$. Therefore, next point is evaluated by $\mathbf{x}_{next} = argmax_{\mathbf{x}}\, a(\mathbf{x})$ balancing the search of places with high variance (exploration) and places with low mean (exploitation).

Among the available acquisition functions [26], *GP Upper Confidence Bound* (GP-UCB) has shown a good performance in *hyperparameter tuning* [28]. This acquisition function can be expressed as:

$$a_{LCB} = \mu(\mathbf{x}) - \kappa\sigma(\mathbf{x}), \tag{1}$$

where κ balances exploration and exploitation. Also, *squared exponential kernel,*

$$K_{SE}(\mathbf{x}, \mathbf{x}') = \theta_0\, exp\{\frac{1}{2}r^2(\mathbf{x}, \mathbf{x}')\} \qquad r^2(\mathbf{x}, \mathbf{x}') = \sum_{d=1}^{D}(x_d - x'_d)^2/\theta_d^2, \tag{2}$$

is often a default choice as covariance function for Gaussian process regression.

2.3 GA-PARSIMONY Methodology

GA-PARSIMONY is a SC methodology based on Genetic Algorithms (GA) to automatically obtain precise overall parsimonious models [23]. Basically, this proposal includes HO, FS, and DT in the GA optimization process.

GA-PARSIMONY has a similar flowchart to other classical GA methods with the exception that this one uses a *parsimonious model selection* process (PMS) arranged in two stages. First, best models are sorted by their fitness function (J), consisting of an error or accuracy metric, and next, individuals with similar Js are rearranged based on their complexities. Therefore, models with less complexity are promoted to the top positions at each generation. This choice of less complex solutions, among those with similar accuracy, fosters the generation of robust solutions with better generalization capabilities.

GA-PARSIMONY has successfully been applied to obtain accurate parsimonious models with the most popular machine learning techniques such as Support Vector Regression (SVR), Random Forest (RF) or Artificial Neural Networks (ANNs) in different fields: mechanical design [10], solar radiation forecasting [1], industrial processes [25], and hotel room demand estimation [30]. Also, a preliminary study with XGboost and high dimensional databases has been developed with different complexity metrics [19]. Although GA-PARSIMONY performed well only with HO, experiments demonstrated that using HO, FS, and PMS is a good choice to obtain better parsimonious solutions when the number of model features is used as complexity measurement.

2.4 Hybrid Method Based on Bayesian Optimization and GA-PARSIMONY

Although GA-PARSIMONY is able to generate accurate and parsimonious models, the implementation of this methodology with large and/or high dimensional database can be too computationally expensive even if parallel computing is used. Thus, a hybrid proposal that combines BO and GA-PARSIMONY is presented in this paper to improve the computational performance (Fig. 1). The main idea is to use BO in a first stage with all features to obtain the best model parameters. Next, GA-PARSIMONY with FS and PMS is used for seeking the best features of the parsimonious model with the fixed parameters obtained in the first step. Finally, another BO process is done with the selected features to find the optimal model parameters.

3 Experiments

3.1 Datasets and Validation Process

The hybrid methodology with XGBoost is evaluated against the use alone of BO or GA-PARSIMONY. Experiments are conducted with six UCI datasets (Table 1).

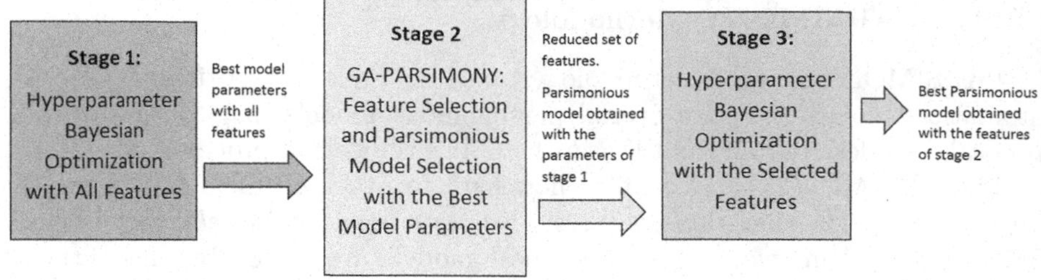

Fig. 1. Hybrid methodology that combines BO and GA-PARSIMONY.

Databases are split into a 80% for validation and a 20% for checking the generalization capability of each model. In particular, the mean of a Root Mean Squared Error ($RMSE$) of a 5 repeated 4-fold CV is performed with the validation dataset ($RMSE_{val}^{mean}$).

3.2 GA-PARSIMONY Settings

The GA optimization is implemented with the following settings. The fitness function selected is $J = RMSE_{val}^{mean}$ while the maximum difference of J to consider similar individuals and promote parsimonious solutions into the re-ranking process is 0.01%. The elitism percentage is set to 25%, the selection method used *random uniform* and crossing is performed via *heuristic blending* [16]. A mutation percentage of 10% is used except for the best two elitists of each generation that are not mutated. The population size is set to $P = 64$ and the maximum number of generations to $G = 100$. However, an early stopping strategy is implemented when the J of the best individual did not decrease more than 0.01% in 10 generations, $G_{early} = 10$.

XGBoost parameters are defined between the following ranges: number of trees, $nrounds = [10,\ 2000]$, maximum depth of a tree, $max\_depth = [2,\ 20]$, minimum sum of instance weight needed in a child, $min\_child\_weight = [1,\ 20]$, *lasso* regularization term on weights, $alpha = [0.0,\ 1.00]$, *ridge* regularization term on weights, $lambda = [0.0,\ 1.00]$, subsample ratio of the training instances, $subsample = [0.60,\ 1.00]$, and subsample ratio of columns when constructing each tree, $colsample\_bytree = [0.80,\ 1.00]$. Random seed is fixed to 1234 and learning rate *eta* to 0.01.

Also, k exponent to transform the dependent variable is used in the following way $y^* = y^k$. In this case, the range set for this parameter is $k = [0.20,\ 1.79]$.

The representation of each individual (i) and generation (g) is a chromosome:

$$\begin{aligned} \lambda_g^i = [&nrounds,\ max\_depth,\ min\_child\_weight,\ alpha, \\ &lambda,\ subsample,\ colsample\_bytree,\ k,\ Q] \end{aligned} \tag{3}$$

where the first seven values are the XGBoost parameters, k is the exponent to transform the dependent variable and Q is a binary-coded array that included the selected features.

3.3 Bayesian Optimization Settings

BO parameter bounds are identical to GA-PARSIMONY settings. The acquisition function selected is the GP-UCB while the covariance function is the squared exponential kernel with $\kappa = 2.576$. The number of initial points is set to 10, and the number of iterations for the optimization process to 50.

3.4 Hybrid Method Settings

The first and third stages of the hybrid method are based on the same BO settings of Sect. 3.3. In the second stage, GA-PARSIMONY perform FS and PMS with the best model parameters obtained in the first stage. Chromosomes at each generation are only defined by the binary-coded array $\lambda_g^i - Q$ because HO is disabled. Except λ_g^i, the rest of GA settings are similar to Sect. 3.2.

All experiments have been implemented in 28-core servers from *Beronia* cluster of the Universidad de La Rioja, and with `R` statistical software [20] and `XGBoost` package [6].

4 Results and Discussion

Table 1 shows the results with six UCI high-dimensional datasets. Among the three methods, GA-PARSIMONY obtains the best $RMSE_{tst}^{mean}$ for all databases but with an important computational effort. Comparing BO with GA-PARSIMONY, a substantial improvement is achieved in *Pol* and *Puma* minimizing $\#FT$ and $RMSE_{tst}^{mean}$. The hybrid methodology generates analogous results than GA-PARSIMONY but with a significant reduction of the elapsed time.

Table 1. Results obtained with the BO, GA-PARSIMONY and the new hybrid proposal. FT stands for the number of features of the best model, $RMSE_{tst}^{mean}$ is the mean testing error and $Time$ the elapsed time in minutes.

Database		*Bayesian Optim.*			*GA-PARSIMONY*				*Hybrid Method*		
Name	# Inst	#FT	Time	$RMSE_{tst}^{mean}$	#Gen	#FT	Time	$RMSE_{tst}^{mean}$	#FT	Time	$RMSE_{tst}^{mean}$
Ailerons	13750	40	295	0.0428	23	13	7949	0.0425	14	4494	0.0425
Bank	8192	32	104	0.0995	35	18	4036	0.0980	20	1636	0.0989
Cpu	8192	21	189	0.0232	20	16	4121	0.0220	16	4373	0.0231
Elevators	16599	18	343	0.0322	39	9	16554	0.0314	12	2799	0.0319
Pol	15000	26	176	0.0476	66	16	13203	0.0400	20	3397	0.0454
Puma	8192	32	209	0.0433	25	4	6168	0.0337	4	3536	0.0332

Figure 2 displays $RMSE_{val}$ and $RMSE_{tst}$ evolution of elitist individuals with GA-PARSIMONY and *Bank* database. Figure 3 shows the same evolution of the second stage of the Hybrid method where GA-PARSIMONY is used without HO. In this second optimization, model parameters are obtained from a previous BO process with all the features.

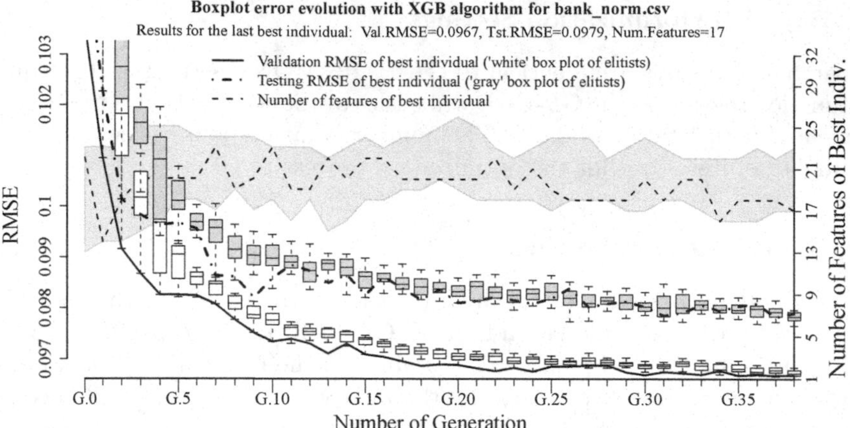

Fig. 2. Evolution of elitist individuals in Bank database using GA-PARSIMONY for HO, FS, DT and PMS. White and gray box-plots represent $RMSE_{val}$ and $RMSE_{tst}$ evolution respectively. The shaded area delimits the maximum and minimum N_{FS}.

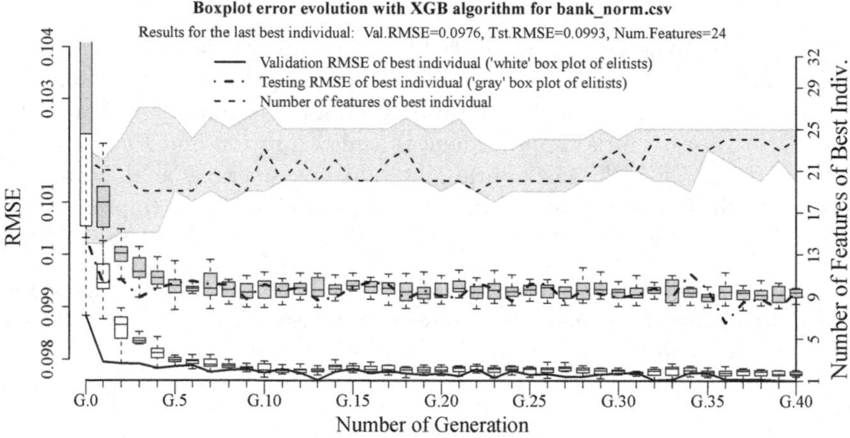

Fig. 3. Evolution of elitist individuals in Bank database using GA-PARSIMONY for FS, DT and PMS (without HO) in the second stage of the Hybrid methodology. White and gray box-plots represent $RMSE_{val}$ and $RMSE_{tst}$ evolution respectively. The shaded area delimits the maximum and minimum N_{FS}.

Table 2 shows *p-values* of a Wilcoxon test of GA-PARSIMONY vs BO and Hybrid proposal. Although, GA-PARSIMONY generates a smaller $RMSE_{tst}^{mean}$ than BO, differences are only statistically significant in *Pol* and *Puma* datasets. However, there is an important reduction of $\#FT$ for all databases, obtaining, as a consequence, parsimonious models with similar or better accuracy.

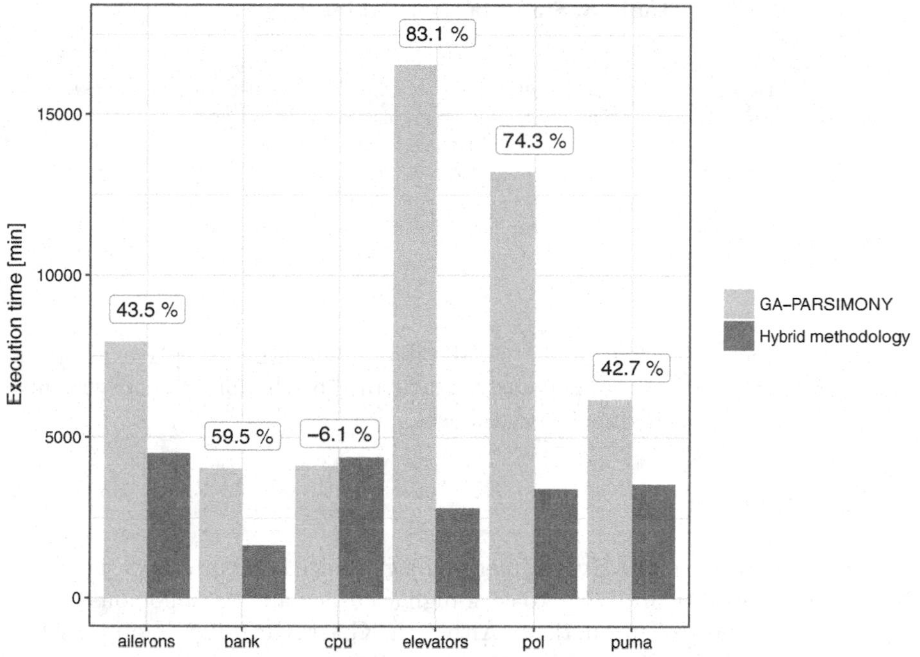

Fig. 4. Execution time between GA-PARSIMONY and the Hybrid methodology.

Table 2. Results of GA-PARSIMONY vs Bayesian Optimization and Hybrid Method

Database	GA-PARSIMONY		Bayesian Optim.			Hybrid Methodology		
Name	$RMSE_{tst}^{mean}$	$RMSE_{tst}^{sd}$	$RMSE_{tst}^{mean}$	$RMSE_{tst}^{sd}$	p-value	$RMSE_{tst}^{mean}$	$RMSE_{tst}^{sd}$	p-value
Ailerons	0.0425	0.000908	0.0428	0.000968	=(0.700)	0.0425	0.000784	=(1.000)
Bank	0.0980	0.001251	0.0995	0.001253	=(0.100)	0.0989	0.001149	=(0.200)
Cpu	0.0220	0.000485	0.0232	0.002806	=(1.000)	0.0231	0.002863	=(0.800)
Elevators	0.0314	0.000709	0.0322	0.000641	=(0.100)	0.0319	0.000679	=(0.400)
Pol	0.0400	0.002797	0.0476	0.002647	+(0.008)	0.0454	0.001483	+(0.030)
Puma	0.0337	0.000420	0.0433	0.001411	+(0.008)	0.0332	0.000648	=(0.200)

With respect to the Hybrid methodology, errors are similar to GA-PARSIMONY except in *Pol* dataset although *p-value* is close to the 95% of confidence level in this dataset.

Stages of Hybrid proposal can be observed in Table 3. In the first step, BO is applied for extracting the best model parameters with all features of the database. Next, in the second stage and with these parameters, FS is performed with GA-PARSIMONY without HO. The *#Gen* is substantially reduced compare to the use of GA-PARSIMONY with FS and HO in five of the six databases. Therefore, the most important reduction in the elapsed time is obtained in this stage. Finally, a second HO is done with the selected features and BO.

Figure 4 shows in boxes the percentage reduction of the execution time achieved with the Hybrid methodology vs GA-PARSIMONY. There is an

Table 3. Stages of the hybrid method

Database	*Stage 1*			*Stage 2*				*Stage 3*		
Name	#FT	Time	$RMSE_{tst}^{mean}$	#Gen	#FT	Time	$RMSE_{tst}^{mean}$	#FT	Time (%)	$RMSE_{tst}^{mean}$
Ailerons	40	295	0.0428	14	14	3926 (43)	0.0425	14	274	0.0425
Bank	32	104	0.0995	13	20	1429 (59)	0.0991	20	103	0.0989
Cpu	21	189	0.0232	26	16	4005 (−6)	0.0231	16	179	0.0231
Elevators	18	343	0.0322	5	12	2123 (83)	0.0319	12	333	0.0319
Pol	26	176	0.0476	17	20	3055 (74)	0.0465	20	167	0.0454
Puma	32	209	0.0433	13	4	3128 (43)	0.0336	4	199	0.0332

important reduction in five of the six databases with the exception of *cpu* in which GA-PARSIMONY stopped early. The hybrid methodology clearly reduces the execution time in the most of databases.

5 Conclusions

This article presents a new Hybrid methodology which combines Bayesian Optimization and GA-PARSIMONY to seek high accuracy and parsimonious models while reducing the execution time. Although, GA-PARSIMONY obtains better models than BO by combining Hyperparameter Optimization (HO), parsimonious model selection (PMS), feature selection (FS), and data transformation (DT), the computational efforts with large and high dimensional databases can be significant. The hybrid proposal uses BO to obtain good initial model parameters previous to the FS, DT and PMS, which are optimized with GA-PARSIMONY without HO. Finally, a second HO is completed with the selected features and BO.

Experiments with six databases demonstrate that the hybrid methodology generates similar parsimonious solutions than the GA-PARSIMONY but with an important reduction of the execution time in five of the six datasets. However, more experiments are needed with additional high dimensional databases to obtain more detailed conclusions.

Acknowledgements. We are greatly indebted to *Banco Santander* for the APPI16/05 fellowship and to the University of La Rioja for the EGI16/19 fellowship. This work used the Beronia cluster (Universidad de La Rioja), which is supported by FEDER-MINECO grant number UNLR-094E-2C-225.

References

1. Antonanzas-Torres, F., Urraca, R., Antonanzas, J., Fernandez-Ceniceros, J., de Pison, F.M.: Generation of daily global solar irradiation with support vector machines for regression. Energy Convers. Manag. **96**, 277–286 (2015)
2. Bergstra, J., Komer, B., Eliasmith, C., Yamins, D., Cox, D.D.: Hyperopt: a python library for model selection and hyperparameter optimization. Comput. Sci. Discov. **8**(1), 014008 (2015)

3. Bischl, B., Lang, M., Kotthoff, L., Schiffner, J., Richter, J., Studerus, E., Casalicchio, G., Jones, Z.M.: MLR: machine learning in r. J. Mach. Learn. Res. **17**(170), 1–5 (2016)
4. Caamaño, P., Bellas, F., Becerra, J.A., Duro, R.J.: Evolutionary algorithm characterization in real parameter optimization problems. Appl. Soft Comput. **13**(4), 1902–1921 (2013)
5. Chen, N., Ribeiro, B., Vieira, A., Duarte, J., Neves, J.C.: A genetic algorithm-based approach to cost-sensitive bankruptcy prediction. Expert Syst. Appl. **38**(10), 12939–12945 (2011)
6. Chen, T., He, T., Benesty, M.: xgboost: extreme gradient boosting (2015). https://github.com/dmlc/xgboost, rpackageversion0.4-3
7. Corchado, E., Wozniak, M., Abraham, A., de Carvalho, A.C.P.L.F., Snásel, V.: Recent trends in intelligent data analysis. Neurocomputing **126**, 1–2 (2014)
8. Dhiman, R., Saini, J.: Priyanka: genetic algorithms tuned expert model for detection of epileptic seizures from EEG signatures. Appl. Soft Comput. **19**, 8–17 (2014)
9. Ding, S.: Spectral and wavelet-based feature selection with particle swarm optimization for hyperspectral classification. J. Softw. **6**(7), 1248–1256 (2011)
10. Fernandez-Ceniceros, J., Sanz-Garcia, A., Antonanzas-Torres, F., de Pison, F.M.: A numerical-informational approach for characterising the ductile behaviour of the t-stub component. part 2: Parsimonious soft-computing-based metamodel. Eng. Struct. **82**, 249–260 (2015)
11. Friedman, J.H.: Greedy function approximation: a gradient boosting machine. Ann. Stat. **29**(5), 1189–1232 (2001)
12. Gorissen, D., Couckuyt, I., Demeester, P., Dhaene, T., Crombecq, K.: A surrogate modeling and adaptive sampling toolbox for computer based design. J. Mach. Learn. Res. **11**, 2051–2055 (2010)
13. Hashem, I.A., Yaqoob, I., Anuar, N.B., Mokhtar, S., Gani, A., Ullah Khan, S.: The rise of big data on cloud computing: review and open research issues. Inf. Syst. **47**, 98–115 (2015)
14. Huang, C.L., Dun, J.F.: A distributed PSO-SVM hybrid system with feature selection and parameter optimization. Appl. Soft Comput. **8**(4), 1381–1391 (2008)
15. Huang, C.J., Chen, Y.J., Chen, H.M., Jian, J.J., Tseng, S.C., Yang, Y.J., Hsu, P.A.: Intelligent feature extraction and classification of anuran vocalizations. Appl. Soft Comput. **19**, 1–7 (2014)
16. Michalewicz, Z., Janikow, C.Z.: Handling constraints in genetic algorithms. In: ICGA, pp. 151–157 (1991)
17. Olson, R.S., Bartley, N., Urbanowicz, R.J., Moore, J.H.: Evaluation of a tree-based pipeline optimization tool for automating data science. In: Proceedings of the Genetic and Evolutionary Computation Conference 2016, GECCO 2016, NY, USA, pp. 485–492. ACM, New York (2016)
18. Perner, P.: Improving the accuracy of decision tree induction by feature preselection. Appl. Artif. Intell. **15**(8), 747–760 (2001)
19. Martinez-de Pison, F.J., Fraile-Garcia, E., Ferreiro-Cabello, J., Gonzalez, R., Pernia, A.: Searching parsimonious solutions with GA-PARSIMONY and XGBoost in high-dimensional databases, pp. 201–210. Springer International Publishing, Cham (2017)
20. Core Team, R.: R: A Language and Environment for Statistical Computing. R Foundation for Statistical Computing, Vienna, Austria (2013)
21. Rasmussen, C.E., Williams, C.K.I.: Gaussian Processes for Machine Learning (Adaptive Computation and Machine Learning). The MIT Press, Cambridge (2005)

22. Reif, M., Shafait, F., Dengel, A.: Meta-learning for evolutionary parameter optimization of classifiers. Mach. Learn. **87**(3), 357–380 (2012)
23. Sanz-Garcia, A., Fernandez-Ceniceros, J., Antonanzas-Torres, F., Pernia-Espinoza, A., Martinez-de Pison, F.J.: GA-PARSIMONY: a GA-SVR approach with feature selection and parameter optimization to obtain parsimonious solutions for predicting temperature settings in a continuous annealing furnace. Appl. Soft Comput. **35**, 13–28 (2015)
24. Sanz-Garcia, A., Fernández-Ceniceros, J., Fernández-Martínez, R., Martínez-De-Pisón, F.J.: Methodology based on genetic optimisation to develop overall parsimony models for predicting temperature settings on annealing furnace. Ironmak. Steelmak. **41**(2), 87–98 (2014)
25. Sanz-García, A., Fernández-Ceniceros, J., Antoñanzas-Torres, F., Martínez-de Pisón, F.J.: Parsimonious support vector machines modelling for set points in industrial processes based on genetic algorithm optimization. In: International Joint Conference SOCO13-CISIS13-ICEUTE13, Advances in Intelligent Systems and Computing, vol. 239, pp. 1–10. Springer International Publishing, Heidelberg (2014)
26. Shahriari, B., Swersky, K., Wang, Z., Adams, R.P., de Freitas, N.: Taking the human out of the loop: a review of bayesian optimization. Technical report, Universities of Harvard, Oxford, Toronto, and Google DeepMind (2015)
27. Snoek, J., Larochelle, H., Adams, R.P.: Practical bayesian optimization of machine learning algorithms. In: Pereira, F., Burges, C.J.C., Bottou, L., Weinberger, K.Q. (eds.) Advances in Neural Information Processing Systems 25, pp. 2951–2959. Curran Associates Inc., Red Hook (2012)
28. Srinivas, N., Krause, A., Kakade, S.M., Seeger, M.W.: Gaussian process bandits without regret: an experimental design approach (2009). CoRR arXiv:abs/0912.3995
29. Thornton, C., Hutter, F., Hoos, H.H., Leyton-Brown, K.: Auto-weka: combined selection and hyperparameter optimization of classification algorithms. In: Proceedings of the 19th ACM SIGKDD International Conference on Knowledge Discovery and Data Mining, KDD 2013, NY, USA. ACM, New York (2013)
30. Urraca, R., Sanz-Garcia, A., Fernandez-Ceniceros, J., Sodupe-Ortega, E., Martinez-de-Pison, F.J.: Improving hotel room demand forecasting with a hybrid GA-SVR methodology based on skewed data transformation, feature selection and parsimony tuning. In: Onieva, E., Santos, I., Osaba, E., Quintián, H., Corchado, E. (eds.) HAIS 2015. LNCS (LNAI), vol. 9121, pp. 632–643. Springer, Cham (2015). doi:10.1007/978-3-319-19644-2_52
31. Vieira, S.M., Mendonza, L.F., Farinha, G.J., Sousa, J.M.: Modified binary PSO for feature selection using SVM applied to mortality prediction of septic patients. Appl. Softw. Comput. **13**(8), 3494–3504 (2013)
32. Winkler, S.M., Affenzeller, M., Kronberger, G., Kommenda, M., Wagner, S., Jacak, W., Stekel, H.: Analysis of selected evolutionary algorithms in feature selection and parameter optimization for data based tumor marker modeling. In: Moreno-Díaz, R., Pichler, F., Quesada-Arencibia, A. (eds.) EUROCAST 2011. LNCS, vol. 6927, pp. 335–342. Springer, Heidelberg (2012). doi:10.1007/978-3-642-27549-4_43
33. Xue, B., Zhang, M., Browne, W.N.: Particle swarm optimisation for feature selection in classification: novel initialisation and updating mechanisms. Appl. Soft Comput. **18**, 261–276 (2014)

Concept Discovery in Graph Databases
A Case Study with Neo4j

Furkan Goz and Alev Mutlu(✉)

Department of Computer Engineering, Kocaeli University, Kocaeli, Turkey
{furkan.goz,alev.mutlu}@kocaeli.edu.tr

Abstract. Concept discovery is one of the most commonly addressed tasks of multi-relational data mining and is concerned with inducing logical definitions of a relation in terms of other relations provided. The problem has long been studied from Inductive Logic Programming and graph-oriented perspectives. In this study, we investigate the problem from graph databases perspective and propose a pathfinding-based method for concept discovery in graph databases. More specifically, we introduce a method that employs Neo4j graph database technology to store data and find the concept descriptors that define the target relation and implements several techniques to further improve the post processing steps of concept discovery process. The experimental results show that the proposed method is superior to state-of-the art concept discovery systems in terms of rule induction time, discovers shorter concept descriptors with high coverage and F1 score, and scales well.

Keywords: Concept discovery · Path finding · Graph database · Neo4j

1 Introduction

Concept discovery is one of the most commonly addressed problems of multi relational data mining. It is concerned with inducing definitions of a relation, called *target relation*, in terms of other relations provided, called *background knowledge*. Given a kinship dataset consisting of relations such as *mother/2*, *husband/2*, and *daughter/2* and *sister/2*, a typical concept discovery system will induce concept descriptors like *mother(A,B):-husband(C,A), daughter(B,C)* and *mother(A,B):-daughter(C,A), sister(C,B)*.

The problem has extensively been studied from Inductive Logic Programming (ILP) and graph-centric perspectives and several methods have been proposed with applications in various domains. In ILP-based approaches data is represented within the first order logic framework and logical operations are utilized to discover valid concept descriptors. In graph-based approaches, data is represented as a graph and methods that fall into this group seek for frequently appearing substructures or paths that contain certain nodes. The main limitations of ILP-based systems include scalability issues [1,2] and the so called local-plateau problem [3]. Graph-based approaches suffer from computationally expensive problems such as substructure isomorphism [4].

F.J. Martínez de Pisón et al. (Eds.): HAIS 2017, LNAI 10334, pp. 63–74, 2017.
DOI: 10.1007/978-3-319-59650-1_6

Recently, graph databases are gathering great interest [5] due to the need of storing and managing graph-like data such as social networks, information-flow networks, and biological networks [6] and are having applications in various domains [7]. In this study, we focus on the concept discovery problem from graph databases perspective and propose a pathfinding method. To this aim, we employ Neo4j as the database engine and implement all the concept discovery and evaluation processes through the functionality provided by Neo4j. Although, the current implementation is limited with working on unary and binary relations, we also provide a road map to handle n-ary relations in last section of this paper. In this study, along with the method we also propose a number of mechanisms and implementation details to further improve the running time of the concept discovery and concept evaluation steps. The method presented in this paper distinguishes from state-of-the-art methods, such as [8,9], as it solely depends on functionalities provided by graph databases, avoids target instance ordering problem and does not require negative target instances.

In order to evaluate the performance and the scalability of the proposed method, a set of experiments is conducted on datasets that belong to different learning problems. The experimental results show that the proposed method is compatible to state-of-the-art methods by means of accuracy, and superior by means of running time. The experimental results also show that the proposed method scales well with the length of the concept descriptors.

The rest of this paper is organized as follows. In Sect. 2, we introduce the concept discovery problem, how graph pathfinding approaches handle it, and its relation to graph databases. In Sect. 3, we introduce the proposed method and introduce several strategies to further improve running of the proposed method. In Sect. 4, we report and discuss the experimental results. In Sect. 5, we conclude the paper and provide future research directions.

2 Background

2.1 Concept Discovery

Concept discovery is concerned with inducing logical definitions of a relation, called *target relation*, in terms of other relations provided, called *background knowledge*. It is one the most commonly addressed tasks of multi-relation data mining [10] and has extensively been studied by Inductive Logic Programming (ILP) community [11]. In ILP-based approaches data is represented within first-order logic framework and logic-based approaches are utilized to discover concept descriptors.

Another direction of research in concept discovery is based on graphs. In graph-based approaches, relational data is represented as a graph and graph algorithms are used to discover and evaluate concept descriptors. In graph-based concept discovery two distinct approaches, namely substructure- and pathfinding-based, are followed. The substructure-based concept discovery methods assume that frequently appearing substructures that involve the target relation are concept descriptors [12,13], hence substructure-based systems look for such patterns in graphs. The pathfinding-based concept discovery methods focus on paths, and assume that finite length paths that connect arguments of the target instances are concept descriptors [3,14].

Richards' and Mooney's work [3] is one of the earliest works on graph-pathfinding concept discovery. In this study, a positive target instance, p/n, is chosen and a graph with n disconnected nodes, each representing an argument of p, is created. Each node is expanded by adding vertices that are related to it until a path is formed between any two arguments of the target relation. Generalized form of a such path is assumed to be candidate concept descriptors.

[15] extends [3] by introducing mode declarations and saturated bottom clauses into graph-based concept discovery process. By means of mode declarations generation of invalid concept descriptors is avoided and the bottom clause bounds the search space.

In [14] a graph pathfinding method called RPBL is presented. RPBL performs depth-limited search on a graph called Structured Instance Space (SIS). In SIS, vertices represent facts and edges connect vertices that have an argument value in common. RPBL works only on unary and binary relations and basically searches for paths that connect a node that represents first argument of a target relation to a node that represents the second argument of the target relation. The concept descriptors are evaluated based on their F1-scores. [16] extends RPBL to discover recursive concept descriptors.

[8] is a graph pathfinding method that stores the data in Neo4j database and benefits from graph traversal algorithms of Neo4j to find paths that connect arguments of the target instances. The method selects a positive target instance, and extends it with one literal at a time. After each expansion, support and confidence of the partial concept descriptors are calculated and those that do not qualify the minimum values are pruned. The related literals are extracted from graph database using the Neo4j's traversal algorithms but the support and confidence are calculated by executing SQL queries on a relational database. [9] extends [8] to handle n-ary relations.

The work proposed in this paper is similar to the ones described above as it is a graph pathfinding method. It distinguishes from [15] as it does not require mode declarations, from [8,9] as it does not employ graph databases just to guide the search but also to evaluate the candidate concept descriptors.

2.2 Graph Databases

Graph databases are mediums where data is stored as graph structures and manipulated by means of graph oriented operations [6]. Graph databases are especially useful when the structure of the data is of more interest than the data itself. Such database systems provide powerful querying mechanisms that can be expressed by graph operations such as path traversals, connectivity and subgraph matching. Graph databases have gained interested in several studies that deal with linked data analysis [17–19].

As the concept discovery problem can be expressed as a connectivity problem and graph databases provide powerful mechanisms for such operations, graph databases are promising systems to effectively solve such problems.

In this study, we employ Neo4j as the data storage and processing engine. It is an open-source system that provides native graph storage and processing mechanisms with an active user and support community [20].

3 The Proposed Method

In this paper, we propose a pathfinding concept discovery method for graph databases. Input to the system is a graph database, minimum support and confidence values, maximum concept descriptor length and the relation whose definition should be learned. Throughout this section we introduce the method based on the graph database instance given in Fig. 1. Although the working dataset is self-explanatory, nodes represent persons and edges represent the relation among them. Direction of edge matters and indicates that starting node of the edge is related to the ending node by means of the edge label, i.e. the edge *son** depicted in Fig. 1 indicates that *arthur* is *son* of *penelope*.

The proposed method consists of two main steps: graph database construction and concept descriptor extraction and evaluation.

- **Graph Construction:** Datasets are usually available either in relation model or as Prolog clauses, hence such a transformation is required. Based on our observation, unary relations generally define a property of an entity. Such relations are represented as a vertex named after the argument name and a self-loop labeled after the relation name. Binary relations generally indicate a relationship named after the relation name and that hold between its arguments. Such relations are represented as two vertices and a directed edge connecting them. Naming is similar to the representation of unary relations. Although not implemented in this study, our observation on various datasets shows that n-ary relation generally keep information about two entities and certain properties that hold between them. Enhancing edges that connect entities of a relation with bundled properties is one possible way to represent such relations. While such transformations may not always be valid, for the datasets used in the experiments we followed such a transformation.
- **Candidate Concept Descriptor Extraction and Evaluation:** Candidate concept description and extraction step involves extracting all paths of length 2 to the *max length* whose starting node is the one that represents the first argument of a randomly picked target instance. Next, these paths are generalized by replacing constants with variables. Neo4j provides mechanisms to traverse the graph either in depth- or in breadth-first search. Although both algorithms have the same computational and space complexities [21], BFS is preferred over DFS when the solution is expected to be close to the root. As in concept discovery one is generally interested in enumerating short length paths, we employed DFS traversal of Neo4j. In Table 1 we list some paths and their generalized version for the target instance $son(colin, victoria)$.

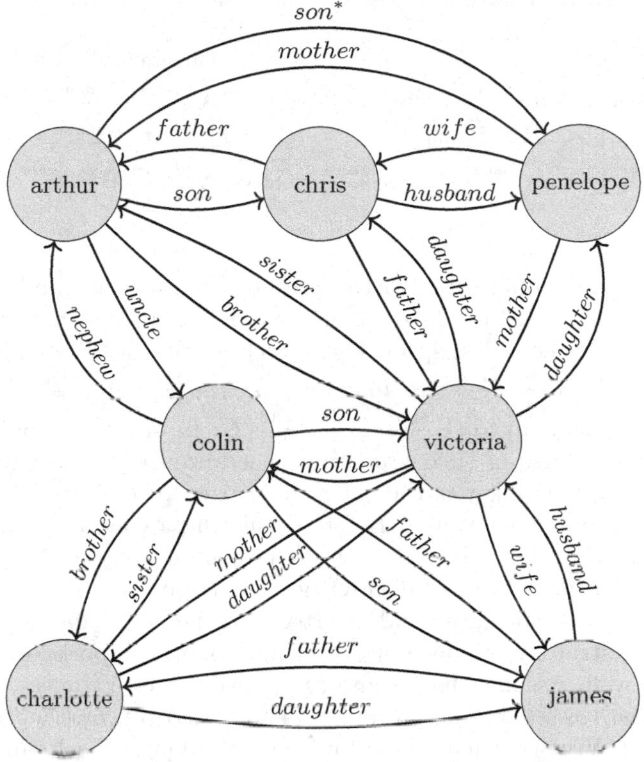

Fig. 1. Kinship graph database instance

Evaluation of concept descriptors is based on their support and confidence values. Support of a concept descriptor is calculated by dividing its support set size to the total number of target instances, where support set refers to the target instances it explains. Confidence of a concept descriptor is calculated by dividing its support set size to the size of its coverage set, where coverage set is the set of instances the concept descriptor explains. Given a start node and a path, Neo4j provides traversal mechanisms to find yielding end nodes. For each candidate concept descriptor and target instance, we set the node that represents the first argument of the target instance as the start node of the concept descriptor as the path and discover the yielding end nodes. If the yielding node is the second argument of the target relation, then that target instance is added to the support set of the candidate concept descriptor, otherwise we check if the start node and the end node pair is a valid background instance and if so we add this fact to the confidence set of the candidate concept descriptor.

Finally F1 score of all candidate concept descriptors whose support and confidence satisfy the minimum values is calculated. Concept descriptors with highest F1 score constitute the solution set.

Table 1. Sample paths and their generalized forms

Path	Generalized path
colin $\xrightarrow{\text{brother}}$ charlotte $\xrightarrow{\text{daughter}}$ victoria	A $\xrightarrow{\text{brother}}$ B $\xrightarrow{\text{daughter}}$ C
colin $\xrightarrow{\text{son}}$ charlotte $\xleftarrow{\text{daughter}}$ victoria	A $\xrightarrow{\text{son}}$ B $\xleftarrow{\text{daughter}}$ C
colin $\xrightarrow{\text{brother}}$ charlotte $\xrightarrow{\text{daughter}}$ james $\xleftarrow{\text{wife}}$ victoria	A $\xrightarrow{\text{brother}}$ B $\xrightarrow{\text{daughter}}$ C $\xleftarrow{\text{wife}}$ D

To improve the running time of the proposed method we implemented two strategies. As indicated in [22], distinct concept descriptors may map to the same generalized concept descriptor. One such example for the running example is: $arthur \xrightarrow{\text{son}} chris \xrightarrow{\text{husband}} penelope$ and $colin \xrightarrow{\text{son}} james \xrightarrow{\text{husband}} victoria$, both of these paths map to $A \xrightarrow{\text{son}} B \xrightarrow{\text{husband}} C$. In order to avoid evaluating support and confidence of such repeating generalized concept descriptors, we keep a hash table where key is the generalized concept descriptor and value is its support and confidence values. Before evaluating a concept descriptor, first it is searched in the hash table. If the search finds an entry for the generalized concept descriptor no action is taken. Otherwise, support and confidence of the concept descriptor is calculated and inserted into the hash table.

The second strategy is concerned with improving support and confidence evaluation, as well. Assume that t_1 and t_2 are two target instances, all paths of t_1 are already processed and no path of t_2 is processed yet. Further assume that c_2 is a path of t_2. When evaluating c_2, if it is not found in the hash table we do not check if the generalized form of c_2 holds for t_1, because if it were so generalized version of c_2 would already be in the hash table. Considering the running example, this situation can be illustrated as follows. All paths of $son(colin, victoria)$ are processed. While processing path $arthur \xrightarrow{\text{uncle}} colin \xrightarrow{\text{son}} victoria \xrightarrow{\text{daughter}} penelope$ that holds for $son(arthur, penelope)$ we do not check if it holds for $son(colin, victoria)$. If it was valid for $son(colin, victoria)$ it would already be in the hash table. Also Fig. 1 shows that there is not such path, by means of edge labels, that connect *arthur* to *penelope*.

4 Experiments

To evaluate the performance of the proposed method, we performed several experiments on datasets that belong to different types of learning problems. In this section, we firstly introduce the datasets used in the experiments and the experimental setting, and later present and discuss the experimental results.

4.1 Datasets and Experimental Setting

Table 2 lists the datasets used in the experiments and the experimental settings. The second column indicates number of relations in the dataset, the third column indicates the number of instances. The last two columns list the minimum

Table 2. Datasets and the experimental setting

Dataset	# Relations	# Instances	Min. Supp.	Min. Conf.
Dunur	9	224	0.2	0.3
Eastbound	12	196	0.1	0.6
Elti	9	224	0.3	0.7
Family	12	744	0.1	0.7
Same generation	2	408	0.3	0.6

support and confidence values concept descriptors should satisfy to be considered as valid.

Eastbound [23] is relational dataset that stores information about trains that either travel east or west. The problem is to induce concept descriptors that define trains that travel east. Elti [24] is a real life dataset that contains kinship relations. In Turkish two females are called elti if they are married to two male siblings. Family dataset [3] contains facts that belong to several family relations. Dunur [24] is an extended version of the Family dataset with a newly added relation called *dunur*. Dunur is a Turkish family relation and two people are called so if they are mother/father-in-law of a couple. Same Generation [24] is yet another kinship dataset which stores information about people that are of the same generation and their parents.

Experiments on Dunur and Eastbound are conducted to observe the performance of the method on datasets that contain transitive relations and facts indirectly related to the target instances. Elti dataset is highly connected and has been used in evaluation of several studies [8,22,25]. Family dataset is considered as a benchmark and has been used in evaluation of several concept discovery systems [3,8,14]. The Same Generation dataset is used to evaluate the performance of the system on the discovery of recursive concept descriptors. The support and confidence values and maximum rule length values are retrieved from [14,24]. The experiments are conducted on machine with Intel Core 2 Quad 2.50 GHz CPU and 4 GB RAM.

4.2 Experimental Results

The proposed method consists of two main steps: (i) graph construction and (ii) concept rule extraction and evaluation. In Table 3 we list the number of nodes, edges and graph construction time for each dataset.

The second step of the method consists of extracting all paths that connect arguments of the target instances, generalizing those paths, calculating their support and confidence values and the F1-score [24]. F1-score is an evaluation metric hypothesis' accuracy and is calculated as $(B^2+1) \times confidence \times support/(support + confidence)$, where B is a user supplied parameter that determines the effect of support and confidence on the overall score. The best

Table 3. Graph properties and graph construction time

Dataset	# Nodes	# Edges	Graph construction time (sec.)
Dunur	24	128	5.60
Eastbound	55	183	6.25
Elti	47	224	6.51
Family	24	112	5.41
Same generation	47	408	5.93

Table 4. Running time and coverage

Dataset	Target R.	C.D. Len.	# C.D.	F1 S.	Coverage	Time (sec.)
Dunur	dunur	3	4	0.53	%100	0.230
Eastbound	eastbound	3	2	1	%100	0.263
Elti	elti	3	8	1	%100	0.243
Same Generation	sg	3	1	1	%100	7.287
Family	aunt	2	2	1	%100	0.177
	brother	2	5	1	%100	0.208
	daughter	2	2	1	%100	0.191
	husband	2	10	0.57	%100	0.201
	father	2	2	1	%100	0.193
	mother	2	2	1	%100	0.196
	nephew	2	2	1	%100	0.194
	niece	2	2	1	%100	0.180
	sister	2	5	1	%100	0.218
	son	2	2	1	%100	0.204
	uncle	2	2	1	%100	0.176
	wife	2	10	0.57	%100	0.192

value of F1-score is 1 and the worst is 0. In the experiments we set the value of B to 1, hence support and confidence have equal weights on the overall score.

In Table 4, we report running time of this step, average of 5 executions, the length and the number of concept descriptors. The F1 S. column lists the lowest F1 score of the concept descriptors that qualify minimum support and minimum confidence values. As the experimental results show, other than the Same Generation data set, candidate concept extraction and evaluation time is well below 1 s and the induced concept descriptors cover all of the target instances. Except for two target relations, F1-score is 1 which implies both precision and recall of the induced concept descriptors are 1. In Table 4, we report the coverage of the solution set, which means that an individual concept descriptor may not achieves full coverage but the solution set covers all of the target instances. As an example, for the Husband relation, the proposed method discovers 10 concept descriptors, 5 have F1-score 0.75 and the remaining 5 have F1-score 0.57. Concept descriptors with F1 score 0.75 defines husbands that either have a son or a daughter or both. The concept descriptors with F1 score 0.57 models the remaining 4 husbands, who do not have a child. Hence no individual concept descriptor covers all of the target instances, but the solution set covers all of the target instances. The same situation holds for the Wife and Dunur relations.

When compared to state-of-the art graph based concept discovery systems, the proposed method is compatible with [16] by means of running time and achieved F1-score, 0.191 s vs. 0.027 s and 0.93 vs. 0.996, respectively, for the Family dataset. Also compared to the same system, the proposed method discovers shorter concept descriptors, i.e. 2 vs. 5.5 on the average for the Family dataset. This is important, as shorter concept descriptors are easier to interpret and longer concept descriptors tend to be overly specific. When compared to [26], the proposed method has shorter running time, 0.191 s vs 1.39 s for the family dataset, and discovers less number of concept of equal length descriptors with the same coverage ratio. Similar discussion also holds for [8]. Table 5 reports these comparisons, P.M. column reports results for the proposed method.

Table 5. Comparison to other systems

Dataset	Elti				Family				Same Gen.			
Metric\System	P.M	[16]	[26]	[8]	P.M	[16]	[26]	[8]	P.M	[16]	[26]	[8]
Running time (sec.)	0.243	NA	2	4	0.191	0.027	1.23	NA	7.287	NA	NA	24
Coverage	%100	NA	%100	%100	%100	NA	%100	%99	%100	NA	NA	%90
F1-Score	1	NA	1	1	0.93	0.99	NA	NA	1	NA	NA	NA

To analyze the scalability of the proposed method, we conducted experiments to observe how running time of the proposed method changes as the length of concept descriptors increase. To this aim, we performed experiments for the father and brother relations for concept descriptors of size from 2 to 9. Figure 2 demonstrates running time of the system with respect to concept descriptor length. As the plot shows, there is a sharp increase in running time for concept descriptors of length larger than 5. Indeed this sharp increase in the running time is due to the sharp increase in the size of the search space. For example, for the father relation, there are 392 paths of length 3 to be evaluated, while there are 142592 and 241920 paths to be evaluated for concept descriptors, respectively, of length 8 and 9. When the running time is divided to the number of paths we get a constant quotient around 0.0002 which indicates that the complexity of the proposed method is linear to the number of paths that connect arguments of the target instances.

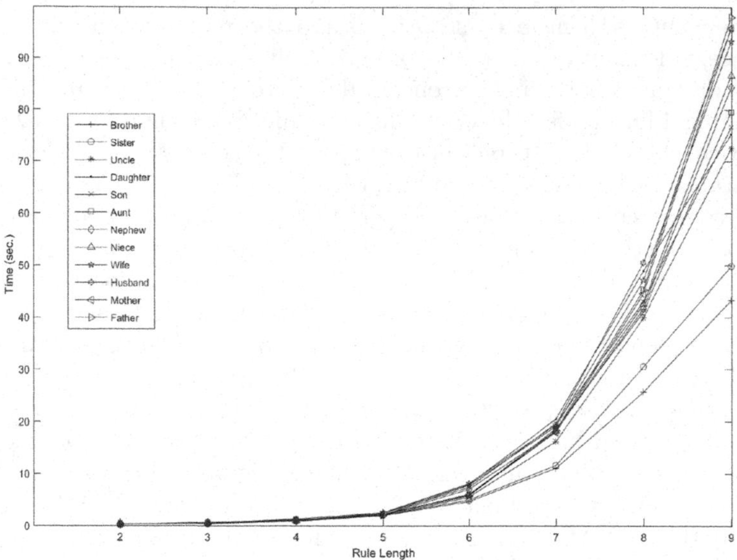

Fig. 2. Scalability: Concept Descriptor Length vs Time

5 Conclusion

In this paper we investigated the concept discovery problem from graph database perspective and introduced a pathfinding method for concept discovery.

The proposed method consists of two main steps: transformation of dataset into a graph database and concept descriptor extraction and evaluation from graph database. The first step is important as most datasets are available either in relational or Prolog format. Although may not be valid for every dataset, we proposed a simple but yet effective methodology to transform relational data to a graph model. To find the concept descriptors, we extract all paths of predefined length that connect arguments of a target instances. Then these paths are generalized and evaluated based on their support and confidence values. Generalized paths that have support and confidence values higher than the thresholds are assumed to be valid concept descriptors. In this study we also implement two hashing based techniques to further improve running time of the proposed method.

The proposed method distinguishes from state-of-the-art methods as all processing is performed by functionalities provided by graph databases. It avoids target instance ordering problem as the evaluation of the concept descriptors are based on their support and confidence rather than covering.

Experimental results show that the proposed method is successful in discovering concept descriptors for datasets that belong to different learning problems. When compared to the state-of-the-art methods it discovers shorter concept descriptors, which makes them more easily interpretable, with comparable coverage, F1 score values and running time. Moreover, the experimental results show that the proposed method scales well with respect to the number of candidate concept descriptors.

Future work includes research problems such as analysis of the mapping procedure proposed for n-ary relations and applicability of the proposed work on datasets that contain attributes from continues domain.

References

1. Fonseca, N.A., Srinivasan, A., Silva, F.M.A., Camacho, R.: Parallel ILP for distributed-memory architectures. Mach. Learn. **74**(3), 257–279 (2009)
2. Rocha, R., Fonseca, N., Costa, V.S.: On applying tabling to inductive logic programming. In: Gama, J., Camacho, R., Brazdil, P.B., Jorge, A.M., Torgo, L. (eds.) ECML 2005. LNCS (LNAI), vol. 3720, pp. 707–714. Springer, Heidelberg (2005). doi:10.1007/11564096_72
3. Richards, B.L., Mooney, R.J.: Learning relations by pathfinding. In: Proceedings of the 10th National Conference on Artificial Intelligence, San Jose, CA, 12–16 July 1992, pp. 50–55 (1992)
4. Cook, D.J., Holder, L.B., Djoko, S.: Knowledge discovery from structural data. J. Intell. Inf. Syst. **5**(3), 229–248 (1995)
5. DB-Engines: Trend of graph dbms popularity. http://db-engines.com/en/ranking_trend/graph+dbms. Accessed 03 Feb 2017
6. Angles, R., Gutiérrez, C.: Survey of graph database models. ACM Comput. Surv. **40**(1) (2008)
7. Miller, J.J.: Graph database applications and concepts with neo4j. In: Proceedings of the Southern Association for Information Systems Conference, Atlanta, GA, USA, vol. 2324 (2013)
8. Abay, N.C., Mutlu, A., Karagoz, P.: A path-finding based method for concept discovery in graphs. In: 6th International Conference on Information, Intelligence, Systems and Applications, IISA 2015, Corfu, Greece, 6–8 July, 2015, pp. 1–6 (2015)
9. Abay, N.C., Mutlu, A., Karagoz, P.: A graph-based concept discovery method for n-ary relations. In: Madria, S., Hara, T. (eds.) DaWaK 2015. LNCS, vol. 9263, pp. 391–402. Springer, Cham (2015). doi:10.1007/978-3-319-22729-0_30
10. Dzeroski, S.: Multi-relational data mining: an introduction. SIGKDD Explor. **5**(1), 1–16 (2003)
11. Muggleton, S., Raedt, L.D., Poole, D., Bratko, I., Flach, P.A., Inoue, K., Srinivasan, A.: ILP turns 20 - biography and future challenges. Mach. Learn. **86**(1), 3–23 (2012)
12. Ketkar, N.S., Holder, L.B., Cook, D.J.: Subdue: compression-based frequent pattern discovery in graph data. In: Proceedings of the 1st International Workshop on Open Source Data Mining: Frequent Pattern Mining Implementations, pp. 71–76. ACM (2005)
13. Matsuda, T., Motoda, H., Washio, T.: Graph-based induction and its applications. Adv. Eng. Inf. **16**(2), 135–143 (2002)
14. Gao, Z., Zhang, Z., Huang, Z.: Learning relations by path finding and simultaneous covering. In: CSIE 2009, 2009 WRI World Congress on Computer Science and Information Engineering, March 31–April 2, 2009, Los Angeles, California, USA, vol. 7, pp. 539–543 (2009)

15. Ong, I.M., Castro Dutra, I., Page, D., Costa, V.S.: Mode directed path finding. In: Gama, J., Camacho, R., Brazdil, P.B., Jorge, A.M., Torgo, L. (eds.) ECML 2005. LNCS (LNAI), vol. 3720, pp. 673–681. Springer, Heidelberg (2005). doi:10.1007/11564096_68
16. Gao, Z., Zhang, Z., Huang, Z.: Extensions to the relational paths based learning approach RPBL. In: First Asian Conference on Intelligent Information and Database Systems, ACIIDS 2009, Dong hoi, Quang binh, Vietnam, 1–3 April, 2009, pp. 214–219 (2009)
17. Cattuto, C., Quaggiotto, M., Panisson, A., Averbuch, A.: Time-varying social networks in a graph database: a Neo4j use case. In: First International Workshop on Graph Data Management Experiences and Systems, GRADES 2013, co-loated with SIGMOD/PODS 2013, New York, NY, USA, 24 June, 2013, p. 11 (2013)
18. Drakopoulos, G., Kanavos, A., Makris, C., Megalooikonomou, V.: On converting community detection algorithms for fuzzy graphs in neo4j. In: CoRR (2016). arXiv:abs/1608.02235
19. Lee, H., Kwon, J.: Efficient recommender system based on graph data for multimedia application. Int. J. Multimed. Ubiquitous Eng. **8**(4) (2013)
20. Neo4j: the worlds leading graph database. https://neo4j.com. Accessed 03 Feb 2017
21. Jiang, B.: Traversing graphs in a paging environment, BFS or DFS? Inf. Process. Lett. **37**(3), 143–147 (1991)
22. Mutlu, A., Senkul, P., Kavurucu, Y.: Improving the scalability of ilp-based multi-relational concept discovery system through parallelization. Knowl. Based Syst. **27**, 352–368 (2012)
23. Larson, J., Michalski, R.S.: Inductive inference of VL decision rules. SIGART Newsl. **63**, 38–44 (1977)
24. Kavurucu, Y., Senkul, P., Toroslu, I.H.: Ilp-based concept discovery in multi-relational data mining. Expert Syst. Appl. **36**(9), 11418–11428 (2009)
25. Kavurucu, Y., Senkul, P., Toroslu, I.H.: Concept discovery on relational databases: new techniques for search space pruning and rule quality improvement. Knowl. Based Syst. **23**(8), 743–756 (2010)
26. Peker, N., Mutlu, A.: A graph-path counting approach for learning head output connected relations. In: Nguyen, N.-T., Manolopoulos, Y., Iliadis, L., Trawiński, B. (eds.) ICCCI 2016. LNCS (LNAI), vol. 9876, pp. 387–396. Springer, Cham (2016). doi:10.1007/978-3-319-45246-3_37

Leveraging Distributed Representations of Elements in Triples for Predicate Linking

Natthawut Kertkeidkachorn[1(✉)] and Ryutaro Ichise[1,2,3]

[1] SOKENDAI (The Graduate University for Advanced Studies), Tokyo, Japan
[2] National Institute of Informatics, Tokyo, Japan
{natthawut,ichise}@nii.ac.jp
[3] National Institute of Advanced Industrial Science and Technology, Tokyo, Japan

Abstract. Knowledge graphs (KGs) play a crucial role in many modern applications. Many open information extraction approaches propose the extraction of triples from natural language text in order to populate knowledge. Nonetheless, most approaches do not consider forming links between the extracted triples and the KG triples, especially for predicates. Predicate linking is used to identify the predicate in a KG that exactly corresponds to an extracted predicate; this allows the avoidance of the heterogeneous problem. Resolving the heterogeneous problem can increase searchability over KGs. Although there have been a few studies that considered linking predicates, most of them have relied on statistical knowledge patterns, which are not able to generate all possible patterns. In this paper, we introduce distributed representations of elements in triples and leverage them for computing the similarity between predicates in order to find links that would not appear in statistical patterns. In the experiment, the results show that leveraging the distributed representations of triple elements can discover links between identical predicates, which cannot be achieved by the statistical pattern approach. As a result, our approach outperformed the traditional baseline for the predicate linking task.

Keywords: Knowledge graph · Predicate linking · Knowledge pattern

1 Introduction

A knowledge graph (KG) is a structured knowledge base that stores knowledge of the relation between entities or between an entity and its property. KGs play an important role in various applications, e.g., question answering, browsing knowledge, and data visualization; A well-known example of KGs is DBpedia [2]. Such KGs contain much useful knowledge, but it is obvious that new knowledge emerges every day. Unfortunately, most new knowledge is published in the form of natural language text, and it is not straightforward to transfer this to a KG. Furthermore, the rate of publication of natural language text is increasing dramatically [7]. As a result, a large amount of knowledge remains available only

F.J. Martínez de Pisón et al. (Eds.): HAIS 2017, LNAI 10334, pp. 75–87, 2017.
DOI: 10.1007/978-3-319-59650-1_7

as text. Consequently, there is an urgent need for a way to populate a KG with knowledge obtained from text.

Recently, many open information extraction approaches have proposed the extraction of triples (subject, predicate, object) from text [3,6,11]. However, those studies have primarily focused on ways to extract the elements of triples, and they do not consider how this information can be linked to entities or predicates in other KGs. Consequently, even once knowledge is added to a KG, it cannot be used efficiently due to this problem of heterogeneity. Although there have been many approaches to forming links between a subject or an object of a triple and its identical entity in a KG, there are only a few studies [1,5,12,13] that have considered linking the predicate to its counterpart in a KG. Furthermore, most proposed approaches to the predicate linking task use statistical knowledge patterns to identify the identical predicate in a KG. Although such an approach could establish many solid links between predicates, due to the sparsity of text, it is enormously difficult to determine all possible patterns for such links.

In this paper, we introduce a novel distributed representation of the elements in triples, and we then leverage them to evaluate the similarity between predicates in order to identify their identical counterparts in a KG when statistical knowledge patterns are missing.

The remainder of this paper is organized as follows. Section 2 explains the terminology used in this study and defines the problem of predicate linking. Section 3 gives a brief survey of work regarding predicate linking. Section 4 presents the details of our approach, and Sect. 5 presents an evaluation of our approach. Our conclusions are presented in Sect. 6.

2 Problem Definition

In this section, we formally define some particular terms, and we formalize the predicate linking task.

Definition 1. *A triple describes the relationship of a set of entities. The elements in a triple consist of the subject (S), predicate (P), and object (O), and the triple is denoted as* (S, P, O).

Definition 2. *A set of text triples* T_t *is a collection of triples that have been extracted from text by any open information extraction system:* $T_t = \{(S_{t_i}, P_{t_j}, O_{t_k}) \mid \exists i, j, k,\ 1 \leq i \leq |S_t|, 1 \leq j \leq |P_t|, 1 \leq k \leq |O_t|\}$ *where* $|S_t|, |P_t|$ *and* $|O_t|$ *are the numbers of unique subjects, predicates, and objects, respectively, that have been extracted from text. For example, given "Barack Obama was born in Hawaii",* $(Barack\ Obama, was\ born\ in, Hawaii)$ *is generated as the text triple.*

Definition 3. *A set of KG triples* T_{KG} *is a collection of triples in KG,* $T_{KG} = \{(S_{KG_x}, P_{KG_y}, O_{KG_z}) \mid \exists x, y, z,\ 1 \leq x \leq |S_{KG}|, 1 \leq y \leq |P_{KG}|, 1 \leq z \leq |O_{KG}|\}$ *where* $|S_{KG}|, |P_{KG}|$ *and* $|O_{KG}|$ *are the numbers of unique subjects, predicates,* *and objects in the KG. For example, given DBpedia as the KG, the sample KG triple is (dbr*[1]*: Barack_Obama , dbo*[2]*: birthPlace, dbr: Hawaii).*

Definition 4. ***Predicate Linking:*** *Given a set of text triples T_t and a set of KG triples T_{KG} as the input, the predicate mapping task is to identify the P_{KG_y} that is equivalent to P_{t_j} denoted by $P_{t_j} \equiv P_{KG_y}$, given $\langle S_{t_i}, O_{t_k} \rangle$, which corresponds to P_{t_j}. For example, given the text triple (Barack Obama, was born in, Hawaii), the predicate "was born in" should be linked to dbo:birthPlace in the context of $\langle$Barack Obama, Hawaii$\rangle$, while given the text triple (Barack Obama, was born in, 1961), it should be linked to dbo:birthDate in the context of $\langle$Barack Obama, 1961$\rangle$.*

3 Related Work

Predicate linking, also known as ontology integration and synonym identification, is to map a predicate to its identical predicate. Most of studies [1,12,13] focus on predicate linking between KG triples. Abedjan et al. [1] proposed the association rule mining to learn associated patterns in KGs and used the patterns to discover identical predicate pairs. Zhao et al. [13] introduced the statistical graph patterns to group candidate predicates and used the string-based similarity approach to verify whether such candidates are identical. Zhang et al. [12] proposed using statistical knowledge patterns to identify identical predicates in the KG. Based upon the results, their approaches [1,12,13] could identify identical predicates between KGs. Nevertheless, it cannot be applied in a straightforward manner for our task, since we focus on forming a link between a predicate in the text triple and its matching counterpart in a KG triple. Generally, text triples are ambiguous and sparse than KG triples. As a result, properties for building the statistical knowledge pattern between text triples and KG triples become missing.

The most applicable study for the predicate linking task in our study is Exners study [5]. Exner et al. uses the state-of-the-art natural language processing (NLP) tool to link entities of text triples to KG entities and determines the statistical pattern of the text predicate and the KG predicate based on each subject-object pair, and then forms a link between identical predicates. Although this approach [5] could avoid the ambiguity of an element in a text triple, generating statistical patterns might not cover all possible patterns; consequently, some statistical patterns are missing.

To overcome this limitation, we aim to leverage the similarity-based approach for linking between text predicates and KG predicates. Generally, the similarity-based approaches, the string-based similarity and the wordnet-based similarity, are used in the ontology matching [4]. Although such approach give reasonable results, they fail to identify identical predicates when surface form of string is sufficiently different due to the use of different vocabularies. For example, considering the triple (Lionel Messi, play for, FC Barcelona), "play for" should be

[1] dbr: http://dbpedia.org/resource/.
[2] dbo: http://dbpedia.org/ontology/.

linked to dbo: team. However, both the string-based similarity and the wordnet-based similarity fail to identify the predicates as identical.

Since the surface form does not adequately represent the vocabulary, we need to learn and represent the vocabulary in the deeper level than just its surface form. Based upon a review, we found that Mikolov et al. [10] proposed a distributed representation of words that can capture both the syntactic and the semantic patterns. *Distributed Representation* is to embed the target word into the dense vector in the low-dimensional vector space as its representation. Inspired by distributed representations of words [10], we introduced a distribution representation of an element in a triple in the continuous vector space. The distributed representation of each of the elements in a triple is learned by the other elements in the same triple. The similarity between the distributions of the elements in a triple can then be leveraged to identify identical predicates.

4 Approach

In this section, the architecture of our approach is described. Our approach takes a set of text triples T_t and a set of KG triples T_{KG} as input, and then as output, it provides a link between the predicate of each text triple and its identical predicate (if any) in the KG. As shown in Fig. 1, our approach has three main components: (1) statistical pattern-based candidate generation (PCG); (2) similarity-based candidate generation (SCG); and (3) candidate selection (CS). The PCG component captures statistical knowledge patterns between text triples and KG triples and then uses these patterns to generate candidate pairs. The SCG component enriches the text triples and KG triples by using bootstrapping prior to embedding their elements in a distributed representations of elements; those vectors are used to compute the similarity between a text predicate and a KG predicate in order to generate predicate candidate pairs. The CS component selects the most suitable predicate candidate. As a result, an identical link is established between a text predicate and a KG triple. The details of each component of our approach are given below.

4.1 Statistical Pattern-Based Candidate Generation

The PCG component extracts statistical patterns of the text predicates and KG predicates and then uses these patterns to link the predicates. As depicted in Fig. 1, PCG consists of two modules: pattern extraction and pattern matching. The details of each module are given below.

Pattern Extraction. The pattern extraction module extracts the statistical patterns of the text predicate and the KG predicate. The strategy is similar to that used by Exner et al. [5] to extract statistical patterns. We begin by mapping the subject and the object of the text triple to the KG by using an entity disambiguation system [9]. Then, if the subject and object of the text triple are similar to the subject and object of the KG triple, respectively, it

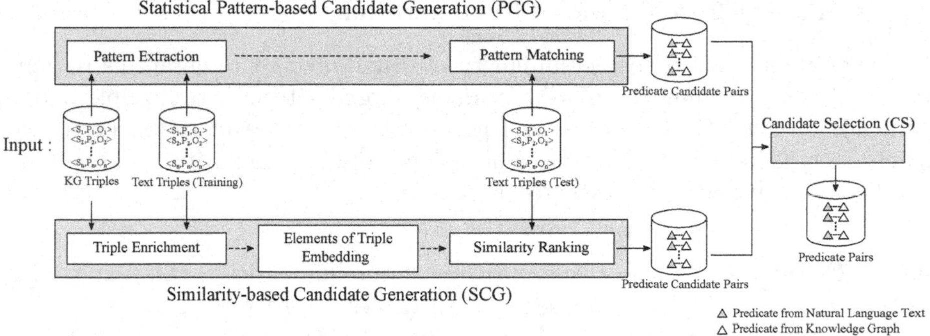

Fig. 1. Architecture of our approach for predicate linking

is assumed that the predicate of the text triple and the predicate of the KG triple are identical. Finally, the types of the subject and object are used as a constraint to generalize the statistical pattern. The types considered in our approach are the 49 top-level types of DBpedia. An example of pattern extraction is as follows. Given the (Barack Obama, was born in, Honolulu Hawaii) and DBpedia triples, the entity disambiguation system maps the given triple to (dbr:Barack_Obama, was born in, dbr:Hawaii). In the second step, we find the DBpredia triple (dbr:Barack_Obama, dbo:birthPlace, dbr:Hawaii), for which the subject and the object are similar to the triple in the first step. In the third step, dbr:Barack_Obama and dbr:Hawaii of the subject and object are generalized to person and place, and then we extract the statistical pattern that (PERSON, was born in, PLACE) is linked to dbo: birthPlace. Note that the same statistical pattern might link to a different KG predicate; in that case, the most frequently linked KG predicate for a given pattern is assumed to be the correct one.

Pattern Matching. The pattern matching module uses the statistical patterns and the text triple to generate the candidate predicate for the linking task. In order to utilize the statistical patterns, we first need to identify the type of the subject and object of the text triple in order to create a new pattern; this is done by any entity type classification system. The new pattern is compared with existing statistical patterns in an attempt to locate an identical pattern; if one is found, a link to the KG predicate is generated. For example, given the text triple (Shinzo Abe, was born in, Tokyo Japan), by using the entity type classification system, the pattern (PERSON, was born in, PLACE) is created. Then, using the statistical pattern generated by the pattern extraction module, the predicate "was born in" in the text triple (Shinzo Abe, was born in, Tokyo Japan) is linked to dbo:birthPlace; this forms the predicate candidate pair.

4.2 Similarity-Based Candidate Generation

The SCG component uses the similarity of distributed representations to generate a predicate candidate pair comprising a predicate in a text triple and a predicate in the KG. As shown in Fig. 1, SCG has three modules: (1) triple enrichment; (2) elements of triple embedding; and (3) similarity ranking. The details of each module are discussed below.

Triple Enrichment. The triple enrichment module enriches the text triples and the KG triples and then integrates all triples in order to create *bootstrapping triples* that will be used in a later module for learning the distributed representations. In this module, only the subject (domain) and range (object) of each triple are enriched. To enrich each text triple, we use the entity type classification system. To enrich a KG triple, we use SPARQL to query the name and the type of the subject and the object of the triple by using the rdfs:[3] label and rdf:type, respectively. As the target for the enrichment, we consider 49 top-level DBpedia types and also include date and number type. Since there is a difference between the types obtained by the entity type classification system and those obtained by the rdf:type property, substring matching is used to match DBpedia types to those provided by the entity type classification system.

Elements of Triple Embedding. The elements of the triple embedding module uses the bootstrapping triples to learn the distributed vector representations of elements in triples. Inspired by the study [10], the idea of the learning representation is to embed an element of a triple into the continuous vector space by using the other elements in the same triple. In the learning process, distributed representations of other elements in a triple are used to predict the target element in the same triples. We use all other elements in a triple to predict the target element in the same triple. Also, since this study focuses on the predicate linking, we concatenate a word sequence of a predicate to create one word for representing that predicate. Formally, given the bootstrapping triple i^{th} denoted by BT_i, e.g. (Barack Obama, was born in, Hawaii), in the set of bootstrapping triples BT, $1 \leq i \leq |BT|$, and a sequence of words of elements, $w_1, w_2, w_3, ..., w_n$ in BT_i (e.g. Barack, Obama, was_born_in, Hawaii), the model is to maximize the following objective function.

$$L = \sum_{i=1; w_e, w_{c_j} \in BT_i}^{|BT|} log\ p(w_e | w_{c_1}, w_{c_2}, w_{c_3}, ..., w_{c_n}) \quad (1)$$

where w_e is the target word of the element in the triple BT_i, w_{c_j} denotes the other elements in the same triple ($w_{c_j} \neq w_e$, $1 \leq j \leq n$) and n is a number of elements in triple BT_i. The conditional probability $p(w_e | w_{c_1}, w_{c_2}, w_{c_3}, ..., w_{c_n})$ is computed by the following softmax function.

[3] https://www.w3.org/TR/rdf-schema/.

$$p(w_e|w_{c1}, w_{c2}, w_{c3}, ..., w_{cn}) = \frac{exp(\bar{v} \cdot v_{w_e})}{\sum_{u=1}^{|W|} exp(\bar{v} \cdot v_u))} \quad (2)$$

where W is the set containing complete words of all elements in bootstrapping triples, v_{w_e} is the distributed representations of the element w_e, $\bar{v}$ is an average distributed representations of $w_{c_j}(v_{w_{c_j}}; w_{c_j} \neq w_e,\ 1 \leq j \leq n)$ and v_u is the distributed representations of the word u $(u \in W)$.

Generally, the computational cost for summing over W is very expensive. Mikolov et al. [10] therefore introduced $Negative\ Sampling$ (NS) to transform the original objective function to the feasible computation one. Based on NS, $log\ p(w_e|w_{c1}, w_{c2}, w_{c3}, ..., w_{cn}$ in Eq. 1 is therefore derived as follows.

$$\log \sigma(\bar{v} \cdot v_{w_e}) \ + \sum_{j=1; w_{ns} \in BT'_{neg_j}}^{|BT'_{neg}|} \log \sigma(-\bar{v} \cdot v_{w_{ns}}) \quad (3)$$

where $\sigma(x) = 1/(1 + exp(-x))$, BT'_{neg_j} is randomly generated triples (negative triples) and $v_{w_{ns}}$ is an distributed representations of w_{ns}, which is the negative sampling of w_e.

Similarity Ranking. The similarity ranking module computes the similarity between a text predicate and the KG predicates, and then the scores are used to form a ranked list of KG predicates. We propose the function $VSim$ for computing the similarity score between a text predicate and a KG predicate:

$$VSim(P_{T_i}, P_{KG_j}) = \delta(\frac{\overrightarrow{P_{T_i}} \cdot \overrightarrow{P_{KG_j}}}{|\overrightarrow{P_{T_i}}||\overrightarrow{P_{KG_j}}|}) + (1-\delta)(\frac{SO(P_{KG_j}) \cdot (\overrightarrow{S_{P_{T_i}}} - \overrightarrow{O_{P_{T_i}}})}{|SO(P_{KG_j})||\overrightarrow{S_{P_{T_i}}} - \overrightarrow{O_{P_{T_i}}}|}) \quad (4)$$

$$SO(P_{KG_j}) = \frac{\sum_{n=1}^{N}(\overrightarrow{S_{P_{KG_n}}} - \overrightarrow{O_{P_{KG_n}}})}{N} \quad (5)$$

where $(S_{P_{T_i}}, P_{T_i}, O_{P_{T_i}})$ are the subject, the predicate and the object of the triple T_i, respectively, T_i is a text triple, P_{KG_j} is a predicate in KG, $S_{P_{KG_{jn}}}$ and $O_{P_{KG_{jn}}}$ are the nth pair of a subject and an object, of which predicate is P_{KG_j} in KG, N is the number of triples in KG, whose predicate is P_{KG_j}, and δ is a parameter that determines the weighting between the predicate similarity and the context similarity.

The idea of $VSim$ is that since the distributed vector representations of identical elements are closed in the same region of the vector space, the cosine between these vectors can be used to measure their similarity; however, the context $\langle subject,\ object \rangle$ might alter the meaning of the predicate and so it must be taken into account. The $VSim$ similarity score function in Eq. 4 therefore consists of two terms: the first term directly computes the similarity between the predicates, while the second term computes the similarity between the contexts; this is done in order to validate the suitability of the predicate with its context. This is based on the assumption that the more the context is suitable, the more important it is that they be linked. Because the first and the second terms in Eq. (4) are different, a parameter is introduced to adjust the weight given to each. Equation (5) computes the average vector representation of the context of P_{KG}.

4.3 Candidate Selection

The CS component selects a predicate from the KG that is a candidate for mapping to the predicate of a text triple. In this component, priority is given to the predicate candidate, which is generated by the PCG component. If such a predicate candidate does not exist, the predicate candidate generated by the SCG component is considered. In the SCG component, the predicate candidate in KG, which provides the highest similarity score for the text predicate, is considered. If the similarity score between the candidate predicate and the text predicate is greater than the threshold θ, then the predicate of the text triple is linked to the candidate.

5 Experiment

In this section, we present the experiment that we conducted to assess the performance of our approach when leveraging distributed representation of elements in triples for the linking predicates on three created benchmark datasets.

5.1 Dataset

In the experiments, 120,000 Wikipedia articles were randomly selected and preprocessed to create text triples. In the preprocessing step, all formatting and any hyperlinks were removed. We then used a co-reference resolution system, the Stanford NLP tool [8], to convert the pronoun in each sentence to its corresponding proper name. Next, text triples were extracted from each sentence by OLLIE [11]. OLLIE is a state-of-the-art open information extraction system that extracts a triple from a sentence by using syntactic and lexical patterns [11]. For the KG triples, we used DBpedia [2], a well-known KG. In this study, the targets of the predicate linking were the 1,313 DBpedia ontology properties.

Based upon the generated text triples, we created three benchmark datasets. The first two datasets (synthetic datasets) were automatically constructed, while the third (gold standard) was manually created by an expert. The synthetic datasets are used for a quantitative evaluation, while the gold standard is used for a qualitative evaluation.

To construct the synthetic datasets, the predicates of the text triples and those in DBpedia were automatically linked. The linking strategy is as follows: if both the subject and the object of a text triple are identical to their respective counterparts in a DBpedia triple, we link the predicate of the text triple to that of the DBpedia triple. Figure 2 shows an example for constructing these datasets. As shown in this figure, the subject and the object of the text triple are identical to the respective parts in the DBpedia triple. Consequently, the

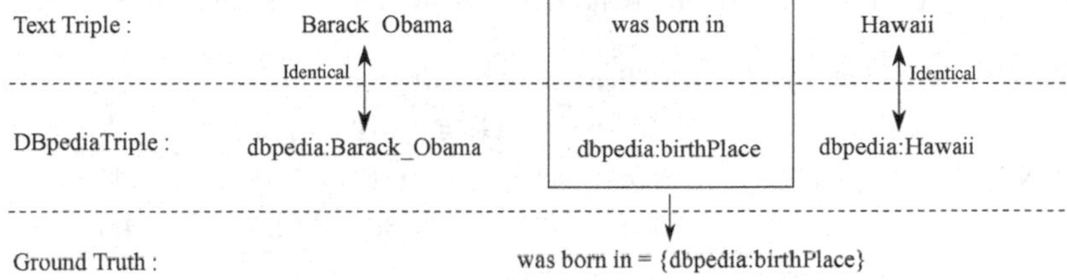

Fig. 2. An example of data construction

predicates, "was born in" and dbpedia:birthPlace, are assumed to be identical. This process was performed using DBpedia Spotlight [9]. Although this strategy establishes many predicate pairs, some of them may be incorrect. For example, consider the text triples (Barack Obama, was born in, USA) and (Barack Obama, lives in, USA) and a KG triple dbr:Obama, dbo:birthPlace, dbr:USA, "was born in" is linked to dbo:birthplace, which is correct, but "lives in" is also linked to dbo:birthplace, which is incorrect. To avoid such problems, we automatically remove any data for which the same subject and object pair results in links to multiple predicates. Our synthetic dataset contains more than 100,000 text triples for which the predicates are each linked to a unique DBpedia predicate. Our synthetic dataset has two characteristics: predicates for which the links form a one-to-one relation between the predicates in the text and those in the KG, and those for which there is a one-to-many relation, where the same text predicate is linked to multiple KG predicates. An example of a one-to-many relation is that "was born in" could be linked to either dbo:birthPlace or dbo:birthDate, based on the context $\langle subject, object\rangle$ in the triple. Given the triple context $\langle BarackObama, HonoluluHawaii\rangle$ and $\langle BarackObama, 1961\rangle$, "was born in" is linked to dbo:birthPlace or dbo:birthDate, respectively. Because of the difference in relations, we separated the synthetic data in two datasets. The first synthetic dataset, SYN(1-1), contains only those predicates that have a one-to-one relation, while the second synthetic dataset, SYN(1-N), has only those that have a one-to-many relation.

To construct the gold standard dataset, we randomly picked text triples and then asked an expert to create the links between the text predicate and the DBpedia predicate. We have made our three benchmark datasets[4] available for download in order to encourage the study of the predicate linking task, as described in this paper. Table 1 presents the statistics of the three benchmark datasets used in the experiments.

The implementation of our approach is as follows. In the pattern extraction module, DBpediaSpotlight [9] is used as the entity disambiguation system. Also, this system is used in the pattern matching module and the triple enrichment module to map the entity (subject or object) of a text triple to an appropriate DBpedia entity. We then use rdf:type to query the type of entity from DBpedia.

[4] http://ri-www.nii.ac.jp/VSim/datasets.zip.

Table 1. Statistic of the datasets in the experiments

Dataset	# Triples	Predicate		Subject	Object	
		# Text	# KG	# Entity	# Entity	# Literal
SYN (1-1)	33,391	30,732	322	17,021	7,317	4,061
SYN (1-N)	84,063	7,503	376	35,036	12,521	14,695
Gold standard	300	186	91	295	239	47

This method is used as the workaround of the entity type classification system. In the elements of triple embedding module, the word2vec library[5] is used for training distributed representations of the elements in triples. In the learning process, we consider a triple as a sequence of words from subject, predicate and object of the triple in order. Therefore, to use all elements of a triple the window size was set as the maximum length of the sequence in bootstrapping triples, while other parameters were set by their default values. In our approach, there are two hyperparameters: the weight δ and the threshold θ. These were set by using a grid search algorithm on the training dataset. The interval of the parameter searching was [0.00, 1.00], and the step interval was 0.01. The hyperparameters that performed best in training were used to test the result. In the experiments, we used a ten-fold cross-validation strategy for the datasets SYN(1-1) and SYN(1-N), and we used a combination of SYN, SYN(1-1), and SYN(1-N) to train the hyperparameter for the gold standard dataset.

5.2 Setting

The experiment evaluated the performance of our approach in the predicate linking task. In the experiment, the linking between a text predicate and a KG predicate is testified whether the approach selects a KG predicate, which corresponding to a text predicate, or not. This is a traditional multi-label classification problem: given the text triple $(S_{t_i}, P_{t_j}, O_{t_k})$, the approach selects $P_{DB_x} \equiv P_{t_j}$ where $P_{DB_x} \in \{P_{DB_1}, P_{DB_2}, P_{DB_3}, ..., P_{DB_n}\}, 1 \leq x \leq n$ as the output.

The statistical knowledge pattern approach in the study [5], which is closely related to our approach, is selected as the baseline. In the experiment, the micro/macro evaluation of precision, recall and F1 are measured to evaluate our approach and the baseline. The macro evaluation averages the performance for each predicate across the dataset, while the micro evaluation aggregates the performance of all predicates in the dataset. The micro/macro F1 are harmonic mean between the micro/macro precision and recall respectively. The micro/macro precision and recall are computed by Eqs. 6 and 7

$$Precision_{micro} = \frac{\sum_{i=1}^{|P_{KG}|} |S_i \cap \hat{S}_i|}{\sum_{i=1}^{|P_{KG}|} |\hat{S}_i|}, \quad Recall_{micro} = \frac{\sum_{i=1}^{|P_{KG}|} |S_i \cap \hat{S}_i|}{\sum_{i=1}^{|P_{KG}|} |S_i|} \qquad (6)$$

[5] https://code.google.com/archive/p/word2vec/.

$$Precision_{macro} = \frac{1}{|P_{KG}|} \sum_{i=1}^{|P_{KG}|} \frac{|S_i \cap \hat{S}_i|}{|\hat{S}_i|}, \quad Recall_{macro} = \frac{1}{|P_{KG}|} \sum_{i=1}^{|P_{KG}|} \frac{|S_i \cap \hat{S}_i|}{|S_i|} \qquad (7)$$

where P_{KG} is the set of predicates in KG, S_i is the set of predicates of text triples, which belong to P_{KG_i} and $\hat{S}_i$ is the set of predicates of text triples, which are predicted as P_{KG_i}.

5.3 Result

Table 2 shows the results of our approach and that of the baseline. The experimental results indicate that in overall our approach, leveraging the distributed representation-based similarity, outperformed the statistical pattern approach. Although the precision results of the baseline are better than our approach due to the nature of statistic knowledge patterns, whose results are highly precise, the recall is relatively low when comparing with our approach. As a result, the F1 results of our approach can outperform the baseline in all datasets. Also, we conduct the statistical testing, t-test, on micro/macro F1 score in order to further investigate the improvements of our results. The statistical test results indicate that our improvements are significant ($\alpha = 0.05$) in all datasets.

The low recall results in the baseline infers that we could not extract the majority of the statistical knowledge patterns due to the sparsity of natural language text, especially in the SYN datasets, the SYN(1-1) and the SYN (1-N) datasets. In the SYN datasets, the variation of predicate in text triples is enormous as shown in the Table 1. Although the statistical knowledge pattern-based approach could efficiently perform well on the limited size of the predicate vocabularies as in the gold standard or between KGs, it still requires a huge amount of the training data to acquire enough knowledge patterns. This result conforms to our hypothesis that it is considerably difficult to extract all possible patterns. Therefore, our approach, leveraging the distributed representation-based similarity, could efficiently discover identical predicates in KG, which could not be achieved by the statistical knowledge patterns.

Table 2. The classification results of our approach the predicate linking task on three benchmark comparing with the baseline

Approach	Dataset	Macro			Micro		
		Precision	Recall	F1	Precision	Recall	F1
Baseline	SYN (1-1)	**1.0000**	0.0241	0.0471	**1.0000**	0.1130	0.2031
Our approach		0.1245	**0.1752**	**0.1456**	0.3720	**0.3228**	**0.3457**
Baseline	SYN (1-N)	**0.1207**	0.0181	0.0315	**0.5029**	0.4256	0.4610
Our approach		0.0592	**0.0585**	**0.0589**	0.4702	**0.4649**	**0.4675**
Baseline	Gold	**0.7217**	0.5600	0.6306	**0.7693**	0.6400	0.6987
Our approach	Standard	0.6902	**0.6660**	**0.6778**	0.7491	**0.7367**	**0.7428**

6 Conclusion

This paper presents novel distributed representations of elements in triples and then leverages them for computing the similarity between a text predicate and a KG predicate to identify identical predicates. The experimental results show that leveraging distributed representation-based similarity metric could help to discover and identify identical KG predicates for text predicates. As a result, our approach could alleviate the problem caused by the limitation of statistical knowledge patterns due to the sparsity of text and improve the discoverability for the predicate linking task.

In the future work, we will apply the predicate linking together with the entity linking in order to populate knowledge in KG from triples, which obtaining by any open information extraction system.

Acknowledgements. This work was partially supported by NEDO (New Energy and Industrial Technology Development Organization).

References

1. Abedjan, Z., Naumann, F.: Synonym analysis for predicate expansion. In: Cimiano, P., Corcho, O., Presutti, V., Hollink, L., Rudolph, S. (eds.) ESWC 2013. LNCS, vol. 7882, pp. 140–154. Springer, Heidelberg (2013). doi:10.1007/978-3-642-38288-8_10
2. Auer, S., Bizer, C., Kobilarov, G., Lehmann, J., Cyganiak, R., Ives, Z.: DBpedia: a nucleus for a web of open data. In: Aberer, K., et al. (eds.) ASWC/ISWC - 2007. LNCS, vol. 4825, pp. 722–735. Springer, Heidelberg (2007). doi:10.1007/978-3-540-76298-0_52
3. Carlson, A., Betteridge, J., Kisiel, B., Settles, B., Hruschka Jr., E.R., Mitchell, T.M.: Toward an architecture for never-ending language learning. In: Proceedings of AAAI (2010)
4. Euzenat, J., et al.: Ontology matching, vol. 18. Springer, Heidelberg (2007)
5. Exner, P., Nugues, P.: Entity extraction: from unstructured text to DBpedia RDF triples. In: The Web of Linked Entities Workshop, pp. 58–69. CEUR-WS (2012)
6. Fader, A., Soderland, S., Etzioni, O.: Identifying relations for open information extraction. In: Proceedings of the Conference on Empirical Methods in Natural Language Processing, pp. 1535–1545. ACL (2011)
7. Kríž, V., Hladká, B., Nečaský, M., Knap, T.: Data extraction using NLP techniques and its transformation to linked data. In: Gelbukh, A., Espinoza, F.C., Galicia-Haro, S.N. (eds.) MICAI 2014. LNCS, vol. 8856, pp. 113–124. Springer, Cham (2014). doi:10.1007/978-3-319-13647-9_13
8. Lee, H., Peirsman, Y., Chang, A., Chambers, N., Surdeanu, M., Jurafsky, D.: Stanford's multi-pass sieve coreference resolution system at the CoNLL-2011 shared task. In: Proceedings of the 15th Conference on Computational Natural Language Learning: Shared Task, pp. 28–34. ACL (2011)
9. Mendes, P.N., Jakob, M., García-Silva, A., Bizer, C.: DBpedia spotlight: shedding light on the web of documents. In: Proceedings of the 7th International Conference on Semantic Systems, pp. 1–8. ACM (2011)
10. Mikolov, T., Sutskever, I., Chen, K., Corrado, G.S., Dean, J.: Distributed representations of words and phrases and their compositionality. In: Proceedings of Advances in Neural Information Processing Systems, pp. 3111–3119 (2013)

11. Schmitz, M., Bart, R., Soderland, S., Etzioni, O.: Open language learning for information extraction. In: Proceedings of the Joint Conference on EMNLP, pp. 523–534. ACL (2012)
12. Zhang, Z., Gentile, A.L., Blomqvist, E., Augenstein, I., Ciravegna, F.: Statistical knowledge patterns: identifying synonymous relations in large linked datasets. In: Alani, H., et al. (eds.) ISWC 2013. LNCS, vol. 8218, pp. 703–719. Springer, Heidelberg (2013). doi:10.1007/978-3-642-41335-3_44
13. Zhao, L., Ichise, R.: Ontology integration for linked data. J. Data Semant. **3**(4), 237–254 (2014)

A Review of Distributed Data Models for Learning

Miguel Ángel Rodríguez[1(✉)], Alberto Fernández[2], Antonio Peregrín[1], and Francisco Herrera[2]

[1] Department of Information Technologies, University of Huelva, Huelva, Spain
{miguel.rodriguez,peregrin}@dti.uhu.es
[2] Department of Computer Science and Artificial Intelligence, University of Granada, Granada, Spain
{alberto,herrera}@decsai.ugr.es

Abstract. This paper deals with aspects of data distribution for machine learning tasks, considering the advantages as well as the drawbacks that are frequently associated with data partitioning and its different models. This study, from the point of view of the distributed data, reviews some of the algorithms that have been used to treat each case, although it is not a review of learning or computation algorithms. Finally, this report looks into the issues that new data partitioning-based models such as MapReduce have brought to distributed learning.

Keywords: Distributed data mining · Data partitioning · MapReduce

1 Introduction

The rise of information technologies has produced a huge amount of data, and mining them is one of the most successful areas of research in computer science. To do so, the use of parallel or distributed computers is a theoretical rational solution to speed up the process, and data then have to be divided into several groups in order to be processed with this kind or hardware.

This kind of resources may be necessary when it is not possible to merge all the data in a single system due to computational resources limitations or exponential growth of the algorithmic time needed to process it.

But the need for more computational power is not the only situation where distributed data must be handled. Data is often originally spread between several locations, and for many reasons, e.g. because of competition or legal issues, they cannot be moved to a single centralized computer or datacentre. This could be the situation of banking entities that may be interested in global knowledge benefits and also avoiding credit card fraud, but they have to safeguard their clients' data.

On the other hand, model combination is the core idea behind classical machine learning methods such as Bagging, Boosting and Stacking [1]. Separate models can be seen as experts and the final model surely will be better if several experts' opinions are combined. As far as we know, all these methods were designed to work in non-distributed environments. They obtain the whole dataset at the beginning of the classification process, so although they are not originally designed to solve inherently distributed data

F.J. Martínez de Pisón et al. (Eds.): HAIS 2017, LNAI 10334, pp. 88–97, 2017.
DOI: 10.1007/978-3-319-59650-1_8

problems, some of their strategies inspire approaches employed in some parallel and distributed learning methods.

Therefore, distributed data mining involves the use of data that are allocated to more than one group, and this fact can lead to different means of learning based on the way data is partitioned. In some cases, it may improve the quality of the model, but also has some drawbacks that have to be taken into account. The main purpose of this document is to propose some taxonomies based on the main properties observed in the distributed data models, and based on them, to characterize their advantages and drawbacks in order to let the reader choose a distribution strategy from a theoretical point of view. To this end, this document provides a brief review of some of the existing contributions on data distribution related to machine learning, mainly on data mining (classification, clustering, regression) but also on data preparation itself as a task to improve the final model (feature selection, prototype selection, etc.).

The document is organized as follows. Section 2 provides the concepts behind data distribution: the influence on data of data partitioning, and the taxonomies of partitioned data models along with reflections. Section 3 focuses on the new models based in MapReduce. Section 4 exposes some thoughts about ongoing issues in modern distributed models and finally Sect. 5 shows some conclusions.

2 Taxonomies of Data Distribution Models

This section initially provides a concise analysis of some of the effects of the process of data distribution. Secondly, we propose some taxonomies based on the review of the different data distribution models found in the specialized literature.

2.1 The Impact of Data Partitioning

When a set of data is partitioned into different subsets this action can vary the distribution of the examples (i.e. values of the characteristics, classes of each instance, etc.) which could be of importance depending on the inherent characteristics of the data set. In this sense, within the scope of the classification we can highlight:

- Sets with *unbalanced classes* [2] have a greater risk of loss of information relative to the minority class.
- *Small disjuncts* [3] are not detectable a priori and might become an important part of instances. The distribution of data may split a small disjunct into several subsets leading to a significant loss of class separability.
- *Multiclass* [4], by definition are a type of data where each class is imbalanced when compared with the rest of the dataset, leading to class separability problems when the data is partitioned into several subsets.
- *Dataset shift* [5], when a dataset is partitioned into smaller subsets, they may have different feature or class distribution that leads the learning algorithm to wrong or inaccurate models.

2.2 Taxonomy Based on Data Partition

Probably, the most obvious classification is the one based on data partitioning, i.e., whether the data in each processing node is the same or a subset of the full dataset:

- Without partitioning: it involves the replication of all instances and features at each node. This model facilitates the application of different pre-processing and learning strategies at each node, but does not help with horizontal scalability [6].
- Partitioned in smaller subsets: commonly, partitioning of the data is performed in order to scale the problem [6], but can also be performed as a strategy to obtain better models. Some studies [7] confirm that a set of algorithms, either with different partitions or by combining different learning algorithms, may improve the quality of the model generated by an algorithm with the complete set of data. Bagging, Boosting and Stacking [1] are the most known techniques that apply it. The partition of the dataset into smaller ones can follow different strategies based on the percentage of shared data between the nodes:
  - Disjoint vs. not disjoint: from the point of view of efficiency and resource management, a set of non-shared information is the optimal distribution, but as mentioned, there could be some drawbacks when performed (loss of important instances for class separability, even fewer instances of the minority class, and dataset shift). The creation of not disjoints sets can be used to get good feature combinations [8] or a better distribution [9] in one of the subsets.

  And also based on the way this division is performed:

- Instances (horizontal) vs. features (vertical):
  - Instance based, or *horizontal*: most of the previous effort devoted to dataset division has been in the area of instance partitioning. To split a dataset into a number of subsets is a natural way of handling a large amount of data. There are some considerations that need to be taken into account. Firstly, the full dataset can be handled without distributed computing by sequential processing [10, 11]. Secondly, the partition process may change the data structure, making more difficult the learning process [5].
  - Feature based, or *vertical:* On one hand, it decreases computational effort due to the reduction of the search space. On the other hand, a good feature combination can improve the learning against noisy instances [8].

2.3 Taxonomy Based on Data Flow Processing

Once a dataset is partitioned in smaller subsets, the learning processes around each subset can be performed not only in parallel but also sequentially. Therefore, we can say that regarding the data flow and the relation of the intermediate results, the following classification can be suggested:

- Incremental: subsets are processed incrementally to complete the model obtained by step n – 1 [10]. A distributed model of this paradigm uses data sets generated in an earlier partial model [12].

- Windowing: the same data is processed by different algorithms at the same time, or a partition is processed each time by the same algorithm [13]. Can be combined with incremental learning.
- Parallel: i.e., each node learns about the assigned data partition. This is the most efficient way from the efficiency point of view, but there are some challenges to be addressed, e.g. the generation of a final model due to the fact that each partition will create its own model based in local data.

2.4 Taxonomy Based on the Data Cooperation Strategies

The learning process over several data partitions can be performed without explicit knowledge of the other partitions or with collaboration while the process is in progress. Based on this criterion, we can find several approaches:

- Collaborative learning, where the nodes share information while the process of learning is ongoing. This can be done by:
  - Meta-information sharing [14]: the nodes interchange meta-information that guides the local model, e.g. it could be a concept in the form of rules, trees or other forms of model representation. [15–18] Are examples of proposals that use rules in this way, inspired in distributed genetic algorithms that periodically share individuals between distributed subpopulations [19].
  - Data sharing: it involves reallocating examples (e.g. misclassified instances of a rule) between nodes, during the learning process. This data redistribution can be centralized [15] by dynamically generating new processing nodes to refine the model, or distributed [17] following strategies of data diffusion.
- Non-collaborative learning, where the global model is created by combining the information generated in the local models. Two strategies can be found:
  - Building a single global model, through the fusion/integration [20] of information of each model (e.g. generating a classifier from different sets of rules). This approach requires processing nodes to share a common representation of the model and feature set. Common descriptive languages are needed that make the fusion of models based on different descriptions possible, such as the distance between instances, decision trees, neural networks or rules [21].
  - Meta-Learning [22], where each local model is used as a black box to get a prediction and then, by using an aggregation process that weights the rating value of each one to give a single value; however, it is expected that the accuracy obtained will decrease accordingly as the number of available instances in the training set used is reduced [23]. This learning model has been extensively used in non-distributed models, including ensembles [7]. Recently, it has inspired a new wave of highly parallel implementations based on the MapReduce [24] paradigm, which brings to its ultimate consequences this separation in learning assisting the work of integration. Due to its current significance, they will described in Sect. 3.

According to the way of determining the final prediction based on local models we can distinguish two approaches. On the one hand, the arbitration model [25] where the predicted class is decided by most of the base classifiers, and on the other, the combination model [26], where the information of each classifier is combined allowing even a hierarchy of multi-models.

3 MapReduce: A Data Distribution Oriented Paradigm

Nowadays, MapReduce is an emergent technology that eases the development of Big Data processing. It is an inherent distributed paradigm based on asynchronous and block independent processing that provides a theoretical unlimited scalability.

Regarding the proposed taxonomies, MapReduce's algorithms could fit naturally as parallelized, since each node works on its own data partition into smaller subsets and its distributed file system means that the location of the subsets determines which node is the one that processes it, and, moreover, this can be defined as non-collaborative learning, as the Map phase runs in parallel without communication between the nodes.

From the standpoint of data partition, we can find the following different proposals:

- Feature based partition: some papers [27, 28] show a greedy implementation on the framework. Other authors propose a Random Forest implementation under the MapReduce paradigm using natively feature subset partitioning [29].
- Instance based partition: inside this approach we can find a set of algorithms dedicated to pre-processing tasks and other ones to machine learning.
  - Pre-processing tasks:
    - Prototype selection: an [23] implementation on MapReduce of evolutionary prototype generation is performed based on the stratification procedure.
    - Data distribution: in the context of MapReduce, [30, 31] proposed an application of SMOTE [32] to later apply Random Forest [8]. [33] propose an extreme oversampling technique. [29] implements a windowing technique to increase the efficiency of the sampling process.
  - Learning techniques: there are some generic libraries [34, 35] with distributed implementations of common learning algorithms, including (but not limited to): various linear models, naïve Bayes, and ensembles of decision trees for classification/regression problems and k-means clustering, but it has yet to be completed. Other specific proposals on learning algorithm are:
    - Classification by Fuzzy Rule Aggregation. [36] implements a scheme of distributed Chi-FRBCS rule generation method and a later fusion of the generated rules in order to generate a global classifier in accordance with the fusion/integration model. [37] shows a set of experiments on a set of datasets applying Chi-FRBCS that shows robustness and scalability.
    - K-nn classification is one of the most widely used methods due to its effectiveness and simplicity. The redesign of this to MapReduce is done by calculating k-neighbours in different partitions, which are then added to generate the list following a fusion/integration model. A second version [38] on Spark implement loops in an iterative way.

4 New Trends in Distributed Data

Mining over distributed data has always been an architecture driven task. As new architectures have been developed, the research community has been able to address new challenges. With no parallel capabilities, the models were based on sequential processing. Later on, the first attempts to parallelize the partition came with the use of MPI and synchronous procedure calls over multi-core processors. Distributed Genetic Algorithms benefited from interprocess communication. But none of these improvements played a changing role, as some bottlenecks related with scalability, learning curve, stability, etc. prevent it. MapReduce paradigm could be one of these game changing issues. It does provide a stable, simple yet powerful platform data oriented architecture. However, it presents difficulties in implementing models out of non-collaborative processes. This section names a few of the improvements that this model could bring to distributed data mining and also points out some of the drawbacks that must be resolved in order for it to become a more mature technology.

4.1 Making the Most of *In-memory* Capability

Most of the processing time in the MapReduce paradigm is dedicated to initial data transformation, which requires access to physical storage. The first extended implementation of this model is Hadoop [39]. This is still widely used by the community, especially in its version 2, which simplifies the design of parallel algorithms.

However, the need to repeatedly access the same data is not feasible in Hadoop and other options have emerged, such as Spark [40], which allows caching of data in memory to avoid accessing the physical layer for retrieving data previously loaded in memory or produced by an earlier process. Although the performance improvement is considerable, to the order of 10 to 100 times faster or even more, the transformation of algorithms to MapReduce primitives remains a critical design point.

Communication in the learning phase cannot be implemented in real time, due to the fact that we cannot guarantee execution of the processes at the same moment. Incremental/windowing learning can be used with a number of MapReduce phases [41], but this is a short-range strategy, as it would require multiple synchronizations at each beginning of a new iteration, and in the case of windowing, the reallocation of data to new processing nodes, resulting in poor algorithm efficiency.

4.2 Allowing Interprocess Communication

The natural way of communication in MapReduce goes from Map to Reduce, but other forms of inter data process communications are possible. Verma [42] proposes a genetic algorithm strategy that performs fitness calculations in the Map while the Reduce parts run the general algorithm. This approach does not imply data partitioning, but it could be adapted easily in a kind of windowing strategy, by calculating the individuals' fitness of a population against each data partition. In order to achieve a theoretical not limited scalability, processes have to avoid centralized coordination by means of distributed independent nodes. In this sense, Elephant56 [43] provides a framework based on the island nodes [19] model and MRPGA [44] proposes specific primitives to connect different processes, allowing a greater level of detail in the communication. There is a lot of improvement in the area of not centralized parallel processing to take advantage of this model.

4.3 Dealing with the Drawback of Data Partitioning

One of the major problems we face in highly distributed datasets is the negative impact on the data partitioning. A study of the intrinsic data properties could determine a strategy of pre-processing that minimizes this impact. An example of this approach may be the non-disjoint redistribution of elements of the minority class to avoid unbalance in the processing nodes. This approach does not reproduce noise or difficult class separability as in over-sampling or under-sampling strategies and is fully coherent with MapReduce.

Other properties are not simple to detect, for example the existence of small disjuncts. As in [17], it is possible to face the problem with a dynamic redistribution of the data taking into account those data misclassified by a first classification, following strategies typical of incremental learning but in a limited form due to the MapReduce limitations.

As stated previously, data shift is applicable to data partitioning, making different non-disjoint distribution increase the size of data in a combinatorial manner, but an intermediate number of sets can be found that minimizes the risk of data fracture. The number and composition of this non-disjoint set is a NP hard problem that has to be addressed. Experience in binarization methods for multiclass datasets [4] has shown that the improvements in results are possible at the expense of the computational cost and space needed to handle a greater number of subsets. However, the process time is kept constant in this model if the number of processors is big enough to handle the data in parallel.

4.4 Dealing with Data Pre-processing

Most of the big data sources acquired nowadays are composed of continuous numerical features. Discretizing the numerical features is a common task in machine learning, in order to decrease the computational complexity or because the learning algorithm needs it in that way. There are few references applied to the discretization in large volumes of data; e.g. [45] implements discretization based on minimum description length (MDL) and analyses the impact of discretization in the scope of Big Data.

Mining hard NP problems may require the use of multiple pre-processing techniques (oversampling, feature selection, etc.) in a coordinated way to achieve quality models with a learning strategy [29].

5 Conclusions

New data distribution-based paradigms have brought new scalability tools into the arena. In this document, we have suggested different taxonomies based on distributed data mining from the standpoint of data partitioning. We have analysed some of the main issues to be faced by new developments in this area that have to be taken into consideration when designing new distributed data based algorithms, and more specifically if planning to use the MapReduce model for this purpose.

Acknowledgements. This work was partially supported by the Spanish Ministry of Education and Science under Project TIN2014- 57251-P.

References

1. Bauer, E., Kohavi, R.: An empirical comparison of voting classification algorithms: bagging, boosting, and variants. Mach. Learn. **36**(1–2), 105–139 (1999)
2. Denil, M., Trappenberg, T.: Overlap versus imbalance. In: Farzindar, A., Kešelj, V. (eds.) AI 2010. LNCS, vol. 6085, pp. 220–231. Springer, Heidelberg (2010). doi: 10.1007/978-3-642-13059-5_22
3. Weiss, G.M., Provost, F.: Learning when training data is costly: the effect of class distribution on tree induction. J. Artif. Intell. Res. **19**, 315–354 (2003)
4. Ally, M.: Survey on multiclass classification methods. Neural Netw. pp. 1–9 (2005)
5. Moreno-Torres, J., Raeder, T., Alaiz-Rodríguez, R., Chawla, N., Herrera, F.: A unifying view on dataset shift in classification. Pattern Recogn. **45**(1), 521–530 (2012)
6. Bekkerman, R., Bilenko, M., Langford, J.: Scaling Up Machine Learning: Parallel and Distributed Approaches. Cambridge University Press, Cambridge (2011)
7. Dietterich, T.G.: Ensemble methods in machine learning. In: Kittler, J., Roli, F. (eds.) MCS 2000. LNCS, vol. 1857, pp. 1–15. Springer, Heidelberg (2000). doi:10.1007/3-540-45014-9_1
8. Breiman, L.: Random forests. Mach. Learn. **45**(1), 5–32 (2001)
9. Chawla, N.V., Japkowicz, N., Kotcz, A.: Editorial: special issue on learning from imbalanced data sets. ACM Spec. Interest Group Knowl. Disc. Data Min. Explor. **6**(1), 1–6 (2004)
10. Schlimmer, J.C., Fisher, D.: A case study of incremental concept induction. In: Fifth National Conference on Artificial Intelligence, pp. 496–501 (1986)
11. Tsoumakas, G., Vlahavas, I.: Effective stacking of distributed classifiers. In: European Conference in Artificial Intelligence, pp. 340–344 (2002)
12. Lazarevic, A., Obradovic, Z.: Boosting algorithms for parallel and distributed learning. Distrib. Parallel Databases **11**(2), 203–229 (2002)
13. Ishibuchi, H., Mihara, S., Nojima, Y.: Parallel distributed hybrid fuzzy GBML models with rule set migration and training data rotation. IEEE Trans. Fuzzy Syst. **21**(2), 355–368 (2013)
14. Provost, F., Hennessy, D.: Distributed machine learning: scaling up with coarse-grained parallelism. In: Proceedings of the 2nd International Conference on Intelligent Systems for Molecular Biology, pp. 340–347 (1994)
15. Giordana, A., Saitta, L.: Learning disjunctive concepts by means of genetic algorithms. In: Proceedings of the International Conference on Machine Learning, pp. 96–104 (1994)
16. Anglano, C., Giordana, A., Bello, G.L., Saitta, L.: An experimental evaluation of coevolutive concept learning. In: Proceedings of the 15th International Conference on Machine Learning, pp. 19–27 (1998)
17. Rodríguez, M., Escalante, D.M., Peregrín, A.: Efficient distributed genetic algorithm for rule extraction. Appl. Soft Comput. **11**(1), 733–743 (2011)
18. Lopez, L.I., Bardallo, J.M., De Vega, M.A., Peregrin, A.: REGAL-TC: a distributed genetic algorithm for concept learning based on regal and the treatment of counterexamples. Soft. Comput. **15**(7), 1389–1403 (2011)

19. Cantú-Paz, E.: A Survey of parallel genetic algorithms. Calculateurs Paralleles, Reseaux et Systems **10**(2), 141–171 (1998)
20. Fayyad, U.M., Djorgovski, S.G., Nicholas, W.: Automating analysis and cataloging of sky surveys. In: Advance in Knowledge Discovery and Data Mining, pp. 471–493 (1996)
21. Peteiro-Barral, G.-B.D.: A survey of methods for distributed machine learning. Proc. Artif. Intell. **2**(1), 1–11 (2013)
22. Chan, P.K., Stolfo, S.J.: Experiments on multistrategy learning by meta-learning. In: Proceedings of the Second International Conference on Information and Knowledge Management, pp. 314–323 (1993)
23. Triguero, I., Peralta, D., Bacardit, J., García, S., Herrera, F.: MRPR: a MapReduce solution for prototype reduction in big data classification. Neurocomputing **150**, 331–345 (2015)
24. Dean, J., Ghemawat, S.: MapReduce: simplified data processing on large clusters. Commun. ACM **51**, 107–113 (2008)
25. Chan, P.K., Stolfo, S.J.: Toward parallel and distributed learning by meta-learning. In: AAAI Workshop in Knowledge Discovery in Databases, pp. 227–240 (1993)
26. Chan, P., Stolfo, S.: Experiments on multistrategy learning by meta-learning. In: Proceedings Second International Conference of Information and Knowledge Management, pp. 314–323 (1993)
27. Peralta, D., Río, S., Ramírez-Gallego, S., Triguero, I., Benítez, J.M., Herrera, F.: Evolutionary feature selection for big data classification: a MapReduce aproach. Math. Probl. Eng. (2015). doi:10.1155/2015/246139
28. Ramirez, S.: Repository of machine learning algorithm over spark (2016). Accessed Jan 2017
29. Triguero, I., Río, S., López, V., Bacardit, J., Benítez, J.M., Herrera, F.: ROSEFW-RF: the winner algorithm for the ECBDL'14 big data competition: an extremely imbalanced big data bioinformatics problem. Knowl. Based Syst. **87**, 69–79 (2015)
30. Río, S., López, V., Benítez, J.M., Herrera, F.: On the use of MapReduce for imbalanced big data using random forest. Inf. Sci. **285**, 112–137 (2014)
31. Río, S.: Repository on imbalanced preprocessing MapReduce (2015). https://github.com/saradelrio/hadoop-imbalancedpreprocessing
32. Luengo, J., Fernández, A., García, S., Herrera, F.: Addressing data complexity for imbalanced data sets: analysis of SMOTE-based oversampling and evolutionary undersampling. Soft. Comput. **15**(10), 1909–1936 (2011)
33. Río, S., Benítez, J.M., Herrera, F.: Analysis of data preprocessing increasing the oversampling ratio for extremely imbalanced big data classification. In: IEEE BigDataSE 2015, vol. 2, pp. 180–185 (2015)
34. Apache Mahout. http://mahout.apache.org. Accessed Jan 2017
35. Meng, X., Bradley, J., Yavuz, B., Sparks, E., Venkataraman, S., Liu, D., Xin, D.: Mllib: machine learning in apache spark. J. Mach. Learn. Res. **17**(34), 1–7 (2016)
36. Río, S., López, V., Benítez, J.M., Herrera, F.: A MapReduce approach to address big data classification problems based on the fusion of linguistic fuzzy rules. Int. J. Comput. Intell. Syst. **8**(3), 422–437 (2015)
37. Fernandez, A., Río, S., Herrera, F.: Fuzzy rule based classification systems for big data with MapReduce: granularity analysis. Adv. Data Anal. Classif. (2016). doi:10.1007/s11634-016-0260-z
38. Maillo, J., Ramírez-Gallego, S., Triguero, I., Herrera, F.: kNN-IS: an iterative spark-based design of the k-nearest neighbors classifier for big data. Knowl. Based Syst. (2016). doi:10.1016/j.knosys.2016.06.012
39. White, T.: Hadoop,The Definitive Guide. OReilly Media Inc., Sebastopol (2012)

40. Zaharia, M., Chowdhury, M., Franklin, M.J., Shenker, S., Stoica, I.: Spark: cluster computing with working sets. In: Proceedings 2nd USENIX Conference on Hot Topics in Cloud Computing, vol. 10, pp. 10–17 (2010)
41. Martín, D., Martínez-Ballesteros, M., Río, S., Alcalá-Fdez, J., Riquelme, J., Herrera, F.: MOPNAR-BigData: un diseno MapReduce para la extracción de reglas de asociación cuantitativas en problemas de Big Data. In: CAEPIA 2015, pp. 979–989 (2015)
42. Verma, A., Llorá, X., Goldberg, D., Campbell, R.: Scaling genetic algorithms using MapReduce. In: Proceedings of the 9th International Conference on Intelligent Systems Design and Applications, pp. 13–18 (2009)
43. Geronimo, D., Ferrucci, L.F., Murolo, A., Sarro, F.: A parallel genetic algorithm based on hadoop MapReduce for the automatic generation of unit test suites. In: IEEE 5th International Conference Software Testing, Verification and Validation, pp. 785–793 (2012)
44. Jin, C., Vecchiola, C., Buyya, R.: MRPGA: an extension of MapReduce for parallelizing genetic algorithms. In: Proceeding of the 4th IEEE International Conference on eScience, pp. 214–221 (2008)
45. Ramírez-Gallego, S., García, S., Mouriño-Talín, H., Martínez-Rego, D., Bolón-Canedo, V., Alonso-Betanzos, A., Benítez, J.M., Herrera, F.: Data discretization: taxonomy and big data challenge. Data Min. Knowl. Disc. **6**(1), 5–21 (2016)

Bio-inspired Models and Evolutionary Computation

Incorporating More Scaled Differences to Differential Evolution

Miguel Cárdenas-Montes(✉)

Centro de Investigaciones Energéticas Medioambientales y Tecnológicas, Madrid, Spain
miguel.cardenas@ciemat.es

Abstract. Differential Evolution is an evolutionary algorithm composed of vectors and based on the application of scaled differences of two vectors over a third one, being all of them different. The variants of this algorithm propose different types of vectors for the scaled difference, and different number of scaled differences, to alter differently-selected vectors. The successful track of Differential Evolution has propitiated numerous variants. These variants use a limited number of vectors for forming the scaled differences and, in general, only one vector for receiving these differences. In this work, new variants with scaled differences using all the population vectors are proposed. These variants are confronted to a wide set of fitness functions and to a set of Differential Evolution variants.

Keywords: Differential evolution · Performance · Optimization

1 Introduction

Since it was proposed in 1995 [1], Differential Evolution (DE) has produced a successful track of applications to real-parameter optimization. DE is a population-based algorithm, in which its elements are termed vectors. It is based on the application of scaled differences of two of more vectors to other different vector, termed base vector. The weight is termed mutation factor, F This successful track has required the creation of new DE-variants [6].

DE-variants have been created through diverse mechanisms: the creation of scaled differences with two or four vectors randomly selected, the variation of the criterion for selecting some of the vectors involved in the scaled differences, or the selection criterion for the base vector. However, in all cases, the scaled differences are not larger than two[1].

In this work, exploratory studies about efficiently enlarging the number of scaled differences are undertaken. Two approaches for incorporating more scaled differences are presented. The first one is termed DE/rand/all, whereas the second one is termed DE/rand/alldiff (Sect. 2.3).

[1] Each scaled difference involves the selection of a pair of vectors. Therefore, two scaled differences mean the selection of four vectors.

F.J. Martínez de Pisón et al. (Eds.): HAIS 2017, LNAI 10334, pp. 101–112, 2017.
DOI: 10.1007/978-3-319-59650-1_9

In DE/rand/all variant, the vectors of the population are selected one by one, and scaled differences are created with the pairs. Once a vector has been selected, it can not be picked up any more. Taking into account that the base vector is the first selection, for a population with a even number of vectors $\frac{N}{2} - 1$ scaled differences can be formed. The initial attempts in which the mutation factor F acts over the $\frac{N}{2} - 1$ scaled differences leaded to a poor performance. For this reason, in DE/rand/all the mutation factor is halved for consecutive scaled differences, so that for the first scaled difference, the mutation factor is F, for the second one is $F/2$, and so on.

For the second DE-variant proposed in this work, DE/rand/alldiff, the scaled-differences and their addition to the base vector are replaced by a sum of the products of the mutation factor divided by the population size, with a binomial distribution of the sign of F, by vectors randomly selected. Each vector can be selected only once. In DE/rand/1 variant, the scaled difference is applied on a base vector. In DE/rand/alldiff, the addition to the base vector is replaced by adding a factor equal to the inverse of the population size, $\frac{1}{pop\,size}$, to all the factors of the product.

In order to ease the handling of the new proposed variants, a matrix notation for DE has been created (Sect. 2.2). This matrix notation allows representing the classical DE-variants as well as the variants proposed in this work. Furthermore, this alternative representation can inspire new DE-variants.

Finally the proposed DE-variants are confronted to the classic DE-variants (Sect. 2.1) as well as to jitter and dither ones for a wide set of benchmark functions (Sect. 2.4).

To the author's knowledge, no similar works have been proposed.

The rest of the paper is organized as follows: Section 2 summarizes the most relevant points in the state-of-the-art and in-detail describes the proposed variants. Results are presented and analysed in Sect. 3. Finally, Sect. 4 contains the conclusions of this work.

2 Methodology

2.1 Differential Evolution and Its Variants

DE is based on altering the population members (vectors) of each generation with other population members, randomly selected, in its turn is modified by the scaled difference of a pair of population members, being all these members distinct. Two operators compose the DE optimizer: the Mutation operator (Eq. 1) and the Crossover operator. The two most popular implementations of the Crossover operator are the Binomial one (Eq. 2) and the Exponential one (Eq. 3). On the other hand, numerous schemas for the Mutation operator have been proposed.

Mutation operator is governed by a parameter, termed mutation factor F, which quantifies the amount of alteration supplied to the base vector. F weights the addition of the scaled difference to the base vector. The vectors produced by the Mutation operator are termed mutant vectors.

On the other hand, the Crossover operator is characterized by a parameter, termed crossover rate C_r. C_r governs how many components from the mutant vector are inherited by the trial vector.

Finally, a selection process is undertaken. It consists of the selection of the most suitable vector between the target vector, vector selected from population in the current generation, and the trial vector.

$$\boldsymbol{v_i} = \boldsymbol{x_1} + F \cdot (\boldsymbol{x_2} - \boldsymbol{x_3}), \quad \boldsymbol{x_1} \neq \boldsymbol{x_2} \neq \boldsymbol{x_3} \tag{1}$$

$$u_i(j) = \begin{cases} v_i(j) \text{ if } rand \leq C_r; \\ x_i(j) \text{ otherwise.} \end{cases} \tag{2}$$

$$u_i(j) = \begin{cases} v_i(j), \text{ for } j = \langle n \rangle_D \ \langle n+1 \rangle_D, \ldots, \langle n+L-1 \rangle_D \\ x_i(j), \ \forall j \in [1, D] \end{cases} \tag{3}$$

From the initial publication [1], numerous variants have been proposed to improve the efficiency of the initial implementation. The original authors of DE even proposed some variants [9]. They try to balance the exploration of the search space and the exploitation of the most suitable candidate solutions. For this purpose diverse combination of vectors are selected for the base vectors as well as for the scaled differences. A detailed review of these variants and other ground-breaking modifications for DE can be found in [6,7,15].

For mentioning the DE-variants, a nomenclature based on the pattern DE/X/Y/Z is frequently used. The two initial letters (DE) correspond to the name of the algorithm, whereas the following ones consecutively correspond to the mechanism to select the base vector (X), the number of vectors involved in the scaled difference (Y), and the crossover operator (Z). Following this nomenclature, the classical DE is DE/rand/1/bin (Eqs. 1, 2). When using the Exponential Crossover operator instead of Binomial one, then the nomenclature is DE/rand/1/exp (Eqs. 1, 3).

In this work the following DE-variants have been analysed[2]. In all the tests, the Binomial Crossover operator is used, and therefore omitted in the nomenclature.

DE/rand/1 Original proposal of DE.
$\boldsymbol{v_i} = \boldsymbol{x_1} + F \cdot (\boldsymbol{x_2} - \boldsymbol{x_3})$

DE/rand/2 In this case, the scaled differences is generated with four vectors.
$\boldsymbol{v_i} = \boldsymbol{x_1} + F \cdot (\boldsymbol{x_2} + \boldsymbol{x_3} - \boldsymbol{x_4} - \boldsymbol{x_5})$

DE/best/1 In this variant, the base vector is not randomly selected, but the best vector of the current generation is used, $\boldsymbol{x_{best}}$.
$\boldsymbol{v_i} = \boldsymbol{x_{best}} + F \cdot (\boldsymbol{x_1} - \boldsymbol{x_2})$

DE/best/2 Similar to DE/best/1, but the number of vectors involved in the scaled difference is doubled.
$\boldsymbol{v_i} = \boldsymbol{x_{best}} + F \cdot (\boldsymbol{x_1} + \boldsymbol{x_2} - \boldsymbol{x_3} - \boldsymbol{x_4})$

---

[2] For the sake of brevity, the symbol corresponding to the crossover operator has been omitted.

DE/current-to-best/1 In this variant, a difference including the best vector in the current generation and the target vector is included. Furthermore, the target vector is used as base vector.
$\boldsymbol{v_i} = \boldsymbol{x_i} + F \cdot (\boldsymbol{x_{best}} - \boldsymbol{x_i}) + F \cdot (\boldsymbol{x_1} - \boldsymbol{x_2})$
This variant and the previous ones were proposed by Price and Storn in [9].

DE/rand-to-best/1 In the scaled differences, a difference including the best vector in the current generation and the base vector is included.
$\boldsymbol{v_i} = \boldsymbol{x_1} + F \cdot (\boldsymbol{x_{best}} - \boldsymbol{x_1}) + F \cdot (\boldsymbol{x_2} - \boldsymbol{x_3})$

DE/rand/2/dir This variant incorporates information of the fitness function. The objective is to guide the evolution towards favourable regions [17].
$\boldsymbol{v_i} = \boldsymbol{x_1} + \frac{\mu}{2} \cdot (\boldsymbol{x_1} - \boldsymbol{x_2} + \boldsymbol{x_3} - \boldsymbol{x_4})$
where $f(\boldsymbol{x_1}) < f(\boldsymbol{x_2})$ and $f(\boldsymbol{x_3}) < f(\boldsymbol{x_4})$.

All the previous variants have steady values of parameters F and C_r, and therefore they can be considered as static variants. However, these parameter can vary along the cycles. In [9] two variants, termed jitter and dither, are proposed with random values for the scaling factor, F. Dither is used when generating a new random F value for each difference vector; whereas if the new random F value is generated for each dimension of each difference vector, then the variant is termed jitter. In [11] a dither schema with F randomly varying between 0.5 and 1 for each vector is proposed.

For comparison purposed, two dither variants are implemented: the first one for which the scaling parameter is generated from a uniform statistical distribution in the range $(0.5, 1.0)$, and the second one for which F is generated from a Gaussian distribution with parameters $N(0.5, 0.25)$ [11]. Also in [11], a schema where F is reduced from 1.0 to 0.5 is proposed. This schema, termed DETVSF (DE with time varying scale factor), aims at promoting the exploration in the initial cycles, and reinforcing the exploitation in the final ones.

Apart from randomly generated scaling factors, they can be modified taking into account the best suited vectors from the previous generations, self-adapting variants [2,12,18,19]. Similarly to randomly generated, this mechanism aims at improving the overall performance.

The efforts in self-adapting variants arise from the initial studies about the importance of the control parameters for the final performance of the variants [20], and specially due to the dispersion of the values for these parameters. In [1] a value for the mutation factor of $F = 0.5$ is proposed. In [8], authors proposed mutation factor in the range $0.5 < F < 0.95$ with $F = 0.9$ as initial choice.

Some works have explored the DE performance when combining several trial-vector generation strategies, namely multi-strategy variants. Examples can be found in CoDE [21] and in EPSDE [22]. Comparisons with self-adapting or multi-strategy variants are not considered in this work, and are proposed as Future Work.

2.2 Matrix Notation for DE

In the matrix notation for DE/rand/1, the population of N vectors of d dimensions is represented by a matrix $\mathcal{P}$ (Eq. 4). $\mathcal{P}$ is formed by arranging the vectors in rows. x_k^i is the i dimension of the k vector, and it corresponds to the element (k, i) of the matrix $\mathcal{P}$.

$$\mathcal{P} = \begin{bmatrix} x_1^1 & \dots & x_1^i & \dots & x_1^d \\ \vdots & \ddots & & \ddots & \vdots \\ x_k^1 & \dots & x_k^i & \dots & x_k^d \\ \vdots & \ddots & & \ddots & \vdots \\ x_N^1 & \dots & x_N^i & \dots & x_N^d \end{bmatrix} \tag{4}$$

The first point to be addressed is the selection of a vector k from $\mathcal{P}$ (Eq. 5). This can be done by the product of a vector S_k and $\mathcal{P}$. Vector S_k is composed of null elements except for one position with a unitary value. By varying the position of the unitary value, distinct vectors can be selected.

$$\boldsymbol{x_k} = S_k \times \mathcal{P} = \begin{bmatrix}0 \dots 1 \dots 0\end{bmatrix}_k \times \begin{bmatrix} x_1^1 & \dots & x_1^i & \dots & x_1^d \\ \vdots & \ddots & & \ddots & \vdots \\ x_k^1 & \dots & x_k^i & \dots & x_k^d \\ \vdots & \ddots & & \ddots & \vdots \\ x_N^1 & \dots & x_N^i & \dots & x_N^d \end{bmatrix} \tag{5}$$

Thus, the difference between two vectors, $\boldsymbol{x_i} - \boldsymbol{x_j}$, can be rewritten as Eq. 6.

$$\boldsymbol{x_i} - \boldsymbol{x_j} = S_i \times \mathcal{P} \; - \; S_j \times \mathcal{P} = S_{ij} \times \mathcal{P} \tag{6}$$

where S_{ij} is a vector with all elements null, except for two elements which take positive and negative unitary values:

$$\begin{bmatrix}\dots 0\; 1\; 0 \dots 0 \; -1\; 0 \dots\end{bmatrix}_{ij} \tag{7}$$

Taking into account this notation and incorporating the mutation factor, Eq. 1 can be rewritten as Eq. 8.

$$\boldsymbol{x_k} + F \cdot (\boldsymbol{x_i} - \boldsymbol{x_j}) = S_k \times \mathcal{P} + F \cdot S_{ij} \times \mathcal{P} = F_{kij}^* \times \mathcal{P} \tag{8}$$

where F_{kij}^* is a vector with dimensionality $1 \times \mathit{Pop.\,size}$ (Eq. 9). The omitted elements in F_{kij}^* are all zeros.

$$F_{kij}^* = \begin{bmatrix}\dots F \dots 1 \dots -F \dots\end{bmatrix} \tag{9}$$

The F_{kij}^* can be vertically stacked, so that a matrix of $\mathit{Popsize} \times \mathit{Popsize}$ is established, $\mathcal{F}^*$. Each row of $\mathcal{F}^*$ is created similarly to Eq. 9, with random positions for the values: 1, F and $-F$.

In this way, the next generation of mutant vectors, $\mathcal{P}_{mutant}$ is produced by the product of the $\mathcal{F}^*$ matrix and the current population $\mathcal{P}_G$ (Eq. 10).

$$\mathcal{P}_{mutant} = \mathcal{F}^* \times \mathcal{P}_G \tag{10}$$

The DE/rand/2 variant can be easily expressed with the $\mathcal{F}^*$ notation (Eq. 9). For this variant, two positions per row of zero values have to be replaced by a F value and a $-F$ value. For other variants involving a larger number of vectors, DE/rand/Y, can also expressed by modifying the number of positions with F and $-F$ values. The DE/best/Y variants are transposed to matrix notation by replacing the S_k vector selector, by the appropriate selector for the best vector of the current generation, S_{best}.

In all these implementations, $\mathcal{F}^*$ keeps the following property $\sum_i \mathcal{F}^*_{ij} = 1$. This property is used as common ground for new DE-variants.

2.3 New Variants for Differential Evolution

The $\mathcal{F}^*$ notation paves the way for new variants of DE. For example, the $\mathcal{F}^*$ notation eases the implementation of a variant involving all the vectors. If the population size is odd, in DE/rand/all all the vectors of the population contribute as base vector or as part of the scaled differences. In this case, $\mathcal{F}^*$ has not zero elements. Conversely, if the population size is even, then one element of the matrix is null. The sum of any row of $\mathcal{F}^*$ is the unit $\sum_i \mathcal{F}^*_{ij} = 1$.

The first attempt for implementing DE/rand/all simply creates as scaled differences as possible with the population. However, this increment in the number of scaled differences carries out a degradation of the performance. For this reason, an alternative implementation, DE/rand/all$\frac{F}{2^n}$, where the mutation factor for the scaled differences are progressively halved is proposed of DE/rand/all (Eq. 11).

$$F^* = \begin{bmatrix} -F \dots & F/2 & \dots & 1 & \dots -F/2 \dots & F \\ \vdots & \ddots & & \ddots & \ddots & \dots \vdots \\ 1 & \dots -F/2 \dots & F/2 \dots & & -F & \dots F \end{bmatrix} \tag{11}$$

In DE/rand/alldiff the elements of matrix $\mathcal{F}^*$ are generated following the schema $(-1)^{B(0.5)} \cdot \frac{0.1*U(0,1)}{pop\,size} + \frac{1}{pop\,size}$, where $U(0,1)$ is a uniform probability distribution and $B(0.5)$ is a binomial distribution of probability 0.5. In this schema the base vector is completely removed, whereas the scaled differences are not longer created by subtracting of pairs of vectors. Conversely, each vector is weighted through the product of fixed and variable factors. The contribution of the base vector is equally distributed among all the vector of the population through the factor $\frac{1}{pop\,size}$. This schema keeps the property $\sum_i \mathcal{F}^*_{ij} = 1$.

2.4 Benchmark Functions

In order to evaluate the new DE-variants, a set of fitness functions are used (Table 1). This set includes both multimodal and monomodal, separable and non-separable functions. These fitness functions have been used in CEC contests [13,14] and also in works where presenting cutting-edge DE-variants [2,3,5,10, 16].

In all the tests performed in this work, a dimensionality of 30 and a population size of 10 vector have been used. Two configurations are used for the number of cycles: 100 and 1000, and the mean and the standard deviation of 25 independent runs per case are shown. Generally, a larger number of cycles leads to higher-quality solutions. However, it is specially interesting when these high-quality solutions can be produced with few cycles, thus CPU-time is saved. As pseudorandom number generator, a subroutine based on Mersenne Twister [4] has been used.

3 Results and Discussion

In this section the performance of the proposed variants are confronted to the a set of classic variants of DE for a set of benchmark functions. Tests with jitter and dither variants are also undertaken.

In Table 2, the numerical results obtained with DE/rand/alldiff variant are compared with the previous best results of the classical DE-variants[3]. Two configurations for the number of cycles are used: 100 and 1000 cycles. This intends to evaluate the DE-variants when trying to produce high-quality solutions with short number of cycles and when enough number of cycles to maximize the performance of the variants are supplied.

As can be appreciated, the DE/rand/alldiff variant outperforms the other static DE-variants in 26 of the 32 cases. They exclude the two configurations of the functions: Rastrigin, Schwefel, and Styblinski-Tang. Two of these functions: Schwefel and Styblinski-Tang, have optimal solution not in $\mathbf{0}$, whereas the third one, Rastrigin function, has the optimal solution in $\mathbf{0}$. For the other 13 functions, including Whitley function which has the optimal solution in $\mathbf{1}$, the DE/rand/alldiff produces better solutions than the other DE-variants included in the test. Concerning the cases where DE/rand/alldiff is outperformed, the DE-variants producing the best results vary from DE/rand/1 and DE/best/2 with 2 cases, and DE/rand/2/dir and DE/rand-to-best/1 with 1 case.

With regard to the performance of DE/rand/all$\frac{F}{2^n}$ (comparing with static DE-variants and DE/rand/alldiff), it only outperforms a single case. For Styblinski-Tang and 1000 cycles, the best mean result obtained is -1111 ± 26, whereas for DE/rand/all$\frac{F}{2^n}$ is -1127 ± 26. Although this is a single case, it corresponds to a function for which the results of DE/rand/alldiff systematically is outperformed by other variants. So that, it is a good candidate to hybridize with other DE-variant, or for studying its features in the exploration-exploitation phases.

Beyond the static DE-variants, further comparisons can be made with dither and jitter variants (Table 3). When comparing with these variants, the

[3] The best DE variant for each configuration and fitness function appears in boldface type.

Table 1. Benchmark functions used in this work.

Name	Function	Search range	Optimum
Ackley	$f(\boldsymbol{x}) = -20\exp(-0.2\sqrt{\frac{1}{n}\sum_{i=1}^{n} x_i^2}) - \exp(\frac{1}{n}\sum_{i=1}^{n} cos(2\pi x_i)) + 20 + \exp$	$[-32.0, 32.0]$	$0\, at\, \mathbf{0}$
Griewank	$f(\boldsymbol{x}) = 1 + \frac{1}{4000}\sum_{i=1}^{D} x_i^2 - \prod_{i=1}^{D} cos(\frac{x_i}{\sqrt{i}})$	$[-600.0, 600.0]$	$0\, at\, \mathbf{0}$
Hyperellipsoid	$f(\boldsymbol{x}) = \sum_{i=1}^{D} i \cdot x_i^2$	$[-5.12, 5.12]$	$0\, at\, \mathbf{0}$
Rana	$f(\boldsymbol{x}) = \sum_{i=1}^{D-1}(x_{i+1} + 1.0) \cdot cos(t_2) \cdot sin(t_1) + cos(t_1) \cdot sin(t_2) \cdot x_i$	$[-100.0, 100.0]$	$0\, at\, \mathbf{0}$
	$t_1 = \sqrt{\lvert x_{i+1} + x_i + 1.0 \rvert}$, $t_2 = \sqrt{\lvert x_{i+1} - x_i + 1.0 \rvert}$		
Rastrigin	$f(\boldsymbol{x}) = 10 \cdot D + \sum_{i=1}^{D}(x_i^2 - 10 \cdot cos(2\pi x_i))$	$[-5.12, 5.12]$	$0\, at\, \mathbf{0}$
Rosenbrock	$f(\boldsymbol{x}) = \sum_{i=1}^{D-1}(x_i - 1)^2 + 100 \cdot (x_{i+1} - x_i^2)^2$	$[-30, 30]$	$0\, at\, \mathbf{0}$
Schaffer's F6	$f(\boldsymbol{x}) = 0.5 + \frac{sin^2(\sqrt{\sum_{j=1}^{D} x_i^2}) - 0.5}{[1 + 0.001 \cdot (\sum_{j=1}^{D} x_i^2)]^2}$	$[-100.0, 100.0]$	$0\, at\, \mathbf{0}$
Schaffer's F7	$f(\boldsymbol{x}) = \frac{1}{n-1}\sum_{i=1}^{D-1}[\sqrt{s_i} \cdot (sin^2(50.0 s_i^{\frac{1}{5}}) + 1)]^2$,	$[-100.0, 100.0]$	$0\, at\, \mathbf{0}$
	$s_i = \sqrt{x_i^2 + x_{i+1}^2}$		
Schwefel	$f(\boldsymbol{x}) = \sum_{i=1}^{D}(-x_i \cdot sin\sqrt{\lvert x_i \rvert}) + 418.982887 \cdot D$	$[-500.0, 500.0]$	$0\, at$ **420.968746**
Schwefel Problem 1.2	$f(\boldsymbol{x}) = \sum_{i=1}^{D}(\sum_{j=1}^{i} x_j)^2$	$[-100.0, 100.0]$	$0\, at\, \mathbf{0}$
Schwefel Problem 2.22	$f(\boldsymbol{x}) = \sum_{i=0}^{D} \lvert x_i \rvert + \prod_{i=0}^{D} \lvert x_i \rvert$	$[-10.0, 10.0]$	$0\, at\, \mathbf{0}$
Schwefel Problem 2.21	$f(\boldsymbol{x}) = \max \lvert x_i \rvert, 1 \leq i \leq D$	$[-100.0, 100.0]$	$0\, at\, \mathbf{0}$
Sphere	$f(\boldsymbol{x}) = \sum_{i=1}^{D} x_i^2$	$[-5.12, 5.12]$	$0\, at\, \mathbf{0}$
Step	$f(\boldsymbol{x}) = \sum_{j=1}^{D}(\lfloor x_i + 0.5 \rfloor)^2$	$[-1000, 1000]$	$0\, at\, \mathbf{0}$
Styblinski-Tang	$f(\boldsymbol{x}) = 0.5 \cdot \sum_{i=1}^{D} x_i^4 - 16x_i^2 + 5x_i$	$[-5, 5]$	$-39.16599 \cdot D$ at $\mathbf{-2.903534}$
Whitley	$f(\boldsymbol{x}) = \sum_{i=1}^{D}\sum_{j=1}^{D}(\frac{(s_{ij})^2}{4000} - cos(s_{ij}) + 1)$	$[-10.24, 10.24]$	$0\, at\, \mathbf{1}$
	$s_{ij} = 100(x_i^2 - x_j)^2 + (1 - x_j)^2$		
Zakharov	$f(\boldsymbol{x}) = \sum_{i=1}^{D} x_i^2 + (\sum_{i=1}^{D} 0.5 \cdot i \cdot x_i)^2 + (\sum_{i=1}^{D} 0.5 \cdot i \cdot x_i)^4$	$[-5, 10]$	$0\, at\, \mathbf{0}$

Table 2. Comparison of DE/rand/alldiff variant with best results of the previous DE-variants. 25 independent runs per case with $F = Cr = 0.5$, for two configurations for the number of cycles: 100 and 1000, and Binomial Crossover operator.

Function	Cycles	Best previous		DE/rand/alldiff
Ackley	100	DE/best/2	6.83 ± 1.46	$\mathbf{0.36 \pm 0.08}$
	1000	DE/best/2	$(5.1 \pm 9.7)10^{-5}$	$\mathbf{(6.5 \pm 0.7)10^{-15}}$
Griewank	100	DE/best/2	17.19 ± 9.88	$\mathbf{0.030 \pm 0.011}$
	1000	DE/best/2	$(0.7 \pm 1.3)10^{-9}$	$\mathbf{(7.5 \pm 5.2)10^{-17}}$
Hyperellipsoid	100	DE/best/2	48.88 ± 22.25	$\mathbf{0.10 \pm 0.05}$
	1000	DE/best/2	$(0.8 \pm 3.1)10^{-8}$	$\mathbf{(1.5 \pm 2.5)10^{-34}}$
Rastrigin	100	DE/best/1	$\mathbf{115.47 \pm 35.91}$	149.97 ± 27.59
	1000	DE/rand/2/dir	$\mathbf{52.29 \pm 19.77}$	86.03 ± 16.04
Rosenbrock	100	DE/best/2	$(48 \pm 20)10^3$	$\mathbf{68.95 \pm 18.02}$
	1000	DE/best/2	$(1.3 \pm 0.8)10^3$	$\mathbf{28.80 \pm 0.16}$
Schaffer's F6	100	DE/rand-to-best/1	$(4925 \pm 58)10^{-4}$	$\mathbf{(3715 \pm 444)10^{-4}}$
	1000	DE/rand/1	0.27 ± 0.11	$\mathbf{0.03724 \pm 0.00007}$
Schaffer's F7	100	DE/rand-to-best/1	25.61 ± 0.80	$\mathbf{4.15 \pm 0.96}$
	1000	DE/rand/1	1.22 ± 1.46	$\mathbf{0.0012 \pm 0.0006}$
Schwefel	100	DE/best/1	$\mathbf{5130 \pm 734}$	9948 ± 398
	1000	DE/rand/1	$\mathbf{1282 \pm 977}$	8891 ± 512
Schwefel P. 1.2	100	DE/current-to-best/1	12766 ± 4593	$\mathbf{99 \pm 47}$
	1000	DE/best/2	4621 ± 1931	$\mathbf{(1.0311 \pm 3.6)10^{-12}}$
Schwefel P. 2.21	100	DE/current-to-best/1	34.07 ± 6.51	$\mathbf{3.80 \pm 1.07}$
	1000	DE/rand/2	22.94 ± 6.96	$\mathbf{(6.8 \pm 3.5)10^{-8}}$
Schwefel P. 2.22	100	DE/rand-to-best/1	18.07 ± 7.00	$\mathbf{0.67 \pm 0.18}$
	1000	DE/best/2	$(0.3 \pm 1.8)10-3$	$\mathbf{(1.2 \pm 0.8)10^{-17}}$
Sphere	100	DE/rand/2/dir	1.99 ± 2.28	$\mathbf{0.008 \pm 0.004}$
	1000	DE/best/2	$(1.7 \pm 3.5)10^{-10}$	$\mathbf{(4.3 \pm 5.9)10^{-36}}$
Step	100	DE/best/2	$(0.16 \pm 0.07)10^6$	$\mathbf{317.16 \pm 181.21}$
	1000	DE/rand/2	1.12 ± 1.63	$\mathbf{0.0 \pm 0.0}$
Styblinski -Tang	100	DE/rand-to-best/1	$\mathbf{-947 \pm 41}$	-670 ± 62
	1000	DE/rand/1	$\mathbf{-1111 \pm 26}$	-838 ± 59
Whitley	100	DE/best/2	$(5 \pm 4)10^6$	$\mathbf{0.48 \pm 0.06}$
	1000	DE/rand/2	1.25 ± 1.78	$\mathbf{0.3590 \pm 0.0006}$
Zakharov	100	DE/rand-to-best/1	93.7 ± 38.3	$\mathbf{1.5 \pm 1.3}$
	1000	DE/best/2	0.41 ± 1.14	$\mathbf{(1.84 \pm 9.03)10^{-10}}$

DE/rand/alldiff variant outperforms the dither and jitter variants in 27 of the 32 cases. With regard to the cases where DE/rand/alldiff is outperformed, the two configuration of Schwefel and Styblinski-Tang functions can be mentioned, as well as the Rastrigin function when using 1000 cycles.

In the previous comparisons, it is appreciated a slight bias toward a better performance when the fitness function has the optimal solution at $\mathbf{0}$. Probably

Table 3. Comparison of DE/rand/alldiff variant with best results of the DE dither and jitter variants. 25 independent runs per case with $F = Cr = 0.5$, for two configurations for the number of cycles: 100 and 1000, and Binomial Crossover operator.

Function	Cycles	Dither Uniform	Dither Gaussian	Jitter	DE/rand/alldiff
Ackley	100	16.07 ± 1.08	8.49 ± 1.62	8.27 ± 1.22	$\mathbf{0.36 \pm 0.08}$
	1000	0.015 ± 0.009	4.65 ± 3.18	2.80 ± 2.28	$\mathbf{(6.5 \pm 0.7)10^{-15}}$
Griewank	100	190.70 ± 57.76	24.65 ± 10.45	25.27 ± 9.79	$\mathbf{0.030 \pm 0.011}$
	1000	$(4.3 \pm 3.3)10^{-5}$	3.06 ± 2.60	2.55 ± 6.057	$\mathbf{(7.5 \pm 5.2)10^{-17}}$
Hyperellipsoid	100	559.09 ± 209.25	108.23 ± 41.46	89.37 ± 35.55	$\mathbf{0.10 \pm 0.05}$
	1000	$(14 \pm 10)10^{-5}$	22.65 ± 26.50	3.87 ± 7.84	$\mathbf{(1.5 \pm 2.5)10^{-34}}$
Rastrigin	100	314.7 ± 26.7	207.3 ± 22.2	235.5 ± 33.7	$\mathbf{149.97 \pm 27.59}$
	1000	165.8 ± 20.0	$\mathbf{30.0 \pm 8.2}$	103.1 ± 23.0	86.03 ± 16.04
Rosenbrock	100	$(441.0 \pm 112.7)10^3$	$(80.9 \pm 39.9)10^3$	$(145.2 \pm 61.9)10^3$	$\mathbf{68.95 \pm 18.02}$
	1000	8621 ± 5030	8013 ± 7775	3438 ± 2235	$\mathbf{28.80 \pm 0.16}$
Schaffer's F6	100	$0.49987 \pm 8 \cdot 10^{-5}$	0.4994 ± 0.0003	0.4996 ± 0.0003	$\mathbf{(3715 \pm 444)10^{-4}}$
	1000	0.38 ± 0.05	0.36 ± 0.10	0.26 ± 0.10	$\mathbf{0.03724 \pm 0.00007}$
Schaffer's F7	100	100.98 ± 10.47	43.62 ± 10.91	49.09 ± 9.36	$\mathbf{4.15 \pm 0.96}$
	1000	4.79 ± 2.01	4.25 ± 2.62	0.79 ± 0.59	$\mathbf{0.0012 \pm 0.0006}$
Schwefel	100	10184 ± 492	$\mathbf{7949 \pm 670}$	9383 ± 495	9948 ± 398
	1000	7862 ± 453	$\mathbf{2459 \pm 586}$	4517 ± 1915	8891 ± 512
Schwefel Problem 1.2	100	126024 ± 34941	64622 ± 12833	76447 ± 20686	$\mathbf{99 \pm 47}$
	1000	67049 ± 18226	10405 ± 5685	22894 ± 10063	$\mathbf{(1.0311 \pm 3.6)10^{-12}}$
Schwefel Problem 2.21	100	81.11 ± 5.18	56.90 ± 8.84	68.72 ± 9.59	$\mathbf{3.80 \pm 1.07}$
	1000	23.41 ± 8.879	45.18 ± 9.13	37.63 ± 7.82	$\mathbf{(6.8 \pm 3.5)10^{-8}}$
Schwefel Problem 2.22	100	848.70 ± 1776.78	16.22 ± 3.58	29.26 ± 8.34	$\mathbf{0.67 \pm 0.18}$
	1000	0.015 ± 0.007	1.73 ± 2.35	0.36 ± 0.80	$\mathbf{(1.2 \pm 0.8)10^{-17}}$
Sphere	100	52.46 ± 18.05	7.80 ± 4.74	6.38 ± 2.04	$\mathbf{0.008 \pm 0.004}$
	1000	$(0.11e \pm 9.14)10^{-6}$	0.98 ± 1.60	0.56 ± 1.01	$\mathbf{(4.3 \pm 5.9)10^{-36}}$
Step	100	$(20.3 \pm 5.8)10^5$	$(2.6 \pm 1.2)10^5$	$(2.4 \pm 0.9)10^5$	$\mathbf{317 \pm 181}$
	1000	1.36 ± 2.33	83705 ± 128632	16079 ± 25020	$\mathbf{0.0 \pm 0.0}$
Styblinski -Tang	100	-570 ± 48	$\mathbf{-905 \pm 48}$	-744.9 ± 60.618	-670 ± 62
	1000	-1101 ± 73	-1072 ± 25	$\mathbf{-1104 \pm 25}$	-838 ± 59
Whitley	100	$(4.0 \pm 3.0)10^9$	$(36.7 \pm 67.9)10^6$	$(28.8 \pm 22.7)10^6$	$\mathbf{0.48 \pm 0.06}$
	1000	2.07 ± 3.43	$(8.5 \pm 20.2)10^6$	$0.24 \pm 0.50)10^6$	$\mathbf{0.3590 \pm 0.0006}$
Zakharov	100	683.8 ± 126.4	437.4 ± 148.3	427.3 ± 93.6	$\mathbf{1.5 \pm 1.3}$
	1000	290.00 ± 113.28	4.53 ± 7.60	5.14 ± 6.45	$\mathbf{(1.84 \pm 9.03)10^{-10}}$

this is due to a greedy behaviour of the DE/rand/alldiff: it is intensive in the exploitation of promising-candidate solutions, but its efficiency for exploring the search space decreases. In order to improve the efficient of this variant in future tests, this greedy behaviour should be corrected by improving the exploratory capacity.

4 Conclusions

In this paper, two new variants of DE are proposed and evaluated: DE/rand/all$\frac{F}{2^n}$ and DE/rand/alldiff. Differently to the variants proposed in the past, these new variants include scaled differences involving all the vectors. In DE/rand/all$\frac{F}{2^n}$ progressively halves the mutation factor, so that the importance of the scaled difference is also reduced. And in DE/rand/alldiff, the base vector and the scaled differences are replaced by weighted contributions of all the vectors in the population. The results state that this last variant outperforms a large set of other DE-variants, including jitter and dither ones, over a wide set of fitness functions.

Furthermore, a matrix notation for generating the mutant vectors population in DE is introduced. This notation helps visualizing the process, at the same time it might inspire new DE-variants.

This work opens diverse lines in relation of Future Work. They include the adaptation of the DE/randalldiff and the DE/rand/all$\frac{F}{2^n}$ to adaptive variation of the mutation factor, statistical studies about the values of the scaled differences for these and other variants, and the generation of new variants based on the matrix notation.

Acknowledgement. The research leading to these results has received funding by the Spanish Ministry of Economy and Competitiveness (MINECO) for funding support through the grant FPA2013-47804-C2-1-R, FPA2016-80994-C2-1-R, and "Unidad de Excelencia María de Maeztu": CIEMAT - FÍSICA DE PARTÍCULAS through the grant MDM-2015-0509.

References

1. Storn, R., Price, K.: Differential evolution - a simple and efficient heuristic for global optimization over continuous spaces. J. Glob. Optim. **11**(4), 341–359 (1997)
2. Zamuda, A., Brest, J.: Self-adaptive control parameters' randomization frequency and propagations in differential evolution. Swarm Evol. Comput. **25**, 72–99 (2015)
3. Peñuñuri-Anguiano, F.R., Cab-Cauich, C.A., Carvente-Muñoz, O., Zambrano-Arjona, M.A., Tapia-González, J.A.: A study of the classical differential evolution control parameters. Swarm Evol. Comput. **26**, 86–96 (2016)
4. Matsumoto, M., Nishimura, T.: Mersenne twister: a 623-dimensionally equidistributed uniform pseudorandom number generator. ACM Trans. Model. Comput. Simul. **8**(1), 3–30 (1999)
5. Mezura-Montes, E., Velazquez-Reyes, J., Coello, C.A.C.: A comparative study of differential evolution variants for global optimization. In: GECCO, pp. 485–492 (2006)

6. Das, S., Suganthan, P.N.: Differential evolution: a survey of the state-of-the-art. IEEE Trans. Evol. Comput. **15**(1), 4–31 (2011)
7. Neri, F., Tirronen, V.: Recent advances in differential evolution: a survey and experimental analysis. Artif. Intell. Rev. **33**(1), 61–106 (2010)
8. Rönkkönen, J., Kukkonen, S., Price, K.V.: Real-parameter optimization with differential evolution. In: Proceedings of the IEEE Congress on Evolutionary Computation, CEC 2005, Edinburgh, UK, 2–4 , pp. 506–513. IEEE (2005)., September 2005
9. Price, K.V., Storn, R.M., Lampinen, J.A.: Differential Evolution a Practical Approach to Global Optimization. Natural Computing Series. Springer, Berlin (2005)
10. Lu, X., Tang, K., Sendhoff, B., Yao, X.: A new self-adaptation scheme for differential evolution. Neurocomput. 146(C), 2–16 (2014)
11. Das, S., Konar, A., Chakraborty, U.K.: Two improved differential evolution schemes for faster global search. In: Genetic and Evolutionary Computation Conference, GECCO 2005, Proceedings, Washington DC, USA, 25–29 , pp. 991–998. ACM (2005)., June 2005
12. Lu, X., Tang, K., Sendhoff, B., Yao, X.: A new self-adaptation scheme for differential evolution. Neurocomputing **146**, 2–16 (2014)
13. Tang, K., Li, X., Suganthan, P.N., Yang, Z., Weise, T.: Benchmark functions for the cec'2010 special session and competition on large-scale global optimization. Technical report, Nature Inspired Computation and Applications Laboratory (NICAL), School of Computer Science and Technology, University of Science and Technology of China (USTC) (2009)
14. Tang, K., Yao, X., Suganthan, P.N., MacNish, C., Chen, Y.P., Chen, C.M., Yang, Z.: Benchmark functions for the CEC 2008 special session and competition on large scale global optimization. Technical report, Nature Inspired Computation and Applications Laboratory, USTC, China (2007)
15. Das, S., Mullick, S.S., Suganthan, P.: Recent advances in differential evolution-an updated survey. Swarm Evol. Comput. **27**, 1–30 (2016)
16. Chen, Y., Xie, W., Zou, X.: A binary differential evolution algorithm learning from explored solutions. Neurocomputing **149**, 1038–1047 (2015)
17. Feoktistov, V., Janaqi, S.: Generalization of the strategies in differential evolution. In: 18th International Parallel and Distributed Processing Symposium (IPDPS 2004), CD-ROM/Abstracts Proceedings, Santa Fe, New Mexico, USA, 26–30. IEEE Computer Society (2004)., April 2004
18. Qin, A.K., Huang, V.L., Suganthan, P.N.: Differential evolution algorithm with strategy adaptation for global numerical optimization. IEEE Trans. Evol. Comput. **13**(2), 398–417 (2009)
19. Qin, A.K., Suganthan, P.N.: Self-adaptive differential evolution algorithm for numerical optimization. In: Proceedings of the IEEE Congress on Evolutionary Computation, CEC 2005, Edinburgh, UK, 2–4 , pp. 1785–1791. IEEE (2005)., September 2005
20. Gämperle, R., Müller, S.D., Koumoutsakos, P.: A parameter study for differential evolution. In: WSEAS International Conference on Advances in Intelligent Systems, Fuzzy Systems, Evolutionary Computation, Press, pp. 293–298 (2002)
21. Wang, Y., Cai, Z., Zhang, Q.: Differential evolution with composite trial vector generation strategies and control parameters. Trans. Evol. Comp. **15**(1), 55–66 (2011)
22. Mallipeddi, R., Suganthan, P.N., Pan, Q.K., Tasgetiren, M.F.: Differential evolution algorithm with ensemble of parameters and mutation strategies. Appl. Soft Comput. **11**(2), 1679–1696 (2011)

Topological Evolution of Financial Network: A Genetic Algorithmic Approach

Ga Ching Lui, Chun Yin Yip, and Kwok Yip Szeto(✉)

Department of Physics, The Hong Kong University of Science and Technology, Clear Water Bay, Kowloon, Hong Kong
phszeto@ust.hk

Abstract. The structure of financial market is captured using a novel time warping method known as discrete time warping genetic algorithm (dTWGA). In contrast to previous studies which estimate the correlations between different time series, dTWGA can be used to analyse time series with different lengths and with data sampled unevenly. Moreover, since coupling between different time series or at different periods of time would be changing over time, the time delay for the influence of a time series to reach another time series would be changing as well, which would not be well captured with correlation measurements. The proposed algorithm is applied on Dow Jones Index (DJI) and its compositions consisting of 30 stocks, and different measurements are performed to observe the evolution of the network structure. It is suggested that there are major topological changes during market crashes, leading to a significant decrease in the size of the network.

Keywords: Financial network · Systemic risk · Time warping · Time series alignment · Genetic algorithm · Minimum spanning tree · Market crash

1 Introduction

There have been rapid developments in network science and graph theory in recent years as the field is gaining more attention, with numerous applications in different sectors ranging from ecology [10], epidermic spreading [3], interbank network [2], to information propagation through social media [17]. In finance, pairwise correlation of financial time series has been used to build a description of the financial network by treating each stock as a node in the network and by using some measurements of the coupling strength as the weight of the edges [4,5,15]. In particular, the hierarchical structure of a financial network is constructed using correlation as a similarity measurement to describe the coupling between different stocks, with close proximity between two stocks representing a positive correlation, while stocks that are very far from the others are negatively correlated [9]. Onnela [12] further applies this methodology to study changes of S&P500 and its components in relation to Black Monday, a financial crisis in 1987. However, there exists limitations with this methodology. For instance, Pearson correlation cannot be used to describe non-linear relations, and thus the

F.J. Martínez de Pisón et al. (Eds.): HAIS 2017, LNAI 10334, pp. 113–124, 2017.
DOI: 10.1007/978-3-319-59650-1_10

network structure described with the above method would not be able to detect interactions of this type. Furthermore, there may be time lags between the occurrence of a price change in a stock and the information of such a change reaching another node to incur certain effects on the price of that node, and would therefore evade the detections made with Pearson correlation. While measuring the cross-correlation with time delay may help determine the time delay and thus rediscover this type of causal relation, the time delay itself may not actually be time-independent and may be affected by the market environment or the investment climate at that time, and therefore non-linear mapping between the two time series is required. In extreme cases, if the time delay becomes negative, then causality between the two stocks is reversed. The third limitation has to do with the length of the time series and the way the data are gathered. For high-frequency trading, the data points are not evenly sampled as transactions are made at different instances [4]. In addition, time series collected for different stocks might not have the same length. Thus, preprocessing of the data points, such as addition or removal of data points, prior to calculating the correlations would be required, and this in turn leads to more assumptions and bias made about the system. In this paper, we are motivated to rectify some of these problems with a new methodology involving genetic algorithm.

Genetic algorithm (GA) is meta-heuristic searching method employed in optimization problems with large searching space. GA has been utilized across different disciplines such as game theory [18], portfolio selection [13], biological time series [7], astrophysics [11] and network optimization [6,8]. In this work, we use GA as a means to recover the coupling between different stocks and this method is called discrete time warping genetic algorithm (dTWGA), which is the discrete version of the method TWGA we have previously proposed [7]. Different from TWGA, dTWGA does not involve the crossover operator. GAs without crossovers have previously been studied, with the example of Mutation Only Genetic Algorithm (MOGA) which involves the use of mutation matrix and can be seen as a generalization of traditional GAs [14]. Making use of dTWGA, the coupling with non-linear time delay can be described and is used to construct a description of the financial market. Topological changes of such network across time is compared with the performance of financial market as a whole. In particular, the network size shrinks significantly at the time of crashes. This paper is organized as follows: The ideas and methodology of dTWGA are explained in Sect. 2. For Sect. 3, the procedure of recovering the network structure is described, and the application is documented in Sect. 4. The results are presented and discussed in Sect. 5, and the paper concludes with Sect. 6.

2 Discrete Time Warping Genetic Algorithm (dTWGA)

Suppose we are given two time series, namely X(t) and Y(t), and the objective of the proposed method dTWGA is to obtain the time mappings $\tau(t)$ such that the overlapping area of the graphs in the time domain for the $X(\tau(t))$ and $Y(t)$ is maximized. Such non-linear transformation is referred to here as time warping.

Discrete TWGA aims to tackle this problem by partitioning the discrete time domain with as few constraints as possible since the determination of constraints requires prior knowledge or domain knowledge of the systems concerned, and we would like to minimize the number of assumptions made. Due to the large solution space, genetic algorithm is used to minimize the sum of absolute pairwise distance of $X(\tau(t_j) = t_i)$ and $Y(t_i)$ across all t_i.

2.1 Solution Representation

Defining the two normalized time series to be $S_i = \{S_i(n)|n = 0, 1, ..., N, N+1\}$ and $S_j = \{S_j(m)|m = 0, 1, ..., M, M+1\}$, where n and m are the time indices, while $\max(S_i) = \max(S_j) = 1$ and $\min(S_i) = \min(S_j) = 0$, a solution in the searching space is encoded in dTWGA to be chromosome k which consists of N time indices such that $C_k = \{C_k[l]|l = 1, 2, ..., N\}$. Each chromosome is of length N instead of $N+1$ because the boundary constraint is imposed such that $S_i(0)$ is always mapped to $S_j(0)$ while $S_i(N+1)$ is always mapped to $S_j(M+1)$. An example of a chromosome is shown in Fig. 1. Two constraints are considered when a population of chromosomes evolves:

Monotonicity: $C_k[l] \leq C_k[l+1] \quad \forall_l$
Boundary: $0 \leq C_k[l] \leq M+1 \quad \forall_l$

To initialize a population of chromosomes, N integers are drawn randomly from a uniform deviate in the closed set $[0, M+1]$ for each chromosome. The N integers are then sorted in ascending order to form a chromosome. N_p chromosomes are produced with this method to form a population such that $k = 1, 2, ..., N_p$ for chromosome C_k.

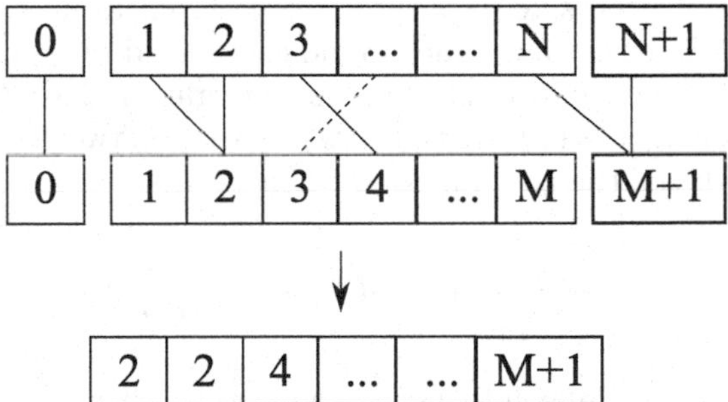

Fig. 1. An example of chromosome of length N representing the mapping of the time indices n and m. The mappings for the two time series are represented by solid line, whereas the dotted line denotes the mapping that is not allowed by the monotonicity requirement. The boundaries are fixed and are therefore not included in the chromosome sequence. This mapping is encoded in the chromosome as shown in the bottom row of numbers in the figure.

2.2 Mutation

For each generation, N_m loci in each chromosome are selected to mutate, except for the fittest chromosome. This is known as elitism, which ensures that the best solution or the fittest chromosome in the population remains in the next generation. The concept of fitness will be clarified in the next section. For a selected position l_m, the original value $C_k(l_m)$ is changed to a random integer drawn from a uniform deviate in $[C_k(l_m - 1), C_k(l_m + 1)]$ unless $l_m = 1$ or N. If $l_m = 1$, an integer is selected from $[0, C_k(2)]$. If $l_m = N$, an integer is selected from $[C_k(N - 1), M + 1]$. This ensures that both monotonicity and boundary constraints are satisfied. A total of $N_m \times (N_p - 1)$ mutates in each generation and this corresponds to the mutation probability of N_m/N. An example of mutation is shown in Fig. 2.

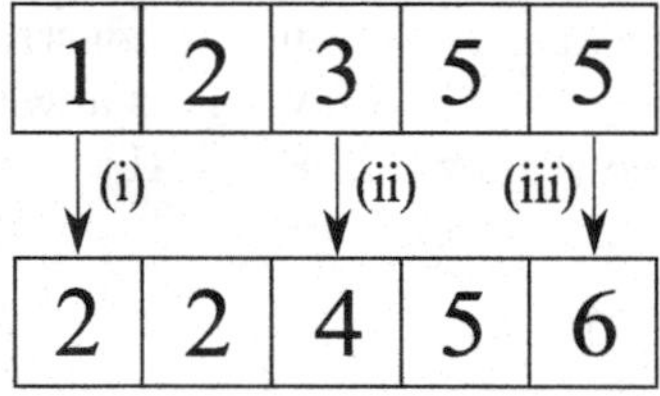

Fig. 2. An example of mutation with $N_m = 3$ and $N = 5$, corresponding to a mutation probability of 0.6. For mutation (i), (ii) and (iii), the modified values are chosen from the closed sets $[0, 2]$, $[2, 5]$ and $[5, 6]$ respectively.

2.3 Fitness

To define concept of fitness, we consider the cost function of chromosome k, denoted as s_k. The fitter chromosomes would correspond to lower values of cost, while the weaker chromosomes would have higher values of cost. Since the objective of this algorithm is to minimize the distance between two time series through time warping, we define the cost function to be

$$s_k = |S_i(0) - S_j(0)| + |S_i(N+1) - S_j(M+1)| + \sum_{l=1}^{N} |S_i(l) - S_j(C_k[l])| \,. \quad (1)$$

Although we simply use absolute norm here, other norms can also be used. By allowing the population to evolve, the cost of the best chromosome would decrease using suitable selection schemes.

2.4 Selection

N_p chromosomes in the population are sorted in ascending order according to the cost function $s_k \leq s_{k+1} \forall_k$. This means that the fitter chromosomes would be assigned with smaller values of k. N_k chromosomes that has the highest cost would be replaced by fitter chromosomes with lower costs. To achieve this, chromosome C_k is removed for $k \geq N_p - N_k$. N_k selections are made in order to replace the removed chromosomes. For each selection, a chromosome is chosen from the fitter chromosomes with $k \leq N_p - N_k$ according to the following probability:

$$P(C_k) = \frac{\sum_{\substack{i=1 \\ i \neq k}}^{N_p - N_k} s_i}{(N_p - N_k - 1) \sum_{j=1}^{N_p - N_k} s_j}. \tag{2}$$

The probabilities defined in (2) are normalized by default. According to the equation, chromosomes with lower costs would have a higher probability to be chosen. The chosen chromosome would replace one of the removed chromosomes, thus lowering the average cost of the population.

2.5 Iteration

The processes of mutation, fitness evaluation, sorting and selection are iterated to produce new generations of chromosomes and to allow the population to evolve until a stopping criteria is reached. In our algorithm, the stopping criteria is defined as the fixed number of generations produced. When the G-th generation is reached, the best chromosome in that population is returned to be the time mapping between the two time series, and the distance $d(S_i, S_j)$ between S_i and S_j is returned to be $s_{k=1}$ in the G-th generation. Since $M = N$ and both are fixed in this work, normalization of the distance is not required. If $M \neq N$, then the distance should be normalized by a constant factor of $N + 2$. A flow chart of this algorithm is shown in Fig. 3.

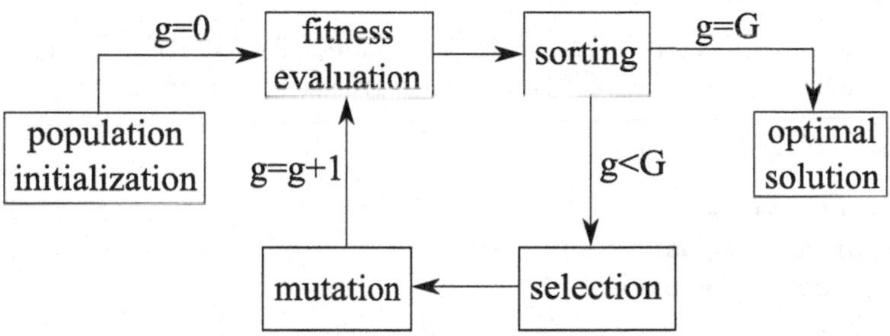

Fig. 3. Flow chart of dTWGA, consisting of operators that maintain monotonicity, with the number of generations reached to be the stopping criteria, and that g denote the number of generations.

3 Financial Network Construction

Given a stock i, consider the time series of stock price P_i, we can detrend the data using log return S_i, which is typically defined as

$$S_i(t) = \ln P_i(t) - \ln P_i(t-1). \tag{3}$$

The network structure of N_s stocks can be captured using dTWGA. The nodes in the graph are the stocks, while the edge weightings between stock i and stock j are given by

$$d_{ij} = \min\left(d(S_i, S_j), d(S_i, -S_j)\right), \tag{4}$$

where $d(S_i, S_j)$ is a measure of positive correlation, while $d(S_i, -S_j)$ is a measure of negative correlation. This measurement is similar to that suggested by Tsinaslanidis [16] for dynamic time warping. By this construction, $d_{ij} = 0$ if $i = j$ and $\forall_{i,j}$, $d_{ij} \geq 0$. As d_{ij} should be the same as d_{ji}, we only need to evaluate $N_s(N_s - 1)/2$ entries in the $N_p \times N_p$ adjacency matrix $\mathbf{D}$, while each entry requires evaluation of two distances using dTWGA, resulting in a weighted, undirected and connected network, of which the topology can be captured using the three measurements described below.

3.1 Minimum Spanning Tree

A minimum spanning tree (MST) refers to an acyclic subgraph with N_p nodes and $N_p - 1$ edges that has the smallest total weight summed over all edges compared to the total weight of other spanning trees. In other words, we may describe the size of an MST, D_{min}, with the tree length:

$$L = \sum_{(i,j)\in D_{min}} d_{ij}, \tag{5}$$

where (i, j) is the edge connecting node i and node j. An MST can be constructed using Kruskal's algorithm which is a type of greedy algorithm:

Pseudo-code of Kruskal's algorithm

```
D_min = empty graph
E = list of all edges
sort E in ascending order
for e in E:
   if (D_min + e) is acyclic:
      add e to D_min
```

We would measure tree length L to characterize a network at different time periods in the later sections.

3.2 Maximum Degree Ratio

In the MST, we are interested in characterizing the largest hub, which has the largest number of nearest neighbours. At crashes, it is expected that the hubs would be more influential to other nodes, and therefore it would be interested to observe the weighted degree of network hubs in MST. We define the maximum degree ratio as

$$\xi(D_{min}) = \frac{\text{weighted degree of node } i}{\text{number of nearest neighbours of node } i}, \tag{6}$$

where node i is the node with the largest number of neighbours in the MST, and the weighted degree is simply the sum of weights of all edges connected to node i in MST.

3.3 Spectrum

We would compare the spectrum at different time periods. Given an adjacency matrix, we denote the eigenvalues to be λ_i, where $i = 1, 2, ..., N_s$, such that $\forall_i$, $\lambda_i \geq \lambda_{i+1}$. In this work, we would only compare the largest eigenvalue λ_1 of matrix $\mathbf{D}$ with the market environment.

4 Experiment

The algorithm is applied to analyse the daily closing price of Dow Jones Index (DJI) and its components consisting of 30 stocks during the period from mid-March in 2008 to the beginning of October in 2016, and the data are obtained from Yahoo [1]. A histogram of log return obtained during this period is plotted in Fig. 4, showing a bell-shaped distribution centred around $S_{dji} = 0$, which is one of the nice properties of using log return, with outliers representing large crashes and sudden increase of stock prices in the financial market. The largest price fluctuation during this period occurs between 2008 and 2009, during which the global financial crisis was triggered. There are also some moderate price fluctuations during 2010, 2011, and 2015 and 2016. To monitor the changes of the financial network, we need to infer the coupling between different stocks. The distances obtained with dTWGA are estimations of the couplings between the components, giving a 30×30 adjacency matrix $\mathbf{D}$ with entries d_{ij}.

A moving window with size w is applied on the time series to obtain the network structure at different time frames. For dTWGA, we are therefore evaluating the distance d_{ij} between $\{S_i(n')|n' = t, t+1, ..., t+w\}$ and $\{S_j(m')|m' = t, t+1, ..., t+w\}$ by (4). By shifting the time axis such that $n = n' - t$ and $m = m' - t$, we can then follow the algorithm described in Sects. 2 and 3 accordingly, with $M = N = w - 2$. For the parameters in this work, the size of population N_p is set to be 8 chromosomes, the number of removed chromosomes in each generation is set to be $N_k = 4$, and the mutation parameter is set to be $N_m = 3$. Here, the window size is set to be $w = 20$, which is around 1 month.

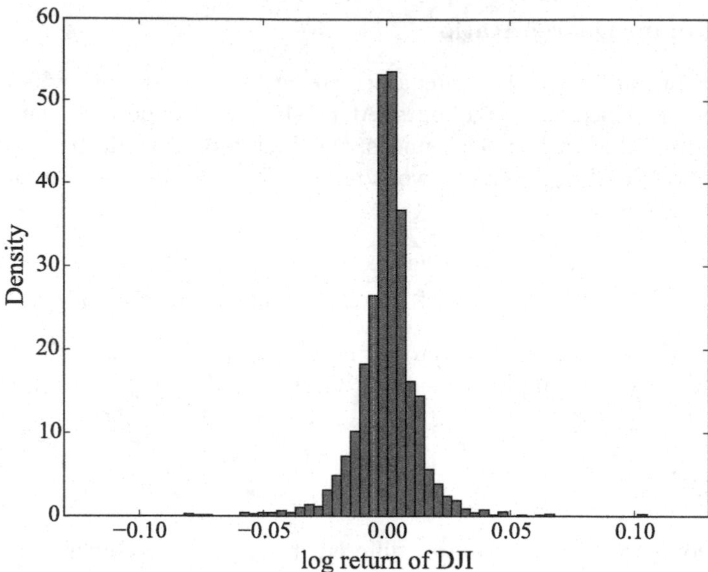

Fig. 4. Histogram of log return of Dow Jones Index (DJI) obtained during the period of mid-March in 2008 to the beginning of October in 2016.

This corresponds to a mutation probability of 1/6. The window size is then increased to $w = 60$ and 100, which corresponds to 3 months and 5 months respectively. After analysing the network at one time frame, the window moves forward in time by 1 time unit. Therefore, the time difference between consecutive moving windows is 1 day, and this allows the evolution of the network topology to be captured. The changes in topology can then be compared with the performance of the market, for which DJI can be used as an indicator to evaluate the performance of all the stocks in the constructed network at different time frames.

5 Results and Discussion

Three variables, namely the largest eigenvalue λ_1, tree length L of the MST and maximum degree ratio ξ, are obtained from the network constructed with dTWGA and compared with the market performance evaluated with the log return of DJI, which is denoted as S_{dji}, at window size $w = 20$. For fair comparison taking into account the effect of averaging, the average of the log return $\langle S_{dji} \rangle$ over the data points taken in a moving window with size w is also plotted in Fig. 5 as an indicator of the average performance of the market.

From Fig. 5, the instances of large decrease of all the three variables λ_1, L and ξ correspond to the large price fluctuations in the year of 2008, 2012, 2015 and 2016 as shown in the time series of S_{dji}. This correspondence becomes more apparent when comparing the trend of the three parameters with the average

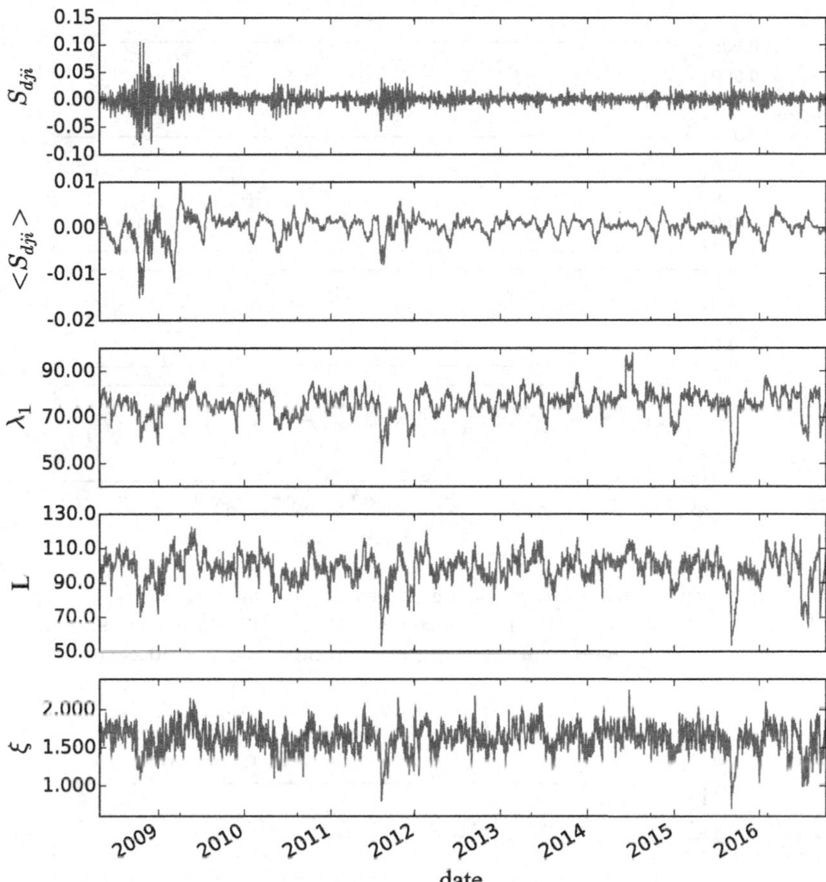

Fig. 5. Comparisons of the log return of Dow Jones index, denotes as S_{dji}, the average of log return in moving window S_{dji}, the largest eigenvalue λ_1 of adjacency matrix $\mathbf{D}$, the tree length L of the minimum spanning tree D_{min} and the maximum degree ratio $\xi(D_{min})$ for window size $w = 20$ as time proceeds.

log return $\langle S_{dji} \rangle$. This suggests that the information of the overall environment of performance in the market can be reflected by information regarding the structure of the index component network. In particular, the tree length of the minimum spanning tree shrinks, indicating that the couplings between the stocks are indeed stronger at the time of crash. The largest eigenvalue has a similar trend compared to that of the tree length of the MST. The maximum degree ratio also decreases at crashes, suggesting the effects asserted by the hub on its neighbours increases and therefore pulls the nodes closer towards it. The window size w is then increased to 60 and 100, corresponding to 3 months and 5 months respectively.

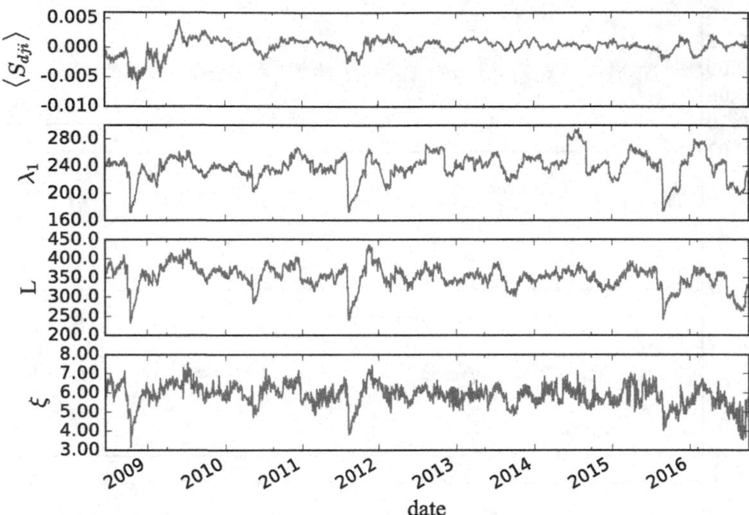

Fig. 6. Comparisons of the average of log return in moving window S_{dji}, the largest eigenvalue λ_1 of adjacency matrix $\mathbf{D}$, the tree length L of the minimum spanning tree D_{min} and the maximum degree ratio $\xi(D_{min})$ for window size $w = 60$ as time proceeds.

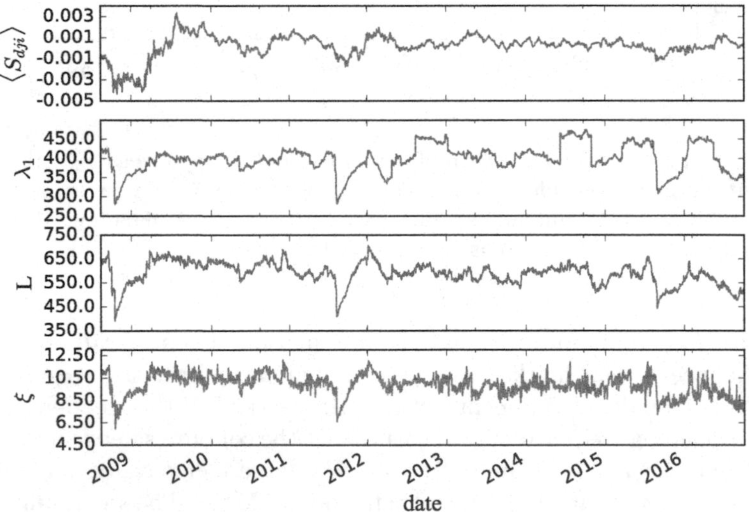

Fig. 7. Comparisons of the average of log return in moving window S_{dji}, the largest eigenvalue λ_1 of adjacency matrix $\mathbf{D}$, the tree length L of the minimum spanning tree D_{min} and the maximum degree ratio $\xi(D_{min})$ for window size $w = 100$ as time proceeds.

By comparing Fig. 5 with Figs. 6 and 7, the prominent features with large peaks and troughs are captured with both settings, of which the latter case with larger windows illustrates the remnant effects of the crashes on the topology of the constructed network over a long period. Another difference with larger window size w is that the effect of noise on signals is reduced since the signals are stronger. This effect is most apparent for maximum degree ratio among the three variables. While moving windows with larger sizes lead to more robust indicators against noise, the remnant effects would make it difficult to differentiate two large price fluctuates occurs in close proximity in time, and thus might not be as useful in predictions.

As demonstrated with the example of DJI, dTWGA can effectively describe the interactions between time series with few assumptions imposed. Further work will be conducted on applying the framework over different indices across different periods. As described in Sect. 2, the entire methodology could be carried over to address unevenly spaced time series, such as those in high frequency trading. Our methodology would also be useful in the studies that merge different types of data collected in different ways, which could be sampled at different instances unlike the daily closing price studied here.

6 Conclusion

In this paper, a novel algorithm dTWGA involving genetic algorithm is proposed. The algorithm is applied to recover the network structure of stocks and the evolution of the network over time is observed. It is found that the size of the network would shrink at large fluctuation of daily log return of stocks, showing increased dependence between the stocks, and the nodes would be pulled towards the node with the largest number of nearest neighbours.

References

1. Yahoo. https://finance.yahoo.com.
2. Boss, M., Elsinger, H., Summer, M., Thurner, S.: Network topology of the interbank market. Quant. Financ. **4**(6), 677–684 (2004)
3. Cai, W., Chen, L., Ghanbarnejad, F., Grassberger, P.: Avalanche outbreaks emerging in cooperative contagions. Nat. Phys. **11**(11), 936–940 (2015)
4. Han, R.Q., Xie, W.J., Xiong, X., Zhang, W., Zhou, W.X.: Market correlation structure changes around the Great Crash. arXiv preprint arXiv:1602.00125 (2016)
5. Laloux, L., Cizeau, P., Bouchaud, J.P., Potters, M.: Noise dressing of financial correlation matrices. Physical review letters 83(7), 1467 (1999).
6. Lin, Y.K., Yeh, C.T.: Maximal network reliability with optimal transmission line assignment for stochastic electric power networks via genetic algorithms. Appl. Soft Comput. **11**(2), 2714–2724 (2011)
7. Lui, G.C., Wu, D., Cheung, K.W., Ma, H.F., Szeto, K.Y.: Time warping of apneic ECG signals using genetic algorithm. In: 2016 IEEE Congress on Evolutionary Computation (CEC), pp. 178–184. IEEE (2016)

8. Luk, P.W.H., Lui, G.C., Szeto, K.Y.: Optimization of systemic stability of directed network using genetic algorithm. In: 2016 IEEE/ACIS 15th International Conference on Computer and Information Science (ICIS), pp. 1–6. IEEE (2016)
9. Mantegna, R.N.: Hierarchical structure in financial markets. Eur. Phys. J. B-Condens. Matter Complex Syst. **11**(1), 193–197 (1999)
10. May, R.M.: Will a large complex system be stable? Nature 238, 413–414 (1972).
11. Metcalfe, T.S., Charbonneau, P.: Stellar structure modeling using a parallel genetic algorithm for objective global optimization. J. Comput. Phys. **185**(1), 176–193 (2003)
12. Onnela, J.P., Chakraborti, A., Kaski, K., Kertsz, J.: Dynamic asset trees and Black Monday. Phys. A: Stat. Mech. Appl. **324**(1–2), 247–252 (2003)
13. Sefiane, S., Benbouziane, M.: Portfolio selection using genetic algorithm. J. Appl. Financ. Banking **2**(4), 143 (2012)
14. Szeto, Kwok Yip, Zhang, Jian: Adaptive genetic algorithm and quasi-parallel genetic algorithm: application to knapsack problem. In: Lirkov, Ivan, Margenov, Svetozar, Waśniewski, Jerzy (eds.) LSSC 2005. LNCS, vol. 3743, pp. 189–196. Springer, Heidelberg (2006). doi:10.1007/11666806_20
15. Tse, C.K., Liu, J., Lau, F.C.: A network perspective of the stock market. J. Empir. Financ. **17**(4), 659–667 (2010). Sep
16. Tsinaslanidis, P., Alexandridis, A., Zapranis, A., Livanis, E.: Dynamic time warping as a similarity measure: applications in finance. In: 13th Annual Conference of Hellenic Finance and Accounting Association (HFAA) (2014)
17. Ver Steeg, G., Galstyan, A.: Information transfer in social media. In: Proceedings of the 21st international conference on World Wide Web, pp. 509–518. ACM (2012)
18. Wu, D., Szeto, K.Y.: Applications of genetic algorithm on optimal sequence for Parrondo games. In: 6th ECTA 2014-Proceedings of the International Conference on Evolutionary Computation Theory and Applications, Part of the 6th International Joint Conference on Computational Intelligence, IJCCI 2014, Rome, Italy, p. 30 (2014)

Optimization of Joint Sales Potential Using Genetic Algorithm

Chun Yin Yip and Kwok Yip Szeto(✉)

Department of Physics, The Hong Kong University of Science and Technology, Clear Water Bay, Kowloon, Hong Kong
phszeto@ust.hk

Abstract. The joint sales potential of a group of nodes in a complex network is defined as the ratio of the number of elements in the union of their second-degree neighbors to that in the union of their first-degree neighbors. A high joint sales potential implies the nodes' high efficiency in disseminating information in the network. Advertisers may want to look for the group of nodes that has the highest joint sales potential and hire them as advertising agents. Due to the impracticality of exhaustive search, this paper presents a mutation-only genetic algorithm for optimizing the joint sales potential of a group of m nodes in an n-node undirected complex network. The algorithm is tested with artificial and real networks and gives satisfactory results. This shows the algorithm's effectiveness in joint sales potential optimization.

Keywords: Advertising strategies · Undirected complex network · Sales potential · Mutation-only genetic algorithm

1 Introduction

For advancements in communication technology like smart phones and social media, we find that a complex network is an effective mathematical tool to describe complex systems like social media [1], interbank [2–4], and ecological systems [5]. In complex networks, objects are represented by nodes, and interactions or relationships between them are represented by edges. A popular topic for research concerns the importance of a node in a complex network. This importance is often formulated as some measures on the "centrality" of the node. Four common measures of centrality are degree centrality, betweenness, closeness, and eigenvector centrality [6]. For instance, PageRank [7] is employed by Google's search engine to determine the importance of a web page on the Internet. Sales potential is another kind of centrality measure and is first introduced by Wang and Szeto [8]. The measure can evaluate a node's efficiency in propagating information in a complex network, so it is applicable in studies of marketing, rumor spreading, contagions, etc.

In an undirected complex network, the sales potential S of a node with an index i is defined as the ratio of its number of second-nearest neighbors to its number of nearest neighbors, i.e. its degree. This is mathematically expressed as

F.J. Martínez de Pisón et al. (Eds.): HAIS 2017, LNAI 10334, pp. 125–136, 2017.
DOI: 10.1007/978-3-319-59650-1_11

$$S = \frac{Size\left(N_2(i)\right)}{Size\left(N_1(i)\right)}, \tag{1}$$

where $Size(N_x(i))$ returns the number of i's x^{th}-nearest neighbors. The number of second-nearest neighbors, or second-degree neighbors, of a node can be viewed as its "influence", while the number of its nearest neighbors, or first-degree neighbors, can be viewed as the "cost" of hiring it to spread the information. This can be understood with an example. Hiring a famous movie star as the agent for an advertisement often incurs a cost proportional to his fame, which may be measured by the number of his followers. In the context of a social network, the number of followers is equivalent to the degree of the node representing the movie star. As for the movie star's influence, one has to regard the number of people he can affect. One way to describe this influence is the number of neighbors, which may include the nearest ones, the next-nearest ones, and so on. Here we simply refer the influence to the number of second-nearest neighbors. (One may do more by studying the number of higher-order neighbors though).

An advertiser always wishes is to hire someone who needs a low cost but has a large (second-degree) influence. An example is hiring the daughter of a famous movie star as an advertising agent. Since she may influence her parent's behaviors and her parent may then influence his followers, the daughter is considered to be influential, while the cost of hiring her is definitely lower than that of directly hiring her parent. As the sales potential of an agent is the ratio of his influence to his cost, sales potential can measure a node's efficiency in disseminating information in the network. This is the logic behind introducing sales potential as a centrality measure.

Very often, an advertiser may like to promote his product in a diverse social network with multiple age groups or ethnicities, so he may wish to hire several agents with a high sales potential. This then requires a generalization of sales potential from one node to a set of nodes. For such purpose, Wang and Szeto [8] also introduce the concept of joint sales potential, which they refer as "combined sales potential". The joint sales potential S_{joint} of a group of m nodes with indices i_j is defined as the ratio of the number of elements in the union of their second-degree neighbors to that in the union of their first-degree neighbors. This is mathematically expressed as

$$S_{joint} = \frac{Size\left(\bigcup_{j=1}^{m}\left(N_2\left(i_j\right)\right)\right)}{Size\left(\bigcup_{j=1}^{m}\left(N_1\left(i_j\right)\right)\right)}. \tag{2}$$

The mission for the advertiser is to find the group of m nodes that has the highest joint sales potential and hire them as advertising agents. Here, the number of agents m is purely subjected to the advertiser's budget. For a network with n nodes, there are C_m^n combinations for the formation of a group of m nodes. As n increases, the number of combinations grows drastically, so an exhaustive search for the highest-joint-sales-potential group becomes impractical. To overcome this problem, genetic algorithm is considered, as it has been shown to be effective in tackling problems with a large solution space across various fields, such as finance [9, 10], control systems [11], and biological time series analysis [12].

In Sect. 2, a mutation-only genetic algorithm (MOGA) is introduced to optimize the joint sales potential of a group of m nodes in an n-node undirected complex network. In Sect. 3, a slightly different MOGA is introduced for studying how mutation operators affect the performance of the algorithm. The two algorithms are tested on artificial and real networks to demonstrate their effectiveness in joint sales potential optimization. The results of the experiment are presented in Sect. 4, followed by discussions in Sect. 5.

2 Algorithm Design

Genetic algorithm makes use of the principle of "survival of the fittest". It treats inanimate data-encoding strings as animate gene-encoding chromosomes. Through "evolution", which is biased towards a fitness function, fitter chromosomes would emerge after some generations. This implies that the information contained in the corresponding data-encoding string is more adapted to the environmental pressure defined by the fitness function.

In this paper, the gene in our genetic algorithm is a node in a network, and a group of nodes forms a chromosome. The aim of the algorithm is to obtain the "fittest" group of m nodes, i.e. an m-gene chromosome, from an n-node undirected complex network (assuming $n \gg m$). The fitness of a chromosome is evaluated with its genes' joint sales potential. (More precisely, that is the joint sales potential of the nodes encoded with the genes.) The higher the genes' joint sales potential is, the fitter the chromosome is, and vice versa.

There are many ways to implement the Darwinian idea of "survival of the fittest" into a genetic algorithm. What we use in this paper is a specific type of genetic algorithm called MOGA, which stands for Mutation-Only Genetic Algorithm [13]. One should not confuse this acronym with multi-objective genetic algorithm. The rationale for choosing a MOGA instead of a simple genetic algorithm (SGA) is that a MOGA is more efficient than an SGA in many cases investigated [13–17]. In an ordinary SGA, we consider a population of C chromosomes, which are of length L and binary encoded. The population at time t is described with a $C \times L$ matrix $A(t)$, which contains entries $A_{ij}(t)$ that denote the value of the j-th locus of the i-th chromosome ($i = 1, \ldots, C; j = 1, \ldots, L$). The convention is to order the rows of A by the fitness $f(t)$ of the chromosomes in descending order so that $f_i(t) \leq f_k(t)$ for $i \geq k$. Traditionally, the population of C chromosomes is divided into three groups. The first group is "survivors", who become the first $C_1 = r_1 C$ rows of $A(t + 1)$. Here, r_1 is a survival ratio between 0 and 1. The second group is "offspring", who are generated from "survivors" by genetic operators such as mutation. They will displace the next $C_2 = r_2 C$ rows in $A(t + 1)$, where r_2 is an offspring ratio between 0 and $1 - r_1$. The third group represented by the remaining $C_3 = C - C_1 - C_2$ rows are randomly generated chromosomes. They ensure the diversity of the population, so the genetic algorithm can continuously explore the solution space. On the other hand, in a general MOGA, we use a $C \times L$ mutation matrix $M(t)$ with elements $M_{ij}(t) \equiv a_i(t) b_j(t)$, where $a_i(t)$ and $b_j(t)$ are between 0 and 1 and are called a row mutation probability and a column mutation probability respectively. The two probabilities are determined with statistics of the fitness and ranking of chromosomes. In fact, an SGA with mutation as the only genetic parameter corresponds to a time-independent MOGA that has no adaptive parameter control. This means that for the SGA, $M_{ij}(t) \equiv 0$ for i between 1 and C_1, k for i between $C_1 + 1$ and C_2, and 1 for i between $C_2 + 1$ and C. Here, k is a time-independent mutation rate between 0 and 1.

Various ingenious methods have been developed to exploit the time-dependent statistics from a population matrix A to compute a time-dependent mutation matrix M. Generalization to crossover operators under the mutation matrix formalism has also been developed [17]. Yet, this paper does not aim at studying the efficiency of variants of MOGA. We just use MOGA as an efficient and simple replacement for SGA. We use a simplified version of MOGA, as we do not intend to compute the mutation matrix. Instead, we realize the mutation operation with assumptions on the form of the sets of nodes that yield high joint sales potential. The following sections describe different phases of the algorithm respectively.

2.1 Initialization

We initialize the population with $C = 3$ chromosomes, by choosing 3 m nodes to form an initial population. The algorithm preferentially chooses low-degree nodes to be a member of the population as they yield a smaller denominator for Eq. (2) and are likely to form a high-joint-sales-potential group. We introduce preferential selection as follows: p nodes are randomly chosen out of the n nodes in the network (where $m < p < n$). The lowest-degree node among the p nodes becomes a gene if the node has not yet been stored in the initial population. The process continues until the population contains 3 m genes. They are then arbitrarily grouped into three m-node chromosomes. The population is now represented with a matrix, in which a row represents a chromosome and the column indicate the gene in the chromosomes.

2.2 Evaluation

The fitness is defined by the joint sales potential of the chromosome. We evaluate the fitness and sort the chromosomes in descending order of their fitness.

2.3 Reproduction

A general genetic algorithm employs two reproduction operators, namely *mutation* and *crossover*. However, this paper uses a mutation-only genetic algorithm in which only *mutation* is implemented. In this phase, a fitter chromosome mutates first. The mutation is determined with several fitness-specific rules.

The Fittest Chromosome (C_1). It does not mutate. It survives to the next generation so that the best solution would not be discarded.

The Second-Fittest Chromosome (C_2). The sales potentials of each of the 3 m genes in the population are calculated. Subsequently, m distinct genes with the highest sales potential are grouped to form chromosome C'. If it is not identical to C_1 or C_2, C'

displaces C_2. This act *exploits* the population. Under an assumption that the intersection between sets of nodes' neighbors is small, the joint sales potential of genes having high sales potential shall also be high. If C' is identical to C_1 or C_2, a random chromosome C'' is generated by preferentially selecting m distinct low-degree nodes to be its genes. (The logic of preferential selection is described in Sect. 2.1) If it is different from C_1 and C_2, C'' displaces C_2. Otherwise, C'' is kept being regenerated until it can displace C_2. This act *explores* the solution space and ensures a genetic variety in the population.

The Third-Fittest Chromosome (C_3). The number of distinct genes in the population d (which must be $\geq m$) is counted. Among the r distinct genes with the highest sales potentials, m genes are picked at random, where r is any arbitrary integer such that $d \geq r \geq m$. For each node represented by the m genes, its highest-degree neighbor's lowest-degree neighbor is selected. The m selected nodes then become the genes of a new chromosome C'. Any duplicated node in C' is replaced with a low-degree node chosen at random. C' displaces C_3 as long as it is not identical to C_1, C_2 or C_3. This act *explores* the solution space under the *guidance* of the present population. With a larger r, the extent of exploration would be larger. In later tests, r is arbitrarily set to be $min(2\,m,d)$. Similar to the case for C_2, if C' is identical to any present chromosomes, a random chromosome C'' is generated by preferentially grouping m distinct low-degree nodes. If it is different from all chromosomes, C'' displaces C_3. Otherwise, C'' is kept being regenerated until it can displace C_3. This act again *explores* the solution space and ensures a genetic variety in the population.

2.4 Evolution

We perform fitness evaluation and mutation for g generations. The m-node group represented by the fittest chromosome at the gth generation is considered to be the optimal m-node configuration for the n-node network (Fig. 1 shows the flow chart of the algorithm.).

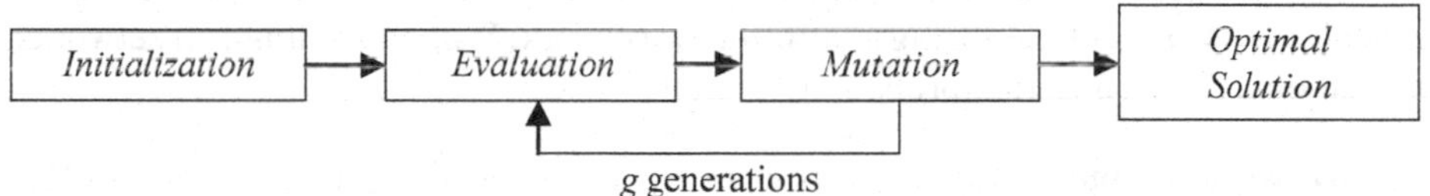

Fig. 1. A flowchart of the algorithm, where g is the assigned number of generations.

3 Testing

To study the performance of the mutation-only genetic algorithm described in Sect. 2, several tests are performed on various undirected networks.

3.1 Sources of Sample Networks

We test our algorithm on two kinds of networks: artificial networks and real networks. A summary of their specifications is tabulated as Tables 1 and 2.

Table 1. Summary of the properties of the three artificial networks.

	ER	*WS*	*BA*
Network type (model)	Random (Erdős-Rényi)	Small-world (Watts-Strogatz)	Scale-free (Barabási-Albert)
n	100	100	100
C_5^n	7.52×10^7	7.52×10^7	7.52×10^7
l	2050	2000	1840
$p = \frac{2l}{n(n+1)}$	0.414	0.404	0.371

Table 2. Summary of the properties of the four undirected real networks.

	Forum	*Science*	*Airport*	*Power*
n	897	16264	500	4941
C_5^n	4.79×10^{12}	9.48×10^{18}	2.55×10^{11}	2.45×10^{16}
l	71380	47594	2980	6594
$p = \frac{2l}{n(n+1)}$	0.177	3.60×10^{-4}	0.0238	5.40×10^{-4}

Artificial Networks. Three undirected networks are created. The first one is a (connected) random network built with the Erdős-Rényi model (*ER*) [18, 19]. It is built upon a 100-node ring and a connection probability of 0.4. The second one is a small-world network built with the Watts-Strogatz model (*WS*) [20]. It has 100 nodes having 40 neighbors each and a rewiring probability of 0.3. The last one is a scale-free network built with the Barabási-Albert model (*BA*) [21]. With a 30-degree node appended each time, it grows from a 40-node ring to a 100-node network. With this setting, all networks have an effective connection probability p around 0.4.

Real Networks. Four sets of network data are downloaded from Tore Opsahl [22]: *Facebook-like Forum Network* (no.2; abbreviated as *Forum*) [23], *Scientific Collaboration* (no.12; abbreviated as *Science*) [24], *US Top-500 Airport Network* (no.14a; abbreviated as *Airport*) [25], and *US Power Grid* (no.15; abbreviated as *Power*) [20]. In *Forum*, each node represents a user in the forum, while a link represents a user's comment in another user's post. In *Science*, a node represents a scientist, while a link between two nodes represents collaborations between the two scientists. In *Airport*, a node represents a US airport, while a link represents any flight between two airports. In *Power*, a node represents a transformer, a substation, or a generator, while a link represents a transmission line. The four networks are originally directed or weighted. Before the test, they are rendered into undirected and non-weighted networks. The numbers of nodes n and links l in the undirected networks are counted, and their effective connection probabilities p are subsequently calculated.

3.2 Effects of Exploration: Guided Versus Random

In order to test the importance of a guided search, we introduce another mutation-only genetic algorithm A', which is designed based on the original algorithm A and is a benchmark algorithm for the test. The working logic of the two algorithms are almost the same, except that for A', C_3 does not undergo a *guided exploration* but a *random exploration* – a chromosome C' is generated by preferentially selecting m low-degree nodes to be its genes and displaces C_3 if it is different from all of the present chromosomes. Otherwise, C' is kept being regenerated until it can displace C_3. The performances of the two algorithms are compared to investigate effects of the exploration method on joint sales optimization.

3.3 Joint Sales Potential Optimization

For each network, both A and A' run for g generations to search for the optimal m-node group configuration, where g is arbitrarily set as 200. The algorithm's performance is tested for $m = 5$, which corresponds to looking for five people who form an influential group. Still, for such a small m, the number of possible configurations, C^n_5, is at least of an order of 10^7, so it is impractical to do an exhaustive search for the optimal solution.

After g generations of evolution, the fittest chromosome is obtained. The generation g' when it first emerged is recorded. Then the joint sales potential of the fittest chromosome is compared with R (standing for "reference"), which is the joint sales potential of the $m = 5$ nodes with the highest sales potential among the n nodes in the network. R would be significantly high if the sets of the m nodes' neighbors have a small intersection. (Particularly, if the intersection is zero, R is the median of the sales potentials of the m nodes, and the median inequality guarantees it to be greater or equal to the smallest one of the m sales potentials.

4 Results

We carry out the test for $t = 5$ trials. The S_f and g' obtained for each network in each trial with both A and A' are tabulated as Tables 3 and 4. Table 3 is for the artificial networks, whereas Table 4 is for the real networks. The average S_f is also computed and compared with the reference value R. Please note that the figures presented in the tables are rounded to three significant figures, except that g' is rounded to integer.

The results show that except for *Science* and *Power*, A can always find a 5-node configuration whose joint sales potential is the same as or larger than the reference R. Therefore, the paper determines that the performance of the algorithm is good and effective in optimizing the joint sales potential of $m = 5$ nodes. However, the results also show that despite the effectiveness of the algorithm, it can be improved by better coordination between *guided* and *random* explorations. For *ER*, *WS*, and *BA*, A often performs better than *A'*. On the contrary, for *Science*, *A'* often finds fitter configurations than *A*. For the remaining networks, the average S_f of *A* and *A'* do not differ significantly, implying that the two algorithms are more or less equally effective.

Table 3. Results obtained for the artificial networks.

		ER		*WS*		*BA*	
R		0.190		0.225		1.21	
Algorithm		*A*	*A'*	*A*	*A'*	*A*	*A'*
S_f / g'	Trial 1	0.389/49	0.266/164	0.406/148	0.338/123	1.34/54	1.21/30
	Trial 2	0.316/72	0.266/21	0.449/105	0.338/51	1.51/87	1.21/13
	Trial 3	0.266/9	0.266/11	0.338/47	0.394/8	1.82/126	1.21/23
	Trial 4	0.389/162	0.266/166	0.338/36	0.338/15	1.51/155	1.21/17
	Trial 5	0.320/40	0.220/11	0.338/19	0.338/12	1.33/78	1.21/13
	Average	0.336/66	0.257/75	0.374/71	0.349/42	1.50/100	1.21/19
% difference of average S_f from R		+76.3%	+34.7%	+66.1%	+55.2%	+24.4%	0

Table 4. Results obtained for the real networks.

		Forum		*Science*		*Airport*		*Power*	
R		89.4		67.5		67.0		16.0	
Algorithm		A	A'	A	A'	A	A'	A	A'
S_f / g'	Trial 1	89.4/7	89.4/53	58.7/142	58.5/174	89.5/6	89.5/7	15.0/181	15.3/111
	Trial 2	91.1/189	89.4/26	67.5/51	60.5/158	89.5/25	127/10	15.3/155	15.3/182
	Trial 3	89.4/46	91.1/21	52.7/92	63.0/167	89.5/10	89.5/14	13.7/43	15.0/75
	Trial 4	89.4/38	91.9/9	58.5/189	62.7/200	67.0/22	89.5/54	15.3/129	15.0/74
	Trial 5	89.4/30	90.8/20	56.0/198	67.5/194	89.5/13	67.0/6	15.3/102	13.7/34
	Average	89.7/62	90.5/26	58.7/134	62.4/179	85.0/15	92.5/18	14.9/122	14.9/95
% difference of average S_f from R		+0.368%	+1.23%	−13.1%	−7.51%	+26.9%	+38.1%	−6.67%	−7.08%

In addition, *g'* in most cases are far less than $g = 200$. This shows that the arbitrary specification of *g* is unlikely a bad choice.

5 Discussion

5.1 Sparsely-Connected Networks

For *Science* and *Power*, *A* does not perform well as it often cannot yield a configuration at least as fit as *R*. The poor performance of the algorithm for these two networks may be due to the networks' extremely low effective connection probabilities. According to Table 2, both *Science* and *Power* have an effective connection probability in an order of 10^{-4}. This extremely small connectivity compared to other networks tested may be the reason behind the poor performance of the algorithm. Indeed, we can anticipate that a guided exploration is inevitably ineffective in a sparsely-connected network. For the lack of links, the exploration process will likely be stuck in a subspace of the solution space and thus the population cannot maintain a good level of genetic diversity. Therefore, it is understandable that the algorithm is defective in optimizing the m-node configuration in a sparsely-connected network like *Science* and *Power*. For networks with such a low connectivity, the intersection between sets of a node's neighbors will probably be very small and therefore negligible. This means that the joint sales potential of a group of nodes will be close to the median of their sales potential. As a result, the optimization problem actually turns into a simple search of m nodes with high sales potential, and an exhaustive search on the nodes would then be feasible.

5.2 Guided or Random Exploration?

It is observed that for all the real networks, A' works at least as well as A or even better than A. This leads to a question: which is more effective, a *guided* exploration or a *random* exploration? When is a *guided* exploration much stronger or weaker than a *random* one?

On one hand, for real networks, performances of the two methods in individual trials are in fact comparable despite the difference in average S_f. Therefore, conclusions on the effect of exploration can hardly be drawn from these tests. On the other hand, for the three densely-connected artificial networks, the average S_f obtained by A is significantly better than those obtained by A', so we conjecture that a guided exploration is more powerful than random search in a densely-connected network in which links are evenly distributed. Indeed, it is logical to expect an abundance of evenly-distributed links can provide a ground for a guided exploration to reach almost everywhere in the solution space.

Nevertheless, we may improve our algorithm by changing the population to one that employs four m-node chromosomes. In this case, the chromosome evaluated to be C_3 undergoes a guided (or random) exploration, and the fourth chromosome, C_4, undergoes the other type of exploration. This four-chromosome algorithm can in principle earn the advantages of both guided and random explorations, but its disadvantage would be a higher required computation power and a longer computation time.

5.3 Number of Generations

In the tests, the number of generation g is arbitrarily set at 200. Although the results show that our choice of g is generally a good one, we also observe that g' can be higher than g for sparsely-connected networks like *Science* and *Power*. This raises another question: would there be an optimal value for g and what is it? What are the factors that determining g'? These questions are beyond the scope of our studies. We prefer to focus on the way we structure our chromosomes with minimal effort so that we can still get reasonably good results on the optimization of the joint sales potential.

5.4 Directed Networks

Currently, the algorithm is designed for optimization in an *undirected* network. However, complex networks in our daily lives are usually directed. For example, if you know a celebrity well but he does not know you, he is your outward neighbor, whereas you are his inward neighbor. Generalizing the algorithm so that it fits a directed network requires a redefinition of sales potential and joint sales potential:

$$S = \frac{Size\left(N_2^{in}(i)\right)}{Size\left(N_1^{in}(i)\right)} \text{ and } S_{joint} = \frac{Size\left(\bigcup_{j=1}^{m}\left(N_2^{in}(i_j)\right)\right)}{Size\left(\bigcup_{j=1}^{m}\left(N_1^{in}(i_j)\right)\right)}, \tag{3}$$

where $Size(N_x(i))$ returns the number of i's x^{th}-nearest inward neighbors, or i's x^{th}-shell in-degree.

6 Conclusion

In this paper, a mutation-only genetic algorithm is designed for optimizing the joint sales potential of a group of $m = 5$ nodes for an n-node undirected complex network. The algorithm first initializes a population of $C = 3$ chromosomes with 3 m genes. Then, it applies different kinds of operations on the chromosomes according to their fitness. The fittest chromosome that the algorithm yields after $g = 200$ generations is considered to be the optimal configuration.

This paper later tests the algorithm with various networks having different properties (Tables 1 and 2). The results are tabulated as Tables 3 and 4. The results are compared with a reference R, which is defined as the joint sales potential of the 5 nodes with the highest sales potential in the target network. It is shown that unless the target network is sparsely-connected, the algorithm can always find a 5-node configuration with a joint sales potential that is the same as or larger than R. Therefore, we can say that we have found an effective algorithm for optimizing the joint sales potential. We also study the relation of the method of exploration to the outcome. Our results show that a guided exploration is significantly better for a densely-connected network with evenly-distributed links. We also note that our algorithm may be improved by a better coordination between *guided* and *random* explorations. For application of our algorithm in advertising, we can apply our algorithm to find the set of the five (or other given number according to the budget allocated) most influential nodes in a complex social network and hire them to be advertising agents with the lowest cost. We can also apply our algorithm for the containment of epidemics. Our algorithm may be used to minimize the damage by proper quarantining those nodes with highest joint sales potential, thereby stopping the spread of disease. These examples suggest that our algorithm may be a useful tool for analyzing big data that have their roots in complex networks.

Acknowledgement. C.Y. Yip acknowledges the support of the Hong Kong University of Science and Technology Undergraduate Research Opportunity Program (UROP) and the discussion of Lui Ga Ching.

References

1. Ver Steeg, G., Galstyan, A.: Information transfer in social media. In: Proceedings of the 21st International Conference on World Wide Web, pp. 509–518. ACM (2012)
2. May, R.M., Levin, S.A., Sugihara, G.: Complex systems: Ecology for bankers. Nature **451**, 893–895 (2008)
3. Eboli, M.: Financial applications of flow network theory. In: Proto, A.N., Squillante, M., Kacprzyk, J. (eds.) Advanced Dynamic Modeling of Economic and Social Systems. SCI, vol. 448, pp. 21–29. Springer, Heidelberg (2013)
4. Haldane, A.G., May, R.M.: Systemic risk in banking ecosystems. Nature **469**, 351–355 (2011)
5. May, R.M.: Networks and webs in ecosystems and financial systems. Philos. Trans. Roy. Soc. Lond. A: Math. Phys. Eng. Sci. **371**, 20120376 (2013)
6. Newman, M.E.J.: Networks: An Introduction. Oxford University Press, Oxford (2010)
7. Page, L., Brin, S., Motwani, R., Winograd, T.: The PageRank citation ranking: Bringing order to the web. Stanford InfoLab (1999)
8. Wang, C.G., Szeto, K.Y.: Sales Potential Optimization on Directed Social Networks: A Quasi-Parallel Genetic Algorithm Approach. In: Chio, C., et al. (eds.) EvoApplications 2012. LNCS, vol. 7248, pp. 114–123. Springer, Heidelberg (2012). doi:10.1007/978-3-642-29178-4_12
9. Sefiane, S., Benbouziane, M.: Portfolio selection using genetic algorithm. J. Appl. Financ. Banking **2**, 143 (2012)
10. Luk, P.W.-H., Lui, G.C., Szeto, K.Y.: Optimization of systemic stability of directed network using genetic algorithm. In: 2016 IEEE/ACIS 15th International Conference on Computer and Information Science (ICIS), pp. 1–6. IEEE (2016)
11. Xia, C., Guo, P., Shi, T., Wang, M.: Speed control of brushless DC motor using genetic algorithm based fuzzy controller. In: Proceeding of the 2004 International Conference on Intelligent Mechatronics and Automation, Chengdu, China, 3rd edn. A Treatise on Electricity and Magnetism, pp. 68–73 (2004)
12. Lui, G.C., Wu, D., Cheung, K.W., Ma, H.F., Szeto, K.Y.: Time warping of apneic ECG signals using genetic algorithm. In: 2016 IEEE Congress on Evolutionary Computation (CEC), pp. 178–184. IEEE (2016)
13. Szeto, K.Y., Zhang, J.: Adaptive genetic algorithm and quasi-parallel genetic algorithm: application to knapsack problem. In: Lirkov, I., Margenov, S., Waśniewski, J. (eds.) LSSC 2005. LNCS, vol. 3743, pp. 189–196. Springer, Heidelberg (2006). doi:10.1007/11666806_20
14. Shiu, K.L., Szeto, K.Y.: Self-adaptive mutation only genetic algorithm: an application on the optimization of airport capacity utilization. In: Fyfe, C., Kim, D., Lee, S.-Y., Yin, H. (eds.) IDEAL 2008. LNCS, vol. 5326, pp. 428–435. Springer, Heidelberg (2008). doi:10.1007/978-3-540-88906-9_54
15. Chen, C., Wang, G., Szeto, K.Y.: Markov chains genetic algorithms for airport scheduling. In: Proceedings of the 9th International FLINS Conference on Foundations and Applications of Computational Intelligence (FLINS 2010), pp. 905–910 (2010)
16. Wang, G., Wu, D., Chen, W., Szeto, K.Y.: Importance of information exchange in quasi-parallel genetic algorithms. In: Krasnogor, N. (ed.) Proceedings of the 13th Annual Conference Companion on Genetic and Evolutionary Computation (GECCO 2011), pp. 127–128. ACM, New York (2011)

17. Law, N.L., Szeto, K.Y.: Adaptive genetic algorithms with mutation and crossover matrices. In: Proceeding of the 12th International Joint Conference on Artificial Intelligence (IJCAI 2007), Hyderabad, India, 6–12 January 2007. Theme: Al and Its Benefits to Society, vol. II, pp. 2330–2333 (2007)
18. Erdos, P., Rényi, A.: On the evolution of random graphs. Publ. Math. Inst. Hung. Acad. Sci. **5**, 17–60 (1960)
19. Albert, R., Barabási, A.-L.: Statistical mechanics of complex networks. Rev. Mod. Phys. **74**, 47 (2002)
20. Watts, D.J., Strogatz, S.H.: Collective dynamics of "small-world" networks. Nature **393**, 440–442 (1998)
21. Barabási, A.-L., Albert, R.: Emergence of scaling in random networks. Science **286**, 509–512 (1999)
22. Tore Opsahl: Datasets. http://toreopsahl.com/datasets/
23. Opsahl, T.: Triadic closure in two-mode networks: Redefining the global and local clustering coefficients. Social Netw. **35**, 159–167 (2013)
24. Newman, M.E.: The structure of scientific collaboration networks. Proc. Natl. Acad. Sci. **98**, 404–409 (2001)
25. Colizza, V., Pastor-Satorras, R., Vespignani, A.: Reaction–diffusion processes and metapopulation models in heterogeneous networks. Nat. Phys. **3**, 276–282 (2007)

Evolutionary Multi-objective Scheduling for Anti-Spam Filtering Throughput Optimization

David Ruano-Ordás[1,2], Vitor Basto-Fernandes[3,4], Iryna Yevseyeva[5], and José Ramón Méndez[1,2(✉)]

[1] Department of Computer Science, University of Vigo, ESEI, Campus As Lagoas, 32004 Ourense, Spain
{drordas,moncho.mendez}@uvigo.es
[2] Centro de Investigaciones Biomédicas (Centro Singular de Investigación de Galicia), Campus Universitario Lagoas-Marcosende, 36310 Vigo, Spain
[3] Instituto Universitário de Lisboa (ISCTE-IUL), University Institute of Lisbon, ISTAR-IUL, Av. das Forças Armadas, 1649-026 Lisbon, Portugal
vitor.basto.fernandes@iscte.pt
[4] School of Technology and Management, Computer Science and Communications Research Centre, Polytechnic Institute of Leiria, 2411-901 Leiria, Portugal
[5] School of Computer Science and Informatics, Faculty of Technology, De Montfort University, Leicester LE1 9BH, UK
iryna.yevseyeva@dmu.ac.uk

Abstract. This paper presents an evolutionary multi-objective optimization problem formulation for the anti-spam filtering problem, addressing both the classification quality criteria (False Positive and False Negative error rates) and email messages classification time (minimization). This approach is compared to single objective problem formulations found in the literature, and its advantages for decision support and flexible/adaptive anti-spam filtering configuration is demonstrated. A study is performed using the Wirebrush4SPAM framework anti-spam filtering and the SpamAssassin email dataset. The NSGA-II evolutionary multi-objective optimization algorithm was applied for the purpose of validating and demonstrating the adoption of this novel approach to the anti-spam filtering optimization problem, formulated from the multi-objective optimization perspective. The results obtained from the experiments demonstrated that this optimization strategy allows the decision maker (anti-spam filtering system administrator) to select among a set of optimal and flexible filter configuration alternatives with respect to classification quality and classification efficiency.

Keywords: Rule-based anti-spam systems · Scheduling · Multi-objective optimization

1 Introduction

SPAM embraces the wide amount of unwanted communications delivered through Internet annoying most users. Some statistics about spam e-mail [1, 2] revealed the real dimension of this trouble. As shown in the work of Statista [1], in the period 2014-2016

F.J. Martínez de Pisón et al. (Eds.): HAIS 2017, LNAI 10334, pp. 137–148, 2017.
DOI: 10.1007/978-3-319-59650-1_12

the percentage of spam deliveries has kept beyond 52.5%. Moreover, Digital Marketing Ramblings (DMR) stated that workers receive an average of 121 messages per day whereupon more than 63 are spam.

During the last years SpamAssassin filtering framework [3] become very popular in the Internet community to fight against spam. It implements a rule-based filtering method designed to combine multiple techniques. Rule-based anti-spam filtering allows the administrator to define ad hoc rules containing logical expression (used as a trigger) together with an associated score (importance in the classification process). Every time an e-mail is received for evaluation, all scores of rules matching the target message are summed. If the summation reaches a value over a predefined threshold (known as *required_score*) the incoming message is classified as spam by the filter. Otherwise, it is labelled as legitimate (also known as ham).

In this context, and given the extensive utilization and increasing significance of rule-based filtering frameworks for the anti-spam domain, several studies have addressed the optimization of parameters (rule scores and scheduling plan) to improve their accuracy [4–7] and classification throughput [8–10]. However, previous works on throughput optimization are based on simple heuristics without taking into account its relation to accuracy. Keeping in mind this background, this work includes a preliminary study of addressing both optimizations in an unified form and using a Multi-objective Evolutionary Algorithm (MOEA).

Due to the high amount of rules being executed by the anti-spam filter (from hundreds to thousands) for the classification of each individual email message, and the difficulty of running a real anti-spam filtering system in the context of optimization experiments, we decided to adopt in this study a recently released configuration simulator [11]. In our formulation, rules to be executed are considered the tasks to perform and computational resources (CPU, RAM and IO) the assets required for rules execution against the email messages to be classified. Moreover, we consider the scores of the rules in the optimization process, because a score of 0 indicates that the rule could be dropped, contributing to reduce the time required to classify a message. Classification time (time required to execute all rules on an email message), false positive (FP) and false negative (FN) errors are the criteria to optimize (minimize) in our study.

The multi-objective problem formulation is characterized by several conflicting goals, for which not simply a single optimum solution, but a set of potential optimal solutions are obtained. These solutions represent the best trade-offs between the objectives and are given to the decision maker to decide which solution matches the trade-off of his/her interest. In multi-objective optimization an optimal solution can only be improved in one objective at the expense of loss in other(s). It is in the best interest of the decision maker that the multi-objective optimization approach provides him/her the ability to select among several optimal solutions with a diversity of trade-offs among the objectives.

In order to evaluate the suitability of the multi-objective approach to the anti-spam filtering throughput optimization problem, and to compare the performance of this type of metaheuristics with best known results in the anti-spam filtering throughput optimization problem, we used NSGA-II [12]. NSGA-II is one of the most popular Evolutionary Multi-Objective Optimization Algorithms (EMOA), has been cited in 9341 papers [13], is among the most cited papers in IEEE Transactions on Evolutionary Computation, has been used in a large variety of multi-optimization problem types, is one of the representative algorithms of EMOA type, and is therefore most suited to be adopted in our study, at this stage of our research hypothesis.

The rest of the paper is structured as follows: Sect. 2 studies current background on filter accuracy and speed optimization, Sects. 3 and 4 present the formulation of our proposal and the experimental results, Sect. 5 provides a detailed discussion of results and finally, Sect. 6 outlines the main outcomes and future work.

2 State of the Art

As mentioned above, previous work on optimization of accuracy and throughput have not been addressed in a joint form. This section includes a description of previous work addressing throughput (Subsect. 2.1) and accuracy (Sect. 2.2) optimization.

2.1 Throughput Optimization

Despite general advices provided by SpamAssassin team [14], the introduction of Wirebrush4SPAM [15] provided some practical advances to really improve the throughput of rule-based filters. Among all proposals, we highlight Smart Filter Evaluation (SFE), parallel rule execution and preventing the execution of rules having a score of 0. SFE provides a lazy evaluation scheme that avoids the evaluation of some rules in specific circumstances. The execution of rules in parallel allows to efficiently combine the execution of rules with high computational requirements (CPU usage) together with rules that imply an I/O operation.

To take more advantage of the above mentioned advances (i.e. achieve the SFE conditions to stop a filter evaluation early and achieve an adequate parallelization of rules), some scheduling heuristics have been introduced [8–10].

Concretely, [8] introduces five scheduling mechanisms (GAV, GDV, PFS, NFS and PSS) to handle the arrangement of the filtering rules according to different sorting criteria designed to take advantage of SFE technique together with the multiprocessing capabilities of current CPUs. The experimental results carried out over several filter configurations demonstrated the suitability of adjusting the rule execution order to save computational resources and achieve a fast filtering (time savings between 13% and 26%).

Nevertheless the growth trend of the e-mail deliveries in the last years forces to continuously increase the spam filtering throughput. To this end, authors in [10] proposed two scheduling strategies (RBM and CEM) for optimizing the time needed to classify new incoming e-mails through an intelligent management of computational resources. To accomplish this task, both strategies use the information about CPU usage and I/O delay of each rule to achieve an adequate execution balance by combining rules that execute I/O operations together with those using intensively CPU resources (perform complex computations). Additionally, in order to increase even more the performance of the previous scheduling strategies, authors in [10] proposed a novel heuristic ensemble method (also called MHE) able to hybridise two individual heuristics to make the most of them. The main difference with previous approaches is that MHE is a heuristic combinatorial scheme instead of a simple heuristic. MHE combines a main heuristic (*h*) with an auxiliary one (*h'*) for sorting rules in those situations in which *h* is not able to break the tie between two rules. Using the MHE criteria, rule r_1 will be executed before any other rule r_2 when Eq. 1 is true. Otherwise r_2 will be executed before r_1.

$$h(r_1) > h(r_2) \vee ((h(r_1) = h(r_2) \wedge h'(r_1) > h'(r_2)) \quad (1)$$

where *h* and *h'* represents the main and auxiliary heuristics respectively.

Due to the definition of the MHE criteria, the user must select both the main heuristic, as well as another one as auxiliary measure.

The results achieved by the RBM and CEM schemes did not improve the performance achieved in [8] due to the high time variability of I/O operations. However, the execution of MHE combined with GDV and RBM allows to filter e-mails up to 10% faster than using any other alternative. This fact enable us to conclude that resource consumption heuristics are the most suitable alternative when used as secondary heuristic.

2.2 Filter Accuracy Optimization

Filter accuracy optimization was early addressed by the SpamAssassin. Evolutionary Algorithms (EA) were used in versions up to 3.0 and after 3.3.0 whilst the rest of the versions used a simple neural network (Perceptron) [16]. EA emerged over other optimization techniques mainly due to their ability to search in large continuous and combinatorial spaces and find approximate (near) optimal solutions [17].

However, due to some limitations of SpamAssassin optimization methods, some interesting proposals emerged from scientific context. Grindstone4SPAM [4] is a set of tools designed to aid in the configuration and deployment of SpamAssassin filters. It includes a rules score optimization tool based on the usage of a Single Objective Evolutionary Algorithm (SOEA). The main limitation of SOEAs is the need of a-priori establishing the criterion for a good solution. In this sense, in some environments the existence of FP errors could be inadmissible, other may prefer reduce the overall number of errors (FP + FN) or adequate balance between them.

With regard to this issue, EA are now widely accepted methods to search for approximations of optimal sets, in particular for dealing with multi-objective problems characterized by several conflicting goals, for which not simply a single optimum solution, but a set of optimal solutions need to be obtained. These solutions represent the trade-offs between the existing objectives, being optimal in the sense of so called Pareto dominance. A Pareto optimal solution can only be improved in one objective at the expense of loss in other(s). Since the population of solutions is used in parallel to solve these problems, the search is directed to not a single optimum but towards multiple Pareto optimal solutions, which is the case of EMOA.

A multi-objective optimization problem can be generically formulated as having *m* objective functions, $f = (f_1, f_2, \ldots, f_m)$, which are simultaneously optimized (minimized or maximized) so that f_k, $k \in \{1, .., m\}$ are real-valued functions evaluated in the multi-objective space. Additionally, constraints (equalities or inequalities) can be considered to impose restrictions on the decision variables. Decision variables are in this context the inputs given to the objective functions. Multi-objective optimization algorithms provide approximations to the set of Pareto optimal solutions that correspond to the set of non-dominated solutions found, based on so called Pareto dominance relation. A Pareto solution dominates any other y alternative ($y, y' \in R^m$) if y is better on at least one objective, and is not worse in the remaining objectives. The selection of a single solution among the set of Pareto optimal solutions is done by the decision maker(s) among the final Pareto optimal solutions given by the EMOA.

Taking into consideration the benefits of EMOAs, several works have analyzed in detail their usage to optimize scores with different problem formulations (scenarios). In [5], the authors provide a detailed comparison between the usage of NSGA-II and SPEA2 to reduce FP and FN errors (2 objectives). This work also compares these results with the ones achieved by using Grindstone4SPAM. Moreover, in [6] multi-objective optimization of classifiers by means of 3D convex-hull-based evolutionary algorithms was applied to different optimization problems, including spam filtering, revealing that several types of EMOA can achieve high quality solution sets when applied to the anti-spam filtering domain. Finally, in [7] authors introduce two different problem formulations with 3 optimization objectives. In the first formulation, rules can be activated or deactivated and the optimization objectives were the minimisation of the number of evaluated rules, FP and FN errors. The second formulation considers a three-way classification scheme and the optimization objectives were the reduction of unclassified samples, FP and FN errors.

Taking into consideration the relevance of EMOAs in literature, this work takes advantage of this type of algorithms to provide an efficient solution to optimize classification throughput and accuracy. Our proposal is introduced in the next section.

3 Problem Formulation and Proposal

In order to study the advantages of applying the EMOA approaches for the multi-objective anti-spam filtering scheduling problem formulation, we defined a scenario where classification quality and classification efficiency are optimized.

In this study, the anti-spam filtering problem is formulated as a multi-objective optimization problem characterized by real-valued objective functions $f(y)$ with values representing the number of false negative errors (FN, spam messages classified as legitimate), number of false positives errors (FP, legitimate messages classified as spam), and classification time (time to evaluate all the rules belonging to the filter).

Note that these objectives are in conflict, since minimizing the number of FP can be done at the expense of increasing the number of FN and vice versa, and reducing the classification time can be achieved by ignoring irrelevant rules of the filter (rules having a score of 0) at the expenses of less accurate messages classification.

Minimization is assumed for all the objectives, which are evaluated with individuals collected from decision space as a two-vector decision variables space $y_1, y_2, .., y_n$ where

$i \in \{1, .., n\}$ and $z_1, z_2, ..., z_n$ where $i \in \{1, .., n\}$. These two vectors are represented by an array of decision variables, y of length n (the total number of filtering rules), where each variable y_i corresponds to the score of one rule, and each variable z_i indicates the order in which the rule must be executed (lower values meaning the rule is executed earlier). The individuals that are part of the initial population are randomly generated with scores in the $[-5, 5]$ real variable range and execution orders a permutation variable in the range [0, n] setting an execution ordering (scheduling plan) for rules execution. Additionally, new individuals are further generated by using the crossover and mutation operators in the same range. The rules scores range $[-5, 5]$ and *required_score* threshold (5) was adopted in our study, because it is a common configuration for the operation of reference rule-based anti-spam filter systems such as SpamAssassin [3] and Wirebrush4SPAM [15].

4 Experimental Study

To carry out the optimization process we design a spam filter comprised by a total of 178 filtering rules (9 belonging to Naïve Bayes techniques and 169 corresponding to Regular Expressions). We decided to avoid rules belonging to network tests (like SPF or RBL/RWL techniques) due to variable latency of the network.

Regarding to the dataset, we have studied a group of well-known corpora available online and distributed following the RFC 2822 [18] format. This RFC was proposed in 2001 and defines the syntax for representing e-mail messages. The raw text representation of messages following this syntax allows to easily parse and extract the required information. Table 1 shows a compilation of corpus following the RFC 2822 format together with relevant information about the size, percentages of spam and ham messages and the existence of duplicate e-mails.

Table 1. Description of popular corpora on spam-filtering

Corpus	Duplicates	Size	%Spam	%Ham
SpamAssassin [19]	x	9332	74.5%	25.5%
CSDMC2010 [20]	x	4327	68.1%	31.9%
2005TRECSpam [21]	✓	92189	57%	43%
2006TRECSpam [21]	✓	37822	65%	35%
2007TRECSpam [21]	✓	75419	66.5%	33.5%
Bruce Guenter [22]	✓	>1000000	100%	0%
Enron [4]	x	517401	0%	100%

As shown in Table 1, the first five corpora are constituted by both spam and legitimate emails while the remaining are single-class datasets (spam or ham) with a huge volume of messages. In order to save computation resources during experimentation without compromising the performance, medium-size datasets are highly recommendable. Taking into account these issues and also guaranteeing the independence of the dataset, the well-known SpamAssassin corpus [19] has been widely used in previous successful research works [4, 5, 11, 14]. In order to ensure the reproducibility of results, we will also use this corpus for the experimental study.

The inclusion of an intelligent classification technique such as Naïve Bayes requires the use of a training corpus. To accomplish this, we divided SpamAssassin corpus into train/test groups following the same spam/ham ratio. Table 2 shows the final distribution used to accomplish our experimental protocol.

Table 2. Final corpus distribution

	Spam	Ham
Training set	5215	1781
Test set	1737	599
Σ	6952	2380

As can be seen from Table 2, 75% of the dataset is used for training Naïve Bayes while the remaining 25% is used for testing purposes.

Additionally, to perform this study, we used RuleSIM, a recent and complete toolkit for simulating the operation of rule-based anti-spam filters [11].

Being one of the reference and general purpose EMOA, one of the most referred in the computer science area in general and in the EMO area in particular, NSGA-II [12] was the algorithm adopted in our experiments. The main purpose of selecting this algorithm is, at this stage, to demonstrate and validate the application of EMOA approaches to the anti-spam classification efficiency domain.

The experiments were performed with jMetal 4.5.2 [23], an optimization framework for the development of multi-objective metaheuristics in Java. NSGA-II population size was set to 100 individuals and a maximum number of 10000 function evaluations was defined. Additionally, the SBX crossover and polynomial mutation operators were used to manipulate the real data decision variables (i.e., rules score vector). For the permutation vector (rules execution order) a jMetal Permutation variable representation was adopted. PMX crossover operator and Swap mutation were used to manipulate the real data decision variables (i.e., rules score vector). The crossover probability was $pc = 0.9$ and the mutation probability was $pm = 1/n$, being n the number of available filtering rules.

Table 3 shows a comparison between the results achieved using throughput heuristics (modifying only the execution scheduling) and a selection of the solutions generated by NSGA-II algorithm (optimizing both classification quality and throughput). Considering NSGA-II solutions as points in a 3D space in the form (*FN*, *FP*, *ExecutionTime*), we included in the table the solution belonging to the pareto front closest to axis origin (0, 0, 0) together with the best ones in each dimension (FN, FP and ExecutionTime). In the former ones, if the evaluation for a certain objective is the same, we selected the one closest to axis origin.

From the results included in Table 3, we can highlight the quality of the solutions generated by NSGA-II. All solutions achieved by NSGA-II outperform the *ExecutionTime* achieved by simple heuristics. Moreover, this algorithm also takes into consideration the minimization of errors.

Table 3. Comparative benchmark results of different optimization strategies

Measure algorithm	FN	FP	Execution time (ms)
Unoptimized	543	0	4315,846
GreaterABSValue			3949,254
GreaterDistanceValue			5920,114
IntelligentBalance			5920,114
NegativeFirst			5920,114
PluginGreaterSignificance			5920,114
PluginOverloadSeparation			3443,162
PluginSeparation			3443,162
PositiveFirst			3443,162
NSGA-II closest to origin	487	7	425,036
NSGA-II best on FP	543	0	435,66
NSGA-II best on FN	459	22	1971,072
NSGA-II best on ExecutionTime	536	3	387,136

In order to analyze in detail the solution space covered by NSGA-II we plotted a 3D-Pareto Front by representing all found non-dominated solutions (optimal solutions such no objective can be improved without sacrificing at least another one). The solutions were plotted following the Eq. 2

$$\left(\frac{FN}{nspam}, \frac{FP}{nham}, executionTime\right) \tag{2}$$

where *nspam* and *nham* stands for the number of spam and ham messages considered in the compilation and *FN*, *FP* and *executionTime* are the target objectives.

Figure 1 shows the hypervolume (HV) of the 3D pareto front with reference point calculated as the maximum of each dimension of the solutions set. As shown in Fig. 1, the Pareto front achieved is an approximated set to the optimal by a finite number of points. The HV shown in grey in Fig. 1, corresponds to a popular EMOA performance indicator, i.e., a bounded size set of points that jointly dominates a maximal part of the objective space relative to a reference point (calculated as the maximum of each dimension of the solutions set).

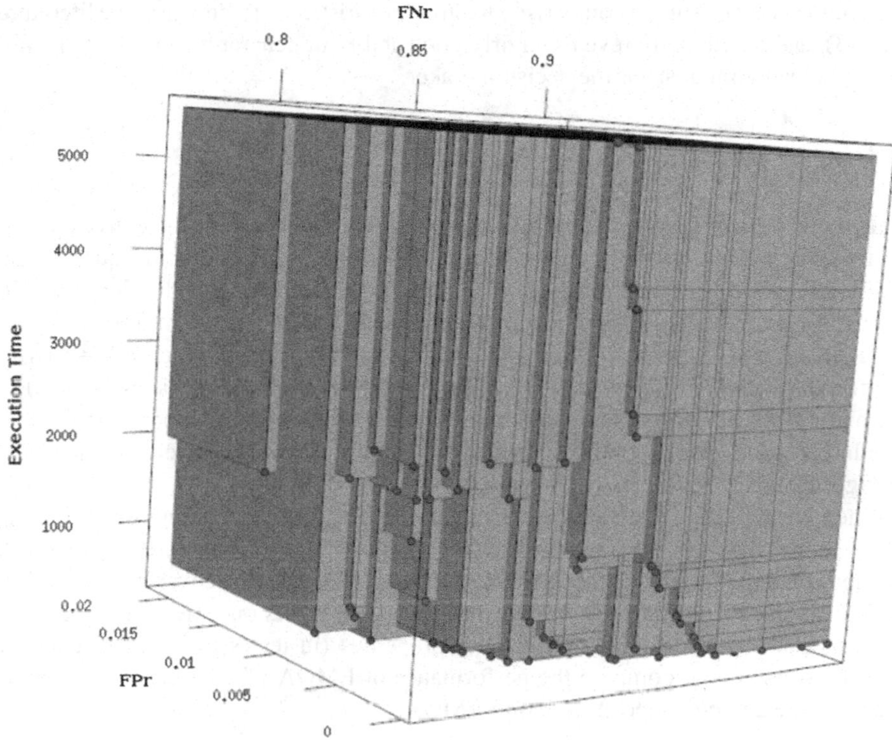

Fig. 1. 3D Pareto Front for NSGA-II execution

HV mean achieved in the experiments was 0,706 in comparison to 1 which represents the absolute optimum, which is a non-existent theoretical optimum.

5 Results Discussion

The optimization problem addressed in this study belongs to the class of optimization problems that is not possible to know the absolute optimum, therefore the results of our study have to be compared with the optimization outcomes of other state of the art algorithms applied in the anti-spam filtering domain.

One of the main advantages of EMO is its ability to provide insights of the conflicts/trade-offs among objectives of a multi-objective optimization problem.

Figure 1 highlights the tradeoff between classification time and quality. It shows that reducing the classification time is possible without significant loss of accuracy up to 1000 ms, and reducing classification time below 1000 ms has a considerable impact in quality, specially expressed by the growth of FN classifications.

We can also observe that NSGA-II provides a variety of solutions for the decision maker to select according to his/her trade-offs of interest. The solutions are distributed in the solution space in a way that allows the decision maker to have a wide range of alternatives. This reveals a good performance of NSGA-II addressing this problem, i.e., it presents the best quality in comparison to other 9 heuristics of reference in the literature (Table 3), and additionally reveals a fairly good ability of generating a variety of solutions of potential interest for the decision maker.

6 Conclusions and Future Work

In this work, we have evaluated the application of evolutionary multi-objective optimization algorithms to optimize rule-based anti-spam filters classification quality and classification time (in other words, anti-spam filters effectiveness and efficiency). To this end, we presented an experimental study using RuleSIM anti-spam filtering simulator and the NSGA-II multi-objective optimization algorithm, which allows us to demonstrate the advantages of EMOA approach in setting rules relevance (scores) to minimize FP and FN spam classifications, and setting rules execution orders that allow fast classification and/or optimal tradeoffs between classification errors rates and messages classification time.

When compared to 9 state of the art heuristics for rules scheduling optimization, NSGA-II revealed the best results in all criteria. Moreover, the EMOA approach provided solutions for anti-spam filter alternative optimal settings, covering a variety of scenarios of use for the anti-spam filter. In future studies it is our intention to perform benchmarks with email corpus with other properties (in terms of size and content/domain), as well as to compare the performance of EMOA of different type, such as indicator-base and decomposition-based EMOA.

Acknowledgements. SING group thanks CITI (Centro de Investigación, Transferencia e Innovación) from University of Vigo for hosting its IT infrastructure.

Funding: This work was partially funded by Consellería de Cultura, Educación e Ordenación Universitaria (Xunta de Galicia) and FEDER (European Union). This work was partially supported by the project Platform of integration of intelligent techniques for analysis of biomedical information (TIN2013-47153-C3-3-R) from the Spanish Ministry of Economy and Competitiveness.

References

1. Statista: The statistics portal, Global spam volume as percentage of total e-mail traffic from January 2014 to September 2016, by month (2016). https://www.statista.com/statistics/420391/spam-email-traffic-share/. Accessed 14 Feb 2017
2. Digital Marketing Ramblings, 73 Incredible e-mail statistics (2016). http://expandedramblings.com/index.php/email-statistics/. Accessed 14 Feb 2017
3. The Apache SpamAssassin Group, The first enterprise open-source spam filter (2003), http://spamassassin.apache.org/. Accessed 14 Feb 2017
4. Méndez, J.R., Reboiro-Jato, M., Díaz, F., Díaz, E., Fdez-Riverola, F.: Grindstone4Spam: an optimization toolkit for boosting e-mail classification. J. Syst. Softw. **85**(12), 2909–2920 (2012). doi:10.1016/j.jss.2012.06.027

5. Yevseyeva, I., Basto-Fernandes, V., Ruano-Ordás, D., Méndez, J.R.: Optimising anti-spam filters with evolutionary algorithms. Expert Syst. Appl. **40**(10), 4010–4021 (2013). doi: 10.1016/j.eswa.2013.01.008
6. Zhao, J., Basto-Fernandes, V., Jiao, L., Yevseyeva, I., Maulana, A., Li, R., Bäck, T., Tang, K.: Emmerich, Michael T. M.: Multiobjective optimization of classifiers by means of 3D convex-hull-based evolutionary algorithms. Inf. Sci. **367–368**, 80–104 (2016). doi:10.1016/j.ins.2016.05.026
7. Basto-Fernandes, V., Yevseyeva, I., Méndez, J.R., Zhao, J., Fdez-Riverola, F.: Emmerich, Michael T. M.: A spam filtering multi-objective optimization study covering parsimony maximization and three-way classification. Appl. Soft Comput. **48**, 111–123 (2016). doi: 10.1016/j.asoc.2016.06.043
8. Ruano-Ordás, D., Fdez-Glez, J., Fdez-Riverola, J., Méndez, J.R.: Effective scheduling strategies for boosting performance on rule-based spam filtering frameworks. J. Syst. Softw. **86**(12), 3151–3161 (2013). doi:10.1016/j.jss.2013.07.036
9. Ruano-Ordás, D., Fdez-Glez, J., Fdez-Riverola, F., Méndez, J.R.: Combining scheduling heuristics to improve e-mail filtering throughput. In: Omatu, S., Malluhi, Qutaibah M., Gonzalez, S.R., Bocewicz, G., Bucciarelli, E., Giulioni, G., Iqba, F. (eds.) Distributed Computing and Artificial Intelligence. AISC, vol. 373, pp. 235–242. Springer, Cham (2015). doi:10.1007/978-3-319-19638-1_27
10. Ruano-Ordás, D., Fdez-Glez, J., Fdez-Riverola, F., Méndez, J.R.: Using new scheduling heuristics based on resource consumption information for increasing throughput on rule-based spam filtering systems. Softw. Pract. Exper. **46**(8), 1035–1051 (2016). doi:10.1002/spe.2343
11. Ruano-Ordás, D., Fdez-Glez, J., Fdez-Riverola, F., Basto-Fernandes, V., Méndez, J.R.: RuleSIM: a toolkit for simulating the operation and improving throughput of rule-based spam filters. Softw. Pract. Exp. **46**, 1091–1108 (2016). doi:10.1002/spe.2342
12. Deb, K., Pratap, A., Agarwal, S., Meyarivan, T.: A fast and elitist multiobjective genetic algorithm: NSGA-II. IEEE Trans. Evol. Comput. **6**(2), 182–197 (2002). doi: 10.1109/4235.996017
13. IEEE Transactions on Evolutionary Computing – Popular Documents, February 2017. http://ieeexplore.ieee.org/xpl/topAccessedArticles.jsp?punumber=4235&sortType=popular_most_cited_by_papers. Accessed 3 April 2017
14. The Apache SpamAssassin Group, How do I get SpamAssassin to run faster? https://wiki.apache.org/spamassassin/FasterPerformance. Accessed 14 Feb 2017
15. Pérez-Díaz, N., Ruano-Ordás, D., Fdez-Riverola, F., Méndez, J.R.: Wirebrush4SPAM: a novel framework for improving efficiency on spam filtering services. Softw. Pract. Exp. **43**(11), 1299–1318 (2013). doi:10.1002/spe.2135
16. The Apache SpamAssassin Group. RescoreMassCheck. https://wiki.apache.org/spamassassin/RescoreMassCheck. Accessed 14 Feb 2017
17. Beasley, D.: Possible applications of evolutionary computation. In: Evolutionary Computation 1: Basic Algorithms and Operators, 1st edn., pp. 4–18. Institute of Physics Publishing, Bristol and Philadelphia (2000)
18. Resnick, P.: RFC2822: Internet Message Format, Network Working Group. https://www.ietf.org/rfc/rfc2822.txt. Accessed 14 Feb 2017
19. The Apache SpamAssassin Group, The Apache SpamAssassin Public Corpus. https://spamassassin.apache.org/publiccorpus/. Accessed 14 Feb 2017
20. CSMINING Group, Spam Emails Datasets. http://csmining.org/index.php/spam-email-datasets-.html. Accessed 14 Feb 2017
21. TREC Spam. Text REtrieval Conference. http://trec.nist.gov/data/spam.html. Accessed 14 Feb 2017

22. Guenter, B.: SPAM archive. http://untroubled.org/spam/. Accessed 14 Feb 2017
23. Durillo, J.J., Nebro, A.J.: jMetal: a java framework for multi-objective optimization. Adv. Eng. Softw. **42**(10), 760–771 (2011). doi:10.1016/j.advengsoft.2011.05.014

A Hybrid Diploid Genetic Based Algorithm for Solving the Generalized Traveling Salesman Problem

Petrica Pop(✉), Matei Oliviu, and Cosmin Sabo

Department of Mathematics and Computer Science, North University Center at Baia Mare, Technical University of Cluj-Napoca, Baia Mare, Romania
{petrica.pop,cosmin_sabo}@cunbm.utcluj.ro, oliviu.matei@holisun.com

Abstract. In this paper, we are addressing the generalized traveling salesman problem, denoted by GTSP, which is a variant of the classical traveling salesman problem (TSP). The GTSP is characterized by the fact that the vertices of the graph are partitioned into a given number of clusters and we are looking for the minimum cost tour that visits exactly one vertex from each cluster. The goal of this paper is to present a novel method for solving the GTSP, namely a hybrid diploid genetic based algorithm. The preliminary computational results on an often set of benchmark instances show that our proposed approach provides competitive solutions compared to the existing state-of-the-arts methods for solving the GTSP.

1 Introduction

This paper focuses on the generalized traveling salesman problem (GTSP), which is a variant of the well-known traveling salesman problem (TSP), where the entire set of vertices is split into sets of vertices called clusters. Given a graph whose vertices are grouped into a number of predefined clusters, the GTSP consists in finding the minimum cost tour visiting exactly one vertex from each cluster. The problem was introduced independently by Henry-Labordere [9] and Srivastava et al. [29].

The GTSP belongs to the class of generalized combinatorial optimization problems, known also as the class of generalized network design problems. This class of problems generalizes the classical combinatorial optimization problems in a natural way and its main features are the following: the vertices of the underlying graph are divided into clusters and the feasibility restrictions of the original problem are expressed in terms of the clusters instead of individual vertices. For more information on the class of generalized combinatorial optimization problems we refer to [3,20].

Taking into account its description, the GTSP is closely related to the following problems:

- *the traveling salesman problem (TSP)* which is perhaps the most well-known and famous combinatorial optimization problem. TSP looks for the most efficient (w.r.t. minimization of the total distance) Hamiltonian tour a salesman

F.J. Martínez de Pisón et al. (Eds.): HAIS 2017, LNAI 10334, pp. 149–160, 2017.
DOI: 10.1007/978-3-319-59650-1_13

can take in order to visit a number of cities. The GTSP reduces to TSP when all the clusters are singletons.
- the problem of finding the minimum cost Hamiltonian tour with the additional constraint that each cluster must be visited exactly once and at least one vertex is visited from each cluster before leaving the cluster. This problem was introduced by Laporte and Nobert [11].
- *the clustered traveling salesman problem (CTSP)* introduced by Chisman [2] and defined on an undirected graph whose vertex set is partitioned into a prespecified number of clusters. The goal of the CTSP is to determine the lowest cost Hamiltonian tour visiting all the vertices and with the additional constraint that the vertices of each cluster are visited consecutively.

The GTSP has several real-world applications such as optimal sequencing of computer files, mail delivery and vehicle routing, warehouse order picking, etc. For more information concerning the applications of the GTSP we refer to Laporte et al. [12,15].

Due to its challenging theoretical aspects and its practical applications, the GTSP has generated a considerable interest over the last five decades being obtained several results concerning complexity aspects, mathematical models, approximation results and heuristic and metaheuristic solution approaches. Integer programming and mixed integer programming models of the GTSP have been described by Fischetti et al. [4,5] and Pop [19,20]. Fischetti et al. [4,5] provided a polyhedral analysis and as well an exact algorithm for GTSP, namely a branch-and-cut algorithm.

The difficulty of obtaining optimal solutions for GTSP led to the development of approximation, heuristic and metaheuristic algorithms. Approximation results have been described by Slavik [27] who provided a polynomial time approximation scheme in the case when the problem has bounded cluster size and Bhattacharya et al. [1] who developed a polynomial time approximation scheme for the problem with grid clustering, i.e. all vertices are situated inside the integer grid, where each grid cell is 1×1 and the Euclidean distance defines the edge cost. Genetic algorithms for solving the GTSP have been proposed by Snyder and Daskin [28], Silberholz and Golden [26], Pop et al. [22] and Matei and Pop [13]. Multi-agent approaches for GTSP have been developed by Pintea et al. [16–18] and Reihaneh and Karapetyan [23] and a discrete particle swarm optimization algorithm was proposed by Tasgetiren [30]. Heuristic and hybrid algorithms for solving the GTSP have been described by Karapetyan and Gutin [7,10], Pop and Iordache [21], Renaud and Boctor [24]. By transforming GTSP instances into standard asymmetric TSP instances, Helsgaun [8] evaluated the performance of the state-of-the-art TSP solver Lin-Kernighan-Helsgaun.

The goal of our paper is to describe a novel hybrid algorithm for solving the GTSP, which is obtained obtained by decomposing the problem into two logical and natural smaller subproblems: an upper-level (global) subproblem and a lower-level (local) subproblem.

Our paper is organized as follows: In Sect. 2 we define the generalized traveling salesman problem. Section 3 describes the developed hybrid diploid genetic based algorithm for solving this problem. The proposed algorithm is applied on a set of often used benchmark instances in Sect. 4, where the obtained results are presented and analyzed. Finally, in the last section, we summarize the obtained results in this paper and future research directions are presented.

2 Definition of the GTSP

In this section we provide a explicit definition of the Generalized Traveling Salesman Problem as a graph theoretic model.

Let $G = (V, E)$ be an undirected graph, which we assume to be strongly connected, with $V = \{v_1, v_2, ..., v_n\}$ as the set of vertices and the set of edges $E = \{e = (v_i, v_j) \mid v_i, v_j \in V, v_i \neq v_j\}$.

The full set of vertices $\{v_1, ..., v_n\}$ is divided into m non-empty subsets, called clusters and denoted by $V_1, ..., V_m$, respecting the following conditions:

1. $V = V_1 \cup V_2 \cup ... \cup V_m$
2. $V_p \cap V_q = \emptyset$ for all $p, q \in \{1, ..., m\}$ and $p \neq q$.

Within this problem we have two kind of edges: edges joining vertices which belong to the same cluster, called intra-cluster edges and edges joining vertices which belong to different clusters, called inter-cluster edges. A nonnegative cost $c(v_i, v_j)$ is attached with each edge $e = (v_i, v_j) \in E$.

The *generalized traveling salesman problem* consists in finding a minimum-cost Hamiltonian tour visiting a subset of vertices which includes exactly one vertex from each cluster (Fig. 1).

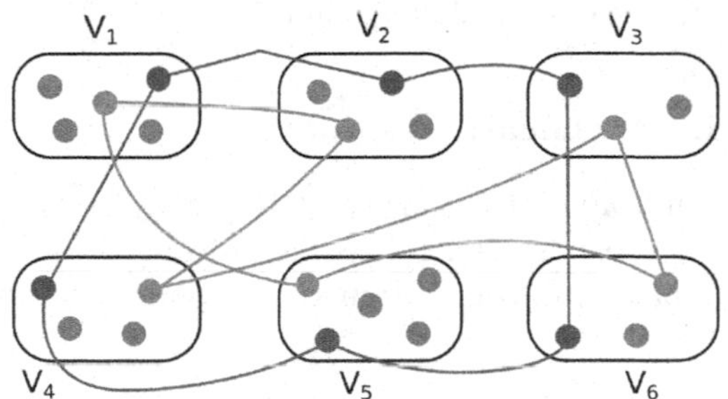

Fig. 1. Two feasible solutions to a GTSP instance

An illustrative scheme of the GTSP defined on an undirected graph with 24 vertices partitioned into 6 clusters and two feasible solutions are shown in the next figure.

The feasible solutions are represented with different colors and are Hamitonian tours visiting exactly one vertex from each of the clusters.

We will call such tours with the property that they are visiting a subset of vertices which includes exactly one vertex from each cluster *generalized tours.*

3 The Hybrid Diploid Genetic Algorithm

In the following we describe the main features of the proposed hybrid diploid genetic algorithm for solving the GTSP, obtained by decomposing the problem into two logical and natural smaller subproblems: an upper-level (global) subproblem which aims at generating the global Hamiltonian tours visiting the clusters (inter-cluster connections) and a lower-level (local) subproblem whose goal is to determine for the above mentioned global Hamiltonian tours the best tour (w.r.t. cost minimization) visiting a subset of vertices which includes exactly one vertex from each cluster.

3.1 The Upper-Level (Global) Subproblem

In order to define the upper-level subproblem, as in the local-global approach described by Pop et al. [20], we denote by G' the graph obtained from G after replacing all the vertices belonging to a cluster V_i, $i \in \{1, ..., m\}$ with a supernode representing it. The graph G' will be called the *global graph*. For convenience, we identify V_i with the supernode representing it and we will denote it by i. Edges of the graph G' are defined between each pair of the global graph vertices $\{1, \ldots, m\}$. By assuming that the graph G is strongly connected it results that the global graph G' is complete.

In the case of the GTSP, we use a diploid genetic algorithm applied to the corresponding global graph in order to provide Hamiltonian tours visiting the clusters. One of the main advantages of using this approach is the considerably decrement of the solution space of the original problem. We will call such a tour visiting the clusters a *global Hamiltonian tour*. In the next figure we present an example of a global tour in the global graph G'.

3.2 The Lower-Level (Local) Subproblem

Having a global Hamiltonian tour visiting the clusters: $(V_{k_1}, V_{k_2}, ..., V_{k_m})$, it is rather easy to find the best generalized Hamiltonian tour w.r.t. cost minimization. To each global Hamiltonian tour corresponds a number of generalized

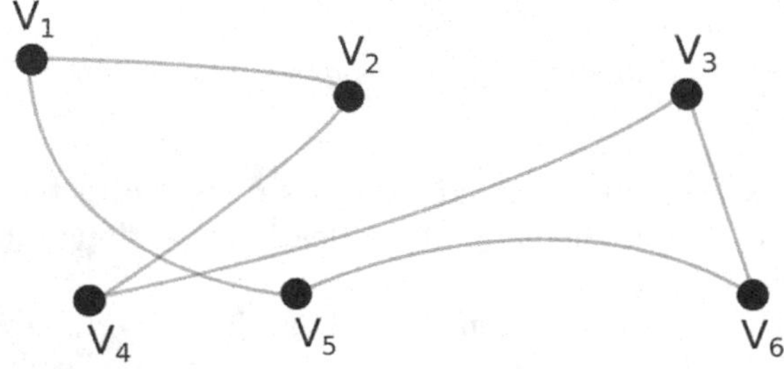

Fig. 2. An example of a global Hamiltonian tour in the global graph G'

Hamiltonian tours and between them there exists one called the best generalized Hamitonian tour that can be found in polynomial time by solving $|V_{k_1}|$ shortest path problems in a constructed layered graph consisting of $m + 1$ layers. For more details we refer to Fischetti et al. [5] and Pop et al. [22].

3.3 The Diploid Genetic Algorithm

Representation

One of the novelties of our approach is the use of a diploid (bi-chromosomal) representation of the individuals that supposes the existence of two chromosomes together. Therefore, unlike the classical individuals, which were synonym with chromosomes, now we talk about individuals consisting of a pair chromosomes. In this way, we mimic the natural diploid individuals [14]. The advantage of this representation is that each individual carries twice as much information as in the classical approach (called also "haploid"). This assures a higher diversity of the potential feasible solutions [6]. An individual is represented as follows:

$$I = (C_1, C_2)$$

where C_i are the chromosomes, with $i \in \{1, 2\}$. Actually, both chromosomes are potential feasible solutions belonging to the space of solutions (i.e. global Hamiltonian tours).

Further we define $C_d \in \{C_1, C_2\}$ as the dominant chromosome if it is the best out of the two chromosomes and $C_r \in \{C_1, C_2\}$ as the recessive chromosome if it is the worst out of the two. Please note that $\{C_d, C_r\} = \{C_1, C_2\}$.

At the level of the global graph, the chromosome associated to each candidate solution is represented as an array of m integer numbers, each number corresponding to the index of a certain cluster. The global Hamiltonian tour is ordered in conformity with the order in which the clusters are visited.

For example, in the case of the feasible solution presented in Fig. 2, the global Hamiltonian tour is $(V_1, V_2, V_4, V_3, V_6, V_5)$ and the corresponding chromosome is represented by the following array: $(1, 2, 4, 3, 6, 5)$.

Fitness function

Let us denote the fitness of the individual by $f(I)$ and subsequently the fitness of the two chromosomes by $f(C_i)$, with $i \in \{1, 2\}$. Of course, according to the definition provided in this section, we have $f(C_d) \leq f(C_r)$.

There are different ways of defining the fitness of an individual:

1. the fitness of the individual is the fitness of the dominant chromosome, that is: $f(I) = f(C_d)$;
2. the fitness of the individual is the fitness of the recessive chromosomes: $f(I) = f(C_r)$;
3. the fitness of the individual is the sum (or average) of the fitness values of the two chromosomes: $f(I) = f(C_1) + f(C_2)$;
4. the fitness of the individual is a weighted average of the fitness values of the two chromosomes: $f(I) = w_1 \cdot f(C_1) + w_2 \cdot f(C_2)$, where $w_i = \frac{f(C_i)}{f(C_1)+f(C_2)}$ with $i \in \{1, 2\}$.

In our approach, we opted for the third possibility, namely the fitness of an individual is the sum of the fitness values of the two chromosomes.

At the solution level, the fitness associated to a feasible solution (i.e. global Hamiltonian tour) is given by the cost of the best corresponding generalized Hamiltonian tour (w.r.t cost minimization). The goal of our problem is to determine the minimum cost global Hamiltonian tour which leads to the best generalized Hamiltonian tour with respect to cost minimization.

Initial population

Our initial population was generated randomly from the space of feasible solutions (global Hamiltonian tours) providing in this way an unbiased initial population.

Crossover

Having two individuals $I_1 = (C_1^1, C_2^1)$ and $I_2 = (C_1^2, C_2^2)$, we can define the recombination operator. For a clear distinction between the crossover at the individual level, respectively at the solution (chromosomes) level, we will define them as *individual crossover* or *macro-crossover* at the individual level, respectively *solution crossover*, *chromosomal crossover* or *micro-crossover* at the solution level.

The macro-recombination is defined in a discrete way, only the chromosomes interchange between the two individuals. Having $I_1 = (C_1^1, C_2^1)$ and $I_2 = (C_1^2, C_2^2)$, the offspring are:

$$O_1 = (C_1^{11}, C_2^{11}) \text{ and } O_2 = (C_1^{22}, C_2^{22}),$$

where C_i^{kk} may be any of the parental chromosomes $\{C_1^1, C_2^1, C_1^2, C_2^2\}$.

At the solution level, a micro-crossover is applied. We select randomly a cut point between 1 and m and then the symbols before the cut point are copied from the first parent into the offspring. Then, starting just after the cut-point, the symbols are copied from the second parent into the offspring, omitting any symbols that were copied already from the first parent. The second offspring is produced by exchanging the role of the parents.

In what it follows, we exemplify the application of the proposed crossover operator in the case of a problem instance consisting of 12 clusters. We assume that we have the following parents and the cutting point was selected randomly between 5 and 6:

$$P_1 = (1\ 11\ 8\ 12\ \ 7\ |\ \ 9\ 4\ 5\ 2\ 10\ 6\ 3)$$
$$P_2 = (2\ 12\ 7\ \ 3\ 10\ |\ 11\ 8\ 4\ 6\ \ 5\ 9\ 1)$$

The offspring are computed by copying first the symbols before the cutting point:

$$O_1 = (1\ 11\ 8\ 12\ \ 7\ |\ \mathrm{x\ x\ x\ x\ x\ x\ x})$$
$$O_2 = (2\ 12\ 7\ \ 3\ 10\ |\ \mathrm{x\ x\ x\ x\ x\ x\ x})$$

and then the indexes of the clusters of the parent P_2 are copied into the offspring O_1 if O_1 does not contain clusters that are already represented in P_1. We observe that the clusters V_{11}, V_8 and V_1 are already represented in O_1 and therefore they are discarded. By exchanging the role of the parents, we obtain the second offspring:

$$O_1 = (1\ 11\ 8\ 12\ \ 7 \mid \mathrm{x}\ \mathrm{x}\ 4\ 6\ 5\ 9\ \mathrm{x})$$
$$O_2 = (2\ 12\ 7\ \ 3\ 10 \mid 9\ 4\ 5\ \mathrm{x}\ \mathrm{x}\ 6\ \mathrm{x})$$

The already existing clusters from the offspring are replaced at random by other clusters which have not been selected:

$$O_1 = (1\ 11\ 8\ 12\ \ 7 \mid 3\ 10\ 4\ 6\ 5\ 9\ \ 2)$$
$$O_2 = (2\ 12\ 7\ \ 3\ 10 \mid 9\ \ 4\ 5\ 1\ 8\ 6\ 11)$$

Mutation
After obtaining the offspring from the crossover algorithm a mutation operator is applied. The mutation operation has a probability to be applied, that is set before solving the problem. The mutation is applied at the level of the chromosome and works as follows: we pick randomly two values from the corresponding array and swap their values.

Selection
In our algorithm we considered a deterministic selection process. The method used is a $(\mu + \lambda)$ selection which works as follows: the best μ individuals are selected from the pool of μ parents and λ offspring. This method is well known to stick in local optima. However, we overcome this shortcoming by using the diploid representation of the individuals.

Genetic parameters
Based on preliminary computational experiments, we have chosen the following values for the genetic parameters: the population size μ has been stated to be three times the number of clusters: $\mu = 3 \cdot m$. A smaller population does not cover the solution space completely enough, whereas a larger one generates quite similar results and raises the computation time without important added value. The intermediate population size λ was set to twice the size of the population: $\lambda = 2 \cdot \mu$. The mutation probability was chosen to be 5% and the maximum number of generations (epochs) in our algorithm was set at 200.

4 Computational Results

In this section we present our preliminary computational results in order to determine the efficiency of our proposed hybrid diploid genetic algorithm for solving the GTSP.

We conducted our computational experiments for solving the GTSP on a set of 30 often used benchmark instances generated from TSPLIB instances [25]. Originally, the set of vertices were not partitioned into clusters and Fischetti et al. [5] proposed a procedure to split the vertices of the graph into clusters, called CLUSTERING. The main idea of their procedure was to set the number of clusters, identify the s farthest vertices from each other and then assign each remaining vertices to its nearest center.

Our proposed solution approach for solving the GTSP has been implemented, and in our experiments we performed 30 independent runs for each instance. The testing machine was an Intel Core 2 Duo 2.4 GHz processor and the algorithm was developed in Java.

In order to study the performance of our proposed solution approach, we compared it with the existing state-of-the-art algorithms from the literature: the memetic algorithm (MA) developed by Gutin and Karapetyan [7], the genetic algorithm approach proposed by Silberholz and Golden [26], the random-key genetic algorithm (RK-GA) described by Snyder and Daskin [28] and the particle swarm optimization algorithm considered by Tasgetiren et al. [30].

The obtained computational results are going to be presented in Table 1 and the corresponding computational times in Table 2. The headers of Table 1 are: the instance name, the errors calculated in per cent of the average solution above the optimal value. It is worth to mention that the exact optimal solutions are known from [5] for a set of 17 of the considered instances and for the rest, we considered the best solutions achieved by Gutin and Karapetyan [7]. There are presented the errors in the case of the memetic algorithm (MA) [7], the genetic algorithm (GA) approach [26], the random-key genetic algorithm (RK-GA) [28] and the particle swarm optimization algorithm (PSO) [30]. The last two columns give the errors of the best solution and average solution above the optimal value.

In Table 2 we report the computational running times necessary to achieve the solutions reported in Table 1. For comparing the running times of all these algorithms, we make use of the correlation relations between the machines used for testing them. According to [7], the computer used for testing the memetic algorithm (MA) [7] and the random-key genetic algorithm (RK-GA) [28] has an AMD Athlon 64 $\times$ 23.0 GHz processor. The computer used for testing the genetic algorithm (GA) [29] has an Intel Pentium 4 3.0 GHz processor and the computer used for particle swarm optimization (PSO) has an Intel Centrino Duo 1.83 GHz processor. The heuristics MA, RK-GA, and PSO have been implemented in C++, with the observation that the MA was implemented in C# but the most time critical fragments have been implemented in C++, while the GA was implemented in Java. Some rough estimation of Java performance in dealing with solving combinatorial optimization problems shows that the C++ implementation could be approximately two times faster than the Java implementation. As a result, we used as in [7] some adjusting coefficients: 3 in the case of GA, 2 in the case of the PSO and 1.6 in the case of the our proposed hybrid diploid genetic algorithm.

Analyzing the reported computational results we observe that our approach outperforms the existing heuristics for solving the GTSP in terms of the achieved solution quality. We were able to improve the existing solutions 9 out of 30 instances. Concerning the computational times necessary to achieve the delivered solutions, ours are larger than those provided by Gutin and Karapetyan [7], but smaller compared to the other considered heuristics.

Some important features of our proposed hybrid diploid genetic algorithm approach:

Table 1. The comparison of the solvers quality

Instance name	Error (%)				Error (%) our aproach	
	MA [7]	GA [26]	RK-GA [28]	PSO [30]	Best solution	Average solution
40d198	0.00	0.00	0.00	0.00	0.00	0.00
40kroa200	0.00	0.00	0.00	0.00	0.00	0.00
40krob200	0.00	0.05	0.01	0.00	0.00	0.00
41gr202	0.00		0.00		0.00	0.00
45ts225	0.00	0.14	0.09	0.04	0.00	0.00
45tsp225	0.00		0.01		0.00	0.00
46pr226	0.00	0.00	0.00	0.00	0.00	0.00
46gr229	0.00		0.03		0.00	0.00
53gil262	0.00	0.45	0.31	0.32	0.00	0.00
53pr264	0.00	0.00	0.00	0.00	0.00	0.00
56a280	0.00	0.17	0.08		0.00	0.00
60pr299	0.00	0.05	0.05	0.03	0.00	0.00
64lin318	0.00	0.00	0.38	0.46	0.00	0.00
80rd400	0.00	0.58	0.60	0.91	0.00	0.00
84fl417	0.00	0.04	0.02	0.00	0.00	0.00
87gr431	0.00		0.30		0.00	0.00
88pr439	0.00	0.00	0.28	0.00	0.00	0.00
89pcb442	0.00	0.01	1.30	0.86	0.00	0.01
107att532	0.01	0.35	0.72		0.00	0.02
107si535	0.00	0.08	0.32		0.00	0.00
113pa561	0.00	1.50	3.57		0.00	0.00
115rat575	0.20	1.12	3.22		0.11	0.14
131p654	0.00	0.29	0.08		0.00	0.01
132d657	0.15	0.45	2.32		0.10	0.16
145u724	0.14	0.57	3.49		0.07	0.12
157rat783	0.11	1.17	3.84		0.09	0.15
201pr1002	0.14	0.24	3.43		0.07	0.16
207si1032	0.03	0.37	0.93		0.00	0.08
212u1060	0.27	2.25	3.60		0.22	0.30
217vm1084	0.19	0.90	3.68		0.10	0.20

- the use of an efficient GA which delivers the global Hamiltonian tours visiting the clusters;
- the use of a diploid representation that assures a high diversity of the potential feasible solutions;
- the use of an efficient method in order to determine the best corresponding generalized Hamiltonian tour for a given global Hamiltonian tour.

Table 2. The comparison of the solvers computational running times in seconds

Instance name	MA [7]	GA [26]	RK-GA [28]	PSO [30]	Our aproach
40d198	0.14	1.63	1.18	1.22	1.12
40kroa200	0.14	1.66	0.26	0.79	0.83
40krob200	0.16	1.63	0.80	2.70	0.56
41gr202	0.21	0.65	3.2		1.34
45ts225	0.24	1.71	0.46	1.42	0.45
45tsp225	0.19	0.55	2.9		1.52
46pr226	0.10	1.54	0.63	0.46	0.45
46gr229	0.25	1.14	4.6		2.33
53gil262	0.31	3.64	0.85	4.51	0.62
53pr264	0.24	2.36	0.82	1.10	0.61
56a280	0.38	2.92	1.14		0.88
60pr299	0.42	4.59	1.74	3.08	1.26
64lin318	0.45	8.08	1.42	8.49	1.12
80rd400	1.07	14.58	3.53	13.55	3.44
84fl417	0.73	8.15	3.17	6.74	2.78
88pr439	1.48	19.06	4.68	20.87	3.75
89pcb442	1.72	23.43	4.26	23.14	3.45
99d493	4.17	35.72	6.34		6.42
107att532	3.45	31.70	8.04		10.58
107si535	1.88	26.35	6.06		6.83
113pa561	3.22	21.08	6.37		5.81
115rat575	4.12	48.48	9.19		5.77
131p654	2.82	32.67	13.23		8.37
132d657	6.82	132.24	15.40		10.67
145u724	11.61	161.82	22.00		18.45
157rat783	15.30	152.15	22.70		26.51
201pr1002	34.83	464.36	63.04		45.86
207si1032	36.76	242.37	34.99		38.44
212u1060	44.76	594.64	65.81		49.12
217vm1084	59.82	562.04	87.38		64.23

5 Conclusions

This paper considers the generalized traveling salesman problem. For solving this optimization problem we developed a hybrid diploid genetic algorithm which is obtained obtained by decomposing the problem into two logical and natural smaller subproblems: an upper-level (global) subproblem and a lower-level (local) subproblem. One important feature of our approach is the use of a diploid (bi-chromosomal) representation of the individuals that assures a higher diversity of the potential feasible solutions. The preliminary computational results show that our hybrid genetic algorithm is robust and compares favorably to existing approaches. The new solution approach yields high-quality solutions within reasonable running-times.

In future, we plan to evaluate the generality and scalability of the proposed solution approach by testing it on larger instances. It would also be promising to investigate the combination of our hybrid diploid genetic algorithm with a local search procedure.

References

1. Bhattacharya, B., Ćustić, A., Rafiey, A., Rafiey, A., Sokol, V.: Approximation algorithms for generalized MST and TSP in grid clusters. In: Lu, Z., Kim, D., Wu, W., Li, W., Du, D.-Z. (eds.) COCOA 2015. LNCS, vol. 9486, pp. 110–125. Springer, Cham (2015). doi:10.1007/978-3-319-26626-8_9
2. Chisman, J.A.: The clustered traveling salesman problem. Comput. Oper. Res. **2**(2), 115–119 (1975)
3. Feremans, C., Labbe, M., Laporte, G.: Generalized network design problems. Eur. J. Oper. Res. **148**(1), 1–13 (2003)
4. Fischetti, M., Salazar-Gonzales, J.J., Toth, P.: The symmetric generalized traveling salesman polytope. Networks **26**(2), 113–123 (1995)
5. Fischetti, M., Salazar-Gonzales, J.J., Toth, P.: A branch-and-cut algorithm for the symmetric generalized traveling salesman problem. Oper. Res. **45**(3), 378–394 (1997)
6. Goldberg, D.E., Smith, R.E.: Nonstationary function optimization using genetic algorithms with dominance and diploidy. In: Proceedings of the Second International Conference on Genetic Algorithms and their application, pp. 59–68 (1987)
7. Gutin, G., Karapetyan, D.: A memetic algorithm for the generalized traveling salesman problem. Natural Comput. **9**(1), 47–60 (2010)
8. Helsgaun, K.: Solving the equality generalized traveling salesman problem using the LinKernighanHelsgaun Algorithm. Math. Prog. Comp. **7**(3), 269–287 (2015)
9. Henry-Labordere, A.L.: The record balancing problem: a dynamic programming solution of a generalized travelling salesman problem. RIRO **B-2**, 43–49 (1969)
10. Karapetyan, D., Gutin, G.: Efficient local search algorithms for known and new neighborhoods for the generalized traveling salesman problem. Eur. J. Oper. Res. **219**(2), 234–251 (2012)
11. Laporte, G., Nobert, Y.: Generalized travelling salesman problem through n sets of nodes: an integer programming approach. Infor. **21**, 61–75 (1983)
12. Laporte, G., Asef-Vaziri, A., Sriskandarajah, C.: Some applications of the generalized travelling salesman problem. J. Oper. Res. Soc. **47**(12), 1461–1467 (1996)
13. Matei, O., Pop, P.C.: An efficient genetic algorithm for solving the generalized traveling salesman problem. In: Proceedings of 6th IEEE International Conference on Intelligent Computer Communication and Processing, pp. 87–92 (2010)
14. Mitchell, M.: An Introduction to Genetic Algorithms. MIT Press (1998)
15. Pintea, C.-M., Chira, C., Dumitrescu, D., Pop, P.C.: A sensitive metaheuristic for solving a large optimization problem. In: Geffert, V., Karhumäki, J., Bertoni, A., Preneel, B., Návrat, P., Bieliková, M. (eds.) SOFSEM 2008. LNCS, vol. 4910, pp. 551–559. Springer, Heidelberg (2008). doi:10.1007/978-3-540-77566-9_48

16. Pintea, C.-M., Pop, P.C., Chira, C.: Reinforcing ant colony system for the generalized traveling salesman problem. In: Proceedings of BIC-TA 2006, pp. 245–252 (2006)
17. Pintea, C.-M., Chira, C., Dumitrescu, D., Pop, P.C.: Sensitive ants in solving the generalized vehicle routing problem. Int. J. Comput. Commun. Control **6**(4), 734–741 (2011)
18. Pintea, C.-M., Pop, P.C., Chira, C.: The Generalized Traveling Salesman Problem solved with Ant Algorithms (2013). arXiv:1310.2350
19. Pop, P.C.: New integer programming formulations of the generalized traveling salesman problem. Am. J. Appl. Sci. **4**(11), 932–937 (2007)
20. Pop, P.C.: Generalized Network Design Problems, Modelling and Optimization. De Gruyter, Germany (2012)
21. Pop, P.C., Iordache, S.: A hybrid heuristic approach for solving the generalized traveling saleasman problem. In: Proceedings of GECCO 2011, pp. 481–488 (2011)
22. Pop, P.C., Matei, O., Sabo, C.: A new approach for solving the generalized traveling salesman problem. In: Blesa, M.J., Blum, C., Raidl, G., Roli, A., Sampels, M. (eds.) HM 2010. LNCS, vol. 6373, pp. 62–72. Springer, Heidelberg (2010). doi:10.1007/978-3-642-16054-7_5
23. Reihaneh, M., Karapetyan, D.: An efficient hybrid ant colony system for the generalized traveling salesman problem. Algorithmic Oper. Res. **7**, 21–28 (2012)
24. Renaud, J., Boctor, F.F.: An efficient composite heuristic for the symmetric generalized traveling salesman problem. Eur. J. Oper. Res. **108**(3), 571–584 (1998)
25. Reinelt, G.: TSPLIB - A traveling salesman problem library. ORSA J. Comput. **3**, 376–384 (1991). http://www.crpc.rice.edu/softlib/tsplib/
26. Silberholz, J., Golden, B.: The Generalized Traveling Salesman Problem: a new genetic algorithm approach. In: Baker, E.K., Joseph, A., Mehrotra, A., Trick, M.A. (eds.) Extending the Horizons: Advances in Computing, Optimization and Decision Technologies. Operations Research/Computer Science Interfaces Series, vol. 37, pp. 165–181. Springer, New York (2007)
27. Slavik, P.: On the approximation of the generalized traveling salesman problem. Working paper, University of Buffalo (1997)
28. Snyder, L.V., Daskin, M.S.: A random-key genetic algorithm for the generalized traveling salesman problem. Eur. J. Oper. Res. **174**, 38–53 (2006)
29. Srivastava, S.S., Kumar, S., Garg, R.C., Sen, P.: Generalized travelling salesman problem through n sets of nodes. CORS J. **7**, 97–101 (1969)
30. Tasgetiren, M.F., Suganthan, P.N., Pan, Q.-K.: A discrete particle swarm optimization algorithm for the generalized traveling salesman problem. In Proceedings of GECCO, pp. 158–167 (2007)

A Novel Hybrid Nature-Inspired Scheme for Solving a Financial Optimization Problem

Alexandros Tzanetos, Vassilios Vassiliadis(✉), and Georgios Dounias

Management and Decision Engineering Laboratory, Department of Financial and Management Engineering, University of the Aegean, 41 Kountouriotou Str., 82100 Chios, Greece
{atzanetos,g.dounias}@aegean.gr, v.vassiliadis@fme.aegean.gr

Abstract. Hybrid intelligent approaches have proven their potential in demanding problem settings. The financial domain provides some challenging problem set-ups, mostly because of non-linearity conditions and conflicting objectives and binding restrictions. In this study, a novel hybrid algorithm, which stems from Nature-Inspired Intelligence, is applied in a specific portfolio optimization problem. The proposed algorithm comprises of an Ant Colony Optimization Algorithm (ACO) for detecting optimal combination of assets and a Gravitational Search Algorithm (GSA), for optimal capital allocation in the portfolio. Results from the proposed hybrid scheme are compared to previous findings, in the same optimization problem and dataset, from another hybrid NII algorithm, namely ACO Algorithm with Firefly Algorithm (FA). Experimental findings indicate that the proposed hybrid scheme yields a promising distribution of fitness values from independent simulation runs. What is more, in terms of best solution found, the proposed hybrid scheme yielded a solution that is 7.2% worst than the benchmark approach's one. However, in terms of execution time, the proposed algorithm was faster. Taking into consideration both the above aspects, the difference of the two hybrid algorithms, in terms of best solution, can be characterized as insignificant. The main aim of the paper is to highlight the advantages of the proposed hybrid scheme, as well as the great potential of Nature-Inspired Intelligent algorithms for the financial portfolio optimization problem.

Keywords: Hybrid NII · Ant Colony Optimization · Gravitational Search Algorithm · Financial portfolio optimization

1 Introduction

The financial portfolio optimization problem poses great challenges for the decision-makers in the financial domain. The best combination of assets and the optimal allocation of the available capital on them, under non-linear objectives and binding restrictions, can be tackled neither by traditional methodologies from the field of statistics and mathematics, nor by individual financial heuristics, applied by the field's experts. In general, portfolio optimization problems are considered as NP-hard problems, i.e. an exact solution cannot be found in polynomial time. The complexity of the optimization problem can be demonstrated by the following example. Consider the situation, where the best combination of 10 stocks out of 100 has to be found. The number of possible

F.J. Martínez de Pisón et al. (Eds.): HAIS 2017, LNAI 10334, pp. 161–172, 2017.
DOI: 10.1007/978-3-319-59650-1_14

combinations sums to $\binom{100}{10} = 1.73 * 10^{13}$. What is more, for each combination of assets, the optimal capital allocation (weights) should be found. It can be easily induced that the number of possible combinations of weights, in the continuous space, tends to infinity. Any known exhaustive search algorithms, or other approach, fail to solve this problem set-up, or even approximate a good-quality solution region [1].

The field of Nature-Inspired Intelligence (NII) algorithms may provide a solution to this problem. NII algorithms are based on the way natural systems work [2]. ACO is a very common example, which stems from the strategy of ants, regarding their searching for food sources. The main advantage of NII techniques is their searching ability, which comprises of strategic components derived from natural paradigms. Hybrid schemes, which combine unique characteristics from individual NII algorithms, are very promising.

The aim of this paper is twofold. Firstly, this study introduces a novel hybrid scheme, which consists of an ACO algorithm for asset selection and a NII component for weight optimization, namely GSA, as the main strategy for optimal capital allocation. The main motivation for proposing this hybrid scheme is the ability of GSA in finding the optimal solution in a framework of continuous optimization. The proposed hybrid algorithm is tested in a portfolio optimization problem framework, as presented in [3], in which another hybrid scheme was applied, namely ACO algorithm and FA. The second objective of this study is to highlight the effectiveness of NII algorithms in detecting heuristic information from a given dataset. This information could be embedded into the hybrid algorithm, a-posteriori as an expert's rule, with the aim of improving the best-so-far solution, or even finding the global optimum.

2 Literature Review

In general, various NII algorithms have been applied to the specific optimization problem. In [8, 9] a Particle Swarm Optimization algorithm is used in order to tackle with different formulations of portfolio optimization. Also, genetic algorithms have been applied to this problem domain.

Hybrid intelligent algorithms have been applied in the financial portfolio optimization domain. In this section, some representative studies are presented in brief. In their study, [4], the authors have applied a genetic algorithm combined with quadratic programming to solve the portfolio optimization problem, with the aim of minimizing the tracking error volatility. This objective is characterized as 'passive portfolio management' and reflects the attitude of risk-averse investors. Findings from this study indicated that the GA strategy allowed several differing threads of the search space to be pursued, which leads to more efficient searching ability. In [5], a genetic algorithm for finding optimal combination of assets combined with simulated annealing for optimal capital allocation is applied to the classical portfolio optimization problem framework, as proposed by Markowitz in his seminal paper [6], i.e. minimization of the portfolio's risk with a constraint on portfolio's expected return. Authors indicated that the combination of evolutionary techniques enhance the abilities of heuristic algorithms such as simulated annealing. More specifically, the proposed hybrid managed to yield a solution with very low variance, compared to results obtained by solely applying simulated annealing. Also, in [7] an ACO algorithm, hybridized with quadratic programming, is implemented in order to minimize the probability of tracking error falling below a defined threshold. In all these papers, hybrid NII schemes have proven their ability in dealing with complex formulations of the financial portfolio optimization problem. Preliminary experimental results highlighted the potential application of hybrid schemes in hard NP-problems, such as financial portfolio optimization.

3 Portfolio Optimization Problem

In this study, the proposed hybrid scheme was applied to a formulation of the portfolio optimization problem, as stated in [3]. The optimization problem can be defined in the multi-objective framework. On the one hand, the aim is to maximize a financial ratio, namely the Sortino ratio [15], which takes into consideration the excess return of the portfolio and the volatility of the portfolio's negative returns. On the other hand, there is a penalty term, in case a portfolio's tracking error volatility (TEV) exceeds a certain threshold. TEV measures the distance between the portfolio's and a benchmark index's returns. In general, TEV is considered as a measure for passive portfolio management strategies [16]. The mathematical formulation of the financial optimization problem is

$$Maximize\ Sortino\ Ratio = \frac{E(r_P) - r_f}{\theta_0(r_P)} \tag{1}$$

s.t.

$$\sum_{i=1}^{N} w_i = 1$$

$$0 \leq w_i \leq 1$$

$$N = 5$$

$$\sqrt{Var(r_P - r_B)} \leq H$$

where,

$E(r_P)$, is the portfolio's expected return

r_f, is the risk-free return ($2{,}8 * 10^{-4}$)

$\theta_0(r_P)$, is the volatility of returns which fall below a certain threshold and equals

w_i, is the percentage of capital invested in the *i-th* asset

N, is the maximum number of assets contained in a portfolio (binding constraint)

r_B, is the benchmark's daily return

H, is the upper threshold for the tracking error volatility (0,0001)

$f(r_P)$, is the probability density function of the portfolio's returns.

4 Combination of Two NII Algorithms for Portfolio Optimization

In this study, a novel hybrid NII scheme, combining ACO and GSA, is proposed for solving the financial portfolio optimization problem. More specifically, the ACO component is used to find optimal combination of assets, whereas GSA is applied for optimal capital allocation (assets' weights). Therefore, the financial portfolio optimization problem is tackled as a dual optimization problem: a discrete optimization as far as the selection of assets is concerned, and a continuous optimization as far as the selection of assets' weights. Results from the proposed hybrid scheme are compared to those from another hybrid NII algorithm, namely ACO with FA, which was presented in [3].

ACO was first introduced by Dorigo [10]. Its main advantage relies on the way real ant colonies search for food in the environment. More specifically, real ants' searching strategy is based on an indirect communication among them, through pheromone trails, which is called stigmergy. The food source with the strongest pheromone trail attracts the majority of the colony. In the portfolio optimization problem, a combination of assets represents a food source, whereas assets may be considered as components of the 'food source'. As a result, artificial ants track the solution space for high-quality components, based on the defined objective function and restrictions. In ACO, the probability of choosing an asset, in order to be incorporated in the portfolio, under construction, is defined in Eq. (1)

$$p_{aj} = \begin{cases} \dfrac{\sum_{i \in P'_\alpha} r_{ij}}{\sum_{i \in P'_\alpha,} \sum_{h \notin P'_\alpha} r_{ih}}, \forall j \notin P'_\alpha \\ 0, \forall j \in P'_\alpha \end{cases} \tag{2}$$

where,

p_{aj}, is the probability of selecting asset j

r_{ij}, is the pheromone value between assets i and j (asset i is already selected in the portfolio)

r_{ih}, is the pheromone value between assets i and h, which represents all the assets not included in the portfolio.

ACO updates the pheromone values through evaporation (2), applied in all cases, and enhancement, applied only to the best solutions (3)

$$r_{ij,t} = (1 - \rho) \times r_{ij,t-1} \tag{3}$$

$$\mathrm{r}_{update} = \frac{1}{e^{ob}} \tag{4}$$

where,

ρ, is the evaporation rate

ob, is the fitness value of *i-th* solution

FA was proposed by Yang [11] and it is considered a swarm-based intelligent meta-heuristic. FA relies on the way fireflies move in the air. In nature, fireflies produce light, through a chemical process, which is the attraction factor. The attractiveness of a position is relative to the brightness of the light. In the portfolio optimization domain, FA is applied for finding the optimal capital allocation. Each artificial firefly is characterized by a specific vector of coordinates in the *n-dimensional* space. The position of each agent is adjusted based on the position of other agents, with the aim of getting towards the best-so-far position, based on the objective value. The movement of an agent's position towards a more attractive one is given by Eq. (4)

$$x_{i,new} = x_{i,old} + b_0 \times e^{-\gamma \times R_{ij}^2} \times \left(x_{j,old} - x_{i,old}\right) + \alpha \times \left(rand - \frac{1}{2}\right) \tag{5}$$

where,

$x_{i,new}$, is the new position of agent i (vector containing coordinates for each dimension)
$x_{i,old}$, is the old position of agent i (vector containing coordinates for each dimension)

$b_0 \times e^{-\gamma \times R_{ij}^2}$, is the attractiveness factor, comprising of b_0 (constant of attractiveness), γ (constant of light absorption), R_{ij}^2 (the Euclidean distance between two agents) which is defined as (5)

$$r_{ij} = \left\| x_i - x_j \right\| = \sqrt{\sum_{k=1}^{d} \left(x_{i,k} - x_{j,k}\right)^2} \tag{6}$$

$\alpha \times \left(rand - \frac{1}{2}\right)$, a component that adds randomness in the process (α denotes the effect of randomness).

ACO is also hybridized with GSA, which is a rather recent NII technique [12]. The popularity of this algorithm has been highlighted in several studies [13, 14]. In GSA, every solution is represented by a mass. This mass increases based on the quality of the solution; better solutions have bigger masses, while worst solutions have smaller masses. For each mass, the force acting on other masses is calculated as:

$$F_{ij}^d(t) = G(t)\frac{M_{pi}(t) \times M_{aj}(t)}{R_{ij}(t) + \varepsilon}(x_j^d(t) - x_i^d(t)) \tag{7}$$

where M_{aj} is the active gravitational mass related to agent j, M_{pi} is the passive gravitational mass related to agent i, $G(t)$ is gravitational constant at time t, ε is a small constant, and $R_{ij}(t)$ is the Euclidian distance between two agents i and j.

To be more stochastic, the total force that acts on agent i in a dimension d can be reconsidered as:

$$F_i^d(t) = \sum_{j=1, j \neq i}^{N} rand_j F_{ij}^d(t) \quad (8)$$

where $rand_j$ is a random number in the interval [0,1]. And by the law of motion, we calculate the acceleration, the velocity and finally the new value of each solution.

$$a_i^d(t) = \frac{F_i^d(t)}{M_{ii}(t)} \quad (9)$$

$$v_i^d(t+1) = rand_i \times v_i^d(t) + a_i^d(t) \quad (10)$$

$$x_i^d(t+1) = x_i^d(t) + v_i^d(t+1) \quad (11)$$

where M_{ii} is the inertial mass of i agent and $rand_i$ is a random number in the interval [0,1].

The gravitational constant, G, is initialized at the beginning of the algorithm and is reduced with time to control the search accuracy:

$$G(t) = G(t_0) \times 1 - \left(\frac{t}{T}\right) \quad (12)$$

where t is the current iteration of the algorithm and T is the maximum number of iterations, so that the gravitational constant decreases linearly.

Furthermore, all masses are considered equal, so that:

$$M_{pi} = M_{aj} = M_{ii} = M_i \quad (13)$$

and we update each solution's mass by the following:

$$m_i(t) = \frac{fit_i(t) - worst(t)}{best(t) - worst(t)} \quad (14)$$

$$M_i(t) = \frac{m_i(t)}{\sum_{j=1}^{N} m_j(t)} \quad (15)$$

where $fit_i(t)$ is the fitness value of the agent i in t iteration, $worst(t)$ is the worst solution of the current iteration and $best(t)$ the best solution of the current iteration (Fig. 1).

In ACO algorithm, population refers to vectors of asset combinations. More specifically, each artificial ant (member of population) corresponds to a unique combination of stocks. The 'weight optimization algorithm', as described below, calculates the amount of capital invested in each portfolio's stocks. In each generation in ACO, population (vectors of asset combinations) is appropriately updated using pheromone information. Thus, new, unique portfolios are found. Their weights are found using FA or GSA, as described below (Fig. 2).

```
Generate initial population of portfolios
Apply algorithm for weight optimization
Evaluate initial population
For i=1:#generations
Construct new portfolios based on pheromone information
Apply algorithm for weight optimization
Evaluate new population
Update pheromone matrix
End
```

Fig. 1. Pseudocode for ACO algorithm

```
Generate initial population of weights
Calculate light intensity (I) for each agent (fitness
evaluation)
For i=1:#generations
For j=1:#pairs of agents
Calculate distance between pair_j
Calculate parameters b and γ
If I_j1< I_j2
Move 1st agent towards 2nd
Evaluate new solution
Else
Move 2nd agent towards 1st
Evaluate new solution
End
End
End
```

Fig. 2. Pseudocode for FA

As mentioned above, FA is used for finding the proper assets' weights. More specifically, for every artificial ant, a number of FA agents (FA population) calculates a vector of weights (amount of capital invested in stock). Afterwards, the solutions are evaluated using the fitness function, and as the algorithm is executed through all generations, new vectors of weights are properly produced, based on FA strategy (Fig. 3).

```
Generate initial population of weights
While stopping criteria not met
Evaluate fitness for each agent
Update the G, best and worst of the population
Calculate mass M for each agent
Update velocities and positions
End
```

Fig. 3. Pseudocode for GSA

GSA performs the same task as FA. Its aim is to find the best allocation of capital for a given combination of assets, provided by ACO. In each iteration, GSA appropriately updates the vectors of weights, moving towards the best solution.

4.1 Differences Between Firefly and Gravitational Search Algorithm

Though there is no clear evidence regarding the superiority of any of the two NII techniques, FA and GSA differ in some extent. Both GSA and FA are attraction-based methods, as stated above. FA is based on the light intensity of each solution (firefly), while GSA is based on the force that is acted between masses (solutions). However, FA is considered a probabilistic method due to a random component in the calculation of the new position. On the other hand, GSA is considered a deterministic method and is based on the interaction of solutions among them and with the best solution so far. In GSA, every mass is updated based on the best and the worst solution and so all the population of solutions is gradually improving. In FA, the population is upgraded via the interaction of every agent, including the best-so-far solution, with each other.

5 Experimental Study

In order to evaluate the performance of the hybrid NII algorithm, a number of independent simulations (80) were executed. Dataset comprised of daily closing stock prices (numerical values) from the S&P's 500, which is a representative benchmark index, not only for the US market. The time period of the study was six months (01/12/2008–01/05/2009), which was a critical period for global markets, due to the severe consequences of the financial crisis. Stock prices reflect, in a large extent, news from various fields (economy, politics etc.). Dataset was obtained from 'Yahoo Finance'.

Results obtained from the independent simulations for ACO-GSA were compared to those presented in [3]. In Table 1, some basic statistical measures of the independent simulations' distribution are presented. What is more, the best-so-far portfolio found, from each method, as well as its fitness value are shown. From Table 1, some interesting points could be aroused. Firstly, ACO-GSA is compared to ACO-FA, in terms of fitness value. The proposed NII hybrid algorithm (namely, ACO-GSA) managed to find a very good solution region, almost as satisfying as the benchmark hybrid scheme (namely, ACO-FA). However, the difference between these two fitness values cannot be considered large, especially if the total execution time is taken into account. ACO-FA needed almost 2.5 days to complete the total amount of the independent simulations, whereas ACO-GSA took only 4 h. Thus, ACO-GSA can give a very good solution in a reasonable amount of time. Based on the statistical measures presented in Table 1, ACO-FA yields a distribution with larger average fitness value, compared to ACO-GSA. This might be an indication that ACO-FA tends to identify better solution regions. Also, in terms of deviation, ACO-FA has a larger standard deviation than ACO-GSA, which practically means that ACO-FA has a more uncertain performance. Another point of interest is the skewness, which indicates whether the distribution leans to the left or right. ACO-FA yields a more promising distribution, due to the larger value of skewness, indicating a higher probability of finding a better solution, or even the global optimum. All in all, it could be stated that ACO-FA seems to be more efficient in searching for the solution space, i.e. has better exploration ability. On the other hand, the advantage of ACO-GSA is that it achieved a rather good solution in a shorter amount of time, which is a promising result. Finally, two benchmark approaches were provided, namely a Monte Carlo – non linear programming approach and a financial heuristic rule. It is worth mentioning that the Monte Carlo algorithm had almost similar performance as ACO-GSA. All in all, it could be stated that the proposed hybrid scheme has a good performance in a short amount of time, which could be its main advantage. In order to obtain more clarified view of the hybrid's performance, a wider set of simulations are needed.

Table 1. Results from independent simulations

	Statistical measures			Best Results Found		
	Mean	Std	Skewness	Sortino ratio	Portfolio	Weights
ACO-FA	0.5024	0.0284	0.8055	0.5996	[81,115,174, 242,438]	[0.0902,0,0.3 202,0.2368,0 .3528]
ACO-GSA	0.4737	0.0257	0.4550	0.5560	[45,144,242, 353,490]	[0.7869,0.03 69,0.1295,0. 0463,0]
Benchmark methods						
Monte Carlo & non linear programmin g[a]				0.5548	[45,242,450, 289,484]	[0.7817,0.21 83,0,0,0]
5 highest capitalization stocks				0.2800	[492,47,3,25 1,204]	[0,0,0.7655,0 ,0.2345]

[a] The non linear algorithm is based on the Levenberg – Marquardt method which combines the Gauss – Newton and the steepest descent method.

6 Financial Implications

The purpose of the hybrid schemes' implementation is to find the global optimum, for the financial optimization problem at hand. However, due to the magnitude of the solution space, i.e. 500 stocks, it is very difficult to detect the global optimum. Therefore, it is more possible to get stuck to a local optimum region. However, this cannot be considered merely as a drawback. Detecting a high-quality region in the vast solution space may be the first step to find the global optimum. This was the case in our study. Through the thorough experimental procedure, described in a previous section, we came up with some interesting findings. More specifically, some assets were chosen, in a systematical way. This could imply that there is the possibility of extracting heuristic information in the dataset. The assets which were included in most cases are: AutoZone Inc. (asset 45), Sun Microsystem (asset 242), Wyeth (485) and Tenet Healthcare Corp. (asset 438). To provide more details about these assets, the following points could be stated:

- Asset 45 was included at almost all best solutions found by the hybrid schemes. Its contribution in the portfolio formulation was at the range [56.45%, 84.07%], which implies that the asset was a driving force in these portfolios. What is more, asset 45 was one of the top five assets, in our dataset, based on the fitness value (Sortino ratio). So, it makes sense, for the intelligent algorithm, to incorporate it.
- Asset 242 was the second most common stock in the solutions found by the hybrid schemes. Its contribution in the portfolio formulation was at the range [10.09% 23.68%]. Though asset 242 was not contributing as much as asset 45, it was included in the overall best-so-far solution found by the hybrid schemes. Another interesting point was that this specific solution did not include asset 45. What is more, this portfolio was well diversified, which can be considered as a requirement in the portfolio management framework.
- Asset 485 was selected in 3 cases with a contribution in the range [32.18%, 42.38%]. This stock was among the best stocks, based on fitness value.
- Asset 438 was selected in 2 cases with a contribution in the portfolios 35.28% and 6.96%. It was included in the best-so-far solution, along with asset 242.
- What is more, the correlation coefficient for each pair of the aforementioned stocks is positive and relatively small.

The results, presented above, highlight the aspect of heuristic information, which can be induced from a dataset by hybrid schemes. So, as a next step, our aim was to incorporate this financial heuristic in the hybrid scheme, in order to investigate whether it improves the best-so-far solution. More specifically, a number of alternative financial heuristic rules, which were incorporated into the hybrid scheme 'ACO - GSA', were tested. The main research focus for these simulations was on the following aspects: how will the decision of including these assets in the solutions, by default, or excluding them from the dataset, affect the ability of the hybrid algorithm to find the global optimum, or at least approximate a high-quality region? Simulations' results are shown in Table 2, below. Based on the results presented in Table 2, some interesting comments could be pointed out. First of all, the inclusion of assets 45, 242 and 483 in the portfolio, enhances the ability of the hybrid algorithm. More specifically, the hybrid algorithm managed to find a new best-so-far solution. The inclusion of these assets guided the hybrid algorithm towards a high-quality solution region. However, it is difficult to know whether the new best-so-far solution is the global optimum in this problem. Secondly, the inclusion of assets 45 and 242 in the portfolios provided the new high-score for this problem setting. As mentioned above, asset 45 is one of the top performers, in terms of fitness function, and asset 242 was systematically selected by the hybrid algorithms in the previous experimental setting (Table 1). Finally, the exclusion of these assets from the dataset only deteriorated the solution, thus guiding the algorithm towards a low-quality solution region. As far as the quantiles of the distributions, from the independent simulations, it seems that in the cases where asset 242 was included, the distribution was more skewed to the right, which is a desirable attribute.

Table 2. Distributional results for financial heuristics

Strategies	Quantiles				Best fitness value
	0.25	0.50	0.75	0.95	
Assets [45, 242] included in all solutions	0.6304	0.6618	0.6724	0.6829	0.6952
Assets [45, 242] excluded from dataset	0.4382	0.4458	0.4550	0.4798	0.4833
Asset 45 included in all solutions	0.5922	0.6067	0.6156	0.6566	0.6696
Assets [45, 242, 438] excluded from dataset	0.4373	0.4439	0.4535	0.4699	0.4905

7 Conclusions

In this study, a novel hybrid scheme, namely ACO with GSA, was applied to a specific formulation of the financial portfolio optimization problem. Results from the proposed scheme were compared to previous findings [3].

The main advantage of the proposed hybrid algorithm is that it has the ability to approximate a very good solution in a short time, in contrast with ACO-FA. Further experimentation could shed more light, regarding the merits of ACO-GSA.

However, the financial implications of the proposed NII hybrid are more interesting. Based on the results presented in the experimental section of this study, it can be stated that these algorithms have the potential of detecting critical heuristic information from the financial dataset. In our case, through a-posteriori iterative experimentation of the proposed NII scheme, a number of financial assets, with guiding performance over the portfolio problem were found. Therefore, this might be a sign for the hybrid scheme, highlighting its importance in formulating financial heuristic rules. However, in order to obtain more robust results, further experimentation both in terms of dataset and portfolio optimization set-up, should be implemented.

References

1. Maringer, D.: Portfolio Management with Heuristic Optimization. Advances in Computational Science. Springer, Heidelberg (2005)
2. Vassiliadis, V., Dounias, G.: Nature-inspired intelligence: a review of selected methods and applications. Int. J. Artif. Intell. Tools **18**(4), 487–516 (2009)
3. Giannakouris, G., Vassiliadis, V., Dounias, G.: Experimental study on a hybrid nature-inspired algorithm for financial portfolio optimization. In: Konstantopoulos, S., Perantonis, S., Karkaletsis, V., Spyropoulos, Constantine D., Vouros, G. (eds.) SETN 2010. LNCS, vol. 6040, pp. 101–111. Springer, Heidelberg (2010). doi:10.1007/978-3-642-12842-4_14
4. Shapcott, J.: Index tracking: genetic algorithms for investment portfolio selection. EPCC-SS92-24, pp. 1–24 (1992)
5. Gomez, M. A., Flores, C.X., Osorio, M.A.: Hybrid search for cardinality constrained portfolio optimization. In: GECCO 2006, pp. 1865–1866 (2006)
6. Markowitz, H.: Portfolio selection. J. Finan. **7**(1), 77–91 (1952)

7. Vassiliadis, V., Thomaidis, N., Dounias, G.: Active portfolio management under a downside risk framework: comparison of a hybrid nature – inspired scheme. In: Corchado, E., Wu, X., Oja, E., Herrero, Á., Baruque, B. (eds.) HAIS 2009. LNCS, vol. 5572, pp. 702–712. Springer, Heidelberg (2009). doi:10.1007/978-3-642-02319-4_85
8. Chen, W., Zhang, R.T., Cai, Y.M., Xu, F.S.: Particle swarm optimization for constrained portfolio selection problems. In: 5th International Conference on Machine Learning and Cybernetics, pp. 2425–2429 (2006)
9. Thomaidis, N.S., Angelidis, T., Vassiliadis, V., Dounias, G.: Active portfolio management with cardinality constraints: an application of particle swarm optimization. New Math. Nat. Comput. **5**(03), 535–555 (2009)
10. Dorigo, M., Stultze, M.: Ant Colony Optimization. The MIT Press, Cambridge (2004)
11. Yang, X.S.: Nature-Inspired Metaheuristic Algorithm. Luniver Press, Bristol (2008)
12. Rashedi, E., Nezamabadi-Pour, H., Saryazdi, S.: GSA: a gravitational search algorithm. Inf. Sci. **179**(13), 2232–2248 (2009)
13. Xing, B., Gao, W.-J.: Gravitational search algorithm. In: Xing, B., Gao, W.-J. (eds.) Innovative Computational Intelligence: A Rough Guide to 134 Clever Algorithms. ISRL, vol. 62, pp. 355–364. Springer, Cham (2014). doi:10.1007/978-3-319-03404-1_22
14. Sabri, N.M., Puteh, M., Mahmood, M.R.: A review of gravitational search algorithm. Int. J. Adv. Soft Comput. Appl. **5**(3), 1–39 (2013)
15. Kuhn, J.: Optimal Risk-Return Tradeoffs of Commercial Banks and the Suitability of Profitability Measures for Loan Portfolios. Springer, Berlin (2006)
16. Sharpe, W.F.: The sharpe ratio. J. Portfolio Manage. **21**(1), 49–58 (1994)

Hypersphere Universe Boundary Method Comparison on HCLPSO and PSO

Tomas Kadavy[(✉)], Michal Pluhacek, Adam Viktorin, and Roman Senkerik

Faculty of Applied Informatics, Tomas Bata University in Zlin, T.G. Masaryka 5555, 760 01 Zlin, Czech Republic
{kadavy,pluhacek,aviktorin,senkerik}@fai.utb.cz

Abstract. In this paper, the hypersphere universe method is applied on Heterogeneous Comprehensive Learning Particle Swarm Optimization (HCLPSO) and a classical representative of swarm intelligence Particle Swarm Optimization (PSO). The goal is to the compare this method to the classical version of these algorithms. The comparisons are made on CEC'17 benchmark set functions. The experiments were carried out according to CEC benchmark rules and statistically evaluated using Friedman rank test.

Keywords: Particle Swarm Optimization · PSO · Heterogeneous · Comprehensive Learning · HCLPSO · Search space boundaries · Roaming particles

1 Introduction

In many applications of optimization, optimized problems have almost every time some boundary restrictions. On benchmark functions, which are typically used for testing, these restrictions can be constant values over dimensions of the problem or can vary over dimensions. Using swarm optimizing technique, for example, Particle Swarm Optimization (PSO) [1], some particles can reach the border of available search space or even try to violate it. In this case, some technique for handling this situation need to be applied to that particle. There are several of them, namely:

- Hard border – particle is clipped to border if it tries to violate,
- Soft border – particle can travel freely, but if the particle is not in the available search space (roaming particle), its position is not evaluated,
- Mirroring – particle bounces from border back to search space,
- Hypersphere universe – method simulates an endless spherical universe.

In this paper last mentioned method, the hyperspherical universe is applied on Heterogeneous Comprehensive Learning Particle Swarm Optimization (HCLPSO) [2]. This PSO modification is already achieving great results on tested functions against canonical version PSO. Also, this recent modification was already used for solve real world problem in [3] with promising results. The results of these algorithms and their modifications are compared on CEC'17 benchmark set [4]. The research questions are:

F.J. Martínez de Pisón et al. (Eds.): HAIS 2017, LNAI 10334, pp. 173–182, 2017.
DOI: 10.1007/978-3-319-59650-1_15

- Can this method, hypersphere universe, improve the performance of HCLPSO?
- Is there a significant difference between classic HCLPSO and modified PSO using hypersphere universe method?

The paper is structured as follows. The PSO is described in Sect. 2. HCLPSO is described in next section, Sect. 3. Then, in Sect. 4, the hypersphere universe method is described, and its utilization with PSO and HCLPSO is explained. The experiment setup is detailed in Sect. 4. Section 5 contains statistical overviews of results and performance comparisons obtained during the evaluation on benchmark set. Discussion and conclusion follow.

2 Particle Swarm Optimization

The main representative of a field of swarm intelligence algorithms is Particle Swarm Optimization (PSO). Ebenhart and Kennedy first published the algorithm itself in 1995 [1]. This algorithm mimics the social behavior of swarming animals in nature. Despite the fact that it is the quite long time from its first appearance, it is still plenty used throughout many optimization problems.

The individuals (particles) of this algorithm are moving in the space of possible solutions of the defined particular problem. Every particle has a position in n-dimensional space of solutions, and this position represents the input parameters of the optimized problem. This position of particles changes over time due to two factors. One of them is the current position of a particle. The second one is the velocity of a particle, labeled as v. Each particle also remembers his best position (solution of the problem) obtained so far. This solution is tagged as the *pBest*, personal best solution. Also, each particle has access to the global best solution, *gBest*, which is selected from all *pBests*. These variables set the direction for every particle and then even a new position in next iteration. PSO usually stops after a defined number of iterations, or a number of FEs (fitness evaluations).

In every step of the algorithm, the new positions of particles are calculated based on previous positions and velocities. The new position of a particle is checked if it still lies in the space of possible solutions. The function of the optimized problem is called Cost Function (CF). The position of a particle is used as input parameters in CF. If the value of CF is better than the value saved in *pBest* of a particle, then the particle saves this new position as his new *pBest*. Also, if this *pBest* has better CF value than the previous *gBest*, then this *pBest* is stored as new *gBest*.

The position of particle x is calculated according to the formula (1)

$$x_{ij}^{t+1} = x_{ij}^{t} + v_{ij}^{t+1} \tag{1}$$

Where $t + 1$ is an actual iteration, t is then the previous iteration, x_{ij} is the position of a i-particle in j-dimension, v is the velocity of a particle.

The velocity of a particle v is calculated according to (2).

$$v_{ij}^{t+1} = w \cdot v_{ij}^{t} + c_1 \cdot r_1 \cdot \left(pBest_{ij} - x_{ij}^{t}\right) + c_2 \cdot r_2 \cdot \left(gBest_j - x_{ij}^{t}\right) \quad (2)$$

Where w is inertia weight [5], c_1 and c_2 are learning factors, and r_1 and r_2 are random numbers of unimodal distribution in the range $<0,1>$.

3 Heterogeneous Comprehensive Learning Particle Swarm Optimization

This algorithm was first presented in 2015 by Lynn and Suganthan [2]. The swarm (population) is divided into two subpopulations. One is enhanced for exploration and the second one is enhanced for exploitation. For both subpopulations, a comprehensive learning (CL) strategy [6] is used to generate example particle $pBest_{fi(j)}$. For detailed information about selecting example particle, see the full paper [2]. The exploration-enhanced subpopulation computes its velocity using formula (3).

$$v_{ij}^{t+1} = w \cdot v_{ij}^{t} + c_1 \cdot r_1 \cdot \left(pBest_{fi(j)} - x_{ij}^{t}\right) \quad (3)$$

The exploitation-enhanced subpopulation computes the velocity by (4).

$$v_{ij}^{t+1} = w \cdot v_{ij}^{t} + c_1 \cdot r_1 \cdot \left(pBest_{fi(j)} - x_{ij}^{t}\right) + \left(gBest_j - x_{ij}^{t}\right) \quad (4)$$

4 Hypersphere Universe Boundary Method

This method, as said before, simulates an endless spherical universe. If a particle violates upper boundary of the search space, the particle than appear in the search space from lower boundary. The upper boundary is neighboring the lower one of corresponding dimension and vice versa. In Fig. 1 is an explanation of this approach.

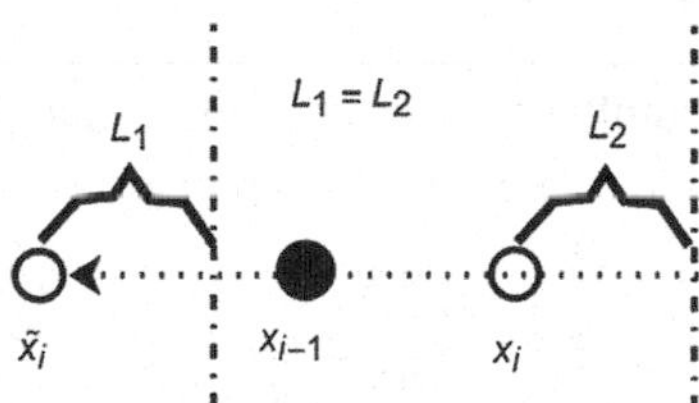

Fig. 1. Explanation of hypersphere universe method. x_{i-1} is the particle position in the last iteration; $\bar{x}_i$ is uncorrected position and x_i is the final correct position.

With this method, a new way of computing velocity appears. Using a formula (2) from classical PSO or formulas (3) and (4) from HCLPSO can cause a situation, where a particle chooses a longer way (vector of particle position and his *pBest* or *gBest*).

The hypersphere universe offers the second option; a particle can travel through a boundary and reach the final destination using shorter vector. In Fig. 2 the *L1* is vector computed using the standard velocity update (2) and vector *L2* is a new vector that appears when the hyperspace method is used.

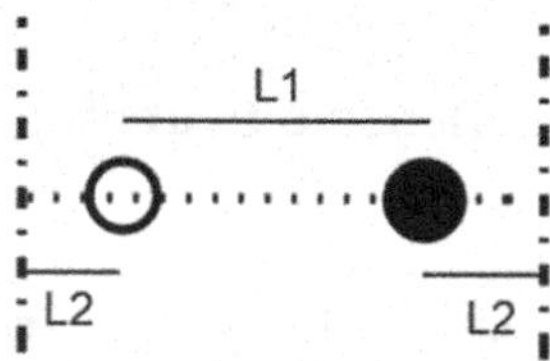

Fig. 2. Two possible velocity vectors in hypersphere universe.

The new velocity formula for this method, which can choose the better (smaller) vector, is defined as (5) for PSO.

$$v_{ij}^{t+1} = w \cdot v_{ij}^{t} + c_1 \cdot r_1 \cdot L_{P,ij}^{t} + c_2 \cdot r_2 \cdot L_{G,ij}^{t} \tag{5}$$

Where $L_{P,ij}^{t}$ and $L_{G,ij}^{t}$ are defined in formula (6).

$$\begin{aligned} L_{P,ij} &= \begin{cases} \hat{L}_{P,ij}, \, if \left|\hat{L}_{P,ij}\right| \leq d \\ \hat{L}_{P,ij} mod(-d), \, if \left(\left|\hat{L}_{P,ij}\right| > d \wedge \left|\hat{L}_{P,ij}\right| > 0\right) \\ \hat{L}_{P,ij} mod(+d), \, if \left(\left|\hat{L}_{P,ij}\right| > d \wedge \left|\hat{L}_{P,ij}\right| \leq 0\right) \end{cases} \\ L_{G,ij} &= \begin{cases} \hat{L}_{G,ij}, \, if \left|\hat{L}_{G,ij}\right| \leq d \\ \hat{L}_{G,ij} mod(-d), \, if \left(\left|\hat{L}_{G,ij}\right| > d \wedge \left|\hat{L}_{G,ij}\right| > 0\right) \\ \hat{L}_{G,ij} mod(+d), \, if \left(\left|\hat{L}_{G,ij}\right| > d \wedge \left|\hat{L}_{G,ij}\right| \leq 0\right) \end{cases} \end{aligned} \tag{6}$$

The d is computed by formula (7) where b^u and b^l stand for upper bound limit and lower bound limit of the search space. The $\hat{L}_{P,ij}$ and $\hat{L}_{G,ij}$ are defined in (8).

$$d = \frac{\left|b^u - b^l\right|}{2} \tag{7}$$

$$\begin{aligned} \hat{L}_{P,ij} &= pBest_{ij} - x_{ij} \\ \hat{L}_{G,ij} &= gBest_{j} - x_{ij} \end{aligned} \tag{8}$$

To use this approach in HCLPSO, a modified version of velocity formula is used. For exploration-enhanced subpopulation, the velocity is (9) and for the second population, exploitation-enhanced one, the formula is (10).

$$v_{ij}^{t+1} = w \cdot v_{ij}^{t} + c_1 \cdot r_1 \cdot S_{P,ij}^{t} \tag{9}$$

$$v_{ij}^{t+1} = w \cdot v_{ij}^{t} + c_1 \cdot r_1 \cdot S_{P,ij}^{t} + c_2 \cdot r_2 \cdot S_{G,ij}^{t} \tag{10}$$

Where $S_{P,ij}^{t}$ and $S_{G,ij}^{t}$ are computed using formula (11).

$$\begin{aligned} S_{P,ij} &= \begin{cases} \hat{S}_{P,ij}, \ if \left|S_{P,ij}\right| \leq d \\ S_{P,ij} mod(-d), \ if \left(\left|\hat{S}_{P,ij}\right| > d \wedge \left|\hat{S}_{P,ij}\right| > 0\right) \\ \hat{S}_{P,ij} mod(+d), \ if \left(\left|S_{P,ij}\right| > d \wedge \left|\hat{S}_{P,ij}\right| \leq 0\right) \end{cases} \\ S_{G,ij} &= \begin{cases} \hat{S}_{G,ij}, \ if \left|S_{G,ij}\right| \leq d \\ \hat{S}_{G,ij} mod(-d), \ if \left(\left|S_{G,ij}\right| > d \wedge \left|S_{G,ij}\right| > 0\right) \\ \hat{S}_{G,ij} mod(+d), \ if \left(\left|S_{G,ij}\right| > d \wedge \left|\hat{S}_{G,ij}\right| \leq 0\right) \end{cases} \end{aligned} \tag{11}$$

The $\hat{S}_{P,ij}$ and $S_{G,ij}$ are defined in (12).

$$\begin{aligned} \hat{S}_{P,ij} &= pBest_{fi(j)} - x_{ij} \\ \hat{S}_{G,ij} &= gBest_{j} - x_{ij} \end{aligned} \tag{12}$$

5 Experimental Setup

The experiments were performed for dimension setting $dim = 10$ and $dim = 30$ on CEC'17 benchmark functions set [4]. This benchmark set can be obtained from web page 'http://www.ntu.edu.sg/home/EPNSugan/'. The maximal number of cost function evaluations is set to 10 000 • *dim* according to the definition for this benchmark set. The population size (*NP*) is set to 40 for all dimensions. The inertia weight is set $w = 0.729$ and learning factors are $c_1 = c_2 = 1.49445$ according to [7] for PSO, settings for HCLPSO remains as in [2]. Every test function is repeated for 51 independent runs, and the results are statistically evaluated. The benchmark set includes 30 functions separated into four categories: unimodal (f_1–f_3), multimodal (f_4–f_{10}), hybrid (f_{11}–f_{20}) and composite (f_{21}–f_{30}). Each function has search space defined in $[-100,100]^{Dim}$, and global minimum is 100 • f_i, where i is an order of test function f.

Four versions of the algorithms were tested. PSO and HCLPSO using hypersphere universe modification and classical versions of these algorithms.

6 Results

The Friedman test [8] was used for statistical comparison of used variants. The JAVA package from 'http://sci2s.ugr.es/keel/multipleTest.zip' was used to evaluate the statistics. The results of each test function from CEC benchmark set were averaged from their 51 independent runs. These average results were utilized for the Friedman test. Both dimensions are tested separately.

The p-value computed by Friedman test for $dim = 10$ is 5.13E−13 and for $dim = 30$ is 4.60E−8. The critical value of the Friedman statistic is at $\alpha = 0.05$ [9], so the rankings of Friedman statistics are valid for both dimensions. The non-parametric Friedman test ranking of the algorithms is in Table 1. The adjusted Bonferroni-Dunn p-values among best performing algorithm and others are shown in Table 2.

Table 1. Friedman ranking of algorithms

Algorithm	Ranking	
	$dim = 10$	$dim = 30$
PSO	2.77	2.60
Modified PSO	3.47	3.63
HCLPSO	1.97	1.87
Modified HCLPSO	1.80	1.90

Table 2. Adjusted p-values of modified PSO and others algorithms

Algorithm	p-value	
	$dim = 10$	$dim = 30$
PSO	0.01E0	0.08E0
Modified PSO	1.72E−6	3.47E−7
HCLPSO	1.85E0	–
Modified HCLPSO	–	2.76E0

Furthermore, some selected examples of mean *gBest* value history are shown in Figs. 3, 4, 5, 6, 7, 8 and 9.

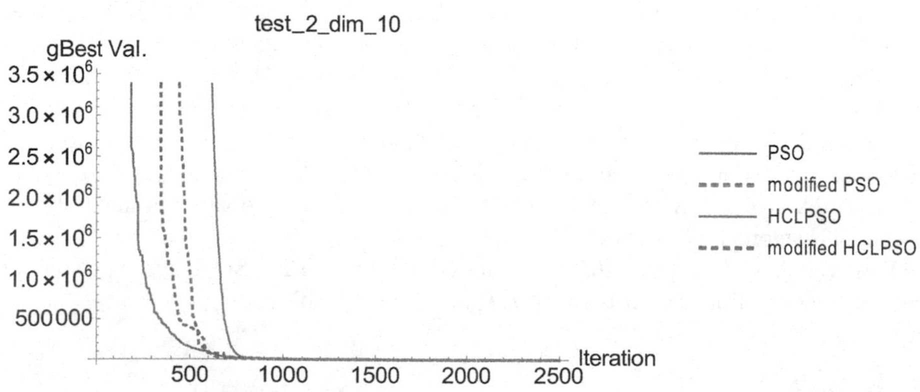

Fig. 3. Comparisons of gBests mean history over 51 runs

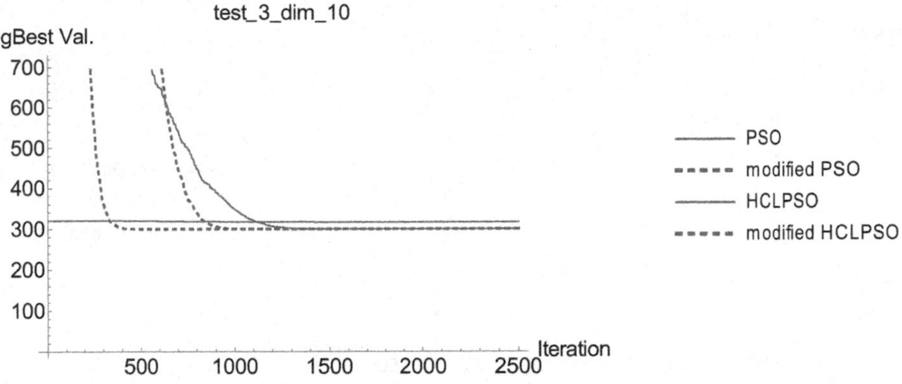

Fig. 4. Comparisons of gBests mean history over 51 runs

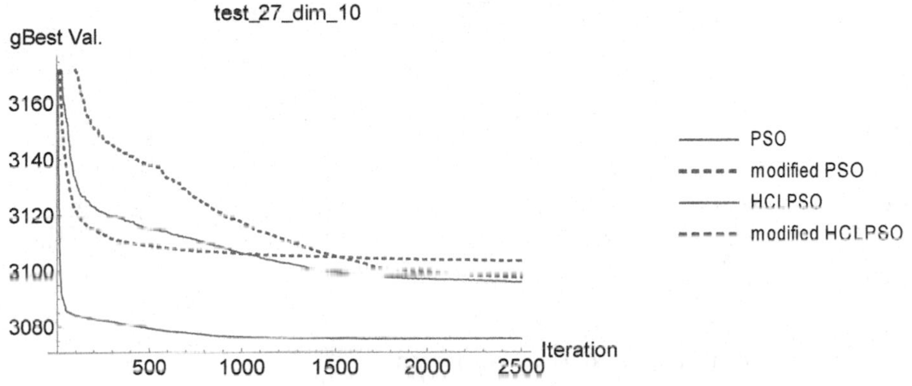

Fig. 5. Comparisons of gBests mean history over 51 runs

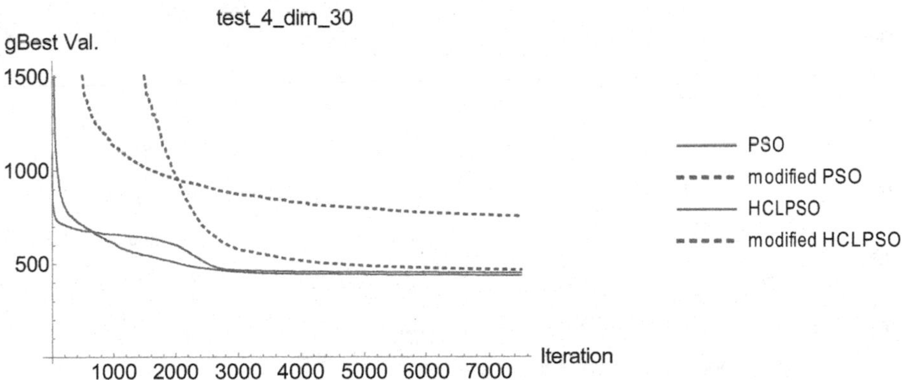

Fig. 6. Comparisons of gBests mean history over 51 runs

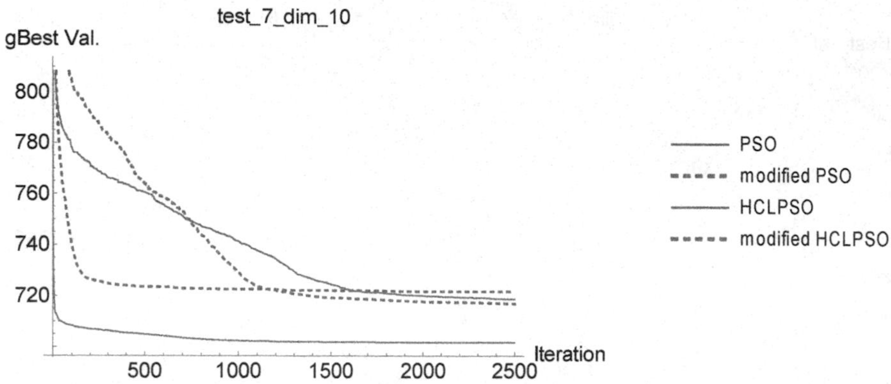

Fig. 7. Comparisons of gBests mean history over 51 runs

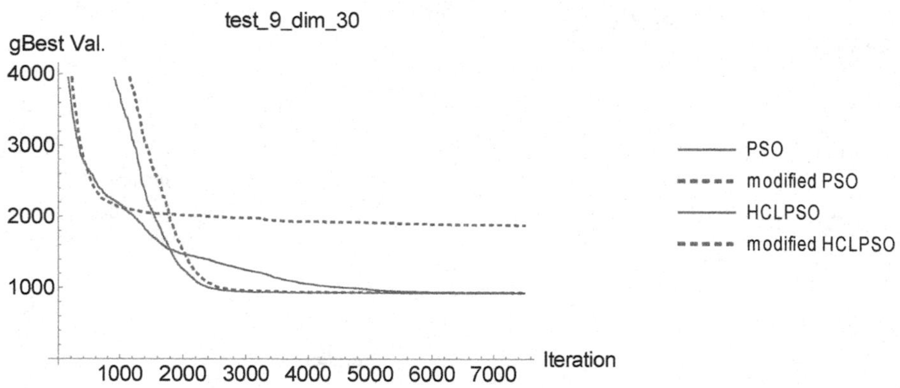

Fig. 8. Comparisons of gBests mean history over 51 runs

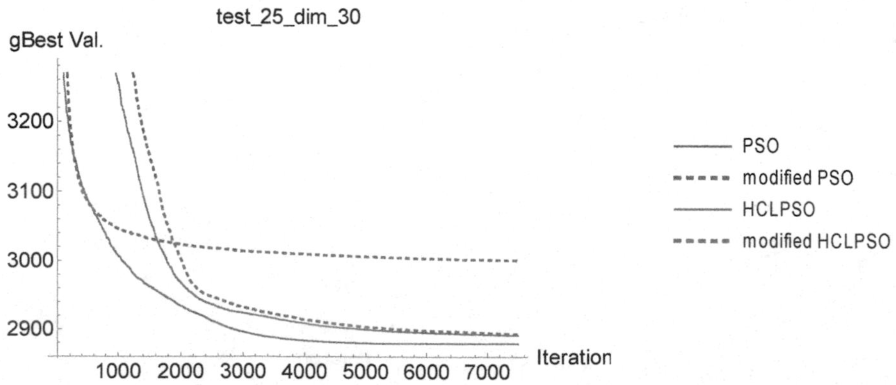

Fig. 9. Comparisons of gBests mean history over 51 runs

7 Results Discussion

The algorithm with the smallest rank value in Table 1 is the best performing one in tested dimension. For *dim* = 10, the best performing one is modified version HCLPSO, HCLPSO using hypersphere universe method. In Table 2, if the p-value is not smaller than significance level 0.03 for Bonferroni-Dunn test, the compared algorithm has no significant difference. With this knowledge, the best performing algorithms for *dim* = 10 are modified HCLPSO and classical HCLPSO. For dim = 30, analogously, the best performing one is classical HCLPSO. However, the modified version HCLPSO and classical PSO have no significant difference from classical HCLPSO, due to p-values in Table 2.

For convergence speed, on Figs. 3 and 5, the fastest seems to be both PSO versions. On Fig. 4, the hyperspherical modification brings better results than classical approach; however, it appears that these algorithms have slower convergence speed. On some tested functions, the modification has even worse results, as on Figs. 5 and 6. On Figs. 8 and 9, the difference of this modification is slight for HCLPSO, thought for PSO is bigger.

8 Conclusion

In this paper, the results of hyperspherical universe modification on PSO and HCLPSO were presented. For comparison was used the CEC'17 benchmark set. The results were statistically tested using Friedman statistic. Based on this results, some conclusions can be made.

The best performing algorithm for both dimension settings (*dim* = 10 and *dim* = 30) is HCLPSO and HCLPSO with hyperspherical universe modification with no significance difference on tested functions. For PSO algorithms, the difference is significant and has a real impact on obtained *gBest* values.

With this results, the answers on research questions are:

- This method seems to have no major impact on *gBest* value for HCLPSO. However, on almost every tested functions, it has slower convergence speed.
- There is significance difference between classical HCLPSO and modified PSO.

The goal of this study was to show and compare differences in performance of the hyperspherical universe method on HCLPSO and PSO. The results of this study will be further used in future studies to suggest possible improvements for controlling the position of particles that violates search space boundaries.

Acknowledgements. This work was supported by Grant Agency of the Czech Republic – GACR P103/15/06700S, further by the Ministry of Education, Youth and Sports of the Czech Republic within the National Sustainability Programme Project no. LO1303 (MSMT-7778/2014. Also by the European Regional Development Fund under the Project CEBIA-Tech no. CZ. 1.05/2.1.00/03.0089 and by Internal Grant Agency of Tomas Bata University under the Projects no. IGA/CebiaTech/2017/004.

References

1. Kennedy, J., Eberhart, R.: Particle swarm optimization. In: Proceedings of the IEEE International Conference on Neural Networks, pp. 1942–1948 (1995)
2. Lynn, N., Suganthan, P.N.: Heterogeneous comprehensive learning particle swarm optimization with enhanced exploration and exploitation. Swarm Evol. Comput. **24**, 11–24 (2015)
3. Lynn, N.: Heterogeneous particle swarm optimization with an application of unit commitment in power system, Singapore. Thesis. School of Electrical and Electronic Engineering. Supervisor Ponnuthurai Nagaratnam Suganthan (2016)
4. Awad, N.H., et al.: Problem Definitions and Evaluation Criteria for CEC 2017 Special Session and Competition on Single-Objective Real-Parameter Numerical Optimization (2016)
5. Kennedy, J.: The particle swarm: social adaptation of knowledge. In: Proceedings of the IEEE International Conference on Evolutionary Computation, pp. 303–308 (1997)
6. Liang, J.J., Qin, A.K., Suganthan, P.N., Baskar, S.: Comprehensive learning particle swarm optimizer for global optimization of multimodal functions. IEEE Trans. Evol. Comput. **10**(3), 281–295 (2006)
7. Eberhart, R.C., Shi, Y.: Comparing inertia weights and constriction factors in particle swarm optimization. In: Proceedings of the 2000 Congress on Evolutionary Computation. CEC00, pp. 84–88. IEEE (2000)
8. Friedman, M.: The use of ranks to avoid the assumption of normality implicits in the analysis of variance. J. Am. Stat. Assoc. **32**, 675–701 (1937)
9. Demsar, J.: Statistical comparisons of classifiers over multiple data sets. J. Mach. Learn. Res. **7**, 1–30 (2006)

PSO with Partial Population Restart Based on Complex Network Analysis

Michal Pluhacek[1(✉)], Adam Viktorin[1], Roman Senkerik[1], Tomas Kadavy[1], and Ivan Zelinka[2]

[1] Faculty of Applied Informatics, Tomas Bata University in Zlin, Nam T.G. Masaryka 5555, 760 01 Zlin, Czech Republic
{pluhacek,aviktorin,senkerik,kadavy}@fai.utb.cz

[2] Faculty of Electrical Engineering and Computer Science, Technical University of Ostrava, 17. listopadu 15, 708 33 Ostrava-Poruba, Czech Republic
ivan.zelinka@vsb.cz

Abstract. This study presents a hybridization of Particle Swarm Optimization with a complex network creation and analysis. A partial population is performed in certain moments of the run of the algorithm based on the information obtained from a complex network structure that represents the communication in the population. We present initial results alongside statistical evaluation and discuss future possibilities of this approach.

Keywords: Swarm intelligence · Particle Swarm Optimization · Complex Network · Hybrid method

1 Introduction

The Particle Swarm Optimization (PSO) [1–4] is among the most prominent members of Swarm Intelligence based algorithms and is widely used in all areas of industrial optimization. PSO belongs among the evolutionary computational techniques (ECT). The techniques are in recent years in the center of interest of the research community. Recently the links between ECTs and complex networks (CN) has been studied [5–8] and successfully applied to improve the performance of the algorithm [9].

In this study, there are presented the possibilities of successful CN creation from PSO algorithm and use of analysis of the network for partial population restart activation. Partial population restart helps the PSO against premature convergence, one of the most well-known weaknesses of the method.

The main aim of this study is to use a computational effortless analysis of CN that does not scale with increasing dimensionality of the problem to keep the population diverse without explicitly computing the diversity of population for the restarting.

The rest of the paper is structured as follows: In Sect. 2, the PSO algorithm is described. The experimental details alongside with methodology for CN creation and first visualization are given in sections three and four. The results are presented in the next section and discussed in the conclusion.

F.J. Martínez de Pisón et al. (Eds.): HAIS 2017, LNAI 10334, pp. 183–192, 2017.
DOI: 10.1007/978-3-319-59650-1_16

2 Particle Swarm Optimization (PSO)

Original PSO [1] takes the inspiration from the flocking behavior of birds. The knowledge of global best found solution (typically noted gBest) is shared among the particles in the swarm. Furthermore, each particle has the knowledge of its own (personal) best found solution (noted pBest). Last important part of the algorithm is the velocity of each particle that is taken into account during the calculation of the particle movement. The new position of each particle is then given by (1), where xit + 1 is the new particle position; xit refers to current particle position and vit + 1 is the new velocity of the particle.

$$x_i^{t+1} = x_i^t + v_i^{t+1} \quad (1)$$

To calculate the new velocity the distance from pBest and gBest is taken into account alongside with current velocity (2).

$$v_{ij}^{t+1} = w \cdot v_{ij}^t + c_1 \cdot Rand \cdot (pBest_{ij} - x_{ij}^t) + c_2 \cdot Rand \cdot (gBest_j - x_{ij}^t) \quad (2)$$

Where:

V_{ij}^{t+1} – New velocity of the ith particle in iteration $t + 1$. (component j of the dimension D)

w – Inertia weight value. Set to typical value 0.7298

v_{ij}^t – Current velocity of the ith particle in iteration t. (component j of the dimension D)

c_1, c_2 – Acceleration constants. Set to typical value 1.49618

$pBest_{ij}$ – Local (personal) best solution found by the ith particle. (component j of the dimension D)

$gBest_j$ – Best solution found in a population. (component j of the dimension D)

x_{ij}^t – Current position of the ith particle (component j of the dimension D) in iteration t

$Rand$ – Pseudo random number, interval (0, 1)

3 Proposed Method

One of the well-known weaknesses of the original PSO (described in previous section) is the tendency for premature convergence into local sub-optima. Partial or full population restarting is one of the possible modifications addressing this issue. The timing of population restart is very critical and often needs computationally expensive measures of population diversity. The computation time also scales dramatically with the dimensionality of the problem.

The various approaches based on complex network analysis [5–9] usually do not scale with the dimensionality of the problem and therefore the computational time is much more acceptable.

In this study, we tried to use the information from the complex network (Eigenvector centrality) to time the partial restart of the population as is described in the following section.

4 Experiment Setup

In the experimental part, a complex network structure was used to store the information about the information in the swarm. A single node in the network represents each particle. An edge is created between two nodes if a particle improved its *pBest* and simultaneously this *pBest* is among the best 10 *pBest* values in the population. In such situation, the connection is created between the nodes representing the particle that improved its *pBest* and node representing particle that discovered the current *gBest*.

A visualization of such network after finished run of the algorithm is presented in Fig. 1. The population size (NP) is set to 40.

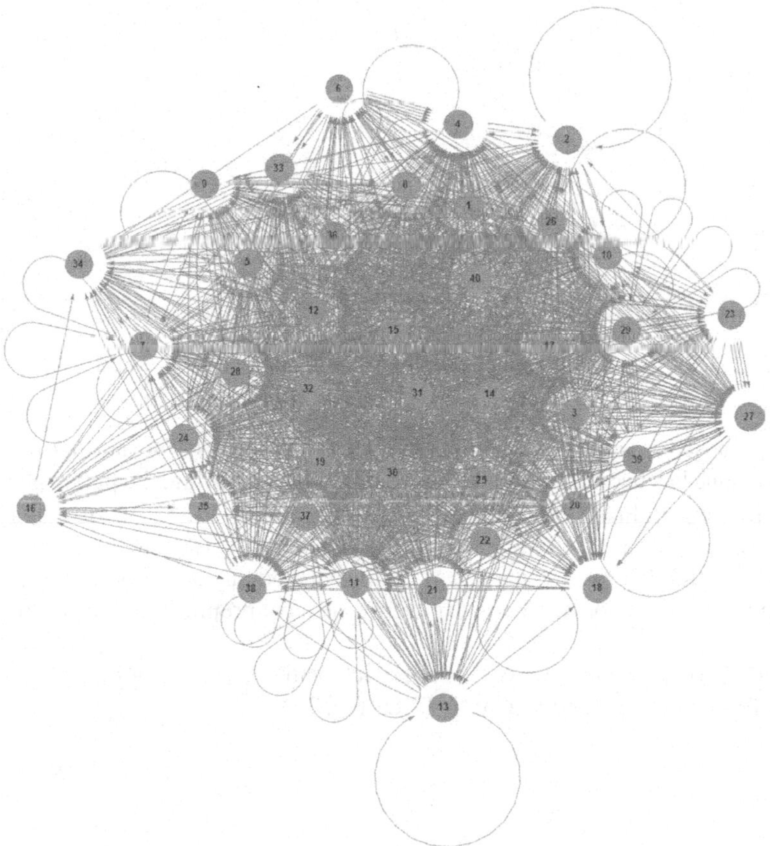

Fig. 1. PSO dynamic as complex network

For each node in the network, the Eigenvector centrality [10] is computed. We can express the value of Eigenvector centrality as weighted sum of centralities of the neighbors of the node in the network (small or non changing value of the centrality may indicate a premature convergence into a local optima and stagnation). These values are then averaged to obtain the mean Eigenvector centrality value for the whole network.

An example of the development of the Eigenvector centrality value for the whole network during the optimization is given in Fig. 2. For the case of classical PSO and Rastrigin test function in dim = 30.

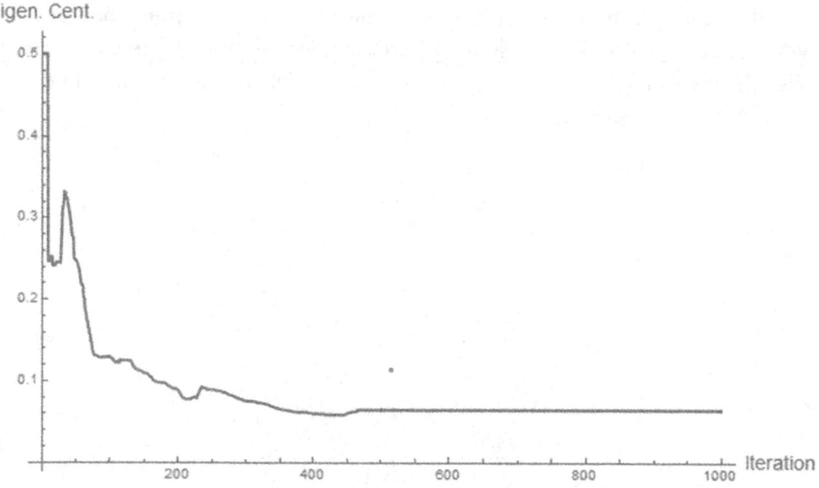

Fig. 2. Mean eigenvector centrality value development – classical PSO

The proposed adaptive mechanism works as follows: If the mean Eigenvector centrality value has decreased after 50 iterations of the algorithm, the partial population restart is performed. In the partial population restart, the NP-5 (35 in this example) worst performing particles are randomly assigned new parameters (positions). The five fittest (best cost function (CF) value) particles remain in the population unaltered. This should encourage the exploration and keep exploiting the most promising region of the search space.

For comparison, the impact of this approach on the Eigenvector centrality is given in Fig. 3 for the same setting as classic PSO (Fig. 2).

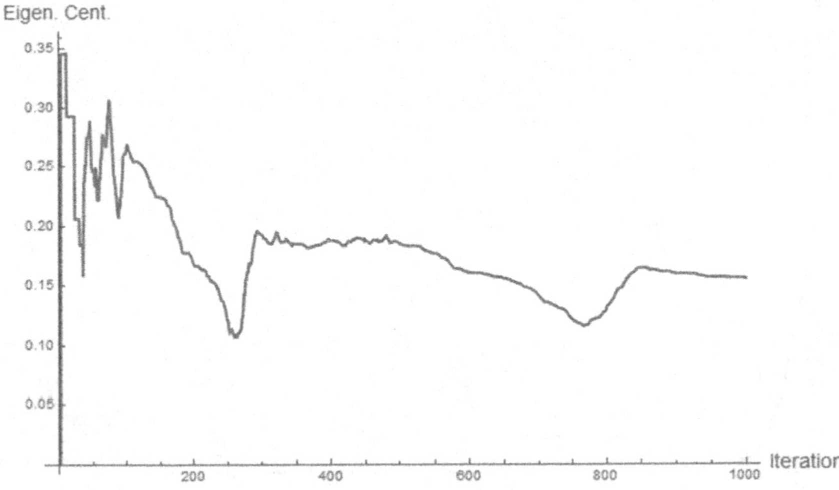

Fig. 3. Mean eigenvector centrality value development – PSO with CN

The effect of the population restarting on the diversity of the swarm is presented in Fig. 4 (In comparison to classical PSO loss of diversity in Fig. 5). The diversity of the swarm is computed as standard deviation of the parameters across the whole population.

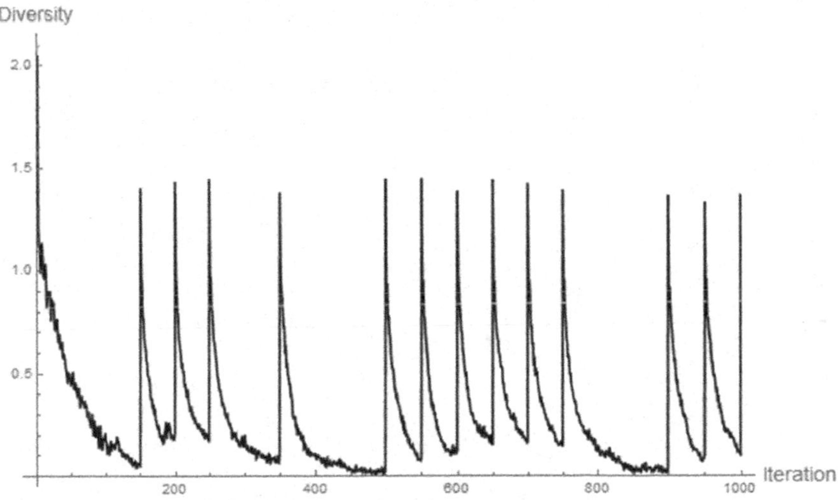

Fig. 4. Population diversity – PSO with CN

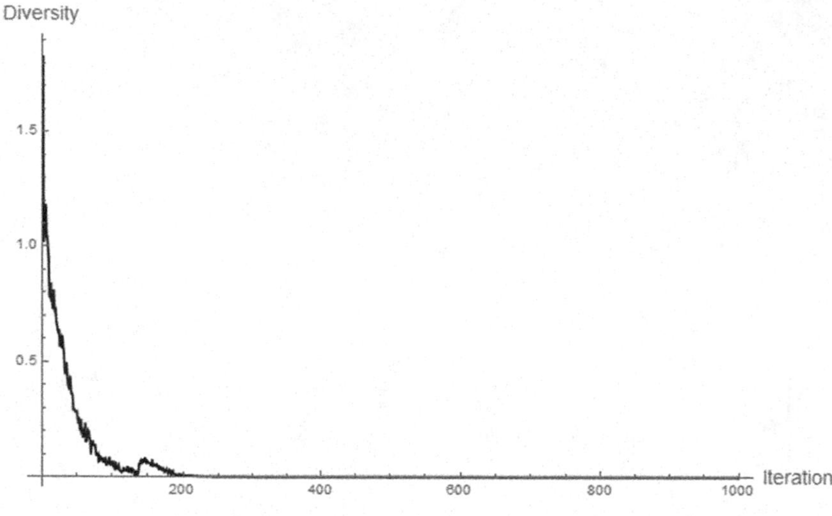

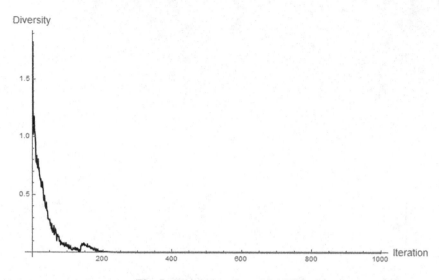

Fig. 5. Population diversity – PSO

Further, the number of newly created connections in the network in each iteration of the algorithm is presented in Fig. 6 (PSO) and Fig. 7 (PSO with CN).

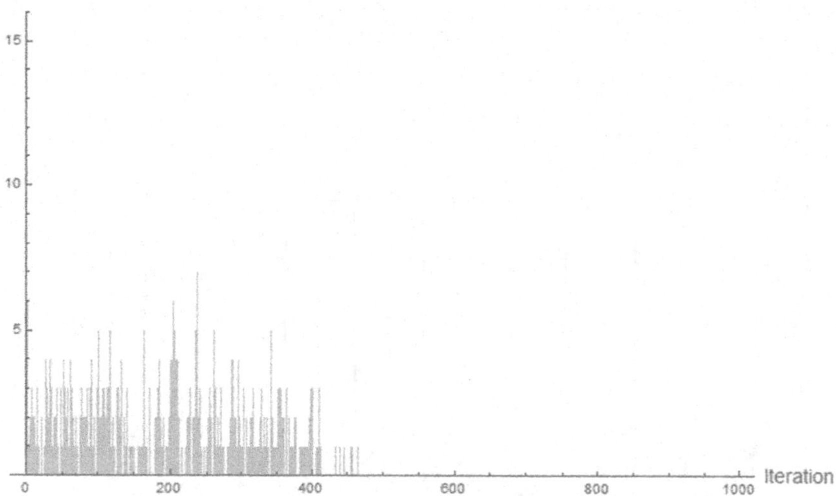

Fig. 6. Newly created links by iterations – PSO

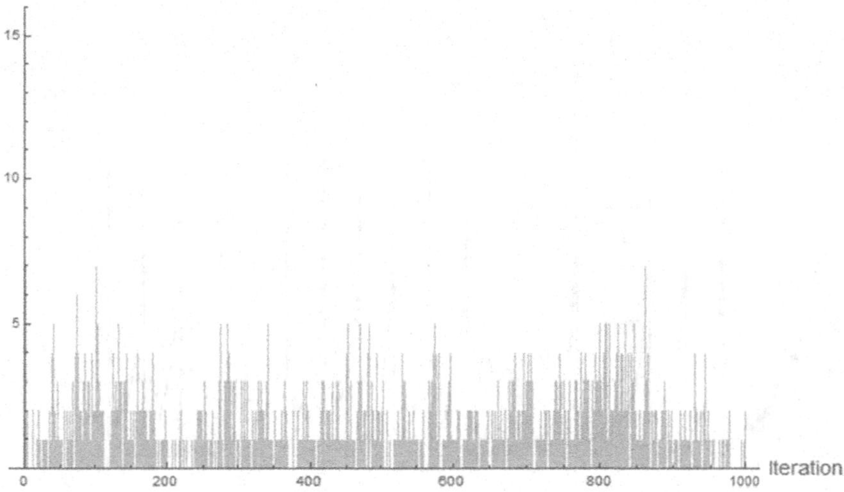

Fig. 7. Newly created links by iterations – PSO with CN

A combined picture (rescaled) of all above mentioned indicators is presented in Figs. 8 and 9.

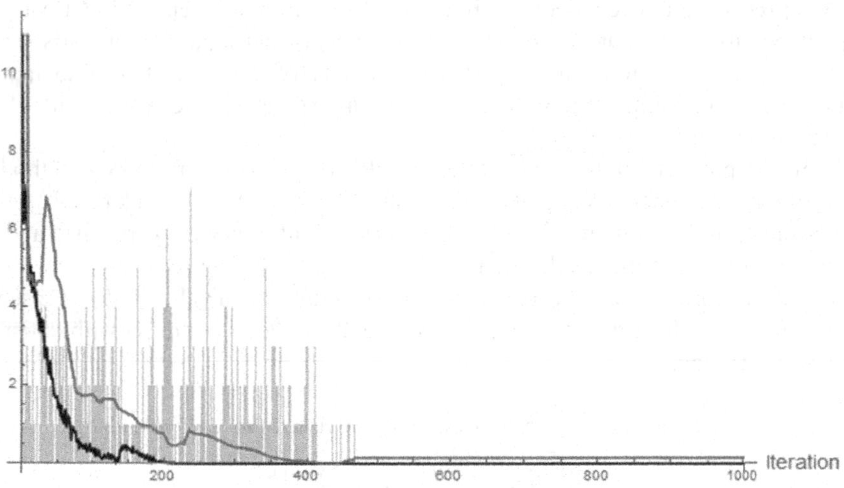

Fig. 8. Combined pictured (diversity and eigenvector centrality values rescaled) – PSO

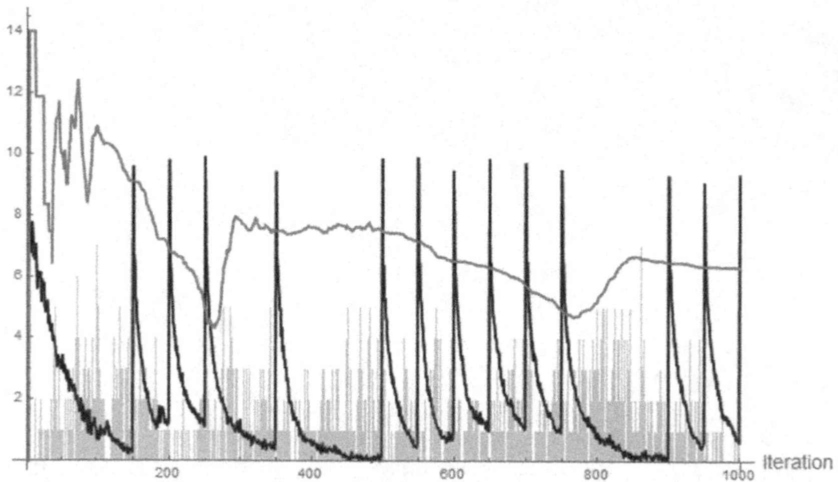

Fig. 9. Combined pictured (diversity and eigenvector centrality values rescaled) – PSO with CN

In above-mentioned figures the various aspect of the proposed method and classic PSO are compared. In Fig. 8, it is clear the fast loss of diversity of classic PSO that leads to local sub-optima trap. Despite that according to the evidence the algorithm keeps improving (creating new connections in the network) the improvement in CF value is marginal because the swarm is converged into very small area. In comparison, the proposed algorithm periodically restarts the diversity of the population allowing the swarm to keep searching in new locations and improving for the whole time of the optimization (See Fig. 9).

Finally we present a numerical results of initial testing of the proposed method on three well known benchmark functions (Rastrign, Schwefel, Rosenbrock [11, 12]) with higher dimensional setting dim = 30. Thirty independent runs were performed and the statistical overviews of the results are presented in Tables 1, 2 and 3 alongside with the *p-values* of standard Mann Whitney statistical test with critical value 0.05. CFE stands for cost function evaluations. If the *p-value* is under 0.05, the results differ with statistical significance (Table 4).

Table 1. Results comparison, *dim* = 30, 30 runs, max. CFE = 40000

Rastrigin	PSO	PSO with CN
Mean	47.6916	40.302
Std. dev.	15.3159	13.7179
Median	44.7731	38.3085
Max	90.5411	77.6066
Min	21.8891	12.9346

Table 2. Results comparison, *dim* = 30, 30 runs, max. CFE = 40000

Schwefel	PSO	PSO with CN
Mean	–7586.94	–7536.27
Std. dev.	482.467	537.876
Median	–7545.45	–7496.2
Max	–6627.58	–6468.46
Min	–8305.12	–8443.39

Table 3. Results comparison, *dim* = 30, 30 runs, max. CFE = 40000

Rosenbrock	PSO	PSO with CN
Mean	22.6806	25.0785
Std. Dev.	1.57739	1.4485
Median	22.3084	24.8171
Max	27.3337	28.7404
Min	20.9915	22.602

Table 4. Mann Whitney statistical test

f	*p-value*
Rastrigin	7.84E–02
Schwefel	7.84E–01
Rosenbrock	3.52E+07

5 Conclusion

In this study, we proposed a complex network analysis tool for timing the partial restarts of the population in the PSO algorithm. The main advantage of the method is that the computational time for the restarting measure does not scale with the dimensionality of the problem. The initial experiments brought mixed results showing the need for future improvements and detailed study of the impact of the population restart on the performance of the method, especially on particular fitness landscapes.

According to the *p-values* of Mann Whitney statistical test the results do not differ with statistical significance however based on the mean and minimal values presented in the tables, there are hints of a promising performance of the proposed method in several cases.

Furthermore, as is presented, the diversity of the population is successfully periodically increased and the algorithm continues to search for the optimal solution. The drawback is the slower convergence speed that causes lack of performance of simple benchmark problems; however, a more complex performance study is our goal for the nearest future to highlight the performance of the proposed method on hybrid and composite benchmark problems and on complex industrial applications that represent a challenge for the heuristic optimization methods.

Acknowledgements. This work was supported by Grant Agency of the Czech Republic – GACR P103/15/06700S, further by the Ministry of Education, Youth and Sports of the Czech Republic within the National Sustainability Programme Project no. LO1303 (MSMT-7778/2014. Also by the European Regional Development Fund under the Project CEBIA-Tech no. CZ. 1.05/2.1.00/03.0089 and by Internal Grant Agency of Tomas Bata University under the Projects no. IGA/CebiaTech/2017/004.

References

1. Kennedy, J., Eberhart, R.: Particle swarm optimization. In: Proceedings of the IEEE International Conference on Neural Networks, pp. 1942–1948 (1995)
2. Shi, Y., Eberhart, R.: A modified particle swarm optimizer. In: Proceedings of the IEEE International Conference on Evolutionary Computation (IEEE World Congress on Computational Intelligence), pp. 69–73 (1998)
3. Kennedy, J.: The particle swarm: social adaptation of knowledge. In: Proceedings of the IEEE International Conference on Evolutionary Computation, pp. 303–308 (1997)
4. Nickabadi, A., Ebadzadeh, M.M., Safabakhsh, R.: A novel particle swarm optimization algorithm with adaptive inertia weight. Appl. Soft Comput. **11**(4), 3658–3670 (2011). ISSN: 1568-4946
5. Zelinka, I., Davendra, D., Enkek, R., Jaek, R.: Do evolutionary algorithm dynamics create complex network structures? Complex Syst. **20**(2), 127–140 (2011). ISSN:0891–2513
6. Zelinka, I.: Investigation on relationship between complex network and evolutionary algorithms dynamics. In: AIP Conference Proceedings, vol. 1389, no. 1, pp. 1011–1014 (2011)
7. Zelinka, I., Davendra, D.D., Chadli, M., Senkerik, R., Dao, T.T., Skanderova, L.: Evolutionary dynamics as the structure of complex networks. In: Zelinka, I., Snasel, V., Abraham, A. (eds.) Handbook of Optimization. ISRL, vol. 38, pp. 215–243. Springer, Heidelberg (2013)
8. Davendra, D., Zelinka, I., Senkerik, R., Pluhacek, M.: Complex network analysis of discrete self-organising migrating algorithm. In: Zelinka, I., Suganthan, P., Chen, G., Snasel, V., Abraham, A., Rossler, O. (eds.) Nostradamus 2014: Prediction, Modeling and Analysis of Complex Systems. Advances in Intelligent Systems and Computing, vol. 289, pp. 161–174. Heidelberg, Springer (2014)
9. Davendra, D., Zelinka, I., Metlicka, M., Senkerik, R., Pluhacek, M.: Complex network analysis of differential evolution algorithm applied to flowshop with no-wait problem. In: 2014 IEEE Symposium on Differential Evolution (SDE), pp. 1–8, 9–12 December (2014)
10. Newman, M.E.J.: The mathematics of networks. New Palgrave Encycl. Econ. **2**(2008), 1–12 (2008)
11. Digalakis, J.G., Margaritis, K.G.: On benchmarking functions for genetic algorithms. Int. J. Comput. Math. **77**(4), 481–506 (2001)
12. Dieterich, J.M., Hartke, B.: Empirical review of standard benchmark functions using evolutionary global optimization. arXiv preprint arXiv:1207.4318 (2012)

Learning Algorithms

Kernel Density-Based Pattern Classification in Blind Fasteners Installation

Alberto Diez-Olivan[1](✉), Mariluz Penalva[1], Fernando Veiga[1], Lutz Deitert[2], Ricardo Sanz[3], and Basilio Sierra[4]

[1] Tecnalia Research and Innovation, Donostia - San Sebastián, Gipuzkoa, Spain
{alberto.diez,mariluz.penalva,fernando.veiga}@tecnalia.com
[2] Airbus Operations GmbH, Bremen, Germany
lutz.deitert@airbus.com
[3] Autonomous Systems Laboratory, Univ. Politécnica de Madrid, Madrid, Spain
ricardo.sanz@upm.es
[4] Department of Computer Sciences and Artificial Intelligence, UPV/EHU, Donostia - San Sebastián, Gipuzkoa, Spain
b.sierra@ehu.eus

Abstract. In this work we introduce a kernel density-based pattern classification approach for the automatic identification of behavioral patterns from monitoring data related to blind fasteners installation. High density regions are estimated from feature space to establish behavioral patterns, automatically removing outliers and noisy instances in an iterative process. First the kernel density estimator is applied on the fastener features representing the quality of the installation. Then the behavioral patterns are identified from resulting high density regions, also considering the proximity between instances. Patterns are computed as the average of related monitoring torque-rotation diagrams. New fastening installations can be thus automatically classified in an online fashion. In order to show the validity of the approach, experiments have been conducted on real fastening data. Experimental results show an accurate pattern identification and classification approach, obtaining a global accuracy over 78% and improving current detection capabilities and existing evaluation systems.

Keywords: Kernel density estimator · Behavioral patterns · Unsupervised classification · Outlier detection · Blind fasteners installation · Machine learning

1 Introduction

Intelligent monitoring of complex industrial processes is a big issue nowadays. The Industry 4.0 revolution is acting as a great driver of the development of new methodologies and technological improvements in the manufacturing industry [1]. One of the big challenges deals with how to optimally and automatically characterize behaviors of interest from monitoring data, and how to use them

F.J. Martínez de Pisón et al. (Eds.): HAIS 2017, LNAI 10334, pp. 195–206, 2017.
DOI: 10.1007/978-3-319-59650-1_17

in an online fashion for fault detection and diagnostics purposes [2,3]. Current techniques and procedures are still based on manual inspections and basic control systems, neither fully exploiting data available nor considering last advantages on data analytics methods and processing capabilities [4].

Benefits derived from adopting such technological advances and methodologies are clear in terms of knowledge management enhancement and time and cost reduction. However, there is still room for improvement in the development and integration of such advanced algorithms. To this concern special attention must be paid to the potential of hybrid methods for fault detection, pattern identification and process parameters optimization [5–8]. They combine two or more algorithms to solve the same problem optimally.

The motivation regarding blind fasteners installation resides in the lack of intelligent strategies for an automatic on-line evaluation of installed blind bolts. When blind fasteners are used to join closed structures their evaluation after installation is not feasible unless by using time and cost intensive equipment (i.e. boroscopes). Even sometimes no evaluation at all is possible. Quite often, these issues are solved by overcalculating the number of fasteners to meet safety requirements thus leading to a weight increase. In any case, much of the benefits of using blind fasteners are not currently being fully exploited. Additional to weight aspects, the increase of the production costs due to overcalculation is also very significant. Safety coefficient being applied will depend on the aircraft area but can reach a value of 2. That means that the number of installed fasteners will be twice that estimated by the design. Considering that a small-medium sized aircraft contains around 85000 fasteners (all types, not just blind ones) and that the price of each fastener is about 30, plus the installation and other consumables cost (drilling, sealant application, fastening) the large economic benefits of an automatic inspection can be foreseen. An on-line evaluation system for blind bolts installation is therefore required. In this work a kernel density-based pattern classification approach for the automatic identification of behavioral patterns from monitoring data related to blind fasteners installation is presented. Patterns found can highly support the online classification of new fasteners.

The rest of the article is organized as follows. Section 2 presents the installation process of the blind fasteners. Section 3 explains the hybrid machine learning approach used to find behavioral patterns and classify fasteners, which relies on Kernel Density Estimation and distance-based classification. In Sect. 4 the test scenario is presented and the experimental results obtained are discussed. Finally, the conclusions achieved in this study and future work are given in the last section.

2 Blind Fasteners Installation

A fastener is a mechanical device used to join or assembly two or more components together. In aircraft manufacturing there is a large variety of fasteners being used. Among them, blind fasteners represent a specific design type allowing the installation just by accessing to the front side of the assembly. This provides cheaper, less complex and easier to automate installation operations. A blind bolt schema can be seen in Fig. 1 [9].

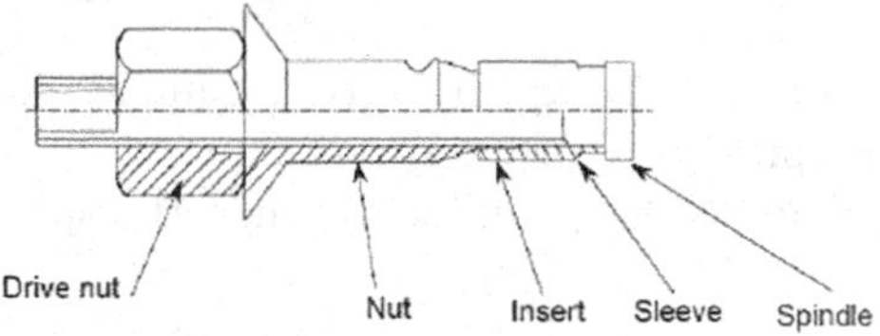

Fig. 1. Blind bolt schema.

An installed blind bolt is classified as correctly or badly installed depending on the representative dimensions of its formed head, namely, the head diameter (J) and the head height (K) as illustrated by Fig. 2.

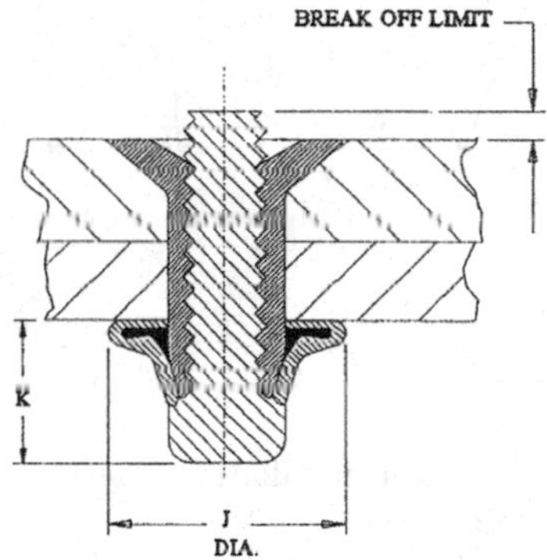

Fig. 2. Representative dimensions of the formed head in an installed blind bolt.

The above mentioned variables, J and K, can be represented into a torque-rotation (rpm) diagram that characterizes the fastening operation. In order to automatically monitor and evaluate the fasteners installation, the torque-rotation diagram appears to be the most straightforward option. In Fig. 3 the fastener installation diagram and the fastener cross-sections for the key torque-rotation diagram points are shown.

The different stages of the installation can be identified through the relevant points in the torque-rotation diagram:

- From 1 to 2 the fastening torque overcomes friction and makes the spindle and the sleeve rotate together. The nut position is fixed through the thrust force applied by the fastening head.

- From 2 to 3 the sleeve does not longer rotate and starts advancing along the spindle towards the back side of the assembly until they get in contact. There is a decrease in the torque value.
- From 3 to 4 the deformation of the sleeve starts as it can no longer advance towards the back side but keeps being pushed to it by the rotating spindle. The torque increases again.
- From 4 to 5 the torque increasing rate becomes higher as the deformation of the sleeve enters the plastic deformation region.
- From 5 to 6 the torque decreases suddenly when the spindle breaks.

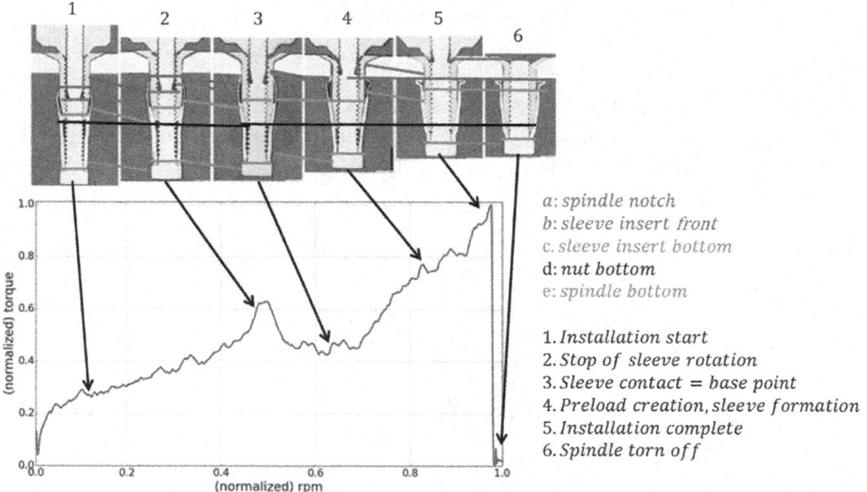

Fig. 3. Torque-rotation (rpm) fastener installation diagram and fastener cross-sections for the relevant torque-rotation diagram points.

Cross sections of the fastener for each relevant point in the installation process also provide helpful information about the operation:

- Line *a* represents the spindle notch position, which advances up to the assembly top side.
- Line *b* represents the sleeve (insert side) front, which advances up to the assembly back side.
- Line *d* represents the nut bottom, which keeps a fixed position.
- Distance *bc* represent the insert length, which first advances up to the back side of the assembly. Once this side is reached, the length decreases due to deformation.
- Distance *ce* represents the sleeve length, which advances up to the back side together with the insert. Once the back side is reached, this length is also expected to decrease though at a rate lower than the one of the insert.

In the following section the proposed approach to automatically find behavioral patterns from data and classify the installation of new blind fasteners is presented.

3 Kernel Density-Based Pattern Classification Approach

In order to automatically classify the installation of blind fasteners a data-driven approach is proposed. It is based on the multivariate density analysis of the head diameter (J) and the head height (K) of the formed heads in a set of installations, and on behavioral patterns identification from high density regions found. Then, a distance-based classification of new monitoring torque-rotation diagrams can be applied.

3.1 Kernel Density Estimation for Behavioral Patterns Identification

Multivariate Kernel Density Estimation (KDE) is a nonparametric technique that allows estimating the density of the data [10,11]. Probability density functions (pdf) are inferred in order to establish the underlying density function and the overall structure of the data. Given a set of m features, $X = \{X_1, ..., X_m\}$ where each feature X_i can take a value from its own set of possible values χ_i, and n feature vectors or instances, $\boldsymbol{x_i} = (x_1, ..., x_m) \in \chi = (\chi_1, ..., \chi_m)$, with $i = 1, ..., n$, the multivariate joint pdf $\hat{f}_h(X)$ can be computed as it is shown in Eq. 1.

$$\hat{f}_h(X) = \frac{1}{n}\sum_{i=1}^{n}\frac{1}{h_1...h_m}G\left(\frac{X_1 - x_{i1}}{h_1}, ..., \frac{X_m - x_{im}}{h_m}\right) \tag{1}$$

being $\boldsymbol{h} = (h_1...h_m)^T$ the vector of bandwidths calculated by the rule of thumb using Scott's Rule [12,13] and G is the multivariate Gaussian kernel function [14] operating on the input features:

$$G(u) = \frac{1}{\sqrt{2\Pi}}e^{\frac{-1}{2}u^2} \tag{2}$$

In our case, and given the fastening torque (J) and the fastener rotation (K) as features, $X = \{J, K\}$, and a set of n instances $\boldsymbol{x_i} = (j_i, k_i)$, the KDE formula becomes:

$$\hat{f}_h(X) = \frac{1}{n}\sum_{i=1}^{n}\frac{1}{h_J, h_K}G\left(\frac{J - j_i}{h_J}, \frac{K - k_i}{h_K}\right) \tag{3}$$

Regions in feature space that show a high density imply a behavior of interest, whereas instances that are isolated, far from any behavior, they can be considered as outliers and therefore they are filtered out. At each step of the process, the instance with the minimum density is removed aiming to eliminate faulty torque-rotation diagrams and noise from patterns to be defined and that will be used to classify new monitoring torque-rotation diagrams. Densities are then recalculated iteratively, using the Scott's factor, $bw = n^{(-1/(m+4))}$, computed in the first iteration for bandwidth selection, until the minimum density obtained at the i-th iteration is over the minimum density at iteration $i+1$. Instances are grouped together to establish a behavioral pattern on the basis of their density and their proximity to each other, using the Euclidean distance [15] (see Eq. 4), normalized between 0 and 1.

$$D(\boldsymbol{x_i}, \boldsymbol{x_j}) = ||\boldsymbol{x_i} - \boldsymbol{x_j}|| = \sqrt{(j_j - j_i)^2 + (k_j - k_i)^2} \tag{4}$$

where $\boldsymbol{x_i}$ and $\boldsymbol{x_j}$ are two instances $\in X = \{J, K\}$.

3.2 Behavioral Patterns Computation

Behavioral patterns are based on torque-rotation diagrams, since they describe the evolution along the time of the fastener installation and it can be monitored in real-time. Having the set of n blind fastener installations, they are first aligned in rotation axis (equivalent to time dimension) to the highest point by cross-correlation. Diagrams are then normalized in both dimensions, the rotation (R) and the torque (T), between 0 and 1 in order to filter out the effect of conditions variation. An example of the resulting torque-rotation diagram, $\boldsymbol{d_i} = (d_1, ..., d_z)$, can be seen in Fig. 3.

For a set S of diagrams a behavioral pattern, $\boldsymbol{p_S} = (p_1, ..., p_z)$, is then simply defined as the average values in fastening torque, J, for every fastener rotation, K, as it is shown in Eq. 5.

$$\boldsymbol{p_S} = \frac{1}{|S|}\sum_{i=1}^{|S|} \boldsymbol{d_i} \tag{5}$$

3.3 Distance-Based Classification

In order to calculate the distance between a pattern, $\boldsymbol{p_S}$, and a torque-rotation diagram, $\boldsymbol{d_i}$, Euclidean metric is computed similarly to Eq. 4, as it can be seen in Eq. 6.

$$D(\boldsymbol{p_S}, \boldsymbol{d_i}) = ||\boldsymbol{p_S} - \boldsymbol{d_i}|| = \sqrt{\sum_{l=1}^{z} (p_{Sl} - d_{il})^2} \tag{6}$$

Then a torque-rotation diagram can be easily classified by its proximity to a behavioral pattern. A maximum distance, D_{max}, to each pattern is established during the training phase. Having a set of k patterns, $\{\boldsymbol{p_1}, ..., \boldsymbol{p_k}\}$, and the corresponding set of maximum distances, $\{D_{max_1}, ..., D_{max_k}\}$, a new diagram $\boldsymbol{d_{new}} \in p_S$ if:

$$D_S = \underset{\{S=1,...,k\}}{\text{argmin}} \; D(\boldsymbol{p_S}, \boldsymbol{d_{new}}) \tag{7}$$

Therefore, new patterns can be found when $D(\boldsymbol{p_S}, \boldsymbol{d_{new}}) > D_{max_S}$, $\forall\ S = 1, ..., k$. The underlying idea is based on proximity and clustering algorithms [16].

The overall algorithm can be seen in Algorithm 1.

Algorithm 1. KDE for behavioral patterns identification

Input: a set of n instances of (J,K) features, $\boldsymbol{x_i} = \{j_i, k_i\}$ and a set of n corresponding torque-rotation diagrams $\boldsymbol{d_i} = (d_1, ..., d_z)$, $i = 1, ..., n$

Compute $\hat{f}_h(X)$ using Eq. 3
Set $min' = 0$
Set $density = \hat{f}_h(X_{|n|})$
Set $bw = n^{(-1/(m+4))}$
$outliers = \{\}$
while $min(density) > min'$ **do**
    $min' = min(density)$
    $\boldsymbol{x_{min'}} \rightarrow outliers$
    Remove $\boldsymbol{x_{min'}}$
    Compute $density - \hat{f}_h(X_{|<n|})$ using Eq. 3
end while
$patterns = \{\}$
for all $\boldsymbol{x_i}$, $i = (1, ..., |<n|)$ **do**
    for all $\boldsymbol{x_j}$, $j = (1, ..., |<n|)$, $j \neq i$ **do**
        if $D(\boldsymbol{x_i}, \boldsymbol{x_j}) < bw$ **then**
            $\boldsymbol{x_j} \rightarrow S$
        end if
    end for
    Compute $\boldsymbol{P_S}$ using Eq. 5
    $\boldsymbol{P_S} \rightarrow patterns$
end for

---

4 Test Scenario

In this section the test scenario to validate the proposed approach is presented. First, the experimental setup is described and then results obtained are shown and discussed. The method accuracy is compared with a k-Means clustering, one of the most popular clustering algorithms to group similar data [17].

4.1 Description of the Experimental Setup

The material used in experimental tests consists of a set of 35 torque-rotation diagrams. They all correspond to fasteners with the same reference and dash (MBF 2313, dash 5), though some variations in their installation conditions exist: grip length, stack thickness, preload and spindle rpm. Despite the small amount of diagrams available, they are representative examples of the main behavioral patterns that can be found in the blind fastener installation process.

Experimental data contained a total of 9 diagrams showing a correct installation. Other 26 diagrams are more or less deviated from admissible limits. The distribution of (J, K) values in normalized feature space can be seen in Fig. 4.

4.2 Results and Discussion

The results obtained allow identifying 3 differentiated high density regions, as it can be seen in Fig. 5. One region contains the 10 faulty torque-rotation diagrams whereas the other regions contains the other 23 diagrams, 9 showing a

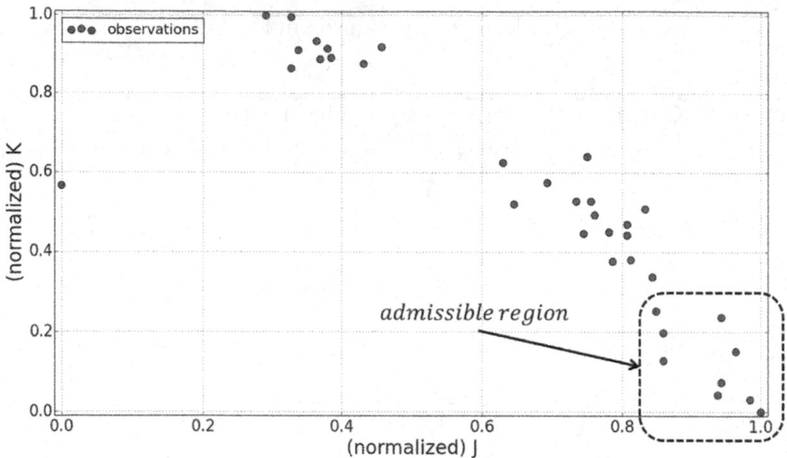

Fig. 4. Data distribution of $(J,\ K)$ values in normalized feature space.

typical normal behavior and 14 corresponding to a faulty behavior but closer to admissible limits.

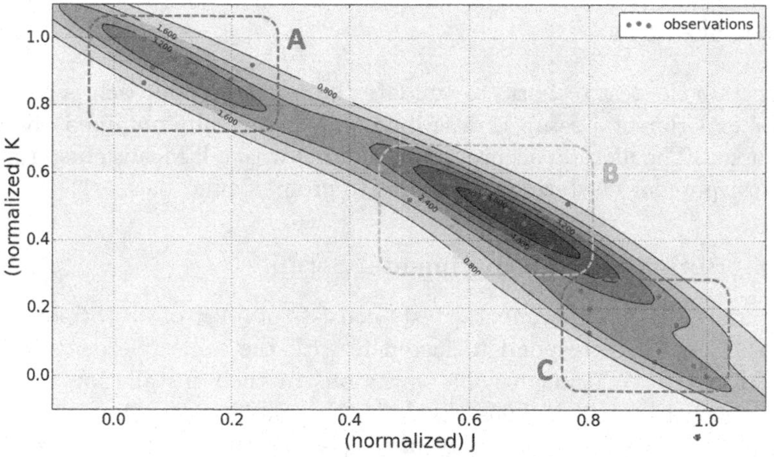

Fig. 5. High density regions found in data.

From computed densities, two outliers are also detected, which corresponds to $(J,\ K)$ pairs isolated in feature space, with low pdf values. They are presented in Fig. 6.

After removing such outliers, three different patterns are obtained: pattern A, representing the faulty diagrams, pattern B, representing a faulty behavior close to admissible limits, and pattern C, containing the normal diagrams. k-Means

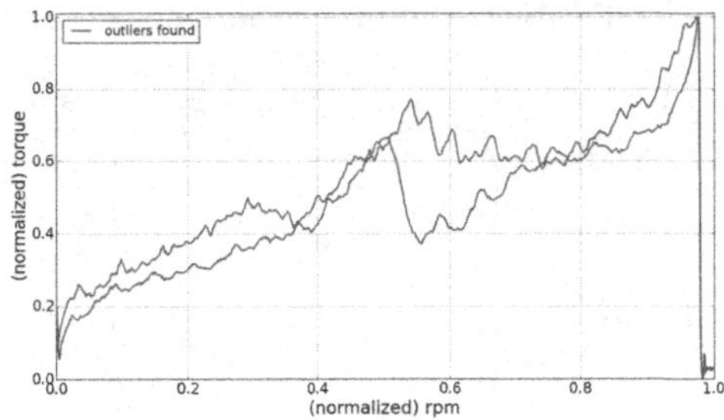

Fig. 6. KDE-based pattern classification approach. Outliers found.

method is also executed with k=3 in order to also find three different groups of similar diagrams in data. The distance metric used is the same Euclidean distance presented in Eq. 6. Resulting patterns slightly differ from those obtained by KDE-based approach. The corresponding (normalized) torque-rotation diagrams obtained by both methods are shown in Fig. 7.

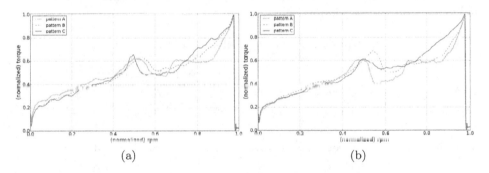

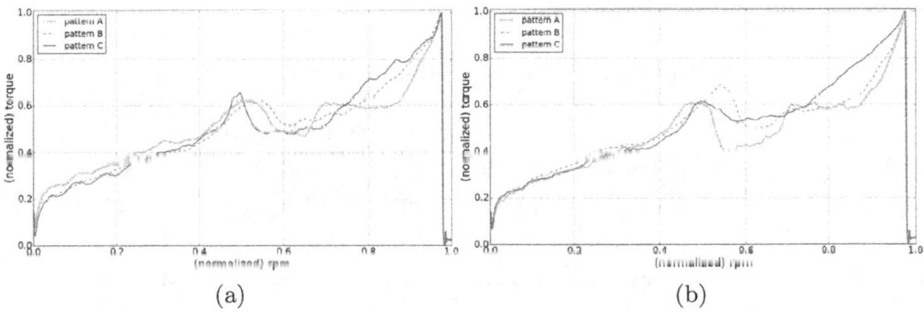

Fig. 7. Patterns found in data by Kernel density-based pattern classification approach (a) and k-Means ($k = 3$) (b).

The differences between the two groups of patterns are evident. Patterns found by both methods share some common features: (i) the varying width and symmetry of the first peak and (ii) the slope evolution between the two peaks. Therefore, they provide a simple analysis basis to identify diagram variations, a critical issue when large amount of diagrams have to be analyzed and characterized.

Torque-rotation diagrams taken from the experimental setup were tested on a 5-fold cross-validation basis, by segmenting the total data set into 5 equal parts. Therefore, the accuracy and generalization of the proposed approach when classifying new diagrams can be tested. The confusion matrix presented in Table 1 is obtained, containing the global results of the 5 folds for both methods.

It can be appreciated that the KDE-based pattern classification outperformed the classification results obtained by k-Means for all patterns. Moreover, most of

Table 1. Confusion matrix.

	Pattern	Predicted A	Predicted B	Predicted C
KDE-based pattern classification	A	**8**	1	1
	B	1	**12**	1
	C	0	3	**6**
k-Means ($k = 3$)	A	**4**	4	2
	B	2	**8**	4
	C	1	7	**1**

the correctly installed blind fasteners, represented by pattern C, are classified as pattern B diagrams in the case of k-Means approach. This may lead to important false positive rates.

In order to evaluate the results, the $Precision = TP/(TP + FP)$, $Recall = TP/(TP + FN)$ and $Accuracy = (TP + TN)/(TP + TN + FP + FN)$ of the classification are calculated, being TP the true positives, FP the false positives, FN the false negatives and TN the true negatives. They are three widely used quality measures in this kind of processes.

Table 2. Precision, recall and accuracy.

		Pattern A	Pattern B	Pattern C	Global results
KDE-based pattern classification	**Precision**	88.89%	75%	75%	**79.63%**
	Recall	80%	85.71%	66.67%	**77.46%**
	Accuracy				**78.79%**
k-Means ($k = 3$)	**Precision**	57.13%	42.14%	14.28%	**37.83%**
	Recall	40%	57.13%	11.1%	**36.07%**
	Accuracy				**39.38%**

As it is shown in Table 2, precision, recall and accuracy are globally above 77%, so the approach accurately establishes patterns from data. Interestingly, the correct classification of diagrams rises above the false positive rate, $FPR = FP/(FP + TN)$, in all patterns, being $FPR = 0.03$ for pattern A, $FPR = 0.2$ for pattern B and $FPR = 0.07$ for pattern C, respectively. In contrast, k-Means obtained a global precision, recall and accuracy below 40%. These results highlights the difficulty and challenging of the given test scenario, containing only 35 representative diagrams, being two of them potential outliers that can highly influence the patterns to be drawn.

5 Conclusions and Future Work

This work presents a kernel density-based pattern approach to automatically and successfully identify patterns and classify them. Experimental results show the potential of the proposed approach in blind fasteners installation. The complexity of such systems and time and cost intensive equipment needed to evaluate installed fasteners, makes their behavior more difficult and challenging to analyze. The most commonly used solution relies on overcalculating the number of fasteners to meet safety requirements. An automatic and online evaluation system for blind bolts installation is therefore required.

It was found that machine learning methods can highly support the traditional classification and evaluation strategies in industrial processes. The proposed kernel density-based pattern classification provides a fully automatic yet accurate evaluation system. Discussed test scenario demonstrated the validity of the approach when analyzing blind fasteners installation, achieving a global precision, recall and accuracy above 77%. Considering the difficulty of the test scenario under study, involving only 35 representative diagrams, being two of them potential outliers that can highly influence the patterns to be drawn, it is still encouraging that the correct classification of diagrams rises above the false positive rate in all patterns. Results achieved were compared to those obtained by k-Means ($k = 3$), giving a global precision, recall and accuracy below 40%.

By taking into account patterns inferred by this approach in an online fashion, new monitoring torque-rotation diagrams can be accurately and automatically classified. The benefits of adopting the proposed solution are clear in terms of material and time saving. It only requires deploying non-expensive sensors (e.g. torque transducers and rotation sensors), and the software that implements the previously identified patterns and the distance-based classification method. Since the approach is fully data-driven, the more data are available the better the robustness of patterns found and the accuracy obtained. Further tests involving more data must be conducted and the same approach should be tested in other similar industrial processes. This will allow improving the accuracy, generalization and robustness of the proposed automatic evaluation system.

Acknowledgements. These results are part of a project that has received funding from the European Unions Horizon 2020 research and innovation programme under grant agreement 686827.

References

1. Madsen, E.S., Bilberg, A., Hansen, D.G.: Industry 4.0 and digitalization call for vocational skills, applied industrial engineering, and less for pure academics. In: 5th World Conference on Production and Operations Management P&OM (2016)
2. Yin, S., Ding, S.X., Zhou, D.: Diagnosis and prognosis for complicated industrial systems—part I. IEEE Trans. Ind. Electron. **63**(4), 2501–2505 (2016)
3. Yin, S., Ding, S.X., Zhou, D.: Diagnosis and prognosis for complicated industrial systems—part II. IEEE Trans. Ind. Electron. **63**(5), 3201–3204 (2016)
4. Severson, K., Chaiwatanodom, P., Braatz, R.D.: Perspectives on process monitoring of industrial systems. Ann. Rev. Control **42**, 190–200 (2016)

5. Diez-Olivan, A., Pagan, J.A., Sanz, R., Sierra, B.: Data-driven prognostics using a combination of constrained k-means clustering, fuzzy modeling and LOF-based score. Neurocomputing **241**, 97–107 (2017). http://dx.doi.org/10.1016/j.neucom.2017.02.024, http://www.sciencedirect.com/science/article/pii/S0925231217302941
6. Serdio, F., Lughofer, E., Zavoianu, A.-C., Pichler, K., Pichler, M., Buchegger, T., Efendic, H.: Improved fault detection employing hybrid memetic fuzzy modeling and adaptive filters. Appl. Soft Comput. **51**, 60–82 (2017)
7. Wang, K., Gelgele, H.L., Wang, Y., Yuan, Q., Fang, M.: A hybrid intelligent method for modelling the edm process. Int. J. Mach. Tools Manuf. **43**(10), 995–999 (2003)
8. Vera, V., Sedano, J., Corchado, E., Redondo, R., Hernando, B., Camara, M., Laham, A., Garcia, A.E.: A hybrid system for dental milling parameters optimisation. In: Corchado, E., Kurzyński, M., Woźniak, M. (eds.) HAIS 2011. LNCS, vol. 6679, pp. 437–446. Springer, Heidelberg (2011). doi:10.1007/978-3-642-21222-2_53
9. Monogram Aerospace Fasteners: MBF2003 Installation and Inspection Specification for Composi-lok II Blind Fasteners, April 2008. http://www.monogramaerospace.com/files/active/0/MBF2003_CLII_Installation.pdf
10. Silverman, B.W.: Density Estimation for Statistics and Data Analysis, vol. 26. CRC Press, Boca Raton (1986)
11. Terrell, G.R., Scott, D.W.: Variable kernel density estimation. Ann. Stat. **20**, 1236–1265 (1992)
12. Scott, D.W.: Multivariate Density Estimation: Theory, Practice and Visualization. John Wiley & Sons, New York (2015)
13. Bashtannyk, D.M., Hyndman, R.J.: Bandwidth selection for kernel conditional density estimation. Comput. Stat. Data Anal. **36**(3), 279–298 (2001)
14. Babaud, J., Witkin, A.P., Baudin, M., Duda, R.O.: Uniqueness of the gaussian kernel for scale-space filtering. IEEE Trans. Pattern Anal. Mach. Intell. **1**, 26–33 (1986)
15. Aggarwal, C.C.: Proximity-based outlier detection. In: Aggarwal, C.C. (ed.) Outlier Analysis, pp. 101–133. Springer, Heidelberg (2013)
16. Kung, S.Y.: Kernel Methods and Machine Learning. Cambridge University Press, Cambridge (2014)
17. Jain, A.K.: Data clustering: 50 years beyond k-means. Pattern Recogn. Lett. **31**(8), 651–666 (2010)

Training Set Fuzzification Towards Prediction Improvement

Eva Volna[✉], Jaroslav Zacek, and Robert Jarusek

Department of Informatics and Computers, University of Ostrava, Ostrava, Czech Republic
{eva.volna,jaroslav.zacek,robert.jarusek}@osu.cz

Abstract. This article presents a method of fuzzification of variables using a histogram. This approach is used when creating an output vector of a training set that forms linguistic variables. An appropriate transformation of an input vector of the training sets was also proposed. Both of the aforesaid procedures were described in detail in the article. An extensive comparative experimental study with the following outcomes was carried out. The neural net which was adapted by the transformed training set showed a significantly better prediction than a neural network which was adapted by a training set without making any changes. The results of this experimental study were analyzed in the conclusion.

Keywords: Continuous distribution · Histogram · Linguistic variable · Neural network · Prediction

1 Introduction

The literature review reveals that neural networks and fuzzy logic theory have a great capability in solving many real-life problems, especially, when it comes to the process of complex decision-making [4]. So, it is beneficial to fuse neural networks and fuzzy set techniques together by substituting the demerits of one technique by the merits of the other. These two techniques can be fused as [8]:

- Application of neural networks for designing fuzzy logic based systems,
- Application of fuzzy logic for designing neural networks based systems.

Many researchers tried to design hybridize-based models to solve complex decision-making problems, such as rough-fuzzy hybridization scheme for case generation [6], recurrent neural network and a hybrid model for prediction of stock return [3], hybridization of neural networks and fuzzy time series for TAIEX forecasting [10], a hybrid model based on ANFIS for stock forecasting [11], fuzzy-neuro approach for sales forecasting of printed circuit board industry [9], etc.

This article presents a method of fuzzification of a training set which is used in a back propagation neural network in order to improve its prediction. An extensive comparative experimental study confirming the intention of our approach was carried out.

F.J. Martínez de Pisón et al. (Eds.): HAIS 2017, LNAI 10334, pp. 207–219, 2017.
DOI: 10.1007/978-3-319-59650-1_18

1.1 Theoretical Background - Continuous Distributions

An overview of basic continuous distributions is shown in Table 1 [7] and in Fig. 1, where *f*(*x*) is the probability density function (pdf), *E*(*x*) is mean or expectation of the distribution, and *V*(*x*) is the variance. There is λ the rate parameter in exponential distribution. There is μ mean, and standard deviation in normal distribution. There is *k* the shape parameter, and the rate parameter in Erlang distribution (Fig. 1).

Table 1. Overview of basic continuous distributions

Distribution	*f*(*x*)	Support	*E*(*x*)	*V*(*x*)
Uniform	$\frac{1}{b-a}$	$a \leq x \leq b$	$\frac{a+b}{2}$	$\frac{(b-a)^2}{12}$
Exponential	$\lambda e^{-\lambda x}$	$x \geq 0$	$\frac{1}{\lambda}$	$\frac{1}{\lambda^2}$
Normal	$\frac{1}{\sigma\sqrt{2\pi}} e^{-\frac{1}{2}\left(\frac{x-\mu}{\sigma}\right)^2}$	$-\infty < x < \infty$	μ	σ^2
Erlang	$\frac{\lambda^k x^{k-1} e^{-\lambda x}}{(k-1)!}$ for $x, \lambda \geq 0$	$0 \leq x < \infty$	$\frac{k}{\lambda}$	$\frac{k}{\lambda^2}$

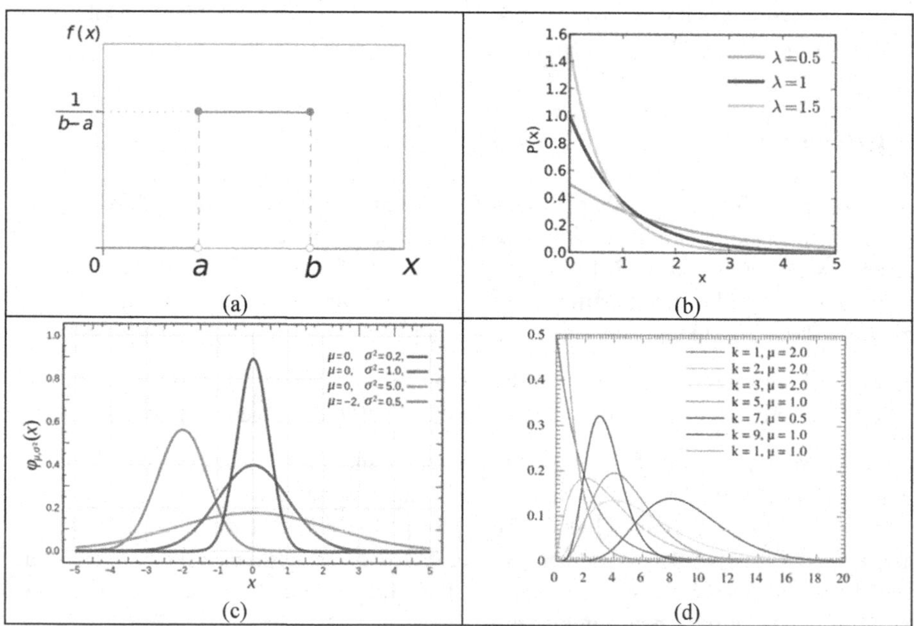

Fig. 1. Continuous distributions (adapted from https://en.wikipedia.org/wiki/). (a) Uniform distribution, (b) Exponential distribution, (c) Normal distribution (The red curve is the standard normal distribution), (d) Erlang distribution. (Color figure online)

1.2 Fuzzification of Variables Using a Histogram

We deal with the evaluating linguistic expressions (possibly with signs) which have the general form [1].

$$\langle \text{linguistic modifier} \rangle \langle \text{atomic term} \rangle \tag{1}$$

where ⟨atomic term⟩ is one of the words *small* (*sm*), *medium* (*me*), and *big* (*bi*) and ⟨linguistic modifier⟩ is an intensifying adverb, such as *extremely* (*ex*), *significantly* (*si*), *very* (*ve*), *rather* (*ra*), *more or less* (*ml*), *roughly* (*ro*), *quite roughly* (*qr*) and *very roughly* (*vr*).

In the data analysis, it is not only important what kind of distribution data is represented, but also whether the curve has only one maximum. It can be seen from the histogram, Fig. 2. In this case, the curve has only one peak, and it resembles to Erlang distribution. The highest rate of sales is around the number 38 according to the histogram. The following procedure applies to fuzzification algorithm:

- Normalization of data into the interval ⟨0, 1⟩. Items larger than 600 are not taken into consideration. So we will set minimum 1 and maximum 600.
- We refine the prediction so that the refinement is greatest in extremes (in this case, the number is 38). For example, the interval is set to 20–40 for values around 38 with expression "significantly small". Conversely, the error does not matter in larger values, therefore the interval 500–600 can be marked with expression "extremely big".

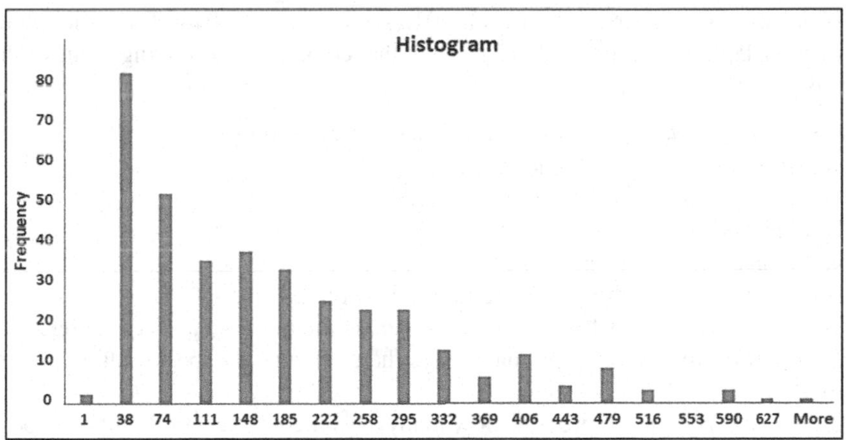

Fig. 2. Histogram - Erlang distribution

If more extremes appear in the histogram, the algorithm has to be adjusted according to these extremes by refining the range of values within them (we use intervals with less variance). Conversely, values that are less represented in the histogram have a greater interval for the linguistic variable.

Studying Fig. 3, it is clear that there cannot be used a full separation of language variables. Data values can be rationally predicted at around 6 values (other values are remote). Therefore, it is necessary to use fewer linguistic variables.

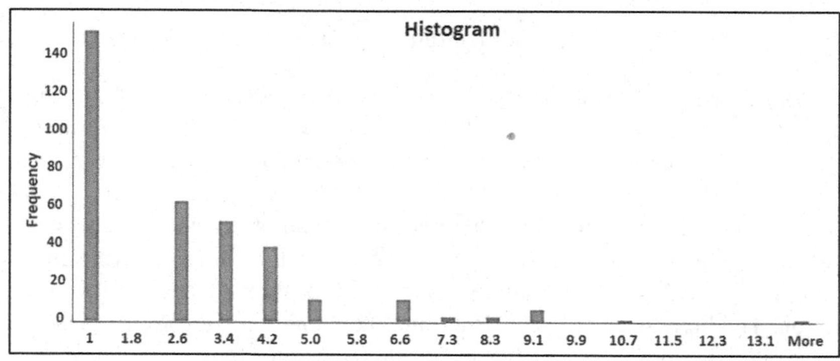

Fig. 3. Histogram of measured values

2 Sales Prediction Using Neural Networks

2.1 Training Set

The experiments were performed with real data, which represented information about the sale of three specific foodstuffs from the assortment of goods *COFFEE, DECAF* and *ALCOHOL* during the period 30 March 2013–31 December 2014. The experimental data for the adaptation included 1917 records that contain the following values. Their format is shown in Table 2.

1. *Warehouse_Code* represents the identifier of a warehouse;
2. *Goods_Code* represents the identifier of goods;
3. *Goods_Name* represents the name of goods;
4. *Day* represents date;
5. *Sale* represents total sales in pieces;
6. *Action* represents, if the goods are in a special offer;
7. *Day_Action* represents how many days there is the goods in a special offer;
8. *Days_Action* represents how many days there are already special offers over the goods;
9. *Days_Out_of_Action* represents how many days there is the goods out of a special offer;
10. *Discount_Percent* represents the percent of goods on sale in a special offer;
11. *Extended_Weekend* represents, if being or not an extended weekend;
12. *Holidays* represents, if being or not holidays;
13. *Alternative_Goods_In_Action* represents if being or not alternative goods within the same range of same producer in a special offer.

Table 2. The format of experimental data (items 1–13 represent the above mentioned inputs)

1	2	3	4	5	6	7	8	9	10	11	12	13
S1	COFF1	COFFEE	2013–03–30	327	1	9	30	0	20	0	0	1
S1	COFF1	COFFEE	2013–03–31	312	1	10	31	0	20	0	0	1
…	…	…	…	…	…	…	…	…	…	…	…	..

Fuzzification of the Output Vector of the Training Set

Figure 4 illustrates a methodology for filtering the output vector of the training set using linguistic variables.

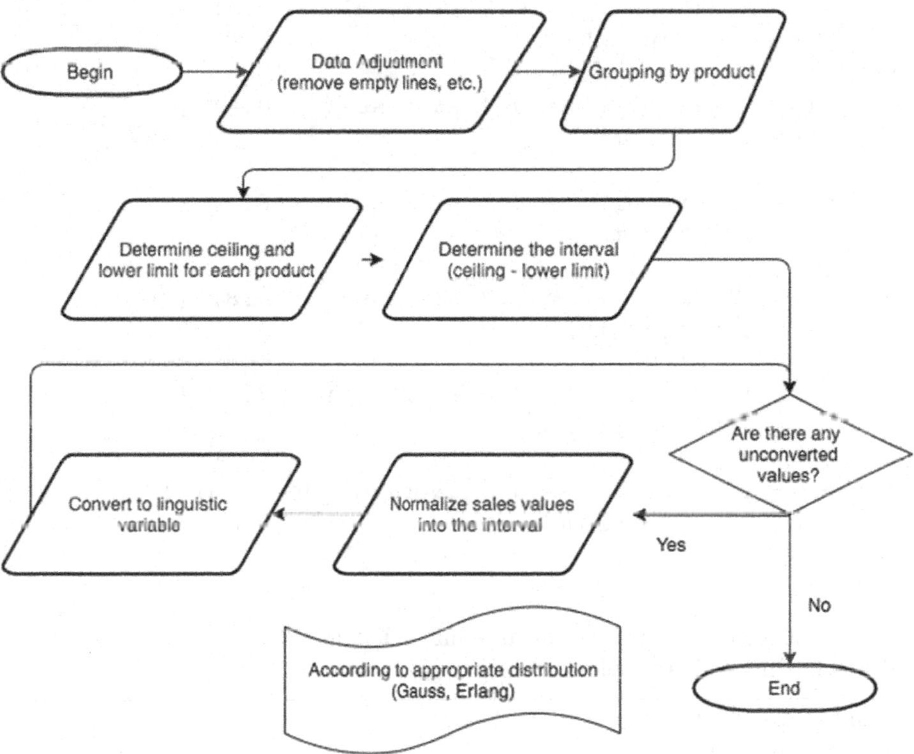

Fig. 4. Methodology for filtering the output vector of the training set using linguistic variables

The item *sale* was fuzzified using normal distribution. Implementation of fuzzification for the item from the assortment of goods *DECAF* was performed as follows:

```
private String convertNumberToLinguistic(
double number, double limit, double lowest)
{
    double result = ((100 * (number-lowest)) / lim-
it)/100d;
    if (result >= 0 && result < 0.1) {
      return "ex sm";
    } else if (result >= 0.1 && result < 0.2) {
      return "si sm";
    }
    else if (result >= 0.2 && result < 0.4) {
      return "vr sm";
    }
    else if (result >= 0.4 && result < 0.6) {
      return "ro me";
    }
    else if (result >= 0.6 && result < 0.7) {
      return "vr me";
    }
    else if (result >= 0.7 && result < 0.8) {
      return "ro bi";
    }
    else if (result >= 0.8 && result < 0.9) {
      return "si bi";
    }
    else if (result >= 0.9 && result <= 1.0) {
      return "ex bi";
    }
```

Therefore, the output vector of the training set includes 8 components representing the following linguistic variables:

1. significantly small (si sm)
2. extremely small (ex sm)
3. very roughly small (vr sm)
4. roughly medium (ro me)
5. very roughly medium (vr me)
6. roughly big (ro bi)
7. significantly big (si bi)
8. extremely big (ex bi)

In the case of the output vector, there was used the transformation of linguistic variables into a sequence of eight bits with the value "1" in an adequate column. For example, if the output value is '*vr sm* ', then the output vector is written in the form (0, 0, 1, 0, 0, 0, 0, 0):

si sm	ex sm	vr sm	ro me	vr me	ro bi	si bi	ex bi
0	0	**1**	0	0	0	0	0

It should be noted that in the case of a forward phase (phase remembering), the neural network answers by a vector of real numbers from the interval ⟨0, 1⟩ to the given pattern, e.g. in this way:

si sm	ex sm	vr sm	ro me	vr me	ro bi	si bi	ex bi
0.01	0.05	**0.89**	0.3	0.01	0.1	0.15	0.05

From the values of individual coefficients can be derived which linguistic variable is predicted according to the neural network.

Transformation of the Input Vector of the Training Set

A separate training set was created for each good. As we used the back propagation neural network with a sigmoid activation function, inputs were transformed into real numbers from the interval ⟨0, 1⟩ One input vector of the training set was created according to the following algorithm.

```
Dictionary<Day_In_a_Week, string> daysDictionary =
        {
            {Day_In_a_Week.Monday,  "1;0;0;0;0;0;0;"},
            {Day_In_a_Week.Tuesday, "0;1;0;0;0;0;0;"},
            {Day_In_a_Week.Wednesday, "0;0;1;0;0;0;0;"},
            {Day_In_a_Week.Thursday,  "0;0;0;1;0;0;0;"},
            {Day_In_a_Week.Friday,  "0;0;0;0;1;0;0;"},
            {Day_In_a_Week.Saturday,  "0;0;0;0;0;1;0;"},
            {Day_In_a_Week.Sunday,  "0;0;0;0;0;0;1;"},
        };
StringBuilder sb = new StringBuilder();
            sb.Append(Day_In_a_Year / 366.0 + ";");
            sb.Append(daysDictionary[Day_In_a_Week]);
            sb.Append(Action + ";");
            sb.Append(Day_Action / 100.0 + ";");
            sb.Append(Days_Action / 100.0 + ";");
            sb.Append(Days_Out_of_Action / 100.0 + ";");
            sb.Append(Discount_Percent / 50.0 + ";");
            sb.Append(Extended_Weekend + ";");
            sb.Append(Holidays + ";");
            sb.Append(Alternative_Goods_In_Action + ";");
```

The input vector of the training set has 6 components which contain the following values:

1. *Day_In_a_Year* (0–366) – normalization on the interval <0, 1> ;
2. *Day_In_a_Week* - *Monday* is represented by a binary number {0, 1};

3. *Day_In_a_Week* - *Tuesday* is represented by a binary number {0, 1};
4. *Day_In_a_Week* - *Wednesday* is represented by a binary number {0, 1};
5. *Day_In_a_Week* - *Thursday* is represented by a binary number {0, 1};
6. *Day_In_a_Week* - *Friday* is represented by a binary number {0, 1};
7. *Day_In_a_Week* - *Saturday* is represented by a binary number {0, 1};
8. *Day_In_a_Week* - *Sunday* is represented by a binary number {0, 1};
9. *Action* is represented by a binary number {0, 1};
10. *Day_Action* is represented by a number from an interval <0, 1> (number of days divided by 100);
11. *Days_Action* is represented by a number from an interval <0, 1> (number of days divided by 100);
12. *Days_Out_of_Action* is represented by a number from an interval < 0, 1 > (number of days divided by 100);
13. *Discount_Percent* is represented by a number from an interval <0, 1> (number of percent divided by 50);
14. *Extended_Weekend* is represented by a binary number {0, 1};
15. *Holidays* is represented by a binary number {0, 1};
16. *Alternative_Goods_In_Action* is represented by a binary number {0, 1}.

A format of the input vectors from the training set is shown in Table 3, which was created by transforming the data from Table 2.

Table 3. Input vectors of the training set

1.	2.	3.	4.	5.	6.	7.	8.	9.	10.	11.	12.	13.	14.	15.	16.
0.24316	0	0	0	0	0	1	0	1	0.09	0.3	0	0.4	0	0	1
0.24590	0	0	0	0	0	0	1	1	0.1	0.31	0	0.4	0	0	1
…	…	..	…	…	…	…	….	…	…	…	..	…	…	…	…

The training set relating to *COFFEE* included **729** patterns, the training set relating to *DECAF* included **728** patterns, **and** the training set relating to *ALCOHOL* included **460** patterns.

2.2 Setting the Parameters of the Neural Network for Experimental Part

In the experimental part, we worked with neural networks that were adapted by back-propagation [2] with the following parameters:

- 16 input neurons;
- 12 hidden neurons;
- 8 output neurons;
- learning rate 0.1–0.2;
- activation function – sigmoid;

Determination of the number of neurons in the input layer and output layer is based on the training set and it is fixed for the whole calculation. the determination of the number of neurons in the hidden layer used the Formula (2) from [5]:

$$N_{hidden} = \sqrt{N_{input} * N_{output}} \tag{2}$$

where

N_{hidden} is the number of neurons in the hidden layer,
N_{input} is the number of neurons in the input layer,
N_{output} is the number of neurons in the output layer.

Within the comparative experimental study were used backpropagation neural networks with the following parameters:

- 16 input neurons;
- 12 hidden neurons;
- 1 output neuron;
- learning rate 0.1–0.2;
- activation function – sigmoid.

The real values of sales x were normalized into the interval $\langle 0, 1\rangle$ according to the Formula (3)

$$x' = \frac{x - min}{max - min} \tag{3}$$

where x' is a normalized output value, *max* is the maximum value of sales of the given goods and *min* is the minimum value of sales of the given goods.

2.3 Experimental Results of a Sale Prediction

The test set included 957 patterns during the period 1 January 2015–31 December 2015. The test set relating to *COFFEE* included **333** patterns, the test set relating to *DECAF* included **361** patterns, **and** the test set relating to *ALCOHOL* included **263** patterns**. The** input and output vectors were transformed with the same procedure as in the case of the training set. The experimental results are shown in Figs. 5, 6 and 7. The success rate prediction *SR* was expressed in percentage according to the Formula (4):

$$SR = 100 * \left(1 - \frac{\sum_{i=1}^{pattern} \sum_{j=1}^{output} \left|x_{ij} - x'_{ij}\right|}{pattern * output}\right) \tag{4}$$

where *pattern* is the number of patterns, *output* the number of output neurons, x the real values of sales, and x' are predicted values of sales. The output values are represented by a number from an interval ⟨0, 1⟩. The success rate of prediction of individual neural networks is shown in Table 4. The presented values represent average values of 10 measurements. The best results were achieved with products whose sales have been in the tens and hundreds of pieces. In contrast, the worst results were achieved in goods, where the number of sold pieces was moving in units (e.g. alcohol).

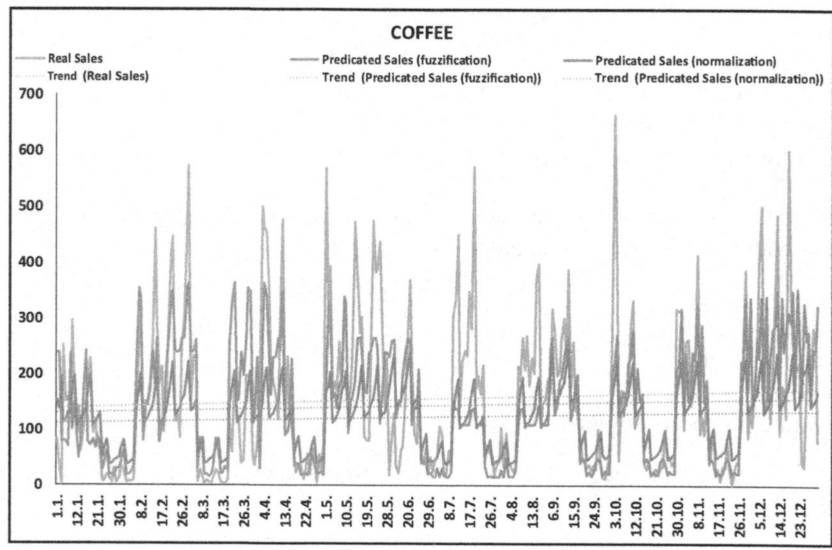

Fig. 5. Predictions of sales regarding *COFFEE* with a trend

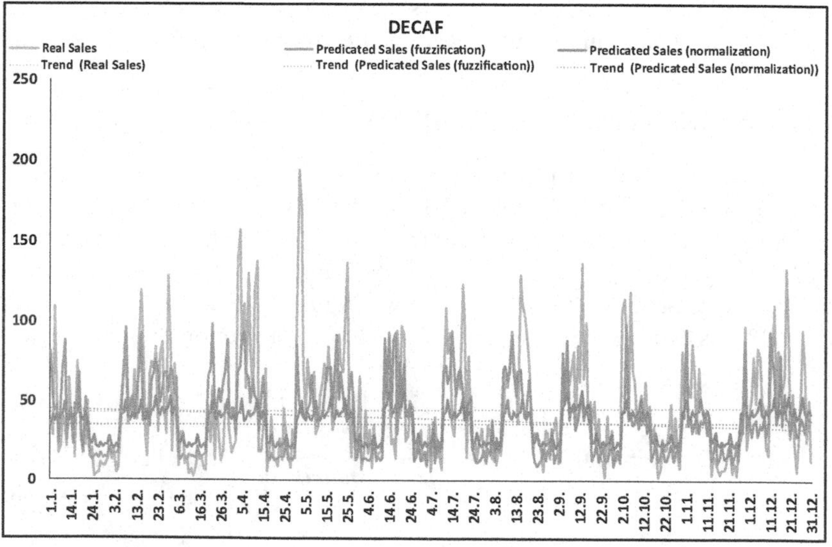

Fig. 6. Predictions of sales regarding *DECAF* with a trend

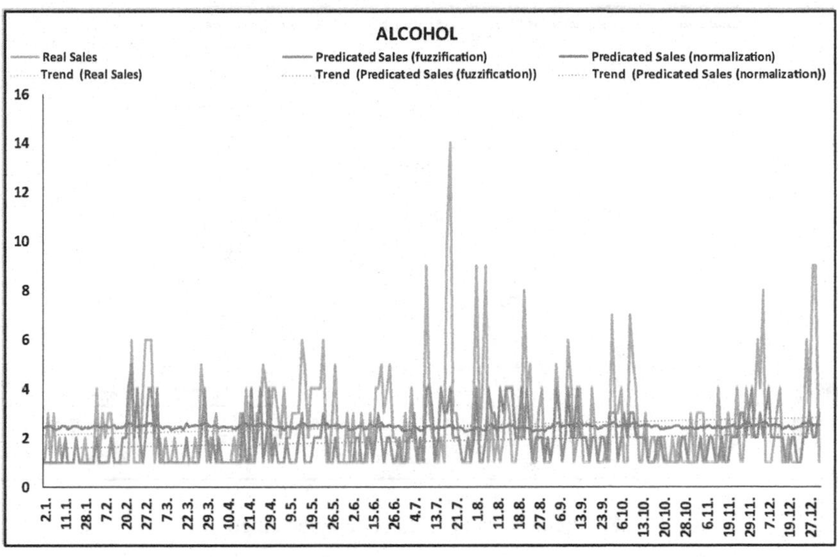

Fig. 7. Predictions of sales regarding *ALCOHOL* with a trend

Table 4. The prediction success of particular neural network models

	COFFEE	*DECAF*	*ALCOHOL*
Fuzzification of outputs	82.48975%	82.89648%	83.52076%
Normalization of outputs	65.30987%	67.94349%	58.12440%

This approach was tested on five different kinds of goods from selected assortments with very similar outputs.

3 Conclusion

This article presents a method of transformation of the input vector of the training set and a method of fuzzification of the output vector. According to the results of comparative experimental studies, which are shown in Figs. 5, 6 and 7 and in Table 4, it can be stated that the neural network which was adapted over fuzzification output vectors showed a significantly better prediction than the neural network which was adapted with a training set without transformations. An advantage of fuzzification is also the fact that only one neural network can be used for more goods, which is obvious from Fig. 8. In a situation where it is necessary to predict thousands of kinds of goods almost in real-time, this approach could be beneficial. In such a situation, the neural network would add information about specific goods, e.g. in the form of a unique code and only the input vector of the neural networks would be extended. The output vectors should consistently reflect sales independent of the particular goods.

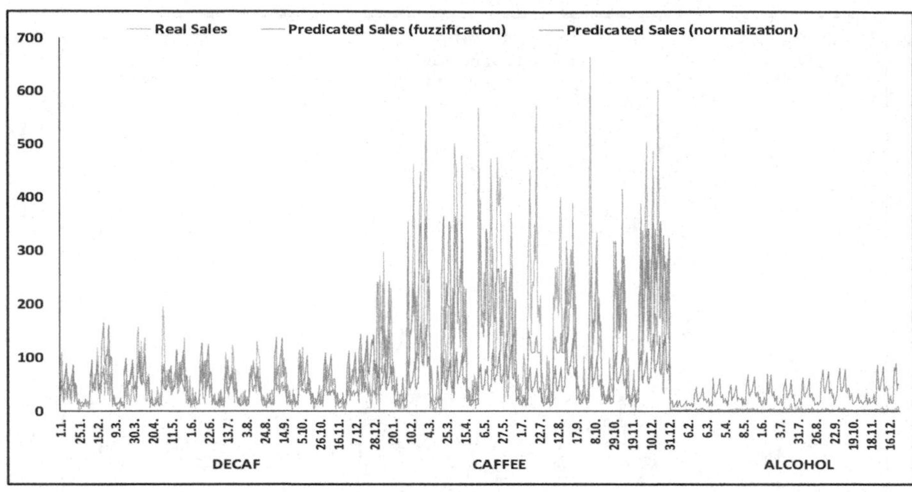

Fig. 8. Predictions of sales of all selected goods

It would also be very interesting to adapt only one neural network over all kinds of goods (this neural network would reflect global trends of sales) and thereafter for each type of goods to adapt a separate neural network (this neural network would reflect movements in sales for a specific goods). By comparing the results of these networks, it would be possible to detect anomalies in the sales of individual goods or global trend, e.g. declining sales of the shop without being dependent on sold goods. Our future work will be carried out in this direction.

Acknowledgments. The research described here has been financially supported by University of Ostrava grant SGS/PRF/2017.

References

1. Dvořák, A., Habiballa, H., Novák, V., Pavliska, V.: The concept of LFLC 2000 - its specificity, realization and power of applications. Comput. Ind. **51**(3), 269–280 (2003)
2. Fausett, L.V.: Fundamentals of Neural Networks. Prentice-Hall Inc., Englewood Cliffs (1994)
3. Rather, A.M., Agarwal, A., Sastry, V.N.: Recurrent neural network and a hybrid model for prediction of stock returns. Expert Syst. Appl. **42**(6), 3234–3241 (2015)
4. Janosek, M., Volna, E., Kotyrba, M.: Knowledge discovery in dynamic data using neural networks. Cluster Comput. **18**(4), 1411–1421 (2015)
5. Masters, T.: Practical Neural Networks Recipes in C++. Academic Press, San Diego (1993)
6. Pal, S.K., Pabitra, M.: Case generation using rough sets with fuzzy representation. IEEE Trans. Knowl. Data Eng. **16**(3), 293–300 (2004)
7. Rumsey, D.J.: Probability for dummies. Wiley, Hoboken (2006)
8. Singh, P.: Neuro-fuzzy hybridized model for seasonal rainfall forecasting: a case study in stock index forecasting. In: Bhattacharyya, S., Dutta, P., Chakraborty, S. (eds.) Hybrid Soft Computing Approaches. SCI, vol. 611, pp. 361–385. Springer, New Delhi (2016). doi: 10.1007/978-81-322-2544-7_12

9. Teoh, H.J., Cheng, C.H., Chu, H.H., Chen, J.S.: Fuzzy time series model based on probabilistic approach and rough set rule induction for empirical research in stock markets. Data Knowl. Eng. **67**(1), 103–117 (2008)
10. Yu, T.H.K., Huarng, K.H.: A bivariate fuzzy time series model to forecast the TAIEX. Expert Syst. Appl. **34**(4), 2945–2952 (2008)
11. Wei, L.Y.: A hybrid ANFIS model based on empirical mode decomposition for stock time series forecasting. Appl. Soft Comput. **42**, 368–376 (2016)

On the Impact of Imbalanced Data in Convolutional Neural Networks Performance

Francisco J. Pulgar(✉), Antonio J. Rivera, Francisco Charte, and María J. del Jesus

Depart of Computer Science, University of Jaén, Jaén, Spain
{fpulgar,arivera,fcharte,mjjesus}@ujaen.es
http://simidat.ujaen.es

Abstract. In recent years, new proposals have emerged for tackling the classification problem based on Deep Learning (DL) techniques. These proposals have shown good results in certain fields, such as image recognition. However, there are factors that must be analyzed to determine how they influence the results obtained by these new algorithms. In this paper, the classification of imbalanced data with convolutional neural networks (CNNs) is analyzed. To do this, a series of tests will be performed in which the classification of real images of traffic signals by CNNs will be performed based on data with different imbalance levels.

Keywords: Deep learning · Convolutional neural network · Image recognition · Imbalanced dataset

1 Introduction

Classification is one of the most widely studied tasks within automatic learning, the fundamental reason being its application to real cases. The objective is to obtain a model that allows the classification of new examples, starting from a set of examples that are correctly labeled [1]. Image classification is a problem that can be solved by applying a classifier.

In recent years, there has been a rise in the use of techniques based on Deep Learning to tackle the classification problem. This heyday was mainly due to two reasons: the large amount of data available and the increase in processing capacity. These DL techniques have provided good results in classification, especially in fields such as image and sound recognition [15,16].

One of the techniques that have obtained better results in the task of image recognition are convolutional neural networks (CNNs) [20]. Given the nature of the convolutions, these networks are able to learn to classify all the types of data where the attributes are distributed continuously along the entrance, as it is given in the images.

Despite the good results obtained with CNN, the fact that these techniques are very recent causes new factors to come into play. One of these is the need to analyze how data imbalance affects the classification performance of this type of

F.J. Martínez de Pisón et al. (Eds.): HAIS 2017, LNAI 10334, pp. 220–232, 2017.
DOI: 10.1007/978-3-319-59650-1_19

tool. Most real data sets show some imbalance degree, thus the importance of studying how this aspect influences classification performance.

Therefore, this study focuses on analyzing the effect of the imbalance of data in the classification of real images of traffic signals using CNN. Our starting hypothesis is that classification performance will improve as the imbalance level decreases. The reason for this hypothesis is a question of similarity with other techniques used in classification, since if the imbalance of data influences the quality of classification using techniques such as traditional neural networks, it could also influence the classification obtained through CNNs. Similarly, the nature of CNNs can be influenced by the imbalance, since the adjustment of the parameters can depend on the different number of examples of the classes.

This paper is structured as follows: Sect. 2 explains how imbalanced datasets influence classification. In Sect. 3 the DL concept is introduced and the CNNs which will be used to classify the images in the experimentation are analyzed in more detail. Section 4 exposes the hypothesis raised in this study. In Sect. 5 we attempt to verify the hypothesis established by CNN classification, starting from data with different degree of imbalance. Lastly, in Sect. 6 some conclusions are drawn.

2 The Imbalance Problem in Classification

Classification is a predictive task that usually uses supervised learning methods [2]. Its purpose is to learn, based on previously labeled data, patterns in order to predict the class to assign to future examples which are not labeled. In traditional classification, datasets are composed of a set of input features and a unique value in the output attribute, the class or label.

In many applications aimed at solving the classification problem there is a significant difference between the number of elements of the different classes, so the probability that an example belongs to each of those classes will also be different. This situation is known as the imbalance problem [3–5]. In many cases, the minority class is the one that has the most interest in the classification and has a greater cost in the case of not doing well.

Most of the standard classification algorithms obtain a good coverage when classifying the elements of the majority class, but the minority class is misclassified frequently. Therefore, these classification algorithms, which obtain good results for a traditional framework, will not necessarily work well with imbalanced data. There are several reasons for this:

- Many of the performance measures used to guide the overall procedure, such as the accuracy rate, disadvantage the minority class.
- The rules that predict the minority class are very specialized and their coverage very low, and therefore are usually discarded in favor of more general rules, that is, those that predict the majority class.
- The treatment of noise can affect the classification of minority classes since, such classes could be treated as noise and discarded erroneously or the actual noise may degrade the classification of the minority classes.

The main obstacle caused by this type of problem is that the classification algorithms are biased toward the majority class and there is a higher Error Rate when trying to classify the minority class. To face this problem, different proposals have emerged in the last years [6], which can be classified as:

- **Data sampling:** In this type of solution it is intended to modify the training set from which the classification algorithm starts. The objective is to obtain training data with a more balanced class distribution, so the classification can be performed in the standard way [7].
- **Algorithmic modification:** The objective pursued in this type of solution is to make an adaptation of the traditional classification algorithms in order to deal with the problem of imbalance in the data [8]. In these cases the data set is not modified, but it is the algorithm itself that adapts.
- **Cost-sensitive learning:** This type of solution can incorporate modifications both at the data level and at the algorithmic level, and is based on penalizing to a greater extent the mistakes made in classifying the minority classes than those committed when classifying the majority classes [9].

When dealing with imbalanced data, there are other factors of the same that must be taken into account, since they can greatly influence the results of the classification obtained. Some of these factors can be overlapping between the classes or noisy data.

3 Deep Learning

The need to extract higher-level information from the data analyzed through learning tools has led to the emergence of new areas of study, such as DL [10]. DL models are based on a deep architecture (multilayer) whose objective is to map the relationships between the characteristics of the data and the expected results [11]. There are some advantages to using DL-based techniques:

- DL models incorporate mechanisms for generating new characteristics by themselves, without having to develop them in an external phase.
- DL techniques improve yield in terms of time spent performing some of the more expensive tasks, such as feature engineering.
- DL-based models have proven successful in dealing with problems in certain fields such as image or sound recognition, improving over traditional techniques [15,16].
- DL-based solutions have a great ability to adapt to new problems.

Due to the good results obtained using DL-based proposals, recently different architectures have been developed, such as, CNN [17] or recurrent neural networks [18]. These architectures have been designed for multiple fields of application, producing very efficient results in the field of image recognition. In Sect. 3.1, we introduce CNN that will be used to perform the experimentation associated with this study.

3.1 Convolutional Neural Network

CNNs are a type of deep neural network based on the way some animals visualize. These networks have been shown to be very effective in certain areas such as image recognition and classification.

CNNs focus on the idea of spatial correlation by applying a series of local connectivity patterns between the neurons of the adjacent layers [19,20]. This implies that, unlike traditional networks where each neuron connects to all the neurons of the previous layer, in the CNNs each neuron only connects to a small region of the previous layer. Another fundamental difference is that the neurons of CNNs are arranged in three dimensions, whereas in the traditional networks they are realized in two dimensions. Figure 1 shows the difference between both types of networks.

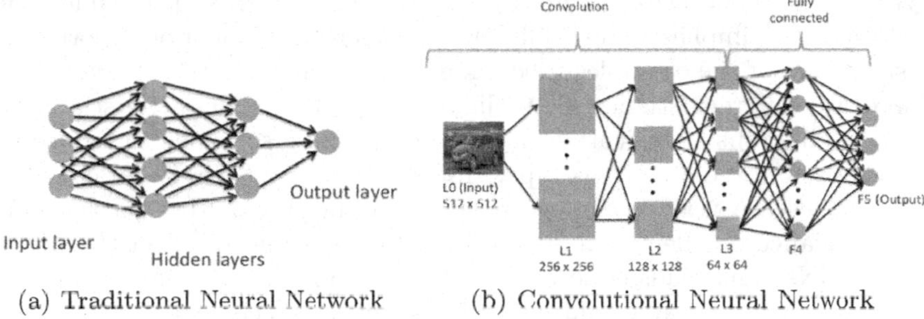

(a) Traditional Neural Network (b) Convolutional Neural Network

Fig. 1. Difference between traditional neural network and CNN.

The architecture of a CNN is based on a sequence of layers, each of them transforming a volume of activations to another by a certain function. There are three types of layers:

- **Convolution layer:** On this layer lies the majority of the computational weight. It is formed by a set of filters that must be learned during the process. Each filter is spatially small, ensuring local connectivity, and scrolls along the entire input, generating a global map of activations. In this way, it is possible for the network to learn filters that activate when there is some determined pattern, for example, edges or curves.
- **Pooling Layer:** This type of layer is normally inserted between several successive convolution layers. The fundamental objective is to reduce the spatial size of the representation by applying the function determined to each slice of the depth of the input independently. In this way a reduction of the height and width is performed but without modifying the depth of the representation. The functions that can be applied are of different types, for example, maximum or average.
- **Fully connected layer:** In this type of layer each of the neurons has complete connections to all the neurons of the anterior layer, differentiated thus from the convolutional layer in which it connects to a local region. The calculations that are performed are the same in both types of layers.

These types of layers that have been listed above are used to form a complex CNN. To do this, layers of different types are stacked according to the model to be constructed.

4 Impact of Imbalanced Data on Convolutional Neural Networks

Once the theoretical principles necessary to establish the bases of this study have been introduced the initial hypothesis is presented, as well as the reasons that lead to this hypothesis. Also, some elements used in the experimentation are presented.

Classification is usually applied to real data. Therefore, the characteristics of this type of data must be taken into account. One of these traits is the imbalance of the data, which implies a great difference between the number of majority and minority classes of the examples used, as we have seen in Sect. 2.

There are different studies [6–9] that show that this characteristic of the data affects different classification models and propose solutions to reduce the effects of classifying data of this type. However, because CNN-based classification techniques are very recent, we have not found any studies on the influence of imbalance on them. We assume that this feature can affect the performance of CNNs. This leads us to propose the initial hypothesis of the work: the classification results obtained through CNNs will be affected by the imbalance of the data.

Section 5 is intended to verify the proposed hypothesis. To do this, a CNN will be used to classify real images of traffic signals, performing different executions in which various sets of examples from the same dataset are used with a decreasing imbalance ratio (IR).

5 Experimentation

The objective of this study is to analyze whether the data imbalance can negatively influence the classification of images made by CNNs. To do this, a set of tests will be performed using data with a different degree of imbalance in them. These data correspond to real images of traffic signals [12], the objective being to correctly classify the signal according to its type. In order to perform the classification a CNN will be used. The network used will be the same for all the experiments performed. Also, it should be noted that no mechanism is used to minimize the effect of the imbalance, since it is intended to analyze how it affects the CNN classification.

5.1 Experimental Framework

In performing this experiment, a traffic signal dataset [12] with a total of 11 910 images belonging to 43 different types of signals or classes has been used. First, it is necessary to perform a pre-processing of the images. This phase has two fundamental objectives: on the one hand, to trim the image in order to select only the traffic signal (Fig. 2); and on the other hand, to scale the images so that all of them have the same size. In this sense, it has been decided to scale them to a size of 32×32 since it is the most widely used in other studies [19].

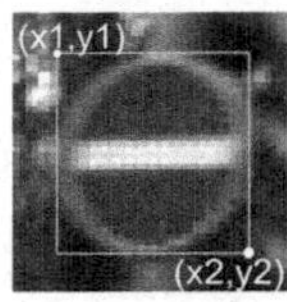

Fig. 2. Example of image crop (source: http://benchmark.ini.rub.de).

Once all the images included in the dataset have been pre-processed. The images corresponding to 10 classes have been selected in order to emphasize the imbalance between the data. Therefore, the classes selected have been the 5 with more examples and the 5 with fewer examples. In this way, we will obtain a subset of the original dataset.

An important aspect to keep in mind when working with imbalanced data is the IR. This measure is defined as the ratio between the number of examples of the majority class and the number of instances of the minority class [13,14].

Another aspect to be taken into account is that the number of images used in each experiment is the same even though the IR of the samples is different. This is important because if the number of examples varies significantly it can affect the results obtained, thus hiding the effects of the imbalance in them. In this way, it has been selected 2 700 images for each execution. The reason for selecting this value is given by the number of images of the minority classes in the original dataset, having 270 examples of the minority classes and about 2 700 of the majority. When balancing the dataset 270 images of each class are selected, so the total number of examples is 2 700, which is kept constant throughout all runs even if the IR changes.

Finally, it should be pointed out that in order to evaluate the efficiency in the classification of the CNN in each case, the Error Rate, Accuracy and Recall will be used.

5.2 CNN Architecture

Although the set of images used will change in distinct executions, the CNN used will be similar in all cases in order to see the effects of the different IRs. This CNN has an architecture whose sequence of layers is as follows:

- **Convolution layer 1:** 32 filters are applied on the original image. These filters are 5×5 size. This creates 32 feature maps.
- **Pooling layer 1:** 32 feature maps are subsampled using max pooling with a pooling window of size 2 and a stride of 2.
- **Convolution layer 2:** This layer applies 64 filters with a size of 5×5 to these subsampled images and generates new feature maps.

- **Pooling layer 2:** The previously generated features maps are subsampled. For this, max pooling with a window of size 2 and a stride of 2.
- **Fully connected layer:** In this layer all the generated features are combined and used in the classifier. This layer has as many individuals as classes have the problem.

In the training process, the cross-entropy error is used to evaluate the network and, later, the back-propagation is used to modify the weights of the network. The configuration chosen is the default setting used in the TensorFlow software[1], considering the initial size of the images and the different output values that the problem may have.

5.3 Results Analysis

In the experiments was carried out to classify the images through a CNN, starting from datasets different IR. In particular, four experiments with IR 1/10, 1/5, 1/3 and 1/1 were performed.

As mentioned in Sect. 5.1 the dataset used has a total of 11 910 images. However, it has also been indicated that each experiment must have a total of 2 700 images, with the aim that all experiments have the same number of examples. Therefore, the first step has been to reduce the number of images of each class proportionally and randomly, in order to reduce the desired number by maintaining the corresponding IR. So, the dataset presents the distribution of examples that can be seen in Table 1 for each case.

Table 1. Train and test examples per experimentation

Class	IR 1/10		IR 1/5		IR 1/3		IR 1/1	
	Train	Test	Train	Test	Train	Test	Train	Test
1	36	11	66	20	98	31	203	67
2	351	115	320	106	288	95	203	67
3	392	130	361	118	325	106	203	67
4	365	121	334	111	301	100	203	67
5	376	125	345	115	311	103	203	67
6	36	11	65	21	97	32	203	67
7	39	13	72	24	108	36	203	67
8	36	11	65	21	97	32	203	67
9	360	120	330	110	297	99	203	67
10	39	13	72	24	108	36	203	67
Total	2030	670	2030	670	2030	670	2030	670

[1] https://www.tensorflow.org/.

Table 1 shows the number of examples of each of the classes in the dataset for each experiment. It can be seen that there are a total of 2 700 images of which 2 030 will be used to train the network and 670 to evaluate the model in all cases. However, it can perceive how the ratio between examples of the majority and minority classes is different. The results obtained in each of the experiments are exposed below.

Results with IR 1/10

The first experiment was carried out to classify the images through a CNN, starting from a dataset with a high degree of imbalance between classes. Table 1 shows the number of examples of each of the classes in the dataset. Similarly, it can be seen how, in this first experiment, there is an IR of approximately 1/10 between the minority and majority classes. Once the dataset is set for experimentation, a CNN is used to perform the classification, obtaining the results presented in Tables 2 and 3.

Table 2 shows the number of test samples per class and the number of errors that the model has made in classifying these examples. Also, in Table 3 it can be seen the Error Rate, Recall and Precision by class. Both tables represent the results for the 4 experiments performed.

Table 2. Number of total and error examples in test per experimentation.

Class	IR 1/10		IR 1/5		IR 1/3		IR 1/1	
	Test	Error	Test	Error	Test	Error	Test	Error
1	11	4	20	4	31	2	67	1
2	115	1	106	3	95	2	67	0
3	130	1	118	2	106	2	67	3
4	121	2	111	0	100	2	67	0
5	125	0	115	2	103	0	67	0
6	11	4	21	2	32	2	67	0
7	13	2	24	0	36	0	67	0
8	11	4	21	1	32	0	67	0
9	120	1	110	1	99	1	67	1
10	13	3	24	0	36	0	67	3
Total	670	22	670	15	670	11	670	8

In this first experiment where the IR is 1/10, the results obtained show the Error Rate per class, with the percentage of global Error being 0.033, since 22 images of a total of 670 are classified badly. Also, the global Accuracy value is 0.963 and the global Recall value is 0.848. These results will serve as a basis for determining whether executions performed with lower imbalance improve them.

Table 3. Results for test dataset

Class	IR 1/10			IR 1/5			IR 1/3			IR 1/1		
	Error	Precision	Recall	Error	Precision	Recall	Error	Precision	Recall	Error	Precision	Recall
1	0.364	**1.000**	0.636	0.200	**1.000**	0.800	0.065	**1.000**	0.935	**0.015**	0.985	**0.985**
2	0.009	0.966	0.991	0.028	0.954	0.972	0.021	0.989	0.979	**0.000**	**1.000**	**1.000**
3	**0.008**	0.963	**0.992**	0.017	0.951	0.983	0.019	0.990	0.981	0.045	**1.000**	0.955
4	0.017	0.983	0.983	**0.000**	**1.000**	**1.000**	0.020	0.990	0.980	**0.000**	0.985	**1.000**
5	**0.000**	0.977	**1.000**	0.017	0.983	0.983	**0.000**	0.956	**1.000**	**0.000**	**0.985**	**1.000**
6	0.364	0.875	0.636	0.095	**1.000**	0.905	0.062	0.968	0.937	**0.000**	0.985	**1.000**
7	0.154	0.917	0.846	**0.000**	0.960	**1.000**	**0.000**	0.947	**1.000**	**0.000**	**1.000**	**1.000**
8	0.364	**1.000**	0.636	0.048	**1.000**	0.952	**0.000**	**1.000**	**1.000**	**0.000**	0.985	**1.000**
9	**0.008**	0.952	**0.992**	0.009	0.991	0.991	0.010	**1.000**	0.990	0.015	0.956	0.985
10	0.231	**1.000**	0.769	**0.000**	**1.000**	**1.000**	**0.000**	**1.000**	**1.000**	0.045	**1.000**	0.955
Total	0.033	0.963	0.848	0.022	0.984	0.958	0.016	0.984	0.980	**0.012**	**0.988**	**0.988**

Results with IR 1/5

The next step is to perform a new execution with a lower IR in concrete, reducing the IR to 1/5. To do this, the first step is to start from the initial dataset that has 11 910 images, and then perform a random deletion of 50% of examples of all major classes. This way we get a dataset with 6 510 images. Once this is done only 2 700 images should be selected, so that all experiments have a similar number.

In Table 1 can be seen as the number of examples per class for this experiment and can be checked that the IR is 1/5. The results obtained from the CNN with this new distribution of examples in the dataset can be seen in Tables 2 and 3.

These results obtained with an IR 1/5 show a decrease of the Error Rate with respect to the experimentation realized with a IR 1/10. The Error value obtained is 0.022, since 15 images of a total of 670 are classified badly. Also, the results show an increase in both Accuracy and Recall. The global Accuracy value obtained is 0.984 and the global Recall value is 0.958. These results reinforce the initial idea, so the next step is to continue to reduce the IR to verify if the improvement is broadened.

Results with IR 1/3

In order to continue to verify the initial hypothesis, the following experimentation focuses on reducing the IR to 1/3. Therefore, starting from the initial dataset with 11 910 images, a random selection of 30% of the examples of each of the majority classes is performed, obtaining a dataset with 4 350 images. Once this is done, and in order to perform all executions with the same number of examples, 2 700 images of that set are selected.

In Table 1, it can be verified that the distribution of examples per class for this experiment has an IR of 1/3, since a greater reduction of the examples of the majority classes has been performed. From this new distribution of the dataset examples, the results shown in the Tables 2 and 3 are obtained using a CNN.

Observing the results for this experiment with an IR value of 1/3, it can be seen that the results continue to improve previous experiments. In this case, a global Error of 0.016 is obtained, since 11 images of a total of 670 are classified badly. Also, the global Accuracy is 0.984 and the global Recall is 0.980. It can be seen that the trend continues to confirm that as the IR of the dataset decreases the classification results obtained through CNN improve. This fact confirms the initial hypothesis, and therefore, it gives rise to a last experiment in which the dataset is completely balanced.

Results with IR 1/1

The objective of the last test is, as it has been mentioned before, to verify the behavior of the CNN starting from a balanced dataset with IR 1/1. Therefore, the first step is to balance the initial dataset of 11 910 images. In order to do so the class with the fewest number of examples is selected and randomly delete examples of the rest of the classes until they match them. In this way, in order to perform the experimentation a dataset with 2 700 images is obtained with the distribution by class that is shown in Table 1.

Tables 2 and 3 show the results obtained using a CNN with the balanced dataset. In this case, the percentage of global Error is 0.012, since 8 images of a total of 670 are classified badly, the global Accuracy is 0.988 and the global Recall is 0.988. These results improve again to those obtained in previous experiments, which confirms the initial hypothesis, since as the imbalance decreases, better results are obtained.

Results Discussion

In the previous subsections, the initial hypothesis established in this study has been confirmed. Next, a visual representation of the results is shown through the Figs. 3 and 4 and a discussion of these results is made.

On the one hand, Fig. 3 shows the Error obtained by class for each of the experiments performed, it can be seen as in all cases, except class 3 and 9, the results obtained with the balanced dataset are the best. On the other hand, Fig. 4 shows the mean Error for each experiment, it can be seen that as IR decreases, better results are obtained.

Analyzing the presented results, different conclusions can be drawn. From the point of view of the overall results, it can be seen that the reduction of the degree of imbalance causes better results to be obtained when classifying with CNN, which confirms the initial hypothesis proposed in this study. If a class-to-class analysis is conducted, it can be seen that the best results are obtained with the balanced dataset for most classes. There are 2 exceptions, meaning classes 3 and 9, where the imbalanced dataset obtains better results. The explanation for this is that both classes are majority classes, so the imbalanced dataset has a greater number of examples of them than the balanced dataset, a fact that affects the classification.

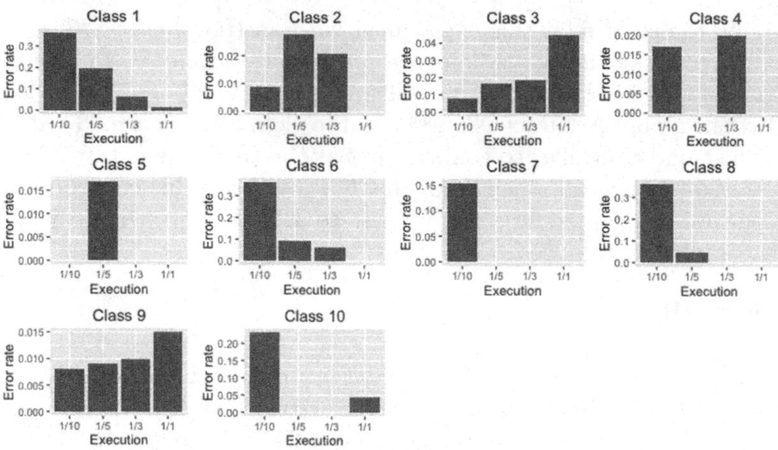

Fig. 3. Error rate for class and execution.

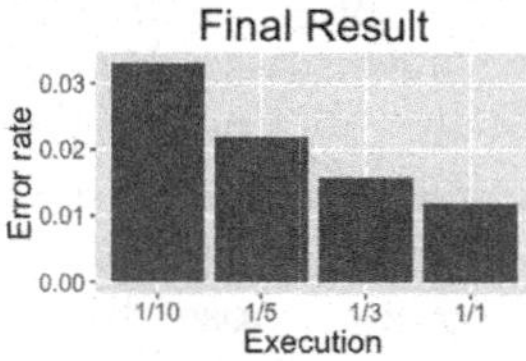

Fig. 4. Average error rate for execution.

Once the results are seen, it can be said that one of the aspects that could most affect the classification is the calculation of weights of the last layer of the network, the fully connected layer that determines the class in a last supervised phase, since the weights obtained could prioritize the majority classes with respect to the minority classes.

Another characteristic of the CNN that could influence the classification is the calculation of the weights corresponding to the different filters in the convolutional layers. These filters move along the different inputs, modifying the weights throughout the process, so that these weights could be overly adapted to the majority classes in cases where there is a greater imbalance. Both this conclusion and the previous one open new avenues of study, with the aim of verifying whether they are fulfilled by a more detailed study.

6 Conclusions

One of the problems that usually arises when trying to tackle the task of classification based on real data is that the data are not balanced, which negatively affects the results obtained with most of the classification models. In this study, a series of tests have been carried out with the aim of demonstrating that this problem also affects the classification by means of CNN.

Tests have shown how, as the imbalance between the data used to classify is minimized, the results obtained through CNN are better. Thus, the hypothesis initially established is fulfilled. These results imply that the distribution of the data must be taken into account when using this type of technique to classify images, since an excessive imbalance can negatively influence the results obtained.

The results derived from this study open up new possibilities for future work. A first approximation to the solution of the problem derived from the use of data intrinsically imbalanced with CNN is the application of classical methods: resampling techniques, cost-sensitive learning or ensembles methods. These techniques aim to reduce the effects of imbalance on the classification algorithms applied later. There is also the possibility of creating new models that combine traditional techniques that face the imbalance with CNN to perform the classification.

However, this is a first approximation to the problem performed with a particular dataset and a given technique, and this fact must be analyzed in more detail in future work.

Acknowledgments. The work of F. Pulgar was supported by the University of Jaén under the Action 15: Predoctoral aids for the encouragement of the doctorate. This work was partially supported by the Spanish Ministry of Science and Technology under project TIN2015-68454-R.

References

1. Duda, R., Hart, P., Stork, D.: Pattern Classification, 2nd edn. Wiley, USA (2000)
2. Kotsiantis, S.: Supervised machine learning: a review of classification techniques. In: Proceedings of the 2007 Conference on Emerging Artificial Intelligence Applications in Computer Engineering: Real Word AI Systems with Applications in eHealth, HCI, Information Retrieval and Pervasive Technologies, pp. 3–24 (2007)
3. Chawla, N.V., Japkowicz, N., Kotcz, A.: Editorial: special issue on learning from imbalanced data sets. SIGKDD Explor. **6**(1), 1–6 (2004)
4. He, H., García, E.A.: Learning from imbalanced data. IEEE Trans. Knowl. Data Eng. **21**(9), 1263–1284 (2009)
5. Sun, Y., Wong, A.K.C., Kamel, M.S.: Classification of imbalanced data: a review. Int. J. Pattern Recogn. Artif. Intell. **23**(4), 687–719 (2009)
6. Galar, M., Fernández, A., Barrenechea, E., Bustince, H., Herrera, F.: A review on ensembles for class imbalance problem: bagging, boosting and hybrid based approaches. IEEE Trans. Syst. Man Cybern. Part C: Appl. Rev. **42**(4), 463–484 (2012)
7. Batista, G.E.A.P.A., Prati, R.C., Monard, M.C.: A study of the behaviour of several methods for balancing machine learning training data. SIGKDD Explor. **6**(1), 20–29 (2004)
8. Zadrozny, B., Elkan, C.: Learning and making decisions when costs and probabilities are both unknown. In: Proceedings of the 7th International Conference on Knowledge Discovery and Data Mining (KDD01), pp. 204–213 (2001)
9. Zadrozny, B., Langford, J., Abe, N.: Costsensitive learning by costproportionate example weighting. In: Proceedings of the 3rd IEEE International Conference on Data Mining (ICDM03), pp. 435–442 (2003)

10. Bengio, Y., Courville, A., Vincent, P.: Representation learning: a review and new perspectives. IEE Trans. Pattern Anal. Mach. Intell. **3**(8), 1798–1828 (2013)
11. Goodfellow, I., Bengio, Y., Courville, A.: Deep learning (2016)
12. Stallkamp, J., Schlipsing, M., Salmen, J., Igel, C.: Man vs. Computer. Neural Netw. **32**, 323–332 (2012)
13. García, V., Sánchez, J.S., Mollineda, R.A.: On the effectiveness of preprocessing methods when dealing with different levels of class imbalance. Knowl. Based Syst. **25**(1), 13–21 (2012)
14. Orriols-Puig, A., Bernad-Mansilla, E.: Evolutionary rule-based systems for imbalanced datasets. Soft Comput. **13**(3), 213–225 (2009)
15. Ciresan, D., Meier, U., Schmidhuber, J.: Multi-column deep neural networks for image classification, Technical Report No. IDSIA-04-12 (2012)
16. McMillan, R.L.: How Skype used AI to build its amazing new language translator, wire (2014)
17. LeCun, Y., Bengio, Y.: Convolutional networks for images, speech, and time-series. In: Arbib, M.A. (ed.) The Handbook of Brain Theory and Neural Networks (1995)
18. Sak, H., Senior, A., Beaufays, F.: Long short-term memory recurrent neural network architectures for large scale acoustic modeling. In: Proceedings of Interspeech, pp. 338–342 (2013)
19. Sermanet, P., LeCun, Y.: Traffic sign recognition with multi-scale convolutional networks. In: Proceedings of International Joint Conference on Neural Networks (2011)
20. LeCun, Y., Kavukcuoglu, K., Farabet, C.: Convolutional networks and applications in vision. In: Proceedings of 2010 IEEE International Symposium on in Circuits and Systems (ISCAS), pp. 253–256 (2010)

Effectiveness of Basic and Advanced Sampling Strategies on the Classification of Imbalanced Data. A Comparative Study Using Classical and Novel Metrics

Mohamed S. Kraiem(✉) and María N. Moreno

Department of Computing and Automation, University of Salamanca, Plaza de los Caídos s/n, 37008 Salamanca, Spain
ing_kriem@yahoo.com

Abstract. The imbalanced class problem is noteworthy given its impact on the induction of predictive models and its constant presence in several application areas. It is a challenge in supervised classification, since most of classifiers are very sensitive to class distributions. Consequently, the predictive model is biased to the majority class, which leads to a low performance. In this paper, we analyze the reliability of resampling strategies through the influence of some factors such as dataset characteristics and the classifiers used for building the models, in order to improve the performance and determine which resampling method will be used according to these factors. Experiments over 24 real datasets with different imbalance ratio, using six different classifiers, seven resampling algorithms and six performance evaluation measures have been conducted aiming at showing which resampling method will be the most suitable depending on these factors.

1 Introduction

Class imbalance is one of the focus topics of many researchers because of its importance and its occurrence in many fields. A dataset containing instances of two classes is said to be imbalanced if one of the classes (the minority one) is represented by a small number of instances in comparison to other class (the majority one) [1]. This type of problem is known as the class imbalance problem and its solution is a challenge in supervised classification. Most of machine learning algorithms are very sensitive to class distributions because the outcome of the prediction model is biased to the majority class and thus the precision for the minority class is usually significantly lower than the precision for the majority class. To address this situation many proposals have been made at level of datasets as well as at level of algorithms. The first can be considered a hybrid approach since the combination of machine learning algorithms with some kind of sampling technique is necessary. Resampling the dataset either replicating the number of minority class examples (oversampling) or removing examples of the majority class (undersampling) is a usual strategy. Other approaches are the combination of ensembles with sampling processing techniques, cost sensitive methods that consider the misclassification costs and algorithm modification for imbalanced data processing.

F.J. Martínez de Pisón et al. (Eds.): HAIS 2017, LNAI 10334, pp. 233–245, 2017.
DOI: 10.1007/978-3-319-59650-1_20

The goal of our work is to conduct a study where the effects of some factors such as imbalanced ratio and machine learning algorithms are analyzed to determine which resampling method will be used to improve the performance according to the influence of these factors. The most commonly used evaluation metrics are applied to compare the results of the models induced from imbalanced datasets that are preprocessed by mean of basic and advanced sampling strategies. In addition, two new performance measures are used in the study: optimized precision and generalized index of balanced accuracy proposed by Ramayana Palade [16] and Garcia et al. [9] respectively.

This paper is organized as following: Some related works are introduced in Sect. 2. Section 3 includes the definition of the basic and advanced resampling strategies tested in the study. In Sect. 4, the metrics used for evaluating the models are presented. The description of the experimental study and the results are given in Sects. 5 and 6 respectively. Finally Sect. 7 is devoted to summarize our conclusions.

2 Related Work

The utility and the quality of each resampling techniques depends on various factors as suggested in [21], including the imbalance ratio between the majority and the minority classes, the characteristics of data sets and the applied classifiers. The effect of the imbalance ratio factor disappears based in the selection and usage of suitable resampling strategy, which can be denoted by obtaining high classifier performance. The effects that prevent from achieving high classifiers performance have been analyzed in previous studies, most of them focused on some lonely factors (data sets, performance metric, resampling strategies), but disregarding the effect of other factors.

Japkowicz and Stephen [22] discussed the performance of random under sampling method and random over sampling method by applying C5.0 decision tree classifier. The impact of some of the factors mentioned above has been analyzed in other previous studies for a specific kind of classifiers [17], but without taking into account their influence on the performance of other types of models. Although there are some others studies about resampling strategies, in these studies the authors do not determine which resampling strategy is the best in general terms, according to specific datasets characteristics and machine learning techniques.

In our study, we concern the relationship between dataset characteristics, learning algorithm and sampling methods. We have studied the behavior of classifiers induced by commonly used machine learning algorithms from very different datasets, each of which is treated with several resampling methods. The goal of the study is to provide a reference that helps to select the best sampling strategy under different conditions.

3 Basic and Advanced Resampling Strategies

3.1 Basic Resampling Strategies

A common approach for dealing with imbalanced data problem is sampling handling. The key idea is to preprocess the dataset to increase or reduce the number of instances in order to minimize the differences between the numbers of instances belonging to each class and to obtain balanced datasets. There are three kinds of strategies, under-sampling, over-sampling and hybrid-sampling. In the first one, instances of the majority class are removed to achieve a balanced distribution of classes. Through this method high percent of data will be lost especially when the imbalance ratio between the majority and the minority class is high. Over-sampling is an approach that increases the number of instances of the minority class by duplicating observations of this class. As the replication of the observations increases the size of the dataset, the required time to build the model increases. In addition, the increasing of the training set can lead to a situation of over-fitting. Under-sampling and over sampling techniques have been tested and studied in different research works concerning learning with decision tree algorithm [5, 6]. The findings of these studies are similar: under-sampling leads to the best result, while over-sampling produces little changes in the performance. In hybrid-sampling, under and over-sampling procedures are combined in different ways

3.2 Advanced Resampling Strategies

In order to avoid some of the problems presented by basic strategies, advanced approaches have been proposed. Some of them are described below.

SMOTE (Synthetic Minority Over-Sampling Technique) is an advanced method for oversampling, proposed by Chawla et al. [2]. This method aims to make the decision border of the minority class more general as well as to prevent over-fitting problem. The procedure involves the generation of new training instances in the minority class by interpolating the existing ones. The procedure involves the identification of the k nearest neighbor for each training instance x of the minority class and the random choice of one (or more) of the neighbors. After that, a random point along the line segment between the instance x and the nearest neighbor is selected and added as a new instance to the training set. SMOTE is an algorithm especially efficient for high imbalanced ratio datasets. High performance of imbalanced datasets can be obtained when combining under-sampling techniques with SMOTE strategy [2].

Tomek Link (T-Link) is another strategy proposed by Ivan Tomek in 1976 as a way of enhancing the nearest neighbor rule. The Tomek link procedure considers two training instances x and y from different classes. The distance between these two instances is denoted by $d(x, y)$, where the values of $d(x, y)$ is called T-link if there is not an instance $z | d(x, y) < d(x, z) \; or \; d(y, z) < d(x, y)$. If two instances are a T-link, then either one of them is as a noise or both of them are in the border of the classes. T-link can be used as a guide for under-sampling or as a technique for data cleaning where the training instances from the majority class are removed. Since T-Link is not specifically designed to return balanced data, in the present paper we will combine SMOTE strategy with T-link method.

One sided selection (OOS) is an under-sampling technique proposed by Kubat and Matwin [4]. In it, D is assumed to be the original dataset. Initially, P contains all positive examples (minority class) from D and one randomly selected negative example (majority class). D is classified with the 1-NN rule by using the examples in P and compare the assigned labels with the original ones. Then, all misclassified examples are moved into P that is now consistent with D while being smaller. All negative examples participating in Tomek links are remove from P. This removes those negative examples that are believed borderline and/or noisy. All positive examples are retained. OSS is an algorithm especially efficient for low imbalanced datasets and inefficient for high imbalanced datasets when it is used in an alone way. In the Present paper we will combine SMOTE with OSS method.

Neighborhood Cleaning Rule (NCL) [3] is an under-sampling technique that uses the Wilson's Edited nearest neighbor rule ENN [13] to identify noise data and remove some training instances from the majority class. The ENN rule identifies the three nearest neighbor (3NN) of each training instance then it removes examples whose class differs from the majority class of at least two of its three NN. Similarly, in the present paper we will combine SMOTE with NCL method.

The condensed Nearest Neighbor rule (CNN) was proposed by Hart (1968) [7] as a method to reduce the storage requirements of the original dataset for the efficient implementation of the nearest neighbor decision rule in pattern classification problems [10]. The basic idea for the rule is: let D denote the original dataset and E the resulting condensed set. The basic idea is to pick an arbitrary point from D and place it in an original empty set E. Then the remaining points in D are classified by the NN-rule using E and those that are classified incorrectly are added to E.

Some modifications of the CNN rule have been proposed by Tomek [10] and Wilson [12]. By preprocessing the data before applying the CNN rule, significant reduction in the storage required can be achieved, while maintaining a low classification error rate [13]. Tomek argues that CNN rule keeps to many points that are not near to the decision boundary because of its arbitrary initialization step. In order to combat this issue, he proposes as his second modification of CNN rule a preliminary pass of D to select a special subset of D called C. Then his method works in the same manner as CNN rule but instead of moving to E data points from the complete D, only data points from C are used.

4 Performance Measures

There are several metrics that allow validate the performance of the predictive models. In binary class problems, there are several types of classifier errors: TP (number of positive examples that are corre̡ctly identified as positive), FN (number of positive examples incorrectly classified as negative), FP (number of negative examples incorrectly classified as positive) and (number of negative examples correctly classified).

The most commonly measure used to evaluate the performance of classifiers is accuracy, but this metric is not suitable when dealing with an imbalanced class datasets. Therefore, other measures need to be considered, which take into account the classification performance of each class independently.

Sensitivity (or recall) and specificity are measures usually adopted to monitor the classification performance on each class separately. The sensitivity, also called true positive rate (TP rate), is the percentage of positive examples that are correctly classified while specificity, also referred to as true negative rate (TN rate), is defined as the proportion of negative examples that are correctly classified.

$$\text{TP rate} = \frac{TP}{TP + FN} \tag{1}$$

$$\text{TN rate} = \frac{TN}{TN + FP} \tag{2}$$

Similarly, the false positive rate (FP rate) and false negative rate (FN rate) are defined:

$$\text{FP rate} = \frac{FP}{TN + FP} \tag{3}$$

$$\text{FN rate} = \frac{FN}{TP + FN} \tag{4}$$

Another measure that is applied to each class separately is precision.

$$\text{Precision} = \frac{TP}{TP + FP} \tag{5}$$

A metric that indicates model performance for each class is F-Measure.

$$\text{F-Measure} = (1 + \beta^2).\frac{Recallxprecision}{(\beta^2 xprecision) + Recall} \tag{6}$$

Where β is the coefficient to adjust the relative importance of precision versus the recall, β is usually set to 1.

Another important performance measure to evaluate classifier on the skew data is G-mean [4]. The idea of G-mean is to test the accuracy on each class by taking the geometric mean of both TP rate and TN rate together (Eq. 8). A low score for G-mean indicates a classifier that is highly biased towards one single class and vice versa. The G-mean score is high when both rates are high.

$$\text{G-mean} = \sqrt{TPrate * TNrate} \tag{7}$$

One of the most popular techniques for the evaluation of classifiers performance in imbalanced data problems is the Receiver Operating Characteristic (ROC) curve [14]. The idea is to represent the performance of classifiers by visualizing the trade-off between true positive rate (T Prate) and false positive rate (FP rate). The perfect performance is obtained when the model achieves 1 for the true positive rate and 0 for the false positive rate. The quantitative representation of a ROC curve is the area under it, known as AUC [15]. The AUC can be computed by using the following equation

$$\text{AUC} = \frac{1 + TPrate - FPrate}{2} \tag{8}$$

AUC and G-mean neglected the negative effect of skewed class, they did not take into account the efficiency of each class.

To remedy this deficiency Ranawana and Palade [16] proposed a new metric called optimized precision (OP).

$$\mathrm{OP} = \mathrm{Accuracy} - \frac{|TNrate - TPrate|}{TNrate + TPrate} \tag{9}$$

The best score for OP is achieved when true negative rate and true positive rate are very close to each other with high overall accuracy.

Recently, Garcia et al. [9] proposed a new performance measure called Generalized Index of Balanced Accuracy (IBA), which can be used and defined for any performance metric (m) as:

$$\mathrm{IBA}\,\alpha(m) = (1 + \alpha \cdot Dom) \cdot m \tag{10}$$

Where *Dom* is an index called dominance that is defined as:

$$(Dom = TPrate - TNrate) \tag{11}$$

The Dom values are within the range $[-1, +1]$, the best value for the Dom when the true positive rate and true negative rate are approximately equal, which produces a value of Dom close to zero. Value of Dom close to zero is good indicator that TP rate and TN rate are completely balanced. In general the value of Dom is weighted by ($\alpha \geq 0$) to reduce its influence on the result of the metric used (m). In practice, the selection of the α value is sensitive and depends on the metric used [8]. The value of α effects to the accurate of overall IBA result, that is the reason why α must be selected properly.

5 Experimental Study

This comparative study aims at determining the best learning algorithm and resampling strategy depending on the characteristics of the datasets.

We checked the effectiveness of several classifiers induced by well-known and popular machine learning paradigms: K-nearest neighbor (KNN) [18], Naïve Bayes [18], Support Vector Machine (SVM) [18], Decision Tree family algorithms (Random Forest, J48 and C5.0) [18]. They were applied over multiple datasets preprocessed by means of the resampling methods described in Sect. 3 in order to determine which classifier and sampling approach present the best behavior for each dataset.

Another goal of this study was to determine the best sampling strategy given a specific classifier and considering the imbalance ratio of the datasets. Therefore, we first compared the effectiveness of the sampling methods when using Random Forest with all datasets and then we analyzed their effect regarding the imbalanced ratio factor. The metrics used in the analysis were classical ones (area under the ROC curve, precision, recall, G-mean and F-measure) and new ones (optimized precision and index of balanced accuracy, which are described in the previous section.

As part of the validation process, we analyzed the statistical significance of the differences between the results produced by the classifiers in the conducted experiments. Non-parametric tests and post-hoc tests are suggested in [19, 20] as statistical tests for algorithms or classifiers performance comparison. We performed Friedman's test because it is more popular and more powerful than other procedures in case of multiple datasets and multiple algorithms.

In all experiments carried out to validate the performance of the classifiers, the training sets included 70% of the total instances and the test set the remainder 30% of them.

6 Experimental Results

6.1 Datasets

There is no consensus in the research community about when a dataset is considered imbalanced. In this paper, we consider a dataset to be imbalanced when imbalance ratio (IR) higher than 1.5.

Table 1. Summary of imbalanced datasets used

Data sets	#inst	#attrib	IR
Glass1	214	9	1.82
Iris0	150	4	2.00
Yeast1	1484	8	2.46
Vehicle3	846	18	2.99
Ecoli1	636	7	3.36
New-Thyroid1	215	5	5.14
Glass6	214	9	6.38
Page-Block0	5472	10	8.79
Glass-0-1-6_Vs_2	192	9	10.29
Glass2	214	9	11.59
Shuttle-C0-Vs-C4	1829	9	13.87
Infection	4615	15	13.89
Page-Blocks-1-3_Vs_4	472	10	15.86
Glass-0-1-6-Vs-5	184	9	19.44
Yeast4	1484	8	28.10
Yeast5	1484	8	32.73
Wineqlty-White3vs7	900	11	44.00
Wineqlty-Red8vs-6-7	855	11	46.50
Wineqlty-White39-Vs5	1482	11	58.28
Shuttle2-Vs-5	3316	9	66.67
Abalone20vs8910	1915	8	72.69
Poker-8-9-Vs-5	2075	10	82.00
Poker-8-Vs-6	1477	10	85.88
Abalone19	4174	8	129.44

According to these criteria, a great variety of imbalanced datasets have been used in this study in order to achieve the objectives described in the preceding section. They have been selected from different sources. The dataset *Infection* contains clinical information from patients hospitalized in one intensive care unit. The other twenty three datasets have been taken from the KEEL dataset repository.

The characteristics of the datasets are summarized in Table 1, where the number of instances (#inst), number of attributes (#attrib) and IR of all them are presented. This table is in ascending order according to the imbalanced ratio (IR).

6.2 Applying Resampling Strategies and Machine Learning Algorithms

The first goal of this work is to compare the results of the six learning algorithms referred in the previous section when they were applied to the 24 datasets preprocessed by means of different resampling methods. Initially, we obtained the AUC metric to evaluate the performance of the classifiers.

We conducted seven experiments, one per each sampling technique (RUS, ROS, SMOTE, SMOTE+OOS, SMOTE+Tomek link, SMOTE+CNN and SMOTE+NCL). Therefore, we obtained 1008 values of AUC, corresponding to the seven experiments where six classification algorithms were applied over 24 different datasets. Given the limitation of space, only a summary of these results is presented in the paper.

Figure 1 shows the average of the AUC values obtained for all the datasets after applying the algorithms: K-nearest neighbor (KNN), Naïve Bayes (NB), Support Vector Machine (SVM), Random Forest (RF), J48 and C5.0.

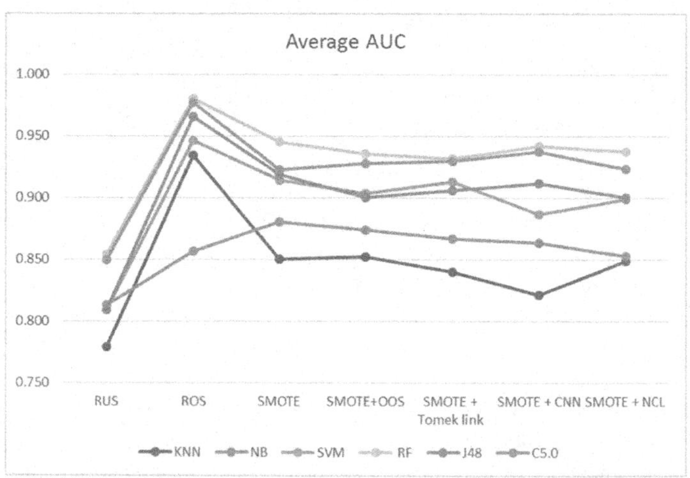

Fig. 1. Average AUC yielded by different classifiers and sampling methods. (Color figure online)

As we can see in the figure, the Random Forest algorithm (yellow line) provides the best values of AUC for all sampling methods. On the other hand, ROS is the best sampling technique for all classifiers with the only exception of Naïve Bayes.

6.3 Statistical Comparison of Classifiers Over Multiple Datasets

Friedman's test was used to perform multiple comparisons aiming at detecting significant differences between the results coming from the classifiers obtained from multiple datasets.

Figure 2 shows post-hoc results using CD (critical distance diagrams) and Fig. 3 shows them using algorithms graph plots, which present the order of classifiers in terms of their AUC. In a CD diagram the classifier in the left extreme is the best. In algorithm graph plots, the best classifiers are denoted by green color. Statistical tests confirm the significant best behavior of Random forest.

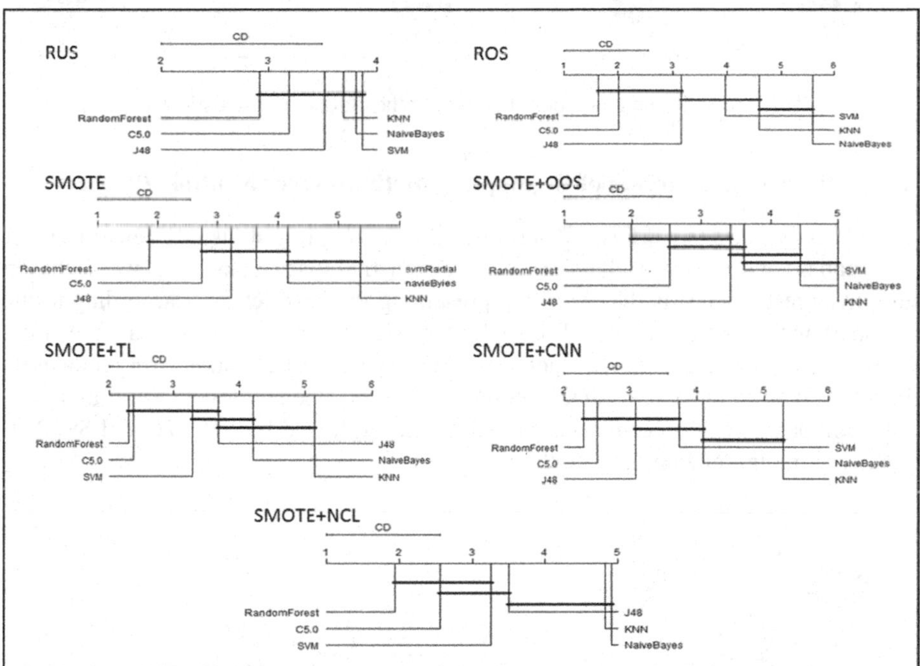

Fig. 2. CD plots for classifiers comparison obtained in the experiments.

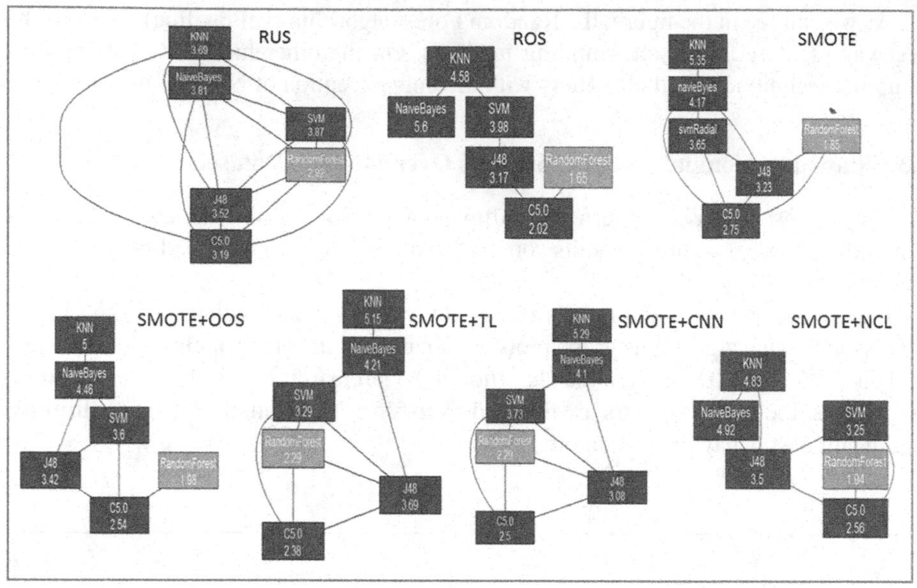

Fig. 3. Algorithms graph plots containing the outcome of statistical tests.

6.4 Statistical Comparison of Resampling Methods Over Multiple Datasets

The second goal of this work is to determine the best sampling strategy given a classifier and a dataset with certain characteristics. Given the space constraint, we focus on Random Forest since it is the algorithm presenting the best behavior according to the previously reported experiments. We applied the significance test to compare the effectiveness of resampling methods when using Random Forest classifier over all datasets (Fig. 4). Test outcome reveals that ROS presents the best behavior with a minimum CD (2.58) compared with other resampling strategies, followed by SMOTE and SMOTE combined with under sampling methods.

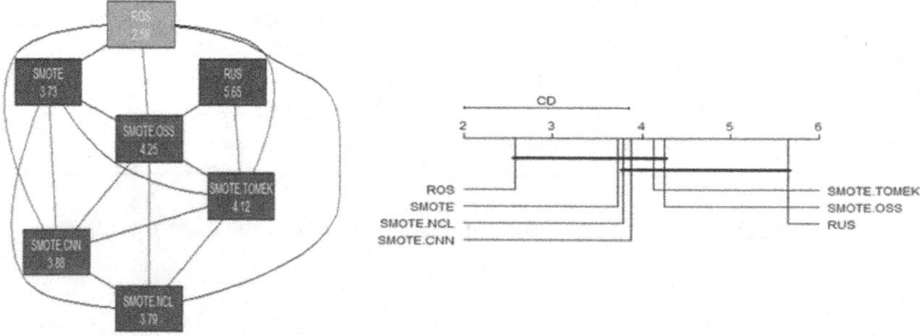

Fig. 4. Statistical test outcome of resampling methods comparison

To complete our study, we analyzed the effectiveness of the sampling approaches regarding the dataset imbalance ratio and taking as reference the Random Forest classifier. Besides AUC, some classical validation metrics as precision, recall, G-mean and F-measure were applied. In addition, two new performance measures were used: optimized precision (OP) and generalized index of balanced accuracy (IBA).

The results of this analysis is summarized in Fig. 5 by means of two Kiviat diagrams. In the figure on the left, the values of AUC are represented in the radial axis, the values of the imbalance ratio for every dataset are placed outside of the external circle, and the sampling strategies are denoted as lines in different colors. We can observe that ROS method produces the best results for high imbalanced datasets while the remainder techniques have a similar performance for low imbalance ratios, with the exception of RUS that has an unequal behavior, which is very poor for some datasets.

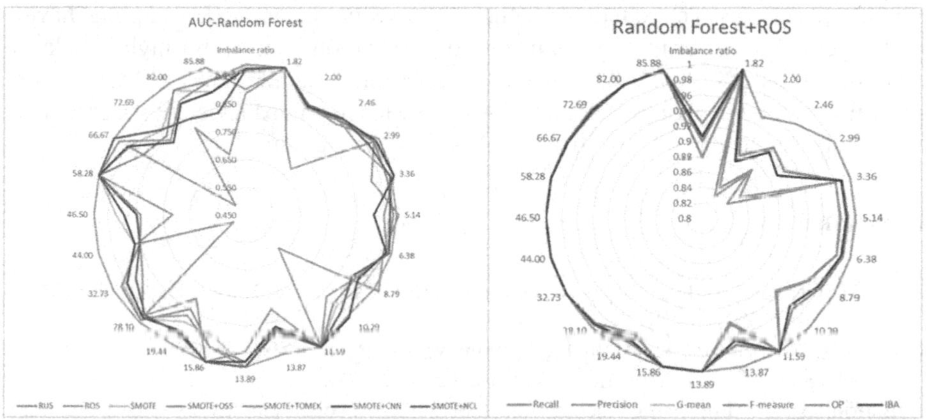

Fig. 5. AUC values of random forest for different sampling methods and datasets with different imbalance ratio (left). Quality metrics of random forest classifier for ROS sampling method and datasets with different imbalance ratio (right).

The rest of the quality metrics of Random Forest classifier used with the ROS strategy are presented in Fig. 5 (right side). The first conclusion concerns the high values of the evaluation metrics, most of them close to 100%. Moreover, the new metrics OP and IBA presents higher values than classical ones as G-mean and F-measure. On the other hand, it can be seen that the combination of Random Forest and ROS yields a value of 100% or very close to it for all the metrics when imbalanced ratios are high.

7 Conclusions

This paper present a comprehensive empirical comparison and analysis of the effect of low and high imbalance ratio datasets on basic and advanced resampling strategies, taking into account different classifiers. In our experiments, the effectiveness of sampling methods is evaluated through the performance of the classifiers obtained when they are applied to datasets with different imbalance ratio, which are preprocessed by those sampling methods. In the study, we used 24 datasets with a wide range of imbalance degree, from low to high imbalance ratio [1.82–129.44], 6 classifiers, among the most popular decision tree family and other popular classifiers and 7 resampling strategies. The performance was evaluated by means of six different metrics and significance tests were applied to confirm the validity of the comparative analysis.

Experimental results have shown that classifiers from the decision tree family (especially Random Forest) present better behavior than the other classifiers in most cases. Another conclusion derived from the obtained results is that over sampling techniques and SMOTE method combined with under sampling techniques, are the most effective when Random Forest is used. This result can be explained the fact that under sampling methods leads to loss of important information on dataset especially when dealing with high imbalance ratio datasets.

Regarding the effect of the imbalance ratio, ROS produces the best results for high imbalanced datasets. The remainder techniques, except random undersampling, have a similar performance for low imbalance ratios. On the other hand, for high imbalance ratio, the results of classical metrics (AUC, precision, recall, G-mean and F-measure) are similar to the novel ones (OP and IBA), while for low imbalance OP shows almost the same behavior than recall and IBA behaves like F-measure.

References

1. He, H., García, E.A.: Learning from imbalanced data. IEEE Trans. Knowl. Data Engine **21**(9), 1263–1284 (2009)
2. Chawla, N., Bowyer, K., Hall, L., Kebelmeyer, W.P.: SMOTE: synthetic minority over sampling technique. J. Artif. Intell. Res. **16**, 321–357 (2002)
3. Laurikkala, J.: Improving identification of difficult small classes by balancing class distribution. In: Quaglini, S., Barahona, P., Andreassen, S. (eds.) AIME 2001. LNCS, vol. 2101, pp. 63–66. Springer, Heidelberg (2001). doi:10.1007/3-540-48229-6_9
4. Kubat, M., Matwin, S.: Addressing the curse of imbalanced training sets: one side selection. In: Fisher, D.H. (ed.) ICML, pp. 179–186. Morgan Kaufmann, San Francisco (1979)
5. Bekkar, M., Alitouche, T.A.: Imbalanced data learning approaches review. Int. J. Data Min. Knowl. Manage. Process (IJDK), **3**(4) (2013)
6. Drummond, C., Holte, R.C.: C4.5, class imbalance and cost sensitivity: why under-sampling beats oversampling. In: Workshop on Learning from Imbalanced Datasets II, held in Conjunction with ICML (2003)
7. Hart, P.E.: The condensed nearest neighbor rule. IEEE Trans. Inf. Theor. **14**, 515–516 (1968)
8. Garcia, V., Sanchez, J.S., Mollineda, R.A.: On the effectiveness of preprocessing methods when dealing with different levels of class imbalance. Elsevier **25**, 13–21 (2012)
9. García, V., Mollineda, R.A., Sánchez, J.S.: Index of balanced accuracy: a performance measure for skewed class distributions. In: Araujo, H., Mendonça, A.M., Pinho, A.J., Torres, M.I. (eds.) IbPRIA 2009. LNCS, vol. 5524, pp. 441–448. Springer, Heidelberg (2009). doi: 10.1007/978-3-642-02172-5_57
10. Toussaint, G.T.: A counterexample to Tomek's consistency theorem for a condensed nearest neighbor decision rule. Pattern Recogn. Lett. **15**, 797–801 (1994)
11. Tomek, I.: A generalization of the K-NN rule. IEEE Trans. SMC **6**, 121–126 (1976)
12. Wilson, D.: Asymptotic properties of nearest neighbor rules using edited data. IEEE Trans. SMC **2**(23), 408–421 (1972)

13. Hand, B.J., Batchelor, B.G.: Experiments on the edited condensed nearest neighbor rule. Inf. Sci. **14**(3), 171–180 (1978)
14. Barley, A.P.: The use of the area under the ROC curve in the evaluation of machine learning algorithms. Pattern Recogn. **30**(7), 359–377 (1997)
15. Jin, H., Ling, C.X.: Using AUC and accuracy in evaluating learning algorithms. IEEE Trans. Knowl. Data Eng. **17**(3), 299–310 (2005)
16. Ranawana, R., Palade, V.: Optimized precision - a new measure for classifier performance evaluation. In: Proceeding of the IEEE Congress on Computational Intelligence, Vancouver, Canada, pp. 2245–2261 (2006)
17. Loyola-Gonzalez, O., Martinez-Trinidad, F.J., Carrasco-Ochoa, J.A.: Study of the impact of resampling methods for contrast pattern based classifiers in imbalanced databases. Neurocomputing **175**, 935–947 (2016)
18. Wu, X., Kumar, V., Quinlan, J.R., Ghosh, J., Yang, Q., Motoda, H., McLachlan, G.J., Ng, A., Liu, B., Yu, P.S., Zhou, Z.H., Steinbach, M., Hand, D.J., Steinberg, D.: Top 10 algorithms in data mining. Knowl. Inf. Syst. **14**, 1–37 (2008)
19. Demsar, J.: Statistical comparison of classifiers over multiple datasets. J. Mach. Learn. Res. **7**, 1–30 (2006)
20. Garcia, S., Herrera, F.: An extension on statistical comparisons of classifiers over multiple datasets for all pairwise comparisons. J. Mach. Learn. Res. **9**, 2677–2694 (2008)
21. Hulse, J.V., Khoshgoftaar, T.M., Naplolitano, A.: Experimental perspectives on learning from imbalanced data. In: Proceedings of the 24th International Conference on Machine Learning, Corvalis, Oregon, pp. 935–942 (2007)
22. Japkowicz, N., Stephen, S.: The class imbalance problem: a systematic study. Intell. Data Anal. **6**(5), 429–449 (2002)

A Perceptron Classifier, Its Correctness Proof and a Probabilistic Interpretation

Bernd-Jürgen Falkowski(✉)

Fachhochschule für Ökonomie und Management FOM,
Karlstrasse 2, 86150 Augsburg, Germany
bernd.falkowski@fh-stralsund.de

Abstract. In this paper a fault tolerant probabilistic kernel version with smoothing parameter of Minsky's perceptron classifier for more than two classes is exhibited and a correctness proof is provided. Moreover it is shown that the resulting classifier approaches optimality. Due to the non-determinism of the algorithm the (approximately) optimal value of a smoothing parameter has to be determined experimentally. The resulting complexity nevertheless allows for an efficient implementation employing for example Java concurrent programming and suitable hardware. In addition a probabilistic interpretation using Bayes Theorem is provided.

Keywords: Perceptron · Classifier for more than 2 classes · Bayes decision

1 Introduction

Recently the analysis of Big Data has become increasingly important. Indeed, implementations of classifying [9] and in particular ranking algorithms [16,17] have been effected in order to perform such diverse tasks as assessing the creditworthiness of banking customers [9], supporting medical doctors in their diagnoses of patients [10], ranking drivers according to their driving behaviour (as made possible by modern navigation systems) [12] or establishing recommender systems for online shops [13]. In [7] an improvement of an old classification algorithm was sketched out that is appealing from an aesthetic point of view due to its elegant simplicity. Here the missing correctness proof is provided. It turns out that geometrical arguments concerning the optimality of a separating hyperplane are of crucial importance. In particular the algebraic characterization of length and angle using the scalar product and the resulting 'Kernel Trick' prove useful. Indeed, without exploiting the vector space structure an efficient implementation that is important for commercial purposes seems hardly possible although the original version of the algorithm does not require it.

In Sect. 2 the original algorithm is again described for the convenience of the reader and in Sect. 3.1 the kernel trick is also again exhibited whilst in Sect. 3.2 the optimal separating hyperplane is discussed in more detail. Section 3.3 is devoted to the Representer Theorem and the Pocket Algorithm. Thus in Sect. 4

F.J. Martínez de Pisón et al. (Eds.): HAIS 2017, LNAI 10334, pp. 246–255, 2017.
DOI: 10.1007/978-3-319-59650-1_21

a correctness proof of the modified Pocket Algorithm can be constructed. A brief probabilistic interpretation of the decision procedure is again given in Sect. 5. A conclusion and outlook in Sect. 6 end the paper.

2 The Perceptron

In their seminal work [14] Minsky and Papert describe a perceptron as a simple classifier by means of a linear threshold function as follows.

Definition 1. *Let $\Phi := \{\phi_1, \phi_2, ..., \phi_m\}$ be a family of (generalized) predicates (in general real valued functions defined on some set of objects). Then the truth-valued function ψ (predicate) is a linear threshold function with respect to Φ if there exists a real number θ and coefficients $\alpha(\phi_1)$, $\alpha(\phi_2)$, ..., $\alpha(\phi_m)$ such that $\psi(x) =$ true if and only if $\sum_{i=1}^{m} \alpha(\phi_i)\phi_i(x) > \theta$. Any predicate that can be defined in this way is said to belong to $L(\Phi)$.*

Now suppose that two disjoint sets of objects S^+ and S^- and a family of generalized predicates Φ on $S = S^+ \cup S^-$ are given. Then one would like to construct a predicate ψ in $L(\Phi)$ such that $\psi(x) =$ true if and only if $x \in S^+$, in other words one would like to construct a ψ in $L(\Phi)$ that separates S^+ and S^-.

As shown by Minsky and Papert this can be done using the following simple program (the Perceptron Learning Algorithm, **PLA**), in which the convenient scalar product notation $\mathbf{A} \cdot \mathbf{\Phi}(x)$ instead of $\sum_{i=1}^{m} \alpha(\phi_i)\phi_i(x)$ is used and $\mathbf{A} := (\alpha(\phi_1), ..., \alpha(\phi_m))$ and $\mathbf{\Phi}(x) := (\phi_1(x), ..., \phi_m(x))$ are considered as elements of $\Re^m$, if a solution exists. (Note here that generalizing to higher dimensions the solution may be considered in geometrical terms as a separating hyperplane. However, the set S is not required to carry a vector space structure although in practical applications this will often be the case.).

Start	Choose any value for $\mathbf{A}$, θ.
Test	If $x \in S^+$ and $\mathbf{A} \cdot \mathbf{\Phi}(x) > \theta$ go to **Test**.
	If $x \in S^+$ and $\mathbf{A} \cdot \mathbf{\Phi}(x) \leq \theta$ go to **Add**.
	If $x \in S^-$ and $\mathbf{A} \cdot \mathbf{\Phi}(x) < \theta$ go to **Test**.
	If $x \in S^-$ and $\mathbf{A} \cdot \mathbf{\Phi}(x) \geq \theta$ go to **Subtract**.
Add	Replace $\mathbf{A}$ by $\mathbf{A} + \mathbf{\Phi}(x)$ and θ by $\theta - 1$. Go to **Test**.
Subtract	Replace $\mathbf{A}$ by $\mathbf{A} - \mathbf{\Phi}(x)$ and θ by $\theta + 1$. Go to **Test**.

Having found a suitable vector $\mathbf{A}^\star$ and a scalar $\theta^\star$ the decision procedure for classification is given by:

Decide $x \in S^+$ if and only if $\mathbf{A}^\star \cdot \mathbf{\Phi}(x) > \theta^\star$.

If there exists a more general partition of $S = \bigcup_{i=1}^{q} S_i$, then one can still construct a suitable classifier as follows. Given $\mathbf{\Phi}$ as above, find a vector $\mathbf{A}^\star := (\mathbf{A}_1^\star, \mathbf{A}_2^\star, \ldots, \mathbf{A}_q^\star)$ and a number $\theta^\star$ such that $\mathbf{A}_i^\star \cdot \mathbf{\Phi}(x) > \mathbf{A}_j^\star \cdot \mathbf{\Phi}(x) + \theta^\star$ for all $j \neq i$ if and only if $x \in S_i$. This problem can be reduced to the one described above by the following definition.

Definition 2. *Define a new vector* $\mathbf{\Phi}_{ij} := (0, ..., 0, \mathbf{\Phi}(x), 0, ..., 0, -\mathbf{\Phi}(x), 0..., 0)$ *containing* $\mathbf{\Phi}(x)$ *in the i-th place and* $\mathbf{\Phi}(x)$ *in the j-th place.*

Indeed, this definition leads to the following program.

Start	Choose any value for $\mathbf{A}$, θ.
Test	If $x \in S_i$ and $\mathbf{A} \cdot \mathbf{\Phi}_{\rm ij}(x) > \theta$ go to **Test**.
	If $x \in S_i$ and $\mathbf{A} \cdot \mathbf{\Phi}_{\rm ij}(x) \leq \theta$ go to **Add**.
	If $x \in S_j$ and $\mathbf{A} \cdot \mathbf{\Phi}_{\rm ij}(x) < \theta$ go to **Test**.
	If $x \in S_j$ and $\mathbf{A} \cdot \mathbf{\Phi}_{\rm ij}(x) \geq \theta$ go to **Subtract**.
Add	Replace $\mathbf{A}$ by $\mathbf{A} + \mathbf{\Phi}_{\rm ij}(x)$ and θ by $\theta - 1$. Go to **Test**.
Subtract	Replace $\mathbf{A}$ by $\mathbf{A} - \mathbf{\Phi}_{\rm ij}(x)$ and θ by $\theta + 1$. Go to **Test**.

Note, in order to avoid confusion, that, by abuse of notation, the same $\mathbf{A}$, θ as above have been used.

Note also that having found a suitable $\mathbf{A}^\star$ and a scalar $\theta^\star$ the decision procedure for classification is of course:

Decide $x \in S_i$ if and only if $\mathbf{A}^\star \cdot \mathbf{\Phi}_{\rm ij}(x) > \theta^\star$ for all $j \neq i$.

The interesting point about this program is the fact that, as already noted by Minsky and Papert, a straightforward error-correcting feedback results in a correct algorithm. Of course, the required existence of a solution is by no means guaranteed in general although, if suitable predicates are used, in many cases a solution can be found, cf. [3]. However, nowadays good generalization properties of the perceptron are of paramount importance and hence it is often preferable to admit a solution that does not separate the S_i completely, see also [2].

3 Kernel Learning

In order to avoid having to deal explicitly with extremely high dimensional spaces that lead to unacceptable CPU times one applies the so-called kernel trick, cf. [19].

3.1 Positive Definite Kernels

If above one starts with the zero vector $\mathbf{0}$ for $\mathbf{A}$ in order to avoid technical complications then it is easily seen that finally $\mathbf{A}$ will have the form

$$\mathbf{A} = (\sum_{k=1}^{m} b_{1k}\mathbf{\Phi}(x_k), \sum_{k=1}^{m} b_{2k}\mathbf{\Phi}(x_k), ..., \sum_{k=1}^{m} b_{qk}\mathbf{\Phi}(x_k))$$

for some coefficients b_{jk}. Hence $\mathbf{A}$ may equally well be described by the vector

$$\mathbf{b} = (\mathbf{b}_1, \mathbf{b}_2, ..., \mathbf{b}_{\rm q})$$

in terms of the b_{ij}. Moreover

$$\mathbf{A} \cdot \mathbf{\Phi}_{\rm ij}(x) = \sum_{k=1}^{m}(b_{ik} - b_{jk})\mathbf{\Phi}(x_k) \cdot \mathbf{\Phi}(x) = \sum_{k=1}^{m}(b_{ik} - b_{jk})K(x_k, x)$$

say, and the update operation is given by

$$\mathbf{A} + \mathbf{\Phi}_{\mathrm{ij}}(\mathrm{x_s}) = (\sum_{\mathrm{k=1}}^{\mathrm{m}} \mathrm{c_{1k}}\mathbf{\Phi}(\mathrm{x_k}), \sum_{\mathrm{k=1}}^{\mathrm{m}} \mathrm{c_{2k}}\mathbf{\Phi}(\mathrm{x_k}), ..., \sum_{\mathrm{k=1}}^{\mathrm{m}} \mathrm{c_{qk}}\mathbf{\Phi}(\mathrm{x_k}))$$

where $x_s \in S_i$ is assumed, and $c_{is} = b_{is} + 1, c_{js} = b_{js} - 1$ and elsewhere $c_{rl} = b_{rl}$. This update operation may of course be described entirely in terms of the vectors $\mathbf{b}$ and $\mathbf{d}_{\mathrm{ij}} = (\mathbf{0}, ...\mathbf{0}, \mathbf{d}_{\mathrm{i}}, \mathbf{0}, ...\mathbf{0}, \mathbf{d}_{\mathrm{j}}, \mathbf{0}..., \mathbf{0})$ that has a 1 as the d_{is} entry, a minus 1 as the d_{js} entry and zeroes elsewhere by

$$\mathbf{b} := \mathbf{b} + \mathbf{d}_{\mathrm{ij}}$$

Thus one is lead to the following definition that formalizes the foregoing considerations.

Definition 3. *A real-valued function $K : S \times S \longrightarrow \Re$ is called a positive definite kernel if for all choices of n, and $x_1, x_2, \ldots, x_n \in S$ the matrix with entries $K(x_i, x_j)$ is symmetric and positive definite.*

Given such a kernel an embedding $\mathbf{\Phi}$ of S in a vector space $H = \Re^S$ (the space of functions from S to $\Re$) may always be constructed by setting $\mathbf{\Phi}(x) := \mathrm{K}(., x)$, considering functions $f = \sum_{j=1}^{m} \gamma_j K(., x_j)$, and defining addition of such functions and multiplication of such a function by a scalar pointwise. If the inner product is defined by $< \mathbf{\Phi}(x), \mathbf{\Phi}(y) >_H := K(x, y)$ and extended by linearity, then a Hilbert space H (the Reproducing Kernel Hilbert space) is obtained by completion as usual, see e.g. [19]. Hence a positive definite kernel is seen to be the abstract version of a scalar product. Of course, given a positive definite kernel one may now discard the set of predicates entirely and arrive at the following algorithm constructing a separating hyperplane, which is obtained from Minsky's original version.

Start	Choose any value for θ. and set $b_{rl} = 0$ for all r,l.
Test	If $x_s \in S_i$ and $\sum_{k=1}^{m}(b_{ik} - b_{jk})K(x_k, x_s) > \theta$ go to **Test**.
	If $x_s \in S_i$ and $\sum_{k=1}^{m}(b_{ik} - b_{jk})K(x_k, x_s) \leq \theta$ go to **Add**.
	If $x_s \in S_j$ and $\sum_{k=1}^{m}(b_{ik} - b_{jk})K(x_k, x_s) < \theta$ go to **Test**.
	If $x_s \in S_j$ and $\sum_{k=1}^{m}(b_{ik} - b_{jk})K(x_k, x_s) \geq \theta$ go to **Subtract**.
Add	Replace $\mathbf{b}$ by $\mathbf{b} + \mathbf{d}_{\mathrm{ij}}$ and θ by $\theta - 1$. Go to **Test**.
Subtract	Replace $\mathbf{b}$ by $\mathbf{b} - \mathbf{d}_{\mathrm{ij}}$ and θ by $\theta + 1$. Go to **Test**.

The above program again computes a weight vector

$$\mathbf{b}^\star = (\mathbf{b}_1^\star, \mathbf{b}_2^\star, ..., \mathbf{b}_{\mathrm{q}}^\star)$$

and a scalar $\theta^\star$ such that the decision procedure is given by:
Decide $x_s \in S_i$ if and only if $\sum_{k=1}^{m}(b_{ik}^\star - b_{jk}^\star)K(x_k, x_s) > \theta^\star$ for all $j \neq i$.

3.2 The Optimal Separating Hyperplane

The algorithm in Sect. 3.1 computes a separating hyperplane in the reproducing kernel Hilbert space, if it exists. However, in this case it is desirable to arrive at a hyperplane that is optimal in the sense that the minimum distance of any point from the plane is maximal, cf. [20]. This can also be achieved by simple feedback if one tests the "worst classified element" instead of an arbitrary one. Details are given in the description of the Krauth/Mezard algorithm, cf. [11]. In fact this amounts to minimizing the (square of the) norm of the weight vector

$$\mathbf{A} = (\sum_{k=1}^{m} b_{1k}\mathbf{\Phi}(x_k), \sum_{k=1}^{m} b_{2k}\mathbf{\Phi}(x_k), ..., \sum_{k=1}^{m} b_{mk}\mathbf{\Phi}(x_k))$$

given by

$$\|\mathbf{A}\|^2 = \sum_{k=1}^{q}\sum_{i=1}^{m}\sum_{j=1}^{m} b_{ki}b_{kj}\mathbf{\Phi}(x_i)\cdot\mathbf{\Phi}(x_j) = \sum_{k=1}^{q}\sum_{i=1}^{m}\sum_{j=1}^{m} b_{ki}b_{kj}K(x_i, x_j)$$

where q is the number of classes. This may be seen as follows. In order to simplify notation consider a training sample from two classes

$$(\mathbf{x_1}, y_1), (\mathbf{x_2}, y_2), \cdots, (\mathbf{x_n}, y_n) \in H \times \{1, -1\}$$

from a Hilbert space H where the $y_i = j$ means that x_i belongs to class j. Assume that a separating hyperplane is to be constructed (the existence being assumed here). More precisely: One wishes to construct a weight vector $\mathbf{w}$ and a cut-off c such that $< \mathbf{w}, x_i > \geq c$ if $y_i = 1$ and $< c$ otherwise. This problem may then be converted into a canonical form as follows. Replace c by $-c_1$ to obtain $< \mathbf{w}, x_i > +c_1 \geq 0$ if $y_i = 1$ and $< \mathbf{w}, x_i > +c_1 < 0$ otherwise. Since there is only a finite number of sample vectors there must exist an $\varepsilon > 0$ such that $< \mathbf{w}, x_i > +c_1 \geq 0$ if $y_i = 1$ and $< \mathbf{w}, x_i > +c_1 < -\varepsilon$ otherwise. Setting $\mathbf{w_1} := \frac{2}{\varepsilon}\mathbf{w}$ and $c_2 := \frac{2}{\varepsilon}c_1 + 1$ one obtains the equivalent problem:

Find a weight vector $\mathbf{w_1}$ and a cut-off c_2 such that

$$< \mathbf{w_1}, x_i > +c_2 \geq 1 \text{ if } y_i = 1 \text{ and } < \mathbf{w_1}, x_i > +c_2 \leq 1 \text{ otherwise.}$$

In this case the minimum distance between the two classes equals $\frac{2}{\|\mathbf{w_1}\|}$. Hence it becomes obvious that minimizing $\|\mathbf{w_1}\|$ or $\|\mathbf{w}\|$ amounts to maximizing the minimum distance to the separating hyperplane that is given by

$$< \mathbf{w_1}, \mathbf{x} > +c_2 = 0.$$

3.3 The Representer Theorem, See [18]

Up to now the main aim has been to construct a discriminant that minimizes the number of errors (in fact even does not allow any errors). However, whilst this is possible in principle unfortunately in practical applications this frequently leads to overfitting. Thus it seems desirable to try to introduce smoothing as for example performed for regularization networks, see [4]. That is to say that instead of attempting to minimize the number of errors only one should simultaneously try to optimize the separating hyperplane. More precisely (applying the simplified notation of the preceding subsection):

One wishes to construct a separating hyperplane minimizing the cost function C given by $C(D, \lambda, \mathbf{w}) = \mathrm{E(D)} + \lambda\|\mathbf{w}\|$ where λ is a positive parameter to be determined experimentally and E(D) is the number of errors arising from the discriminant. Of course, it is by no means clear, that such a minimum can be reached by perceptron learning. However, a first hint is provided by the following theorem.

Theorem 1. *Let X be a nonempty set and K a positive definite real valued kernel on $X \times X$ with corresponding reproducing kernel Hilbert space H. Given a training sample*

$$(\mathbf{x_1}, \mathrm{y_1}), (\mathbf{x_2}, \mathrm{y_2}), \cdots, (\mathbf{x_n}, \mathrm{y_n}) \in \mathrm{H} \times \{1, -1\}$$

a strictly monotonically increasing function $g : [0, \infty] \rightarrow \Re$ and an arbitrary empirical risk function $E : (X \times \Re^2) \rightarrow \Re$, then for any $f^\star \in H$ minimizing

$$E((\mathbf{x_1}, \mathrm{y_1}, \mathrm{f}(\mathbf{x_1})), (\mathbf{x_2}, \mathrm{y_2}, \mathrm{f}(\mathbf{x_2}), \ldots, (\mathbf{x_m}, \mathrm{y_m}, \mathrm{f}(\mathbf{x_m})) + \mathrm{g}(\|\mathbf{w}\|)$$

$f^\star$ admits a representation of the form $f^\star(x) = \sum_{j=1}^{m} w_j K(x, x_j)$

The Pocket Algorithm. As pointed out above one would like an algorithm that correctly classifies the maximal number of elements in S^+ and S^- leaving aside the question of optimality of the separating hyperplane for the time being. Gallant proposed a variant of the **PLA** capable of computing a good approximation to this perfect linear separation. The crucial idea of this algorithm is to store the best weight vector found so far in perceptron learning (in a pocket) while continuing to update the weight vector itself. If a better weight vector is found it replaces the one currently stored and the algorithm continues.

Start	Choose any value for $\mathbf{w}$. Set the stored $\mathbf{w}_s = \mathrm{w}$, and set the history of $\mathbf{w}_s$ to $h_s = 0$. Set the number of consecutively successfully tested vectors to $h = 0$ as well.
Test	If $h > h_s$ replace $\mathbf{w}_s$ by $\mathbf{w}$, h_s by h and set $h = 0$. Go to **Update**
Update	Update $\mathbf{w}$ according to the **PLA**

For details see [8].

In view of the preceding sections it is tempting to use the cost function C described above as a ratchet. Of course, now the number of errors will not be zero in general at the minimum of the target function. Nevertheless the kernel version of the modified pocket algorithm still works and a correctness proof based on the representer theorem will be provided in the next section.

4 Correctness Proof of the Modified Pocket Algorithm

(1) Because of the representer theorem any suitable function minimizing the empirical risk (number of errors) whilst reducing the danger of overfitting by introducing a smoothing parameter is given by a seprating hyperplane for the correctly classified samples. Moreover this separating hyperplane should be optimal in the geometrical sense described above.

(2) Since there is only a finite number of training sample vectors only a finite number of perceptron weight vectors $(\mathbf{w_1}, \mathbf{w_2}, \ldots, \mathbf{w_n})$ can be reached, cf. [2], Minsky's Cycling Theorem.

(3) Starting from any such weight vector $\mathbf{w_i}$ there is a non-zero probability that by perceptron learning an approximately optimal weight vector $\mathbf{w}$ can be reached. Let $S := \{\mathbf{y_1}, \mathbf{y_2}, \ldots, \mathbf{y_t}\}$ be the set of training samples that are correctly classified by the approximately optimal weight vector $\mathbf{w}$. Then because of the perceptron learning theorem, and because of the Krauth/Mezard algorithm, see [11], $\mathbf{w_i}$ will converge in finite time to $\mathbf{w}$, if only certain training samples from S are selected. However, there is a non-zero probability that precisely this sequence of training samples will be chosen by random selection. Thus let $P(\mathbf{w}|\mathbf{w_j})$ denote the probability that $\mathbf{w}$ is reached from $\mathbf{w}_\mathrm{j}$. In addition set $P(\mathbf{w}) := \min_\mathrm{j} \mathrm{P}(\mathbf{w}|\mathbf{w_j})$.

(4) If $\mathbf{w}$ has been reached there is a non-zero probability $P(S)$ that, if "runs" (successive correct classifications) are generated by random selection, only samples from S are chosen as training samples. As a consequence there is a probability $P(\mathbf{w}|\mathrm{S})$ to reach $\mathbf{w}$ first and thereafter generate a run with optimal target function value, which satisfies

$$P(\mathbf{w}|\mathrm{S}) \geqq \mathrm{P}(\mathbf{w}) * \mathrm{P}(\mathrm{S}) > 0$$

(5) Finally after $\mathbf{w}$ has been reached r times the probability that no run with optimal target function value has been generated by $\mathbf{w}$ is given by

$$(1 - P(\mathbf{w}|\mathrm{S})^\mathrm{r}) \leqq (1 - \mathrm{P}(\mathbf{w}) * \mathrm{P}(\mathrm{S}))^\mathrm{r}.$$

Since the right hand side of the inequality converges to zero with increasing r the correctness of the algorithm is now guaranteed.

5 Probabilistic Interpretation of the Decision Procedure

The decision procedure described above may under certain conditions be interpreted as Bayes decision. Indeed, assume that the class conditional densities belong to the family of exponential distributions (which includes a number of well-known distributions) of the general form

$$p(\mathbf{\Phi}(\mathrm{x})|\mathbf{x} \in \mathrm{S_i}) = \exp(\mathrm{B}(\mathbf{e}_\mathrm{i}) + \mathrm{C}(\mathbf{\Phi}(\mathrm{x})) + < \mathbf{e}_\mathrm{i}, \mathbf{\Phi}(\mathrm{x}) >)$$

where $\mathbf{x}$ is now a vector in some Euclidean space and the $\mathbf{e}_\mathrm{i}$ are parameter vectors. Then the posterior probabilities can be computed using Bayes theorem.

Theorem 2. *If the class conditional densities belong to the family of exponential distributions and $B(\mathbf{e}_\mathrm{i}) + \ln(\mathrm{P}(\mathrm{S}_\mathrm{i}))$ is independent of i the decision procedures derived above will give the Bayes decision.*

Proof. Setting $\mathbf{A}_\mathrm{i}^\star := \mathbf{e}_\mathrm{i}$ and $-\theta^\star := B(\mathbf{e}_\mathrm{i}) + \ln(\mathrm{P}(\mathrm{S}_\mathrm{i}))$ the posterior probabilities can be computed using Bayes theorem as

$$p(\mathbf{x} \in \mathrm{S}_\mathrm{i}|\mathbf{\Phi}(\mathbf{x})) = \frac{\exp(\mathrm{a}_\mathrm{i})}{\sum_\mathrm{j}\exp(\mathrm{a}_\mathrm{j})}$$

with

$$a_i =< \mathbf{A}_\mathrm{i}^\star, \mathbf{\Phi}(\mathbf{x}) > -\theta^\star$$

Hence it becomes clear that, provided that the assumed class conditional density is appropriate and that the above substitutions are justified, deciding that an $\mathbf{x}$ belongs to S_i if a_i is maximal is also the Bayes decision since the a posteriori probability is maximal in this case.

The kernel version of a_i, say k_i is then given by

$$k_i = \sum_{k=1}^{m} b_{ik}^\star K(\mathbf{x}_\mathbf{k}, \mathbf{x}) - \theta^\star$$

and again deciding that an $\mathbf{x}$ belongs to S_i if b_i is maximal is the Bayes decision. □

In this context also note that the function given in the equation above describes a generalization of the logistic sigmoid activation function which is known as the normalized exponential or softmax activation function. This function represents a smooth version of the winner-takes-all activation model, For further details see e.g. [1].

6 Conclusion and Outlook

An elegant and compact probabilistic algorithm relying on straightforward error correcting feedback has been presented (derived essentially from Minsky's original perceptron learning algorithm) and a correctness proof has been provided. A probabilistic interpretation of the output has been given using Bayes' theorem. Good generalization properties due to the introduction of a smoothing parameter appear to be likely as indicated by preliminary experimental results exhibited in [7]. This seems rather important in view of a possibly large Vapnik-Chervonenkis bound, see [21], arising from a high dimensional image of the feature maps, see [3]. Whilst the currently needed CPU times to execute the kernel version of the algorithm are still in the region of several hours the possibility of parallelization (using for example Java concurrent programming, see e.g. [5]) allows significant improvements if suitably sophisticated hardware is employed. Indeed, employing a virtual machine with eight CPUs and using Java concurrent programming a simplified version of the algorithm only required computing times of approximately twenty minutes which is certainly feasible in a commercial environment. This resulted essentially from executing the ratchet part of the algorithm in parallel threads and could certainly still be improved by for example using graphic cards.

Thus it seems that an algorithm has been obtained that is not only very appealing from an aesthetic point of view but could also quite successfully be used in commercial and academic applications. Of course, in order to prove the commercial viability extensive experimental work is still necessary.

Nevertheless, it appears rather remarkable that an old algorithm, that originally was probably mainly of academic interest, gives rise to a variety of derived algorithms (e.g. ranking see [6], classification as above) that also admit probabilistic interpretations under certain special conditions. Moreover it seems that this approach can also be used for unsupervised learning in the context of clustering, see [15]. It will be interesting to see how much further the above results can be extended in the direction just indicated.

Acknowledgements. The author is indebted to M. Stern for help with some problems concerning the Java system.

References

1. Bishop, C.M.: Pattern Recognition and Machine Learning. Springer, New York (2006)
2. Block, H.D., Levin, S.A.: On the boundedness of an iterative procedure for solving a system of linear inequalities. In: Proceedings of AMS (1970)
3. Cover, T.M.: Geometrical and statistical properties of systems of linear inequalities with applications in pattern recognition. IEEE Trans. Electr. Comput. **14**, 326–334 (1965)
4. Evgeniou, T., Pontil, M., Poggio, T.: Regularization networks and support vector machines. In: Smola, A.J., Bartlett, P.L., Schölkopf, B., Schuurmanns, D. (eds.) Advances in Large Margin Classifiers. MIT Press, Cambridge (2000)
5. Falkowski, B.-J.: Parallel implementation of certain neural network algorithms. In: Ruan, D., Montero, J., Martinez, L., D'hondt, P., Kerre, E. (eds.) Computational Intelligence in Decision and Control, Proceedings of the 8th International FLINS Conference. World Scientific, Singapore (2008)
6. Falkowski, B.-J.: Minsky revisited, fault tolerant perceptron learning with good generalization properties. In: Miller, L. (ed.) Proceedings of 30th international Conference on Computers and their Applications (CATA 2015). ISCA Publications (2015)
7. Falkowski, B.-J.: A perceptron classifier and corresponding probabilities. In: Ferraro, M.B., Giordani, P., Vantaggi, B., Gagolewski, M., Gil, M.Á., Grzegorzewski, P., Hryniewicz, O. (eds.) Soft Methods for Data Science. AISC, vol. 456, pp. 213–220. Springer, Cham (2017). doi:10.1007/978-3-319-42972-4_27
8. Gallant, S.I.: Perceptron-based learning algorithms. IEEE Trans. Neural Netw. **1**(2), 179–191 (1990)
9. Hands, D.P., Henley, W.E.: Statistical classification methods in consumer credit scoring: a review. J. R. Stat. Soc. Ser. A **160**(3), 523–541 (1997)

10. Kononenko, I.: Machine learning or medical diagnosis: history, state of the art, and perspective. AI Med. **23**, 89–109 (2001)
11. Krauth, W., Mezard, M.: Learning algorithms with optimal stability in neural networks, J. Phys. A: Math. Gen. **20** (1987)
12. Meiring, G.A.M., Myburgh, H.C.: A review of intelligent driving style analysis systems and related AI algorithms, senses MDPI (2015)
13. Melvile, D., Webb, G.: Recommender systems. In: Samuel, C., Web, G. (eds.) Encyclopedia of Machine Learning. Springer, USA (2013)
14. Minsky, M.L., Papert, S.: Perceptrons, Expanded edn. MIT Press, Cambridge (1990)
15. Rojas, R.: Neural Networks. Springer, Berlin (1996)
16. Shashua, A., Levin, A.: Ranking with large margin princple: two approaches. In: NIPS, vol. 14 (2003)
17. Shivani, A., Partha, N.: Generalization bounds for ranking alogorithms via algo rithmic stability. J. Mach. Learn. Res. **10**, 441–474 (2009)
18. Schölkopf, B., Herbrich, R., Smola, A.J.: A generalized representer theorem. In: Helmbold, D., Williamson, B. (eds.) COLT 2001. LNCS, vol. 2111, pp. 416–426. Springer, Heidelberg (2001). doi:10.1007/3-540-44581-1_27
19. Shawe-Taylor, J., Cristianini, N.: Kernel Methods for Pattern Analysis. CUP, New York (2004)
20. Smola, A.J., Bartlett, P.L., Schölkopf, B., Schuurmanns, D.: Introduction to large margin classifiers. In: Smola, A.J., Bartlett, P.L., Schölkopf, B., Schuurmanns, D. (eds.) Advances in Large Margin Classifiers. MIT Press, Cambridge (2000)
21. Vapnik, V.N.: Statistical Learning Theory. Wiley, New York (1998)

Parallel Implementation of a Simplified Semi-physical Wildland Fire Spread Model Using OpenMP

D. Álvarez[1(✉)], D. Prieto[1], M.I. Asensio[1,2], J.M. Cascón[2,3], and L. Ferragut[1,2]

[1] Departamento de Matemática Aplicada, Universidad de Salamanca, Casas del Parque 2, 37008 Salamanca, Spain
{daalle,dpriher,mas,ferragut}@usal.es

[2] I. U. de Física Fundamental y Matemáticas, Universidad de Salamanca, Casas del Parque 1, 37008 Salamanca, Spain

[3] Departamento de Economía e Historia Económica, Universidad de Salamanca, Edificio FES, Campus Miguel de Unamuno, 37007 Salamanca, Spain
casbar@usal.es

Abstract. We present a parallel 2D version of a simplified semi-physical wildland fire spread model based on conservation equations, with convection and radiation as the main heat transfer mechanisms. This version includes some 3D effects. The OpenMP framework allows distributing the prediction operations among the available threads in a multicore architecture, thereby reducing the computational time and obtaining the prediction results much more quickly. The results from the experiments using data from a real fire in Galicia (Spain) confirm the benefits of using the parallel version.

Keywords: OpenMP · Parallel computing · Performance · Wildland fire model

1 Introduction

Wildland fires caused by natural or human factors remain a major threat to our forests. Therefore, the real-time simulation of wildland fire spread has direct applications in prevention, fire-fighting planning, and prescribed burn planning.

There are numerous mathematical models designed to predict the spread and spatial behaviour of wildland fire events according to the nature of their construction. The types of models range from empirical models based on statistical correlations of observed fire behaviour, to theoretical or physical models based on the fundamental understanding of the physics and chemistry that govern combustion and heat transfer, covering a wide range of intermediate models: semi-physical, semi-empirical, etc. The names and classifications vary depending on the author; see for example [18,19,22–24]. The empirical models are simple, but applicable only to systems in which the conditions are identical to those used in formulating

F.J. Martínez de Pisón et al. (Eds.): HAIS 2017, LNAI 10334, pp. 256–267, 2017.
DOI: 10.1007/978-3-319-59650-1_22

and testing the models. Physical models are much more complex; their computational cost is high and their validation is extremely difficult, although they may be extrapolated to a wide variety of fire situations. Advances in computational power and spatial data analysis have improved the computational efficiency of complex models, whereby simplified physical or semi-physical models can now provide reliable and effective simulations, being considered a serious alternative to the widely used semi-empirical models.

The simulation response time of a wildland fire spread model is critical. The prediction provided by the model must obviously be much faster than the real evolution of the simulated fire event if it is to be useful for fire-fighting planning. The results of the simulation should also be reliable. Data assimilation is a technique that improves the accuracy of the predictions [8]. This method is used to feed current data into a model while it is still in simulation mode by using sequential statistical estimation. Data assimilation uses statistical methods to periodically adjust the model state, incorporating new data, with the aim of improving the simulation's accuracy. The computational cost of data assimilation is high, as it involves a large number of simulations. Data assimilation has been used previously in fire spread simulation; see for example [10,16]. In addition, a models's validation process includes certain steps that again involve numerous simulations, such as sensibility analysis, and especially parameter adjustment.

Today, thanks to the myriad of different types and varietiesy of data received from satellite images, real-time sensors and many other sources, the models have become more complex, with the main aim being to improving simulation accuracy. Nevertheless, a serious drawback of using such a large amount of data is the time required to compute them all and generate a prediction under demanding time constraints. It is thus of the utmost importance to significantly reduce model's simulation response time.

Thanks to advances in computation, it is becoming more common to find models exploiting multicore architectures, regardless of the model's nature. This enables computational-intensive models to generate simulations in competitive time. Techniques such as OpenMP allow fully exploiting the performance of a single machine, as it enables all the cores to be used at the same time [14]. Moreover, the GPU's advantages can exploited to improve this performance using CUDA [4]. In addition, MPI is a powerful framework that allows a task distribution over several resources in a cluster for the best performance. It is common to find a hybrid OpenMP - MPI integration [7] that achieves satisfying results in the shortest amount of time.

This paper is organized as follows: Sect. 2 presents an overview of the fire model optimized in this research. Section 3 details the technique used in the parallel version of the model using the OpenMP framework. Experiments and the performance study of the proposed parallel model are discussed in Sect. 4. Finally, the conclusions and future research are summarised in Sect. 5.

2 The Model

The simplified semi-physical wildland fire spread model used in this research has been proposed by Ferragut *et al.* [11]. This model is based on principles of energy and mass conservation and takes into account convection and radiation as the main heat transfer mechanisms. Although the model's equations are defined on a 2D domain, the model considers some 3D effects, such as non-local radiation from the flames above the vegetal layer, for tackling with the effect that wind and slope have over flame tilt. The model also uses a multivalued operator representing enthalpy to consider the influence of fuel moisture content and heat absorption by pyrolysis. The model has been modified with several improvements, see [9,10], with the current model version being called *Physical Forest Fire Spread* (PhFFS) [20]. The version we present here computes the radiation term by numerical integration [11], and provides a maximum improvement in computational cost with the use of parallel computation.

The model's non-dimensional simplified equations are,

$$\partial_t e + \beta \mathbf{v} \cdot \nabla e + \alpha u = r \quad \text{in } S \times (0, t_{max}), \tag{1}$$

$$e \in G(u) \quad \text{in } S \times (0, t_{max}), \tag{2}$$

$$\partial_t c = -g(u) c \quad \text{in } S \times (0, t_{max}). \tag{3}$$

We complete the problem with homogeneous Dirichlet boundary conditions and the following initial conditions,

$$u(x, y, 0) = u_0(x, y) \quad \text{in } S, \tag{4}$$

$$c(x, y, 0) = c_0(x, y) \quad \text{in } S. \tag{5}$$

The spatial domain S represents the surface where the fire occurs, defined by the mapping,

$$S : d \longmapsto \mathbb{R}^3$$
$$(x, y) \longmapsto (x, y, h(x, y))$$

where $h(x, y)$ is a known function representing the topography of surface S and $d = [0, l_x] \times [0, l_y] \subset \mathbb{R}^2$ is a rectangle representing the projection of surface S. Topography is one of the data layers that the model needs, and takes from a *Geographical Information System* (GIS), see Fig. 1.

The unknowns, $e = \frac{E}{MCT_\infty}$, dimensionless *enthalpy*, $u = \frac{T - T_\infty}{T_\infty}$, dimensionless *temperature of the solid fuel* and $c = \frac{M}{M_0}$, dimensionless *mass fraction of solid fuel*, are bidimensional variables defined in $S \times (0, t_{max})$, where t_{max} is the time of study. The physical quantities E $(J\, m^{-2})$, T (K) and M $(kg\, m^{-2})$ are *enthalpy*, *temperature* of the solid fuel and *fuel load* respectively.

M_0 $(kg\, m^{-2})$ is the *initial solid fuel load*, that defines the initial condition and it is provided by two data layers, fuel load and fuel type, which the model also takes from a GIS; see Fig. 1. Fuel load layer shows where there is fuel and where there is not (roads, rivers, barren areas, firewalls set by firefighters...). Fuel type layer shows the spatial distribution of different fuel types, as initial fuel load and other model input variables depend on fuel type. The model can be fed by different fuel classifications, such as the well-known BEHAVE fuel models [2], the more recent Scott and Burgan dynamic fuel models [21], or even monitored data whenever available. C $(J\, K^{-1}\, kg^{-1})$ is the *heat capacity of solid*

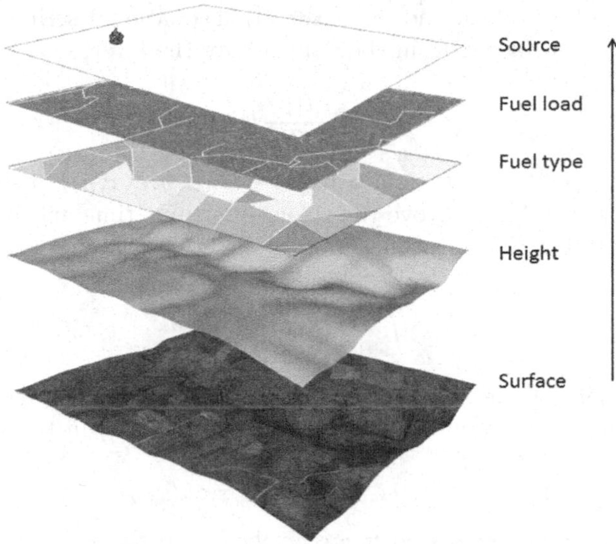

Fig. 1. Layers gathered from a surface as input data by the model.

fuel, that also depends on fuel type. The temperature initial condition locates the fire source by another data layer (see Fig. 1).

T_∞ (K) is a reference temperature given by the *ambient temperature*, which together with wind direction and intensity are the meteorological data the model uses. The model considers wind effect in two different ways: through the convective term itself, and through the flame tilt caused by wind that affects the radiation term. The convective term, $\beta\mathbf{v}\cdot\nabla e$ in the energy conservation equation represents the energy convected by the gas pyrolyzed through the elementary control volume, where the *surface wind velocity*, $\mathbf{v}$, is re-scaled by a *correction factor* β. For a detailed explanation of the model parameter β see [20]. Wind velocity $\mathbf{v}$ can be collected from meteorological stations located close to the fire, or it can be computed by a wind model [5,6,12].

The model also takes into account the energy lost by natural vertical convection through the term αu in the energy conservation equation. This term is related to the *natural convection coefficient* $\alpha = \frac{H[t]}{MC}$, where H $(J\,s^{-1}\,m^{-2}\,K^{-1})$ is a model parameter representing natural convection, and $[t]$ is a time scale.

The expression $e \in G(u)$ represents a multivalued operator that models the influence of solid fuel moisture content, and depends on *fuel moisture content* M_v (kg of water/kg of dry fuel), on *dimensionless pyrolysis temperature* u_p, both related to fuel type, and on *latent heat evaporation* Λ_v.

The right-hand side of the mass conservation equation represents the loss of solid fuel due to combustion. $g(u)$ is null when $u < u_p$ and constant γ otherwise, with this constant being inversely proportional to the *half time of combustion* $t_{1/2}(s)$ of each type of fuel, $\gamma = \frac{\ln 2[t]}{t_{1/2}}$.

The right-hand side of the energy conservation equation describes the thermal radiation reaching surface S from the flame above the layer,

$$r = \frac{[t]}{MCT_\infty} R \tag{6}$$

R represents the incident energy at a point $\mathbf{x} = (x, y, h(x, y))$ of surface S due to radiation from the flame above the surface per unit time and per unit area, obtained by summing the contribution of all directions $\boldsymbol{\Omega}$, that is

$$R(\mathbf{x}) = \int_{\omega=0}^{2\pi} I(\mathbf{x}, \boldsymbol{\Omega}) \boldsymbol{\Omega} \cdot \mathbf{N} \, d\omega, \tag{7}$$

where ω is the solid angle and $\mathbf{N}$ is the unit outer vector normal to surface S. This term is computed by numerical integration (see [11]) in the following 3D domain,

$$D = \{(x, y, z) \colon x, y \in d, h(x, y) < z < h(x, y) + \delta\},$$

and each contribution depends on *flame height* F and *flame temperature* T_f for each type of fuel, through the differential equation that describes total radiation intensity I at any position along a given path Ω in a grey medium, which may be written, ignoring scattering, as

$$\frac{dI}{ds} + a(s)I(s) = a(s)I_b(s). \tag{8}$$

I_b is the black body total radiation intensity, and is governed by the Stefan-Boltzmann law, corresponding to the integral over all wavelengths of the emissive power of a black body

$$I_b = \frac{\sigma}{\pi} T^4, \tag{9}$$

where $\sigma = 5.6704 \times 10^{-8} Js^{-1}m^{-2}K^{-4}$ is the Stefan-Boltzmann constant, and temperature T reaches flame temperature T_f. a is the *radiation absorption coefficient* inside the flame, and it is the third model parameter.

The numerical solution of Eqs. (1), (2) and (3) is based on $P1$ finite element approximation on a regular mesh for spatial discretisation and a Crank-Nicolson finite difference scheme for time discretisation, combined with a Euler half-step for the radiation term, and the characteristic method for the convective term. For each time step, the corresponding discretised expressions for temperature, enthalpy and fuel load can be computed separately for each spatial node, so their calculation can be parallelised. The radiation term (Eq. 7) is computed with numerical integration, solving the intensity ordinary differential (Eq. 8) with a second-order BDF finite difference method. In order to reduce computation time, the equations are only resolved using the *active nodes* placed around the perimeter where the fire occurs, as the operations only affect the nodes involved in the fire front, and not all the nodes in the domain.

3 Parallel Model Implementation

Modern computer architectures are commonly designed with multicore-processors to work at the same time. So it is increasingly common to find programs working in parallel mode, taking advantage of this feature. OpenMP [15] is an *Application Programming Interface* (API) that provides all the language extensions needed for developing parallel applications. While the MPI framework [17] is the leading technique for parallel programming in highly-parallel systems or clusters, OpenMP framework also provides the potential to develop high-performance applications, as it allows creating threads for working simultaneously on the same computer.

Our model is developed in C++, and has three main parts:

1. *Preprocessing()*. This function initializes the model and reads the data from the initial domain, including layers, input variables and model parameters.
2. *Solve()*. This function computes the simulation from the previously acquired data.
3. *Postprocessing()*. This function saves the simulation results.

Firstly, the sequential version of the model was analysed using the **Gprof** tool [13] to locate the most time-consuming functions in the code. The analysis reports an 84.1% execution time for FireSimulator:Solve() function. As this function represents the bulk of the program, achieving a better performance focused on improving this function using OpenMP. We therefore analyse the callgraph report looking for loops potentially parallelizables in the *Solve()* function. Some of these methods present a considerable number of shared variables or other inconveniences in the loop (such as loop breaking) which mean they cannot become a parallel region. After a careful review of the analysis, the parallelisable code represents approximately an 85% execution time, and the remaining 15% corresponds to the sequential code.

As Amdahl's law [1] concludes, the theoretical speed-up in latency of a program is limited by the part of the application that cannot be parallelised. The minimum execution time we could then obtain using a parallel version of the program is shown in Eq. (10), where t_{seq} represents the execution time in sequential mode, and N_{th} the number of threads used. In addition, Eq. (11) expresses the maximum speed we could obtain. When the number of threads N_{th} tends to infinity, the limit of the speed-up is reached, and the equation value is $1/0.15 = 6.67$.

$$t_{par}(N_{th}) = 0.15 * t_{seq} + \frac{0.85}{N_{th}} * t_{seq} \tag{10}$$

$$S_{N_{th}} = \frac{t_{seq}}{0.15 * t_{seq} + \frac{0.85}{N_{th}} * t_{seq}} = \frac{1}{0.15 + \frac{0.85}{N_{th}}} \tag{11}$$

After recoding the *for* loops into the model algorithms for independent iterations, the OpenMP language directives have been used to achieve parallelism. In this way, the **#pragma omp parallel for** directive enables the distribution of a task among the available threads speeding-up the execution. The scheduling of the iterations is *dynamic*: each thread executes a chunk of iterations then requests another chunk until none remains to be distributed. This method allows accessing consecutive elements in arrays containing the input variables. Besides that, the data-sharing attribute clause is *shared*; so the array of input variables and the results are shared among all threads. This configuration leads to a negligible increment in the global memory when the application runs in parallel mode.

A parallel implementation of the algorithms in our model requires identifying both major operations: matrix initialisation and basic matrix operations such as addition, subtraction or multiplication. Accordingly, each thread retrieves a chunk of elements, performs the assigned tasks and saves the result in a final shared matrix where all the elements are independent.

The sequential *Solve()* function is outlined in Algorithm 1. The *for* loops included in the following members of the *Solve()* function have been distributed among the available threads in a parallel version for a better performance.

Algorithm 1. Sequential *Solve()* function in the model. Sections 1 to 7 have been parallelised into threads.

Solve() {

1. Comp. of the initial values in the domain: {- *1.Parallel loop* -}
   - u_0: Dimensionless solid fuel temperature.
   - c_0: Dimensionless fuel mass fraction.
   - e_0: Dimensionless enthalpy.
2. For each simulation epoch:
   (a) Comp. of the node convection in the 2D domain. {- *2.Parallel loop* -}
   (b) Comp. of the 3D temperature for radiation comp. {- *3.Parallel loop* -}
   (c) Set active nodes in 2D domain. {- *4.Parallel loop* -}
   (d) Comp. of the radiation (for each active node):
      i. Solve the numerical integration (Eq. 7). {- *5.Parallel loop* -}
      ii. Solve the intensity ODE (Eq. 8). {- *6.Parallel loop* -}
      iii. Update values u, e, c. {- *7.Parallel loop* -}

}

---

4 Experiments and Results

4.1 Real Case Study

The topographic data used in our experiments were taken from an area in Osoño (Galicia), situated in the northwest of Spain, where a real fire occurred in August, 2009. The wildfire ignited at 3.45 p.m. (local time) on August 17th, 2009. Despite the firefighters' efforts to bring the fire under control in the early hours, it was not stabilised until the following day at 3.45 a.m. Finally, the fire was extinguished at 9.10 p.m. on August 18th, burning a total area of 224 *ha*.

The simulation area is a surface of 3.315 *m* x 2.740 *m*, where the altitude ranges from 540 *m* to 680 *m* above sea level. The average slope ranges from 6.56% at the initial point to 2.86% at the end. The fire spread over an irregular surface with discontinuous slopes, watersheds, river basins and even firebreaks. Fuel data were collected from the IFN4 database, with fuel type distribution according to BEHAVE classification [3]. Weather data were gathered from a nearby weather station 3.750 *m* from the fire ignition, providing ambient temperature and wind data. The initial wind speed was about 11.45 km/h, increasing to 17.26 km/h, and moving from the west to the north.

The input layers in the domain are therefore transformed into an array of 663 × 548 nodes, as the model considers a 5 m cell size. The model must operate over four layers, with more than 363, 000 nodes per layer, to solve the system of equations detailed in Sect. 2. Moreover, the real input variables and parameters detailed above must be resolved by the model, along with the numerical integration in the nodes placed around the fire area to provide the simulation result.

4.2 Performance Analysis/Evaluation

The main objective pursued in this research is to evaluate the potential benefit of using the parallel version of the model rather than the sequential version. To achieve this, our parallel version has been developed as detailed in Sect. 3 and compiled by GCC 5.4.0 using the *-O3* compilation flag with OpenMP 4.0. The experiments have been run on a workstation with a Xeon Broadwell Processor E5-1650 v4 at 3.60 GHz with six cores and 12 threads, 15 MB of cache memory and a memory of 16 GB of DDR4/2400 MHz ECC Reg. To prevent the processor from handling the frequency and obtain an adequate correlation of the data, the *Intel SpeedStep* and *Turbo Boost* technologies have been disabled.

By taking data on the Osoño fire as input data, each test was performed at least five times, increasing the number of the threads from one (sequential) to 12, as this is the maximum number of threads supported by the workstation. For the parallel time analysis, only the execution time of the *Solve()* function is considered. Table 1 summarises the average execution time collected from one to four hours of fire spread simulation time.

Table 1. *Solve()* function execution time in seconds obtained for every hour simulated.

Hour	Number of threads											
	Seq.	2	3	4	5	6	7	8	9	10	11	12
1	93.8	51.8	37.3	29.8	28.5	24.2	21.0	19.8	19.5	19.0	17.5	18.0
2	229.6	130.2	86.4	74.6	62.4	54.3	48.4	46.7	44.4	43.7	41.7	42.4
3	434.4	228.5	157.2	122.6	107.9	88.8	82.8	77.8	75.2	73.8	73.0	72.5
4	653.3	355.1	241.7	186.0	154.8	137.1	126.1	118.3	113.5	111.3	109.4	108.8

The results gathered from the experiments show how the execution time depends on the number of threads involved. Hence, whereas the sequential execution of one hour using one thread (sequential) took 93.8 s, this time decreased according to the number of threads configured in the simulation until the best time of 17.5 s was reached when 11 threads were used. In this case, the execution time running in parallel t_{par} among 11 threads is up to 18.75% of the sequential runtime t_{seq}.

Speed-up, which is defined as the ratio of sequential time t_{seq} to parallel execution time t_{par}, is detailed in Table 2.

Table 2. *Solve()* function Speed-up obtained from one to four hours of fire spread simulation.

Hour	Number of threads										
	Seq.	2	3	4	5	6	7	8	9	10	11	12
1	1	1.81	2.51	3.15	3.28	3.87	4.46	4.72	4.79	4.92	5.33	5.19
2	1	1.76	2.66	3.08	3.67	4.22	4.74	4.91	5.17	5.25	5.50	5.41
3	1	1.90	2.76	3.54	4.02	4.89	5.24	5.58	5.78	5.89	5.95	5.99
4	1	1.84	2.70	3.51	4.22	4.73	5.14	5.52	5.75	5.87	5.97	6.00

The model's parallelisation recorded a considerable difference in performance depending on the number of threads configured in the simulation, as detailed in Table 2. This table shows how the execution time for one hour of simulation significantly improves when the first six threads were used and therefore, a 74.15% (3.87) speed-up increase over the sequential time was raised. The remaining improvement, around 6%, was achieved when the rest of the threads were used: from six threads with 74.15% (3.87) over the sequential time to 11 threads with 81.25% (5.33). However, the results between 10–12 threads may fluctuate by less than 1%, and are not therefore meaningful because the operating system also keeps running, and affects the optimal number of threads for the best results.

As detailed in Sect. 3, the theoretical maximum speed-up we could obtain when the number of threads tends to infinity is defined in Eq. 11, and its value is $1/0.15 = 6.67$. The results gathered from four hours of fire spread simulation using 12 threads provide a 6.00 x maximum speed-up over the sequential time, which is not far from the theoretical speed.

Furthermore, in order to check how the increase in threads influences the increase in speed-up , the *parallel efficiency* $E_{N_{th}} = (t_{seq}/t_{par})/N_{th}$ (%) is evaluated, where N_{th} is the number of threads involved.

Figure 2 summarises the speed-up and parallel efficiency of four hours of fire spread simulation. In this case, the speed-up increases linearly until six threads that matches with the number of the cores of the workstation. A slight increase in the speed-up has then been observed according to the number of threads (from 7 to 12) configured in the runtime. This effect is due to *Hyper-Threading*

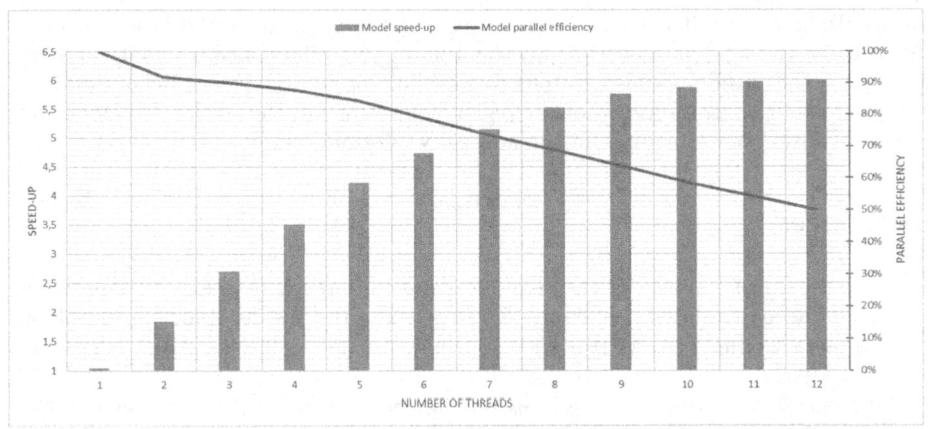

Fig. 2. Speed-up and parallel efficiency for four hours of fire spread simulation.

technology that allows running the concurrent scheduling of two processes per core. At this point, efficiency decreases from around 80% using six threads to 50% when 12 threads are involved. As Amdahl's law describes, when the number of threads increases, a parallel overhead appears causing a deterioration of speed-up and parallel efficiency. This drop in performance is due to the OpenMP programming methodology's loop-scheduling overhead when the model's loops are parallelised.

5 Conclusions and Further Research

This research describes a parallel version of a simplified semi-physical wildland fire spread model using OpenMP. This model's sequential version is analysed and improved using the **#pragma omp parallel for** directive to develop a parallel version. In this way, all the independent loop iterations can be distributed among the available threads to speed-up the execution. The experimental results for a simulation of a real fire in Osoño show an improvement in the speed-up when the parallel version of the model is used. Nevertheless, performance efficiency decreases in step with the number of threads involved in the simulation. However, our improved parallel model computes simulations much more quickly: one hour of fire spread can be simulated in less than 50 s, and four hours in about four minutes.

Although our model is under continuous development, we are currently working on improving the performance reported in this work by using the CUDA framework to run the model on GPU. Future work on the model will also include a new approach for working on a cluster or in a highly-parallel system combining OpenMP and MPI frameworks. Furthermore, we are also studying other models, including wind models [12], which may exploit parallelisation capabilities for a better performance.

Acknowledgement. This work has been partially supported by the Department of Education of the regional government, the Junta of Castilla y León, Grant contract: SA020U16. The authors are also grateful to Arsenio Morillo Rodríguez chief of the *forest prevention and valorization area* of the regional government, the *Xunta de Galicia*, for his technical support providing all the necessary information about the *Osoño* fire.

References

1. Amdahl, G.M.: Validity of the single processor approach to achieving large scale computing capabilities. In: Proceedings of the April 18–20, 1967, Spring Joint Computer Conference, AFIPS 1967 (Spring), pp. 483–485, New York, NY, USA. ACM (1967)
2. Anderson, H.E.: Aids to determining fuel models for estimating fire behavior. General Technical Report INT-122, U.S. Department of Agriculture, Forest Service, Intermountain Forest and Range Experiment Station (1982)
3. Andrews, P.L.: BEHAVE: fire behavior prediction and fuel modeling system-BURN subsystem, Part 1. U.S. Department of Agriculture, Forest Service, Intermountain Research Station Ogden, UT (1986)
4. Arca, B., Ghisu, T., Spataro, W., Trunfio, G.A.: GPU-accelerated optimization of fuel treatments for mitigating wildfire hazard. Procedia Comput. Sci. **18**, 966–975 (2013)
5. Asensio, M.I., Ferragut, L., Simon, J.: A convection model for fire spread simulation. Appl. Math. Lett. **18**(6), 673–677 (2005). Special issue on the occasion of MEGA 2003
6. Cascón, J.M., Engdahl, Y.A., Ferragut, L., Hernández, E.: A reduced basis for a local high definition wind model. Comput. Methods Appl. Mech. Eng. **311**, 438–456 (2016)
7. Cencerrado, A., Artés, T., Cortés, A., Margalef, T.: Relieving uncertainty in forest fire spread prediction by exploiting multicore architectures. Procedia Comput. Sci. **51**, 1752–1761 (2015)
8. Esvensen, G.: Data Assimilation, The Ensemble Kalman Filter. Springer, Heidelberg (2009)
9. Ferragut, L., Asensio, M.I., Cascón, J.M., Prieto, D.: A simplified wildland fire model applied to a real case. In: Casas, F., Martinez, V. (eds.) Advances in Differential Equations and Applications, pp. 155–167. Springer International Publishing, Cham (2014)
10. Ferragut, L., Asensio, M.I., Cascón, J.M., Prieto, D.: A wildland fire physical model well suited to data assimilation. Pure Appl. Geophys. **172**(1), 121–139 (2015)
11. Ferragut, L., Asensio, M.I., Monedero, S.: Modelling radiation and moisture content in fire spread. Commun. Numer. Methods Eng. **23**(9), 819–833 (2007)
12. Ferragut, L., Asensio, M.I., Simon, J.: High definition local adjustment model of 3D wind fields performing only 2D computations. Int. J. Numer. Methods Biomed. Eng. **27**(4), 510–523 (2011)
13. Graham, S.L., Kessler, P.B., Mckusick, M.K.: Gprof: a call graph execution profiler. In: SIGPLAN Notices, vol. 17, no. 6, pp. 120–126 (1982)
14. Innocenti, E., Silvani, X., Muzy, A., Hill, D.R.C.: A software framework for fine grain parallelization of cellular models with OpenMP: application to fire spread. Environ. Model. Softw. **24**(7), 819–831 (2009)

15. Itzkowitz, M., Mazurov, O., Copty, N., Lin, Y.: An OpenMP runtime API for profiling. Sun Microsystems, Inc., OpenMP ARB White Paper. http://www.compunity.org/futures/omp-api.html
16. Mandel, J., Bennethum, L.S., Beezley, J.D., Coen, J.L., Douglas, C.C., Kim, M., Vodacek, A.: A wildfire model with data assimilation. Math. Comput. Simul. **79**, 584–606 (2008)
17. MPI Forum. Message Passing Interface (MPI) Forum Home Page, December 2009. http://www.mpi-forum.org/
18. Pastor, E., Zárate, L., Planas, E., Arnaldos, J.: Mathematical models and calculation systems for the study of wildland fire behaviour. Prog. Energy Combust. Sci. **29**(2), 139–153 (2003)
19. Perry, G.L.W.: Current approaches to modelling the spread of wildland fire: a review. Prog. Phys. Geogr. **22**(2), 222–245 (1998)
20. Prieto, D., Asensio, M.I., Ferragut, L., Cascón, J.M.: Sensitivity analysis and parameter adjustment in a simplified physical wildland fire model. Adv. Eng. Softw. **90**, 98–106 (2015)
21. Scott, J.H., Burgan, R.E.: Models, standard fire behavior Fuel : a comprehensive set for use with Rothermel's surface fire spread model. General Technical Report RMRS-GTR-153, U.S. Department of Agriculture, Forest Service, Rocky Mountain Research Station (2005)
22. Sullivan, A.L.: Wildland surface fire spread modelling, 1990–2007. 1: physical and quasi-physical models. Int. J. Wildland Fire **18**(4), 349–368 (2009)
23. Sullivan, A.L.: Wildland surface fire spread modelling, 1990–2007. 2: empirical and quasi-empirical models. Int. J. Wildland Fire **18**(4), 369–386 (2009)
24. Sullivan, A.L.: Wildland surface fire spread modelling, 1990–2007. 3: simulation and mathematical analogue models. Int. J. Wildland Fire **18**(4), 387–403 (2009)

A Study on the Noise Label Influence in Boosting Algorithms: AdaBoost, GBM and XGBoost

Anabel Gómez-Ríos(✉), Julián Luengo, and Francisco Herrera

Department of Computer Science and Artificial Intelligence,
University of Granada, CITIC-UGR, 18071 Granada, Spain
anabelgrios@correo.ugr.es, {julianlm,herrera}@decsai.ugr.es

Abstract. In classification, class noise alludes to incorrect labelling of instances and it causes the classifiers to perform worse. In this contribution, we test the resistance against noise of the most influential boosting algorithms. We explain the fundamentals of these state-of-the-art algorithms, providing an unified notation to facilitate their comparison. We analyse how they carry out the classification, what loss functions use and what techniques employ under the boosting scheme.

Keywords: Class noise · Boosting · Classification

1 Introduction

In Data Mining, we want to extract helpful knowledge from great amounts of data. In this extraction process high quality data is mandatory in order to obtain valuable results. However, it is common that real world data is far from being perfect. In classification, one kind of corruption in the data is noise and it can affect the labels assigned to the instances, changing the class the instances belong, or the input attributes, affecting the input feature's values of the instances. We will focus on the former kind of noise that appears in the labels, usually known as class or label noise. The presence of noise in real data causes the classifiers to perform worse and it is the reason why it is important to use algorithms able to handle certain levels of imperfections in the data.

Boosting is one of the most prominent classification techniques in the state-of-the-art, providing the best accuracy levels at many problems. However, the most known boosting algorithm, AdaBoost, has already been proved to be sensitive against noise [5,12,14]. We want to explore if some of the most recent boosting algorithms, which perform better than AdaBoost, show the same noise sensitivity problem.

In this contribution, we will focus on the comparison of the basics among AdaBoost and state-of-the-art boosting algorithms: Generalized Boosted Models (GBM) [8,9], and eXtreme Gradient Boosting (XGBoost) [4], which hasn't been done yet. We will compare their robustness against noise too, taking into account

F.J. Martínez de Pisón et al. (Eds.): HAIS 2017, LNAI 10334, pp. 268–280, 2017.
DOI: 10.1007/978-3-319-59650-1_23

AdaBoost as a baseline classic approach. In order to compare the robustness, we will test the accuracy of the algorithms at diverse levels of artificial class noise, 5%, 10% and 20%, introduced in 21 different datasets. Then we will use the Equalized Loss of Accuracy (ELA) metric [16] to measure the robustness of the algorithms.

The rest of the paper is organized as follows: in Sect. 2 we set the background of this study, including previous works to make AdaBoost works better with class noise, transforming it into a noise robust algorithm. In Sect. 3 we introduce the most known boosting algorithms: AdaBoost, GBM and XGBoost, and we perform a comparison between them. In Sect. 4 we present the experimental study, along with the accuracy and ELA values of the considered algorithms. Finally, some conclusions and future work are commented in Sect. 5.

2 Class Noise. Preprocessing vs. Robust Methods

When dealing with real world data in classification, a common problem is the presence of noise in the form of alterations of some values in the data. We need to be careful and not misrecognize noisy examples as outliers or good examples. There are two types of noise: *class noise*, when the corruptions affects the labels of the instances, and *attribute noise*, when it appears in the input attributes of the instances. Noise can affect learning in several ways: if attribute noise appears in instances located in class boundaries, it is probable that instances belonging to a class intrude the area of another class. This will guide to misleaded classification models. Class noise can affect the decisions made in supervised learning, leading to more complex and larger models which can overfit the data. This implies less accuracy, more building time and changes in the interpretability of the model built [10].

When it comes to class noise, we can find three main approaches to deal with it if we don't have an expert to double-check the data. These three approaches are [10]: robust learners, data polishing methods and noise filters. The first of them is based on building learners which are able to deal with noise explicitly. Data polishing methods and noise filters works at data level, relabelling or removing, respectively, the instances marked as noise. Both of them are independent from the classifier but they are time consuming and noisy filters imply loss of information which can be useful to build a good learner. Robust learners, while harder to design, do not suffer from these problems.

How can we obtain robust learners against noise? A classic example is C4.5. It avoids the overfitting caused by the isolated instances, which are usually noisy, by pruning the decision tree generated. Pruning is one simple way to construct robust learners, but there are several alternatives, like training different classifiers instead of one, using the advantages of each one. We can also model the noise distribution and modify the weights of the instances with a high probability of being a noisy instance. Another strategy is to use semi-supervised methods to detect misclassified instances and prevent the models to be influenced by the unlabelled examples by using the dataset without the labels first. A good review about these noise coping strategies is presented in [6].

Boosting is one of the most successful classification techniques, but we already know that boosting algorithms are very sensitive to noise. This has been studied specially in AdaBoost [5,12,14]. AdaBoost usually excessively increases the weight for noisy instances. There are previous works trying to overcome this limitation, like ORBoost, which removes the instances with unusually high weights [11], or HABOND, which re-labels or removes the noisy instances based on some thresholds [2]. There are also previous works fixing this problem by building a robust AdaBoost which doesn't remove noisy instances but limits the weights, so that AdaBoost doesn't focus on them [3,13,17].

3 Boosting Methods. Most Influential vs. State-of-the-Art

Boosting [7] is a well-known supervised learning algorithm, based on the reiterated use of a weak classifier. This weak classifier only has to perform slightly better than a random classifier. We need to feed it with different training sets in order to force it to deduce something new from the data every time we use it. Therefore, it will obtain different results every time, which will be combined to get a good final model. These deductions are made sequentially, i.e. boosting uses all the information about the data obtained before to train again the weak classifier. This implies that boosting focuses in the misclassified examples in the previous step, allowing the algorithm to classify the harder instances.

In this section we suppose we have a dataset $\{(\mathbf{x}_i, y_i)\}_1^n$ of n input examples with m variables $\mathbf{x}_i = (\mathbf{x}_{i1}, \ldots, \mathbf{x}_{im})$, $i \in \{1, 2, \ldots, n\}$ and a output variable $\mathbf{y} = (y_1, \ldots, y_n)$. In Sect. 3.1 we analyse the most influential boosting algorithm, AdaBoost. In Sects. 3.2 and 3.3 we analyse more recent and more used boosting algorithms: GBM and XGBoost, respectively. Lastly, in Sect. 3.4 we provide a comparison between these three algorithms.

3.1 AdaBoost

AdaBoost [7] is the most influential, classical and well-known boosting algorithm. It handles a distribution, denoting the weights of every instance. This distribution, D_t, will change in every iteration t, i.e. every time AdaBoost calls the weak classifier. The weights will tell AdaBoost which instances have to be in more consideration than others: larger weight in a instance implies that instance has been misclassified, so it need more attention in the next call to the weak classifier (the weights will be set equally for all the instances at the beginning). Every time AdaBoost trains a weak classifier, it returns a weak hypothesis, h_t, and we want to select a h_t that minimizes the weighted error

$$\varepsilon_t = \Pr_{i \sim D_t}[h_t(\mathbf{x}_i) \neq y_i]. \tag{1}$$

Then, AdaBoost chooses a parameter, α_t, which measures the weak hypothesis importance. That way, the more accuracy h_t gets, the more importance we assign to it. Originally, Freund and Schapire defined this parameter as

$$\alpha_t = \log\left(\frac{1 - \varepsilon_t}{\varepsilon_t}\right), \tag{2}$$

which distributes half of the weight among misclassified examples and the other half among well-classified examples.

Breiman [1] defined α_t as

$$\alpha_t = \frac{1}{2}\log\left(\frac{1-\varepsilon_t}{\varepsilon_t}\right), \tag{3}$$

which distributes more weight among well-classified examples than among misclassified examples.

After that, AdaBoost updates the distribution for every example $\mathbf{x}_i$ with label y_i, taking into account α_t and h_t:

$$D_{t+1}(i) = \frac{D_t(i)}{Z_t} \times \begin{cases} \exp(-\alpha_t) & \text{if } h_t(\mathbf{x}_i) = y_i \\ \exp(\alpha_t) & \text{if } h_t(\mathbf{x}_i) \neq y_i, \end{cases} \tag{4}$$

where Z_t is a normalization factor chosen so that D_t sums one.

When all the iterations T have finished, AdaBoost returns a final hypothesis

$$H(\mathbf{x}) = \text{sign}\left(\sum_{t=1}^{T} \alpha_t h_t(\mathbf{x})\right). \tag{5}$$

Originally, AdaBoost was proposed for binary classification only, but there are extensions to the multi-class classification problem, like AdaBoost M.1 [1]. The difference between them is that AdaBoost M.1 uses the indicator function, $\mathbf{I}(\cdot)$, when calculating the errors of the weak classifier and when updating the distribution. Specifically, the weight update turns out to be

$$D_{t+1}(i) = D_t(i)\exp\left(\alpha_t \mathbf{I}(h_t(\mathbf{x}_i) \neq y_i)\right) \tag{6}$$

and after that the weights D_{t+1} are normalized to sum one, just like in AdaBoost.

The weak classifier can be implemented with any classification algorithm. However, it is usually implemented using unprunned classification trees, because unprunned trees provide different models if the data are varied. In particular, `adabag` [1], which is the `R` package we will use, uses classification trees.

3.2 GBM

In GBM [8,9,15], we want to find a function $F^*(\mathbf{x})$ that maps every $\mathbf{x}$ to its class y, so we can predict the output $\widehat{y}$, so that the expected value of a loss function $L(F(\mathbf{x}), y)$ is minimized

$$F^*(\mathbf{x}) = \arg\min_{F(\mathbf{x})} E_{\mathbf{x},y}[L(F(\mathbf{x}), y)]. \tag{7}$$

GBM approximates this function by an additive expansion of J functions using regression trees $h(\mathbf{x}; \mathbf{a})$ [9]:

$$\widehat{F}(\mathbf{x}) = \sum_{j=1}^{J} h(\mathbf{x}; \mathbf{a}_j). \tag{8}$$

The current version of the GBM package in R CRAN implements several loss functions and models, like the Cox Proportional Hazard or the quantile regression, always following the approach described in [8]. Here we are going to focus in the AdaBoost distribution implementation and the multinomial distribution, which is the AdaBoost multi-class version.

As we have just said, GBM works with regression trees instead of classification trees, so inside the general algorithm for any loss function we want to find a regression function $\widehat{F}(\mathbf{x})$ that minimizes the loss function expectation. GBM does this iteratively using a stochastic gradient descent scheme: in every iteration j, it fits a regression tree over the loss function's negative gradient evaluated at the current function $\widehat{F}_j(\mathbf{x})$ using only a randomly selected subset from the original dataset. Then it computes, for the regression tree obtained, the optimal node predictions. Then it adds these predictions to the current function (for each feature $\mathbf{x}$, it adds to the node in which $\mathbf{x}$ would fall the optimal prediction for that node) using a shrinkage parameter to reduce the movement. The full algorithm is described in [15], Fig. 2. The boosting scheme is clear: in every iteration, GBM trains a weak classifier with the information obtained until that moment (it uses the current function $\widehat{F}_j(\mathbf{x})$) and adds the information from the weak classifier to the current function, updating it.

After this loop, we have a regression function $\widehat{F}(\mathbf{x})$ and we need the output labels for the new examples given to the model. Generally speaking, GBM transforms $\widehat{F}(\mathbf{x})$ into probabilities: for each $\mathbf{x}$, the probability that $\mathbf{x}$ belongs to each class. Then it chooses the class with higher probability. The way this is done depends on the number of classes, and therefore, the distribution used.

For AdaBoost distribution (two classes), it uses the exponential loss function:

$$L(F(\mathbf{x}), y) = \exp\left(-2yF(\mathbf{x})\right)), \quad y \in \{-1, 1\}, \tag{9}$$

where

$$F(\mathbf{x}) = \frac{1}{2} \log \left(\frac{\Pr(y = 1|\mathbf{x})}{\Pr(y = -1|\mathbf{x})} \right). \tag{10}$$

However, the GBM package works with labels in $\{0, 1\}$, so minimizing L is equivalent to minimize $L_1(F(\mathbf{x}), y) = \exp\left(-2(y-1)F(\mathbf{x})\right) \;\; y \in \{0, 1\}$, which is the function implemented in the package.

Using this loss function, GBM returns a regression function $\widehat{F}(\mathbf{x})$ and computes the probability that $\mathbf{x}$ belongs to class 0:

$$p_0(\mathbf{x}) = \frac{1}{1 + \exp\left(-2\widehat{F}(\mathbf{x})\right)}. \tag{11}$$

It isn't necessary to compute the probability that $\mathbf{x}$ belongs to class 1: if $p_0(\mathbf{x})$ is less than 0.5, then it assigns class 1 to $\mathbf{x}$.

For the multinomial distribution (K classes), it uses the loss function [8]:

$$L(\{F_k(\mathbf{x}), y_k\}_1^K) = -\sum_{k=1}^{K} y_k \log \left[\frac{\exp\left(F_k(\mathbf{x})\right)}{\sum_{l=1}^{K} \exp\left(F_l(\mathbf{x})\right)} \right], \tag{12}$$

where y_k works like an indicator function: $y_k = 1$ if class $= k$ and $y_k = 0$ in any other case, and

$$F_k(\mathbf{x}) = \log\left(p_k(\mathbf{x})\right) - \frac{1}{K}\sum_{l=1}^{K} \log\left(p_l(\mathbf{x})\right), \tag{13}$$

where

$$p_k(\mathbf{x}) = Pr(y_k = 1|\mathbf{x}) = \frac{\exp\left(F_k(\mathbf{x})\right)}{\sum_{l=1}^{K} \exp\left(F_l(\mathbf{x})\right)} \in [0, 1]. \tag{14}$$

This way, GBM computes K regression functions $\widehat{F_1}, \ldots, \widehat{F}_K$ as we explained before, and calculates the probability that every $\mathbf{x}$ belongs to every class $k \in \{1, \ldots, K\}$ through $p_k(\mathbf{x})$. After that, we assign to each $\mathbf{x}$ the class corresponding to the highest probability.

3.3 XGBoost

In XGBoost [4], like in GBM, we want to find a function $F^*(\mathbf{x})$ that maps $\mathbf{x}$ to y in order to predict the output $\widehat{y}$. XGBoost approximates $F^*(\mathbf{x})$ by an additive expansion of J regression trees too (h belonging to the space of regression trees):

$$\widehat{F}(\mathbf{x}) = \sum_{j=1}^{J} h(\mathbf{x}, \mathbf{a}_j), \tag{15}$$

but instead of minimizing just a loss function L, in every iteration j it minimizes

$$L'(\widehat{F}_j(\mathbf{x}), y) = L(h(\mathbf{x}, \mathbf{a}_j), y) + \Omega(h(\mathbf{x}, \mathbf{a}_j)), \tag{16}$$

where $\Omega(h(\mathbf{x}, \mathbf{a}_j))$ is a function that punishes the complexity of the regression tree. XGBoost follows a iterative scheme like GBM, predicting trees with the current function obtained at the moment in each iteration, but XGBoost uses the first and second order gradient of the loss function L instead of just the first order gradient when calculating the tree in each iteration. It also uses a shrinkage parameter to reduce the optimal node predictions done in each iteration j before it adds this predictions to the current function $\widehat{F}_j$. Moreover, it uses row subsampling, like GBM, and column sumsampling. This three last techniques, along with the function Ω, allows XGBoost to avoid overfitting.

Besides that, XGBoost implements a lot of features in order to give a fast and scalable algorithm, like parallel and distributed computing, a tree learning algorithm for handling sparse data, an approximate algorithm for split finding when the data does not fit into memory, and so on. All of them can be seen in [4]. Here we are going to focus on how it carries out the binary and multiclass classification.

For binary classification it uses the logistic loss function:

$$L(p(\mathbf{x}), y) = y \log\left(p(\mathbf{x})\right) + (1 - y) \log\left(1 - p(\mathbf{x})\right), \tag{17}$$

where $y \in \{0,1\}$ and $p(\mathbf{x}) = \frac{1}{1+\exp(-F(\mathbf{x}))}$, so

$$L(F(\mathbf{x}), y) = y \log\left[\frac{1}{1+\exp(-F(\mathbf{x}))}\right] + (1-y)\log\left[\frac{\exp(-F(\mathbf{x}))}{1+\exp(-F(\mathbf{x}))}\right], \quad (18)$$

and $p(\mathbf{x})$ give us the way to transform the output regression function $\widehat{F}(\mathbf{x})$ into probabilities.

For multi-class classification with K classes it uses, like GBM, a loss function of the form

$$L(p_k(\mathbf{x}), y) = -\sum_{k=1}^{K} y_k \log(p_k(\mathbf{x})) \ , \quad (19)$$

where y_k works again like an indicator function: $y_k = 1$ if $\mathbf{x}$'s label is k and 0 in any other case, and

$$p_k(\mathbf{x}) = \frac{\exp(F_k(\mathbf{x}))}{\sum_{l=1}^{K} \exp(F_l(\mathbf{x}))}. \quad (20)$$

Again, $p_k(\mathbf{x})$ gives a way to change from the regression function obtained at the end of the iterations for every class k, $F_k(\mathbf{x})$, to probabilities, so XGBoost chooses for every instance $\mathbf{x}$ the class with higher probability.

3.4 Comparison Among AdaBoost, GBM and XGBoost

In Table 1 we summarize the main differences among AdaBoost as implemented in adabag package, GBM and XGBoost commented before.

Table 1. Differences among AdaBoost, GBM and XGBoost.

	Base classfiers	Ways to prevent overfitting	Loss function for binary classification	Loss function for multi-class classification
AdaBoost (adabag)	Classification trees	Row subsampling	$\sum_{i:h_t(\mathbf{x}_i)\neq y_i} D_t(i)$	$\sum_{i:h_t(\mathbf{x}_i)\neq y_i} D_t(i)$
GBM	Regression trees	Row subsampling Shrinkage parameter	$L = \exp(-2(y-1)F(\mathbf{x}))$	$L = -\sum_{k=1}^{K} y_k \log\left[\frac{\exp(F_k(\mathbf{x}))}{\sum_{l=1}^{K}\exp(F_l(\mathbf{x}))}\right]$
XGBoost	Regression trees	Row subsampling Shrinkage parameter Column subsampling Regularization term in the objective function	$L = y\log(p(\mathbf{x})) + (1-y)\log(1-p(\mathbf{x}))$, $p(\mathbf{x}) = \frac{1}{1+\exp(-F(\mathbf{x}))}$	$L = -\sum_{k=1}^{K} y_k \log\left[\frac{\exp(F_k(\mathbf{x}))}{\sum_{l=1}^{K}\exp(F_l(\mathbf{x}))}\right]$

4 Comparative Study with Noise

In this section we test the robustness of AdaBoost with Freund's and Breiman's weights, GBM and XGBoost. To do this, we have separated the study in binary problems and multi-class problems, due to the differences between the loss functions shown in Sect. 3. In Sect. 4.1 we fix the environment and parameters for the experiments. In Sects. 4.2 and 4.3 we show the results obtained for the binary and multi-class case, respectively.

4.1 Parameters Used in the Experiments

We have used eleven datasets for binary classification and ten datasets for multi-class classification. The datasets chosen can be seen in Table 2 and can be downloaded from the KEEL-dataset repository[1]. In every dataset a percentage of class noise is introduced in the training sets: 5%, 10% and 20%. The noise is introduced by choosing instances randomly and changing their class to another one. This is a Noise Completely at Random mechanism (NCAR), which is the more disruptive one, and allow us to study the noise effect more easily [10]. Five different seeds have been used to introduce the noise, generating five different versions of the noisy sets. This results in 336 different datasets in which we perform a 5-fold cross validation in order to measure the accuracy. Therefore, we have carried out 1680 experiments for each algorithm.

The categorical variables have been transformed into binary variables in order to be used with XGBoost R package.

Table 2. Number of attributes (#At) and number of examples (#Ex).

Binary				Multi-class			
Dataset	Acronym	#At	#Ex	Dataset	Acronym	#At	#Ex
Heart	HEA	13	270	balance	BAL	4	625
Ionosphere	ION	33	351	car	CAR	6	1728
Monk-2	MON	6	432	contraceptive	CON	9	1473
Phoneme	PHO	5	5404	hayes-roth	HAY	4	160
Pima	PIM	8	768	iris	IRI	4	150
Ring	RIN	20	7400	segment	SEG	19	2310
Sonar	SON	60	208	splice	SPL	60	3190
Spambase	SPA	57	4597	newthyroid	NEW	5	215
Twonorm	TWO	20	7400	wine	WIN	13	178
WDBC	WDB	30	569	vehicle	VEH	18	846
German	GER	20	1000				

[1] http://keel.es/datasets.php.

The metric used to measure the robustness of the algorithms is ELA (Equalized Loss of Accuracy) [16], which has the following definition:

$$\text{ELA}_{x\%} = \frac{100 - \text{Acc}_{x\%}}{\text{Acc}_{0\%}}, \tag{21}$$

where $\text{Acc}_{x\%}$ denotes percentage of accuracy at a noise level $x\%$. That way, the smaller the ELA metric, the greater the robustness of the algorithm.

In general, we have tried to modify as less parameters as possible. The modified parameters can be seen in Table 3. The default numbers of iterations in GBM and AdaBoost (and therefore, the default number of trees generated) is 100. XGBoost doesn't set a default number of iterations, so we must give a value to the `nrounds` parameter. We have done an experiment with the datasets described in Table 2 and 20 is a good value. In AdaBoost, we need to set the `control` parameter to `minsplit=0` so it doesn't try to split a tree with no observations.

Table 3. Parameters fixed for every algorithm.

	Binary	Multi-class
AdaBoost	`coeflearn = "Freund"` or `"Breiman"` `control = (minsplit = 0)`	`coeflearn = "Freund"` or `"Breiman"` `control = (minsplit = 0)`
GBM	`distribution = "adaboost"`	`distribution = "multinomial"`

XGBoost	`objective = "binary:logistic"`
	`nrounds = 20`
		`objective = "multi:softmax"`
		`nrounds = 20`
		`num_class =` number of classes

4.2 Analysis of Results: Binary Case

Table 4 shows the complete accuracy results obtained in the experiments and Table 5 shows the ELA metric. The best accuracy or ELA value among the four algorithms is highlighted in each table. The row ALG refers to the algorithm considered: BRE means AdaBoost with Breiman's weights, FRE means Freund's weights and XGB is XGBoost. First of all, at noise level 0% (that is, without artificial noise introduced) XGBoost has more accuracy in half of the cases along with AdaBoost with Breiman's weights. When these two are not the algorithms with the highest accuracy, AdaBoost with Freund's weights is the technique with the best performance. However, there isn't large differences between the two aforementioned techniques and Adaboost with Freund's weights. Only GBM presents a differentiated behaviour, being the one with the least accuracy.

Regarding to the ELA metric, some interesting points can be made. If we compare Freund's and Breiman's weights for AdaBoost, Breiman's weights have less ELA value in most cases, which means AdaBoost with Breiman's weights is more robust than AdaBoost with Freund's weights, probably because Breiman distributes less weight between the wrongly classified examples. In particular,

Table 4. Accuracy obtained in binary datasets.

Noise	0%				5%				10%				20%			
ALG	BRE	FRE	GBM	XGB	BRE	FRE	GBM	XGB	BRE	FRE	GBM	XGB	BRE	FRE	GBM	XGB
HEA	79.63	80.74	55.56	**81.48**	78.30	78.44	56.59	**79.56**	74.67	73.56	59.11	**77.41**	69.85	68.00	63.70	**71.78**
ION	91.46	**92.03**	64.10	90.32	91.98	**92.26**	64.10	91.68	88.85	88.61	64.10	**89.18**	82.63	81.43	64.22	**83.65**
MON	**100.0**	**100.0**	61.11	**100.0**	94.91	94.26	71.82	**99.40**	91.39	89.86	66.77	**98.06**	84.59	81.34	63.12	**91.02**
PHO	84.38	83.75	70.65	**85.70**	86.19	85.72	70.65	**87.67**	85.26	84.69	70.65	**86.42**	83.80	83.12	70.65	**84.17**
PIM	73.83	73.71	65.10	**74.61**	72.53	70.52	65.10	**74.28**	70.94	70.08	65.10	**72.48**	67.43	65.08	65.10	**69.07**
RIN	**97.18**	97.01	69.09	95.31	**95.13**	93.58	69.73	95.08	93.97	90.58	65.56	**94.56**	**93.29**	86.39	66.18	92.41
SON	**83.67**	81.75	53.37	77.39	**81.61**	81.51	55.38	79.13	**80.19**	78.95	59.34	76.16	**75.08**	73.76	56.64	72.21
SPA	95.04	**95.43**	60.58	94.61	**94.30**	93.34	60.58	94.24	93.41	91.54	60.58	**93.60**	**92.36**	90.12	60.58	91.38
TWO	**96.42**	96.38	80.14	95.15	94.95	93.75	79.15	**95.07**	93.55	90.31	77.38	**94.02**	**92.18**	85.88	67.74	91.66
WDB	**97.54**	97.01	62.74	96.31	96.17	**96.20**	62.74	95.43	**94.90**	94.20	62.74	93.81	88.30	86.85	62.74	**88.89**
GER	74.10	73.00	70.00	**74.80**	72.72	72.00	70.00	**72.82**	72.18	70.40	70.00	**72.44**	67.30	65.10	70.00	**69.30**

Table 5. ELA in binary datasets.

Noise	5%				10%				20%			
ALG	BRE	FRE	GBM	XGB	BRE	FRE	GBM	XGB	BRE	FRE	GBM	XGB
HEA	27.26	26.70	78.13	**25.09**	27.70	28.74	63.78	**25.01**	30.15	32.00	59.39	**28.22**
ION	9.51	**9.24**	50.81	9.70	15.11	15.45	55.13	**14.50**	17.88	19.14	51.79	**17.15**
MON	6.09	7.02	52.81	**0.78**	9.06	10.63	54.85	**2.06**	15.98	19.36	46.02	**9.44**
PHO	14.16	14.72	46.78	**12.80**	19.89	20.97	41.93	**18.15**	19.55	20.81	39.28	**18.88**
PIM	27.74	29.80	49.83	**26.16**	52.78	52.65	68.53	**49.80**	39.84	42.30	60.69	**38.18**
RIN	**5.11**	6.73	31.31	5.16	6.29	9.81	48.69	**5.71**	**7.13**	14.62	40.55	8.04
SON	19.29	**19.20**	40.70	21.80	**21.10**	23.18	44.15	25.43	**32.14**	33.50	73.67	36.45
SPA	7.16	8.24	70.95	**7.06**	7.21	9.19	61.49	**7.08**	**7.64**	9.88	64.50	8.02
TWO	5.98	7.47	29.51	**5.76**	8.74	13.15	34.74	**8.01**	**8.04**	14.55	46.70	8.75
WDB	**4.58**	4.64	69.81	5.91	**5.36**	6.08	61.50	6.54	12.14	13.64	46.49	**11.67**
GER	**27.97**	28.86	47.82	28.22	37.54	40.55	42.86	**36.84**	39.38	43.02	40.15	**36.55**

at noise level 20% Breiman's weights have less ELA value in all datasets. If we compare the four algorithms at noise level 20%, AdaBoost with Breiman's weights has the best ELA values in four datasets.

If we compare GBM with the others algorithms, GBM has higher ELA values for all datasets at all noise levels, so GBM is the least robust algorithm.

Finally, considering XGBoost and the rest of the algorithms, we can observe that XGBoost is slightly better in more than half of the cases at noise level 5%. At noise level 10%, is the best algorithm in almost all datasets, only surpassed by AdaBoost with Freund's weights in two datasets. At noise level 20% XGBoost is again the best algorithm is most datasets. This means XGBoost is the most robust algorithm among the algorithms considered for binary datasets, probably because the methods to avoid overfitting it uses, which allows XGBoost to focus less than the other algorithms on misclassified instances. This is specially useful as noise increases.

Table 6. Accuracy obtained in multi-class datasets.

Noise	0%				5%				10%				20%			
ALG	BRE	FRE	GBM	XGB	BRE	FRE	GBM	XGB	BRE	FRE	GBM	XGB	BRE	FRE	GBM	XGB
BAL	82.88	81.12	74.72	**83.84**	**85.54**	83.94	72.51	81.22	**84.93**	84.13	71.33	80.29	**82.85**	82.75	72.22	76.51
CAR	**99.02**	98.90	70.02	98.32	95.52	95.47	70.02	**96.77**	94.58	94.32	70.02	**95.53**	92.07	91.91	70.02	**92.35**
CON	55.06	**56.82**	50.92	55.26	**55.48**	55.30	50.17	54.60	54.81	**55.13**	50.94	53.74	54.88	**55.13**	50.58	52.59
HAY	81.77	**82.54**	57.49	81.03	**83.58**	83.58	56.77	80.71	80.90	**81.81**	55.89	79.07	**78.01**	75.56	56.91	76.50
IRI	95.33	95.33	**96.67**	95.33	90.93	90.80	**94.80**	92.93	90.00	88.93	**94.80**	91.33	**91.87**	87.20	94.00	84.13
SEG	95.84	**95.97**	70.74	95.41	95.32	94.92	82.63	**96.94**	92.98	91.83	80.26	**95.54**	91.62	91.11	80.47	**93.39**
SPL	94.04	93.08	83.41	**94.36**	92.10	**92.60**	83.15	91.85	**90.72**	90.59	83.40	90.46	82.44	79.62	81.08	**84.07**
NEW	95.35	**96.28**	91.63	95.35	94.33	94.42	90.14	**94.60**	90.79	90.51	89.49	**92.19**	87.72	83.91	90.51	**88.65**
WIN	93.78	**94.89**	92.10	93.78	95.38	94.71	94.93	**95.72**	**94.23**	93.45	94.93	93.68	86.72	85.95	**93.25**	87.06
VEH	77.54	**78.13**	58.87	76.24	75.67	**76.50**	59.88	75.15	74.75	**74.89**	58.25	74.75	72.39	**73.05**	60.33	70.99

Table 7. ELA in multi-class datasets.

Noise	5%				10%				20%			
ALG	BRE	FRE	GBM	XGB	BRE	FRE	GBM	XGB	BRE	FRE	GBM	XGB
BAL	**14.61**	16.24	39.26	19.10	**27.37**	27.93	56.31	35.67	20.98	**20.90**	48.31	28.99
CAR	4.70	4.75	31.01	**3.39**	5.65	5.92	42.38	**4.68**	8.43	8.69	35.94	**8.11**
CON	46.69	**46.42**	54.38	47.62	48.18	**47.29**	53.27	49.33	58.19	**57.43**	83.96	62.19
HAY	20.62	**20.34**	77.81	23.68	20.88	**19.77**	68.81	23.17	**21.99**	24.44	70.50	23.50
IRI	10.74	10.98	**7.36**	8.25	13.54	15.01	**7.99**	11.62	**8.37**	13.19	8.68	16.65
SEG	5.60	6.22	32.54	**3.96**	7.39	8.56	32.58	**4.71**	8.69	9.23	24.37	**6.95**
SPL	8.10	**7.63**	26.86	8.47	**12.52**	12.89	23.71	12.75	21.18	25.12	25.33	**19.00**
NEW	5.73	5.64	14.08	**5.49**	16.73	16.70	20.64	**14.14**	15.02	19.50	16.50	**14.01**
WIN	4.85	5.55	5.25	**4.49**	**6.02**	6.82	7.17	6.62	14.12	15.10	**8.09**	13.71
VEH	25.51	**24.41**	43.78	26.06	26.92	**26.46**	45.33	26.92	35.61	**34.49**	67.38	38.05

4.3 Analysis of Results: Multi-class Case

Table 6 shows the complete accuracy results and Table 7 shows the ELA metric, obtained for the multi-class case. The best accuracy or ELA value among the four algorithms is highlighted in each table. The row ALG refers to the algorithm considered: BRE means AdaBoost with Breiman's weights, FRE means AdaBoost with Freund's weights and XGB is XGBoost. In this case at noise level 0% AdaBoost with Freund's weight is the best algorithm. However, there isn't large differences among AdaBoost with Freund's weights, XGBoost and AdaBoost with Breiman's weights, as all of them show good accuracy.

When we take the ELA measure into account, GBM obtains the highest ELA values in the majority of data sets again, becoming the least robust algorithm against noise. As we can see, when comparing Freund's weights and Breiman's weights in AdaBoost algorithm, there is not an outstanding algorithm. Lastly, between XGBoost and AdaBoost with Breiman's weights, XGBoost has less ELA values in more than half of the cases, although the differences aren't specially large. If we compare the four algorithms trough all levels of noise, XGBoost has better ELA values in at least the same number of datasets as the next best algorithm in every level of noise. In particular, at noise level 20%, XGBoost is the least affected by noise, which makes XGBoost the most robust algorithm among those considered for multi-class datasets too.

5 Conclusions and Future Work

In this first study we have described and compared for the first time three of the most important boosting paradigms. We have tested the robustness of these algorithms by calculating its accuracy in 21 different datasets and by using the ELA metric. XGBoost has turned out to be the most robust algorithm in both binary and multi-class datasets. However, this behaviour is better supported by the results in the binary case.

As future work, different ways to obtain a more robust algorithm can be explored. The influence of the number of classes in the loss of accuracy when the noise is introduced, using more multi-class datasets with more variety in the number of classes (here the majority of the multi-class datasets have three classes) can be studied deeper. The influence of the loss functions in the robustness of the algorithms should be analyzed. Lastly, the robust modifications designed for Adaboost should be exported to the best algorithm against noise found in this study, XGBoost, studying if it improves its robustness. We should explore how missing labels or label updating in data streams can affect the algorithm accuracy.

Acknowledgments. This work was supported by the National Research Project TIN2014-57251-P and Andalusian Research Plan P11-TIC-7765.

References

1. Alfaro, E., Gámez, M., García, N.: Adabag: an R package for classification with boosting and bagging. J. Stat. Softw. **54**(2), 1–35 (2013). https://www.jstatsoft.org/article/view/v054i02
2. Álvarez, P.M., Luengo, J., Herrera, F.: A first study on the use of boosting for class noise reparation. In: Martínez-Álvarez, F., Troncoso, A., Quintián, H., Corchado, E. (eds.) HAIS 2016. LNCS, vol. 9648, pp. 549–559. Springer, Cham (2016). doi:10.1007/978-3-319-32034-2_46
3. Cao, J., Kwong, S., Wang, R.: A noise-detection based AdaBoost algorithm for mislabeled data. Pattern Recogn. **45**(12), 4451–4465 (2012)
4. Chen, T., Gestrin, C.: A scalable tree boosting system. In: Proceedings of the 22nd ACM SIGKDD International Conference on Knowledge Discovery and Data Mining, pp. 785–794. ACM (2016)
5. Dietterich, T.G.: An experimental comparison of three methods for constructing ensembles of decision trees: Bagging, boosting, and randomization. Mach. Learn. **40**(2), 139–157 (2000)
6. Frénay, B., Verleysen, M.: Classification in the presence of noise: a survey. IEEE Trans. Neural Netw. Learn. Syst. **25**(5), 845–869 (2014)

7. Freund, Y., Schapire, R.E.: Foundations and algorithms. MIT press, Cambridge (2012)
8. Friedman, J.H.: Greedy function approximation: a gradient boosting machine. Ann. Stat. **29**(5), 337–374 (2002)
9. Friedman, J.H.: Stochastic gradient boosting. Comput. Stat. Data Anal. **38**, 367–378 (2002)
10. García, S., Luengo, J., Herrera, F.: Data Preprocessing in Data Mining. Springer, New York (2015)
11. Karmaker, A., Kwek, S.: A boosting approach to remove class label noise. Int. J. Hybrid Intell. Syst. **3**(3), 169–177 (2006)
12. McDonald, R.A., Hand, D.J., Eckley, I.A.: An empirical comparison of three boosting algorithms on real data sets with artificial class noise. In: Windeatt, T., Roli, F. (eds.) MCS 2003. LNCS, vol. 2709, pp. 35–44. Springer, Heidelberg (2003). doi:10.1007/3-540-44938-8_4
13. Miao, Q., Cao, Y., Xia, G., Gong, M., Liu, J., Song, J.: RBoost: label noise-robust boosting algorithm based on a nonconvex loss function and the numerically stable base learners. IEEE Trans. Neural Netw. Learn. Syst. **27**(11), 2216–2228 (2015)
14. Rätsch, G., Onoda, T., Mller, K.R.: Soft margins for AdaBoost. Mach. Learn. **42**(3), 287–320 (2001)
15. Ridgeway, G.: Generalized Boosted Models: A guide to the gbm package. Update **1**(1), 1–15 (2007)
16. Sáez, J.A., Luengo, J., Herrera, F.: Evaluating the classifier behaviour with noisy data considering performance and robustness: the equalized loss of accuracy measure. Neurocomputing **176**, 26–35 (2016)
17. Sun, B., Chen, S., Wang, J., Chen, H.: A robust multi-class AdaBoost algorithm for mislabeled noisy data. Knowl. Based Syst. **102**, 87–102 (2016)

rNPBST: An R Package Covering Non-parametric and Bayesian Statistical Tests

Jacinto Carrasco[1(✉)], Salvador García[1], María del Mar Rueda[2], and Francisco Herrera[1]

[1] Department of Computer Science and Artificial Intelligence, University of Granada, Granada, Spain
jacintocc@correo.ugr.es, {salvagl,herrera}@decsai.ugr.es
[2] Department of Statistic and Operational Research, University of Granada, Granada, Spain
mrueda@ugr.es

Abstract. Statistical tests has arisen as a reliable procedure for the validation of results in many kind of problems. In particular, due to their robustness and applicability, non-parametric tests are a common and useful tool in the process of design and evaluation of a machine learning algorithm or in the context of an optimization problem. New trends in the field of statistical comparison applied to the field of algorithms' performance comparison indicate that Bayesian tests, which provides a distribution over the parameter of interest, are a promising approach.

In this contribution rNPBST (*R Non-Parametric and Bayesian Statistical tests*), an R package that contains a set of non-parametric and Bayesian tests for different purposes as randomness tests, goodness of fit tests or two-sample and multiple-sample analysis is presented. This package constitutes also a solution which integrates many of non-parametric and Bayesian tests in a single repository.

Keywords: Non-parametric tests · Bayesian tests · R · Software

1 Introduction

In the development of machine learning and optimization algorithms there is an increasing need of validation and examination of uncertainty. Statistical tests are the recommended approach to ensure that conclusions obtained from the corresponding experiments are not biased by researcher intention or given by chance [15].

There are multiple tests that can be used with this purpose and can be categorized into two main categories: frequentist [20] and Bayesian tests [6]. The first group is subdivided in parametric, which will be not the subject of study in this contribution, and non-parametric tests [12]. Non-parametric tests do not have the strict conditions that parametric ones have, but it turns into a lower ability to find the existent differences between algorithms when conditions are fulfilled [16]. These prerequisites are usually the normality or the homoscedasticity, that

F.J. Martínez de Pisón et al. (Eds.): HAIS 2017, LNAI 10334, pp. 281–292, 2017.
DOI: 10.1007/978-3-319-59650-1_24

can be checked by non-parametric tests such as Kolmogorov-Smirnov test, as well as other properties of the distribution of the data, like the randomness of a sample. For the comparison of algorithms' performance, Wilcoxon Signed-Rank for two algorithms or Friedman test for the comparison of multiple algorithms are the usual methods. Beyond the descriptive overview about the statistical tests, an `R` package is proposed on this contribution as a collection of non-parametric and Bayesian statistical tests accessible from `R`. It also contains the functionality to plot the distribution of the parameter of interest for Bayesian tests, what helps to the understanding of these tests and synthesizes the information given by Bayesian tests.

This contribution is organized as follows. In Sect. 2 necessary statistical concepts and different statistical tests are described. In Sect. 3 we include an overview of principal methods and tests included in the R package and some examples of the use of the package. Section 4 concludes the contribution.

2 Statistical Background

In Sect. 2.1, basic statistical concepts are described. Next, in Sect. 2.2, the usual frequentist tests applied in the algorithms comparison are mentioned, with a special interest in non-parametric tests. The Bayesian tests for the comparisons between algorithms are included in Sect. 2.3.

2.1 Preliminary Concepts

In inferential statistics, we are interested in obtaining reliable predictions from data and it is necessary to avoid reaching erroneous conclusions by random effects. The main concepts we will use are [20]:

- The results of the algorithms involved in the comparison constitute a **sample**. It may represents the performance in one or many problems of one or many algorithms. From a statistical perspective, this sample comes from an unknown distribution and will be used to infer valuable information.
- When we talk about a **parameter** of interest, or the distribution of a parameter, we mean the measure used to evaluate the difference between the algorithms results or the goodness of fit of the sample with respect to a distribution.
- A frequentist approach to infer information consists in the calculation of a **statistic**, i.e. an estimator of a characteristic of the sample.
- The **distribution** from which we get the sample is unknown so the statistic will be used to estimate the parameter of interest.
- As we are interested in statistical comparisons, we must also pay attention to tests properties. So we define a **type I error** as rejecting $\mathcal{H}_0$ when it is true and a **type II error** when $\mathcal{H}_0$ is not rejected and it is false.
- The main measure to compare the test T quality is the **power**, i.e. the probability of rejecting $\mathcal{H}_0$. We are interested in a greater power with the same type I error, which is represented by the parameter of significance α.

2.2 Frequentist Tests

Frequentis tests are the most common tool in algorithms' performance comparison until now [9]. Here a non effect hypothesis, called null hypothesis ($\mathcal{H}_0$) and an alternative hypothesis ($\mathcal{H}_1$) are stated. Then, using the sample, we compute the probability of obtain a sample as far from null hypothesis as ours assuming $\mathcal{H}_0$ is true, this is called the p-value [20]. Then, if the obtained probability is lower than a fixed value α (usually 0.05), $\mathcal{H}_0$ is rejected, otherwise, there is no evidence enough for null hypothesis to be rejected.

Parametric Tests. They assume that our sample comes from a distribution from a known family of distributions, being the most usual the Gaussian distribution. The normality assumption usually leads to a more powerful test when it is satisfied. The main tests belonging to this section are the well known t-test for compare two paired sample and ANOVA in the comparison of multiple algorithms. In both tests the null hypothesis consists in the equivalence of the performance of the implied algorithms.

Non Parametric Tests. Non parametric tests do not assume that a sample comes from a distribution of a known family [18], so they have less restrictive conditions about sample distribution, such as symmetry o continuity. Consequently, non-parametric tests are more robust than parametric ones.

A safe use of an ANOVA or t-test implies that we certainly know that the sample comes from a normal distribution normality, so we can use the goodness of fit tests to at least, not dismiss that hypothesis. Examples of goodness of fit tests are Kolmogorov-Smirnov, Shapiro-Wilk and D'Agostino-Pearson tests [19].

The recommended test for the comparison of algorithms depends on the number of algorithms and different scenarios involved:

Sign and Signed-Rank Wilcoxon tests. Sign test is a non-parametric analogous for simple t-test and Wilcoxon test is the analogous for paired t-test. They use median instead of the mean as the parameter of interest of the distribution.

Friedman test. This is a non-parametric analogous for ANOVA test. The comparison is made between k algorithms in n datasets or benchmark functions. The statistic is computed from algorithms rankings for every problem. The more powerful Iman-Davenport proposal is based on this test.

Friedman Aligned-Ranks test. This upgrade of the simple Friedman test takes account of differences of performance among problems.

Post-hoc tests. Once the null hypothesis $\mathcal{H}_0$ is rejected, i.e. there are significant differences between algorithms performance, our purpose is to pinpoint exactly where the differences are. An adjustment of the p-values is needed in order to maintain the control over the family-wise error rate. Some examples of post-hoc tests are Bonferroni-Dunn, Holm, Holland, Hochberg or Li [9,11,13].

2.3 Bayesian Tests

A distinct approach is the Bayesian proposal made by Benavoli et al. [3]. The main idea is not to make a null hypothesis about the parameter of interest and the corresponding null hypothesis statistical test (NHST) but obtain a probability distribution of the parameter.

NHST Comparison. According To Benavoli [5], the main differences between the two approaches could be emphasize:

- In frequentist tests, decisions about a test significance are dichotomies based on the comparison between p-value and the significance level α. In Bayesian statistic, there is not a fixed threshold for the rejection of the null hypothesis but a distribution of the parameter from which we can get the probability of the null hypothesis being true.
- There is a common misunderstanding in the application of the NHST. The p-value does not represent the probability of the null hypothesis being true given the data, but the probability of obtaining a sample as far from the null hypothesis as the data assuming $\mathcal{H}_0$ is true. Usually the question we want to answer is the first one and this is which Bayesian statistic tests returns.
- A common critique made about NHST is that effect size and sample size are not distinguished. This implies that an effect as small as we want can be identified as significant if we add enough instances to the sample. Since the sample size depends on the researcher, they could be tempted to vary the number of observations until the desired result is obtained.
- A NHST does not offers information when null hypothesis is not rejected. In this situation we should not say that there is not a difference but we should say that we do not have evidence enough to reject the null hypothesis. However, in a Bayesian test, the distribution of the parameter is informative although it did not indicate a great difference between algorithms.
- The process to make inference in Bayesian statistics sets up a prior probability model (based on the information we got or with a non-informative prior distribution), calculates and interprets the posterior distribution reliant on the data, and a model evaluation.

Correlated Bayesian t-test. This is a Bayesian version of t-test used to compare the results of two machine learning algorithms in a k-fold cross-validation partition [8]. This test takes account of correlation among the folds. Data is considered to come from a multivariate Gaussian where the covariance matrix depends on the correlation ρ between folds. As ρ can not be estimated from data, the heuristic suggested by Nadeau and Bengio [17] is adopted and $\rho = \frac{n_{test}}{n_{tot}}$. Assuming a Normal-Gamma distribution as prior distribution of the difference between algorithms, we obtain a Student distribution as the posterior distribution of the parameter μ, i.e., the difference between means. We must also consider the possibility that there is no significant difference between performance, so a region of practical equivalence (rope) $[r_{min}, r_{max}]$ is defined for μ and probabilities of algorithms relationships are considered in terms of rope, for example for a_1, a_2 algorithms involved in the comparison, $P(a_1 \gg a_2) = P(\mu > r_{max})$ or $P(a_1 = a_2) = P(\mu \in \text{rope})$. The rope allows us to make automatic decisions, although we must be conscious that this implies that we are coming back to loose information and dichotomies. However, in this occasion the interpretation of the probabilities are direct and the limits for decisions can vary according to the context.

Bayesian Sign Test. The Bayesian version of non-parametric sign test uses the Dirichlet Process (DP) [4]. This can be seen as a probability distribution over a family of probability distributions, so inference is made in two steps:

- First we get the posterior probability density function as a linear combination of Dirac's deltas centred on the observations, whose weights comes from a Dirichlet distribution.
- Then, we approach the previous posterior probability function as a posterior probability from we can compute the probability of the belonging of the parameter to each region of interest.

Bayesian Signed Rank Test. The Bayesian version of signed-rank has the same statistical background that the Bayesian sign test. It also uses the DP as a method to make inference from the data. The differences lie in the fact that signed rank test uses two samples and the comparison between them in the compute of the probabilities of the possible relationships between algorithms. In this test we do not obtain a simple formula for the posterior distribution but we can get it by sampling the weights for a Dirichlet distribution.

3 rNPBST Package

This Section contains a description of the developed `R` package. In Sect. 3.1 we describe `JavaNPST`, the basis of the package presented in this contribution and the modifications made to use this package from `R`. Section 3.2 contains the descriptions of the datasets included in the `R` package and an illustration of the use of the package for the comparison of algorithms, mainly focusing on the Bayesian methods, due to the fact that they are not included in any available package in `R`, like `scmamp`, developed by Calvo and Santaf [7], which performs frequentist tests for the comparison among algorithms. Also authors of the Bayesian tests have a Github repository with these tests implemented in `Julia`.

3.1 Description

JavaNPST. The `rNPBST` package has been developed initially as a wrapper of the `Java` library `JavaNPST` developed by Derrac et al. [10]. It is an open Java library which integrates an extensive set of non-parametric statistical tests of different families and with different purposes.

In the original Java package only non-parametric tests were included but we added some attractive Bayesian tests and associated visualization methods using ggplot and ggtern [14]. Moreover, some of the tests implemented in the JavaNPST package made use of tables of distributions, here these tables are available for users as a R data file (a file with extension .rda that contains an R object which can be easily restored in an R session). Tests are classified into 11 classes according to the main purpose of the tests or the type of data that we have (Table 1).

rNPBST package is a Github[1] repository and can be installed using devtools package and executing in R:

```
devtools::install_github("JacintoCC/rNPBST")
```

3.2 Examples of Use

Comparative Study. To illustrate the use of some of the tests, we present a comparative study among 5 classic algorithms of machine learning for classification problems. Algorithms included in the comparison are mentioned in Table 2. The results of each algorithm's performance in the different datasets are stored in the package as an R object with a matrix shape that we can load in our R session. The name of the data frame for each algorithm is also in Table 2. Results across different partitions are summarized in the results dataset. The measure used in the performance of the algorithms in each dataset is the standard accuracy. The datasets used to obtain these measures are the 5-dob-cv partitions [2] of some of the available datasets[2] for classification in the KEEL repository [1] and the already made partitions that can be found in this repository.

Test of goodness of fit. In the description of parametric tests, we mentioned that these tests require to check like normality. We can use one of the family of goodness of fit tests to, at least, not reject the normality of a population to ensure a safe use of parametric tests. We could also perform this check of normality with chi-squared, Kolmogor-Smirnov or Anderson-Darling tests:

```
> lill.test <- lilliefors.test(results.rf[1, ]) lill.test$parameters
> mean sd 0.26553804 0.02756517 lill.test$p.value Asymptotic p-value
> <= 1
```

As we could expect from a small sample of the distribution of the accuracy of an algorithm in a dataset, there is no evidence enough to reject the normality test.

[1] http://www.github.com.

[2] Abalone, australian, automobile, balance, breast, bupa, car, cleveland, crx, dermatology, german, glass, hayes-roth, heart, ionosphere, led7digit, letter, lymphography, mushroom, optdigits, satimage, spambase, splice, tic-tac-toe, vehicle, vowel, wine, yeast and zoo.

Table 1. Tests included in the current version of `rNPBST`

Family	Test
Test of randomness	Number of runs
	Runs Up and Down
	Runs Up and Down (Median)
	Von Neumann
Tests of goodness of fit	Chi-Squared
	Kolmogorov-Smirnov
	Lilliefors
	Anderson-Darling
One-sample and paired-samples	Confidence Quantile
	Population Quantile
	Sign test Wilcoxon Signed-Ranks
Two-Sample general procedures	Wald-Wolfowitz
	Median test
	Control Median
	Kolmogorov-Smirnov
Scale problem	David-Barton
	Freund-Ansari-Bradley
	Mood
	Klotz
	Siegel-Tukey
	Sukhatme
Location problem	Wilcoxon Rank-Sum
	van der Waerden
Equality of independent samples	Extended Median test
	Kruskal-Wallis
	Jonckheere-Terpstra
	Charkraborti-Desu
Association for bivariate samples	Kendall
	Daniel Trend
Association in multiple classifications	Friedman
	Friedman Aligned-Rank
	Page
	Concordance Coefficient
	Incomplete Concordance
	Partial Correlation
Association of count data	Contingency Coefficient
	Fishers exact test
	McNemar
	Multinomial Equality test
	Ordered Equality test
Bayesian	Correlated Bayesian t-test
	Bayesian Sign test
	Bayesian Signed-Rank test

Table 2. Algorithms

Algorithm	Description	Data object
`multinom`	Logistic regression from `nnet` package	`results.lr`
`knn`	From `class` library. Parameters $k = 1$, $l = 0$	`results.knn`
`randomForest`	From `randomForest` library parameters `mtray` $= \sqrt{p}$	`results.rf`
`nnet`	Neural network from `nnet` library	`resuts.nnet`
`naiveBayes`	Naïve Bayes classificator from `e1071` package	`results.nb`

Paired-sample analysis. For a parametric comparison between two algorithms we could use the Wilcoxon Rank-Sum test. The results are included in Table 3 to illustrate the use of `htest2Tex`.

```
lr.vs.knn <- cbind(results$logistic.regression, results$KNN) wrs <-
 wilcoxonRankSum.test(lr.vs.knn) htest2Tex(wrs)
```

Table 3. Wilcoxon Rank Sum test

Wilcoxon Rank Sum test		
data.name		lr.vs.knn
Statistic		665.00
p.value	Asymptotic Left Tail	0.001565
	Asymptotic Right Tail	0.998512
	Asymptotic Double Tail	0.003129

The null $\mathcal{H}_0 : \mu_{LR} = \mu_{KNN}$ can be rejected because the asymptotic p-value is less than 0.05, so this test finds a difference between these two algorithms. In order to determine which one gets the better results, we look up the p-values for directional alternatives and we conclude that logistic regression gets better results here given that we can not reject $\mathcal{H}_l$ when the alternative hypothesis is $\mathcal{H}_1 : \mu_{LR} > \mu_{KNN}$.

Test of analysis in multiple comparisons. As we described in Sect. 2, the null hypothesis in Friedman test is the equivalence of the means of the different algorithms, then, a low p-value implies that null hypothesis can be rejected.

```
> friedman.test(results)
Friedman test

data:  results
s = 2812.000, q = 39.056, p-value = 6.789e-08
```

Correlated Bayesian t-test. In this test, we use as input the results of **random forest** and **knn** algorithms for one dataset each time, with the output of Bayesian t-test we can plot the distribution of the difference between the algorithms:

```
> btt <- correlatedBayesianT.test(results.rf[1, ],
                                  results.knn[1, ])
> btt$probabilities
        left         rope        right
4.962298e-05 4.407245e-04 9.995097e-01
> plotPosterior(btt, c("RF","KNN"),"abalone")
```

The posterior distribution of the parameter of interest shows how we can assure with a 99.9% of probability that **random forest** outperforms **knn** in this dataset. The distribution of the difference is showed in Fig. 1 for abalone and letter datasets. In this second one, although **random forest** also outperforms **knn**, there is a higher probability of both algorithms obtaining the same results with respect to the first dataset.

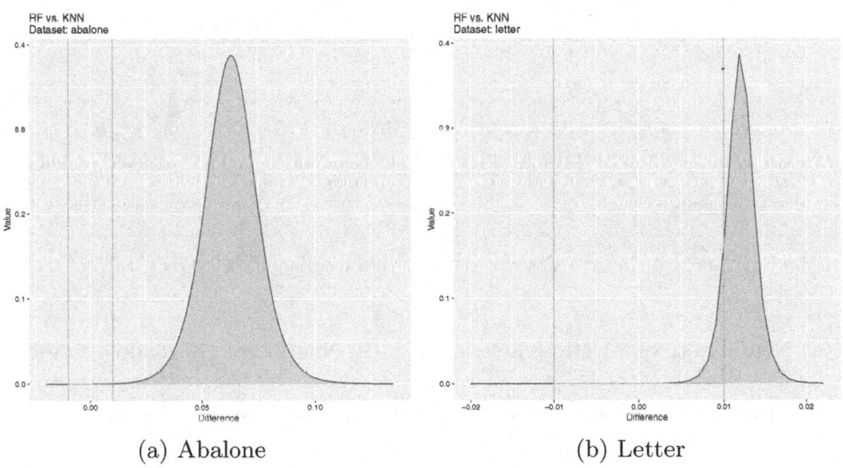

(a) Abalone (b) Letter

Fig. 1. Distribution of RF and KNN accuracy

Bayesian Sign test. For this test we use the averaged results of two algorithms in every available dataset.

```
> bst <- bayesianSign.test(results$neural.network,
                           results$logistic.regression)
> bst$probabilities
     left      rope     right
0.4827586 0.1379310 0.3793103
> plotSimplex(bst$sample)
```

The greater probability corresponds with logistic regression outperforming neural network, although we can check that the differences are small. In Fig. 2a sample from the posterior distribution is plotted and we can easily see how there is a higher concentration of point in the left region, that corresponds with logistic regression outperforming neural network. In Fig. 2b the comparison between neural network and random forest. There is even a greater concentration in left region, so we can assure that there exists a higher probability of `random forest` outperforming `neural network`.

Bayesian Signed-Rank test. We repeat the previous comparisons using the Bayesian Signed-Rank test.

```
> bsrt <- bayesianSignedRank.test(results$neural.network,


  results$logistic.regression)
> bsrt$probabilities
     left        rope       right
0.860733333 0.001433333 0.137833333
> plotSimplex(bst$sample)
```

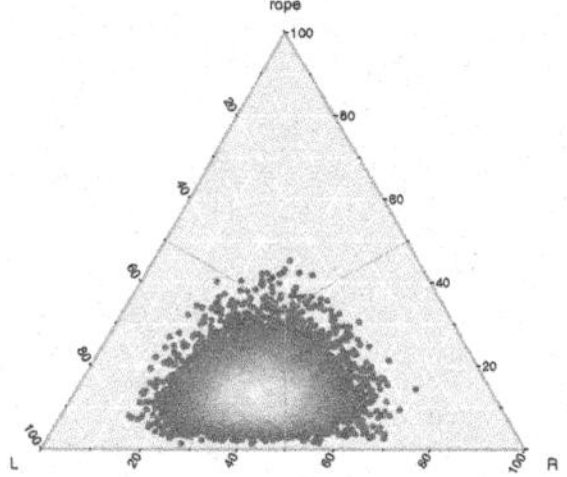

(a) Neural net. vs logistic regression

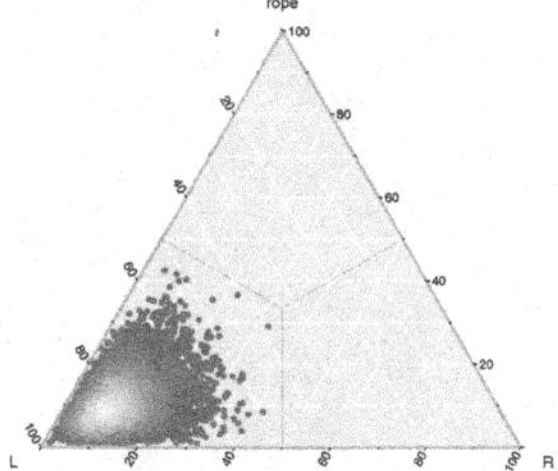

(b) Neural net. vs random forest

Fig. 2. Sample from posterior distribution in Bayesian Sign test

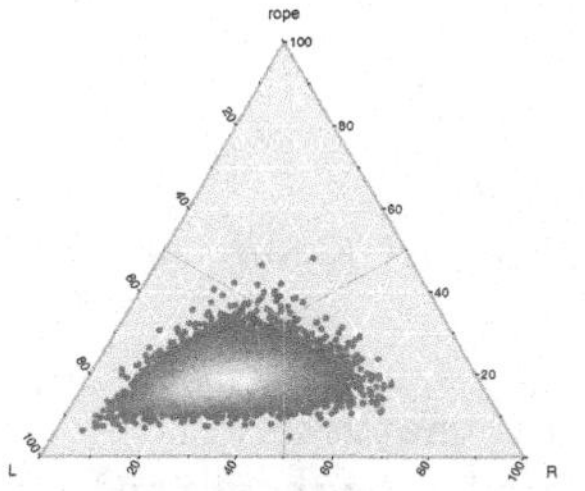

(a) Neural net. vs logistic regression

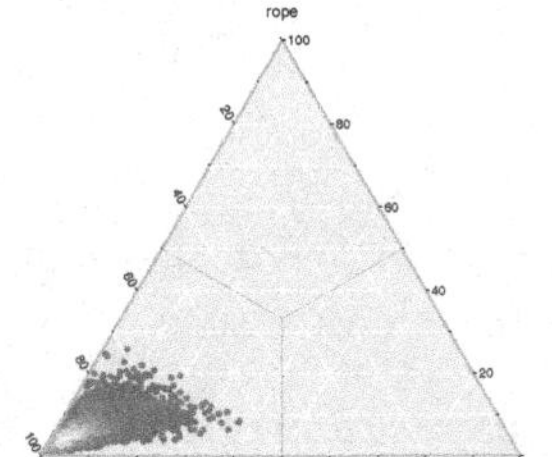

(b) Neural net. vs random forest

Fig. 3. Sample from posterior distribution in Bayesian Signed-Rank test

The posterior probability for the left region is higher than this probability in Bayesian Sign test, so we have a great certainty for this comparison using Bayesian Sign-Rank test. As is seen in Fig. 3, the distribution is shifted to the left, so a higher power is expected for this test with respect to Bayesian Sign test.

4 Conclusions

The experimental inherent nature of machine learning and the quick growth of the number of algorithm proposals leads to the need of a clear method to compare these algorithms' performance and a software tool which facilitate this procedure. In this contribution we present the `rNPBST` package, whose main goal is the compilation of existent non-parametric tests from the base of `JavaNPST` library and adding new tests such as Bayesian tests.

`rNPBST` provides an `R` interface for non-parametric and Bayesian tests in order to get all common tests in a single package for researchers interested in comparing new algorithms or practitioners interested in non-parametric or Bayesian tests. In the future, the package will be maintained with the addition of new tests.

Acknowledgments. This work was supported by the Spanish National Research Projects TIN2014-57251-P and MTM2015-63609-R, and the Andalusian Research Plan P11-TIC-7765.

References

1. Alcalá, J., Fernández, A., Luengo, J., Derrac, J., García, S., Sánchez, L., Herrera, F.: Keel data-mining software tool: data set repository, integration of algorithms and experimental analysis framework. J. Multiple-Valued Logic and Soft Comput. **17**(2–3), 255–287 (2010)
2. Alpaydin, E.: Combined 5 x 2cv f test for comparing supervised classification learning algorithms. Neural Comput. **11**, 1885–1892 (1998)
3. Benavoli, A., Campos, C.P.: Statistical tests for joint analysis of performance measures. In: Suzuki, J., Ueno, M. (eds.) AMBN 2015. LNCS, vol. 9505, pp. 76–92. Springer, Cham (2015). doi:10.1007/978-3-319-28379-1_6
4. Benavoli, A., Corani, G., Mangili, F., Zaffalon, M., Ruggeri, F.: A Bayesian Wilcoxon signed-rank test based on the Dirichlet process. In: Proceedings of the 31th International Conference on Machine Learning, ICML 2014, Beijing, China, 21–26 June 2014, JMLR Workshop and Conference Proceedings, vol. 32, pp. 1026–1034 (2014). http://JMLR.org
5. Benavoli, A., Corani, G., Demsar, J., Zaffalon, M.: Time for a change: a tutorial for comparing multiple classifiers through bayesian analysis. CoRR abs/1606.04316 (2016)
6. Bernardo, J.M., Smith, A.F.: Bayesian Theory (2001)
7. Calvo, B., Santafe, G.: scmamp: Statistical comparison of multiple algorithms in multiple problems. The R Journal Accepted for Publication (2015)
8. Corani, G., Benavoli, A.: A bayesian approach for comparing cross-validated algorithms on multiple data sets. Mach. Learn. **100**(2–3), 285–304 (2015)

9. Demšar, J.: Statistical comparisons of classifiers over multiple data sets. J. Mach. Learn. Res. **7**, 1–30 (2006)
10. Derrac, J., García, S., Herrera, F.: Javanpst: Nonparametric statistical tests in java. ArXiv e-prints, January 2015
11. Derrac, J., García, S., Molina, D., Herrera, F.: A practical tutorial on the use of nonparametric statistical tests as a methodology for comparing evolutionary and swarm intelligence algorithms. Swarm Evol. Comput. **1**(1), 3–18 (2011)
12. Dietterich, T.G.: Approximate statistical tests for comparing supervised classification learning algorithms. Neural Comput. **10**(7), 1895–1923 (1998)
13. Garcia, S., Herrera, F.: An extension on "statistical comparisons of classifiers over multiple data sets" for all pairwise comparisons. J. Mach. Learn. Res. **9**, 2677–2694 (2008)
14. Hamilton, N.: ggtern: An Extension to 'ggplot2', for the Creation of Ternary Diagrams (2016). https://CRAN.R-project.org/package=ggtern, R package version 2.1.4
15. Japkowicz, N., Shah, M.: Evaluating Learning Algorithms: A Classification Perspective. Cambridge University Press, New York (2011)
16. Luengo, J., García, S., Herrera, F.: A study on the use of statistical tests for experimentation with neural networks: analysis of parametric test conditions and non-parametric tests. Expert Syst. Appl. **36**(4), 7798–7808 (2009)
17. Nadeau, C., Bengio, Y.: Inference for the generalization error. Mach. Learn. **52**(3), 239–281 (2003)
18. Pesarin, F., Salmaso, L.: Permutation Tests for Complex Data: Theory. Applications and Software. Wiley, Hoboken (2010)
19. Pizarro, J., Guerrero, E., Galindo, P.L.: Multiple comparison procedures applied to model selection. Neurocomputing **48**(1), 155–173 (2002)
20. Sheskin, D.J.: Handbook of Parametric and Nonparametric Statistical Procedures. CRC Press, Boca Raton (2003)

Solve Classification Tasks with Probabilities. Statistically-Modeled Outputs

Andrey Gritsenko[1,2,3](✉), Emil Eirola[4], Daniel Schupp[3], Edward Ratner[3], and Amaury Lendasse[1,2,4]

[1] Department of Industrial Engineering, The University of Iowa, Iowa City, USA
andrey-gritsenko@uiowa.edu
[2] Iowa Informatics Initiative, The University of Iowa, Iowa City, USA
[3] Lyrical Labs LLC, Iowa City, USA
[4] Arcada University of Applied Sciences, Helsinki, Finland

Abstract. In this paper, an approach for probability-based class prediction is presented. This approach is based on a combination of a newly proposed Histogram Probability (HP) method and any classification algorithm (in this paper results for combination with Extreme Learning Machines (ELM) and Support Vector Machines (SVM) are presented). Extreme Learning Machines is a method of training a single-hidden layer neural network. The paper contains detailed description and analysis of the HP method by the example of the Iris dataset. Eight datasets, four of which represent computer vision classification problem and are derived from Caltech-256 image database, are used to compare HP method with another probability-output classifier [11,18].

Keywords: Classification · Machine learning · Extreme learning machines · Gaussian mixture model · Multiclass classification · Probabilistic classification · Histogram distribution · Image recognition

1 Introduction

There are many algorithms that can be successfully used for multiclass classification problems, e.g. Extreme Learning Machines (ELM) [1,7,17] and Artificial Neural Networks in general. The standard procedure is to convert class labels into numerical 0/1 binary variables, effectively transforming classification problem into a regression task. When a new sample is fed through the network to produce a result, the class is assigned based on which numerical output it the highest. Such approach leads to good performance in terms of precision and classification accuracy, though, numeric outputs as such are not always meaningful. In many real world multiclass classification problems misclassification penalty may be considerably higher or expensive depending on certain results. One such example is in website filtering based on user-defined categories, where Artificial Neural Networks are used to classify previously uncategorized sites [27]. For such problems, it would be preferable if probabilistic models could be built to add

F.J. Martínez de Pisón et al. (Eds.): HAIS 2017, LNAI 10334, pp. 293–305, 2017.
DOI: 10.1007/978-3-319-59650-1_25

confidence to classification results and evaluate the possibility of misclassification. This paper presents a method that converts outputs of a standard classifier into probabilities by building histograms of hits (correct predictions) and misses (misclassification) - Histogram Probability method.

The paper is structured as follows: Sect. 2 briefly introduces state-of-the-art probabilistic methods for classification tasks and states some of their drawbacks. A short description of all the methods used in the experiments section is given in Sect. 3, with Sect. 3.4 providing the detailed explanation of the proposed Histogram Probability method for probabilistic outputs as well as some of its improvements. A new metric allowing to treat probabilistic outputs in a more intuitive way is proposed in Sect. 4. Section 5 presents ten datasets and describes how experiments have been conducted over those datasets. Discussion on the results and analysis are given in Sect. 6, followed by conclusions in Sect. 7.

2 Previous Works

Despite the great benefit that could be obtained with probabilistic classification, only limited work has been done, so far. The most popular classification method with probabilistic outputs is called Naive Bayes Classifier (NBC) [19] and is based on Bayes' Theorem to compute conditional probabilities. Though this theorem works well in probability theory, NBC assumes that input variables are conditionally independent given the class label, in other words, we should know the probability of occurrence of a certain class. Obviously, that this knowledge usually cannot be obtained for real-world problems and thus NBC cannot be considered as a reliable probability classifier. Another approach to obtain probability estimates (also multiclass probability estimates) is to map classifier outputs into some mapping function [28,31]. The main drawback of this approach is that the knowledge of a mapping function to use is required, which is not always possible [28]. The Histogram Probability method allows to avoid drawbacks of other methods providing statistically-modeled classifier outputs.

3 Methodology

3.1 Extreme Learning Machines

Extreme Learning Machines (ELMs) [7] are single hidden-layer feed-forward Neural Networks where only the output weights are optimised, and all the weights between the input and hidden layer are assigned randomly (Fig. 1). Due to its fast computational speed and theoretical guarantees [7], the method recently received an active development both theoretically [15,21,23], including optimally pruned modification of ELM [24,25,29], and in applications [7,26].

Training of Extreme Learning Machines is performed by finding the least-squares solution to the matrix equation:

$$\mathbf{H}\boldsymbol{\beta} = \mathbf{T}, \quad \text{where} \quad H_{ik} = h(\boldsymbol{w}_k \cdot \boldsymbol{x}_i), \tag{1}$$

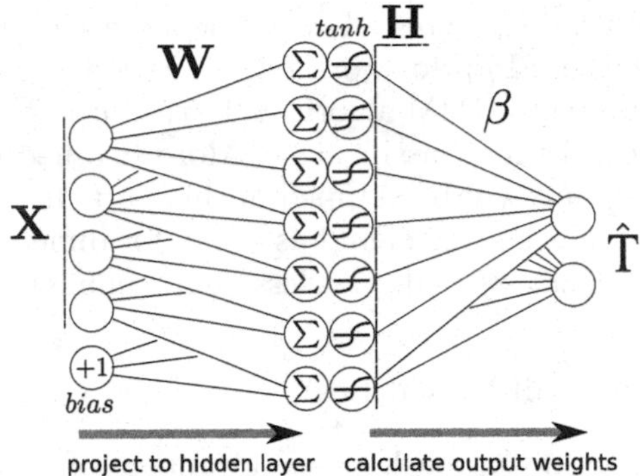

Fig. 1. Extreme learning machine with multiple outputs. Hidden layer weights **W** are fixed, only output layer weights β are calculated.

where **T** is the matrix of targets formed from classification targets using one-hot encoding [18], h - activation function of hidden neurons, H_{ik} - value of k-th hidden neuron for i-th training sample. It has been shown in [7] that this feed-forward neural network with single hidden layer has the properties of universal approximator. The number of neurons in the hidden layer is the only tunable hyper-parameter in ELM model and it can be trained with zero error when the number of hidden neurons is equal to the number of training samples. To avoid overfitting of ELM model cross-validation is used. Due to linear properties of ELM's output layer, Leave-One-Out (LOO) Cross-Validation can be efficiently applied using a closed form of LOO Mean Square Error given by Allen's Prediction Sum of Squares (PRESS) [2].

3.2 Support Vector Machines

In general, SVM's are used to train a separating hyperplane to separate a set of feature vectors into two classes [8]. More recent advances allow for multiclass classification [20], but the proposed method here uses the classic two-class formalization [30]. The hyperplane w is chosen to maximize the gap between the feature vectors of the different classes. The implementation [8] is adopted for efficiency. For the purpose of this multiclass classification problem, a series of one-vs-many SVMs are trained, one for each class. These SVMs are designed to yield a binary decision (which would be in-class or out-of-class), but the distance of the vector to the separating hyperplane can also be computed. The distance is useful for the histogram method, to be discussed in the following section.

3.3 Gaussian Mixture Models

Mixtures of Gaussians can be used for a variety of applications by estimating the density of data samples [4, 12]. A Gaussian Mixture Model can approximate any distribution by fitting a number of components, each representing a multivariate normal distribution. In prior work [11] a method was proposed to obtain probabilistic results applying GMM algorithm to the outputs of ELM previously trained in a standard way for classification. More detailed description of this method is given in [18] and will be skipped in this part. It is worth noting that in this method ELM could be considered as a way for dimensionality reduction, as usually the number of classes in data is less then number of features/variables.

3.4 Histogram Probability Method

Overview. The proposed approach takes advantage of a continuous decision function by binning the resulting decision space, it uses training data to build a model of class distributions [32]. The HP method provides probabilistic outputs by building two types of histograms of classification outputs. Depending on the choice of multi-class classification (MCC) algorithm to obtain classification outputs the implementation of the HP method can slightly differ.

Methodology. For a certain multi-class problem, some classification algorithm is trained. Obtained classification outputs then serve as basis for histograms used to derive probabilistic outputs. At first, the maximum $\max \hat{\mathbf{T}}_{train}$ and minimum $\min \hat{\mathbf{T}}_{train}$ value among all classification outputs are found. The range $\left[\min \hat{\mathbf{T}}_{train}; \max \hat{\mathbf{T}}_{train}\right]$ is then to be divided into bins. Worth noting that the number of bins should be chosen carefully corresponding the complexity of classification problem. Also, too small number of bins would result in loosing features of distribution, while too large number could be a reason for sparse histograms.

Considering the given partition, two types of histograms are built for each class. The first histogram, called *IN*-class, assembles all classification outputs corresponding to a certain class; while the second, *OUT*-class, histogram is built with classification outputs corresponding to all other classes:

$$\hat{T}_{ij} \mapsto \begin{cases} \mathrm{IN}_{C_k} & \text{if } j = k \\ \mathrm{OUT}_{C_k} & \text{if } j \neq k \end{cases}, \; k = \text{correct class}\,(i)\,, \tag{2}$$

where $\hat{T}_{ij}$ – is classification output value of sample i for the corresponding class C_j, k identifies correct class for sample i, IN_{C_k} and OUT_{C_k} stand for *IN*-class and *OUT*-class histograms for class C_k, respectively, and they represent the frequency, with which a classifier provides classification outputs for class C_k (*IN*-class histogram) and other classes (*OUT*-class histogram) in a certain range, when C_k is the correct class. If a MCC task is solved by applying *one-vs-all* classification scheme, e.g. a set of n one-vs-all SVMs for n-class classification problem ($n > 2$), then *IN*-class and *OUT*-class histograms could be built for each SVM separately. That means that $\max \hat{\mathbf{T}}_{train}$ and $\min \hat{\mathbf{T}}_{train}$ are to be defined separately for each SVM. Considering that the number of classes in the problem can be rather big and/or ratio of classes can be different (unbalanced classification problems), *IN*-class and *OUT*-class histograms are to be normalized according to the ratio of a certain class:

$$\overline{\mathrm{IN}}_{C_k} = \frac{\mathrm{IN}_{C_k}}{size\,(C_k)} \text{ and } \overline{\mathrm{OUT}}_{C_k} = \frac{\mathrm{OUT}_{C_k}}{\sum_{j=1}^{M} size\,(C_j)}, \quad j \neq k,\ k = 1, \ldots, M, \quad (3)$$

where M is the number of classes in the problem. Now, histograms display relative frequencies and show proportions of classification outputs that fall in a certain range. With the respect to the used classification algorithm, probabilistic output for a given sample i, which has a classification output value $\hat{T}_{ij}$ for j class respectively, is computed as follows

$$p(C_j \mid \hat{T}_{ij}) = \frac{\overline{\mathrm{IN}}_{C_j}(\hat{T}_{ij})}{\overline{\mathrm{IN}}_{C_j}(\hat{T}_{ij}) + \overline{\mathrm{OUT}}_{C_j}(\hat{T}_{ij})}, \quad (4)$$

where $\overline{\mathrm{IN}}_{C_j}(\hat{T}_{ij})$ and $\overline{\mathrm{OUT}}_{C_j}(\hat{T}_{ij})$ stand for the frequencies of corresponding bins, which classification output value $\hat{T}_{ij}$ falls into. Equation (4) does not guarantee that for each sample i probabilities along all the classes would sum up to 1. The main reason is that for each class these probabilities are calculated independently of the information about other classes. In order to treat results of Eq. (4) as probabilities for each sample they should be normalized.

Implementation Details of the Method (by the Example of the Iris Dataset). A detailed explanation of the proposed probability output classification method is presented hereafter by the example of the *Iris* dataset [22], and summarized in Algorithm 1. Assume, for a certain ELM implementation some classificatoin output values were obtained. All of the output values are in the interval [−0.32; 1.33]. This interval does not depend on the accuracy of the model and can differ for different experiments, even when the same input data and the same number of neurons in the hidden layer are used, e.g. in the current example the accuracy of ELM algorithm was 94%, which can be noticed by well-separated *IN*-class and *OUT*-class histograms. SVM algorithm was implemented as well, whose output was also used to build histograms. Output values, which represent the distance from data samples to a hyperplane, for the current SVM implementation are disposed in the range of [−4.42; 6.1].

These intervals of classification outputs were divided into 20 bins each to build *IN*-class and *OUT*-class histograms for each class, using Eq. (3) (see Fig. 2, x axis shows classification outputs increase from left to right). Hereafter, *IN*-class histograms are represented in blue color and *OUT*-class histograms are represented in red color. The number of bins was chosen empirically so that on one hand, the features of distribution would retain, and on the other hand, the histograms itself would not be sparse. The same number of bins was used for other datasets mentioned in this paper.

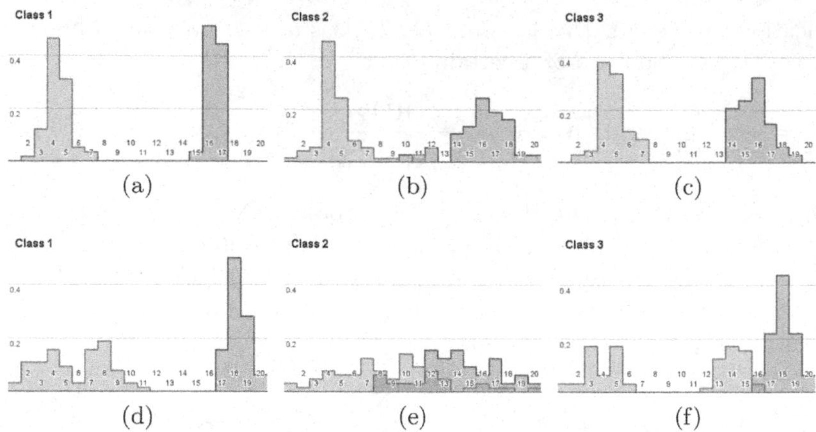

Fig. 2. *IN*-class and *OUT*-class histograms for each class, built based on ELM outputs (a, b, c) and SVM outputs (d, e, f). (Color figure online)

Improvement 1. According to the methodology, value of a particular bin for both *IN*-class and *OUT*-class histograms can be zero, if for all samples there was no one output in a specified range. This usually happens only for well separated classes, while in practice another situation is more frequent (see Fig. 2b, c, d, e), when either *IT*-class or *OUT*-class values equal to 0. On the other hand, *IN*-class and *OUT*-class histograms are built based on training data. Thus, there is no guarantee that for test data there wouldn't be any output value that falls into the bin with zero frequency. Obviously, using Eq. (4) in this case becomes meaningless or even impossible (when classification output value falls into zero-value bin for both histograms). In order to avoid such unreliable results and improve the overall reliability of the method, it is proposed to use the Cauchy distribution to fill the values of zero-value bins (Fig. 3). For each such zero-value bin a value of probability density function (PDF) of corresponding Cauchy distribution is calculated

$$f\left(x, x_0, \gamma\right) = \frac{1}{\pi\gamma\left[1 + \left(\frac{x - x_0}{\gamma}\right)^2\right]} = \frac{1}{\pi\gamma}\frac{\gamma^2}{\left(x - x_0\right)^2 + \gamma^2}, \tag{5}$$

where argument for the Cauchy distribution PDF x – is the consecutive number of the corresponding bin (from 1 to 20), parameters of the Cauchy distribution *location* x_0 and *scale* γ – are the mean value and the standard deviation of the histogram distribution for a given class, respectively. The choice of the Cauchy distribution was made because it fits and retains features of histogram values distribution better that other tested distributions (Gaussian, Poisson, Student's t-distribution).

Improvement 2. According to the Eq. (4) probability of the certain class is calculated regardless of the output value until it belongs to a certain bin. It

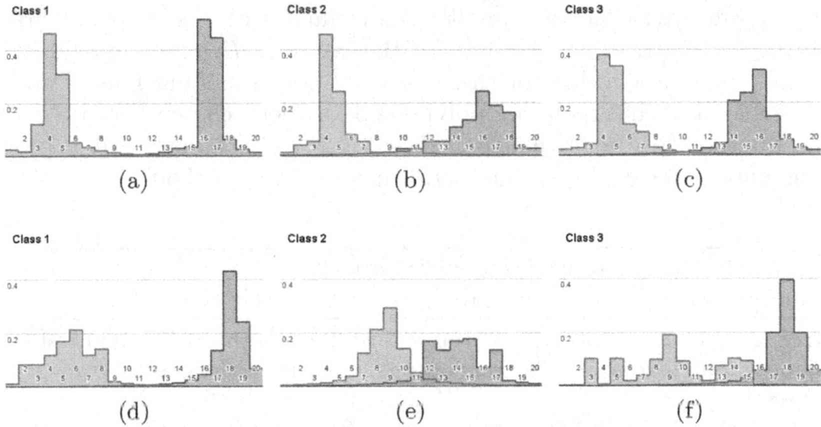

Fig. 3. *IN*-class and *OUT*-class histograms after modification using Cauchy distribution for ELM-based outputs (a, b, c) and SVM-based outputs (d, e, f).

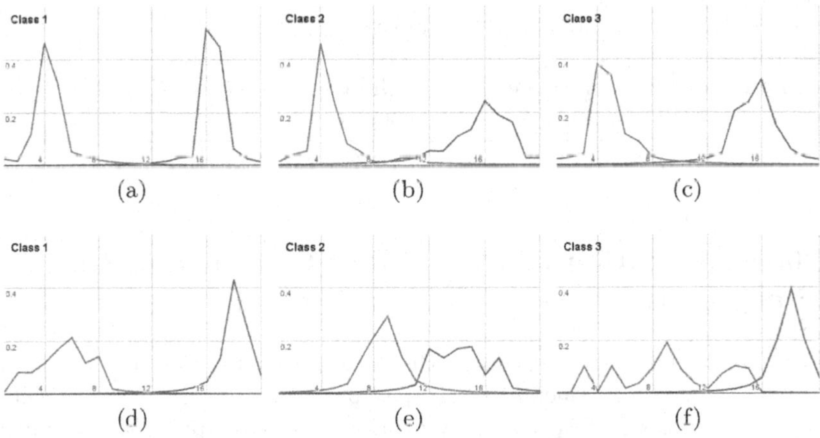

Fig. 4. *IN*-class and *OUT*-class histograms after using Lagrange interpolation for ELM-based outputs (a, b, c) and SVM-based outputs (d, e, f).

means that for two values, one of which is located in the center of a bin and other is close to its edge, probability would be the same. Obviously, that is a very rough estimate, especially for standalone bins with high values (Fig. 2). To reduce this negative impact and make probability distribution smoother, the Lagrange interpolating polynomial [9] is used (Fig. 4). Here, for any classification output value x, *IN*-class and *OUT*-values are computed using Lagrange interpolating polynomial for two interpolation points that are chosen as centers of two closest bins

$$L(x) = \sum_{k=0}^{1} L_k(x)\, y_k = \frac{x - x_1}{x_0 - x_1} y_0 + \frac{x - x_0}{x_1 - x_0} y_1. \tag{6}$$

For output values x, which are smaller than value of the center of the first bin and greater than value of the center of the last bin, *IN*-class and *OUT*-class values are equated to values of the centers of corresponding bins. Two-point version of Lagrange interpolating polynomial has been chosen because it is the simplest interpolating algorithm that is very easy to implement, still it provides sufficient improvement in resulting performance of the method.

Algorithm 1. Finding unseen data class probabilities based on trained classification model (with proposed improvements to the basic method)

Require: Targets $\mathbf{T}$, classification output values $\hat{\mathbf{T}}$ for both training and test sets
1: Compute the range of classification output values for training set
2: **For each** class C **do**
3: Build *IN*-class and *OUT*-class histograms from corresponding classification output values (Eq. (2))
4: Replace histogram values in 0-value bins using Cauchy distribution (Eq. (5))
5: Use Lagrange two-point interpolating polynomial to switch from probabilities' histograms (Eq. (6))
6: Normalize *IN*-class and *OUT*-class histograms (Eq. (3))
7: **End for**
8: Calculate $p(C_i \mid \hat{T}_{ij})$ for each class for each sample in test set (Eq. (4))
9: **Return** Probabilities $p(C_i \mid \hat{T}_{ij})$ normalized for each sample

4 Characterization of Probability Output and Its Interpretation

There are many measures to estimate the accuracy of non-probabilistic learning algorithms [34], while the lack of interest in probabilistic classification methods has resulted in a lack of accepted methods to evaluate probabilistic outputs. The most well known Mean Square Error estimation is usually used to evaluate accuracy of probabilistic methods, though this approach may discard the meaning of probability output [11]. The primary method for assessing the accuracy of probabilistic predictions is Brier score [6] proposed for binary problems. For MCC problems the Brier score (BS) can be generalized as follows:

$$\mathrm{BS}(C_k) = \frac{1}{N}\sum_{i=1}^{N}(p(C_k \mid x_i) - o(C_k \mid x_i))^2, \tag{7}$$

where, for a given class C_k, $p(C_k \mid x)$ is the probability that sample x_i belongs to class C_k and $o(C_k \mid x)$ is defined to be 1 if the actual label of x_i is C_k and 0 otherwise. The other way to interpret output of a MCC method is to compute accuracy - treat a class with the highest output value as the predicted class and compute how often the predicted class match the correct class. Still these evaluation methods either do not use features of probabilistic outputs or have sufficient drawbacks, e.g. Brier score heavily weights outliers and has to be computed for each class separately. The proposed approach is to evaluate *how far* the correct class ends up from the predicted class with the highest probability output by measuring its *score* $s = (\hat{p}_{\max} - \hat{p}_{\text{correct}})$, where $\hat{p}_{\max}$ and $\hat{p}_{\text{correct}}$ are respectively the highest probability output value and the probability output value for the correct class, and *rank* r. In order to have an equivalent measurements of rank for problems with different number of classes, rank values are scaled into $[0; 1)$ interval $r = (rank_{\text{correct}} - 1)/M$ where $rank_{\text{correct}}$ is the rank of the correct class in a descending-ordered probability output vector, M – number of classes in MCC problem; by definition, score values are scaled into $[0; 1]$ interval. To evaluate the performance of a multi-class probabilistic classification method the average score S and rank R are used (N - number of samples):

$$S = \frac{1}{N}\sum_{i=1}^{N} s_i, \quad R = \frac{1}{N}\sum_{i=1}^{N} r_i. \tag{8}$$

5 Experiments

The experimental part consists in the comparison of the proposed probability-output methods for classification problems over eight different datasets (see Table 1), including the *Iris* dataset that is used as an example dataset for the detailed explanation of HP method. This and next three datasets are collected from the UCI ML Repository [22]. The last four datasets are based on Caltech-256 Object Category Dataset [16] and represent different feature descriptors, used to generate datasets. *SURF* features [3] are used to generate *PHOW* dataset, *Color*, *Gabor* [14] and histogram of oriented gradients (*HOG* [10]) features are used to generate datasets of the same names. The original datasets are subject to random permutation followed by splitting in the ratio 2:1, with larger subsets used for training and smaller for testing. In case of unbalanced datasets, ratio of classes is preserved in training and test subsets. Finally, for each problem, both training and test subsets are normalized using the mean and the variance of original training subset. Compared methods include ELM (Sect. 3.1), SVM (Sect. 3.2), ELM-GMM (Sect. 3.3) and ELM-GMMr (version of ELM-GMM, where GMM is trained only on correct predictions of ELM), ELM-HP and SVM-HP (HP method (Sect. 3.4) applied to classification outputs of ELM and SVM). All of the methods are implemented using OpenCV library for computer vision and machine learning [5]. The current SVM implementation is based on [13], and optimal C-parameter for SVM models is chosen empirically using bisection search. Optimal number of neurons for ELM models is chosen using PRESS Leave-One-Out cross-validation technique [2]. For Gaussian Mixture Models methods, the BIC criterion [33] is used to choose the optimal number of Gaussian components. The comparison is performed in two ways. At first, training time and accuracy (percentage of correct predictions) are compared for all of the above-mentioned methods (Table 2). Table 3 presents comparison results of probability output methods in terms of rank and score (Sect. 4).

Table 1. Information about used datasets

Dataset	# of features	# of classes	Balanced classes	Samples		Neurons	
				Train	Test	Max	Mean
Iris	4	3	Yes	100	50	50	17
Wine	13	3	No	118	60	60	35
Image Segmentation (IS)	18	7	Yes	1540	770	700	496
First-Order Theorem Proving (FOTP)	51	6	No	4078	2040	1000	765
Caltech-256 PHOW feature	50	10	Yes	600	300	200	72
Caltech-256 Color feature	3600	10	Yes	600	300	200	117
Caltech-256 Gabor feature	2500	10	Yes	600	300	200	88
Caltech-256 HOG180 feature	1700	10	Yes	600	300	200	129

Table 2. Comparison of the accuracy (mean value and std, in percents) and training time (in seconds) for presented methods

Dataset	ELM		ELM-GMM		ELM-GMMr		ELM-HP		SVM		SVM-HP	
	Time	Acc	Time	Acc	Time	Acc	Time	Acc	Time	Acc	Time	Acc
Iris	0.02	94.02	0.05	94.64	0.05	94.02	0.02	**94.64**	0.87	**98.00**	0.87	97.00
		3.16		3.86		3.83		2.82		0.64		0.70
Wine	0.06	94.23	0.11	92.83	0.11	93.83	0.06	**95.77**	0.61	96.75	0.61	**98.39**
		3.14		3.44		3.09		1.63		0.11		0.12
IS	20.67	**95.06**	44.24	94.47	22.09	94.82	20.74	95.03	12.21	**84.64**	12.21	80.86
		0.72		0.49		0.51		0.84		0.91		0.89
FOTP	95.12	**54.10**	109.92	52.09	109.91	53.38	95.32	53.54	600.43	**40.41**	600.43	26.66
		0.77		0.57		0.64		0.88		7.40		6.90
PHOW	17.46	**30.43**	17.55	25.27	17.48	25.97	17.49	29.40	37.12	40.40	37.12	**44.75**
		1.99		2.66		2.89		1.31		3.10		2.90
Color	18.44	**23.04**	18.51	20.63	18.46	21.13	18.58	21.37	849.15	**29.69**	849.15	26.25
		2.14		1.91		1.83		2.08		3.90		3.20
Gabor	17.73	17.25	17.79	13.17	17.79	13.56	17.81	**17.57**	164.69	24.38	164.69	**24.69**
		1.98		2.63		2.54		2.42		3.80		3.30
HOG180	17.37	**30.61**	17.59	26.43	17.46	26.60	17.67	28.87	1460.17	51.88	1460.17	**53.44**
		2.32		1.98		2.01		1.73		3.50		2.70

6 Results and Analysis

For each dataset, the best performance is marked in bold (groups of ELM- and SVM-based methods assessed separately). The analysis of Table 2 reveals that ELM-HP method has better performance for 2 datasets, worse performance for 2 datasets, and for 4 datasets the difference in accuracy is not statistically significant, when compared to ELM. Concerning other ELM-based probabilistic methods, ELM-GMM and ELM-GMMr show slightly worse accuracy for almost all datasets. In terms of computational time, ELM-GMM and ELM-GMMr take

Table 3. Evaluation of probabilistic methods in terms of 'rank-score' estimation

Dataset	ELM-GMM		ELM-GMMr		ELM-HP		SVM-HP	
	Rank	Score	Rank	Score	Rank	Score	Rank	Score
Iris	0.023	0.054	0.027	0.066	0.023	0.031	**0.010**	**0.009**
Wine	0.037	0.082	0.034	0.073	0.026	0.028	**0.015**	**0.011**
IS	0.009	0.044	**0.008**	0.041	0.012	**0.022**	0.051	0.052
FOTP	0.199	0.301	**0.194**	0.394	0.198	0.198	0.350	**0.074**
PHOW	0.297	0.445	0.312	0.620	0.273	0.277	**0.201**	**0.198**
Color	0.337	0.553	0.339	0.663	**0.336**	0.363	0.345	**0.241**
Gabor	0.373	0.476	**0.356**	0.472	0.377	0.306	0.365	**0.279**
HOG180	0.289	0.506	0.298	0.616	0.269	0.327	**0.201**	**0.198**

significantly longer time only for 2 datasets when compared to the base method. For several datasets, applying HP method to the outputs of ELM results in a slight increase of computational time when comparing the combined method to the base method. It also can be stated that computational time of SVM-HP method is basically the same as of SVM method, though accuracy may increase (observed for 4 out of 8 datasets).

From the results presented in Table 3, it can be implied that combination of ELM and HP methods in the majority of cases (5 out of 8) shows better results than ELM-GMM(r), both for 'rank' and 'score' measures. In comparison with SVM based HP method, ELM-HP results have significantly higher 'score' value for almost all datasets. Though no relation can be found between generalized properties of data and performance of methods (both in terms of standard accuracy and rank-score metric), a strong relationship can be observed between 'rank' values and corresponding accuracies: higher accuracy correlates with the lower 'rank' value, based on the analysis of the experiments results.

7 Conclusions and Further Works

Histogram Probability method - is a newly proposed method that allows the obtaining of probability estimates from classifier's outputs for multiclass problems, using statistics behind these outputs. The advantage of this method, is that it uses outputs for all classes (for each class, two histograms are built) when computing probability. Thus, it considers not only the output for correct class, but outputs for other classes as well. This approach makes Histogram Probability method extremely useful for complex multiclass problems. The main innovation of the proposed Histogram Probability method is that neither any assumptions are have to be made (like in Bayes classifiers), nor knowledge of mapping function is required (mapping approach). From the analysis of experiments, it is be concluded that time cost of HP method computations can be neglected as insufficient when compared to time cost of base method computations. Additionally, a new criteria have been proposed - the score and the ranking - in order to evaluate probability outputs in more intuitive way. From the analysis and discussion of the experimental results, it can be concluded that newly proposed Histogram Probability method is reliable when probabilistic outputs need to be obtained. The choice of a base method (ELM or SVM) can be done considering the difference in computational time for those methods. Hyperparameters of base methods (number of neurons or C-value) have to be chosen and tuned carefully with respect to the generalized properties of data, as the performance of both HP and GMM probabilistic methods fully depend on the performance of base methods. In the future, the proposed methodology has to be improved in terms of computational time in order to target Big Data problems. Furthermore, the new proposed criteria have to be further developed and potentially merged into a new single global criterion.

References

1. Akusok, A., Bjork, K.M., Miche, Y., Lendasse, A.: High performance extreme learning machines: a complete toolbox for big data applications. Access, IEEE (2015)
2. Allen, D.M.: The relationship between variable selection and data agumentation and a method for prediction. Technometrics **16**(1), 125–127 (1974)
3. Bay, H., Tuylelaars, T., Van Gool, L.: Surf speeded up robust features. In: 9th European Conference on Computer Vision, vol. 61, no. 2, pp. 346–359 (2006)
4. Bishop, C.M.: Pattern Recognition and Machine Learning. Springer, New York (2006)
5. Bradski, G.: The OpenCV Library. Dr. Dobb's Journal of Software Tools (2000)
6. Brier, G.W.: Verification of forecasts expressed in terms of probability. Mon. Weather Rev. **78**, 1–3 (1950)
7. Cambria, E., et al.: Extreme learning machines. IEEE Intell. Syst. **28**(6), 30–59 (2013)
8. Change, C.C., Lin, C.J.: LIBSVM: a library for support vector machines. ACM Trans. Intell. Syst. Technol. (2011)
9. Dahlquist, G., Björck, Å.: Numerical Methods. Dover Books on Mathematics. Dover Publications, USA (2003)
10. Dalal, N., Triggs, B.: Histograms of oriented gradients for human detection. In: CVPR, pp. 886–893 (2005)
11. Eirola, E., et al.: Extreme learning machines for multiclass classification: refining predictions with gaussian mixture models. In: Rojas, I., Joya, G., Catala, A. (eds.) IWANN 2015. LNCS, vol. 9095, pp. 153–164. Springer, Cham (2015). doi:10.1007/978-3-319-19222-2_13
12. Eirola, E., Lendasse, A., Vandewalle, V., Biernacki, C.: Mixture of gaussians for distance estimation with missing data. Neurocomputing **131**, 32–42 (2014)
13. Fabian, P., et al.: Scikit-learn: machine learning in python. J. Mach. Learn. Res. **12**, 28252830 (2011)
14. Fogel, I., Sagi, D.: Gabor filters as texture discriminator. Biol. Cybern. **61**(2), 103–113 (1978)
15. Frénay, B., van Heeswijk, M., Miche, Y., Verleysen, M., Lendasse, A.: Feature selection for nonlinear models with extreme learning machines. Neurocomputing **102**, 111–124 (2013)

16. Griffin, G., Holub, A., Perona, P.: Caltech-256 object category dataset. Technical report, CNS-TR-2007-001, California Institute of Technology (2007)
17. Gritsenko, A., Akusok, A., Miche, Y., Björk, K.M., Baek, S., Lendasse, A.: Combined nonlinear visualization and classification: ELMVIS++C. In: The 2016 International Joint Conference on Neural Networks (IJCNN), pp. 2617–2624, IEEE World Congress on Computational Intelligence, July 2016
18. Gritsenko, A., Eirola, E., Schupp, D., Ratner, E., Lendasse, A.: Probabilistic methods for multiclass classification problems. In: Cao, J., Mao, K., Wu, J., Lendasse, A. (eds.) Proceedings of ELM-2015, vol. 7, pp. 375–397. Springer, Berlin (2016)
19. Hand, D.J., Yu, K.: Idiot's bayes - not so stupid after all? Int. Stat. Rev./Revue Internationale de Statistique **69**(3), 385–398 (2001)
20. Hsu, C.W., Lin, C.J.: A comparison of methods for multiclass support vector machines. IEEE Trans. Neural Netw. **13**(2), 415–425 (2002)
21. Lendasse, A., Akusok, A., Simula, O., Corona, F., Heeswijk, M., Eirola, E., Miche, Y.: Extreme learning machine: a robust modeling technique? Yes! In: Rojas, I., Joya, G., Gabestany, J. (eds.) IWANN 2013. LNCS, vol. 7902, pp. 17–35. Springer, Heidelberg (2013). doi:10.1007/978-3-642-38679-4_2
22. Lichman, M.: UCI ML Repository (2013). http://archive.ics.uci.edu/ml
23. Miche, Y., van Heeswijk, M., Bas, P., Simula, O., Lendasse, A.: TROP-ELM: a double-regularized ELM using LARS and Tikhonov regularization. Neurocomputing **74**(16), 2413–2421 (2011)
24. Miche, Y., Sorjamaa, A., Bas, P., Simula, O., Jutten, C., Lendasse, A.: OP-ELM: optimally pruned extreme learning machine. IEEE Trans. Neural Netw. **21**(1), 158–162 (2010)
25. Miche, Y., Sorjamaa, A., Lendasse, A.: OP-ELM: theory, experiments and a toolbox. In: Kůrková, V., Neruda, R., Koutník, J. (eds.) ICANN 2008. LNCS, vol. 5163, pp. 145–154. Springer, Heidelberg (2008). doi:10.1007/978-3-540-87536-9_16
26. Nian, R., He, B., Zheng, B., Van Heeswijk, M., Yu, Q., Miche, Y., Lendasse, A.: Extreme learning machine towards dynamic model hypothesis in fish ethology research. Neurocomputing **128**, 273–284 (2014)
27. Patil, A.S., Pawar, B.: Automated classification of web sites using naive bayesian algorithm. In: Proceedings of the International MultiConference of Engineers and Computer Scientists, vol. 1, pp. 519–523 (2012)
28. Platt, J.C.: Probabilistic outputs for support vector machines and comparisons to regularized likelihood methods. In: Advances in Large Margin Classifiers, pp. 61–74. MIT Press (1999)
29. Pouzols, F.M., Lendasse, A.: Evolvin fuzzy optimally pruned extreme learning machine for regression problems. Evolving Syst. **1**(1), 43–58 (2010)
30. Press, W.H., Teukolsky, S.A., Vetterling, W.T., Flannery, B.P.: Numerical Recipes 3rd Edition: The Art of Scientific Computing, 3rd edn. Cambridge University Press, New York (2007)
31. Robertson, T., Wright, F., Dykstra, R.: Order Restricted Statistical Inference. Probability and Statistics Series. Wiley, Chichester (1988)
32. Schupp-Omid, D.R., Ratner, E., Gritsenko, A.: Object categorization using statistically-modeled classifier outputs, August 2016. http://www.freepatentsonline.com/y2017/0046615.html, U.S. Patent Application 2017/0046615 A1, Appl. No. 15/237048
33. Schwarz, G.: Estimating the dimension of a model. Ann. Stat. **6**(2), 461–464 (1978)
34. Westgard, J.O., Carey, R.N., Wold, S.: Criteria for judging precision and accuracy in method development and evaluation. Clin. Chem. **20**(7), 825–833 (1974)

FRB-Dialog: A Toolkit for Automatic Learning of Fuzzy-Rule Based (FRB) Dialog Managers

David Griol(✉), Aracel Sanchis de Miguel, and José Manuel Molina

Computer Science Department, Carlos III University of Madrid,
Avda. de la Universidad, 30, 28911 Leganés, Spain
{david.griol,araceli.sanchis,josemanuel.molina}@uc3m.es

Abstract. This paper describes a toolkit designed to automatically develop dialog managers for spoken dialog system based on evolving Fuzzy-rule-based (FRB) classifiers. The *FRB-dialog* toolkit allows to develop dialog managers selecting the next system action by considering a set of dynamic rules that are automatically obtained by means of the application of the FRB classification process. Our approach bridges the gap between the academic and industrial perspectives for developing dialog systems, taking into account the data supplied by the user throughout the complete dialog history without causing scalability problems, and also considering confidence measures provided by the recognition and understanding modules.

Keywords: Conversational interfaces · Spoken dialog management · Evolving classifiers · Fuzzy-rule based systems · Human-machine interaction

1 Introduction

Spoken dialog system (SDS) support conversational interaction by means of speech. Typically these interfaces operate following these steps, that are usually modularized in different system components: automatically recognize the user utterance (Automatic Speech Recognition, ASR), interpret the recognized words (Spoken Language Understanding, SLU), decide how to proceed (Dialog management, DM), formulate a response (Natural Language Generation, NLG) and convert it into a spoken output (Text-To-Speech synthesis, TTS) [10].

Continuous advances in the field of spoken dialog systems make the processes of design, implementation and evaluation of dialog management strategies more and more complex. The motivations for automating dialog learning are focused on the time-consuming process that hand-crafted design involves and the ever-increasing problem of dialog complexity. Statistical models can be trained from real dialogs, modeling the variability in user behaviors. Although the construction and parameterization of the model depend on the expert knowledge of the task, the final objective is to develop dialog systems that have a more robust behavior, better portability, and are easier to adapt to different user profiles or tasks.

F.J. Martínez de Pisón et al. (Eds.): HAIS 2017, LNAI 10334, pp. 306–317, 2017.
DOI: 10.1007/978-3-319-59650-1_26

However, commercial systems have not yet adopted the new statistical perspective proposed in the academic settings, which would allow straightforward adaptation of these interfaces to various application domains. In this paper, we propose a toolkit designed to bridge the gap between the academic and industrial perspectives in order to develop dialog systems using an academic paradigm for the dialog manager while employing the industrial standards for the rest of modules of the system. The dialog managers developed by means of the *FRB-dialog* toolkit are based on the selection of the next system action by means of an online classifying method based on Evolving Fuzzy Systems (EFS) [2]. The use of EFS allows us to cope with huge amounts of data, process streaming data on-line in real time, and evolve the structure of a dialog model that defines an activity based on the human-computer interaction for each specific application domain.

After this introduction, the remainder of the paper is organized as follows. Section 2 describes existing approaches for the development of dialog managers, paying special attention to statistical approaches. Section 3 describes the methodology followed by the proposed toolkit for dialog management. Section 4 describes the application of our proposal to develop a statistical dialog manager for a dialog system providing railway information. Finally, Sect. 5 presents the conclusions and suggests some future work guidelines.

2 Related Work

Although dialog management is only a part of the development cycle of spoken dialog systems, it can be considered one of the most demanding tasks given that this module encapsulates the logic of the speech application [19]. The selection of a specific system action depends on multiple factors, such as the output of the speech recognizer (e.g., measures that define the reliability of the recognized information), the dialog interaction and previous dialog history (e.g., the number of repairs carried out so far), the application domain (e.g., guidelines for customer service), knowledge about the users, and the responses and status of external back-ends, devices, and data repositories. Given that the actions of the system directly impact users, the dialog manager is largely responsible for user satisfaction. This way, the design of an appropriate dialog management strategy is at the core of dialog system engineering.

The simplest dialog management strategy is programmatic dialog management, in which a generic program implements the application with an interaction model based on finite-state machines. The user actions determine the transitions between the system responses, which are the nodes of the finite-state machine. Users' actions represent the user responses to the system prompts, which are usually coded in recognition grammars. These early applications only supported strict directed dialog interaction, in which at each turn the system directs the user by proposing a small number of choices, which also result in a limited grammar or vocabulary at each turn. Directed dialog was efficient in terms of accuracy and cost of development.

Unlike the finite-state approach, frame-based dialog managers do not have a predefined dialog path but use a frame structure comprised of one slot per piece of information that the system can gather from the user. In this approach, the system interprets speech in order to acquire enough information to perform a specific action. One of the main advantages is that it can capture several data at once and the information can be provided in any order (more than one slot can be filled per dialog turn and in any order), thus supporting mixed-initiative dialogs.

Statistical approaches for dialog management present several important advantages. Rather than maintaining a single hypothesis for the dialog state, they maintain a distribution over many hypotheses for the correct dialog state. In addition, statistical methodologies choose actions using an optimization process, in which a developer specifies high-level goals and the optimization works out the detailed dialog plan.

Automating dialog management is useful for developing, deploying and re-deploying applications and also reducing the time-consuming process of hand-crafted design. In fact, the application of machine learning approaches to dialog management strategy design is a rapidly growing research area. Machine-learning approaches to dialog management attempt to learn optimal strategies from corpora of real human-computer dialog data using automated "trial-and-error" methods instead of relying on empirical design principles [15]. The main trend in this area is an increased use of data for automatically improving the performance of the system.

Statistical models can be trained with corpora of human-computer dialogs with the goal of explicitly modeling the variance in user behavior that can be difficult to address by means of hand-written rules [15]. Additionally, if it is necessary to satisfy certain deterministic behaviors, it is possible to extend the strategy learned from the training corpus with handcrafted rules that include expert knowledge or specifications about the task [18,20].

The most widespread methodology for machine-learning of dialog strategies consists of modeling human-computer interaction as an optimization problem using Markov Decision Processes (MDP) and reinforcement methods [9,17]. The main drawback of this approach is that the large state space of practical spoken dialog systems makes its direct representation intractable [20]. Partially Observable MDPs (POMDPs) outperform MDP-based dialog strategies since they provide an explicit representation of uncertainty [14]. This enables the dialog manager to avoid and recover from recognition errors by sharing and shifting probability mass between multiple hypotheses of the current dialog state.

Other interesting approaches for statistical dialog management are based on modeling the system by means of Hidden Markov Models [4], stochastic Finite-State Transducers [13], or using Bayesian Networks [11,12]. Also [8] proposed a different hybrid approach to dialog modeling in which n-best recognition hypotheses are weighted using a mixture of expert knowledge and data-driven measures by using an agenda and an example-based machine translation approach respectively.

Our methodology for dialog management (Sect. 3) is based on the estimation of a statistical model from the sequences of the system and user dialog acts obtained from a set of training data. The next system response is selected by means of a classification process that considers the complete history of the dialog, which is one of the main advantages regarding the previously described statistical methodologies for dialog management. The evolving neuro-fuzzy classifiers that are proposed in this paper for its application on dialog management (*eClass* family [2]) are recursive, non-iterative, incremental and thus computationally light and suitable for real-time applications. These classifiers can be used to evolve an initial dialog model which has been previously defined but which needs to be modified because of the evolving nature of a dialog manager.

An *eClass* learns new rules from new data gradually preserving/inheriting the rules learned already. Thus, *eClass* can be defined as a self-developing classifier which has both their parameters but also (more importantly) their structure self-adapting on-line. For this reason, these classifiers can deal with the problem of classification of streaming data, which is essential for dialog management. An additional important advantage of these classifiers is the clear representation of the decisions that are taken by the dialog manager.

As it is explained in [2], the main differences between *eClass* family and a conventional Fuzzy Rule-Based (FRB) classifier are:

- the open structure of the rule-base: *eClass* self-develops on-line starting "from scratch", while in a conventional FRB classifier it is determined offline and then fixed.
- the online learning mechanism which takes into account this flexible rule-base structure.

Due to those characteristics, these classifiers have been applied to many other different environments. In [7], *eClass* is applied to IR spectral data of exfoliative cervical cytology, which has considerable potential in clinical settings. In [1], eClass is used to recognize and simultaneous classify the landmarks in real time for mobile robots. In [3], these classifiers are used for analyzing social networks emerging from phone calls of mobile users.

3 The FRB-Dialog Toolkit: Fuzzy-Rule-Based Dialog Systems

Figure 1 summarizes the previously described five main tasks usually integrated in a spoken dialog system. As can be observed, the dialog manager receives as input the semantic interpretation of a text string recognized by the ASR module. This information also includes confidence scores generated by the ASR and NLU modules.

Our proposal is focused on slot-filling dialog systems, for which dialog managers use a structure comprised of one slot per piece of information that the system can gather from the user. This data structure, which we call *Dialog Register* (*DR*), keeps the information provided by the user (e.g., slots) throughout

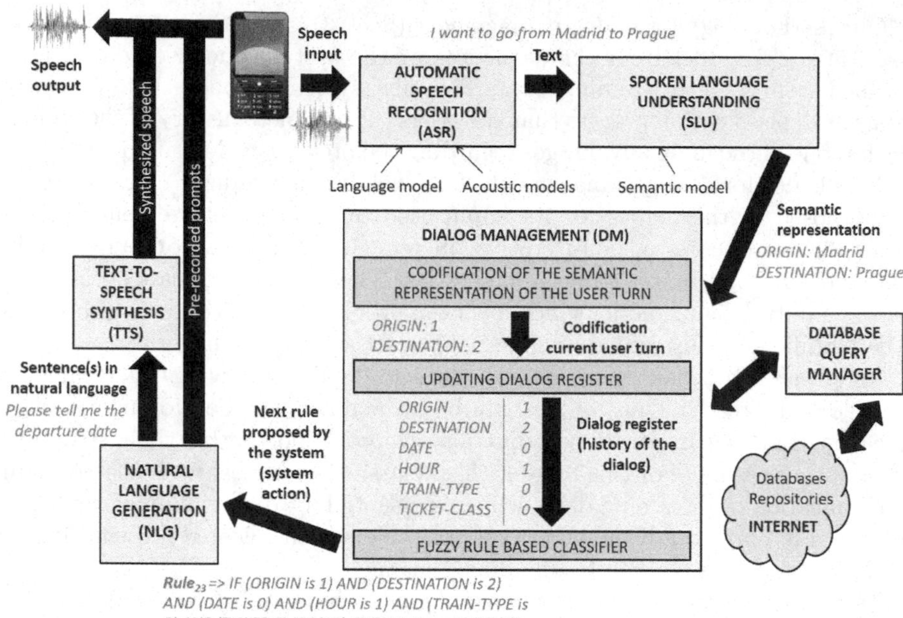

Fig. 1. Modular architecture of a spoken dialog system showing the proposed dialog management technique

the previous history of the dialog. The system can capture several data at once and the information can be provided in any order (more than one slot can be filled per dialog turn and in any order), thus supporting mixed-initiative dialogs in which the system asks the user a series of questions to gather information, and then consults an external knowledge source.

As described in Fig. 1, the dialog manager must consider the values for the slots provided by the user throughout the previous history of the dialog to select the next system action. For the dialog manager to take this decision, we have assumed that the exact values of the attributes are not significant. They are important for accessing databases and for constructing the output sentences of the system. However, the only information necessary to predict the next action by the system is the presence or absence of concepts and attributes. Therefore, the codification we use for each concept and attribute provided by the NLU module is in terms of three values, $\{0, 1, 2\}$, according to the following criteria: (i) (0): The value for the slot has not been provided; (1) The value is known with a confidence score that is higher than a given threshold; (2): The value of the slot has a confidence score that is lower than the given threshold.

We propose to determine the next system action by means of a classification process. The *FRB-Dialog* toolkit employs the *eClass0* (evolving Classifier) for the definition of the classification function. The toolkit allows training these classifiers from a labeled corpus of training dialogs, which can be provided to the toolkit or be automatically generated by it using a specific module based on a recently developed automatic dialog simulation technique [6].

After training the classifier, a set of fuzzy rules is generated describing the values of the observed features for the classification of each class (i.e., system action):

$$Rule_i = IF(Feature_1\ is\ P_1)\ AND \ldots AND(Feature_n\ is\ P_n) THEN\ Class\ =\ c_i$$

where i represents the number of rule; n is the number of input features (observations corresponding to the different slots defined for the semantic representation of the user's utterances); the vector $Feature$ stores the observed features, and the vector P stores the values of the features of one of the prototypes (coded in terms of three possible values, $\{0, 1, 2\}$) of the corresponding class $c_i \in$ {set of different classes}. Each class is then associated to a specific system action (response).

The following steps are carried out by the developed dialog managers after each user turn:

1. The values of the different slots provided by the NLU module for the current user turn is coded in terms of the previously described three possible values. Confidence scores also provided by this module are used to determine data reliability (e.g., in Fig. 1 the value of the associated confidence scores are used to code "Madrid" as a 1 and "Prague" as a 2).
2. The previous Dialog Register is updated with the new values for the slots determined in the previous step. In the example that Fig. 1 shows, the Dialog Register contains the slots ORIGIN, DESTINATION, DATE, HOUR, TRAIN-TYPE, and TICKET-CLASS. The previous *DR* containing just a 1 value for the HOUR slot is updated with the ORIGIN and DESTINATION values.
3. The classifier determines the fuzzy rule to be applied (i.e., next system action that will be translated into a sentence in natural language by the NLG module). The cosine distance is used to measure the similarity between the new sample to be classified and the rest of prototypes. For instance, the rule corresponding to the system action "Ask for a date" is selected in Fig. 1.

The *eClass0* model consists of several fuzzy rules per class (the number of rules depends on the heterogeneity of the input data of the same class). During the training process, a set of rules is formed from scratch using an evolving clustering approach to decide when to create new rules. The inference in *eClass0* is produced using the "winner takes all" rule and the membership functions that describe the degree of association with a specific prototype are of Gaussian form.

The *potential* (Cauchy function of the sum of distances between a certain data sample and *all* other data samples in the feature space) is used in the partitioning algorithm. However, in these classifiers, the potential (P) is calculated recursively (which makes the algorithm faster and more efficient). The potential of the kth data sample (x_k) is calculated by means of Eq. 1 [2]. The result of this function represents the *density* of the data that surrounds a certain data sample.

$$P(x_k) = \frac{1}{1 + \frac{\sum_{i=1}^{k-1} distance(x_k, x_i)}{k-1}} \quad (1)$$

where *distance* represents the distance between two samples in the data space.

The potential can be calculated using the euclidean or the cosine distance. In this case, cosine distance (*cosDist*) is used to measure the similarity between two samples; as it is described in Eq. 2.

$$cosDist(x_k, x_p) = 1 - \frac{\sum_{j=1}^{n} x_{kj} x_{pj}}{\sqrt{\sum_{j=1}^{n} x_{kj}^2 \sum_{j=1}^{n} x_{pj}^2}} \quad (2)$$

where x_k and x_p represent the two samples to measure its distance and n represents the number of different attributes in both samples.

Note that the resolution of Eq. 1 requires all the accumulated data sample available to be calculated, which contradicts to the requirement for real-time and on-line application needed in the proposed problem. For this reason, in [2] it is developed a recursive expression for the cosine distance. The proposed formula is as follows:

$$\begin{aligned} P_k(z_k) &= \frac{1}{2 - \frac{1}{(k-1)\sqrt{\sum_{j=1}^{n}(z_k^j)^2}} B_k}; k = 2, 3... \\ where: \ B_k &= \sum_{j=1}^{n} z_k^j b_k^j \ ; \ b_k^j = b_{(k-1)}^j + \sqrt{\frac{(z_k^j)^2}{\sum_{l=1}^{n}(z_k^l)^2}} \\ and \ b_1^j &= \sqrt{\frac{(z_1^j)^2}{\sum_{l=1}^{n}(z_1^l)^2}} \ ; \ j = [1, n+1]; \ P_1(z_1) = 1 \end{aligned} \quad (3)$$

where z_k represents the kth data sample (x_k) and its corresponding label ($z = [x, Label]$). Using this expression, it is only necessary to calculate *(n + 1)* values where n is the number of different subsequences obtained; this value is represented by b, where $b_k^j, j = [1, n]$ represents the accumulated value for the kth data sample.

In this case, a specific system action can be represented by several rules, depending on the heterogeneity of the samples that represent the same action. Thus, a class could be represented by one or several prototypes. The different prototypes that represent a system action are obtained from the input data and they are updated constantly. However, as it has previously explained, a initial rule-base can be defined (if necessary) by hand as start point of the classifier. In this sense, new prototypes are created or existing prototypes are removed if necessary.

4 Example of a Practical Application

Figure 2 shows an excerpt of a dialog for a system designed to provide railway information [5]. The set of task-dependent concepts and attributes defined for the semantic representation consists of the possible queries that users can make (*Timetables*, *Fares*, *Train-Type*, *Trip-Time*, or *Services*) and ten attributes that they must provide to complete these queries (*Origin*, *Destination*, *Departure-Date*, *Arrival-Date*, *Departure-Hour*, *Arrival-Hour*, *Class*, *Train-Type*, *Order-Number*, and *Services*). Users can also provide three task-independent dialog acts (*Affirmation*, *Negation*, and *Not-Understood*). A total of 51 system responses were defined for the task (classified into confirmations of concepts and attributes, questions to require data from the user, and answers obtained after a query to the database).

Using the previously described codification for the concepts and attributes, when a dialog starts (in the greeting turn) all the values are initialized to "0". The information provided by the users in each dialog turn is employed to update the previous values and obtain the current ones, as Fig. 2 shows.

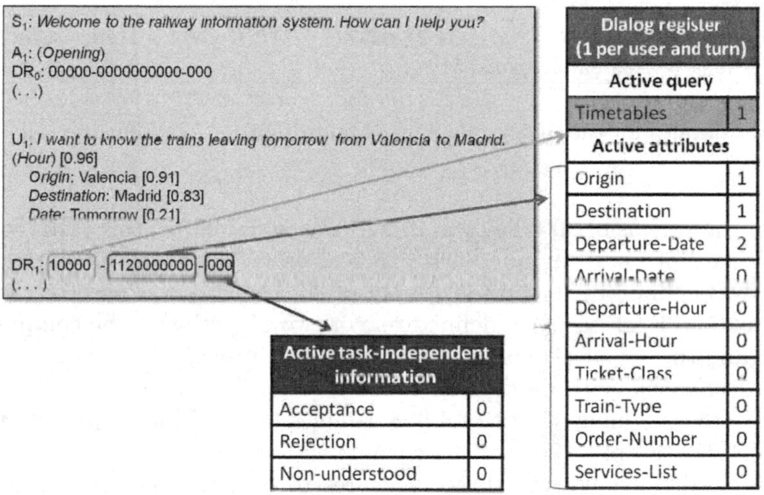

Fig. 2. Excerpt of a dialog with its correspondent representation of the task-dependent and active task-independent information for one of the dialog turns

This figure shows the semantic interpretation and confidence scores (in brackets) for a user's utterance provided by the NLU module. In this case, the confidence score assigned to the attribute *Date* is very low. Thus, a "2" value is added in the corresponding position for this attribute. The concept (*Hour*) and the attribute *Destination* are recognized with a high confidence score, adding a "1" value in the corresponding positions.

The set of features for the classifier includes the codification of the different concepts and attributes that can be provided by the user, the last system turn (A_1), and the task-independent information provided in the last user turn (none in this case). The set of rules for the task obtained with *eClass0* has then the structure described in Fig. 3. Using these rules, the dialog manager would select the class $'SystemResponse23'$, which corresponds to a system confirmation of the departure date. This process is repeated to predict the next system response after each user turn.

$FRB - RailwayTask(eClass0):$

IF ($Timetables$ is 1) AND ($Fares$ is 0) $AND \cdots AND$ ($Not - Understood$ is 0)
$THEN\ Class =' SystemResponse1'$

IF ($Timetables$ is 0) AND ($Fares$ is 0) $AND \cdots AND$ ($Not - Understood$ is 1)
$THEN\ Class =' SystemResponse1'$

IF ($Timetables$ is 0) AND ($Fares$ is 1) $AND \cdots AND$ ($Not - Understood$ is 2)
$THEN\ Class =' SystemResponse2'$

...
IF ($Timetables$ is 1) AND ($Fares$ is 2) $AND \cdots AND$ ($Not - Understood$ is 1)
$THEN\ Class =' SystemResponse51'$

Fig. 3. Set of rules for the dialog manager obtained with *eClass0* for the railway task

An initial corpus of 900 dialogs (10.8 h) was acquired for this task by means of the Wizard of Oz technique with 225 real users, for which an initial dialog strategy was defined by experts [5]. A set of 20 scenarios was used to carry out the acquisition. Each scenario defined one or two objectives to be completed by the user and the set of attributes that they must provide. The corpus consists of 6,280 user turns, with an average number of 7.7 words per turn. The corpus was split into a training subset of 4,928 samples (80% of the corpus) and a test subset of 1,232 samples (20% of the corpus).

We defined the following three measures to evaluate the statistical dialog model: (i) *Matching*: percentage of responses provided by the system that match exactly the initial dialog strategy defined by the experts; (ii) *Coherence*: percentage of responses that are coherent with the current dialog state but do not match the initial strategy; and (iii) *Error*: percentage of responses that could cause a dialog failure.

We have test the behavior of our proposal comparing it with different definitions of the classification function used to determine the next system response. In this work, we have used three approaches for the definition of the classification function: a multilayer perceptron (MLP), a multinomial naive Bayes classifier, and finite-state classifiers. We also defined three types of finite-state classifiers: bigram models, trigram models, and Morphic Generator Grammatical Inference (MGGI) models [16].

Table 1 shows the results obtained. As it can be observed, the Fuzzy-rule-based classifier provides satisfactory results in terms of the percentage of correct responses selected (*Matching* and *Coherence* measures) and responses that could cause the failure of the dialog (*Error* measure). With regard the rest of classifiers, the MLP classifier is the one providing the closest results to our proposal. The table also shows that among the finite-state model classifiers, the bigram and trigram classifiers are worse than the MGGI classifier, this is because they cannot capture long-term dependencies. The renaming function defined for the MGGI classifier seems to generate a model with too many states for the size of the training corpus, therefore, this classifier could be underestimated.

Table 1. Results of the evaluation of the different classification functions

Dialog manager	*Matching*	*Coherence*	*Error*
Fuzzy-rule-based (FRB) classifier	76.7%	89.2%	5.6%
MLP classifier	76.8%	88.8%	5.8%
Multinomial classifier	63.4%	76.7%	10.6%
Bigram classifier	28.8%	37.3%	42.2%
Trigram classifier	31.7%	42.1%	44.1%
MGGI classifier	46.6%	67.2%	24.8%

Secondly, we have evaluated our proposal with the acquisition of 100 dialogs by means of a user simulator [5]. We considered the following measures: (i) Dialog success rate (*Success*); (ii) Average number of turns per dialog (nT); (iii) Confirmation rate (*Confirmation*); and (iv) Error correction rate (ECR). The confirmation rate was computed as the ratio between the number of explicit confirmation turns and the total number of turns in the dialog. The ECR was computed as the number of errors detected and corrected by the dialog manager divided by the total number of errors.

Table 2. Results of the evaluation with the user simulator

Fuzzy-rule-based (FRB) dialog manager	
Success	93.5%
nT	13.8
Confirmation	22%
ECR	0.87%

The results presented in Table 2 show that in most cases the automatically learned dialog model has the capability of correctly interacting with the user. The dialog success depends on whether the system provides the correct data for every objective user's query. All of the objectives defined are achieved in 93.5% of the dialogs. The analysis of the main problem detected in the acquired dialogs shows that, in some cases, the system did not detect the introduction of data with a high confidence value due to errors generated by the ASR that were not detected by the dialog manager. However, the evaluation confirms a good operation of the approach since the information is correctly given to the user in the majority of cases. The confirmation and error correction rates have also a remarkable impact on the described system performance.

5 Conclusions and Future Work

In this paper, we have presented a toolkit based on a novel statistical methodology for the development of dialog managers for spoken dialog systems. The selection of the following system response is based on a classification process that takes into account the previous history of the dialog.

The most important contribution of our work consists of the use of Evolving Fuzzy Systems (EFS) to complete this classification, which is then modeled as a dynamic and evolving phenomenon. As a result of the application of our proposal, the dialog model is modeled by a set of automatically obtained dynamic rules that are applied to select the next system response. The use of EFS allows us to cope with huge amounts of data, and process streaming data on-line in real time. Thus, the dialog model is designed as a changing model which constantly reflect the changes in the way the dialog system interacts with its users.

We have described a application of our proposal for the *eClass0* classifier. Task-dependent information is isolated from the model taking into account whether the user has provided a given piece of information related to the task and also the confidence scores that the recognition and understanding modules have assigned to this piece of information. This allows not only to cope with the situations observed the training corpus, but also to manage unseen situations by selecting the most convenient system action.

For future work, we plan to evaluate the *FRB-dialog* toolkit considering the opinions of a group of experts in the field to whom it will be offered for testing. We want to also consider extending the definition of the Dialog register with additional features related to the users' emotional state. Also we will release the toolkit for the community via *GitHub*, so that it can be freely employed to evaluate different spoken dialog systems in several interaction contexts.

Acknowledgements. This work was supported in part by Projects TRA2015-63708-R and TRA2016-78886-C3-1-R.

References

1. Angelov, P., Zhou, X.: Evolving fuzzy classifier for novelty detection and landmark recognition by mobile robots. In: Nedjah, N., dos Santos Coelho, L., de Macedo Mourelle, L. (eds.) Mobile Robots: The Evolutionary Approach. SCI, vol. 50, pp. 89–118. Springer, Heidelberg (2007)
2. Angelov, P., Zhou, X.: Evolving fuzzy-rule-based classifiers from data streams. IEEE Trans. Fuzzy Syst. **16**(6), 1462–1475 (2008)

3. Baruah, R., Angelov, P.: Evolving social network analysis: a case study on mobile phone data. In: Proceedings of EAIS 2012, pp. 114–120 (2012)
4. Cuayáhuitl, H., Renals, S., Lemon, O., Shimodaira, H.: Human-computer dialogue simulation using hidden markov models. In: Proceedings of ASRU 2005, pp. 290–295 (2005)
5. Griol, D., Callejas, Z., López-Cózar, R., Riccardi, G.: A domain-independent statistical methodology for dialog management in spoken dialog systems. Comput. Speech Lang. **28**(3), 743–768 (2014)
6. Griol, D., Carbó, J., Molina, J.: An automatic dialog simulation technique to develop and evaluate interactive conversational agents. Appl. Artif. Intell. **27**(9), 759–780 (2013)
7. Kelly, J., Angelov, P., Trevisan, J., Vlachopoulou, A., Paraskevaidis, E., Martin-Hirsch, P., Martin, F.: Robust classification of low-grade cervical cytology following analysis with atr-ftir spectroscopy and subsequent application of self-learning classifier eclass. Anal. Bioanal. Chem. **398**(5), 2191–2201 (2010)
8. Lee, C., Jung, S., Kim, K., Lee, G.G.: Hybrid approach to robust dialog management using agenda and dialog examples. Comput. Speech Lang. **24**(4), 609–631 (2010)
9. Levin, E., Pieraccini, R., Eckert, W.: A stochastic model of human-machine interaction for learning dialog strategies. IEEE Trans. Speech Audio Process. **8**(1), 11–23 (2000)
10. McTear, M.F., Callejas, Z., Griol, D.: The Conversational Interface: Talking to Smart Devices. Springer, Switzerland (2016)
11. Meng, H.H., Wai, C., Pieraccini, R.: The use of belief networks for mixed-initiative dialog modeling. IEEE Trans. Speech Audio Process. **11**(6), 757–773 (2003)
12. Paek, T., Horvitz, E.: Conversation as action under uncertainty. In: Proceedings of UCAI 2000, pp. 455–464 (2000)
13. Planells, J., Hurtado, L., Sanchis, E., Segarra, E.: An online generated transducer to increase dialog manager coverage. In: Proceedings of Interspeech 2012 (2012)
14. Roy, N., Pineau, J., Thrun, S.: Spoken dialogue management using probabilistic reasoning. In: Proceedings of ACL 2000, pp. 93–100 (2000)
15. Schatzmann, J., Weilhammer, K., Stuttle, M., Young, S.: A survey of statistical user simulation techniques for reinforcement-learning of dialogue management strategies. Knowl. Eng. Rev. **21**(2), 97–126 (2006)
16. Segarra, E., Hurtado, L.: Construction of language models using morfic generator grammatical inference MGGI methodology. In: Proceedings of Eurospeech 1997, pp. 2695–2698 (1997)
17. Singh, S., Kearns, M., Litman, D., Walker, M.: Reinforcement learning for spoken dialogue systems. In: Proceedings of NIPS 1999, pp. 956–962 (1999)
18. Suendermann, D., Pieraccini, R.: One year of contender: what have we learned about assessing and tuning industrial spoken dialog systems? In: Proceedings of SDCTD 2012, pp. 45–48 (2012)
19. Wilks, Y., Catizone, R., Worgan, S., Turunen, M.: Some background on dialogue management and conversational speech for dialogue systems. Comput. Speech Lang. **25**, 128–139 (2011)
20. Young, S., Gasic, M., Thomson, B., Williams, J.: POMDP-based statistical spoken dialogue systems: a review. In: Proceedings of IEEE 2013, Montreal, Canada, pp. 1–18 (2013)

Radial-Based Approach to Imbalanced Data Oversampling

Michał Koziarski[1](✉), Bartosz Krawczyk[2], and Michał Woźniak[1]

[1] Department of Systems and Computer Networks,
Wrocław University of Science and Technology, Wrocław, Poland
{michal.koziarski,michal.wozniak}@pwr.edu.pl

[2] Department of Computer Science, Virginia Commonwealth University,
Richmond, VA, USA
bkrawczyk@vcu.edu

Abstract. The difficulty of the many practical decision problem lies in the nature of analyzed data. One of the most important real data characteristic is imbalance among examples from different classes. Despite more than two decades of research, imbalanced data classification is still one of the vital challenges to be addressed. The traditional classification algorithms display strongly biased performance on imbalanced datasets. One of the most popular way to deal with such a problem is to modify the learning set to decrease disproportion between objects from different classes using over- or undersampling approaches. In this work a novel preprocessing technique for imbalanced datasets is presented, which takes into consideration the mutual density class distribution. The proposed approach has been evaluated on the basis of the computer experiments carried out on the benchmark datasets. Their results seem to confirm the usefulness of the proposed concept in comparison to the state-of-art methods.

Keywords: Machine learning · Classification · Imbalanced data · Oversampling · Radial basis functions

1 Introduction

Most of commonly used machine learning algorithms work under an underlying assumption that classes have roughly equal number of instances in the training set. However, in many real-life scenarios it is difficult, or even impossible, to gather representative collections of instances of similar size from all of classes [11]. We may deal with a predominant group of objects being abundant and easy to gather, and with a significantly smaller group to instances of which we have an limited access [1]. Therefore, we need to create an efficient learning system using the imperfect data at our disposal. Such an imbalanced distribution will significantly affect the training process of a classifier, as it is usually guided by predictive accuracy. This solution assumes uniform importance of all training instances, thus leading to a classifier being biased towards the majority class.

F.J. Martínez de Pisón et al. (Eds.): HAIS 2017, LNAI 10334, pp. 318–327, 2017.
DOI: 10.1007/978-3-319-59650-1_27

When concentrating on more abundant case classifier is more likely to obtain higher accuracy rates, thus making such a model preferable from the canonical point of view. However, the minority class is usually the more important one and thus we want to maximize the predictive performance on it. This has lead to development of a number of approaches for balancing the classes or alleviating the bias during training step [4]. Let us now review quickly three most important groups of methods in this domain.

Preprocessing approaches are applied directly on the training set, before a classifier is being trained [14]. They aim at manipulating instances in such a way that will lead to obtaining a balanced dataset. One may achieve this by either undersampling the majority class, or oversampling the minority one. Randomized methods are the most basic ones, characterized by a low computational complexity and ease of usage. However, they may actually have a harmful effect on the dataset. Random undersampling may lead to discarding instances that are essential to forming correct class boundary or lie in specific subregions of the target class. Random oversampling may multiply noisy or corrupted instances, thus shifting the actual class distribution. Therefore, in recent years one may see significant developments in this area that propose a more guided approach for balancing classes.

Algorithm-level approaches aim at modifying the classifier learning procedure in order to make it skew-insensitive. This requires an in-depth understanding of the modified methods, as well as of the actual learning difficulty that causes the poor performance on minority class. Here, cost-sensitive approaches are popular, as they allow to easily modify any learning method by adding a separate misclassification penalty for each class [8]. This should improve minority class recognition, as classifier will be much more penalized for misclassification of minority instance. Another potential solution include usage of one-class classifiers [3]. Here, we create a data description of the target class (one selected by the user) and treat the remaining one as outliers. While we sacrifice knowledge about one of the classes, we gain a skew-insensitive classifier that captures unique properties of its target.

Hybrid solutions use advantages of the mentioned approaches and combine them with other methodologies, mainly ensemble learners [16]. They take advantage of increased predictive power, diversity and ability to capture complex data offered by combined classifiers and augment it with tackling imbalance at the level of each classifier. Popular approaches include combination of Bagging or Boosting with preprocessing.

Despite these developments there still exists a need for introducing more efficient and robust methods for learning from imbalanced data. Especially interesting recent direction is taking into account the properties of individual instances in the minority class.

In this paper, we introduce a novel oversampling technique that uses radial functions for estimating the potential of instances. We propose to use them to model mutual class distributions and analyze the learning difficulty associated with each instance. Our solution is able to select which objects should be subject to oversampling, instead of blindingly using all of them. By analyzing the differences in potential at a given point, we are able to predefine the nature of minority class instances use it to guide the artificial instance injection procedure. This allows for a more meaningful capturing of the minority class underlying distribution. Additionally, as our solution does not rely on neighborhood calculation, it is suitable for applications in high-dimensional datasets. Experimental study conducted on a number of benchmarks prove that the proposed radial-based oversampling is able to return satisfactory performance.

2 Radial-Based Approach to Oversampling

By far the most prevalent approach to imbalanced data oversampling is Synthetic Minority Oversampling Technique (SMOTE) [6] algorithm and its numerous extensions [5,7,9,12]. However, while widely used and empirically tested, SMOTE and its derivatives are not devoid of weaknesses. In the remainder of this section we discuss possible shortcomings of neighborhood-based oversampling strategies. Afterwards, we propose an alternative approach that aims at mitigating described issues. We describe how radial basis functions can be used to estimate mutual class density. Finally, we propose a novel algorithm, Radial-Based Oversampling, which takes advantage of this density estimation approach to guide the oversampling process in an informed manner.

2.1 Shortcomings of Neighborhood-Based Approaches

Conceptually simplest approach to imbalanced data oversampling is duplicating existing instances randomly, up to the point of achieving balanced class distributions. However, it leads to minority class distribution being highly focused in a small area, in which the original observations were present. Because of that, learning on data modified in such manner is prone to overfitting. SMOTE algorithm was designed specifically do address this issue. Instead of duplicating existing instances, SMOTE and its derivatives are based on creating new, synthetic samples. This family of methods relies on finding nearest, same-class neighbors of a given minority instance. Afterwards, new samples are being generated between the given target and one of its neighbors. This approach can be interpreted as finding the regions in which new samples can be synthesized, and these regions are lines connecting nearest minority neighbors. Since synthetic observations are spread out, SMOTE is less prone to overfitting than random oversampling. Furthermore, new objects can be synthesized in regions previously not containing minority samples. Because of that, this approach tends to move the decision border in favor of minority class, a behavior often desirable in case of highly imbalanced data.

The underlying assumption being made in SMOTE is that the regions between nearest minority neighbors are suitable for generating new instances. While often being the case, this assumption does not always hold true. An example of data distribution not meeting this requirement is presented in Fig. 1.

In presented case minority instances form several small clusters, divided by a large cluster of majority objects. Nearest minority neighborhood is therefore spread apart, which leads to generation of synthetic samples overlapping the majority cluster. This issue is so prevalent that it was addressed with several post-oversampling cleaning strategies, most notable being Tomek links [13] and Edited Nearest Neighbor Rule [15]. However, even applying such post-processing is not always sufficient to properly clean the resulting distribution. Furthermore, since sizes of minority clusters vary, it is not clear what size of neighborhood k should be chosen. Even the choice of $k = 1$ would not, however, be sufficient to fully remedy the issue of overlapping the majority cluster. To make the matters worse, it cannot be picked dynamically for different minority instances: SMOTE algorithm requires single choice of k for whole object space. Both of the mentioned issues, that is: synthetic samples overlapping existing majority instances and inability to pick number of neighbors dynamically, are deeply rooted in the fact that SMOTE does not take into the account presence of majority instances. Regions in which synthetic samples are generated are based solely on the minority class distribution, and this information is simply not sufficient in all cases.

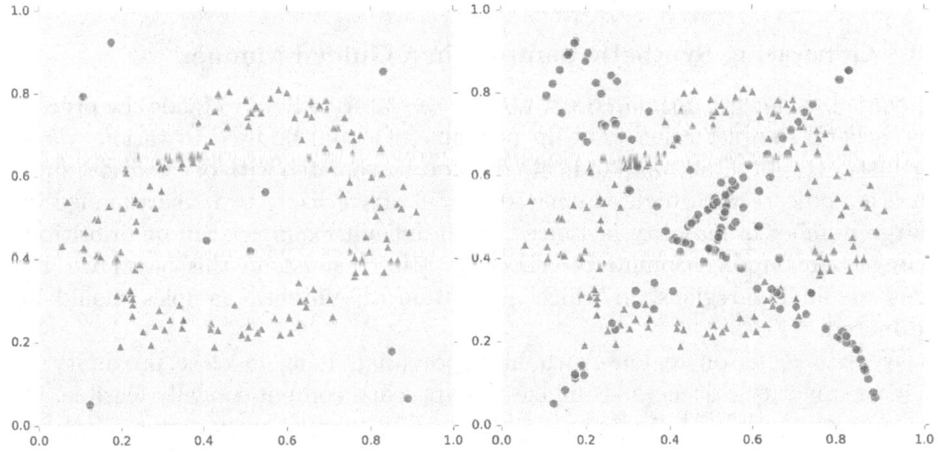

Fig. 1. Possible difficult case for SMOTE before (on the left) and after (on the right) generating synthetic samples. Due to varying sizes of minority objects clusters, it is not clear what number of neighbors k should be chosen. Even choosing $k = 1$ would lead to generating synthetic samples overlapping cluster of majority objects.

2.2 Estimating Difficulty with Radial Basis Functions

Instead of relying on nearest neighbors in process of generating new samples, in this paper we will investigate the possibility of density-based approach. Intuitively, our goal is similar to SMOTE techniques: we try to find the regions, in which generating synthetic samples is justified. However, contrary to SMOTE, we will take into account placement of majority objects. By doing so, our hope is to reduce the amount of synthetic samples placed in regions densely packed with majority instances.

To this end we will employ radial basis functions (RBFs). RBFs are real-valued functions, value of which depends on the distance of the point from the origin. Common example of such function is Gaussian RBF. Given distance r and parameter ε, Gaussian RBF can be defined as

$$\phi(r) = e^{-(\varepsilon r)^2}. \tag{1}$$

To estimate the mutual class density in a given point in space, also referred to as a potential, we will sum the values of RBFs for all the instances, with sign determined by the class of the particular instance. Throughout this paper we will use a convention that for majority objects value of RBF will be added, whereas for the minority objects it will be subtracted. Observing high potential in a given point will therefore correspond to high confidence in the fact that it belongs to the majority class. Furthermore, observing minority objects with high potential might indicate that they will be hard to classify correctly, since it is likely to be surrounded by multiple majority instances.

2.3 Generating Synthetic Samples in a Guided Manner

Mutual class density estimated with RBFs can later be used to guide the process of synthetic samples generation. In principle, it could be used in various ways. For instance, potential could indicate difficulty associated with observation, since minority objects with high associated potential are likely to be surrounded by a large number of majority instances. Such difficult examples can be prioritized during oversampling, similar to ADASYN [10]. Instead, in this paper we will focus on finding regions, in which generation of synthetic samples should be conducted.

We will focus on regions with high potential, lying in close proximity to existing minority instances. To make the approach computationally feasible, we will employ modified hill climbing procedure to maximize the potential of the synthetic samples. Optimization will start at a position of randomly chosen, existing minority instance. Whole procedure will last limited number of steps to prevent placing new instances too deeply into the majority objects clusters. Finally, to spread synthetic samples more evenly, we will allow optimization procedure to stop early with a small probability. Pseudocode of the final algorithm has been presented in Algorithm 1. An illustration of both confidence estimation with radial basis function and the conducted oversampling has been presented in Fig. 2.

3 Experimental Study

Experimental investigations, backed up with statistical analysis of the results, were conducted to evaluate the practical usefulness of the proposed oversampling

Algorithm 1. Radial-Based Oversampling algorithm

```
Input: collections of majority objects M and minority objects m
Parameters: spread of radial basis function γ, optimization step size, number of
   iterations per synthetic sample, probability of early stopping p
Output: collection of synthetic minority objects S

function RBO(M, m, γ, step size, iterations, p):
initialize empty collection S
while |m| + |S| < |M| do
   point ← randomly chosen object from m
   for i ← 1 to iterations do
      break with probability p
      translated ← point translated by step size in random direction
      if potential(translated, M, m, γ) > potential(point, M, m, γ) then
         point ← translated
      end if
   end for
   add point to S
end while
return S

function potential(point, M, m, γ):
result ← 0
for all majority points M_i do
   result ← result + e^(-(||M_i - point||_1 / γ)^2)
end for
for all minority points m_i do
   result ← result - e^(-(||m_i - point||_1 / γ)^2)
end for
return result
```

strategy. In the remainder of this section we describe set-up of the study, present obtained results and discuss achieved outcomes.

3.1 Set-up

Proposed strategy of dealing with data imbalance, Radial-Based Oversampling (RBO), has been compared with two state-of-the-art oversampling algorithms: SMOTE [6] and ADASYN [10]. Additionally, the baseline case was considered, in which no resampling was applied prior to classification. To assess the robustness to the choice of learner, several classification algorithms were considered, namely: k-nearest neighbors (k-NN), support vector machine with radial basis function kernel (SVM) and CART decision tree (CART).

Following parameters were used in combination with the RBO method: γ coefficient, corresponding to the spread of radial basis function, was set to 0.05. Step size used during hill climbing optimization was set to 0.001. Number of

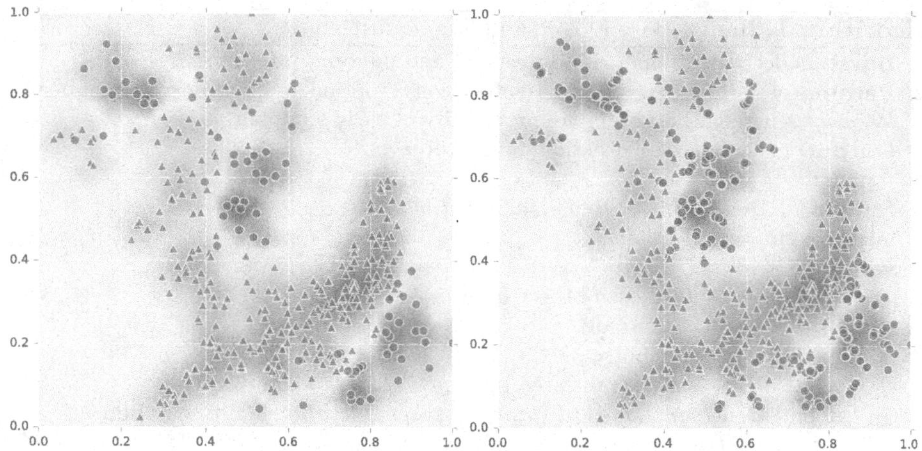

Fig. 2. On the left: confidence estimation conducted using radial basis functions. Of particular interest are minority objects (in blue) lying in regions of high confidence in majority class (in red). On the right: modified data distribution with synthetically generated samples. (Color figure online)

iterations per synthetic sample was set to 500. Finally, the probability of stopping the optimization early was set to 0.02. Meanwhile, both baseline methods, SMOTE and ADASYN, used 5 nearest neighbors to construct the synthetic samples. In all cases new samples were generated up to the point of balancing the distributions.

Evaluation was performed on 10 datasets taken from KEEL [2] repository. They were chosen to cover varying levels of imbalance and their details are presented in Table 1. During the evaluation datasets were partitioned using a 5-folds stratified cross validation. Prior to classification data was normalized to range from 0 to 1. No further preprocessing was applied.

3.2 Results

In order to properly analyze the behavior of examined methods on imbalanced data, several metrics were considered: accuracy, precision, recall, F-measure and geometric mean (G-mean). To assure statistical validity of the results Friedman test was conducted and average rankings on all the datasets were reported. They were presented in Table 2. Additionally, detailed results of F-measure for all datasets were presented in Table 3.

Oversampling strategy proposed in this paper achieved performance comparable to SMOTE method. Using ADASYN led to best results on tested datasets as far as recall was considered, at the cost of slightly lower precision. These trends were alike for all considered classifiers, suggesting robustness to the choice of base learner. Overall, performance of all three resampling algorithms was similar. This leads us to believe that further work on radial-based oversampling strategies is a promising research direction.

Table 1. Details of datasets used during the experimental study.

No	Name	IR	Features	Samples
1	glass1	1.82	9	214
2	wisconsin	1.86	7	220
3	yeast1	2.46	8	1484
4	vehicle0	3.25	18	846
5	ecoli1	3.36	7	336
6	new-thyroid1	5.14	5	215
7	segment0	6.02	19	2308
8	page-blocks0	8.79	10	5472
9	vowel0	9.98	13	988
10	abalone19	16.4	8	731

Table 2. Average rankings of various performance measures, computed for k-NN/SVM/CART classifiers. Method proposed in this paper, Radial-Based Oversampling (RBO), was compared with SMOTE and ADASYN algorithms, as well as the baseline case in which no oversampling was applied.

Measure	None	SMOTE	ADASYN	RBO
Accuracy	**1.8/2.3/1.8**	2.6/2.6/2.8	3.1/2.4/2.7	2.4/2.6/2.6
Precision	**1.4/2.2/1.7**	2.5/2.4/2.9	3.2/2.8/2.8	2.7/2.6/2.6
Recall	4/4/3.8	2.3/2.2/2.2	**1.5/1.4/1.4**	2.1/2.3/2.5
F-measure	2.7/4/2.6	**2.4/2**/2.7	2.5/**2/2.1**	**2.4/2**/2.6
G-mean	4/4/3.5	2/2.3/2.4	**1.9/1.6/1.9**	2.1/2.1/2.2

Table 3. Values of F-measure achieved on specific datasets, computed for k-NN/SVM/CART classifiers.

Dataset	None	SMOTE	ADASYN	RBO
1	0.67/0.00/0.66	0.70/0.56/0.64	**0.72**/0.53/**0.67**	**0.72/0.57/0.67**
2	**0.96/0.96**/0.90	**0.96/0.96**/0.92	**0.96/0.96/0.93**	**0.96/0.96**/0.92
3	0.49/0.11/**0.52**	**0.57**/0.58/**0.52**	0.56/0.58/0.50	0.54/**0.59/0.52**
4	**0.86**/0.00/**0.89**	0.84/0.68/0.86	0.85/**0.71/0.89**	0.85/0.69/0.85
5	**0.82**/0.72/0.74	0.78/0.75/0.74	0.78/**0.76**/0.74	0.77/0.75/**0.77**
6	0.89/0.62/0.90	**0.96/0.93/0.92**	0.94/**0.93**/0.90	0.95/**0.93**/0.89
7	**0.98**/0.57/**0.98**	0.97/**0.89/0.98**	0.97/0.66/0.97	0.97/0.88/**0.98**
8	**0.77**/0.55/**0.84**	0.76/**0.67**/0.82	0.76/0.61/0.83	**0.77/0.67**/0.80
9	0.97/0.00/0.92	**0.99**/0.76/0.90	**0.99/0.80/0.93**	**0.99**/0.76/0.90
10	0.00/0.00/0.00	**0.04/0.04/0.03**	**0.04/0.04/0.03**	0.03/0.03/0.02

4 Conclusions and Future Directions

In this paper we proposed a novel approach to imbalanced data oversampling. It relied on using radial basis functions to estimate classification difficulty of minority objects. An inspiration for it lied in addressing possible shortcomings of existing oversampling strategies, which we described in this paper. Results of conducted experimental evaluation seem to confirm possible usefulness of the proposed approach.

Proposed method, while capable of achieving performance comparable to other state-of-the-art oversampling algorithms, is relatively simple and can be improved upon. First of all, it is not clear whether maximization of potential is the optimal choice. Usually it corresponds to generating new minority objects in areas of the lowest certainty. In some cases it might be preferable to generate safer objects instead, especially so if preserving high precision is an important factor. Secondly, results of experimental study conducted in this paper indicate that oversampling with ADASYN leads to better results than SMOTE. This corresponds to focusing on difficult minority objects while generating synthetic samples. Incorporating such mechanism into the Radial-Based Oversampling might therefore improve performance of the method. Thirdly, in the proposed approach we considered only mutual class density, difference between the potential of majority and minority classes. In some cases it might be insufficient to describe the difficulty of classification in a particular point in space. For instance, neighborhood of an object could be densely packed with both minority and majority instances. Opposite potentials could cancel themselves out, leading to the same final value as in the case of a single object with no nearby observations. To mitigate this issue, probability distributions of individual classes could be incorporated into the oversampling procedure. Finally, in presented form radial-based approach to oversampling is computationally expensive, since at every iteration potential is computed based on all existing objects. However, since influence of far-away points is usually negligible, this operation could be significantly sped up by focusing only on nearest instances.

Acknowledgements. This work was supported by the Polish National Science Center under the grant no. UMO-2015/19/B/ST6/01597 as well as the PLGrid Infrastructure.

References

1. Ahmed, F., Samorani, M., Bellinger, C., Zaïane, O.R.: Advantage of integration in big data: Feature generation in multi-relational databases for imbalanced learning. In: 2016 IEEE International Conference on Big Data, BigData 2016, Washington DC, USA, 5–8 December 2016, pp. 532–539 (2016)
2. Alcalá, J., Fernández, A., Luengo, J., Derrac, J., García, S., Sánchez, L., Herrera, F.: KEEL data-mining software tool: Data set repository, integration of algorithms and experimental analysis framework. J. Multiple-Valued Logic Soft Comput. **17**(2–3), 255–287 (2010)

3. Bellinger, C., Sharma, S., Japkowicz, N.: One-class versus binary classification: Which and when? In: 11th International Conference on Machine Learning and Applications, ICMLA, Boca Raton, FL, USA, 12–15 December 2012, vol. 2. pp. 102–106 (2012)
4. Branco, P., Torgo, L., Ribeiro, R.P.: A survey of predictive modeling on imbalanced domains. ACM Comput. Surv. **49**(2), 31:1–31:50 (2016)
5. Bunkhumpornpat, C., Sinapiromsaran, K., Lursinsap, C.: Safe-level-SMOTE: safe-level-synthetic minority over-sampling technique for handling the class imbalanced problem. In: Theeramunkong, T., Kijsirikul, B., Cercone, N., Ho, T.-B. (eds.) PAKDD 2009. LNCS, vol. 5476, pp. 475–482. Springer, Heidelberg (2009). doi:10.1007/978-3-642-01307-2_43
6. Chawla, N.V., Bowyer, K.W., Hall, L.O., Kegelmeyer, W.P.: SMOTE: synthetic minority over-sampling technique. J. Artif. Intell. Res. **16**, 321–357 (2002)
7. Chawla, N.V., Lazarevic, A., Hall, L.O., Bowyer, K.W.: SMOTEBoost: improving prediction of the minority class in boosting. In: Lavrač, N., Gamberger, D., Todorovski, L., Blockeel, H. (eds.) PKDD 2003. LNCS, vol. 2838, pp. 107–119. Springer, Heidelberg (2003). doi:10.1007/978-3-540-39804-2_12
8. Domingos, P.M.: Metacost: a general method for making classifiers cost-sensitive. In: Proceedings of the Fifth ACM SIGKDD International Conference on Knowledge Discovery and Data Mining, San Diego, CA, USA, 15–18 August 1999, pp. 155–164 (1999)
9. Han, H., Wang, W.-Y., Mao, B.-H.: Borderline-SMOTE: a new over-sampling method in imbalanced data sets learning. In: Huang, D.-S., Zhang, X.-P., Huang, G.-B. (eds.) ICIC 2005. LNCS, vol. 3644, pp. 878–887. Springer, Heidelberg (2005). doi:10.1007/11538059_91
10. He, H., Bai, Y., Garcia, E.A., Li, S.: ADASYN: adaptive synthetic sampling approach for imbalanced learning. In: IEEE International Joint Conference on Neural Networks, IJCNN 2008. (IEEE World Congress on Computational Intelligence), pp. 1322–1328. IEEE (2008)
11. Porwik, P., Doroz, R., Orczyk, T.: Signatures verification based on PNN classifier optimised by PSO algorithm. Pattern Recogn. **60**, 998–1014 (2016)
12. Ramentol, E., Caballero, Y., Bello, R., Herrera, F.: SMOTE-RSB*: a hybrid preprocessing approach based on oversampling and undersampling for high imbalanced data-sets using SMOTE and rough sets theory. Knowl. Inf. Syst. **33**(2), 245–265 (2012)
13. Tomek, I.: Two modifications of CNN. IEEE Trans. Syst. Man Cybern. **6**(11), 769–772 (1976)
14. Triguero, I., Galar, M., Merino, D., Maillo, J., Bustince, H., Herrera, F.: Evolutionary undersampling for extremely imbalanced big data classification under apache spark. In: IEEE Congress on Evolutionary Computation, CEC 2016, Vancouver, BC, Canada, 24–29 July 2016, pp. 640–647 (2016)
15. Wilson, D.L.: Asymptotic properties of nearest neighbor rules using edited data. IEEE Trans. Syst. Man Cybern. **2**(3), 408–421 (1972)
16. Wozniak, M., Graña, M., Corchado, E.: A survey of multiple classifier systems as hybrid systems. Inf. Fusion **16**, 3–17 (2014)

Visual Analysis & Advanced Data Processing Techniques

Simulation of a Directional Process by Means of an Anisotropic Buffer Operator

M. Dolores Muñoz(✉) and María N. Moreno García

Department of Computing and Automatic, University of Salamanca,
Plaza de la Merced, s/n, Salamanca, Spain
{mariado,mmg}@usal.es

Abstract. Geographic information systems have usually implemented a module that allows areas to be delimited by an isotropic buffer. In this kind of buffer, the generating polygon is a circle, which implies a constant distance from the border of the buffer to the object. The simulation of anisotropic processes, in contrast, requires the use of generating polygons which determine directionally non-uniform areas of influence. In this paper, a review of how some of the commercial GISs address the problem of anisotropy is presented, concluding that commercial GIS have modules that allow to perform spatial analysis. However, the anisotropic analysis tools are not sufficiently developed, being restricted to implementations based on the study of distance costs. In addition, we proposed a method to check the anisotropy and the creation of a generator oval that allows to delimit zones of influence that represent phenomena with anisotropic characteristics.

Keywords: Anisotropic image analysis · Geographic Information Systems · Anisotropic buffer · Visualization

1 Introduction and Previous Concepts

A buffer operator, also called the buffering or influence zone, is commonly found in commercial GIS (Geographic Information Systems) products such as the ESRI [7] Spatial Analyst extension, Idrisi, Mapinfo or ERDAS. It is defined as the geometric space of the points that are at a smaller or similar distance to a given object (point, polyline or polygon) [5]. This definition is isotropic or directionally uniform, since the distance of the object to the edge of the buffer is constant in any direction of the plane. In [12, 15], a Case-Based Reasoning (CBR) system is presented in which an isotropic buffer operator is applied to calculate the area of an oil slick and a forest fire, respectively, for prediction and visualization tasks. The use of the buffer operator improves the quality of the data used by the system and as a consequence the quality of the results obtained. The rest of the paper is organized as follows. Section 2 presents the concept of anisotropy in different fields. In Sect. 3 the treatment of directional aspects by commercial GIS is described. The cost analysis in commercial GIS is explained in Sect. 4. Section 5 is devoted to proposing the visualization of the process of the expansion. Finally, conclusions are drawn in Sect. 6.

F.J. Martínez de Pisón et al. (Eds.): HAIS 2017, LNAI 10334, pp. 331–341, 2017.
DOI: 10.1007/978-3-319-59650-1_28

2 Anisotropy

The word anisotropy is the combination of three words with their own meanings: AN (negative particle), iso (same or equivalent) and trope (figure). Thus, it is defined as "unequal behaviour in the different directions of space." [10]. Anisotropy is one of the most important qualities in human spatial vision. It is based on the biological fact of being citizens of the earth's crust, unable to fly autonomously or dive freely in the deep sea. This biological situation entails a perception of space that it is not homogeneous with respect to vertical and horizontal dimensions.

We stand on a vertical axis and symmetry along this axis gives us enormous adaptive advantages, as far as energy consumption is concerned, to move as well as to maintain balance. These conditions help us understand the forces acting on the space in which we move.

2.1 Vertical Anisotropy

Human vision shows anisotropy in the vertical dimension due to the effects exerted on all bodies by gravitational force, and horizontally (left/right) because of the structural and functional asymmetry in the human brain [11]. Anisotropy is a perceptual property of our visual field that has a great influence on our way of seeing objects. Its visual effect makes humans perceive an image differently depending on its location. Therefore, our perception of an object depends on whether it is located on the right or on the left, or in the lower or upper visual field. This effect can be observed by rotating an object 180° to the left (Fig. 1).

Fig. 1. Vertical anisotropy

The number 3 has a characteristic design. It is formed by two open lobes, which, in most cases, are slightly different.

By inverting the position of the number, the larger lobe, which is usually at the bottom, takes on a prominent role which makes it seem deformed. This disparity is a manifestation of anisotropy in the vertical axis.

2.2 Horizontal Anisotropy

To justify the phenomenon of perceptual disparity between the right and left side of our visual field, the following factors have been considered [11]:

- The habit of following the direction of reading.
- The problem is that people from countries that read upside down or vertically do not present directional anisotropy. However, anisotropy also occurs in the illiterate.
- The differences between the two lobes of the brain.
- Differences in functionality and perceptive intensity between both eyes: as with the hands, we are always left or right handed when it comes to vision. Left-handed people usually look from left to right. That is why newspaper adverts cost double if they are located on odd pages rather than on even pages.

Horizontal anisotropy causes the same things to generate different sensations, which are often polarized, depending on whether they are located on the right or on the left.

Vermeer's work "The Street", shown in Fig. 2, is a good example of how the perception of the same form undergoes significant variations depending on whether you are located in one area or another. We have the sensation that we see the alley more or less, which is more or less the space next to brick building.

Fig. 2. The street Vermer's work

2.3 Anisotropy, A Characteristic of Minerals

A mineral is defined as a natural chemical combination or as a native chemical element constituting the earth's crust, and having almost always the same crystal structure. Two of its fundamental properties, which therefore define the crystalline environment, are homogeneity and anisotropy. When two equal portions of a crystalline material with the same orientation in space show no difference in chemical quality, it is said to preserve a homogeneous structure.

Anisotropy in this case can be defined as the characteristic according to which certain properties of a crystal depend on the orientation that it has at a given time. Thus, electrical conductivity, heat, thermal expansion, speed of propagation of light, etc. are very different depending on the direction in which the characteristic is manifested. In the case of the propagation of light inside a quartz crystal, for example, its speed depends on the direction that the rays follow inside, because structurally, the distance between the neighboring nodes of a crystalline network varies according to the direction, and consequently, also the properties of the crystal.

The crystalline substances whose physical properties vary with direction are called anisotropic, and are classified within the vector physical properties, that is to say, those which are represented by vectors indicating direction, intensity and orientation.

3 Anisotropy Testing

There are phenomena that have certain characteristics which change according to the direction from which they have been observed. When this happens, these phenomena are said to have a spatial behavior. To describe these phenomena linear statistics cannot be used, but certain tools which provide directional statistical analysis shall be used instead. Directional statistics deals with data representing vectors in the plane or in 3D space.

The study of the spatial behavior of a phenomenon can be carried out by analyzing the mean value of every variable under study and with the results obtained, extrapolate all of them in order to be able to know the overall behavior of the phenomenon. For it, the homogeneity degree in local and global effects is studied, allowing to assume some kind of pattern, limiting this way the number of parameters and ensuring a more manageable model [13].

The next step consists of identifying the directional component that determines an anisotropic phenomenon using tools that allows us to represent a particular and differentiated treatment of the linear variables, such as the descriptive statistics and the methods of correlation analysis.

A common practice used to analyze the spatial dependence is to estimate the spatial correlation at different distances, i.e. to examine the structure of the spatial covariance of the pattern.

The most commonly used technique is the self-correlation test based on any statistic designed for it, such as Lagrange's, Moran's I, Geary's C or Geti's G multipliers.

Another element of circular statistics, which allows us to represent the information for descriptive purposes only, is the standard ellipse.

4 Cost Analysis in GIS

Commercial GIS have modules that allow spatial analysis; however, anisotropic analysis tools are not sufficiently developed, and are restricted to implementations based on the cost distance study.

The Idrisi GIS [16] product, developed by Clark Laboratories, incorporates a calculation module called anisotropic Varcost that can be used to model the effects of anisotropic friction associated with movement across a surface. Similar capabilities (called weighted distance functions) have been incorporated to ArcGIS version 9 [2, 7]. AccessMod (developed by the World Health Organization together with the network of centers of excellence) is an extension of ArcView 3.x, and uses the same Cost Distance isotropic module for spatial analysis as ArcView 3.x. and ArcGIS 9.

This function is also available in version 3 of ArcView and MAP ArcGIS 9 through a dynamic library written in C++ (dll) based on the Boost [3] library, constructed such that it can directly link AccessMod modules. MAPA isotropic combines information from both layers of digital terrain models, like the layers represented by linear vectors (roads and rivers).

Grass GIS [9] includes R.spread to allow simulation of anisotropic expansions through an ellipse and create a corresponding raster map to accumulate the time invested in generating the expansion surface.

4.1 The Idrisi GIS

Idrisi [16] provides two modules for calculation of anisotropic cost called Varcost and Disperse.

Some cost studies not only consider the cost generated by the movement, but also take into account the forces and frictions that impede or facilitate the displacement. When either Varcost or Disperse are used, anisotropic forces and friction through a vector are represented. To model the anisotropic cost, two images are used, one in which the magnitude of forces and friction are represented and another which stores the direction of the forces and friction expressed as degrees azimuthal.

Because the analysis may reflect the consequences of applying different forces at the same time, there are two other modules that allow us to represent the combination of forces and friction: Resultant and Decomp. Resultant takes information from an image representing the torque force/friction and generates another force/friction image representing the vector resulting from these actions. Resultant can be used to combine forces on friction and produce an image of a single variable (address) that can be used as input for Varcost or Disperse.

$$d(\alpha) = fricción\_efectiva = fricción\_patrón^{f(\alpha)} \tag{1}$$

Where $f(\alpha) = 1/cos^k\ \alpha$, where k is a coefficient defined by the user and α the angle difference between the direction in which the phenomenon reaches its maximum friction value and the actual direction of action (Fig. 3).

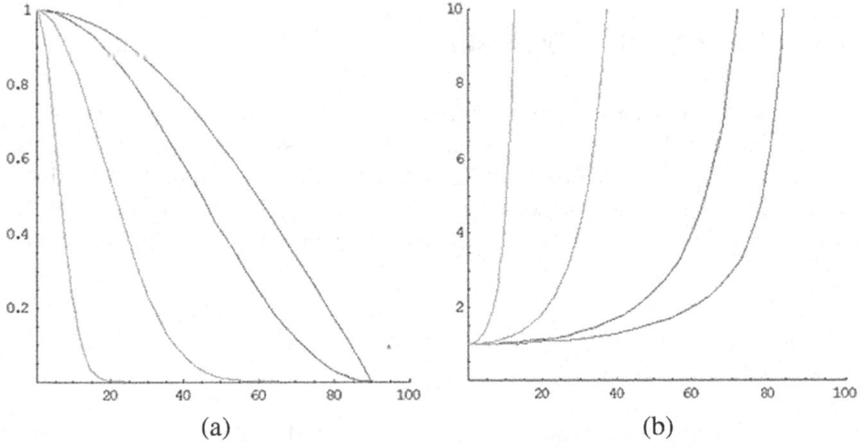

Fig. 3. (a) Function $f(\alpha) = cos^k\ \alpha$ (b) Function $f(\alpha) = 1/cos^k\ \alpha$

An extremely high exponent would produce zero friction. Independently of the exponent, using the anisotropic function returns negative values for the angles between 90° and 270°.

With Disperse, the same logic applies but in this case the anisotropic function is different:

$$d(\alpha) = efective\_friction = pattern\_friction * f(\alpha) \tag{2}$$

where $f(\alpha) = 1/cos^k\ \alpha$. The purpose of this function is to modify the friction to achieve maximum value at angle 0 with progressive increases in frictions, reaching infinite value for the 90° angle.

Figure 4 shows the values returned by the function *f*, for the case of the Disperse and Varcost functions.

$$efective\_friction = pattern\_friction * f \tag{3}$$

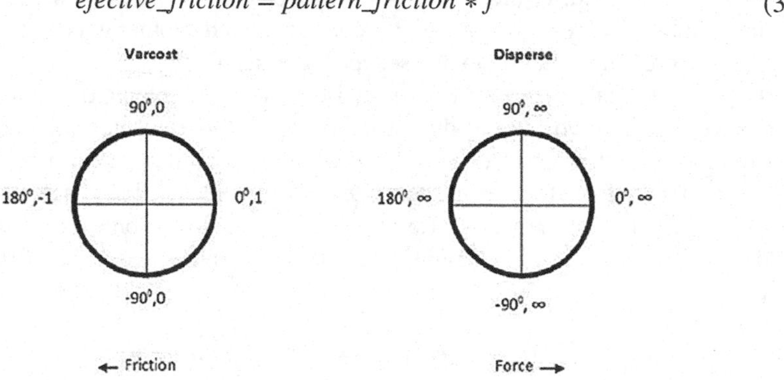

Fig. 4. Behaviour of the functions Varcost and Disperse in Idrisi

Where *f* is a function defined by the user.

5 Visualization of the Expansion

Let suppose we are studying the dispersion of a gas and we want to represent its expansion. It is to be expected that the behaviour of the expansion does not follow an established pattern, so that it cannot be considered as a directional uniform process, since the area affected by the gas will depend on changes in the direction of the wind. If we consider the time periods t_1, t_2, …, t_n, the expansion will be given by the following formula:

$$E = \bigcup_{i=1}^{n} E_i(l_i, \theta_i) = \bigcup_{i=1}^{n} E_i(v_i \cdot t_i, \theta_i) \tag{4}$$

Because the Minkowski property of the sum, where P is the image from which we start, the above formula gives rise to:

$$E = P \oplus \left[G(l_1, \theta_1) \oplus G(l_2, \theta_2) \oplus \ldots \oplus G(l_n, \theta_n)\right] = P \oplus G_t \quad (5)$$

The produced expansion would be the result of the sum of the n partial expansions, which can be considered as a single expansion in which the generating polygon G_t is given by the following expression:

$$g_t(\Phi) = \sum_{i=1}^{n} l_i \cdot \mathrm{Exp}\left[\frac{\mathrm{k}}{2}\left[\mathrm{Cos}(\Phi - \theta_i) - 1\right]\right] \quad (6)$$

The following figure shows in a graphical way a set of expansions (Fig. 5).

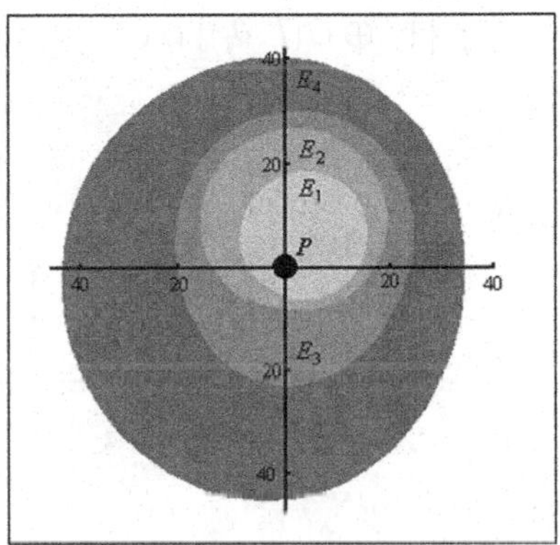

Fig. 5. Expansion of point P.

The fact that different forces cause significant changes over the same period of time prevents us from representing the expansion using the sum of Minkowski as we have seen previously.

At the moment in which the expansion begins, there may be one or several forces that are causing this expansion. In addition, we must take into account if the force/s is/are kept constant while studying the expansion of the phenomenon.

As seen in [14], in the case of different forces are acting and they keep constant over time, it is necessary to divide the zone of influence of the expansion into parts and to apply the sum of Minkowski.

Another case to consider will be one in which you consider that only a force acts. Let's see an example to explain how it works:

Suppose the expansion begins with different forces that remain constant over time.

Figure 6 shows the primary polygon of vertices P = {(5, 15), (15, 12), (20, 7), (7, 4), (5, 15)}. The surface on which this is included is divided into cells, each of which possesses a value of dominant direction and speed or the external forces that act on it. When at least one side of P is included in cells of different values, the buffer cannot be calculated applying the Minkowski sum. The generation of the influence area requires:

(a) Segmentation of each side of the image into as many segments as cells occupied, so that after the division, each of the resulting segments possesses a single value of v an θ.
After this operation the polygon is described as P = {(5, 15), (11, 13.2), (15, 12), (18, 9), (20, 7), (11, 5), (7, 4), (6.09, 9)}, after adding the vertices (11, 13.2), (18, 9), (11, 5) and (6.09, 9).

(b) The Minkowski sum [12, 15] to be performed on each of the segments s_j of the image, using $G(lj,\theta_j)$ as generating polygons in each segment where l_j and θ_j are the values of velocity per unit of time and dominant direction in its containing cell c; the sum should be circumscribed to this cell.

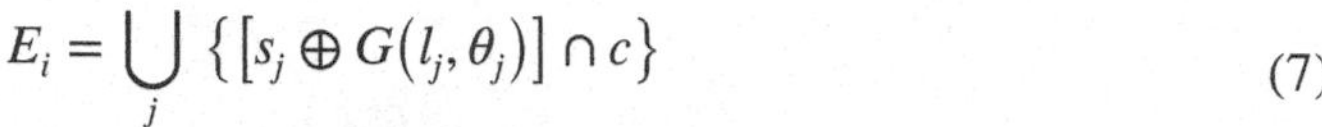

$$E_i = \bigcup_j \{[s_j \oplus G(l_j, \theta_j)] \cap c\} \tag{7}$$

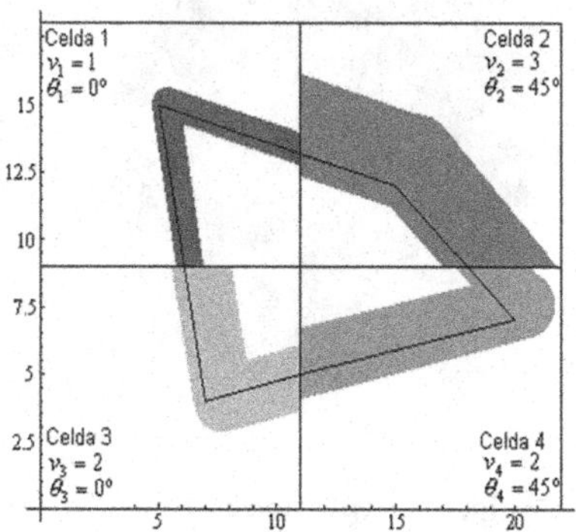

Fig. 6. Generating areas of influence

When only one force acts at the time the expansion occurs, it is to be expected that there will be changes over time in the direction and/or speed of the external forces, which will cause the spot to take different shape Therefore, the generating polygon finds areas with different values of v_i and/or θ_i, which makes it necessary to use as many generating polygons as different pairs (v_i, θ_i) the expansions find. The simplest case is shown in Fig. 7. We can see that in the period i = 1, the expansion of point P is the result of the expansions in cell 1 and in cell 2:

$$E_1 = E_{1,1} + E_{1,2} = Z1 + Z2 + Z3 \tag{8}$$

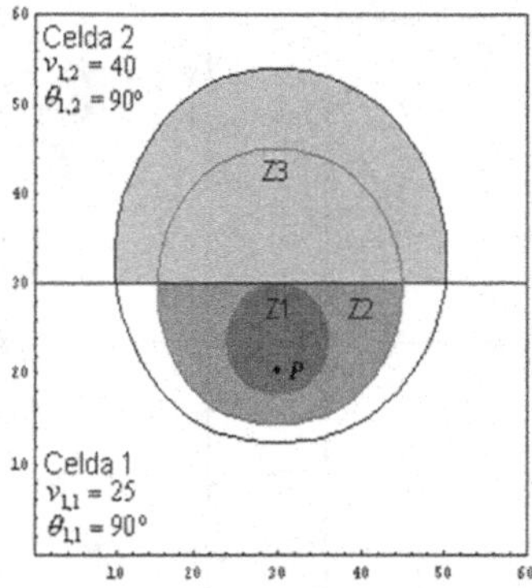

Fig. 7. The expansion E of point P is the result of the expansions of cell 1 and cell 2

The exclusive expansion in cell 1 (area Z1) takes place from the initial moment $t = 0$ to the moment $t = t_c$, starting from which expansion takes place in both cells. Simultaneously, the expansion in cell 1 behaves typically during the whole period, and for that reason, assuming t_1 as the unit of time:

$$E_{1,1} = \left(P \oplus G\left(l_{1,1}, \theta_{1,1}\right)\right) \cap \text{cell } 1 = \text{Z1} + \text{Z2} \tag{9}$$

In cell 2, the expansion will depend on moment t_c:

$$E_{1,2} = \left(P \oplus G\left(v_{1,1}, v_{1,2}, \theta_{1,1}, \theta_{1,2}, t_c\right)\right) \cap \text{cell } 2 = \text{Z3} \tag{10}$$

$P \oplus G\left(v_{1,1}, v_{1,2}, \theta_{1,1}, \theta_{1,2}, t_c\right)$ the generating polygon of polar radius being

$$\begin{aligned} g(\Phi) = {} & v_{1,1} \cdot t_c \cdot \text{Exp}\left[\frac{\text{k}}{2}\left[\text{Cos}\left(\Phi - \theta_{1,1}\right) - 1\right]\right] \\ & + v_{1,2} \cdot \left(1 - t_c\right) \cdot \text{Exp}\left[\frac{\text{k}}{2}\left[\text{Cos}\left(\Phi - \theta_{1,2}\right) - 1\right]\right] \end{aligned} \tag{11}$$

The values of Fig. 7 are shown in Table 1.

Table 1. Expansion values shown in Fig. 7

	$0 < t \leq t_c$	$t_c < t \leq 1$
$E_{1,1}$	$P \oplus G(25, 90°) = \text{Z1}$	$(P \oplus G(25, 90°)) \cap \text{Cell } 1 = \text{Z2}$
$E_{1,2}$	————	$(P \oplus G(25, 40, 90°, 90°, 0.4)) \cap \text{Cell } 2 = \text{Z3}$

Figure 8 shows different examples of variations in the velocity and/or direction of the forces. The expansions in each cell are those given by Eqs. (9), (10) and (11). Although for didactic reasons the procedure has been described by taking a point as the primary image, this is expandable to primary images of the polyline and polygon type.

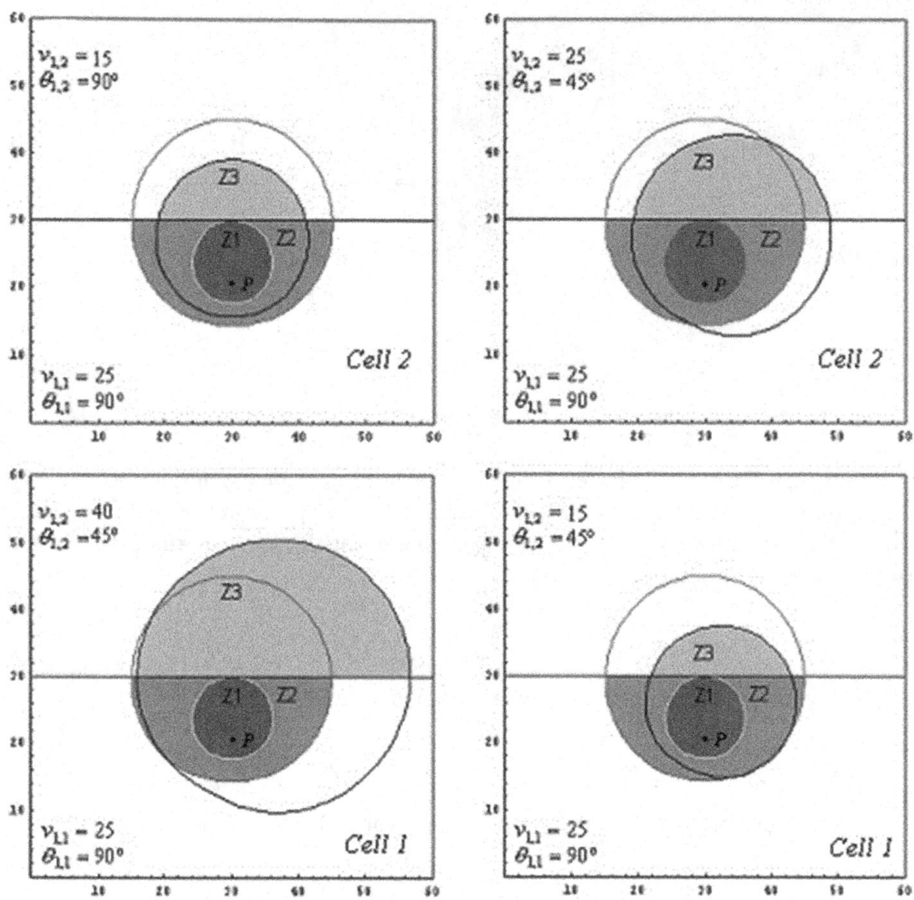

Fig. 8. Examples of expansion of different cells based on changes in the speed and direction of forces

When the expansion starts with different forces that change over time, to solve it, we first perform the segmentation described above and then we act in the same way we did when the expansion started with a single force but applied to the new set of points.

6 Conclusions

In this paper we have addressed the problem of the simulation and visualization of anisotropic phenomena expansions, by proposing a method for the design of generating ovals in which the surface is distributed in a Normal way around its dominant direction. A study of the state of the art of anisotropy and a review of how different commercial GIS deal with the directional treatment of a process, have been made, concluding that the directional aspect of a phenomenon is not implemented in commercial GIS. We propose the creation of a generator oval that allows to delimit zones of influence that have anisotropic characteristics.

References

1. Bailey, T.C., Gatrell, A.C.: A Review of: Interactive Spatial Data Analysis. Longman, Harlow (2007)
2. Black, M., Ebener, S., Najera, P., Viaurre, M., El Morjani, Z.: Using GIS to measure physical accessibility to health care. In: Proceedings of the International Health Users Conference (2004)
3. Boost, B.: Boost C++ Libraries (2015). http://www.boost.org. Accessed 17 Feb 2017
4. Casciola, G., Montefuscoa, L.B., Morigi, S.: The regularizing properties of anisotropic radial basis functions. Appl. Math. Comput. **190**(2), 1050–1062 (2007)
5. Chou, Y.H.: Exploring Spatial Analysis in GIS. Onward Press, Santa Fe (1997)
6. Cressie N.: Statistics for Spatial Data. Wiley, New York (1993)
7. Esri. The Gis software leader (2015). http://www.esri.com. Accessed 17 Feb 2017
8. Getis A. Homogeneity and Proximal Databases in Spatial Analysis and GIS. Taylor & Francis, London (1994)
9. Grass GIS (2015). https://grass.osgeo.org/documentation/manuals/. Accessed 17 Feb 2017
10. Mardia, K., Jupp, P.: Directional Statistics. Wiley, New York (1999)
11. Martinez, J.: Introducción a la lógica virtual (2008) (Spanish). https://composicionarqdatos.files.wordpress.com/2008/09/introduccion-a-la-logica-visual_juan-martinez-val.pdf. Accessed 17 Feb 2017
12. Mata, A., Muñoz, M.D., Corchado, E., Corchado, J.M.: Isotropic Image Analysis for improving CBR forecasting. J. Math. Imaging Vis. **42**, 212–224 (2012)
13. Molina, A., Feito, F.R.: A method for testing anisotropy and quantifying its direction in digital images. Comput. Graph. **26**, 771–784 (2002)
14. Molina, A., Muñoz, M.D.: Simulation and visualization of anisotropic expansion phenomena. In: 5th Agile Conference on Geographical Information Science (2002)
15. Muñoz, M.D., Mata, A., Corchado, E., Corchado, J.M.: (OBIS) isotropic image analysis for improving a predicting agent based systems. Expert Syst. Appl. **40**, 5011–5020 (2013)
16. Ronald, J.: Idrisi Kilimanjaro Guía para SIG y Procesamiento de Imágenes. Clack Labs, Córdoba (2003)

Visual Clustering Approach for Docking Results from Vina and AutoDock

Génesis Varela-Salinas[1], Carlos Armando García-Pérez[2(✉)], Rafael Peláez[3], and Adolfo J. Rodríguez[1]

[1] Unidad Académica Multidisciplinaria Reynosa-Rodhe, Universidad Autónoma de Tamaulipas (UAT), Ciudad Victoria, México
genesisvyvyvs@gmail.com

[2] Centro de Biotecnología Genómica, Instituto Politécnico Nacional, Mexico City, México
carlosgarcia@usal.es

[3] Química Farmacéutica, Universidad de Salamanca, Salamanca, Spain

Abstract. AutoDock Tools allows the analysis of docking files and is used to represent clustering conformations, yet it analyses only one docking file at a time and the method applied to represent the clustering complicates the visualization of clustering conformations. The creation of a plugin called PyDRA for the molecular visualizer PyMOL resolves that problem and allows to simultaneously process more than one docking file for the two types of file format from AutoDock 4.2 and Vina 1.1 (dlg and pdbqt). Moreover, this plugin facilitates the visualization of conformations through two clustering methods. The first method is a K-RMSD algorithm, which is based on the clustering through RMSD and enables the interactive visualization groups through a treemap. And the other one is based on a hierarchical clustering algorithm, using an algorithm of average distances which generates a dendrogram that offers the possibility to explore sequentially the groups that illustrate best the docking. The results obtained with the visualization methods implemented showed that the treemap, due to the implemented colour bar, facilitates to identify the clusters that have a greater affinity to the protein at a glance, and to determine which of the clusters hold a greater number of elements, on the other hand, the dendrogram shows a detailed analyses of the hierarchical clustering, which also enables the user to distinguish the clustering regardless the size of the window, as well as to differentiate each cluster and conformation in order to gain insight of docking results of Autdock and Vina. The fact that both visualizations are connected to PyMOL increases its ability of discernment.

Keywords: PyMOL · Molecular docking · K-RMSD · Hierarchical clustering · Python

1 Introduction

Molecular docking is a computational technique frequently used by scientists and investigators from different areas to predict molecular interactions, for example, the development of drugs [1]. If the geometry of two molecules is complementary and

F.J. Martínez de Pisón et al. (Eds.): HAIS 2017, LNAI 10334, pp. 342–353, 2017.
DOI: 10.1007/978-3-319-59650-1_29

involves favourable biochemical interactions, these molecules potentially can be connected in vitro or in vivo [2]. Nevertheless, this method may result in a false positive or a false negative. That is why it is preferable to conduct a simulation first which helps us to predict the affinity of one molecule to the other. At present, there are different type of programs to perform docking simulations, from which the most used ones are AutoDock [3], AutoDock Vina [4], GOLD [5], FlexX [6], Fred [7], DOCK [8], and ICM [9]. The most popular ones are AutoDock and AutoDock Vina.

Through a genetic algorithm, AutoDock determines a series of conformations which allow it to conduct calculations of free binding energy. Then, these conformations are clustered using a RMSD function. At this point, a molecular visualizer is necessary to monitor the obtained results. AutoDock has its own visualizer called AutoDock Tools [10] which employs a bar graph in order to analyse the formed cluster. This type of graph is limited to analyse groups with similar scores as they appear all together and therefor are difficult to analyse. A possible alternative is PyMOL, which allows developers to create plugins to improve and extend the capacity of the visualizer [11]. To exploit this possibility of PyMOL, a plugin called PyDRA (Python Docking Results Analyser) was developed to process result files from AutoDock and Vina (dlg or pdbqt). This tool performs two types of clustering, one uses a K-RMSD function (K-Root mean square deviation) [12], the other is a hierarchical clustering through an agglomerative algorithm (AGNES agglomerative nesting) [13]. PyDRA is available at: http://visualanalytics.land/cgarcia/pydra.html

The rest of this work is organized as follows. In Sect. 2, we explain the K-RMSD and the hierarchical clustering algorithms, furthermore, the visualization methods used to display the obtained clusters. Afterwards, Sect. 3 describes the results of the plugin for the clustering algorithms and the visual analytical techniques used. Finally, Sect. 4 presents the conclusions of this work.

2 Materials and Methods

PyDRA was developed with Python which is a language based on classes, which facilitates object-oriented programming [14]. Moreover, it possesses different packages like Numpy, which simplifies the usage and declaration of arrays, lists, and matrices [15]. Besides, the graphic packages Tkinter and Matplotlib [16] have been applied for the graphic interface of the plugin and for the visualization of the clustering results through displays.

2.1 Graphical User Interface

In this section, we present a detailed description of the three processes that PyDRA performs. The first one consists of a matrix construction which handles file parsing from Autodock, the second one involves the clustering methods, and the third one is regarding to the visual analyses of the clustering results.

The three parts are as follows:

1. Coordinate matrix construction. The plugin is able to process files with results from AutoDock (dlg) and Vina (pdbqt). The conformations of every file are transformed into coordinate matrices.
2. Clustering method selection. For each transformed file one clustering method is applied, which can be the K-RMSD, based on the distance of the square root, or the hierarchical method, which applies an agglomerative algorithm based on average distance.
3. Clustering visualizations. Each clustering method employs a different visualization to represent its results. The hierarchical method uses a dendrogram which shows different clusters within each level. The K-RMSD method redefines the visualization of the treemap in which each square represents one cluster. Both visualizations are connected to PyMOL to facilitate the analysis of the clusters that were created by both methods.

2.2 Information Extraction

Since PyDRA is able to process docking results from AutoDock and Vina (dlg or pdbqt), to perform the clustering methods it is necessary to mine specific data from both types of files.

Dlg files

The name of the file will be used as label in the visualization in order to know the name of the file that is analysed. Each file contains a predefined number of conformations and they can vary from 10 to 100. Moreover, AutoDock labels the binding energy as Estimated Free Energy of Binding from each conformation, therefore its value is mined. Finally, the Cartesian coordinates X, Y, and Z are extracted from each conformation and labelled as ATOM. This data is used to create a matrix with each conformation that is processed by the algorithms.

Pdbqt files

As well as with the dlg files, the name of the file will be used as label in the visualization. Each file contains nine conformations by default. Vina labels the binding energy as REMARK VINA RESULT, therefore its value is extracted. Finally, the Cartesian coordinates X, Y, and Z are extracted from each conformation, and, in contrast to AutoDock files, with Vina they can be defined with the label ATOM or HETATM. This data is used to create a matrix with each conformation that is processed by the algorithms.

2.3 Clustering Algorithms

The first step for both algorithms consists of extracting the coordinates of the conformations and treat them as vectors:

```
vector of vectors conformations_data
var counter := 0;
var x, y, z;
for model in line:
if model starts_with("DOCKED")
if "MODEL" in model:
    counter := 1
    var model_number := model split(:)[1]
    array atoms := []
   else if "Estimated Free Energy of Binding" in model:
    var free_binding_energy = model[16:62]
  else if "ATOM" in model:
    if counter == 1:
      x := model[39:46]
      y := model[47:55]
      z := model[55:62]
        atoms.append(x,y,z)
  else if "BEGIN_RES" in model:
    if counter == 1:
      conformations_data.append(model_number, free_binding_en-
ergy, atoms)
      counter := 0
  else if "ENDMDL" in model:
    if counter == 1:
      conformations_data.append(model_number, free_binding_en-
ergy, atoms)
      counter := 0
end for
```

K-RMSD

The K-RMSD algorithm [12] is based on the calculations of distances (differences) that exist between different elements of a data set. The RMSD is the most commonly used quantitative measure of similarity between two superimposed atomic coordinates. The RMSD calculation is performed through function (1).

$$\mathrm{RMSD}(A,B) = \sqrt{\frac{1}{n}\sum_{i=1}^{n}(A_{ix}-B_{ix})^2+\left(A_{iy}-B_{iy}\right)^2+(A_{iz}-B_{iz})^2} \quad (1)$$

Where A and B represent two conformations of the same type, n is the total number of atoms in the structure, and (x, y, z) represent the coordinates in space of each atom.

The steps of the algorithm are as follows:

1. Arrange from greater to lesser binding affinity (free_binding_energy) of the conformations to the active site according to the result from the Docking programme.
2. K-RMSD grouping:

```
array treemap := []
var threshold := 2.0
begin while conformations_data > 0:
  array grup := []
  conformation1 := conformations_data[0]
  for conformation2 in conformations_data:
    var rmsd := cal_rmsd(conformation1, conformation2)
    if rmsd <= threshold:
      grup.append(conformation2)
      conformations_data.remove(conformation2)
    treemap.append(grup)
end while

function cal_rmsd (array conformation1, array conformation2):
  sum := 0
  begin for conf1,conf2 in (conformation1.getCoords(),confor-
mation2.getCoords()):
    sum+= ((conf1.getX()-conf2.getX())**2.0) + ((conf1.getY()-
conf2.getY())**2.0) + ((conf1.getZ()-conf2.getZ())**2.0)
  end for
  var rmsd = sqrt(sum/conf1.getCoords.lenght())
      return rmsd
end function
```

AGNES

In contrast to partitional algorithms, like K-RMSD, the hierarchical algorithms do not have predefined clusters, but they are built according to a function distance that indicates the degree of similarity between the elements of a data set. To obtain similarity among the molecules, it is necessary to measure the distance between the positions of their atoms [17]. For this plugin the Euclidian (2) distance and the average distance [18] were used to bind among clusters. In order to calculate the average distance of all elements of both clusters we used function (3).

$$\sqrt{\sum_{i=1}^{n} (P_i - Q_i)^2} \quad (2)$$

$$(R, Q) = \frac{1}{|R||Q|} \sum_{\substack{i \in R \\ i \in Q}} d(i,j) \quad (3)$$

The algorithm to perform the hierarchical clustering is as follows:

1. Apply the Euclidian distance (2) to each vector and create a similarity matrix,

```
matrix similarity_matrix := []
var conf_length := conformations_data.lenght()
begin for i in (0, conf_length):
  for j in (i, conf_length):
    var euclidean_distance:= Euclidean_distance (confor-
mations_data[i], conformations_data[j])
    similarity_matrix[i][j] = euclidean_distance
  end for
end for

begin function Euclidean_distance (array conformations_data[i],
array conformations_data[j]):
sum := 0
begin for conf1,conf2 in (conformation1.getCoords(),confor-
mation2.getCoords()):
  sum+= ((conf1.getX()-conf2.getX())**2.0) + ((conf1.getY()-
conf2.getY())**2.0) + ((conf1.getZ()-conf2.getZ())**2.0)
end for

  distance := sqrt(sum/conf1.getCoords.lenght())
  return distance
end function
```

2. Bind the two elements that have the shortest distance in the similarity matrix (similarity_matrix),
3. Calculate the new similarity matrix with the function (3) of distance. Then, bind both elements/clusters of short distance, until all elements/clusters are grouped:

```
matrix reduced_matrix:= []
begin for i in reduced_matrix[0].lenght:
  for j in reduced_matrix[0][0].lenght:
    reduced_matrix[i][j]:= similarity_matrix[i][j]
  end for
end for

begin while reduced_matrix[0].lenght > 2 :
  reduced_matrix:= join_clusters(similarity_matrix, reduced_ma-
trix)
end while

begin function join_clusters (similarity_matrix, reduced_ma-
trix):
  var conformation1:= 0
  var conformation2:= 0
  begin for i in reduced_matrix[0].length
    for j in reduced_matrix[i][0].length
      var distance:= reduced_matrix[i][j];
      if reduced_matrix [i][j] < small:
        conformation1 = i
        conformation2 = j
    end for
  end for
  new_reduced_matrix:= [len(reduced_matrix), len(reduced_ma-
trix)]
```

```
   begin for i in new_reduced_matrix[0].length
      for j in new_reduced_matrix[i][0].lenght
         if i == conformation2
            new_reduced_matrix [i][j]:= Upgma_distance(similar-
ity_matrix, conformation2, i)
         if j == conformation1
            new_reduced_matrix [i][j]:= Upgma_distance(similar-
ity_matrix, conformation1, j)
         else
            new_reduced_matrix [i][j]:= Upgma_distance(similar-
ity_matrix, i, j)
   end for
end for

return new_reduced_matrix

end function

function distanciaUpgma(matrix similarity_matrix, var i, var j):
   var sum:= 0
   var result:= 0
   sum := similarity_matrix[i] + similarity_matrix[j])
         result = (sum/(similarity_matrix.length[i] * similar-
ity_matrix.length[j]))
   return result
end function
```

2.4 Visualization

Two types of visualizations were designed to analyse the clusters. On the one hand, the concept of treemap visualization [19, 20] was employed to visualise the obtained clusters from the K-RMSD method, on the other hand, a dendrogram was used to visualise the hierarchical clustering.

Treemap

The treemap is used to represent hierarchical information [19], nevertheless, during this work it was used as a partitional visualization because a treemap would allow an organized representation of the clusters found by the K-RMSD algorithm.

The package squarify [21] served to create the treemap visualization, which makes it possible to determine the exact size of each square and position in space. The size depends on the number of elements that each cluster contains, and based on that, it is positioned at the corresponding place. Apart from the clustering, the following aspects have been taken into consideration for the visualization:

1. The colour bar helps the user to identify the binding range of values from greater to less affinity. Besides, each square is assigned a colour according to the clusters that contain conformations with the best binding value to the protein.
2. The interaction between PyMOL and the visualization is conducted through the selection of squares in the treemap. For example, when selecting a square, its cluster conformations appear in the PyMOL visualizer.

Dendrogram
Applying the dendrogram, it is possible to visualize all elements at the same time and to analyse how they have been clustered hierarchically based on the calculation of distance between them. Moreover, due to the tool the user can select all elements, a cluster, or only one element through the selection of a vertical line from the dendrogram. The PyMOL visualizer is linked directly to the dendrogram, that means, by selecting a line, the conformations that belong to that cluster are shown. In addition, for visual support, a horizontal bar was implemented to help to identify and to separate the levels of the dendrogram.

3 Results and Discussion

For demonstration purposes, the plugin was applied to a set of derivative compounds of a docking process. The set contained a total number of 40 results, dlg and pdbqt files. Twenty dlg files with 100 conformations per compound and 20 pdbqt files with approximately nine to ten conformations per compound.

PyDRA was loaded with 20 dlg files and hierarchical clustering was used for the analysis since it is easier for the user to visualize how the conformations have been clustered. The same files were analysed with AutoDock Tools to do a comparison between the results from both tools (Figs. 1 and 2).

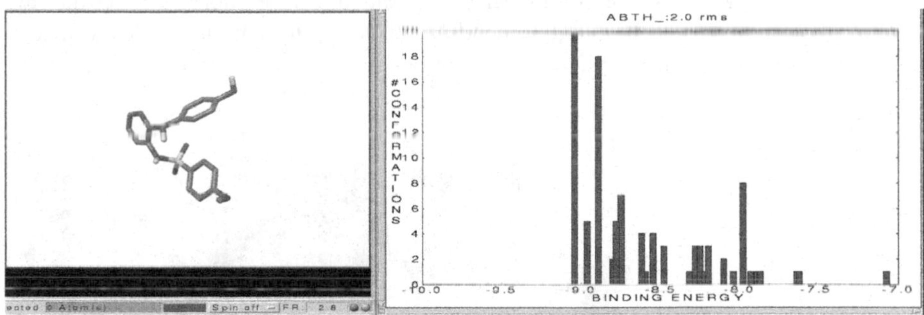

Fig. 1. Visualization by AutoDock Tools to analyse docking results. The bars represent groups of conformations. The accumulation of bars complicates the analysis.

One of the differences that can be observed is shown in Fig. 1, where the clustering is visualized in a bar graph, in which each bar represents a group, and in Fig. 2, where the dendrogram that employs the plugin is visualized, showing each conformation at the bottom. Figure 1 is an example of an inefficient representation of clustering due to the superposition of the majority of bars. Besides, the visualization of the dendrogram enables the user to distinguish the clustering regardless the size of the window. Figure 2 shows a detailed analysis of the hierarchical clustering, allowing the user to distinguish each cluster and conformation in order to gain insight of docking results of Autdock and Vina.

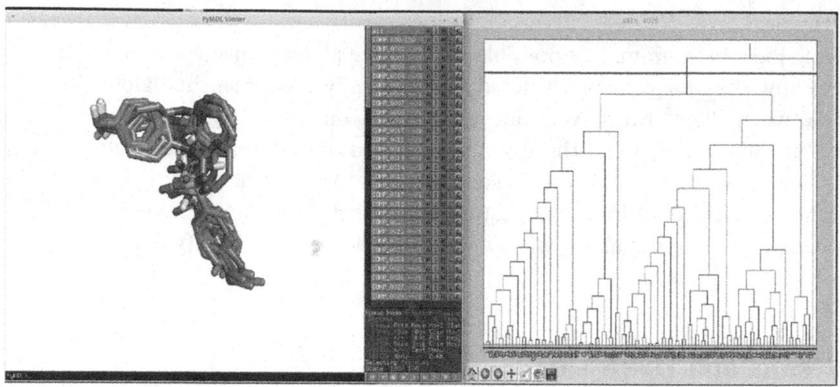

Fig. 2. Visualization of results from AutoDock, clustered hierarchically using the AGNES method, and represented with a dendrogram. (Color figure online)

Figure 3 shows a treemap with the obtained clusters after the clustering of results from Vina through the K-RMSD method. Each square of the treemap represents a cluster of conformations whose distance is the same or less to the one established by the user (2.0 Å in this case). Also, the bottom part of the treemap shows a colour bar from greater to less affinity (blue to red). Also, Fig. 3 shows that using a treemap as a visualization method for the K-RMSD clustering, helps to easily recognize the groups with greater affinity due to the colour bar implemented. Furthermore, the fact that the treemap gives a size to each square depending on the group length enables to distinguish the groups with more or less conformations.

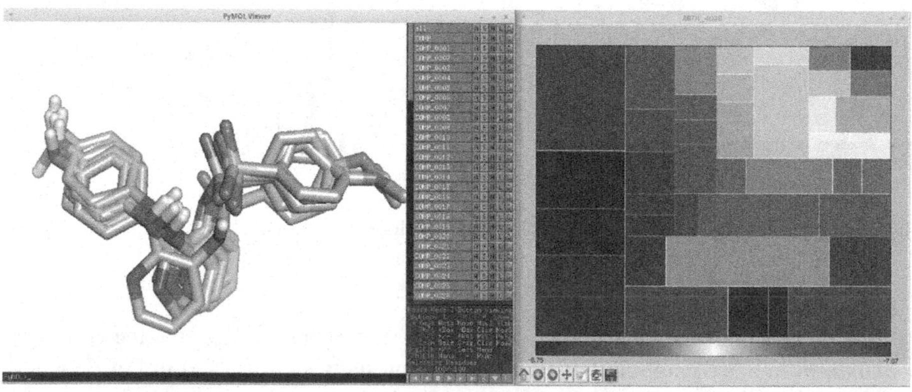

Fig. 3. Visualization of the clustering in a treemap obtained through the K-RMSD method which uses the plugin, showing the clusters of conformations in the PyMOL visualizer. (Color figure online)

In Fig. 4 the method from AutoDock Tools is applied for the results from Vina in pdbqt format. This tool shows all the conformations it has employed without any

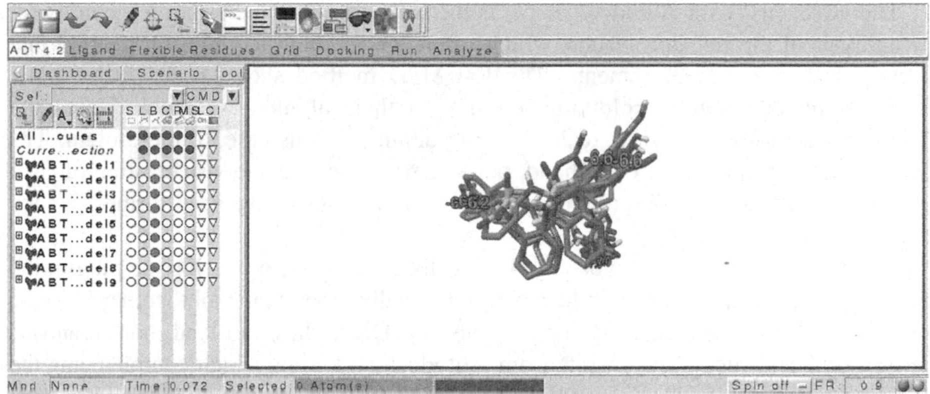

Fig. 4. Results of Vina shown in the visualizer from AutoDock Tools.

clustering, which is why the user should select one conformation and compare it one by one with all of the others to analyse the conformations that might be similar, and create the clusters manually. This would be time-consuming when there are a lot of results to analyse.

As mentioned before, the visualization methods of the plugin, treemap for the K-RMSD method (see Fig. 3) and dendrogram for the hierarchical clustering (see Fig. 2), vary in number and group size. The treemap allows to identify the clusters that have a greater affinity to the protein at a glance, due to the colour bar. Moreover, it allows to determine which of the clusters hold a greater number of elements. Nevertheless, one disadvantage of the treemap is the difficulty to identify the number of conformations inside the cluster, consequently, it is necessary to select and visualize it with PyMOL. Furthermore, this disadvantage disappears applying the dendrogram visualization, as can be seen in Fig. 2. This visualization determines easily which conformations bind to form each cluster, as well as it allows to analyse a small group of two or even one element, or even a big group in detail. To sum up, the treemap can be applied for the analysis of clusters considering their affinity to the protein, since each cluster is identified with a colour depending on its affinity (blue showing a greater and red less affinity). But to identify how many conformations are similar, it is preferable to use the dendrogram.

4 Conclusion and Future Work

This work established that the visualization method used by AutoDock Tools to analyse results employing the RMSD clustering is not the most viable option. This method raises difficulties distinguishing the clusters, since they superpose each other. Therefore, due to PyDRA, applying a treemap for the visualization of the clustering through K-RMSD allows the analysis without that disadvantage. Moreover, PyDRA offers an alternative using a dendrogram to represent the hierarchical method, which allows an uncomplicated differentiation of the formed clusters and their elements inside.

The advantage over Autodock Tools is the inclusion of two clustering methods for the analysis of the docking results, which offers the freedom to choose a method that meets the necessary requirements. The K-RMSD method shows each cluster separately, being labelled by colour depending on their affinity, which simplifies the identification of clusters with greater binding affinity, in this case, to the protein. The hierarchical method, on the other hand, benefits from the separate visualization of each element and the detailed observation of the way the clusters have been formed at each level.

One of the main reasons to use PyMOL is the possibility to develop the plugin, the manipulation, and the interaction between the visualization, which all together increase and extend the analysis capacity. For example, PyDRA allows to load more than one file at a time and recognises results from Autodock and Vina, which complements the manipulation and visualization of the molecular structure through PyMOL in a comprehensive and simple way.

The future work, we aim to improve the visualization methods allowing to perform a comparison between the clusters. Furthermore, the potential of PyDRA can be improved by letting to analyse the docking results thru the algorithms K-RMSD and Hierarchical simultaneously.

References

1. Li, H., Leung, K.-S., Wong, M.-H., Ballester, P.J.: Improving autodock vina using random forest: the growing accuracy of binding affinity prediction by the effective exploitation of larger data sets. Mol. Inform. **34**, 115–126 (2015)
2. Shi, J., Tu, W., Luo, M., Huang, C.: Molecular docking and molecular dynamics simulation approaches for identifying new lead compounds as potential AChE inhibitors. Mol. Simul. **43**, 102–109 (2017)
3. Morris, G.M., Huey, R., Lindstrom, W., Sanner, M.F., Bele, R.K., Goodsell, D., Olson, A.J.: AutoDock version 4.2. J. Comput. Chem. **30**, 2785–2791 (2009)
4. Trott, O., Olson, A.J.: AutoDock Vina: improving the speed and accuracy of docking with a new scoring function, efficient optimization, and multithreading. J. Comput. Chem. **31**, 455–461 (2009)
5. Verdonk, M.L., Cole, J.C., Hartshorn, M.J., Murray, C.W., Taylor, R.D.: Improved protein-ligand docking using GOLD. Proteins: Struct. Funct. Bioinf. **52**, 609–623 (2003)
6. Kramer, B., Rarey, M., Lengauer, T.: Evaluation of the FLEXX incremental construction algorithm for protein-ligand docking. Proteins Struct. Funct. Genet. **37**, 228–241 (1999)
7. McGann, M.: FRED pose prediction and virtual screening accuracy. J. Chem. Inf. Model. **51**, 578–596 (2011)
8. Ewing, T.J.A., Makino, S., Skillman, A.G., Kuntz, I.D.: DOCK 4.0: search strategies for automated molecular docking of flexible molecule databases. J. Comput. Aided Mol. Des. **15**, 411–428 (2001)
9. Azam, S., Abbasi, S.: Molecular docking studies for the identification of novel melatoninergic inhibitors for acetylserotonin-O-methyltransferase using different docking routines. Theor. Biol. Med. (2013)

10. Morris, G.M., Huey, R., Lindstrom, W., Sanner, M.F., Belew, R.K., Goodsell, D.S., Olson, A.J.: AutoDock4 and AutoDockTools4: automated docking with selective receptor flexibility. J. Comput. Chem. **30**, 2785–2791 (2009)
11. Schrödinger, LLC: The PyMOL Molecular Graphics System, Version ~ 1.8 (2015)
12. García-Pérez, C., Peláez, R., Therón, R., López-Pérez, J.L.: JADOPPT: Java based AutoDock Preparing and Processing Tool. Bioinformatics **14**, btw677 (2016)
13. Seifert, B., Ritz, M., Csősz, S.: Application of exploratory data analyses opens a new perspective in morphology-based alpha-taxonomy of eusocial organisms. Myrmecological News (2014)
14. Bogdanchikov, A., Zhaparov, M., Suliyev, R.: Python to learn programming. J. Phys. Conf. Ser. **423**, 12027 (2013)
15. Milano, F.: A python-based software tool for power system analysis. In: 2013 IEEE Power & Energy Society General Meeting, pp. 1–5. IEEE (2013)
16. Singh, M.K., Gautam, R., Gatebe, C.K., Poudyal, R.: PolarBRDF: a general purpose Python package for visualization and quantitative analysis of multi-angular remote sensing measurements. Comput. Geosci. **96**, 173–180 (2016)
17. Tan, P., Steinbach, M., Kumar, V.: Data mining cluster analysis: basic concepts and algorithms. In: Introduction to Data Mining (2013)
18. Dega, R.K.Y., Ercal, G.: A comparative analysis of progressive multiple sequence alignment approaches using UPGMA and neighbor joining based guide trees. Int. J. Comput. Sci. Eng. Inf. Technol. **5** (2015)
19. Mahipal, J., Sha, K.: Tree-map: a visualization tool for large data. In: Graph Search and Beyond, p. 39 (2015)
20. Johnson, B., Shneiderman, B.: Tree maps: a space-filling approach to the visualization of hierarchical information structures. In: Proceeding Visualization 1991, pp. 284–291. IEEE Comput. Soc. Press (1991)
21. Learson, U.: Squarify. https://pypi.python.org/pypi/squarify

Establishing a Cooperation Between RadViz and SOM to Improve the Analyst Visual Experience

Rosa Matias(✉)

ESTG - Polytechnic Institute of Leiria, Leiria, Portugal
rosa.matias@ipleiria.pt

Abstract. Radial Visualization (RadViz) is an information visualization technique for visual data exploration and data analysis. RadViz transforms multidimensional data into two dimensional features. A circle is drawn and, then, respectively, dimensions and instances become axes and points. It aims to enable human identification of similarities among instances stored in datasets. RadViz has a dimension arrangement problem since different radial axes disposal produce different point arrangements misleading, the expert user, about the most appropriate for interpretation. In this work, the results produced by an automated method (*Self Organizing Maps* (SOM)) and a visual metaphor (RadViz) are committed into a strict cooperation through a middle layer. The middle layer main objective is to identify an appropriate dimension arrangement. We propose that the dimension arrangement should be computed at the multidimensional space by analyzing reference vectors produced by SOM. The reference vectors are analyzed so that similar dimensions become neighbors. Later the achieved dimension arrangement is communicated to RadViz for rendering proposes and used to render the instances. Expert users can analyze all neurons, a combination of neurons or isolated neurons. The dimension arrangement represents a relational and universal order established for dimensions. In summary, the system inspects and proposes axes arrangement on-the-fly as users adds and removes neurons and dimensions.

Keywords: Visual Analytics · Radial Visualization · Self Organizing Maps

1 Introduction

The human visual system has amazing visual interpretation capabilities when presented with appropriate visual artifacts. A messy and clutter image is like an abstract painting made by an artist, hard to comprehend and liable to interpret. In organizations is common sense that crowding of data overlaps exponentially the analysis capacity and as a consequence precious knowledge is hidden. It is also a widespread idea that knowing interesting and peculiar facts at high levels of abstractions is a competitive advantage in a global and competitive world. A dataset stores raw data and its structure has either instances and dimensions. To analyze a dataset expert users can apply automated methods, visual methods or a pipeline with both. The gap between automated and visual methods is enormous but complementary. Automated methods take

F.J. Martínez de Pisón et al. (Eds.): HAIS 2017, LNAI 10334, pp. 354–366, 2017.
DOI: 10.1007/978-3-319-59650-1_30

profit of today's computational capabilities and are essential because datasets seems like data pumps. They are black boxes since what happens between the input and the output is unknown. Visual methods allow ad-hoc data exploration and increases the ability to submit and confirm user's hypotheses taking profit of humans cognition, perception and background knowledge. They are white boxes since allow ah-doc data exploration. However the exploratory flexibility turns it hard to infer easily the most deeply hidden patterns.

Visual Analytics is the science of analytical reasoning supported by interactive visual interfaces [1–3]. It is a science to the cooperation between automated and visual methods. It allows decision makers to combine their flexibility, creativity, and background knowledge with the enormous storage and processing capabilities of today's computers to gain insight into complex problems [3]. By combining those complementary resources (computational capabilities, visual capabilities and users cognition) the probability of Eureka moments is higher. *Bertini and Lalanne* [4] made a study analyzing research work related to the integration between automated and visual methods and identified four major integration categories [4], which are (i) Visualization (**VIS**), systems where only visual methods are applied; (ii) Computationally Enhanced Visualization (**V++**), systems where both visual and automated methods are applied but the visual method has a high importance and automated methods are employed to help the visual method work better; (iii) Mining Enhanced Methods (**M++**), systems where both visual and automated methods are employed but the automated method has a higher importance and visual methods are employed to explore results; and (iv) Integrated Visualization and Mining (**VM**), systems where both visual and automated methods are integrated but it is not possible to identify the most important one, the most fundamental to illuminate the users minds.

This work takes into consideration the definitions made by *Bertini and Lalanne* [4] and is an example of an Integrated Visualization and Mining system where both methods categories are equally important. Basically it is M++ and V++ system because the models identified by an automated method are explored by a visual method enabling the identification of patterns (M++), and, results produced by the automated method are processed to help the visual method display results in an accurate way (V++). This work assumes that the combination between automated and visual methods depends on their natures. For each pairs (automated, visual) particular mechanisms of cooperation have to be identified to take profit of both. This can include the development of particular mechanisms and algorithms. Of course the problem nature might also influence the combination. As a prove of concepts this work combines RadViz (visual method) and SOM (automated method). A middle layer is garnished with enough intelligence so that SOM results can be analyzed to identify the best way to display results in RadViz.

Next RadViz and its native limitations are presented. Then the architecture of the cooperation mechanism followed by the involved algorithms. Lastly some results are presented and conclusions taken.

2 The Visual Method: RadViz

RadViz is a geometric visualization technique that translates datasets to a visual representation for human readability and interpretation [5]. RadViz is based on Hooke's law. A circle is drawn and dimensions and instances of datasets became axes and points (respectively). In the circle and attached to the end of axes there are springs applying strengths proportional to values in corresponding dimensions. The translation converts instance belonging to the dataset into equilibrium points in a circle through Eq. (1). A_i represents the dimension i and α represents the separation angle between axes which are equally separated. Considering n dimensions, α is computed as follow: $\alpha = 360°/n$.

$$F_{(x,y)} = \begin{cases} \mathrm{x} = \sum_{i=0}^{n} A_i \times \cos(i \times \alpha) \\ \mathrm{y} = \sum_{i=0}^{n} A_i \times \sin(i \times \alpha) \end{cases} \tag{1}$$

Figure 1 show an equilibrium point rendered from a four dimensional instance (A1, A2, A3, A4) with the values [0.85, 0.25, 0.25, 0.85]. The equilibrium point is drawn in fourth quadrant since dimensions A1 and A4 carry out high values than A2 and A3. RadViz is a simple geometric technique to analyze and identify relationships among multidimensional datasets [6]. An interesting characteristic of RadViz is that axes whose spring apply higher forces pushes near points and it places data items with similar values close together so that data aggregations can be discovered [7]. No meanwhile its native implementation has some disadvantage [6, 7], namely:

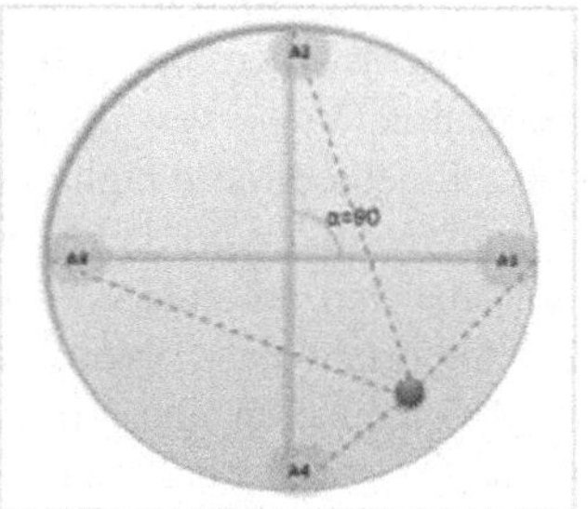

Fig. 1. An equilibrium point

1. **Overlap Problem**. It may occur that two very different instances may be drawn close to each other due to mathematical coincidence not because they are similar. Accurate ways of translations between spaces are needed as well as mechanism to distinct those instances. If a clustering algorithm was previously applied then, certainly, those instances will belong to different clusters and can be distinguished through symbols, colors or other thematic elements. Then filter mechanisms can help removing and adding clusters and instances from analysis;
2. **Visual Clutter Problem**. RadViz may render images hard to interpret and with clutter when datasets have too many instances. As in the overlap problem, clustering, filter and themes can help reduce the problem;
3. **Dimensional Arrangement Problem**. The combination of axes disposal create a multitude of axes arrangements that can create multiple images confusing users about the best for interpretation. The dimensional arrangement problem was formalized by *Ankest et al.* [8] and can be resolved by maximizing similarity between dimensions located near to each other. However, the dimension similarity identification is considered a problem with complexity $O(n^2)$ [6, 8]. The dimension

arrangement problem is common to other geometric information visualization techniques like Parallel Coordinate Plot [9].

2.1 The Dimension Arrangement Problem

In this section, the dimension arrangement problem is explained using a simple example. An synthetic multidimensional dataset with four dimensions $\{A_1, A_2, A_3, A_4\}$ and ten objects (instances) was created to contextualize the reader (Table 1).

Table 1. The synthetic multidimensional dataset

Object/Dimension	A1	A2	A3	A4
O1	0,82	0,83	0,21	0,24
O2	0,86	0,12	0,81	0,72
O3	0,80	0,76	0,96	0,68
O4	0,30	0,55	0,24	0,95
O5	0,27	0,05	0,03	0,76
O6	0,79	0,46	0,92	0,89
O7	0,99	0,69	0,53	0,65
O8	0,29	0,66	0,50	0,34
O9	0,83	0,46	0,36	0,92
O10	0,48	0,58	0,54	0,94

Applying Eq. (1) to the same object over different axes arrangements give rise to different point (X, Y) locations because through different arrangements the same dimension is assigned to different angles. This aspect can be proved for a few selected arrangements presented in Table 2.

Of course if for each object the point location depends on the dimension arrangement then the visual displays is also different. Figures 2, 3, 4 and 5 present those different displays. In Fig. 5 objects O8 and O9 are very close to each other so they seem similar. However, another arrangement does not confirm those similarities, for instance, in Fig. 2 the same objects O8 and O9 are distant and so seem dissimilar. Without more information the conclusions about similarities cannot be inferred with

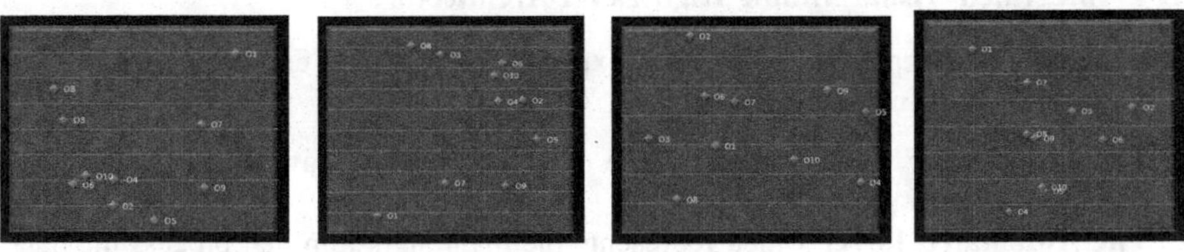

Fig. 2. A1, A2, A3, A4 **Fig. 3.** A4, A3, A2, A1 **Fig. 4.** A4, A1, A3, A2 **Fig. 5.** A3, A1, A2, A4

Table 2. Computing equilibrium points (X, Y) through different arrangements

First Arrangement				Second Arrangement				Third Arrangement				Fourth Arrangement			
A1	A2	A3	A4	A4	A3	A2	A1	A4	A1	A3	A2	A3	A1	A2	A4
0°	90°	180°	270°	0°	90°	180°	270°	0°	90°	180°	270°	0°	90°	180°	270°

	First X	First Y	Second X	Second Y	Third X	Third Y	Fourth X	Fourth Y
O1	0,61	0,59	−0,59	−0,61	0,03	−0,01	−0,62	0,59
O2	0,05	−0,60	0,60	−0,05	−0,09	0,74	0,69	0,14
O3	−0,16	0,07	−0,07	0,16	−0,28	0,04	0,21	0,12
O4	0,06	−0,39	0,39	−0,06	0,71	−0,25	−0,32	−0,65
O5	0,24	−0,71	0,71	−0,24	0,73	0,22	−0,02	−0,49
O6	−0,12	−0,43	0,43	0,12	−0,02	0,33	0,45	−0,10
O7	0,46	0,04	−0,04	−0,46	0,12	0,29	−0,16	0,33
O8	−0,21	0,32	−0,32	0,21	−0,15	−0,37	−0,16	−0,06
O9	0,47	−0,46	0,46	−0,47	0,56	0,37	−0,10	−0,09
O10	−0,06	−0,36	0,36	0,06	0,40	−0,10	−0,04	−0,46

thoroughness. This is a disadvantage of visual methods. Ad-doc exploration does not fit a model leaving some uncertainty that needs meticulous confirmation. In summary, maybe O8 and O9 are similar. Another interesting fact is that arrangements with opposite axes orders give rise to symmetric images (see Figs. 2 and 3).

3 An Integrated Visual and Mining System

This section explains the system architecture, equations and algorithms implemented in the middle layer.

3.1 Integrated Visual Mining High Level Architecture

The system has independent layers that expose interfaces and exchange information and services. In summary the layers are:

- **The Data Layer** which represents the data source where raw data is stored persistently and was previously treated;
- **The Automated Layer** which represents the main algorithm that process the data source and produces results that are stored for further analysis;

- **The Middle Layer** which eliminates the gap between automated and visual methods enhancing their cooperation. The automated and visual methods do not communicate directly but through this intelligent software component. In this system this layer is responsible for the identification of axes arrangements;
- **The Visual Layer** which represents the visual method responsible for rendering data in agreement with suggestions;
- **The User Layer (Interface + User Layer)**, a layer where actions are performed by expert users forcing the system to work and execute the desired actions. Those actions are garnished by cognition and expert users background knowledge. All other layers perform efforts to respond to the triggered actions.

Figure 6 shows the existing system high level architecture with a sequence of actions represented by numbered circles which and are explained next. First data is loaded and analyzed by the algorithm and results stored persistently (circles 1 and 2). An analyst wishes to analyze results and ask for them using the application system interface (circle 3). The visual method receives the requests and sends then to the middle layer asking data as well as information about the better way to display them (circle 4). The middle layer verify if the requests have already been computed verifying their presence in the knowledge base repository (circles 5 and 6). This avoids having to compute them once and again. If requests are in the knowledge base they are sent to the visual method API for rendering proposes (circles 7 and 8). If not the middle layer consults the results produced by the algorithm, infers an optimized display, stores it in knowledge base (circles 5′ and 6′) and finally sends it to display (circles 7 and 8) (Figure 7).

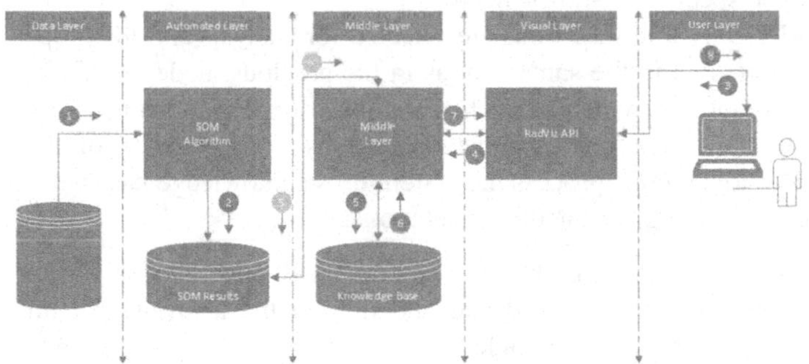

Fig. 6. Integrated visual data mining high level architecture

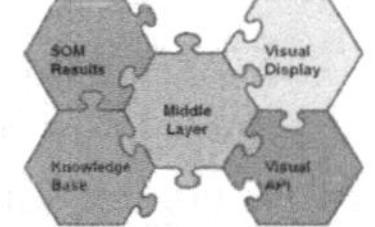

Fig. 7. The missing piece

The middle layer is like the missing piece in a puzzle that connects all other components. It is the missing piece to integrate automated and visual methods. This piece can be substituted at any time or garnished with more functionalities.

3.2 Discovering the Dimension Arrangement

In this section it is explained how the middle layer computes an appropriate dimension arrangement. All the work is supported by the following observation:

Observation 1: IF [8] says that the dimension arrangement problem could be resolved by maximizing similarities between dimensions located near to each other AND [6, 8] say that finding similarities between dimensions is computational expensive because all instances are considered AND [6] says that there are error-prone problems with the translation between multidimensional and two dimensional spaces THEN ***after processing the data using a clustering algorithm an appropriate dimension arrangement should be identified by analyzing only representative entities, for instances, reference vectors associated with neurons. The similarities between dimensions much be maximized so that similar ones became neighbors. Then after the proper dimension arrangement is achieved consider to use it as a guide to draw instances as well in RadViz.***

As users remove and add neurons and dimensions from the analysis new axes arrangements are generated. With this in mind the following execution modes of execution can co-exist:

1. **Isolated neuron mode**. An isolated neuron and respective objects are been analyzed and the proper neuron axes arrangement are extrapolated to guide its instances rendering;
2. **All neurons mode**. All neurons and respective instances are been analyzed and axes arrangement is obtained through their overall combinations. Points are colored in agreement to their respective assigned neurons;
3. **Some neurons mode**. Only a few neurons are selected for analysis and the proper axes arrangement is obtained in the same way as in the previous mode, but taking into consideration only those few neurons. These on-the-fly explorations gives rise to an exponential number of neurons combination, and, as a consequence, of axes arrangements. In order to help this process the system uses a knowledge base where it stores arrangements avoiding repeatedly calculations.

The execution operation modes can be further combined with another factor: dimensions (attributes) can also be removed and added from the analysis. All this possible combinations can be observed in Table 3.

Table 3. Possible neurons/dimensions combination

Neurons/Dimensions	All dimensions	Some dimensions
Isolated neuron	X	X
All neurons	X	X
Some neurons	X	X

Next the mathematical formulation is presented for each mode of execution. Nerveless common issues are presented first.

Common Issues
Considering a Dataset D with $\underline{n}$ dimensions (attributes) and $\underline{m}$ instances (objects). Appling the SOM algorithm to the Dataset D will produce a collection of $\underline{x}$ neurons.

$$SOM : \text{Dataset} \overset{\text{yields}}{\rightarrow} \{N_1, \ldots, N_X\} \tag{2}$$

Collection of x Neurons. A neuron N_i has both a collection $\underline{n}$ attributes and of h instances following property $0 \leq h \geq m$. The collection of attributes is given by

$$Attributes(N_i) = \{A_{i1}, \ldots, A_{in}\} \tag{3}$$

The neuron n attributes and the collection of instances by

$$Instances(N_i) = \{O_{i1}, \ldots, O_{ih}\} \tag{4}$$

The neuron h instances.

One Neuron Mode
This section presents how the proper axes arrangement of an isolated neuron (the neuron e) is obtained. Basically a $1 \times n$ vector is achieved with the strengths carry out by each n attributes. The vector is sorted and the corresponding vector with dimension positions obtained. For each attribute in the weight vector, its strength is computed using Eq. (5) and consists on the division of the dimension contribution by the overall contribution (all dimensions).

$$F(A_{ei}) = \frac{A_{ei}}{\sum_{j=1}^{n} A_{ej}} \tag{5}$$

The sorted vector S is obtained by applying the previous formula to all dimensions in neuron e (see Eq. (6)).

$$S = Sort(F(A_e)) = Sort([F(A_{e1}), \ldots, F(A_{en})]) \tag{6}$$

Using the sorted vector S the corresponding vector X with dimension positions (axes positions) is obtained and communicated to the visual method for rendering proposes.

Algorithm 1. Compute a neuron forces (name: **ANF**)

```
Input:
     The neuron weight vector (V)
     The number of dimensions (n)
Output:
     The strengths vector (F)
sum ← 0
for i=0 to n do
    sum ← sum + V[i]
end for
for i=0 to n do
    F[i] ← V[i]/sum
end for
F ← sort(F)
return F
```

All Neurons Mode

This approach is similar to the previous plus the fact that all neurons ($\underline{x}$ neurons) are considered. In this case the force performed by each of the $\underline{x}$ neurons is given by a $x \times n$ matrix, where $\underline{x}$ is the number of neurons and $\underline{n}$ the number of dimensions. The matrix is presented in Eq. (7).

$$F(N) = \begin{bmatrix} F(A_{11}) & \cdots & F(A_{1n}) \\ \vdots & \ddots & \vdots \\ F(A_{x1}) & \cdots & F(A_{xn}) \end{bmatrix} \tag{7}$$

The overall force made by each attribute is also a vector like the one in the previous section but computed in a distinct way. It is the sum with the contribution in each dimension for all neurons Eq. (8).

$$F(N)(A_i) = \sum\nolimits_{j=0}^{x} A_{ji} \tag{8}$$

Next, is presented a visual perspective of the computation and its associated and final vector.

$$F(N) = \left\{ \frac{\begin{bmatrix} F(A_{11}) & \cdots & F(A_{1n}) \\ \vdots & \ddots & \vdots \\ F(A_{x1}) & \cdots & F(A_{xn}) \end{bmatrix}}{\frac{\left[\sum_{j=0}^{x} A_{i1} \ldots\ldots\ldots \sum_{j=0}^{x} A_{in}\right]}{\left[F(A_1) \ldots\ldots\ldots F(A_n)\right]}} \right. \tag{9}$$

The vector is sorted given rise to $\underline{S}$ and next is necessary to identify the corresponding dimensions. Basically is necessary for each value identify the corresponding dimension position.

$$S = Sort(F) = Sort([F(A_1), \ldots, F(A_n)]) \tag{10}$$

Algorithm 2. Compute neurons forces (name:**NF**)

```
Input:
     The neurons weights matrix (M)
     The number of dimensions (n)
Output:
     The strengths vector(F)
FMatrix
for i=0 to x do
     FMatrix[i] ← ANF(M[i],n) // Algorithm 1.
end for
for i=0 to n do
     sum ← 0
     for j=0 to x do
          sum ← sum + FMatrix[i][j]
     end for
     F[i] ← sum
end for
F ← sort(F)
return F
```

Some Neurons Mode
This modes of operand is similar to the all neurons explained lastly. But the neurons used to compute the strengths are a subset of the overall neurons. Equations are similar however the number of neurons is smaller and in agreement with $0 < n' \leq x$.

4 Integrated Visual Mining eXplorer (iVMX)

In the context of this work an application was developed whose foundations is the architecture in Fig. 6. The application name is Integrated Visual Mining eXplorer (iVMX) and the user interface have a control area, a radial display and a raw data display. For space reasons only some images with results are presented and for the UCI Iris

Table 4. Results iVMX Obtained by Applying SOM

Index	Color	#Instances	Species
0	Brown	24	*(24) Iris-Versicolor*
1	Orange	50	*(50) Iris-Septosa*
2	Rose	40	*(40) Iris-Virginica*
3	Green	35	*(26) Iris-Versicolor* *(9) Iris - Virginica*

dataset. Table 4 presents SOM results applied to the well known UCI Iris Dataset [10]. Four neurons were asked each one was generated with a different identification, color and total number of assigned instances. After analyzing raw data we concluded neuron 0 represents Iris-Verticolor, neuron 1 the Iris-Septosa, neuron 2 the Iris-Virginica and neuron 3 both Iris-Versicolor (26 instances) and Iris-Virginica (9 instances).

Index	Color	CountInstances	Show
0	ffa07c7c	24	☑
1	ffcc842a	50	☑
2	ffd66f6a	40	☑
3	ffa6ea5a	35	☑

Fig. 8. Control component (Color figure online)

In the graphical interface, through checkboxes neurons are added and removed from analysis (Fig. 8). The results of a sequence of add and remove actions are presented from Figs. 9, 10, 11, 12, 13 and 14. Table 5 shows the corresponding system suggested DA for each figure (from the lowest to the highest).

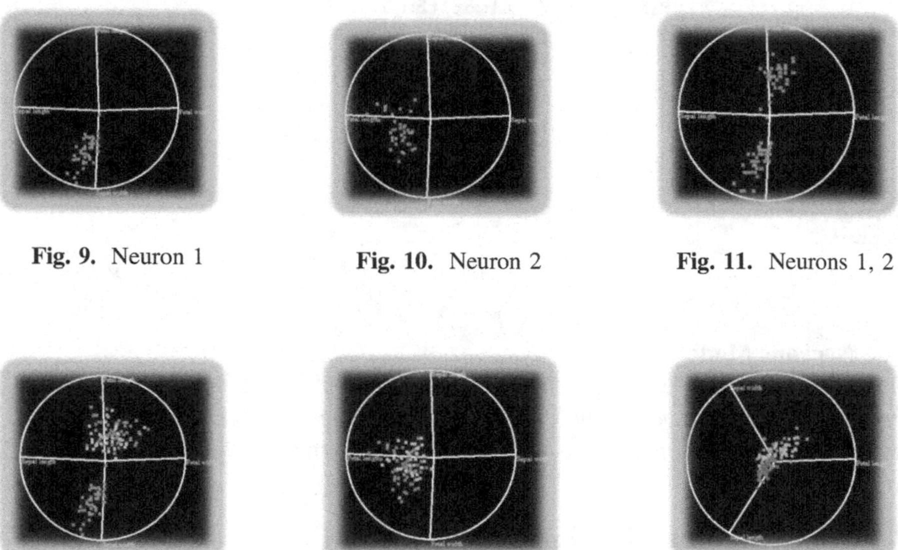

Fig. 9. Neuron 1 **Fig. 10.** Neuron 2 **Fig. 11.** Neurons 1, 2

Fig. 12. All neurons **Fig. 13.** Neurons 0, 2, 3 **Fig. 14.** Remove axis

In Fig. 9 an isolated neuron and respective instances are displayed (actions based on Algorithm 1 were persecuted). An isolated cluster rendering can be profit to discover outliers and analyze the structure without others influence. The system proposes a dimension arrangement with the sequence: [*Pedal Width (PW)*, *Pedal Length (PL)*, *Sepal Length (SL)*, *Sepal Width (SW)*] (for neuron 1). The proposed dimension arrangement can be considered an universal relationship order where SW > SL > PL > PW. Also taking into consideration the work [11], SL > PW and SW $\ggg$ PL since instances where drawn at the bottom of the third quadrant. *Sepal Length* and *Sepal With* are the strongest dimensions (*Iris-Septosa*). Figure 10 another isolated neuron is presented; in this case instances are associated with *Iris-Virginica*.

Table 5. Dimensions universal arrangements for isolated neurons

Fig. 9	Pedal Width	Pedal Length	Sepal Length	Sepal Width
	-			+
Fig. 10	Sepal Width	Sepal Length	Pedal Length	Pedal Width
	-			+
Fig. 11	Pedal Length	Pedal Width	Sepal Length	Sepal Width
	-			+
Fig. 12	Pedal Width	Pedal Length	Sepal Length	Sepal Width
	-			+
Fig. 13	Sepal Width	Sepal Length	Pedal Length	Pedal Width
	-			+
Fig. 14		Pedal Length	Pedal Width	Sepal Length
	-			+

The universal order or the identified proper dimension arrangement is [*Sepal Width, Sepal Length, Pedal Length, Pedal Width*], where SW > SL > PL > PW. Indeed the system has classified these last two neurons (1 and 2) has been different and their arrangements are inverse. So those species are clearly different. Figure 11 presents the two neurons together having an universal order [*Pedal Length, Pedal Width, Sepal Length, Sepal Width*]; comparing with Fig. 9 only *Pedal With* and *Pedal Length* have exchange places in this proposed dimension arrangement. Neuron 1 and *Sepal With* and *Sepal Length* influences more deeply the combination of these two neurons. This order expresses that for neuron 1 SL > PL and SW ⋙ PL and for neuron 2 PL > SL and PW > SW with universal order PL > PW > SL > SW. Figure 12 presents all neurons and the dimension arrangement still the same as in Fig. 9. Figure 14 shows display after removing a dimension of the analysis (*Septal Width*). Each combinations neurons/dimensions has its universal order dimension arrangement.

5 Conclusion and Future Work

This paper considers scenarios associated to visual data exploration and analysis of results produce by clustering algorithms. It is proposed an architecture for an Integrated Visualization and Mining system where a middle layer is responsible for the cooperation between results of an automated method and a visual method. The middle layer is garnished with enough intelligence, analyze results, proposes rendering layouts to the visual method for a more profit display illuminating the path for users. In particular the middle layer looks over neurons produced by SOM algorithm and sends suggestions to RadViz about axes arrangement. The most important contribution of the middle layer is in the resolution of RadViz dimension arrangement problem. The guidelines for the resolution are: (i) identify axes arrangement at multidimensional space; (ii) analyze only representative entities; and (iii) use the axes arrangement as a guide to render instances. The system achieves dimension arrangement by means of the following modes of operation: (i) isolated neuron; (ii) group of neurons; or (iii) all neurons.

Similarity of neurons dimensions is computed using their overall contribution and them their neighborhood is maximized obtaining an universal order (relational order is established between dimensions). Users may not want to see all the clustered data because datasets are too big creating messing images with clutter problems. Seeing cluster by cluster or groups clusters might be an interactive approach. Many combinations automated/visual methods can be explored and take profit of each other capacities and data. But certainly that can also depend on the nature of data analysis problems. In future works neuron cohesion and separation will be taken into consideration in order to join or collapse them.

References

1. Cook, K.A., Thomas, J.J.: Illuminating the path: The research and development agenda for visual analytics (No. PNNL-SA-45230). Pacific Northwest National Laboratory (PNNL), Richland, WA (US) (2005)
2. Keim, D., Andrienko, G., Fekete, J.-D., Görg, C., Kohlhammer, J., Melançon, G.: Visual analytics: definition, process, and challenges. In: Kerren, A., Stasko, John T., Fekete, J.-D., North, C. (eds.) Information Visualization. LNCS, vol. 4950, pp. 154–175. Springer, Heidelberg (2008). doi:10.1007/978-3-540-70956-5_7
3. Keim, D.K., Mansmann, F., Thomas, J.: Visual analytics: How much visualization and how must analytis? SIGKDD Explor. Newslett. **11**, 5–8 (2010)
4. Bertini, E., Lalanne, D.: Surveying the complementary role of automatic data analysis and visualization in knowledge discovery. In: ACM SIGKDD Workshop on Visual Analytics and Knowledge Discovery: Integrating Automated Analysis with Interactive Exploration (VAKD 2009), New York, USA (2009)
5. Hoffman, P., Grinstein, G., Pinkney, D.: Dimensional anchors: a graphic primitive for multidimensional multivariate information visualizations. In: Proceedings of New Paradigms in Information Visualization and Manipulation (NPIV), Kansas City, Missouri, USA (1999)
6. Caro, L.D., Frias-Martinez, V., Frias-Martinez, E.: Analyzing the role of dimension arrangement for data visualization in RadViz. In: Advances in Knowledge Discovery and Data Mining: 14th Pacific-Asia Conference, Hyderabad, India (2010)
7. Aquila, L.D., Santucci, G., Bertini, E.: SpringView: coorperation of RadViz and parallel coordinates for view optimization and cutter reduction. In: International Conference on Coordinated and Multiple View in Exploratory Visualization, London (2005)
8. Ankest, D., Berchtold, S., Keim, D.A.: Similarity clustering of dimensions for an enhanced visualization of multidimensional data. In: IEEE Symposium on Information Visualization (1998)
9. Lui, S., Maljovec, B., Wang, B., Bremer, P.-T., Pascucci, V.: Visualizing high-multidimensional data: advances in the past decade. IEEE Trans. Vis. Comput. Graph. **23** (3), 1249–1268 (2015)
10. Fisher: Center of machine learning and intelligent systems (1936). https://archive.ics.uci.edu/ml/datasets/Iris/. Accessed Jan 2017
11. Nováková, L., Stepánkova, O.: Visualization of trends using RadViz. Intell. Inf. Syst. **37**, 355–369 (2011)

Quantification and Visualization of a Heritage Conservation in a Quito Neighbourhood (Ecuador)

Taras Agryzkov[1], José Luis Oliver[2], Javier Santacruz[1], Leandro Tortosa[1], and José F. Vicent[1(✉)]

[1] Departamento de Ciencia de la Computación e Inteligencia Artificial, Universidad de Alicante, Ap. Correos 99, 03080 Alicante, Spain
jvicent@ua.es

[2] Departamento de Expresión Grafica, Composición y Proyectos, Universidad de Alicante, Ap. Correos 99, 03080 Alicante, Spain

Abstract. This paper focuses on the process of quantification and visualization of a heritage conservation study in a neighbourhood of Quito (Ecuador). The first part of the paper consists of collecting real information about different features of every building in the urban network of the mentioned neighbourhood. The information collected is then quantified by means of a data matrix that allows us to obtain an indicator of the heritage conservation of every parcel studied. In order to better understand the preservation of the neighbourhood, an analysis and visualization of the obtained indicators is carried out. The visualization is based on a non-linear interpolation of the vertices of a grid using a chromatic scale. This type of visualization provides a smooth graphic that helps us to represent areas that are more or less interesting from the point of view of the heritage conservation state.

Keywords: Data visualization · Interpolation · Data analysis · Heritage conservation

1 Introduction

At the end of the 19th century and the beginning of the 20th century the city of Quito (Ecuador) and, specifically, the southern part of the city was growing rapidly and needed a global urban plan to control the process [14]. Thus, about 1940, urban planners were commissioned to design a new Master Plan for the city [1]. The plan proposed to create a new suburb (Villaflora) in the south side, that follows the garden city model. The buildings of Villaflora are neither old enough nor artistic enough to be included as part of the city's patrimony in a traditional sense, its interest and patrimonial importance lies in its own urban model [8,12].

There are two main reasons for using graphic displays of datasets: either to present or to explore data [3,4]. A correct and clear graphical representation of a dataset plays a crucial role for further analysis of the data.

F.J. Martínez de Pisón et al. (Eds.): HAIS 2017, LNAI 10334, pp. 367–378, 2017.
DOI: 10.1007/978-3-319-59650-1_31

Furthermore, geographical information differentiates from other kinds of data as it refers to objects or phenomena with a specific location in space [10]. Because of this particular characteristic the precise location of objects can be visualised and the resulting maps can lead to further study as you can see in [6]. Maps are nowadays regarded as a form of scientific visualisation and for an extensive literature review about data visualisation it can be seen [5,13,15,16]. The Milestones Project [7] is about the History of Cartography, Statistical Graphics, and Data Visualisation. Detailed and exhaustive information about techniques and advances in the field, from old times to the present, can be found at datavis.ca.

The main objective of the paper is twofold: the quantification and analysis of heritage conservation values and their visualization. That is to say, we want to use visualization techniques with the aim of establishing areas, within the network, where there is a greater probability of locating people interested in cultural and heritage preservation of the neighbourhood under study.

To achieve this objective we organize the paper as follows: In Sect. 2, we describe the fieldwork develop in a neighbourhood of Quito (Ecuador), as well as the quantification of the dataset obtained. In Sect. 3, we perform a brief analysis of the fieldwork's results. Some visualizations of the heritage conservation numerical results is made in Sect. 4. Finally some conclusions are summarized.

2 Dataset and the Quantification Process

In order to measure the patrimonial value of the Villaflora neighbourhood (see Fig. 1), we need to define a framework that allows us to identify and understand the relevant elements.

To obtain the data, a fieldwork was carried out during the summer of 2016. In this fieldwork we obtained information for each one of the parcels in the urban layout of the neighbourhood. We have tried to perform a quantification process from different theoretical concepts (more exactly, indicators) related to the heritage conservation of all the parcels (see [11] for a detailed description).

The urban area object of this study has 719 parcels and, in order to better organize the fieldwork, the urban layout was divided into sectors and fact sheets were produced for each parcel. Thus, for instance, we can see in Fig. 2 the fact sheet corresponding to parcel number 27 of sector 3. On the left side of this image, we can see a photo of the parcel analysed, the central part shows the location of the parcel in the sector and the right part of the image summarizes the numerical data associated with the analysed indicators.

The final objective of this quantification process, based on the study of indicators, is to be able to establish a numerical value for each parcel, which summarizes the degree of heritage conservation at the present time. This value will be denoted hereafter as HC (Heritage Conservation).

To develop this process, we define a $n \times k$ *data matrix* which we denote by DM. It has n rows representing the n parcels studied, and each of its k columns represent indicators. More specifically, an element $dm_{ij} \in DM$ is the value we attach to the indicator k_j at parcel i.

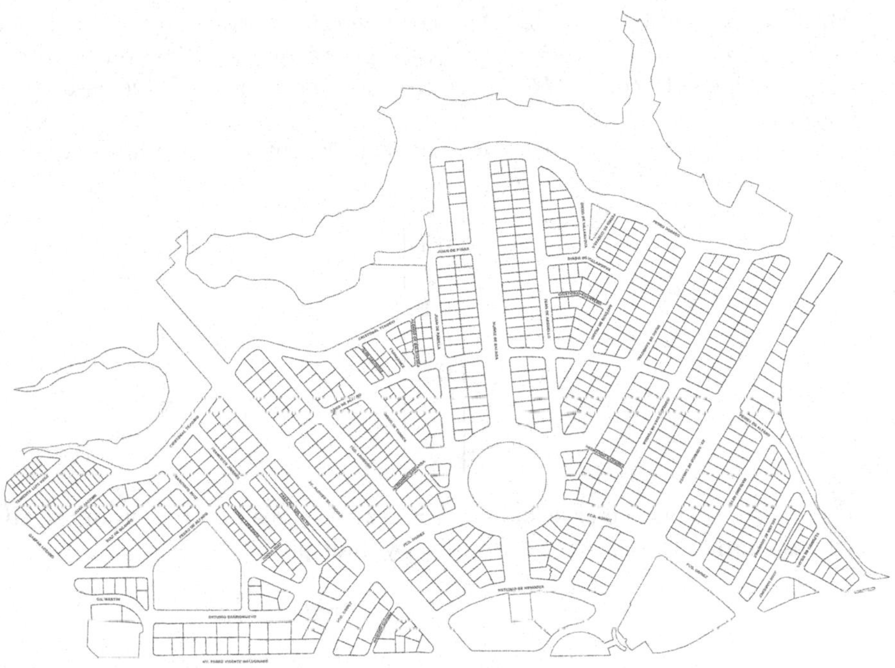

Fig. 1. Villaflora neighbourhood.

Taking into account a similar methodologies in heritage conservation as [9] and considering the morphology of Villaflora, we have quantified, for every parcel, the following indicators (k_i):

k_1 Form of the roof
k_2 Cover material
k_3 Coating
k_4 Colour
k_5 Windows
k_6 Ornaments
k_7 Fences
k_8 Scale
k_9 Volume

However, if we establish $\{k_1, k_2, \ldots, k_9\}$ indicators associated to the different parcels, not all of them have the same relevance or influence in the study of the heritage conservation. Therefore, we assign a weight to each indicator studied. We construct a vector $\boldsymbol{v}$ of $k \times 1$ size, where the element that occupies the row i is the multiplicative factor associated with the property or characteristic k_i.

Now, we multiply

$$DM \cdot \boldsymbol{v} = \boldsymbol{HC}.$$

With this, we obtain a vector $\boldsymbol{HC}$ (Heritage Conservation) of $n \times 1$ size that contains the values we assign to every parcel of the neighbourhood. In particular, an element $HC_i \in \boldsymbol{HC}$ is the heritage conservation value associated to the parcel i.

Following similar methodologies we use as a weight vector $\boldsymbol{v}$ associated to the different indicators k_i:

$$\boldsymbol{v} = \begin{bmatrix} 1 \\ 0.7 \\ 0.6 \\ 0.9 \\ 0.5 \\ 0.9 \\ 1 \\ 1 \\ 1 \end{bmatrix}.$$

For instance, taking the case shown in Fig. 2 let us see how to obtain the HC value corresponding to this parcel. Simply, by multiplying

$$dm_{27} \cdot \boldsymbol{v} = \begin{bmatrix} 7 \; 7 \; 5 \; 2.5 \; 5 \; 6 \; 7 \; 7 \; 7 \end{bmatrix} \begin{bmatrix} 1 \\ 0.7 \\ 0.6 \\ 0.9 \\ 0.5 \\ 0.9 \\ 1 \\ 1 \\ 1 \end{bmatrix} = [44.1]$$

so, we have the HC value associated to the parcel number 27, $HC(27) = 44.1$.

3 Analysis of the Results

Once the quantification process has been determined, the calculations have been carried out with the aim of obtaining the HC values of each of the parcels in which the urban layout has been divided.

The classic measures of basic statistics give, for the 795 parcels, the following parameters:

Range	Mean	Median	1st Qu	3rd Qu	SD
$[0, 76]$	18.85	6.9	0	31	22.5

Analyzing the data obtained from the fieldwork, we can observe the following characteristics:

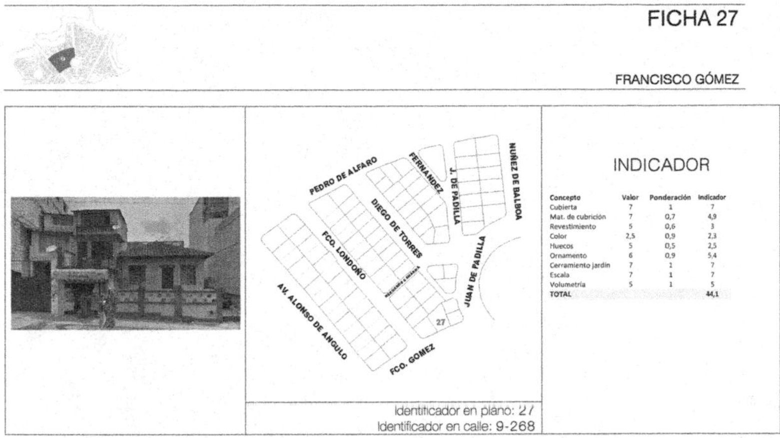

Concepto	Valor	Ponderación	Indicador
Cubierta	7	1	7
Mat. de cubrición	7	0,7	4,9
Revestimiento	5	0,6	3
Color	2,5	0,9	2,3
Huecos	5	0,5	2,5
Ornamento	6	0,9	5,4
Cerramiento jardín	7	1	7
Escala	7	1	7
Volumetría	5	1	5
TOTAL			44,1

Fig. 2. Fact sheet of parcel 27 of sector 3.

- The number of parcels with HC in the range $[0, 5[$ is 356, that represents more than 44%. This gives an idea of the degree of degradation of the current architectural construction.
- There are 5 parcels with maximum HC values, representing about 6%.
- Although the maximum value of HC is 76, the arithmetic average is 18.85. This is a low value as a result of 45% of null HC.
- The median is 6.9 with a frequency of 27.
  A large dispersion can been observed, since the standard deviation is 22.5.

In Fig. 3 all HC values corresponding to the parcels of the studied area have been represented. The number shown in the graph corresponds to an identifier of each parcel. In the image a high number of parcels with $HC = 0$ is clearly observed. On the other hand, the differences in the sizes of the identification numbers are related to the number of parcels with value $HC = 0$ that is around the parcel represented. Thus, if we take as a reference parcel 291 from the top of the chart, we conclude that it is parcel number 291, which has a high HC value and is surrounded by other parcels whose value $HC = 0$.

4 Visualization of the Numerical Results

Since these HC indicators do not provide any visual information, we need to transform these values into a chromatic scale that easily allows us to visualize the importance of each parcel. In the chromatic scale used, blue tones represent low HC values and red tones represent a range close to the maximum value.

In Fig. 4 a visualization of the values obtained by each parcel can be observed.

There is an area, on the left side of the image, where elements that have a high HC value are concentrated. We also highlight the large number of parcels

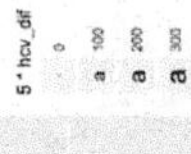

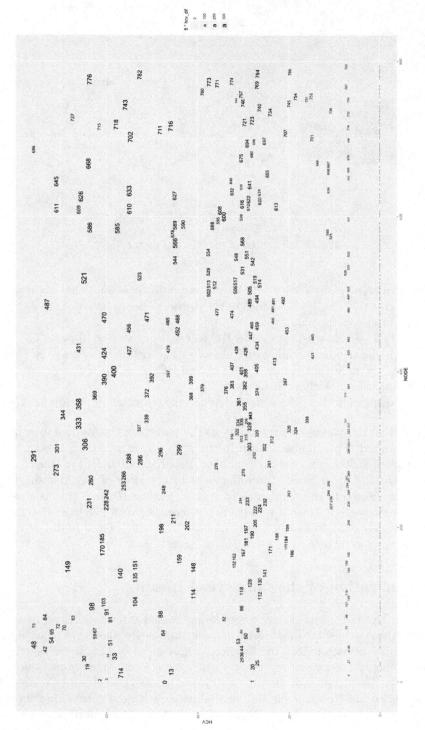

Fig. 3. HC values for the 795 parcels studied.

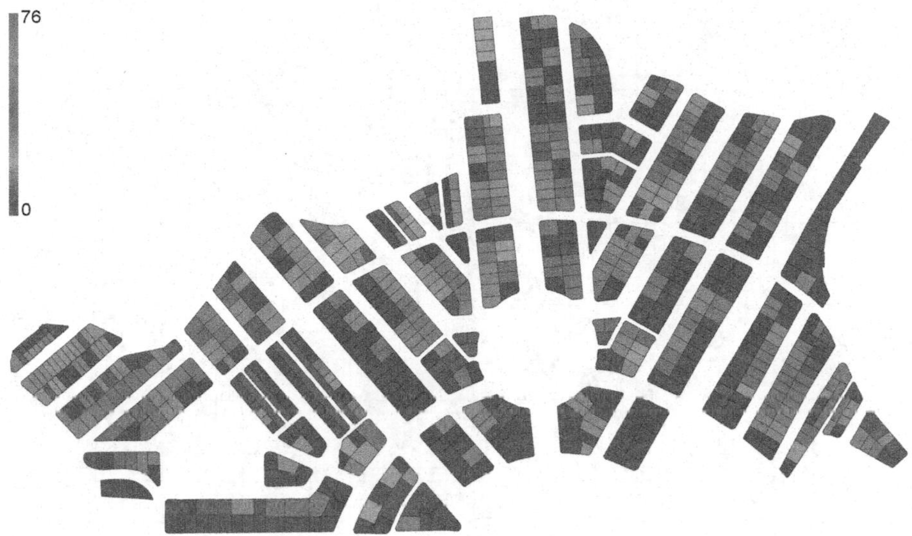

Fig. 4. Graphical display of the HC values for each building. (Color figure online)

with $HC = 0$, meaning that there are blocks of buildings where degradation, from the point of view of heritage conservation, is very important.

The data visualization followed by the model presented in this section does not divide the space by following a geometric criterion, but considers the fact that the data to be visualized are geopositioned. We represent every parcel of the neighbourhood with a geolocated point in the plane, specifically the centre of the parcel. With this representation, we have a point cloud (see Fig. 5) with an HC value associated to each point.

This section presents four types of graphics to visualize the HC values, paying special attention to the characteristics and particularities of each one. All of these graphics have two common features in terms of the display. On the one hand a gradient chromatic scale is used in which the colour intensity is proportional to the amount of data, the red colour represents the highest values and the blue colour represents the lowest values. On the other hand a non-linear interpolation is performed, specifically the so-called cosine interpolation.

The common process to obtain the different visualizations can be summarized in the following steps:

1. Obtaining the point cloud. Every parcel is represented as a point in the plane, in particular the centre of the parcel (see Fig. 5).
2. Assignment of the HC values. Each parcel has an HC value that we assign to the corresponding point of the cloud.
3. Definition of the grid. We define a grid with 2546 (67×38) cells of 15×15 (m) size, with the aim of covering all of the space in the neighbourhood (see Fig. 5).
4. Data assignment to the vertices of the grid. For each vertex of the grid we assign the data located in an area defined by a circle of 30 m radius and with

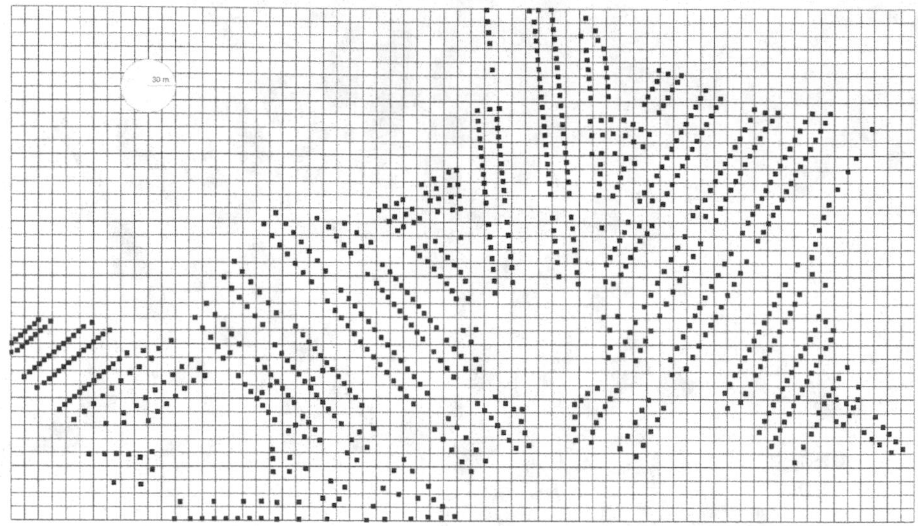

Fig. 5. Point cloud with grid.

centre each vertex itself. With this, each point of the grid has an associated value.

5. Interpolation. With the values assigned to the vertices of the grid, a non-linear interpolation is perform. We have used is the so-called cosine interpolation (adapted for 2D) [2]:

$$v = (1 - y)(v_1 f_1 + v_2 f_2) + y(v_3 f_1 + v_4 f_2)$$

where v_i are the values associated with each of the four vertices of the grid and

$$f_1 = \frac{1 + \cos(\pi x)}{2}, \quad f_2 = \frac{1 - \cos(\pi x)}{2},$$

for

$$0 \leq x \leq 1, \quad 0 \leq y \leq 1.$$

In Fig. 6, each vertex of the grid has associated the number of HC values. This type of visualization represents the density of parcels of the neighbourhood under study. As we can see in Fig. 6, the maximum value is 22 and it occurs in the left side of the image, which has a higher concentration of parcels, regardless of the HC value of each one. We must see this image if we want to establish areas where there is a greater concentrations of buildings.

Figure 7 represents the study of the arithmetic average of HC values associated to each vertex of the grid. As it can be seen, the maximum value is 76 and it occurs in the left part of the image but slightly displaced towards the centre. Summarizing, we must see this image if we want to establish areas where there is a greater probability of locating interesting parcels from the heritage conservation point of view.

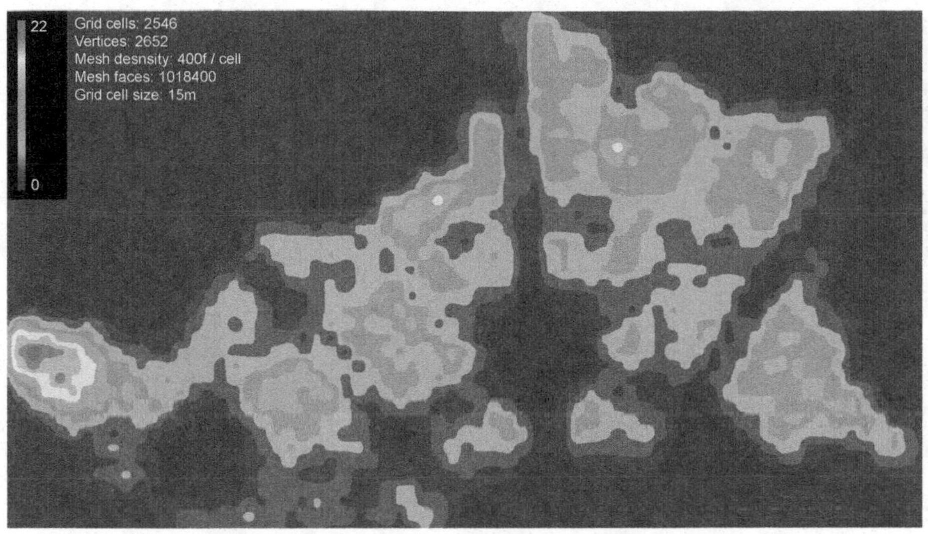

Fig. 6. Interpolation of the quantity of HC values.

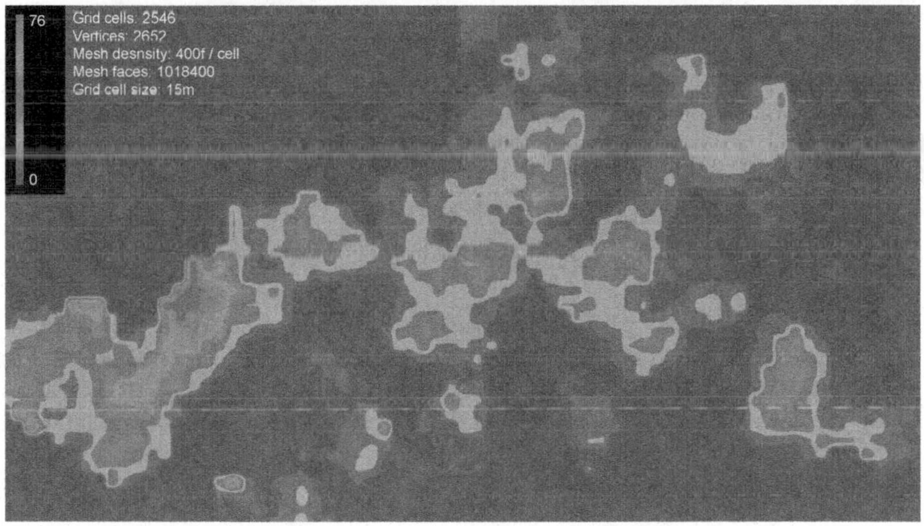

Fig. 7. Interpolation of the arithmetic average of HC values.

Figure 8 is related to Fig. 6 and it represents the standard deviation of the arithmetic average of HC values of the grid. This image shows zones of contrast between high and low values of HC. In this case the maximum value for the standard deviation is 38, that gives an idea of the dispersion degree. There are multiple points in which we can find together parcels of very high patrimonial value and others with a very low value. While in Fig. 7 represents the arith-

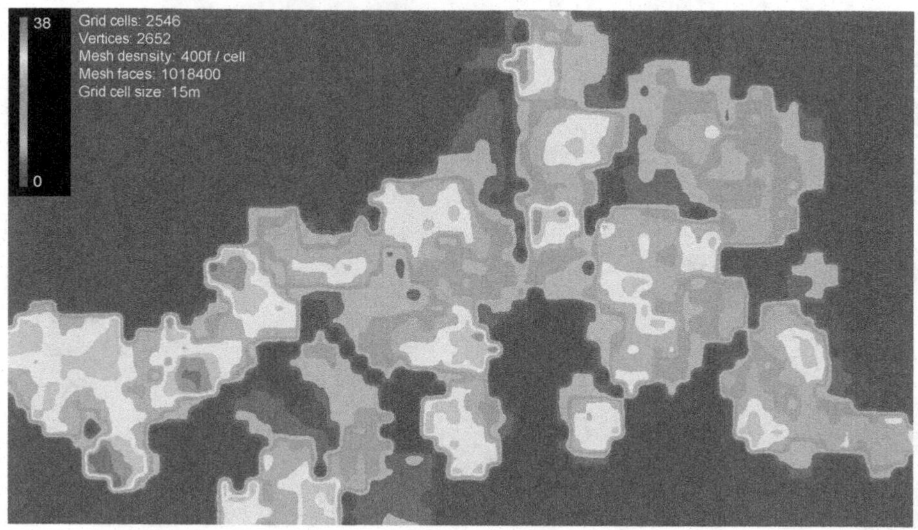

Fig. 8. Interpolation of standard deviation of HC mean values.

metic average of the HC values assign to every node of the grid, in Fig. 8 the interpretation in totally different since it represents the dispersion of HC values.

Finally, Fig. 9 shows a data heterogeneity analysis associated to the vertices of the grid. This analysis is carried out by studying the frequency of intervals of values within a range for each vertex. The process is similar to that of constructing a histogram and follows the next steps:

1. We divide the range of values into 10 intervals (according to the Sturgets criterion).
2. For each vertex of the grid, we quantify the number of intervals that have at least one data. As a result we obtain a measure which represents the diversity of HC values associated to each vertex of the grid.
3. The sum of elements of each interval, having at least one value, is calculated. Then this sum is divided by the total number of intervals (10), so we perform a normalization of the result.

This process allows us to identify the number of different classes of values associated to each vertex of the grid. In other words, identify if the data associated with a vertex are homogeneous or heterogeneous. Figure 9 shows that, especially in the centre, several areas exist with high heterogeneity and this means low uniformity regarding the heritage conservation.

The visualization process allows us to understand the heritage conservation features of the neighbourhood under a global perspective. In addition, the different types of visualization presented allow us the possibility of introduce modifications in the buildings of the urban network, with the aim to evaluate the effect of such modifications over the whole network.

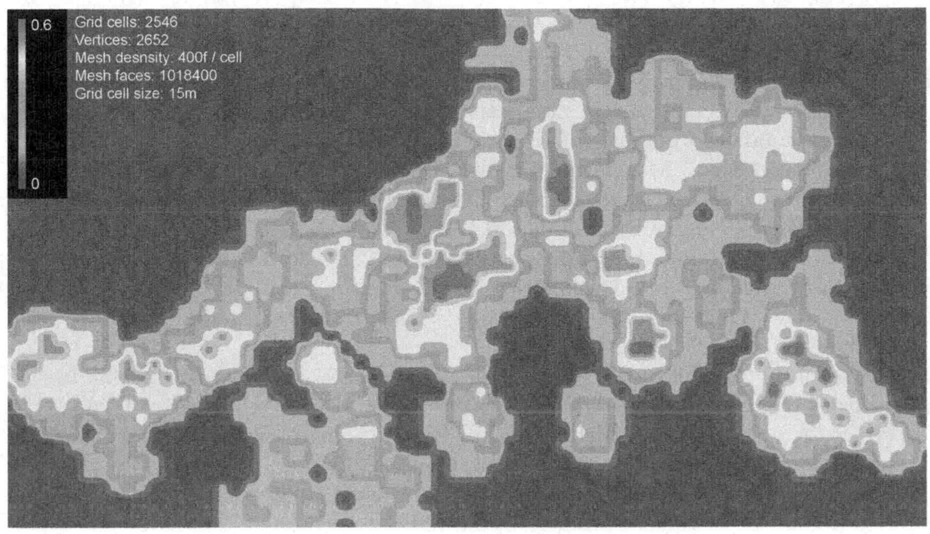

Fig. 9. Heterogeneity based on interpolation.

5 Conclusion

In this paper we present a quantification and visualization process with the aim of studying the heritage conservation of neighbourhood buildings. In this process, the first part consists of collecting information about different features of every building of the urban network of the neighbourhood of Villaflora in Quito (Ecuador). Then, the information collected is quantified with the goal of obtaining an indicator of the heritage conservation of every parcel studied. An analysis and visualization of the indicators is carried out, in order to better understand the heritage conservation. We perform different visualizations based on a non-linear interpolation of the vertices of a grid. This type of visualization provides smooth graphics that help us to represent areas that are more or less interesting from the point of view of the heritage conservation state.

Acknowledgement. This work was partially supported by the Spanish Government, Ministerio de Economía y Competitividad, grant number TIN2014-53855-P.

References

1. Achig, L.: El proceso urbano de Quito, pp. 57–72. Flacso, Quito (1983)
2. Agbinya, J.I.: Interpolation using the discrete cosine transform. Electron. Lett. **28**(20), 1927–1928 (1992)
3. Chen, C.H., Hardle, W., Unwin, A.: Handbook of Data Visualization. Springer, Berlin (2008)
4. Chua, A., Marcheggiani, E., Servillo, L., Vande Moere, A.: FlowSampler: visual analysis of urban flows in geolocated social media data. In: Aiello, L.M., McFarland, D. (eds.) SocInfo 2014. LNCS, vol. 8852, pp. 5–17. Springer, Cham (2015). doi:10.1007/978-3-319-15168-7_2

5. Ciuccarelli, C., Lupi, G., Simeone, L.: Visualizing the Data City. Springer, Heidelberg (2014)
6. Dimitrova, T., Tsois, A., Camossi, E.: Developmenmt of a web-based geographical information system for interactive visualization and analysis of container itineraries. Int. J. Comput. Inf. Technol. **3**(1) (2014)
7. Friendly, M., Sigal, M., Harnanansingh, D.: The milestones project: a database for the history of data visualization. In: Visible Numbers: The History of data Visualization. Ashgate Press, London (2012). Chapter 10
8. Garces, K.: La ciudad de Quito y los otros, pp. 226–234. Flacso, Quito (2006)
9. Gehl, J.: Cities for People. Island Press, Washington (2010)
10. Kraak, M.J., Ormeling, F.: Cartography - Visualization of Spatial Data, 3rd edn. Pearson Education, Essex (2010)
11. Oliver, J.L., Agryzkov, T., Tortosa, L., Vicent, J.F., Santacruz, J.: The use of network theory in heritage cities. World Acad. Sci. Eng. Technol. **11**, 21–26 (2017)
12. Ponce, A.: La Mariscal. Historia de un barrio modern en Quito en el siglo XX. Instituto Metropolitano de Patrimonio, Quito (2011)
13. Rozenblat, C., Melacon, G.: Methods for Multilevel Analysis and Visualization of Geographical Networks. Springer, Berlin (2013)
14. Salvador, J.: Historia de Quito, pp. 270–290. Fonsal, Quito (2009)
15. Telea, A.C.: Data Visualization Principles and Practice, 2nd edn. CRC Press, London (2014)
16. Yau, N.: Data Points - Visualization that Means Something, 3rd edn. Wiley, Indiana (2013)

An Enhanced Hierarchical Traitor Tracing Scheme Based on Clustering Algorithms

Faten Chaabane[(✉)], Maha Charfeddine, and Chokri Ben Amar

REGIM-Lab.: REsearch Groups in Intelligent Machines, ENIS, University of Sfax, BP 1173, 3038 Sfax, Tunisia
faten.chaabane@ieee.org

Abstract. The easiness of using and manipulating digital media content has a volte face. In fact, although average users can simply be familiar with some manipulations such as a simple duplication, these manipulations can be dangerous with dishonest users whose target is illegal. Manipulating and duplicating digital media content via the Internet and Peer to Peer networks is available even to average users but can be used to unauthorized purposes with dishonest customers. Henceforth, facing the loss caused by unauthorized treatments and protecting the digital content become challenging to the media industry and research has led to different mechanisms of digital content protection. The aim of the multimedia distribution platforms, even Video on demand platforms, is to propose a suitable structure to the embedded fingerprints to ensure an efficient and fast tracing process in multimedia distribution platforms involving great number of users. The Tardos code has been the most popular tracing code due to its efficient tracing detection performance. One main challenge of the existing Tardos-based tracing approaches was to face the decoding complexity and the computational costs of the tracing process.

Hence, the tracing scheme we propose to improve in this paper was proposed previously as a group-based scheme which enables to construct groups of users according to a multi-level hierarchy. Based on clustering algorithm, we propose to construct groups of users' fingerprints, and then to apply the tracing process. The main target is to show how deep is the impact of using a clustering algorithms in the hierarchical tracing scheme.

Keywords: Tracing · Traitors · Tardos · Clustering · Hierarchical

1 Introduction

The tracing traitors was proposed to fight the copyright infringement of multimedia contents through the internet and Peer to Peer networks. It consists in hiding a fingerprint in each release of the media content before its distribution to only purchasers. More than one approach was proposed in the literature to provide efficient tracing codes, ranging from signal processing-based approaches [21]

F.J. Martínez de Pisón et al. (Eds.): HAIS 2017, LNAI 10334, pp. 379–390, 2017.
DOI: 10.1007/978-3-319-59650-1_32

to cryptology-based approaches [2,19]. The well-known probabilistic code called Tardos code has been proposed in [19] and has attracted increasing interest due to its short code length with an adjustment of the error probability [18]. Despite its fair compromise between the code length and the detection rate, the Tardos code still requires improvement with regard to its complexity decoding. This weakness is unequivocal in the case of multimedia distributing systems which involve a large size of audience and are expected to use a low complex pirates' retrieving process. The fingerprinting schemes based on Tardos code have witnessed a flurry of research efforts. This part surveys the current state of the art in traitor tracing approaches based on Tardos code. Some approaches focus on applying shifts to the Tardos code itself. Whereas, few other attempts have been made to ameliorate its tracing process by using a group-based property. According to [22], the group-based tracing scheme mainly consists in grouping users having common characteristics according to the assumption that they have more probability to cooperate together. Henceforth, this type of scheme may reduce the Tardos users' search space and consequently the complexity of its decoding step.

As a first example, in [1], a two-level hierarchical structure was proposed for the fingerprint generation process. Assigning users to a group was made randomly without considering any relationships inter or in groups. The main target was to minimize the complexity of the Tardos tracing decoding process.

In [12], the idea was to focus on the hierarchical structure proposed by [22], not for independent Gaussian signals but for Tardos-based fingerprints. Despite the good detection rates proven in this technique, the main weakness was the important length of the tracing code. In the same context, and according to the identifier multi-level hierarchical structure we proposed previously, it was necessary to find a suitable tracing strategy which enables a first group selection and then user accusation in the retrieved group. According to related work, we have focused on rising to the challenge of improving robustness results and accusation rates of Tardos code. Thus, we tried to reduce its complexity computation by proposing a multi-level hierarchical fingerprint in [5]. Henceforth, we will study in this paper the impact of clustering algorithm used to generate the groups of fingerprints on the two-level tracing scheme proposed in [6] as an accurate tracing strategy to our hierarchical fingerprints. The paper is organized as follows: in Sect. 2, we remind the scheme of the multi-level hierarchical fingerprint we proposed in [5]. In Sect. 3, we detail the structure of the improved tracing scheme. Section 4 presents the experimental assessment, and finally we conclude.

2 The Proposed Multi-level Fingerprint Generation Step

The majority of the traitor tracing field agree upon the fact that the whole fingerprinting system includes three main steps: the fingerprint generation step, their embedding into the media content and the tracing process [15]. According to related work, we have focused on rising to the challenge of improving robustness results and accusation rates of Tardos code. Thus, we try to reduce

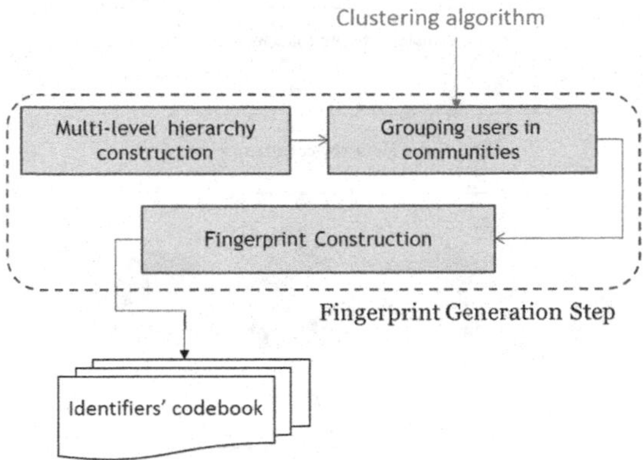

Fig. 1. Details of the fingerprint generation step.

its complexity computation by proposing a multi-level hierarchical fingerprint. Then, we embed it by an original robust watermarking technique which has proven good robustness and imperceptibility results compared to other existing approaches [9,10,17,20]. For multimedia distribution platform integrating a Tardos serialization system, one key constraint in the tracing scheme is the required computational costs to compute the scores S_j of all considered users, which is around $O(n \times m)$ operations, where n is the number of users and m is the codeword length. Through this part, we propose to involve a clustering step, as shown in Fig. 1 to construct our multi-level hierarchical fingerprint. The only requirement is the codeword length of users' fingerprints which is constrained by the applied watermarking technique used in the tracing scheme [7] and the number of groups defined by the hierarchy. The result of the generation step as shown in Fig. 1 is a codebook of codewords; a set of clustering-based identifiers.

2.1 The Hierarchy Construction Step

Reducing the search space of dishonest users by assigning a user to a specific group as depicted in Fig. 2 represents a suitable solution to face the Tardos accusation costs. The user assignment to a group can be used to counter different types of coalitions: temporal, geographic, social, etc. In the hierarchy, each chosen constraint corresponds to a level. We will detail each selected constraint separately.

Thus, according to this study made in [3], we embrace a multi-level hierarchy in the fingerprint generation step. Each criterion is represented by a level in the hierarchy. The first level is the time level where we assume that the most important period for a video life in a VOD platform is about 4 months [8,16]. Hence, we consider two groups of two-month-duration: in the first one, users' curiosity is moderately important and increases gradually to reach the maximal audience interest and in the second one it decreases to reach the minimal bound in the fourth one. A second level in the hierarchy represents the geographic criterion

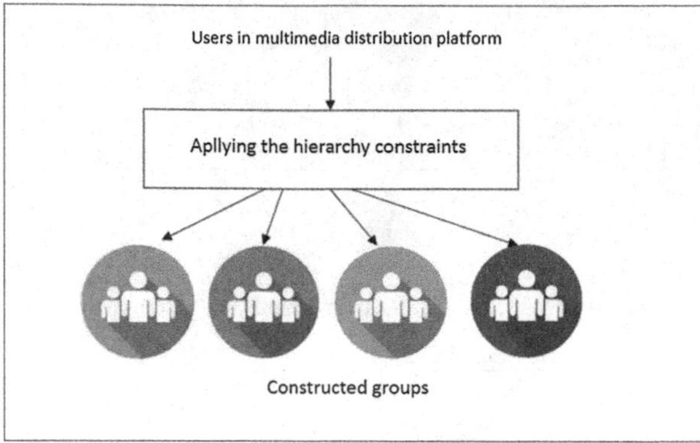

Fig. 2. Applying group-based properties to construct groups of users.

where we propose to divide platform users to two essential regions: Zone_A where the piracy phenomenon is very important, especially in Asia and Africa continents, and Zone_B where the piracy phenomenon is less important especially in Europe, America and Austria. We divide each continent to two groups of the main large countries in the third level. In the last levels, we are interested in social criteria, such as the age and the gender ones, etc. Once the hierarchy is fixed, we construct the users' fingerprints or codewords. Then, we apply a clustering step to construct groups of identifiers. Hence, The resulting fingerprint for each user is the concatenation of his community identifier concatenated to his personal identifier which is encoded with Tardos code.

$$Final_{identifier} = id_{level1} + id_{level2} + .. + id_{levelk} + personal_{id} \tag{1}$$

2.2 The Group-Based Construction Involving Clustering Step

According to [4,5], the generation of group identifier using the K-means clustering algorithm has proved the most efficient group detection rates. We remind that this clustering step consists in computing iteratively the Euclidean distance between each fingerprint and the group center. For each iteration, groups are constructed according to the minimal computed distance. Once this distance is unchanged, the algorithm converges and we have the final K clustered groups of fingerprints. Thus, the resulting modified user identifier is the concatenation of his clustered group identifier and his personal identifier as follows: $ModifiedUser_{id} = group_{id} + personal_{id}$ with $group_{id} = id_{clusteredgroup}$. Once the clusters are obtained, the traitor tracing process is applied. The retrieved fingerprint is treated to check the detection success.

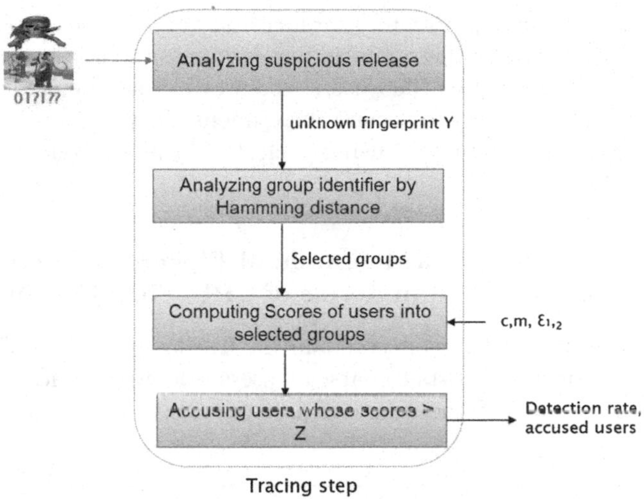

Fig. 3. Details of the tracing step.

3 The Tracing Process Using Multi-level Hierarchical Fingerprint

One key requirement in the fingerprinting system is the tracing process: when the supplier detects a copy with unknown fingerprint Y, he tries to trace back colluders by analyzing the extracted fingerprint Y, retrieving its similarity to a group identifier and hence tracing individual colluders. The tracing is performed here by the Tardos code. As shown in Fig. 3, group selection is based on computing Hamming distance between the ID_{group} of the suspicious copy and the other groups' identifiers. The selected groups are the closest to the extracted one; namely groups having the smallest Hamming distance to the ID_{group} of the suspicious copy. Then, the tracing process continues with the Tardos tracing step, the score S_j is computed per user only in selected groups. The user whose score exceeds the threshold Z [14] is thus accused. The detection rate of the proposed system is then computed to check its efficiency.

4 Experiments and Discussion

The real challenge of a traitor tracing scheme is to cover the gap between theoretical and practical results. Optimizing the fingerprinting code parameters and preserving the robustness even if the collusion size increases are the most important requirements of a traitor tracing scheme. In this contribution, we propose to construct a multi-level hierarchical fingerprint whose structure should improve the Tardos accusation process in terms of time consumption and tracing performance. To validate this multi-level structure, we propose to evaluate its impact on the tracing process when considering different collusion attacks and varying collusion size. In all the experiments, we focus on varying the number of levels by comparing the multi-level hierarchical fingerprint to the non-hierarchical one. We propose, thus, to generate 1000 users' codewords with 5 colluders in a first example and 8 colluders in the second experiment. In a second set of experiments, we validate the impact of using a clustering algorithm on the tracing performance.

4.1 Evaluation of the Multi-hierarchical Fingerprint Versus the Non Hierarchical One in Terms of CPU Time Consumption

It is undeniable that one key constraint in the Tardos-based tracing scheme is the required computational costs to parse all users' codewords and compute their corresponding scores before the accusation.

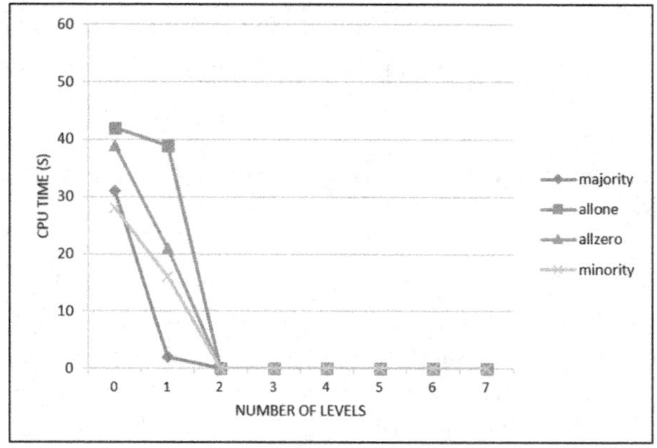

Fig. 4. CPU time consumption by hierarchical structures for different collusion attacks and for collusion size $c=5$

To show the outperformance of the proposed multi-level hierarchy when addressing the time consumption during the accusation process, we propose to compute the required CPU time to trace colluders for different collusion attacks and two collusion sizes $c=5$ and $c=8$. The time consumption in computed for varying hierarchical structures, ranging from hierarchy of one level to hierarchy of seven levels. The non-hierarchical structure is referred by a number of levels equal to zero. As illustrated in Figs. 4 and 5, the time consumption is reduced significantly when the number of hierarchical levels is increasing. For the non-hierarchical structure, it exceeds 30 s for the majority vote attack for the two collusion size, nevertheless it is close to 0.1 s since the second level for $c=5$ and below 2 s since the fourth level. Regarding the payoff in time when using the hierarchical structure, it exceeds 95% and 60% since the second level for the two curves. Now, when regarding the collusion size, it is clear that the tracing process spends more time to retrieve 8 colluders than for 5 colluders. Indeed,

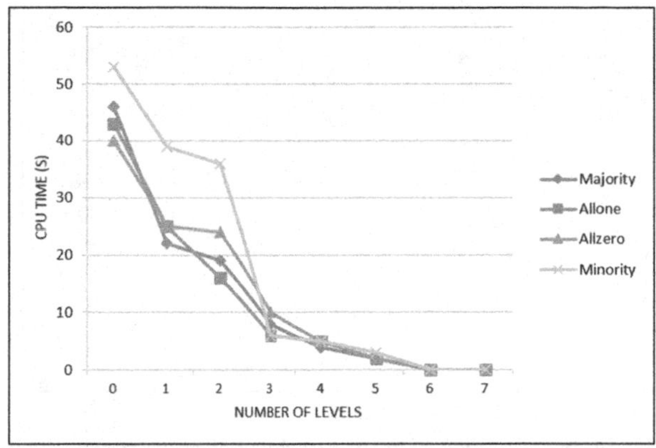

Fig. 5. CPU time consumption by hierarchical structures for different collusion attacks and for collusion size *c=8*

for *c=8*, the CPU time becomes close to 0.1 s in the sixth level. The impact of the collusion attack on the required CPU time is also an important point. In fact, from the two figures, we notice that some attacks such as the Minority vote attack has deeper effect on the time than the others. This can be proved by the fact that time values are the most important for this attack. However, with the hierarchical structure, this required time is also reduced significantly.

When studying the CPU time criterion, we notice that the hierarchical structure provides an important reduction in the time consumption of the tracing process. This can be explained by the fact that according to this structure, users are grouped together and hence the search space of the Tardos code is reduced to only the selected groups.

4.2 Evaluation of the Multi-hierarchical Fingerprint Versus the Non Hierarchical One in Terms of Positive False Alarm

Now, another important point to evaluate the tracing performance is the positive false alarm probability, the probability of accusing falsely an innocent.

As shown in Figs. 6 and 7, the probability of falsely accusing innocents is also reduced when the number of levels is increasing. For the non-hierarchical structure, the pfa is very important and exceeds 0.5 for the majority of collusion attacks. However, it is closer to 0 since the third level for *c=5* and the sixth level for *c=8*. When studying the pfa rates, we also notice that some collusion attacks have deeper effect on the accuracy of the detection rates than others. In our experiments, the minority attack has the highest values of pfa. These values are also reduced with hierarchical structure. The behavior of the pfa curve can be explained by the fact that the hierarchical structure keeps more accuracy to the accusation process. Parsing groups susceptible to contain colluders prevents from accusing falsely innocent users. The whole experimental assessments were made with the proposed assumption that users belong to the

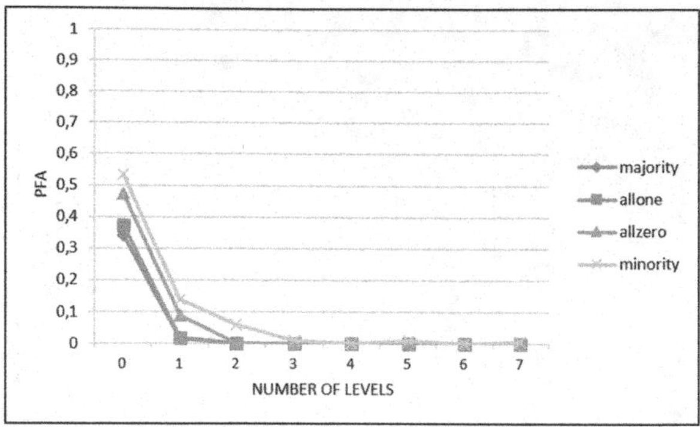

Fig. 6. Probability of false positive of hierarchical structures for different collusion attacks and for collusion size *c=5*

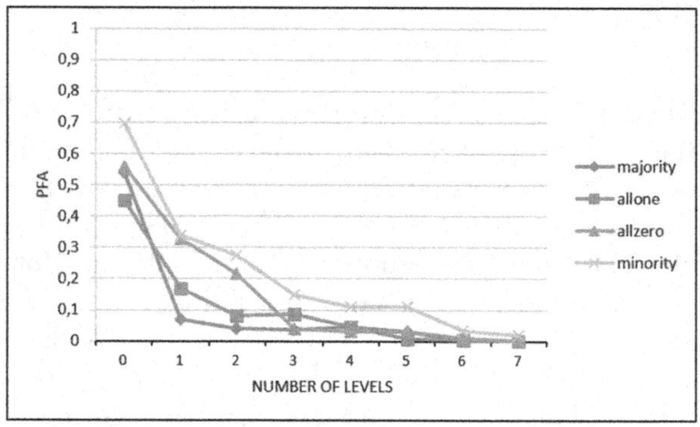

Fig. 7. Probability of false positive of hierarchical structures for different collusion attacks and for collusion size *c=8*

same group. In case of having users in different groups, the proposed tracing algorithm is executed for all the selected groups (having a minimal Hamming distance). Retrieving one colluders is fairly sufficient to stop the tracing process. Otherwise, the tracing process continues to parse all the selected groups. If users belong to all the groups of the hierarchy, the tracing process is executed for all the groups because they have the similar Hamming distance, and hence we are in the worst case (which is in contrast with our assumption). In this context, in a last part of this paper, we focus on the group-based property of our hierarchy. In fact, this property is applied randomly to groups of fingerprints; the groups are constructed with no constraints. In [24], group of users are constructed by applying a clustering algorithm to the group identifier. Data clustering process in traitor tracing context can be assimilated to an unsupervised data analysis process whose goal is to partition unlabeled users' identifiers into groups of similar characteristics, called clusters. In this part of paper, we propose to study the users' grouping step by involving a clustering step to construct our multi-level hierarchical fingerprint. The only requirement is the codeword length of users' fingerprints which is constrained by the applied watermarking technique used in the tracing scheme [7].

4.3 Comparison of the Proposed Fingerprinting Approach to Other Hierarchical Techniques

Compared to non hierarchical fingerprints, the experimental assessments prove that the multi-level hierarchical fingerprints have good robustness to collusion attacks and are able to provide good detection rates in fewer time. Now, when regarding the existing hierarchical tracing approaches, it is obvious that they belong to different classes: code-based tracing classes and signal-based ones. Hence, we propose to report the most interesting experimental results able to allow us to compare them to the proposed approach. Looking at the different results reported in Table 1, we compare the tracing complexity of respectively [1,12,22,23]. The smallest decoding complexity is shown for both the proposed technique and [23].

Table 1. Comparative tracing complexity results to some existing hierarchical techniques

Hierarchical technique	Tracing complexity
[22]	$O(N \times l)$
[1]	$O(c_g \times \sqrt{N} \times l)$
[12]	$O(c_g \times n_g \times m)$
[23]	$O(m)$
The proposed technique	$O(\mathbf{m})$

Now, if we compare the experimental results related to the detection rate for [23], we notice that the majority vote attack is the only assessed collusion attack. We use the same experimental parameters proposed in [23]. We set the number of users n to 10^3, the number of groups to 8 and the number of colluders to 5. Compared to the CPU tracing time value of the [23] required to retrieve the 5 colluders whose value is about 10^{-1} s, the CPU time value required by the proposed technique is close to 10^{-2} s for a 3-hierarchical structure (the number of levels is tied to the number of groups).

4.4 Robustness to Collusion Attacks Between Different Groups

According to the experiments conducted in [5], we have proved that K-means which has provided the best recognition rate compared to the other clustering algorithms. Hence, we propose to test it for collusion including more than one group. As depicted in Fig. 8(a) and (b), the group recognition rate is enhanced when using the K-means clustering algorithm. In fact, we vary the group participation rate in the collusion attack, and we show that the K-means clustering algorithm is able to detect at least 37.5% of colluders for a group participation which exceeds 40%. For the non hierarchical structure, the group recognition is null for all group participation size which proves that the tracing detection for this structure is not able to detect colluders belonging to different groups.

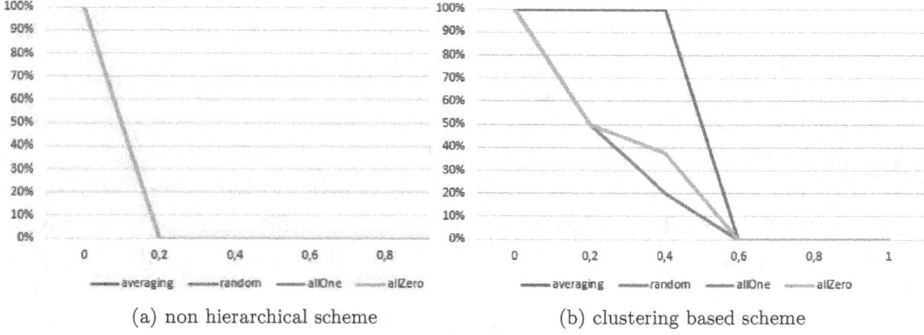

(a) non hierarchical scheme (b) clustering based scheme

Fig. 8. Robustness to different attacks: averaging, random, allOne, allZero.

Another important point is to compare the group detection capacity of the proposed technique to other group-based existing techniques. Moreover, due to the diversity of experimental assessments, we propose to report the main important and available experimental results in respectively [12,13,22,23]. Looking at the different results reported in Table 2, we notice that, for all the group-based techniques, the group detection capacity under the averaging collusion attack decreases with the increase of the group participation rate, called Group rate. Moreover, the proposed technique based on K-means algorithm shows good detection rate compared to the other existing techniques. Furthermore, we have proved previously that the group-based technique we propose provide a good compromise between the detection rate, the CPU time tracing and the decoding complexity. In this section, we have detailed the first contribution we propose in traitor tracing field. We have constructed a multi-level hierarchical fingerprint in order to apply a group-based tracing process which has proven a significant reduction of tracing and computational costs of the Tardos code even compared to other hierarchical existing tracing approaches.

Table 2. Comparative group detection capacity results to some existing group-based techniques

Technique	Group rate=0.1	Group rate=0.2	Group rate=0.25	Group rate=0.3
[22]	0.5	X	X	X
[13]	≤ 0.9	≤ 0.35	X	X
The proposed technique	**1**	**0.5**	**0.45**	**0.1**

5 Conclusion

In this paper, we presented the group-based fingerprinting system we propose for traitor tracing in multimedia distribution platform. The construction of fingerprints is based on a multi-level hierarchy where each level corresponds to a constraint inspired from the threat channel in the platform. The aim from this construction is to reduce the search space of the Tardos code and hence to reduce the complexity of the Tardos decoding step even in case of great number of users. We have also proposed to use a clustering step to enhance the group-based property which has improved the tracing results. We performed a detailed analysis of the proposed system performance according to two criteria: the robustness to collusion attacks and the tracing time criterion. The proposed fingerprinting system was evaluated for different collusion sizes. We also assigned an important consideration to the comparison of the performance of the proposed hierarchical system with non hierarchical one.

References

1. Akashi, N., Kuribayashi, M., Morii, M.: Hierarchical construction of Tardos code. In: International Symposium on Information Theory and Its Applications 2008, ISITA 2008, pp. 1–6 (2008)
2. Boneh, D., Kiayias, A., Montgomery, H.W.: Robust fingerprinting codes: a near optimal construction. In: Proceedings of the 10th ACM Workshop on Digital Rights Management, Chicago, Illinois, USA, 4 October 2010, pp. 3–12 (2010)
3. Chaabane, F., Charfeddine, M., Amar, C.B.: A multimedia tracing traitors scheme using multi-level hierarchical structure for Tardos fingerprint based audio watermarking. In: SIGMAP 2014 - Proceedings of the 11th International Conference on Signal Processing and Multimedia Applications, Vienna, Austria, 28–30 August 2014, pp. 289–296 (2014)
4. Chaabane, F., Charfeddine, M., Amar, C.B.: Clustering impact on group-based traitor tracing schemes. In: 15th International Conference on Intelligent Systems Design and Applications (ISDA), Marrakesh, Morocco, 14–16 December 2015, pp. 440–445 (2015)
5. Chaabane, F., Charfeddine, M., Amar, C.B.: Novel two-level tracing scheme using clustering algorithm. J. Inf. Assur. Secur. **11**(4), 179–189 (2016). 11p
6. Chaabane, F., Charfeddine, M., Puech, W., Amar, C.B.: A two-stage traitor tracing strategy for hierarchical fingerprints. Multimedia Tools Appl. (2016)
7. Charfeddine, M., Elarbi, M., Koubaa, M., Amar, C.B.: DCT based blind audio watermarking scheme. In: SIGMAP, pp. 139–144 (2010)
8. Choi, J., Reaz, A.S., Mukherjee, B.: A survey of user behavior in VOD service and bandwidth-saving multicast streaming schemes. IEEE Commun. Surv. Tutorials **14**(1), 156–169 (2012)
9. Elarbi, M., Charfeddine, M., Masmoudi, S., Amar, M.: Video watermarking algorithm with BCH error correcting codes hidden in audio channel. In: IEEE Symposium on Computational Intelligence in Cyber Security, CICS 2011, Paris, France 11–15 April 2011, pp. 164–170 (2011)
10. El'arbi, M., Koubaa, M., Charfeddine, M., Amar, C.B.: A dynamic video watermarking algorithm in fast motion areas in the wavelet domain. Multimedia Tools Appl. **55**(3), 579–600 (2011)

11. Furon, T., Pérez-Freire, L.: Worst case attacks against binary probabilistic traitor tracing codes. CoRR abs/0903.3480 (2009)
12. Hamida, A.B., Koubàa, M., Nicolas, H.: Hierarchical traceability of multimedia documents. In: Computational Intelligence in Cyber Security, pp. 108–113 (2011)
13. He, S., Wu, M.: Collusion-resistant video fingerprinting for large user group. IEEE Trans. Inf. Forensics Secur. **2**(4), 697–709 (2007)
14. Laarhoven, T., de Weger, B.: Optimal symmetric Tardos traitor tracing schemes. CoRR abs/1107.3441 (2011)
15. Liu, K.: Multimedia Fingerprinting Forensics for Traitor Tracing. EURASIP Book Series on Signal Processing and Communications. Hindawi Publishing Corporation, Cairo (2005)
16. Liu, N., Cui, H., Chan, S.H.G., Chen, Z., Zhuang, Y.: Dissecting user behaviors for a simultaneous live and VOD IPTV system. TOMCCAP **10**(3), 23 (2014)
17. Mejdoub, M., Fonteles, L.H., Amar, C.B., Antonini, M.: Fast indexing method for image retrieval using tree-structured lattices. In: International Workshop on Content-Based Multimedia Indexing, CBMI 2008, London, UK, 18–20 June 2008, pp. 365–372 (2008)
18. Peikert, C., shelat, A., Smith, A.: Lower bounds for collusion-secure fingerprinting. In: Proceedings of the Fourteenth Annual ACM-SIAM Symposium on Discrete Algorithms, pp. 472–479 (2003)
19. Tardos, G.: Optimal probabilistic fingerprint codes. In: STOC, pp. 116–125 (2003)
20. Wali, A., Ben Aoun, N., Karray, H., Ben Amar, C., Alimi, A.M.: A new system for event detection from video surveillance sequences. In: Blanc-Talon, J., Bone, D., Philips, W., Popescu, D., Scheunders, P. (eds.) ACIVS 2010. LNCS, vol. 6475, pp. 110–120. Springer, Heidelberg (2010). doi:10.1007/978-3-642-17691-3_11
21. Wang, Z.J., Wu, M., Zhao, H., Liu, K.J.R., Trappe, W.: Resistance of orthogonal Gaussian fingerprints to collusion attacks. In: 2003 International Conference on Multimedia and Expo, 2003, ICME 2003. Proceedings, vol. 1, pp. I-617–I-620, July 2003
22. Wang, Z.J., Wu, M., Trappe, W., Liu, K.J.R.: Group-oriented fingerprinting for multimedia forensics. EURASIP J. Appl. Signal Process. **2004**(14), 2153–2173 (2004)
23. Ye, C., Ling, H., Zou, F., Lu, Z.: A new fingerprinting scheme using social network analysis for majority attack. Telecommun. Syst. **54**(3), 315–331 (2013)
24. Yong, Z., Aixin, Z., Songnian, L.: DCT fingerprint classifier based group fingerprint. In: 2014 International Conference on Audio, Language and Image Processing (ICALIP), pp. 292–295, July 2014

Generation of Reducts Based on Nearest Neighbor Relations and Boolean Reasoning

Naohiro Ishii[1(✉)], Ippei Torii[1], Kazunori Iwata[2], Kazuya Odagiri[3], and Toyoshiro Nakashima[3]

[1] Aichi Institute of Technology, Toyota, Japan
{ishii,mac}@aitech.ac.jp
[2] Aichi University, Nagoya, Japan
kazunori@vega.aichi-u.ac.jp
[3] Sugiyama Jyogakuen University, Nagoya, Japan
{odagiri,nakasima}@sugiyama-u.ac.jp

Abstract. Dimension reduction of data is an important issue in the data processing and it is needed for the analysis of higher dimensional data in the application domains. Rough set is fundamental and useful to reduce higher dimensional data to lower one. Reduct in the rough set is a minimal subset of features, which has the same discernible power as the entire features in the higher dimensional scheme. It is shown that nearest neighbor relation with minimal distance proposed here has a fundamental information for classification. In this paper, the nearest neighbor relation plays a fundamental role for generation of reducts using the Boolean reasoning. Then, two reduct generation methods based on the nearest neighbor relation with minimal distance are proposed here, which are derived from Boolean expression of nearest neighbor relations and their operations.

Keywords: Reduct · Nearest neighbor relation · Indiscernibility matrix · Boolean reasoning · Classification

1 Introduction

Rough sets theory firstly introduced by Pawlak [1, 2] provides us a new approach to perform data analysis, practically. Up to now, rough set has been applied successfully and widely in machine learning and data mining. The need to manipulate higher dimensional data in the web and to support or process them gives rise to the question of how to represent the data in a lower-dimensional space to allow more space and time for efficient computation. Thus, dimension reduction of data still remains as an important problem. An important task in rough set based data analysis is computation of the attributes or feature reducts for the classification. By Pawlak's [1, 2] rough set theory, a reduct is a minimal subset of features, which has the discernibility power as using the entire features. Skowlon [3, 4] developed the reduct derivation by using the Boolean expression for the discernibility of data. But, generating reducts is a computationally complex task in which the computational complexity may grow non-polynomially with the number of attributes in data set [3, 5]. So, a new concept for the efficient generation

F.J. Martínez de Pisón et al. (Eds.): HAIS 2017, LNAI 10334, pp. 391–401, 2017.
DOI: 10.1007/978-3-319-59650-1_33

of reducts is expected. In this paper, first, nearest neighbor relation with minimal distance between different classes proposed here has a basic information for classification. We have developed further analysis for the generation of reducts by using the nearest neighbor relations and the Boolean reasoning. Second, we propose here a new reduct generation methods based on the nearest neighbor relation with minimal distance and the Boolean reasoning, in which indiscernibility matrix of data is newly defined. Then, the generation methods of the nearest neighbor relation are useful for the classified data with groups.

2 Boolean Reasoning of Reducts

Skowron proposed to represent a decision table in the form of the discernibility matrix [3, 4]. This representation has many advantages, in particular it enables simple computation of the core, reducts and other concepts [1–3]. The discernibility matrix is computed for pairs of instances and stores the different variables(attributes) between all possible pairs of instances that must remain discernible.

Definition 1. The discernibility matrix $M(T)$ is defined as follows. Let $T = \{U, A, C, D\}$ be a decision table, with $U = \{x_1, x_2, \ldots, x_n\}$, set of instances. A is a subset of C called condition, and D is a set of decision classes. By a discernibility matrix of T, denoted by $M(T)$, which is $n \times n$ matrix defined as

$$\begin{aligned} c_{ij} = \{a \in C : a(x_i) \neq a(x_j) \\ \wedge (d \in D, d(x_i) \neq d(x_j))\}\, i,j = 1,2,\ldots n, \end{aligned} \tag{1}$$

where U is the universe of discourse, C is a set of features or attributes.

Definition 2. A discernibility function f_A for A is a propositional formula of m Boolean variables, $a_1^*, \ldots, a_m^*$, corresponding to the attributes $a_1, \ldots, a_m$, defined by

$$f_A(a_1^*, \ldots, a_m^*) = \bigwedge_{1 \leq j < i \leq m} \bigvee_{c \in c_{ij}^*, c_{ij}^* \neq \phi} c_{ij} \tag{2}$$

where $c_{ij}^* = \{a^* : a \in c_{ij}\}$ [3]. In the sequel, a_i is used instead of a_i^*, for simplicity.

It can be shown that the set of all prime implicants of f_A determines the set of all reducts, which are derived from the Boolean Eq. (2). The Boolean Eq. (2) is the Boolean conjunctive normal form. This equation is simplified to the Boolean disjunctive normal form by using the Boolean absorption law. An example of decision table of the data set is shown in Table 1.

The left side data in the column in Table 1 as shown in, $\{x_1, x_2, x_3, \ldots x_7\}$ is a set of instances, while the data $\{a, b, c, d\}$ on the upper row, shows the set of attributes of the instance. The contents of each row in Table 1 shows numeral values of the corresponding instance. The class shows that the corresponding instance belongs to the numeral class value +1 or -1.

Table 1. Decision table of data example (instances)

Attribute	a	b	c	d	Class
x_1	1	0	2	1	+1
x_2	1	0	2	0	+1
x_3	2	2	0	0	−1
x_4	1	2	2	1	−1
x_5	2	1	0	1	−1
x_6	2	1	1	0	+1
x_7	2	1	2	1	−1

In Table 2, the discernibility matrix of the decision table in Table 1 is shown. In case of instance x_1, the value of the attribute a, is $\mathrm{a}(x_1) = 1$. That of the attribute b, is $\mathrm{b}(x_1) = 0$. Since $\mathrm{a}(x_1) = 1$ and $\mathrm{a}(x_5) = 2$, $\mathrm{a}(x_1) \neq \mathrm{a}(x_5)$ holds.

Table 2. Discernibility matrix of the decision table in Table 1

	x_1	x_2	x_3	x_4	x_5	x_6
x_2	—					
x_3	a,b,c,d	a,b,c				
x_4	b	b,d	—			
x_5	a,b,c	a,b,c,d	—	—		
x_6	—	—	b,c	a,b,c,d	c,d	
x_7	a,b	a,b,d	—	—	—	c,d

The discernibility function is represented by taking the combination of the disjunction expression of the discernibility matrix. In Table 2, the item (b, c, d) in the second row and the first column, implies $b+c+d$ in the Boolean sum expression, which shows the attribute b or c or d appears for the discrimination between instances x_1 and x_3 [3]. By using nearest neighbor relation, generation of reducts is developed in the next session, in which nearest neighbor plays an important role on the discernibility matrix.

2.1 Nearest Neighbor Relation with Minimal Distance

Nearest neighbor relation with minimal distance is introduced here. The relation with minimal distance plays an important role in the generation of reducts. The nearest neighbor relation with minimal distance implies the items in the discernibility matrix, which have the minimal distance between the different classes. In Table 2, The shaded item (a, b) makes the minimal distance, $\sqrt{2}$ between x_1 and x_7, since the distance x_1 in the class +1 and x_7 in the class −1 becomes $\sqrt{2}$. Also, the same minimal distance, is $\sqrt{2}$ computed between x_3 in the class −1 and x_6 in the class +1. Similarly, it is computed between x_5 and x_6. These three items in Table 2 are shown in the shaded items. Boolean characteristics are derived in the discernibility matrix in Table 2 in the following Sect. 3. Pair instances which are located nearest to different classes are picked up to make nearest neighbor relation. They are called to be in the nearest neighbor relation with minimum distance.

3 Generation of Reducts Based on Nearest Neighbor Relation and External Set

We can define a new concept, a nearest neighbor relation with minimal distance, δ. Instances with different classes are assumed to be measured in the metric distances for the nearest neighbor classification [6, 8–11]. The advantage of the proposed generation of reducts is to use nearest neighbor relations on the discernibility matrix and their related data, while the conventional methods use all data on the discernibility matrix. [3, 7]. Thus, the nearest neighbor relation is in the subset on the discernibility matrix.

Definition 3. A nearest neighbor relation with minimal distance is a set of pair of instances, which are described in

$$\{(x_i, x_j) : d(x_i) \neq d(x_j) \wedge |x_i - x_j| \leq \delta\}, \tag{3}$$

where $|x_i - x_j|$ shows the distance between x_i and x_j and δ is the minimal distance.

Then, x_i and x_j in the Eq. (3) are called to be in the nearest neighbor relation with minimal distance δ. To find minimal nearest neighbor relation, the divide and conquer algorithm [12] is applied to the array of instances in Table 1 with the search of the nearest data so as to be classified to different classes. In Fig. 1, $x_4 \rightarrow x_7 \rightarrow x_1$ ... are searched using the algorithm with distance circles, iteratively.

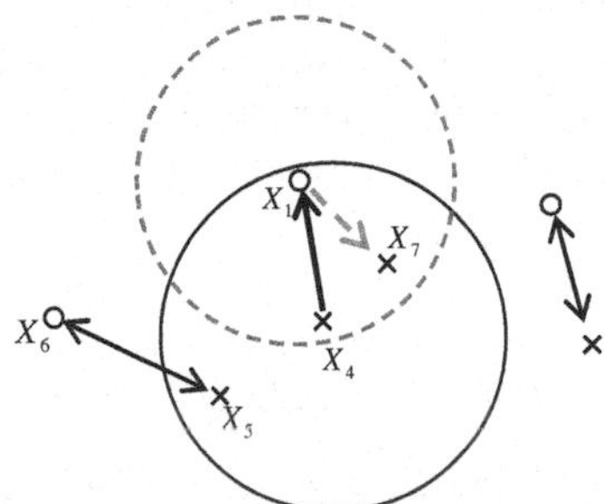

Fig. 1. Search of nearest neighbor relations

In Table 1, $(x_6, x_7), (x_5, x_6), (x_1, x_7)$ and (x_3, x_6) are elements of the relation with a distance $\sqrt{2}$. Thus, a nearest neighbor relation with minimal distance $\sqrt{2}$ becomes

$$\{(x_6, x_7), (x_5, x_6), (x_1, x_7), (x_3, x_6)\} \tag{4}$$

Here, we want to introduce the nearest neighbor relation on the discernibility matrix. Assume that the set of elements of the nearest neighbor relation are $\{nn_{ij}\}$. The following characteristics are shown. Respective element of the set $\{nn_{ij}\}$ corresponds to the term in Boolean sum expression [3]. As an example, the item (a, b, c) of discernibility matrix in the set $\{nn_{ij}\}$ corresponds to a Boolean sum $(a + b + c)$. The following lemmas are derived easily.

Lemma 1. Respective Boolean term consisting of the set $\{nn_{ij}\}$ becomes a necessary condition to be reducts in the Boolean expression.

This is trivial, since the product of respective Boolean term becomes reducts in the Boolean expression.

Lemma 2. Boolean product of respective terms corresponding to the set $\{nn_{ij}\}$ becomes a necessary condition to be reducts in the Boolean expression.

This is also trivial by the reason of Lemma 1. Thus, the relation between Lemmas 1 and 2 is described as

Lemma 3. Reducts in the Boolean expression are included in the Boolean term of Lemma 1 and the Boolean product in Lemma 2.

Figure 2 shows that nearest neighbor relation with classification is a necessary condition in the Boolean expression for reducts, but not sufficient condition. The distance δ of the nearest neighbor relation in the Eq. (3) is compared with the distance δ' of the relation in the following theorem.

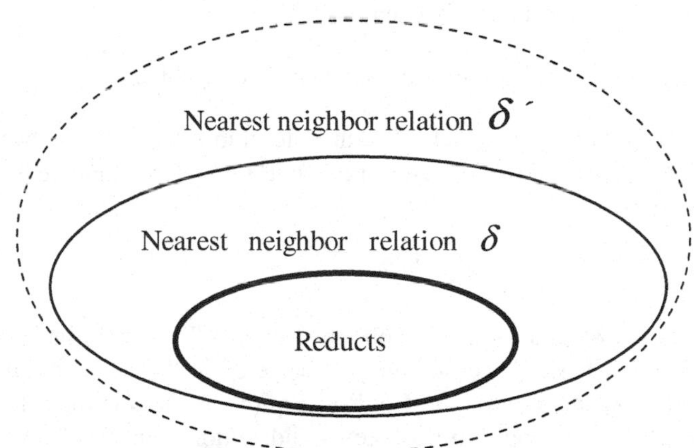

Fig. 2. Boolean condition of nearest neighbor relations and reducts

Theorem 4. If the distance δ is greater than the δ', i.e., $\delta > \delta'$ in the Eq. (3), the Boolean expression of the case of δ' includes that of δ.

This is by the reason that the Boolean expression of the nearest neighbor relation is consists of the Boolean product of variables of the relation. The number of variables in the distance δ' are less than that of δ. Thus, the nearest neighbor relation with distance δ' includes the ellipse of δ in Fig. 2.

Two sets of attributes (variables), (A) and (B) are defined to extract reducts from the nearest neighbor relation $\{nn_{ij}\}$.

(A): Set of elements in the discernibility matrix includes those of any respective element in $\{nn_{ij}\}$ and those of elements absorbed by $\{nn_{ij}\}$ in the Boolean expression.

(B): Set of elements in the discernibility matrix, which are not absorbed from those of any respective element in $\{nn_{ij}\}$, which is called here set (B) or external set.

The Boolean sum of attributes is absorbed in the Boolean sum element with the same fewer attributes in the set $\{nn_{ij}\}$. As an example, the Boolean sum of $(a+b+c)$ in the set (A) is absorbed in the Boolean sum of $(a+b)$ in the set $\{nn_{ij}\}$.

Lemma 5. Within set (B), the element with fewer attributes (variables) plays a role of the absorption for the element with larger attributes (variables).

Then, the absorption operation is carried out within set (B).

Theorem 6. Reducts are derived from the nearest neighbor relation by the absorption of variables in set (B) terms in the Boolean expression.

In the relation (x_1, x_7) in Table 1, the x_1 in the class +1 is nearest to the is x_7 in the class -1. Similarly, (x_5, x_6) and (x_6, x_7) are nearest relations. Then, variables of the set (A) in these relations are shown in shading in Table 2 of the discernible matrix. The Boolean product of these four terms becomes

$$(a+b)\cdot(b+c)\cdot(c+d) = b\cdot c + b\cdot d + a\cdot c, \tag{5}$$

which becomes a candidate of reducts. The third term in the Eq. (5) is absorbed by the product of variable {b} of the set (B) and the Eq. (5). The final reducts Boolean equation becomes

$$b\cdot c + b\cdot d \tag{6}$$

Thus, reducts $\{b,\ c\}$ and $\{b,\ d\}$ are obtained finally. To search final reducts in the Eq. (5), the following Boolean reasoning is considered at the class (A) of the nearest neighbor relations. At the step of the Boolean Eq. (4), some dominant Boolean variables are searched from the bottom up. The candidate dominant Boolean variables are shown in Fig. 3. From the Eq. (5), three Boolean minterms $b\cdot c$, $b\cdot d$ and $a\cdot c$ are derived from the nearest neighbor relations. The common variables are candidates of the dominant variables between three terms.

From the set (B), the dominant variables are searched in Table 2. Thus, the variable (b) is searched from the set (B), which is not in the set (A).

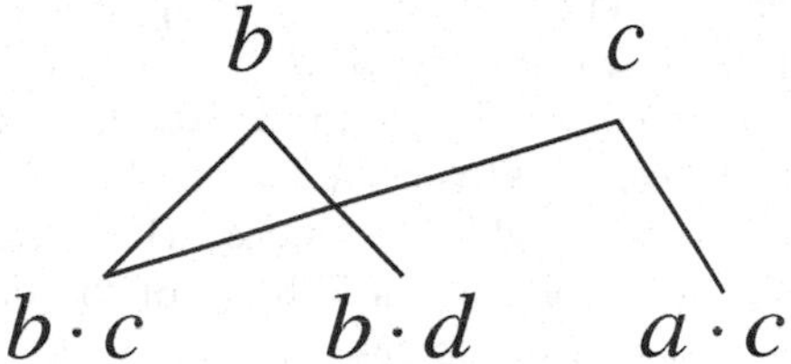

Fig. 3. Dominant boolean variables of the set (A)

4 Generation of Reducts Based on Nearest Neighbor Relation and Indiscernibility Matrix

In this section, we propose another generation method of reducts, which is based on nearest neighbor relation and indiscernibility matrix proposed here. To test the sufficiency condition for the candidate reducts, which are derived from the nearest neighbor relation on the discernibility matrix, a new indiscernibility matrix is proposed here. The indiscernibility matrix is computed for pairs of instances and stores the same variables between all possible pairs of instances.

Definition 4. Indiscernibility matrix is defined to be $IM(T)$, which is $n \times n$ matrix defined as

$$c_{ij} = \{a \in C : a(x_i) = a(x_j) \\ \wedge (d \in D, d(x_i) \neq d(x_j))\} \quad i,j = 1,2,\ldots n, \tag{7}$$

where U is the universe of discourse, C is a set of features or attributes.

The difference between $M(T)$ in the Eq. (1) and $IM(T)$ in the Eq. (7), is shown in the following. Attributes $a(x_i) \neq a(x_j)$ holds in $M(T)$, while $a(x_i) = a(x_j)$ holds in $IM(T)$. The example of the indiscernible matrix $IM(T)$ for Table 1 of decision table T is shown in Table 3. Indiscernibility shows the instance x_i in the row has the same variables at the instance x_j in the column, in which x_i and x_j belong to the different classes. For example, the instance x_2 in the class +1 and the instance x_4 in the class −1, cannot be discriminated by only variables a and c, since they are the same variables. Since the Boolean operation in the element of the indiscernible matrix is AND, the

Table 3. Indiscernibility matrix of the decision table in Table 1

	x_1	x_2	x_3	x_4	x_5	x_6
x_2	—					
x_3	—	d				
x_4	a,c,d	a,c	—			
x_5	d	—	—	—		
x_6	—	—	a,d	—	a,b	
x_7	c,d	c	—	—	—	a,b

element (a, c, d) between x_1 and x_4 shows Boolean product $a \cdot c \cdot d$. The Boolean product $a \cdot b \cdot c$ also implies $a \cdot c$ or $c \cdot d$ or $a \cdot d$.

In the Sect. 2, the nearest neighbor relation is derived from Table 1. In the relation (x_1, x_7) in Table 1, the x_1 in the class +1 is nearest to the is x_7 in the class −1. Similarly, (x_5, x_6) and (x_6, x_7) are nearest neighbor relations. Then, variables of the nearest neighbor relations are shown in shading in Table 2 of the discernible matrix. The Boolean product of these four terms becomes

$$(a+b) \cdot (b+c) \cdot (c+d) = b \cdot c + b \cdot d + a \cdot c \tag{8}$$

In the three minterms in the above Boolean Eq. (8), the minterm $a \cdot c$ in Eq. (8) is checked in the indiscernibility matrix Table 3. The $(a \cdot c)$ is found between x_1 and x_4, also between x_2 and x_4. The minterm $a \cdot c$ cannot discriminate instances between x_1 and x_4, also between x_2 and x_4. Then, the minterm $a \cdot c$ is removed from the Eq. (8). Thus, the implicant

$$b \cdot c + b \cdot d \tag{9}$$

is obtained, which is the same derived in the Eq. (6). Thus, reducts $\{b, c\}$ and $\{b, d\}$ are obtained. Another example is shown in Table 4.

Table 4. Decision table of another data (instances)

Attribute	a	b	c	d	Class
x_1	1	0	2	1	+1
x_2	1	1	2	0	+1
x_3	1	2	0	0	−1
x_4	1	2	2	1	−1
x_5	2	1	0	1	−1
x_6	2	1	1	0	+1
x_7	2	1	2	1	−1

The nearest neighbor relations are computed in data of instances Table 4 as the method developed in Sect. 2. Then, the relations become

$$(x_1, x_7), (x_2, x_4), (x_2, x_7), (x_5, x_6) \text{ and } (x_6, x_7) \tag{10}$$

are shown in Table 5, in which the shadowed variable data in the element make nearest neighbor relations. Thus, Boolean data of the nearest neighbor relations become

$$(a, b), (a, d), (b, d) \text{ and } (c, d) \tag{11}$$

The Boolean product of respective Boolean sum becomes

$$\begin{aligned} (a+b) \cdot (a+d) \cdot (b+d) \cdot (c+d) &= (a + b \cdot d) \cdot (d + b \cdot c) \\ &= a \cdot d + b \cdot d + a \cdot b \cdot c \end{aligned} \tag{12}$$

Table 5. Discernibility matrix of the decision table in Table 4

	x_1	x_2	x_3	x_4	x_5	x_6
x_2	—					
x_3	b,c,d	b,c				
x_4	b	b,d	—			
x_5	a,b,c	a,c,d	—	—		
x_6	—	—	a,b,c	a,b,c,d	c,d	
x_7	a,b	a,d	—	—	—	c,d

Table 6. Indiscernibility matrix of the decision table in Table 4

	x_1	x_2	x_3	x_4	x_5	x_6
x_2	—					
x_3	a	a,d				
x_4	a,c,d	a,c	—			
x_5	d	—	—	—		
x_6	—	—	d	—	a,b	
x_7	c,d	b,c	—	—	—	a,b

Next, the indiscernibility matrix in Table 4 is shown in Table 6.

The minterm $a \cdot d$ in Eq. (12) exists in the indiscernibility matrix in Table 6, which is shown in the shadow. The (a, c, d) in Table 6, implies Boolean product, $a \cdot c$ or $c \cdot d$ or $a \cdot d$. The Boolean product $a \cdot d$ in the Eq. (12) must be removed, since $a \cdot d$ exists in two elements in the matrix $IM(T)$ in Table 6. Thus, the Boolean implicant for reducts for data in Table 4 becomes

$$b \cdot d + a \cdot b \cdot c$$

Thus, reducts become $\{b, d\}$ and $\{a, b, c\}$.

4.1 Relation Between External Set and Indiscernibility Matrix

For the one generation method of reducts, set (A) and set (B) called external set are defined in Sect. 3 and the other generation method uses indiscernibility matrix in Sect. 4. The set (B) in Table 2, becomes $\{b, (b, d)\}$, which is remained after Boolean absorption by the set of nearest neighbor relations. In the set (B), the variable (b, d) is expressed in Boolean sum $(b + d)$. The variable b of Boolean product with $(b + d)$ becomes by Boolean absorption law,

$$b \cdot (b + d) = b + b \cdot d = b$$

Thus, the variable b represents the set (B). The variable b multiplied by the Boolean form of the set (A) derived from the nearest neighbor relation becomes

$$b \cdot (a \cdot c + b \cdot c + b \cdot d) = b \cdot c + b \cdot d$$

The element variable (a, c, d) in indiscernibility table, which is placed in the same element in discernibility matrix, removes the Boolean minterm $a \cdot c$. Thus, the final implicant in the Boolean form becomes

$$b \cdot c + b \cdot d$$

This shows the obtained reducts are $\{b, c\}$ and $\{b, d\}$.

Theorem 7. The Boolean absorption of the variables in the set (B) multiplied by the Boolean forms derived from the nearest neighbor relations generate reducts, which are also generated by directly removing Boolean variables in the indiscernibility matrix from the Boolean forms of the nearest neighbor relations.

5 Conclusion

Nearest neighbor relation developed here is the set of pair elements with minimal distance, which classify between different classes. Reduct is introduced as the minimal set for the data classification in the rough set theory. We proposed two methods of generation of reducts. First, this paper develops the role of the nearest neighbor relations for the generation and the data classification of the reducts from the point of Boolean reasoning. The generations of reducts are based on the nearest neighbor relation proposed in this paper. First, the data in the discernibility matrix are classified to the set absorbed by Boolean minterms of the nearest neighbor relation and the external set not absorbed by them. Second, the Boolean implicant of the nearest neighbor relations are made. Then, the minterms are removed, if the variables of them exist in the indiscernibility matrix developed in this paper. Thus the obtained implicant becomes reducts. Generations of reducts based on the nearest neighbor methods are useful for the classified data with different groups.

References

1. Pawlak, Z.: Rough Sets. Int. J. Comput. Inf. Sci. **11**, 341–356 (1982)
2. Pawlak, Z., Slowinski, R.: Rough set approach to multi-attribute decision analysis. Eur. J. Oper. Res. **72**, 443–459 (1994)
3. Skowron, A., Rauszer, C.: The discernibility matrices and functions in information systems. In: Intelligent Decision Support Handbook of Application and Advances of Rough Sets Theory, pp. 331–362. Kluwer Academic Publishers, Dordrecht (1992)
4. Skowron, A., Polkowski, L.: Decision algorithms, a survey of rough set theoretic methods. Fundamenta Informatica **30**(3-4), 345–358 (1997)
5. Meghabghab, G., Kandel, A.: Search Engines, Link Analysis, and User's Web Behavior. Springer, Heidelberg (2008)
6. Cover, T.M., Hart, P.E.: Nearest neighbor pattern classification. IEEE Trans. Inf. Theor. **13**(1), 21–27 (1967)

7. Susmaga, R.: Experiments in incremental computation of reducts. In: Rough Sets in Knowledge Discovery, vol. 1, pp. 530–553. Physica-Verlag (1998)
8. Preparata, F.P., Shamos, M.I.: Computational Geometry. Springer, New York (1993)
9. Ishii, N., Morioka, Y., Bao, Y., Tanaka, H.: Control of variables in reducts - kNN classification with confidence. In: König, A., Dengel, A., Hinkelmann, K., Kise, K., Howlett, Robert J., Jain, Lakhmi C. (eds.) KES 2011. LNCS, vol. 6884, pp. 98–107. Springer, Heidelberg (2011). doi:10.1007/978-3-642-23866-6_11
10. Ishii, N., Torii, I., Bao, Y., Tanaka, H.: Modified reduct nearest neighbor classification. In: Proceedings of ACIS-ICIS, pp. 310–315. IEEE Computer Society (2012)
11. Ishii, N., Torii, I., Mukai, N., Iwata, K., Nakashima, T.: Classification on nonlinear mapping of reducts based on nearest neighbor relation. In: Proceedings of ACIS-ICIS, pp. 491–496. IEEE Computer Society (2015)
12. Levitin, A.V.: Introduction to the Design and Analysis of Algorithms. Addison Wesley, Boston (2002)

Extraction of Outliers from Imbalanced Sets

Pavel Škrabánek[1(✉)] and Natália Martínková[2,3]

[1] Faculty of Electrical Engineering and Informatics, University of Pardubice, Studentská 95, 532 10 Pardubice, Czech Republic
pavel.skrabanek@upce.cz

[2] Institute of Vertebrate Biology, Czech Academy of Sciences, Květná 8, 603 65 Brno, Czech Republic
martinkova@ivb.cz

[3] Institute of Biostatistics and Analyses, Masaryk University, Kamenice 3, 625 00 Brno, Czech Republic

Abstract. In this paper, we presented an outlier detection method, designed for small datasets, such as datasets in animal group behaviour research. The method was aimed at detection of global outliers in unlabelled datasets where inliers form one predominant cluster and the outliers are at distances from the centre of the cluster. Simultaneously, the number of inliers was much higher than the number of outliers. The extraction of exceptional observations (EEO) method was based on the Mahalanobis distance with one tuning parameter. We proposed a visualization method, which allows expert estimation of the tuning parameter value. The method was tested and evaluated on 44 datasets. Excellent results, fully comparable with other methods, were obtained on datasets satisfying the method requirements. For large datasets, the higher computational requirement of this method might be prohibitive. This drawback can be partially suppressed with an alternative distance measure. We proposed to use Euclidean distance in combination with standard deviation normalization as a reliable alternative.

Keywords: Outlier analysis · Distance based method · Global outlier · Single cluster · Mahalanobis distance · Biology

1 Introduction

Data mining reveals new, valuable and non-trivial information in large datasets [14]. It is a process of discovering interesting patterns and knowledge in the data that is not immediately apparent. Various data mining approaches help to specify the patterns in the data mining tasks. Examples include characterization and discrimination, mining of frequent patterns, associations and correlations, classification and regression, clustering analysis, and outlier analysis [10].

The outlier analysis has an important position among data mining approaches. Hawkins specified an intuitive definition of the term *outlier* as: 'Within a given dataset, the outlier is an observation which deviates so much

F.J. Martínez de Pisón et al. (Eds.): HAIS 2017, LNAI 10334, pp. 402–412, 2017.
DOI: 10.1007/978-3-319-59650-1_34

from other observations as to arouse suspicions that it was generated by a different mechanism' [11]. The other observations are usually called *inliers*, *normal data* or *normal observations*. Throughout the text, a predetermined battery of *features* characterizes an observation.

The outlier analysis is used in a wide variety of domains such as the financial industry, quality control, fault diagnosis, intrusion detection, web analytics, and medical diagnosis [2]. The most typical application of the outlier analysis is data cleaning. However, in many applications, outliers are more interesting than inliers. Fraud detection is a classic example, where attention focuses on the outliers, because these more likely represent cases of fraudulent behaviour [12].

The outlier analysis distinguishes three categories of outliers that require specific analytical approaches: *global outliers*, *contextual outliers* (known also as *conditional outliers*), and *collective outliers* [10]. A global outlier is an observation that deviates significantly from the rest of the dataset, whereas a contextual outlier deviates from inliers only with respect to a specific context. The term collective outlier is used for a subset of observations. A subset of observations forms a collective outlier if the subset as a whole deviates significantly from the entire dataset.

To identify outliers, the outlier detection methods create models of normal patterns in the data (so called *data model* or simply *model*), and then compute an *outlier score* of a given observation on the basis of the deviations from the normal patterns [2]. The outlier detection methods utilize *clustering models*, *distance-based models*, *density-based models*, *probabilistic* and *statistical models*, *classification models*, and *information theoretic models* [2,10].

The selection of the model and outlier score calculation is data-specific and relies on assumptions of information contained in the data. For example, classification models require datasets of labelled observations. Methods based on other models, e.g. statistical models or distance-based models, can be applied to both labelled as well as unlabelled datasets.

The correct choice of the method from the perspective of the data model determines results of the outlier analysis [2]. For example, application of a method based on a statistical model, which expects a uniform distribution of inliers, would be inappropriate for a dataset with the zipf distribution.

In biology, animal group behaviour studies generate specific datasets of observable variables pre-selected in the experimental design [5,18]. Typically, such datasets are unlabelled and may contain numerical as well as categorical data. Given the complexity of animal behaviour, feature space of the observed variables will not be exhaustive on an individual level and determinants of group behaviour will exhibit subtle trends. From amongst the data mining approaches, the outlier analysis provides functionality to identify observations putatively generated by an alternative mechanism, which makes the analysis suitable for application in animal group behaviour research. In order to ensure a simple and reliable recognition of the outliers in such a dataset, we developed an outlier detection method. Our method detects global outliers using a distance-based model. Here, we introduce the method for numerical data.

2 Methods

2.1 Analysis of the Problem

A dataset considered for application with the proposed method contains inliers that form one multidimensional cluster, while the outliers span at a distance from the cluster centre. The outliers may or may not form small clusters. The total number of observations in the dataset range from tens to hundreds of observations. Further, distribution of inliers may significantly vary among various datasets. The data contains no prior knowledge about the outliers, and the information embodied in the outliers is the object of interest. These datasets may include both numerical and categorical data; however, the proposed method is intended for datasets composed of numerical data.

The first step in developing a new outlier detection method is identification of the outlier category. Following the above stated setup, the proposed method detects global outliers. The second step, selection of the model for inliers, delineates the direction of the development process. Herein, we use backward selection to select the proper model. Information-theoretic models are impropriate for the defined datasets, because of the expected type of features. Without prior knowledge about the outliers, the new detection method cannot be based on a classification model. As different datasets may have different distributions of inliers, usage of a probabilistic, density-based or a statistical model is inadvisable. Consequently, the method has to be based on one of the remaining model types; clustering or distance-based models.

Both clustering models and distance-based models represent appropriate choices for the new outlier detection method given the data. Between them, distance-based methods enable a higher granularity of analysis as compared to clustering methods. This property of distance-based methods provides a more refined ability to distinguish between weak and strong outliers in noisy data sets [2]. Hence, the presented method has been developed on a distance-based model.

2.2 Description of the Method

Let $X = \{\mathbf{x}_1, \ldots, \mathbf{x}_n\}$ be a set of n observations $\mathbf{x}$. The i-th observation $\mathbf{x}_i$, where $i \in I$ and $I = \{1, \ldots, n\}$, is a d-dimensional real vector $\mathbf{x}_i = (x_{i1}, \ldots, x_{id})$ of features $x \in \mathcal{F}$, where x_{ik} is the k-th feature of the i-th observation, and $\mathcal{F}$ is a feature space. Let us expect that the majority of the observations, say m, belongs to inliers. The remaining p observations correspond to outliers. A subset of all outliers in the set X will be denoted as O.

The presented method belongs to the group of outlier detection methods based on a distance model. It assumes two attributes in the observations $\mathbf{x} \in X$:

(I) inliers form one predominant cluster and the outliers are at distances from the centre of the cluster,
(II) the number of inliers is much higher than the number of outliers ($m >> p$).

In order to design the separation method, the outlier score had to be properly formulized. For this purpose, an appropriate similarity measure had to be chosen. Similarity of two observations, say $\mathbf{x}_i$, $\mathbf{x}_j \in X$, was assessed using a distance measure. In order to ensure a comparable level of impact for all the features $x \in \mathcal{F}$, the observations should be compared with normalized data or the measure should be unitless and scale-invariant. In our solution, we used Mahalanobis distance [4,7]. This measure is unitless and scale-invariant. For the observations $\mathbf{x}_i, \mathbf{x}_j$, the Mahalanobis distance is defined as

$$d\left(\mathbf{x}_i, \mathbf{x}_j\right) = \sqrt{(\mathbf{x}_i - \mathbf{x}_j)\mathbf{S}^{-1}(\mathbf{x}_i - \mathbf{x}_j)^\top}, \tag{1}$$

where $\mathbf{S}$ is a covariance matrix, and $\top$ symbolizes transposition.

Considering the properties of the datasets expressed via the assumptions (I) and (II), we proposed to formulate the outlier score J for the i-th observation as the sum of distances between the i-th observation and the others, i.e.

$$J_i = \sum_{\forall j \in I} d\left(\mathbf{x}_i, \mathbf{x}_j\right). \tag{2}$$

The distance-based methods usually take into account distances between an evaluated observation and its k nearest neighbours. Nevertheless, the outlier score (2) considers all n distances. An example demonstrates rationalization for the formulation of the score. In Fig. 1, the number of distances is identical regardless of whether an inlier (Fig. 1a) or an outlier (Fig. 1b) is evaluated; however, distributions of their values differ. For the outliers, longer distances appear more frequently than for inliers. This holds for an arbitrarily chosen inlier and outlier, since inliers form a single cluster and $m >> p$.

The specific properties of the dataset lead to the conclusion that the greater the number of nearest neighbours which are included in the analysis, the larger the difference between scores of inliers and outliers. Consequently, inclusion of all observations in the comparison results in higher sensitivity of the method. The associated increase in computational complexity of the method is irrelevant for the expected dataset sizes. For larger datasets, a GPU optimized variant of the method may be developed [3].

Observations evaluated using the outlier score (2) can be easily classified as outliers or inliers using a threshold value t. In our case, the unusual structure of the dataset X inspired the analytical expression of t. Indeed, values of the score for inliers are markedly smaller than for outliers. Considering this fact and the fact that $m >> p$, median of the score's values $\hat{J}$ adequately describes inliers. On the basis of the median and the smallest score values, the range of score values of inliers can be estimated. Thus, the threshold value can be expressed as

$$t = \varepsilon.[\hat{J} - \min_{\forall i \in I} J_i] + \hat{J}, \tag{3}$$

where the parameter ε is used as a tuning parameter. Each observation with a score equal to or greater than the threshold value t is expected to be an outlier.

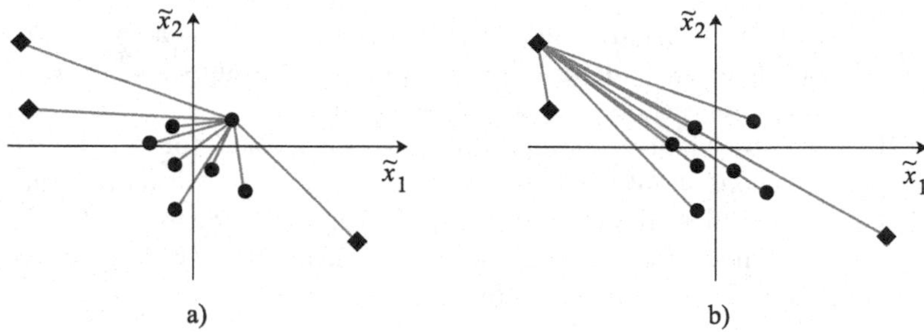

Fig. 1. Demonstration of the idea behind the outlier score by evaluation of: (a) an inlier, and (b) an outlier. In both figure panels, three outliers (diamonds) and seven inliers (circles) are plotted on a two-dimensional centred, rotated and standardized feature space $\tilde{x}_1, \tilde{x}_2 \in \tilde{\mathcal{F}}$. The distance between two observations is symbolized using a red line. (Color figure online)

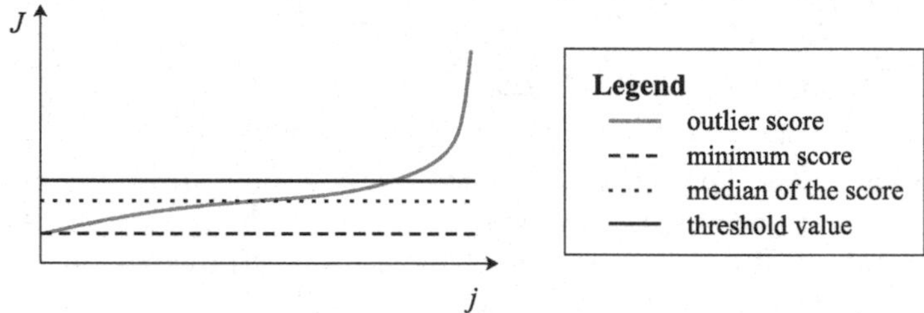

Fig. 2. Visualization of the score J as a function j where j are indexes of the observations sorted according to J in the ascending order. Threshold for outlier classification t is placed at a point with rapid change in score trend

The presented method has one tuning parameter ε, and its setting significantly predetermines the output of the method. We proposed a visualization method in order to estimate the accurate value for ε. The visualization displays a continuous line connecting scores J for $\forall \mathbf{x} \in X$, where the scores are sorted in ascending order. The line is approximately exponential. The initial lag phase with gradual increase in J, includes inliers, and the subsequent exponential phase includes outliers. Using the graph, an expert can estimate the boundary between inliers and outliers and accordingly the threshold value determining ε (Fig. 2).

For datasets satisfying the assumptions, the right placement of the auxiliary line is straightforward. However, the more the dataset X deviates from the ideal, the deeper understanding of the data is necessary for the appropriate placement.

2.3 Algorithmic Expression of the Method

The proposed method can be realized as a function, here presented as a pseudocode (Algorithm 1). The function has two inputs and two outputs. The inputs are the set of observations X and the tuning parameter ε. The outputs are a set of all outliers O and a set of outliers indexes I_o in the original set X.

Algorithm 1. Extraction of Exceptional Observations

function EEO(X, ε)

Input: Set of n observations $X = \{\mathbf{x}_1, \ldots, \mathbf{x}_n\}$, constant ε specifying the limit for outliers

Output: Set O of all outliers and set of their indexes I_o in X

$J_i \leftarrow \sum_{\forall j \in I} d(\mathbf{x}_i, \mathbf{x}_j), \forall i \in I$ ▷ Evaluation of observations using the criterion

$t \leftarrow \varepsilon.[\hat{J} - \min_{\forall i \in I} J_i] + \hat{J}$ ▷ Threshold value for exceptional observations

$I_o \leftarrow \{i : i \in I \text{ where } J_i \geq t\}$ ▷ Indexes of exceptional observations

$O \leftarrow \{\mathbf{x}_i : i \in I_o\}$ ▷ Set of exceptional observations

return O, I_o

end function

2.4 Experimental Evaluation of the Method

We used 44 previously published datasets for evaluation of the proposed method [8]. The datasets originated from areas such as biology, medicine, criminology or astronautics. They contained three types of features: R - real numbers, I - integers, and N - nominal values. The datasets consisted of labelled samples with two classes. All datasets were imbalanced with an imbalance ratio $IR = m/p$, where $IR \in [1.82, 129.44]$. We expected that the minority class represented outliers, while the majority class consisted of inliers.

We adapted three performance measures used in binary classification to evaluate results obtained from our method. Namely, we considered *sensitivity* (Se), *specificity* (Sp), and their geometric mean (G) [8,15]. For the outlier analysis, they can be expressed as

$$Se = \frac{|TO|}{|TO| + |FI|}, \qquad Sp = \frac{|TI|}{|TI| + |FO|}, \qquad G = \sqrt{Se \cdot Sp}, \tag{4}$$

where $|TO|$ is the number of correctly recognized outliers (true outliers), $|FO|$ is the number of inliers labelled as outliers (false outliers), $|TI|$ is the number of correctly recognized inliers (true inliers), $|FI|$ is the number of outliers labelled as inliers (false inliers).

We evaluated our method (extraction of exceptional observations, EEO) for two values of ε. Within the first experiment, we estimated the value of ε from the graph (as per Fig. 2). This value was denoted as $\hat{\varepsilon}$. In the second experiment, we searched for an optimal setting (ε^*) using genetic algorithms [16]. The genetic algorithms used the objective function as $\max G(\varepsilon)$. We applied the MATLAB function ga, with no constraints and default settings [1].

3 Results

Due to the presence of nominal variables, EEO could not be applied on datasets 'abalone19' and 'abalone9–18'. Further, it was unsuccessful on datasets 'ecoli-0_vs_1' and 'segment0', in which some features had constant values for all observations. The obtained results are summarized in Table 1. In general, sensitivity of

EEO with manual estimation of $\hat{\varepsilon}$ was lower than for ε^*, established from labelled data with genetic algorithms in lieu of higher specificity. This was accompanied by higher, and thus more conservative, values of $\hat{\varepsilon}$.

To estimate the performance of EEO amongst existing outlier detection methods, we compared our method with Chi et al.'s method with 3 and 5 labels (Chi-3 and Chi-5) [6], Ishibuchi et al.'s method (Ish05) [13], E-Algorithm (E-Alg) [19], Fernández et al.'s method (HFRBCS) [8], and C4.5 decision tree (C4.5) [17]. We adopted the evaluation results published in [8]. The evaluation results using G are summarized for all expected methods, including the EEO with optimal and manual setting of ε, in Table 2.

4 Discussion

The proposed EEO method was tested on 44 datasets previously used for algorithm testing [8]. The datasets differed in the imbalance ratio, in the number of features and their type (Table 1). However, from the viewpoint of EEO testing, many of these datasets did not meet the assumptions that the inliers form one multidimensional cluster (I) and the number of inliers is much higher than the number of inliers (II). This is apparent when displaying the first two principal components of observation scores with their class labels [9]. The dataset 'shuttle-c0-vs-c4' fully met the assumptions (Fig. 3b), and EEO was successful in outlier detection ($G \approx 98$). The datasets 'ecoli-0-1-3-7_vs_2-6', 'shuttle-c2-vs-c4', and 'Wisconsin' similarly showed nearly ideal class assignment with respect to inliers (data not shown). On these datasets, EEO exhibited excellent results according to all three measures (4) both for $\hat{\varepsilon}$ and ε^*. The performance of EEO is fully comparable to all evaluated methods. In fact, EEO provides considerably better separation on 'ecoli-0-1-3-7_vs_2-6' dataset than any other considered method (Table 2).

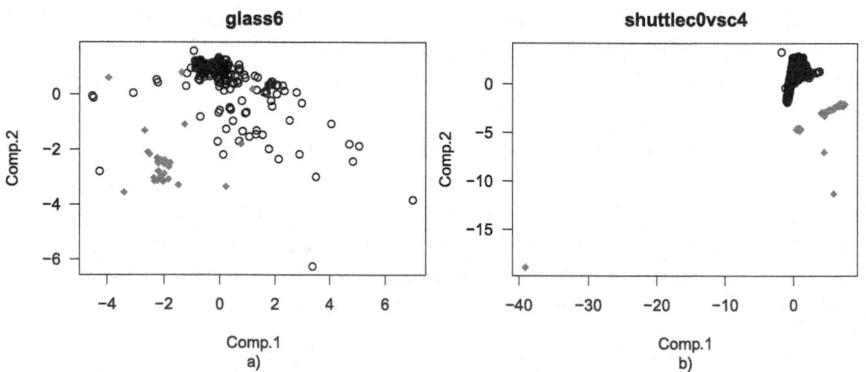

Fig. 3. Example of (a) inappropriate and (b) ideal datasets. The outliers (red diamonds) and inliers (black circles) are plotted in a two-dimensional centred, rotated and standardized feature space using the first two principal components. (Color figure online)

Table 1. Evaluation of EEO on test datasets using sensitivity Se, specificity Sp, and their geometric mean G. In first four columns, basic information about datasets is listed. It includes name, feature type (R - real numbers, I - integers, and N - nominal values), number of observations n, and imbalance ratio IR. The remaining columns consist of evaluation results for estimated and suboptimal setting of ε, respectively.

Information about datasets				EEO with $\hat{\varepsilon}$				EEO with ε^*			
Name	R/I/N	n	IR	ε	Se	Sp	G	ε	Se	Sp	G
abalone19	7/0/1	4174	129.44	-	-	-	-	-	-	-	-
abalone9-18	7/0/1	472	16.4	-	-	-	-	-	-	-	-
ecoli-0_vs_1	7/0/0	220	1.86	-	-	-	-	-	-	-	-
ecoli-0-1-3-7_vs_2-6	7/0/0	281	39.14	0.60	71.43%	86.13%	78.44%	2.47	71.43%	98.91%	84.05%
ecoli1	7/0/0	336	3.36	0.70	20.78%	83.78%	41.72%	0.04	59.74%	55.98%	57.83%
ecoli2	7/0/0	336	5.46	0.90	9.62%	86.97%	28.92%	0.26	57.69%	64.79%	61.14%
ecoli3	7/0/0	336	8.6	0.90	8.57%	87.04%	27.31%	0.06	65.71%	55.15%	60.20%
ecoli4	7/0/0	336	15.8	0.90	65.00%	90.82%	76.83%	0.75	70.00%	87.34%	78.19%
glass0	9/0/0	214	2.06	1.30	10.00%	68.75%	26.22%	−0.30	51.43%	25.69%	36.35%
glass-0-1-2-3_vs_4-5-6	9/0/0	214	3.2	1.30	52.94%	84.66%	66.95%	0.88	86.27%	83.44%	84.84%
glass-0-1-6_vs_2	9/0/0	192	10.29	1.60	17.65%	77.71%	37.03%	−0.21	88.24%	37.71%	57.69%
glass-0-1-6_vs_5	9/0/0	184	19.44	1.40	22.22%	78.86%	41.86%	0.85	55.56%	69.71%	62.23%
glass1	9/0/0	214	1.82	1.30	19.74%	73.19%	38.01%	−0.22	56.58%	34.78%	44.36%
glass2	9/0/0	214	11.59	1.00	11.76%	85.28%	31.67%	0.12	41.18%	55.84%	47.95%
glass4	9/0/0	214	15.47	1.30	46.15%	77.11%	59.66%	0.59	92.31%	66.67%	78.45%
glass5	9/0/0	214	22.78	1.30	22.22%	75.61%	40.99%	0.88	55.56%	67.80%	61.38%
glass6	9/0/0	214	6.38	1.30	65.52%	82.16%	73.37%	0.87	96.55%	76.76%	86.09%
haberman	0/3/0	306	2.78	0.60	14.81%	95.11%	37.54%	0.13	46.91%	66.22%	55.74%
iris0	4/0/0	150	2	0.80	10.00%	81.00%	28.46%	−0.22	86.00%	30.00%	50.79%
new-thyroid1	4/1/0	215	5.14	0.70	65.71%	83.89%	74.25%	0.31	80.00%	74.44%	77.17%
new-thyroid2	4/1/0	215	5.14	0.70	65.71%	83.89%	74.25%	0.23	82.86%	71.11%	76.76%
page-blocks0	4/6/0	5472	8.79	0.70	85.87%	83.88%	84.87%	0.69	86.05%	83.68%	84.85%
page-blocks-1-3_vs_4	4/6/0	472	15.86	0.70	53.57%	78.60%	64.89%	0.46	71.43%	71.40%	71.41%
pima	8/0/0	768	1.87	0.90	20.15%	88.40%	42.20%	0.10	61.57%	67.20%	64.32%
segment0	19/0/0	2308	6.02	-	-	-	-	-	-	-	-
shuttle-c0-vs-c4	0/9/0	1829	13.87	0.70	100.00%	95.96%	97.96%	0.77	100.00%	97.01%	98.49%
shuttle-c2-vs-c4	0/9/0	129	20.5	0.50	100.00%	88.62%	94.14%	0.97	100.00%	96.75%	98.36%
vehicle0	0/18/0	846	3.25	0.50	16.08%	90.42%	38.13%	0.05	53.27%	60.59%	56.81%
vehicle1	0/18/0	846	2.9	0.40	9.68%	82.83%	28.31%	−0.02	48.85%	46.10%	47.46%
vehicle2	0/18/0	846	2.88	0.40	18.35%	85.83%	39.68%	0.14	31.65%	65.61%	45.57%
vehicle3	0/18/0	846	2.99	0.40	10.85%	83.28%	30.06%	−0.12	70.75%	37.54%	51.54%
vowel0	10/3/0	988	9.98	0.40	48.89%	86.64%	65.08%	0.20	68.89%	72.72%	70.78%
wisconsin	0/9/0	683	1.86	0.50	97.07%	88.51%	92.69%	1.15	93.72%	94.37%	94.05%
yeast-0-5-6-7-9_vs_4	8/0/0	528	9.35	0.50	37.25%	81.34%	55.05%	0.30	54.90%	72.54%	63.11%
yeast1	8/0/0	1484	2.46	0.50	18.41%	78.58%	38.04%	−0.03	48.48%	45.31%	46.87%
yeast-1_vs_7	7/0/0	459	14.3	0.70	40.00%	85.31%	58.42%	0.24	53.33%	66.67%	59.63%
yeast-1-2-8-9_vs_7	8/0/0	947	30.57	0.70	40.00%	83.32%	57.73%	0.39	53.33%	72.30%	62.10%
yeast-1-4-5-8_vs_7	8/0/0	693	22.1	0.70	10.00%	82.50%	28.72%	−0.13	73.33%	40.57%	54.55%
yeast-2_vs_4	8/0/0	514	9.08	0.60	50.98%	84.45%	65.61%	0.18	84.31%	69.76%	76.69%
yeast-2_vs_8	8/0/0	482	23.1	0.60	70.00%	81.82%	75.68%	1.20	65.00%	93.94%	78.14%
yeast3	8/0/0	1484	8.1	0.50	25.15%	80.02%	44.86%	−0.01	69.33%	51.40%	59.69%
yeast4	8/0/0	1484	28.1	0.50	45.10%	80.32%	60.19%	0.16	78.43%	62.11%	69.79%
yeast5	8/0/0	1484	32.73	0.70	34.09%	86.74%	54.38%	0.06	100.00%	55.69%	74.63%
yeast6	8/0/0	1484	41.4	0.70	22.86%	86.34%	44.42%	−0.04	91.43%	47.83%	66.13%

Table 2. Comparison of EEO with other approaches for outlier detection. The geometric mean G of sensitivity and specificity was used as an overall comparison value. Results obtained by EEO are in bold on relevant datasets that meet designed criteria (inliers form a predominant cluster with outliers spanned from it and the number of inliers is greater than the number of outliers)

Dataset	Chi-3	Chi-5	Ish05	E-Alg	HFRBCS	C4.5	EEO	
							$\hat{\varepsilon}$	ε^*
abalone19	62.69%	66.71%	66.09%	0.00%	70.19%	15.58%	-	-
abalone9-18	63.93%	66.47%	65.78%	32.29%	67.56%	53.19%	-	-
ecoli-0_vs_1	92.27%	95.56%	96.70%	95.25%	93.63%	67.95%	-	-
ecoli-0-1-3-7_vs_2-6	71.04%	49.57%	71.31%	73.65%	71.48%	71.21%	**78.44%**	**84.05%**
ecoli1	85.28%	86.05%	85.71%	77.81%	84.18%	76.10%	41.72%	57.83%
ecoli2	88.01%	87.64%	87.00%	70.35%	87.62%	91.60%	28.92%	61.14%
ecoli3	87.58%	91.61%	85.39%	78.54%	90.81%	88.77%	27.31%	60.20%
ecoli4	91.27%	92.11%	86.92%	92.43%	93.02%	81.28%	76.83%	78.19%
glass0	64.06%	63.69%	69.39%	0.00%	76.57%	78.14%	26.22%	36.35%
glass-0-1-2-3_vs_4-5-6	85.83%	85.94%	88.56%	82.09%	88.37%	90.13%	66.95%	84.84%
glass-0-1-6_vs_2	40.84%	56.17%	41.18%	0.00%	58.37%	48.91%	37.03%	57.69%
glass-0-1-6_vs_5	71.48%	75.59%	88.77%	65.14%	77.96%	72.08%	41.86%	62.23%
glass1	64.90%	64.91%	59.29%	0.00%	73.66%	75.11%	38.01%	44.36%
glass2	47.67%	49.24%	43.55%	9.87%	54.84%	33.86%	31.67%	47.95%
glass4	84.96%	81.75%	78.27%	83.38%	70.39%	83.71%	59.66%	78.45%
glass5	81.56%	64.33%	89.96%	50.61%	68.73%	86.70%	40.99%	61.38%
glass6	83.87%	78.13%	86.27%	90.23%	86.95%	83.00%	73.37%	86.09%
haberman	58.91%	60.40%	62.65%	4.94%	57.08%	61.32%	37.54%	55.74%
iris0	100.00%	98.97%	100.00%	100.00%	100.00%	98.97%	28.46%	50.79%
new-thyroid1	87.44%	95.38%	89.02%	88.52%	95.58%	97.98%	74.25%	77.17%
new-thyroid2	89.81%	96.34%	94.21%	88.57%	99.72%	96.51%	74.25%	76.76%
page-blocks0	79.91%	87.25%	32.16%	64.51%	91.40%	94.84%	84.87%	84.85%
page-blocks-1-3_vs_4	91.92%	92.93%	94.53%	94.12%	98.64%	99.55%	64.89%	71.41%
pima	66.80%	66.78%	71.10%	55.01%	68.72%	71.26%	42.20%	64.32%
segment0	94.99%	95.88%	42.47%	95.33%	97.51%	99.26%	-	-
shuttle-c0-vs-c4	99.12%	98.71%	99.16%	98.40%	99.12%	99.97%	**97.96%**	**98.49%**
shuttle-c2-vs-c4	89.99%	78.34%	99.17%	100.00%	97.49%	99.15%	**94.14%**	**98.36%**
vehicle0	86.41%	84.93%	75.94%	39.07%	88.92%	91.10%	38.13%	56.81%
vehicle1	70.92%	71.88%	64.89%	3.09%	71.76%	69.28%	28.31%	47.46%
vehicle2	85.54%	87.19%	67.82%	43.83%	90.61%	94.85%	39.68%	45.57%
vehicle3	69.22%	63.13%	63.12%	0.00%	66.80%	74.34%	30.06%	51.54%
vowel0	98.37%	97.87%	89.03%	89.63%	98.82%	94.74%	65.08%	70.78%
wisconsin	88.91%	43.58%	95.78%	96.01%	88.24%	95.44%	**92.69%**	**94.05%**
yeast-0-5-6-7-9_vs_4	78.91%	75.99%	79.49%	59.99%	73.18%	74.88%	55.05%	63.11%
yeast1	67.69%	69.66%	51.41%	0.00%	71.71%	70.86%	38.04%	46.87%
yeast-1_vs_7	80.05%	63.02%	53.15%	27.55%	70.74%	67.73%	58.42%	59.63%
yeast-1-2-8-9_vs_7	76.12%	69.26%	48.55%	50.00%	69.37%	64.13%	57.73%	62.10%
yeast-1-4-5-8_vs_7	62.40%	58.76%	40.80%	0.00%	62.49%	41.19%	28.72%	54.55%
yeast-2_vs_4	86.80%	86.39%	70.85%	80.92%	89.32%	85.09%	65.61%	76.69%
yeast-2_vs_8	72.75%	78.76%	72.83%	72.83%	72.47%	78.23%	75.68%	78.14%
yeast3	90.13%	89.33%	77.06%	81.99%	90.41%	88.50%	44.86%	59.69%
yeast4	82.99%	83.07%	71.36%	32.16%	82.64%	65.00%	60.19%	69.79%
yeast5	93.41%	93.64%	94.94%	88.17%	94.20%	92.04%	54.38%	74.63%
yeast6	87.50%	87.73%	88.42%	51.72%	84.92%	80.38%	44.42%	66.13%

Good results were obtained also on other datasets, e.g. on 'glass6' (Fig. 3a), 'new-thyroid1', or 'yeast-2_vs_8'. Here, a majority of the inliers were concentrated near the cluster center; however, many inliers (their number was similar to the total number of outliers) were interspersed with the outliers. In such cases, estimation of ε became vague and perfect separation was not possible. Thus, the good EEO results on these datasets were coincidental and the presented method was not suited for them.

While the threshold values t for outlier detection can be directly set from the sorted distance visualization, estimating ε will represent a good practice in data reporting. The ε value defines the position of the outliers relative to the median, providing a data-independent approximation on outlier distribution comparable between studies.

The presented method was based on the Mahalanobis distance (1). While the distance was efficient for the proposed problem, we found the method to be computationally extravagant. Thus, we suggest an alternative approach based on the Euclidean distance for application where computational intensity would be of concern. The Euclidean distance in combination with standard deviation normalization [14] might provide equally good results while its time-complexity would be considerably lower.

5 Conclusion

The outlier analysis has the potential to mine valuable information from a complex dataset, but its sensitivity and specificity is dependent on both suitability of the method and the model, to the data. We designed EEO for the specifics of animal group behaviour observations, where the outliers could reveal alternative mechanisms determining group behaviour. Our testing on varied imbalanced sets demonstrated that the utility of the method is wider. The EEO was able to correctly classify outliers in datasets from engineering, microbiology or medicine. We therefore conclude that global outliers may be detected with EEO based on the threshold estimated from sums of pairwise Mahalanobis distances in datasets across fields that form one predominant multidimensional cluster with outliers distanced from it.

Acknowledgments. The work was supported by the University of Pardubice (PŠ) and the Czech Science Foundation grant number 17-20286S (NM).

References

1. MATLAB: Global optimization toolbox (R2016a) (2016). https://www.mathworks.com/help/gads/index.html
2. Aggarwal, C.C.: Outlier Analysis. Springer, New York (2013)
3. Angiulli, F., Basta, S., Lodi, S., Sartori, C.: GPU strategies for distance-based outlier detection. IEEE Trans. Parallel Distrib. Syst. **27**(11), 3256–3268 (2016)
4. Brereton, R.G.: The Mahalanobis distance and its relationship to principal component scores. J. Chemometr. **29**(3), 143–145 (2015)

5. Broom, D.M., Fraser, A.F.: Domestic Animal Behaviour and Welfare, 4th edn. CABI, Wallingford (2015)
6. Chi, Z., Yan, H., Pham, T.: Fuzzy Algorithms: With Applications to Image Processing and Pattern Recognition, vol. 10. World Scientific, Singapore (1996)
7. Deza, M.M., Deza, E.: Encyclopedia of Distances, 3rd edn. Springer, Heidelberg (2014)
8. Fernndez, A., del Jesus, M.J., Herrera, F.: Hierarchical fuzzy rule based classification systems with genetic rule selection for imbalanced data-sets. Int. J. Approximate Reasoning **50**(3), 561–577 (2009)
9. Gower, J., Lubbe, S., Roux, N.: Understanding Biplots. Wiley, New York (2010)
10. Han, J., Kamber, M., Pei, J.: Data Mining, 3rd edn. Morgan Kaufmann, San Francisco (2012)
11. Hawkins, D.M.: Identification of Outliers. Springer, Netherlands (1980)
12. Hawkins, S., He, H., Williams, G., Baxter, R.: Outlier detection using replicator neural networks. In: Kambayashi, Y., Winiwarter, W., Arikawa, M. (eds.) DaWaK 2002. LNCS, vol. 2454, pp. 170–180. Springer, Heidelberg (2002). doi:10.1007/3-540-46145-0_17
13. Ishibuchi, H., Yamamoto, T.: Rule weight specification in fuzzy rule-based classification systems. IEEE Trans. Fuzzy Syst. **13**(4), 428–435 (2005)
14. Kantardzic, M.: Data Mining: Concepts, Models, Methods, and Algorithms, 2nd edn. Wiley, Hoboken (2011)
15. Kohl, M.: Performance measures in binary classification. Int. J. Stat. Med. Res. **1**(1), 79–81 (2012)
16. Reeves, C.R., Rowe, J.E.: Genetic Algorithms: Principles and Perspectives: A Guide to GA Theory. Kluwer Academic Publishers, Norwell (2002)
17. Salzberg, S.L.: C4.5: programs for machine learning by J. Ross Quinlan. Morgan Kaufmann Publishers, Inc., 1993. Mach. Learn. **16**(3), 235–240 (1994)
18. Ward, A., Webster, M.: Sociality: The Behaviour of Group-Living Animals. Springer International Publishing, Heidelberg (2016)
19. Xu, L., Chow, M.Y., Taylor, L.S.: Using the data mining based fuzzy classification algorithm for power distribution fault cause identification with imbalanced data. In: 2006 IEEE PES Power Systems Conference and Exposition. pp. 1228–1233, October 2006

Data Mining Applications

Context-Aware Data Mining: Embedding External Data Sources in a Machine Learning Process

Oliviu Matei[1,3(✉)], Teodor Rusu[2], Andrei Bozga[1], Petrica Pop-Sitar[3], and Carmen Anton[3]

[1] Holisun srl, Baia Mare, Romania
{oliviu.matei,andrei.bozga}@holisun.com
[2] University of Agricultural Sciences and Veterinary Medicine, Cluj-Napoca, Romania
rusuteodor23@yahoo.com
[3] Technical University of Cluj-Napoca, North University Centre of Baia Mare, Cluj-Napoca, Romania
{petrica.pop,oliviu.matei}@cunbm.utcluj.ro, carmen.anton@profinfo.edu.ro

Abstract. The article presents a data mining system capable of predicting the soil moisture using local data, provided by weather stations in real time, as well as context-related, publicly available data from web portals. We have proven that the quality and quantity of context data is very important for improving the accuracy of the predictions, comparing with classical scenario, in which only the local data is used.

Keywords: Context-aware data mining · Internet of things · Ambience intelligence

1 Introduction

Weather is a key factor in agricultural productivity, despite technological advances, such as improved varieties, genetically modified organisms, and irrigation systems. The effect of climate on agriculture is related to variabilities in local weather rather than in global climate patterns. The classical weather prediction schemes are easily offset and do not provide a good local accuracy, as the weather varies even on short distances. However, a well informed agricultural production is needed, especially taking into account that by 2030, the food production will be outnumbered by the population of the world [5].

In this article, we focus on predicting soil moisture in real-time, so the farmers can take actions when needed, with no delays. Matei et al. [10] presented a data mining system capable of gathering weather data from several weather stations and predicting the moisture of the soil for the next day, all in real time. The system has been tested in real-life conditions, with ten stations working in Transylvanian Plain. They have proven that the prediction accuracy is very high and the system can be used in agriculture as a mature platform in any

F.J. Martínez de Pisón et al. (Eds.): HAIS 2017, LNAI 10334, pp. 415–426, 2017.
DOI: 10.1007/978-3-319-59650-1_35

geo-climate conditions. Further more, we want to use also some context data for improving the accuracy of the predictions. The real-time predictions are important for overcoming the negative effects of the weather to come, as various weather conditions (temperatures below zero degrees or hail in May) require different interventions, which may take a lot of time for large areas.

With the rapid expansion of the connectivity to Internet [?], innovative improvements to machine learning have been developed, such as the use of the context knowledge. Context-aware computing is often mentioned as a key component of Weiser's vision of ubiquitous computing [26]. Scholze et al. [17] developed self-learning production systems based on context-aware services designed by Ning et al. [13]. Vajirkar et al. [22] used context-aware data mining for wireless medical applications. Adamovicius and Tuzhilin [1] propose a context-aware recommendation system which uses data mining. They discuss the general notion of context and how it can be modeled in recommender systems. Furthermore, they three algorithms - contextual prefiltering, post-filtering, and modeling - for embedding contextual information into the recommendation process, discuss the possibilities of combining several context-aware recommendation techniques into a unified approach.

Baldauf et al. [3] makes a good survey of the common architecture principles of context-aware systems and derive a layered conceptual design framework, used also in our experiments. The hybridization of the data from various sources has been inspired by Alvarado et al. [2].

Pedreschi et al. [14] introduce a discrimination-aware data mining. Their approach leads to a precise formulation of the redlining problem along with a formal result relating discriminatory rules with apparently safe ones by means of background knowledge. Singh et al. [18] propose a context-aware data mining framework, where context is represented in an ontology, is automatically captured during data mining process, and allows the adaptive behavior to carry over to powerful data mining. Wallace and Stamou [24] explain the relation between context, user interest and the multiple relations; furthermore, they present a clustering algorithm that is able to mine user interests from multi-relational data sets.

Regarding weather prediction, this has been part of daily life since ever for its economic importance [11]. Gutman et al. [8] comes up with a model for agricultural weather predictions. Sivakumar [19] has an extensive study on the climate prediction and agriculture, discussing trends, opportunities and challenges. A similar research with the one reported in this article is the one carried out by Meinke and Stone [12].

The article is structured as follows. Section 2 discusses the concept of context-aware data mining. Section 3 describes the experimental setup, followed by Sect. 4 which summarizes the results along with the discussions. And, finally, Sect. 5 shows the conclusions of the work.

2 What is Context-Aware Data Mining?

Unlike the classical DM processes, context-aware data mining (CADM) integrates also context data, which is expected to improve the quality of the machine learning algorithms. With respect to this, we consider, actually, a data hybridization, rather than an algorithmic one. This data can be collected from various sources and is related to the context of the process.

The CADM respects the stages of a classical data mining (DM) process (see Fig. 1), namely:

1. reading the data;
2. preprocessing the data;
3. applying a machine learning algorithm.

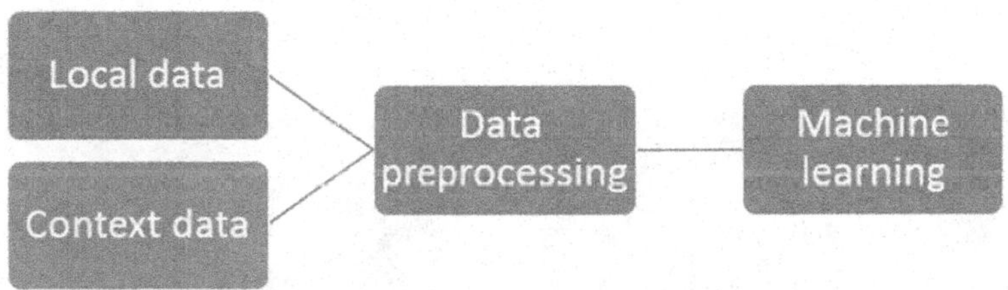

Fig. 1. The context-aware data mining process

Taking into account the changes in the context (environment) should bring in more data and information and hence it is expected to improve the quality of data mining. However, it is also expected a relationship between the availability and quality of the context, respectively the quality of the DM output. On the other hand, a large amount of context data would increase the computational time and may also overwhelm the DM process as well as the significance of the main (local) data.

3 Experimental Setup

The experiments rely on two types of data: the ones available on the weather stations (see Sect. 3.1), respectively the one, context-related, available publicly, detailed in Sect. 3.2.

3.1 Local Data Sources

The concept of context-aware data mining is applied on weather data collected from an agricultural weather stations (MAN-H21-002 HOBO) [16] located at the site of HOLISUN company, with the GPS coordinates (47.6345063, 23.5932327).

The stations operate in the range [−20° *to* 50°C] with alkaline batteries, respectively [−40° *to* 70°C] with lithium batteries. They accommodate up to four smart sensors (including multiple-parameter sensors) and communicates on a 3.5 mm serial port [23].

The experimental setup is based on the one presented by Matei et al. [10]. The station (see Fig. 2) stores electronically the temperature data from ground at three depths (10, 30, 50 cm) and moisture at 10 cm depth. The sensors are:

temperature sensor (S-TMB-M002) uses 12-Bit representation. The measurement range is [−40°C, 100°C]. The accuracy is ±0.2°C in the range [0°, 50°C]. The response time is less than 3 min.

moisture sensors EC-5 (S-SMC-M005) is 12-bit A/D. It provides ±3% accuracy in typical soil conditions, and ±2% accuracy with soil-specific calibration. Readings are provided directly in volumetric water content. This sensor is designed to maintain low sensitivity to salinity and textural effects.

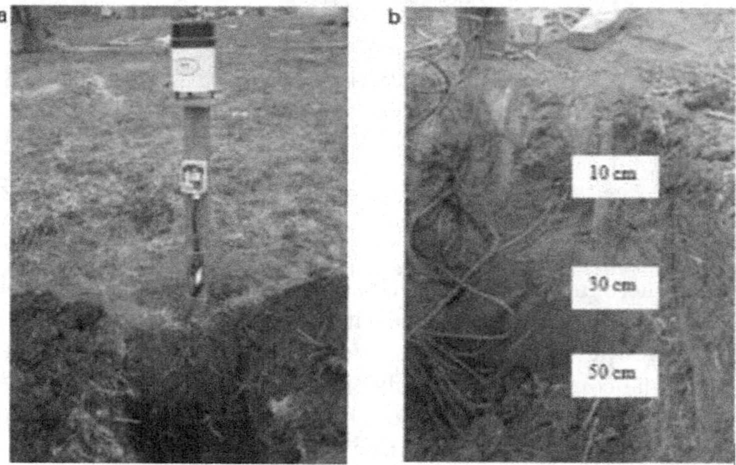

Fig. 2. (a) HOBO-MAN-H21-002 stations, (b) The temperature sensors at −10 cm, −30 cm and −50 cm

The collected data is stored in a table of a relational database, and looks like in Table 1. In both of them, M is the moisture in the soil at −10 cm, and T_x is the temperature in the soil at x cm, were $x \in \{-10, -30, -50\}$. The prefixes A and SD show that the values are the averages, respectively standard deviations.

3.2 Context Data Sources

In this set of experiments, the external data sources are the weather websites: vremea.net, yr.no and freemeteo.ro. Each of them provide the forecasts for 24 h

Table 1. The format of the local data

Timestamp	M	T_10	T_30	T_50
12.28.09 11:29:03 AM	0.3061	4.662	3.195	1.317
12.28.09 11:39:03 AM	0.3061	4.662	3.196	1.289
12.28.09 11:49:03 AM	0.3053	4.663	3.195	1.289

regarding: the temperature, air humidity and precipitations. We computed the average and standard deviation for each prediction. This assures a pretty high accuracy with respect to the limits (minimum and maximum) of the value interval over the day.

Please notice that these values refer entirely to the context (related to the air) where the research site is (see Sect. 3.1), not to the soil conditions. Another possibility would be to collect the air-related data, such as air humidity and air temperature, for which specialized sensors would be needed.

For each source, the weather prognoses are collected three times a day, at: 9:00, 13:00 and 18:00. Further on, we compute:

- average and standard deviation of the air temperature (T_A and T_SD);
- average and standard deviation of the air humidity (H_A and H_SD);
- average and standard deviation of the air precipitations (P_A and P_SD).

Table 2 shows a snapshot of the public data .

Table 2. A snapshot of the public data, for 3 days

Date	Source	T_A	T_SD	H_A	H_SD	P_A	P_SD
7/14/2016	freemeteo.ro	22.875	6.173279	69.125	17.26584	0.625	1.653595
7/14/2016	vremea.net	24.5	3.316625	57	10	0.025	0.066144
7/14/2016	yr.no	25.125	3.257204	68.625	15.75546	0.2	0.287228
7/15/2016	freemeteo.ro	19.8125	4.171612	73.75	16.81331	0.9375	1.59956
7/15/2016	vremea.net	18.75	4.683748	72	16.70329	1.0625	2.811111
7/15/2016	yr.no	20.75	3.072051	73.5	11.46734	0.3125	0.631343
7/16/2016	freemeteo.ro	21.5	4.387482	74.5	17.74824	0.25	0.433013
7/16/2016	vremea.net	21.875	4.428247	58	8.558621	0	0

3.3 Experimental Scenarios

The weather station has been monitored in the interval 14th of July 2016 – 15th of November 2016. We have tested several machine learning algorithms on several intervals, in two scenarios:

1. using the data only from the sensors of the weather station;
2. using not only the data from the sensors, but also predictions from public sources (www.yr.no, www.vremea.net and www.freemeteo.ro).

Further on, we present each step of the DM process.

3.4 Data Preprocessing

As the local data is recorded every 10 min, there are 144 records for each sensor daily. Therefore, for reducing the amount of data, and still preserving its representation power, the average and standard deviation are computed for every day. This way, two values are considered for each sensor per day (instead of 144). Several advantages come out, such as:

- reduction of the computational resources;
- reduction of noise and errors which come along with any measurement set;
- improvement of the prediction quality.

After this stage, in which the data is structured like in Table 1, it becomes like in Table 3.

Table 3. The new data format, using the average and standard deviation of the daily records

Date	$A\ M$	$SD\ M$	$A\ T_{10}$	$SD\ T_{10}$	$A\ T_{30}$	$SD\ T_{30}$	$A\ T_{50}$	$SD\ T_{50}$
28.12.2010	0.308	0.002	4.631	0.034	3.147	0.033	1.341	0.038
29.12.2010	0.308	0.001	4.493	0.048	2.983	0.064	1.087	0.091
30.12.2010	0.306	0.049	4.329	0.061	2.765	0.041	0.833	0.0005

3.5 Machine Learning Algorithms

Although more machine learning algorithms have been tested, only the following ones are worth to be reported and, therefore, are detailed here.

Gaussian process is a stochastic process consisting of random values associated with every point in a range, distributed normally (Gaussian distribution). That said, every finite collection of those random variables has a multivariate normal distribution [15]. Formally, a Gaussian process generates data located throughout some domain such that any finite subset of the range follows a multivariate Gaussian distribution [7].

Polynomial regression is a form of linear regression in which the relationship between the independent variable x and the dependent variable y is modeled as an n-th order polynomial [6].

The **Relevance Vector Machine (RVM)** uses Bayesian inference for regression and classification [21]. The RVM has an identical functional form to the support vector machine, but provides probabilistic classification. However the Bayesian formulation of the RVM avoids the set of free parameters of the SVM (that usually require cross-validation-based post-optimizations). This means that over-training is highly improbable and that helps for generalizing the model.

The **k-Nearest Neighbor (k-NN)** algorithm is based on learning by analogy, more precisely, by comparing a given test example with training examples that are similar to it [25]. Each set is considered an n-dimensional space, where n represents the number of attributes. When a new example is fed to the algorithm, k-nearest neighbor algorithm searches the space for the k training examples (points) that are closest to this new example. These k points are the k "nearest neighbors" of the unknown example. "Closeness" is defined in terms of a distance metric, such as the Euclidean distance [20]. The k-nearest neighbor algorithm is one the simplest and most used of all machine learning algorithms because it is very powerful and easy to understand and use.

3.6 Experimental Environment

The tool used for data mining is RapidMiner, a well-known environment for such tasks. The process is depicted in Fig. 3. It consists of mainly three stages: input data, time windowing and the machine learning sequence.

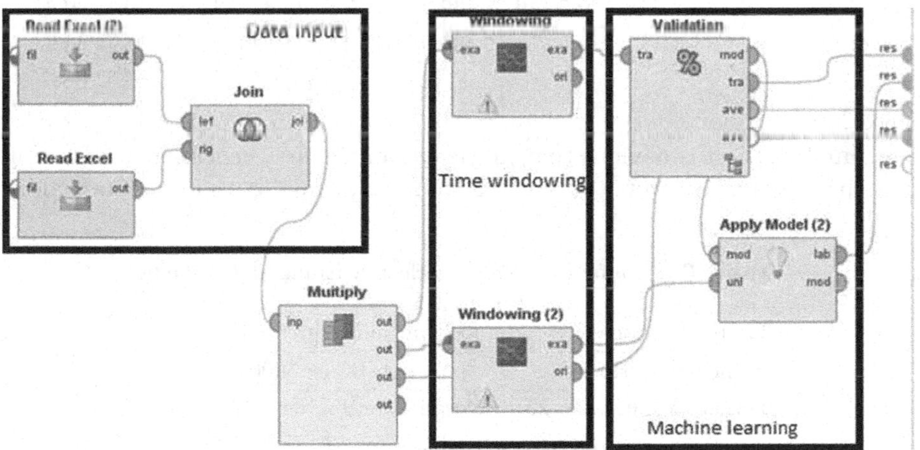

Fig. 3. The DM process designed in RapidMiner

4 Experimental Results

Several benchmarks have been run starting with 20.08.2016, as more data became available. For technical reasons, the publicly available weather predictions were

Table 4. The availability of data over the benchmark time interval

Availability	20.08.2016	21.09.2016	04.10.2016	01.11.2016	15.11.2016
Context-related data	20	44	57	81	95
Sensor data	37	70	83	110	124
Ratio	54.05%	62.85%	68.67%	73.63%	76.61%

not available for each day, therefore some predictions are missing, as summarized in Table 4.

The accuracies of the two approaches are summarized in Table 5. Columns *SA* refer to the accuracies in the case of stand alone DM, whereas columns *CA* refer to the results in the case of context aware DM.

Table 5. The accuracies of the algorithms in the whole time interval

Algorithm	20.08.2016		21.09.2016		01.11.2016		15.11.2016	
	SA	CA	SA	CA	SA	CA	SA	CA
Gaussian process	38.9	25.9	44.7	24.7	48.1	48.6	46.4	46.6
Polynomial regression	33.3	3.7	39.8	16.6	22	12.6	33.8	32.1
Relevance vector machine	42.6	0	25.9	0	26.1	0.2	34.5	36.8
k-NN	40.7	46.3	39.8	16.2	40.3	16.8	40.1	40.8
Average	35.5	15.56	34.95	12.875	34.125	19.55	38.7	38.94

From Table 5, it is obvious that in the case of the first benchmark, almost all algorithms performed worse on context-aware data mining than on stand alone

Table 6. Parameters of the machine learning algorithms

Gaussian process	Polynomial regression
kernel type: rbf	max iterations: 5000
kernel length scale: 2.0	replication factor: 1
max basis vectors: 100	max degree: 5
ϵ tolerance: 10^{-7}	min coefficient: -100.0
	max coefficient: 100.0
Relevance vector machine	**k-nearest neighbour**
kernel type: rbf	k: 2
kernel length scale: 3	measure: Euclidean distance
min $\delta \log \alpha$: 0.001	
α max: 10^{12}	

data mining because the large number of days for which there are no predictions (54.05%). The only algorithms that performed better is k-NN.

The context-aware DM keeps performing worse than the stand-alone DM until the benchmark of 15.11.2016, when it is the first time when the accuracy of the context-aware DM is better than the accuracy of the stand-alone DM. Therefore the percentage of available predictions from publicly available sources needed to be more than 73.63%.

These results have been obtained with the configurations of the algorithms shown in Table 6.

4.1 Discussions

Figure 4 draws the accuracies of the two DM processes, along with the percentage of available context data. The stand-alone DM accuracy is slowly increasing over time as the quantity of data increases. In the other hand, the context-aware DM accuracy increases drastically as the quantity of context data is available.

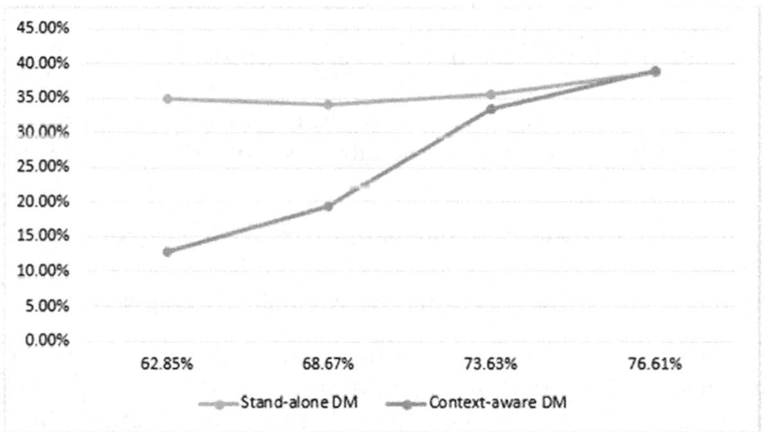

Fig. 4. The accuracies of the stand-alone, respectively context-aware DM

Computing the correlation between the availability of the context and the accuracy of the context-aware DM, it turns out that it is 0.984, which means that the quality of the DM process is highly correlated with the availability of the data.

However external data sources used, the accuracy of the data mining prediction was not influenced. This is because the three predictions are very similar, as shown in Fig. 5. The three sources are very low variations (less than 2%) reported to their average.

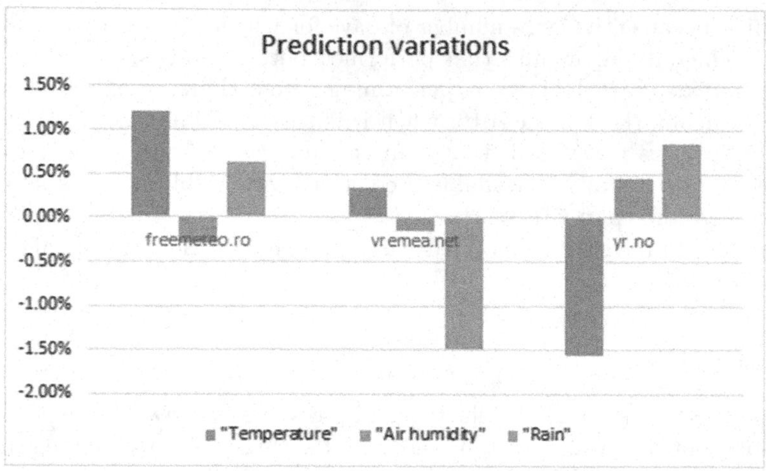

Fig. 5. Variations of the three predictions (www.freemeteo.ro, www.vremea.net, www.yr.no) with respect to the average

5 Conclusions and Future Developments

The article explores the impact of the context data on the accuracy of data mining processes. The model was applied for predicting the soil moisture in two scenarios:

1. based on the data provided by the sensors (installed in the soil) of a weather stations,
2. respectively using also weather predictions publicly available.

The accuracy of the context-aware data mining increases as the quantity of the available context data increases. At this moment, the process is very dependent on the existence (and quality) of the context data. In this specific case, a percentage of 76.61 available data was the threshold after which the context-aware accuracy was better than the stand-alone accuracy. This means that simply bringing context data in the mining process does not assure an improved accuracy. However, at this moment we do not know what should be the quality of the context data. It is important to define metrics or indicators on this aspect.

The context-aware data is used in sub-semantic intelligent systems, rather than using knowledge-based models, such as the ones proposed by Kamal Uddin et al. [9] and Berri et al. [4].

5.1 Future Developments

As we have shown so far, the context-aware DM is very sensitive to the quantity of available context data, which may be a huge drawback when this data is scarce, which may be often the case. Therefore, a next research should focus on the methods and techniques for reducing the dependency of the context-aware DM of the availability of the data.

Another issue which needs to be investigated further represents the ways of increasing the accuracy of context-aware DM by reducing the quantity of context data.

Yet another research direction would be to determine the underlying relationships between the context-aware DM and the context data, along with its structure.

And finally, as both context-aware data mining, as well as collaborative data mining [?] are improvements of the classical approach in the context of Interent of Things, respectively Industry/Agriculture 4.0 [?]. However as both have been introduced and research rather recently, there is no study focused on comparing and/or using them together.

Acknowledgment. This paper was performed under the frame of the Partnership in priority domains - PNII, developed with the support of MEN-UEFISCDI, project no. PN-II-PT-PCCA-2013-4-0015: Expert System for Risk Monitoring in Agriculture and Adaptation of Conservative Agricultural Technologies to Climate Change.

References

1. Adomavicius, G., Tuzhilin, A.: Context-aware recommender systems. In: Recommender Systems Handbook, pp. 191–220. Springer, Boston (2015)
2. Alvarado, B., Ariel, I., Van Gent, R.P.: Context aware data presentation. US Patent 8,412,675, 2 April 2013
3. Baldauf, M., Dustdar, S., Rosenberg, F.: A survey on context-aware systems. Int. J. Ad Hoc Ubiquit. Comput. **2**(4), 263–277 (2007)
4. Berri, J., Benlamri, R., Atif, Y.: Ontology-based framework for context-aware mobile learning. In: Proceedings of the 2006 International Conference on Wireless Communications and Mobile Computing, pp. 1307–1310. ACM (2006)
5. Cohen, J.E.: Human population grows up. Sci. Am. **293**(3), 48–55 (2005)
6. Edwards, J.R., Parry, M.E.: On the use of polynomial regression equations as an alternative to difference scores in organizational research. Acad. Manage. J. **36**(6), 1577–1613 (1993)
7. Goodman, N.: Statistical analysis based on a certain multivariate complex Gaussian distribution (an introduction). Ann. Math. Stat. **34**(1), 152–177 (1963)
8. Gutman, G., Ignatov, A.: The derivation of the green vegetation fraction from NOAA/AVHRR data for use in numerical weather prediction models. Int. J. Remote Sens. **19**(8), 1533–1543 (1998)
9. Kamal, M., Puttonen, J., Scholze, S., Dvoryanchikova, A., Lastra, J.L.M.: Ontology based context sensitive computing for FMS optimization. Assembly Autom. **32**(2), 163–174 (2012)
10. Matei, O., Rusu, T., Petrovan, A., Mihut, G.: A data mining system for real time soil moisture prediction. In: Proceedings of INTER-ENG 2016, Procedia Engineering. Elsevier (2017)
11. Maunder, J.: R.W. Katz and A.H. Murphy, economic value of weather and climate forecasts. Climatic Change **45**(3), 601–606 (2000)

12. Meinke, H., Stone, R.C.: Seasonal and inter-annual climate forecasting: the new tool for increasing preparedness to climate variability and change in agricultural planning and operations. Climatic Change **70**(1–2), 221–253 (2005)
13. Ning, K., Scholze, S., Marques, M., Campos, A.R., Neves-Silva, R., O'Sullivan, D.: A service oriented framework for context aware knowledge enhancing. IFAC Proc. Volumes **43**(17), 9–15 (2010)
14. Pedreshi, D., Ruggieri, S., Turini, F.: Discrimination aware data mining. In: Proceedings of the 14th ACM SIGKDD International Conference on Knowledge Discovery and Data Mining, pp. 560–568. ACM (2008)
15. Rasmussen, C.E.: Gaussian processes in machine learning. In: Bousquet, O., Luxburg, U., Rätsch, G. (eds.) ML-2003. LNCS, vol. 3176, pp. 63–71. Springer, Heidelberg (2004). doi:10.1007/978-3-540-28650-9_4
16. Rusu, T., Weindorf, D., Haggard, B., Moraru, P.I., Cacovean, H., Sopterean, M.: Soil moisture and temperature monitoring for sustainable land and water management in Transylvanian plain, Romania. In: Geophysical Research Abstracts, vol. 13 (2011)
17. Scholze, S., Stokic, D., Kotte, O., Barata, J., Di Orio, G., Candido, G.: Reliable self-learning production systems based on context aware services. In: 2013 IEEE International Conference on Systems, Man, and Cybernetics (SMC), pp. 4872–4877. IEEE (2013)
18. Singh, S., Vajirkar, P., Lee, Y.: Context-based data mining using ontologies. In: Song, I.-Y., Liddle, S.W., Ling, T.-W., Scheuermann, P. (eds.) ER 2003. LNCS, vol. 2813, pp. 405–418. Springer, Heidelberg (2003). doi:10.1007/978-3-540-39648-2_32
19. Sivakumar, M.: Climate prediction and agriculture: current status and future challenges. Climate Res. **33**(1), 3–17 (2006)
20. Smola, A.J., Schölkopf, B.: A tutorial on support vector regression. Stat. Comput. **14**(3), 199–222 (2004)
21. Tipping, M.: Relevance vector machine, US Patent 6,633,857, 14 October 2003
22. Vajirkar, P., Singh, S., Lee, Y.: Context-aware data mining framework for wireless medical application. In: Mařík, V., Retschitzegger, W., Štěpánková, O. (eds.) DEXA 2003. LNCS, vol. 2736, pp. 381–391. Springer, Heidelberg (2003). doi:10.1007/978-3-540-45227-0_38
23. Veloz, Y., Zalewski, J.: Hobo weather system (2008)
24. Wallace, M., Stamou, G.: Towards a context aware mining of user interests for consumption of multimedia documents. In: 2002 IEEE International Conference on Multimedia and Expo 2002, ICME 2002 Proceedings, vol. 1, pp. 733–736. IEEE (2002)
25. Weinberger, K.Q., Blitzer, J., Saul, L.: Distance metric learning for large margin nearest neighbor classification. Adv. Neural Inf. Process. Syst. **18**, 1473 (2006)
26. Weiser, M.: Some computer science issues in ubiquitous computing. Commun. ACM **36**(7), 75–84 (1993)

Single and Blended Models for Day-Ahead Photovoltaic Power Forecasting

Javier Antonanzas[1,3], Ruben Urraca[1,3], Alpha Pernía-Espinoza[1,3], Alvaro Aldama[1,3], Luis Alfredo Fernández-Jiménez[2], and Francisco Javier Martínez-de-Pisón[1,3](✉)

[1] EDMANS Group, University of La Rioja, Logroño, Spain
fjmartin@unirioja.es, edmans@dim.unirioja.es
[2] Department of Electrical Engineering, University of La Rioja, Logroño, Spain
[3] Department of Mechanical Engineering, University of La Rioja, Logroño, Spain
http://www.mineriadatos.com

Abstract. Solar power forecasts are gaining continuous importance as the penetration of solar energy into the grid rises. The natural variability of the solar resource, joined to the difficulties of cloud movement modeling, endow solar power forecasts with a certain level of uncertainty. Important efforts have been carried out in the field to reduce as much as possible the errors. Various approaches have been followed, being the predominant nowadays the use of statistical techniques to model production.

In this study, we have performed a comparison study between two extensively used statistical techniques, support vector regression (SVR) machines and random forests, and two other techniques that have been scarcely applied to solar forecasting, deep neural networks and extreme gradient boosting machines. Best results were obtained with the SVR technique, showing a nRMSE of 22.49%. To complete the assessment, a weighted blended model consisting on an average weighted combination of individual predictions was created. This blended model outperformed all the models studied, with a nRMSE of 22.24%.

Keywords: Solar power forecasting · Extreme gradient boosting · Deep neural networks · Weighted blended model

1 Introduction

The Paris Agreement, which limits greenhouse gas emissions to avoid global temperature rise above 2 °C with respect to pre-indrustrial levels, will force the massive use of renewable energies. The integration in the grid of these energy sources, sometimes intermittent (i.e. wind or solar photovoltaic) poses many challenges for grid managing.

Focusing on solar energy, solar radiation presents variability, explained by diurnal and annual changes, which can be accurately described by physical equations, but solar radiation forecasts also have a certain level of uncertainty, mainly

F.J. Martínez de Pisón et al. (Eds.): HAIS 2017, LNAI 10334, pp. 427–434, 2017.
DOI: 10.1007/978-3-319-59650-1_36

derived from cloud induced changes, which are very difficult to predict. Thus, solar power forecasts have an inherent error, which limits the integration of photovoltaic (PV) energy for the sake of stability of the grid. This fact has motivated many research studies worldwide.

PV production forecasts can be obtained using a physical model of the plant, for which solar radiation predictions are needed. The difficulty to characterize the elements of the PV plant has boosted the use of statistical models, which do not need any internal information of the plant. Hybrid models also appear to foster the benefits of individual techniques. As detailed in [3], over 70% of the studies found in the bibliography used statistical techniques. There are various statistical techniques used for solar power forecasts, such as artificial neural networks (ANN) [2], support vector regression (SVR) machines [11], random forests (RF) [1] or linear stationary models [9], among others.

Forecasts can also be classified according to the effective time horizon of the predictions. Most of the studies focus on day ahead (DA) predictions, which can be used by market agents in the DA market, where most of the energy is traded. Intra-day (ID) predictions, which cover a time horizon between 1 and 6 h, are useful for trading in ID markets. Forecasts for time horizons of less than 1 h are denominated as nowcasts. Each type of predictions require different sources of inputs. In that way, DA forecasts are best fed with numerical weather predictions (NWP), ID forecasts benefit from solar radiation predictions derived from satellite images and nowcasting normally requires sky images.

In this work, we propose a comparison study between extreme gradient boosting (XGB) machines, deep neural networks (DNN), RF and SVR to produce DA forecasts. The first two techniques have not yet been extensively applied to solar power forecasts. The benefits of combining several models were also addressed through the construction of an ensemble model. That model consisted on a weighted blended combination of the predictions of the aforementioned models.

2 Data

Hourly production values from a 1.86 MW PV plant for the years 2009–2010 were used. This period covers all sky conditions and hence, models could be tested in all situations. The PV plant has dual tracker systems and is located in the north of Spain. Production forecasts were adapted to the regulation of the Iberian electricity market. Gate closure time of the DA market is at 12:00 local.

NWP of global horizontal irradiance (GHI), air temperature, relative humidity and wind speed were obtained for the location of interest. They were downloaded from the Meteogalicia website. This meteorological service runs the weather research and forecasting (WRF) model twice a day (00:00 and 12:00 UTC). For this study, DA predictions made with the 00:00 UTC run were used, because the 12:00 run was not available by gate closure time. The spatial resolution of forecasts is 12 km. Deterministic variables of the Sun position (solar elevation and solar azimuth) and the extraterrestrial irradiance were also used.

The two-day persistence of production was also added to the input set. The one-day persistence could not be used because by 12:00 local (when forecasts are issued), the production of the entire day is not available yet.

3 Method

In this Section, the four individual techniques used for predictions are detailed. Besides, the construction of the blended model is explained.

3.1 Extreme Gradient Boosting

Extreme gradient boosting (XGB) [6] is derived from gradient boosting machines (GBM). Models are created by a combination of several "weak" learners (whose predictions are only a bit better than random guessing) following a gradient learning algorithm to build a "strong" learner. Normally, regression trees are selected as weak learners. The strategy is as follows. First, a weak learner is fit to the data. Then, another learner is fit to the residuals of the previous learner. This process is repeated until a stopping condition is fulfilled. The weighted mean of weak learners generates the prediction.

Nevertheless, boosting has some problems associated to the technique, the main one being the risk of overfitting. Controlling model complexity is a way to limit overfitting. XGB addresses this issue with an objective function that reduces complexity and the same time, limits computational effort.

$$Obj^{(t)} = \sum_{i=1}^{n} l(y_i, \hat{y}_i) + \sum_{i=1}^{t} \Omega(f_i), \tag{1}$$

where l is the predictive term (user specified) and γ the regularization term (based on the number of leaves of the tree and the scores of each leaf). l and γ are later combined, under the following expression:

$$Obj^{(t)} = -\frac{1}{2} \sum_{j=1}^{T} \frac{G_j^2}{H_j + \lambda} + \gamma T, \tag{2}$$

where G and H are obtained from the Taylor series expansion of the loss function, λ is the L2 regularization parameter and T, the number of leaves.

Bayesian optimization was applied to obtain the best configuration of the internal parameters of the technique. The number of rounds varied in the range [10–3000], *max_depth*, in the range [1–8], *min_child_weight*, in the range [1–50] and λ and γ, in the range [0.1–1].

3.2 Random Forests

Random forests (RF) were introduced by [5] and have proven successful results when applied to solar power forecasts. They are based on an ensemble of regression trees which, as above mentioned, have the disadvantage of overfitting to the training data set. The high variance derived from overfitting can be reduced by averaging results of several random trees. Nevertheless, trees are still very correlated. For this reason, the bagging technique is introduced, in which trees are grown with bootstrap samples of the entire data set. To further reduce correlation, a random subset of variables is used in each tree, and RF are obtained.

Several variables were optimized via bayesian optimization. The bounds for the search were [100–10000] for the number of trees n_{trees}, [2–7] for m_{try}, [1–100] for the node size and [1–100] for the maximum number of nodes. Bias correction and replacement could be also present or not in the models.

3.3 Deep Neural Networks

Deep neural networks belong to the family of feed-forward ANN. They characterize for having more than one layer of hidden units between input and output [4]. They are able to cope with complex non-linear problems. The structure of the selected DNN consists on three hidden layers. As in ANN, DNN may produce overfitting to the training data set due to the addition of layers. For this reason, a dropout regularization was applied. With this method, some of the units are randomly omitted from the hidden layers.

3.4 Support Vector Machines

Support Vector Machines have already been successfully used in solar power prediction [7] and have become the second most applied technique in the field, according to [3]. Hence, they represent a proper benchmark to the proposed techniques. [10] firstly introduced them for classification purposes, although SVM can also be applied for regression, where they are denominated support vector regression (SVR) machines. SVR stand out for a strong generalization capacity, because of the use of a loss function which is not that sensitive to outliers compared to the least squares method, the traditional one. Besides, they are also able to cope with non-linear problems.

A general multiple linear regression equation is represented as

$$f(x) = \langle w, x \rangle + b, \tag{3}$$

where x is the set of inputs, w the weight vector, $\langle w, x \rangle$, the dot product between w and x, and b the bias. As above-mentioned, SVR computes w in an alternative way, i.e.

$$\begin{aligned} & minimize \;\; C \sum_{i=1}^{N} (\xi_i + \xi_i^*) + \tfrac{1}{2}||w||^2 \\ & subject\,to \begin{cases} y_i - (\langle w, x_i \rangle + b) \leq \varepsilon + \xi_i \\ (\langle w, x_i \rangle + b) - y_i \leq \varepsilon + \xi_i^* \\ \xi_i, \xi_i^* \geq 0 \end{cases} \end{aligned} \tag{4}$$

The first term regulates model accuracy. The use of the absolute error limits the sensitivity to outliers. Besides, the errors found inside a tolerance band designated by ε are canceled. Model complexity may be regulated as well. The trade off between these two parameters (accuracy and complexity) is controlled trough a cost parameter C.

SVR machines are suitable to work with non-linear problems. To cope with this data and allow a linear fitting, variables are transformed to a higher dimensional feature space. The radial basis function was used for that purpose.

$$K(x_i, x) = e^{-\gamma||x_i - x||^2}, \gamma > 0, \tag{5}$$

where γ is a predefined value that controls the width of the Gaussian function.

Three parameters must be controlled to obtain a good fit of the model and optimize results, ε, C and γ. Bayensian optimization was performed to obtain the best model. C was varied in the range $[10^{-3}–10^{3}]$, γ, in the range $[10^{-3}–10^{0}]$ and ε, in the range $[10^{-2}–10^{0.1}]$.

3.5 Models

Figure 1 summarizes the structure of the forecasting algorithm. Single models were created as follows. Ten different configurations were created for each technique. Fifty iterations were performed, resulting in sixty different models. Every model (60 for each technique), with the exception of SVR, was initialized with ten different random seeds, what is denoted as "random committee". This is performed to increase model robustness. The random committee was not applied to SVR models because they are not based on random initial parameters. The error of each model configuration was obtained as the average of the ten predictions made with the random committee (except for SVR). Year 2009 was used to train the models. Simple validation was performed during the odd weeks of 2010. The configuration with the smallest RMSE in the validation set was considered the optimum. Then, models were tested during the even weeks of 2010.

3.6 Blending

Blending consists of combining two or several models to foster their strengths and improve model accuracy. Blending has already been successfully applied to power forecasting models [8].

In this study, once a model was optimized for each technique, a fifth model was constructed, based on a combination of them. Hourly predictions of each model were weighted, combined and optimized with the Broyden–Fletcher–Goldfarb–Shanno (BFGS) algorithm, as depicted in Fig. 1. Optimization was performed in two steps. First, the weights of each model were obtained with the validation set, which could range [0–4]. Thus, the relative importance of each model to the ensemble prediction was obtained. Then, the weighted predictions were averaged to generate the final prediction. Several average configurations were tested, such as the arithmetic mean, harmonic mean, geometrical mean and power means of index p [0.5–9]. Each of the possible combinations were evaluated in terms of nRMSE with the validation set. The combination of weights and average type that produced the smaller nRMSE was considered to be the optimum.

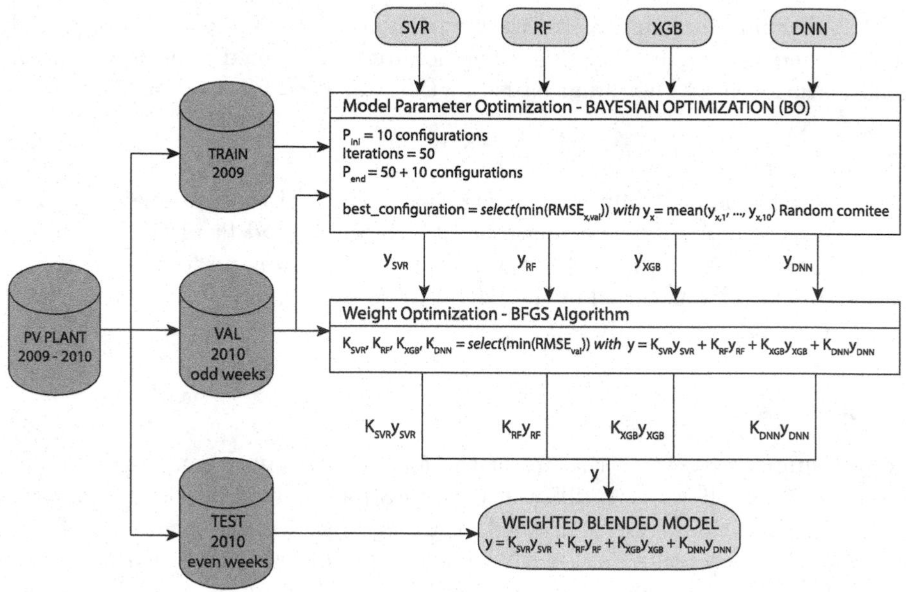

Fig. 1. Model construction and selection. x comprises each of the configurations.

3.7 Software

Calculations were made with the freely distributed statistical software `R`. Various packages were used, such as the `zoo`, to work with time series, the `solaR` package, to obtain solar variables and the `xgboost`, `e1071`, `randomForest` and `deepnet` packages to generate the model under the studied techniques.

4 Results

Table 1 lists the error metrics obtained with each of the models. SVR stood out for having the best predictions among the single models, showing a nRMSE of 22.49%. According to RMSE, second best was RF, which showed a small bias. However, both XGB and DNN had a great positive bias, ascending to 45.61 kWh for the former technique. Compared to the two-day persistence of production, used as baseline, all proposed model could beat it, improving by large its performance. Nevertheless, the baseline remained as the model with lowest bias.

However, if models are ranked according to the MAE, a different classification is obtained. SVR maintained its first position, with a MAE of 322.61 kWh, but the DNN model, which had the greatest RMSE, showed smaller MAE than RF and XGB. This reflects the importance of making a complete assessment of performance metrics prior to selecting a technique to issue forecasts.

Table 1. Error metrics for various models during test period (even weeks of 2010).

Model	MAE (kWh)	RMSE (kWh)	nRMSE (%)	MBE (kWh)
Two-day persistence	420.94	595.41	32.86	6.28
DNN	336.46	426.29	23.53	34.42
SVR	322.61	407.54	22.49	–10.11
RF	340.42	412.57	22.77	–11.33
XGB	341.57	417.15	23.02	45.61
Blended	323.40	403.00	22.24	7.57

Table 2. Weights of the blended model

	DNN	SVR	RF	XGB
Weigths	0.59	2.59	0.02	0.80

Nevertheless, when results of the blended model are taken into account, it outperforms all single models, with a nRMSE of 22.24%. This proves that a correct combination of single models may enhance prediction accuracy. The blended model also showed the smallest bias (7.57 kWh), although it had a slightly superior MAE than the single SVR model.

According to Table 2, the most important contribution to the blended model was that of the SVR model, which coincided to be the best performing single model. Second best results in Table 1 were obtained by the RF model. However, the contribution of that model to the blended one was insignificant. Contrarily, XGB, which showed worse results, ended having more relevance in the blended model. Both RF and XGB are based on regression trees. The reason for this situation could be that XGB predictions have smaller correlation to SVR forecasts than RF do and thus, in a blended model, XGB can contribute with more information, eclipsing RF. The greater importance of DNN, which was the model with worse results, in the blended model compared to RF may also be explained by the aforementioned argument. Besides, the best performing average method was the arithmetic mean.

5 Conclusions and Future Work

Solar power forecasts are necessary to safely integrate into the grid the intermittent production coming from the PV plants. Variability caused by cloud movement increases the uncertainty of forecasts, which leads to errors in predictions. Production forecasts are useful for grid operators and for plant managers who bid in the electricity market. In the present study, different statistical models were trained to forecast DA power production for a PV plant located in the North of Spain. NWP of various meteorological variables were added to the input set to enhance predictions. Besides, a blended model was constructed with a weighted combination of single-technique predictions. Results show that among the single models, best performing one was SVR, with a nRMSE of 22.49%, showing also the smallest bias (with the exception of the two-day persistence of production). Second best was RF, followed by XGB, with nRMSE of 22.77% and 23.02%, respectively. All models clearly outperformed the two-day persistence of production, used as a baseline. However, when the blended model was considered, it outperformed all single models, bottoming the nRMSE to 22.24%. The weights assigned to each model reveal the great importance of the SVR predictions in the ensemble model, being the participation of RF negligible. The best ensemble model was obtained when predictions were averaged with the geometrical mean.

Acknowledgments. J. Antonanzas and R. Urraca would like to acknowledge the fellowship FPI-UR-2014 granted by the University of La Rioja. This work used the Beronia cluster (Universidad de La Rioja), which is supported by FEDER-MINECO grant number UNLR-094E-2C-225.

References

1. Almeida, M.P., Perpinan, O., Narvarte, L.: PV power forecast using a nonparametric PV model. Solar Energy **115**, 354–368 (2015)
2. Almonacid, F., Perez-Higueras, P.J., Fernendez, E.F., Hontoria, L.: A methodology based on dynamic artificial neural network for short-term forecasting of the power output of a PV generator. Energy Convers. Manage. **85**, 389–398 (2014). http://dx.doi.org/10.1016/j.enconman.2014.05.090
3. Antonanzas, J., Osorio, N., Escobar, R., Urraca, R., Martinez-de Pison, F.J., Antonanzas-Torres, F.: Review of photovoltaic power forecasting. Solar Energy **136**, 78–111 (2016). http://dx.doi.org/10.1016/j.solener.2016.06.069
4. Bengio, Y.: Learning deep architectures for AI. Found. Trends Mach. Learn. **2**, 1–127 (2009)
5. Breiman, L.: Random forests. Mach. Learn. **45**(1), 5–32 (2001)
6. Chen, T., He, T.: XGBoost: eXtreme gradient boosting. R package version 0.4–2 (2015)
7. Da Silva Fonseca Junior, J.G., Oozeki, T., Ohtake, H., Shimose, K., Takashima, T., Ogimoto, K.: Regional forecasts and smoothing effect of photovoltaic power generation in Japan: an approach with principal component analysis. Renew. Energy **68**, 403–413 (2014). http://dx.doi.org/10.1016/j.renene.2014.02.018
8. Hossain, R., Maung, A., Oo, T., Ali, A.B.M.S.: Hybrid prediction method for solar power using different computational intelligence algorithms. Smart Grid. Renew. Energy **4**, 76–87 (2013)
9. Li, Y., Su, Y., Shu, L.: An ARMAX model for forecasting the power output of a grid connected photovoltaic system. Renew. Energy **66**, 78–89 (2014). http://dx.doi.org/10.1016/j.renene.2013.11.067
10. Vapnik, V., Lerner, A.: Pattern recognition using generalized portrait method. Autom. Remote Control **24**, 774–780 (1963)
11. Wang, F., Zhen, Z., Mi, Z., Sun, H., Su, S., Yang, G.: Solar irradiance feature extraction and support vector machines based weather status pattern recognition model for short-term photovoltaic power forecasting. Energy Buildings **86**, 427–438 (2015). http://dx.doi.org/10.1016/j.enbuild.2014.10.002

Integration of Case Based Reasoning in Multi-agent System for the Real-Time Container Stacking in Seaport Terminals

Ines Rekik[1(✉)], Sabeur Elkosantini[2], and Habib Chabchoub[3]

[1] LOGIQ Research Unit, University of Sfax, Sfax, Tunisia
ines.rekik.86@gmail.com
[2] Industrial Engineering Department, King Saud University, Riyadh, Saudi Arabia
selkosantini@ksu.edu.sa
[3] International School of Business, Sfax, Tunisia
Habib.chabchoub@gmail.com

Abstract. In seaport terminals, Container Stacking Problem (CSP) consists of determining the exact storage location of incoming containers in the storage area. During the stacking process, many unexpected events and disturbances may occur and, then, scheduled position of containers must be modified. In this paper, we suggest a new multi-agent architecture based on the Case Based Reasoning mechanism for modeling the container storage process in an uncertain and disturbed environment. The suggested multi agent system is based on three agents: interface agent, container agent and evaluation agent. Computational experiments show that integration of Case Based Reasoning in Multi Agent System seems to be effective for the real-time container stacking in seaport terminals.

Keywords: Multi-agent system · Case based reasoning · Disturbances management · Container stacking system

1 Introduction

With the continuous development of seaport terminals and the significant increase of containers exchange flows between ports, various types of problems have emerged and attracted increasing attention in recent research. These problems can cause downtime or wasted movements during the process of unloading-storage-loading containers and an imbalance of transport flows of goods requiring transportation of empty containers. One of the most difficult of these problems is the Container Storage Problem (CSP). CSP consists of determining the temporary storage location of containers in the storage area of a terminal on their arrival to the port.

Several research works have been conducted to develop Decision Support Systems (DSS) for the management of container storage operations, which are referred to as Container Terminal Operating Systems (CTOS) [4–6]. However, existing real-time CTOSs suffer limitations with respect to several aspects related to knowledge management, distributed control and the efficiency of used real-time stacking strategies

F.J. Martínez de Pisón et al. (Eds.): HAIS 2017, LNAI 10334, pp. 435–446, 2017.
DOI: 10.1007/978-3-319-59650-1_37

particularly in presence of dangerous containers [8, 9], and disturbances management [1]. Unfortunately, most of the existing multi-agent based CTOSs consider one storage rule for all types of incoming containers and for all situations without taking into account the real-time change in the terminal. It is generally well admitted that there is no storage rule that is globally better than all the others [2].

This paper presents an agent based model for the control of container stacking in an uncertain and disturbed environment. The proposed system combines Case Based Reasoning (CBR) and multi-agent system for the selection of the allocation decision. To the best of the author's knowledge, this paper is the first adopting the CBR mechanism for container stacking in seaport terminals.

The remainder of this paper is organized as follows: Sect. 2 introduces the CSP and gives a brief survey on existing studies related to CSP and to disturbances management in the stacking systems. Section 3 presents the global architecture of the proposed multi-agent approach. Section 4 describes the different agents constituting this system. Finally, Sect. 5 presents the interactions and the communication between the different agents for determining the appropriate exact storage location.

2 Problem Description

2.1 Container Stacking Problem (CSP)

CSPs include the process of storing or retrieving containers in a stack so as to ensure the proper conduct of the rest of operations within the terminal. The container stacking operation consists on determining the temporary storage location of containers in the storage area (named the storage yard) in a terminal on their arrival to the seaport terminal.

A storage yard consists of a number of areas perpendicular or parallel to the berth called blocks. Each block is characterized by a number of bays, which represent the length of the block, a number of rows, which represent its width, and a number of tiers, which represent its height (see Fig. 1).

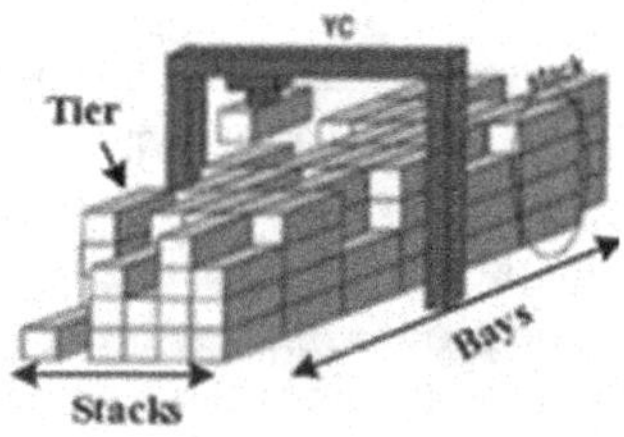

Fig. 1. A stacking block

To improve terminals performance, several staking rules (strategies) have been developed in the literature. The efficiency of each rule varies from terminal to terminal [3]. According to [1], stacking rules are categorized into three main families:

- Block Stacking Rules (BlSR): deal with the selection of the "appropriate" block for incoming containers (import or export containers). These rules include dedicated

areas, Role Separation of Blocks, Role Separation of Rows, Role Separation of Bays, No Restriction, the Different Priorities on Blocks for Different Berths, and the Maximum Number of Internal Trucks and Road Trucks in a Block.
- Bay Stacking Rules (BSR): are responsible for the selection of a bay from the pre-selected block. Several bay stacking rules have been studied in the literature, such as Concentrated Location Principle and Sequence rule.
- Slot Stacking Rules (SSR): are related to the selection of the exact storage location in the assigned bay of the assigned block. Several stack (or slot) stacking rules have been studied in the literature including the Random rule, Levelling rule, Closest Position rule, Maximum Remaining Stack height rule.

Several approaches have been used in the literature to solve CSPs. Optimization approaches [4] and centralized artificial intelligence approaches [5] have been widely used in the literature. Few research studies, in contrast, have attempted to use Multi Agent Systems (MAS) to address the CSP. For example, [6] have developed a MAS denoted COSAH (COntainer Stacking via multi-Agent approach and Heuristic method) that allows simulating, solving and optimizing the amount of storage space for handling incoming and outgoing containers within a fluvial or maritime port. This approach is intended to minimize the expected total number of rehandles while respecting the dynamic spatio-temporal constraints. Similarly, [7] proposed also a Multi-Agent approach via market-based allocation to plan and coordinate the different processes within a terminal by mapping the objects and resources used in the terminal. Hamidou et al. [8] have developed a hybrid architecture, combining Cellular Automaton and a Multi-Agent System to handle dangerous containers in order to minimize the safety distance between two dangerous containers and while taking into account the dynamic arrival and departure of containers. They have considered the storage constraints and rules for each class of dangerous containers. However, their architecture was restricted only to one unique block of many rows.

2.2 Disturbances Management

In a storage yard, the assignment of specific storage positions for incoming containers can't be pre-planned due to the high uncertainties and the unexpected (disruptive) events (equipment (blocks, bays, stacks) breakdown, breakage of materials (yard cranes), a fault in a container placing, container retrieve, dangerous container arrival) that may occur. A disruptive event here is defined as a significant change in the allocation plan and that can lead to deadlock or failure situations. Thus, the storage location for inbound containers is made on real-time basis.

The literature review conducted and briefly presented in this paper revealed that there are still limitations of exiting DSS with regards to different aspects. Firstly, we noted that there are no generic approaches treating disturbances management. Indeed, most of existing studies are limited to a restricted number of disturbances (dynamic arrival and departure of containers in most studies). Therefore, the development of a reactive system monitoring in a real time manner the stacking operation remain a relevant global research direction. Secondly, few works have developed distributed Multi-Agent Systems for determining the online exact location of containers [6]. Finally, there is only one work [9], as far as we know, from existing agent based studies used intelligent agents that learn from past experience. In this study, the authors proposed a knowledge based system for the real time container stacking. In this context, there is no work adopting the Case Based Reasoning (CBR) for the container stacking control system.

3 Suggested System Architecture

This section introduces the used CBR system, including cases representation and case bases, and its integration into a multi-agent system.

3.1 Case Representation

A *case* represent knowledge related to a situation of a container as well as the appropriate assignment rule that can be adopted to determine the position of the associated container. In this article, cases having the following structure:

$$Case:\ < Knowledge, Decision > \tag{1}$$

Where *Knowledge* is an attribute describing all characteristics related to a container to be stored and *Decision* is the exact position of this container. *Knowledge* represents all knowledge related to the containers to be stored. It is structured as represented in the following vector:

$$Knowledge:\ < Container, Terminal, Event, [disturbance] > \tag{2}$$

The first part of the knowledge is related to containers. In this work, such knowledge is represented by the following vector:

$$Container\ Knowledge:\ < Origin, Destination, Date\ in, Date\ out, Container\ Type > \tag{3}$$

The attribute Container Type is an integer. Three types of containers are considered in this article: regular (1), open top (2), and dangerous (3).

The system should also have a detailed representation of the actual configuration of the storage space and available positions in all blocks. This knowledge is formalized by:

$$Terminal\ Knowledge:\ < N_{i,j}^{k}, T_{i,j}^{k} > \tag{4}$$

Where $N_{i,j}^{k}$ represents the number of containers in the ith stack of the jth bay of the kth block and $T_{i,j}^{k}$ is its type.

The system has also to identify the types of events and disturbances. An event is characterized by its type and its cause:

$$Event\ Knowledge:\ < Event\ Type, Cause > \tag{5}$$

Three event types are identified: Allocation request and Re-allocation requests, Retrieval requests and Disturbance events. Such events can be generated by the detection of a disturbance, the need for the retrieval of a container or a request from another agent to treat. Finally, the system should also collect data and knowledge related to disturbance if it is detected. A disturbance is characterized by its type and degree of gravity (which should be indicated by the decision maker). Thus, a disturbance is represented by the following vector:

$$Disturbance\ Knowledge\!: < Disturbance\ Type, gravity > \tag{6}$$

There are three types of disturbances: resources disturbances (yard crane breakage), equipment disturbances (blocks breakdown etc.) and containers disturbances (fault in container placing, container breakdown, a change in a container's date out etc.).

The attribute *Decision* of the case representation (see Eq. 1) is described by three attributes representing the stacking rules used for the determination of the strategy to be adopted to determine the position of the position:

$$Decision\!: < BlSR, BSR, SSR > \tag{7}$$

Where *BlSR* is the id of the block stacking rule representing the strategy to be adopted by the system to determine the block, *BSR* is the id of the bay stacking rule representing the strategy to be adopted by the system to determine the bay, and *SSR* is the id of the stack stacking rule representing the strategy to be adopted by the system to determine the stack.

3.2 Case Base

The suggested system integrates a continuous learning mechanism by the use of two types of case base:

- $CB^{Bad} = \{Case_i^{bad}\}, i = 1..n$: A case base storing bad cases where n is the number of bad cases. This case base will allow the system to avoid some decisions that were tested in the past and that have provided bad results. $Case_i^{bad}$ is a bad case that have not improved the performance of the port in a previous experience.
- $CB^{Good} = \{Case_i^{Good}\}, i = 1..m$: A case base storing good cases, where m is the number of good cases. This case base will allow the system to quickly select some decisions that were tested in the past and have provided good results.

3.3 Case Retrieval

When a new container requiring the determination of position is detected, the system needs to find the most similar case in order to find the best decision and avoid bad ones. This steps is performed by calculating the distance between a $Case_i$ stored in a case base and a *Sit* where *Sit* is a vector representing the knowledge of the container to be stacked. The Euclidian distance is used for the similarity measure. An unweighted measure is used in this article. The case with the lowest value of the distance is considered as the most similar.

Two distance measures are introduced. The first determines the distance between a situation and a case from CB^{Good} (see Eq. 8) and the second measure calculates the similarities between a case and cases from CB^{Bad} (see Eq. 9)

$$Dist\left(Sit, Case_i^{Good}\right) = \sum\nolimits_{j=1}^{p} \left|Sit.Knowledge.att_j - Case_i^{Good}.Knowledge.att_j\right| \quad (8)$$

Where p is the number of attributes of the knowledge part of a case (see Eq. 2), $Sit \cdot Knowledge \cdot att_j$ is the jth attribute of the part Knowledge of the situation Sit and $Case_i^{Good} \cdot Knowledge \cdot att_j$ is the jth attribute of the part Knowledge of the case $Case_i^{Good}$.

$$\begin{aligned} Dist\left(Case, Case_i^{Bad}\right) = & \sum\nolimits_{j=1}^{p} \left|Case.Knowledge.att_j - Case_i^{Bad}.Knowledge.att_j\right| \\ & + \sum\nolimits_{k=1}^{3} \left|Case.Decision.att_k - Case_i^{Bad}.Decision.att_k\right| \end{aligned} \quad (9)$$

Where $Case \cdot Decision \cdot att_k$ is the id of the kth stacking rules (see Sect. 3.1).

3.4 Overview of the Suggested Architecture

For the design of our MAS based CTOS, we have used O-MaSE (Organization based Multi-agents System Engineering) methodology presented in [10] and including the analysis phase, the conception phase and the implementation phase. This methodology takes into account the system dynamics. It conceives also a MAS as an agent society where each agent has specific goals and plays a specific role. Thus, the purpose of this method is to construct an organizational agent based on the meta-models of the organization. The analysis and the design of our proposed system led us to define three types of agents (see Fig. 2):

- Container Agent (CA): determines the location of each incoming container.
- Evaluation Agent (EA): evaluates the efficiency of an allocation decision. This agent is solicited particularly by the container agent.
- Interface Agent (IA): detects and analyzes, in a real time way, the different requests of containers allocation/retrieval and also the unexpected events and disturbances from the common environment.

The interface agent IA collects data from different sensors in the terminal (such as RFID), analyzes them and then sends an allocation or re-allocation request to CA for the determination of the position of the incoming container. In the suggested architecture (see Fig. 2), the decision making process of CA relies on a CBR system using the two suggested case bases: CB^{Bad} and CB^{Good} (see Subsect. 3.5). The exact position of each container is then sent to the EA for assessment considering a set of performance criteria. The EA sends a request to the CA to change the allocation solution if it is rejected by

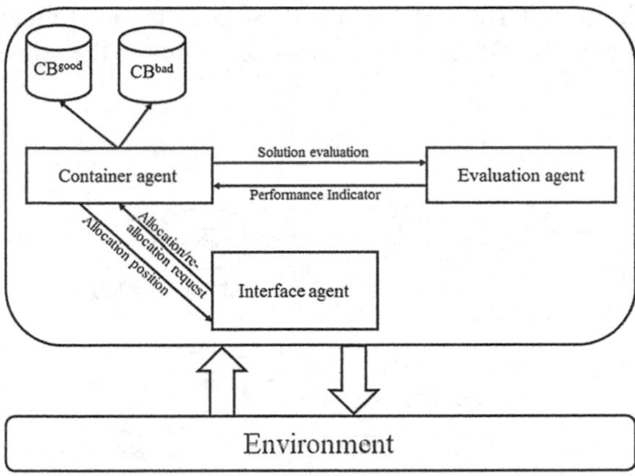

Fig. 2. Multi-agent architecture

the EA. Otherwise, a message is sent to the IA to inform the decision makers about the exact position of the incoming container.

3.5 Agents Description

As shown in previous section, the suggested Multi-Agent System is composed of three agents (Interface agent, Container agent and Evaluation agent) which communicate with each other and with the external environment in order to make an allocation/re-allocation decision. The goals and behaviors of the different agents constituting our system are detailed in the following subsections.

Interface Agent (IA)
The Interface agent (IA) detects and analyses, in a real time way, the different events (container's allocation/retrieval requests, disturbances) from the terminal. It captures the knowledge related to the detected events (type of event, cause, and gravity), the terminal configuration and the corresponding container (type of container, date in, date out and type). This agent plays also the role of the HMI (Human Machine Interface) where the final allocation decision is represented. As soon as an event is detected, one of the following requests are sent to Container Agent (CA): Allocation request, Re-allocation request, and Disturbance detected request.

Container Agent (CA)
The container agent (CA) is an intelligent agent as it is able to reason before acting. The main objective of this agent consists on selecting the most appropriate exact position of the incoming container by using the Case Based Reasoning mechanism. The case base allows the system to quickly select some decisions that were tested in the past. For achieving this goal, the CA uses the two types of case bases: CB^{Good} and CB^{Bad}. The decision making process implemented in the CA relies on a suggested two-steps methodology for determining the exact position of containers: the first is the determination

of the stacking rule using CBR and the second step is the determination of the exact position of containers in blocks, bays and stacks according to the selected stacking rule (see Fig. 3).

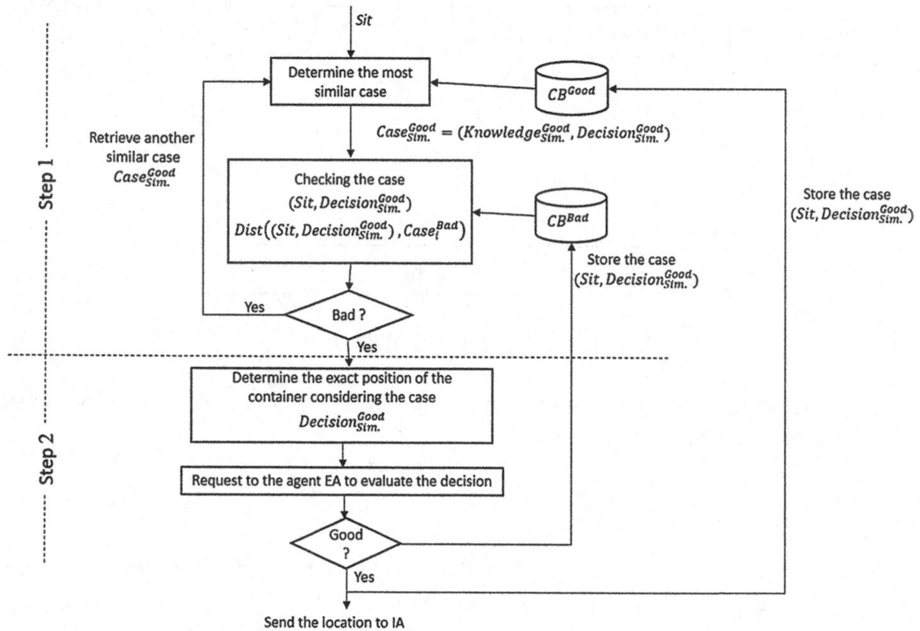

Fig. 3. Suggested learning mechanisms of the agent CA

The decision making process includes the following steps:

- Step 1: stacking rules identification:
  - Sub-step 1.1: When the CA receives a request from IA with all knowledge related to the container to be stacked. The agent starts by checking in CB^{Good} if such situation *Sit* is encountered in the past $\left(Dist\left(Sit, Case_i^{Good}\right) = 0\right)$ using the similarity measure (see Eq. 8). In that a case, CA activates the second step of the decision making process and determines the exact position according to the selected stacking rules then it sends the exact position of the container to IA to allocate the container. Otherwise, the agent search for the most similar case, refereed to by $Case^{Good}_{Sim.}$ and represented by the vector $\left(Knowledge^{Good}_{Sim.}, Decision^{Good}_{Sim.}\right)$, i.e. the distance is less than a fixed threshold.
  - Sub-step 1.2: the agent checks in CB^{Bad} if the decision of the determined most similar case $Decision^{Good}_{Sim.}$ is not good for the container to be located. Indeed, the agent calculates the similarity between $Case_i^{Bad}$ and the new case formed by knowledge related to the situation *Sit* and the decision $Decision^{Good}_{Sim.}$ (see Eq. 9), i.e. the following case (Sit, $Decision^{Good}_{Sim.}$).

- Sub-step 1.3: if the distance is less than a fixed threshold, the decision is considered as bad. In that case, sub-step 1.1 is called to determine another decision coming from another case. Otherwise, the decision is sent to the EA to evaluate the performance (see next subsection) of the decision considering the all knowledge of the incoming container represented by the attribute *Sit*.
- Sub-step 1.4: if the performance of the decision is evaluated as bad, a new case (Sit, $Case^{Good}_{Sim.}.Decision$) is added to CB^{Bad} and another *Allocation request* is sent to CA to determine another decision. Otherwise, the decision is considered as good and a new case ($Sit, Decision^{Good}_{Sim.}$) is added to CB^{Good}. Then, Step 2 is called

– Step 2: Considering the three stacking rules, the agent identify the location of the container and sends to IA to inform operators.

This suggested learning mechanism allow the agent CA to continuously learn from experience and reduce requests to EA for the evaluation of new decisions which can take time. This mechanisms is presented in the Fig. 3.

Evaluation Agent (EA)
The evaluation agent (EA) evaluates the stacking position sent by the CA considering the following performance indicator:

$$P(d_1, q, d_2, h) = \alpha d_1 + \beta q + \gamma d_2 + \delta h \tag{10}$$

Where $P(d_1, q, d_2, h)$ represents the weighted sum of four criteria: d_1 which represents the distance separating the given block from the gate; q represents the waiting queue in front of the given block; d_2 represents the distance separating the given stack from the gate; and h represents the remaining stack height. α, β, γ and δ represent the related weights. The weight related to each criterion varies according to the type of the incoming container; three cases are considered in our paper:

- In case of open top container, the remaining stack height has the highest weight.
- In case of dangerous container the distance to gate has the highest weight.
- In case of regular or empty container, the waiting queue has the highest weight.

In other word, in order to optimize the yard space and retrieval time, open top containers require the highest positions in a bay since we can't place another container above them, but dangerous containers require the closest positions since they do not generally stay too long in the yard. Finally, regular containers do not have an influencing criterion which dominates regarding the other criterion.

4 Agents Communication

The Communication between agents defines the relationships between the various agents of a system by means of messages exchange respecting a certain sequence [11]. The different interactions between agents can be represented by the protocol diagram (see Fig. 4) in O-MaSE.

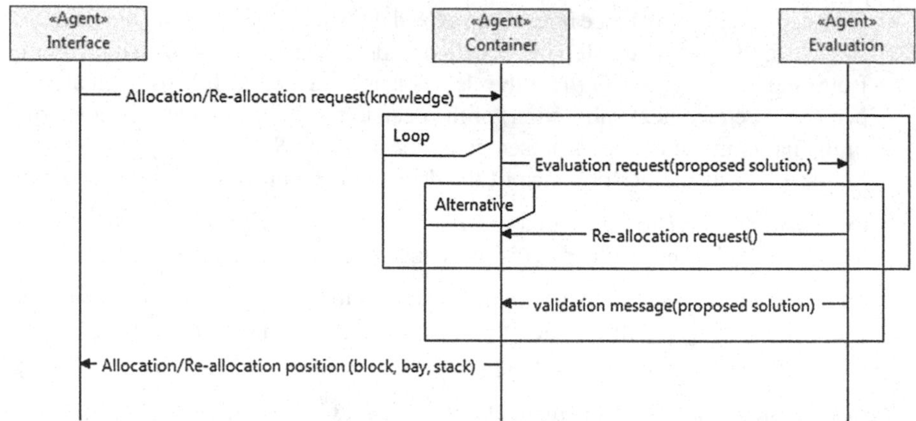

Fig. 4. Protocol diagram of an allocation/re-allocation request

The proposed multi-agent system uses three types of requests when they exchange messages including:

- *Allocation request*: activated when an incoming container arrives to the yard and searches for a position where it can be stored.
- *Re-allocation request*: is sent from an agent to another in order to ask to select another position.
- *Disturbance detected request*: activated when a disturbance, such as a yard crane breakdown or a locked block, occurs during the stacking process. In this article, disturbances are categorized into three categories: resources disturbances (yard crane breakage), equipment disturbances (blocks breakdown etc.) and containers disturbances (fault in container placing, container breakdown, container's date out change etc.).

5 Implementation and Assessment

The proposed system was implemented using the multi-agent platform JADE (Java Agent DEvelopement framework). This approach was evaluated relying on the data collected from the certified ISO Tunisia Sfax seaport in Tunisia. The port has a capacity of 83 000 TEUs and a storage area of 28 hectares. The presented port contains 30 blocks. Each block is made up of 5 bays and each bay contains 4 stacks (the maximum stack height is 4). In this work, we have simulated the arrival of three kinds of containers: regular, dangerous (with different class of goods) and open top. We assumed that only one container at a time enters the yard to be stored.

For the assessment of our system, we have defined three scenarios with different initial configurations and different arrival and departure rates of containers: scenario 1 with an empty yard at the beginning of the planning horizon (simulation of 1500 incoming containers); scenario 2 with a 50% utilization rate of the yard capacity (simulation of 500 incoming containers); and scenario 3 with an 80% utilization rate of the yard capacity (simulation of 200 incoming containers). For the assessment of our proposed approach, we compared its performance to the fuzzy logic strategy implemented in [5] with regards to the performance measure presented by the Eq. 10. The computational results are shown in Figs. 5 and 6.

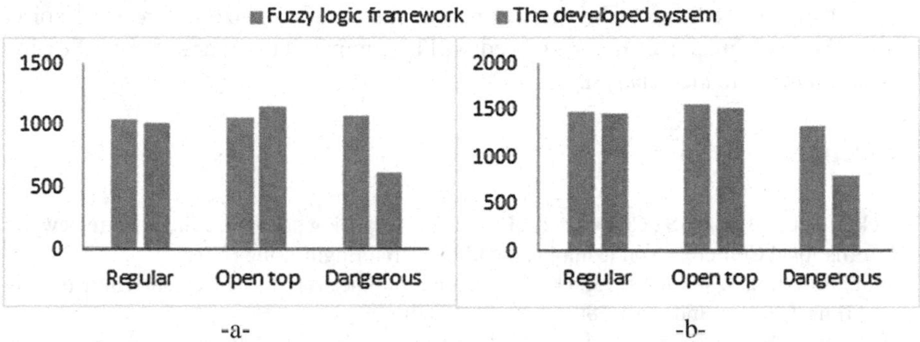

Fig. 5. Experimental results for the empty yard scenario (a) and for the 50% congestion scenario (b)

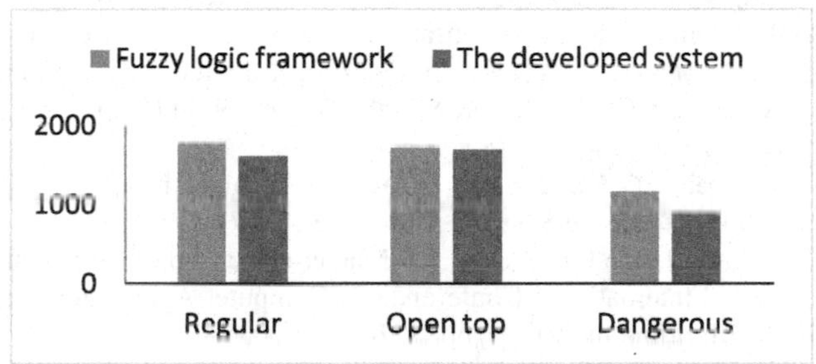

Fig. 6. Experimental results for the 80% congestion scenario

The conducted experiment shows that, the integration of Case Based Reasoning in the Multi Agent System in the real time container stacking problem can be efficient compared to the fuzzy logic strategy especially in presence of dangerous containers. Although the similarity between the two approaches for both regular and open top container staking, the developed system provides best results for the stacking of dangerous container in all scenarios. However, an in-depth statistical analysis of the system with regards to other scenarios and systems is necessary.

6 Conclusion and Future Work

In this paper, a new Multi Agent architecture for the real time container stacking in seaport terminals is presented. The allocation structure is based on a set of learning mechanisms (based on Case Based Reasoning (CBR)) allowing the system to learn from past encountered good and bad decisions. In this context, a CBR system is developed and integrated in the proposed MAS. The proposed approach allows also the control of the storage system in a real time manner by including the different unexpected events and disturbances that may occur during the allocation process. To improve the suggested system, we will suggest a case adapting mechanism to replace the case updating mechanism integrated in the container agent. Moreover, we will suggest in the future the use of condensing and editing techniques to reduce the case base size and remove noise. Finally, the performance of the suggested will be compared to other systems allowing an in-depth performance analysis.

References

1. Rekik, I., Elkosantini, S., Chabchoub, H.: Container stacking problem: a literature review. In: International Conference on Computers and Industrial Engineering (2015)
2. Mouelhi-Chibani, W., Pierreval, H.: Training a neural network to select dispatching rules in real time. Comput. Ind. Eng. **58**(2), 249–256 (2010)
3. Asperen, E.V., Borgman, B., Dekker, R.: Evaluating impact of truck announcements on container stacking efficiency. Flex. Serv. Manuf. J. **25**, 543–556 (2013)
4. Zhang, C., Wu, T., Zhong, M., Zhen, L., Miao, L.: Location assignment for outbound containers with adjusted weight proportion. Comput. Oper. Res. **52**, 84–93 (2014)
5. Ries, J., González-Ramírez, Rosa G., Miranda, P.: A fuzzy logic model for the container stacking problem at container terminals. In: González-Ramírez, R.G., Schulte, F., Voß, S., Ceroni Díaz, J.A. (eds.) ICCL 2014. LNCS, vol. 8760, pp. 93–111. Springer, Cham (2014). doi:10.1007/978-3-319-11421-7_7
6. Gazdar, M.K., Korbaa, O., Ghedira, K., Yim, P.: Container handling using multi-agent architecture. Int. J. Inf. Database Syst. **3**(3), 685–693 (2007)
7. Henesey, L., Wernstedt, F., Davidsson, P.: Market-driven control in container terminal management. In: 2nd International Conference on Computer Applications and Information Technology in the Maritime Industries, pp. 377–386 (2003)
8. Hamidou, M., Fournier, D., Sanlaville, E., Serin, F.: Management of dangerous goods incontainer terminal with MAS model. In: The 15th International Conference on Harbor, Maritime & Multimodal Logistics, Athènes, Greece, September 2013
9. Rekik, I., Elkosantini, S., Chabchoub, H.: Toward a knowledge based multi-agent architecture for the reactive container stacking in seaport terminals: application to the port of Sfax in Tunisia. In: Rutkowski, L., Korytkowski, M., Scherer, R., Tadeusiewicz, R., Zadeh, L.A., Zurada, J.M. (eds.) ICAISC 2016. LNCS, vol. 9692, pp. 718–728. Springer, Cham (2016). doi:10.1007/978-3-319-39378-0_61
10. Deloach, S.A.: Engineering organization based multiagent systems. In: 4th International Workshop on Software Engineering for Largescale Multiagent Systems (SELMAS 2005), pp. 109–125 (2005)
11. Guessoum, Z.: Modéles et Architectures d'agents et de systèmes multi-agents adaptatifs. Université Pierre et Marie Curie, Thèse de doctorat (2003)

Experimental Evaluation of Straight Line Programs for Hydrological Modelling with Exogenous Variables

Ramón Rueda Delgado[1(✉)], Luis G. Baca Ruiz[1], Patricia Jimeno-Sáez[2], Manuel Pegalajar Cuellar[1], David Pulido-Velazquez[3], and Mara Del Carmen Pegalajar[1]

[1] Department of Computer Science and Artificial Intelligence, University of Granada, C/. Pdta. Daniel Saucedo Aranda s.n., Granada, Spain
ramon92@correo.ugr.es, bacaruiz@ugr.es, {manupc,mcarmen}@decsai.ugr.es

[2] Department of Civil Engineering, Catholic University of San Antonio, Campus de los Jerónimos s/n, Guadalupe, 30107 Murcia, Spain
pjimeno@ucam.edu

[3] Instituto Geológico y Minero de España, Urb.Alczar del Genil, 4. Edificio Zulema Bajo, 18006 Granada, Spain
d.pulido@igme.es

Abstract. The estimation of the future streamflows is one of the main research topics in hydrology and a very important task for water resources management. The aim of this work is to use symbolic regression in order to model the hydrological balance. Specifically, we use genetic programming to solve the symbolic regression problem. Nevertheless, in this work we use Straight Line Programs instead of trees to encode algebraic expression. Results shows that this representation for algebraic expressions could improve the results in both accuracy and computational time.

Keywords: Genetic programming · Straight line programs · Symbolic regression · Modeling hydrological balance

1 Introduction

Streamflow data are essential for flood and drought mitigation, operation of reservoirs, design and operation of water infrastructure, water supply, environmental conservation or hydropower generation [4,9]. It is required to hold robust and reliable streamflow models that can be used to infer hidden information in streamflows as well as accurate prediction models, to mitigate the impacts and risks of basins under drought conditions.

This paper addresses the development and comparison of techniques for water resources modeling, focusing on computational models to ease the automatic inference of regression hypotheses of real streamflow datasets. With the long-term aim of a better resource management under water scarcity conditions,

F.J. Martínez de Pisón et al. (Eds.): HAIS 2017, LNAI 10334, pp. 447–458, 2017.
DOI: 10.1007/978-3-319-59650-1_38

this study analizes classic and recent regression representation models able to approximate the real streamflow in six catchments, using the symbolic regression paradigm [7].

Traditionally, symbolic regression problems have been addressed using tree representations to model a regression hypothesis, and using global search procedures such as Genetic Programming [12] to find a model that best fits an output dataset considering other input variables. In this work, we use tree representation as a baseline method, but we also test the recently proposed Straight Line Program (SLP) as a promising model representation for regression hypotheses. In addition, we use a hybrid Genetic Programming approach to perform the search of the best tree/SLP that models streamflow data, using a local search method (least squares estimation) to approximate the regression hypothesis parameters for each candidate tree/SLP during the search procedure. Having this into consideration, our problem description is as follows:

The testbed encompasses 6 subbasins in the Alto-Genil basin in Granada (Southeast of Spain). The amount of the total streamflow in a basin is composed of two main components: surface water and groundwater. The amount of streamflow is related to climate data (rainfall and temperature) and basin characteristic (physical features). A large number of rainfall-runoff models have been developed to explore the relationships between precipitation and streamflow. Among these model, some of them as the Sacramento model [6], the Témez model [19], the HBV-96 model [13] and the SWAT model [3]. Other aspects such as evapotranspiration, infiltration, velocity of groundwater flow, etc. also affect in the modelling of a specific basin streamflow. Thus, as we pursue to find an accurate streamflow model specially adapted for a particular basin, we should consider how these external parameters affect the specific basin under study. Moreover, the data sampling rate or data granularity is also a key factor: The velocity of groundwater flow is slower than superficial flow, so that the effect of rain does not affect the basin total streamflow instantly, but with a delay that can be perceived depending on the granularity of the data sampling. Thus, models applied over daily sampled data are not presumably as affected by a recent rainflow as models applied over monthly sampled data, due to the groundwater flow speed.

For this reasons, our dataset is composed by monthly and daily streamflow datasets containing precipitation (P), temperature (T) and surface waterflow measurements (X) as inputs, and our goal is to find an accurate particularized regression model for the whole streamflow (Y) in each basin, considering both surface and groundwater flows. Thus, a complete model of a basin has a potential form of $Y = f(X, T, P, w)$, where f is an unknown function (regression hypothesis model), and w are the model parameters, which are also unknown. However, the influence of T and P for each basin might differ substantially depending on further considerations such as the data granularity (daily, monthly) and terrain properties, as it was mentioned previously, therefore providing different regression models particularized for each basin.

Under this problem formulation, our analysis suggests that the problem has two components: A feature selection stage to know which input data parameters affect to each basin, and a regression hypothesis induction for each dataset. This problem could be easily solved using universal approximation models such as traditional neural networks or support vector machines, between others, as it has been studied previously in the literature [4]. However, in our problem it is also important to have a high expressivity in the resulting model, so that Earth Science experts could validate the regression hypothesis and infer streamflow properties from the interred formulae. For this reason, in our experimentation we test: (a) the regression hypothesis representation that can provide the most accurate results in the function approximation problem, considering tree and SLP representation, and (b) the capabilities of the approach to make an automatic feature selection in the datasets.

This paper is organized as follows: Sect. 2 introduces symbolic regression and the traditional tree representation for regression hypotheses, as well as the genetic programming procedure to find the best candidate regression hypothesis. Section 3 explains the Straight Line Program model for symbolic regression, and the genetic operators for genetic programming search. After that, Sect. 4 describes the experimentation performed, and Sect. 5 concludes.

2 Symbolic Regression

Regression analysis [1,20] is a mathematical methodology used to fit a functional model between dependent and independent variables. The components of regression analysis (Formula 1) are: a function f, a set of input data $\bar{x} = x_1, x_2, x_3, ..., x_n$, a set of output data $\bar{y} = y_1, y_2, y_3, ..., y_m$ and a set of dependent parameters $\bar{w} = w_1, w_2, w_3, ..., w_k$, where only $\bar{x}$ and $\bar{y}$ are known in advance, and f is a regression hypothesis function stated by the researcher. The objective here is to find the optimal values for $\bar{w}$ that minimizes an error measure $(||\bar{y} - f(\bar{x}, \bar{w})||)$.

$$\bar{y} = f(\bar{x}, \bar{w}) \tag{1}$$

An alternative that solve the problem, is symbolic regression [7], which works under the assumption that the function f is also unknown and not stated by the researcher in advance, and its purpose is to estimate both and approximation $f'(\bar{x}, \bar{w} \approx f(\bar{x}, \bar{w}))$, and the values of $\bar{w}$. Symbolic regression optimization required of global state-space search algorithms like metaheuristics (specifically, genetic programming [10,14,16,17]). Genetic programming [12] is a supervised learning technique that mimics the biological evolution and is the most used technique in the literature to solve the problem of symbolic regression. Traditionally, the representation for the function f'' is a tree representation [15].

Figure 1 shows an example of how the algebraic expression $(f''(x, \bar{w}) = x^{w_1} + cos(w_2 * x) + w_3 + (cos(w_2 * x)))$, where $\bar{w} = (w_1, w_2, w_3) = (4, 8, 3))$, is encoded into a tree.

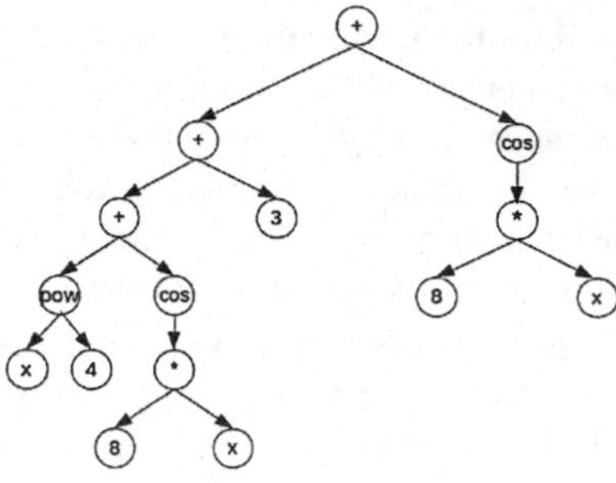

Fig. 1. Tree structure

Further reading about traditional symbolic regression problem solving using genetic programming can be found in Ref. [12]. In this work, we use Straight Line Programs as an alternative to encode algebraic expressions in genetic programming, in order to improve the results obtained with classical models.

3 Straight Line Programs for Symbolic Regression

Straight Line Grammars [5] are a type of grammars that can generate exactly one expression given a series of production rules. Because of this, straight line grammars production rules contains no cycles for a language word generation. Straight Line Programs (SLP) [2] are based on Straight Line Grammars and have been used in the literature to solve geometry problems [8], polynomial equations [11] and document clustering [18] among other problems. The representation of SLP can be achieved using a table where each row represents a production rule containing combinations of a set of atomic operators $O = o_1, o_2, ..., o_n$, a set of terminal symbols $T = t_1, t_2, ..., t_m$ and references to other rows of the table.

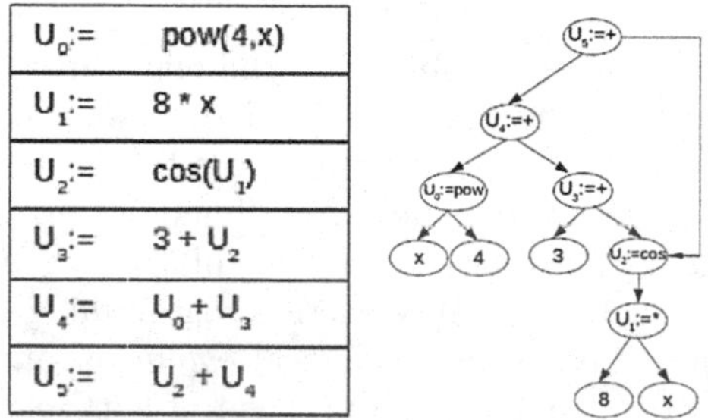

U_0:=	pow(4,x)
U_1:=	8 * x
U_2:=	cos(U_1)
U_3:=	3 + U_2
U_4:=	U_0 + U_3
U_5:=	U_2 + U_4

Fig. 2. SLP representation

Figure 2 shows how the expression ($\tilde{f}(x, \bar{w}) = x^4 + cos(8*x) + 3 + (cos(8*x))$) is encoded by a Straight Line Program. We emphasize that SLP is a linear structure (Fig. 2(a)) that encode a non-linear structure (Fig. 2(b)). The main advantage of Straight Line Programs against trees is the possibility to reuse subexpressions in the own structure since it can model non-cyclic graphs, while traditional tree representation cannot fulfill this capability. Figure 3 faces the same algebraic expression represented by trees and SLP. Here, the size of the SLP is considerably smaller than the tree representation, since the SLP allows us to reuse some subexpressions.

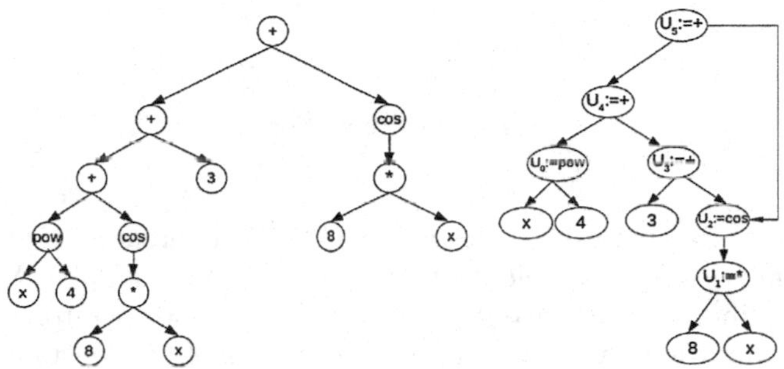

Fig. 3. Tree vs SLP representation

The use of Straight Line Programs in our genetic algorithm starts out with the initialization of each SLP with randomly generated algebraic expressions followed by the evolutionary cycle. This cycle starts with a tournament selection to select two individuals of the population for recombination. A crossover operator (Fig. 4(a)) is applied in the previously selected individuals, selecting a random row from each individual and combining the subtables in order to generate two new children (Fig. 4(b)).

FATHER

U_0:=	$X - K_0$
U_1:=	K_1 / X
U_2:=	$K_0 * K_1$
U_3:=	$X * X$
U_4:=	$U_0 * U_1$
U_5:=	$U_3 - U_2$
U_6:=	$U_5 + U_4$

K = 4

MOTHER

U_0:=	$X * K_1$
U_1:=	K_0 / K_0
U_2:=	$X + X$
U_3:=	K_0 / X
U_4:=	$U_1 + U_0$
U_5:=	$U_3 + U_2$
U_6:=	U_5 / U_4

t = 5

SON 1

U_0:=	$X * K_1$
U_1:=	K_0 / K_0
U_2:=	$X + X$
U_3:=	$X - K_0$
U_4:=	K_1 / X
U_5:=	$U_3 + U_4$
U_6:=	U_5 / U_4

Fig. 4. On the left is shown the best individuals selected (parents) to apply the crossover operator. On the right is shown the individual obtain to combine the genetic material of the two parents

After that, a mutation operator is applied over the two new individuals generated, in order to avoid premature convergence of the algorithm. This mutation operator selects a random row of the table in a specific individual and it

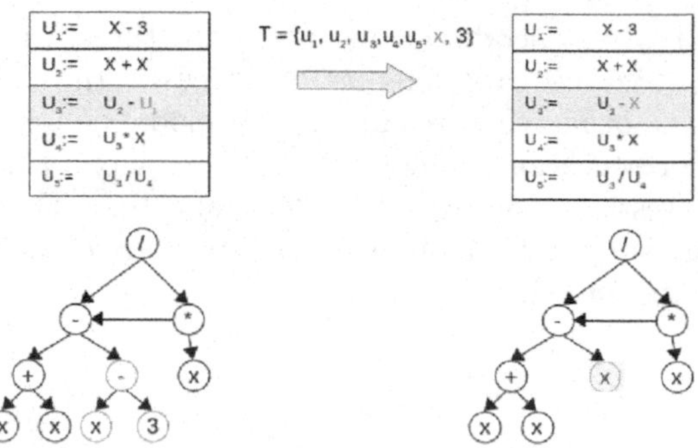

Fig. 5. SLP mutation

exchanges one of its operators, terminal symbols or references to other rows of the table by another random element (see Fig. 5 as an example). We refer the reader to [2] to find more detailed information about these operators. When both crossover and mutation have been applied, the values of the constants are calculated by *least squares estimation* as well as the quality of each individual using the Mean Square Error (MSE) as fitness. After that, the generation replacement takes place and a new evolutionary cycle begins.

4 Experiments

In this section we show the experiments carried out to approximate the total flow of 6 subbasins located in the region of Granada (Spain): Colomera (r_1), Cubillas (r_2), Darro (r_3), Velillos (r_4), remaining Colomera component (r_5), and remaining Western component (r_6), considering the rainfall (x_1), temperature (x_2) and surface flow (x_3) as inputs to calculate the total streamflow as output. An additional purpose of the experimentation is to identify the exogenous variables (specifically, temperature and rainfall) that affect each subbassin, in order to make a preliminary experimentation to know if symbolic regression can be used as a feature selection method also. The data were measured from 1991 to the present day. We have four monthly-sampled datasets (around 400 instances), and two daily-sampled datasets (around 10000 data instances).

To perform the experimentation, we have divided each dataset in 2 subsets: calibration (70%) and test (30%). We want to compare the results obtained with the two representations described in this work: trees and SLP. We have tested different experimental configurations, but the best combination found in order to solve the problem presented in this work is shown in Table 1. We do not show all the settings of preliminary experimentation due to the page limitation of this work.

Table 1. Experimental configuration genetic algorithm

	Tree	SLP
Population size	70	70
Tree depth/SLP size	5	20
Crossover rate	0.9	0.9
Mutation rate	0.1	0.1
Function set F	+, −, *, /, sin, cos,	log, tan, exp, pow, min, max, sqrt
Model parameters W	w_1, w_2, w_3, w_4, w_5	w_1, w_2, w_3, w_4, w_5
Input variables	x_1, x_2, x_3	x_1, x_2, x_3
Stopping criterion: Number of evaluations	35000	35000

We run 30 experiments so that statistical analyses could be carried out in the results. The results obtained in the experimentation are shown in Tables 2 and 3 for monthly and daily sampling rates respectively, where *AF, BF, WF, AT, BT* means *Average Fitness, Best Fitness, Worst Fitness, Average Time (seconds), Best Time (seconds)* respectively. Regarding these results, we can conclude that our initial hypothesis has been fulfilled; since Straight Line Program provide better results than trees and in a shorter time. Since SLPs have a linear structure and can reuse its own information, it could avoid local optima and explore a larger search space. In addition to this, although Trees have obtained a good approach, we emphasize that SLPs requires less computational power since the average time of execution is far less than trees.

Table 2. Symbolic regression experiment monthly results

	SGA-Tree					GGA-SLP				
	AF	BF	WF	AT	BT	AF	BF	WF	AT	BT
r_1	0.3285	0.2132	0.6708	3.68e+03	3.43e+03	0.3263	0.1694	0.5675	965.32	701.487
r_2	1.3028	1.1967	1.5304	3.83e+03	3.61e+03	1.2662	1.0958	1.504	1.16e+03	552.273
r_3	0.3472	0.3329	0.3552	3.64e+03	3.3e+03	0.3445	0.3248	0.359	1.14e+03	767.5193
r_4	1.6617	1.4311	1.9687	3.67e+03	3.52e+03	1.6986	1.4249	2.1148	1.1298e+03	844.8791
r_5	0.5217	0.4476	1.2184	366e+03	3.45e+03	0.4746	0.418	0.5286	1.18e+03	765.2859
r_6	0.073	0.0663	0.0797	4.01e+03	3.54e+03	0.0785	0.0664	0.1671	1.02e+03	590.45

Table 3. Symbolic regression experiment daily results

	SGA-Tree					GGA-SLP				
	AF	BF	WF	AT	BT	AF	BF	WF	AT	BT
r_1	5.848e-04	3.61e-04	0.0014	4.78e+03	4.35e+03	4.627e-04	3.328e-04	7.468e-04	20.9e+03	1.13e+03
r_4	0.0028	0.0025	0.0032	5.31e+03	5 e+03	0.0028	0.0025	0.0036	2.18e+03	1.307e+03

Table 4. Neural network experiment daily and monthly results

	AF	BF	WF	AT	BT
r_1	34.89	6.7224	40.401	0.5307	0.1172
r_2	9.6878	4.999	13.223	0.1418	0.105
r_3	1.174	0.3618	1.629	0.1438	0.099
r_4	17.994	5.167	28.746	0.469	0.111
r_5	1.1441	0.5281	1.679	0.134	0.098
r_6	0.1226	0.081	0.165	0.134	0.098
r_1	0.1	0.09	0.105	2.845	0.527
r_4	0.127	0.073	0.248	3.453	0.331

In order to compare the results obtained with other approximation techniques in the literature, we have used a feed forward neural network with 15 neurons, whose results are shown in Table 4. Being compared with the results of Tables 2 and 3, we can conclude that Symbolic Regression has obtained a more accurate model for each problem than neural networks. This suggests that the inner feature selection carried out by the SLPs and trees can help to not only find out the relevant variables of a problem, but also to reduce the search space and improve accuracy.

Figures 6 to 7 shows the flow modeling for each river with both tree (left) and SLP (right) representations. Red line shows the real data and blue line shows our flow modeling. A non-parametric Kruskal-Wallis test with 95% confidence suggests that there are significant differences between the results of the error distributions, and therefore SLP can avoid local optima and find better solutions than traditional tree representations. According to Table 5, we also emphasize that our initial hypothesis about automatic feature selection can be demonstrated: whereas the rainfall variable is not used in the daily modeling of the flow, we can see the relationship between the rainfall, temperature and surface flow in the monthly-sampled data. Thus in this preliminary research, we conclude that the SLP representation requires less computational power for the genetic programming search, but also that the resulting algebraic expressions could be more accurate than using trees. Moreover, it opens a new research line where SLP and symbolic regression could be used to simultaneously make an input variable feature selection and regression hypothesis induction. This work will be studied in depth in a future research.

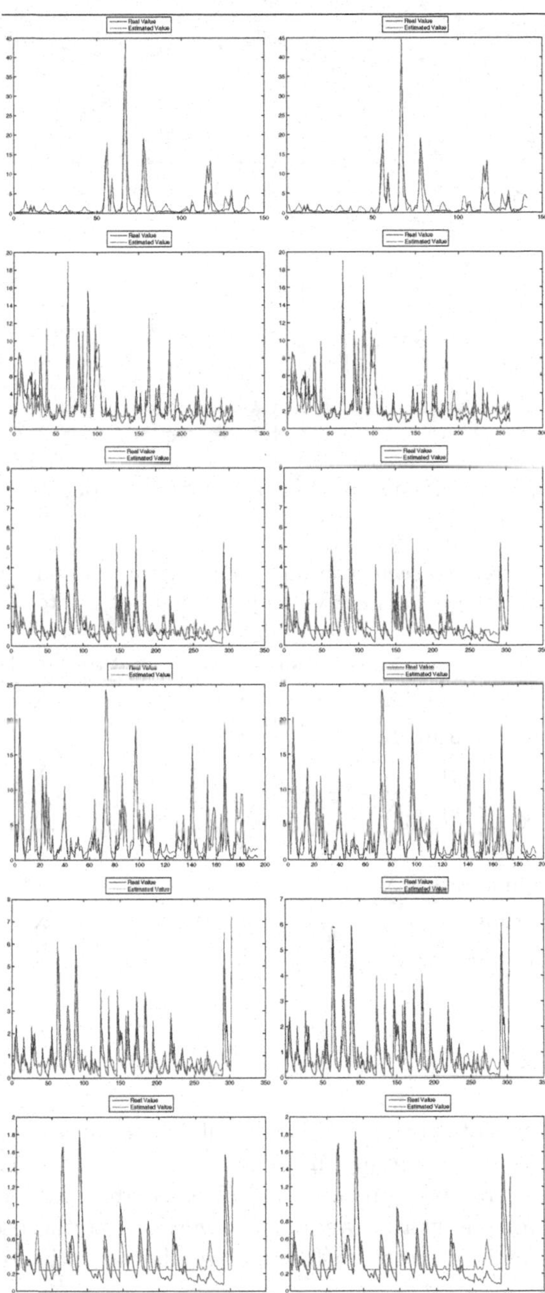

Fig. 6. Results using Tree (left) and SLP (right) representation, for datasets r_1 to r_6 (monthly sample rate)

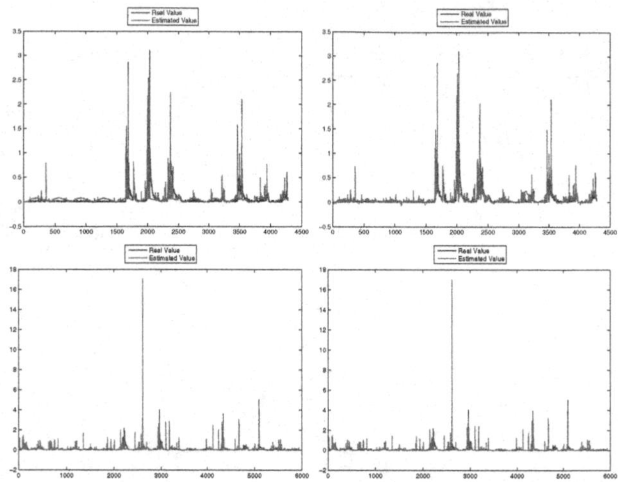

Fig. 7. Results using Tree (left) and SLP (right) representation, for datasets r_1 and r_4 (daily sample rate)

Table 5. Features selected for each river and sampling rate. A mark X shows that the resulting regression hipothesis uses the variable to calculate the total streamflow.

Dataset	x_1 (rainfall)	x_2 (temperature)	x_3 (surface flow)
r_1 (monthly sampling rate)	X	X	X
r_2 (monthly sampling rate)	X	X	X
r_3 (monthly sampling rate)	X		X
r_4 (monthly sampling rate)	X	X	X
r_5 (monthly sampling rate)	X	X	X
r_6 (monthly sampling rate)	X		X
r_1 (daily sampling rate)		X	X
r_4 (daily sampling rate)		X	X

5 Conclusions

In this paper we have studied the use of different alternatives to encode algebraic expressions in genetic programming in order to solve symbolic regression in flow modeling. The two representations used in this work are trees and Straight Line Programs. As in previous works, we want to verify that the use of new alternatives (SLP) to classic structures (trees) have the potential to obtain better results.

As we can see in the previous section, Straight Line Programs has obtained better results than trees and in a shorter time. This fact is due to the linear representation of Straight Line Programs versus the non-linear representation of trees. Using SLP instead of trees, the genetic algorithm is able to leave local optima and find the best solution.

According to the results obtained, we can conclude that the use of symbolic regression with a specific representation to encode algebraic expressions is able to model the flow of the river and select the relevant variables of the problem.

Acknowledgements. This work has been supported by the project TIN201564776-C3-1-R.

References

1. Alberto, M.R.: Programación genética: La regresión simbólica. Entramado **3**, 76–85 (2007)
2. Alonso, C.L., Montaña, J.L., Puente, J., Borges, C.E.: A new linear genetic programming approach based on straight line programs: some theoretical and experimental aspects. Int. J. Artif. Intell. Tools **18**(5), 757–781 (2009). http://dx.doi.org/10.1142/S0218213009000391
3. Arnold, J.G., Srinivasan, R., Muttiah, R.S., Williams, J.R.: Large area hydrologic modeling and assesment part i: model development. J. Am. Water Resour. Assoc. **34**(1), 73–89 (1998)
4. Awchi, T.A.: River discharges forecasting in northern Iraq using different ANN techniques. Water Resour. Manage. **28**(3), 801–814 (2014)
5. Benz, F., Kötzing, T.: An effective heuristic for the smallest grammar problem. In: Proceedings of GECCO (Genetic and Evolutionary Computation), pp. 487–494 (2013)
6. Burnash, R.J.C., Ferral, R., McGuire, R.A.: A generalized streamflow simulation system-conceptual modeling for digital computers. National Weather Service and California Department of Water Resources (1973)
7. Chen, Q., Xue, B., Zhang, M.: Generalisation and domain adaptation in GP with gradient descent for symbolic regression. In: 2015 IEEE Congress on Evolutionary Computation (CEC), pp. 1137–1144, May 2015
8. Giusti, M., Heintz, J., Morais, J., Morgenstem, J., Pardo, L.: Straight-line programs in geometric elimination theory. J. Pure Appl. Algebra **124**(1), 101–146 (1998). http://www.sciencedirect.com/science/article/pii/S0022404996000990
9. Huang, W.C., Yang, F.T.: Streamflow estimation using kriging. Water Resour. Res. **34**(6), 1599–1608 (1998)
10. Icke, I., Bongard, J.C.: Improving genetic programming based symbolic regression using deterministic machine learning. In: 2013 IEEE Congress on Evolutionary Computation, pp. 1763–1770, June 2013
11. Krick, T.: Straight-line programs in polynomial equation solving (2002)
12. Langdon, W.B.: Genetic Programming — Computers Using "Natural Selection" to Generate Programs, pp. 9–42. Springer, Boston (1998)
13. Lindstrom, G., Johannson, B., Persson, M., Gardelin, M., Bergstrom, S.: Development and test of the distributed HBV-96 hydrological model. J. Hydrol. **201**, 272–288 (1997)
14. Maarten, K.: Improving Symbolic Regression with Interval Arithmetic and Linear Scaling, pp. 70–82. Springer, Berlin (2003)
15. McKay, B., Willis, M.J., Barton, G.W.: Using a tree structured genetic algorithm to perform symbolic regression, pp. 487–492, September 1995

16. Oliver Morales, C., Rodríguez Vázquez, K.: Symbolic Regression Problems by Genetic Programming with Multi-branches. Springer, Heidelberg (2004). http://dx.doi.org/10.1007/978-3-540-24694-7_74
17. Pospíchal, J., Varga, Ľ., Kvasnička, V.: Symbolic Regression of Boolean Functions by Genetic Programming. Springer, Heidelberg (2013). http://dx.doi.org/10.1007/978-3-642-30504-7_11
18. Sequera, J., del Castillo Diez, J., Sotos, L.: Document clustering with evolutionary systems through straight-line programs slp. Intell. Learn. Syst. Appl. **4**(4), 303–318 (2012)
19. Temez, J.R.: Modelo matemático de transformación precipitación-aportación. ASINEL (1977)
20. Tosun, N., Özler, L.: A study of tool life in hot machining using artificial neural networks and regression analysis method. J. Mater. Process. Technol. **124**(12), 99–104 (2002). http://www.sciencedirect.com/science/article/pii/S0924013602000869

Integration of Immune Features into a Belief-Desire-Intention Model for Multi-agent Control of Public Transportation Systems

Salima Mnif[1(✉)], Saber Darmoul[2], Sabeur Elkosantini[1,2], and Lamjed Ben Said[1]

[1] SMART Lab, High Institute of Management of Tunis, University of Tunis, Tunis, Tunisia
mnifsalima@yahoo.fr, lamjed.bensaid@isg.rnu.tn

[2] Department of Industrial Engineering, College of Engineering, King Saud University, Riyadh, Kingdom of Saudi Arabia
{sdarmoul, selkosantini}@ksu.edu.sa

Abstract. There is a growing need to develop monitoring and control systems to maintain the performance and the quality of service of Public Transportation Systems (PTS) at acceptable levels, especially in case of traffic disturbances, such as accidents or congestion. Despite the use of Multi-Agent Systems (MAS) to control PTS, many existing systems still rely on centralized control architectures, and do not offer generic agent behavior models. Many Belief-Desire-Intention (BDI) models were developed as generic agent decision-making processes, but existing developments still lack detailed descriptions of models instantiation and implementation. This article introduces a new framework for the implementation of the Belief-Desire-Intention (BDI) model for the development of an agent based decision support system for the control of public transportation systems. The suggested framework uses a set concepts and mechanisms inspired from biological immunity. Through a simulation case study, we have presented an example of implementation of the suggested BDI framework.

Keywords: Multi-agent systems · Belief-Desire-Intention model · Immune concepts · Public transportation system control

1 Introduction

The monitoring and control of Public Transportation Systems (PTS) in urban areas is a complex challenge. Public transportation authorities struggle to maintain performance and quality of service at acceptable levels, especially in the case of traffic disturbances, such as accidents and congestion. Many Public Transportation Control Systems (PTCS) were developed based on different artificial intelligence paradigms [1–3]. Davidsson et al. [1] particularly pointed out that 64% of the research conducted in the

F.J. Martínez de Pisón et al. (Eds.): HAIS 2017, LNAI 10334, pp. 459–470, 2017.
DOI: 10.1007/978-3-319-59650-1_39

field of public transportation monitoring and control focused on the development of multi-agent system (MAS) architectures. Despite the ability of MAS to distribute control, 30% of research articles used MAS to develop centralized architectures.

Despite the fact that agent based decision support systems (DSS) require the development of agent behavior models [4], only few references suggested explicit agent behavior models. For example, [5] developed an agent based DSS to control an urban transportation system. In there system, environment representation, agents' objectives and decision-making processes are modeled and implemented using Case Based Reasoning. Balbo and Pinson [6] presented an agent-based PTCS named SATIR that monitors the public transportation system activity in real-time and assists the regulator under normal and disrupted conditions. They suggested a representation of the environment and a distributed decision making process without using an explicit agent behavior model. Cheikh and Hammadi [7] suggested an agent based PTCS that includes different types of agents with different behaviors. Ezzedine et al. [8] combined Petri nets and MAS for an agent oriented PTCS considering the interaction with the human regulator to monitor the PTS.

A large number of agent decision-making models can be found in the literature, each inspired by different aims and research questions. Balke and Gilbert [4] reviewed 14 agent decision-making models. Many of them integrate social and affective dimensions which are not appropriate for the development of agent based PTCS. Among these decision-making models, the Belief-Desire-Intention (BDI) model supports the development of reasoning systems for complex tasks in dynamic environments [9]. Despite its wide use, the BDI model has a high level of abstraction that complicates its implementation in computer applications. It is important to note that existing literature still lacks implementation guidelines of such generic agent behavior models.

This article suggests a new framework for the implementation of the Belief-Desire-Intention (BDI) model for the development of an agent based decision support system for the control of public transportation systems. The suggested framework uses a set concepts and mechanisms inspired from biological immunity. Through a simulation case study, we have presented an example of implementation of the suggested BDI framework.

2 Belief-Desire-Intention Model

The BDI model is commonly used to develop agent based simulation or decision support systems [4]. Bajo et al. [10] noted that the BDI model has the advantages of being intuitive, able to simply identify the decision-making process and the way to perform it. The BDI model includes the following concepts (see Fig. 1):

- Beliefs are the agent's perception to its state or environment. Accordingly, the agent should have a knowledge model of the environment;
- Desires represent the goals that the agent aims to accomplish;
- Intentions represent the set of decisions that an agent can execute;

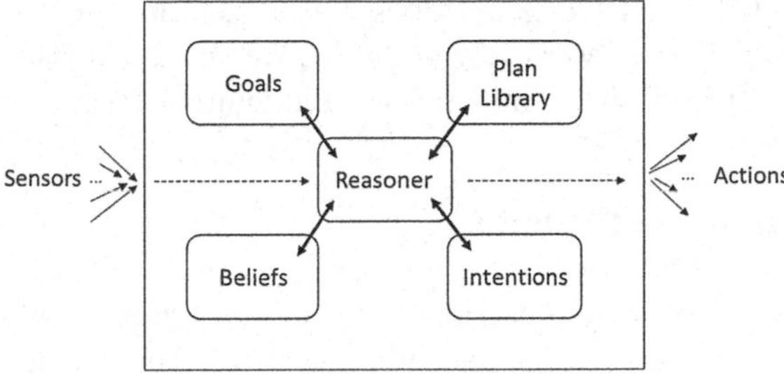

Fig. 1. BDI model [11]

- Plan library is a set of plans. Each plan defines a set of actions that are expected to contribute to achieving a goal in specific situations.
- Reasoner is the engine that ties together the previous four components. Its main objective is to select the appropriate plan to be executed by the agent from the set of plans.
- Percepts represent elementary information perceived by an agent from the environment by using sensors.

BDI agents are typically able to reason about their plans dynamically. They are able to reason about their own internal states, i.e. reflect upon and modify their own beliefs, desires and intentions [4]. The control loop of a BDI agent is shown in Fig. 2. Let π be an agent plan, *B* an agent belief and *I* an agent intention. According to the BDI model, an agent perceives by collecting data from the environment (*getPercept()*) and updates its beliefs accordingly (*update(B,p)*). Then, the agent generates a set of desires given its beliefs and current intentions (*wish(B, I)*). The most valuable and achievable desires must be identified taking into account the beliefs, desires and current intentions (*focus (B, D, I)*). Given agent's beliefs and intentions, the function *plan (B, I)* returns a plan from the plan library to achieve the agent's current intentions.

```
B:=B0;I:=I0; /* Initial beliefs and intentions
π := null; /* π is the plan to be performed
While alive do
  P := getPercept();
  B := update(B,p);
  D := wish(B, I);
  I := focus(B, D, I);
  π  := plan (B, I);
  execute (π);
end while
```

Fig. 2. Pseudo code of the BDI control loop

As it can be noted, the BDI model does not present any explicit way of implementation of the overall framework. Accordingly, we suggest a framework to implement the BDI model based on the integration of immune features.

3 Biological Immune Systems

The Biological Immune System (BIS) reacts to disease-causing elements called *pathogens*, such as viruses, bacteria, and other parasites. The BIS recognizes specific features called *antigens* that are present at the surface of pathogens. When an antigen enters into the body, it stimulates a subset of immune cells, named *B-cells* able to secrete substances called *antibodies*, which bind to antigens, block them and lead to their elimination. An antibody identifies antigens using its surface receptors, called *paratopes*. Furthermore, an antibody is not activated unless its receptors bind to the antigen with an *affinity* that exceeds *an affinity threshold*. The BIS relies on the *self/non-self discrimination principle* to distinguish between foreign/disease causing elements (pathogens and antigens) and elements belonging to the body (self). According to this phenomenon, when an antibody recognizes a self-cell, it is destroyed in order not to react to body cells. Such a principle is called the negative selection mechanism.

As soon as a non-self-cell such as an antigen is detected, the body activates the immune response. Then, lymphocytes are generated and are divided into two main types of cells: effector cells and memory cells [12, 13]. Effector cells have a short lifetime and are created for the immediate defense of the organism. Memory cells are long-lived cells that circulate through the host organism. This concept is called the *immunological memory*. When confronted with the presence of an antigen that was previously recognized, memory cells are able to launch a rapid and effective response.

Many concepts and mechanisms were extracted from the BIS and applied in order to create effective computational solutions to complex problems in a wide range of engineering areas [14]. However, to the best of authors' knowledge, only a few research exists on the investigation of AIS in the field of public transportation [15]. Usually, Artificial Immune Systems (AIS) often use the idea of memory cells to retain good solutions to the problem under consideration. In our case, we rely on immune memory, and on the mechanism of affinity to control public transportation systems.

4 Immune Modelling

Similarly to the BIS, which protects the body from disease causing elements, a PTCS should protect public transportation systems from disturbances affecting pre-established schedules. In this paper, a pathogen represents a disturbance that affects the transportation system, such as a bus delay, a technical problem or successive buses. An antibody represents a corrective decision that could be recommended to regulate the system, such as "hold at a station" or "skip stations". The immune response must determine the best action that will regulate the system using an immune memory and which is considered as the first immune response. Table 1 synthesizes the suggested analogies.

Table 1. Analogies between biological and public transportation systems.

Biological immune system	Public transportation system
Body	Public transportation network
Pathogen	Disturbances affecting a bus
Antigen	An attribute that characterize a special feature of a disturbance
Antibody	Unitary control decision
B-cells	Control decisions
Memory cells	Stored control decisions
Paratope	A feature triggering a control decision
Affinity	Adequacy between the correction action and the detected disturbance
Immune memory	Database
Negative Selection	Bus network monitoring and disturbance detection
Immune response	Immune memory based algorithm

4.1 Pathogen Representation

In this work, a pathogen is a disturbance that refers to any kind of event that affects a single bus. Therefore, if there are several disturbed buses, a pathogen will be created for each one. The pathogen includes knowledge describing the affected bus (kind of the disturbance, load of the bus, etc.) and the disturbance itself. A pathogen is a vector of 12 antigens, where each antigen characterizes a specific feature of a disturbance:

$$Pg = \left\langle \begin{array}{l} Ag_1 = B_{ij}, Ag_2 = L_j, Ag_3 = S_{kj}, Ag_4 = P, Ag_5 = R, Ag_6 = C, Ag_7 = Ea_{ijk}, \\ Ag_8 = De_{ijk}, Ag_9 = D, Ag_{10} = N_{i,j}, Ag_{11} = N_{i+1,j}, Ag_{12} = WP_{i,k+1,j} \end{array} \right\rangle \quad (1)$$

Where

- Ag_i is the ith antigen
- B_{ij} is the disturbed bus i of the line j.
- L_j is bus line j
- S_{kj} is the station k of line j where the disturbance occurred
- P is the period of the day when the disturbance occurred (1 for rush hour and 0 for an off-peak hour)
- R is the availability of a of alternative/extra buses at the depot (1 for available and 0 for not)
- C is the cause of the disturbance (1 for accident or technical problem, 2 for traffic congestion, 3 for absence of driver, and 4 for the cause bad weather),
- Ea_{ijk} refers to earliness of the bus i in the station k of the jth line. It is equal to 1 if the bus arrives to the station before the scheduled time; 0 otherwise.
- De_{ijk} refers to delay. It is equal to 1 if the bus arrives to the station after the scheduled time; 0 otherwise
- D is the duration of the earliness or the delay (in minutes),
- N_{ij} is the number of passengers in the disturbed bus while

- $N_{i+1,j}$ is the number of passengers in the following bus,),
- $WP_{i,k+1,\ j}$ is the number of waiting passengers for the bus i in the next station k + 1 of the line j.

4.2 Pathogen Detection

To detect a pathogen, performance index is introduced, named $PBus_i$ (see Eq. 2). $PBus_i$ is an aggregation of two type of performance indicators: the delay/earliness of the bus at a station and the served passengers.

$$PBus_i(S_{kj}) = W_1TD_i(S_{kj}) + W_2TE_i(S_{kj}) + W_3NS_i(S_{kj}) \tag{2}$$

Where $TD_i(S_{kj})$ is the total delay of the bus i from the first station until the station $S_{kj}, TE_i(S_{kj})$ is the total earliness of the bus i from the first station until the station $S_{kj}, NS_i(S_{kj})$ is the number of non served passengers by the bus i rom the first station until the station S_{kj}, W_1, W_2 and W_3 are weights associated to $TD_i(S_{kj})$, $TE_i(S_{kj})$ and $NS_i(S_{kj})$ respectively. Their sum is equal to 1.

4.3 Antibody Representation

Antibodies represent different types of control decisions. An antibody can be combined with other antibodies to obtain hybrid control decisions. We consider six different decisions, which are listed below:

- Half-turn online (HTOL): it consists in eliminating a part of the trip. The vehicle will continue at the opposite direction.
- Direct online (DOL): make a vehicle continue its trip ensuring only the stops of descent for on-board passengers.
- Skip stations (SS): speeding up buses by skipping stations (one or more)
- Hold at a station (HS): delaying the bus, at a given station, that are ahead of its planned timetable.
- Injection of a bus (IB): it consists in injecting a new bus in the network to strengthen the number of buses in the network.
- Exchange of a bus (EB): it consists in replacing an existing bus that is not able to continue its travel.

4.4 B-Cell Representation

B-cells represent the control decisions applied for a disturbed bus. Hence, the system must create a B-cell for each detected antigen. Equation 3 illustrates our definition of B-cells. The receptor part of B-cells is a precondition that has the same structure as the pathogen. The paratopes part includes a set of Boolean variables associated to control decisions to define their implication in the control strategy. If an antibody is activated, its associated paratope is assigned the value 1; otherwise it is assigned the value 0.

$$Bcell = \langle \text{Receptors}, Antibodies, Paratopes \rangle \tag{3}$$

4.5 Immune Memory

Similarly to the BIS, the suggested PTCS memorizes a set of control decisions for some disturbances. We introduce an Immune Memory DataBase (IMDB) including a set of memory B-cells.

$$IMDB = \{Bcell_1, Bcell_2, \ldots, Bcell_k\} \tag{4}$$

To create the initial Immune Memory DataBase (IMDB), we adopted a Simulation Optimization (SO) technique using a suggested negative selection algorithm presented in a previous paper [16]. A first run of a simulation is required to create the set of patterns R including most representative pathogens. Then, we use SO to determine the optimal combination of antibodies that minimize total delay of buses for each antigen of the set R. Finally, both obtained antigens of the set R and antibodies constitutes the memory B-cells of the IMDB.

4.6 B-Cell/Antigen Affinity

The affinity refers to the similarity degree between the disturbance and a control decision. The Manhattan distance measure is adopted. The Manhattan distance is more efficient than Euclidean distance in parallel and distributed systems. Moreover, Manhattan distance has demonstrated a better performance in presence of noisy data, which is always the case in public transportation systems [17]. The affinity is then determined using the Eq. (5):

$$Affinity(Bcell, Ag) = \frac{\sum_{i=1}^{Length(Ag)} \delta_i}{Length(Ag)} \tag{5}$$

Where

$$\begin{cases} \delta_i = 1 \text{ if Bcell.Paratope[i]} = Pg.Ag_i \\ \delta_i = 0 \text{ otherwise} \end{cases} \tag{6}$$

4.7 Immune Memory Algorithm

The Immune Memory Algorithm (IMA) builds a reaction strategy for detected disturbances. The suggested PTCS memorizes a set of control decisions for some disturbances that the system is able to recognize. The suggested IMA works according to the following steps:

- Step 1 – Read and collect data: the algorithm performs measurement data acquisition from the network. In this paper, measurement data is related to the number of passengers in the disturbed bus, the number of passenger in the following bus, the availability of a bus and difference between the scheduled timetable and exact position of the bus.
- Step 2 – Data analysis: the algorithm analyzes collected data in order to detect possible disturbances. Indeed, the evaluation of the performance of the bus is calculated using the Eq. 2.
- Step 3 – Selection of the appropriate control decision: the algorithm selects from the immune memory IMDB the control strategy (B-cell) that can deal with the disturbance (antigen). For that, the algorithm calculates the affinity measure between the detected disturbance and memory B-cells stored in the IMDB to determines the appropriate control decision for detected disturbance using the affinity measure. Thus, the algorithm selects the control decision with the highest value of affinity. The considered affinity measure in this paper is the Manhattan distance presented in the Sect. 4.5.
- Step 4 – the control decision (B-cell) with the highest affinity degree will be considered as the decision to the disturbed bus.
- Go to step 1 for data acquisition.
- Steps 1 to 4 are repeated each T (sampling period) seconds. It is worth noting that data acquisition is performed in the beginning of a sampling period, while the determined control decision is applied at the beginning of next sampling period.

5 Integration of Immune Features in BDI Model

According to the generic BDI model presented in Sect. 2 and the suggested immune modeling, we suggest a matching between BDI concepts and developed immune features (see Table 2).

The presented immune concepts and algorithms are integrated into a BDI model. Thus, the developed BDI model presented in the Fig. 3 includes the following components:

- Percepts: antigens are used to represent the different data collected from the public transportation system using sensors;
- Beliefs: the pathogen knowledge model of the Eq. 1 is used to provide an abstract representation of the public transportation system.
- Desires: agents of the suggested PTCS have many objectives that can be accomplished and which are: analyze data, detect disturbance, determine control decision or update control decision.

Table 2. Matching between BDI concepts and immune features

BDI concepts	Immune features
Percepts	Antigens
Beliefs	Pathogens
Desires	Goals such as pathogen detection, affinity calculation or control decision determination
Intentions	Antibodies
Plan	B-cells
Plan library	Immune memory
Reasoner	Immune Memory Algorithm

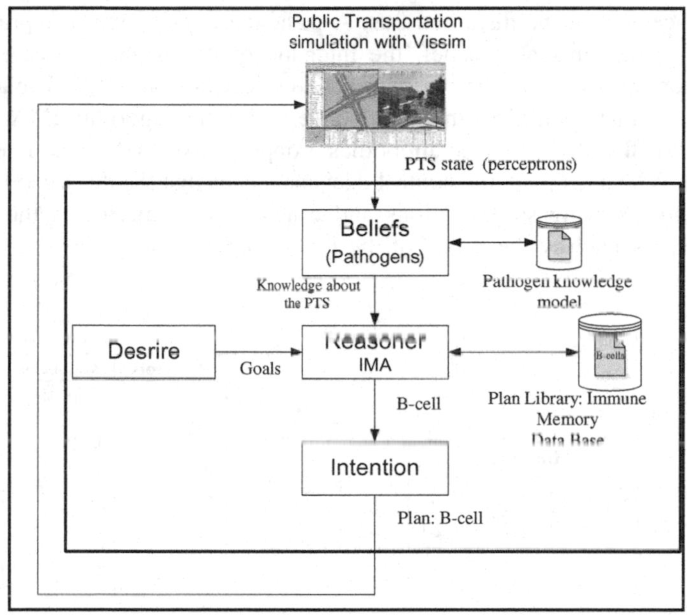

Fig. 3. The BDI model

- Intention: Antibodies are used to represent different type of decisions to be determined by the agent.
- Plan: B-cells are used to represent the combination of actions (antibodies) to tackle a detected disturbance.
- Reasoner: The suggested Immune Memory Algorithm (IMA, see Sect. 4.7) is used to determine the control strategy (plan) for the detected disturbance.

6 A Test Case Scenario

The objective of this section is to show an example of implementation of the suggested model. Let us consider a bus (with a bus no. 1) that has to serve the bus line no. 5 including 15 stop stations. An agent based PTCS is developed in which each agent implements the suggested BDI model and has to monitor and control a bus. An agent is then associated to the bus no. 1. The initial intention of the agent is to collect and monitor the bus. When a disturbance is detected, which represents a new belief, the agent updates its beliefs. Let us assume that the disturbance is detected in the station no. 4. The disturbance is caused by a traffic congestion and results in a delay of 8 min detected at station no. 4. The disturbance occurs at a rush hour. There are 20 passengers on-board the disturbed bus, 12 passengers on-board the following bus, and 5 passengers waiting at the next station. Finally, there is one free bus available at the depot for possible replacement of the disturbed bus. A pathogen is then created represented by Fig. 4(a). Regarding this new belief, the intention of the agent is to determine the appropriate control decision. The reasoner has to select from the IMDB (plan library) the B-cell (plan) that neutralizes the disturbance. Using the algorithm IMA, the agent retrieves the B-cell with 2 activated antibodies: skipping stations (SS) and injection of a new bus (IB). With such plan, the control decision means that the disturbed bus should continue without serving some stations and a new bus is injected in the line. The decision in represented by the B-cell of the Fig. 4(b).

Pathogen											
B_{ij}	L_i	S_{kj}	P	R	C	Ea_{ijk}	De_{ijk}	D	N_{ij}	$N_{i+1,j}$	$Wp_{i,k+1,j}$
1	*5*	4	*1*	1	*2*	*0*	1	*8*	20	12	5

a

B-cell			
Receptors		Antibodies	Paratopes
B_{ij}	1	1. HTOL	0
L_j	5	2. DOL	0
S_{kj}	4	3. SS	1
P	1	4. HS	0
R	1	5. IB	1
C	2	6. EB	0
Ea_{ijk}	0		
De_{ijk}	1		
D	8		
N_{ij}	20		
$N_{i+1,j}$	12		
$Wp_{i,k+1,j}$	5		

b

Fig. 4. The detected pathogen (a) and the determined B-cell (b)

The suggested model is implemented with Python programming language and using PTV VISSIM 7 [18], a traffic simulation software. We have also simulated another scenario in which we simulated a traffic congestion which has affected the scheduled timetable of some buses. This disturbance occurs just before the station number 3 starting after 25 min. The bus number 2 is the first to be affected by this disturbance. Finally, we have simulated a 10 waiting passengers in stations number 5, 7, 8, 9 and 10. No waiting passengers are simulated in station 4 and only one passenger in station 6. Figure 5 illustrates the obtained results. The Fig. 5 presents the deviation between the theoretical and the real timetables of the bus number 2. We can note that the situation is improved after the activation of the developed PTCS. Indeed, the disturbed bus have skipped two stations: number 4 and number 6 (see Fig. 5). The bus have continued to serve stations from station number 7. No injected bus was decided by the developed PTCS for the disturbed bus.

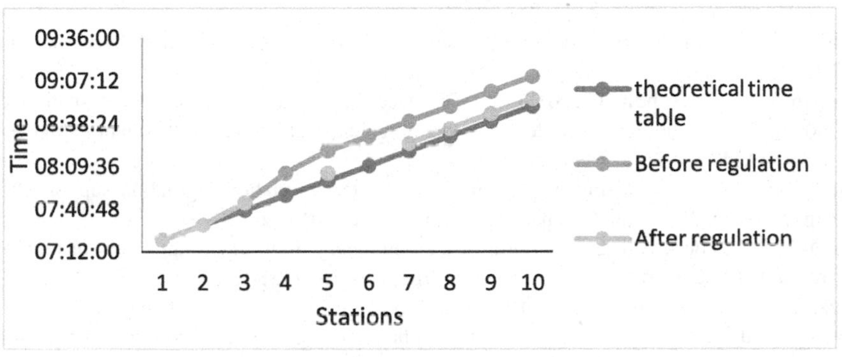

Fig. 5. Obtained results

7 Conclusion

The main contribution of this article is the development of a set of concepts and mechanisms borrowed from immunity for the development of a distributed decision making mechanism. Moreover, the article introduces a new framework for the implementation of the Belief-Desire-Intention (BDI) model for the development of an agent based decision support system for the control of public transportation systems. Indeed, BDI model is one of the most widely used architectures for the development of agents based decision support systems. It integrates the rational and cognitive aspects of human behavior, including beliefs, desires, and intentions. However, BDI model, as many others generic agent models, was, however, presented in such a high level of abstraction that complicated its implementation in computer applications. Moreover, such model is not used for the development of PTCS. The suggested framework is based on the integration of suggested immune features into BDI for the description of the different concepts of BDI model. An example of implementation is discussed. The suggested PTCS will be extended in future works by other immune mechanisms to allow the system to learn and update the immune memory. Moreover, an in-depth assessment of the suggested system is required which will be the focus of next works.

Acknowledgement. The authors extend their appreciation to the Deanship of Scientific Research at King Saud University for funding this work through research group No (RG-1438-056).

References

1. Davidsson, P., Henesey, L., Ramstedt, L., Törnquist, J., Wernstedt, F.: An analysis of agent-based approaches to transport logistics. Transp. Res. Part C Emerg. Technol. **13**(4), 255–271 (2005)
2. Chen, B., Cheng, H.H.: A review of the applications of agent technology in traffic and transportation systems. IEEE Trans. Intell. Transp. Syst. **11**(2), 485–497 (2010)
3. Bazzan, A.L.C., Klügl, F.: A review on agent-based technology for traffic and transportation. Knowl. Eng. Rev. **29**(3), 375–403 (2013)
4. Balke, T., Gilbert, N.: How do agents make decisions? A survey. J. Artif. Soc. Soc. Simul. **17**(4), 1 (2014)
5. Bouamrane, K., Tahon, C., Beldjilali, B.: Decision making system for regulation of a bimodal Urban transport system, associating classical and multi-agent approaches. INFORMATICA **16**(3), 1–30 (2005)
6. Balbo, F., Pinson, S.: Using intelligent agents for transportation regulation support system design. Transp. Res. Part C Emerg. Technol. **18**(1), 140–156 (2010)
7. Cheikh, S.B., Hammadi, S.: An optimized evolutionary multi-agent approach for regulation of disrupted Urban transport. Int. J. Mod. Eng. Res. **3**(6), 3841–3851 (2013)
8. Ezzedine, H., Trabelsi, A., Kolski, C.: Modelling of an interactive system with an agent-based architecture using petri nets, application of the method to the supervision of a transport system. Math. Comput. Simul. **70**(5–6), 358–376 (2006)
9. Bordini, R.H., Hübner, J.F., Wooldridge, M.J.: Programming Multi-agent Systems in AgentSpeak using Jason. Wiley (2007)
10. Bajo, J., Borrajo, M.L., De Paz, J.F., Corchado, J.M., Pellicer, M.A.: A multi-agent system for web-based risk management in small and medium business. Expert Syst. Appl. **39**(8), 6921–6931 (2012)
11. Norling, E., Sonenberg, L.: Creating interactive characters with BDI agents. In: Australian Workshop on Interactive Entertainment, p. 8, Febuary 2004
12. Perelson, A., Weisbuch, G.: Immunology for physicists. Rev. Mod. Phys. **69**(4), 1219–1268 (1997)
13. Hofmeyr, S.A.: An interpretative introduction to the immune system. In: Segel, L.A., Cohen, I.R. (eds.) Design Principles for the Immune System and Other Distributed Autonomous Systems, pp. 3–28. Oxford University Press, New York (2001)
14. Dasgupta, D., Yu, S., Nino, F.: Recent advances in artificial immune systems: models and applications. Appl. Soft Comput. **11**(2), 1574–1587 (2011)
15. Darmoul, S., Elkosantini, S.: Artificial immunity to control disturbances in public transportation systems: concepts, mechanisms and a prototype implementation of a knowledge based decision support system. Knowl.-Based Syst. **68**, 58–76 (2014)
16. Mnif, S., Elkosantini, S., Darmoul, S., Ben Said, L.: An immune memory and negative selection based decision support system to monitor and control public bus transportation systems. In: 4th IFAC Conference on Intelligent Control and Automation Sciences, vol. 49, no. 5, pp. 143–148 (2016)
17. Lau, H.Y.K., Wong, V.W.K.: An immunity-based distributed multiagent-control framework. IEEE Trans. Syst. Man Cybern. Part A Syst. Hum. **36**(1), 91–108 (2006)
18. PTV, G.: VISSIM Simulation Software (2015). http://vision-traffic.ptvgroup.com/en-uk/home/. Accessed 28 Sept 2015

A Multi-Agent System to Improve Mobile Robot Localization

Cristian Peñaranda(✉), Vicente Julian(✉), Javier Palanca(✉), and Vicente Botti(✉)

Departamento de Sistemas Informáticos y Computación (DSIC), Universitat Politècnica de València, Camino de Verá s/n. 46020, Valencia, Spain
{cpenaranda,vinglada,jpalanca,vbotti}@dsic.upv.es

Abstract. This paper provides a way to solve the problem of localization in mobile robots using a MAS approach. Typically, the robot localization has been resolved in static environments by adding sensors that help the robot, but this is not useful in dynamic environments where the robot moves through different rooms or areas. The novelty of this dynamic scenario is that each room is composed of external devices that report the position where the robot is. In this paper, we propose a multi-agent system using the SPADE MAS platform to improve the location of mobile robots in dynamic scenarios. To do this, we are going to use some of the advantages offered by the SPADE platform such as presence notification and subscription protocols in order to design a friendship network between sensors/devices and the mobile robots.

Keywords: Multi-Agent System · Mobile robots · Open systems

1 Introduction

Over the last few years, a great evolution of mobile robot applications has been observed. Current mobile robots are very complex machines which include a lot of components that in some circumstances are difficult to synchronize. For this reason, it is quite common for mobile robot applications that the level of complexity gets increased due to a good coordination and/or synchronization of the different elements for sensorization and actuation. This problem complicates the achievement of their objectives. One of the most well-known problems is the positioning problem of a mobile robot inside a building.

In this paper, we used a humanoid robot NAO[1], which has been developed by Aldebaran Robotics. The robot has a coordinates system to know its own position. The problem is that the robot is not very accurate when it performs several movements. In such situations it is very common for the robot to have a significant deviation between its actual position and the robot's belief of its position according to its sensors. Besides, when it performs several complex tasks,

[1] www.ald.softbankrobotics.com.

F.J. Martínez de Pisón et al. (Eds.): HAIS 2017, LNAI 10334, pp. 471–482, 2017.
DOI: 10.1007/978-3-319-59650-1_40

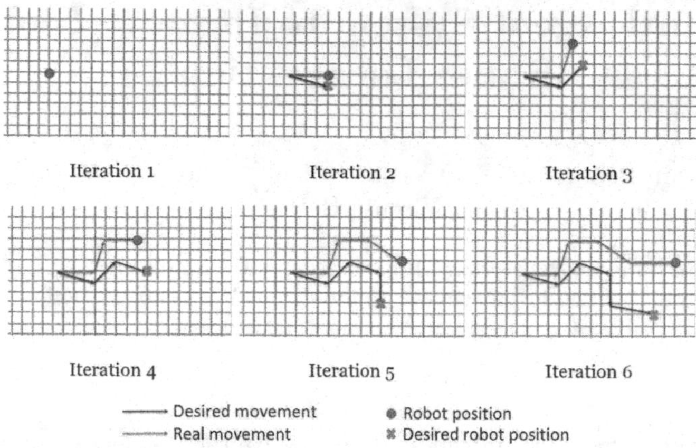

Fig. 1. NAO robot movement.

which are composed of different movements along different rooms, the robot gets big mistakes due to its lack of knowledge about its real position, as we can see in Fig. 1. Our goal is to provide an agent-based framework that gives a mobile robot, which is moving through different areas or rooms inside a building, a flexible and dynamic way to obtain its correct position.

This location problem may appear due to two causes. The first one is due to the type of floor used. Each material exerts a kinetic friction between the robot and the ground and, depending of this kinetic friction, the robot movement is more or less accurate. The second one depends on the components that the robot employs for its movements. These components usually make little errors that may affect the robot movement and may make it believe that it is in a different position than the real one.

Several previous works have done different studies taking into account this problem. Specifically, they have focused on two approaches: the first one tries to locate the robot position using fixed devices that know the robot position in the environment [1,2,6,7]. These studies satisfy the main objective of locating the robot, but they are oriented to a single static room. Besides, the information given by the external devices is critical, hence the works that follow this approach do not tolerate possible failures of these devices such as incorrect operations or changes in the environment that difficult the detection of the robot (for example, a new obstacle between the device and the robot). The second approach satisfies the main objective using only the internal robot sensors [4,5,8]. The robot calculates its position depending on the detected objects of the environment and its distance from the detected objects. This solution may not work correctly in a dynamic environment, because the robot can not calculate its global position when there are obstacles in the environment that are changing their position or even new obstacles appear. Therefore, this work proposes a hybrid approach which tries to solve the problem of the robot positioning when it has to perform several tasks in different rooms of a building with changing conditions as new objects, failures of external devices, changes in the available sensorization, etc. Also, the proposed system could tolerate and fix possible deviations committed by the external devices, either due to an internal malfunction or due to obstacles that difficult the detection of the robot.

The proposed approach is based on the use of a multi-agent system (MAS). Intelligent agents offer a great opportunity to solve different types of distributed problems. For that reason, we are going to use a Multi-Agent System (MAS) to help the robot to know its real position when it performs several movements inside a building. The Multi-Agent System (MAS) provides the distribution, dynamism and flexibility needed to solve this problem. Besides, the proposed solution can be used to help any mobile robot to know their position and also to allow new devices that know the robot position to be added or removed.

The rest of the paper is organized as follows. Section 2 describes the developed MAS. Section 3 shows the experiments and the final performance achieved using the proposed (MAS). Finally, some conclusions and future work are presented.

2 Multi-Agent System Proposal

As commented before, the main contribution of this paper is to provide an agent-based framework that allows us a flexible and dynamic way to obtain the correct position of a mobile robot which moves through different areas or rooms inside a building. The framework has been implemented using the SPADE platform [3]. The use of an agent-oriented approach allowed us to obtain a flexible and distributed solution where different sensing devices can be added or deleted in the (MAS) in a transparent way. The platform follows FIPA and XMPP/Jabber standards [3] and it is also the first platform based on XMPP instant messaging.

Agents developed in SPADE are implemented using Python, which is one of the most used programming languages for the development of applications for the NAO robot. Also, the SPADE platform incorporates different features that are interesting for this work, such as: a transparent use of the publish and subscribe event protocol following the PubSub protocol (which is supported by the platform) and the use of presence notification that allows the system and the different agents to know, in real-time, which agents are connected in the platform.

The use of the SPADE platform allows us to use it as a component that connects the different agents that control sensing devices, called *device agents*, with the agent that controls the robot, which is called the *robot agent*. The device agents can be used to manage the different sensing devices which are placed in the environment. Thus, each sensing device can have a different way to obtain and calculate the position of the robot, depending on its physical sensor component and its location algorithm. Next section describes in more detail this kind of agent.

2.1 Device Agent

The device agent has been designed as a set of different behaviors which are shown in Fig. 2. The first one is the **Service Behavior** which activates the services offered by the device and periodically publishes information about the robot position through these services (this is done using the PubSub protocol[2]). Note that, the number of activated services depend on the number of sensors that the device incorporates. That is, a device agent can be an aggregation of different sensors available through the same device. Finally, for each offered service, the device agent also includes a **Position Calculation Behavior** which calculates the robot position using the available data of a specific sensor (camera, sonar, etc.) and its own algorithm.

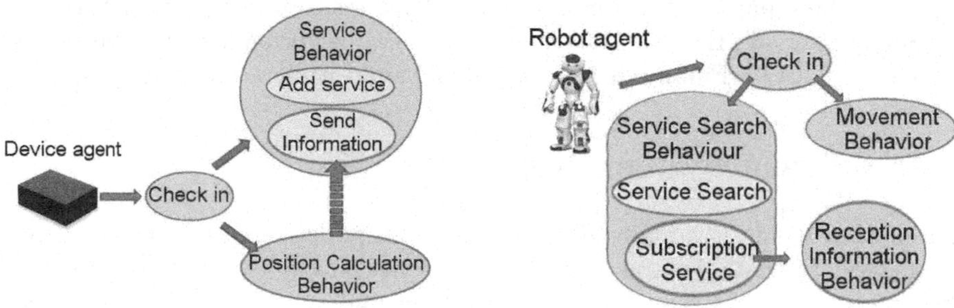

Fig. 2. Device agent behaviors.

Fig. 3. Robot agent behaviors.

For camera sensors, the calculation of the robot position is done following an algorithm which searches the robot position in the environment, using the OpenCV[3] library. The developed algorithm depends directly on the device position and the employed sensor. So each device agent can have a different **Position Calculation Behavior** for each sensor. To ease the position calculation, the environment has been divided into fields (identified by two coordinates x and y), which reduces drastically the number of possible positions of the robot in the experimentation environment.

2.2 Calculating Position with OpenCV

Different algorithms that detect the robot position have been developed depending on the different devices that we use. In this paper, we used two types of

[2] The PubSub protocol allows agents to subscribe to events published by other agents. Agents receive the information that another agent publishes if they are subscribed to the event.

[3] http://www.opencv.org/.

Fig. 4. Robot positioning with VGA camera.

devices: VGA cameras and infrared cameras that detect the depth of the environment. Scenario was divided into fields where different sensing devices can locate the robot position.

First, a vertical search is performed to detect the position x of the robot. In this search the algorithm obtains the position in which the robot gets the largest area. This initial part is similar in VGA and infrared cameras. Then, the algorithm performs a horizontal search that detects the position y. This algorithm is different in VGA and infrared cameras because Infrared cameras perform an in-depth search and easily find the robot position. But, VGA cameras look for the robot from the camera's closest position to the farthest one and stores the position in which the robot appears first, if the area that gets exceeds a certain threshold. This threshold has been set to improve the accuracy of these cameras. An example of the use of this algorithm is shown in Fig. 4, where the darker lines are the x and y position that have been detected by a normal camera.

2.3 Robot Agent

The robot agent incorporates a set of different behaviors as can be observed in Fig. 3. The first one is the **Service Search Behavior** which is in charge of collecting information periodically about the different available services (offered by the available device agents). If one service is found, the robot agent sends a subscription request to the found service. Each subscription activates in the robot a new behavior named **Reception Information Behavior** that is in charge of collecting the necessary information in order to calculate the robot position. Finally, the robot agent also incorporates the **Movement Behavior** which is responsible for moving the robot around the environment.

Thanks to the presence notification feature of the SPADE platform, the robot agent can know the current status of each device agent, knowing whether the device agent is connected or not to the platform. Thereby, the robot agent can modify its subscription related to this agent. This allows the robot agent to have the subscription list always updated with the device agents that are currently available in the environment.

2.4 Trust Model

One of the problems that the robot agent can have in order to use the information given by the device agents is the reliability of that information. Sensors can have some percentage of error in the calculation of the robot position. Moreover, this error can increase due to the changing conditions of the environment. According to this, a trust model has been incorporated to the proposal. This model allows the robot agent to assign a level of trust for each device agent, that can be adapted during the execution of the system. Note that the robot also has a self-trust value, because it has an internal coordinates system that is also used as a sensor device. The problem is that this system is not very accurate and leads the robot to make errors in its movements. The trust model on each agent is used by the robot agent to calculate its position, as explained in the next section.

Initially, a new device agent will have the highest possible trust value. This value can be decreased or increased depending on the information about the robot position given by the device to the robot agent. As the robot moves, the robot agent can adjust the trust value assigned to each device agent following the Table 1. Since the environment is divided in a grid, the robot agent calculates the difference between the calculated position and the position returned by the device and adjusts the trust value depending on the difference obtained in previous steps and the last difference obtained. On the one hand, if the difference obtained is 0 it increases the trust value in λ when the previous difference is also 0. When the previous difference is more than 0 it increases the trust value in θ. On the other hand, the trust value decreases θ if the current difference is 1 and the previous is more than 0 or λ if the current difference is more than 1. Note that the trust value can not be increased more than its maximum value (1) or be decreased less than its minimum value (0).

2.5 Position Calculation

The **Movement Behavior** commented in Sect. 2.3 is responsible for the movement of the robot around the environment depending of the information obtained in the **Reception Information Behavior**. First, the agent robot calculates the robot position following the Eq. 1, that depends of the information returned by each device agent (p), the trust value of each device agent (β) and a factor (α)

Table 1. Summary of the values to adjust the trust model

Previous difference	Current difference	Trust modification
0	0	$+\lambda$
>0	0	$+\theta$
0	1	None
>0	1	$-\theta$
-	>1	$-\lambda$

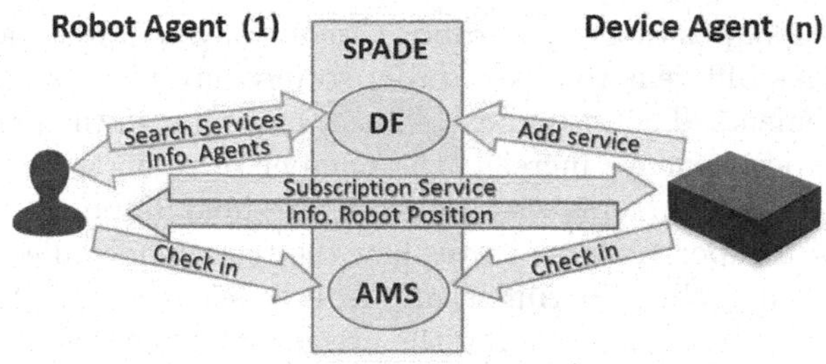

Fig. 5. General scheme of the proposed system.

that takes into account the arrival time of the returned information. This factor will be larger the less time has passed from the reception of the information. Then, the robot only stops when the result of this calculation matches with the desired position. If the calculated position is not the target position, the robot will try again to move to the desired position until it reaches the target position.

$$\hat{P}_{\{x,y\}} = \frac{\sum_{i=0}^{d} \alpha_i \cdot \beta_i \cdot P_{i\{x,y\}}}{\sum_{i=0}^{d} \alpha_i \cdot \beta_i} \tag{1}$$

A general view of the above commented agents can be seen in Fig. 5. Figure also shows the exchange of messages between the two agent classes. From a perspective of the MAS, agents are initially registered in the Agent Management System (AMS). After this initial step, the device agent registers the offered services in the Directory Facilitator (DF). Then, the robot agent tries to search the available services and subscribes to them following the PubSub standard. Finally, the device agent periodically publishes information about the robot position; the robot agent receives this information in order to determine the correct position of the robot.

3 Experimentation

Before starting the different tests, the robot movement was verified in different environments with different floors and we concluded that for these experiments the kinetic friction was lower in the wooden floor. Therefore, a scenario with wooden floor was developed and was divided into fields. Then different sensing devices where installed in the scenario to locate the robot position. Specifically, these sensing devices were VGA cameras and infrared cameras that can detect the depth of the environment. Besides, the OpenCV library has been used to calculate the robot position following the algorithm explained in Sect. 2.2.

In order to evaluate the developed system, four experiments have been designed using different cameras as sensing devices. The first experiment evaluates how the number of available devices affect in the calculation of the robot position. To evaluate this aspect the experiment increases in each test the number of cameras in a room. In this experiment we have employed cameras that always know the real position of the robot without any error. In the experiment the robot performs different routes in order to measure the error made by the robot in its movements. The second experiment is similar to the previous experiment. In this experiment we increase the number of cameras used in a room, but, in this case, we use cameras with an error threshold in the calculation of the position. The third experiment evaluates how the trust model affects in the proposed (MAS). Besides, this experiment allows us to show how the trust assigned to each device agent is adapted during the execution of the system. Finally, the last experiment is an experiment that analyses the results obtained when the robot is moving through different rooms of a building.

Note that the euclidean distance was used to calculate the error in each experiment using the field where the robot was and the field where the robot was supposed to be. Besides, each experiment has been repeated ten times, and both the average error obtained in each movement of the robot and the average standard error have been calculated and showed in each figure.

3.1 First Experiment Using Cameras Without Error

In this experiment, the robot performs different routes to measure the error made using different cameras which know the real robot position (without error). Each route is performed several times by the robot increasing the number of available cameras in each repetition.

The first route is a simple movement where the robot tries to do a circle (Fig. 10, path *a*). The results obtained can be seen in Fig. 6. As we can see, the robot accumulates the obtained error when it moves without the help of the cameras, achieving a maximum error value of 0.8 fields. The error is reduced until a value of 0.5 fields when we introduce a new camera (37.5% of improvement than without cameras). Finally, the error is completely eliminated introducing a second camera.

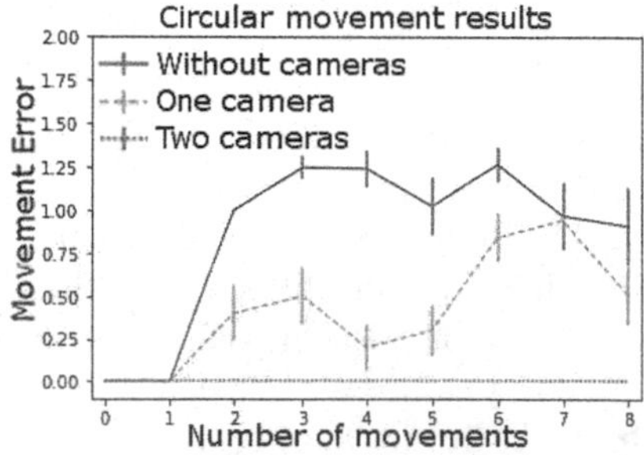

Fig. 6. Circular movement results.

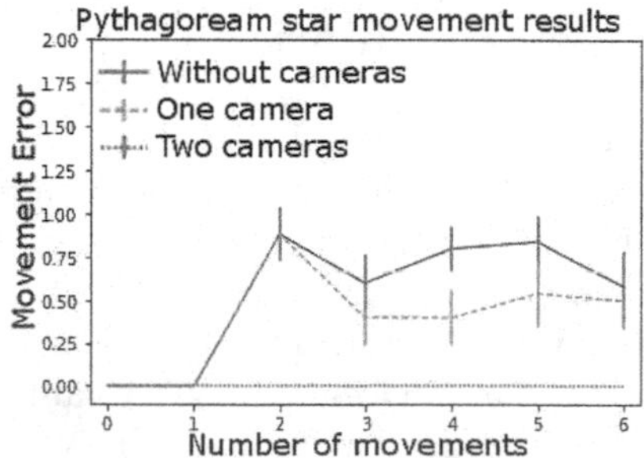

Fig. 7. Pythagorean star movement results.

Other route used is a movement that simulates a star with 5 points, showed in the path *b* of Fig. 10 (Pythagorean Star). This route contains fewer movements than the previous route, but their movements contain higher angles which make the robot movement harder. In Fig. 7, we can see the results of this experiment, which are quite similar than in the previous route. The robot accumulates an error without the help of the device agents until it achieves an error of 0.6 fields. This error is reduced when a new camera is introduced in the system. It finally achieves an error of 0.5 fields (16.67% of improvement than without cameras). In this case the error has not been significantly reduced compared to the previous route. Finally, with two cameras the error is completely eliminated.

Finally, route *c* from Fig. 10 was tested. In this case the robot performs a greater number of movements. The obtained results are very similar to those obtained in the previous routes as can be seen in Fig. 8. Without using sensing devices, the robot accumulates an error of 1.4 fields. The error is reduced until it reaches a value of 1.2 fields (14.29% better than without cameras) when we introduce the first camera. Finally, the error disappears again when two cameras are used.

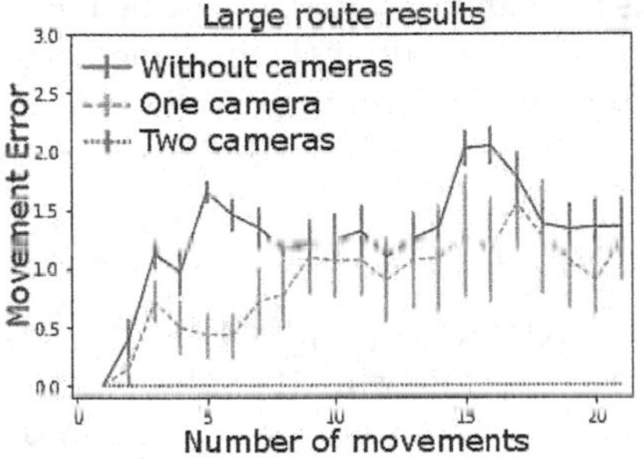

Fig. 8. Large route results.

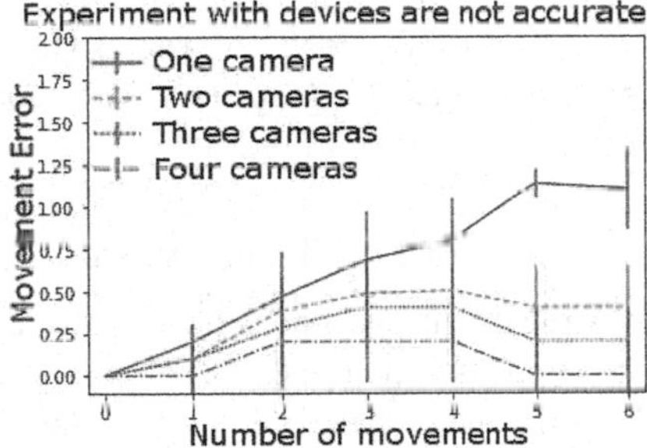

Fig. 9. Results of the experiment with non ideal cameras.

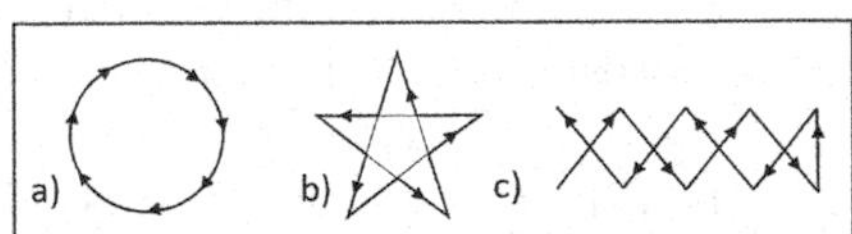

Fig. 10. Different routes used in the experiments.

3.2 Second Experiment Using Cameras with Error

The use of cameras that always know the real robot position without error is not possible in a real scenario. Devices can produce errors in their calculations due to several reasons, such as: the sensors are not effective enough or because different changes have been introduced in the environment that hinder sensor effectiveness. So, we decided to perform new experiments where the number of cameras have an associated error. As in the previous experiments, the number of cameras is increased in each test. In this case, the number of analysed routes has been reduced. The robot only performs the movements that simulate the Pythagorean Star because we consider that is the route with the highest probability of error during the movements of the robot. Moreover, we used cameras with a random error between 10% and 30% in their robot position calculation.

Figure 9 shows the results obtained in this experiment. We can see the error obtained by the robot while the number of cameras gets increased. The robot obtains worse results when a new device agent, which has an associated error, is introduced in the experiment. Specifically, the robot gets an error of 1.1 fields (the robot got an error 0.6 fields without the help of the device agents). However, the error is reduced when the number of cameras is increased until it performs the movement without error with 4 cameras. As the cameras introduce some kind of error, the robot does not reach the desired position in all of the intermediate steps in many of the tests (using 4 cameras), but the final accumulated error is low enough (only 0.2 fields).

3.3 Study of the Trust Model

This experiment evaluates how the trust model affects in the proposed MAS. The robot agent assigns trust values to all the device agents following the table shown in Table 1. These trust values are used to calculate the robot position taking into account that the information provided by device agents will be more important if their trust is higher. So, a correct assignment of the trust to the different device agents is critical. Moreover, the experiment also shows how the trust assigned to each device agent is adapted according to changes in the environment.

The experiment has been executed using 4 cameras with an associated error shown in Fig. 11. The error of camera 4 and camera 1 are exchanged in the movement number ten. As commented before, initially all the device agents (and also the robot agent) have the maximum trust assigned. Note that, as explained in Sect. 2.4, the robot also has a self-trust value. This is because it has a coordinates system that is used as a sensing device too. The problem is that this system is not accurate when the robot makes mistakes in its movement, and that is why the robot keeps a trust value also for its own coordinates system.

As can be seen in the figure, this trust is continuously decremented in the case of cameras 4 and 3 and the robot agent. This is because they have a higher error assigned. However, when the robot reaches the movement number ten, their trusts begin to change, increasing the trust in the case of camera 4 until it reaches the maximum and decrementing the trust of the camera 1 until it reaches the minimum value.

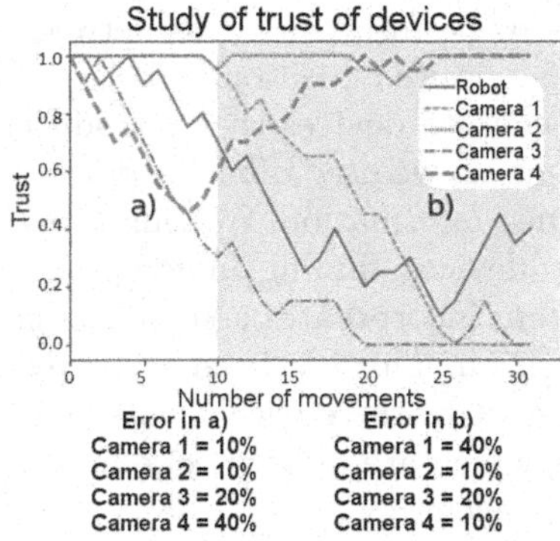

Fig. 11. Study of the trust model.

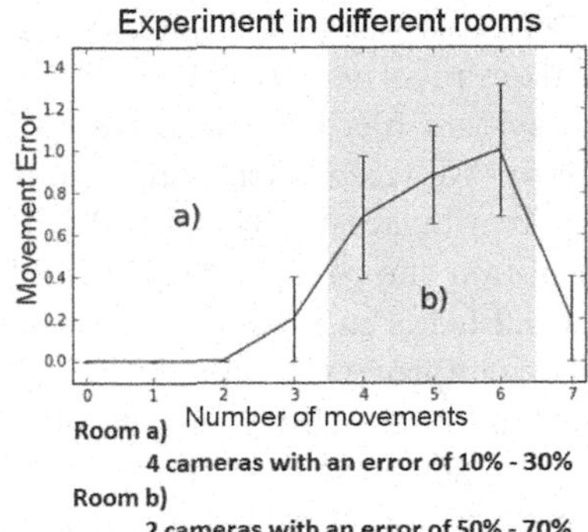

Fig. 12. Experiment with different rooms.

3.4 Fourth Experiment with Movements Through Different Rooms

The last one is an experiment whose results can be seen in Fig. 12. In this case, we want to analyse the results obtained when the robot is moving though different rooms and some device agents can appear or disappear. The experiment has been designed with two rooms. The first one is a room (a) with 4 cameras with an error between 10%–30%. The second room (b) is a less informed room with 2 cameras with an error of 50%–70%. We are trying to demonstrate how the robot is able to reach the desired position on the first room in most of the cases, but its error begins to increase when the robot enters the second room. In addition, the accumulated error of the second room is reduced when the robot returns to the first room. As in previous experiments, in the figure we can see the error obtained in each movement and the standard mean error.

4 Conclusions

In this paper, we have designed a MAS to help a mobile robot to know its real position when it performs several movements in a building with several rooms. As before commented, this problem occurs due to two causes: the flooring used that exerts a frictional force on the robot and the mistakes caused by the internal robot components. According to this, we have proposed a new distributed, dynamic and flexible solution that can be used to help any mobile robot and which allows anyone to include any external device that can provide information about the robot position.

We have reached different experiments to evaluate the proposed solution. We introduced the robot into an environment with perfectly accurate devices which know the exact robot position in the first experiment. The robot did different routes and we found that results improve as more devices are introduced into the

(MAS). This is because the robot agent believes to be in a consensus between the position returned by each device agent and the desired position.

The system has been also tested using not accurate devices that introduce some error. We tried to simulate a real environment, so we used different devices with an error between 10% and 30% in their returned information. We found that we can obtain the real position using four of these devices, finding an acceptable error of 0.2 fields in most cases. Besides, the system incorporates a trust model in order to improve the calculation of the real position. This has been evaluated with a study of the trust assigned by the robot agent to the device agents. The robot agent assigned more trust to device agents which are more precise and it adapted trust values according to changes in their accuracy.

According to the proposed evaluation, the implemented MAS can help to know the robot position in an environment with one or more rooms, with changes in the environment and with changes in the external devices used by the robot for the calculations of its position. Besides, this solution allows us to incorporate different device agents and appropriately adjusts their trusts.

As future work, we want to test different types of sensing devices that the ones used in our tests. Then, we will study how the movement error of the robot evolves as the devices and the robot reach a consensus. Moreover, in this paper we used only one robot, but in future work we will use a bigger team of robots that cooperate to obtain a result that is beneficial for all.

Acknowledgements. This work was supported by the project TIN2015-65515-C4-1-R of the Spanish government.

References

1. Canedo-Rodríguez, A., Alvarez-Santos, V., Regueiro, C.V., Iglesias, R., Barro, S., Presedo, J.: Particle filter robot localisation through robust fusion of laser, wifi, compass, and a network of external cameras. Inf. Fusion **27**, 170–188 (2016)
2. Fernández, I., et al.: Guidance of a mobile robot using an array of static cameras located in the environment. Auton. Robots **23**(4), 305–324 (2007)
3. Gregori, M.E., Cámara, J.P., et al.: A Jabber-based multi-agent system platform. In: Proceedings of the Fifth International Joint Conference on Autonomous Agents and Multiagent Systems, pp. 1282–1284. ACM (2006)
4. Lee, N., Kim, C., Choi, W., Pyeon, M., Kim, Y.: Development of indoor localization system using a mobile data acquisition platform and bow image matching. KSCE J. Civ. Eng. **21**(1), 418–430 (2017)
5. Martín Rico, F., Matellán Olivera, V., González-Careaga, R., Barrera González, P., et al.: Visual based localization for a legged robot (2006)
6. Sánchez, E.M., Alcobendas, M.M., Noguera, J.F.B., et al.: A reliability-based particle filter for humanoid robot self-localization in robocup standard platform league. Sensors **13**(11), 14954–14983 (2013)
7. Pizarro, D., Mazo, M., Santiso, E., et al.: Localization of mobile robots using odometry and an external vision sensor. Sensors **10**(4), 3655–3680 (2010)
8. Se, S., Lowe, D.G., Little, J.J.: Vision-based global localization and mapping for mobile robots. IEEE Trans. Rob. **21**(3), 364–375 (2005)

Spanish Road Fork Traffic Analysis and Modelling

Irene Díaz, José Ramón Villar(✉), and Enrique de la Cal

Computer Science Department, University of Oviedo, Oviedo, Spain
{sirene,villarjose,delacal}@uniovi.es

Abstract. This study focuses on the analysis of traffic data concerning road crashes, with the aim of extracting relevant knowledge in order to choose the location of intelligent road guardrails. To do so, historical data of the accidents in Spanish roads since 2011 have been gathered from the Dirección General de Tráfico and analyzed afterwards. After a preliminary stage, where association rule mining algorithms were performed, this study focuses on Decision Tree classifiers to determine the relationships among the features in the accidents yearly dataset. These relationships are related to the intrinsic connections between features. Some interesting relationships have been found, specially for the T or Y shape road fork type. Future work will deploy a severity index using both the victims and vehicles, so relationships due to conditions and severity can be extracted. As long as the extracted rule set varies for each year, it might be useful as well to determine invariants in the trees, which is led as future work.

Keywords: Intelligent guardrails · Applied intelligence · Traffic analysis

1 Introduction

In the last 15 years, there have been a high number of published studies focusing on traffic accident data. The idea is, in short, to discover knowledge from the traffic data, so improvements in security can be performed. Olga et al. proposed a decision support system to determine accident black spots based on different partial evaluation functions used all together [1]. Despite the fact neither the functions nor the mixing of the function outcomes were sufficiently described, the suggestion that ensembles of classifiers or regressions in order to obtain more robust and general solutions. Similarly, Luca et al. proposed several specific variables -like the vehicle speed and some parameters from the location- to estimate the possible number of accidents at the current location. This study was concerned with the road design, promoting a better and safe design; data from 2004 to 2008 corresponding to the south of Italy was used for validating the approach. Finally, a study of how the accidents are modified according to the traffic security system was presented in [2]. To determine these relationships, the authors analyzed the location data before and after the accident, in an effort to find the most representative factors according to the severity of the accident.

F.J. Martínez de Pisón et al. (Eds.): HAIS 2017, LNAI 10334, pp. 483–493, 2017.
DOI: 10.1007/978-3-319-59650-1_41

Several projects have been funded to develop road design computer aided programs -SAFE, [3], or [4]-, to locate traffic barriers and guardrails -SAVeRS, [5,6]. In Spain we can mention the project proposed in [7], focused on the road design for the Andalucia regional government. Several local governments have deployed some of these projects when designing roads.

This research is embedded in a research project to design intelligent traffic retention systems for the Spanish road network. The aim of this study is to extract the most promising relationships between variables in the accident database for the Spanish roads; this database has been published by the Spanish Traffic Agency, containing records since year 2008. Although the project focuses on avoiding vehicles to run out of the road in road crosses, this research pays attention to all the accident types as a preliminary study for extracting knowledge that relates types of accidents with road characteristics.

The organization of this paper is as follows. In the next section, some riskiness indexes used and the published data mining approaches in the literature are related. Section 3 introduces the database Sect. 3.1 and discusses the algorithm and method to extract the relationships. In Sect. 4 the experimental results are shown. Finally, some conclusions and future work are drawn.

2 Related Issues in Traffic Accident Analysis

As stated before, the main part of the studies estimate the number of accidents or the number of deaths as the riskiness rank of a road section; afterwards, the security elements are chosen and placed. Nevertheless, the difficulty in proposing an index with generalization capabilities leads to the design of riskiness indexes for specific problems. For instance, Pardillo et al. [8] proposed an index to evaluate the riskiness of running out of the road, including data about the ditches, their slope, the distances between the security elements and the road lines. Gathering information about the road infrastructure and about the accidents and their severity, the authors defined a riskiness index to group the road segments in 5 main groups. Similarly, Agarwal et al. analyzed the data concerning the road typology and surroundings, so that an hierarchy could be found among them considering the accidents [9]. In the same way, Jalayer et al. proposed a riskiness index according to local environment of local road segments [10].

More related with Internet of Things, Rosolino et al. proposed a riskiness index for the road, the road topology and environment and the road surface to be shared with the mobile devices beforehand, so the drivers could get aware of the current driving conditions [11]. Nevertheless, a very interesting index can be developed considering the historical evolution of this riskiness index.

Data mining has also been applied in this context [7] with the aim to evaluate the road section in order to decide and select the most relevant security enhancements. For instance, Principal Component Analysis and Neural Networks have been used to model the relationships between the traffic accident data and the generated losses [12]. Principal Components were used to find the most interesting transformed dimensions, while neural networks -trained with back propagation and wavelets as the neuron activation functions were proposed-modelled the losses.

Neural networks have been also proposed in [13] to measure the risk of accident for running out of the road. To do so, several riskiness indexes -together with traffic flow density, the section length, and the wealth income of the area as relevant variables- were analyzed for the studied road sections, fetching the ratio of deaths as the value to estimate. Rujun et al. [14] also proposed neural networks in their study to relate the death ratio and the economic losses. In all these cases, the obtained models are black box models, and no extra knowledge could be extracted from them.

Different solutions proposed using logit models -either binomial or multinomial models as in [15,16]-, or clustering together with association rule mining [17–19]. In [15], the study aimed to identify the cross-median and Median rollover crash severity. In [17–19], the focus is in finding the relevant factors that increase the risk of several different groups of accidents. Finally, the study in [16] aimed to identify the most relevant factors of running out of the road accidents.

Actually, [20] determined the main problems to solve in order to reduce the accident rate and to increase the security in the roads. However, the published works in the literature suggest that each specific problem has developed its own solution, either for the design of roads, location of security barriers, etc. At the same time, Roque et al. [21] showed that the differences in the road infrastructure, weather, vehicle population among the different countries make impossible to proposed general solutions for neither road design nor accident rate estimation [21]. After this study, not only the solutions should be specific for each problem due to the divide and conquer approach, but also because the variability of the available data, its dimensions and the variable types and cardinalities makes it impossible to provide general solutions. Therefore, this study focuses on analyzing the dataset and finding interesting relationships among the variables before any further and complex modeling task.

3 Finding Relations Between Variables

3.1 The Spanish Accidents Database

From the study published in [7], we contacted the Dirección General de Tráfico (DGT, [22]), which is the Spanish Agency for the traffic security. The DGT publishes every year a report of the accidents in the Spanish roads; these datasets are publicly available at [22]. In this work we have considered the data of accidents in Spain from 2008 to 2013 (both included). Table 1 shows the number of accidents per year, while some of the 26 input variables in the dataset are described in Table 2; for each variable, the set of allowed predefined values is included.

This database contains three main tables -namely, accidents, vehicles and victims-. The main table is the accident table, while the vehicles is the description of the vehicles involved in each accident. The victims table includes information about the injured and murdered people in each accident. These two latter tables

Table 1. Accidents per year, from the DGT dataset.

Year	2008	2009	2010	2011	2012	2013
Number of accidents	93161	88251	85503	83027	83115	89519

can be used for computing a severity index for each accident that can be used in further research; however, for this study we focus only on the relations between features to discover factors involved in accidents, without considering a severity index. More specifically, the relations of the variable *Road fork kind* with the remaining features will be analyzed, aiming to determine which are the most important features for the accidents in each type of road fork. The different kinds of road forks are shown in Table 3.

3.2 Extracting the Relations

At a first sight, the problem seemed to be easily addressable using frequent patterns and association rule mining (ASM). Therefore, the initial stage of this phase was performing ASM on the data [23]. This method produced a fairly bast amount of rules, typical for the ASM, that need further filtering and processing. However, either no suitable method for filtering and finding meaningful rules was found, or the set of rules included only elemental ones. Consequently, an alternative has been proposed.

The strategy followed to extract knowledge from the accident databases is based on first studying the main factors affecting accidents at an intersection year by year. To obtain these factors, an analysis of the rules extracted from different Decision Trees Classifiers has been performed. In a second step, the rules associated to each different intersection across the years are mined in order to obtain the more frequent rule sets: once the rules per year are identified, the final rule set includes those rules that have support by 3 years at least.

The prediction of accidents depending on crosses and intersections is modeled in this problem as a Machine Learning (ML) problem. As the final goal of the work is to provide an understandable output to be used by traffic analysts, we focus our attention in approaches based on tree models, due to their performance and great interpretability. At this concern, tree based models has been chosen to build classification trees. Starting with a sample population consisting of n observations (accidents in this model) belonging to C classes (the five kind of intersections detailed in Table 3), a given model will classify these observations into k terminal groups; each group is labelled with a class. In general, Tree-based ML models and algorithms work in the following described two-stage procedure:

- Grow a tree using forward selection using a top-down approach (from root to leaves).
- At each step find the best split according to some impurity measure. The node associated to the maximal impurity reduction is then selected.

Table 2. Excerpt of the variables included in the dataset, with their defined allowed values.

Variable	Value	Variable	Value
Hour	1 h periods from a day	Road elements	No available data (0)
Week day	Monday(1) to Sunday(7)		Nothing remarkable (1)
Province	52 Spanish provinces		Zebra-cross or island (3)
Region	18 Spanish regions		Middle road island (4)
Area	Road (1)		Central stop lane (5)
	Urban Area (2)		Left-turn traffic circle (6)
	Side Street (3)		Other (7)
	Detour (4)	Priority	No available data (0)
Grouped area	Intercity road (1)		Traffic officer (1)
	City road (2)		Traffic Lights (2)
Road	Road identifier		STOP sign (3)
Road owner	National (1)		GIVE WAY sign (4)
	Regional (2)		Road markings only (5)
	Provincial (3)		Zebra-crossing sign (6)
	Municipal (4)		Other signalization (7)
	Other (5)		None (8)
Road kind	Motorway (1)	Roadbed	Dry and Clean (1)
	Highway (2)		Shaded (2)
	Motored-vehicle road (3)		Damped (3)
	Road w slow lane (4)		Frozen (4)
	Road wout slow lane (5)		Snowed (5)
	Byway (6)		Muddy (6)
	Side road (7)		Loose gravel (7)
	Road fork (8)		Oily (8)
	Other (9)		Other (9)
Stretch of road	No sense -is a fork- (0)	Luminosity	Day light (1)
	Straight line (1)		Twilight (2)
	Soft curves (2)		Night: good lighting (3)
	Strong curves wout traffic signs (3)		Night: bad lighting (4)
	Strong curves w traffic signs wout speed limit (4)		Night: no lighting (5)
	Strong curves with traffic signs w speed limit (5)		

Table 3. Different road forks considered in the dataset.

Road fork type	Code
T or Y shape	1
X or + shape	2
Acceleration lane	3
Diverting lane	4
Roundabout	5

- Stop when a node has less than m examples or the node is pure enough, that is, all the nodes have (almost) the same outcome, obtaining the k terminal groups.
- Prune the tree back, obtaining a less complex model with good performance.
- Obtain a rule per path from the root to each leaf.

Different combinations of metrics, splits, stopping conditions and pruning methods lead to different approaches. In this work, considering both interpretability and performance, C5.0 ([24,25]) and recursive partitioning (PART) [26] are selected as classifiers. The performance of these classifiers is measured in terms of the well known measures Precision, Recall, F_1 and Accuracy [27]. Finally, although the modelling process seems strange from the ML point of view, facing the problem as a classification problem will find the rules that match as many examples as possible; therefore, a relationship between features will be proposed. For sure, there is no sense in deploying these classifiers, but the found relations can help in a second phase of the project.

4 Experiment Results

4.1 Parameter Settings

The performance and rules obtained by tree decision learners depends highly on the chosen set of parameters. Besides, this parameter setting must be aware of the high dimensionality of the problem. For instance, allowing a small minimum number of elements per leaf (let's say 5) may cause over-fitting while at the same time will produce very huge trees.

Therefore, a carefully selection and parameter tuning have been performed. To do so, for both C5.0 and PART, an analysis of the performance has been done for those parameters related with the tree size, more specifically:

- *The Confidence factor (C)*, which controls the tree pruning. C is varied from 0.01 to 0.25 -from more to less prunning capabilities-.
- *The Minimum number of examples per leaf (minCases)*, allowed to vary $\in \{25, 50, 100, 200\}$.

Furthermore, 10 fold cross validation (10fCV) has been introduced for the statistical comparison of the results. In this 10fCV, all the samples in the dataset were grouped in ten different sets, using one of them from testing while keeping the remaining for training. The best parameter configuration found so far were $C = 0.1$, $minCases = 200$ for C5.0, while $C = 0.1$, $minCases = 100$ were found for PART. The mean values of the classification indexes on the 10fCV are shown in Table 4 for these best parameter configurations; as can be seen, the C5.0 outperforms the PART algorithm.

Table 4. Classifiers performance per year. The comparisons are performed using well-known classification performance measurements.

Year	C5.0 (C = 0.1, minCases = 200)				PART (C = 0.1, minCases = 100)			
	Precision	Recall	F1	Accuracy	Precision	Recall	F1	Accuracy
2008	0.63	0.64	0.61	0.71	0.62	0.63	0.61	0.63
2009	0.63	0.64	0.61	0.71	0.61	0.62	0.59	0.62
2010	0.58	0.61	0.57	0.69	0.60	0.62	0.60	0.62
2011	0.58	0.59	0.56	0.68	0.60	0.61	0.59	0.61
2012	0.59	0.61	0.57	0.69	0.60	0.61	0.58	0.60
2013	0.59	0.60	0.57	0.70	0.58	0.58	0.57	0.58

4.2 Results

Tables from 5, 6, 7, 8 and 9 show the rules associated to each road fork. These rules are supported by at least three years. Table 5 shows the induction rules whose consequence is T or Y road fork. From this rule set it is possible to deduce that accidents in T or Y road forks are produced in City roads (Grouped area = 2) without sidewalk (Sidewalk = NO). Priority regulation, restricted visibility, traffic volume and roadbed conditions are also variables to take into account. Among all the regions in Spain, Catalonia (region = 9) seems to produce more accidents in a T or Y road fork. Note that although the rules obtained by C5.0 or PART are not the same, the variables as well as their values are more or less the same.

Table 6 shows the rules obtained for studying accidents in a X or + road fork. City roads (Grouped area = 2) are more likely to have an accident when the road fork is X or + (especially city roads (Area = 2)). Note also that priority regulations represent an important factor to work with. In particular, No available data, Traffic Lights and No priority regulations (see Table 2) are important to study accident behavior in X or + road forks. On the other hand, the behavior of an accident in a X or + road fork is different among regions, being region = 1 (Andalucía) obtained by two methods (PART and C5.0) as a highlighted factor. Surprisingly, low traffic volume and good atmospheric conditions are other factors obtained by at least one method as a factor of accident in an X or + road fork. No special actions or local roads (Road owner = 4) are also important factors to take into account. In this case, there is only one rule supported by at least 3 years in case of C5.0.

For acceleration lanes (see Table 7), accidents are produced in motorways (road kind=1) and they also depend on priority regulations. In particular acceleration lanes with traffic lights, stop signs, road markings (only) or none regulation are the most common configuration where accidents were registered.

For diverting lanes (Table 8), the accidents are produced in highways (Road kind = 1) without priority regulations (Priority regulation = 8). Note that in

Table 5. Rules obtained by the different methods for T or Y Road fork

C5.0
Grouped Area = 2 AND *Region* = 9
Sidewalk = *NO*
Priority regulation = 8 AND Road elements ! = 7
Grouped Area = 2 AND Road kind = 9
Priority regulation= 0 AND *Sidewalk* = *NO*
Priority regulation = 8 AND Roadbed condition $\in \{1, 2, 3, 6, 7, 8, 9\}$
Priority regulation $\in \{0, 1, 2, 5, 6, 7, 8\}$
Roadbed condition$\in \{1, 2, 3, 6, 7, 9\}$ AND Restricted visibility $\in \{3, 4, 5, 7, 8\}$
Grouped Area = 2
Grouped Area = 2 AND Roadbed condition $\in \{1, 2, 4, 5, 6\}$
PART
Roadbed condition $\in \{1, 4\}$
Road $\in \{5, 9\}$
Region = 9
Traffic volume = 1
Special measure = 1
Priority regulation $\in \{0, 2, 3, 5, 6, 8\}$
Road kind $\in \{5, 6\}$
Grouped Area = 2
Restricted visibility = 8

Table 6. Rules obtained by the different methods for X or + Road fork

C5.0
Priority regulation $\in \{0, 1, 2, 3, 8\}$
PART
Roadbed elements $\in \{0, 1, 3\}$
Road = 9
Priority regulation $\in \{0, 2, 3, 4, 8\}$
Region = 1
Traffic volume = 1
Grouped Area = 2
Restricted visibility = 8
Special measure = 4
Road kind $\in \{5, 9\}$

Table 7. Rules obtained by the different methods for acceleration lanes

C5.0
Priority regulation $\in \{2, 3, 5, 7\}$
PART
Road kind = 1

Table 8. Rules obtained by the different methods for diverting lanes

C5.0
No common rules across years
PART
Priority regulation = 8 Road kind = 2

Table 9. Rules obtained by the different methods for roundabouts

C5.0
Special actions $\in \{3, 4\}$ Priority regulation = 4 Priority regulation = 4 AND Road kind $\in \{3, 4, 5, 6, 7, 9\}$
PART
Priority regulation $\in \{3, 4\}$ Road kind $\in \{2, 5, 9\}$ Grouped area = 1 Road $\in \{5, 9\}$

this case the rules obtained by C5.0 across the different years are different each other.

Regarding Rounds (see Table 9), intercity roads (Grouped area = 1) are those more likely to suffer accidents inside rounds. In addition, roads without slow lane appear as a reason for accidents in a round. In fact, this reason is highlighted by the two methods for this type of road (road kind = 5). Mean while, the variable Special actions set to the value "No special actions" plays an important role as well; it seems that special actions, such as Reversible lines, don't have relevance in the accident rate, perhaps because the drivers are more focused on the road.

5 Conclusions and Future Work

In this work we have presented a first approach to study the behavior of accidents in road forks. The approach presented is based on producing induction rules from the accident database released by the Spanish Agency for guaranteeing the traffic security from 2008 to 2013 (both included). Induction rules are obtained by training different machine learners (considering different parameter configurations), in particular C5.0 and PART. The final induction rule set is obtained considering only those rules obtained at least 3 years. The method allows to identify those relevant variables (or combination of variables) for accidents in road forks and to characterize different road forks. With this information, it is possible to act on road forks in order to prevent accidents.

As future work, we plan to introduce new learners to make the rule set broader. In addition we will try to characterize the different accident kinds and to include more information to our data base to study new factors affecting accidents. Furthermore, the relationships with the different tables in the DGT database should also be analyzed. To do so, a severity index needs to be selected in order to extract more relevant rules.

Acknowledgments. This research has been funded by the Interconecta call of the European Union Structural Funds (FEDER) INTERCONECTA CDTI project ABECATIM (SOL-00082271/ITC-20151039).

References

1. Olga, B., Luca, P.: Tools for assessing the safety impact of interventions on road safety. Procedia Soc. Behav. Sci. **53**, 682–691 (2012)
2. Park, J., Abdel-Aty, M., Lee, J.: Use of empirical and full bayes before-after approaches to estimate the safety effects of roadside barriers with different crash conditions. J. Saf. Res. **58**, 31–40 (2016)
3. Roque, C., Cardoso, J.L.: Observations on the relationship between European standards for safety barrier impact severity and the degree of injury sustained. IATSS Res. **37**, 21–29 (2013)
4. Strandroth, J.: Validation of a method to evaluate future impact of road safety interventions, a comparison between fatal passenger car crashes in Sweden 2000 and 2010. Accid. Anal. Prev. **76**, 133–140 (2015)
5. Torre, F.L., Erginbas, C., Williams, G., Thomson, R., Hemmings, G., Stefan, C.: Guideline for the selection of the most appropriate roadside vehicle restraint system (2015). http://www.saversproject.com
6. Torre, F.L., Erginbas, C., Thomson, R., Amato, G., Pengal, B., Stefan, C., Hemmings, G.: Selection of the most appropriate roadside vehicle restraint system - the SAVeRS project. Transp. Res. Procedia **14**, 4237–4246 (2016)
7. Martín, L., Baena, L., Garach, L., López, G., de Oña, J.: Using data mining techniques to road safety improvement in Spanish roads. Procedia Soc. Behav. Sci. **160**, 607–614 (2014)
8. Pardillo-Mayora, J.M., Domínguez-Lira, C.A., Jurado-Piña, R.: Empirical calibration of a roadside hazardousness index for Spanish two-lane rural roads. Acci. Anal. Prev. **42**, 2018–2023 (2010)
9. Agarwal, P.K., Patil, P.K., Mehar, R.: A methodology for ranking road safety hazardous locations using analytical hierarchy process. Procedia Soc. Behav. Sci. **104**, 1030–1037 (2013)
10. Jalayer, M., Zhou, H.: Evaluating the safety risk of roadside features for rural two-lane roads using reliability analysis. Acci. Anal. Prev. **93**, 101–112 (2016)
11. Rosolino, V., Teresa, I., Vittorio, A., Carmine, F.D., Antonio, T., Daniele, R., Claudio, Z.: Road safety performance assessment: a new road network risk index for info mobility. Procedia Soc. Behav. Sci. **111**, 624–633 (2014)
12. Li, S., Zhao, D.: Prediction of road traffic accidents loss using improved wavelet neural network. In: Proceedings of the IEEE 10 Conference on Computers, Communications, Control and Power Engineering TENCON 2002 (2002)
13. Liyan, Q., Chunfu, S.: Macro prediction model of road traffic accident based on neural network and genetic algorithm. In: Proceedings of the Second International Conference on Intelligent Computation Teclmology and Automation, pp. 354–357 (2009)

14. Rujun, Y., Xiuqing, L.: Study on traffic accidents prediction model based on RBF neural network. In: Proceedings of the IEEE International Conference on Information Engineering and Computer Science (ICIECS) (2010)
15. Hu, W., Donnell, E.T.: Severity models of cross-median and rollover crashes on rural divided highways in Pennsylvania. J. Saf. Res. **42**, 375–382 (2011)
16. Roque, C., Moura, F., Cardoso, J.L.: Detecting unforgiving roadside contributors through the severity analysis of ran-off-road crashes. Acci. Anal. Prev. **80**, 262–273 (2015)
17. Kumar, S., Toshniwal, D.: Analysing road accident data using association rule mining. In: Proceedings of the IEEE International Conference on Computing, Communication and Security (ICCCS) (2015)
18. Kumar, S., Toshniwal, D.: A data mining framework to analyze road accident data. J. Big Data **2**(26), 1–18 (2015). doi:10.1186/s40537-015-0035-y
19. Äyrämö, S., Pirtala, P., Kauttonen, J., Naveed, K., Kärkkäinen, T.: Mining road traffic accidents. Technical report, University of Jyväskylä, Department of Mathematical Information Technology (2009)
20. Elvik, R.: Problems in determining the optimal use of road safety measures. Res. Transp. Econ. **47**, 27–36 (2014)
21. Roque, C., Cardoso, J.L.: Safeside: a computer-aided procedure for integrating benefits and costs in roadside safety intervention decision making. Saf. Sci. **74**, 195–205 (2015)
22. de Tráfico, D.G.: Dirección general de tráfico, sección de estadística. series históricas. http://www.dgt.es/es/seguridad-vial/estadisticas-e-indicadores/accidentes-30dias
23. Agrawal, R., Srikant, R.: Fast algorithms for mining association rules in large databases. In: Proceedings of the 20th International Conference on Very Large Data Bases VLDB 1994, pp. 487–499 (1994)
24. Quinlan, R.J.: C4.5: programs for machine learning. Mach. Learn. **16**(3), 235–240 (1994)
25. Quinlan, R.J.: Data Mining Tools See5 and C5.0 (2000)
26. Witten, I.H., Frank, E., Hall, M.A.: Data Mining: Practical Machine Learning Tools and Techniques, 3rd edn. Morgan Kaufmann Publishers Inc., San Francisco (2011)
27. Díaz, I., Ranilla, J., Montañés, E., Fernández, J., Combarro, E.F.: Improving performance of text categorisation by combining filtering and support vector machines. J. Am. Soc. Inf. Sci. Technol. **55**(7), 579–592 (2004)

Application of the Systems Dynamics Approach to Model Inventive Problems

Jesús Delgado-Maciel[1], Guillermo Cortes-Robles[1(✉)], Emilio Jiménez Macias[2], Cuauhtémoc Sánchez-Ramírez[1], and Jorge García-Alcaraz[3]

[1] Instituto Tecnológico de Orizaba, Avenida Oriente 9 No. 852 Col., Emiliano Zapata, 94320 Orizaba, Veracruz, Mexico
jdelgadom@ito-depi.edu.mx, {gcortes,csanchez}@itorizaba.edu.mx
[2] Universidad de La Rioja Avenida de La Paz, 93 26006 Logroño, Spain
emilio.jimenez@unirioja.es
[3] Department of Industrial Engineering and Manufacturing, Institute of Engineering and Technology, Autonomous University of Ciudad Juarez, Avenida Del Charro 450 Norte, Col. Partido Romero, Ciudad Juárez, Chihuahua, Mexico
jorge.garcia@uacj.mx

Abstract. The Theory of Inventive Problem Solving (TRIZ) has a broad range of application in today's industry. Many companies have assimilated this problem-solving approach and unveiled new technological resources for add value and impel the innovation process. Nevertheless, the appropriation effort of TRIZ also revealed several research opportunities; one that has particular significance is the complexity for modeling inventive problems. Typically, TRIZ proposes to model problems through Functional Analysis, Root-Cause Analysis, and other graphical tools. However, these tools are inadequate to represent how one conflict changes in time. Hence, it is not possible to observe the effect of one solution on the system. An approach particularly appropriate to model a system in a period is the System Dynamics Modeling. This article has the purpose of demonstrating that the modeling tools of the System Dynamics can represent inventive problems. In this process, both techniques obtain something useful. In the first place, TRIZ gains a modeling tool, and on the other hand, the System Dynamics Modeling explores the possibility to enrich their problem-solving toolbox. The objective of this article is to demonstrate that it is possible to model any inventive problem through the System Dynamic Modeling approach.

Keywords: Inventive problems modeling · System dynamics simulation · TRIZ

1 Introduction

The Theory of Inventive Problem Solving (TRIZ) identifies an inventive problem (frequently called non-routine or innovation problems) when some of the following situations produce an impasse: (1) If available knowledge cannot provide a satisfactory solution, and a tradeoff emerges (Salamatov 1999), and (2) If at least one critical step to a solution as well as the solution itself is unknown (Savransky 2000).

F.J. Martínez de Pisón et al. (Eds.): HAIS 2017, LNAI 10334, pp. 494–506, 2017.
DOI: 10.1007/978-3-319-59650-1_42

TRIZ proposes then a set of modeling and problem-solving tools that deal efficiently with inventive problems. The usefulness of TRIZ is an active research field in the present industrial and academic context. As any other problem-solving approach, TRIZ has several opportunities that have the potential to produce more efficient problem-solving tools. According to (Rantanen and Domb 2008), the combination of TRIZ with other tools, techniques or methodologies is a successful improvement strategy that produces a synergy where both techniques increase their performance (Cortes et al. 2009). Under this logic, this article deal with one of the TRIZ drawback: how to model in time the complex relations that cause an inventive problem?

Currently, TRIZ can formulate inventive problems through some fundamental mechanism. The most frequent problem models are contradictions, functions, and trends of evolution. It is important to notice that this article focuses on modeling contradictions and essential functions, due to the frequency of use in reported articles (Chechurin and Borgianni 2016). Nonetheless, TRIZ examines a conflict from a static point of view. The TRIZ Toolbox is unable to model a conflict and their intrinsic relation taking into account the time dimension. However, there is a technical approach useful to analyze a system in time: The System Dynamics Modeling (SD). This article evaluates the potential of combining both methods to model conflicts and connect the problem formulation with at least one TRIZ tool. The article has four sections. Section two briefly describes the TRIZ theory and a research opportunity. Section three demonstrate that with SD it is possible to model the problem archetypes of TRIZ. Section four discusses the feasibility to combine TRIZ with System Dynamics. The last section presents the conclusion of this work.

2 Background

The Theory of Inventive Problem Solving (TRIZ)

The particular knowledge capitalization process behind TRIZ is probably the most significant difference with other tools or techniques for problem-solving (e.g. Synectics, trial and error, and brainstorming, among others). TRIZ has a knowledge-base which lies in five fields: (1) The synthesis of valuable information about the work of great inventors, (2) An analysis of several methods for problem-solving, (3) The history of technical systems evolution, (4) A massive patents review, and finally, (5) The scientific literature. As a result, TRIZ provides a philosophy background, and a set of mechanisms to reuse the knowledge-base that is useful to assists the innovation process. The TRIZ toolbox deals well with inventive problems. Next paragraph briefly explains each type of conflict.

1. A contradiction exists when one component, one useful parameter, or the entire system must offer two different and mutually exclusive states to reach an objective. For instance, the total volume of a car must increase to assure the passenger's comfort but simultaneously should be as small as possible to reduce air friction. TRIZ distinguishes two basic kinds of contradictions: physical and technical. Physical contradictions use the separation principles as solving strategy, while technical contradictions make use of an arrangement called contradiction matrix (Altshuller 1999).
2. According to TRIZ, all technical system exists to provide at least one main useful function (MUF). Then, each system component interacts with each other to produce

a desirable effect or MUF. The interactions that take place in a system are the key element for a TRIZ tool named as Substance-Field Analysis (SFA). This tool exposes that a minimal and controllable technical system capable of performing a function has three fundamental elements: two substances and one field (Rantanen and Domb 2008, Fey and Rivin 2005). The problem formulation of the SFA has a graphical model as a requisite. The user must identify the similarity between the problem model with a set of patterns named as Standard Solution. The user selects the most similar model, which proposes one solving strategy to transform the system.
3. TRIZ proposes a set of trends of evolution (ToE) that are useful to explore the future stages of a service, product, process, and even an organizational structure (Altshuller 1999, Kwatra and Salamatov 2013).

The synthesis of the ToE was an extent knowledge capitalization effort. The classification and study of thousands of patents produced enough evidence to state an essential TRIZ foundation: a set of trends of evolution can explain the past transitions of any technical systems to figure out the future state. The application of the ToE in different systems is a very active research field, due to the amount of information necessary to identify the most suitable evolution trend.

Despite the utility of the modeling and solving TRIZ tools, still no possible to model a problem in time. In other words, the TRIZ tools produce a static vision of a problem. In consequence, it is not feasible to observe how the system containing the conflict will change in or what will be the effect of removing one conflict in the system, neither to distinguish between two potential solutions. Nevertheless, there is an approach that deals well with the TRIZ lack of dynamism: The System Dynamics Modeling and Simulation. Several research works apply System Dynamics focused on the innovation process. For instance, (Timma et al. 2015) propose a model of innovation diffusion for energy efficiency solutions in households. The same article combines empirical study with system dynamics modeling. (Samara et al. 2012) Integrate the systemic approach, the computer modeling, and the simulation discipline into a holistic and dynamic structure. The case study considers the National Investigation System (NIS) in Greece. (Kreng and Jyun 2013) Propose a multi-generation diffusion model based on system dynamics, which takes into account the dynamic market potential with a competitive relationship among generations and products. The use of System Dynamics for explaining the innovation process is a research topic with intense activity. However, it is important to underline that the search in several databases did not produce any result about the combination of TRIZ with System Dynamics.

The SD initially called Industrial Dynamics was proposed by J. Forrester in the 60's (Forrester 1961). SD is a method for studying and managing complex systems, which combines a conceptual framework, some methods, and philosophy to analyze the complex relations within a system and understand how the system changes over time (Forrester 1988, Sterman 2000). This article proposes a combination of both approaches where TRIZ obtains a dynamic modeling tool, and SD acquires the capacity to solve inventive problems via the TRIZ toolbox. Hence, the synergy creates value for both techniques. Table 1 shows a comparison between TRIZ and DS. The potential advantages of the synergy are the focus of this table.

Table 1. Comparison between TRIZ and DS

Advantage	TRIZ	DS
Modeling complex problems	Yes	Yes
Conflict resolution	Yes	No
Solving inventive problems	Yes	No
Allows the user to perform simulations	No	Yes
Uses mathematical models	No	Yes

The work of (Altshuller 1999, Salamatov 1999, Forrester 1961) are the basis to create a synergy between TRIZ and SD. To combine both techniques, the simplest strategy has three stages: (1) definition and identification of variables, (2) analysis of archetypes, and (3) development of the simulation model. The objective of this article is circumscribed for the moment to demonstrate the feasibility to model any inventive problem described in the form of contradictions or functions. (Salamatov 1999, Fey and Rivin 2005) describe nine typical configurations of inventive problems. These archetypes use a graphical representation to illustrate the effect or effects that a variable, component or system has on another. These archetypes are the guide for exploring the possibility to model problems via the System Dynamics Modeling. Each case contains three elements: the graphical model of each conflict, the Forrester diagram (Forrester 1988), and the differential equations of the case. Next section breaks down each archetype. Table 2 contains the graphical nomenclature.

Table 2. Nomenclature used in the TRIZ archetypes

Analysis	Nomenclature	Analysis	Nomenclature
1) Application	——→	4) Harmful effect	——→
2) Desired effect	- - - - - - - - - →	5) Inexistent effect	━━━→
3) Insufficient desired effect	∿∿∿→	6) Transformation of model	— — — — — —
7) Excessive	⟹	8) Uncontrolled effect	- · - · - · - · →

The subjacent research hypothesis of this work explains that: if it is possible to model an inventive problem, then it will be possible to link the conflict with at least one TRIZ tool to solve it. Next section depicts the modeling perspective of this article and suggests a potential solving tool.

3 Case Studies: Modeling Inventive Problems with SD

3.1 Case 1: Counter Action

"A produces the desired effect on B (solid arrow), but there is a partial or continual negative reaction of B (wave arrow). Thus, it is necessary to maintain or increase the positive effect on B without the adverse effect."

A significant increase in the horsepower of a combustion car engine demands a more robust engine and more cylinders. The impact is a powerful car. However, when the power increases, the energy consumption, and the cost also growth.

This conflict has several formulations: (1) The engine should be robust but lighter (physical contradiction). (2) The engine should augment its power but not to increase its operational cost. (3) The engine must increase its power without affecting the car weight. Then, each situation produces a different problem formulation. However, the graphical model acts as a generic model. The contradiction matrix or the set of inventive principles could solve this problem. (Figs. 1, 2, 3, 4, 5, 6, 8 and 9).

$$\frac{d(E_f)}{dt} = (P - E) \Rightarrow E_f(t) = E_f(t_0) + \int_0^t (P - E)dt \tag{1}$$

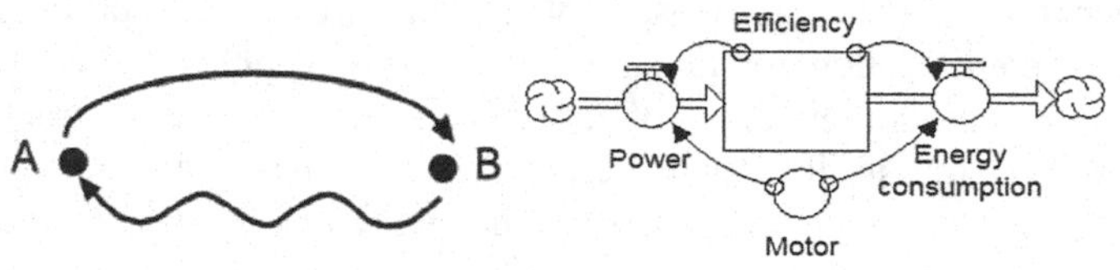

Fig. 1. Counter action

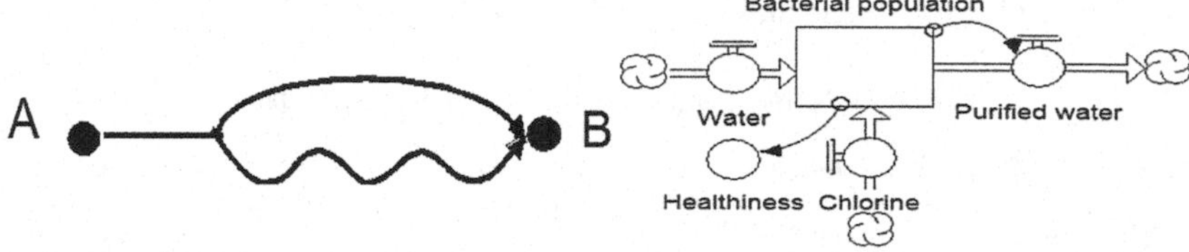

Fig. 2. Coupled effect in the entire system

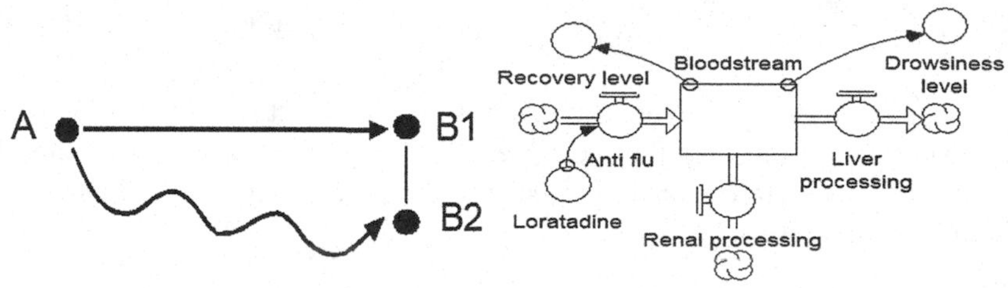

Fig. 3. Coupled effect in two components

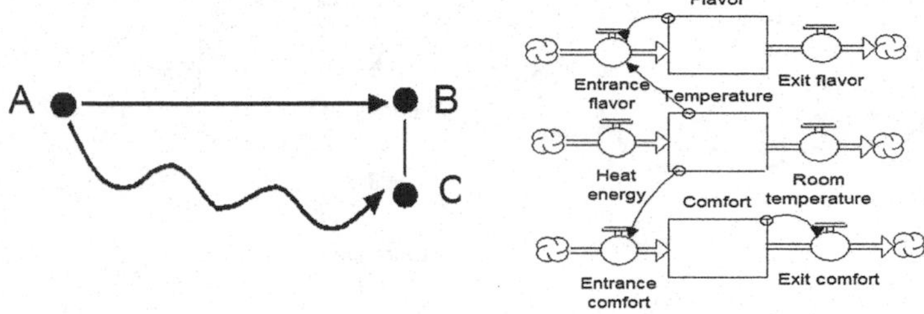

Fig. 4. Coupled effect in a system with several components

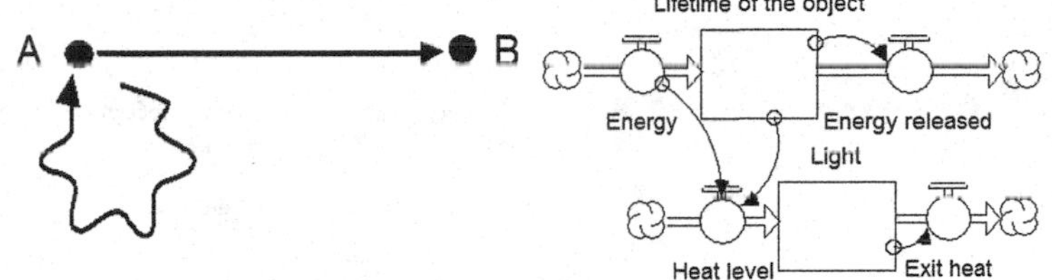

Fig. 5. Coupled effect with negative feedback

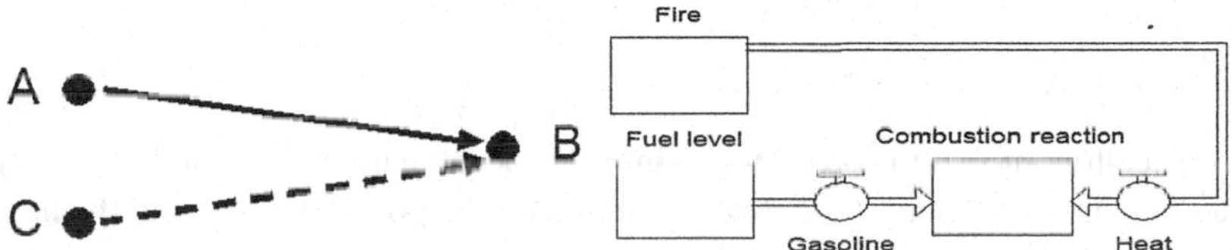

Fig. 6. Incompatible effect

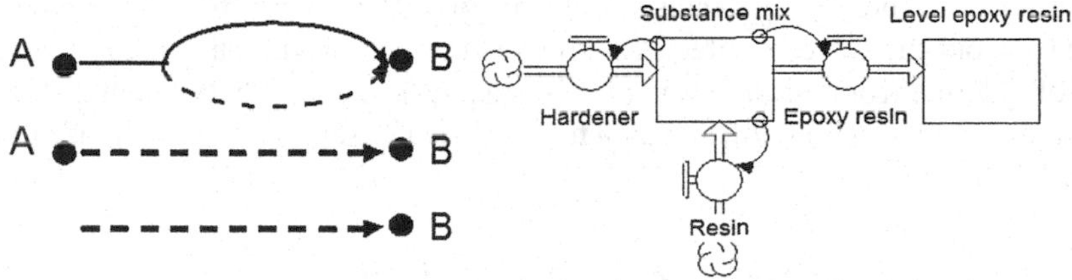

Fig. 7. Inaction

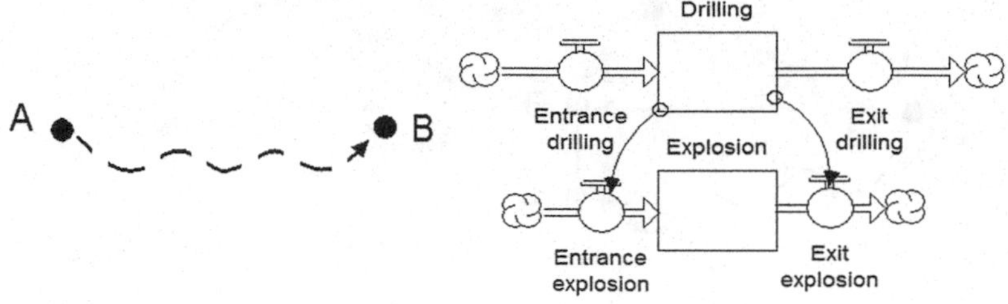

Fig. 8. 'Silence'

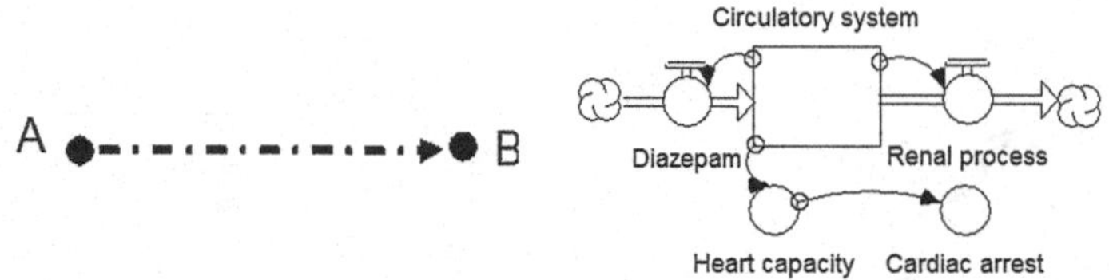

Fig. 9. Excessive effect

Where: E_f = Efficiency of a car engine, P = Power and E = Energy consumption.

3.2 Case 2: Coupled Effect

"The useful effect of A on B produces a simultaneous negative effect on B. The conflict appears when it is necessary to increase or maintain the positive effect, but the negative effect should be eliminated."

The addition of chlorine to water reduces the bacterial population. However, in high concentration chlorine makes water unhealthy, modifies taste, and increase the water purification cost. Thereby, it is indispensable to guarantee the positive effect and simultaneously avoid the adverse effect. Enterprises use activated charcoal to remove the excess of chlorine from purified water. This is a physical contradiction, but the conflict could be modeled as a function and then to use the set of separation principles or the 76 Standard Solutions.

$$\frac{d(B)}{dt} = (W + C - P) \Rightarrow B(t) = B(t_0) + \int_0^t (W + C - P)dt \tag{2}$$

Where: B = Bacterial population, C = Percentage of chlorine, W = Water to be purified and P = Purified water.

3.3 Case 3: Coupled Effect in Different Subsystem

"This causal relation is similar to preceding one. The effect of A on B is useful in one part or component of B but harmful for another part, or component of B. Some actions must be in place to eliminate the negative effect on B2 while the positive effect on B1 remains or get improved."

The anti-flu has a formulation that diminishes the influenza symptoms. An active substance in the anti-flu is loratadine, which reduces the symptoms, but produces somnolence incapacitating the patient for certain activities. Medical laboratories reduce this negative impact by shrinking the amount of loratadine. However, it is imperative to assure the dose to guarantee the anti-flu main useful function (Baumann et al. 2014). This conflict could be formulated via the technical contradiction and potentially solved with the contradiction matrix.

$$\frac{d(B)}{dt} = (A - R - L) \Rightarrow B(t) = B(t_0) + \int_0^t (A - R - L)dt \tag{3}$$

Where: B = Bloodstream, A = Anti-flu, R = Renal processing and L = Liver processing.

3.4 Case 4: Coupled Effect in System with Several Components

"In a system involving several components, A has a positive effect on B but produces a simultaneous negative effect on C. It is necessary to eliminate or reduce the negative effect and preserve or improve the useful effect without damaging the system."

The traditional coffee-maker raises the water temperature in a range between 90–95 °C to extract the flavor and coffee fragrance. Nevertheless, at this temperature, the user finds difficult to manipulate the mug or cup. This is a physical contradiction: temperature must be near to 95 °C to enjoy a great coffee but must be as low as possible to hold the cup comfortably. Again, this is a physical contradiction. The separation principles can guide the solving process.

$$\frac{d(T)}{dt} = (H - R) \Rightarrow T(t) = T(t_0) + \int_0^t (H - R)dt \tag{4}$$

$$\frac{d(F)}{dt} = (E_f - e_f) \Rightarrow F(t) = F(t_0) + \int_0^t (E_f - e_f)dt \tag{5}$$

$$\frac{d(C)}{dt} = (E_c - e_c) \Rightarrow C(t) = C(t_0) + \int_0^t (E_c - e_c)dt \tag{6}$$

Where: E_f & E_c = Inflow of information, e_f & e_c = Information output flow, F = Flavor, R = Room temperature, H = Heat energy, C = Comfort and T = Temperature.

3.5 Case 5: Coupled Effect with a Negative Feedback

"The useful effect of A on B produces a harmful effect on A. Thus, it is necessary to eliminate the negative effect but maintain or increase the useful effect."

An incandescent light bulb produces its main useful function when electric current flows through a tungsten filament to reach a brilliant white color (more than 3000 °C). Under this condition, tungsten filament losses matter and gets deteriorated. This is essentially a physical contradiction as the case 4.

$$\frac{d(L_0)}{dt} = (E - E_r) \Rightarrow L_0(t) = L_0(t_0) + \int_0^t (E - E_r)dt \tag{7}$$

$$\frac{d(L)}{dt} = (H - E_h) \Rightarrow L(t) = L(t_0) + \int_0^t (H - E_h)dt \tag{8}$$

Where: L_0 = Lifetime of the object (light bulb), E = Energy, H = Heat level, E_h = Exit heat, E_r = Energy released and L = Quantity of Lumens used.

The physical contradiction exposes that is necessary a high temperature for obtaining a brilliant white color in the light bulb, but a low temperature to avoid damage.

3.6 Case 6: Incompatible Effect

"The useful effect of A on B is excluding the useful effect of C on B. It is necessary to provide the effect of C on B without changing the effect of A on B. A mutually exclusive relation could also be present in the system."

The engine combustion chamber produces a controlled explosion to transform energy from a chemical reaction to mechanical energy. The fuel and the fire (ignition spark) are mutually exclusive in the rest of the system (the car). This conflict is easily model as a function. Hence, the 76 Standard Solutions can guide the solving process.

$$\frac{d(F)}{dt} = -H \Rightarrow F(t) = F(t_0) - \int_0^t Hdt \tag{9}$$

$$\frac{d(F_l)}{dt} = -G \Rightarrow F_l(t) = F_l(t_0) - \int_0^t Gdt \tag{10}$$

$$\frac{d(C)}{dt} = (G + H) \Rightarrow C(t) = C(t_0) + \int_0^t (G + H)dt \tag{11}$$

Where: F = Fire, C = Combustion reaction, Fl = Fuel level, H = Heat and G = Gasoline.

3.7 Case 7: Inaction

"This relation has several interpretations. The first one is that A has a single effect on B. Nevertheless, two different effects are demanded. The second interpretation explains that A has no the desired effect on B, or that it is necessary to change B, but the mechanism to execute the transformation is not known. Finally, the relation exposes that it is a need to provide the effect of B, but the complexity of A should not increase."

This case has three interpretations. The example in Fig. 7 depicts only the first one, in which A has a single effect on B, but the execution of the function demands two different effects. For instance, the epoxy resin consists of a reactive polymer that forms a mix with a catalytic substance frequently named as a hardener. Both materials react and create a polyepoxide useful to protect a surface or an object, due to their mechanical properties and chemical resistance. The catalytic needs to interact with the polymer but simultaneously, it must guarantee the right proportion in the mix for obtaining the proper quality attributes. The problem formulation corresponds to a technical contradiction: the amount of substance versus the accuracy of measurement. The contradiction matrix recommends a set of inventive principles to solve this conflict.

$$\frac{d(S)}{dt} = (H + R - L) \Rightarrow H(t) = H(t_0) + \int_0^t (H + R - L)dt \tag{12}$$

$$\frac{d(L)}{dt} = E_r \Rightarrow L(t) = L(t_0) + \int_0^t E_r dt \tag{13}$$

Where: S = Substance mix, H = Hardener, E_r = Epoxy resin, R = Resin and L = Level epoxy resin.

3.8 Case 8: 'Silence'

"The information or interaction between A and B does not exist. A mechanism to collect information or to implement a useful action is necessary. Essentially, the conception of this interaction is a creative process."

The use of columns and metal bars underground to gain strength in the mechanical structures of buildings is very common. The insertion of the column in the ground brings into light a problem: the column must have a pointed end to facilitate the insertion, but it must present the opposite state to ameliorate the mechanical resistance. The transition from one state (insertion) to another desirable state (flat shape) is a physical contradiction, and the strategy for executing this change is unknown (Fey and Rivin 2005). In this case, the use of the Substance-Field Analysis is desirable.

$$\frac{d(D)}{dt} = (E_d - e_d) \Rightarrow D(t) = D(t_0) + \int_0^t (E_d - e_d)dt \tag{14}$$

$$\frac{d(E)}{dt} = (E_e - e_e) \Rightarrow E(t) = E(t_0) + \int_0^t (E_e - e_e)dt \tag{15}$$

Where: E_d & E_e = Inflow of information, e_d & e_c = Information output flow, E = Explosion and D = Drilling.

3.9 Case 9: Excessive Effect

"The effect of A on B is not controllable; the control process is unknown, or the mechanism to make controllable the effect is not known."

The use of Diazepam in patients suffering from anxiety is a common control medication. However, a small positive variation in the dose can produce severe damages in the patient and even to trigger a cardiorespiratory arrest, due to the suppression of some fundamental functions in the nervous system. Also, a small reduction in the dose cannot produce the desired effect. Hence, the control mechanism still under research.

$$\frac{d(C)}{dt} = (D - R) \Rightarrow C(t) = D(t_0) + \int_0^t (D - R)dt \tag{16}$$

Where: C = Circulatory system, D = Quantity of diazepam and R = Renal process.

4 Discussion

Section three shows that it is possible to model the underlying archetype problems of the TRIZ theory and simulate the relations among the constituent parts. The synergy between TRIZ and SD produces value for each component. TRIZ profits the analytical support of SD through a set of differential equations. This benefit also covers one of the TRIZ drawbacks: the need for a formal modeling structure. Thus, a model can unveil the hidden relations within a system, and this ability is not available in traditional modeling approaches such as Functional Analysis, Cause-Effect Diagram, and Cause-Root Analysis. In these methods, each component and their relations are assumed as an independent element. In complex systems, there is more than one problem, thereby, SD it is the right technique to use due to a flexible modeling tool: the Causal Loop Diagram. This graphic tool outlines the most important relations in a conflict and outlines the repercussions that any change of the model variables on the system.

The modeling capacities of SD enables a new technological resource in TRIZ: the ability to simulate the system behavior or a scenario in time. Hence, if there are several inventive problems in a system, which is a common condition, through simulation will be possible to select the problem which has the stronger influence. The evaluation of potential solving paths is also another advantage. The TRIZ toolbox can assist the user to delimitate the solution space (e.g. the Ideal Final Result, or the 76 Standard Solution), and SD brings up with the mechanism to evaluate the possible effect of a particular solving path. The synergy also amplifies the SD capabilities. The simulation and the modeling framework do not have an appropriate tool for dealing with inventive problems. Hence, the solver must face this kind of challenges using traditional problem-solving techniques (e.g. brainstorming, the trial and error method, the six thinking hats, among others), which have a psychological foundation, instead of technological basis. Another benefit is the access to the TRIZ knowledge-base that has a transversal application through the TRIZ problem archetypes. The modeling strategies in SD recognizes only two classes of effect among variables: (1) Positive if variable V1 increases, then V2 also increases. (2) Negative if variable V1 increases, then V2 decreases. The terminology of the TRIZ archetypes will provide more flexibility to the modeling structure of SD. The problem archetypes described in this section represent an area of opportunity with multiple applications. The system dynamics modeling of inventive problems allows the user to analyze various conflicts that may arise in engineering and management areas such as logistics, manufacturing, among others. The advantage of SD over other techniques is the ability to analyze the whole system as a single object and the impact of one variable on the others simultaneously. The methodology of SD includes the creation of a model with a graphical interface, which allows the user to manipulate the variables to facilitate decision making.

5 Conclusion and Future Work

The nine cases that compose section three have as purpose to illustrate that it is feasible to combine the modeling approach of the System Dynamics with the underlying problem archetypes of the TRIZ theory. The set of cases exposes that it is possible to model inventive situations and then connect the conflict with the TRIZ toolbox. The combination of TRIZ with SD produces benefits for both elements and generates a more flexible and powerful problem-solving tool. Probably, the most significant advantage is a formal structure to model inventive problems and simulate their relations with the goal to observe how the system changes in time. This ability is not present in TRIZ. SD also gets improved if assimilates the TRIZ toolbox. In this scenario, the user builds a system model, then he formulates the conflict, and finally, TRIZ suggests a solving strategy. The user simulates this solution and recommends or not the solution. There are several research opportunities as future work: (1) to configure out a flexible methodology to combine the TRIZ tools with SD. (2) The service domain has many challenges and TRIZ is recently exploring this field. The cases presented in this article demonstrate that the synergy between TRIZ and SD can model inventive problems based on the dynamic simulation tools. The future work suggests implementing this synergy to solve systems with a greater degree of complexity. There are processes of manufacture and services as well as the design of new products with many conflicts, which be modeled as inventive problems. Those problems demand an analysis of their behavior over time. Therefore, it is concluded that the combination between TRIZ and SD generates new benefits for both techniques, and creates a new field of application with novel technological resources.

Acknowledgement. The National Council of Science and Technology (CONACYT), the Public Education Secretary (SEP) through PRODEP, and the Tecnologico Nacional de Mexico sponsored this work. Additionally, the ROPRIN working group (Network of Optimization in Industrial Processes) supported this work.

References

Altshuller, G.: The Innovation Algorithm: TRIZ, Systematic Innovation and Technical Creativity. Technical Innovation Ctr., Massachusetts (1999)

Baumann, L., Grant, G., Anoopkumar, S., Kavanagh, J., et al.: Drowsiness and motor responses to consecutive daily doses of promethazine and loratadine. Clin. Neurophysiol. **125**(12), 2390–2396 (2014). doi:10.1016/j.clinph.2014.03.026

Cortes, G., Negny, S., Le Lann, M., et al.: Case-based reasoning and TRIZ: a coupling for innovative conception in chemical engineering. Chem. Eng. Process. Process Intensification **48**(1), 239–249 (2009). doi:10.1016/j.cep.2008.03.016

Chechurin, L., Borgianni, Y.: Understanding TRIZ through the review of top cited publications. Comput. Ind. **82**, 119–134 (2016). doi:10.1016/j.compind.2016.06.002

Fey, V., Rivin, E.: Innovation on Demand: New Product Development Using TRIZ. Cambridge University Press, New York (2005)

Forrester, J.: Industrial Dynamics. The MIT Press, Cambridge (1961)

Forrester, J.: Principles of Systems. Productivity Press, Portland (1988)

Kreng, V., Jyun, B.: An innovation diffusion of successive generations by system dynamics — an empirical study of Nike Golf Company. Technol. Forecast. Soc. Chang. **80**(1), 77–87 (2013). doi:10.1016/j.techfore.2012.08.002

Kwatra, S., Salamatov, Y.: Trimming, Miniaturization and Ideality via Convolution Technique of TRIZ. Springer, Krasnoyarsk (2013)

Rantanen, K., Domb, E.: New Problem Solving Applications for Engineers and Manufacturing Professionals. CRC Press, New York (2008)

Salamatov, Y.: TRIZ: The Right Solution at the Right Time: A Guide to Innovative Problem Solving. Insytec BV, Krasnoyarsk (1999)

Samara, E., Georgiadis, P., Bakouros, I., et al.: The impact of innovation policies on the performance of national innovation systems: a system dynamics analysis. Technovation **32**(11), 624–638 (2012). doi:10.1016/j.technovation.2012.06.002

Savransky, S.: Engineering of Creativity: Introduction to TRIZ Methodology of Inventive Problem Solving. CRC Press, New York (2000)

Sterman, J.: Business Dynamics: Systems Thinking and Modeling for a Complex World. McGraw-Hill Education, Boston (2000)

Timma, L., Bariss, U., Blumberga, A., Blumberga, D., et al.: Outlining innovation diffusion processes in households using system dynamics. case study: energy efficiency lighting. Energy Procedia **75**, 2859–2864 (2015). doi:10.1016/j.egypro.2015.07.574

A Soft Computing Approach to Optimize the Production of Biodiesel

Marina Corral Bobadilla[1(✉)], Roberto Fernandez Martinez[2], Ruben Lostado Lorza[1], Fatima Somovilla Gomez[1], and Eliseo P. Vergara Gonzalez[1]

[1] Mechanical Engineering Department, University of La Rioja, Logroño, Spain
marina.corral@unirioja.es
[2] Department of Electrical Engineering, University of the Basque Country UPV/EHU, Bilbao, Spain

Abstract. There is an increasing global concern for environmental protection for the conservation of non-renewal natural resources. It needs to be obtain an alternative, renewable and biodegradable combustible like biodiesel. Waste cooking oil is a potential replacement for vegetable oils in the production of biodiesel. Biodiesel is synthesized by direct transesterification of vegetable oils, which is controlled by several inputs or process variables, including the dosage of catalyst, process temperature, mixing speed, mixing time, humidity and impurities of waste cooking oil. This study proposes a methodology to improve the production of biodiesel based on the use of soft computing techniques to predict several features of biodiesel production. The method selected a group of regression models based on Support Vector Machines (SVM) techniques to perform a prediction of several properties of a biodiesel sample taking into account a configuration of 7 test inputs. This test inputs were: molar ratio, dosage of catalyst, temperature, mixing speed, mixing time, humidity and impurities. Then and based on these inputs, the features to predict were: yield, turbidity, density, viscosity and high heating to obtain a better understanding of the process. Finally, considering the samples of the design of experiments studied, it has been observed that SVM models, based on a radial basic function kernel, record accurate results, with the best performance in four of the five features, improving in all the cases the accuracy obtained using linear regression.

Keywords: Biodiesel · Waste cooking oil · Soft computing techniques · Support vector machines

1 Introduction

There is an increasing global concern for environmental protection for the conservation of non-renewal natural resources. It needs to be obtain an alternative, renewable and biodegradable combustible like biodiesel. Biodiesel can be used in all conventional diesel engines, delivers similar performances to petroleum diesel, and requires almost no modifications in fuel handling and delivery systems. Biodiesel, which is, defined a substitute for or an additive to diesel fuel is derived from oils and fats of plants and

F.J. Martínez de Pisón et al. (Eds.): HAIS 2017, LNAI 10334, pp. 507–518, 2017.
DOI: 10.1007/978-3-319-59650-1_43

animals [1]. Waste cooking oil could be a potential replacement for vegetable oils for the production of biodiesel due to its low raw material cost and because it solves the disposal problem [2, 3]. The quantity of waste cooking oil that any generates annually is immense, and the methods of disposal of waste cooking oil are problematics, as may contaminate the water in the environment. The production of biodiesel from waste cooking oil is one of the best ways to utilize it efficiently and economically. The most common method for producing biodiesel is transesterification (See Fig. 1), in which, according to stoichiometry, 1 mol of triglyceride react with 3 mol of alcohol in the presence of catalyst (Sodium Hydroxide: NaOH), producing a mixture of fatty acid alkali esters (biodiesel) and glycerol [4, 5]. The transesterification process is influenced by several process variables. The type and dosage of catalyst, process temperature, agitation speed, agitation time, water content and impurities, are the main variables that affect biodiesel yield [6, 7]. On the other hand, the most studied properties of biodiesel generated are usually: yield (η), density (ρ), viscosity (μ) and higher heating value (HHV) [8]. For example, higher density (ρ) and viscosity (μ) of biodiesel poses some acute problems when used in unmodified engine and should be taken into account [9]. The water content in fuels can be classified in free, emulsionated, and soluble water and can cause problems such as water accumulation and microbial growth in fuel tanks and transportation equipment. The water content in the fuel can be estimated by turbidity experiments [10]. Higher heating value (HHV) provides the calorific power that the fuel can provide when it is burned [11], while yield (η) represents the amount of fuel that is obtained from the waste cooking oil used [12]. The present work deals with transesterification of waste cooking oil using NaOH as a base catalyst in different process conditions.

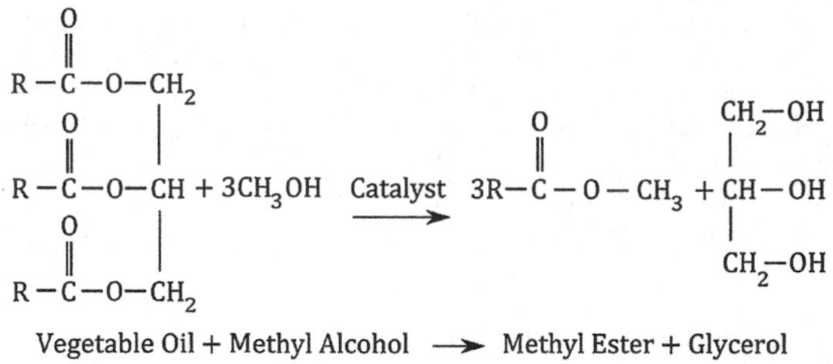

$$
\begin{array}{l}
R-\overset{\overset{O}{\|}}{C}-O-CH_2 \\
R-\overset{\overset{O}{\|}}{C}-O-CH + 3CH_3OH \xrightarrow{\text{Catalyst}} 3R-\overset{\overset{O}{\|}}{C}-O-CH_3 + \begin{array}{l} CH_2-OH \\ CH-OH \\ CH_2-OH \end{array} \\
R-\overset{\overset{O}{\|}}{C}-O-CH_2
\end{array}
$$

Vegetable Oil + Methyl Alcohol → Methyl Ester + Glycerol

Fig. 1. Transesterification process of biodiesel production.

The use of models based on soft computing and machine learning methods has proven to be useful for solving engineering and optimization problems [13, 14]. In the field of biodiesel production, some researchers have used regression models based on data mining techniques to model and optimize some of the most influential factors in the transesterification process. Thus, for example, in [15], the molar ratio, catalyst amount, and reaction temperature in biodiesel production were studied as operational conditions using Artificial Neural Networks (ANN) to estimate the biodiesel yield.

Others researchers [16] have employed ANN and Genetic Algorithm to optimized process parameters for biodiesel production. The authors believe that investigation of several features of biodiesel production using regression techniques based on Support Vector Machines (SVM) has never been published in open literature.

The present work investigates the possibility and capability of using regression techniques based on SVM to perform a prediction of several properties of a biodiesel sample.

The dosage of catalyst, process temperature, mixing speed, mixing time, humidity and impurities of waste cooking oil are the input variables that were considered in this work. The outputs that were studied are: yield, turbidity, density, viscosity and high heating value. Using the parameters mark as inputs and the results obtained when they are submitted to the 56 test, a regression techniques based on SVM used with different kernel were used for modeling output variables. Also, ordinary linear regression (LR) was applied to compare this linear technique with the previous nonlinear technique and show the influence on the non-linearity. The regression models proposed were trained from the data obtained based on the Design of Experiments (DoE), using repeated cross-validation [17, 18]. Subsequently, these proposed models were tested with additional data chosen randomly from the whole space of possibilities to identify their degree of generalization.

2 Methodology

2.1 Design of Experiments and Design Matrix

The statistical DoE is a structured and systematized method of experimentation in which all factors are varied simultaneously over a set of experimental runs in order to determine the relationship between the factors affecting the output response of the process. DoE [19] is used in experimental tasks to minimize the number of experiments and to obtain an adequately amount of detail to support a hypothesis. In general, the hypothesis is that a number of controllable variables (inputs or design factors) and uncontrollable variables (noise factors) determine the number of responses (outputs) with a continuous and differentiable function. Several methods have been proposed to develop DoE, but all of them involve the construction of a design matrix (inputs) and measuring the outputs or responses of the experiments [20]. In this study, the input parameters used for the experiments are methanol/oil molar ratio (M), catalyst (C), temperature (T), speed (S), time (t), humidity (H) and impurities (I). The experimentally selected factors for optimization and their respective ranges were as follows: methanol/oil molar ratio (6:1–9:1), quantity of NaOH catalyst (1–2 wt%), reaction temperature (20–40 °C), reaction speed (500–1000 rpm), humidity (0–3 wt%) and impurities (0–3 wt%). These ranges are provided in Table 1, and were adopted to cover the intervals that commonly are utilized in literature [21–25]. The outputs studied are: yield, turbidity, density, viscosity and high heating value. The design (Table 1) was performed using Central Composite Design (CCD) [26], which is a fractional three-level design that reduces the number of experiments in comparison with a full three-level design. Reducing the number of experiments in this case is important due to the difficultly involved in preparing each experiment's initial samples. According to the input parameters and levels included in Table 1 and using the R statistical analysis tool [27], 56 experiments were generated with their corresponding inputs (Table 2).

Table 1. Input parameters and levels

Input	Notation	Magnitude	Levels		
			–1	0	1
Molar ratio	M		6/1	7.5/1	9/1
Catalyst	C	wt%	1	1.5	2
Time	t	min	20	30	40
Speed	S	rpm	500	750	1000
Temp	T	°C	20	30	40
Humidity	H	wt%	0	1.5	3
Impurity	I	wt%	0	1.5	3

Table 2. Design matrix and samples obtained following the CCD DoE

Inputs							
Sample	Molar ratio	Catalyst (wt%)	Time (min)	Speed (rpm)	Temp (°C)	Humidity (wt%)	Impurity (wt%)
1	7.5	1.5	30	500	20	0	1.5
2	7.5	1.5	30	1000	20	0	1.5
…	…	…	…	…	…	…	…
55	7.5	1	40	750	30	3	1.5
56	7.5	2	40	750	30	3	1.5

2.2 Materials

Waste cooking oils of domestic origin were collected from various local restaurants and used as raw materials to prepare biodiesel by NaOH catalyzed transesterification. The reagents used during the synthesis were: methanol 98% (GR for analysis, Merck) and NaOH (GR for analysis, Merck).

2.3 Experimental Procedure

The waste cooking oils collected were filtered to remove any insoluble impurities and heated at 100 °C to remove most of the moisture. Experiments were conducted in a laboratory scale setup, with the desired of the oil heated to the required temperature using a water bath and a magnetic hot plate stirrer with a temperature controller. The speed of the stirrer was kept constant throughout each experiment. The amounts of NaOH and methanol were then added to the oil. The heating and stirring were stopped after the reaction had reached the preset reaction time. This biodiesel then was added to glass containers and subsequently were analyzed to determine the yield (η), turbidity (Turb), density (ρ), viscosity (μ) and higher heating value (HHV).

2.4 Biodiesel Characterization

The biodiesel yield can be calculated by using Eq. (1) [28].

$$\text{Yied} = \frac{weight\ of\ product(g)}{weight\ of\ rawoil(g)} \times 100 \tag{1}$$

In addition to yield, the following variables were determined in the final biodiesel product: turbidity measurements were carried out with a 2100 Q Turbidimeter, kinematic viscosity values were determined with Cannon–Fenske viscometers at a temperature of 40 °C following the standard ASTM D445 method [29]. Density measurements were carried out using a pycnometer according to ASTM D941 [30] The HHV of the biodiesel was obtained in a bomb calorimeter (Parr-1351), according to the ASTM D2015 standard method [31].

2.5 Support Vector Machines

There are numerous regression techniques inherently based on a nonlinear nature. One of the most intensively studied and applied are SVM thanks to its performance as a universal approximation [32–34]. This technique is based on a kernel-based algorithm that have sparse solutions, where the predictions for new inputs depend on the kernel function evaluated at a subset of instances during a training stage. The goal of this technique is to find a function that minimizes the final error in Eq. 2.

$$y(x) = w^T \cdot \phi(x) + b \tag{2}$$

Where $y(x)$ is the predicted value, w is the vector with the parameters that define the model, b indicates the value of the bias and $\phi(x)$ is the function that fixes the feature-space transformation.

In this method, the error function used in simple linear regression (Eq. 3) is replaced by a ε-insensitive error function (Eq. 4) which assign zero to values when the target and the predicted value difference is less than ε and keep the value of the error function otherwise. With the idea of minimize Eq. 5, that also assign a cost (C) to the difference with the target.

$$\frac{1}{2}\sum_{n=1}^{N}[y_n - t_n]^2 + \frac{\lambda}{2}\|w\|^2 \tag{3}$$

$$E_\epsilon(y(x) - t) = \begin{cases} 0, & if|y(x) - t| < \epsilon \\ |y(x) - t| - \epsilon, & otherwise \end{cases} \tag{4}$$

$$C\sum_{n=1}^{N} E_\epsilon(y(x_n) - t_n) + \frac{1}{2}\|w\|^2 \tag{5}$$

Where $y(x)$ is the predicted value from Eq. 2, t is the searched target function, ϵ defines the margin where the function does not penalize and C define the cost of the penalization. The process is optimized and finally the initial function (Eq. 2) became the more complex function (Eq. 6).

$$y(x) = \sum_{n=1}^{N} (\alpha_i - \alpha_i^*) \langle x_i \cdot x \rangle + b \tag{6}$$

Where α is a solution of the optimization problem obtained through Lagrangian theory [32], and α_i and α_i^* are Lagrange multipliers that represent the support vectors. Also, the function makes a transformation of the data to a higher dimensional feature space to improve the accuracy of the nonlinear problem. In this way, the final function became like Eq. 7.

$$y(x) = \sum_{n=1}^{N} (\alpha_i - \alpha_i^*) k(x_i, x) + b \tag{7}$$

Also, in this case three kernels functions are used: linear (Eq. 8), polynomial (Eq. 9) and Gaussian Radial Basis Function (RBF) (Eq. 10).

$$k(x_i, x) = x_i^T x \tag{8}$$

$$k(x_i, x) = \langle x_i \cdot x \rangle^d \tag{9}$$

$$k(x_i, x) = e^{-\frac{\|x_i - x\|^2}{2\sigma^2}} \tag{10}$$

R statistical software environment v2.15.3 was used to program the proposed methodologies, to develop the regression models [27, 35].

The SVM models were trained using 50 times repeated 10 fold cross-validation, as their calculation times were not very high and allowed using the entire training dataset obtained from the DoE, with 56 entries, for creating the models. This method involved dividing the initial database into 10 subsets, building the model with 9 subsets and calculating the error with the other partial sample of the dataset. This procedure was repeated 50 times obtaining other errors. Finally, the error was calculated as the arithmetic mean of all the errors of the process. Once the different algorithms were trained during some of the most significant parameters were tuned, a selection was made of those with the best predictive performance. The coefficients indicative of the error used to evaluate the accuracy of the predictions were the Root Mean Square Error (RMSE) and the correlation between real and predicted values.

Also, once the most accurate models were selected they were tested with new samples, 11 new experiments were performed in the laboratory to test the real degree of generalization of the selected models.

3 Results

3.1 Analysis of the Uncertainty

An analysis of variance ANOVA was performed to assess the uncertainty in the experimental measurements based on the proposed DoE. The five outputs studied on the experiments were analyzed against the input variables.

The p-values obtained show low values for two of the variables, especially with catalyst and molar ratio, which indicates that the observed relationships are statistically significant. Thus, when the p-value is lower than 0.1, it is considered — with a low level of uncertainty — that the null hypothesis, that the model has no predictive capability, can be confident rejected. For example, in this case 'catalyst' satisfies this condition in three cases, for the features η, μ and HHV (Table 3).

Table 3. Results obtained from the analysis of variance of the five output features.

	η		Turb		ρ		μ		HHV	
	p-value		p-value		p-value		p-value		p-value	
Molar ratio	0.09459	.	0.08468	.	0.03046	*	0.07618	.	0.07549	.
Catalyst	4.91e-06	***	0.10095		0.31188		0.00050	***	0.00049	***
Time	0.85788		0.99890		0.31188		0.45523		0.45600	
Speed	0.63687		0.53505		0.57979		0.45992		0.45890	
Temp	0.69014		0.57371		0.35746		0.47761		0.47506	
Humidity	0.99206		0.27337		0.92636		0.00411	**	0.00406	**
Impurity	0.46221		0.14076		0.71178		0.53145		0.53015	

Significant codes according to p-value: '***' 0.001, '**' 0.01, '*' 0.05, '.' 0.1

3.2 Models Developed

Once the main variables had been selected, the next process involved the training, validation and testing of models.

Creation of regression models that predict some significant features of a biodiesel production process was based on classical machine learning techniques based on SVM. Also, and to have the possibility to compare linear and nonlinear techniques, LR was perform too. In this case, the method was conducted in the following way: Firstly, the 56 experiments were performed according to the proposed DoE. The dataset obtained from the experiments were normalized between 0 and 1. Thereafter, these 56 instances were used to train the models using 50 times repeated 10 fold cross-validation. During this training, and to have the possibility to compare the accuracy of the models, the RMSE and the correlation between real and predicted values were obtained. At the same time, during this training, a tuning of the most important parameters of each algorithm was performed to improve the prediction capability. For example in Fig. 2 is shown the RMSE of the output feature 'μ' during the training of a SVM with a RBF kernel when parameters like the cost and σ are varying. In this case the most accurate model was built with a cost equal to 1.4 and a σ equal to 0.2.

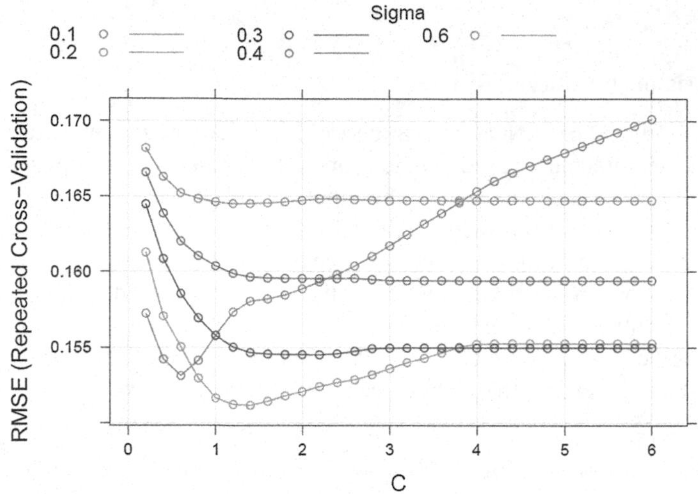

Fig. 2. Results obtained from the training period (50 times repeated cross-validation) using SVM with a RBF kernel to predict the feature 'μ'. Values of the most accurate configuration: Cost = 1.2 and sigma = 0.2.

Besides, and to be able to test the models with new and previously unused data during the training, the new 11 experiments were performed and tested. These new instances were chosen randomly trying to cover the whole space of possibilities of the problem out of previous DoE, and in that way have the chance of avoid overtraining on the models.

The results obtained are shown in Tables 4, 5, 6, 7 and 8 (in bold letters the most accurate and selected one).

Table 4. Results obtained during training and testing stage for yield.

η				
	Training (Cross validation)		Testing	
	RMSE (%)	Correlation	RMSE (%)	Correlation
SVM (Linear kernel)	23.64	34.56	25.76	71.94
SVM (Polynomial kernel)	23.59	34.56	25.83	71.79
SVM (RBF kernel)	**22.71**	**83.03**	**25.41**	**51.53**
LR	23.49	38.73	21.38	69.56

In most of the cases a lower RMSE in training and testing implied higher correlation, so these conditions fixed the models that were chosen. But in other cases the experts selected the model according to the results obtained in all criteria. For example, in the cases of μ and HHV, the selected models haven't got lower errors, but it was due to some outliers (Fig. 3) that once removed, the prediction of the selected models improved the other ones, so finally these ones were selected.

Table 5. Results obtained during training and testing stage for turbidity.

Turb				
	Training (Cross validation)		Testing	
	RMSE (%)	Correlation	RMSE (%)	Correlation
SVM (Linear kernel)	11.56	1.71	10.43	56.96
SVM (Polynomial kernel)	**11.64**	**1.64**	**10.43**	**57.15**
SVM (RBF kernel)	11.56	35.53	10.58	0.01
LR	15.75	17.35	12.72	0.01

Table 6. Results obtained during training and testing stage for density.

ρ				
	Training (Cross validation)		Testing	
	RMSE (%)	Correlation	RMSE (%)	Correlation
SVM (Linear kernel)	15.61	13.73	45.45	2.62
SVM (Polynomial kernel)	15.64	13.02	44.91	4.77
SVM (RBF kernel)	**15.50**	**36.10**	**44.91**	**4.77**
LR	16.81	14.86	44.57	0.91

Table 7. Results obtained during training and testing stage for viscosity.

μ				
	Training (Cross validation)		Testing	
	RMSE (%)	Correlation	RMSE (%)	Correlation
SVM (Linear kernel)	15.14	31.01	14.72	7.69
SVM (Polynomial kernel)	14.07	33.43	15.49	5.82
SVM (RBF kernel)	**15.18**	**86.05**	**16.64**	**18.35**
LR	14.96	37.11	18.47	9.44

Table 8. Results obtained during training and testing stage for higher heating value.

HHV				
	Training (Cross validation)		Testing	
	RMSE (%)	Correlation	RMSE (%)	Correlation
SVM (Linear kernel)	15.22	31.06	14.67	7.31
SVM (Polynomial kernel)	14.03	33.30	15.44	5.35
SVM (RBF kernel)	**15.13**	**88.55**	**16.96**	**17.90**
LR	14.88	37.17	18.44	9.18

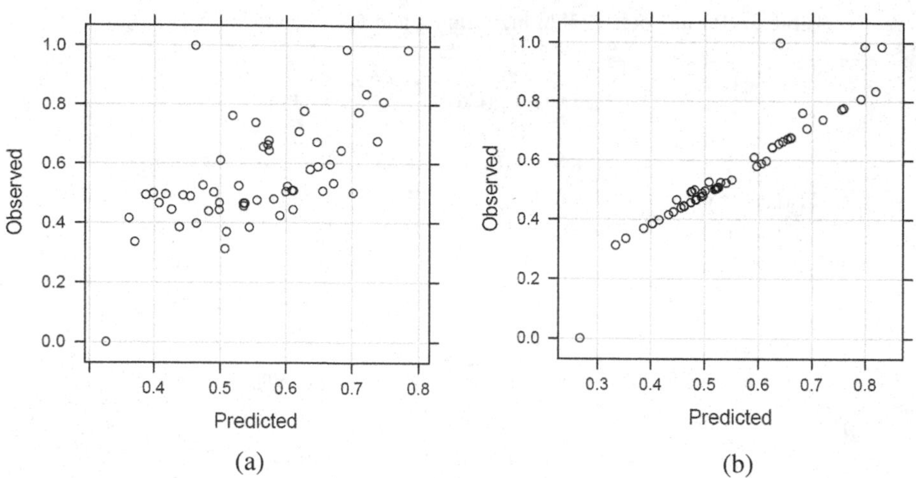

Fig. 3. Correlation between real and predicted values for HHV in two cases: (a) LR and (b) SVM (RBF kernel)

4 Conclusions

Biodiesel is an alternative and interesting combustible because it can be produced from vegetable and waste oils, and it is compatible with diesel engines either used as a pure substitute or blended with diesel. These facts make of great significance the knowledge obtained from models of several features of biodiesel production from waste cooking oil by transesterificación, using NaOH as the catalyst.

Based on the proposed methodology, a nonlinear process like the production of biodiesel can be modeled based on the use of soft computing techniques, obtaining models that during this work have been effectively verified by the validation of experimental data. The knowledge provided by the models can be really helpful for biodiesel producers to optimize the process, since the obtained errors are not really high.

Also, this work shows how a training-testing with parameter tuning methodology allow to obtain the most accurate results, although in some cases like in the prediction of μ and HHV, an appropriate analysis and interpretation of the results can improve the results of the modeling process.

Acknowledgements. The authors wish to thanks the University of the Basque Country UPV/EHU for its support through Project US15/18 OMETESA and to the La Rioja Government through Project ADER 2014-I-IDD-00162.

References

1. Betiku, E., Okunsolawo, S.S., Ajala, S.O., Odedele, O.S.: Performance evaluation of arti-ficial neural network coupled with generic algorithm and response surface methodology in modeling and optimization of biodiesel production process parameters from shea tree (Vitellaria paradoxa) nut butter. Renew. Energy **76**, 408–417 (2015)
2. Yan, J., Zheng, X., Li, S.: A novel and robust recombinant Pichia pastoris yeast whole cell biocatalyst with intracellular over expression of a Thermomyces lanuginosus lipase: prepa-ration, characterization and application in biodiesel production. Bioresour. Technol. **151**, 43–48 (2014)
3. Phan, A.N., Phan, T.M.: Biodiesel production from waste cooking oils. Fuel **87**, 3490–3496 (2008)
4. Singh, A.K., Fernando, S.D., Hernandez, R.: Base catalyzed fast transesterification of soybean oil using ultrasonication. Energy Fuel. **21**, 11–61 (2007)
5. Serio, M.D., Ledda, M., Cozzolino, M., Minutillo, G., Tesser, R., Santacesaria, E.: Transesterification of soybean oil to biodiesel by using heterogeneous basic catalysts. Ind. Eng. Chem. Res. **45**(9), 3009–30014 (2006)
6. Shahid, E.M., Jamal, Y.: Production of biodiesel: a technical review. Renew. Sustain. Energy Rev. **15**, 4732–4745 (2011)
7. Borges, M.E., Díaz, L.: Recent developments on heterogeneous catalysts for biodiesel pro-duction by oil esterification and transesterification reactions: a review. Renew. Sustain. Energy Rev. **16**, 2839–2849 (2012)
8. Uddin, M.R., Ferdous, K., Uddin, M.R., Khan, M.R., Islam, M.A.: Synthesis of biodiesel from waste cooking oil. Chem. Eng. Sci. **1**, 22–26 (2013)
9. Tesfa, B., Mishra, R., Gu, F., Powles, N.: Prediction models for density and viscosity of biodiesel and their effects on fuel supply system in CI engines. Renew. Energy **35**, 2752–2760 (2010)
10. Fregolente, P.B.L., Fregolente, L.V., Maciel, M.R.W.: Water content in biodiesel, diesel, and biodiesel–diesel blends. J. Chem. Eng. Data **57**, 1817–1821 (2012)
11. Sivaramakrishnan, K., Ravikumar, P.: Determination of higher heating value of biodiesels. Int. J. Eng. Sci. Technol. **3**, 7981–7987 (2011)
12. Çaylı, G., Küsefoğlu, S.: Increased yields in biodiesel production from used cooking oils by a two step process: comparison with one step process by using TGA. Fuel Process. Technol. **89**, 118–122 (2008)
13. Yuste, A.J., Dorado, M.P.: A neural network approach to simulate biodiesel production from waste olive oil. Energy Fuels **20**, 399–402 (2006)
14. Yin, F., Li, W., Yao, C.: Optimization for biodiesel production technology based on genetic algorithm–neural network. Chem. Ind. Eng. Prog. **8**, 42–47 (2008)
15. Moradi, G.R., Dehghani, S., Khosravian, F., Arjmandzadeh, A.: The optimized operational conditions for biodiesel production from soybean oil and application of artificial neural networks for estimation of the biodiesel yield. Renew. Energy **50**, 915–920 (2013)
16. Rajendra, M., Jena, P.C., Raheman, H.: Prediction of optimized pretreatment process parameters for biodiesel production using ANN and GA. Fuel **88**, 868–875 (2009)
17. Fernandez, R., Okariz, A., Ibarretxe, J., Iturrondobeitia, M., Guraya, T.: Use of decision tree models based on evolutionary algorithms for the morphological classification of reinforcing nano-particle aggregates. Comput. Mater. Sci. **92**, 102–113 (2014)
18. Fernandez, R., Martinez de Pisón, F.J., Pernía, A.V., Lostado, R.: Predictive modelling in grape berry weight during maturation process: comparison of data mining, statistical and artificial intelligence techniques. Span. J. Agric. Res. **9**(4), 1156–1167 (2011)

19. Fisher, R.A.: The Design Of Experiments (1935)
20. Box, G.E., Behnken, D.W.: Some new three level designs for the study of quantitative vari-ables. Technometrics **2**(4), 455–475 (1960)
21. Atapour, M., Kariminia, H.R., Moslehabadi, P.M.: Optimization of biodiesel production by alkali-catalyzed transesterification of used frying oil. Process Saf. Environ. Prot. **92**, 179–185 (2014)
22. Farag, H., El-Maghräby, A., Taha, N.A.: Optimization of factors affecting esterification of mixed oil with high percentage of free fatty acid. Fuel Process. Technol. **92**, 507–510 (2011)
23. Silva, G.F., Camargo, F.L., Ferreira, A.L.: Application of response surface methodology for optimization of biodiesel production by transesterification of soybean oil with ethanol. Fuel Process. Technol. **92**, 407–413 (2011)
24. Hamze, H., Akia, M., Yazdani, F.: Optimization of biodiesel production from the waste cooking oil using response surface methodology. Process Saf. Environ. Prot. **94**, 1–10 (2015)
25. El-Gendy, N.S., El-Gharabawy, A.A., Amr, S.S., Ashour, F.H.: Response surface optimiza-tion of an alkaline transesterification of waste cooking oil. Int. J. ChemTech Res. **8**, 385–398 (2015)
26. Montgomery, D.C.: Design and Analysis of Experiments. Wiley, Hoboken (2008)
27. R Core Team: R: A Language and Environment for Statistical Computing. R Foundation for Statistical Computing, Vienna, Austria (2013). http://www.R-project.org/
28. Leung, D.Y.C., Guo, Y.: Transesterification of neat and used frying oil: optimization for biodiesel production. Fuel Process. Technol. **87**, 883–890 (2006)
29. ASTM D445: Standard Test Method for Kinematic Viscosity of Transparent and Opaque Liquids
30. ASTM D941: Standard Test Method for Density and Relative Density of Liquids by Lipkin Bicapillary Pycnometer
31. ASTM D240: Standard Test Method for Heat of Combustion of Liquid Hydrocarbon Fuels by Bomb Calorimeter Standard Test Method for Gross Calorific Value of Coal and Coke by the Adiabatic Bomb Calorimeter
32. Vapnik, V., Golowich, S.E., Smola, A.: Support vector method for function approximation, regression estimation, and signal processing. Adv. Neural Inf. Proc. Syst. **9**, 281–287 (1997)
33. Clarke, S.M., Griebsch, J.H., Simpson, T.W.: Analysis of support vector regression for approximation of complex engineering analyses. J. Mech. Des. **127**, 1077–1087 (2005)
34. Bishop, C.M.: Pattern Recognition and Machine Learning. Springer, New York (2006)
35. Kuhn, M.: Contributions from Jed Wing, Steve Weston, Andre Williams, Chris Keefer, Allan Engelhardt, Tony Cooper, Zachary Mayer, Brenton Kenkel, the R Core Team, Michael Benesty, Reynald Lescarbeau, Andrew Ziem and Luca Scrucca. caret: Classification and Regression Training. R package version 6.0-41 (2015)

Market Trends and Customer Segmentation for Data of Electronic Retail Store

Carlos Rodriguez-Pardo(✉), Miguel A. Patricio(✉), Antonio Berlanga(✉), and Jose M. Molina(✉)

Applied Artificial Intelligence Group, University Carlos III of Madrid, Madrid, Spain
{carlos.rodriguez,miguelangel.patricio, antonio.berlanga,josemanuel.molina}@uc3m.es

Abstract. Data analysis is comprised of a set of processes that allows a key support for making better decisions. The ability to analyse data in the field of retail trade allows companies to obtain valuable information such as understanding the profile of customers who demand a particular type of product, optimizing the price of certain products, identifying customers interested in such products and analysing the best way to approach them. This paper will present results obtained during the development of an analysis process on the data of an electronic retail store. The analysis will show the results obtained and validated by end users using different visualization techniques. Finally, the result of applying client segmentation using self-organized maps and the interpretation of their results in a visual way will be discussed.

1 Introduction

Nowadays, we are living in a deep digital revolution, where the priorities and needs of the companies are conditioned by the offers and technological solutions of the market. One of these transformation factors is the concept of Business Analytics. The business analysis capabilities of companies are making profound transformations in society and it is giving companies the opportunity to be more competitive. The possibility of having tools that allow the capture of information and its analysis, as well as the possibility of optimizing information and studying the data in real time are already a reality [1].

In recent years, retail companies have adopted the ability to collect large volumes of data on their customers' activities. Nevertheless, obtaining relevant information about the behaviour of their customers is not a simple task. Companies have the capacity to collect information, however, they do not have the tools or capacities for understanding the data, the identification of outliers, or the visualization of significant results, among others. By analysing large volumes of data using modelling techniques, these companies can identify patterns of customer behaviour, recognize valuable leads, and identify meaningful trends.

The purpose of this work is to carry out an analysis of the profiling of customers of an e-commerce platform through the use of data analysis, visualization and segmentation techniques. This paper will present results obtained during the

F.J. Martínez de Pisón et al. (Eds.): HAIS 2017, LNAI 10334, pp. 519–530, 2017.
DOI: 10.1007/978-3-319-59650-1_44

development of an analysis process on the data of an electronic retail platform. In the analysis process, one of the most important tasks is the choice of visualization models used for representation of the results, which will be utilised by management teams to support decision making. The visualization of data is intimately related to the correct management of data and information. Let us not forget that data represents one of the main values of any organization and, therefore, its correct administration is of great importance in the corporate strategy. Incorrect display of data can lead to negative business decisions. The results presented in this work are related to those visualization models validated by the end user, which have been the basis of their business strategy. In this work, the client's behaviour is analysed considering variables such as the gender of the client, the platform used, the date of acquisition, the price, and the category of the product purchased. For the segmentation aspect we propose the use of Artificial Intelligence techniques. More specifically, models of neuronal networks based on self-organized maps will be used.

2 Related Work

The amount and diversity of data that both smart-phones and their users produce have increased significantly throughout the last few years. That tendency will likely strengthen during the next years. According to the Cisco VNI Mobile Forecast, which studies the use of mobile data during the last years, and uses that information to predict how much mobile data will be consumed until the end of the decade, mobile data traffic is expected to increase from 3.7 exabytes in 2015, to 30.6 in 2020 [2]. This vast amount of data provides an incomparable opportunity to study the behaviour and characteristics of societies, customers, business, etc.

A similar tendency can be appreciated with on-line retail stores. The increasing trust in electronic payment systems, and the popularisation of on-line shopping, have created a new opportunity for retail business. Gathering some information of the customers, that can be obtained through their registration in the store, and using machine learning and data mining techniques, it is possible to identify groups of customers that behave similarly, and to discover purchasing patterns by aggregating data from all the customers of a on-line store.

Several attempts have been made throughout the years, and the analysis of the possibilities of applying data mining methods to this kind of data does not cease to grow. This article will give a brief outlook at some of the most recent articles [3–7] that tried to fulfil this task, giving priority at those that were similar in scope to our proposal.

For instance, in "A data mining approach for segmentation-based importance - performance analysis (SOM–BPNN–IPA): a new framework for developing customer retention strategies" [8], the authors propose a framework that uses "Importance-performance analysis" (IPA) as the basis for the task of improving customer satisfaction. They utilize self-organizing maps as a mean of performing the customer segmentation task, and, inside each segment or cluster, they apply Back-Propagation Neural Networks to compute the importance of service attributes, with the goal of maximizing customer satisfaction inside each segment. That way, they can compute new, different IPAs for every segment. After that has been done, new customer retention strategies can be developed for every segment. Their framework combines machine learning and data mining methods with measuring techniques usually applied in marketing.

The need for advanced, collaborative-based data visualization systems and techniques has been deeply analysed in the literature. Examples of visualization frameworks and techniques can be found in many articles [9–12], that propose several techniques for properly displaying multidimensional data. Many data analysis frameworks and platforms, such as the programming language R, already give support for state-of-the-art data visualization libraries. That is the case, for example, of the well-known library ggplot2, which has been used for many of the graphs included in this article.

It has been seen so far that data is regarded as a fundamental requirement to perform customer segmentation, and that customer segmentation can improve decision making and resources allocation. Customer segmentation can be done using data visualization and machine learning techniques, as well as other methods. To complement those conclusions, we propose a real case study of visualization and clustering techniques.

3 Summary of the Data

We used a set of data obtained from a electronic retail store, consisting of approximately ~300000 purchases made during 2015 and 2016. The information related with those purchases included information about customers (genre, postal code, etc.), the platform where the purchase was made (Android, Web, iPhone, etc.), the price of the product and a set of categories that contained information about the type of product that was purchased.

The variables that were used in the analysis are summarized in the following table. Those variables are always related to a particular purchase made by a particular user and were obtained after a pre-processing of the variables. For instance, the date in which the product was purchased was transformed into different, more intuitive variables, such as "month of the year", or "day of the week". Some other, less informative, variables are not included in this analysis, as they appeared in a insufficient amount of rows, or were too specific to give real information about the customer, like the postal code (Table 1).

Of course, the distribution of each categorical variable was not even throughout the data. To visualize those differences, we have included histograms that summarizes those distributions.

Several things can be noticed. In the fist histogram, it is obvious that the most common category is "Well-being". This category includes purchases of services related to health and beauty. Secondly, it is clear that, even though the gender of many of the users was unknown, those of whom their gender is known, are mostly female. Most of the sales are made during the Monday to Thursday

Table 1. Variables in the data set

Variable	Type	Possible values	Description
Platform	Categorical	{Android, iPhone, iPad, Web, Mobile}	Device used to purchase the product. Iphone, Android and Ipad indicate the native application of the store in those devices, whereas Mobile relates to the web browser of the smartphone.
Gender	Categorical	{Male, Female, Not Defined}	The gender of the person that purchased the product.
Price	Numeric	$(0, 689]$ €	The price in euros (€) of the product that was purchased
Weekday	Numeric	1–7	Day of the week in which the purchase was made. 1 corresponds to Monday, 2 to Tuesday, etc.
Month	Numeric	1–12	Month of the year in which the purchase was made. 1 corresponds to January, 2 to February, etc
Year	Numeric	2015–2016	Year in which the purchase was made. The data set only included those two years
Weekend	Categorical	{Yes, No}	"Yes" if the purchase was made on a Friday, Saturday or Sunday, "No" otherwise.
Category	Categorical	{Well-being, Bars and Restaurants, Outdoor activities, Holidays, Retail, Other products}	Classification of the product sold, inside the product distribution of the store

period of the week. Finally, it is notable that most of the purchases are made using the web browser, and that almost no purchases are made using the iPad native application (Fig. 1).

It would also be interesting to see how purchases are distributed according to the price of the product that was purchased. In the next graph, purchases of products worth more than 200 € were omitted, as they only constitute the 1.81% of the total and hinder the correct visualization of the data (Fig. 2).

In the density graph above, it can be seen that most of the purchases are made of products worth less than 50 €, and that there is a peak around the multiples of 10. This is because, like in any other store, prices tend to be rounded to the power of 10.

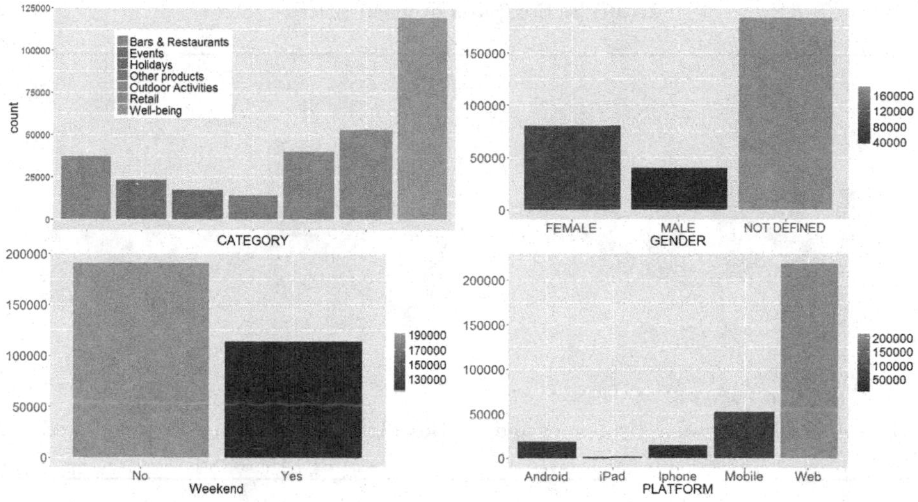

Fig. 1. Categorical data distribution

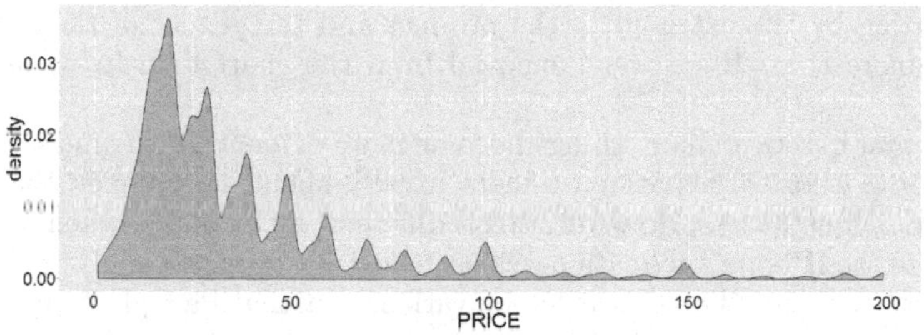

Fig. 2. Price density graph

The distribution of the data set in a simple way has been seen, so far, in a simple way. However, a deeper, more complex visualization is required to be able to fully understand and make sense of the problem.

4 Visualization Techniques

It would be interesting to find out what gender tends to expend more money, and if each gender uses the different devices in a distinct way. The following graph combines box plots for every platform, and differentiates each gender. This way, both the median and the variance of the prices that each gender in each platform expends can be easily visualized. We limited the chart to prices of less than 50 € so that both the medians and variances are as visible as possible, and *notches* were added for comparing medians. If the notches of two boxes do not overlap, there is a strong evidence that the medians of the groups are different.

Table 2. Box plots of mean prices

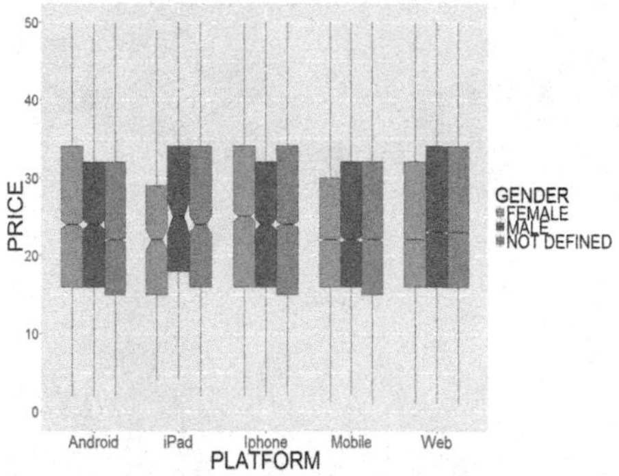

Box-plots differentiating by gender and platform	Box-plots differentiating by gender and category

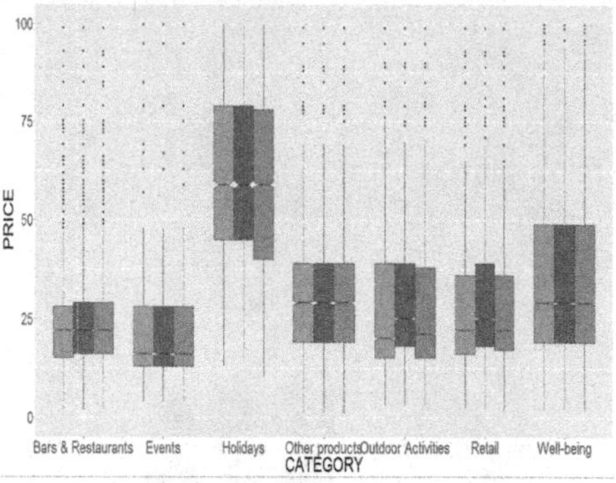

Using the same type of graph, one can examine how different the prices are, differentiating by the category of the product and the gender of the customer. Prices of more than 100 € were removed from the chart to help visualization (Table 2).

In the graph above, many things become more evident. In the most common platform, the website, female customers usually spend less money than make users or not defined users. However, this is different, for example, when purchases are made in the iPhone application, where female customers usually spend more money per purchase. There is a lot of variance in the iPad platform because there is very few purchases made using that platform.

Even though the differences between genders are blurred in this graph, it is obvious that the category related to holidays contains the most expensive purchases. This category is related with hotel reservations and transportation tickets, which are usually more expensive than 50 €. The categories "events" and "bars and restaurants" are usually related with less valuable goods. We can notice other differences. For instance, male customers usually expend more money than female customers in two particular categories: retail and outdoor activities.

It has been seen so far that the category of the product and the platform used to perform the purchases are factors that may change the price spent in every purchase, and that each gender behaves differently. However, we think that it is not only important the mean price spent in each product according to all those variables, but also the amount of products purchased in every category. To answer that question, a histogram was plotted, separating, for each gender, the amount of purchases related to every particular category. Above the bars, we included the numeric amount of purchases, and the height of every bar is proportional to the percent of purchases of that category, of customers of the

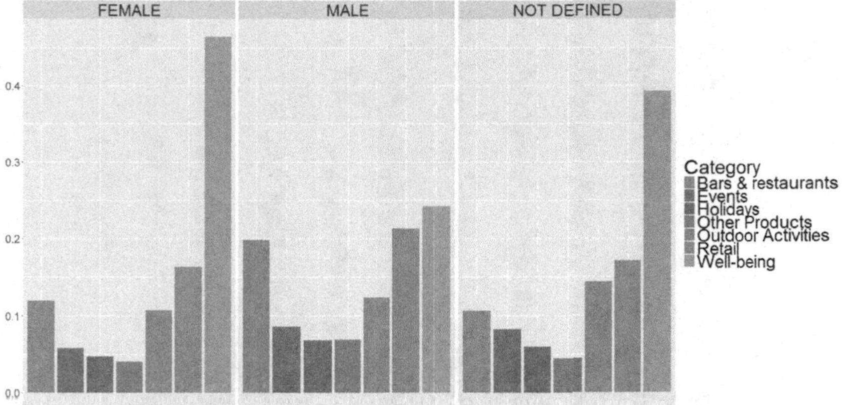

Fig. 3. Histogram of categories, separated by gender

gender specified on top of the graph. Colours were used to help the visualization of the graph (Fig. 3).

With the help of this graph, some knowledge can be obtained. Female customers are particularly prone to purchasing products of the "well-being" category, and that male customers are more likely to buy products of the "Bars and restaurants" and "Retail" categories. It also becomes easier to see that the "not defined" gender, that stores purchases made by customers who did not want to specify their gender, is approximately proportional to the weighted arithmetic mean of male and female users.

It can be expected that customers that buy more than one product behave differently than those who repeat purchases. It would also be interesting to visualize the relationship between prices of products, the amount of purchases made for a given price range, and the amount of purchases made by an individual customer for that given price range. This relationship can be problematic to visualize, and that is why we propose the following graph. We have computed the mean price of the purchases of each individual customer, and have differentiated customers depending on how many purchases they made in the store. For every customer, it is plotted in the graph the point {Amount of purchases, mean price of those purchases}. Right after this, to help the visualization, those points were grouped into hexagons, which are coloured depending on the amount of points they contain. For example, if an hexagon is painted in red, it means that, for the price range and the amount of purchases that the hexagon refers to, there is a significantly greater amount of purchases at that range than in an hexagon painted in blue. Customers that bought more than 10 products and mean prices of more than 100 € have been omitted, as they burdened the visualization (Fig. 4).

Once the graph is presented, its meaning becomes more clear. There is a significant concentration of purchases made in the ≈20 € range, by customers who only made one purchases in the store. Moreover, most of the customers

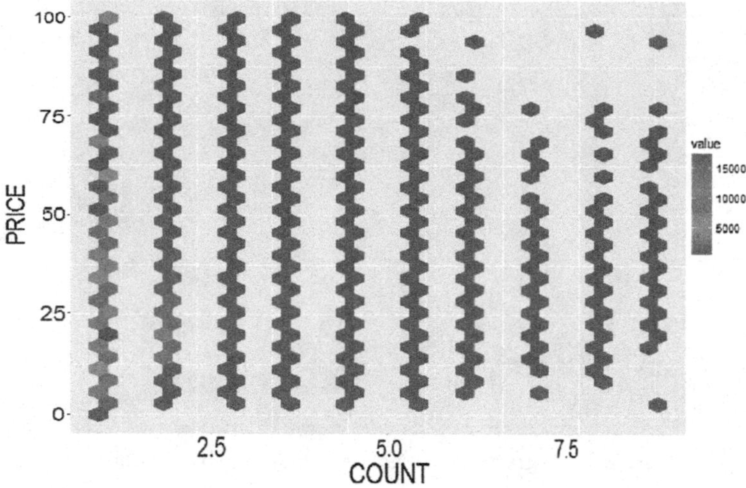

Fig. 4. Purchases density graph

only purchased once in the store, which can be helpful to understand what kind of clients this store has: Clients that register to buy once, or, at much, twice, products with prices that are usually lower than 50 €.

There is still a variable has not been properly analysed yet: time. The original data set included the time when was the purchase made, and that variable was found to be particularly important. It would give a lot of information to see how customers behave throughout the two years that the data set includes. That can be done by visualizing the mean price spent by every customer, differentiating by their gender, throughout 2015 and 2016. The next graph, limited to products worth less than 50 €, uses locally weighted scatterplot smoothing to plot the evolution of prices. It also includes a density plot that is helpful to see higher concentration of purchases of a given price at a given time. The darker the background of the graph, the higher the concentration of purchases at that point (Fig. 5).

It is clear that both genders tend to behave similarly during time. This indicates that time does not affect differently to women and men. However, it does make an influence on the mean price and the amount of products sold. There are higher concentrations of purchases during the fist months of 2015 and right by the end of that year. We can also see that, around August and September of both years, the mean price of the purchases is lower than, for instance, during May and April.

Following parametric analysis, clustering using Self-Organizing Maps can be made. First introduced by Teuvo Kohonen in 1982, SOMs are a powerful clustering and high-dimensional visualization tool that is framed inside the Artificial Neural Networks branch of machine learning. They make use of a series of centroids that are placed in a grid, which "learns" the original structure of the

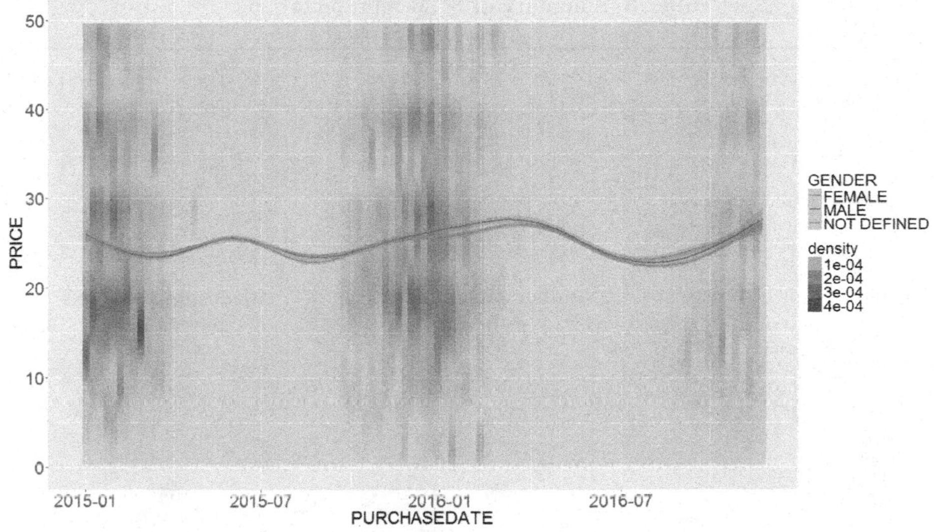

Fig. 5. Purchases evolution through time

input data. This way, centroids that are close in the grid will have more similar characteristics than those centroids that are apart in the grid. Every centroid represents several input data points.

After training the SOM, it can be visualized what variables are more important and helpful to separate some purchases from others. As most of the users have only purchased one product in the store, it has not been included as input for the SOM the amount of products purchased by an individual customer. The characteristics of the SOM that was used are the following: 20×20 centroids, using an hexagonal, non toroidal, topology. It was trained during 500 iterations and learning rate $\alpha \in [0.15, 0.01]$, decreasing linearly with every iteration. The neighbourhood used was circular, and extended to about 2/3 of the whole map. The results of the SOM training can be visualized in following Table 3.

In the table below, the first row represents general information about the training process of the SOM and about the grid obtained. Clearly, both the number of samples per centroid and the mean distance of each centroid to its neighbours are considerably homogeneous. In the second row, that refers to categorical variables, it is evident that the data is strongly separable according to the gender of the customer, to the platform in which the purchases are made and the category of each product. The last row, that refers to time variables, shows that the data can be easily separated depending on the year and day of the week in which the purchases are made, but that the month of the year is not such a relevant variable. This particular method can be very convenient when parametric approaches do not provide enough information to perform the customer segmentation task.

Table 3. Summary of SOM representation

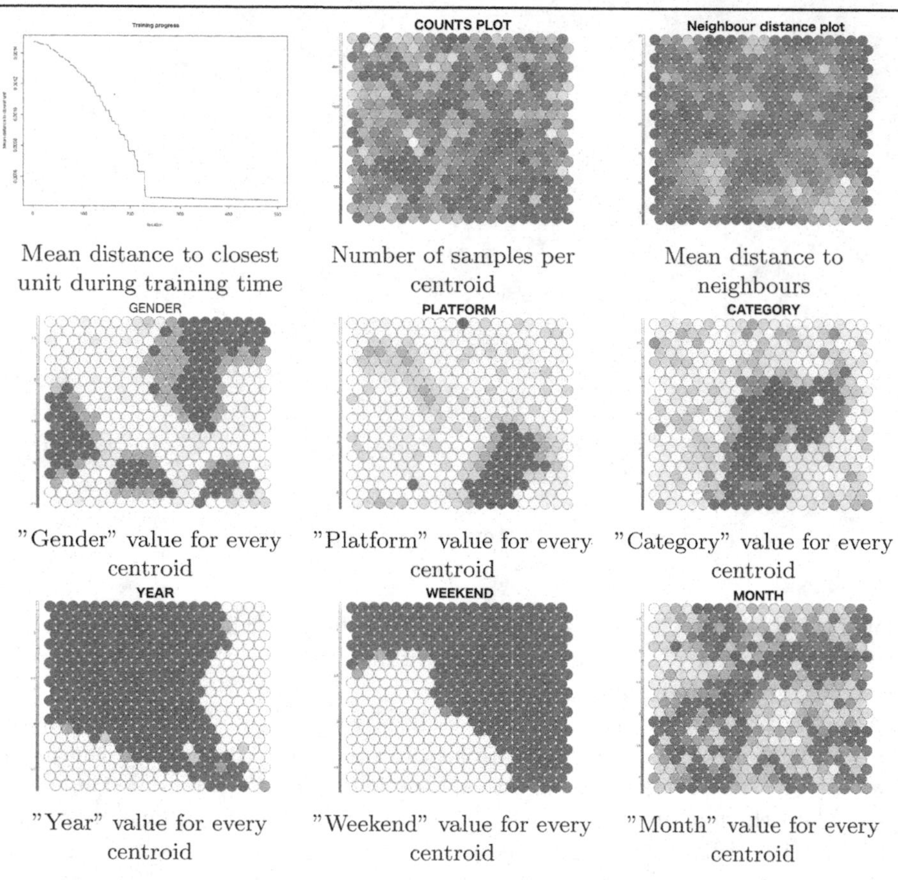

Mean distance to closest unit during training time

Number of samples per centroid

Mean distance to neighbours

"Gender" value for every centroid

"Platform" value for every centroid

"Category" value for every centroid

"Year" value for every centroid

"Weekend" value for every centroid

"Month" value for every centroid

5 Customer Segmentation

The analysis has identified, so far, different behavioural patterns among customers, depending on several variables. These some of those variables that should be taken into account to create the segments:

- **Gender:** Even though there are no significant differences between genders in their mean expenditure through time, it can be seen that the type of products they typically purchase are notably different. This means, that, for every product category, it is expected that female and male customers behave differently, are more or less prone to spend a different amount of money per product, and to have divergent likelihoods to buy or not a product given a particular category. Therefore, male and female customers should be treated as different customer segments and create specific strategies for each gender.

- **Day of the week:** In the dataset, it was notable that customers that purchase during the weekends behave differently, in price, number of purchases and the type of products they purchase, than those who purchase products from Monday to Thursday. This means that two different segments can be created: one for those who buy products during the weekends and those who do not.
- **Category:** Both SOM and the parametric analysis have shown that there are product categories that have unique behaviours, while there are others that tend to behave in a similar way. This means that different customer segments should be created for those categories that do not behave in the typical way, and another, aggregated segment, for those categories that are alike.
- **Platform:** SOM has shown that customers that purchase their products in mobile platforms behave differently to those who do so in the web page of the store. Moreover, those who use iPhones show different patterns to those who use Android smart-phones or tablets. This creates another opportunity to create unique customer segments, according to the platform they use to purchase their products.

More things can be noticed after the analysis. For example, customers in 2015 behaved differently than in 2016, and, inside every year, there are divergent purchasing patterns. This indicates that the analysis of the data of one year may not be valid for another year.

6 Conclusions and Future Work

This paper has analysed several ways to construct customer segments: Using different visualization techniques and using neural networks to automatically create customer clusters. These methods have given valuable information about the data set that regular analysis, like computing the mean, variance, and other statistical values, would not have provided. With them and a fair amount of data, some basic clusters can be built, which can improve decision making for marketing campaign formulations. Nevertheless, the data that has been evaluated, which only included purchases of two different years, showed that each year had different purchasing patterns. This means that customer segmentation should be done frequently, as new data is gathered and customer behaviour develops. With a bigger amount of data, new, more complex, segments could be discovered automatically, taking into account more specific variables, such as the postal code of the customer, or more specific product categories. The clustering, segmentation and visualization techniques described in this article have been validated by the end user, and have been used as the basis for their strategic decision-making.

Acknowledgments. This work was partially funded by projects MINECO TEC2014-57022-C2-2-R, TEC2012-37832-C02-01.

References

1. Hebert, D., Anderson, B., Olinsky, A., Hardin, J.M.: Time series data mining: a retail application. Int. J. Bus. Anal. (IJBAN) **1**(4), 51–68 (2014)
2. Cisco: Cisco Visual Networking Index: Global Mobile Data Traffic Forecast Update, 2015–2020. Technical report (2016)
3. Muley, M., Joshi, A.: Application of data mining techniques for customer segmentation in real time business intelligence. Int. J. Innov. Res. Adv. Eng. **2**(4), 106–109 (2014)
4. Ismail, M., Ibrahim, M.M., Sanusi, Z.M., Nat, M.: Data Mining in Electronic Commerce: Benefits and Challenges, pp. 501–509, December 2015
5. Cuadros, A.J., Domínguez, V.E.: Customer segmentation model based on value generation for marketing strategies formulation. Estudios Gerenciales **30**(130), 25–30 (2014)
6. Dzobo, O., Alvehag, K., Gaunt, C.T., Herman, R.: Multi-dimensional customer segmentation model for power system reliability-worth analysis. Int. J. Electr. Power Energy Syst. **62**, 532–539 (2014)
7. Floh, A., Zauner, A., Koller, M., Rusch, T.: Customer segmentation using unobserved heterogeneity in the perceived-value-loyalty-intentions link. J. Bus. Res. **67**(5), 974–982 (2014)
8. Hosseini, S.Y., Ziaei Bideh, A.: A data mining approach for segmentation-based importance-performance analysis (SOM-BPNN-IPA): a new framework for developing customer retention strategies. Serv. Bus. **8**(2), 295–312 (2014)
9. Tam, N.T., Song, I.: Big data visualization. In: Kim, K., Joukov, N. (eds.) ICISA 2016. LNEE, vol. 376, pp. 399–408. Springer, Singapore (2016)
10. Chi, E.H.: A taxonomy of visualization techniques using the data state reference model. In: Proceedings of the IEEE Symposium on Information Visualization 2000, INFOVIS 2000, vol. 94301(Table 2), pp. 69–75 (2000)
11. Dos Santos, S., Brodlie, K.: Gaining understanding of multivariate and multidimensional data through visualization. Comput. Graph. (Pergamon) **28**(3), 311–325 (2004)
12. Langseth, J., Aref, F., Alarcon, J., Lindner, W.: Real-time data visualization of streaming data (2016)

Smart Drivers' Guidance System Based on IoT Technologies for Smart Cities Application

Imen Masmoudi(✉), Wiam Elleuch, Ali Wali, and Adel M. Alimi

REGIM-Lab: Research Groups in Intelligent Machines,
National Engineering School of Sfax, University of Sfax, BP 1173, 3038 Sfax, Tunisia
imen.masmoudi@ieee.org

Abstract. Finding an available parking place is becoming an exhaustive task due to the increasing amount of cars and vehicles, especially in the metropolitan cities. The search for an available parking place through the roads and parking stations is a major waste of time and efforts, mainly in pic hours when parking places are almost full. This problem can be felt mainly around city centres, hospitals, shopping complexes and many other crowded stations and roads. This can also accentuate the problem of traffic congestion and aggravate the task of the drivers.

In this paper, we propose a smart multi agent parking management system exploring the Internet of Things (IoT) technologies and aiming at providing smart urban service to the citizens. The presented system supplies the drivers with the real time information about the availability of parking spaces through the parking stations, and ensures the task of guidance through the roads. In addition to the parking availability, our system takes into consideration the factor of traffic congestion, while guiding the drivers. We collect the Global Positioning System (GPS) data from the already circulating vehicles through the town and we exploit the real time information to improve our system of guidance.

1 Introduction

Recent advances in communication technologies and network infrastructure give the opportunity to develop new smart solutions to solve many challenging problems annoying the citizens' lives in large cities. A smart city should be equipped with basic infrastructure to provide a good quality of life, a clean and sustainable environment through the application of some smart solutions. Thereby, it became interesting to apply the concept of IoT in the context of smart cities and urban life in order to benefit from the progress of the communication technologies and to exploit it to develop new and smart public services.

In particular, modern cities have an increasing need for advanced intelligent transportation systems to overcome the lacks in this field. The most challenging problems that can annoy the drivers in the modern cities are the search for an available parking space or being stuck in a traffic congestion. Hence the need for a smart parking lot management system to efficiently guide drivers to find available parking spaces and identify their positions. Such smart parking systems

F.J. Martínez de Pisón et al. (Eds.): HAIS 2017, LNAI 10334, pp. 531–542, 2017.
DOI: 10.1007/978-3-319-59650-1_45

will have a significant impact on the transport field in terms of environment impact and time management.

The public and private security is also having a rising interest in the metropolitan cities. We notice that nowadays, the cities are almost covered with the installed video surveillance cameras, and that the majority of vehicles are equipped with GPS devices. So the idea to explore these already installed and connected devices such as the video surveillance cameras that are installed in the parking stations as well as the GPS devices that are installed in the vehicles circulating through the city. We collect the issued data in order to provide drivers with useful information about parking availability through the town as well as the information about the traffic congestions.

This paper is organised as follows: Sect. 2 provides an overview of the existent approaches for parking vacancies detection. Section 3 presents a multi agent architecture for our proposed system then details the three principal modules of parking vacancies detection, traffic congestion detection and the smart service presented as a mobile phone application. In Sect. 4, we evaluate the performance of our proposed system. And finally we conclude with Sect. 5.

2 Related Work

In recent years, thanks to the growing interest in the field of intelligent transport systems, many solutions and approaches were proposed trying to propose new solutions in order to help the drivers and to reduce the impact of this problem. A bibliographical study was firstly performed aiming at identifying the existing approaches proposition solutions that guide drivers to the vacant parking places.

In the last years, several research works propose new solutions based on the IoT technologies in order to benefit from the technological progress. The system presented in [14] provides users with the possibility of recommendation, car park reservation, outdoor and indoor car park navigation. This system relies on a module ESP8266 that is integrated with ultrasound sensors to detect whether a parking lot is occupied or not in an indoor context.

The authors of [6,13] present an IoT based smart parking systems. The detection of the presence of cars is performed with ultrasonic sensors and an on-site deployment of an IoT module used to monitor the state of each parking space. The approach of [15] presents also a sensor based min max algorithm for vacancies detection. The authors of [5] introduce a smart service relying on the IoT and integrates ultrasound sensors to detect the vacant spaces.

We can notice that these proposed systems are using sensor-based techniques such as ultrasound and infra-red-light sensors for the detection of the parking vacancies. They consider these sensors as the connected devices to apply the concept of IoT. In our context, we are interested to the video surveillance cameras as the connected devices because there is an increasing interest in the use of the approaches based on the vision techniques thanks to their high performances with a low cost solution.

Several other approaches were proposed which are based on vision techniques. The method of [1] is able to detect the presence of cars in parking lots based on fast integral channel features and machine learning techniques. The authors of [2] rely on a Convolutional Neural Network classifier running on-board of a smart camera. The system proposed in [16] performs also a deep learning technique to learn and consequently recognize the vehicles in order to detect the parking vacancies. The approach of [7] learnt the appearances of the objects which are present in the video scene and recognize pedestrians and vehicles in order to detect parking vacancies.

Almost all the newly proposed approaches based on the vision techniques are focusing on the vacancies detection from the video streams and neglect the phase of drivers' guidance.

In this paper we propose a new multi agent system that combines the two main phases of a parking management system. The first phase of parking vacancies detection is obtained based on the video surveillance streams and the vision techniques and is able to cover several number of parking stations in the city. The second phase of drivers' guidance is performed thanks to the collected data from the GPS devices installed in the vehicles. Finally we provide a central information system able to guide the drivers to the available parking places while avoiding the traffic congestion.

3 Proposed System

In this section, we aim at proposing a parking management system which is able to satisfy the needs of a smart city in the context of the IoT. We explore a network of interconnected video surveillance cameras and parking stations to provide an intelligent service to the drivers in order to facilitate their task and improve the exploitation of the parking resources. In our approach, we propose a multi agent system for Parking Lots Management, based on vision techniques.

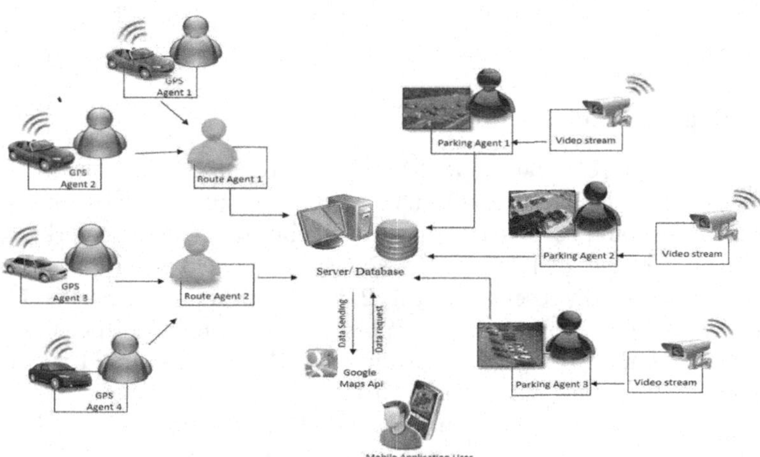

Fig. 1. General multi agent architecture of the proposed system

The system presented in this paper combines two main phases of the parking vacancies detection based on vision techniques and the service of drivers' guidance with traffic congestion avoidance, as presented in Fig. 1. The elaboration of such a system requires a distributed and extended architecture to cover as much as possible the huge amount of information collected from the parking stations as well as from the GPS devices. So the need for a multi agent architecture in order to exploit the interesting capacities of the agents and consequently to satisfy the needs at a city level. This architecture will enable as to provide a smart service to the citizens.

This system ensures the detection of vacant parking places based on the already installed video surveillance cameras, as was proposed in [10,11]. The proposed approach should cover an important number of parking places as well as an important number of parking stations to face the needs of the drivers in a city level. Thus we adapt a multi agent architecture where each parking station is considered as a Parking Agent PA. Each PA agent controls the state of its corresponding station and provides the real time state about the number of vacant places to the server.

The second phase of drivers' guidance relies on the already extracted state of vacancies of each parking station, as well as the real time information about the traffic congestion through the roads of the city. This information is obtained, as presented in [3] thanks to the GPS data collected from thousands of vehicles circulating on public roads. Considering this huge number of vehicles, we represent each vehicle as a GPS Agent GA that sends its geographical coordinates to the corresponding Route Agent RA responsible for the route link where the vehicle is circulating. The RA will explore the information about the speed of the vehicles in order to compute and inform the central server whether there is a congestion or not.

Finally, a mobile phone application is developed in order to provide a smart service to the drivers allowing them to simply be informed about the existent traffic congestions or to be guided to the available parking spaces while avoiding the traffic jams.

3.1 Parking Vacancies Detection

In this section we present the proposed architecture for parking vacancies detection. This approach should be adapted for outdoor parking stations with different dispositions and should cover an important number of configured parking lots in divers stations in order to elaborate a global state of the existent vacant parking places at a city level. As presented in Fig. 2, we opt for a multi agent architecture to detect the parking vacancies. We represent each configured parking station with a Parking Agent PA and it is considered as the one who updates the global state of parking vacancies within this station.

As a first step of configuration, we provide a new parking model aiming at overcoming the major problems of perspective distortion and inter spaces distortion. We propose to do not configure each parking space separately and to model the whole row of parking spaces as a single 3D cube covering several

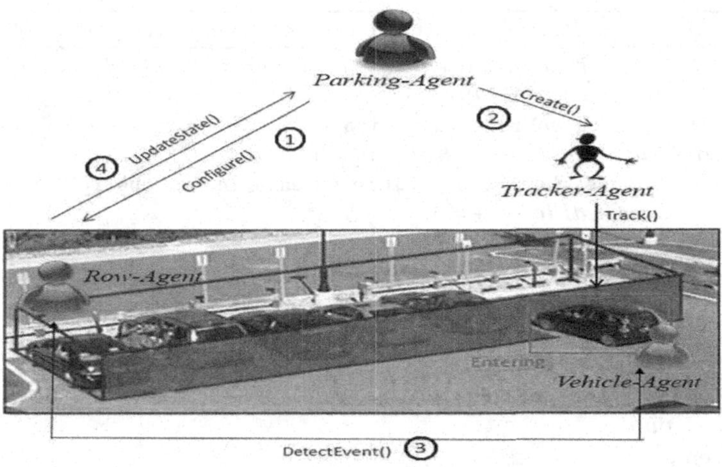

Fig. 2. Multi agent architecture for parking vacancies detection

number of places. This model inspired from the one proposed in [8], but instead of the individual configuration of each parking space, we configure a whole row as a 3D cube and are interested to the vertical on-street surface as presented in Fig. 2. According to this proposed model, the PA affects a Row Agent RA for each parking row which will be responsible for the vacancies detection and the update of the real time state about these vacancies within the station.

As a second step, based on the video steams issued from the video surveillance camera installed in the parking station, the PA triggers a step of adaptive background subtraction followed by a step of objects in motion tracking. Each detected vehicle in motion inside the scene, will be represented with a Vehicle Agent VA that tracks its state and position over time.

The detection and the tracking of the vehicles in motion in conjunction with the proposed model as well as the adoption of the multi agent architecture, will permit to detect the parking vacancies based on the performed events without the need to a preliminary training phase. The RA will cooperate with the different detected VA in order to detect the events of entering and leaving within the 3D cube as soon as they happen. And we define principally four configured events:

- Vehicle Out: The vehicle is in motion inside the scene but not interfering with any configured parking row;
- Vehicle Entering: The vehicle is crossing a vertical On-Street Row surface of the parking model and is entering to a parking space;
- Vehicle In: The vehicle is inside a configured parking row;
- Vehicle Leaving: The vehicle is getting out of the parking row and is crossing the On-Street Row surface to go out to the street.

Based on these detected events, each configured RA in the parking space will be able to determine the number of vacant places as well as the occupied ones, then it will update its own state to the PA as detailed in Algorithm 1.

Algorithm 1. Vacancies estimation based on events' detection

```
Function VacancyDetection (Vehciles, TotalPlaces, OccupiedPlaces)
    for i=1 to Vehicles.size do
        /* for each vehicle in motion                                   */
        if Vehciles[i].state == Entering then
            /* Case where the vehicle is entering to the row cube       */
            OccupiedPlaces += 1;
        else
            if Vehciles[i].state == Leaving then
                /* Case where the vehicle is leaving the row cube       */
                OccupiedPlaces −= 1;
            else
                /* No changes                                           */
            end
        end
    end
    Vacancies = TotalPlaces − OccupiedPlaces;
    return Vacancies ;
```

This *PA* is responsible for the generation of the final state of parking vacancies within its station and to send this state to the central server.

3.2 Traffic Congestion Detection

This section is devoted to present our elaborated approach to detect the traffic congestion in public roads in real time. Our research work is relying on a huge number of vehicles from different types that are circulating in urban and rural regions and each of these vehicles is equipped with a GPS device.

In order to guarantee the privacy of the drivers and the vehicles' owners, only the movements of the vehicles are captured. GPS receivers send the necessary geographical information as well as the timestamp information to the central servers using the General Packet Radio Service (GPRS) protocol. This real time data received from the vehicles contains GPS data sequences presented in the standard format Recommended minimum specific GPS/Transit data (GPRMC) [3]. Each sentence specifies the real time information about the *GA* and it contains principally:

1. Spatial information: it indicates the geographical information such as the latitude, the longitude and the orientation of the vehicle;
2. Temporal information: it specifies the timestamp which is a temporal information indicating the time and date of the reception of this data;
3. Speed information: it gives the speed of the vehicle at this instant.

According to our proposed architecture, each GPS Agent *GA*, embedded in a circulating vehicle, sends its spatio-temporal data to the server approximately each one minute. Based on the information about the speed of the vehicles received from the GA, we can elaborate a knowledge about the behaviour of the drivers as well as the real time states of the routes [4]. This information can be classified into four classes according to the range of speed as presented in Fig. 3. This information can be disabled on the map in order to give a graphical presentation of the drivers to inform them about the traffic congestions. In this case, the presence of vehicles that are circulating with a speed low than 15 km/h, indicates a high probability of a traffic congestion.

Fig. 3. Real time speed of vehicles

In addition to the graphical presentation of these speeds, it is important to have a relevant information about the existence of a traffic jams in the specific routes. To achieve this goal, we implement a Route Agent RA responsible for the establishing of the real time state of a given route and for giving the exact information about the existence of a traffic congestion. This RA is defined as a segment of route delimited with two geographical points and it should compute the rate of traffic congestion within this route link, at an instant t, as presented in Eq. (1):

$$C = 1 - \frac{Speed_{avr}}{Speed_{max}}. \tag{1}$$

Where:

$Speed_{avr}$ is the average speed of the vehicles that are circulating within this route link;

$Speed_{max}$ is the maximal allowed speed, in our case we opt for the speed of 110 km/h.

3.3 Driver's Guidance

In this section, we present the second phase of the parking management system which is the drivers' guidance. We propose a mobile phone application in order to provide a relevant smart service to the citizens and specially the drivers. This will permit to save time and efforts and to improve the quality of live. The proposed service aims principally at facilitating the task of the drivers by finding the available places and guiding them directly to the target. It aims also at reducing the problem of traffic congestion by providing the drivers with the optimal way to the destination while avoiding the traffic jams.

We develop a mobile phone application presenting an interactive interface to the users. It provides an interactive map with the different configured parking stations. Each configured Parking-Agent provides the real time state of parking vacancies of its corresponding station to the central server in order to update the global state at a city level. These real time informations will be displayed on the map, and the user is able to consult the number of remaining vacant parking places of each configured station as well as other general informations such as its name and address [9].

The goal of this mobile phone application is to drive the users directly to the optimal parking station that responds to their needs. In addition to the real time information about the remaining vacant parking spaces in each parking station, we suggest to introduce other relevant parameters to improve the task of drivers' guidance. The suggested route to the parking station in destination is acquired thanks to the Google API, and we can so obtain the necessary distance to reach the station by car.

Another parameter to be considered is the traffic congestion through this corresponding way. This information is obtained from the already calculated rate in Sect. 3.2.

Table 1. Considered parameters for drivers' guidance

Parameter's name	Description	Values
D_i	The distance of the route i between the departure point and destination	In kilometre
V_i	The number of vacant parking spaces in the corresponding station i	Decimal
C_i	The rate of the traffic congestion through the route i	Between 0 and 1

Thanks to these adopted parameters we can provide the drivers with real time states about the parking vacancies and we can guide them to the optimal parking station as we recommend a classification of the relevant ones according to three main parameters which are detailed in Table 1.

Once these parameters are selected, we should provide drivers with relevant informations and determine which parking station is the most convenient to his preferences. To make this decision, we combine these criteria and we propose a new solution able to calculate a score S_i to each parking station. According to the Eq. (2), we affect to each parking station a corresponding score computed based on the three parameters. This score gives an idea about the priority of the parking station and its degree of interest. The parking station having the lowest score is considered as the best station meeting the driver's need.

$$S_i = D_i + C_i + \frac{1}{V_i}. \tag{2}$$

4 Experimental Results

In this section, we aim at proving the performance of our proposed system. Firstly, the performed tests are interested to the capacity of our approach of parking vacancies detection to be adapted with different parking dispositions. These tests were performed based on the database VIRAT [12] which presents video record of five different parking dispositions.

Table 2 proves that, thanks to our proposed model in conjunction with the vision approach, whatever is the position of the camera and the disposition of the vehicles, we can surmount the most challenging situations and principally the problems of perspective distortion and inter spaces occlusion.

Table 2. Performance under different parking dispositions

Parking station	FPR	FNR	Accuracy	Recall	Precision
Parking station 1	0.12	0.02	96.62 %	97.65 %	98.58 %
Parking station 2	0.31	0.03	92.66 %	96.28 %	95.33 %
Parking station 3	0.26	0.02	95.26 %	97.19 %	96.7 %
Parking station 4	0.06	0.19	94.2 %	98.2 %	94.3 %
Parking station 5	0.22	0.05	91.6 %	94.7 %	95.1 %

A comparative study is presented in Table 3 which presents average measurements of several implemented approaches and demonstrate the good performance of our proposed approach for vacancies detection.

Table 3. Comparative study of performance

	F-measure	Recall: R	Precision: P
Approach of [8]	0.91	0.93	0.90
Approach of [11]	0.93	0.95	0.92
Our approach	0.95	0.96	0.95

Other tests were performed to prove the ability of our system to provide a smart service to the drivers and to guide them directly to the optimal parking station while avoiding the traffic congestion. The Table 4 presents a case where the driver has the choice between four different parking stations. The characteristics of each station are detailed, and we calculate the obtained score for each one based on the already presented Eq. (2).

Table 4. Parking stations' classification and recommendation to the drivers

Parking station	Distance	Vacancy	Congestion	Score	Order of stations
PS_1	0.5	10	0.2	0.8	1
PS_2	0.3	13	0.5	0.87	3
PS_3	0.7	20	0.1	0.85	2
PS_4	1	7	0	1.14	4

We can notice that the parking station PS_2 is the nearest station to the user and presents the highest number of vacant parking places. Despite that, our system does not consider this station as the more relevant one and promotes the parking stations PS_1 and PS_3 because of the problem of traffic congestion. So, we try to guide the driver to the nearest parking station with important number of parking places while avoiding to pass through traffic congestions. These obtained results are also represented graphically in our mobile phone application, as schematized in Fig. 4.

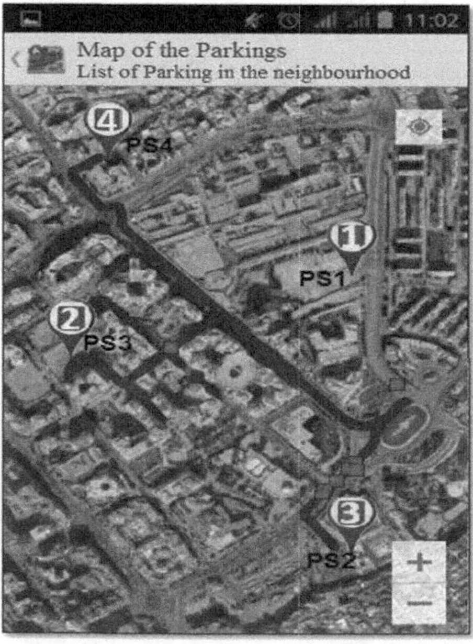

Fig. 4. Drivers' guidance application

The displayed map orders the parking stations according to their priority obtained thanks to the calculated scores. It displays principally the route to the more relevant parking station as a first choice to the driver as well as the other possible routes. It displays also the points of traffic congestion in order to inform the driver of their locations.

5 Conclusion

In this paper, we propose a new smart drivers' guidance system trying to help the drivers to find an available parking place in a simple way based on a mobile phone application. This system is able to cover several number of parking stations in the city and to collect the information about the traffic congestion from thousands of different types of vehicles circulating through the road of the city. This ability is guaranteed thanks to the adoption of a multi agent architecture which permit to elaborate a distributed and flexible system.

The developed mobile phone application presents a smart service to the drivers. It displays the list of configured parking stations via an interactive interface and gives relevant information about the parking vacancies for each station. This smart service provides to its users an ordering of these stations based on several parameters such as the distance, the number of vacant places and the traffic congestion. It aims at guiding the drivers to the optimal parking station while avoiding the parking jams.

Acknowledgements. The authors would like to acknowledge the financial support of this work by grants from General Direction of Scientific Research (DGRST), Tunisia, under the ARUB program.

The research and innovation are performed in the framework of a thesis MOBIDOC financed by the EU under the program PASRI.

References

1. Ahrnbom, M., Strm, K., Nilsson, M.: Fast classification of empty and occupied parking spaces using integral channel features. In: 2016 IEEE Conference on Computer Vision and Pattern Recognition Workshops (CVPRW), pp. 1609–1615, June 2016
2. Amato, G., Carrara, F., Falchi, F., Gennaro, C., Vairo, C.: Car parking occupancy detection using smart camera networks and deep learning. In: 2016 IEEE Symposium on Computers and Communication (ISCC), pp. 1212–1217, June 2016
3. Elleuch, W., Wali, A., Alimi, A.M.: Mining road map from big database of GPS data. In: 2014 14th International Conference on Hybrid Intelligent Systems, pp. 193–198, December 2014
4. Elleuch, W., Wali, A., Alimi, A.M.: Collection and exploration of GPS based vehicle traces database. In: 2015 4th International Conference on Advanced Logistics and Transport (ICALT), pp. 275–280, May 2015
5. Grodi, R., Rawat, D.B., Rios-Gutierrez, F.: Smart parking: parking occupancy monitoring and visualization system for smart cities. In: SoutheastCon 2016, pp. 1–5, March 2016

6. Khanna, A., Anand, R.: IoT based smart parking system. In: 2016 International Conference on Internet of Things and Applications (IOTA), pp. 266–270, January 2016
7. Màrmol, E., Sevillano, X.: Quickspot: a video analytics solution for on-street vacant parking spot detection. Multimedia Tools Appl. **75**, 17711–17743 (2016)
8. Masmoudi, I., Wali, A., Alimi, A.M.: Parking spaces modelling for inter spaces occlusion handling. In: 22nd International Conference in Central Europe on Computer Graphics, Visualization and Computer Vision, pp. 119–124, June 2014
9. Masmoudi, I., Wali, A., Jamoussi, A., Alimi, A.M.: Trajectory analysis for parking lots vacancy detection system. IET Intell. Transp. Syst. (2014)
10. Masmoudi, I., Wali, A., Jamoussi, A., Alimi, A.M.: Architecture of parking lots management system for drivers' guidance. In: IEEE International Conference on Systems, Man, and Cybernetics, SMC 2015, pp. 2974–2978, October 2015
11. Masmoudi, I., Wali, A., Jamoussi, A., Alimi, A.M.: Vision based parking lot management system with anomalies detection while parking. In: IET Computer Vision (2015)
12. Oh, S., Hoogs, A., Perera, A., Cuntoor, N., Chen, C.C., Lee, J.T., Mukherjee, S., Aggarwal, J.K., Lee, H., Davis, L., Swears, E., Wang, X., Ji, Q., Reddy, K., Shah, M., Vondrick, C., Pirsiavash, H., Ramanan, D., Yuen, J., Torralba, A., Song, B., Fong, A., Roy-Chowdhury, A., Desai, M.: A large-scale benchmark dataset for event recognition in surveillance video. In: CVPR (2011)
13. Ramaswamy, P.: Iot smart parking system for reducing green house gas emission. In: 2016 International Conference on Recent Trends in Information Technology (ICRTIT), pp. 1–6, April 2016
14. Tsai, M.F., Kiong, Y.C., Sinn, A.: Smart service relying on internet of things technology in parking systems. J. Supercomput., 1–24 (2016). http://dx.doi.org/10.1007/s11227-016-1875-8
15. Tsaramirsis, G., Karamitsos, I., Apostolopoulos, C.: Smart parking: an IoT application for smart city. In: 2016 3rd International Conference on Computing for Sustainable Global Development (INDIACom), pp. 1412–1416, March 2016
16. Valipour, S., Siam, M., Stroulia, E., Jägersand, M.: Parking stall vacancy indicator system based on deep convolutional neural networks. CoRR abs/1606.09367 (2016)

Machine Learning of Optimal Low-Thrust Transfers Between Near-Earth Objects

Alessio Mereta, Dario Izzo(✉), and Alexander Wittig

Advanced Concepts Team, European Space Agency,
Keplerlaan 1, 2201AZ Noordwijk, The Netherlands
{Alessio.Mereta,Dario.Izzo,Alexander.Wittig}@esa.int

Abstract. During the initial phase of space trajectory planning and optimization, it is common to have to solve large dimensional global optimization problems. In particular continuous low-thrust propulsion is computationally very intensive to obtain optimal solutions. In this work, we investigate the application of machine learning regressors to estimate the final spacecraft mass m_f after an optimal low-thrust transfer between two Near Earth Objects instead of solving the corresponding optimal control problem (OCP). Such low thrust transfers are of interest for several space missions currently being developed such as NASA's NEA Scout.

Previous work has shown machine learning to greatly improve the estimation accuracy in the case of short transfers within the main asteroid belt. We extend this work to cover also the more complicated case of multiple-revolution transfers in the near Earth regime. In the process, we reduce the general OCP of solving for m_f to a much simpler OCP of determining the maximum initial spacecraft mass m^* for which the transfer is feasible. This information, along with readily available information on the orbit geometries, is sufficient to learn the final mass m_f for the same transfer starting with any initial mass m_i. This results in a significant reduction of the computational cost compared to solving the full OCP.

Keywords: Machine learning · Regression · Astrodynamics · Near earth objects · Low thrust transfers

1 Introduction

In the early phase of space missions design the careful selection of the trajectory of the spacecraft is paramount. The availability of an efficient trajectory determines many further mission parameters, and can enable missions otherwise not feasible due to restrictions on the available fuel mass or cost.

In order to obtain optimal trajectories compatible with the overall mission parameters, such as propulsion system and available fuel mass, a complex global optimization problem must be solved. It consists of a large discrete combinatorial part, typically involving questions such as the selection of possible targets or

F.J. Martínez de Pisón et al. (Eds.): HAIS 2017, LNAI 10334, pp. 543–553, 2017.
DOI: 10.1007/978-3-319-59650-1_46

flyby sequences, as well as a continuous part due to the optimal control of the spacecraft during the travel from one target to the next.

With impulsive chemical propulsion it is possible to approximate the effect of propulsion by discrete instantaneous changes in the spacecraft velocity. Combined with efficient methods for the solution of Lambert's problem (computing an inertial orbit connecting two points in space), this leads to an overall relatively compact search space that can be handled efficiently by current global optimizers to obtain good solutions also for quite challenging problems with reasonable computational effort [1].

Chemical propulsion, however, is not the most efficient propulsion method in terms of fuel consumption. Low-thrust methods such as electric propulsion have a much higher specific impulse, meaning they deliver a higher impulse per fuel mass and thus allow lighter spacecraft carrying less propellant. This advantage comes at the cost of very long time scales over which the acceleration is applied. Solar electric engines produce very little thrust (on the order of 1–100 mN) but are operated continuously over months.

This means that the optimal control problem (OCP) for moving from one target to the next also becomes continuous instead of discrete. The solution now consists of a function indicating the thrust direction as well as the thrust magnitude as a function of time. The optimal trajectory is the trajectory requiring the least amount of fuel mass to reach a target and match its velocity within a given transfer time.

There are several numerical and mathematical methods for solving this OCP. Direct methods transform the continuous problem into a non-linear programing problem by discretizing the trajectory into short arcs of constant thrust magnitude and direction and imposing appropriate boundary conditions [2,3]. Indirect methods use a technique from control theory known as Pontryagin's principle [4], which transforms the problem into a two-point boundary value problem to be solved.

Unfortunately, both methods are computationally difficult to solve. In the context of the global trajectory optimization problem, an efficient way to estimate the fuel consumption of a given low-thrust transfer allows much faster evaluation of the feasibility of a given trajectory. Once a potentially feasible trajectory has been identified by the optimization process, it can then be refined using a full solver for the OCP. The goal is therefore to obtain the final mass m_f of a spacecraft after a particular transfer as a function of the initial mass m_i, the initial and final positions $\boldsymbol{r}_i$ and $\boldsymbol{r}_f$, and velocities $\boldsymbol{v}_i$ and $\boldsymbol{v}_f$, and the transfer time ΔT without solving the associated OCP.

Previous work [5] has shown that machine learning techniques are very successful in estimating the optimal m_f for relatively short transfer arcs (typically a quarter or half a turn) between asteroids in the main belt an order of magnitude better than the Lambert estimate in Eq. 3.

In this paper, we apply the same ideas to the regime of Near-Earth objects (NEOs). There are several important differences in this regime compared to the main asteroid belt. NEOs have a significantly shorter period, around 1 year as opposed to about 3–6 years, due to their proximity to the Sun. Transfers between NEOs are thus not only short arcs but can be more complicated including several revolutions around the Sun. This results in a more complicated structure of the solutions to the OCP, which now feature several thrust and coast arcs with a pronounced bang-bang control structure (see Fig. 1). Due to these differences, we will see that the simple indicators used in [5] are not applicable any more.

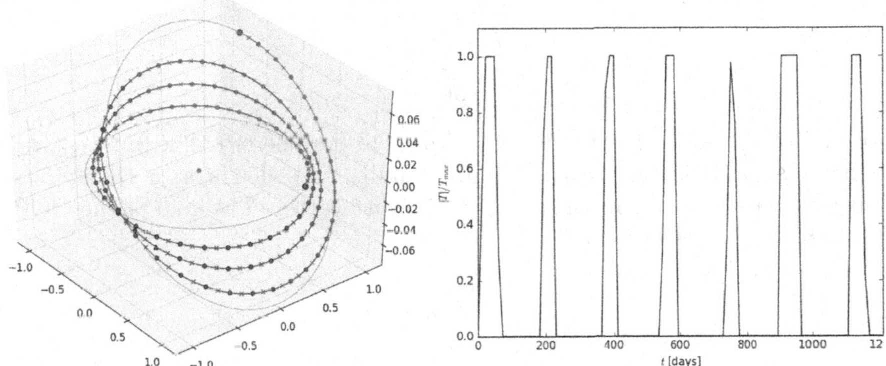

Fig. 1. Example of an optimal trajectory involving multiple revolutions (*left*) with thrust arcs highlighted in red, and the corresponding bang-bang control profile (*right*). (Color figure online)

The rest of this paper is structured as follows: in Sect. 2 we describe the optimal control problem and the generation of a database of low thrust trajectories between NEOs used in the training. Section 3 will present the algorithms and analyze the attributes used for the machine learning, the results of which are presented in Sect. 4. We conclude with some remarks and an outlook on possible future work in Sect. 5.

2 Generation of Optimal Low-Thrust Trajectories

In this section we first give a short presentation of the spacecraft dynamics and the OCP we need to solve. We then proceed to describe our method for generating a database of optimal transfers used in the training.

For the remainder of this work, we assume a small spacecraft (CubeSat) of initial dry mass of $m_{sc} = 20\,\text{kg}$ and an electric low-thrust propulsion system with specific impulse $I_{sp} = 3000$ s and a maximum thrust of $T_{max} = 1.7$ mN. The mission of the spacecraft is to visit several NEOs starting from a parking orbit around Earth. The mission is similar to actual space missions currently being developed such as NASA's NEA Scout [7], although we use solar electric propulsion instead of solar sails.

2.1 Spacecraft Dynamics

The motion of the spacecraft is modeled as a restricted two-body problem of the spacecraft around the Sun. The spacecraft of initial mass m_i is located at position $\boldsymbol{x}_i$ with velocity $\boldsymbol{v}_i$ at time t_i. We want to reach the final position $\boldsymbol{x}_f$ with velocity $\boldsymbol{v}_f$ at time t_f.

The equations of motion are given by

$$\ddot{\boldsymbol{x}} = -\mu \frac{\boldsymbol{x}}{|\boldsymbol{x}|^2} + \boldsymbol{u}(t)/m, \tag{1}$$
$$\dot{m} = -\frac{|\boldsymbol{u}(t)|}{I_{sp} g_0},$$

where $\mu \approx 1.327 \cdot 10^{20}\,\mathrm{m}^3/\mathrm{s}^2$ is the gravitational parameter of the Sun, I_{sp} is the specific impulse of the low-thrust engine, and $g_0 \approx 9.8066\,\mathrm{m/s}^2$ is the standard gravity on Earth. The control $\boldsymbol{u}(t)$ is the thrust vector. The goal of the OCP is to find the control $\boldsymbol{u}(t)$ minimizing

$$S = \int_{t_i}^{t_f} |\boldsymbol{u}(t)| \; dt, \tag{2}$$

subject to the constraints

$$\begin{aligned}
\boldsymbol{x}(t_i) &= \boldsymbol{x}_i, \\
\dot{\boldsymbol{x}}(t_i) &= \boldsymbol{v}_i, \\
\boldsymbol{x}(t_f) &= \boldsymbol{x}_f, \\
\dot{\boldsymbol{x}}(t_f) &= \boldsymbol{v}_f, \\
|\boldsymbol{u}(t)| &\leqslant T_{max} \quad \forall t \in [t_i, t_f], \\
m_f &\geqslant 0.
\end{aligned}$$

Note that we impose that the final mass $m_f = m(t_f)$ of the spacecraft at time t_f must be positive, but no further restriction is placed on the amount of propellant on the spacecraft. Furthermore, note that minimizing Eq. 2 is equivalent to maximizing m_f.

To solve this problem, we use a direct collocation method based on the Sims-Flanagan model [3]. In this model the trajectory is discretized into a number of segments and on each segment the low thrust is approximated by a small impulsive transfer in the middle of the segment. Solving the resulting non-linear programming problem (NLP) using e.g. SNOPT [6] yields discrete values for the control $\boldsymbol{u}(t)$ along the trajectory, as well as the optimal final mass m_f.

While approximate analytical and heuristic expressions have been proposed to estimate m_f, they only work for short transfer arcs and can be quite inaccurate. The simplest method for estimating m_f is assuming it the same as the impulsive Δv from a Lambert transfer:

$$m_{f_L} = m_i \exp \frac{-\Delta V_L}{I_{sp} g_0}. \tag{3}$$

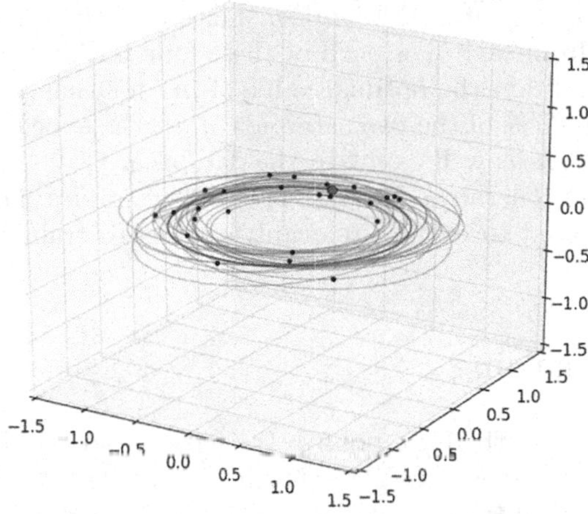

Fig. 2. Orbits of the selected asteroids for the mission (*black*) and Earth (*blue*). (Color figure online)

However, while already quite inaccurate in general, in our particular application to multi-revolution transfers this estimate will be shown to be practically useless.

2.2 Training Database Generation

We begin by selecting possible targets from the catalog of known asteroids. To obtain asteroids in an Earth-like orbit, we require that $0.8 < a < 1.2$, $i < 5°$, and $e < 0.4$. This yields 24 asteroids, and we also include Earth itself as the 25th object in the list. Figure 2 shows the orbits of all selected asteroids with the orbit of Earth.

To construct our database of training data, we start by randomly selecting two objects from the list of targets. Next, we select a random initial epoch t_i between the year 2020 and 2025, as well as a transfer time $\Delta T = t_f - t_i$ in the interval $[60, 1500]$ days. No transfer is expected to be feasible below 60 days, and due to mission constraints we are not interested in transfer times longer than about 4 years.

With this information, we solve a simplified OCP to the original one given above. Instead of fixing the initial mass and maximizing for the final mass, we simply maximize the initial mass. This yields the maximum initial mass m^* of a spacecraft that can still make the given transfer within the limitations of the propulsion system. Note that this problem is significantly easier to solve than the original OCP, since there will be no coast arcs. This fixes the thrust magnitude to T_{max} (always on), and leaves only the thrust direction to be determined while removing all but one inequality constraint from the problem.

If m^* is less than the dry mass m_{sc} of our spacecraft, we discard this data point, since in that case obviously there is no possible transfer compatible with our mission requirements. Otherwise, we continue to generate entries in our database by dividing the interval $[0.3m^*, m^*]$ into four equal parts and selecting one random value from each. For each of these four initial masses m_i, we solve the initial OCP to obtain the optimal value of m_f for that particular transfer. We then store the indices of the two asteroids i_0, i_1, the epoch and transfer time t_i and tof, m_i and m_f as well as m^* in the database.

In this fashion we generate a database of 60,000 examples of optimal transfers, from which we proceed to extract relevant features to train a set of standard regressors.

3 Machine Learning

In Fig. 3 we visualize all the data points (trajectories) in the database. The left plot reports the ratio between the ΔV (which is directly related to the fuel mass) required for the optimal trajectory and the ΔV^* for the maximum initial mass trajectory. This quantity appears correlated with the ratio m_i/m^*, as is clear from the darker region of the plot. This finding is in agreement with the results in [5].

On the right side of Fig. 3, the final mass m_f is plotted against the maximum initial mass m^* (*blue*), displaying again a clear correlation. Since this figure contains data points for any initial mass m_i, there is a wide band structure. Highlighting only data points corresponding to a narrow range of m_i (*red*), here between 0.5 m^* and 0.55 m^*, suggests a nearly linear correlation for fixed m_i.

3.1 Regression Algorithms

From the database of trajectories we randomly select 50,000 entries to use as the training set, and 10,000 as the test set. The split is performed not at the

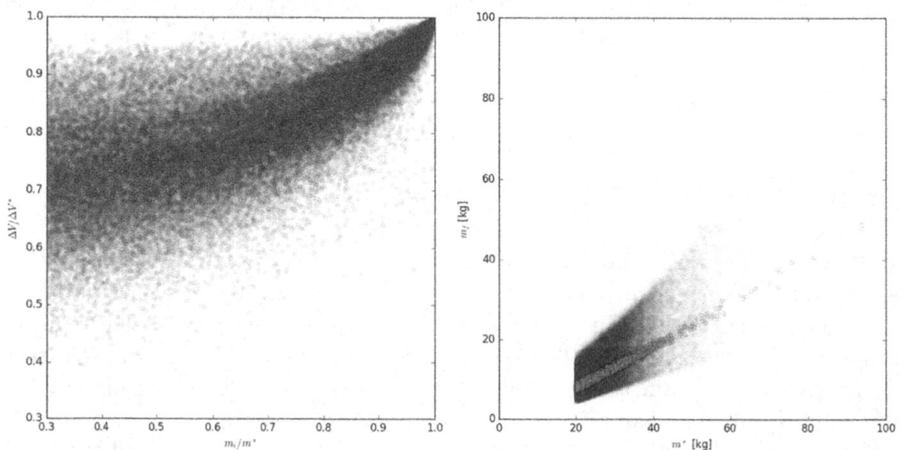

Fig. 3. Visualization of the training data. (Color figure online)

level of a single trajectory, but of a single choice of $\{i_1, i_2, t_i, \Delta T\}$. This ensures that trajectories differing only in m_i are inserted together in either one of the two sets.

We train a set of regressors on the training set, using the Python Machine Learning library *scikit-learn* [8]. For each of them we evaluate the Mean Absolute Error (MAE) and Root Mean Square Error (RMSE) on our test set. We use both base estimators (Decision Trees) and meta-estimators, namely Extra Trees, Random Forest, Gradient Boosting, Bagging and AdaBoost.

For ensemble methods the base estimators are Decision Trees and the number of estimators is set to 1000. The other parameters are optimized by grid search using 5-fold cross-validation. As a result, for Gradient Boosting we set a maximum depth of 6 and a learning rate of 0.1. For AdaBoost a square loss is used, with a learning rate of 1.2. All the other parameters are set to their default, since any change results in a degradation of performance.

We also experiment with a Neural Network regressor, implemented using the library Lasagne [9]. The architecture consists of 2 hidden layers of 80 units each with *ReLu* activations, and an output layer of a single linear unit. Training is performed with 500 epochs of Stochastic Gradient Descent using a batch size of 16 and a learning rate of 10^{-3}.

3.2 Attributes

In order to perform regression to learn the optimal final mass m_f, domain knowledge suggests a number of possible attributes, listed in Table 1.

Table 1. Possible attributes considered to learn m_f

Attribute	Description
m_i	Initial mass
ΔT	Transfer time
$\boldsymbol{r}_i, \boldsymbol{v}_i$	Starting position and velocity
$\boldsymbol{r}_f, \boldsymbol{v}_f$	Arrival position and velocity
$\cos\theta$	Cosine of the inclination between starting and arrival orbit
$\lvert\Delta a\rvert$	Difference between semi-major axes of the orbits
$\lvert\Delta e\rvert$	Difference between eccentricities of the orbits
m^*	Maximum initial mass
m^*_D	MIMA
m^*_L	Maximum initial mass using the Lambert transfer

This list includes some obvious choices: in order to solve the original OCP, knowledge of the initial mass m_i, the transfer time ΔT, and the initial and final states $\boldsymbol{r}_i$, $\boldsymbol{v}_i$ and $\boldsymbol{r}_f$, $\boldsymbol{v}_f$ is strictly required.

We also include some other readily available orbital parameters. These relate directly to the geometrical shape of the departure and target orbits, and thus are expected to be a good measure of how different the two orbits are and hence how complicated the transfer is.

None of these attributes, however, encode any information on the actual OCP that needs to be solved. We therefore expect that it is necessary to also include some information related to the solution of the OCP, without, of course, actually specifying the solution. This is why we include the value m^*, the maximum initial mass making the specified transfer feasible. While this is not the solution m_f to the full OCP we want to solve, as mentioned before we still need to solve a simpler reduced OCP to obtain m^*.

To avoid solving the reduced OCP, [5] introduces two approximations for m^*: the commonly used cost of the impulsive Lambert transfer m_L^* given by Eq. 3, and the new Maximum Initial Mass Approximation (MIMA) m_D^*, a simple analytical expression that in their case results in a relevant improvement over m_L^*. We also include these in the possible set of attributes.

3.3 Feature Selection

We perform a preliminary tree-based feature selection based on the Extra Trees Regressor from *scikit-learn*. Such analysis shows that, unsurprisingly, the most informative attribute is m_i, followed by m^* and ΔT. After that, also the three orbital parameters $\cos\theta$, Δa, and Δe carry some relevant information.

The starting and arrival states, or any combination of them, does not contribute to the learning. While mathematically sufficient for solving the OCP (together with the constant maximum thrust T_{max}, ΔT and m_i), the relationship between those inputs and the final mass m_f is highly non-linear and hence non-trivial.

More surprisingly, given their previous success, both approximators m_L^* and m_D^* turn out to be utterly uninformative as well. This result can be explained by the relatively short transfers considered in [5], usually requiring less than one revolution. For multi-revolution trajectories such as those considered in our case, neither one of the two measures has any correlation to m^*. This is particularly obvious when plotting both values against m^* in Fig. 4. It is therefore currently unavoidable to solve the simplified OCP for m^* numerically each time when querying the model.

Based on this analysis, we select the following features to perform our experiments, while training each regressor to predict the target variable m_f:

$$\{\Delta T,\ m_i,\ m^*,\ cos\theta,\ |\Delta a|,\ |\Delta e|\}.$$

In order to investigate the impact of m^* on the performance we also run the same experiments excluding it from the input features.

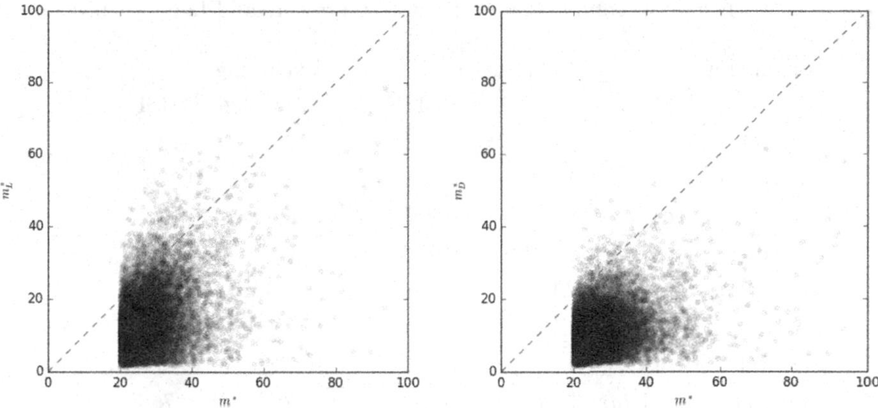

Fig. 4. Correlation of correct m^* from OCP with estimated m_L^* via Lambert (*left*) and m_D^* via MIMA (*right*). The truncation of m^* at 20 kg is due to the database generation described in Subsect. 2.2.

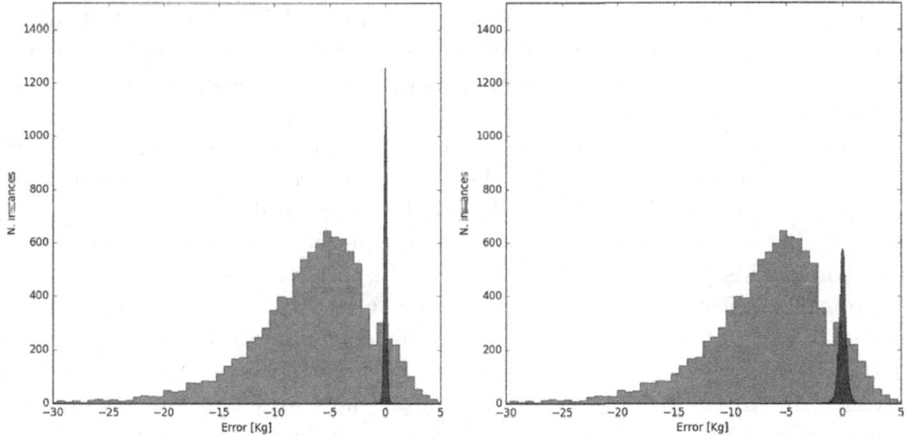

Fig. 5. The distribution of the prediction error for the best (*left, blue*) regressor Gradient Boosting and the worst regressor Decision Tree (*right, blue*). The Lambert baseline is shown in both cases for comparison (*green*). (Color figure online)

4 Results

Our baseline for comparisons is the simple impulsive Lambert transfer cost estimate given in Eq. 3. Since our transfers include multi-revolution transfers, we compute the ΔV_L^i and corresponding $m_{f_L}^i$ for Lambert transfers with i revolutions (in our case $i = 0, 1, \ldots, 5$) and take the minimum

$$m_{f_L} = \min_i m_{f_L}^i.$$

Table 2. Performance comparison of different regressors and Lambert baseline

Algorithm	Including m^*		Excluding m^*	
	MAE [kg]	RMSE [kg]	MAE [kg]	RMSE [kg]
Decision Tree	0.236	0.315	0.477	0.742
Extra Trees	0.147	0.195	0.425	0.596
Random Forest	0.154	0.205	0.376	0.533
Gradient Boosting	0.097	0.134	0.231	0.347
Bagging	0.154	0.205	0.376	0.533
AdaBoost	0.149	0.201	0.315	0.454
Neural Network	0.120	0.161	0.328	0.469
Lambert's predictor	*6.98*	*8.76*	*6.98*	*8.76*

As expected, the regressors easily outperform this basic Lambert estimate, which is vastly wrong. Figure 5 shows a histogram of the error in the final mass m_f (computed against the numerical solution of the OCP) over the test set for the best regressor (Gradient Boosting), the worst regressor (Decision Tree), and the Lambert baseline. It is clear that even the worst regressor outperforms the Lambert baseline estimate by an order of magnitude.

Table 2 shows the performance of each algorithm trained with its default parameters. Also quantitatively, it is clear that all learning algorithms improve on Lambert, whether m^* is included in the attributes or not. It must be pointed out, however, that this is basically due to the horrible performance of the Lambert estimator for this problem.

Typical spacecraft such as the one considered in this work, carry on the order of 3–5 kg of propellant. The average fuel consumption for the transfers in our database is 3.41 kg with a standard deviation of 1.45 kg. This means that even an error in the final mass of 0.3 kg after the transfer means a 10% error in the required fuel mass. This is why the improvement between the results including m^* in the learning and those excluding it is very important. While it seems small compared to the Lambert baseline, the improvement relative to the typical transfer cost is still substantial.

5 Conclusions

We have shown that also in the case of multi-revolution transfers between NEOs the machine learning approach is vastly superior to the commonly used impulsive Lambert estimate. We did not perform any particular tuning of the parameters of the learning algorithms to achieve this result.

To obtain realistically usable results, however, we were not able to eliminate entirely the need for solving an OCP. But the problem is reduced to solving a significantly easier OCP for m^* instead of the direct solution of m_f.

In future work we propose to remove this requirement by training a more sophisticated regressor to also learn the full solution of the OCP without the need of m^*.

References

1. Izzo, D., Becerra, V.M., Myatt, D.R., Nasuto, S.J., Bishop, J.M.: Search space pruning and global optimisation of multiple gravity assist spacecraft trajectories. J. Glob. Opt. **38**(2), 283–296 (2007)
2. Izzo, D.: PyGMO and PyKEP: open source tools for massively parallel optimization in astrodynamics (the case of interplanetary trajectory optimization). In: Proceedings of the Fifth International Conference on Astrodynamics Tools and Techniques, ICATT (2012)
3. Sims, J.A., Flanagan, S.N.: Preliminary design of low-thrust interplanetary missions. In: AAS/AIAA Astrodynamic Specialist Conference (1999)
4. Pontryagin, L.S., Boltyanskii, V.G., Gamkrelidze, R.V., Mishchenko, E.F.: The Mathematical Theory of Optimal Processes. Interscience, New York (1962). English translation
5. Hennes, D., Izzo, D., Landau, D.: Fast approximators for optimal low-thrust hops between main belt asteroids. In: IEEE Symposium Series on Computational Intelligence (2016)
6. Gill, P.E., Murray, W., Saunders, M.A.: SNOPT: an SQP Algorithm for Large-Scale Constrained Optimization. SIAM Rev. **47**(1), 99–131 (2005)
7. NASA NEA Scout. https://www.nasa.gov/content/nea-scout/
8. Pedregosa, F., et al.: Scikit-learn: machine learning in Python. J. Mach. Learn. Res. **12**, 2825–2830 (2011)
9. Dieleman, S., et al.: Lasagne: first release (2015). http://dx.doi.org/10.5281/zenodo.27878

Neuronal Electrical Behavior Modeling of Solar Panels

Jose Manuel Lopez-Guede(✉), Jose Antonio Ramos-Hernanz, Julian Estevez, Asier Garmendia, and Manuel Graña

Computational Intelligence Group, Basque Country University (UPV/EHU), San Sebastian, Spain
jm.lopez@ehu.es

Abstract. In this paper authors model the electrical behavior of a commercial solar panel composed of solar cells connected in series through an Artificial Neural Network (ANN) with one hidden layer. The real solar panel that has been used as proof of concept is of the commercial model ATERSA A55, and it is placed at the Faculty of Engineering of Vitoria-Gasteiz (Basque Country University, Spain). The resulting model consists on one input (V_{PV}) and one output (I_{PV}), since the standard deviation of the temperature and irradiance magnitudes in the used dataset was residual.

1 Introduction

Solar energy [1] is very suitable to be used in urban centers due to its accommodation possibilities and because it prevents the emission of contaminant subproducts [2] where it is placed. It is very interesting to know the electrical behavior (the relation between the supplied voltage V_{PV} and current I_{PV}) of their components in order to optimize their performance.

There are two main trends when modeling the electrical behavior of solar elements: the theoretical and the empirical approaches. The methods that belong to the theoretical approach have the common characteristic of using the characteristic equation [3] (see Subsect. 2.1) with a different number of degrees of freedom, being the more outstanding difference among them the number of parameters that are used by each model. In this way there are theoretical models based on the double diode equivalent circuit with 7 parameters (a_1, a_2, R_S, R_{SH}, I_{0_1}, I_{0_2} and I_{PH}) [4–6]. A number of simplifications can be carried out on that complete model, obtaining a 5 parameters model based on a single diode equivalent circuit, being the parameters a, R_S, R_{SH}, I_0 and I_{PH} [7–9]. More simplifications can be done ($R_{SH} = \infty$ in such a way that $I_{SH} = 0$) in order to obtain a 4 parameters model [10], or even more ($R_S = 0\,\Omega$ or $I_{PH} = I_{SC}$), obtaining a 3 parameters model [11,12].

The other above mentioned main trend are the empirical methods, which share the common characteristic of learning the electrical behavior of the solar elements from their actual data. Among these methods there are authors that

F.J. Martínez de Pisón et al. (Eds.): HAIS 2017, LNAI 10334, pp. 554–564, 2017.
DOI: 10.1007/978-3-319-59650-1_47

obtain empirical models from theoretical data as [13] and authors that use polynomial interpolation of real data as in [3].

In this paper we are addressing the problem of designing accurate models of the electrical behavior of the solar elements from their actual data using artificial neural networks (ANN) due to their potential advantages (see Subsect. 2.2), and a more formal description of this problem will be given in Sect. 3, where it will be posed. After carrying out a number of experiments, we have reached the first quite accurate empirical model of the Atersa A55 solar panel, with a Root Mean Square Error (RMSE) of 0.036 A.

The paper is structured as follows. Section 2 provides a background on solar elements modeling (both solar cells and panels), and on artificial neural networks (ANN). Section 3 poses formally the objective of the paper. The detailed description of the experimental setup which has been designed in order obtain an accurate neuronal model of solar panels is given in Sect. 4, while Sect. 5 discusses the obtained results. Finally, the more outstanding conclusions are given in Sect. 6.

2 Background

As we have stated in the previous section, we are facing the problem of designing an accurate neural model of solar panels. In this section we provide the necessary background to frame the problem and the solution on the scope of solar elements and artificial neural networks.

2.1 Characterization of Solar Elements

The ideal solar cell can be modeled as a current source with an anti-parallel diode. Once the cell is exposed to light the generated direct current varies linearly with the solar radiation. Some authors have improved the model taking into account the effects of a shunt resistor and other one in series, as shown in Fig. 1. That equivalent circuit can be used either for an individual cell, a panel that consists of several cells or for a matrix that is the union of several panels. The main involved magnitudes are the photogenerated current or photocurrent I_{PH}, the current of the diode I_D, the series resistance R_S and the shunt resistance R_{SH}.

The first way of characterizing a solar element (a cell in this case) is analyzing the circuit of Fig. 1, where it is easy to relate the current I_{PV} and the voltage V_{PV} provided by the solar cell through Eq. (1) [14], which is expanded in Eq. (2) [12]:

$$I_{PV} = I_{PH} - I_D - I_{SH}, \tag{1}$$

$$I_{PV} = I_{PH} - I_0 \left(e^{\frac{q(V_{PV}+I_{PV}R_S)}{aKT}} - 1 \right) - \frac{V_{PH} + I_{PH}R_S}{R_{SH}}, \tag{2}$$

where T is the cell temperature [°C], K is the Boltzmann's constant (1.38×10^{-23} [j/K]), a is the diode ideality factor, q is the charge of the electron

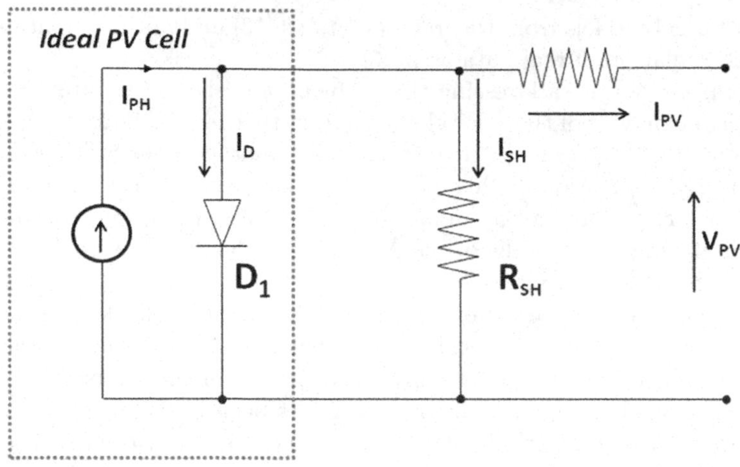

Fig. 1. Schematic of an ideal solar cell

(1.6×10^{-19} [C]) and I_0 is the saturation current of the diode [A]. A number of manufacturing structural parameters of the solar cell are involved in Eq. (2), i.e., R_{SH}, R_S, a, I_D and I_{PH}.

The second way of characterizing a solar element (a panel in this case) is through its characteristic curves. Figure 2 shows the characteristic curves IV, PV and PI showing the relations between pairs of the more relevant magnitudes of a solar panel when operating at a given temperature and irradiation. If any of these two factors changes, the obtained curves will be different. The inferior abscissa axis represents the working voltage V_{PV} of the panel, while in the upper one and in the left ordinate axis there is current delivered by the solar panel I_{PV}. Finally, the power supplied by the solar panel is in the right ordinate axis.

As these are theoretical models and the enumerated parameters (for the first model) and the curves (for the second model) are the standard ones for a solar panel commercial model, it is only possible to obtain approximate values when dealing with a specific solar panel. The individual small errors for one solar cell could be relevant when dealing with large solar panels or large solar farms.

2.2 Artificial Neural Networks

One of the more outstanding utilities Artificial Neural Networks (ANN) [15] is the modeling of dynamic systems [16], which could be arbitrary complex. There are several types of ANNs, each one with different characteristics that make them more suitable for solving specific problems. Anyway, independently of their type all ANNs have several relevant properties in order to face the problem that is being addressed in this paper. The first one is the learning capability, i.e., they can learn complex non-linear black box models if such models are adequately designed with appropriate inputs and output and the adequate training algorithm is used. The second property is relative to their generalization

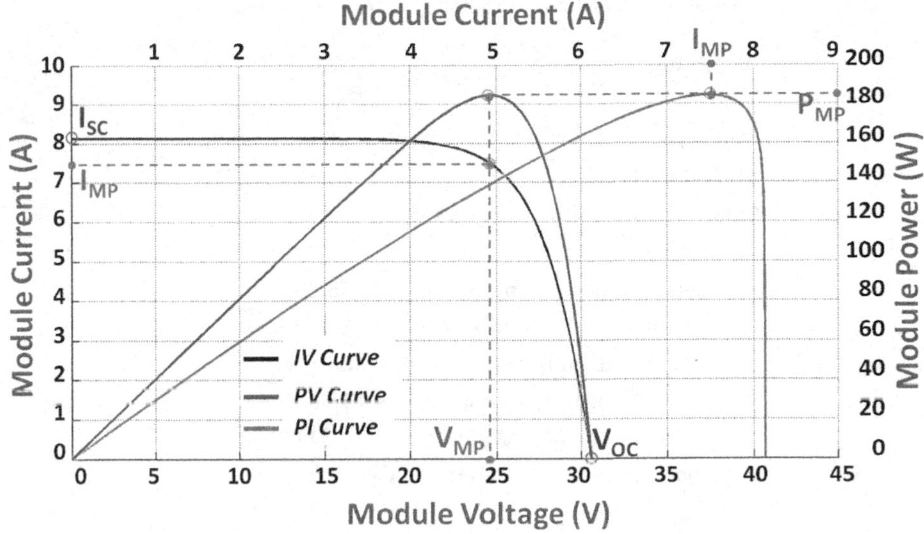

Fig. 2. Main characteristic curves of the ATERSA A-55 solar panel

capabilities, which in short means that if the training algorithm and the training patterns have been carefully chosen, the behavior of the ANNs in new situations probably will be adequate. The last property is with regard to their calculation capacity, which confers them real time capabilities since they have an inherent parallel internal structure. Due to these main properties and to other minor ones, ANNs have found a wide field of application in a number of areas [17,18].

3 Statement of the Problem

The problem that we are facing in this paper is to design a model of the solar panel installed at the Faculty of Engineering of Vitoria-Gasteiz (University of the Basque Country, Spain), based on the ANN approach. The main requirement is that the model should be as accurate as possible compared to the collected data, but there are other minor requirements for that model design:

- It is desirable a very small human intervention. It means that the engineer or practitioner must not develop a long and tiring tuning process.
- It is also desirable the model to be easy to adjust without computational burden.
- It should be useful a model with a very fast response, in such a way that as it needs a very small amount of time to give an approximate response, it could be used in intensive simulations.
- It would be convenient that such model could be adjusted again when new collected data were available without discarding the previous acquired knowledge.

Table 1. ATERSA A55 solar panel characteristics

Attribute	Value
Model	Atersa A-55
Cell type	Monocrystalline
Maximum Power [W]	55
Open Circuit Voltage Voc [V]	20,5
Short circuit Current Isc [A]	3,7
Voltage, max power Vmpp [V]	16,2
Current, max power Impp [A]	3,4
Number of cells in series	36
Temp. Coeff. of Isc [mA/°C]	1,66
Temp. Coeff. of Voc [mV/°C]	−84,08
Nominal Operation Cell Temp. [°C]	47,5

As summary, we are going to model in the simplest suited way the behavior of the solar panel as a black box, trying to use only one input (V_{PV}) and one output (I_{PV}).

4 Experimental Design

This section is devoted to explain the experimental design that has been implemented in order to get the objective of the paper. Subsection 4.1 gives a summary of the more outstanding characteristics of the solar panels that were used in the experimental part. The data recording process is explained in Subsect. 4.2, while Subsect. 4.3 describes the neuronal training process.

4.1 Solar Panels Specifications

Solar panels ATERSA A55 (637 × 527 × 35) are professional panels, not only for small systems but also for large installations. As its specifications show in Table 1, they are composed of monocrystalline silicon cells that guarantee power production from dawn to dusk. The performance of solar cells is usually evaluated under the standard test condition (STC), where an average solar spectrum at AM 1.5 is used, the irradiance is normalized to 1,000 W/m^2, and the cell temperature is defined as 25 °C. In Fig. 3 we can see the placement of the real solar panels on the roof of the Faculty of Engineering of Vitoria-Gasteiz.

4.2 Data Gathering

In order to obtain an empirical model, it is mandatory to have a representative dataset of all working points of the element to be modeled. The measurement

Table 2. Mean and Standard deviation of the Temperature and Irradiance of the gathered data

	Mean ($\bar{x}$)	Standard deviation (σ)
Temperature °C	8.15	0.71
Irradiance W/m^2	51.14	0.06

task to collect data to train the artificial neural network is carried out through the data logger Sineax CAM because it allows a continuous measurement and recording of measured data. Besides, its I/O interface can be configured according to specific requirements. In this case, the selected parameters to register are the panel voltage, the panel current, temperature and irradiance. The adaptation to this task is carried out through the CB-Manager software.

4.3 Model Training Process

In order to build a neural model the first step is to fix the structure of the neural network to train. In this case we chose a feed-forward artificial neural network. As it was explained in Sect. 3, we want a model consisting on only one input (V_{PV}) and one output (I_{PV}) in order to make it as simple as possible. After analyzing the gathered data, we found that the temperature and the irradiance are quite constant values as can be seen in Table 2 due to their very small standard deviation, so the initial idea of building a model with only one input and one output has been supported by that evidence (Fig. 4).

Fig. 3. ATERSA A-55 solar panels

Fig. 4. Real used devices during the data logging process

Table 3. Main parameters of the training process

Training parameter	Value
Initial μ	10^{-3}
μ decrease factor	10^{-1}
μ increase factor	10^{1}
Maximum μ	10^{10}
Minimum performance gradient	10^{-7}
Maximum validation failures	6

Given the very simple specification of the model, i.e., there is only one target value associated with each input value, the network has only one neuron in both the input and the output layers. With regard to the number of hidden layers, after carrying out a number of trials in a heuristical search we have decided to have only one layer, and that hidden layer will have ten neurons, defining a quite reduced ANN. The last element to fix is the activation function of both the hidden and output layers. In the hidden layer the tan-sigmoid activation function is used, while the linear activation function in the output layer.

A very relevant aspect of the training process is the training algorithm that is used. In this case the Levenberg-Marquardt algorithm was chosen due to speed reasons, and the used parameters are specified in Table 3.

The last aspect to decide is how to use the gathered data in order to carry out the learning process. In this case, all the input data appear at once in a batch. They are used directly as were recorded, avoiding to run any normalization nor preprocess. Both the input and target vectors have been divided into three sets using interleaved indices as follows generating a partition where the 60% are used for training, the 20% are used for validation and the remaining 20% are used as a completely independent test of network generalization.

5 Results

This section is devoted to discuss the results that we have obtained following the training process described in Sect. 4. In this discussion we will pay more attention to the accuracy of the model than to the training process, which has finished when the validation error increased for ten iterations at iteration 20.

The prediction capabilities of the trained model are assessed through Fig. 5, where we can see that the network response is reasonable because the predicted outputs tracks the targets even with the test dataset, in fact the Root Mean Square Error (RMSE) is 0.036 A. In Fig. 5 there are some small errors that could be explained by the following circumstances:

- The dataset used to train the network is composed of raw and non-preprocessed data (un-normalized data).
- In a number of cases, we found that in both the training and test datasets, for a unique value of the input (V_{PV}) there are several targets (I_{PV}). This circumstance reveals that this learning process involves a multivaluated function.
- We also should keep in mind that the temperature and irradiance magnitudes have been discarded in order to build a simple model. However, it is a fact

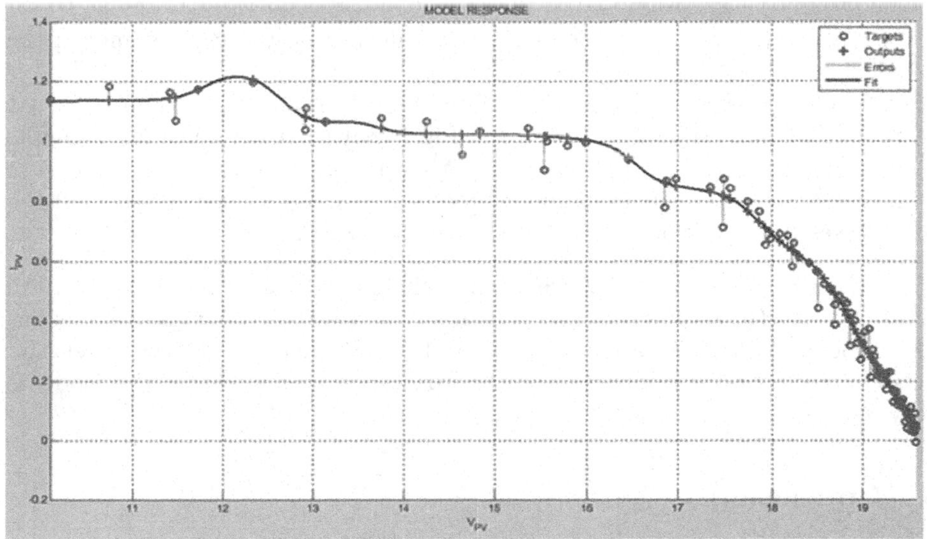

Fig. 5. Model response using the test dataset

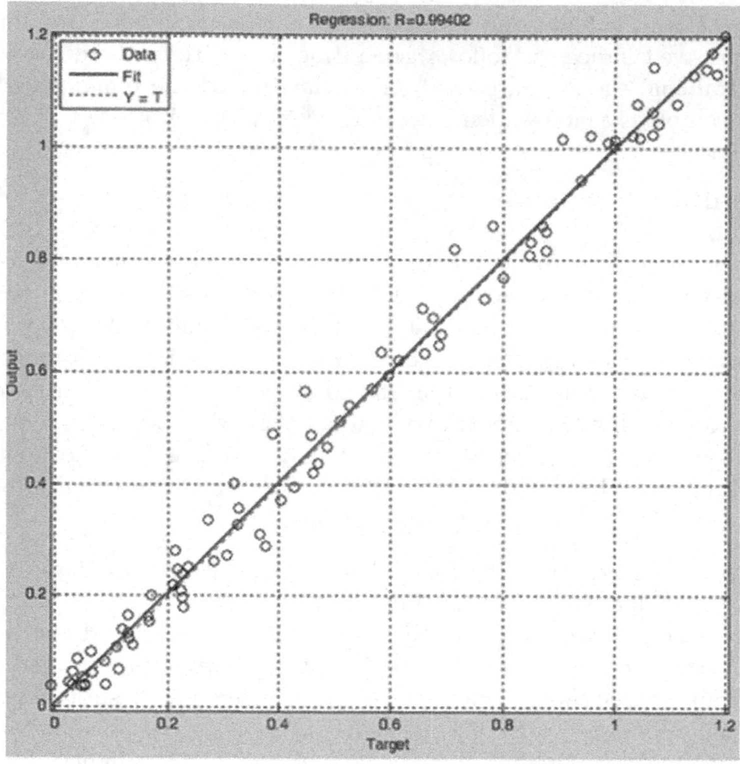

Fig. 6. Correlation coefficient of the trained model

of matter that they exert some kind of influence on the performance of the solar panels.

- It is clear that the distribution of the sample data of the dataset is not properly balanced. It is easy to see in Fig. 5 that there are much more sample data for input values $V_{PV} > 17.5\,\text{V}$ than for input values $V_{PV} \leq 17.5\,\text{V}$; however for an adequate training process it is more convenient that all the samples were uniformly distributed over the input range.

Finally, we can see that the correlation coefficient (R-value) obtained with the total response (including training, validation and test partitions) is over 0.99, as Fig. 6 shows. Taking into account that $R = 1$ is equivalent to a perfect correlation between the network responses and the targets, we conclude that the model is very accurate.

6 Conclusions

The paper has started reviewing the state-of-the-art on the field of modeling solar panels, where it has been clearly explained that current the two main trends are the modeling based on theoretical models and on empirical data, that is the way that has been chosen in this paper. In Sect. 2 we have given a brief background on characterization of photo voltaic cells and on ANN. As we stated in Sect. 3 the main objective of the work described in the paper is to design an accurate neuronal model of the electrical behavior of a solar panel installed at the Faculty of Engineering of Vitoria-Gasteiz (Basque Country University, Spain). So, we have given a complete specification of the experimental design to get it in Sect. 4, providing the used solar panels specification, the data gathering and the ANN training processes. Finally, in Sect. 5 we discussed the obtained results, which can be summarized by the fact of obtaining a Root Mean Square Error (RMSE) of 0.036 A and a R value larger to 0.99, both using the test dataset.

This paper has been a first proof of concept of the modeling that can be carried out using a neuronal approach of solar panels, using specifically the model ATERSA A55 for the experiments. As has been stated in the discussion part of the paper, the obtained results are promising and the small errors that have been detected when the obtained model is tested are reasonable and easily explained. So, more efforts should be done to tackle each one of the factors that are detected as responsible of such small errors, most of them linked to the used datasets, being the more outstanding the non use of temperature and irradiance as input of the model. Besides, a comparison with other models could be appropriate.

Acknowledgments. The research was supported by the Computational Intelligence Group of the Basque Country University (UPV/EHU) through Grant IT874-13 of Research Groups Call 2013–2017 (Basque Country Government).

References

1. Singh, G.K.: Solar power generation by pv (photovoltaic) technology: a review. Energy **53**, 1–13 (2013). http://www.sciencedirect.com/science/article/pii/S0360544213001758
2. Kilkis, B.: District energy systems: theory and applications. J. Polytech. **14**(2), 149–154 (2011)
3. Ramos Hernanz, J.A., Lopez Guede, J., Belver, I.Z., Lopez, P.E., Zulueta, E., Barambones, O., Echavarri, F.O.: Modelling of a photovoltaic panel based on their actual measurements. Int. J. Tech. Phys. Prob. Eng. (IJTPE) **6**(4), 37–41 (2014)
4. Miceli, R., Orioli, A., Gangi, A.D.: A procedure to calculate the i-v characteristics of thin-film photovoltaic modules using an explicit rational form. Appl. Energy **155**, 613–628 (2015). http://www.sciencedirect.com/science/article/pii/S0306261915007953
5. Elbaset, A.A., Ali, H., Sattar, M.A.-E.: Novel seven-parameter model for photovoltaic modules. Sol. Energy Mater. Sol. Cells **130**, 442–455 (2014). http://www.sciencedirect.com/science/article/pii/S0927024814003778
6. Muhsen, D.H., Ghazali, A.B., Khatib, T., Abed, I.A.: Parameters extraction of double diode photovoltaic module model based on hybrid evolutionary algorithm. Energy Convers. Manag. **105**, 552–561 (2015). http://www.sciencedirect.com/science/article/pii/S0196890415007694

7. Bastidas-Rodriguez, J., Petrone, G., Ramos-Paja, C., Spagnuolo, G.: A genetic algorithm for identifying the single diode model parameters of a photovoltaic panel. Math. Comput. Simul. (2015). http://www.sciencedirect.com/science/article/pii/S0378475415002220
8. Villalva, M., Gazoli, J., Filho, E.: Modeling and circuit-based simulation of photovoltaic arrays. In: Brazilian Power Electronics Conference: COBEP 2009, pp. 1244–1254 (2009)
9. Soto, W.D., Klein, S., Beckman, W.: Improvement and validation of a model for photovoltaic array performance. Sol. Energy **80**(1), 78–88 (2006). http://www.sciencedirect.com/science/article/pii/S0038092X05002410
10. Gonzaez-Longatt, F.: Model of photovoltaic in matlabtm. In: 2do Congreso Iberoamericano de Estudiantes de Ingeniería Eléctrica, Electrónica y Computación (II CIBELEC 2005), Puerto la Cruz-Venezuela (2006)
11. Bandou, F., Arab, A.H., Belkaid, M.S., Logerais, P.-O., Riou, O., Charki, A.: Evaluation performance of photovoltaic modules after a long time operation in saharan environment. Int. J. Hydrogen Energy **40**(39), 13839–13848 (2015). http://www.sciencedirect.com/science/article/pii/S0360319915010034
12. Ramos-Hernanz, J., Campayo, J., Larranaga, J., Zulueta, E., Barambones, O., Motrico, J., Gamiz, U.F., Zamora, I.: Two photovoltaic cell simulation models in matlab/simulink. Int. J. Tech. Phys. Prob. Eng. (IJTPE) **4**(1), 45–51 (2012)
13. Karamirad, M., Omid, M., Alimardani, R., Mousazadeh, H., Heidari, S.N.: Ann based simulation and experimental verification of analytical four-and five-parameters models of pv modules. Simul. Model. Pract. Theory **34**, 86–98 (2013). http://www.sciencedirect.com/science/article/pii/S1569190X13000166
14. Gow, J., Manning, C.: Development of a photovoltaic array model for use in power-electronics simulation studies. IEE Proc. Electr. Power Appl. **146**(2), 193–200 (1999)
15. Widrow, B., Lehr, M.: 30 years of adaptive neural networks: perceptron, madaline, and backpropagation. Proc. IEEE **78**(9), 1415–1442 (1990)
16. Narendra, K., Parthasarathy, K.: Identification and control of dynamical systems using neural networks. IEEE Trans. Neural Netw. **1**(1), 4–27 (1990)
17. Fang, W., Quan, S., Xie, C., Tang, X., Wang, L., Huang, L.: Maximum power point tracking with dichotomy and gradient method for automobile exhaust thermoelectric generators. J. Electron. Mater. **45**(3), 1613–1624 (2016). http://dx.doi.org/10.1007/s11664-015-4130-9
18. Gautam, A., Soh, Y.C.: Stabilizing model predictive control using parameter-dependent dynamic policy for nonlinear systems modeled with neural networks. J. Process Control **36**, 11–21 (2015). http://www.sciencedirect.com/science/article/pii/S0959152415001870

A Proposal to Enhance Human-Machine Interaction by Means of Multi-agent Conversational Interfaces

David Griol(✉), Araceli Sanchis de Miguel, and José Manuel Molina

Computer Science Department, Carlos III University of Madrid,
Avda. de la Universidad, 30, 28911 Leganés, Spain
{david.griol,araceli.sanchis,josemanuel.molina}@uc3m.es

Abstract. Conversational interfaces have become a hot topic during the last years. Major research groups and technology companies have been making huge investments in research into technologies such as Artificial Intelligence, deep neural networks, machine learning, and natural language understanding with the aim of creating intelligent assistants that will enable users to interact with information and services in a natural, conversational way. However, most of the current conversational interfaces use hand-crafting dialog strategies and architectures tightly coupled to the application domain and are not adapted to the specific requirements and preferences of each user. In this paper, we propose a multi agent architecture to develop user-adapted conversational interfaces. Our proposal considers two types of agents. Expert agents access different knowledge sources, and decision agents coordinate them to provide a coherent response to the user. We describe our proposal and its practical application to develop a conversational interface that provides bus schedule information.

Keywords: Conversational interfaces · Multi-agent systems · Human-agent interaction · Spoken interaction · Statistical methodologies

1 Introduction

With the advances in Language Technologies and Natural Language Processing, conversational interfaces have begun to play an increasingly important role in the design of human-machine interaction systems in a number of devices and intelligent environments [7]. These interfaces can be defined as computer programs that engage the user in a dialog that aims to be similar to that between humans [6,8,10].

The increased number of applications of conversational interfaces for an enhanced human-machine interaction is supported by recent major advances in Artificial Intelligence (big data and deep learning to cite just two), language technologies (e.g., automatic speech recognition, natural language processing, and use of the semantic web), and device technologies (more powerful smartphones, use of sensors and context information, and increased connectivity).

F.J. Martínez de Pisón et al. (Eds.): HAIS 2017, LNAI 10334, pp. 565–576, 2017.
DOI: 10.1007/978-3-319-59650-1_48

Natural human-computer interaction is a complex problem that requires work on multiple levels, such as speech recognition, natural language processing, dialog management, and speech synthesis. However, most of the natural language conversational interfaces are oriented to solve restricted problems in which the knowledge is stored in just one type of source (e.g., relational databases, ontologies, etc.) and hand-crafting dialog strategies tightly coupled to the application domain are used to offer exactly the same system's behavior for every user.

Thus, one of the core aspects of developing adaptive conversational interfaces is to design flexible dialog management strategies and architectures portable across domains and applied to systems with varying complexity. The dialog strategy defines the system conversational behavior in response to user utterances and environmental states that, for example, can be based on observed or inferred events or beliefs.

On the one hand, this has motivated the research community to find ways for automating dialog learning by using statistical models trained with real conversations. Statistical approaches can model the variability in user behaviors and allow exploring a wider range of strategies. Although the construction and parametrization of the model depends on expert knowledge of the task, the final objective is to develop conversational interfaces that have a more robust behavior, better portability, and are easier to adapt to different user profiles or tasks. These approaches facilitate the development of multi-domain systems, easily extensible and able to automatically adapt the interaction considering users' specific requirements and preferences.

On the other hand, classical architectures to develop these interfaces defined within the research community include valuable examples like Galaxy [11], used as a testbed for the research and development of several dialog systems in different domains (e.g., automobile classified ads [3], restaurant guide [15], and weather information [4]), different languages [14], and different access mechanisms [3,4,15]. This architecture, created as a reference for the DARPA Communicator Program, is based on the client-server paradigm and the introduction of a "hub" to receive and transmit the messages generated by the different modules of the system.

However, as recently described in [2], many of these systems are not interactive or offer limited interactivity. Users are often not satisfied with the lack of memory of the dialog manager and the requirement of using the same dialog strategy and same system actions in every dialog. In addition, most of these systems are not able to deal with heterogeneous data sources at the same time and in a non-obtrusive way.

In this paper we describe a proposal to address these problems by means of a multi-agent architecture that allows to develop conversational interfaces portable across domains and varying complexity. In our proposal, a set of expert agents specialized in specific domains facilitates the access to different information sources, and a series of decision agents coordinate them to provide a coherent user-adapted response. The selection of these specific system actions depends on multiple factors, such as the output of the speech recognizer (e.g., N-best options and confidence measures), the previous dialog history (e.g., number of errors detected, sequence of system actions, number of previous confirmations), the application domain (e.g., guidelines for customer service), knowledge about the users and their emotional state, and the responses and status of external back-ends, devices, and data repositories.

The remainder of the paper is organized as follows. In Sect. 2 we describe the motivation of our proposal and review main approaches focused on key aspects related to it. Section 3 details our proposed multi-agent architecture to develop adaptive conversational interfaces. Section 4 describes the application of our proposal in the CMU Let's Go spoken dialog system and presents the results of the evaluation of our proposal for this practical system. Finally, Sect. 5 presents the conclusions and suggests some future work guidelines.

2 Related Work

The spoken dialog industry has reached a maturity based on standards that pervade technology to provide high interoperability, which makes it possible to divide the market in a vertical structure of technology vendors, platform integrators, application developers, and hosting companies [7,10].

The design practices of conventional commercial conversational interfaces are currently well established in industry. In these practices, voice user interface (VUI) experts handcraft a detailed dialog plan based on their knowledge about the specific task and the business rules (e.g., to verify the user's identity before providing certain information). In addition, designers commonly define the precise wording for the system prompts according to the dialog state and context, and also the expected types of user's utterances for each turn.

This standard procedure to develop commercial conversational interfaces can be represented as a graph that describes the set of dialog states and tables containing the details of each state. This way, commercial applications are usually implemented as directed dialogs, in which users are restricted and guided to provide specific pieces of information, thus restricting the possible user responses and minimizing the probability of speech recognition errors. This way, each interaction is designed to accept a restricted set of expected user reactions to the specific prompt played at that particular turn, providing the speech recognizer with an appropriately designed grammar with a small list of options.

On the other side, spoken dialog research has been moving on a parallel path trying to attain naturalness and freedom of communication. This way, current research lines include very important topics that can be classified into the following three categories:

- Understanding human-human communication and the differences with human-computer interaction (HCI): understand the mechanisms of human dialog through linguistically motivated studies on human-human corpora.
- Designing interfaces for usable systems: develop general design principles that, once applied, would result in usable human-machine user interfaces based on speech recognition and speech synthesis technology.

– Developing these usable systems: formalize programming styles, models, engines and tools which can be used to build effective dialog applications.

Some authors [2,7,9] have recently state that to achieve these important objectives, a good natural language conversational interface should: be easy to configure and use; use heterogeneous data sources; make its capabilities and limitations evident to users; offer recommendations sufficiently justified; be robust to possible failures; provide responses quickly and with accuracy; be multimodal; be domain-independent and also from the database management system, languages, hardware and software; handle linguistic phenomena (e.g. anaphora, ellipsis, ambiguity, or incomplete sentences). In addition, the system must be interactive (including a memory and a dialog manager to engage in conversation with users and modify or revise requests), versatile (i.e., able to work with heterogeneous data sources at the same time), and also consider valuable information such as the user's emotional state and previous uses to decide the next system action.

As described in the introduction section, we address these objectives by means of multi-agent architecture in which two kinds of agents cooperate to decide the next systems actions. Expert agents are specialized in accessing different knowledge sources, and decision agents coordinate them to provide a coherent answer to the user. As it will be described in Sect. 3, the decisions taken to develop the different modules of these agents have been carefully taken so that the proposal can be domain-independent and applied to systems with varying complexity.

3 Proposed Architecture

Figure 1 shows the proposed client-server multi-agent architecture to develop user-adapted multi-domain conversational agents. Two types of agents have been defined: expert agents and decision agents. Our proposal is based on [2]. We extend this contribution by means of: (i) the incorporation of a domain-independent dialog management methodology that allows the selection of user-adapted system responses by means of a classification process; (ii) the integration of a module to model user's intention into the architecture of the expert agents. This module is based on a statistical methodology to predict the user's dialog act(s) for the current dialog state and consider this prediction in the dialog management process; (iii) the proposal of open-source solutions for speech recognition and synthesis; (iv) the proposal of a statistical methodology for the practical implementation of the decision agents and the selection of the final response of the conversational system.

Expert agents provide information about specific domains, and their access is carried out by means of decision agents, which manage the answers provided by the different expert agents to provide a coherent response to the user. Decision agents could be organized hierarchically to make the integration process easier.

Given that it is a multi-agent architecture, it is easily scalable. Several expert agents are aimed to different purposes. Each agent is an expert doing its own

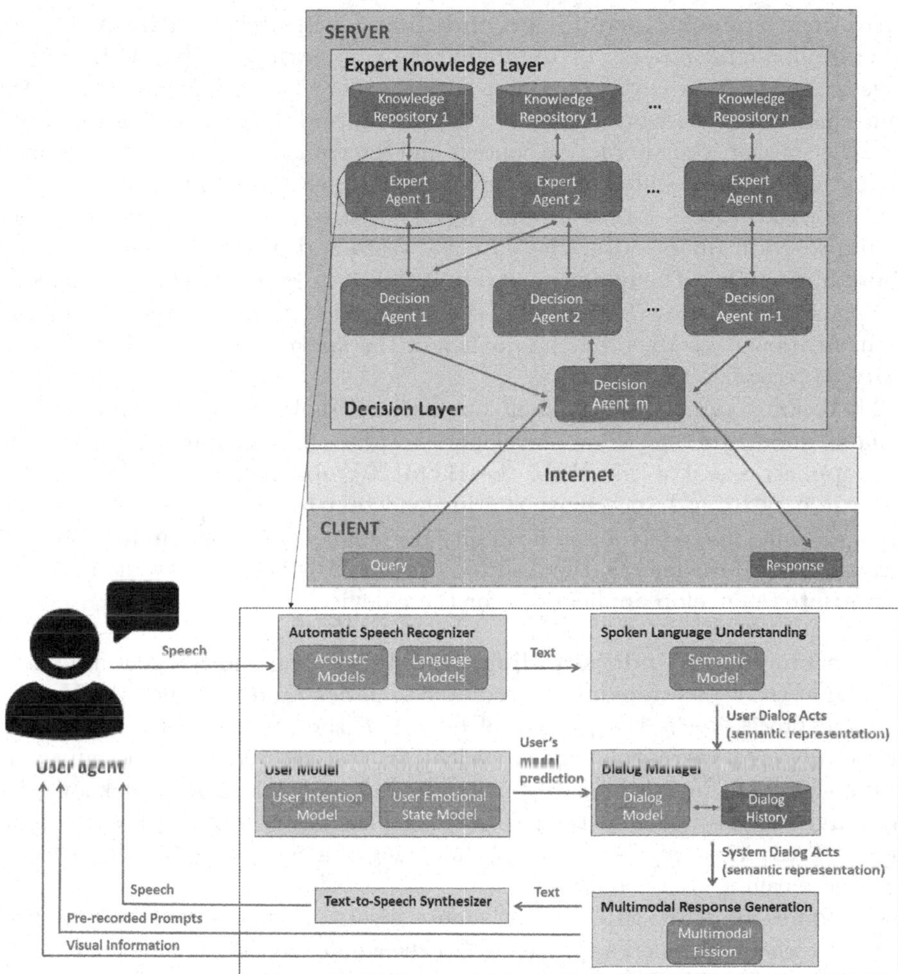

Fig. 1. Proposed multi-agent architecture to develop enhanced conversational interfaces

work, and it does not have to know anything about all the other expert agents. They are able to access, process and abstract the information of heterogeneous data sources and architectures to work wit reusable high-level semantic interpretations independent from the database management system.

3.1 Expert Agents

Each expert system consists of six main modules that respectively carry out the following tasks: automatic speech recognition (ASR), spoken language understanding (NLU), user modeling (UM), dialog management (DM), multimodal language generation (NLG), and text-to-speech synthesis (TTS). The following subsections summarize our proposal to develop these modules.

Automatic Speech Recognition and Text-to-Speech Synthesis. Speech recognition is the process of obtaining the text string corresponding to an acoustic input. It is a very complex task as there is much variability in the input characteristics, which can differ depending on the linguistics of the utterance, the speaker, the interaction context and the transmission channel. Different applications demand different complexity of the speech recognizer.

TTS is the process of transforming written text to speech. Synthesized speech has improved in quality over the past few years and in many cases can sound almost human-like. The quality and intelligibility of synthesized speech play an important role in the acceptability of speech-based systems, as users often judge a conversational interface by the quality of the spoken output rather than its ability to recognize what they say.

There are a number of different open-source tools as well as commercially available products that allow developers to add speech input and output to their applications. For the Web, the HTML5 Web Speech API (Web SAPI) makes it easy to add speech recognition and text-to-speech synthesis to Web pages, allowing fine control and flexibility in versions of Chrome from version 25 onward. For mobile devices, the Android Speech APIs is an open source solution appropriate to develop applications for these devices.

Spoken Language Understanding. Once the conversational agent has recognized what the user uttered, it is necessary to understand what he said. Natural language processing is the process of obtaining the semantic of a text string. It generally involves morphological, lexical, syntactical, semantic, discourse and pragmatical knowledge. In a first stage lexical and morphological knowledge allow dividing the words in their constituents distinguishing lexemes and morphemes. Semantic analysis extracts the meaning of a complex syntactic structure from the meaning of its constituents.

Compared to ASR, SLU is much more diverse as it embraces a variety of different technologies and approaches. On the whole, statistical techniques dominate the research literature, but there are still many proponents of handcrafted approaches, particularly in industry where designers wish to have greater control over the output of their systems and how this output is obtained.

The choice of a particular approach depends on the task to be performed by SLU. For example, it may be important to perform fairly low level tasks such as normalizing the input before going on to higher-level tasks. Extracting the meaning may in some cases only require identifying keywords in the input while in other cases a deeper understanding may be required. A number of spoken language understanding platforms take the approach of intent recognition and entity extraction, including Api.ai, Wit.ai, Amazon Alexa, and Microsoft LUIS.

User Modeling. The methodology that we have developed for modeling the user's intention considers user intention as the predicted next user action to fulfill their objective in the dialog. It is computed taking into account the information provided by the user during the dialog and the last system turn.

The formal description of the proposed model is as follows. Let A_i be the output of the dialog system (the system answer) at time i, expressed in terms of dialog acts. Let U_i be the semantic representation of the user intention. We represent a dialog as a sequence of pairs (A_i, U_i), where A_1 is the system greeting (the first dialog turn), and U_n is the last user turn.

The objective of the user intention recognizer at time i is to select an appropriate user answer U_i. This selection is a local process for each time i, which takes into account the sequence of pairs that precede time i and the system answer at time i. The selection of the most likely user intention $\widehat{U}_i$ at each time i, is made using the following maximization rule: $\widehat{U}_i = argmax_{U_i \in U} P(U_i|UR_{i-1}, A_i)$, where the set U contains all the possible user answers, and UR_i is what we call the *user register* at time i.

The user register is a data structure that, on the one hand, contains information about concepts and attribute values provided by the user throughout the previous dialog history. On the other hand, it contains information regarding the user profile: id, gender, experience, skill level, most frequent objective of the user, a reference to the location of all the information regarding the previous interactions and the corresponding objective and subjective parameters for that user, and the parameters of the user neutral voice.

To recognize the user intention, we assume that two different sequences of states are equivalent if they lead to the same UR and that the exact values for the attributes provided by the user are not significant to determine the user intention. Therefore, the values of the attributes in the UR are coded in terms of three values: 0 (not provided), 1 (provided with high confidence), and 2 (provided with low confidence).

Dialog Management. There is not a universally agreed upon definition of the tasks that the dialog management module has to carry. Traum and Larsson [13] state that dialog managing involves four main tasks: (i) updating the dialog context, (ii) providing a context for interpretations, (iii) coordinating other modules and (iv) deciding the information to convey and when to do it. Thus, the dialog manager has to deal with different sources of information such as the NLU results, database queries results, application domain knowledge, knowledge about the users and the previous dialog history. Its complexity depends on the task and the dialog flexibility and initiative.

The methodology that we propose for the multimodal data fusion and dialog management processes considers the set of input information sources (spoken interaction, external context acquisition, and user intention modeling) by means of a machine-learning technique that extends our proposal for user modeling [5]. In a similar way, we propose the definition of a data structure to store the values for the different input information sources received by the dialog manager along the dialog history. The information stored in this data structure, that we called Interaction Register (IR), is coded in terms of previously described three values, $\{0, 1, 2\}$ for each field.

The information in the IR at each time i is thus generated considering the values extracted from the inputs to the dialog manager along the dialog history.

Each slot in the IR can be usually completed by means of an input modality or by the use of the external context. If just one value has been received for a specific dialog act, then it is stored at the corresponding slot in the IR using the described codification. Confidences scores provided by the modules processing each input modality are used in case of conflict among the values provided by several modalities for the same slot. Thus, a single input is generated for the dialog manager to consider the next system response. The predicted user dialog act and emotional state are also incorporated as additional slots of the IR. After applying the above considerations, the selection of the best system response A_i is given by $\hat{A}_i = \text{argmax}_{A_i \in \mathcal{A}} P(A_i|IR_{i-1}, A_{i-1})$.

As in our proposal for user modeling, we propose the use of a classification process to determine the next system response given the single input that is provided by the interaction register after the fusion of the input modalities and also considering the previous system response. This way, the current state of the dialog is represented by the term (IR_i, A_{i-1}), where A_{i-1} represents the last system response. The values of the output of the classifier can be viewed as the a posteriori probability of selecting the different system responses given the current situation of the dialog.

Natural Language Generation. Natural language generation is the process of obtaining texts in natural language from a non-linguistic representation. It is usually carried out in five steps: content organization, content distribution in sentences, lexicalization, generation of referential expressions and linguistic realization. It is important to obtain legible messages, optimizing the text using referring expressions and linking words and adapting the vocabulary and the complexity of the syntactic structures to the user's linguistic expertise. The simplest approach consists in using predefined text messages (e.g. error messages and warnings). Although intuitive, this approach completely lacks from any flexibility. The next level of sophistication is template-based generation, in which the same message structure is produced with slight alterations. In some cases, the methods of canned text and templates are not sufficient for generating an appropriate response. For example, statistical approaches have been proposed if the contents to be output need to be structured in such a way that it is easy for the user to understand.

3.2 Decision Agents

The previously described process allows to model every task in which the dialog manager takes its decisions based only in the information provided by the user in the previous turns and its own model. This is the case of most slot-filling conversational systems. In other systems, the dialog manager generates the following system answer taking into account also the information generated by the results of the queries to the data repositories or module that controls the application (which we will note as the *Application Manager*, *AM*). For example, the *AM* can validate restrictions, apply privacy policies or carry out computations which define the next system response (for instance, select a different system action depending on the result of a query to the databases of the application). Thus, the output of this module has to be taken into account for the selection of the best system action. For this reason, we have decided that for this kind of tasks, decision agents are required for the selection of the next system action.

The decision agent generates the final system answer ($\hat{A}_{2_i}$) taking into account the response provided by the corresponding expert agent ($\hat{A}_{1_i}$) and the information provided by the AM (AM_i): $\hat{A}_{2_i} = \text{argmax}_{A_{2_i} \in \mathcal{A}_2} P(A_i|AM_i, A_{1_i}$. The final system action is provided to the user by means of the multimodal response generation and TTS processes of the expert agent selected to generate the $\hat{A}_{1_i}$ response.

4 Practical Application

Let's Go is a spoken dialog system developed by the Carnegie Mellon University to provide bus schedule information in Pittsburgh at hours when the Port Authority phones are not carried out by operators (7 pm to 7 am on weekdays and 6 pm to 7 am on weekends). The information provided by the system covers a subset of 5 routes and 559 bus stops. In 2009, a corpus of 338 dialogs acquired with real users was distributed among the scientific community as a common testbed for the 2010 Spoken Dialog Challenge (SDC) initiative [1].

We have chosen the Let's Go task to evaluate our proposal for several reasons. Firstly, the corpus available was gathered from a real task in an operative dialog system that provided its service to real users. This poses a challenge to build realistic user models and find new dialog strategies that are at least as good as the hand-crafted system. Secondly, Let's Go is a common ground for experimentation and evaluation within the dialog system community, which therefore makes our results directly comparable to the alternatives presented by other authors, and this is why it has been intensively used by researchers in the last years [12].

A total of 16 categories of user dialog acts were defined. Four of the dialog acts are used to model where the user is leaving from (monument, pair of road names, neighborhood, or stop). The four dialog acts used for modeling the place of arrival are similar. Six dialog acts are used for describing the user's required time of travel (next bus or specific times). The *meth* node describes whether the user is asking for a bus with some constraints, is finished or wants to restart. The dialog act *disc* models how the user issues "discourse" actions, which relate to only one turn in a dialog.

A total of 36 system dialog acts were defined. These dialog acts can also be classified into 5 groups: *formal* (dialog formalities like "welcome"), *results* (presentation of search results), *queries* (request for values to fill slots), *statusreports* (when the system reports about its status, e.g. "looking up database"), *error* (error messages), and *instructions* (instructions to the user how to speak to the system).

Regarding the languages and technologies, the core of the multi-agent system has been implemented in Java. The Android Speech APIs have been used for automatic speech recognition and the Api.ai platform to develop the spoken language understanding module. The user intention, emotional state and dialog models have been learned using the previously described training corpus containing 338 dialogs. Finally, the responses provided by the conversational system are transformed into speech using Nuance Loquendo TTS.

To assess the benefits of our proposal, we have compared the developed multi-agent system with the initial system developed for the Let's Go task [1]. In order to do so, 30 recruited users participated in the evaluation, aged 21 to 69 (mean 37.2), 69% male. A total of 120 dialogs was recorded from the interactions of the recruited users, 15 users employed the multi-agent system and 15 users employed the baseline version of the system. The users were provided with a brochure describing the scenarios that they were asked to complete and main functionalities of the system. A total of 38 scenarios was defined to specify a set of objectives that had to be fulfilled by the user at the end of the dialog and they were designed to include and combine the complete set of services provided by the system.

We considered the following high-level measures for the comparative assessment: (i) Dialog success rate; (ii) Dialog length: average number of turns per dialog, number of turns of the shortest dialog, number of turns of the longest dialog, and number of turns of the most observed dialog; (iii) Different dialogs: percentage of different dialogs with respect to the total number of dialogs, and number of repetitions of the most observed dialog; (iv) Turn length: average number of actions per turn; (v) Participant activity: number of turns in the most observed, shortest and longest dialogs; (vi) Confirmation rate, computed as the ratio between the number of explicit confirmation turns and the total number of turns in the dialog; and (vii) Error correction rate, computed as the number of errors detected and corrected by the dialog manager divided by the total number of errors.

Table 1 presents the results of the evaluation. As can be observed, both systems could interact correctly with the users in most cases. However, the multi-agent system obtained a higher success rate, improving the initial results by a value of 5% absolute. Using the multi-agent system, the average number of required turns is also reduced from 12.1 to 9.3.

These results show that improving the dialog strategy made it possible to reduce the number of necessary system actions to attain the dialog goals for the different tasks. In addition, the results show a higher variability in the dialogs generated with the multi-agent system as there was a higher percentage of different dialogs and the most observed dialog was less repeated. There was also a slight increment in the mean values of the turn length for the dialogs collected with the multi-agent system due to the better selection of the system actions in the improved strategy.

The confirmation and error correction rates were also improved by using the multi-agent system as it required less data from the user, thus reducing the number of ASR errors. A problem occurred when the user input was misrecognized but it had high confidence score, in which case it was forwarded to the dialog manager. However, as the success rate shows, this problem did not have a remarkable impact on system performance.

Table 1. High-level dialog measures obtained for the multi-agent and baseline systems. Dialog success rate (M_1), Average number of turns per dialog (M_2), Percentage of different dialogs (M_3), Repetitions of the most observed dialog (M_4), Average number of actions per turn (M_5), Number of user turns of the most observed dialog (M_6), Confirmation rate (M_7), Error correction rate (M_8)

	Baseline system	Multi-agent system
M_1	89.0%	94.0%
M_2	12.1	9.3
M_3	77.8%	87.2%
M_4	6	3
M_5	1.2	1.5
M_6	5	4
M_7	39%	36%
M_8	0.88%	0.93%

5 Conclusions and Future Work

In this paper, we have contributed a multi-agent architecture that can be used to develop adaptive conversational interfaces. In our proposal, a set of expert agents specialized in concrete domains facilitate the access to different knowledge sources, and a set of decision agents interact with the expert agents to coordinate them and provide a user-adapted response to the user. The decisions taken to develop the different modules of these agents have been carefully designed so that the proposal can be portable across domains and applied to develop conversational systems with varying complexity. To adapt the interaction, our proposal integrates a statistical methodology for user modeling that anticipates the next user turn during the dialog and also allows considering their emotional state as valuable information sources for the dialog management process. This module selects the next system response taking into account these predictions and the history of the dialog up to the current dialog state.

For future work we plan to apply the proposed technique to other tasks in order to see whether it can be used for comparison between several user models and dialog management techniques. We also intend to extend the evaluation of the system considering user profiles and satisfaction measures that complement the proposed adaptation and the statistical measures employed.

Acknowledgments. This work was supported in part by Projects TRA2015-63708-R and TRA2016-78886-C3-1-R.

References

1. Black, A., Burger, S., Langner, B., Parent, G., Eskenazi, M.: Spoken dialog challenge 2010. In: Proceedings of SLT 2010, pp. 448–453 (2010)

2. Eisman, E., Navarro, M., Castro, J.: A multi-agent conversational system with heterogeneous data sources access. Expert Syst. Appl. **53**, 172–191 (2016)
3. Glass, J., Polifroni, J., Seneff, S.: Multilingual language generation across multiple domains. In: Proceedings of ICSLP 1994, pp. 983–986 (1994)
4. Goddeau, D., Brill, E., Glass, J., Pao, C., Phillips, M., Polifroni, J., Seneff, S., Zue, V.: Galaxy: A human language interface to online travel information. In: Proceedings of ICSLP 1994. pp. 707–710 (1994)
5. Griol, D., Callejas, Z., López-Cózar, R., Riccardi, G.: A domain-independent statistical methodology for dialog management in spoken dialog systems. Comput. Speech Lang. **28**(3), 743–768 (2014)
6. Lee, G., Kim, H.K., Jeong, M., Kim, J.: Natural Language Dialog Systems and Intelligent Assistants. Springer, Switzerland (2015)
7. McTear, M.F., Callejas, Z., Griol, D.: The Conversational Interface: Talking to Smart Devices. Springer, Switzerland (2016)
8. Ota, R., Kimura, M.: Proposal of open-ended dialog system based on topic maps. Procedia Technol. **17**, 122–129 (2014)
9. Pazos, R., Gonzalez, J., Aguirre, M., Martinez, J., Freire, H.: Natural language interfaces to databases: an analysis of the state of the art. In: Castillo, O., Melin,P., Kacprzyk, K. (eds.) Recent Advances on Hybrid Intelligent Systems. SCI, vol. 451, pp. 463–480. Springer, Heidelberg (2013)
10. Pieraccini, R.: The Voice in the Machine: Building computers that understand speech. MIT Press, Cambridge (2012)
11. Polifroni, J., Seneff, S.: GALAXY-II as an Architecture for Spoken Dialogue Evaluation. In: Proceedings of LREC 2000, pp. 725–730 (2000)
12. Schmitt, A., Ultes, S., Minker, W.: A parameterized and annotated spoken dialog corpus of the CMU let's go bus information system. In: Proceedings of LREC 2012, pp. 3369–3375 (2012)
13. Traum, D., Larsson, S.: The information state approach to dialogue management. In: Current and New Directions in Discourse and Dialogue, pp. 325–353. Kluwer (2003)
14. Wang, C., Glass, J., Meng, H., Polifroni, J., Seneff, S., Zue, V.: Yinhe: a mandarin chinese version of the galaxy system. In: Proceedings of Eurospeech 1997 (1997)
15. Wang, C., Seneff, S.: Lexical stress modeling for improved speech recognition of spontaneous telephone speech in the JUPITER domain. In: Proceedings of EuroSpeech 2001 (2001)

Finding Communities in Recommendation Systems by Multi-agent Spatial Dynamics

Leire Ozaeta and Manuel Graña(✉)

Computational Intelligence Group, Dept. CCIA,
University of the Basque Country, Leioa, Spain
manuel.grana@ehu.eus

Abstract. We have designed a multi-agent dynamic systems that move in a virtual space according to repulsive and attractive forces that are defined from the complex network structure. In our approach we consider that each agent does not have access to the information about the general structure of the network, because it is non attainable to have a complete representation of the network inside each agent, but only searches for its first order connections. The links to each of its neighbors conditions the movement of the agent, pulling it by attractive forces. This dynamical system reaches an stable global state where agents tend to form clusters that correspond to high order connections in the network. We apply this approach to Amazon's similar product's network, based in the "client who bought this also bought that" feature looking for hidden product communities that break through the immediate categorization of products given a catalog. We report preliminary results of simulations carried out in Netlogo.

1 Introduction

Complex networks are widely used to represent a broad spectrum of systems ranging from the World Wide Web to biological networks, social networks [10] or the emerging Internet of Things [5]. Anything that can be modeled as a graph whose nodes are mapped to entities that can be objects or people, and whose edges represent relationships between entities [4,6]. There are a number of global properties that can be computed for diverse applications, such as the propagation of effects that can be diseases in the population, or influence in social systems, or local measures such as the centrality of a node. For example, trust prediction in social networks endowed with some kind of web of trust applies predictive modeling by machine learning. In general many such computational problems are combinatorial in nature, so that they computational complexity makes them intractable as the size of network increases. Hence, many research efforts have been directed to the proposal of heuristics (or meta-heuristics) for their approximate solution. Usually, computing these properties is posed as an optimization problem, e.g. the minimal subset of nodes with the influence maximization. Then, the exact solution of problem corresponds to the global optimum of the

F.J. Martínez de Pisón et al. (Eds.): HAIS 2017, LNAI 10334, pp. 577–587, 2017.
DOI: 10.1007/978-3-319-59650-1_49

cost function modeling the problem, which often requires NP-complete computational effort, or exponential in the number of the nodes, so that scalability of the approaches is seriously compromised when the number of nodes grows. Taking into consideration social networks, the number of nodes has grown in the last years to the order of billions. Approximate solutions aim to get good local optima in an affordable computational time. Often it is not possible to provide guarantees about how close to the global optimum found by the heuristics are these local optima.

Communities are subsets of the set of nodes sharing some property. The straightforward graph-theoretical based definition of a community is a subset of nodes that define a completely connected subgraph. It is also possible to relax the conditions on the density of the subgraph to find diverse degrees of approximation to such communities. Less evident communities appear making induction from attributes of the nodes or the edges of a meta-network based on similarity measures computed over these attributes. In this regard, community discovery is not very different from clustering. Recommendation systems follow this approach in order to offer likely alternatives to the users. Finally, hidden communities may appear when we deal with higher order connections, i.e. when we consider that two nodes are connected if there is a path of arbitrary length between them. This is the kind of communities we are dealing with in this paper.

Intended Contribution. The aim of the work in this article, is to propose a multi-agent dynamic system whose simulations provide a visual representation of hidden communities existing in a graph when high order connections (paths of length greater than one) are considered. We demonstrate the approach on the network extracted from the Amazon recommendation system, where edges are defined on the basis of the "client that bought this also bought that" feature, so that edges represent non causal concurrent purchases. Each agent corresponds to a product, and has information about its nearest neighbors in the graph of recommendations. Every agent has position in a virtual space, and it is moving according to the spatial proximity of its recommendation nearest neighbors. The system dynamics tends to form spatial clusters of related products, regardless of their geodesic distance over the recommendation graph. We report results showing significant hidden communities from the recommendation graph, with strong second order connections and agents with multiple but weak connections to numerous communities. Random starts demonstrates the robustness of the approach, where membership to communities repeats in several repetitions regardless of initial position of agents.

The paper contents are as follows: Sect. 2 gives an overview of related works in the literature. Section 3 describes the multi-agent system model and how the network is mapped into it to discover hidden communities. Section 4 describes the experimental designs of our simulations and describes the dataset over which we have demonstrated the approach. Section 5 provides some preliminary results of the analysis. Finally, Sect. 6 gives some conclusions.

2 State of the Art

The identification of communities in complex networks is a non trivial problem that has been attacked in many different ways, because exhaustive search methods are impractical and local methods are more computationally efficient leading to good approximate results. The use of agents was already proposed by [2], who proposed a kind of modular computational approach, decomposing the graph and feeding the parts to independent agents who processed the subgraphs concurrently. Local processing provided interesting results at the global level for some kind of sparse networks.

The use of heuristics to obtain approximate good solutions in a reasonable time has been a strong research track. The use of self-organized bio-inspired agents with local knowledge of the graph structure has been proposed [3] achieving good results with very simple agent definitions. However, this approach is more like a colony of agents traveling over the graph, which poses problems of scalability and distributed processing of the data collection. Another swarm based approach is described in [6], where some kind of friendship relation is propagated through the graph by swarm agents that posses some kind of graph reasoning intelligence based on the local structures of the graph. This swarm intelligence is able to decompose the graph autonomously in order to produce a local processing, which is robust to community overlapping allowing multiple community membership. A more graph theory based approach in [11] looks for the core nodes in the potential communities, so that community detection is an expansion from the core node, which are detected on the basis of conventional graph centrality measures. Centrality distances are also used in [8] to find out communities, however their approach is not amenable to parallel processing, and it has low scalability. Another such graph theoretical approaches is proposed in [1], using measures of node closeness in order to achieve overlapping community detection. These measures are computed by independent agents feeding of partitions of the network. Seed node analysis is carried out in [7] in a process much like a influence maximization process.

Evolutionary algorithms have been also applied to overlapping community detection, as metaheuristics for the search of optimal partitions of the graph. In [9] multi cultural population algorithms are proposed with good results. A multi-agent genetic algorithm has been also proposed [4] where a decomposition of the network is feed to evolutionary agents living in a lattice-like structure and carrying their search concurrently for local communities.

3 Model

Our multi-agent system model assume a collection of N agents $A = \{a_i\}_{i=1}^N$, each agent a_i is characterized by spatial position in a virtual space $P_i \in \mathbb{R}^2$, and it is endowed with a list of similar agents $\{S_i \subseteq A\}_{i=1}^N$, and a list of objective agents $\{O_i \subseteq A\}_{i=1}^N$. The dynamics of the system are as follows:

1. In the initial configuration, the agents are randomly placed in the virtual arena at positions $P_i(0)$. The list of objectives of each agent $O_i(0)$ is initialized with all the similar agents in the S_i list, ordered from nearest agent to farthest in the virtual space. A list of linked agents is empty at the beginning $L_i(0) = \emptyset$.
2. Simulation is carried out in discrete time steps. At each time instant t the new positions of the agents are recomputing according to the following rules:
   (a) Each agent selects an objective agent $o_i(t)$, which is the first element of O_i. Then it moves towards it according to the following equation

   $$P_i(t+1) = P_i(t) + \Delta(P_i, P_o, L_i(t)),$$

   where P_o is the position of the selected object agent o_i, and $\triangle(P_i, P_o, L_i)$ computes the motion vector in the next step taking into account the agent position, the position of the objective agent P_o, and the ties to previously linked agents L_i. This function tries to move the agent towards the objective but trying to remain close to the linked agents. It has this expression:

   $$\triangle(P_i, P_o, L_i) = (1-\gamma)(P_i - P_o) + \gamma \sum_{k \in L_i} (P_i - P_k) + \eta,$$

   where $\gamma \in [0,1]$ is the weight of the attraction of the linked agents, and η is a random perturbation following a normal distribution $\mathcal{N}(0,\sigma)$.
   (b) Agent a_i and its objective $o_i(t)$ become linked when their proximity is below certain threshold, i.e. $\|P_i(t+1) - P_o\| < \theta$. Then the objective agent is removed from the list of objectives $O_i(t+1) = O(t) - \{o_i(t)\}$, and a tie is included in the set of links $L_i(t+1) = L_i(t) \cup \{o_i(t)\}$. These ties are visualized as white edges linking the agents in the system configuration visualization.
   (c) When an agent has reached all its targets, i.e. $O_i(t) = \emptyset$, then the motion equation is simplified to

   $$\triangle(P_i, L_i) = \gamma \sum_{k \in L_i} (P_i - P_k) + \eta,$$

   where $\gamma \in [0,1]$ and η are defined as before.
3. Simulation stops when some time limit is reached or when all the agents have achieved all the objectives.

The agents behavior is similar to a game of collecting prices that are moving targets. However, prices are not collected in a bag forcing them to remain attached to the collector, because there are no winners o losers, there is no subordination of one agent to another. The only effect is that having collected a prices, there some restriction of movement due to a kind of affective link, that pulls the linked agents to be together. Therefore "popular" agents have a lower degrees of freedom, they are dragged by their prices. Hence, as the game evolves agents move more slowly and eventually become almost static even if they have not picked all the target prices. The random perturbation in the dynamics may remain the only motion force in the system when it becomes stagnant. It is nevertheless introduced in order to disentangle ties and to add some ability to perform random motions for improved exploration of the space.

In the visualization of the system behavior the agents with empty O_i list are assigned the red colour except if they have more than 20, 50, or 100 links when they are assigned the orange, yellow, and white colour respectively. Also, the links are visualized as white edges,

Given a graph $G = (V, E)$ where $V = \{v_i\}_{i=1}^{N}$ is the set of nodes, and $E \subseteq V \times V$ the edges between nodes, each agent represents a node, so that we define a bijective map is defined between the sets A and V. The nearest neighbors of a vertex v_i are given by $NN_i = \{k \,|(v_i, v_k) \in E\}$, in our approach they become the similar agents $S_i = NN_i$. Under this settings, the multi-agent system dynamics work towards finding communities based on the high order connections between nodes. In other words, the agents move into space in order to create clusters, and they are dragged by their attraction to neighborhoods of greater order by the link term in the definition of the $\triangle ()$ function. Eventually, in the stationary state, agents are grouped according those high order neighbourhoods.

The main advantage of the approach is that it is able to find global properties of the graph G using only local information known by each node. Therefore the system has good scalability properties.

4 Experimental Design

We have taken the experimental dataset from KONECT (Koblenz Network Collection)[1] which is a repository of large network datasets of all kinds, made public in order to foster research in network science and related fields. KONECT contains 235 network datasets of various types (directed, undirected, bipartite, weighted, unweighted, signed and rating networks). Those networks belong to many different areas such as social networks, recommendation systems, hyperlink networks, authorship networks, physical networks, interaction networks and communication networks.

For our experimental work we use the Amazon (MDS) dataset from KONECT. This graph is defined from a co-purchase network based in the "customers who bought this also bought" feature. This network represents non causal concurrent purchases that do not necessarily need to pair products by their nature, as a client is not very likely to buy two different product of the same exact nature, as can be two toasters of a different brand. Nodes represent sold products and the undirected edges between two nodes shows that the corresponding products have been frequently bought together.

The network has a low connectivity degree with a total of 334,863 products as vertices and 925,872 co-purchases as edges. The average number of co-purchases

[1] http://konect.uni-koblenz.de/.

(nearest neighbours) of a product is 5.53. Taking into account network size, we divided it into sub-networks with a maximum of 5,000 edges. These sub-networks had an average number of 3,648.18 (±126.61) vertices and an average connectivity degree of 2.27. Unfortunately, the downloadable dataset does not provide information about the frequency of each purchase or the nature of the products, which prevent us from studying the results under the view of degree of similarity between products or labeling the clusters.

In our experiments we apply our approach to observe the grouping of related products in order to find clusters based in non evident similarities, where product similarity is understood as proximity in the network, and hidden second level connections. The simulations were implemented and carried out in Netlogo, in an torus shaped arena with no close walls, where the next patch to the one further to a wall is the one in the same level from the opposite side, left-right and up-down. We carried out 5 runs for each 5,000 link subnetwork selection and used a proximity threshold of 1 patch. In our very first trials we observe that the system did not allow all the product to achieve connection with all their objectives in a reasonable time, so we run the models until more than 100 ticks were passed without a new link being created. From each simulation we extracted the most connected nodes to compare them with their connection degree in the network, as well as agent number, link number and total of ticks to achieve the certain stability degree. Implementation code will be made available at the research group site www.ehu.es/ccwintco.

5 Results

Our results show two particular groups of agent regarding their final situation:

- members of a compact community, i.e. a community with a strong degree of high order connectivity, and
- in-between agents that are linked to several different communities, apart from agents without clear membership to one group or another. The final position of each agent varied widely from run to run, however the membership to the particular groups remained remarkably invariant.

The two kinds of agents that can be identified at the end of each run as follows:

- the first kind are visualized as red dots, correspond to agents that have achieved to link their products to all their similar products, and particularly there are some that built up tight clusters around them, i.e. "popular" agents.
- The other kind of agents are visualized as blue dots, correspond to agents that have not achieved to link their products to all their similar products.

To observe the link creation during the executions we measured the number of connections over time as to get the system's connectivity's evolution. As it can be seen in the Fig. 1 the number of connections increased quite fast in the first 250 ticks before it softens to converge below the total number of links that

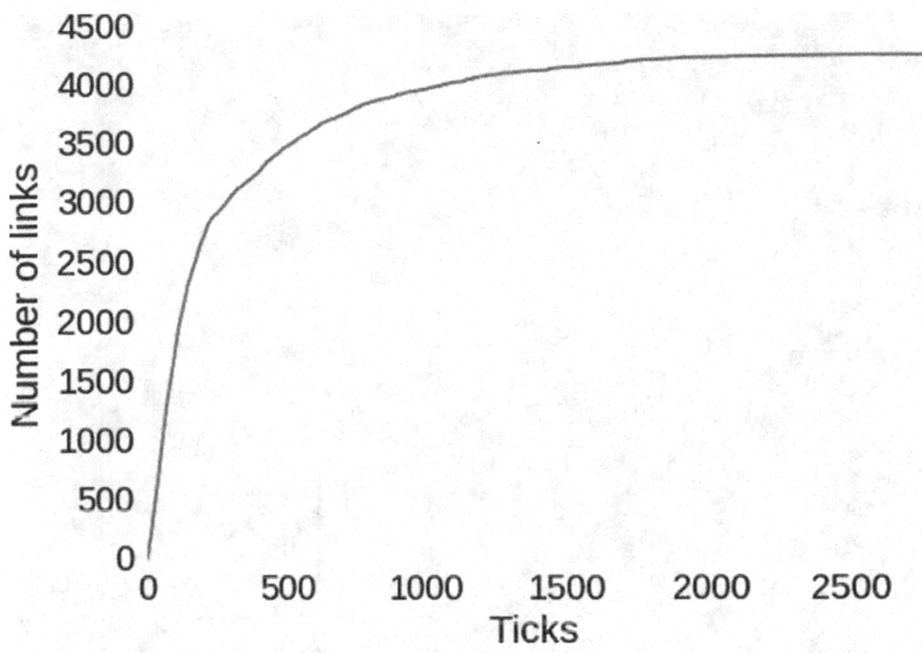

Fig. 1. Number of links created over time.

could be expected. In our simulations the system ended with a high connectivity, achieving the 87.342% of links between products.

Said connectivity was distributed as follows: the 16.91% of the agents remain "un-connected", not being able to establish all the links to similar products. The 1.016% of the agents had a number of connection between 20 and 50, creating small communities. The 0.164% had between 50 and 100 connections and the 0.032% of the agents had more than 100 products connected to them, creating stronger communities that could act as "gravity centers" for less connected products. This more "popular agents" are represented with orange, yellow, and white dots respectively.

Following an example realization is given in Figs. 2, 3, and 4 which are subjected to some postprocessing in order to enhance their clarity. As it can be seen in the Fig. 2 the blue, "un-connected", agents are not grouped and are distributed without clear structure across all the arena. Red, "connected" agents, however, are mostly distributed in more compact groups, many of them with a central "popular" nodes of orange, yellow, or even white color. The clusters created by the connected agents are more clearly seen in Fig. 3 where the "un-connected" agents are removed. In order to achieve even a more clear visualization of the clusters, and define their shape better, we removed the agents in any patch with less than three agents on them. This is observable in Fig. 4, where the clusters are clearly defined. Notice that some popular agents disappear because they are

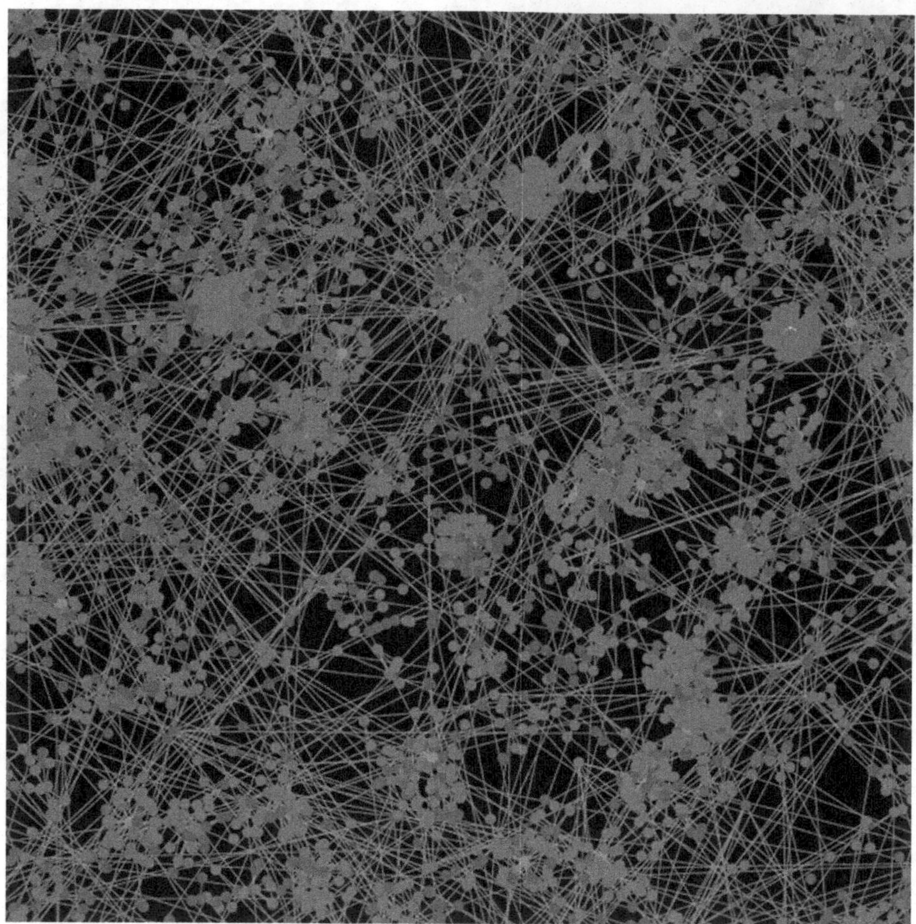

Fig. 2. Final configuration of a multi-agent systems simulation showing all connections. (Color figure online)

the only ones in their patch though they are surrounded by their community in the neighboring spatial patches.

Our claim that we are achieving high order connection communities is visually reflected in the abundance of the white edges that link similar products that have been found the agents but that have not impede the agents to move to other communities composed of agents which are not nearest neighbors, hence the high order communities emerge from the system dynamic interaction. We are carrying out detailed analysis regarding the connectivity properties of the stable states, to test numerically this hypothesis.

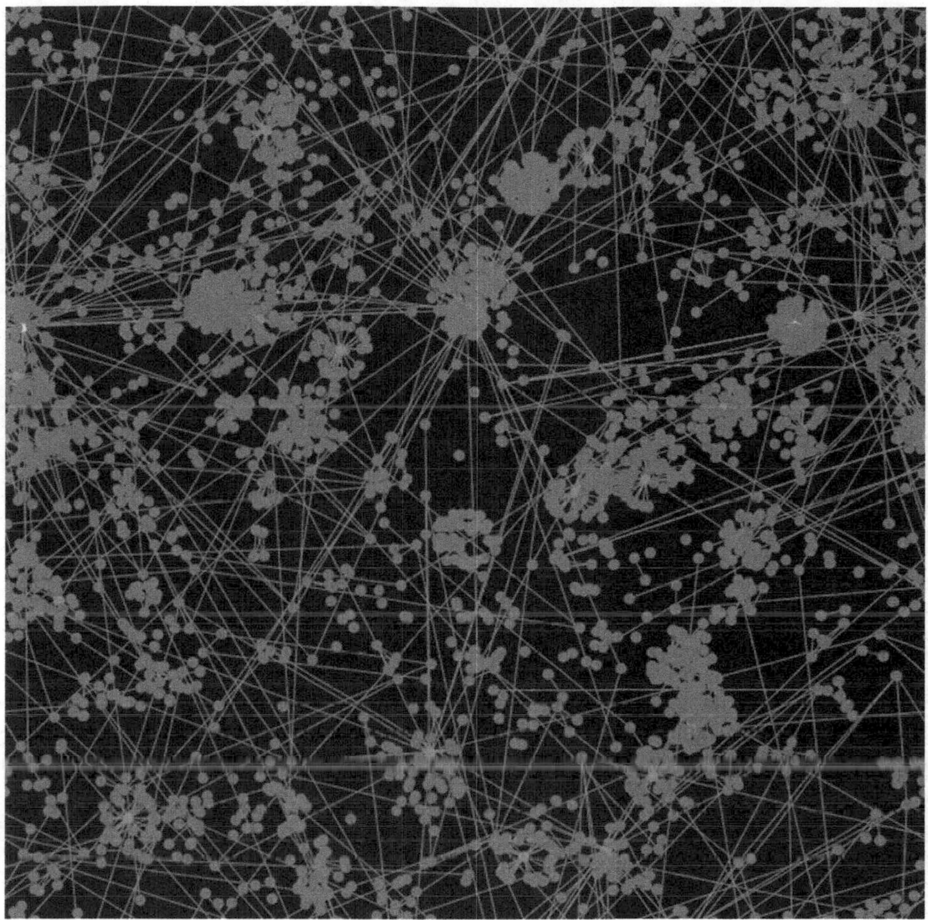

Fig. 3. Final configuration of a multi-agent systems simulation showing all connections removing connections and connections that are not totally connected. (Color figure online)

6 Discussion and Conclusions

Even with the lack of information about the nature of each product our model shows that the products can be arranged in clusters based on their proximity and that, in this clusterization, some products will not be able to reach all their closest neighbors of the original graph, while others will be hard-linked to even those which are second level connections in the network. This reveals hidden communities of products, mostly reunited around a particularly node that acts as central product, and identifies "versatile" products, that are linked to different communities and do not show a closeness to even it's first level connections in the original network. This information can be useful to e-commerce sites, as

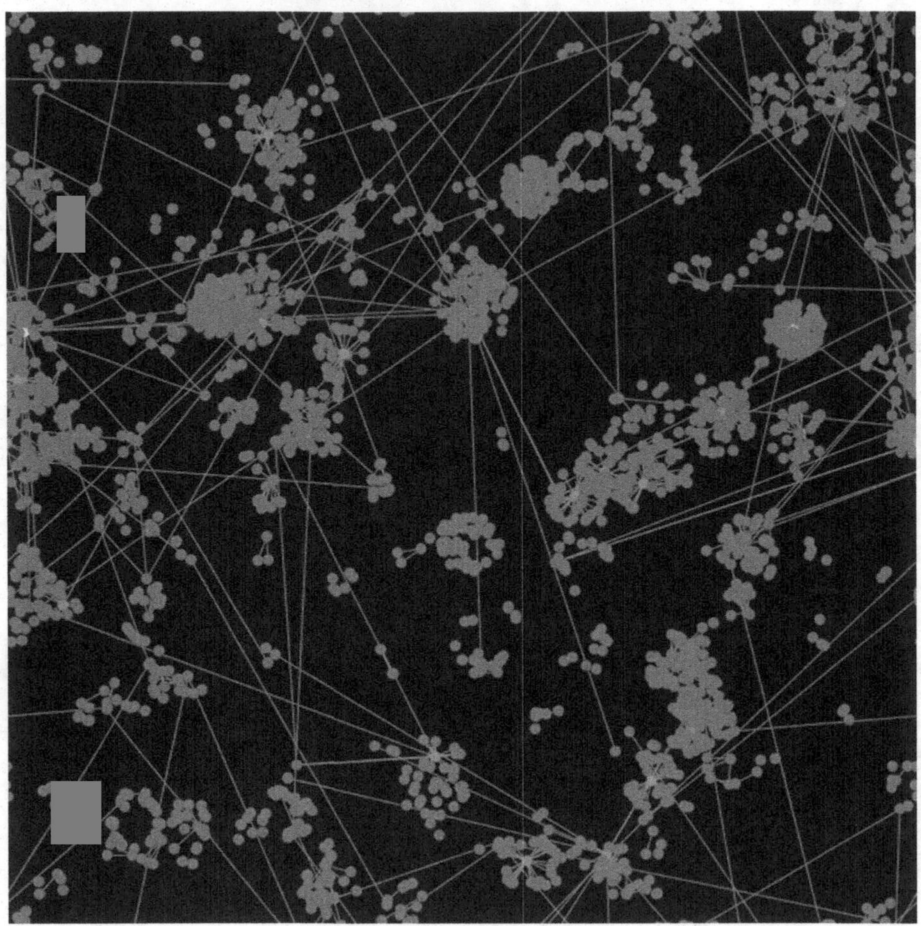

Fig. 4. Final configuration of a multi-agent systems simulation without totally connected products or patches with less than 3 agents on them

their "client who bought this also bought" system could be improved based on if the product is part of a hidden community, and therefore less probable for it to be connected to other products outside it's local community, or a stand-in-the-middle product, connected to different communities. This could help provide the client more accurate recommendations that are not evident from the purchase graph, improving the chances of offering relevant products.

Acknowledgments. Leire Ozaeta has been supported by a Predoctoral grant from the Basque Government.

References

1. Badie, R., Aleahmad, A., Asadpour, M., Rahgozar, M.: An efficient agent-based algorithm for overlapping community detection using nodes' closeness. Phys. Aysica A **392**, 5231–5247 (2013)
2. Clauset, A.: Finding local community structure in networks. Phys. Rev. E **72**, 026132 (2005)
3. Guo, X., Huang, J.: A self-organization method for discovering communities in a distributed network. In: 2013 Ninth International Conference on Natural Computation (ICNC), pp. 90–94. IEEE (2013)
4. Li, Z., Liu, J.: A multi-agent genetic algorithm for community detection in complex networks. Phys. A **449**, 336–347 (2016)
5. Misra, S., Barthwal, R., Obaidat, M.S.: Community detection in an integrated internet of things and social network architecture. In: Global Communications Conference (GLOBECOM 2012), pp. 1647–1652. IEEE (2012)
6. Rees, B.S., Gallagher, K.B.: Overlapping community detection using a community optimized graph swarm. Soc. Netw. Anal. Min. **2**(4), 405–417 (2012)
7. Whang, J.J., Gleich, D.F., Dhillon, I.S.: Overlapping community detection using neighborhood-inflate seed expansion. IEEE Trans. Knowl. Data Eng. **28**(5), 1272–1284 (2016)
8. Wu, L., Bai, T., Wang, Z., Wang, L., Hu, Y., Ji, J.: A new community detection algorithm based on distance centrality. In: 10th International Conference on Fuzzy Systems and Knowledge Discovery (FSKD 2013), pp. 898–902. IEEE (2013)
9. Zadeh, P.M., Kobti, Z.: A multi-population cultural algorithm for community detection in social networks. Procedia Comput. Sci. **52**, 342–349 (2015)
10. Zardi, H., Romdhane, L.B., Guessoum, Z.: A multi-agent homophily-based-approach for community detection in social networks. In: IEEE 26th International Conference on Tools with Artificial Intelligence (ICTAI 2014), pp. 501–505. IEEE (2014)
11. Zhang, T., Wu, B.: A method for local community detection by finding core nodes. In: Proceedings of the 2012 International Conference on Advances in Social Networks Analysis and Mining (ASONAM 2012), pp. 1171–1176. IEEE Computer Society (2012)

Ensemble Trend Classification in the Foreign Exchange Market Using Class Variable Fitting

Andrew Kreimer(✉) and Maya Herman(✉)

Department of Mathematics and Computer Science,
The Open University of Israel, Ra'anana, Israel
kreimer.andrew@gmail.com, maya@openu.ac.il

Abstract. We present a method for ensemble classification of trends in the foreign exchange market using historical data, technical analysis and class variable fitting. We have implemented a complete closed source algorithmic trading platform in Java and MQL. In contradiction to standard concrete price prediction or trend classification, we apply ensemble trend classification and search for optimal class variable. We use single timeframe in contradiction to multiple timeframes analysis approach. We show substantial profitably applying the trading strategies derived by our approach. This paper has two main objectives. The first, to present a new trend definition by expanding the search space for more efficient trading strategies. The second, is to present a new algorithmic trading platform and provide a live trading historical performance rather than back testing results. While previous works in the field tend to incorporate single trading strategy, we show a method for finding multiple trading strategies for various assets.

Keywords: Data Mining · Ensemble classifier · Foreign exchange market · Trend classification · Algorithmic trading

1 Introduction

The Foreign Exchange market is the biggest market in the world in terms of daily traded volume. The huge impact on countries and economies highlights this market as a key point in assessing an economy [11, 16]. The problem we are addressing is the effective trading in the foreign exchange market.

Previous works in the field incorporate several well-known approaches such as price prediction, multiple timeframe analysis and trend classification using technical analysis [1–3, 5, 18, 20]. Trend classification using Machine Learning is a well-known approach in FX (Foreign Exchange) and stock markets analysis. Previous works showed various profitable trading strategies for investment in local currency pairs [2, 17].

Many works have shown significant abilities to predict prices based on historical data analysis [2, 3, 7, 17]. Concrete price prediction in the stock market is another approach for investment [5]. Such methods are usually applicable in HFT (High-Frequency Trading), otherwise market spreads, latency and volatility sum up to losing trading strategies [9, 14]. In this paper we show that trend classification is a long term trading strategy that can be applied for investment in the foreign exchange market.

F.J. Martínez de Pisón et al. (Eds.): HAIS 2017, LNAI 10334, pp. 588–599, 2017.
DOI: 10.1007/978-3-319-59650-1_50

Previous works in the field have shown that multiple time frame analysis is vital for prediction improvement. Multiple timeframe analysis is a well-known method for technical analysis, both for manual and algorithmic trading in FX and stock markets. Previous works showed substantial profitability using such methods, even though replication of features increases dataset cardinality and complexity in real-time trading [17].

The purpose of this paper is to present an effective method for investment in the foreign exchange market by fitting the class variable. In contradiction to the approaches presented in the literature, we span a wider search space testing several class variables, eventually finding better trading strategies. We support our findings by real trading and substantial profitability.

The paper is organized as follows; Sect. 2 overviews our methodology for the problem solving. Section 3 provides concrete platform implementation details. Section 4 presents results of a real trading application. Section 5 provides conclusion and discussion of future improvement and extension.

2 Methodology

The developed system is comprised of two core components: batch offline ETL (Extract Transform Load) and real-time trading engine. The offline batch process is responsible for historical data retrieval and persistence, data preprocessing, feature selection and data mining. Weekly batch process retrieves more than 100 GB of historical data for the past 10 years. Multiple flat files are created for each desired currency pair and Data Mining methods are applied to find the most promising models. Finally, the models are deployed to a shared location for the online trading engine access.

The online trading engine is responsible for concrete live trading using models created by the offline component. In active market hours, the engine receives streams of data: prices, indicators and various key factors. The engine decides for the best next action: what asset to buy or sell. After decision has been made, the engine executes the trade using internal trading API supported by the trading platform. Figure 1 describes the component flows.

Offline flow describes data retrieval and persistence in some DBMS, flat files etc. Then data preprocessing and mining are performed. Eventually the offline flow creates a series of models to be used by the online flow. The offline batch ETL process runs once a week.

Online flow describes the foreign exchange market as a sequence of streams waiting for decision: whether to buy or sell and which assets. Relying on the previously built models, the online flow decides on the best next action and executes a trade or closes a position. All of the trading is logged in the trading platform.

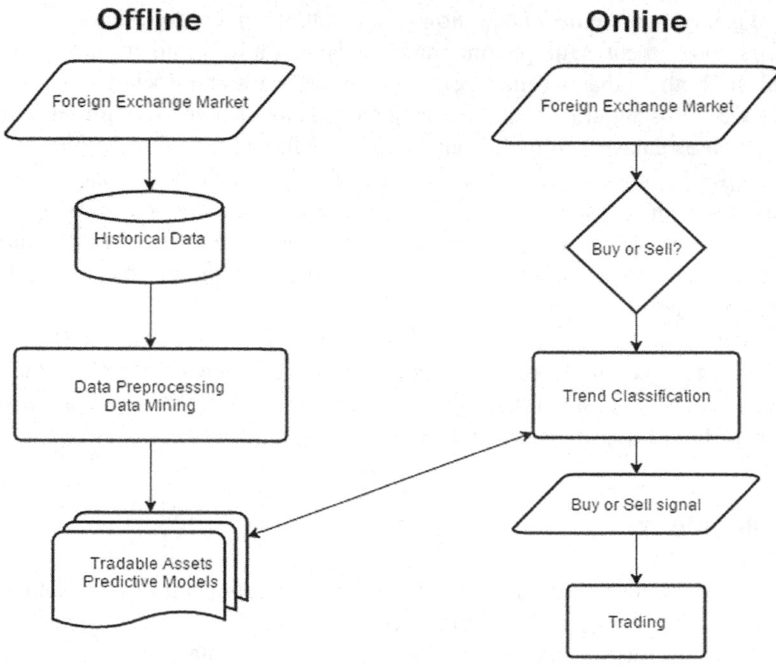

Fig. 1. Offline batch ETL and online trading engine flows.

2.1 Ensemble Classifier

Classification is a Data Mining technique widely used in several enterprise domains such as marketing automation, spam filtering, insurance and trading. The main challenge of a classification algorithm is to find the best generalization function of raw instances and have the smallest error possible when encountering previously unseen instances. Ensemble classifier, sometimes called meta-classifier is a combination of several classifiers which allows better generalization and decision making [10, 15].

Usually ensemble classifier performs majority vote or averages probabilities to make a decision. Wider span of classifier categories provides better classification and generalization abilities. Due to limited number of classifiers, we have been using averaging of probabilities.

Our trading system consists of an ensemble of standard classifiers such as Random Forest with 100 trees and maximum depth set to 10, Logistic Regression with L2 regularization and max iterations set to 100 and Bayesian Network with TAN (Tree Augmented Naïve Bayes) as the structure search algorithm has been incorporated. Note that all of the base classifiers come from completely different classification methods, which have been incorporated in FX market related problems solely, but not as an ensemble. Random Forest is an ensemble classifier build from randomly constructed forests of classification trees. Using random feature subset selection, we avoid over-fitting and allow higher rate of generalization [15]. Logistic Regression is a fast learning classifier incorporating minimization of target loss function. LR performs data normalization and converts nominal attributes to binary attributes (dummy values) using one hot encoding. LR tends to converge faster than other classifiers, although wider data sets in terms of attributes consume higher memory [15]. Bayesian Network is a discrete classification model consisting of DAG and conditional probability tables (CPT) for each feature. Various structure learning techniques are available: K2, TAN, Simulated Annealing, Hill Climbing and more [4].

2.2 Features

We incorporate several widely used technical indicators both in foreign exchange and stocks trading. Technical analysis is a well-known method for assessing tradable assets. Moving averages are a simple aggregation of several past periods for each time slice. Eventually we have a time series of averages. RSI (Relative Strength Index) is a representation of overbought and oversold price levels, usually targeting values higher than 70 as a short signal and values lower than 30 as a long signal. CCI (Commodity Chanel Index) is another bounded indicator with extreme levels of +100 and −100. Bollinger Bands calculate standard deviation for the given period and usually referred to as a price bound. Prices tend to fluctuate mainly within the bands [12].

In this work we have been using all of the available technical indicators supported by the MetaTrader 4 [12] platform to extract wide verity of features. For multiple views of the same market state, we have been using several periods for each indicator such as 7, 14, 21 etc. rather than multiple timeframes [16]. We have been incorporating more than 400 features and feature selection methods such as information gain, gain ratio and correlation, filtering more than 200 features for each dataset [21, 22].

2.3 Data Source

We have been testing several data sources for historical data: Yahoo Finance [19], MetaTrader 5 Terminal [13] and FXCM API [8]. The main principle of Data Mining is that the data source and data quality are key elements of a successful trading system. Yahoo Finance provides daily historical data for all tradable stocks in AMEX, NYSE, NASDAQ, TASE and more. There are 250 trading days in one year. Historical data for the past 10 years is bounded by 2500 records (daily time frame) which are not enough for a proper knowledge discovery [10, 15]. FXCM Java API provides DMA (Direct Market Access) and historical prices. The API supports several timeframes but is limited by the number of records [8]. MetaTrader 5 platform provides free and public FX data for historical periods of more than 10 years in all time frames. In our experiment we have been using MetaTrader 5 as the main data source [13].

2.4 Data Preprocessing

We perform a series of transformations, data sanity checks and data integrity checks. Feature Engineering is incorporated via generation of new nominal features such as key levels of several technical indicators or relations between several moving averages.

We have tested supervised discretization using MDL (Minimum Description Length) or unsupervised binning, eventually adding custom made features as they were better. Normalization is applied for all numerical price like features as prices of different currency pairs and indicators have extremely different cardinalities and ranges. Let us describe several key features engineered in our use case.

Several well-known indicators such as CCI, RSI and Stochastic have over bought and over sold extremes. We have used a manual discretization for the key extreme levels such as 20 and 80 for Stochastic, −100 and +100 for CCI and 30/70 for RSI. Notice that supervised discretization lead to ambiguous extreme levels which tended to over-fit certain market conditions [11, 16].

We incorporate several MA (Moving Average) periods and describe the relations between them: MA A is above MA B or vice versa. We add close price and MA relations: price is above both MAs, price is below both etc. This feature engineering methodology was applied to various MA periods and types such EMA (Exponential Moving Average) etc.

2.5 Defining Class Variable

Standard classification tasks incorporate deterministic class variable. Many use cases provide an obvious target question we are trying to solve. Marketers want to know the estimated CTR (Click Trough Rate). Email services want to classify spam emails. Insurance companies want to estimate the probability of an incident for a given client. The vast majority of papers in the field of predicting the market prices tend to estimate the concrete price or classify the trend [5, 17].

In contrast to the deterministic class variable, in our use case we can optimize for the best trading strategy by searching the best fitted class variable. Trend can be defined in several ways and we can search for the best performance. Notice that in contradiction to the standard trend definition, we are not limited, moreover we turn the problem to be a closed space search optimization in order to find the best trading model.

Zigzag is a lagging technical indicator which encapsulates market fluctuations using calculation of market drop and rise for given levels [11, 16]. Zigzag indicator has 3 input parameters: depth, deviation and back step. The stock market version has only depth and deviation. By modifying the possible combinations, we can find the best class variable and eventually the best trading strategy. Encapsulating in between the high and lows of Zigzag indicator, we create an artificial trend definition. Applying several combinations of period, fluctuation and tradable asset, we are searching for the best fitted models to be used in our real-time trading engine.

We define our binary class variable (Uptrend/Downtrend) as minimum and maximum points of the ZigZag indicator for a specified period. Any maximum point is regarded as an initial short position entry signal and a down trend, until a paired bottom is met. Minimum points of ZigZag are an initial long position entry signal and an uptrend, until the respective maximum point is met and vice versa.

2.6 Data Mining

Dealing with time series data is completely different than non-time dependent instances. We avoid random sampling and cross validation techniques and rely only on custom train and test splits of variable size. We avoid validation sets by constant classifier hyper parameters. We have incorporated several split groups to simulate real market situations. Notice that training is earlier data in time and testing is the most up to date market data. Cross validation or random sampling can deeply influence classifier performance and make a biased illusion of perfect models [14].

We perform batch learning and find optimal assets and models to trade with. Our guideline metrics were AUC, precision and recall [10]. Precision and recall are calculated as the mean for each class category. We search over several trend definitions, keeping models having AUC of no less than 0.95, precision of minimum 0.85 and minimum recall of 0.85. Notice that in our live trading scenario it is very important to have higher recall than higher precision. Higher recall guarantees a better trading performance as a result of constant position in the market. Lower recall and higher precision leads to a poor trading performance comparable to tossing a coin.

3 Implementation

Our trading system relies on several modules. The core decision making element encapsulates ETL and data preprocessing batch jobs written in Java. There are several jobs for data retrieval, data preprocessing and data mining. Our core Machine Learning library is WEKA (Waikato Environment for Knowledge Analysis) [21]. In real time market trading, the classification module provides probabilities for market trends in any given asset (in our use case those are currency pairs). A trading engine performs concrete live trading by external API provided by the broker. The trading engine is implemented in MQL (MetaQuotes Language) under MetaTrader 4 trading terminal [6, 12]. Figure 2 describes a model view controller design pattern (MVC) in our use case.

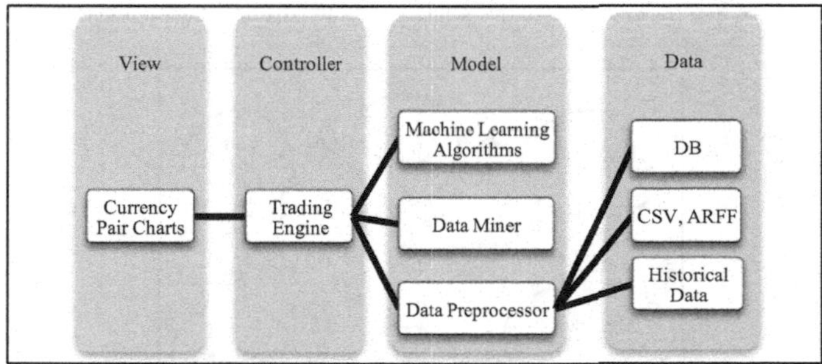

Fig. 2. MVC of an algorithmic trading platform.

- View – Currency pair charts provided by the trading platform. Shows entry and exit points of past orders and current positions. This functionality is provided by the build in charts in MetaTrader 4.
- Controller – A trading engine that connects the model with view. Takes real-time decisions and executes live trading. Implemented in MQL (C like).
- Model – Encapsulates various Machine Learning algorithms as a single ensemble classifier. Performs data preprocessing and transformations regarding the offline batch jobs. Interoperates with several data sources. Mainly uses WEKA for Machine Learning tasks.
- Data – The system is compatible with various data sources such as DBMS, flat files or API. In our use case the data is retrieved by the MetaTrader 5 platform [13].

In contrast to standard Algorithmic Trading methodologies which rely on HFT (High- Frequency Trading), low latency and DMA (Direct Market Access), we incorporate simple infrastructure and rely on single AWS (Amazon Web Services) machine for the trading and single PC for ETL and batch Data Mining. In contrast to standard Algorithmic Trading market execution techniques which rely on fast trading and high number of trades in small amounts such as HFT (High-Frequency Trading), we apply long term trading approach by entering a trade every 4 h. Notice that our method is applicable for retail investors.

4 Experimental Results

Our experiments are comprised of several stages. We begin with massive Data Mining and class variable fitting, then we trade using the best models that were found and finally we compare results and expand to new assets. Eventually we build a generalized and complete method for algorithmic trading investment. Figure 3 presents the iterative optimization method for finding best trading strategies. The optimization stopping criteria is a significant profitability and desired metrics bounds (as described in Sect. 4.1).

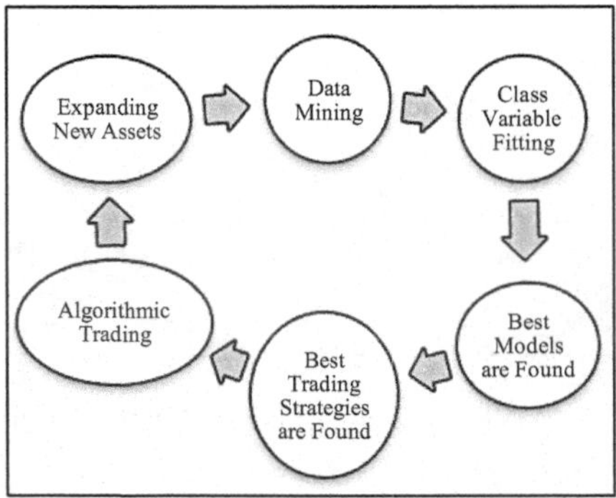

Fig. 3. An iterative optimization method for finding best trading strategies.

The goal of our experiment is to show the efficiency of a trading strategy relying on trend classification using Machine Learning algorithms. Particularly we contradict the concrete price prediction and multiple time frame analysis showing a strong Markov property in the foreign exchange market. We have implemented a complete trading platform for real time trend classification. We have been evaluating the trading strategy using real trading on demo and live accounts with substantial profitability.

Our difference in the problem solution relies on concrete live trading versus back-testing. We apply single time frame for trend classification. Our tests adding more features for multiple time frames showed lower metrics and performance. Eventually we showed that multiple time frames provide less knowledge about the class variable, meaning that the foreign exchange market holds the Markov property: when classifying the current trend, we rely only on the previous timestamp data.

4.1 Model Selection

Let us define the optimal class variable fitting as a closed search problem. In our case we have been incorporating several timeframes and classes to find best fitted models. We have been searching for different dataset sizes, spanning historical periods of several months up to ten years, incorporating several custom made recursive splits: splitting the data set to 90%–10% train-test respectively, followed by another 90%–10% split of the train set alone. We repeat the train-test split for three times in order to converge to a standard split of 70%–30%. This way we create multiple hold out datasets and simulate real time market conditions. Notice that bigger training set is more likely to represent real market condition during real-time trend classification. Also notice that no random split was incorporated as we have been dealing with ascending time series data.

Figure 4 shows H4 EURUSD graph class fitting. Each line represents different split of train and test datasets according to our model selection routine. Notice that the best class is found at the 28–35 period zone, and all of the train-test splits converged closer relative to other class variables such as ClassZZ24Trend or ClassZZ42Trend.

Model selection comparison and class variable fitting show hidden optimal fit zones for various assets. Figure 4 shows gradual period increase and AUC raise until a breakpoint and the optimal class variable period are found. Each line represents different holdout split for training and testing without any classifier parameters change to avoid over-fitting and leakage of biased knowledge into the learning process [15]. We can summarize that such a closed form search leads to finding optimal trading strategies.

4.2 Live Trading

We show a substantial profitably of real market trading 20 currency pairs on H4 charts. We have been using major currency pairs and all possible crosses for USD, EUR, CHF, JPY, CAD, AUD and NZD. The trading was running 5 days a week, 24 h a day starting on 13.03.2016 and ending on 13.06.2016. We have been applying stop loss of 1000

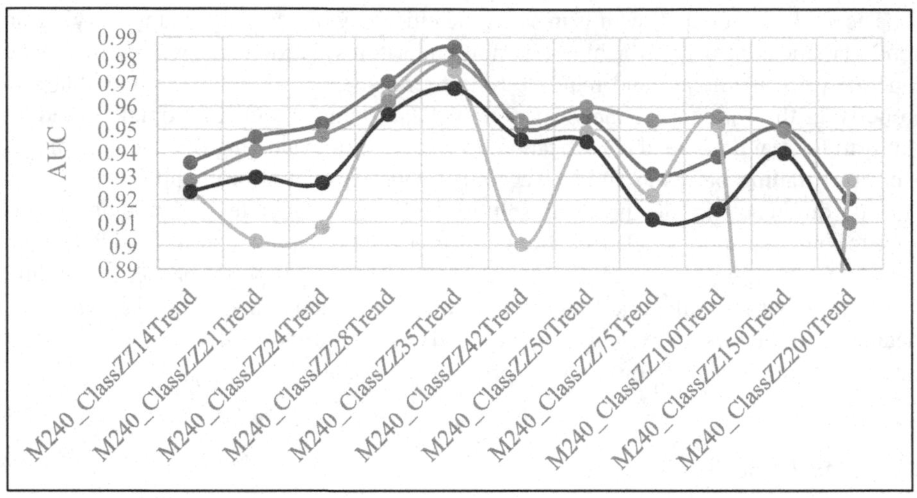

Fig. 4. EURUSD H4 class variable fitting (each line is different train-test split).

pips, take profit of 1000 pips and no more than 10 consecutive trades. We gained 65% profitable shorts, 62% profitable longs and showed ROI of 30% based on 35 K pips profit with maximum drawdown of 15%, average loss of 132 pips, average profit of 131 pips, profit factor of 1.67 and Sharpe ration of 0.22 on 985 trades, indicating a profitable trading system [11, 16]. Pip is the standard smallest currency pair change, usually expressed as 1/1000 for 4/5 digit pairs such as EURUSD and 1/100 for 2/3 digit pairs such as USDJPY.

Figure 5 shows the daily account balance for the period we have been trading in. Notice the positive slope and divergence of balance vs. equity.

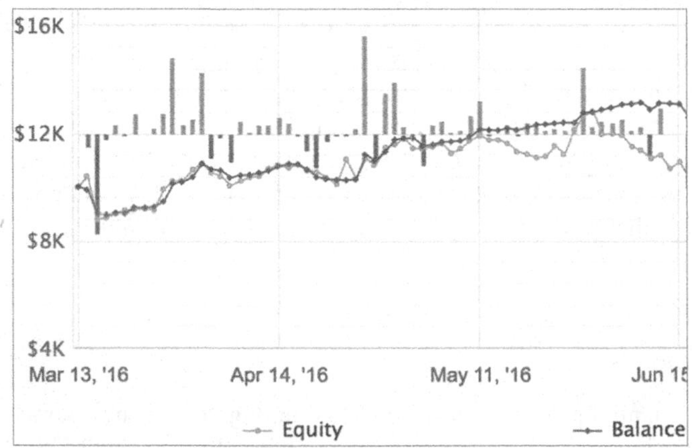

Fig. 5. Daily balance (March–June 2016).

Figure 6 shows a sample real-time classification of trends in the EURUSD 5-minute graph. Each timestamp (black bar) represents a 5-minute slice. Each red arrow represents a strong short signal whereas each blue arrow represents strong long signal. Notice that a consecutive position entry is vital in order to get a higher precision and recall, hence such a trading strategy requires high liquidity.

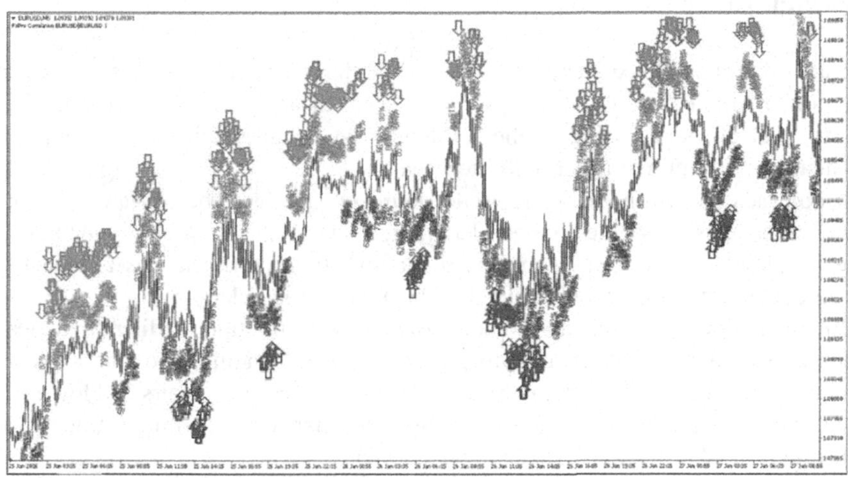

Fig. 6. Predicted trend (red is short and blue is long) vs. real market (black). (Color figure online)

4.3 Running Time

We have been exposed to computational complexity issues in our real time trend classification. First experiments began with 30 min of calculation for decision making on 1 h graph. After several improvements we have reduced the running times to 15 min, 3 min and eventually to no more than 10 s. Our key improvements rely on reducing nominal attributes cardinality to avoid one hot encoding or dummy variables [10]. Notice that real-time classification time deeply varies as a function of instance to be classified. Usually linear models have concrete upper bounds for the real-time classification, while classification trees are subject to instance location within the model.

4.4 Risk Assessment

Let us analyze the risk involved in our trading methodology by analyzing maximum number of losing trades and Monte Carlo simulation benchmarking. Our trading strategy exposes the trading account to a risk of losing 40% of the trades. Trading with 20 currency pairs, 10 trades for each pair, we have 200 maximum positions in our trading account. Trading 985 trades with loss probability lower than 40%, we can bound the probability of multiple losses by the Binomial distribution: $X \sim B(200, 0.4)$. The probability for loosing half of the trades: $P(X \geq 100) < 0.0027$.

Using Monte Carlo simulation benchmarking with 60% win probability with initial capital of 10000, 1000 trades and 10000 trials, revealed 12400 profit mean with 370 profit SD, representing 24% ROI. This simulation is similar to what we have done in the real trading simulation as expected.

5 Conclusions

This paper described the key approaches for algorithmic trading strategies such as price prediction, multiple timeframe analysis and technical analysis. We have presented a case study of efficient trading in the foreign exchange market using ensemble trend classification and optimal trend definition search.

In contradiction to the standard trend definition, we have been searching for the optimal trend class variable in bounded period space. Also, we have incorporated single timeframe in contrast to the usual multiple timeframe analysis approach and showed concrete trading results instead of back-testing simulations.

Our methodology reveals an efficient way to create multiple trading strategies for various assets. We have been avoiding high-frequency trading, showing substantial profitability in the foreign exchange market for multiple currency pairs and low latency trading. This methodology is completely different than the algorithmic trading standards, thus available for retail traders and investors.

In the aspect of algorithmic trading, the model can be extended by additional features and feature engineering. Latency can be reduced by using FIX protocol and DMA trading. Expansion of the stock market is vital having the same data quality level. In the aspect of real-time classification, the model should be extended to faster and distributed solutions such as Python or C++. More classifiers can be added to the ensemble leading to a more accurate trade execution. In the aspect of model selection, we could expand to other metrics and evaluation criteria such as portfolio profitability, alpha and beta.

References

1. Ameen, A.A.: Do Japanese candlestick patterns help identify profitable trading opportunities? M.Sc. thesis, The British University in Dubai (2013)
2. Baasher, A.A., Fakhr, M.W.: Forex trend classification using machine learning techniques. Recent Res. Appl. Inform. Remote Sens. **8**, 41–47 (2012). ISBN: 978-1-61804-039
3. Blackledge, J., Murphy, K.: Forex Trading using MetaTrader 4 with the Fractal Market Hypothesis (2011)
4. Bouckaert, R.R.: Bayesian network classifiers in weka for version 3-5-7. Artif. Intell. Tools **11**(3), 369–387 (2008)
5. Brailovskiy, L., Herman, M.: Prediction of financial time series using Hidden Markov Models. In: The Second ASE International Conference on, Big Data Science and Computing, Stanford University, June 2014. ISBN: 978-1-62561-000-3
6. Chan, L.C., Wong, W.K.: Expert advisor development on MT4/MT5 for automated algorithmic trading on EURUSD M1 data. Finamatrix J., September 2013

7. Cumming, J., Alrajeh, D., Dickens, L.: An Investigation into the Use of Reinforcement Learning Techniques within the Algorithmic Trading Domain (2015)
8. FXCM java API. http://www.dailyfxforum.com/forums/481-Java-Trading-API-Support/
9. Johnson, B.: Algorithmic Trading & DMA: An Introduction to Direct Access Trading Strategies. 4Myeloma Press, London (2010)
10. Larose, D.T.: Data Mining Methods & Models. Wiley, Hoboken (2006)
11. Lien, K.: Day Trading and Swing Trading the Currency Market: Technical and Fundamental Strategies to Profit from Market Moves. Wiley, Hoboken (2008)
12. MetaTrader 4 forex trading platform. http://www.metatrader4.com/
13. MetaTrader 5 forex trading platform. http://www.metatrader5.com/
14. Narang, R.K.: Inside the Black Box: A Simple Guide to Quantitative and High Frequency Trading. Wiley, Hoboken (2013)
15. Russel, S., Norvig, P.: Artificial Intelligence: A Modern Approach. Prentice Hall, Upper Saddle River (2003)
16. Schlossberg, B.: Technical Analysis of the Currency Market: Classic Techniques for Profiting from Market Swings and Trader Sentiment. Wiley, Hoboken (2006)
17. Talebi, H., Hoang, W., Gavrilova, M.L.: Multi-scale foreign exchange rates ensemble for classification of trends in forex market. Procedia Comput. Sci. **29**, 2065–2075 (2014)
18. Wright, J.H.: Bayesian model averaging and exchange rate forecasts. J. Econometrics **146** (2), 329–341 (2008)
19. Yahoo Finance: http://finance.yahoo.com/
20. Yazdi, S.H.M., Lashkari, Z.H.: Technical analysis of forex by MACD indicator. Int. J. Humanit. Manage. Sci. (IJHMS) **1**(2), 159–165 (2013)
21. Hall, M., Frank, E., Holmes, G., Pfahringer, B., Reutemann, P., Witten, I.H.: The WEKA data mining software: an update. SIGKDD Explor. **11**, 10–18 (2009)
22. BestParents: Open source project. https://github.com/algonell/BestParents

A Personality-Based Recommender System for Semantic Searches in Vehicles Sales Portals

Fábio A.P. Paiva[1(✉)], José A.F. Costa[2], and Cláudio R.M. Silva[2]

[1] Federal Institute of Rio Grande do Norte, IFRN, Parnamirim, Brazil
fabio.procopio@ifrn.edu.br

[2] Federal University of Rio Grande do Norte, UFRN, Natal, Brazil
jafcosta@gmail.com, claudio.rmsilva@gmail.com

Abstract. This work proposes a personality-based recommender system to implement semantic searches on Internet Vehicles Sales Portals. The system is based on a typical recommender system architecture that has been extended to combine a hybrid recommendation approach with a machine learning classifier technique (k-NN). It proposes a combination of the Five Factor Model (Big Five Model) with a correlation between car fronts and power and sociability perceptions. A prototype was implemented to answer the semantic searches considering personality-based user's profiles and a set of Brazilian cars. After each search, a questionnaire was provided for the users to verify how successful the recommendations were for them. The prototype received web searches during a period of 15 days. The final report showed that 77.67% of the users accepted the personality-based recommendations, what indicates that the proposed approach could be promising to improve the quality of the recommendations on the user's point of view.

Keywords: Recommender system · Personality traits · Semantic searches

1 Introduction

A recent report [1] has estimated that a massive part of car sales portals users (90%) gather information on the Internet when they think about to buy a car. Considering this group of 90%, something between 20% to 30% of them have visited several web portals in order to compare the information supplied in the different websites before choosing a specific car. Vehicles sales portals offer services that involve more than simple web searches. Some services may be so complex that they could be considered semantic web search services.

Semantic search aims to determine the contextual meaning of the words that a user is using for searching [2]. In general, search engines are evolving towards semantic search in two different ways. The first way is the use of tags or label parts of a webpage. The other way is the use of hybrid approaches using computational intelligence techniques. One of these hybrid approaches is the hybrid recommender system guided by semantic information [3].

F.J. Martínez de Pisón et al. (Eds.): HAIS 2017, LNAI 10334, pp. 600–612, 2017.
DOI: 10.1007/978-3-319-59650-1_51

Recommender systems are filtering systems that seek to predict preferences that user would give to an item. They have emerged as one successful approach to tackle the problem of information overload [4,5]. Recommender systems have become extremely common and they have been applied in a variety of applications. Some of these recommender systems may use optimization techniques such as the ones used by Machine Learning [6], Swarm Intelligence [7] or combinations of them to make smarter recommendations.

A hybrid recommender system typically combines content-based and collaborative methods, but it may also includes other techniques such as the ones used in machine learning or data mining to provide learning functionalities. There are many approaches in the literature considering hybrid recommender systems that are capable of learning in some degree along its operation to provide better recommendations. According to literature, they have used techniques such as Naive Bayes [8], Clustering [9], Neural Networks [10] etc.

Some studies have considered addressing the recommendation problem from the users' psychological characteristics. Personality is an important aspect that influences people's behavior and their interests. These studies have shown a promising opportunity for recommender systems to enhance recommendation quality and user's experience. The question is how to incorporate personality to cars in the context of car sales portal recommender systems.

A possible alternative may be in the recent researches [11–13] about human sensitivity to features in human faces and their information on sex, age, emotions and intentions. In [12], for example, it is demonstrated that automotive features and proportions do covary with trait perception in a manner similar to that found with human faces.

This work proposes a personality-based recommender system to implement semantic web searches to find "best buy opportunities" about cars. The prototype is based on a typical recommender system architecture that has been adapted to include a recommendation engine that combines a hybrid recommendation approach with a machine learning algorithm. The work uses k-Nearest Neighbors (k-NN) to classify the users' personality traits (Five Factor Model) and a correlation between car fronts and personal preferences, according to [12].

The paper is organized as follows: in Sect. 2, it is provided a brief background in order to introduce the basic concepts. Section 3 presents the functionalities of the proposed recommendation engine. Section 4 presents the scenario used for the experiments and discusses the results obtained. Finally, in Sect. 5, the final considerations are presented to conclude the work.

2 Background

Recommender systems provide suggestions of personalized items for users according to their interests. "Item" is a general term used to represent what the system recommends. For example, recommendations are related to many decision-making processes, such as what book to read, what movie to watch, or what vehicle to buy.

In [4], it is proposed a taxonomy that may be used to distinguish recommendation techniques. They are classified in six different categories: (1) collaborative, (2) content-based, (3) demographic, (4) knowledge-based, (5) community-based and (6) hybrid. However, in recent years, several papers have used a new recommendation technique known as personality-based recommendation.

Some researchers [14,15] have considered incorporating personality aspects into recommender systems to personalize recommendations and enhance both recommendation quality and users' experience. Other researches [16–18] believe that machine learning is the answer for the main research problems in recommender systems such as cold start, data sparsity and over-specialization. Cold start refers to the difficulty in bootstrapping the recommender systems for new users or new items. Data sparsity occurs when users in general rate only limited number of items. Over-specialization occurs when the recommended items are similar to those previously rated by the user.

Machine learning is a subfield of computer science that improves computer algorithms with the ability to learn without being explicitly programmed [19]. There are several approaches to combine machine learning with recommender system [20–22]. According to a review [23], the most used algorithms to improve recommender systems are: bayesian networks, decision tree, matrix factorization-based algorithms, artificial neural networks, neighbor-based algorithms and rule learning. The choice for the best machine learning algorithm will depend on the specific application of the recommender system to be developed. This work considers a recommendation engine improved with a machine learning algorithm known as k-NN. It is used as a classifier, so that the output data is associated to a personality traits group.

A semantic search is normally defined as a kind of data searching technique in which a query aims not only to find keywords matches, but to determine essentially the contextual meaning of the words that a user is considering for searching.

Personality is defined as a set of consistent behavior patterns and intrapersonal processes that characterizes individuals and impact on their thinking process and decision making. There are several studies [12,15,24,25] that propose to use personality traits to increase the performance of recommender systems.

In [12], for example, there is an approach that is based on the assumption that every human is unique and all of them have common and individual traits. It considered a methodology in which these individuals were asked to report the characteristics, emotions, personality traits, and attitudes they attribute to car fronts, and then used geometric morphometrics and multivariate statistical methods to determine and visualize the corresponding shape information according these characteristics. The research proved that automotive shapes do covary with trait perception in a manner similar to that found with human faces.

Other approaches use a Five Factor Model personality traits [26] to implement personality-based recommended systems [15,24,25] considering five dimensions used to describe human personality. These dimensions are labeled OCEAN: Openness, Conscientiousness, Extraversion, Agreeableness and Neuroticism.

The main problem with these approaches is that they cannot accurately predict any single specific behavior, since human behavior is based on many dimensions. It is limited and does not help in the understanding of culturally-specific, gender specific and age-specific personality expressions. These limitations suggest that a combination of different approaches should be to implement personality aspects in recommender systems.

3 Proposed Method for Recommendation

This work considers a typical architecture [27] as the starting point to develop a variant approach in which a recommendation engine component is changed to incorporate machine learning capabilities that enable semantic searches behind the car sales portal. It is a hybrid approach to recommend items that considers content-based and collaborative-based recommendations combined with a k-NN algorithm to implement a Recomendation Engine Component that is based on a personality-based context in which semantic searches that are constrained to the personality traits of the users and the cars available in the user's countries.

The recommendation component computes the degree of the users' interest in order to estimate how a vehicle may be interesting for them, according to Eq. 1. A vehicle is considered interesting when the value of the interest exceeds a certain threshold θ ($\theta = 3.0$). The degree of interest is computed based on the priorities defined for the users' profile and it considers the following attributes which are obtained from benchmarks portal: (1) vehicle purchasing price, (2) fuel consumption, (3) insurance price, (4) depreciation index, (5) satisfaction index with authorized dealer, (6) reparability index, (7) standard equipment, (8) reselling price, (9) the vehicle using cost, (10) vehicle warranty and (11) price of auto parts. Equation 1 is used to compute the degree of interest of the user u related to vehicle v.

$$\varphi(u,v) = \frac{\sum_{i=1}^{n} b_i * p_i}{\sum_{i=1}^{n} p_i} \tag{1}$$

where b_i is the evaluation value which is defined by the benchmark portal to attribute i, p_i the weight of the priority that the user associated to attribute i. As the vehicles are evaluated according to 11 benchmarks, then we have defined $n = 11$. Personality-based recommendation utilizes the personality scores to calculate the similarity between users. For this, the recommendation engine component implements k-NN algorithm to find k nearest users, i.e., those with the shortest distance. The metric used to determine the neighborhood of user u is the Euclidean Distance according to Eq. 2.

$$d(u,w) = \sqrt{(p_u^1 - p_w^1)^2 + (p_u^2 - p_w^2)^2 + ... + (p_u^n - p_w^n)^2} \tag{2}$$

where $d(u, w)$ represents the distance between users u and w. Here, the neighborhood of the user u is determined for $k = 3$ and n is the number of attributes used to represent the vector of the user's personality. This vector is defined by the Five Factor Model as $p_u = (p_u^O, p_u^C, p_u^E, p_u^A, p_u^N)$ for user u and, therefore, $n = 5$. In this work, $p_u^O, p_u^C, p_u^E, p_u^A, p_u^N$ represent the values in the dimension of Openness, Conscientiousness, Extraversion, Agreeableness and Neuroticism respectively.

To complement the recommendation process, the component builds a list D containing vehicles that can be used to add diversity in recommendations that are offered for users. The list D is presented as Eq. 3:

$$D = \{v_i | v_i \in G \wedge \varphi(u, v_i) > \theta\} \tag{3}$$

where v_i is a vehicle used to add diversity into recommendation list, G is a set that represents vehicles which the user has sympathy, u is the user who receives recommendations containing diversity, and $\varphi(u, v_i)$ is the interest of u by v_i.

Generally, typical car sales portals perform searches within their databases considering simple attributes such as price, model, mileage, manufacture year and brand. However, other attributes can be used to improve the quality of the recommendations such as reselling price, depreciation index, insurance price, reparability index etc. There is an essential difference between the typical car sales portals and the prototype that is proposed here. The proposed prototype is supposed to collect information from other portals such as car sales ads to increase the possibility of finding updated good offers. Another difference is that the proposed prototype uses ontologies. An ontology defines common vocabulary for people who need to share information in the domain. The use of ontology is a good alternative for sharing understanding of the structure of information among people or software agents, enabling the reuse of the domain knowledge and separating the domain knowledge from the operational knowledge.

The prototype uses also a web robot to extract ads from known car sales portals. Next, it populates the ontologies that represent the necessary information to enable the recommendation. In order to identify good offers for users, the prototype is integrated with three kinds of portals such as references, benchmarks and ads portals. A car sales reference portal centralizes and shares information about minimum, average and maximum price for different cars available in Brazil. They are used as a reference to evaluate the acceptable prices for a specific vehicle searched on the market. A benchmark portal is used to compare cars according to a set of features. This comparison information estimates the better cost-benefit analysis necessary for recommendations. The car sales portals are used to offer ads representing business opportunities for new and used vehicles. For each kind of service, some famous portals in Brazil have been chosen such as FIPE (www.fipe.org.br), QuatroRodas (www.quatrorodas.abril.com.br), OLX (www.olx.com.br), and iCarros (www.icarros.com.br).

FIPE portal is used here as a reference to evaluate the average price of a specific vehicle. QuatroRodas portal is used here to acquire benchmarks. It evaluates many vehicles categories. The evaluation considers the following criteria:

vehicle purchasing price, fuel consumption, insurance price, depreciation index, parts replacements, satisfaction index with authorized dealer, reparability index, standard equipment, reselling price, vehicle using cost, vehicle warranty and price of auto parts. OLX and iCarros portals are used here to provide car sales ads. OLX portal hosts ads in several categories including vehicles. iCarros portal is a specialized in ads to buy and sell new and semi-new vehicles.

A Recommendation Engine is a component inside a typical recommender system architecture that is used to predict items on which a user may be interested in using different techniques based on several different knowledge sources. This component depends on the type of necessary recommendation inside a real application of the architecture.

Figure 1 presents the basic functionality for the new recommendation engine. It shows three subcomponents that implement the recommendation process in three steps to generate two groups of recommendations. They are: (a) ads that match the restrictions defined by the current search and user's preferences (content-based filtering) – moreover, a similarity analysis is performed with information gathered from personality tests for Five Factor Model dimensions (collaborative filtering); (b) ads that match the classifier that associate users according to their preferences to car front shapes and that associate cars [12].

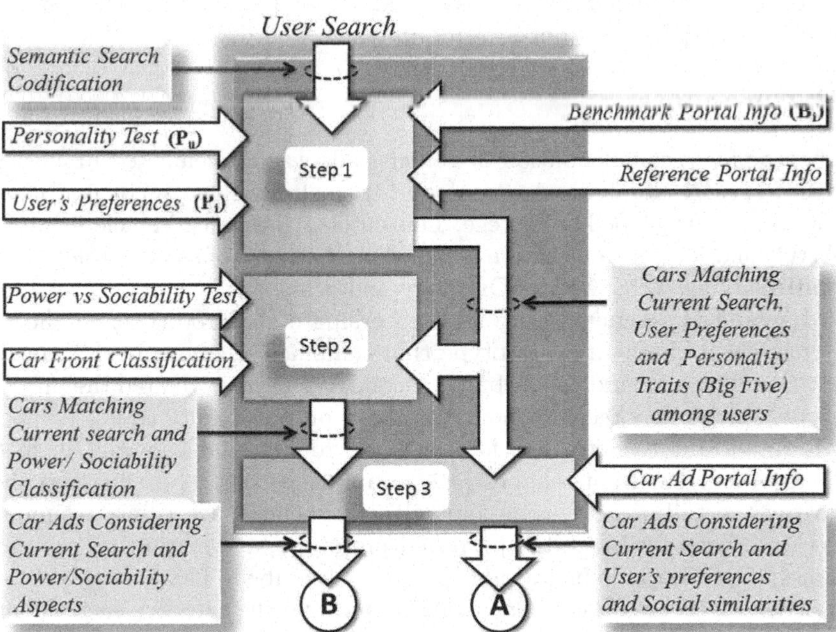

Fig. 1. Recommendation engine component funcionality.

In the first step, the parameters for the search are received from the Internet portal interface. These parameters will be used according to the user's profile and the personality information previously collected from the user. The main objective of this step is to identify a car (or set of cars) that matches the semantic search initially provided on Internet portals. In order to accomplish this objective, the system accesses the benchmark and reference information available on defined links for specialized portals.

Imagine, for example, that the user is asking the following question in the first step: "What is the best sedan for me, considering my profile information, budget (R$ 50,000.00) and personality traits?". The first step is supposed to select, among all the available cars in the sedan category, those cars that are compatible with the budget and personality traits of similar users according to Big Five Model.

In the second step, the main objective is to find alternatives that could improve car recommendations with other personality aspects such as power/sociability association with car front shapes. In order to accomplish this objective, two sets of information are previously collected: (a) information about the users' preference for a degree of variation in a power/sociability personality test; (b) information about how Brazilian cars are classified in an similarity analysis with the cars classified in reference [12]. The output of this step is a car (or set of cars) that complements the set initially provided by step one.

In the last step, a data mining procedure is made on Internet to collect ads for the cars recommended after steps one and two. The final output is supplied to the user by the Internet portal using dynamic web pages.

4 Experiments

A prototype for recommendation of vehicles ads was implemented in Java language and MySQL database. An ontology that includes concepts related to vehicles domain was developed in Protégé. This ontology is named Vehicle Ads Ontology (VAO) and its implementation is based on the reuse of some ontologies such as GoodRelations, Vehicle Sales Ontology and Schema.

Two sets of experiments were used to evaluate the prototype. In the first, the users evaluated a hybrid prototype that combines collaborative filtering and content-based recommendations. In the second, the users evaluated the proposed prototype which offers recommendations based on personality traits.

It is important to note that for each car front available in Brazil, in this work one of four car fronts shapes (1 – narrow and short; 2 – wide and short; 3 – narrow and tall; and 4 – wide and tall) is associated according to similarity aspects. In order to validate the proposed prototype, a scenario that represents a common situation in vehicles sales portal is described. This scenario consists of a user who searches for car ads belonging to a specific category such as hatch, sedan, sport car etc. The implementation of this scenario is shown in Fig. 2.

When the user indicates the year of manufacture (Fig. 2C), the prototype queries the references portal and returns the average price of the vehicle on the national market (Fig. 2D). Next, the user indicates the price range that he/she intends to pay for the selected car (Fig. 2E). Finally, ads portals integrated into the prototype are visited and a recommendation list is produced.

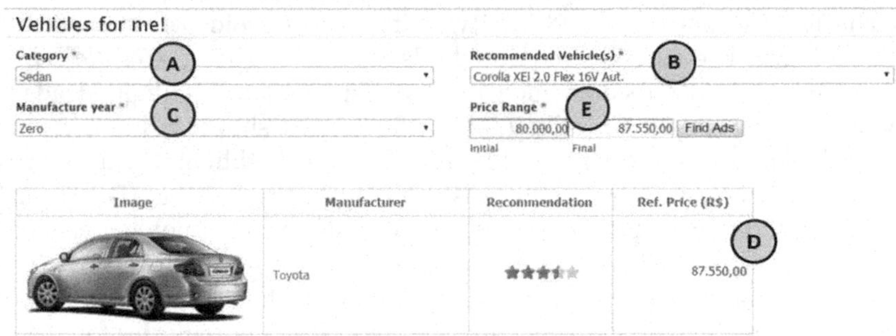

Fig. 2. Searching ads for Toyota Corolla XEi 2.0.

Advertisements for me!

Image	Description	Price	Advertisement
	Toyota Corolla XEi 2.0 Flex 16V Aut. 2016 | 0 Km Automático	R$ 82799	Preview
	Toyota Corolla XEi 2.0 Flex 16V Aut. 2016 | 0 Km Automático	R$ 82990	Preview
	Toyota Corolla XEi 2.0 Flex 16V Aut. 2016 | 0 Km Automático	R$ 84900	Preview
	Toyota Corolla XEi 2.0 Flex 16V Aut. 2016 | 0 Km Automático	R$ 84900	Preview
	Toyota Corolla XEi 2.0 Flex 16V Aut. 2016 | 0 Km Automático	R$ 84900	Preview
	Toyota Corolla XEi 2.0 Flex 16V Aut. 2016 | 0 Km Automático	R$ 84990	Preview
	Toyota Corolla XEi 2.0 Flex 16V Aut. 2016 | 000 Km Automático	R$ 85880	Preview
	Volksvagen Golf Tsi 1.4 Highline Aut. 2014 | 12357 Km Automático	R$ 83990	Preview
	Volkswagen Golf Highline 1.4 Tsi 2014 | 22000 Km Automático	R$ 87300	Preview

9 advertisements recommended for you.

Fig. 3. Ads list containing diversity in recommendation.

In order to complement this list, the prototype uses the acquired knowledge about the user to increase the diversity of items and avoid over-specialization. As seen in Fig. 2, the user has requested ads related to *Toyota Corolla XEi 2.0*. However, in Fig. 3, the recommendation list displays two highlighted ads that are related to *Volksvagen Golf Tsi 1.4*. The first 7 cars shown in Fig. 3 represent the ads related to user's query, as Fig. 1A. The two highlighted cars represent ads related to the user's personality aspects, according to Fig. 1B. Regarding these highlighted ads, it can be seen that (a) Golf car does not belongs to the sedan category, (b) Golf car was not chosen in the user's query and, (c) the recommended ads do not offer new cars according to the user's query. However, the prototype considered that these ads may be good opportunities for the user.

An expert in vehicles domain has defined that Golf car can be represented by *car front 3*. Therefore, the recommendation component learned that the user sympathizes with cars that can be associated to this specific car front. Moreover, it calculated the degree of user's interest and verified that Golf car could be interesting.

To perform the experiments, 243 participants (158 males and 85 females) used the prototype. They are aged from 30–60 with different education levels such as PhD, master and bachelor. Each participant (user) created his/her profile. It contains user's information and also 11 attributes that represent the priorities that a user has in relation to the features of a car.

The participants also answered one questionnaire containing 10 questions from BFI-10 Test [28] to assess the values related to five personality dimensions (OCEAN), according to Five Factor Model. They were also invited to select an image that represents a car front which he/she has more sympathy.

An expert in vehicles domain was invited to create a mapping for representing the relationship between the car front and cars. The purpose of this mapping is to enable a strategy which identifies cars that can please the user, even if he/she is not interested in buying them or he/she does not know them. This strategy is implemented using the Eq. 3. It has been used to complement the recommendation list in order to add diversity for recommended items.

According to [29], the user's satisfaction measures the success of a recommender system. Commercial systems measure user's satisfaction by the number of products purchased (and not returned), while noncommercial systems may just ask users how satisfied they are [30]. In [31], the authors used a questionnaire survey to examine how usefulness, novelty and usability are related to the user's satisfaction.

In order to evaluate the user's satisfaction, we invited the participants who answered both the questionnaire related to BFI-10 Test and the form in which they selected a car front that represents his/her sympathy. Unfortunately, only 68.31% (109 males and 57 females) were willing to participate again.

Each user has been instructed to request vehicles recommendations belonging to three categories such as hatch, sedan and sport car. After three recommendation lists are offered to the user (one for each category), he/she is invited to answer another questionnaire containing only five questions. The goal is to

Table 1. Users' satisfaction regarding the recommendations.

Question	Hybrid prototype		Prototype based on personality traits	
	Yes	No	Yes	No
Q1	62.96%	37.04%	88.59%	11.41%
Q2	64.60%	35.40%	75.94%	24.06%
Q3	—	—	74.67%	25.33%
Q4	58.02%	41.98%	69.61%	30.39%
Q5	44.85%	55.15%	68.31%	31.69%

evaluate the user's satisfaction with the prototype. The questions are: *(Q1) I consider the suggested vehicles ideal for me*, *(Q2) The recommended ads meet my expectations*, *(Q3) The highlighted ads are useful for me*, *(Q4) In general, the prototype meets my expectations* and *(Q5) I would use the prototype again*. The answers to these questions are stored into a database to evaluate the user's satisfaction. The results that evaluate the users' satisfaction are presented in Table 1.

The question *Q1* aims to identify the user's satisfaction related to vehicles that have been suggested as appropriate for his/her profile. These suggestions are based on Eqs. 1 and 2. *Q2* aims to verify if the prototype has been able to extract from ads portals offers that meet the user's expectations. *Q3* aims to evaluate if the diversity which is computed using Eq. 3 has satisfied the user. Finally, the questions *Q4* and *Q5* verify the user's satisfaction about the prototype.

Questions *Q1* and *Q2* have shown the user's satisfaction about the recommendations of vehicles and ads according to his/her profile. The results shown in Table 1 are satisfactory. The evaluation shows that more than 75% of the participants were satisfied by the offered recommendations. We regard that to the hability that the recommendation component has to evaluate vehicles based on benchmarks from specialized portals. However, traditional portals recommend vehicles based on simple features such as price, model, brand, mileage etc.

Question *Q3* aims at evaluating the user's satisfaction when the diversity is applied to the recommendation list. Almost 70% of the participants consider that the diversity of items were useful for the search. Five cars were associated to each car front. Furthermore, we have to evaluate if the quantity of cars associated to the car front is suitable or it might still need some adjustments on this quantity. Thus, new experiments and more participants are extremely important.

Finally, the last two questions show the user's evaluation about the prototype and his/her perspective to use it again, respectively. The results show that more than 68% of the participants evaluated the prototype satisfactorily and that, on another opportunity, they will use it again.

5 Conclusion

This work presented a personality-based recommender system to enable semantic searches to find "best buy" opportunities about cars for sale on the Internet. The prototype combined a hybrid recommendation approach (content-based and collaborative one) with a machine learning algorithm known as k-NN. The results indicate that the proposed approach is promising to improve the quality of the recommendations, even though they may be improved to obtain better satisfaction numbers in the final report.

A possible future approach should consider other personality aspects associated with the reputation of the different vehicles according to the common sense of the users, since in some cases this reputation may result from other sources that are independent from the car front shapes and their dimensions.

References

1. McDonald, M.: Internet reshapes how dealers sell used cars (2012). http://wardsauto.com/dealerships/internet-reshapes-how-dealers-sell-used-cars. Accessed 05 Feb 2014
2. Grimes, S.: Breakthrough analysis: two + nine types of semantic search (2010). http://www.informationweek.com/software/informationmanagement/breakthrough-analysis-two-+-nine-types-ofsemantic-search/d/d-id/1086310. Accessed 09 Feb 2017
3. Zhuhadar, L., Nasraoui, O.: A hybrid recommender system guided by semantic user profiles for search in the e-learning domain. J. Emerg. Technol. Web Intell. **2**(4), 272–281 (2010)
4. Burke, R.: Hybrid web recommender systems. In: Brusilovsky, P., Kobsa, A., Nejdl, W. (eds.) The Adaptive Web. LNCS, vol. 4321, pp. 377–408. Springer, Heidelberg (2007). doi:10.1007/978-3-540-72079-9_12
5. Manchale, P., Bilal, M.: Curated content based recommender system. Int. J. Comput. Sci. Eng. **2**(4), 66–72 (2013)
6. Hariri, N., Castro-Herrera, C., Mirakhorli, M., Cleland-Huang, J., Mobasher, B.: Supporting domain analysis through mining and recommending features from online product listings. IEEE Trans. Softw. Eng. **39**(12), 1736–1752 (2013)
7. Wasid, M., Kant, V.: A particle swarm approach to collaborative filtering based recommender systems through fuzzy features. Procedia Comput. Sci. **54**, 440–448 (2015)
8. Miyahara, K., Pazzani, M.J.: Improvement of collaborative filtering with the simple Bayesian classifier. Inf. Process. Soc. Jpn. **43**(11), 3429–3437 (2002)
9. Pham, M.C., Cao, Y., Klamma, R., Jarke, M.: A clustering approach for collaborative filtering recommendation using social network analysis. J. UCS **17**(4), 583–604 (2011)
10. Vassiliou, C., Stamoulis, D., Martakos, D., Athanassopoulos, S.: A recommender system framework combining neural networks & collaborative filtering. In: Proceedings of the 5th WSEAS International Conference on Instrumentation, Measurement, Circuits and Systems, pp. 285–290 (2006)
11. Matthews, G., Deary, I.J., Whiteman, M.C.: Personality Traits, 2nd edn. University Press, Cambridge (2003)

12. Windhager, S., Slice, D., Schaefer, K., Oberzaucher, E., Thorstensen, T., Grammer, K.: Face to face: the perception of automotive designs. Human Nat. **19**(4), 331–346 (2008)
13. Windhager, S., Booksteina, F.L., Grammera, K., Oberzauchera, E., Saidd, H., Slicee, D.E., Thorstensenb, T., Schaefera, K.: Cars have their own faces: cross-cultural ratings of car shapes in biological (stereotypical) terms. Evol. Hum. Behav. **33**(2), 109–120 (2012)
14. Nunes, M.A.S., Hu, R.: Personality-based recommender systems: an overview. In: Proceedings of the Sixth ACM Conference on Recommender Systems, RecSys 2012, pp. 5–6. ACM, New York (2012)
15. Tintarev, N., Dennis, M., Masthoff, J.: Adapting recommendation diversity to openness to experience: a study of human behaviour. In: Proceedings of User Modeling, Adaptation, and Personalization, pp. 190–202 (2013)
16. Ericson, K., Pallickara, S.: On the performance of distributed clustering algorithms in file and streaming processing systems. In: Fourth IEEE International Conference on Utility and Cloud Computing (UCC 2011), pp. 33–40. IEEE (2011)
17. Ericson, K., Pallickara, S.: On the performance of high dimensional data clustering and classification algorithms. Future Gener. Comput. Syst. **29**(4), 1024–1034 (2013)
18. Panda, M., Patra, M.R., Dehuri, S.: Building recommender systems for network intrusion detection using intelligent decision technologies. In: Intelligent Techniques in Recommendation Systems: Contextual Advancements and New Methods, pp. 49–62. IGI Global (2015)
19. Samuel, A.L.: Some studies in machine learning using the game of checkers. IBM J. Res. Dev. **3**(3), 210–229 (1959)
20. Kelley, P.G., Hankes Drielsma, P., Sadeh, N., Cranor, L.F.: User-controllable learning of security and privacy policies. In: Proceedings of the 1st ACM Workshop on AISec, pp. 11–18. ACM (2008)
21. Marović, M., Mihoković, M., Mikša, M., Pribil, S., Tus, A.: Automatic movie ratings prediction using machine learning. In: MIPRO: Proceedings of the 34th International Convention 2011, pp. 1640–1645. IEEE (2011)
22. Takács, G., Pilászy, I., Németh, B., Tikk, D.: Scalable collaborative filtering approaches for large recommender systems. J. Mach. Learn. Res. **10**, 623–656 (2009)
23. Portugal, I., Alencar, P., Cowan, D.: The use of machine learning algorithms in recommender systems: a systematic review. arXiv:1511.05263 (2015)
24. Roshchina, A., Cardiff, J., Rosso, P.: TWIN: personality-based intelligent recommender system. J. Intell. Fuzzy Syst. **28**(5), 2059–2071 (2015)
25. Wu , W., Chen, L.: Implicit acquisition of user personality for augmenting movie recommendations. In: Proceedings of User Modeling, Adaptation and Personalization, Dublin, Ireland, pp. 302–314 (2015)
26. Gosling, S.D., Rentfrow, P.J., Swann, W.B.: A very brief measure of the big-five personality domains. J. Res. Pers. **37**, 504–528 (2003)
27. Paiva, F.A.P., Costa, J.A.F., Silva, C.R.M.: A hierarchical architecture for ontology-based recommender systems. In: Proceedings of the Computational Intelligence and 11th Brazilian Congress on Computational Intelligence (2013)
28. Rammstedt, B., John, O.P.: Measuring personality in one minute or less: a 10-item short version of the big five inventory in English and German. J. Res. Pers. **41**(1), 203–212 (2007)

29. Ziegler, C.-N., McNee, S.M., Konstan, J.A., Lausen, G.: Improving recommendation lists through topic diversification. In: Proceedings of the 14th International Conference on World Wide Web, pp. 22–32. ACM, New York (2005)
30. Herlocker, J.L., Konstan, J.A., Terveen, L.G., Riedl, J.T.: Evaluating collaborative filtering recommender systems. ACM Trans. Inf. Syst. **22**(1), 5–53 (2004)
31. Swearingen, K., Sinha, R.: Beyond algorithms: an HCI perspective on recommender systems. In: Proceedings of Workshop on Recommender Systems, vol. 13, No. 5–6, pp. 393–408 (2001)

Hybrid Intelligent Applications

A Hybrid System of Deep Learning and Learning Classifier System for Database Intrusion Detection

Seok-Jun Bu and Sung-Bae Cho(✉)

Department of Computer Science, Yonsei University, Seoul, South Korea
{sjbuhan, sbcho}@yonsei.ac.kr

Abstract. Nowadays, as most of the companies and organizations rely on the database to safeguard sensitive data, it is required to guarantee the strong protection of the data. Intrusion detection system (IDS) can be an important component of the strong security framework, and the machine learning approach with adaptation capability has a great advantage for this system. In this paper, we propose a hybrid system of convolutional neural network (CNN) and learning classifier system (LCS) for IDS, called Convolutional Neural-Learning Classifier System (CN-LCS). CNN, one of the deep learning methods for image and pattern classification, classifies the queries by modeling normal behaviors of database. LCS, one of the adapted heuristic search algorithms based on genetic algorithm, discovers new rules to detect abnormal behaviors to supplement the CNN. Experiments with TPC-E benchmark database show that CN-LCS yields the best classification accuracy compared to other state-of-the-art machine learning algorithms. Additional analysis by t-SNE algorithm reveals the common patterns among highly misclassified queries.

1 Introduction

Relational database management system (RDBMS) has been used for the high performance data storage. Many companies and organizations depend upon the database to safeguard sensitive data [1]. Because the value of some of these data is worth millions, it is necessary to guarantee the strong protection of the data. An important component of a strong security framework able to protect sensitive data in database is an intrusion detection system (IDS) [2].

The attacks on RDBMS can be categorized in insider and outsider attacks. Outsider attacks, such as SQL-injection, can be usually mitigated by defensive programming techniques; insider threats, however, are much more difficult to detect and are potentially more dangerous [3, 4]. The IDS proposed so far seems insufficient to detect and handle a class of intrusion, especially insider attack, since these solutions lack the learning and adaptation capabilities [5]. In particular, 0-day attacks (attacks that previously unseen) may cause a major security hole in IDS.

With the capability of adaptation, the machine learning approach can address the issue. The state-of-the-art method used random forest algorithm to generalize and classify the role of each query [6]. The method models the pattern of authorized queries

F.J. Martínez de Pisón et al. (Eds.): HAIS 2017, LNAI 10334, pp. 615–625, 2017.
DOI: 10.1007/978-3-319-59650-1_52

and classifies a new query according to each role, but the information loss in dimension reduction left a room to improve the intrusion detection performance.

In this paper, we propose a hybrid system, called Convolutional Neural-Learning Classifier System (CN-LCS), for IDS composed of convolutional neural network (CNN) and learning classifier system (LCS). Different from Dam's work [7], we exploit a deep learning method of CNN. CN-LCS can classify sparse and high-dimensional feature vectors of queries from database using automatic feature selection ability from genetic algorithm and convolution-pooling operations. Convolutional neural network, one of the deep learning methods for image and pattern classification [8], is used for modeling normal behaviors of database queries. Experiments with TPC-E benchmark database will show the superiority of the CN-LCS compared to other state-of-the-art machine learning algorithms.

The rest of the paper is organized as follows. Section 2 discusses the related works and Sect. 3 describes the proposed CN-LCS architecture in detail. Section 4 presents the results from experiments on role-based access control (RBAC) model from TPC-E benchmark database. In addition, some analyses by t-SNE algorithm reveal the general patterns among misclassified queries.

2 Related Works

A lot of research works have been developed in IDS domain. In this section, we introduce various research works based on machine learning approach to compare with the proposed CN-LCS. Most of the methods before the year of 2000 were proposed without machine learning algorithms. Lee et al. proposed signature-based approach based on predefined blacklist of queries [1]. Hu et al. used classification rules with the rationale that an item update does not happen alone and is accompanied by a set of other events recorded in the database log [9]. A data dependency miner was designed for mining data correlations, and a sinuous IDS was developed as a result.

On the other hand, IDS using machine learning approach is gaining more and more attention in the field of database anomaly detection because of the high detection accuracy, efficiency, and automation features [10]. Barbara et al. used hidden Markov model (HMM) to capture the change in database's normal behavior over time [11]. Several machine learning algorithms have been adopted in IDS since 2005. Valeur et al. used Bayesian model to detect anomalous queries and showed almost 0% false positive rate on manually created attacks [12]. Ramasubramanian et al. used artificial neural network (ANN) to model the behaviors of misuse-based intrusion [13]. They showed that database behaviors can be modeled successfully using machine learning algorithms.

Kamra et al. used naive Bayes classifier to classify anomalous queries without feature selection [14]. Also, support vector machine (SVM) and multi-layered Perceptron (MLP) were adopted to detect SQL-injection attacks [5, 15]. Ronao et al. used a combination of principal component analysis (PCA) and random forest (RF) for the task of query feature selection and database anomaly detection [2]. PCA produced a compact and meaningful set of features from queries and RF achieved a relatively good performance. Table 1 shows the summary of these methods.

Table 1. Related works for the IDS using machine learning algorithms

Authors	Methods	Description
Barbara [11]	Hidden markov model	Create an HMM for each cluster
Valeur [12]	Bayesian model	SQL grammar generalization
Ramasubramanian [13]	Artificial neural network, genetic algorithm	GA used to speed-up the training process of ANN
Kamra [14]	Naive bayes	Take into account imbalanced SQL query access
Pinzon et al. [5, 15]	Support vector machine	Agent-based intrusion detection
Ronao [2]	Principal component analysis, random forest	PCA is performed before RF

3 The Proposed System

In this section, we present the architecture of CN-LCS and the two main components: rule discovery component to select and filter out features from queries based on learning classifier system, and the intrusion detection component to classify the role of each query based on convolutional neural network.

3.1 System Overview

Role-based access control (RBAC) is essential to database security. RBAC provides a methodology for regulating an individual user's query to database based on her role.

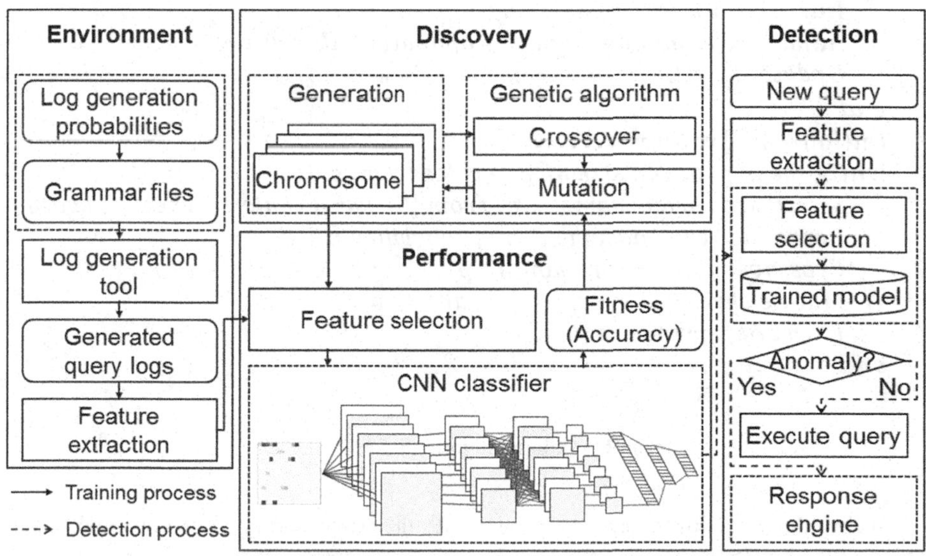

Fig. 1. System architecture of the proposed IDS of CN-LCS

The IDS based on RBAC profiles is considered as a standard classification problem [2]. Figure 1 shows the proposed CN-LCS architecture.

During the training phase in Fig. 2, n queries collected from database log with its own role are fed to environment and the features are extracted to form feature vector $F = (x_1, y_1), \ldots, (x_n, y_n)$. Since the features extracted form fairly sparce vectors, they should be selected before the classifier is learnt [16]. The discovery component has the key part in feature selection using LCS. p chromosomes encoded in generation [G] are partial solutions to the overall feature selection task. Each chromosome consists of a simple rule that forms 1-dimensional array of binary code (0, 1) in the length of features. The element of rule decides if the corresponding element in feature vector will be used in input, or filtered as 0. The selected features are then fed into CNN, where the convolution and pooling operations are done to distort the given pattern of normal behavior of queries, and extract the representative values from it. The model using convolution and pooling operations is mainly used for image classification and achieved the highest accuracy in various competitions [17, 18]. The accuracy of each trial on chromosome is considered as fitness, and genetic operations are applied to get better partial solution for feature selection.

Initialize $CN - LCS$ *parameters;*
Initialize $[G]$ *with random s chromosomes;*
Extract $F = (x_1, y_1), \ldots, (x_n, y_n)$ *from query logs;*
for *each training iteration* ***do***
    for *each chromosome* s_j ***do***
        for *each training instance* (x_i, y_i) ***do***
            Filtering the effective feature from x_i *with* s_j
        end
        Initialize a CNN classifier C;
        Adjust C weights using backpropagation algorithm;
        Update the fitness of chromosome s_j *with* C_{acc}*;*
    end
    Initialize $[G']$ *to empty;*
    while *the population size of* $[G']$ *is less than s* ***do***
        Select two chromosome c_r, c_r' *from* $[G]$ *using roulette wheel selection;*
        Reproduce chromosome c_r *by probability* p_r*;*
        Crossover c_r, c_r' *by probability* p_c*;*
        Mutate chromosome c_r *by probability* p_m*;*
        Insert offsprings in $[G']$*;*
    end
end

Fig. 2. Training algorithm for CN-LCS

During the detection phase, the model with the corresponding chromosome which achieved the highest fitness is selected. Features are extracted for a newly arrived query and selected according to the fitness. The trained CNN classifies if the query is anomalous, so that the response engine alarms to administrator and drops the query. Otherwise, it is executed in database.

3.2 Rule Discovery by Learning Classifier System

The main purpose of genetic algorithm used in rule discovery component is filter out noise from each training data instance. The multiple criteria to be optimized include the accuracy of classification, cost and risk associated with classification which in turn depends on the selection of features used to describe the patterns [19]. Given feature vectors $F = (x_1, y_1), \ldots, (x_n, y_n), x_i$ from instance i is the feature extracted from a query. The binary-encoded chromosomes carrying schema H decide whether the feature from feature vector instance x_i is used or not. Given the probabilities of crossover p_c and mutation p_m, the probability of disruption p is calculated as follows:

$$p = \frac{\delta(H)}{1-1} p_c + o(H) p_m \tag{1}$$

where $\delta(H)$ is the defining length and o(H) is the order of a schema, and l is the length of the chromosome. The short, low-order schema with above-average fitness increases exponentially, given by:

$$m(H, t+1) \geq \frac{m(H, t) f(H)}{a_t} [1 - p] \tag{2}$$

where m(H, t) is the number of strings belonging to scheme H at generation t, f(H) is the observed average fitness of schema H and a_t is the observed average fitness at generation t [20].

Each encoded chromosome carrying schema is a partial solution of automated feature selection and can be a supplementation to the following classifier. Gradient based learning algorithms mathematically well-founded for unimodal search spaces can get caught in local minima of the error function [19]. The features F extracted manually from database log often form a noisy or irrelevant vector of features. The learning algorithm used gets slow down significantly due to the large number of dimensions of the noisy feature space, and also produces lower classification accuracy due to learning irrelevant information [21].

3.3 Intrusion Detection by Convolutional Neural Network

While noise from the training instance x_i is filtered out from discovery component of CN-LCS, the large length of the x_i is still problematic. In order to handle data in a high dimensionality, we need to reduce the dimensionality [22].

Convolution and pooling operations, which can be used to reduce spectral variations and model spectral correlations that exist in patterns, are used for the task [23].

Given feature vector (x_i, y_i), the output c^l_{xy} from the lth convolutional layer performs the convolution operation with y^{l-1} which froms the $l-1$ st layer using $m \times m$ filter w:

$$c^l_{xy} = \sum\nolimits_{a=0}^{m-1} \sum\nolimits_{b=0}^{m-1} w_{ab} y^{l-1}_{(x+a)(y+b)} \tag{3}$$

The summary statistic of nearby outputs is derived from c^{l-1} by max-pooling operation. The output p^l_{xy} from the lth pooling layer performs the max-pooling operation with $k \times k$ area in $N \times N$ output vector, where T is pooling stride:

$$p^l_{xy} = \max c^{l-1}_{xy \times T} \tag{4}$$

Several convolutional and pooling layers can be stacked on top of the another to form a deep neural network architecture, and the proposed CN-LCS uses two pairs of convolution and pooling layers to prevent the model from overfiting in training dataset or degradation problem [24].

Distorted and pooled features from stacked convolutional and pooling layers are flattened to form feature vectors $p^l = [p_1, \ldots, p_I]$, where I is the number of units in the last pooling layer, as input to the fully-connected layer:

$$h^l_i = \sum_j w^{l-1}_{ji} \left(\sigma\left(p^{l-1}_i\right) + b_i \right) \tag{5}$$

where w^{l-1}_{ji} is weight between the ith node from $l-1^{st}$ st layer and the jth node from the lth layer, σ is the activation function used in the layer, and b_i is the bias term.

The output of the last layer, the softmax layer, is the inferred query role $\hat{y}_i$ where R is the total number of roles, and L is the last layer index:

$$p(\hat{y}_i | x_i) = argmax \frac{exp(p_{L-1} w_L + b_L)}{\sum_{k=1}^{R} exp(p_{L-1} w_k)} \tag{6}$$

Network weight update and error cost minimization are done by backpropagation algorithm to x_i, and mapped with y_i after forward propagation is performed using Eqs. (3)–(6).

The CNN classifier is implemented as thirty-two 2×2 convolution filters and 2×2 pooling, and 128-64-11 nodes for fully-connected layer, from bottom-to-top, to build shallow but practical size of network.

4 Experimental Results

In this section, we explain the dataset and experimental environments. We also show how CN-LCS performs in accordance with generations, and compare with other machine learning methods. For the fairness of evaluation, 10-fold cross validation was conducted.

4.1 Environments

The schema and standard transactions of the TPC-E benchmark database were used for the experiments. 11 read-only and read/write transactions were treated as roles, as if it were obtained from an RBAC model. We generated 1,000 normal queries for each role, with a total of 11,000 queries for each of our training dataset. The accuracy of classifying anomalous queries increases in proportion to the performance of classifying normal queries.

The generated queries parsed as query clause are separated, such as projection clause, selection attribute clause, and others, line-by-line. From these parsed queries, we extracted query features, represented by the vector. Counting features, which are features that count the presence of an element in a query clause, and ID features, which denote the position of an element in the query clause, are extracted from a parsed queries [6]. All features use the decimal encoding scheme for their final values.

A total of 277 features were extracted given the TPC-E schema. Since the nearest full squares is 289, 12 features were padded as 0 to each instance x_i and reshaped in 17×17 2-dimensional pattern as shown in Fig. 3. Experimental results showed 2D-CNN converges faster than 1D-CNN. It is advantageous to reduce the number of iterations even a little, though the final classification performance was similar, since CN-LCS algorithms create a large number of CNN's in proportion to the size of population per generation.

Fig. 3. Visualization of feature vectors from queries

The proposed CN-LCS is implemented with Tensorflow that is a very efficient library for matrix multiplication using GPU [25]. We used four NVIDIA GTX1080 to run a large number of CNN's trained with the CN-LCs algorithm.

4.2 Results and Analysis

The best and average classification accuracies per generation are shown in Fig. 4. 30 generations were tested and each of generation consists of 50 populations, thereby 1500 CNN's were created.

As the generation went by, overall accuracy of classification increased, whereas slight performance degradation was occurred in generations 20 to 25. This may be attributed to the accidental disruption of schema occurred due to genetic operation. The best model achieved in generation 28, resulting in the test accuracy of 94.64%.

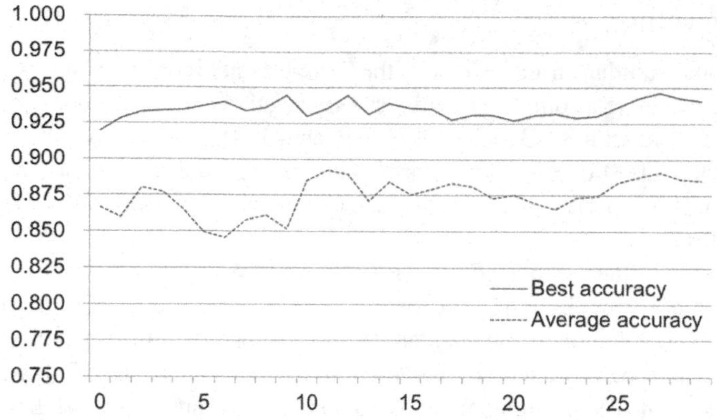

Fig. 4. The best and average accuracies (fitness) per generation

Figure 5 is the boxplot with other classification methods after 10-fold cross validation. The proposed CN-LCS achieved the highest accuracy and MLP has the lowest accuracy. We also replaced the CNN in CN-LCS with a shallow MLP, with 128-64-11 nodes bottom-to-top, to compare with our model. It is observed that the MLP adopted to the CN-LCS algorithm immediately improved.

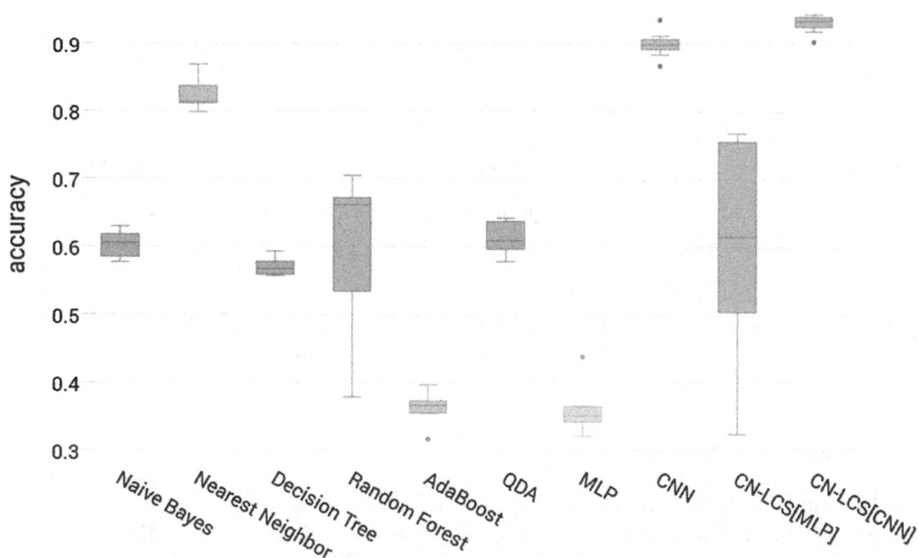

Fig. 5. Comparison of 10-cross validation accuracy with other classifiers

Figure 6 shows the confusion matrix of classification from model which achieved the test accuracy of 93.36%, indicating a similar accuracy with 10-fold cross validation average. Notice that classes 0 to 5 are read-only roles (SELECT commands only) and

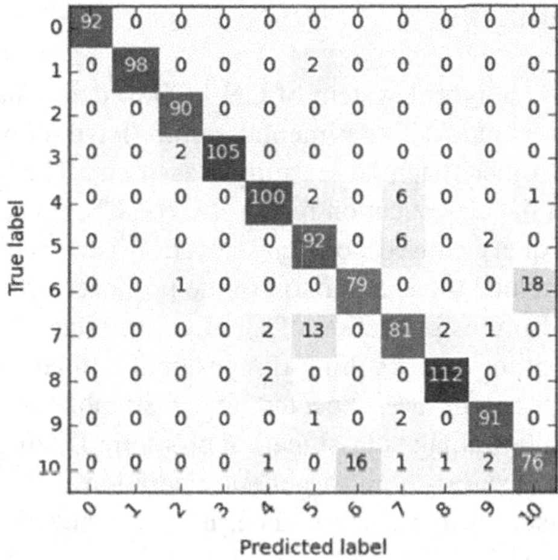

Fig. 6. Confusion matrix of the CN-LCS

the remaining is read/write roles. Among read/write roles, classes 6 and 10 were highly confused with each other. We noticed that both roles include SELECT and INSERT commands. This confusion is caused by overlapping between the two roles; INSERT commands are commonly associated with a SELECT command.

Figure 7 shows the overlap between SELECT and INSERT commands, plotted the last output activation of CNN using t-SNE dimension reduction algorithm [26]. t-SNE algorithm is a dimension reduction technique that is capable of retaining the local structure of the data while also revealing some important global structure. Each point represents each query, the distance between points is similarity, and the color represents its role. The queries which consists of SELECT and INSERT commands are messily mapped in upper left and center parts.

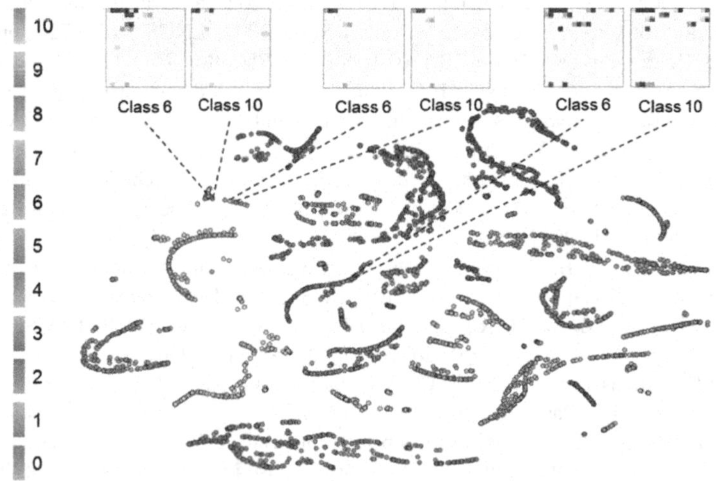

Fig. 7. The activations visualized from the last layer by t-SNE (Color figure online)

5 Concluding Remarks

In this paper, we propose a hybrid system of CN-LCS to detect intrusions on database, especially against insider attack. Experimental results have shown that the proposed CN-LCS outperformed other machine learning classifiers. The t-SNE algorithm was used for the analysis on the classification result of CN-LCS, revealing that the overlaps between commands in query caused poor classification performance.

Future works will include the comparison of the proposed CN-LCS with other LCS implementations, and also the application of CN-LCS to other fields. Feature selection using genetic algorithm and high-dimensional feature modeling using convolution-pooling operations are expected to be suitable for pattern recognition, especially in high-resolution image classification problem. Distinguishing the temporal decline in classification accuracy due to genetic operation during learning is another issue to explore. To ensure stable performance, it is also necessary to change or tune the genetic operators used in CN-LCS.

Acknowledgements. This work was supported by Defense Acquisition Program Administration and Agency for Defense Development under the contract (UD160066BD).

References

1. Lee, S.Y., Low, W.L., Wong, P.Y.: Learning fingerprints for a database intrusion detection system. In: Gollmann, D., Karjoth, G., Waidner, M. (eds.) ESORICS 2002. LNCS, vol. 2502, pp. 264–279. Springer, Heidelberg (2002). doi:10.1007/3-540-45853-0_16
2. Ronao, C.A., Cho, S.-B.: Mining SQL queries to detect anomalous database access using random forest and PCA. In: Ali, M., Kwon, Y.S., Lee, C.-H., Kim, J., Kim, Y. (eds.) IEA/AIE 2015. LNCS, vol. 9101, pp. 151–160. Springer, Cham (2015). doi:10.1007/978-3-319-19066-2_15
3. Jin, X., Osborn, S.L.: Architecture for data collection in database intrusion detection systems. In: Jonker, W., Petković, M. (eds.) SDM 2007. LNCS, vol. 4721, pp. 96–107. Springer, Heidelberg (2007). doi:10.1007/978-3-540-75248-6_7
4. Mathes, S., Petropoulos, M., Ngo, H.Q., Upadhyaya, S.: A data-centric approach to insider attack detection in database systems. In: International Workshop on Recent Advances in Intrusion Detection, pp. 382–401 (2010)
5. Pinzon, C.I., De Paz, J.F., Herrero, A., Corchado, E., Bajo, J., Corchado, J.M.: idMAS-SQL: intrusion detection based on MAS to detect and block SQL injection through data mining. Inf. Sci. **231**, 15–31 (2013)
6. Ronao, C.A., Cho, S.-B.: Random forests with weighted voting for anomalous query access detection in relational databases. In: Rutkowski, L., Korytkowski, M., Scherer, R., Tadeusiewicz, R., Zadeh, L.A., Zurada, J.M. (eds.) ICAISC 2015. LNCS, vol. 9120, pp. 36–48. Springer, Cham (2015). doi:10.1007/978-3-319-19369-4_4
7. Dam, H.H., Abbass, H.A., Lokan, C., Yao, X.: Neural-based learning classifier systems. IEEE Trans. Knowl. Data Eng. **20**, 26–39 (2008)
8. LeCun, Y., Bengio, Y., Hinton, G.: Deep learning. Nature **521**, 436–444 (2015)
9. Hu, Y., Panda, B.: A data mining approach for database intrusion detection. In: Proceedings of the 2004 ACM Symposium on Applied Computing, pp. 711–716 (2004)

10. Rajput, I.J., Shrivastava, D.: Data mining based database intrusion detection system: a survey. Int. J. Eng. Res. Appl. **2**, 1752–1755 (2012)
11. Barbará, D., Goel, R., Jajodia, S.: Mining malicious corruption of data with hidden markov models. In: Gudes, E., Shenoi, S. (eds.) Research Directions in Data and Applications Security. ITIFIP, vol. 128, pp. 175–189. Springer, Boston, MA (2003). doi:10.1007/978-0-387-35697-6_14
12. Valeur, F., Mutz, D., Vigna, G.: A learning-based approach to the detection of SQL attacks. In: Julisch, K., Kruegel, C. (eds.) DIMVA 2005. LNCS, vol. 3548, pp. 123–140. Springer, Heidelberg (2005). doi:10.1007/11506881_8
13. Ramasubramanian, P., Kannan, A.: A genetic-algorithm based neural network short-term forecasting framework for database intrusion prediction system. Soft. Comput. **10**, 699–714 (2006)
14. Kamra, A., Ber, E.: Survey of machine learning methods for database security. In: Kamra, A., Ber, E. (eds.) Machine Learning in Cyber Trust, pp. 53–71. Springer, USA (2009)
15. Pionzon, C., De Paz, J.F., Herrero, A., Corchado, E., Bajo, J.: A distributed hierarchical multi-agent architecture for detecting injections in SQL queries. In: Herrero, Á., Corchado, E., Redondo, C., Alonso, Á. (eds.) Computational Intelligence in Security for Information Systems, pp. 51–59. Springer, Berlin (2010)
16. Hinton, G.E., Salakhutdinov, R.R.: Reducing the dimensionality of data with neural networks. Science **313**, 504–507 (2006)
17. Krizhevsky, A., Sutskever, I., Hinton, G.E.: ImageNet classification with deep convolutional neural networks. In: Advances in Neural Information Processing Systems, pp. 1097–1105 (2012)
18. Szegedy, C., Liu, W., Jia, Y., Sermanet, P., Reed, S., Anguelov, D., Rabinovich, A.: Going deeper with convolutions. In: Proceedings of the IEEE Conference on Computer Vision and Pattern Recognition, pp. 1–9 (2015)
19. Yang, J., Honavar, V.: Feature subset selection using a genetic algorithm. In: Feature Extraction, Construction and Selection, pp. 117–136 (1998)
20. Goldberg, D.E., Holland, J.H.: Genetic algorithms and machine learning. Mach. Learn. **3**, 95–99 (1988)
21. Oreski, S., Oreski, G.: Genetic algorithm-based heuristic for feature selection in credit risk assessment. Expert Syst. Appl. **41**, 2052–2064 (2014)
22. Van Der Maaten, L., Postma, E., Van den Herik, J.: Dimensionality reduction: a comparative. J. Mach. Learn. Res. **10**, 66–71 (2009)
23. Sainath, T.N., Mohamed, A.R., Kingsbury, B., Ramabhadran, B.: Deep convolutional neural networks for LVCSR. In: Acoustics, Speech and Signal Processing, pp. 8614–8618 (2013)
24. He, K., Zhang, X., Ren, S., Sun, J.: Deep residual learning for image recognition. In: Proceedings of the IEEE Conference on Computer Vision and Pattern Recognition, pp. 770–778 (2016)
25. Abadi, M., Barham, P., Chen, J., Chen, Z., Davis, A., Dean, J., Kudlur, M.: Tensorflow: a system for large-scale machine learning. In: Proceedings of the 12th USENIX Symposium on Operating Systems Design and Implementation (2016)
26. Maaten, L.V.D., Hinton, G.: Visualizing data using t-SNE. J. Mach. Learn. Res. **9**, 2579–2605 (2008)

Evolutionary Computing for the Sustainable Management of Educative Institutions

Juan-Ignacio Latorre-Biel[1(✉)] and Emilio Jiménez-Macías[2]

[1] Public University of Navarre, Campus of Tudela, 31500 Tudela, Spain
juanignacio.latorre@unavarra.es

[2] University of La Rioja, 26006 Logroño, Spain
Emilio.jimenez@unirioja.es

Abstract. Educative institutions consist of systems that can be considered as discrete event systems and show a complex behavior. The management of this kind of institutions may be very demanding, particularly if the planning and scheduling of educative activities are complemented by environmental and financial issues, such as programs of energy consumption efficiency, waste reduction and control, or rationalizing the use of the center resources. In order to cope with some of these issues, it is proposed a methodology that combines mathematical modeling, optimization based on genetic algorithms for searching the best solution in the solution space, and discrete event systems simulation. In order to carry out with all these tasks, a modeling paradigm has been considered to describe the educative institution. The institution is modelled using Petri nets following a top-bottom approach. This process is performed by the development of a low-detailed Petri net model of the global system and, in an additional step, the subsystems can be detailed by expanding their models. The Petri net model will present some parameters, representing the decision variables, which act as freedom degrees of the system and constitute the focus of the management board of the educative center.

Keywords: Sustainable management · Educative institution · Petri nets · Discrete event simulation · Genetic algorithm

1 Introduction

1.1 The Management of an Educative Institution

The management of educative institutions should lead to policies that profit efficiently from commonly limited resources. A traditional justification of this objective is to achieve financial savings. However, this justification is not the only one and even it might be discussed if it is the most important one.

In effect, the management of an educative institution should lead by example all the members of the educative community, including the pupils or students, teachers or professors, administration, and services staff. In particular, practicing actions committed with sustainability is a key factor in the education of the future's leaders and decision-makers in our society. In this context, it is convenient to take special care to

F.J. Martínez de Pisón et al. (Eds.): HAIS 2017, LNAI 10334, pp. 626–637, 2017.
DOI: 10.1007/978-3-319-59650-1_53

tasks related to responsible consumption of resources, such as energy or paper, reuse of certain materials, recycling, and waste management [1, 2].

In addition to the educative and financial motivations, pursuing sustainable policies are supported by a broad social concern, as well as national and international regulations. In order to put into practice this approach, it is convenient to be aware of the time scope of a given decision, since it may fall into one of three different categories: operational, tactical, or strategic management. These categories range from the day-to-day management to a period of several years, when it may be decided to change the heating system, the insulation of a building, or the building itself.

Nevertheless, the strategic decisions should be made taking into consideration not only long-term objectives of reduction of resources consumption or waste generation but also short-term goals achieving educative objectives. As a consequence of the previous considerations, the management of an educative institution is a challenging task, where it can be very complicated to take into account all the decision variables and all the factors that influence the outcome of the decisions made.

For this reason, the availability of a decision support system can be of great help to the decision-makers in the management of an educative institution.

1.2 Decision Making Support for the Management of an Educative Institution

The approach proposed in this paper for developing an appropriate decision support system consists of combining the following elements:

(a) Petri net model of the educative institution. Petri nets constitute a broadly used modeling paradigm for the description of discrete event systems (DES) [3–6], while an educative institution can be interpreted as a DES. Moreover, a Petri net model can be applied as both, an analytic as well as a simulation model. For this reason, the same mathematical description can be used for analyzing the structure and the behavior of the original educative institution [7].

(b) Optimization problem statement. The objectives to be achieved should be quantified and their relative importance, weighted [8]. Of course, while financial objectives can be easily transformed into numbers, other, such as educative objectives are much more subjective. Anyway, it is always possible to find quantitative indicators of the achievement of educative goals. In fact, the application of quality assurance systems to educative institutions, imply the search of these indicators, values of reference, and continuous improvements for meeting the expected values. The decision making support can be carried out by the solution of the optimization problem, leading to one or several solutions [9] that might be chosen by the decision makers.

(c) Metaheuristic of genetic algorithms. The finding process of a feasible and promising solution for the optimization problem, discarded an exhaustive search in the solution space, can be developed by means of a guided search aiming at finding promising regions to explore. The means to guide the search is a genetic algorithm. However, other techniques, such as ant colony, or tabu search can alternative be used.

(d) Discrete event simulation. The degree of achievement of the objectives quantified in the objective function of the optimization problem statement, require to know beforehand the evolution of the Petri net associated to a given solution of the decision problem. One possibility to carry out this calculation consists of simulating the behavior of the model of the system by the simulation of the Petri net [8].

1.3 Life Cycle Assessment Applied to a Decision Making Support System

One of the most specifically oriented handicap in the application of this methodology consists of quantifying the objectives of the educative institution management. As it has been mentioned previously, the most subjective goals can be quantified by indicators, which might already be defined in the quality assurance system of the institution.

Other objectives, related to the environmental and financial impact of the educative institution activities can be evaluated by the application of the methodology of Life Cycle Assessment (LCA). This methodology facilitates the calculation of the environmental impact of activities performed by humans in a given application, such as, in this case, the activities in an educative institution [10]. LCA presents an integral approach from "cradle to grave", meaning that the complete life cycle of the institution can be in the analysis scope of this methodology [11]. In this approach, inputs such as energy and raw materials are considered, as well as their return to the earth [12].

The application of LCA to an educative institution, requires measures of inputs and outputs, of resources and waste, and provides with quantitative results about the environmental implications of the activities. It can be concluded that certain improvements can be carried out to reduce the environmental impact of the analyzed system and reach the sustainability objectives of the institution [13]. The usefulness of this methodology to evaluate non-implemented strategies is limited, since it is based on real data. For this reason, a decision making support tool, such as the one presented in this document, although based on LCA, outperforms it in predictive power [14].

The rest of the paper is organized as follows. The next section describes the modeling formalisms, the Petri nets, used to describe the model of the system in a quantitative representation. Section 3 discusses the Petri net model of an educative institution, while Sect. 4 details the underlying algorithm to the decision Support System, as well as the applied metaheuristic. Section 5 is devoted to conclusions.

2 Modeling Formalism

Discrete event systems, such as an educative institution, may present very complex behavior. Not only for the number of actors that participate in the organizations' activities but also for the number of simultaneous processes that may evolve at a given time and can compete for shared resources or meet and collaborate in the consecution of their objectives. In an educative institution, an example of shared resources are the classrooms or other spaces of the center, while processes can be lessons, administrative work, meetings, talks, cleaning, recess, etc.

2.1 Generalized Petri Nets

In this context, the choice of Petri nets as modeling paradigm, is a natural decision, since this family of formalisms is especially suited for the description of discrete event systems with complex behaviors [15], while representing explicitly the interrelation between subsystems and processes [16]. An interesting feature of Petri nets is that in addition to its graphical nature, this formalism can be translated automatically into its matrix-based form. This algebraic description of a Petri net is particularly suited for its mathematical use for structural analysis, performance evaluation, or transformation from one formalism to an equivalent representation using another more suited formalism for a given application, just to give three examples [17]. A definition of a marked Petri net or Petri net system can be found in [15].

2.2 Static Structure and Dynamic Behavior in a Petri Net

In a Petri net model, there are some important elements that represent different features of the discrete event system. As it has been seen in the definition, there are two type of nodes: places and transitions. The first ones, called places and depicted by circles, represent the state variables, while the second ones, called transitions and depicted by rectangles or bars, represent the feasible evolution of the system's state.

The marking of a Petri net is depicted by black dots, called tokens, inside the places. The marking of a Petri net represents the values of its state variables. Places, transitions, and directed arcs, compose the static structure and can be represented by the incidence matrix. The description of the evolution of a Petri net model is given by its marking, represented alternatively by a vector, whose elements are the number of tokens in each place of the net. The evolution of the Petri net from a given state to another one can be performed once the conditions of this evolution are met. Then, the evolution of the net is performed by the firing of a transition of the net. These conditions are represented in a Petri net by the correspondence between the number of tokens in the input places of a firable transition and the weight of the arc linking the each one of these input places with the transition.

Tokens in an educative institution may represent very diverse actors, such as a student, parent or a member of the staff. All these actors may share places, since any of them may be present in, let us say, a given classroom.

Nevertheless, there are other elements of the institution, such as resources, which may be described by tokens. Examples are paper, electricity, gas, combustible for a central heating, and also waste. Designing a Petri net model including all these elements require a careful definition of the units that are associated to every token. For example, a certain place may represent the room, where paper is stored and a token may represent a box with, let us say 2500 sheets of paper. However, the consumption of paper in a class of 1 h and 20 students might be about 50 sheets of paper. In this case, the unit associated to a single token can be a single sheet of paper, 10 of them or even 50 sheets. It is a decision of the designer of the Petri net. The higher the number of tokens present in the Petri net, the more computational resources will require to handle the model of the system, for example for performing a simulation.

Some types of tokens may not be allowed to share the same place, for example a young pupil and a bottle of toxic cleaning products. However, other tokens, such as teachers and pupils, would certainly share a common place very frequently. If the tokens are represented by "black" dots, it is not possible to distinguish them. Tokens of different type would perform different tasks in different places, such as a teacher, a primary school pupil, or a vocational training student. In order to overcome this limitation it is convenient to assign some label to the tokens that would allow to identify the tokens of the same type and distinguish them from other type of tokens.

2.3 Colored Petri Nets

The identification of a certain type of token may be performed by the assignment of certain attributes. This idea leads to the concept of the so called high-level Petri nets, and more in particular to a subclass of this type of nets, which is called colored Petri nets. In this particular formalism, a color is just any attribute that can be associated to a given token to identify it.

Colored Petri nets have been extensively applied to many application fields with success. Moreover, this formalism counts of many theoretical results, as well as practical tools, that make them very useful to model a discrete event system, such as an educative institution. A definition of colored Petri nets can be found in [18].

3 Model of the Educative Institution

3.1 Top-Bottom Modeling Approach

The model of a generic educative institution presents some assumptions in the schedule and the organization of the staff. However, it can easily be adapted to other centers that follow different policies. For example, the day schedule is divided in three class periods interrupted by two recesses. The total time spent by the members of the educative community (students, teachers or professors, and staff) is 6 h, including both recesses. That implies 6 classes of less than 1 h duration each.

The modeling approach followed in the development of the Petri net model is called top-bottom. It is based in the idea of developing, as a first step, a low-detailed model of the whole discrete event system. This system is represented in Fig. 1. The complete system may be composed of different subsystems, which can be refined in successive steps. In this case, the detailed sub-models correspond to expansions of certain nodes, places, of the Petri net describing the complete educative institution.

This approach presents several advantages as indicated below:

(a) On the first hand, the modeling process is systematic and can spare complexity and difficulty in every step of the model building.
(b) On the other hand, it is possible to stop the modeling process at any level of detail or abstraction desired by the modeler. It has to be considered that the more detailed the model, the more computational effort would require to handle it, for example for performance evaluation.

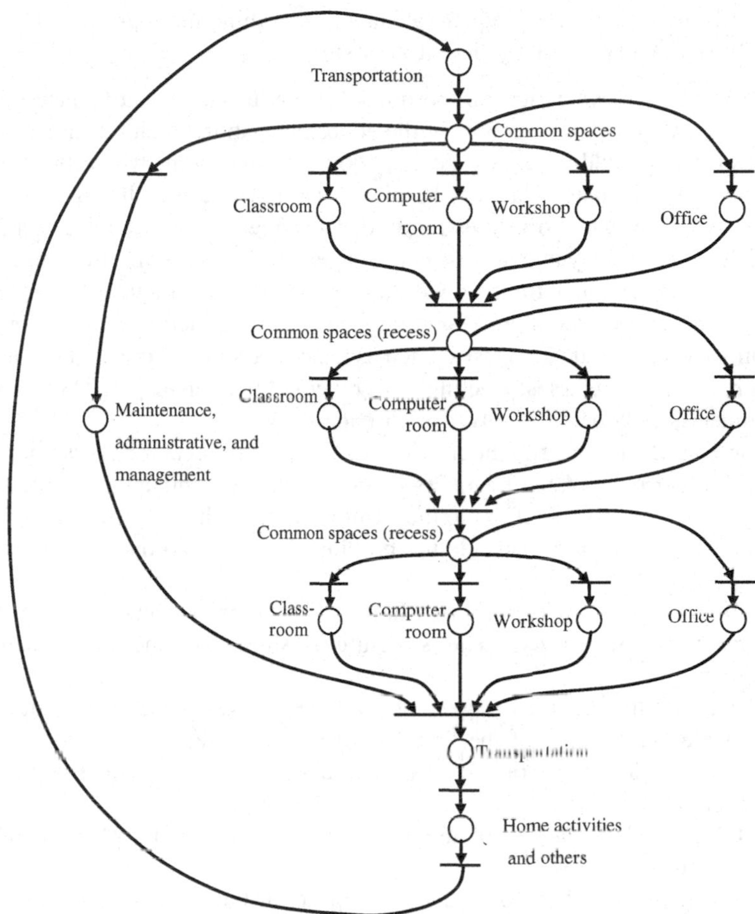

Fig. 1. Petri net model of a generic educative institution.

(c) As an additional advantage, the model can be easily decomposed for the sake of clarity. This fact, facilitates the use of a Petri net as a means of transmitting the specifications and formal features of a given discrete event system.

3.2 Low-Detailed Global Model of an Educative Institution

Figure 1 shows the outcome of a first stage in building a low-detailed model for a generic educative institution, where a complete day of work can take place.

In this model, the daily activities of the different members of the educative community have been represented explicitly. In particular, colored tokens in the net may represent students of different levels, teachers and professors, parents, as well as members of the management staff, and members of the administration and services staff, including janitors or maintenance technicians.

The model represents eight sequential stages, describing the sequence of actions in the timetable that carry out the different actors:

(a) The daily activities begin with the transportation to the educative institution.
(b) After the arrival of the members of the educative institution and their access to the corresponding building, every person moves to the room, where the first daily activity will take place. Among the places that have been included in the model, there are classes and workshops for students and teachers, and offices for staff. In fact, the students may attend classes in conventional classrooms, in computer labs, or even in vocational training workshops, where they might use professional equipment. Teachers and professors may have teaching activities or perform other administrative or educative tasks, such as the correction and preparation of exams, the preparation of classes, meeting with other teachers, managing staff, or parents of students, even being involved with paperwork.
(c) At the end of the first two hours of classes, the first break or recess begin. It is expected that most of the members of the educative community, all the students and some of the other staff, go to the common areas to have some leisure time, for example to the cafeteria, outside the building, or to rest rooms, just to give some examples.
(d) The following stage is another two hours of class, of the same duration than the classes before the recess. The structure is similar to the one described in paragraph (b).
(e) At the end of the previous stage, a second recess takes place. Its duration can be the same as in the case of the first one or not, depending on the policies of the institution. Again, most of the people would move to common spaces to have some leisure time.
(f) The third and last classes, of the same duration and taking place in the same spaces than before.
(g) At the end of the school day, the participants in the activities of the educative institution use different transportation means to return to their homes. As it will be seen in a more detailed model of this stage, different transportation means have been considered, since they may have very different impacts on the environment.
(h) The last stage is a global place, representing all the activities performed from the end of the school day to the beginning of the following one.

For the sake of clarity and simplicity, not all the feasible actions have been represented in this low-detailed model. In fact, if there are empty spaces, such as common areas, classrooms, workshops or offices, the cleaning staff or the maintenance technicians might develop their work there. For this reason, a richer model would include the feasible transitions of tokens from the place labelled "Maintenance, administrative, and management" to other places representing empty spaces. In the present model, it has been considered that either the staff carry out their activities in a common place, labelled "Maintenance, administrative, and management", or in the other spaces, such as classrooms or offices.

3.3 Detailed Petri Nets of Model Subsystems

A second step in the development of an analytical and simulation model for an educative institution, consists in detailing some of the places of the global Petri net, representing different subsystems.

The first place that will be detailed is in fact a pair of them, both labelled "Transportation". This important process, from an environmental point of view, have been developed for classifying the members of the educative community according to the transportation means they use.

This model has been depicted in Fig. 2 and takes into account five different transportation means: walk, bicycle, motorbike, car, and bus. The choice of one of this vehicles by every person can be modelled by means of a stochastic parameter.

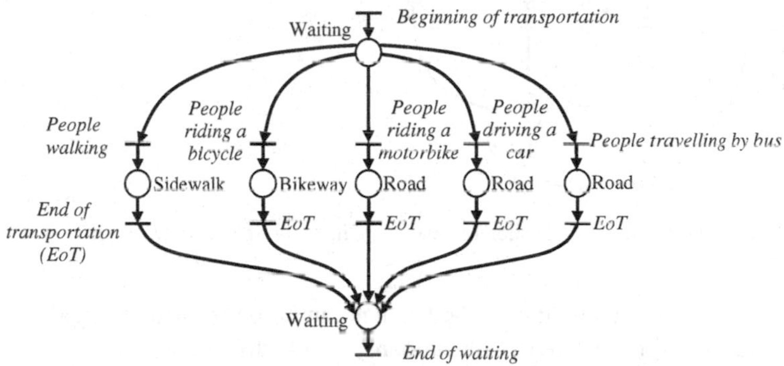

Fig. 2. Petri net model of the transportation process

In order to model realistically the different means of transportation, statistical information of the particular educative institution that is being modelled should be very useful. In effect, the proportion of persons traveling by each different means may have a significant influence in the environmental impact of the process as a whole. Among the statistical information, which is interesting for the evaluation of the environmental impact, it is possible to consider the distance covered, as well as the length of the route and the density of the traffic.

Next subsystem to be detailed in a Petri net model are the activities of a teacher or professor in a classroom, computer lab, or workshop. It has been represented in Fig. 3 and describe the tasks that a teacher or professor can develop during a class. A workshop and a computer lab allow a richer variety of activities than a conventional classroom and this has been taken into account in the developed Petri net, trying to apprehend all the activities from the three types of spaces.

Petri net of Fig. 3 includes a place, where the teacher or professor monitors the students, waiting for the development of a more specific task. The teacher can decide what to do next, from starting an explanation, help a single student or a group of them, while the rest of the class complete a certain activity, carrying out the correction of exercises or administrative tasks.

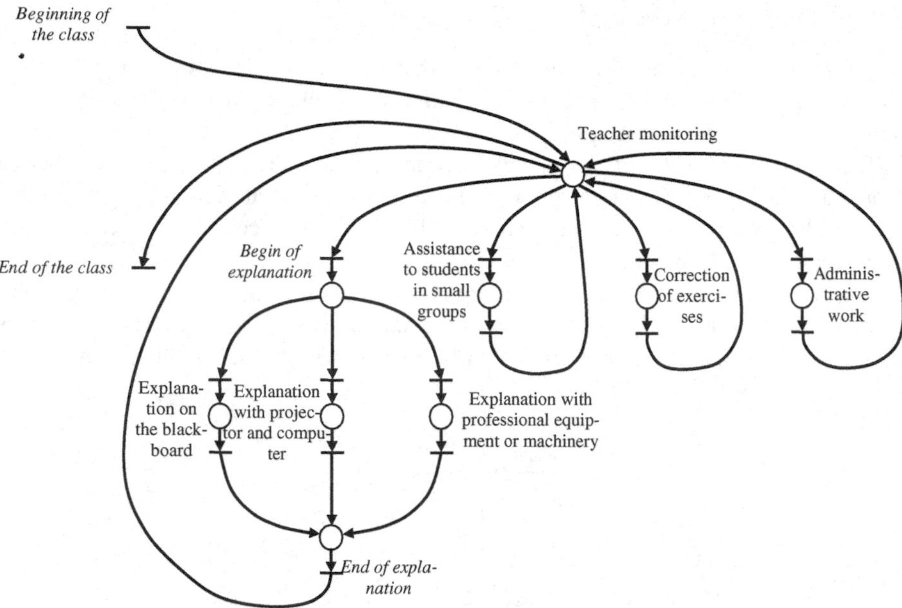

Fig. 3. Tasks developed by a teacher or professor in a classroom or workshop with students

Additionally, the explanation of the teacher can be performed by means of the use of different technologies, such as a blackboard, a projector connected to a computer, or professional machinery or devices in a workshop of vocational training, where chemical products, metal parts, or other materials can be used.

The depicted activities have been selected by the authors as the most representative, frequent, and with a higher environmental impact. Moreover, a limited range of feasible activities allows a tradeoff between simplicity and realistic modeling.

Last example of subsystem of the global Petri net detailed in the second modeling stage according to the bottom-up approach is depicted in Fig. 4. This is a link between the global net represented in Fig. 1 and the detailed tasks to be performed by a teacher, represented in Fig. 3. In Fig. 4, several paths for the tokens classify the different actors of the educative processes that may develop activities in a classroom, computer lab or workshop. The places associated to every professional category or student can be detailed in subnets, such as the one represented in Fig. 3.

4 Decision Making Support

The goal of an educative center model, as described in the previous section, consists of the development of a decision support tool for the management of the institution.

The Petri net model of the system contains a set of parameters (initial markings, timing associated to transitions, elements of the incidence matrices, and priorities in actual conflicts). This model is a very flexible component for decision making, since

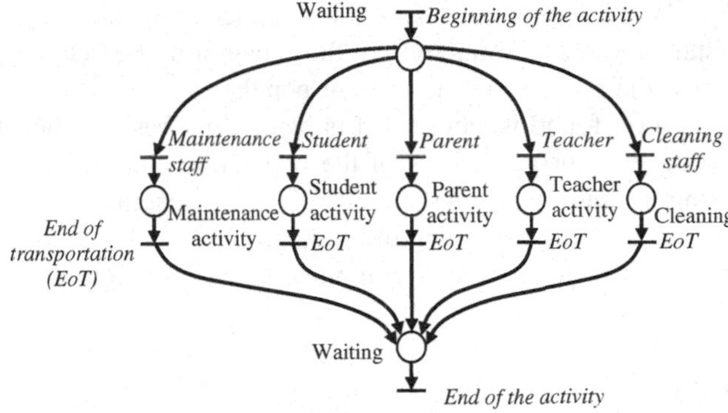

Fig. 4. Actors of the educative institution performing tasks in a classroom or workshop

any of these parameters can be considered decision variable in a certain situation. As a consequence, the model can represent a wide range of scenarios, with different decision makers, from the manager to any institution member willing to test the outcome of a certain decision. This feature is rarely found on other decision support tools.

A decision making process based on the proposed methodology starts with the definition of the specifications of the decision problem. It is necessary to specify the set of decision variables, parameters of the Petri net model that can be controlled by the decision maker. The rest of the parameters of the model are uncontrollable, meaning that the decision maker cannot change their values. Additionally, the objectives of the decision making process should be specified and a formula to quantify the degree of their achievement should be given. These formulas can be named objective functions.

A decision consists of choosing, from the pool of solutions, a combination of values for the choice variables. The proposed methodology chooses a small amount of feasible solutions, reduced when compared to the solution space size, associates numbers quantifying their quality or degree of achievement of the objectives, and compares them to decide which tested solutions are the best for solving the problem.

The way to calculate the quality values consists of evaluating the objective functions as the evolution of the Petri net model from a given feasible solution is simulated. Discrete event system simulation is, then, used for calculating one or several performance or quality parameters for a given solution.

One critical factor in obtaining good solutions is the selection of the set of tested solutions among the complete solution space. A manual selection may be unsuccessful due to the size of the solution space and the fact that intuition may fail in complex environments. Additionally, experienced and resolute decision makers are difficult and expensive to hire. As a consequence an automatic search by means of a genetic algorithm has been chosen for selecting feasible solutions to be tested.

A combination of a genetic algorithm with discrete event simulation can be described in the following steps:

Stage 1. Define and adjust the parameters of the genetic algorithm.
Stage 2. Select randomly an initial population of solutions from the solution pool.

Stage 3. Assess the quality of each solution by calculating the objective function. This stage requires a simulation of the behavior of the Petri net associated to each feasible solution in the present population.

Stage 4. Best solution found is stored if it is better than best solution found so far.

Stage 5. Eliminate the worst solutions of the population and replace them with the offspring of the remaining ones. This new generation is built up from operations such as crossover and mutation.

Stage 6. Finish if the stop criterion is complied. Otherwise, continue from step 3.

5 Conclusions

In this paper, a methodology based in evolutionary computing, discrete event system modeling and simulation, and optimization has been presented for the development of a decision support system applied to the management of an educative institution.

A tradeoff should be found between accuracy in the description of the real system and simplicity, since a too detailed model implies unaffordable computer resources.

The model can be enriched with stochastic parameters, statistical data for the transportation of the members of the educative community, and real data from the application of the life cycle assessment methodology to the educative institution.

The authors believe that the proposed methodology is very promising and can assist the management of an educative institution in a positive way, since it can take into account financial, environmental, and social issues, which are difficult to conjugate and can be skipped if this approach or a similar one also based in the intensive use of artificial intelligence is considered.

As future research lines, the authors propose the integration of the elements and the development of a tool with real data of a particular educative institution in order to adjust its features and test the quality of the proposed decision making support tool.

References

1. Otero-Prego, M., Latorre-Biel, J.I., Azofra-Rojo, D., Jiménez-Macías, E.: Management of resources and wastes in a network of schools modelled by Petri nets. In: Bruzzone, A.G., Jiménez, E., Longo, F., Merkuryev, Y. (eds.) Proceedings of the 24th European Modeling & Simulation Symposium, EMSS 2013, Athens, Greece, 25–27 September 2013, pp. 424–429 (2013)
2. Otero-Prego, M., Latorre-Biel, J.I., Martínez-Cámara, E., Jiménez-Macías, E.: Sustainable design for a centre of vocational training. A Petri net approach. In: Bruzzone, A.G., Jiménez, E., Longo, F., Merkuryev, Y. (eds.) Proceedings of the 24th European Modeling & Simulation Symposium, EMSS 2013, Athens, Greece, 25–27 September 2013, pp. 430–435 (2013)
3. Latorre-Biel, J.I., Jiménez-Macías, E., Blanco-Fernández, J., Martínez-Cámara, E., Sáenz-Díez, J.C., Pérez-Parte, M.: Decision support system, based on the paradigm of the Petri nets, for the design and operation of a dairy plant. Int. J. Food Eng. **11**(6), 767–776 (2015). doi:10.1515/ijfe-2015-0063

4. Latorre-Biel, J.I., Jiménez-Macías, E., Blanco-Fernández, J., Sáenz-Díez, J.C.: Optimal design of an olive oil mill by means of the simulation of a Petri net model. Int. J. Food Eng. **10**(4), 573–582 (2014). doi:10.1515/ijfe-2013-0066
5. Latorre-Biel, J.I., Jiménez-Macías, E., Blanco-Fernández, J., Sáenz-Díez, J.C.: Decision support in the rioja wine production sector. Int. J. Food Eng. **9**(3), 267–278 (2013). doi:10.1515/ijfe-2013-0032
6. Latorre, J.I., Jiménez, E.: Modelling, analysis, and simulation of manufacturing processes with alternative structural configurations by parametric Petri nets. Adv. Sci. Lett. **19**(2), 665–669 (2013). doi:10.1166/asl.2013.4767
7. Latorre-Biel, J.I., Jiménez, E.: Modeling, simulation, and optimization with Petri nets as disjunctive constraints for decision-making support. An overview. Simul. Notes Eur. SNE **26**(2), 75–82 (2016). doi:10.11128/sne.26.on.10333
8. Latorre-Biel, J.I., Jimenez-Macias, E.: Simulation-based optimization of discrete event systems with alternative structural configurations using distributed computation and the Petri net paradigm. Simul.: Trans. Soc. Model. Simul. Int. **89**(11), 1310–1334 (2013). doi:10.1177/0037549713505761
9. Latorre-Biel, J.I., Jimenez-Macias, E., Perez-Parte, M.: The optimization problem based on alternatives aggregation Petri nets as models for industrial discrete event systems. Simul.: Trans. Soc. Model. Simul. Int. **89**(3), 346–361 (2013). doi:10.1177/0037549712464410
10. Baumann, H., Tilman, A.: The Hitch Hicker's Guide to LCA: An Orientation in Life Cycle Assessment Methology and Application. Student Literature, Lund (2004)
11. Curran, M.A.: Environmental Life Cycle Assessment. McGraw-Hill, USA (1996)
12. Environmental Protection Agency: Life Cycle Assessment: Principles and Practice. National Risk and Research Laboratory, Cincinnati, Ohio, USA (2006)
13. Hertwich, E.G.: Life cycle approaches to sustainable consumption: a critical review. Environ. Sci. Technol. **39**(13), 4673–4684 (2005). doi:10.1021/es0497375
14. Jiménez, E., Martínez, E., Blanco, J., Pérez, M., Graciano, C.: Methodological approach towards sustainability by integration of environmental impact in production system models through LCA. Application to the Rioja wine sector. In: Simulation: Transactions of the Society for Modeling and Simulation International. Special Issue of Simulation: Modelling Sustainability for Third Millennium (2012). doi:10.1177/0037549712464409
15. Silva, M.: Introducing Petri nets. In: Di Cesare, F. (ed.) Practice of Petri Nets in Manufacturing, pp. 1–62. Chapman & Hall, London (1993). doi:10.1007/978-94-011-6955-4_1
16. Latorre-Biel, J.I., Jiménez, E., García-Alcaraz, J.L., Sáenz-Díez J.C., Blanco-Fernández, J., Pérez de la Parte, M.: Modular constructions of compact Petri Net models. In: International Journal of Simulation and Process Modelling Special Issue on: Integrating Modelling and Simulation Tools and Methodologies in Real-World Complex Systems for Solving Multidisciplinary Problems (In press)
17. Latorre-Biel, J.I., Jiménez-Macías, E., Pérez-de-la-Parte, M., Sáenz-Díez, J.C., Martínez-Cámara, E., Blanco-Fernández, J.: Compound Petri nets and alternatives aggregation Petri nets: two formalisms for decision-making support. Adv. Mech. Eng. **8**(11) (2016). doi:10.1177/1687814016680516
18. Latorre-Biel, J.C., Jiménez-Macías, E., Pérez de la Parte, M., Blanco-Fernández, J., Martínez-Cámara, E.: Control of discrete event systems by means of discrete optimization and disjunctive colored PNs: application to manufacturing facilities. Abstr. Appl. Anal. **2014** (3), 1–16 (2014). doi:10.1155/2014/821707

NCRIO: A Normative Holonic Metamodel for Multi-agent Systems

Ezzine Missaoui[1(✉)], Belhassen Mazigh[2], Sami Bhiri[3], and Vincent Hilaire[4]

[1] ENSI, University of Manouba, Manouba, Tunisia
ezzine.missaoui@gmail.com
[2] Department of Computer Sciences, FSM, Monastir, Tunisia
belhassen.mazigh@gmail.com
[3] OASIS-ENIT, Tunis, Tunisia
samibhiri@gmail.com
[4] Univ Bourgogne Franche-Comt,
UTBM IRTES-SET EA 7274/IMSI, 90010 Belfort Cedex, France
vincent.hilaire@utbm.fr

Abstract. Increasing collaborative work and distributing information creates a request for large-scale and flexible systems in regulated environments. A promising approach in the field of multi-agent system is the design and development of complex, hierarchical and critical systems. These systems require both a hierarchical structure that allows to make together different levels of abstraction within the same system and require the maintenance of social control of the various entities involved in these systems by using social norms. Several proposals on normative models for multi-agent systems have been made in order to design agent societies in norms-based environments. However, they are not adapted to support holonic systems, i.e. those who allow to model complex organizations involving several levels simultaneously. In this paper, we propose a new metamodel, called NCRIO (Norm, Capacity, Role, Interaction, and Organization), for the design of normative holonic multi-agent systems (NHMAS). This metamodel is an extension of the CRIO (Capacity, Role, Interaction, and Organization) metamodel, which allows the design of holonic multi-agent systems (HMAS). The NCRIO metamodel retains the properties of the HMASs and adds normative concepts (Norms and Contracts) to maintain social control in these systems. This new metamodel allows the design for complex (which require a hierarchical structure) and critical (which require social control) systems.

Keywords: Agent oriented software engineering · Model Driven Architecture · Holon · Holonic multi-agent systems · Crio metamodel · Norms · Normative approach

1 Introduction

The management of collaborative work and decentralized processes in complex systems (Intelligent transportation systems, Smart City Management System,

F.J. Martínez de Pisón et al. (Eds.): HAIS 2017, LNAI 10334, pp. 638–649, 2017.
DOI: 10.1007/978-3-319-59650-1_54

etc.), is a problem whose complexity is frequently linked to the lack of coordination and control of the various entities involved.

Holonic multi-agent systems (HMAS) [1,2] is a paradigm for the design of complex systems. In effect, this paradigm offers new strategies to analyze, design and implement such systems. HMASs are considered as societies composed of autonomous and independent entities, called holons [3] - groups of agents, which interact in order to solve a problem or collectively performs a task. According to Koestler, holon [3] is a self-similar structure that is stable, coherent and which consists of several holons as substructures. A holon is a component which can be seen both as a component part of a higher level element, and as a whole composed of other holons. Therefore, the notion of holon makes it possible to describe systems of hierarchical nature [4]. A holon has the same properties assigned to agents such as autonomy, social empowerment and proactivity. The holonic approach [2] is used to develop applications in complex domains characterized by a hierarchical structure, facilitate holarchic modeling, encourage modularity and reuse of models. HMASs involve heterogeneous and autonomous holons whose interactions must conform to certain social norms [7] and shared conventions to ensure the social control of the system.

Norms (permissions, obligations and prohibitions) [6,7] can be used in multi-agent systems [5] to define behavioral models. Norms specify behaviors that agents should follow in order to achieve the objectives of the system. The use of norms induces a positive impact on the coordination by reducing the uncertainty of the interactions due to the autonomy of holons (decides of its own process if it runs or not a required action). The main interest of norms is to compromise between the need for autonomy and the need for control.

Several proposals on normative models for multi-agent systems have been made in order to design agent societies in environments governed by norms. However, they are not adapted to support holonic systems, i.e. those who allow to model complex organizations involving several levels simultaneously.

Our contribution consists in effectively combining the advantages of these two approaches - the holonic approach [1,2] and the normative approach [7, 8], whose objective is to propose a new normative holonic approach, to ensure regulation, cooperation, coordination and social control in holonic multi-agent systems, and maintain consistency in these systems. The purpose of this paper is not to describe the methodological process, but rather it provides abstractions of our new normative holonic metamodel, NCRIO, that will become the basis of this process. This metamodel is an extension of the CRIO metamodel [9], which allows the design of HMAS. Our NCRIO metamodel retains the properties of HMAS systems and adds normative concepts (Norms and Contracts) to maintain social control in these systems.

The rest of this paper is organized as follows: Sect. 2 presents a motivating example; Sect. 3 makes an overview of works on normative model and Sect. 4 will detail our normative holonic metamodel. The last section concludes our paper and gives same future works.

2 Motivating Example

In this section, we present a motivating example, the design of Smart City Management System, which will be used throughout this paper to illustrate our normative holonic metamodel for MAS.

Smart City is an innovative city that uses the Information and Communication Technology (ICT). The ICT covers all areas of smart city such as government facilities, buildings, traffic, electricity, health, water and transport. Smart City must include: intelligent energy, smart buildings, intelligent transportation, intelligent management of the water and the waste, smart security and safety, intelligent health care and intelligent education. Smart City has a lot of features: (i) improved comfort in buildings (heating, air conditioning, ventilation and electric lighting); (ii) help to the surveillance and the security in the building; (iii) managing power consumption and helping to reduce energy consumption; (iv) improvement of the energy efficiency of buildings.

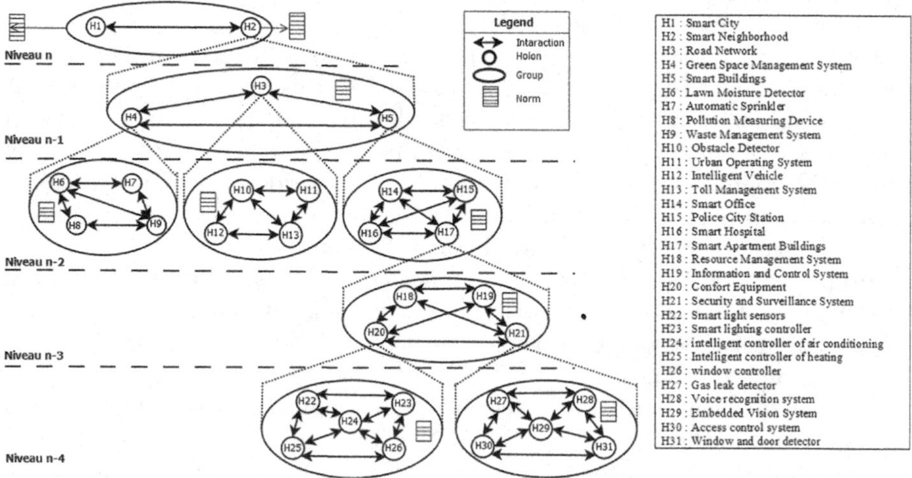

Fig. 1. Normative holonic structure of Smart City Management System

Smart city is composed of multiple heterogeneous and complex entities interacting with each other. In order to meet the needs of all these entities, the smart city must anchor its development in respect of a set of social norms and shared agreements. The smart city management system is a hierarchical system and requires social control. The normative Holonic metamodel, NCRIO, proposed in this paper allows the modeling of this type of system, which requires a hierarchical structure and social control.

From a holonic point of view, we can decompose smart city into several smart neighborhoods. In the same way, a smart neighborhood can be decomposed into a set of organizations (road network, green space management system, smart buildings). This holarchy of the smart city is described in Fig. 1. At the highest level (level n), the holon smart city is composed of smart neighborhoods. A smart neighborhoods is composed of three sub-holons: the road network, the management of the green space system and the smart buildings. At the level the lowest (level n–5) are intelligent sensors and meters, digital media and information devices, where n is the number of levels, here n = 5 levels.

From a normative point of view, we define a set of norms that govern behavior patterns for a smart city. Smart city is modeled as a set of holonic organizations that define several roles. Norms are integrated into the actions and guide the execution of actions of the holons to achieve the appropriate objectives. Smart city control requires a set of norms that specify what actions are necessary in certain situations. An informal specification of some norms in the smart city management system is reported below:

Norm 1: Smart City is obliged to respect the environment (green space) by reducing the production of waste.
Norm 2: Smart City is obliged to improve surveillance, safety and comfort of users.
Norm 3: Smart City is obliged to reduce energy consumption.

3 Related Work

Much work has been done on the normative models to design complex and dynamic agent organizations. For example, the work described in [10] provides a service-oriented methodology, called GORMAS [10], which defines a set of activities for the analysis and design of organizational systems, including the design of the norms that govern the behavior of the entities of the system. Other, normative model was proposed in [11], called Moise+. This last specifies a set of constraints for agents along three dimensions: a structural, functional and deontic specification. The Moise+ model is an attempt to unify the structural and functional specification of a MAS by a deontic phase. The above mentioned models present some limits when supporting normative MAS. They do not cover different types of norms (regulative, constitutive and procedural).

Recently, new proposals on normative models were made to design methodologies for the analysis and design of normative open MAS, like the ROMAS methodology [12]. This methodology is focused on the analysis and design processes for developing open organizational MAS where agents interact by means of services, and where social and contractual relationships are formalized using norms. This methodology presents certain limits, it only offers support to one norm level. It does not consider the different levels of abstraction.

In the field of normative holonic multi-agent systems, only one work was proposed, that of Massimo Cossentino et al. in [13]. This work presents an idea to integrate Moise+ [11] models with ASPECS [14] methodology, to provide abstractions and manage the normative aspect of an organization. They made an extension of ASPECS to include the elements of Moise+ model. This extension allows to define models not only from the point of view of the holonic agent, but also the point of view of the normative organization. This last present certain limits. It does not consider the existence of procedural and constitutive norms, but only give support to the regulative dimension of norms.

In this paper, we propose a new normative holonic metamodel, called NCRIO. We take the CRIO metamodel as starting point and extends him by adding normative aspects (norms and contracts). This metamodel inherits the concepts of Organization, Role, Interaction, Capacity and also adds the Norm and Contract concepts.

4 Normative Holonic Metamodel Proposal: NCRIO Metamodel

A metamodel is a formal specification of an abstraction to identify, formulate and describe a problem and its possible solution. NCRIO metamodel is a normative holonic metamodel for modeling of hierarchical systems in environments governed by norms. It is obtained from the integration and extension of the metamodel CRIO by adding normative aspects. CRIO was designed to the modeling of HMAS. NCRIO metamodel allows to define norms related to organizations and roles.

NCRIO is based on the MDA (Model Driven Architecture) approach [15], which is a software development approach, proposed and supported by the OMG (Object Management Group). The MDA approach considers three levels of models: (1) Computation Independent Model (CIM) focuses on the environment of the system and the specification of the needs which the system will have to satisfy. The details of the structure and the functioning of the system are hidden or indefinite; (2) Platform Independent Model (PIM) concentrates on the functioning of a system while hiding necessary details for its implementation on a particular platform. This type of model describes the part of the complete specification that does not change from a platform to another; (3) Platform Specific Model (PSM) combines the PIM with a model describing the details of the use of a specific implementation platform. In the logic of the MDA approach, NCRIO metamodel offers three levels of domains: the problem domain, agency domain and the solution domain. Our new extended metamodel (problem domain, agency domain, and solution domain) are shown in Figs. 2, 4 and 6. We used the green color to make distinctions of the new concepts of the NCRIO metamodel to highlight the differences with existing CRIO metamodel.

4.1 Problem Domain

This domain corresponds to the CIM model defined in the MDA approach, because it contains the necessary elements for the description of the problem from a normative holonic point of view independently of a specific solution. Figure 2 presents the UML diagram of the problem domain of the NCRIO metamodel.

The problem domain of NCRIO metamodel allows the modelling of the problem in terms of norm, organization, role, capacity and interaction. An Organization is defined by the aggregation of a set of roles. Each organization is associated with at least one functional need that corresponds to the objective it must satisfy. Functional requirements define the features of the system to be designed. Non-Functional Requirements define the properties of the system to be designed. A Role is an abstraction of a behavior in the context of an organization. Interactions occurring between roles within an organization are described in an interaction scenario that is usually represented by a UML sequence diagram. The normative environment is considered as a set of norms which govern the behavior of each entity, and a set of contracts which formalize the relationships between these entities. The normative context of each entity is specified by the set of norms which directly affect the behavior of this entity. In this domain, the norms are associated with organizations and roles, the function of which is to prescribe a set of constraints related to the membership in an organization or the fulfillment of the role. Concepts introduced in the problem domain allow to raise a first decomposition of the system in the form of an organizational hierarchy. Each of these organizations aims to satisfy one or several functional needs. Figure 3 illustrates this process of hierarchical decomposition of a smart city management system. Each need is associated with a global behavior in charge of satisfying it. This behavior is represented by an organization and each organization is then decomposed into a set of interacting roles. The decomposition process stops when the roles identified at a given level of abstraction are considered simple and easily implantable. For example, roles 'window and door detector' and 'window controller' at level n–4 are considered sufficiently simple.

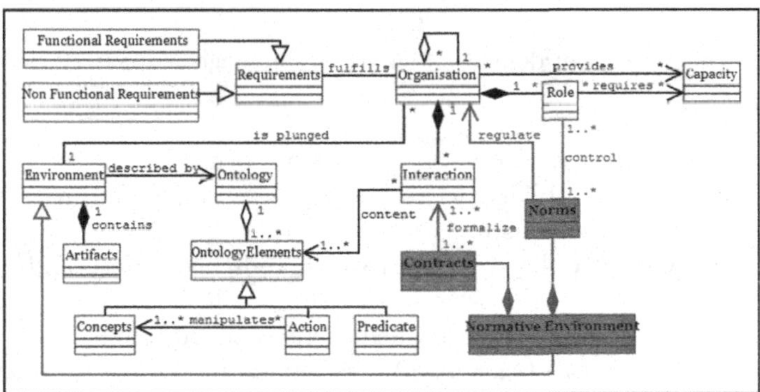

Fig. 2. Problem domain of NCRIO metamodel (Color figure online)

Since norms are associated with hierarchical organizations or roles, the normative context of an organization (set of norms) is also specified in a hierarchical structure using successive refinements. Refinement allows to develop the normative context of a system in an incremental way starting from an abstract context which constitutes a specification of the system. Refinement allows keeping the properties of more abstract normative contexts. During the refinement, new norms can be added. For example, in the case of Fig. 3, the normative context

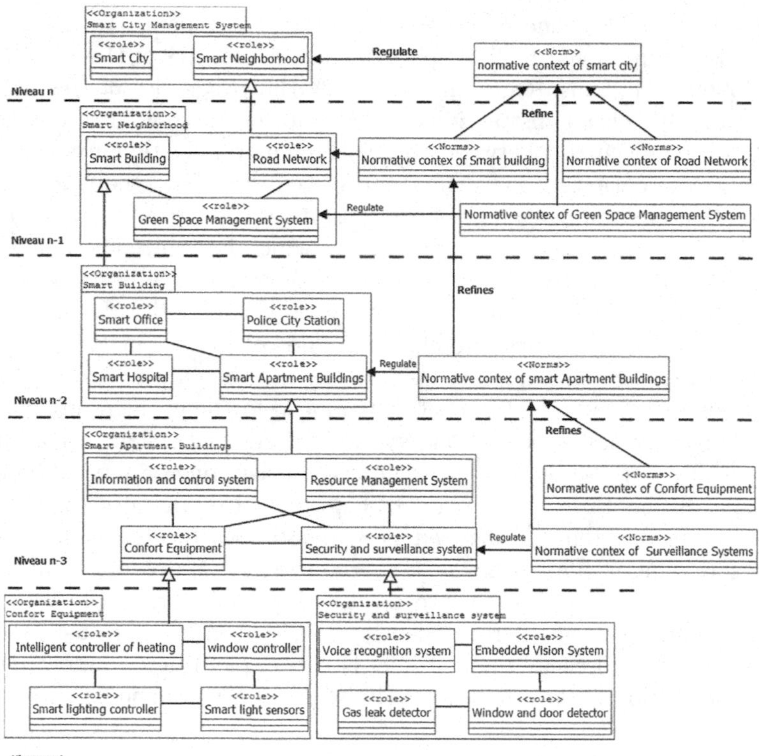

Fig. 3. Problem domain of smart city management system

of level n (abstract level) is composed of a set of norms:
Norm 1: Smart City is obliged to respect the environment (green space) by reducing the production of waste.
Norm 2: Smart City is obliged to improve surveillance, safety and comfort of users.
Norm 3: Smart City is obliged to reduce energy consumption.
These norms, of level n (abstract level), are refined in level n–1. During refinement, new norms are introduced. For example in level n–4, the lowest level of our example - Smart city, several norms are added.

4.2 Agency Domain

This domain corresponds to the PIM model defined in the MDA approach, because it describes the model of agents society, in charge to offer a solution to the previously modelled problem. It defines the concepts of norm, agent, holon, group and service. It provides a set of the necessary means to give an organizational hierarchy of the system. Figure 4 shows the UML diagram of the agency domain of NCRIO metamodel.

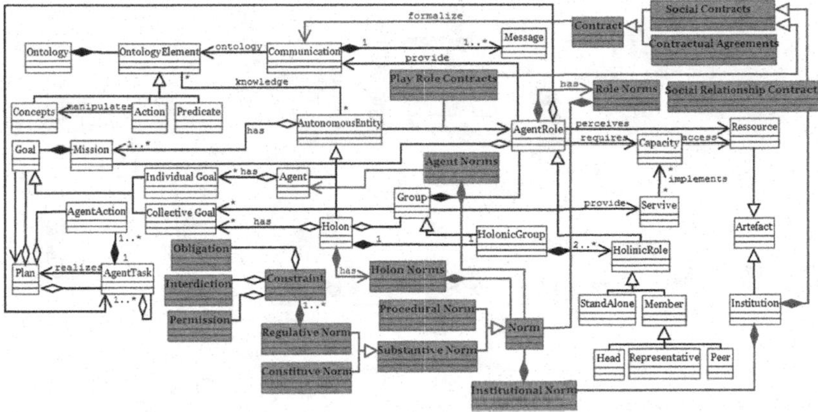

Fig. 4. Agency domain of NCRIO metamodel (Color figure online)

Within the agency domain, organizations stemming from the problem domain are instantiated in the form of groups. The roles which composed these organizations are also instantiated in the form of agent's roles. A role requires capacities to define its behavior, but it can also make them available to other roles by publishing a service. Each agent which plays a specific role acquires a set of rights, obligations and restrictions bound to this role. Therefore, it is necessary that the design architecture allows the definition of the set of norms associated to each specific role. These types of norms are called role norms.

The normative context of an organization of agents is formed by a set of norms which can be defined by the organization or institution [19]. These norms are classified into two main categories: **(i) Substantive norms**: allows the definition of the legal behavior of the system in terms of constitutive and regulative norms [16]. Constitutive norms [17] can be seen as an institutional constraint. These norms define the institutional level. An institution is thus represented by a set of rules. These rules are defined in separation the world in two: social (institutional) world and 'brute' (physical) world. Constitutive norms are defined using the logical operator **COUNT-AS** [20]. This operator is defined as follows: *a 'brute' fact X COUNT-AS an institutional fact Y in a given context C.* It allows to formally establish the link between a 'brute' fact and an institutional fact in a given institution S. Institutional facts are interpretations of 'brute' facts. For example (Fig. 5), in the Comfort Equipment institution, the brute fact '*open the window*' corresponds to the institutional fact to create a draft in case of a high temperature, or, in the institution Surveillance System, this fact is interpreted as to renew the air in case of gas leak. The institution is used to talk about specific organizations, or abstract schemes designed to regulate the interactions between holons, or to refer to the description of shared concepts and rules that regulate an institutional reality. Regulative norms define the set of constraints of a norm which defines a model of behavior for the agents. A constraint is the expression of an obligation, prohibition or permission for a property (the object of

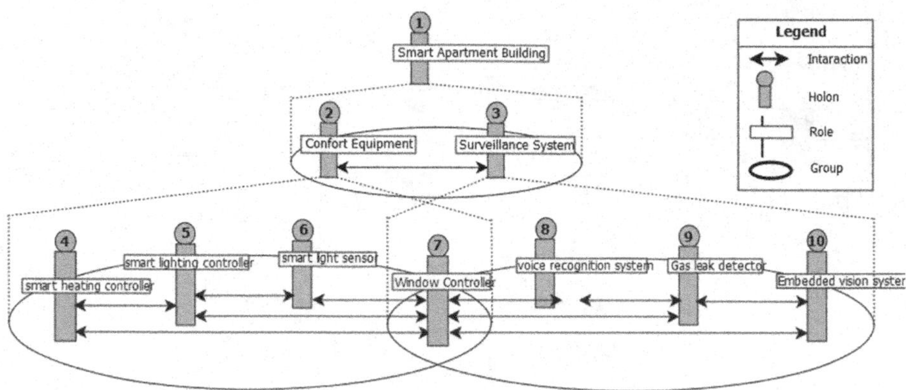

Fig. 5. Agency domain of Smart Apartment Buildings management system of smart city management system

the constraint). A constraint assigns a deontic value to a property. These norms generally refer to more abstract concepts defined by the constitutive norms. **(ii) Procedural norms**: aim to achieve the social order specified in terms of substantive norms. These norms define the mechanisms of the application in terms of punishments and rewards carried out by representative holon of the NHMAS. The norms that regulate behavior, in a specific institution, or a group of entities, are called institutional norms.

Our metamodel involves two types of contracts: (i) Social contracts: can be defined as a statement of intention which governs the behavior between organizations and individuals. The social contracts are used to formalize the relations between an agent playing role and his organization, or between two agents. (ii) Contractual arrangements: represent the commitments between several entities to formalize an exchange services or products.

The process of agentification of the organizational hierarchy is illustrated by Fig. 5. To build the application holarchy, the organizations that make up the system are instantiated as groups. A set of holons is then created at each level, each of them playing one or more roles in one or more groups. The organizational hierarchy is therefore directly associated with a hierarchy of holons (or holarchy). The norms governing the behavior of these holons are also described, using the the following template:

< *norm* >::= < *entity* > 'IS' < *deontic_concept* > 'TO' < *norm_description* >
< *entity* >::= 'Holon' | 'Agent'
< *deontic_concept* >::= 'OBLIGED' — 'FORBIDDEN' | 'PERMISSION'
< *norm_description* >::= {< *action* >< *sanction* >}
| {< *action* >< *temporal_situation* >< *sanction* >}
| {< *action* > 'IF'< *condition* >< *sanction* >}
| {< *action* >< *temporal_situation* >'IF'< *condition* >< *sanction* >}
< *action* >::=< *entity* > 'EXECUTE' < *exec* >
< *temporal_situation* >::= BEFORE < *situation* >
| AFTER < *situation* >
| BETWEEN (< *situation* >, < *situation* >)
< *exec* > ::= < *class* > . < *method* > (< *parameters* >)
< *condition* >::=< *variant* >< *operator* >< *variant* >

| < *normative_result* > (< *norm* >)
< *normative_result* >::= FAILED — SATISFIED
> *operator* >::= > | < | >= | <= | = | ⊆
< *variant* >::= < *atomic* > | < *formula* > | value
< *atomic* >::= variable | identifier.attribute
< *formula* >::= identifier(<args>)
< *sanction*::= < *punishments* >< *rewards* >
| < *punishments* >
| < *rewards* >
< *punishment* >::=< *authority* > 'PUNISHES' < *action* >
| < *authority* > 'PUNISHES' < *expression* >
< *reward* >::=< *promoter* > 'REWARDS' < *action* >
| < *promoter* > 'REWARDS' < *expression* >
< *authority* >::= < *entity* >
< *promoter* >::= < *entity* >

For example, specifying Norm 4, if room temperature is higher than expected temperature and the outside temperature is higher than the temperature of the room so the controller of the window is obliged to close the window and the controller of the air-conditioner is obliged to open the air-conditioner; the template for this norm would be:

Specifying Norm 4: ((< *the_controller_of_the_window* > 'IS' < *OBLIGED* > 'TO' < *close_the_window* >) 'AND' (< *the_controller_of_the_air − conditioner* > 'IS' < *OBLIGED* > 'TO' < *open_the_air − conditioner* >)) 'IF' ((< *room_temperature* > *expected_temperature* >) 'AND' (< *outside_temperature* > *room_temperature* >))

Norm 4 states the obligation of executing an action if a condition is true. It is a regulative norm.

4.3 Solution Domain

This domain corresponds to the PSM model defined in the MDA approach, because it depends on a particular implementation platform. The solution domain defines a set of concepts relatively close to those introduced into the agency domain of NCRIO metamodel. The concepts introduced into this domain are partially described in the UML diagram of the Fig. 6. To implant normative

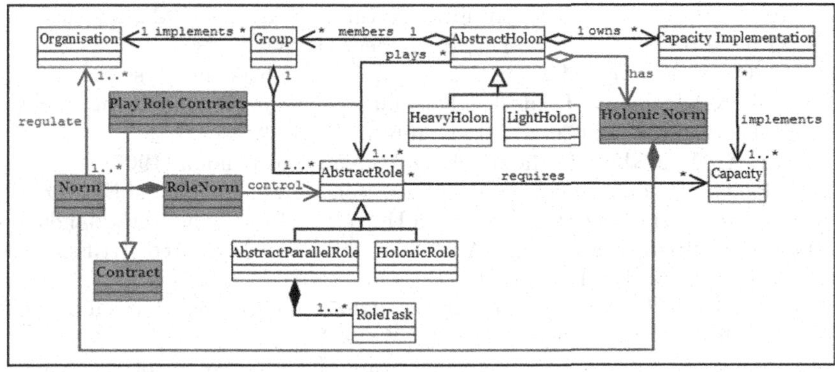

Fig. 6. Solution domain of NCRIO metamodel (Color figure online)

holonic models, we need a platform that can handle the notion of holon, the norm concept and to provide an operational representation of normative models combining several levels of abstraction. The SARL platform [18] integrates all these concepts. This latter was implanted so as to provide directly the concepts on the basis of the design holonic multi-agent systems.

Our objective consists to integrate the norm and contract concepts in the SARL platform which already supports the analysis, design and implementation of holonic MAS.

5 Conclusions and Future Work

In this paper, we have proposed a new normative holonic metamodel, called NCRIO. This metamodel is based on the MDA approach and provides three domains: problem domain, agency domain and the solution domain. He takes the CRIO metamodel as starting point and extends by adding normative aspects: norm and contract. This new metamodel, NCRIO, allows the design for complex (which require a hierarchical structure) and critical (which require social control) systems. We have used the NCRIO metamodel to properly specify the two aspects (Normative and Holonic) of a MAS in the design of smart city management system, used as an example here.

As future work, this work must be extended to define some rules and well defined steps leading the user to the progressively model complex system. The NCRIO metamodel will be the base of a new normative Holonic methodology, because it offers all the necessary abstractions for the modelling of these types of systems. The concepts proposed in this paper will be integrated into the SARL platform which already supports the analysis, design, and implementation of holonic MAS.

References

1. Rodriguez, S., Hilaire, V., Gaud, N., Galland, N., Koukam, A.: Holonic multi-agent systems. Self-Organising Software From Natural to Artificial Adaptation. Natural Computing, pp. 238–263. Springer, Heidelberg (2011)
2. Gerber, C., Siekmann, J.H., Vierke, G.: Holonic multi-agent systems. Technical Report DFKIRR- 99–03, Deutsches Forschungszentrum für Künztliche Inteligenz - GmbH, Postfach 20 80, 67608 Kaiserslautern, FRG (1999)
3. Koestler, A.: The Ghost in the Machine. Hutchinson, London (1967)
4. Mella, P.: The Holonic Revolution: Holons, Holarchies and Holonic Networks: The Ghost in the Production Machine. Pavia University Press, The Netherlands (2009)
5. Ferber, J.: Multi-Agent Systems: An Introduction to Distributed Artificial Intelligence. Addison-Wesley, London (1999)
6. Boella, G., Torre, L., Verhagen, H.: Introduction to normative multiagent systems. Comput. Math. Organ. Theor. **12**(2–3), 71–79 (2006)
7. Hollander, C.D., Wu, A.S.: The current state of normative agent-based systems. J. Artif. Soc. Soc. Simul. **14**(2), 6 (2011)

8. Garbay, C., Badeig, F., Caelen, J.: Normative multi-agent approach to support collaborative work in distributed tangible environments. In: Proceedings of the ACM 2012 Conference on Computer Supported Cooperative Work Companion, CSCW 2012, pp. 83–86. ACM, New York (2012)
9. Cossentino, M., Gaud, N., Galland, S., Hilaire, V., Koukam, A.: A holonic metamodel for agent-oriented analysis and design. In: Mařík, V., Vyatkin, V., Colombo, A.W. (eds.) HoloMAS 2007. LNCS (LNAI), vol. 4659, pp. 237–246. Springer, Heidelberg (2007). doi:10.1007/978-3-540-74481-8_23
10. Argente, E., Botti, V., Julian, V.: GORMAS: an organizational-oriented methodological guideline for open MAS. In: Gleizes, M.-P., Gomez-Sanz, J.J. (eds.) AOSE 2009. LNCS, vol. 6038, pp. 32–47. Springer, Heidelberg (2011). doi:10.1007/978-3-642-19208-1_3
11. Hubner, J., Sichman, J., Boissier, O.: Moise+: towards a structural, functional, and deontic model for MAS organization. In: Proceedings of the First International Joint Conference on Autonomous Agents and Multiagent Systems: Part 1, p. 502. ACM (2002)
12. Garcia, E., Giret, A., Botti, V.: ROMAS Methodology. In: Cossentino, M., Hilaire, V., Molesini, A., Seidita, V. (eds.) Handbook on Agent-Oriented Design Processes, pp. 331–369. Springer, Berlin (2014)
13. Cossentino, M., Hilaire, V., Lodato, C., Lopes, S., Ribino, P., Seidita, V.: ńNorm-Governed HMAS Metamodel Applied to Logistics, ż chez International Workshop on AGENT ORIENTED SOFTWARE ENGINEERING (2013)
14. Cossentino, M., Gaud, N., Hilaire, V., Galland, S., Koukam, A.: ASPECS: an agent-oriented software process for engineering complex systems - how to design agent societies under a holonic perspective. Auton. Agents Multi-Agent Syst. **2**(2), 260–304 (2010)
15. Object Management Group (OMG): MDA Guide, v1.0.1, OMG (2003)
16. Boella, G., der Torre, L.: Constitutive norms in the design of normative multiagent systems. In: Toni, F., Torroni, P. (eds.) CLIMA 2005. LNCS (LNAI), vol. 3900, pp. 303–319. Springer, Heidelberg (2006). doi:10.1007/11750734_17
17. Boella, G., van der Torre, L.: Regulative and constitutive norms in normative multiagent systems. In: KR2004: Principles of Knowledge Representation and Reasoning, pp. 255–265. AAAI Press (2004)
18. Rodriguez, S., Gaud, N., Galland, S.: SARL: a general-purpose agent-oriented programming language. In: 2014 IEEE/WIC/ACM International Joint Conferences on Web Intelligence (WI) and Intelligent Agent Technologies (IAT), vol. 3, pp. 103–110 (2014)
19. Dignum, V., Dignum, F.: Modelling agent societies: co-ordination frameworks and institutions. In: Brazdil, P., Jorge, A. (eds.) EPIA 2001. LNCS, vol. 2258, pp. 191–204. Springer, Heidelberg (2001). doi:10.1007/3-540-45329-6_21
20. Searle, J.R.: Speech Acts. Cambridge UP, London (1969)

Forecasting Satellite Trajectories by Interpolating Hybrid Orbit Propagators

Iván Pérez[1(✉)], Montserrat San-Martín[2], Rosario López[3], Eliseo P. Vergara[1], Alexander Wittig[4], and Juan Félix San-Juan[1(✉)]

[1] Scientific Computing Group (GRUCACI), University of La Rioja, 26006 Logroño, Spain
{ivan.perez,eliseo.vergara,juanfelix.sanjuan}@unirioja.es

[2] Scientific Computing Group (GRUCACI), University of Granada, 52005 Melilla, Spain
momartin@ugr.es

[3] Scientific Computing Group (GRUCACI), Center for Biomedical Research of La Rioja, 26006 Logroño, Spain
rlgomez@riojasalud.es

[4] Advanced Concepts Team, European Space Agency, 2200 Noordwijk, AG, The Netherlands
Alexander.Wittig@esa.int

Abstract. A hybrid orbit propagator based on the analytical integration of the *Kepler problem* is designed to determine the future position and velocity of any orbiter, usually an artificial satellite or space debris fragment, in two steps: an initial approximation generated by means of an integration method, followed by a forecast of its error, determined by a prediction technique that models and reproduces the missing dynamics. In this study we analyze the effect of slightly changing the initial conditions for which a hybrid propagator was developed. We explore the possibility of generating a new hybrid propagator from others previously developed for nearby initial conditions. We find that the interpolation of the parameters of the prediction technique, which in this case is an additive Holt-Winters method, yields similarly accurate results to a non-interpolated hybrid propagator when modeling the J_2 effect in the *main problem* propagation.

1 Introduction

The propagation of perturbed orbits is a well-known problem which implies having to tackle a set of three second-order or six first-order differential equations, so as to determine the position and velocity of an orbiter at a given final time t_f from its situation at an initial instant t_1.

As these equations are not directly integrable, there are three well-established techniques aimed at providing a solution to the problem. Each of these methods can be characterized in terms of the formulation of the equation of motion, the integration method used to obtain the solution to this equation, which can be numerical or analytical, and, finally, the perturbation model taken into account.

F.J. Martínez de Pisón et al. (Eds.): HAIS 2017, LNAI 10334, pp. 650–661, 2017.
DOI: 10.1007/978-3-319-59650-1_55

General perturbation theories apply perturbation methods to the determination of an analytical solution. Such solution, which is an explicit function of time and some physical constants, allows for a fast determination of the coordinates at t_f. In addition, being an analytical expression, it embeds the dynamics of the problem. Nevertheless, in order to avoid extreme complexity, the analytical solution is usually a low-order approximation in which only the most relevant forces are considered.

Special perturbation theories, in contrast, perform a numerical integration of the problem. They have the advantage of allowing for the consideration of any effect into the model, even the complex ones, thus leading to highly accurate solutions. Nonetheless, the disadvantage lies in the necessity to take small integration steps, which implies long computational time.

Semianalytical techniques take advantage of both theories. They allow for the consideration of complex perturbing effects into the model, which is simplified by means of analytical methods so as to remove the short-period component. Consequently, the new equations of motion can be numerically integrated through longer steps, resulting in reduced computational time.

More recently, the *hybrid propagation methodology* has been presented. It is based on the combination of any of the aforementioned integration methods and a forecasting technique. The former generates an initial solution, which is approximate because of the assumed simplifications and inaccuracies in the perturbation models. The latter makes use of forecasting techniques, based on either statistical time series models [7,8] or machine learning methods [5], in order to provide, once adjusted with a set of real observations that include the dynamics neglected in the initial approximation, a prediction of its error. The sum of this error prediction and the initial solution generates the final result.

The forecasting component of a hybrid propagator needs a set of control data, deduced from precise observations or accurately computed coordinates, so that the statistical or machine learning technique can model dynamics not present in the first stage of the method.

Nevertheless, a grid of hybrid propagators for a set of relatively close initial conditions can be constructed, in such a way that hybrid propagators for intermediate cases can be directly deduced from the grid, with no need for control data. By doing so, the study of initial conditions in the surroundings of an orbiter can be easily handled with no need to recompute the parameters of the forecasting component of the hybrid method.

In this paper we will consider the so-called *main problem* of the artificial satellite theory, that is, the *Kepler problem* only perturbed by the flattening of the Earth. We will create a hybrid propagator, composed of a general perturbation theory derived from the *Kepler problem* plus an additive Holt-Winters method modeling the J_2 effect, for a certain orbiter. In order to handle both eccentricity and inclination small variations, we will construct a grid of hybrid propagators around the studied satellite. After that, we will prove that the forecasting component of the hybrid propagator, when eccentricity and/or inclination slightly vary, can be directly derived from the grid by simply interpolating the parameters of the Holt-Winters method.

The outline of the paper is divided into seven sections. Section 2 presents the principles of the hybrid propagation methodology, whereas Sect. 3 focuses on the use of an exponential smoothing technique, the Holt-Winters method, as the forecasting stage of hybrid propagators. The described concepts are applied to the creation of a hybrid propagator for a certain satellite in Sect. 4. With the aim of studying its surroundings, a grid of initial conditions, together with its corresponding hybrid propagators, is created around the studied satellite in Sect. 5. Section 6 illustrates how to develop new hybrid propagators for nearby initial conditions through the interpolation of parameters from other propagators in the grid. Finally, Sect. 7 summarizes the conclusions of the study and future lines of research.

2 Hybrid Propagation Methodology

The hybrid propagation methodology is aimed at estimating the position and velocity of an orbiter, which can be an artificial satellite or a fragment of space debris, at a given final time t_f, $\hat{\boldsymbol{x}}_f$, starting from the known position and velocity at an initial instant t_1, $\boldsymbol{x}_1$. It is worth noting that any set of canonical or non-canonical variables can be used for this purpose.

In a first stage, an integration method $\mathcal{I}$ is used to calculate an initial approximation of $\hat{\boldsymbol{x}}_f$:

$$\boldsymbol{x}_f^{\mathcal{I}} = \mathcal{I}(t_f, \boldsymbol{x}_1). \tag{1}$$

The integration method is applied to a mathematical model that not always describes the physical phenomena exactly. Moreover, when the general perturbation theory or semianalytical techniques are used, only the most important forces and low-order approximations are usually considered; otherwise cumbersome expressions would be obtained. Due to all these facts, $\boldsymbol{x}_f^{\mathcal{I}}$ is an initial approximation that needs to be complemented in a second stage in order to obtain $\hat{\boldsymbol{x}}_f$.

The information that this second stage needs to model and reproduce, that is, the missing dynamics, has to be deduced from a *control interval* $[t_1, t_T]$, with $t_T < t_f$. Throughout this interval both the initial approximation $\boldsymbol{x}_i^{\mathcal{I}}$ and the exact position and velocity $\boldsymbol{x}_i$ are assumed to be known, for example by means of precise observations or intensive and accurate numerical propagations. Therefore, the error due to the missing dynamics for any instant in the control interval can be expressed as

$$\boldsymbol{\varepsilon}_i = \boldsymbol{x}_i - \boldsymbol{x}_i^{\mathcal{I}}, \tag{2}$$

and the time series of the errors of each of the six variables during the control interval, which we will call *control data*, can be constructed as $\boldsymbol{\varepsilon}_1, \ldots, \boldsymbol{\varepsilon}_T$.

The processing of this time series, by means of either statistical techniques or machine learning methods, allows for the modeling of its behavior and, more importantly, its prediction at any time outside the control interval. Therefore, an estimation of the error at the final instant t_f, $\hat{\boldsymbol{\varepsilon}}_f$, can be determined, and thus the desired value of $\hat{\boldsymbol{x}}_f$ can be calculated as

$$\hat{\boldsymbol{x}}_f = \boldsymbol{x}_f^{\mathcal{I}} + \hat{\boldsymbol{\varepsilon}}_f. \tag{3}$$

3 Exponential Smoothing Method for Time Series Forecasting

Exponential smoothing methods consider a time series ε_t as the combination of three components: the trend μ_t, or secular variation, the seasonal component S_t, or periodic oscillation, and the irregular or non-predictable component ν_t. In the case of an additive composition, ε_t can be expressed as

$$\varepsilon_t = \mu_t + S_t + \nu_t. \tag{4}$$

In particular, the Holt-Winters method [10] considers a linear trend with level A and slope B:

$$\mu_t = A + Bt. \tag{5}$$

According to this method, and taking into account that ν_t cannot be predicted, the next value of a time series can be estimated from past values as

$$\hat{\varepsilon}_t = A_{t-1} + B_{t-1} + S_{t-s}, \tag{6}$$

where s is the period of the seasonal component, and A, B, and S can be determined from previous values according to the following recurrences

$$\begin{aligned} A_t &= \alpha(\varepsilon_t - S_{t-s}) + (1-\alpha)(A_{t-1} + B_{t-1}), \\ B_t &= \beta(A_t - A_{t-1}) + (1-\beta)B_{t-1}, \\ S_t &= \gamma(\varepsilon_t - A_t) + (1-\gamma)S_{t-s}, \end{aligned} \tag{7}$$

in which α, β, and γ are three smoothing parameters with values in the interval $[0, 1]$.

Algorithm 1. Holt-Winters

Require: s, c, h, and $\{\varepsilon_t\}_{t=1}^{T}$
Ensure: $\hat{\varepsilon}_{T+h|T}$
Estimate the values of $A_0, B_0, S_{-s+1}, \ldots, S_{-1}, S_0$
for $t = 1$; $t \le T$; $t = t + 1$ **do**
    $A_t = \alpha(\varepsilon_t - S_{t-s}) + (1-\alpha)(A_{t-1} + B_{t-1})$
    $B_t = \beta(A_t - A_{t-1}) + (1-\beta)B_{t-1}$
    $S_t = \gamma(\varepsilon_t - A_t) + (1-\gamma)S_{t-s}$
    $\hat{\varepsilon}_t = A_{t-1} + B_{t-1} + S_{t-s}$
end for
Select `error_measure` $\in$ {MSE, MAE, MAPE} and express it as a function of the smoothing parameters
Obtain the smoothing parameters that minimize `error_measure` using the L-BFGS-B method
Calculate $A_T, B_T, S_{T-s+1}, \ldots, S_{T-1}, S_T$ for the optimum smoothing parameters
$\hat{\varepsilon}_{T+h|T} = A_T + hB_T + S_{T-s+1+h \bmod s}$
return $\hat{\varepsilon}_{T+h|T}$

Algorithm 1 shows how to apply the Holt-Winters method to the prediction of future time series values. The inputs to the algorithm are the amount of data per revolution, s, the number of revolutions in the control interval, c, the number of time steps after the control interval for which the time series value has to be predicted, h, and the control data, $\{\varepsilon_t\}_{t=1}^{T}$, with $T = s \times c$. The output is $\hat{\varepsilon}_{T+h|T}$, that is, the forecast of the time series at the final instant $t_f = t_{T+h}$, based on the last control data, ε_T.

The algorithm starts by estimating the initial parameters A_0, B_0, $S_{-s+1}, \ldots,$ S_{-1}, and S_0, which is accomplished through a classical additive decomposition into trend and seasonal variation over the three first revolutions. A linear regression over the trend provides the initial level A_0 and slope B_0, whereas the seasonal component yields the values of $S_{-s+1}, \ldots, S_{-1}$, and S_0.

Then, an iterative process takes place by applying Eqs. (6) and (7) to the control interval (lines 2–7). As a result, the expressions of the parameters A_t, B_t, S_t, and the single-step time series prediction $\hat{\varepsilon}_t$ are obtained as functions of the smoothing parameters α, β, and γ.

After that, an error measure is selected among mean square error, MSE, mean absolute error, MAE, and mean absolute percentage error, MAPE.

The selected error measure applied to the control interval yields an expression which is a function of the smoothing parameters. Then, an optimization method is necessary to determine the values of the smoothing parameters that minimize this error measure. The limited memory algorithm L-BFGS-B [4], which is a variation of the BFGS method [9], allows to impose restrictions on the smoothing parameters, and hence is the algorithm that has been used.

Once the optimal smoothing parameters have been found, the time series parameters A_T, B_T, $S_{T-s+1}, \ldots, S_{T-1}, S_T$ are determined for the last period of the control interval, from which the forecasted time series value at the final instant, that is, h epochs ahead, $\hat{\varepsilon}_f = \hat{\varepsilon}_{T+h|T}$, can be calculated (line 11).

4 Application of the Hybrid Propagation Methodology

In this section, the described hybrid methodology is applied to the propagation of an orbit with the following initial conditions: semi-major axis $a = 7228$ km, eccentricity $e = 0.06$, and inclination $i = 49°$. The first stage of the method is an analytical theory derived from the *Kepler problem*, that is, considering no perturbations at all, whereas the second part is an additive Holt-Winters method, designed to model the perturbation caused by the flattening of the Earth, which corresponds to the J_2 term in its gravitational potential. Therefore, the complete hybrid propagator is adapted to the *main problem* of the artificial satellite theory; consequently, its results will be compared with those obtained from a highly accurate numerical integration of the *main problem* by means of a high-order Runge-Kutta method.

The solution to the *Kepler problem* provided by the analytical expression in the first stage of the hybrid propagator is characterized by constant values in all the classical orbital elements, except in the mean anomaly, whose values evolve following the orbiter angular position. In contrast, when the J_2 effect is considered, no orbital element remains constant, so that, in general, secular, short-period, and long-period effects can be found in the evolution of orbital elements. The goal of the Holt-Winters method in the second stage of the hybrid propagator is the modeling and reproduction of such dynamics. The difference between the initial Kepler solution and the desired *main problem* solution translates into a position error of about 14500 km after 20 days of propagation, which represents approximately the distance between the apogee and perigee of the orbit.

The hybrid methodology can be applied to any set of variables, although Delaunay variables (l, g, h, L, G, H) will be used in this case. The first step consists in preparing the control data, which is composed of two time series: the initial approximations generated by the analytical expression derived from the *Kepler problem*, and the accurate solutions calculated by means of a high-order Runge-Kutta method. The last time series could be substituted for a set of precise observations in case they were available. The subtraction of both data sets yields the time series of the error, which contains the dynamics missing from the initial approximation. It is worth noting that the control data set should be large enough so as to include any pattern to be modeled by the second stage of the method. In this case, a control interval of ten revolutions has been chosen, which represents a time span of nearly 17 h, taking into account that the aforementioned orbital elements correspond to an orbital period of 101.926 min. The sampling rate for the time series has been taken equal to 12 samples per orbiter revolution, which corresponds to a sampling period of 101.926/12 = 8.494 min.

Before processing data, angular variables are homogenized to the interval $(-\pi, \pi]$ by adding or subtracting complete spins to values outside this interval. An univariate Holt-Winters model is considered for the time series of the error of each Delaunay variable, except for ε_t^H, which is 0 in this case, which means that the analytical approximation is perfect for this variable, and hence there is no need to complement it in the second stage of the hybrid propagator.

Then, a preliminary analysis of the five remaining time series is performed through the study of their sequence graphics, periodograms, and autocorrelation functions (ACF). This analysis reveals the existence of three main seasonal components, with periods a third, a half, and one Keplerian period, that is, 33.976, 50.964, and 101.926 min, although the last one is the most remarkable and includes the others.

Next, Algorithm 1 is applied, selecting MSE as the error measure needed to determine the optimal values for the smoothing parameters α, β, and γ.

Once the five Holt-Winters models corresponding to Delaunay variables l, g, h, L, and G have been created, they are integrated into the hybrid propagator so as to evaluate its accuracy through the comparison with a precise numerical propagation by means of a high-order Runge-Kutta method.

Table 1 compares the position error, after different propagation spans, between the analytical approximation, which only considers the *Kepler problem*, and the hybrid propagation, which models the *main problem*. As can be

Table 1. Distance error (km) after propagating the studied satellite.

Propagation span	Analytic method (Kepler)	Hybrid method (Kepler + J_2)
1 day	1197.10	0.45
2 days	2379.94	0.83
7 days	7900.47	3.63
30 days	14504.69	13.73

seen, the latter presents reduced errors, even after 30 days of propagation, which implies that the forecasting part of the hybrid method has been able to model most of the J_2 effect.

5 Creation of a Grid from Control Data

After developing a hybrid propagator for the studied satellite, the effect of a slight change in the initial conditions will be analyzed. For that purpose, small variations in eccentricity and inclination will be considered. We construct a grid of initial conditions around the studied satellite, modifying its eccentricity in 0.5×10^{-2} steps and its inclination in 1° steps, as shown in Fig. 1.

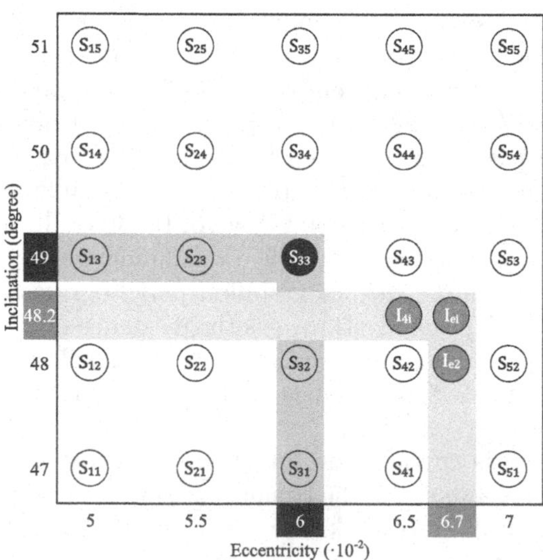

Fig. 1. Grid of initial conditions S_{ei} constructed around the studied satellite S_{33}, and intermediate initial conditions I.

Next, we develop a new hybrid propagator for each initial condition S_{ei} in the grid, following the steps described in the previous section for the studied

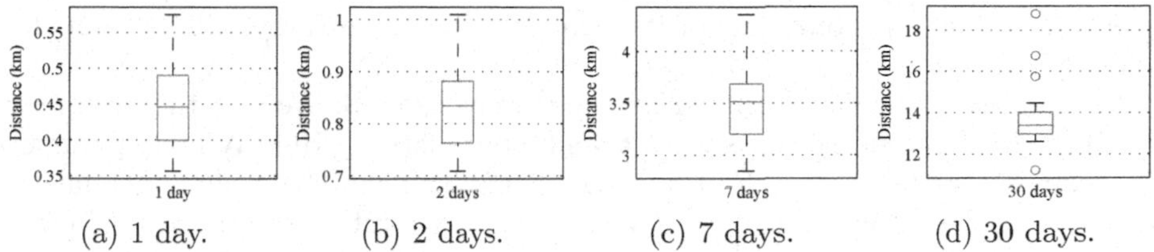

(a) 1 day. (b) 2 days. (c) 7 days. (d) 30 days.

Fig. 2. Boxplots of distance errors corresponding to the hybrid propagation of the grid initial conditions at different propagation horizons.

satellite S_{33}. It is worth noting that control data are necessary for that process. Our final objective, in the next section, will be to verify the possibility to develop new hybrid propagators for initial conditions within the margins of the grid without having to follow the complete process, and hence with no need for control data.

We finish the creation of the grid hybrid propagators by analyzing their position errors with respect to the accurate numerical integration of their initial conditions. Figure 2 shows their distribution after different propagation spans by means of boxplot graphics. It can be seen that their average values agree with those shown in Table 1 for the studied satellite S_{33}.

In general, the distributions of the position errors are symmetrical, showing little dispersion and only a few outliers in the case of a 30-day propagation horizon. All the initial conditions have similar dynamic behavior, which leads to the homogeneity of the obtained position errors. Such results constitute an appropriate scenario for the adaptation of the developed hybrid propagators to nearby initial conditions.

6 Propagation of New Orbits

At this point, hybrid propagators for the studied satellite S_{33} and its surrounding grid S_{ei} have been developed. Now, we want to propagate nearby initial conditions I which occupy intermediate positions within the limits of the grid (Fig. 1).

The analytical theory in the first stage of the hybrid propagators is the same for all the cases. However, each set of initial conditions requires an individual Holt-Winters model in the forecasting stage of its hybrid propagator, aimed at modeling and predicting the effect of the J_2 perturbation under its particular conditions. In order to take advantage of the nearby hybrid propagators developed in advance, and also to avoid the need for control data, a new strategy is proposed: the interpolation of the parameters A_T, B_T, $S_{T-s+1}, \ldots, S_{T-1}, S_T$ of the intermediate I Holt-Winters models from those corresponding to the studied satellite S_{33} and its surrounding grid S_{ei}.

Several interpolation methods have been compared. Some of them only allow for one-dimensional interpolation, while others permit multi-dimensional interpolation. We perform comparisons on I_{e2}, which only needs one-dimensional interpolation because only one of its elements, the eccentricity, differs from the values in the grid.

In the first place, a *weighted average* technique is used. We take the inverse of the difference in eccentricity as weight, and interpolate I_{e2} Holt-Winters parameters from those of S_{12}, S_{22}, S_{32}, S_{42}, and S_{52}, which share the same inclination with I_{e2}. In the second place, the *linear regression* method is applied, deducing I_{e2} parameters from the nearest straight lines to S_{12}, S_{22}, S_{32}, S_{42}, and S_{52} parameters. The third interpolation approach is performed through *Lagrange polynomials*, by deducing I_{e2} parameters from the fourth-order polynomials passing through S_{12}, S_{22}, S_{32}, S_{42}, and S_{52} parameters. As it is known, the order of the Lagrange polynomials would increase if more initial conditions were available on the grid. Finally, *spline interpolation* is used. This is the only considered method that permits multi-dimensional interpolation. The two-dimensional spline interpolation implemented in the Akima package [3] of the R programming language [6], which will be the method to be applied to the case of I_{ei} because both its eccentricity and inclination differ from all the initial conditions present on the grid, is based on Refs. [1,2].

Table 2. Position error (km) after the interpolated hybrid propagation of the intermediate initial conditions I_{e2} through different interpolation methods.

Propagation span	Weighted average	Linear regression	Lagrange polynomial	Spline
1 day	9.070	1.772	2.021	0.469
2 days	18.440	3.563	4.070	0.836
7 days	66.222	12.460	14.237	3.498
30 days	272.777	48.653	55.715	13.598

Table 2 presents the results obtained for each of the four aforementioned interpolation methods by means of the position error of the interpolated hybrid propagators developed for I_{e2}. As can be seen, spline interpolation leads to the best results for all the propagation spans, followed by linear regression, Lagrange polynomial, and, finally, the weighted average technique, which yields the worst results.

The analysis of these interpolation methods applied to the other set of intermediate initial conditions that requires one-dimensional interpolation, I_{4i}, yields the same conclusions; therefore spline is selected as the interpolation method to be used. Then, an interpolated hybrid propagator is also developed for I_{ei}, making use of two-dimensional spline interpolation, as mentioned previously.

Figure 3 represents the position errors obtained for the spline-interpolated hybrid propagation of the three intermediate initial conditions, and compares them with the distributions of the corresponding position errors for the hybrid propagation of the grid initial conditions (Fig. 2). As could be expected, due to the homogeneous behavior of all the initial conditions in the grid, the position errors of the intermediate cases are very similar to the grid average.

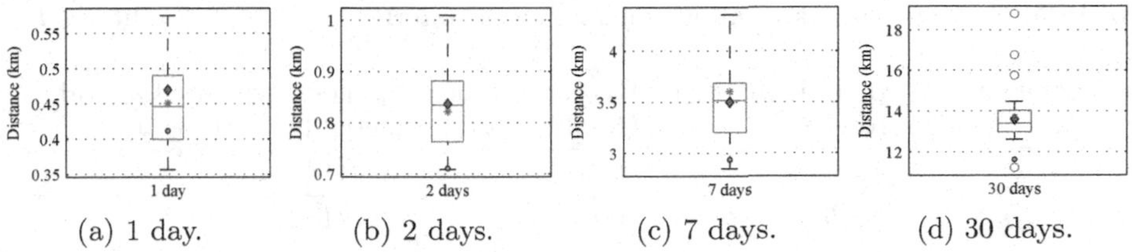

(a) 1 day. (b) 2 days. (c) 7 days. (d) 30 days.

Fig. 3. Position errors of the spline-interpolated hybrid propagation of the three intermediate initial conditions against the boxplot distributions of their corresponding grid position errors. Diamond, circle and star represent the initial conditions I_{e2}, I_{ei}, and I_{4i}, respectively.

The case of the two-dimensional interpolation in eccentricity and inclination, I_{ei}, is remarkable because of its especially low errors, to the extent that it constitutes a low-error outlier for a propagation horizon of 30 days.

Tables 3, 4, and 5 compare the results of propagating the three sets of intermediate initial conditions I_{e2}, I_{4i}, and I_{ei} through the mere analytic, the hybrid, and the spline-interpolated hybrid methods. In general, it can be verified that the latter propagators outperform the non-interpolated hybrid ones, especially in the case of the two-dimensionally spline-interpolated hybrid propagator for I_{ei}.

Table 3. Position error (km) after propagating the intermediate initial conditions I_{e2}.

Propagation span	Analytic method (Kepler)	Hybrid method (Kepler + J_2)	Spline-interpolated hybrid method (Kepler + J_2)
1 day	1244.061	0.600	0.409
2 days	2472.668	0.840	0.836
7 days	8165.104	3.711	3.498
30 days	14504.581	14.982	13.598

Table 4. Position error (km) after propagating the intermediate initial conditions I_{4i}.

Propagation span	Analytic method (Kepler)	Hybrid method (Kepler + J_2)	Spline-interpolated hybrid method (Kepler + J_2)
1 day	1232.193	0.533	0.451
2 days	2449.259	0.819	0.821
7 days	8098.784	3.828	3.601
30 days	14510.092	15.090	13.691

Table 5. Position error (km) after propagating the intermediate initial conditions I_{ei}.

Propagation span	Analytic method (Kepler)	Hybrid method (Kepler + J_2)	Spline-interpolated hybrid method (Kepler + J_2)
1 day	1240.220	0.561	0.411
2 days	2465.050	0.823	0.711
7 days	8143.626	3.724	2.936
30 days	14506.802	14.950	11.619

7 Conclusion and Future Work

In this work, we have presented an advance in the hybrid propagation methodology. Hybrid propagators are composed of an integration theory plus a forecasting technique. The latter is developed from control data so as to complement the approximation generated by the former by modeling and reproducing the missing dynamics. We have explored the possibility of deducing the forecasting stage directly from other hybrid propagators developed for surrounding initial conditions. This approach avoids the need for control data, and makes it possible to have a grid of hybrid propagators prepared in advance for a region of initial conditions of interest. We have verified that the spline interpolation of the parameters of an additive Holt-Winters forecasting method from nearby hybrid propagators yields similar accuracy, or even better, to a non-interpolated hybrid propagator. The study has been conducted using the *main problem* of the artificial satellite theory as the propagation model, with the forecasting stage modeling the complete J_2 effect.

At present, we are testing the hybrid propagation methodology considering neural networks instead of the Holt-Winters algorithm as time series forecasters. During the second semester of 2017, a competition organized by the European Space Agency will be launched through the Advanced Concepts Team competition website, KELVINS,[1] in order to encourage the machine learning community to get involved and participate in the problem.

Acknowledgments. This work has been funded by the Spanish State Research Agency and the European Regional Development Fund under Project ESP2016-76585-R (AEI/ERDF, EU). Support from the European Space Agency through Project Ariadna Hybrid Propagation (ESA Contract No. 4000118548/16/NL/LF/as) is also acknowledged.

References

1. Akima, H.: A method of bivariate interpolation and smooth surface fitting for irregularly distributed data points. ACM Trans. Math. Softw. **4**(2), 148–159 (1978)

[1] https://kelvins.esa.int/.

2. Akima, H.: Algorithm 761: scattered-data surface fitting that has the accuracy of a cubic polynomial. ACM Trans. Math. Softw. **22**(3), 362–371 (1996)
3. Akima, H., Gebhardt, A., Petzold, T., Maechler, M.: akima: interpolation of irregularly and regularly spaced data. R Foundation for Statistical Computing (2015). http://CRAN.R-project.org/package=akima, R package version 0.5-12
4. Byrd, R.H., Lu, P., Nocedal, J., Zhu, C.: A limited memory algorithm for bound constrained optimization. SIAM J. Sci. Comput. **16**(5), 1190–1208 (1995)
5. Pérez, I., San-Juan, J.F., San-Martín, M., López-Ochoa, L.M.: Application of computational intelligence in order to develop hybrid orbit propagation methods. Math. Probl. Eng. Article ID 631628, 11 (2013)
6. R Core Team: R: A language and environment for statistical computing. R Foundation for Statistical Computing, Vienna, Austria (2015). https://www.R-project.org
7. San-Juan, J.F., San-Martín, M., Pérez, I.: An economic hybrid J_2 analytical orbit propagator program based on SARIMA models. Math. Probl. Eng. Article ID 207381, 15 (2012)
8. San-Juan, J.F., San-Martín, M., Pérez, I., López, R.: Hybrid perturbation methods based on statistical time series models. Adv. Space Res. **57**(8), 1641–1651 (2016). Advances in Asteroid and Space Debris Science and Technology - Part 2
9. Shanno, D.F.: Conditioning of quasi-Newton methods for function minimization. Math. Comput. **24**(111), 647–656 (1970)
10. Winters, P.R.: Forecasting sales by exponentially weighted moving averages. Manage. Sci. **6**(3), 324–342 (1960)

Detecting Potential Design Weaknesses in SHADE Through Network Feature Analysis

Adam Viktorin, Michal Pluhacek, Roman Senkerik, and Tomas Kadavy(✉)

Faculty of Applied Informatics, Tomas Bata University in Zlin, T.G. Masaryka 5555, 760 01 Zlin, Czech Republic
{aviktorin, pluhacek, senkerik, kadavy}@fai.utb.cz

Abstract. This preliminary study presents a hybridization of two research fields – evolutionary algorithms and complex networks. A network is created by the dynamic of an evolutionary algorithm, namely Success-History based Adaptive Differential Evolution (SHADE). Network feature, node degree centrality, is used afterward to detect potential design weaknesses of SHADE algorithm. This approach is experimentally tested on the CEC2015 benchmark set of test functions and future directions in the research are proposed.

Keywords: Differential evolution · SHADE · Complex network · Centrality

1 Introduction

Differential Evolution (DE) is one of the most powerful tools for numerical optimization since its discovery in 1995 [1]. Therefore, the field of DE has been thoroughly studied by a large number of researchers all over the world and the primary goal is to develop a DE variant, which would outperform the current state-of-art algorithms. This leads to an overwhelming quantity of DE based algorithms that emerge every year. Luckily, an overview of current variants has been done in [2, 3] and most recently [4].

A late trend in DE sector is in adapting control parameters of the algorithm – population size *NP*, scaling factor *F* and crossover rate *CR* to the given optimization task. An algorithm from this family usually tries to overcome the No Free Lunch (NFL) theorem [5] and simultaneously provides almost setting-free optimization algorithm, which does not require a user with expert knowledge in the field. The typical examples of such algorithms are SDE [6], jDE [7], MDE_pBX [8], SaDE [9], JADE [10], SHADE [11] and L-SHADE [12].

Over the years, DE variants have won almost every single-parameter numerical optimization competition [13–16] and especially Success-History based Adaptive Differential Evolution (SHADE) and L-SHADE (SHADE with Linear decrease in population size) variants were successful in recent years [17–20]. Adaptive DE algorithms were also successfully used in various real-world applications – vehicle routing problem [21], automatic test case generation [22], underwater glider path planning [23], high-rise building design [24].

F.J. Martínez de Pisón et al. (Eds.): HAIS 2017, LNAI 10334, pp. 662–673, 2017.
DOI: 10.1007/978-3-319-59650-1_56

There are still plenty of challenges in understanding the algorithm properties like control parameters [25] and their online effects [26] and there is a lot of room-for-improvement in DE scheme design [27]. One of the ways to address these issues might be in hybridization of complex networks and DE and extraction of the possibly useful network properties, like in [28]. Therefore, this paper proposes a method to translate the dynamic of the SHADE algorithm into the complex network and one of the network features (node degree centrality) is analyzed in order to provide additional insight. This insight is used to detect possible weak spots of the SHADE algorithm design.

The remainder of this paper is structured as follows: Sects. 2 and 3 are dedicated to DE and SHADE algorithms, Sect. 4 describes the network design. Section 5 depicts experiment settings, Sect. 6 discusses results and the last section includes the concluding remarks.

2 Differential Evolution

The DE algorithm is initialized with a random population of individuals ***P***, that represent solutions of the optimization problem. The population size *NP* is set by the user along with other control parameters – scaling factor *F* and crossover rate *CR*.

In continuous optimization, each individual is composed of a vector $\boldsymbol{x}$ of length *D*, which is a dimensionality (number of optimized attributes) of the problem, and each vector component represents a value of the corresponding attribute, and of objective function value $f(\boldsymbol{x})$.

For each individual in a population, three mutually different individuals are selected for mutation of vectors and resulting mutated vector $\boldsymbol{v}$ is combined with the original vector $\boldsymbol{x}$ in crossover step. The objective function value $f(\boldsymbol{u})$ of the resulting trial vector $\boldsymbol{u}$ is evaluated and compared to that of the original individual. When the quality (objective function value) of the trial individual is better, it is placed into the next generation, otherwise, the original individual is placed there. This step is called selection. The process is repeated until the stopping criterion is met (e.g. the maximum number of objective function evaluations, the maximum number of generations, the low bound for diversity between objective function values in population).

The following sections describe four steps of DE: Initialization, mutation, crossover and selection.

2.1 Initialization

As aforementioned, the initial population ***P***, of size *NP*, of individuals is randomly generated. For this purpose, the individual vector $\boldsymbol{x}_i$ components are generated by Random Number Generator (RNG) with uniform distribution from the range which is specified for the problem by *lower* and *upper* bound (1).

$$\boldsymbol{x}_{j,i} = U\left[lower_j, upper_j\right] \quad \text{for } j = 1, \ldots, D \tag{1}$$

where *i* is the index of a current individual, *j* is the index of current attribute and *D* is the dimensionality of the problem.

In the initialization phase, a scaling factor value F and crossover value CR has to be assigned as well. The typical range for F value is [0, 2] and for CR, it is [0, 1].

2.2 Mutation

In the mutation step, three mutually different individuals $\boldsymbol{x}_{r1}, \boldsymbol{x}_{r2}, \boldsymbol{x}_{r3}$ from a population are randomly selected and combined in mutation according to the mutation strategy. The original mutation strategy of canonical DE is "rand/1" and is depicted in (2).

$$\boldsymbol{v}_i = \boldsymbol{x}_{r1} + F(\boldsymbol{x}_{r2} - \boldsymbol{x}_{r3}) \tag{2}$$

where $r1 \neq r2 \neq r3 \neq i$, F is the scaling factor value and $\boldsymbol{v}_i$ is the resulting mutated vector.

2.3 Crossover

In the crossover step, mutated vector $\boldsymbol{v}_i$ is combined with the original vector $\boldsymbol{x}_i$ and produces trial vector $\boldsymbol{u}_i$. The binary crossover (3) is used in canonical DE.

$$u_{j,i} = \begin{cases} v_{j,i} & \text{if } U[0,1] \leq CR \text{ or } j = j_{rand} \\ x_{j,i} & \text{otherwise} \end{cases} \tag{3}$$

where CR is the used crossover rate value and j_{rand} is an index of an attribute that has to be from the mutated vector $\boldsymbol{v}_i$ (ensures generation of a vector with at least one new component).

2.4 Selection

The selection step ensures, that the optimization progress will lead to better solutions because it allows only individuals of better or at least equal objective function value to proceed into next generation $G + 1$ (4).

$$\boldsymbol{x}_{i,G+1} = \begin{cases} \boldsymbol{u}_{i,G} & \text{if } f(\boldsymbol{u}_{i,G}) \leq f(\boldsymbol{x}_{i,G}) \\ \boldsymbol{x}_{i,G} & \text{otherwise} \end{cases} \tag{4}$$

where G is the index of current generation.

The whole DE algorithm is depicted in pseudo-code below.

```
Algorithm pseudo-code 1: DE
Set NP, CR, F and stopping criterion;
G = 0, xbest = {};
Randomly initialize (1) population P = (x1,G,…,xNP,G);
Pnew = {}, xbest = best from population P;
while stopping criterion not met
  for i = 1 to NP do
    xi,G = P[i];
    vi,G by mutation (2);
    ui,G by crossover (3);
    if f(ui,G) < f(xi,G) then
      xi,G+1 = ui,G;
    else
      xi,G+1 = xi,G;
    end
    xi,G+1 → Pnew;
  end
  P = Pnew, Pnew = {}, xbest = best from population P;
end
return xbest as the best found solution
```

3 Success-History Based Adaptive Differential Evolution

In SHADE, the only control parameter that can be set by the user is population size *NP*, other two (*F, CR*) are adapted to the given optimization task, a new parameter *H* is introduced, which determines the size of *F* and *CR* value memories. The initialization step of the SHADE is, therefore, similar to DE. Mutation, however, is completely different because of the used strategy "current-to-*p*best/1" and the fact, that it uses different scaling factor value F_i for each individual. Mutation strategy also works with a new feature – external archive of inferior solutions. This archive holds individuals from previous generations, that were outperformed in selection step. The size of the archive retains the same size as the size of the population by randomly discarding its contents whenever the size overflows *NP*.

Crossover is still binary, but similarly to the mutation and scaling factor values, crossover rate value CR_i is also different for each individual.

The selection step is the same and therefore following sections describe only different aspects of initialization, mutation and crossover.

3.1 Initialization

As aforementioned, initial population $\boldsymbol{P}$ is randomly generated as in DE, but additional memories for F and CR values are initialized as well. Both memories have the same size H and are equally initialized, the memory for CR values is titled $\boldsymbol{M}_{CR}$ and the memory for F is titled $\boldsymbol{M}_F$. Their initialization is depicted in (5).

$$M_{CR,i} = M_{F,i} = 0.5 \text{ for } i = 1, \ldots, H \tag{5}$$

Also, the external archive of inferior solutions $\boldsymbol{A}$ is initialized. Since there are no solutions so far, it is initialized empty $\boldsymbol{A} = \emptyset$ and its maximum size is set to NP.

3.2 Mutation

Mutation strategy "current-to-*p*best/1" was introduced in [9] and unlike "rand/1", it combines four mutually different vectors, therefore $pbest \neq r1 \neq r2 \neq i$ (6).

$$\boldsymbol{v}_i = \boldsymbol{x}_i + F_i\left(\boldsymbol{x}_{pbest} - \boldsymbol{x}_i\right) + F_i(\boldsymbol{x}_{r1} - \boldsymbol{x}_{r2}) \tag{6}$$

where $\boldsymbol{x}_{pbest}$ is randomly selected from the best $NP \times p$ best individuals in the current population. The p value is randomly generated for each mutation by RNG with uniform distribution from the range $[p_{min}, 0.2]$. where $p_{min} = 2/NP$. Vector $\boldsymbol{x}_{r1}$ is randomly selected from the current population and vector $\boldsymbol{x}_{r2}$ is randomly selected from the union of current population $\boldsymbol{P}$ and archive $\boldsymbol{A}$. The scaling factor value F_i is given by (7).

$$F_i = C\left[M_{F,r}, 0.1\right] \tag{7}$$

where $M_{F,r}$ is a randomly selected value (by index r) from $\boldsymbol{M}_F$ memory and C stands for Cauchy distribution, therefore the F_i value is generated from the Cauchy distribution with location parameter value $M_{F,r}$ and scale parameter value 0.1. If the generated value $F_i > 1$, it is truncated to 1 and if it is $F_i \leq 0$, it is generated again by (7).

3.3 Crossover

Crossover is the same as in (3), but the CR value is changed to CR_i, which is generated separately for each individual (8). The value is generated from the Gaussian distribution with mean parameter value of $M_{CR,r}$, which is randomly selected (by the same index r as in mutation) from $\boldsymbol{M}_{CR}$ memory and standard deviation value of 0.1.

$$CR_i = N\left[M_{CR,r}, 0.1\right] \tag{8}$$

3.4 Historical Memory Updates

Historical memories $\boldsymbol{M}_F$ and $\boldsymbol{M}_{CR}$ are initialized according to (5), but its components change during the evolution. These memories serve to hold successful values of F and CR used in mutation and crossover steps. Successful in terms of producing trial individual better than the original individual. During one generation, these successful values are stored in corresponding arrays $\boldsymbol{S}_F$ and $\boldsymbol{S}_{CR}$. After each generation, one cell of $\boldsymbol{M}_F$ and $\boldsymbol{M}_{CR}$ memories is updated. This cell is given by the index k, which starts at 1 and increases by 1 after each generation. When it overflows the size limit of memories H, it is again set to 1. The new value of k-th cell for $\boldsymbol{M}_F$ is calculated by (9) and for $\boldsymbol{M}_{CR}$ by (10).

$$M_{F,k} = \begin{cases} \text{mean}_{WL}(\boldsymbol{S}_F) & \text{if } \boldsymbol{S}_F \neq \emptyset \\ M_{F,k} & \text{otherwise} \end{cases} \tag{9}$$

$$M_{CR,k} = \begin{cases} \text{mean}_{WA}(\boldsymbol{S}_{CR}) & \text{if } \boldsymbol{S}_{CR} \neq \emptyset \\ M_{CR,k} & \text{otherwise} \end{cases} \tag{10}$$

where $\text{mean}_{WL}()$ and $\text{mean}_{WA}()$ are weighted Lehmer (11) and weighted arithmetic (12) means correspondingly.

$$\text{mean}_{WL}(\boldsymbol{S}_F) = \frac{\sum_{k=1}^{|\boldsymbol{S}_F|} w_k \cdot S_{F,k}^2}{\sum_{k=1}^{|\boldsymbol{S}_F|} w_k \cdot S_{F,k}} \tag{11}$$

$$\text{mean}_{WA}(\boldsymbol{S}_{CR}) = \sum_{k=1}^{|\boldsymbol{S}_{CR}|} w_k \cdot S_{CR,k} \tag{12}$$

where the weight vector $\boldsymbol{w}$ is given by (13) and is based on the improvement in objective function value between trial and original individuals.

$$w_k = \frac{\text{abs}\left(f(\boldsymbol{u}_{k,G}) - f(\boldsymbol{x}_{k,G})\right)}{\sum_{m=1}^{|\boldsymbol{S}_{CR}|} \text{abs}\left(f(\boldsymbol{u}_{m,G}) - f(\boldsymbol{x}_{m,G})\right)} \tag{13}$$

And since both arrays $\boldsymbol{S}_F$ and $\boldsymbol{S}_{CR}$ have the same size, it is arbitrary which size will be used for the upper boundary for m in (13). Complete SHADE algorithm is depicted in pseudo-code below.

Algorithm pseudo-code 2: SHADE

```
Set NP, H and stopping criterion;
G = 0, x_best = {}, k = 1, p_min = 2/NP, A = Ø;
Randomly initialize (1) population P = (x_1,G,…,x_NP,G);
Set M_F and M_CR according to (5);
P_new = {}, x_best = best from population P;
while stopping criterion not met
  S_F = Ø, S_CR = Ø;
  for i = 1 to NP do
    x_i,G = P[i];
    r = U[1, H], p_i = U[p_min, 0.2];
    Set F_i by (7) and CR_i by (8);
    v_i,G by mutation (6);
    u_i,G by crossover (3);
    if f(u_i,G) < f(x_i,G) then
      x_i,G+1 = u_i,G;
      x_i,G → A;
      F_i → S_F, CR_i → S_CR;
    else
      x_i,G+1 = x_i,G;
    end
    if |A|>NP then randomly delete an ind. from A;
    x_i,G+1 → P_new;
  end
  if S_F ≠ Ø and S_CR ≠ Ø then
    Update M_F,k (9) and M_CR,k (10), k++;
    if k > H then k = 1, end;
  end
  P = P_new, P_new = {}, x_best = best from population P;
end
return x_best as the best found solution
```

4 Network Design

The network is designed during the mutation step in SHADE algorithm. Each individual in a population is a node of the network and undirected edges ($e_{i,pbest}$, $e_{i,r1}$, $e_{i,r2}$) are created between active individual $\boldsymbol{x}_i$ and 3 individuals present in mutation ($\boldsymbol{x}_{pbest}$, $\boldsymbol{x}_{r1}$, $\boldsymbol{x}_{r2}$) only if the trial individual succeeds in selection step (mutation and crossover produced better individual than active individual) forming a sort of communication between individuals.

A new network is created for each generation, therefore there is a maximum of $3 \times NP$ edges in the network (all individuals in a population were enhanced). Node degree centrality c_i of i-th node is a sum of edges connected to that node.

5 Experimental Setting

Node degree centralities were extracted for each of 51 independent runs of SHADE algorithm on 15 test functions from CEC2015 benchmark set. Stopping criterion was set to 10,000 $\times$ *D*, where *D* is the dimensionality of the problem – 10. The settings of SHADE algorithm were – population size *NP* = 100 and historical memory size *H* = 10.

The primary assumption was that individuals with better objective function values are the ones leading the evolution (greedy approach) and therefore, centralities of these individuals should be among the highest. In order to test that assumption, ranking methods for objective function values and centralities were implemented.

Each individual in a population is extended by *ofvRank*, which corresponds to the number of individuals, that have worse (higher) objective function value than this individual, resulting in *ofvRank* = 99 for the best individual in the population and *ofvRank* = 0 for the worst one. Similar *cenRank* was introduced for centrality ranking, where *cenRank* is the number of individuals that have lower node degree centrality than the current individual, therefore individual represented by a node with highest centrality degree will have *cenRank* = 99 and the individual represented by a node with the lowest centrality degree will have *cenRank* = 0.

According to the previously mentioned assumption, there should be a positive correlation between *ofvRank* and *cenRank*. Such correlation history was recorded for each generation on each test function and is presented in the next section.

6 Results and Discussion

The correlation history was recorded for 15 test functions (2 simple unimodal, 7 simple multimodal, 3 hybrid and 3 composition) in 10 dimensions and 3 typical behavior patterns are depicted in right parts of Figs. 1, 2 and 3. Each correlation graph is accompanied by the convergence graph for given function. All graphs depict the average value with 95% confidence interval in lighter color.

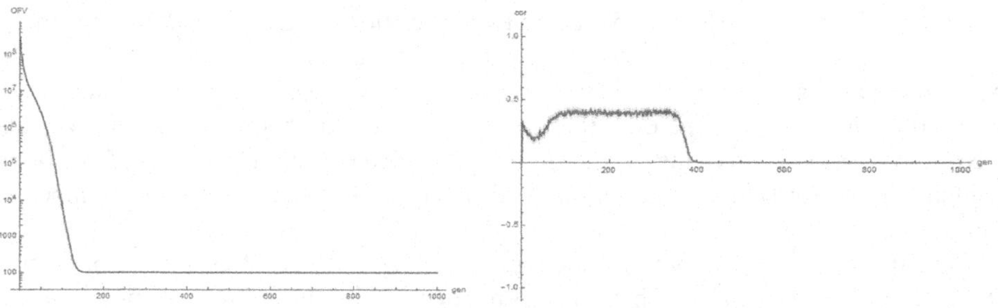

Fig. 1. Left – average convergence graph of 51 runs on *f*1 test function in 10*D*. Right - average correlation on *f*1 test function in 10*D*. Typical behavior for *f*1, *f*2 and *f*15. (Color figure online)

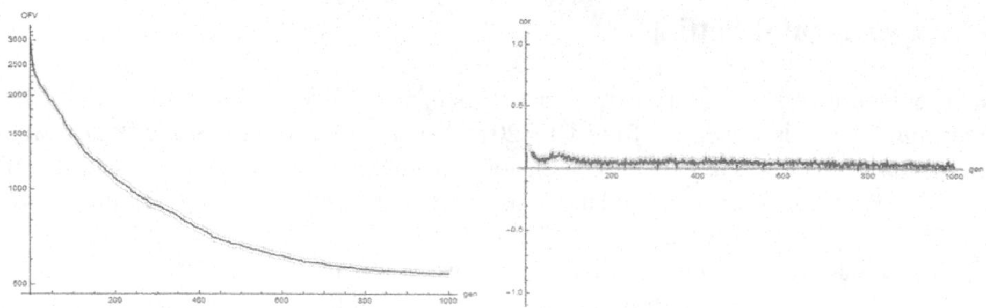

Fig. 2. Left – average convergence graph of 51 runs on *f*5 test function in 10*D*. Right - average correlation on *f*5 test function in 10*D*. Typical behavior for *f*3, *f*4, *f*5, *f*7, *f*9, *f*12 and *f*13.

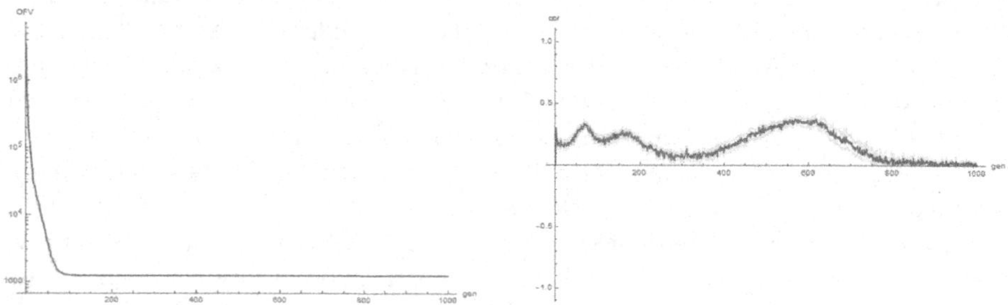

Fig. 3. Left – average convergence graph of 51 runs on *f*10 test function in 10*D*. Right - average correlation on *f*10 test function in 10*D*. Typical behavior for *f*6, *f*8, *f*10, *f*11 and *f*14.

For the first case (Fig. 1), there is a direct link between convergence and correlation of rank methods. While there is a convergence, the correlation of *ofvRank* and *cenRank* is around 0.4 and goes to 0 after the convergence phase. This behavior can be seen on 3 of the test functions – *f*1, *f*2 and *f*15 (shown is *f*1). The first two functions are easily solvable by SHADE and *f*15 is a function with fast convergence to local optima. Therefore, the fast convergence is common for these 3 functions.

The second case (Fig. 2) describes the typical behavior of 7 test functions – *f*3, *f*4, *f*5, *f*7, *f*9, *f*12 and *f*13 (shown is *f*5). There the correlation has a high peak in the starting phase of the evolution but decreases down to approximately 0 in later phases even when the convergence still continues. This behavior suggests that the best individuals in the population are not the ones that communicate often, therefore these individuals are not the ones who drive the evolution towards global optima. This group of functions contains the majority of simple multimodal functions, one hybrid, and one composite function.

The third case (Fig. 3) presents the typical behavior of 5 test functions – *f*6, *f*8, *f*10, *f*11 and *f*14 (shown is *f*10). There the correlation is high in the starting phase of the evolution and later fluctuates until the convergence stops, then it decreases to 0. This behavior suggests a change in preferred individuals during the evolution when sometimes it is desirable to use greedy approach and sometimes not. This group contains 2 simple multimodal functions, 2 hybrid functions, and 1 composite function.

These results suggest that the greedy approach used in "current-to-*p*best/1" mutation strategy might not be the most efficient and rather than using a set of best (in terms of objective function value) individuals for the $\boldsymbol{x}_{pbest}$, it could be preferred to use a set given by another common characteristic (potentially one of the network features, e.g. node degree centrality or clustering coefficient). The same goes for a greedy approach to the linear decrease in population size, where the worst individuals are removed from the population during evolution. Findings in this paper suggest that there might be individuals with worse objective function value who might still provide a good search direction. Also, this research supports the idea that there is still a lot of room-for-improvement and the hybrid approach with complex networks is one of the promising candidates for future study.

Correlation and convergence graphs for all 15 test functions can be found on https://owncloud.cesnet.cz/index.php/s/K97jdCiBFzAKR0l.

7 Conclusion

This preliminary study presented a hybridization of complex network and state-of-art DE variant – SHADE in order to detect potential weaknesses of this evolutionary algorithm. The correlation between objective function value ranking and node degree centrality ranking was studied on 15 test functions from CEC2015 benchmark set.

Findings in this paper suggest that the greedy approach of mutation strategy and the linear decrease in population size, which uses objective function value as the measure of a quality of an individual is a possible weak spot in the algorithm and might be replaced by another metric, e.g. various network feature.

The future research will be aimed at improvement of the algorithm through the use of complex network features as a replacement of the objective function metric in a greedy environment and at a thorough analysis of such algorithm.

Acknowledgements. This work was supported by Grant Agency of the Czech Republic – GACR P103/15/06700S, further by the Ministry of Education, Youth and Sports of the Czech Republic within the National Sustainability Programme Project no. LO1303 (MSMT-7778/2014). Also by the European Regional Development Fund under the Project CEBIA-Tech no. CZ.1.05/2.1.00/03.0089 and by Internal Grant Agency of Tomas Bata University under the Projects no. IGA/CebiaTech/2017/004.

References

1. Storn, R., Price, K.: Differential Evolution-A Simple and Efficient Adaptive Scheme for Global Optimization Over Continuous Spaces, vol. 3. ICSI, Berkeley (1995)
2. Neri, F., Tirronen, V.: Recent advances in differential evolution: a survey and experimental analysis. Artif. Intell. Rev. **33**(1–2), 61–106 (2010)
3. Das, S., Suganthan, P.N.: Differential evolution: a survey of the state-of-the-art. IEEE Trans. Evol. Comput. **15**(1), 4–31 (2011)

4. Das, S., Mullick, S.S., Suganthan, P.N.: Recent advances in differential evolution–an updated survey. Swarm Evol. Comput. **27**, 1–30 (2016)
5. Wolpert, D.H., Macready, W.G.: No free lunch theorems for optimization. IEEE Trans. Evol. Comput. **1**(1), 67–82 (1997)
6. Omran, M.G.H., Salman, A., Engelbrecht, Andries P.: Self-adaptive differential evolution. In: Hao, Y., et al. (eds.) CIS 2005. LNCS, vol. 3801, pp. 192–199. Springer, Heidelberg (2005). doi:10.1007/11596448_28
7. Brest, J., Greiner, S., Bošković, B., Mernik, M., Zumer, V.: Self-adapting control parameters in differential evolution: a comparative study on numerical benchmark problems. IEEE Trans. Evol. Comput. **10**(6), 646–657 (2006)
8. Islam, S.M., Das, S., Ghosh, S., Roy, S., Suganthan, P.N.: An adaptive differential evolution algorithm with novel mutation and crossover strategies for global numerical optimization. IEEE Trans. Systems Man Cybern. Part B (Cybern.) **42**(2), 482–500 (2012)
9. Qin, A.K., Huang, V.L., Suganthan, P.N.: Differential evolution algorithm with strategy adaptation for global numerical optimization. IEEE Trans. Evol. Comput. **13**(2), 398–417 (2009)
10. Zhang, J., Sanderson, A.C.: JADE: adaptive differential evolution with optional external archive. IEEE Trans. Evol. Comput. **13**(5), 945–958 (2009)
11. Tanabe, R., Fukunaga, A.: Success-history based parameter adaptation for differential evolution. In: 2013 IEEE Congress on Evolutionary Computation (CEC), pp. 71–78, IEEE, June 2013
12. Tanabe, R., Fukunaga, A.S.: Improving the search performance of SHADE using linear population size reduction. In: 2014 IEEE Congress on Evolutionary Computation (CEC), pp. 1658–1665, IEEE, July 2014
13. Das, S., Abraham, A., Chakraborty, U.K., Konar, A.: Differential evolution using a neighborhood-based mutation operator. IEEE Trans. Evol. Comput. **13**(3), 526–553 (2009)
14. Mininno, E., Neri, F., Cupertino, F., Naso, D.: Compact differential evolution. IEEE Trans. Evol. Comput. **15**(1), 32–54 (2011)
15. Mallipeddi, R., Suganthan, P.N., Pan, Q.K., Tasgetiren, M.F.: Differential evolution algorithm with ensemble of parameters and mutation strategies. Appl. Soft Comput. **11**(2), 1679–1696 (2011)
16. Brest, J., Korošec, P., Šilc, J., Zamuda, A., Bošković, B., Maučec, M.S.: Differential evolution and differential ant-stigmergy on dynamic optimisation problems. Int. J. Syst. Sci. **44**(4), 663–679 (2013)
17. Brest, J., Maučec, M.S., Bošković, B.: iL-SHADE: improved L-SHADE algorithm for single objective real-parameter optimization. In: 2016 IEEE Congress on Evolutionary Computation (CEC), pp. 1188–1195, IEEE, July 2016
18. Viktorin, A., Pluhacek, M., Senkerik, R.: Success-history based adaptive differential evolution algorithm with multi-chaotic framework for parent selection performance on CEC2014 benchmark set. In: 2016 IEEE Congress on Evolutionary Computation (CEC), pp. 4797–4803, IEEE, July, 2016
19. Poláková, R., Tvrdík, J., Bujok, P.: L-SHADE with competing strategies applied to CEC2015 learning-based test suite. In: 2016 IEEE Congress on Evolutionary Computation (CEC), pp. 4790–4796, IEEE, July 2016
20. Awad, N.H., Ali, M.Z., Suganthan, P.N., Reynolds, R.G.: An ensemble sinusoidal parameter adaptation incorporated with L-SHADE for solving CEC2014 benchmark problems. In: 2016 IEEE Congress on Evolutionary Computation (CEC), pp. 2958–2965, IEEE, July 2016
21. Viktorin, A., Hrabec, D., Pluhacek, M.: Multi-chaotic differential evolution for vehicle routing problem with profits. In: Proceedings-30th European Conference on Modelling and Simulation, ECMS 2016. European Council for Modelling and Simulation (ECMS) (2016)

22. Szenkovits, A., Gaskó, N., Jakab, H.: Optimizing test input generation for reactive systems with an adaptive differential evolution. In: 2016 18th International Symposium on Symbolic and Numeric Algorithms for Scientific Computing (SYNASC), pp. 214–218, IEEE, September 2016
23. Zamuda, A., Sosa, J.D.H., Adler, L.: Constrained differential evolution optimization for underwater glider path planning in sub-mesoscale eddy sampling. Appl. Soft Comput. **42**, 93–118 (2016)
24. Ekici, B., Chatzikonstantinou, I., Sariyildiz, S., Tasgetiren, M.F., Pan, Q.K.: A multi-objective self-adaptive differential evolution algorithm for conceptual high-rise building design. In: 2016 IEEE Congress on Evolutionary Computation (CEC), pp. 2272–2279, IEEE, July 2016
25. Karafotias, G., Hoogendoorn, M., Eiben, Á.E.: Parameter control in evolutionary algorithms: trends and challenges. IEEE Trans. Evol. Comput. **19**(2), 167–187 (2015)
26. Zamuda, A., Brest, J.: Self-adaptive control parameters' randomization frequency and propagations in differential evolution. Swarm Evol. Comput. **25**, 72–99 (2015)
27. Tanabe, R., Fukunaga, A.: How far are we from an optimal, adaptive DE? In: Handl, J., Hart, E., Lewis, Peter R., López-Ibáñez, M., Ochoa, G., Paechter, B. (eds.) PPSN 2016. LNCS, vol. 9921, pp. 145–155. Springer, Cham (2016). doi:10.1007/978-3-319-45823-6_14
28. Viktorin, A., Pluhacek, M., Senkerik, R.: Network based linear population size reduction in SHADE. In: 2016 International Conference on Intelligent Networking and Collaborative Systems (INCoS), pp. 86–93, IEEE, September 2016

Multiobjective Reliability-Based Design Optimization Formulations Solved Combining NSGA-II and First Order Reliability Method

Luis Celorrio(✉)

Universidad de La Rioja, Logroño, La Rioja, Spain
luis.celorrio@unirioja.es

Abstract. Uncertainties are inherent in realistic structural optimization problems. For example, geometric variables and material properties are uncertain parameters and have to be accounted to ensure safety and quality. A manner of considering uncertainties in structural design is using constraints written in terms of probability of failure or reliability index in the optimization problem.

Usually structural optimization problems consider constraints as restrictions and optimize the cost or the weight of the structures. However, several types of problems can be formulated in the field of Optimization under Uncertainty. This paper presents a computer program to solve two type of problems: In the first one, a bi-objective problem is solved, where the probability of system failure has been added as the second objective to the original cost objective. The second problem consists in optimising simultaneously two more performances or objective functions subject to reliability constraints. This formulation is named Multiobjective Reliability Based Design Optimization (MO-RBDO).

Reliability analysis is carried out using a gradient based First Order Reliability Method (FORM). This structural reliability assessment method has shown efficient. An analytical example and a classical ten bar truss illustrate the application of this algorithm.

Keywords: Fusion of soft computing and hard computing · Evolutionary multiobjective optimization · Decision making · NSGA-2 · System reliability

1 Introduction

A large research effort has been developed in the field of Structural Optimization. Early studies and develops started considering deterministic parameters and design variables. Because of the improvement of computational power during the last years a special topic in the field of structural optimization has appeared: Structural Optimization under Uncertainty. Uncertainties are inherent in realistic structures. Geometric variables, material properties, loads, including the mathematical model representing the structure are uncertain and these uncertainties have to be accounted for in the design process to ensure safety and quality. Structural optimizations problems include constraints. These constraints are named limit states or performance functions and are usually expressed in term of stress or nodal displacements. A failure occurs when a limit state is violated or exceeded. When design variables and parameters are considered uncertain and are

F.J. Martínez de Pisón et al. (Eds.): HAIS 2017, LNAI 10334, pp. 674–685, 2017.
DOI: 10.1007/978-3-319-59650-1_57

modelled as random variables, these constraints are probabilistic and are written in terms of probability of failure. Typical problems consist of a large number of random design variables and parameters with several probabilistic limit state functions, which are usually implicit functions of the random variables and require a large number of calls to a finite element analysis software simulating a complex mechanical model.

The process of design optimization enhanced by the addition of reliability constraints is referred as Reliability-Based Design Optimization (RBDO) [1, 2]. Typical RBDO problems minimises a single objective function subject to a fixed level of reliability for the reliability constrains. However, more meaningful design optimization problems can be formulated when several objectives are optimised. This paper considers two types of problems.

The first type of problems appears frequently in design optimization. A structural designer sometimes acts as a Decision Maker (DM) considering the cost of the optimum design for different values of reliability and deciding about the level of reliability more profitable taking into account legal, quality and budget requirements. A simple manner to obtain a trade-of between cost and system reliability is solving a Bi-objective Optimization problem with the probability of system failure added as the second objective to the original cost objective. Deb *et al.* have solved this problem applying the well-known Fast Non-dominated Sorting Genetic Algorithm (NSGA-II) as Multiobjective Optimization (MOO) algorithm and the FastRIA method to compute the probability of failure of each reliability constraints [3].

The second type of problems consists of enhancing the concept of RBDO considering several objectives subject to reliability constraints. This formulation is named Multiobjective Reliability Based Design Optimization (MO-RBDO). The difference between RBDO and MO-RBDO consists in the fact that a single objective function is optimized in RBDO problems. On the other hand, several objective functions are considered in MO-RBDO problems.

The MO-RBDO formulation has been used to solve optimization under uncertainty problems in the automotive industry [4, 5]. For example, Cid-Montoya *et al.* consider the optimal design of a bumper in a car where probabilistic constraints are related with crashworthiness tests [5]. These constraints stem from EuroENCAP standard: the norm about safety requirements and test for the automotive industry in the European Union.

It is well known that metaheuristic based optimization algorithms like Genetic Algorithms, Evolutionary Algorithms, Particle Swarm Optimization, Ant Colonies, etc. have demonstrated their efficiency in finding good approximations to global optimum in engineering applications with deterministic variables and parameters. For example, Genetic Algorithms has been applied to solve RBDO problems with discrete random design variables [6–8]. Now, optimization problems are multiobjective. Then, we can extend these metaheuristic algorithms to their multiobjective version to solve them.

A large research has been carried out in multiobjective optimization field, showing the ability of some Multiobjective Genetic Algorithms to simultaneously obtain an approximate Pareto front in the objective space and a Pareto set in the design variables space. Therefore, MOGA have been the most popular metaheuristic approaches to multiobjective or multi-criteria design [9]. There is a multitude of MOGA methods. Some algorithms consider the concept of Pareto dominance and uses a ranking based on non-dominated solutions. The population is ranked according to a dominance rule, and then each solution is assigned to a fitness value based on its rank in the population [10].

The present work contributes to solve the two types of problems described. A computer program has been implemented to solve multiobjective structural optimization problems under uncertainty. The algorithm implemented combines the efficient NSGA-II algorithm developed by Deb *et al.* [5, 12] to carry out the Multiobjective Optimization (MOO) and a gradient-based method in the inner loop to compute the reliability indexes. NSGA-II uses a crowding distance method to obtain a uniform spread of solutions along the best-known Pareto front. Also, NSGA-II includes a constraint handle based in the concept of constrained dominance.

Reliability constraints are evaluated by Reliability Index Approach (RIA) based First Order Reliability Method (FORM). This approximated method computes the Reliability Indexes β for each constraint using a gradient based optimization named Hasofer-Lind-Rackwitz-Fiessler (HL-RF) method. We refer the reader to the books [13, 14] where structural reliability methods (FORM, SORM, etc.) are described. This RIA-based FORM method produces more accurate results than the FastRIA method used by Deb *et al.* in [3]. Also, several probabilistic distributions can be considered for the random design variables. A more realistic problem can be solved because coefficients of variation have been assigned to random design variables instead of constant standard deviations. In the case of difficulties of convergence at the structural reliability assessment, new individuals are selected from the current population.

The rest of the paper is organized as follow. Section 2 explains briefly the formulation of RBDO problems. Section 3 describes two types of problems in the field of Multiobjective Optimization under Uncertainty. Section 4 analyses a classical analytical example, frequently used as benchmark test in the literature about RBDO [1, 2], reformulated as a bi-objective optimization problem where the second objective function is the reliability of a series system consisting of three performance functions. In Sect. 5 we apply the MO – RBDO formulation to the classical ten bar truss. Two objectives are minimised: the weight of the truss and the displacement at the tip node, subject to ten stress-based reliability constraints. Finally, conclusions are outlined in Sect. 6.

2 RBDO Formulation

Reliability Based Design Optimization consists in solving a constrained optimization problem where constraints are formulated as probability constraints. In practical applications constraints are expressed as reliability constraints. RBDO methods are usually applied in mechanical and structural design because parameters (loads, material properties, node locations, etc.) and design variables (geometrical dimensions, topological variables) are uncertain [1, 2, 15].

The most common mathematical formulation of a RBDO problem is:

$$\begin{aligned} &\min_{\mathbf{d},\boldsymbol{\mu}_{\mathbf{X}}} f(\mathbf{d},\boldsymbol{\mu}_{\mathbf{X}},\boldsymbol{\mu}_{\mathbf{P}}) \\ s.t.\quad &P_{fi} = P[g_i(\mathbf{d},\mathbf{X},\mathbf{P}) \le 0] \le P_{fi}^t, i = 1,\ldots,n \\ &\mathbf{d}^L \le \mathbf{d} \le \mathbf{d}^U, \quad \boldsymbol{\mu}_{\mathbf{X}}^L \le \boldsymbol{\mu}_{\mathbf{X}} \le \boldsymbol{\mu}_{\mathbf{X}}^U \end{aligned} \tag{1}$$

where $\mathbf{d} \in R^k$ is the vector of deterministic design variables. $\mathbf{d}^L$ and $\mathbf{d}^U$ are the lower and upper bounds of vector $\mathbf{d}$, respectively. $\mathbf{X} \in R^m$ is the vector of random design variables, that is, random variables whose mean values, $\boldsymbol{\mu}_{\mathbf{X}}$ are design variables. $\boldsymbol{\mu}_{\mathbf{X}}^L$ and $\boldsymbol{\mu}_{\mathbf{X}}^U$ are the lower and upper bounds of vector $\boldsymbol{\mu}_{\mathbf{X}}$. $\mathbf{P} \in R^q$ is the vector of random parameters. $\boldsymbol{\mu}_{\mathbf{P}}$ is the mean value of $\mathbf{P}$. $f(\cdot)$ is the objective function, n is the number of reliability constraints, k is the number of deterministic design variables, m is the number or random design variables and q is the number of random parameters. $g_i(\mathbf{d},\mathbf{X},\mathbf{P})$ is the i-th limit state function. P_{fi} is the probability of violating the i-th probabilistic constraint and P_{fi}^t is the target probability of failure for the i-th probabilistic constraint.

Limit state functions are defined in a way that $g_i(\cdot) \le 0$ represents the failure domain. Then, the probability of failure for the i-th limit state function P_{fi} could be computed using the multivariate integral:

$$P_{fi} = \int_{g_i(\mathbf{d},\mathbf{X},\mathbf{P}) \le 0} f_{\mathbf{X}}(\mathbf{x})d\mathbf{x} \tag{2}$$

where $f_{\mathbf{X}}(\mathbf{x})$ is the joint probability density function random variables $\mathbf{X}$. The close-form solution of this integral is not usually available. Numerical solutions have been obtained only until dimension 4 or 5. Simulation methods based in Monte Carlo Simulation need a large computing time and generally are not used. Approximate reliability methods as FORM and (Second Order Reliability Method) SORM are often used [1, 13, 14].

FORM provides an accurate value for P_{fi} of each reliability constraint. However, it cannot converge with highly nonlinear performance functions. Usually constraints are written in term of the reliability index β_i. This index is related with the probability of failure by $P_{fi} \approx \Phi(-\beta_i)$, where Φ is the normal standard Cumulative Distribution Function (CDF).

In the problem (1) there is only a unique objective with several probabilistic constraints. These constraints usually are component level constraints, involving a single failure mode. However, it is possible to consider a RBDO problem with only a system level constraint, taking into account the failure of system composed by several components in series. In this case the problem formulation is:

$$\begin{aligned} &\min_{\mathbf{d},\boldsymbol{\mu}_{\mathbf{X}}} f(\mathbf{d},\boldsymbol{\mu}_{\mathbf{X}},\boldsymbol{\mu}_{\mathbf{P}}) \\ s.t.\quad &P_{fsys} = P\left[\bigcap_{i=1}^{n} g_i(\mathbf{d},\mathbf{X},\mathbf{P}) \le 0\right] \le P_{fsys}^t \\ &\mathbf{d}^L \le \mathbf{d} \le \mathbf{d}^U, \quad \boldsymbol{\mu}_{\mathbf{X}}^L \le \boldsymbol{\mu}_{\mathbf{X}} \le \boldsymbol{\mu}_{\mathbf{X}}^U \end{aligned} \tag{3}$$

This type of problem is more interesting for the DM, because he or she usually considers the mechanical system as a whole. The metric of interest for the DM is the system reliability R, defined as $R = 1 - P^t_{fsys}$.

3 Multiobjective Optimization Under Uncertainty

The formulation of RBDO has been extended to consider more complex problems involving multiple and often conflicting objectives. Two types of these problems are considered in this paper. In the first problem, a multiobjective optimization under uncertainty problem contains the initial objective function (structural cost or weight) and n additional objective functions. Each additional objective is intended to minimize the probability of failure corresponding a performance function. The reliability constraints of the original RBDO problem are rewritten here as objective functions. The formulation is stated:

$$\begin{aligned} &\min_{\mathbf{d},\boldsymbol{\mu}_\mathbf{X}} f(\mathbf{d}, \boldsymbol{\mu}_\mathbf{X}, \boldsymbol{\mu}_\mathbf{P}) \\ &\min_{\boldsymbol{d},\boldsymbol{\mu}_X} \left(P_{f1}(\boldsymbol{d}, \boldsymbol{\mu}_X, \boldsymbol{P}), P_{f2}(\boldsymbol{d}, \boldsymbol{\mu}_X, \boldsymbol{P}), \ldots, P_{fn}(\boldsymbol{d}, \boldsymbol{\mu}_X, \boldsymbol{P})\right) \\ &\text{where} \quad P_{fi}(\boldsymbol{d}, \boldsymbol{\mu}_X, \boldsymbol{P}) = P[g_i(\boldsymbol{d}, \boldsymbol{\mu}_X, \boldsymbol{P}) \le 0] \\ &s.t. \quad \boldsymbol{\mu}_X^L \le \boldsymbol{\mu}_X \le \boldsymbol{\mu}_X^U; \quad \boldsymbol{d}^L \le \boldsymbol{d} \le \boldsymbol{d}^U \end{aligned} \tag{4}$$

Now this problem has $n+1$ objective functions and no constraints, except bound constraints for design variables. This problem is very difficult to solve and specific methods could be applied.

In the practice, the DM needs a global vision of the problem and is interested in knowing how the cost changes for various reliability levels. Therefore, a simpler problem with two objectives is formulated. The first objective is the cost or weight of the structures and the second objective is the probability of failure of the system:

$$\begin{aligned} &\min_{\mathbf{d},\boldsymbol{\mu}_\mathbf{X}} f(\mathbf{d}, \boldsymbol{\mu}_\mathbf{X}, \boldsymbol{\mu}_\mathbf{P}) \\ &\min_{\boldsymbol{d},\boldsymbol{\mu}_X} P_{F_{Sis}}(\boldsymbol{d}, \boldsymbol{\mu}_X, \boldsymbol{P}) \\ &s.t. \quad \boldsymbol{\mu}_X^L \le \boldsymbol{\mu}_X \le \boldsymbol{\mu}_X^U; \quad \boldsymbol{d}^L \le \boldsymbol{d} \le \boldsymbol{d}^U \end{aligned} \tag{5}$$

where $P_{F_{Sis}}(\boldsymbol{d}, \boldsymbol{\mu}_X, \boldsymbol{P})$ is the probability of failure of the series system.

To solve this type of problems, we have used a double loop method. An Evolutionary Multiobjective (EMO) algorithm implements the optimization at the outer loop. Specifically, a Multiobjective Genetic Algorithm named NSGA-II has been used [11]. A system reliability analysis at the inner loop computes the probability of failure of the series system.

Several methods have been proposed to determine this probability of failure. Usually approximate methods are used. A simple approximate method consists in replacing the $P_{F_{Sis}}$ by the maximum of the probabilities of failure at component level, that is:

$$P_{F_{Sis}}(\boldsymbol{d}, \boldsymbol{\mu_X}, \boldsymbol{P}) = \max\left(P_{f1}(\boldsymbol{d}, \boldsymbol{\mu_X}, \boldsymbol{P}), P_{f2}(\boldsymbol{d}, \boldsymbol{\mu_X}, \boldsymbol{P}), \ldots, P_{fn}(\boldsymbol{d}, \boldsymbol{\mu_X}, \boldsymbol{P})\right) \tag{6}$$

Then, the second objective is a min-max objective. More accurate results can be obtained considering the Ditlevsen's bounds or second order bounds [13, 14]. The probability of failure of a series system is bounded by the equation below:

$$P_1 + \sum\nolimits_{i=1}^{J} max\left\{0, \left(P_i - \sum\nolimits_{j=1}^{i-1} P_{ji}\right)\right\} \le P_{F_{Sis}} \le \sum_{i=1}^{J} P_i - \sum_{i=2}^{J} \max_{j|j<i} P_{ji} \tag{7}$$

where P_i is $P_{fi}(\boldsymbol{d}, \boldsymbol{\mu_X}, \boldsymbol{P}) = P[g_i(\boldsymbol{d}, \boldsymbol{\mu_X}, \boldsymbol{P}) \le 0]$ and the P_{ji} is the joint probability of failure of the constraints j e i and is computed with the equation:

$$P_{ji} = \Phi\left(-\beta_j, -\beta_i, \rho_{ji}\right) \tag{8}$$

where ρ_{ij} is the correlation coefficient between the failure modes j e i:

$$\rho_{ji} = \frac{\boldsymbol{u}_j^* \cdot \boldsymbol{u}_i^*}{\left\|\boldsymbol{u}_j^*\right\| \left\|\boldsymbol{u}_i^*\right\|} \tag{9}$$

and Φ is the CDF of a standard normal distribution. It is worth to note that the values of the bounds depend of the arrangement of the failure modes. Because that, the probabilities of failure at component level have been ordered in descending order. Then $P_{F_{Sis}}$ is approximated by the upper bound of the true probability of failure. More accurate values of $P_{F_{Sis}}$ could be computed by sampling. Mahadevan *et al.* [16, 17] consider a multimodal Adaptive Importance Sampling method to compute the system reliability. However, this method involves a large computational effort.

In the second type of problems, several objective functions are optimized subject to reliability constraints at component level. This problem is known as the MO-RBDO problem [3, 18]. The formulation of a MO-RBDO problem is stated below:

$$\begin{aligned} &\min_{\mathbf{d}, \boldsymbol{\mu}_\mathbf{X}} (f_1(\mathbf{d}, \boldsymbol{\mu}_\mathbf{X}, \boldsymbol{\mu}_\mathbf{P}), f_1(\mathbf{d}, \boldsymbol{\mu}_\mathbf{X}, \boldsymbol{\mu}_\mathbf{P}), \cdots, f_n(\mathbf{d}, \boldsymbol{\mu}_\mathbf{X}, \boldsymbol{\mu}_\mathbf{P})) \\ &s.t. \quad P_{fi} = P[g_i(\mathbf{d}, \mathbf{X}, \mathbf{P}) \le 0] \le P_{fi}^t, i = 1, \ldots, n \\ &\qquad \mathbf{d}^L \le \mathbf{d} \le \mathbf{d}^U; \quad \boldsymbol{\mu}_\mathbf{X}^L \le \boldsymbol{\mu}_\mathbf{X} \le \boldsymbol{\mu}_\mathbf{X}^U \end{aligned} \tag{10}$$

4 Analytical Example

In this section an analytical bi-objective optimization problem is solved. The first objective is the cost function and the second objective is the probability of failure of a series system composed by three failure modes. The problem has only two objective functions and two design variables for the sake of doing a graphical representation of the Pareto front and Pareto set of solutions.

The formulation of the analytical example is:

$$\begin{aligned} \min_{\boldsymbol{\mu_X}} f(\boldsymbol{\mu_X}) &= \mu_{X_1} + \mu_{X_2} \\ \max_{\boldsymbol{\mu_X}} \ & \beta_{SIS}(\mu_{X_1}, \mu_{X_2}) \\ s.t. \quad 0 \le \mu_{X_1} \le 10; & \quad 0 \le \mu_{X_2} \le 10 \end{aligned} \tag{11}$$

where β_{SIS} is the reliability index at system level. It is related with the probability of failure at the system level by $P_{F_{SIS}} \approx \Phi(-\beta_{SIS})$. Two random variables X_1 y X_2 are considered and their mean values are the design variables:

$$\begin{aligned} X_1 &\sim Normal(\mu_{X_1}, CoV = 0.6) \\ X_2 &\sim Normal(\mu_{X_2}, CoV = 0.6) \end{aligned} \tag{12}$$

The limit state functions or performance functions included in the reliability constraints are:

$$\begin{aligned} g_1(\boldsymbol{X}) &= X_1^2 X_2/20 - 1 \\ g_2(\boldsymbol{X}) &= (X_1 + X_2 - 5)^2/30 + (X_1 - X_2 - 12)^2/120 - 1 \\ g_3(\boldsymbol{X}) &= 80/(X_1^2 + 8X_2 + 5) - 1 \end{aligned} \tag{13}$$

NGSA-II was used to solve the problem. Design variables were codified as real numbers. Therefore, Simulated Binary Crossover (SBX) and Polynomial Mutation operators were considered [10]. The values of the algorithm parameters are $P_c = 0.9$ and $P_m = 1/n$ where $n = 2$ (the number of design variables), and so, $P_m = 0.5$. Other parameters are: distribution index for crossover, $\eta_c = 20$ and distribution index for mutation, $\eta_m = 20$, population size = 80, max number of generations = 200.

The Pareto front is represented in the Fig. 1. A monotonically increment of the reliability index with respect to cost is shown. Also, the slope of the front decrease when the cost increased. This plot is an important tool for the DM. For example, an increment of the cost in two points from 4 to 6 involves an increment of more than 8

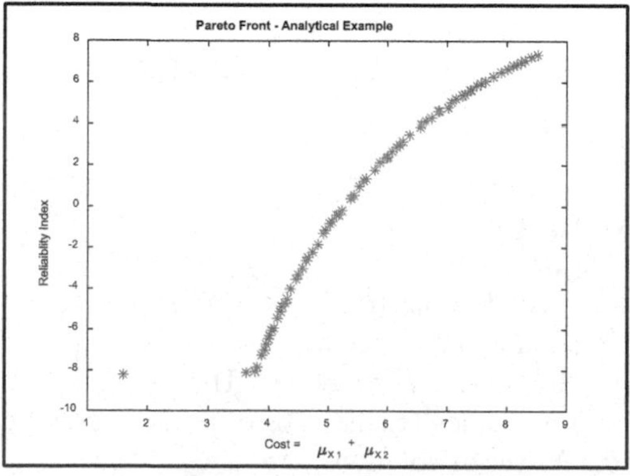

Fig. 1. Pareto front in the objective function space.

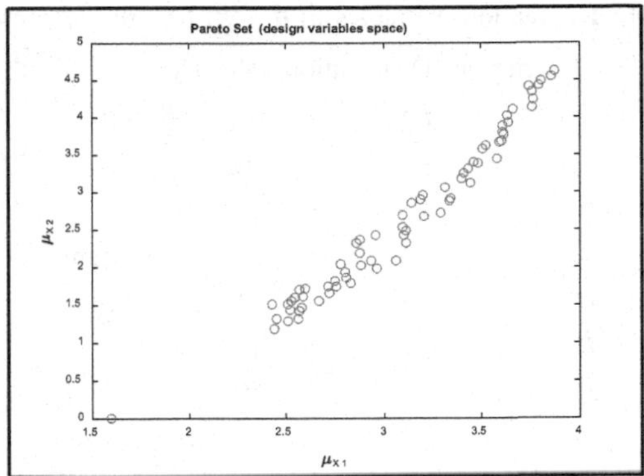

Fig. 2. Pareto Set for the analytical example.

points in β_{SIS}. However, an increment from 6 to 8 in the cost only represents an increment of 4 points in β_{SIS}. Then, the DM can take the decision about the final cost of the system. Pareto set in design variables space is shown in Fig. 2. The figure shows a simultaneous increment in both design variables for increased values of the system reliability index.

5 Ten Bar Truss Example

In this example the classical ten bars truss is considered. The material used is steel and the elastic modulus E and yield stress σ_y are random variables. Nodal displacements and element forces are computed using Finite Element Analysis under the hypothesis of linear analysis and elastic material. Figure 3 shows this structure.

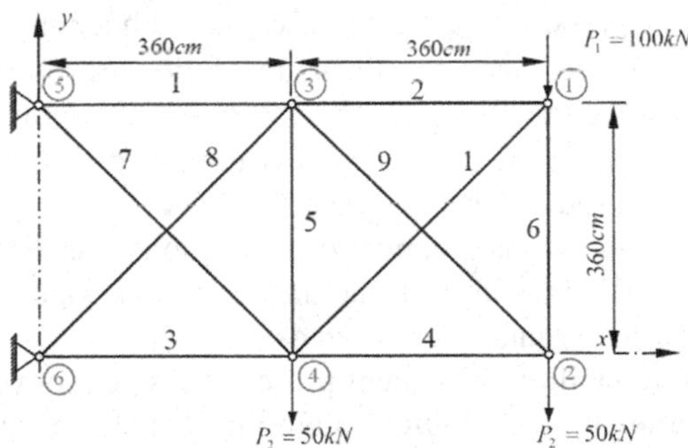

Fig. 3. Ten bar truss

The bars are grouped in 3 groups. Bars in the same group have the same cross sectional area. Then, the mean values of these areas are the design variables of the problem. Group 1 contains horizontal bars, group 2 contains vertical bars and group 3

Table 1. Random variables in the ten bar truss example

Random variable	Description	Distribution	Mean value	CoV or σ^2
X_1	A_1	LN	μ_{X_1}	0.05
X_2	A_2	LN	μ_{X_2}	0.05
X_3	A_3	LN	μ_{X_3}	0.05
X_4	E	LN	21000.0 kN/cm^2	1050 kN/cm^2
X_5	σ^a	LN	21.0 kN/cm^2	1 kN/cm^2
X_6	P_1	LN	100.0 kN	20 kN
X_7	P_2	LN	50.0 kN	2.5 kN

contains diagonal bars. Also, vertical loads are applied in nodes 1, 2 and 4 and are lognormal random variables. The random variables of the problem are collected in Table 1.

The formulation of the MO-RBDO problem for the ten bars truss is:

$$\begin{gathered} \min V(\mathbf{d}, \boldsymbol{\mu}_\mathbf{X}, \boldsymbol{\mu}_\mathbf{P}) \\ \min q_{2y}(\mathbf{d}, \boldsymbol{\mu}_\mathbf{X}, \boldsymbol{\mu}_\mathbf{P}) \\ s.t. \quad \beta_i \geq \beta_i^t = 3.7, \quad i = 1, \cdots, 10 \\ 20 \leq \mu_{X_j} \leq 80, \quad j = 1, 2, 3. \end{gathered} \tag{14}$$

The objectives are the volume (weight) of the structure and the mean value of the vertical displacement in the node 2. Reliability constraints are formulated as stress constraints:

$$g_i(\mathbf{d}, \mathbf{X}, \mathbf{P}) = 1 - \frac{|\sigma_i(\mathbf{d}, \boldsymbol{\mu}_\mathbf{X}, \boldsymbol{\mu}_\mathbf{P})|}{\sigma_i^a(\mathbf{d}, \boldsymbol{\mu}_\mathbf{X}, \boldsymbol{\mu}_\mathbf{P})} \quad i = 1, \cdots, 10 \tag{15}$$

where σ_i^a is the maximum stress allowed and takes the value of the Euler's critical stress for the bars in compression to take into account the buckling state limit. A target reliability index $\beta_i^t = 3.7$ was stated for all the reliability constraints.

This problem was solved applying the NSGA-II for the optimization at the outer loop. Reliability assessment at the inner loop was computed with a RIA-based FORM method. The parameters used were: $P_c = 0.9$, $P_m = 0.33$, $\eta_c = 20$ and $\eta_m = 20$. The population size was 80 and the max number of generations was 200. These values was selected after several runs with different parameters. Initial population was uniformly distributed between the lower and upper bounds.

It could occur that reliability assessment process does not converge for individuals of the current population because FORM algorithm could not converge, especially, with highly nonlinear limit state functions and with some marginal probability distributions for random design variables. If that case occurred, reliability indexes would not be available and constraints could not be computed. The solution adopted consists of rejecting these individuals and select other individuals from the current parent population to enter the parent population for the next generation.

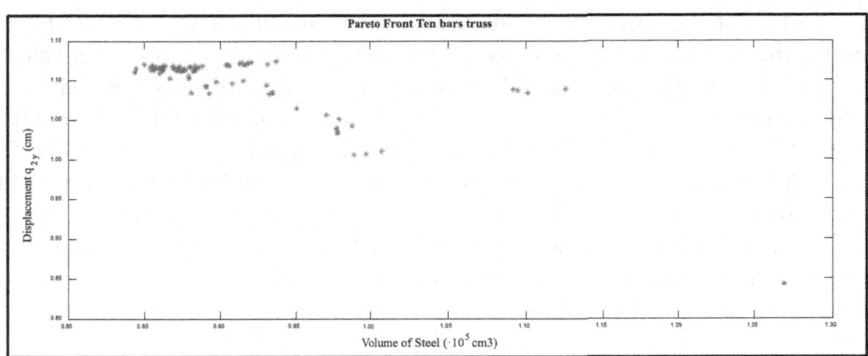

Fig. 4. Pareto front in the objective function space.

Reliability assessment has carried out directly with the exact limit state functions because the mechanical model is not very complex. In the case of large mechanical models, the calls to a finite element package running a numerical model suppose a prohibited computational effort. Then, metamodels or surrogate models are usually used to approximate the limits state functions. For example, surface response, Support Vector Regression (SVR), Artificial Neural Networks (ANN), Radial Basis Functions (RBF) and others.

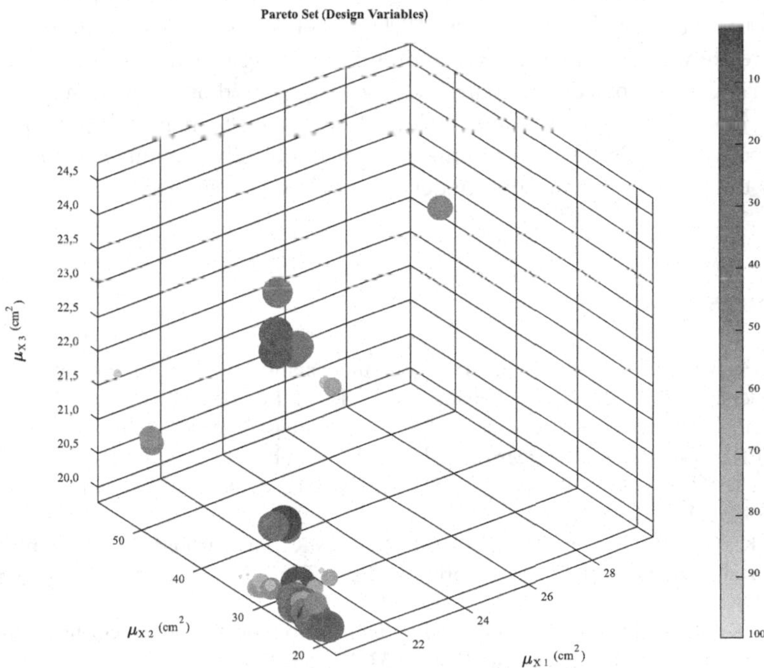

Fig. 5. Pareto set for the ten bar truss problem. Colourbar shows the rank of the solutions (Color figure online)

Pareto front in the space of objective functions is shown in Fig. 4. Horizontal axis represents the total volume of the truss. Vertical axis corresponds to the mean value of the vertical displacement of node 2. It is worth to note that the response, that is, the vertical displacement is a random variable and its variance could be high. Pareto front shows that the mean value of displacement decreases from 1.12 cm to 1 cm with a little increment of steel volume from $0.85 \cdot 10^5$ cm^3 to $1 \cdot 10^5$ cm^3. However, next reduction of vertical displacement to 0.84 cm involves a very large increment of the volume ($1.27 \cdot 10^5$ cm^3). With this in mind the DM could decide about the design to manufacture. Figure 5 shows the Pareto set in the design variables space. The colourbar represents the rank of the solutions.

6 Conclusions

Two problems about Multiobjective Optimization under uncertainty have been formulated and solving using the computer program developed. In both cases a Multiobjective Genetic Algorithm named NSGA – II carried out the design optimization in the outer loop. Reliability assessment was developed in the inner loop with FORM using the HLRF algorithm.

These problems are very useful to the DM. When the problems are solved, the DM can see a plot representing the trade-of between both objectives (cost and reliability level) that supports his or her decision.

Optimization methodologies do not guarantee that the global optimum will be obtained for every optimization problem. However, the optimization algorithms proposed here are well suited for at least finding better designs within an extensive design parameter space compared with a preliminary design based on engineering judgement.

More research work on the application of other metaheuristics algorithms such as Multiobjective Particle Swarm Optimization, Multiobjective Immune Algorithms and others in the field of Optimization under Uncertainty is ongoing.

References

1. Celorrio-Barragué, L.: Efficient methodology in reliability based design optimization applied to structures (Ph.D. thesis), Universidad de La Rioja, Logroño (2010)
2. Celorrio Barragué, L.: Development of a reliability-based design optimization toolbox for the FERUM software. In: Hüllermeier, E., Link, S., Fober, T., Seeger, B. (eds.) SUM 2012. LNCS (LNAI), vol. 7520, pp. 273–286. Springer, Heidelberg (2012). doi:10.1007/978-3-642-33362-0_21
3. Deb, K., Gupta, S., Daum, D., Branke, J., Mall, A.K., Padmanabhan, D.: Reliability-based optimization using evolutionary algorithms. IEEE Trans. Evol. Comput. **13**(5), 1054–1074 (2009)
4. Sinha, K.: Reliability-based multiobjective optimization for automotive crashworthiness and occupant safety. Struct. Multidisc. Optim. **33**(3), 255–268 (2007)

5. Cid Montoya, M., Costas, M., Díaz, J., Romera, L.E., Hernández, S.A.: Multi-objective reliability-based optimization of the crashworthiness of a metallic-GFRP impact absorber using hybrid approximations. Struct. Multidisc. Optim. **52**(4), 827–843 (2015)
6. Celorrio, L.: Reliability-based design optimization of structures combining genetic algorithms and finite element reliability analysis. In: Herrero, Á., Sedano, J., Baruque, B., Quintián, H., Corchado, E. (eds.) 10th International Conference on Soft Computing Models in Industrial and Environmental Applications. Advances in Intelligent Systems and Computing, vol. 368, pp. 143–152. Springer, Heidelberg (2015)
7. Celorrio-Barragué, L.: Reliability-based optimization of steel structures using genetic algorithms and nonlinear finite elements. In: CMMoST 3rd International Conference on Mechanical Models in Structural Engineering, Sevilla (2015)
8. Beck, J.L., Chan, E., Irfanoglu, A., Papadimitriou, C.: Multi-criteria optimal structural design under uncertainty. Earthq. Eng. Struct. Dyn. **28**, 741–761 (1999)
9. Konak, A., Coit, D.W., Smith, A.E.: Multi-objective optimization using genetic algorithms: a tutorial. Reliab. Eng. Syst. Saf. **91**(9), 992–1007 (2006)
10. Deb, K.: Multi-objective Optimization using Evolutionary Algorithms. Wiley, New York (2001)
11. Deb, K., Pratap, A., Agarwal, S., Meyarivan, T.: A fast and elitist multiobjective genetic algorithm: NSGA-II. IEEE Trans. Evol. Comput. **6**(2), 182–197 (2002)
12. Baskar, S., Tamilselvi, S., Varshini, P.R.: A MATLAB code for NSGA-II algorithm. File Exchange - MATLAB Central, Version 1.0, 24 February 2015
13. Thoft-Christensen, P., Baker, M.J.: Structural Reliability Theory and Its Applications. Springer, Heidelberg (1982)
14. Melchers, R.E.: Structural Reliability Analysis and Prediction, 2nd edn. Wiley, UK (1999)
15. Aoues, Y., Chateauneuf, A.: Benchmark study of numerical methods for reliability-based design optimization. Struct. Multidisc. Optim. **41**, 277–294 (2010)
16. Zou, T., Mahadevan, S.: Versatile formulation for multiobjective reliability-based design optimization. J. Mech. Des **128**(6), 1217–1226 (2005)
17. Zou, T., Mahadevan, S., Mourelatos, Z.P.: Reliability-based evaluation of automotive wind noise quality. Reliab. Eng. Syst. Saf. **82**(2), 217–224 (2003)
18. Coelho, R.F., Bouillard, P.: Multi-objective reliability-based optimization with stochastic metamodels. Evol. Comput. **19**(4), 525–560 (2011)

Hybridization of Analytic Programming and Differential Evolution for Time Series Prediction

Roman Senkerik[1(✉)], Adam Viktorin[1], Michal Pluhacek[1], Tomas Kadavy[1], and Ivan Zelinka[2]

[1] Faculty of Applied Informatics, Tomas Bata University in Zlin, Nam T.G. Masaryka 5555, 760 01 Zlin, Czech Republic
{senkerik, aviktorin, pluhacek, kadavy}@fai.utb.cz
[2] Faculty of Electrical Engineering and Computer Science, Technical University of Ostrava, 17. Listopadu 15, 708 33 Ostrava-Poruba, Czech Republic
ivan.zelinka@vsb.cz

Abstract. This research deals with the hybridization of symbolic regression open framework, which is Analytical Programming (AP) and Differential Evolution (DE) algorithm in the task of time series prediction. This paper provides a closer insight into applicability and performance of the hybrid connection between AP and different strategies of DE. AP can be considered as a powerful open framework for symbolic regression thanks to its usability in any programming language with arbitrary driving evolutionary/swarm based algorithm. Thus, the motivation behind this research, is to explore and investigate the applicability and differences in performance of AP driven by basic canonical strategy of DE as well as by the state of the art strategy, which is Success-History based Adaptive Differential Evolution (SHADE). An experiment with three case studies has been carried out here with the several time series consisting of GBP/USD exchange rate, where the first 2/3 of data were used for regression process and the last 1/3 of the data were used as a verification for prediction process. The differences between regression/prediction models synthesized by means of AP as a direct consequences of different DE strategies performances are briefly discussed within conclusion section of this paper.

Keywords: Analytic programming · Differential evolution · SHADE · Time series prediction

1 Introduction

This paper provides an insight into hybridization of symbolic regression open framework, which is Analytical Programming (AP) [1], and Differential Evolution (DE) [2] algorithm in the task of time series prediction.

The most current intelligent methods are mostly based on soft computing, representing a set of methods of special algorithms, and belonging to the artificial

F.J. Martínez de Pisón et al. (Eds.): HAIS 2017, LNAI 10334, pp. 686–698, 2017.
DOI: 10.1007/978-3-319-59650-1_58

intelligence paradigm. The most popular of these methods are fuzzy logic, neural networks, evolutionary algorithms (EA's) and symbolic regression approaches like genetic programming (GP). Currently, EA's together with symbolic regression techniques are known as a powerful set of tools for almost any difficult and complex optimization problems. One of such a challenging problem is naturally the regression/prediction of data/time series. In recent years, it attracts the researches' attention, and it has been solved by GP or hybrid mutual connection of EA's, GP, fuzzy systems, neural networks and more complex models [3–5].

The organization of this paper is following: Firstly, the related works and motivation for this research is proposed. The next sections are focused on the description of the concept of AP and used DE strategies. Experiment design, results and conclusion with discussion follow afterwards.

2 Related Works and Motivation

Analytical Programming (AP) is a novel approach to symbolic structure synthesis which uses EA for its computation. Since it can utilize arbitrary evolutionary/swarm based algorithm and it can be easily applied in any programming language, it can be considered as powerful open framework for symbolic regression. AP was introduced by I. Zelinka in 2001 and since its introduction; it has been proven on numerous problems to be as suitable for symbolic structure synthesis as Genetic Programming (GP) [6–10]. AP is based on the set of functions and terminals called General Functional Set. The individual of an EA is translated from individual domain to program domain using this set (more in the next section).

Currently, DE [11–14] is a well-known evolutionary computation technique for continuous optimization purposes solving many difficult and complex optimization problems. A number of DE variants have been recently developed with the emphasis on adaptivity/selfadaptivity. DE has been modified and extended several times by means of new proposals of versions; and the performances of different DE variant instance algorithms have been widely studied and compared with other evolutionary algorithms. Over recent decades, DE has won most of the evolutionary algorithm competitions in major scientific conferences [15–22], as well as being applied to several applications.

This research is an extension and continuation of the previous successful experiment with connection of state of the art Success-History based Adaptive Differential Evolution (SHADE) [22] algorithm and AP on regression of simple functions.

Since the open AP framework has been used recently only with basic and canonical versions of SOMA algorithm, Simulated Annealing, and many other algorithms as well as mostly with one basic strategy of DE, our motivation was to provide a closer insight into connection between AP and both canonical and state of the art powerful strategies of DE. The motivation can be summarized in following points:

- To show the results of DE driven AP for time series regression/prediction problems. This research encompasses three case studies.
- To investigate the differences in performances of AP driven by basic canonical strategy of DE and state of the art SHADE.

3 Analytic Programming

The basic functionality of AP is formed by three parts – General Functional Set (GFS), Discrete Set Handling (DSH) and Security Procedures (SPs). GFS contains all elementary objects which can be used to form a program, DSH carries out the mapping of individuals to programs and SPs are implemented into mapping process to avoid mapping to pathological programs and into cost function to avoid critical situations.

3.1 General Function Set

AP uses sets of functions and terminals. The synthesized program is branched by functions requiring two and more arguments and the length of it is extended by functions which require one argument. Terminals do not contribute to the complexity of the synthesized program (length) but are needed in order to synthesize a non-pathological program (program that can be evaluated by cost function). Therefore, each non-pathological program must contain at least one terminal.

Combined set of functions and terminals forms GFS which is used for mapping from individual domain to program domain. The content of GFS is dependent on user choice. GFS is nested and can be divided into subsets according to the number of arguments that the subset requires. GFS_{0arg} is a subset which requires zero arguments, thus contains only terminals. GFS_{1arg} contains all terminals and functions requiring one argument, GFS_{2arg} contains all objects from GFS_{1arg} and functions requiring two arguments and so on, GFS_{all} is a complete set of all elementary objects. For the purpose of mapping from individual to the program, it is important to note that objects in GFS are ordered by a number of arguments they require in descending order.

3.2 Discrete Set Handling

DSH is used for mapping the individual to the synthesized program. Most of the EAs use individuals with real number encoded individuals. The first important step in order for DSH to work is to get individual with integer components which are done by rounding real number values. The integer values of an individual are indexes into the discrete set, in this case, GFS and its subsets. If the index value is greater than the size of used GFS, modulo operation with the size of the discrete set is performed. An illustrative example of mapping is given in (1).

$$\begin{gathered} Individual = \left\{ \begin{matrix} 0.12, 4.29, 6.92, 6.12, 2.45, \\ 6.33, 5.78, 0.22, 1.94, 7.32 \end{matrix} \right\} \\ Rounded\ individual = \{0, 4, 7, 6, 2, 6, 6, 0, 2, 7\} \\ GFS_{all} = \{+, -, *, /, sin, cos, x, k\} \\ \boldsymbol{Program}\text{:}\mathbf{sin}\boldsymbol{x} + \boldsymbol{k} \end{gathered} \tag{1}$$

The objects in GFS_{all} are indexed from 0 and the mapping is as follows: The first rounded individual feature is 0 which represents + function in GFS_{all}. This function requires two arguments and those are represented by next two indexes – 4 and 7, which are mapped to function *sin* and constant *k*. The *sin* function requires one argument which is given by next index (rounded feature) – 6 and it is mapped to variable *x*. Since there is no possible way of branching the program further, other features are ignored and synthesized program is *sin x* + *k*.

3.3 Security Procedures

SPs are used in AP to avoid critical situations. Some of the SPs are implemented into the AP itself and some have to be implemented into the cost function evaluation. The typical representatives of the later are checking synthesized programs for loops, infinity and imaginary numbers if not expected (dividing by 0, square root of negative numbers, etc.).

The most significant SP implemented in AP is checking for pathological programs. Pathological programs are programs which cannot be evaluated due to the absence of arguments in the synthesized function. For example, individual with rounded features of {5, 5, 5, 5, 5} would be mapped to program cos(cos(cos(cos(cos_)))) which lacks constant or variable at the empty position denoted by _ and thus represent a pathological program. Such situation can be avoided by a simple procedure which checks remaining positions (parameters) of the individual during mapping and according to that maps rounded individual features to subsets of GFS_{all} which do not require too many arguments.

3.4 Constants Handling

The constant values in synthesized programs are usually estimated by second EA (meta-heuristic) or by non-linear fitting, which can be very time-demanding. Alternatively it is possible to use the extended part of the individual in EA for the evolution of constant values. The important task was to determine, what is the correct size of an extension (2).

$$k = l - floor((l - 1)/max\_arg) \tag{2}$$

Where *k* is the maximum number of constants that can appear in the synthesized program (extension) of length *l* and *max_arg* is the maximum number of arguments needed by functions in GFS. Also the *floor()* is a common floor round function. The final individual dimensionality (length) will be *k* + *l* and the example might be:

- Program length *l* = 10
- GFS: {+ , -, *, /, *sin*, *cos*, *x*, *k*}
- GFS maximum argument *max_arg* = 2
- Extension size *k* = 10 – *floor*((10-1) /2) = 6
- Dimensionality of the extended individual *k* + *l* = 16

This means, that the EA will work with individuals of length 16, but only first 10 features will be used for indexing into the GFS and the rest will be used as constant values.

While mapping the individual into a program, the constants are indexed and later replaced by the value from individual. Simple example can be seen in (3). Individual features in bold are the constant values. It is worthwhile to note that only features which are going to be mapped to GFS are rounded and the rest is omitted.

$$\begin{gathered} Individual = \left\{ \begin{matrix} 5.08, 1.64, 6.72, 1.09, 6.20, \\ 1.28, \mathbf{0.07}, \mathbf{3.99}, \mathbf{5.27}, \mathbf{2.64} \end{matrix} \right\} \\ Rounded\ individual = \{5, 2, 7, 1, 6, 1\} \\ GFS_{all} = \{+, -, *, /, sin, cos, x, k\} \\ \boldsymbol{Program}\text{:}\mathbf{cos}(\boldsymbol{k1} * (\boldsymbol{x} - \boldsymbol{k2})) \\ \boldsymbol{Replaced}\text{:}\mathbf{cos}(\mathbf{0.07} * (\boldsymbol{x} - \mathbf{3.99})) \end{gathered} \tag{3}$$

The first index to GFS_{all} is 5, which represents *cos* function, its argument is chosen by next index – 2 representing function * which needs two arguments. Arguments are indexed 7 and 1 – constant *k1* and function -. After this step, two arguments are needed and only two features are left in the program part of the individual. Therefore, the security procedure takes place and those last two features are indexed into GFS_{0arg}. Thus indexes 6 and 1 are mapped to variable *x* (6 mod size(GFS_{0arg}) = 0) and constant *k2*. The synthesized program is therefore *cos(k1 * (x – k2))*. The constants are replaced by the remaining features 0.07 and 3.99 respectively.

4 Differential Evolution

This section describes the basics of canonical DE strategy and SHADE strategy. The original DE [1] has four static control parameters – number of generations *G*, population size *NP*, scaling factor *F* and crossover rate *CR*. In the evolutionary process of DE, these four parameters remain unchanged and depend on the user initial setting. SHADE algorithm, on the other hand, adapts the *F* and *CR* parameters during the evolution. The values that brought improvement to the optimization task are stored into according historical memories M_F and M_{CR}. SHADE algorithm thus uses three control parameters – number of generations *G*, population size *NP* and size of historical memories *H*. The concept of basic operations in DE and SHADE algorithms is shown in the following sections, for a detailed description of either the canonical DE refer to [1] or for feature constraint correction, update of historical memories and external archive handling in SHADE see [22].

4.1 Canonical DE

In this research, we have used canonical DE “best/1/bin” (4) mutation strategy and binomial crossover (5).

Mutation Strategies and Parent Selection
In canonical forms of DE, parent indices (vectors) are selected by classic pseudo-random number generator (PRNG) with uniform distribution. Mutation strategy "best/1/bin" uses only two random parent vectors with indexes *r1*, *r2*, and best individual solution in current generation, where $r1 = U[1, NP]$, $r2 = U[1, NP]$, and $r1 \neq r2 \neq best$. Mutated vector $\boldsymbol{v}_{i,G}$ is obtained with the help of static scaling factor F as follows:

$$\boldsymbol{v}_{i,G} = \boldsymbol{x}_{best,G} + F(\boldsymbol{x}_{r1,G} - \boldsymbol{x}_{r2,G}) \tag{4}$$

Crossover and Elitism
The trial vector $\boldsymbol{u}_{i,G}$ which is compared with original vector $\boldsymbol{x}_{i,G}$ is completed by crossover operation (5). CR_i value in canonical DE algorithm is static, i.e. $CR_i = CR$.

$$\boldsymbol{u}_{j,i,G} = \begin{cases} \boldsymbol{v}_{j,i,G} & \text{if } U[0,1] \leq CR_i \text{ or } j = j_{rand} \\ \boldsymbol{x}_{j,i,G} & \text{otherwise} \end{cases} \tag{5}$$

Where j_{rand} is randomly selected index of a feature, which has to be updated ($j_{rand} = U[1, D]$), D is the dimensionality of the problem.

The vector which will be placed into the next generation $G + 1$ is selected by elitism. When the objective function value of the trial vector $\boldsymbol{u}_{i,G}$ is better or equal than that of the original vector $\boldsymbol{x}_{i,G}$, the trial vector will be selected for the next population. Otherwise, the original will survive. (6).

$$\boldsymbol{x}_{i,G+1} = \begin{cases} \boldsymbol{u}_{i,G} & \text{if } f(\boldsymbol{u}_{i,G}) \leq f(\boldsymbol{x}_{i,G}) \\ \boldsymbol{x}_{i,G} & \text{otherwise} \end{cases} \tag{6}$$

4.2 Success-History Based Adaptive Differential Evolution

The differences between canonical DE and SHADE strategy are given in following subsections.

Mutation Strategies and Parent Selection
In the original version of SHADE algorithm [22], parent selection for mutation strategy is carried out by the PRNG with uniform distribution. The mutation strategy used in SHADE is "current-to-*p*best/1" and uses four parent vectors – current *i*-th vector $\boldsymbol{x}_{i,G}$, vector $\boldsymbol{x}_{pbest,G}$ randomly selected from the $NP \times p$ best vectors (in terms of objective function value) from current generation G. The p value is randomly generated by uniform PRNG $U[p_{min}, 0.2]$, where $p_{min} = 2/NP$. Third parent vector $\boldsymbol{x}_{r1,G}$ is randomly selected from the current generation and last parent vector $\boldsymbol{x}_{r2,G}$ is also randomly selected, but from the union of current generation G and external archive A. Also, vectors $\boldsymbol{x}_{i,G}$, $\boldsymbol{x}_{r1,G}$ and $\boldsymbol{x}_{r2,G}$ has to differ, $\boldsymbol{x}_{i,G} \neq \boldsymbol{x}_{r1,G} \neq \boldsymbol{x}_{r2,G}$. The mutated vector $\boldsymbol{v}_{i,G}$ is generated by (7).

$$v_{i,G} = x_{i,G} + F_i\left(x_{pbest,G} - x_{i,G}\right) + F_i\left(x_{r1,G} - x_{r2,G}\right) \quad (7)$$

The i-th scaling factor F_i is generated from a Cauchy distribution with the location parameter $M_{F,r}$ (selected randomly from the scaling factor historical memory M_F) and scale parameter value of 0.1 (8). If $F_i > 1$, it is truncated to 1 also if $F_i \leq 0$, Eq. (8) is repeated.

$$F_i = C\left[M_{F,r}, 0.1\right] \quad (8)$$

Crossover and Elitism

SHADE algorithm uses the very same crossover (5) and elitism (6) schemes as canonical DE with following differences. *CR* value is not static, CR_i is generated from a normal distribution with a mean parameter value $M_{CR,r}$ (selected randomly from the crossover rate historical memory M_{CR}) and standard deviation value of 0.1 (9). If the CR_i value is outside of the interval [0, 1], the closer limit value (0 or 1) is used. The crossover compare rule is given in (9).

$$CR_i = N\left[M_{CR,r}, 0.1\right] \quad (9)$$

Also the elitism process is almost identical to that described in (7), with the addition of historical archive. If the objective function value of the trial vector $\boldsymbol{u}_{i,G}$ is better than that of the current vector $\boldsymbol{x}_{i,G}$, the trial vector will become the new individual in new generation $\boldsymbol{x}_{i,G+1}$ and the original vector $\boldsymbol{x}_{i,G}$ will be moved to the external archive of inferior solutions *A*. Otherwise, the original vector remains in the population in next generation and external archive remains unchanged.

Due to the limited space here, for the detailed information about historical memory update processes for *F* and *CR* parameters, please refer to [22].

5 Experiment Design

For the purpose of performance comparison of AP driven by two different DE strategies, an experiment with time series prediction has been carried out. Time series consisting of 300 data-points of GBP/USD exchange rate has been utilized. To support the robustness of the performance comparisons, the experiment encompasses of three case studies:

- Case study 1: The entire dataset was used: The first 2/3 of data (200 points) were used for regression process and the last 1/3 of the data (100 points) were used as a verification for prediction process.
- Case study 2: Snapshot No. 1 of the time series (data points 51–200). The first 100 points for regression and 50 points for prediction.
- Case study 3: Snapshot No. 2 of the time series (data points 151–300). The first 100 points for regression and remaining 50 points for prediction.

The parameter settings for both canonical DE and SHADE were following: Population size of 75, canonical DE parameters $F = 0.5$ and $Cr = 0.8$; SHADE parameter $H = 20$. The maximum number of generations was fixed at 2000 generations. The cost function (CF) was defined as a simple difference between given time series and the synthesized model given by means of AP (10) on regression interval.

$$CF = \sum_{i=1}^{nreg} |dataTS_i - dataAP_i| \tag{10}$$

Where *nreg* represents the length of the time series regression part (*nreg* data points), *dataTS* given time series data; and *dataAP* synthesized model given by AP.

Setting for AP was following:

- Max length of the individual (max *D*) = 150, where all max. 150 positions were used for functions, no constants were synthesized here.
- GFS_{All} = {+ , -, *,/ abs, cos, x^3, exp, ln, log10, mod, x^2, sin, sigmoid, sqrt, tan, a^b, x}

Experiments were performed in the environment of *Java* and *Wolfram Mathematica.* Overall, 30 independent runs for each DE strategy were performed.

6 Results

Simple statistical results of the experiments are shown in comprehensive Tables 1, 2 and 3 for all 30 repeated runs of both DE strategies. These tables contain basic statistical characteristics for the cost function values like: *minimum, maximum, mean, median and standard deviation*. The last presented attribute is noted as "*Avg. CFE Best Sol.*" which stands for the average cost function evaluations required for finding the best solution for all 30 independent run of particular DE strategy. The bold values depict the best obtained results (except the last attribute).

Table 1. Simple statistical comparisons for both DE strategies and 30 runs, case study 1.

DE Strategy	Min	Max	Mean	Median	Std. Dev.	Avg. CFE Best Sol.
DE "best/1/bin"	0.9170	15.1072	3.1951	1.5175	4.2162	10142
SHADE	**0.7641**	**3.4694**	**1.2658**	**1.1264**	**0.6335**	42238

Statistical non-parametric tests have been performed for compared pair of DE strategies. Wilcoxon Signed Rank test with the significance level of 0.05 has been used. The p-values for alternative hypothesis "unequal" are depicted in Table 4.

For the graphical comparisons of case study 1, it have been selected the best (Fig. 1 - left) obtained results as well as the best 5 successive results given by both DE strategies (Fig. 1 - right). The best results for the case studies 2 and 3 are depicted in Fig. 2. Synthesized prediction models given by means of AP are depicted in (11) as the illustrative example of the AP outputs for the best results of particular DE strategy within the case study 1.

Table 2. Simple statistical comparisons for both DE strategies and 30 runs, case study 2.

DE Strategy	Min	Max	Mean	Median	Std. Dev.	Avg. CFE Best Sol.
DE "best/1/bin"	**0.2744**	1.3526	0.4840	0.4353	0.2579	5744
SHADE	0.3196	**0.4841**	**0.4066**	**0.4063**	**0.0351**	36982

Table 3. Simple statistical comparisons for both DE strategies and 30 runs, case study 3.

DE Strategy	Min	Max	Mean	Median	Std. Dev.	Avg. CFE Best Sol.
DE "best/1/bin"	**0.4440**	7.7090	1.1181	0.7868	1.3882	7862
SHADE	0.4635	**0.7904**	**0.6619**	**0.6638**	**0.0882**	53987

Table 4. p-values for Wilcoxon non-parametric tests, all case studies.

	Case study 1	Case study 2	Case study 3
DE "best/1/bin" vs. SHADE	0.0008	0.819194	0.002749

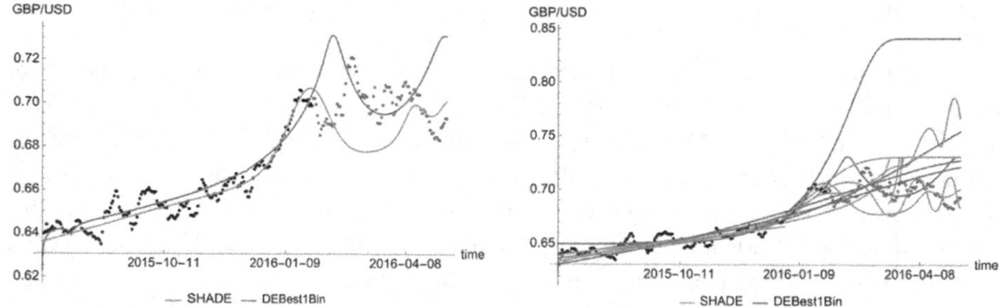

Fig. 1. Comparison of the best results (left) and successive five best results (right) given by two different DE strategies and AP framework for time series prediction problem of GBP/USD exchange rate. Black points (200) used for regression, red points (100) as reference for prediction. Case study 1.

Possible missing/discrete areas in plots of complex symbolic formulas are present due to the numerical instabilities occurring in Plot function in *Wolfram Mathematica SW.*

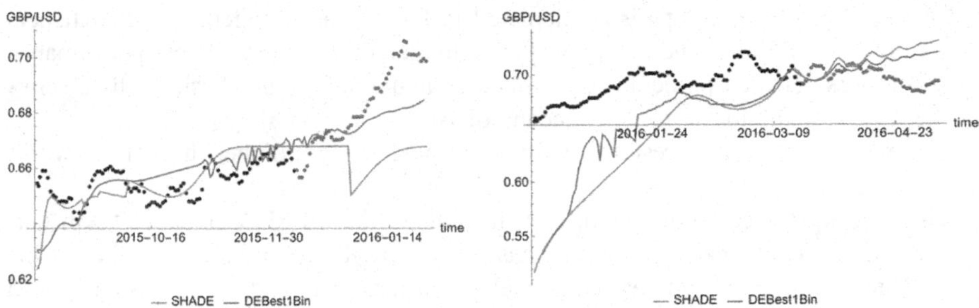

Fig. 2. Comparison of the best results given by two different DE strategies and AP framework for time series prediction problem of GBP/USD exchange rate. Black points (100) used for regression, red points (50) as reference for prediction, Case study 2 – left; Case study 3 – right

DE/best/1/Bin:

$$1 \Big/ \left(1 + e^{-\frac{1}{1+e^{-\sqrt{\mathrm{Abs}\left[\mathrm{Tan}\left[\mathrm{Tan}\left[x1^{\mathrm{Cos}[2\,x1+\mathrm{Abs}[\mathrm{Tan}[x1]]]-\mathrm{Cos}\left[x1^{\frac{\sqrt{\mathrm{Abs}\left[\mathrm{Log}\left[\frac{1}{2}\mathrm{Abs}[\mathrm{Log}[\mathrm{Abs}[x1+\mathrm{Abs}[x1]]]]\right]\right]}}{\sqrt{\mathrm{Log}[10]}}}\right]}\right]\right]\right]}}}} \right) \tag{11}$$

SHADE:

$$\frac{1}{1+e^{-\left(\frac{1}{1+e^{-x1}}\right)^{\mathrm{Sin}\left[\mathrm{Cos}\left[x1^{3\left(\sqrt{\mathrm{Abs}[x1]}+\mathrm{Cos}\left[x1+\left(\left(e^{2\,x1}\right)^{x1}+x1\right)\mathrm{Tan}[x1]\right]\right)}\right]\right]}}}$$

7 Conclusion and Results Analysis

This paper presented an insight into performance of hybridization between AP and different strategies of DE. Since AP has been proven as a powerful open framework for symbolic regression thanks to its usability in arbitrary programming language with arbitrary driving evolutionary/swarm based algorithm, the motivation behind this research, was to explore the level of applicability and to investigate the differences in performance of AP hybridized with basic canonical DE strategy as well as by the state of the art SHADE strategy. Therefore, no comprehensive comparison to other methods (GP, EP, NNs etc.) was performed. The findings can be summarized as follows:

- Average required time per one run of any DE strategy was around 3 min (for maximum of 150 000 cost function evaluations). Considering the "*Avg. CFE Best Sol.*" values in Tables 1, 2 and 3, we can roughly estimate, that SHADE required approx. 1 min for good solution, and canonical DE approx. 10–15 s.

- Obtained graphical comparisons depicted in Figs. 1 and 2 together with statistical data in Tables 1, 2, 3 and 4 support the claim that there are significant performance differences between particular DE strategies in the task of synthesizing time series regression/prediction models by means of AP.
- Complexity of the best results (synthesized models) was higher than of the worse results.
- The primary logical assumption, that the state of the art SHADE variant will outperform the canonical DE strategy has been partially confirmed, nevertheless the graphical outputs of synthesized models, statistical data and paired tests revealed different aspects in performance comparisons.
- *Case study 1*: Here, all the statistical data and paired tests lend weigh to the argument that SHADE strategy performed significantly better than canonical DE.
- *Case study 2*: The simple statistical data presented in the Table 2 shows the mixed results between SHADE and canonical DE. The canonical DE variant has found the best CF value, nevertheless remaining statistical features in Table 1 supports the apparent claim that SHADE has performed better. However, the Wilcoxon test shows, that there is no significant difference between DE strategies.
- *Case study 3*: Both SHADE strategy and canonical DE strategy show similar mixed results structure as in the previous case. Nevertheless the Wilcoxon test and simple statistical data show in favor of SHADE.
- The possible confirmation of aforementioned claims is supported by the recorded parameter noted in Tables 1, 2, and 3 as "*Avg. CFE Best Sol.*". Its very low value for "best/1/bin" strategy shows the possibility of very fast and premature convergence to local extremes in high dimensional complex search space. Whereas markedly higher values for SHADE strategy confirms the longer searching process before stagnation/not-updating of the best result.
- An interesting phenomenon was discovered within this experimental research. It seems to be a very good choice to hybridize the AP and powerful state of the art DE strategy, to obtain a very good synthesized model structure fitting and predicting the data with higher accuracy. Even though from the statistical point of view, there are mixed/similar characteristics with much simpler strategy (the lowest found cost function values – case studies 2 and 3). The mutual connection of AP and SHADE was able to quickly search in very complex high dimensional space for fine individual (solution) structure for discrete set handling process inside AP resulting in good synthesized model structure securing not only the regression phase, but also with the tendencies for approximate prediction of the time series.

Acknowledgements. This work was supported by Grant Agency of the Czech Republic - GACR P103/15/06700S, further by project NPU I No. MSMT-7778/2014 by the Ministry of Education of the Czech Republic and also by the European Regional Development Fund under the Project CEBIA-Tech No. CZ.1.05/2.1.00/03.0089, partially supported by Grant SGS 2017/134 of VSB-Technical University of Ostrava; and by Internal Grant Agency of Tomas Bata University under the projects No. IGA/Cebia-Tech/2017/004.

References

1. Zelinka, I., Davendra, D., Senkerik, R., Jasek, R., Oplatkova, Z.: Analytical programming - a novel approach for evolutionary synthesis of symbolic structures. In: Kita, E. (ed.) Evolutionary Algorithms. InTech, Rijeka (2011)
2. Storn, R., Price, K.: Differential evolution – a simple and efficient heuristic for global optimization over continuous spaces. J. Glob. Optim. **11**(4), 341–359 (1997)
3. Wang, W.-C., Chau, K.-W., Cheng, C.-T., Qiu, L.: A comparison of performance of several artificial intelligence methods for forecasting monthly discharge time series. J. Hydrol. **374** (3), 294–306 (2009)
4. Santini, M., Tettamanzi, A.: Genetic programming for financial time series prediction. In: Miller, J., Tomassini, M., Lanzi, P.L., Ryan, C., Tettamanzi, Andrea G.B., Langdon, William B. (eds.) EuroGP 2001. LNCS, vol. 2038, pp. 361–370. Springer, Heidelberg (2001). doi:10.1007/3-540-45355-5_29
5. Pallit, A., Popovic, D.: Computational Intelligence in Time Series Forecasting. Springer, Heidelberg (2005)
6. Koza, J.R.: Genetic Programming: On the Programming of Computers by Means of Natural Selection, vol. 1. MIT press, Massachusetts (1992)
7. Zelinka, I., Oplatková, Z., Nolle, L.: Boolean symmetry function synthesis by means of arbitrary evolutionary algorithms-comparative study. Int. J. Simul. Syst. Sci. Technol. **6**(9), 44–56 (2005)
8. Oplatková, Z., Zelinka, I.: Investigation on artificial ant using analytic programming. In: Proceedings of the 8th Annual Conference on Genetic and Evolutionary Computation, pp. 949–950. ACM (2006)
9. Zelinka, I., Chen, G., Celikovsky, S.: Chaos synthesis by means of evolutionary algorithms. Int. J. Bifurcat. Chaos **18**(04), 911–942 (2008)
10. Senkerik, R., Oplatkova, Z., Zelinka, I., Davendra, D.: Synthesis of feedback controller for three selected chaotic systems by means of evolutionary techniques: analytic programming. Math. Comput. Model. **57**(1–2), 57–67 (2013)
11. Price, K.V., Storn, R.M., Lampinen, J.A.: Differential Evolution - A Practical Approach to Global Optimization. Natural Computing Series. Springer, Heidelberg (2005)
12. Neri, F., Tirronen, V.: Recent advances in differential evolution: a survey and experimental analysis. Artif. Intell. Rev. **33**(1–2), 61–106 (2010)
13. Das, S., Suganthan, P.N.: Differential evolution: a survey of the state-of-the-art. IEEE Trans. Evol. Comput. **15**(1), 4–31 (2011)
14. Das, S., Mullick, S.S., Suganthan, P.N.: Recent advances in differential evolution–an updated survey. Swarm Evol. Comput. **27**, 1–30 (2016)
15. Brest, J., Greiner, S., Boskovic, B., Mernik, M., Zumer, V.: Self-adapting control parameters in differential evolution: a comparative study on numerical benchmark problems. IEEE Trans. Evol. Comput. **10**(6), 646–657 (2006)
16. Qin, A.K., Huang, V.L., Suganthan, P.N.: Differential evolution algorithm with strategy adaptation for global numerical optimization. IEEE Trans. Evol. Comput. **13**(2), 398–417 (2009)
17. Zhang, J., Sanderson, A.C.: JADE: adaptive differential evolution with optional external archive. IEEE Trans. Evol. Comput. **13**(5), 945–958 (2009)
18. Das, S., Abraham, A., Chakraborty, U.K., Konar, A.: Differential evolution using a neighborhood-based mutation operator. IEEE Trans. Evol. Comput. **13**(3), 526–553 (2009)
19. Mininno, E., Neri, F., Cupertino, F., Naso, D.: Compact differential evolution. IEEE Trans. Evol. Comput. **15**(1), 32–54 (2011)

20. Mallipeddi, R., Suganthan, P.N., Pan, Q.-K., Tasgetiren, M.F.: Differential evolution algorithm with ensemble of parameters and mutation strategies. Appl. Soft Comput. **11**(2), 1679–1696 (2011)
21. Brest, J., Korošec, P., Šilc, J., Zamuda, A., Bošković, B., Maučec, M.S.: Differential evolution and differential ant-stigmergy on dynamic optimisation problems. Int. J. Syst. Sci. **44**(4), 663–679 (2013)
22. Tanabe, R., Fukunaga, A.S.: Improving the search performance of SHADE using linear population size reduction. In: 2014 IEEE Congress on Evolutionary Computation (CEC), pp. 1658–1665. IEEE (2014)

Adjust the Thermo-Mechanical Properties of Finite Element Models Welded Joints Based on Soft Computing Techniques

Roberto Fernández Martinez[1(✉)], Rubén Lostado Lorza[2], Marina Corral Bobadilla[2], Rubén Escribano Garcia[3], Fátima Somovilla Gomez[2], and Eliseo P. Vergara González[2]

[1] Department of Electrical Engineering, University of Basque Country UPV/EHU, Bilbao, Spain
roberto.fernandezm@ehu.es

[2] Department of Mechanical Engineering, University of La Rioja, Logroño, Spain

[3] Built Environment and Engineering, Leeds Beckett University, Leeds, UK

Abstract. An appropriate characterization of the thermo-mechanical behavior of elastic-plastic Finite Element (FE) models is essential to ensure realistic results when welded joints are studied. The welded joints are subject to severe angular distortion produced by an intense heat concentration on a very small area when they are manufactured. For this reason, the angular distortion and the temperature field, which the joints are subjected, is very difficult to model with the Finite Element Method (FEM) when nonlinear effects such as plasticity of the material, radiation and thermal contacts are considered. This paper sets out a methodology to determine the most appropriate parameters needed for modelling the thermo-mechanical behavior in welded joints FE models. The work is based on experimental data (temperature field and angular distortion) and the combined use of Support Vector Machines (SVM) and Genetic Algorithms (GA) with multi-objective functions. The proposed methodology is applied for modelling Butt joint with single V-groove weld manufactured by Gas Metal Arc Welding (GMAW) process when the parameters of speed, current and voltage are, respectively, 6 mm/sec 140 amps and 26 V.

Keywords: Finite element method · Genetic algorithms · Support vector machines · Welding temperature distribution · Angular distortion · Multi-objective optimization

1 Introduction

Welded joint components are widely used in many industrial applications, therefore knowing the manufacturing process can help significantly to the industry. The regions near to the weld line, when manufacturing such joints, are subjected to severe thermal cycles due to the intense concentration of heat in a small area. These thermal cycles generate changes in the microstructure and in the mechanical properties, and cause residual stresses that produce important angular distortions on welded joints [1].

F.J. Martínez de Pisón et al. (Eds.): HAIS 2017, LNAI 10334, pp. 699–709, 2017.
DOI: 10.1007/978-3-319-59650-1_59

Furthermore, these thermal cycles are substantially affected by the way the welds have been manufactured and the welding process parameters [2]. During decades, the Finite Element Method (FEM) has been used as an alternative in an attempt to reduce the costs during the design phase of the welded joints. Generally, the Finite Element (FE) models welded joints require a large number of parameters, which are difficult to adjust when the chosen methodology is based solely on test error. Many authors have studied the temperature field and the angular distortion separately in FE models to study welded joints. For example, [3] studied the welding temperature distribution in Gas Tungsten Arc Welding (GTAW) process. In this case, the FEM was applied to predict temperature distributions throughout the plates welded using ABAQUS software, and was validated experimentally with thermocouples. Other researchers have based their studies of welded joints with FEM on the angular distortion instead of the temperature fields. For example in [4], the combination of FE models and experiments was applied to study the effects of arc distance and welding parameters to control the residual angular distortion in Tungsten Inert Gas (TIG). The conduction and convection phenomenon and the elastic-plastic material behavior were the parameters considered on the welded joints FE models.

The current paper presents a methodology to determinate the most appropriate parameters for modelling the thermo-mechanical behavior in welded joints FE models on the basis of experimental data (temperature field and angular distortion). The work is focused in Butt joint single V-groove weld manufactured by Gas Metal Arc Welding (GMAW) when the parameters of speed, current and voltage are, respectively, 6 mm/sec 140 amps and 26 V. The process is based on the combined use of Support Vector Machines (SVM) to predict critical features of the process and Genetic Algorithms (GA) with multi-objective functions to adjust the variables that define the FE models.

2 Experimental Data and FE Model Proposed

During the manufacturing process with GMAW, the plates that composed the welded joint studied had the dimension 60 × 80 × 6 mm, and were composed by low carbon steel ST37. The gas mixture used was 80% Argon (Ar) and 20% Carbon Dioxide (CO_2), and the parameters of speed, current and voltage considered were, respectively, 6 mm/sec, 140 amps and 26 V. Also, the plates to be welded were mounted on a refractory surface, and one of the plates was fixed by a clamp. In these conditions, the forces that produced the angular distortion of the welded joint were the gravity and the force of thermal shrinkage. The temperature field was recorded during the manufacture of the welded joint using a thermographic camera (Thermovision 570 AGEMA infrared system AB) every two seconds during a period of 100 s, while the angular distortion was measured on the most distorted edge using a coordinate-measuring machine (model Zeiss PMC 850). To avoid possible errors in the temperature field measurement produced by the transient event on starting and completion of the welding process, only the central points of the weld cord were taken into consideration. In this case, the locations P_1, P_5, P_6, P_{10}, P_{11} and P_{15} were not taken into consideration, and only the locations P_2, P_3, P_4, P_7, P_8, P_9, P_{12}, P_{13} and P_{14} were considered. Figure 1(a) shows the temperature field obtained experimentally during the experiment after 6 s, and Fig. 1(b) shows the temperature field obtained after 20 s. In addition, the FE models proposed in the current work were formulated parametrically to determine the temperature field and the angular distortion of the butt welded joints with MSC Marc software. These FE models were composed by a weld bead, a pair of plates and a refractory surface. They considered coupled thermal-mechanical fields and temperature dependent material of the ST37 steel [4]. The FE simulations proposed used the technique of birth and death of elements to model the addition of weld metal on the parts to weld [5].

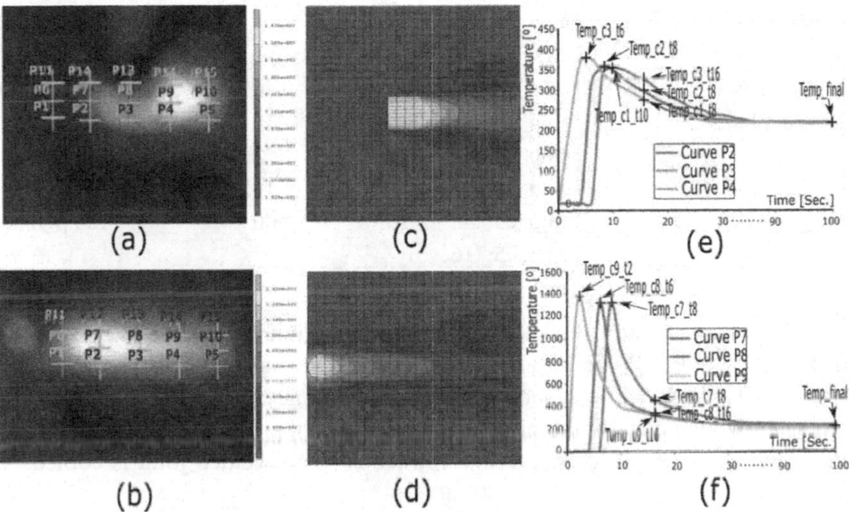

Fig. 1. Temperature field obtained experimentally and by FE model respectively at 6 s time ((**a**) and (**c**)) and 9 s time ((**b**) and (**d**)). Temperature curves vs time for points P_2; P_3 and P_4 (**e**) and P_7; P_8 and P_9 (**f**).

A total of thirteen different parameters of the welded joint FE models were taken into consideration. They were: The thermal conduction phenomena considering six parameters based on the different pairs of contacts that made up the welded joints (melt_point; contac_p_init; contac_p_center; contac_p_end; contact_p1_p2; contact_p2_ap). Also, the weld flux for all FE models was assumed to be a double ellipsoidal shaped [6] and it was defined by four parameters that defined the shape of the ellipsoid (forward_lenght; rear_lenght; width; deep). In addition, the phenomenon of thermal convection was modelled using three different film coefficient parameters (face_film; face_film2; face_film3) [7]. Finally, the radiation was taken into consideration in the FE model and applied in the weld bead and the surrounding areas. Figure 1(c) shows the temperature field obtained from the FE models proposed after 6 s and Fig. 1(d) shows the temperature field obtained after 9 s in order to compare with those temperatures obtained experimentally.

Since the number of temperature samples from each of the 9 points studied during the welding process is very high (one sample every two seconds during a period of

100 s), the problem was simplified taking just the most significant points in each curve of temperature. These selected points are shown in Table 1.

Table 1. Selected final features: defined by the location in the weld and the time when the temperature was measured.

Location	Sample time (seconds)	Feature name	Location	Sample time (seconds)	Feature name
P_2	10	Temp_c1_t10	P_9	6	Temp_c6_t6
	16	Temp_c1_t16		16	Temp_c6_t16
P_3	8	Temp_c2_t8	P_{12}	8	Temp_c7_t8
	16	Temp_c2_t16		16	Temp_c7_t16
P_4	6	Temp_c3_t6	P_{13}	6	Temp_c8_t6
	16	Temp_c3_t16		16	Temp_c8_t16
P_7	10	Temp_c4_t10	P_{14}	2	Temp_c9_t2
	16	Temp_c4_t16		16	Temp_c9_t16
P_8	4	Temp_c5_t4	All	100	Temp_final
	16	Temp_c5_t16			

Also, Fig. 1(e), (f) show the temperature curves vs time obtained experimentally for points P_2, P_3, P_4, P_7, P_8 and P_9 and the temperature values of the selected points according to Table 1. Table 2 shows the corresponding experimental values of temperatures obtained at each of the nine points studied in their respective times as well as the distortion angle obtained by thermal retraction when welded joint is cooled.

Table 2. Experimental values at each of the nine points studied in their respective times.

Feature	Exp. Data	Feature	Exp. Data	Feature	Exp. Data
Distort_Angle	4.93°	Temp_c7_t8	1300.0 °C	Temp_c5_t16	280.0 °C
Temp_c1_t10	355.0 °C	Temp_c8_t6	1300.0 °C	Temp_c6_t16	283.7 °C
Temp_c2_t8	355.3 °C	Temp_c9_t2	1340.0 °C	Temp_c7_t16	465.6 °C
Temp_c3_t6	376.9 °C	Temp_c1_t16	323.0 °C	Temp_c8_t16	334.9 °C
Temp_c4_t10	350.0 °C	Temp_c2_t16	293.7 °C	Temp_c9_t16	322.0 °C
Temp_c5_t4	400.0 °C	Temp_c3_t16	273.1 °C	Temp_final	216.8 °C
Temp_c6_t6	380.0 °C	Temp_c4_t16	312.5 °C	–	–

In addition and due that the simulation time for each of the welded joint FE models proposed were not excessive (around 2 h), the Design of Experiments (DoE) was performed using a Fractional Factorial Design to generate the design matrix (dataset) which was formed by 2048 FE simulations. This dataset was composed by the thirteen inputs and the corresponding twenty outputs (angular distortion and temperature points) obtained from the FE simulations.

2.1 Analysis of Features Significance

The dataset obtained from the DoE and the FE simulations was analysed to determine which variables were the most significant to define the outputs of the problem. This point was performed with three different analyses, which were:

- Using an analysis of linear variance (ANOVA test) [8]
- Using an analysis of nonlinear variance (Kruskal-Wallis test) [9, 10]
- Using a backpropagation filter (random forest selection function) [11]

The following stages of the methodology were applied to the selected features according to these three methods, as well as for the entire set of variables analysed in the problem.

2.2 Support Vector Machines

There are numerous regression techniques inherently based on a nonlinear nature. One of the most intensively studied and applied are SVM thanks to its performance as a universal approximation [12]. This technique is based on a kernel-based algorithm that have sparse solutions, where the predictions for new inputs depend on the kernel function evaluated at a subset of instances during a training stage where a repeated cross validation is performed.

The goal of this technique is to find a function that minimizes the final error in Eq. 1.

$$y(x) = w^T \cdot \phi(x) + b \tag{1}$$

Where $y(x)$ is the predicted value, w is the vector with the parameters that define the model, b indicates the value of the bias and $\phi(x)$ is the function that fixes the feature-space transformation.

The process is optimized and finally the initial function (Eq. 1) became the more complex function (Eq. 2).

$$y(x) = \sum_{n=1}^{N} (\alpha_i - \alpha_i^*) \langle x_i \cdot x \rangle + b \tag{2}$$

Where α is a solution of the optimization problem obtained through Lagrangian theory.

Also, the function makes a transformation of the data to a higher dimensional feature space to improve the accuracy of the nonlinear problem. In this way the final function became like Eq. 3.

$$y(x) = \sum_{n=1}^{N} (\alpha_i - \alpha_i^*) k(x_i, x) + b \tag{3}$$

Where in this case three kernels functions were used: linear (Eq. 4), polynomial (Eq. 5) and Gaussian Radial Basis Function (RBF) (Eq. 6).

$$k(x_i, x) = x_i^T x \tag{4}$$

$$k(x_i, x) = \langle x_i \cdot x \rangle^d \tag{5}$$

$$k(x_i, x) = e^{-\frac{\|x_i - x\|^2}{2\sigma^2}} \tag{6}$$

R statistical software environment v2.15.3 was used to program the proposed methodologies, to develop the regression models and to perform the optimization based on GA [13].

2.3 Model Selection Criteria

The SVM models were trained using 50 times repeated 10 fold cross-validation using the entire training dataset obtained from the DoE, with 2048 entries, to create the models. This method involves dividing the initial database into 10 subsets, building the model with 9 subsets and calculating the error with the other partial sample of the dataset. This procedure is repeated 50 times obtaining other errors. And finally, the error is calculated as the arithmetic mean of all the errors of the process [14–16].

Once the different algorithms were trained during some of their most significant parameters were tuned, a selection was made of those with the best predictive performance. The coefficients indicative of the error used to evaluate the accuracy of the predictions were the RMSE and its standard deviation.

2.4 Optimization Based on Genetic Algorithms

Once the regression model with the best generalization capacity was selected, the optimal parameters for defining the welded joint FE models were performed applying evolutionary optimization techniques based on GA [7, 17], and was conducted as follows: firstly, a number of 1000 individuals or combinations of the 13 inputs were randomly generated and named as the initial generation. Subsequently, and based on these individuals, the 20 outputs were obtained applying the most accurate model according to previous results. Two objective functions were analyzed in this case: the objective function $Jtemp_j$ implemented to adjust the nine curves of temperature (Eq. 7), and the objective function *Jangle*, implemented to adjust the angular deformation (Eq. 8). Both functions are combined affected by the same weight.

$$Jtemp_j = \sum_{i=0}^{n} \frac{\left| T_{FEM(i)} - T_{EXP(i)} \right|}{T_{EXP(i)}} \tag{7}$$

$$Jangle = \frac{\left| \propto_{FEM} - \propto_{EXP} \right|}{\propto_{EXP}} \tag{8}$$

Where $T_{FEM(i)}$ are FE models temperature measurements, $T_{EXP(i)}$ are experimental temperature measurements, n is the number of points where temperature is measured, $\propto_{FEM}$ is the FE models angular deformation, and $\propto_{EXP}$ is the experimental angular deformation.

The next generations were generated using selection, crossover and mutation. The new generation was comprised as follows:

- 25% comprised the best individuals from the previous generation.
- 60% comprised individuals obtained by crossover.
- The remaining 15% is obtained by random mutation.

Finally the best combination of values of each feature was selected and tested to determinate the final error of the methodology.

3 Results

3.1 Analysis of Features Significance

First an analysis of variance ANOVA was performed to assess the uncertainty in the experimental measurements based on the proposed DoE. All the final outputs were analyzed against the input variables. The p-values that obtained low values were selected since indicate that the observed relationships were statistically significant. Subsequently a nonparametric Kruskal-Wallis test was performed by ranks in the same way than the previous technique in order to select some features. Table 3 shows the results of both techniques for the output feature "Distort_Angle".

Finally, a feature selection using search backwards selection algorithms were performed. In this case, the selected attributes according to the RMSE obtained for the output feature "Distort_Angle" are those corresponded to the number 12 (see Table 4) with a value of RMSE = 0.01956.

Table 3. Results obtained from the ANOVA analysis and the Kruskal-Wallis analysis for the feature "angle" (only significant features are shown). Significant codes according to p-value: '***' 0.001, '**' 0.01, '*' 0.05, '.' 0.1.

ANOVA analysis			Kruskal-Wallis analysis		
Feature	p-value		Feature	p-value	
melt_point	5.80e-05	***	melt_point	2.755e-09	***
contac_p_init	<2.2e-16	***	contac_p_init	<2.2e-16	***
contac_p_center	<2.2e-16	***	contac_p_center	<2.2e-16	***
contac_p_end	0.04841	*	contac_p_end	0.02151	*
rear_lenght	0.08133	.	rear_lenght	0.06186	.

Table 4. Results obtained using the backwards selection algorithm for the feature "angle" (Selected set of features in bold letters).

Number of features	RMSE	Rsquared	RMSESD	RsquaredSD
1	0.24532	0.4820	0.0042429	0.0137015
2	0.10301	0.9783	0.0029787	0.0016687
...	...	...	...	...
12	**0.01956**	**0.9993**	**0.0008958**	**0.0001080**
13	0.02654	0.9988	0.0010458	0.0002229

3.2 SVM

The creation of regression models that predict the temperature on several points of the welded joint and also the angular distortion was based on machine learning techniques based on SVM. Also, and in order to compare linear and nonlinear techniques, a linear regression (LR) was also performed. In this case, the method was conducted in the following way: Firstly, the 2048 experiments were performed according to the proposed DoE. The dataset obtained from the experiments was normalized between 0 and 1. Thereafter, these 2048 instances were used to train the models using 50 times repeated cross-validation. During the training process, the RMSE and its standard deviation were also obtained while a tuning of the most important parameters of each algorithm was performed to improve its prediction capability.

The process was repeated four times, one per each of the feature selection method previously mentioned. For example, the results obtained when all the features were used in the process are shown in Table 5. For each feature selection method, one model was selected subsequently, and from the four models selected, the most accurate one was chosen. In that way, only the most accurate model per each output variable was selected and used in the following processes.

From each of the selected models, the tuned parameters that allow the model its most accurate behavior was obtained. For example, for the feature "angle" the best performance happened when ANOVA group of features was used, and the selected values from the tuning of parameters were a cost of 0.04 and a degree of the polynomial applied in the kernel was 2. In this case the RMSE was equal to 2.46% and its standard deviation was 0.06%.

3.3 Adjustment Based on Genetic Algorithms

The adjustment process to find the best combination of inputs to optimize both objective functions was performed minimizing their error based on the experimental data obtained experimentally (see Table 2).

The minimization of the objective functions generates the values that are shown in Table 6. These values indicate the closest values to the real behavior of the Butt joint single V-groove weld manufactured by GMAW. With these values, a new FE model was simulated to observe the real effectiveness of the methodology. In this case, RMSE equal to 12.35% was obtained comparing the new FE model simulated with the optimal

Table 5. Results obtained during training stage for the output variables (in bold letters the most accurate and selected ones) (values in %)

Feature	LR		SVM (Linear)		SVM (Polynomial)		SVM (RBF)	
	RMSE	SD	RMSE	SD	RMSE	SD	RMSE	SD
Angle	11.64	0.18	13.09	0.91	**2.64**	**0.04**	3.20	0.02
Temp_c1_t10	4.87	0.17	5.36	0.33	**2.73**	**0.02**	2.96	0.03
Temp_c2_t8	5.11	0.10	5.17	0.09	**3.82**	**0.02**	4.23	0.01
Temp_c3_t6	5.48	0.17	6.14	0.28	**2.91**	**0.03**	3.03	0.03
Temp_c4_t10	4.94	0.18	5.44	0.33	**2.73**	**0.01**	2.94	0.01
Temp_c5_t4	2.50	0.08	**3.68**	**0.01**	**3.68**	**0.01**	4.34	0.01
Temp_c6_t6	5.49	0.19	6.23	0.32	**2.88**	**0.02**	3.03	0.03
Temp_c7_t8	14.75	0.20	17.92	1.01	**2.97**	**0.01**	3.54	0.04
Temp_c8_t6	13.31	0.08	17.07	1.84	**2.87**	**0.05**	3.40	0.04
Temp_c9_t2	**0.88**	**0.02**	5.33	1.04	3.76	1.60	5.38	1.07
Temp_c1_t16	4.69	0.16	4.88	0.24	**2.50**	**0.04**	2.65	0.03
Temp_c2_t16	5.22	0.13	5.38	0.13	**2.70**	**0.03**	3.03	0.02
Temp_c3_t16	4.84	0.14	5.12	0.27	**2.57**	**0.02**	2.69	0.04
Temp_c4_t16	4.71	0.16	4.89	0.24	**2.51**	**0.04**	2.65	0.01
Temp_c5_t16	5.22	0.14	5.37	0.18	**2.70**	**0.04**	3.03	0.02
Temp_c6_t16	4.85	0.15	5.21	0.17	**2.57**	**0.05**	2.69	0.02
Temp_c7_t16	15.46	0.18	18.17	0.78	**1.78**	**0.02**	2.39	0.01
Temp_c8_t16	5.27	0.19	5.32	0.17	**1.48**	**0.03**	1.88	0.01
Temp_c9_t16	18.88	0.26	21.37	0.62	**1.93**	**0.03**	2.66	0.01
Temp_final	3.97	0.15	3.99	0.17	**2.28**	**0.02**	2.62	0.04

Table 6. Results obtained from the minimization of the objective functions for each input feature

Input variable	Obtained value from GA adjustment	Input variable	Obtained value from GA adjustment
melt_point	1423.11	face_film2	0.0003
contac_p_init	275.42	face_film3	0.0008
contac_p_center	239.71	forward_lenght	1.00
contac_p_end	150.90	rear_lenght	5.00
contact_p1_p2	83.48	width	23.40
contact_p2_ap	4.06	depth	4.43
face_film	0.0008		

values obtained from the adjustment process against the experimental data. This indicates that the methodology proposed to find the best combination of parameters is effective.

4 Conclusions

This work presents a methodology for determining the most appropriate parameters for modelling the thermo-mechanical behavior in welded joints FE models on the basis of experimental data (temperature field and angular distortion). The work is focused in Butt joint single V-groove weld manufactured by Gas Metal Arc Welding (GMAW). The process is based on the combined use of Support Vector Machines (SVM) to predict critical features of the process and Genetic Algorithms (GA) with multi-objective functions to adjust the variables that define the FE models. In this case, a value of 12.35% for the RMSE was obtained comparing the FE model with the optimal parameters obtained from the adjustment against the experimental data applying this methodology. This indicates that the methodology proposed to find the best parameters in Butt joint single V-groove weld manufactured by GMAW is effective when the parameters of speed, current and voltage are, respectively, 6 mm/sec 140 amps and 26 V.

Acknowledgements. The authors wish to thanks to the University of the Basque Country for its support through the project US15/18 OMETESA and to the University of La Rioja for its support through Project ADER 2014-I-IDD-00162.

References

1. Olabi, A.G., Lostado L.R., Benyounis, K.Y.: Review of microstructures, mechanical properties, and residual stresses of ferritic and martensitic stainless - steel welded. In: Comprehensive Materials Processing, vol. 6. Welding and Bonding Technologies (2014)
2. Macherauch, E., Kloos, K.H.: Origin, measurements and evaluation of residual stresses. Residual Stress Sci. Technol. **1**, 3–26 (1987)
3. Attarha, M.J., Sattari-Far, I.: Study on welding temperature distribution in thin welded plates through experimental measurements and finite element simulation. J. Mater. Process. Technol. **211**(4), 688–694 (2011)
4. Zhang, H., Zhang, G., Cai, C., Gao, H., Wu, L.: Fundamental studies on in-process controlling angular distortion in asymmetrical double-sided double arc welding. J. Mater. Process. Technol. **205**(1), 214–223 (2008)
5. Gannon, L., Liu, Y., Pegg, N., Smith, M.: Effect of welding sequence on residual stress and distortion in flat-bar stiffened plates. Mar. Struct. **23**(3), 385–404 (2010)
6. Goldak, J., Chakravarti, A., Bibby, M.: A new finite element model for welding heat sources. Metall. Trans. B **15**(2), 299–305 (1984)
7. Lostado, R., Fernandez Martinez, R., Mac Donald, B.J., Villanueva, P.M.: Combining soft computing techniques and the finite element method to design and optimize complex welded products. Integr. Comput. Aided Eng. **22**(2), 153–170 (2015)
8. Bailey, R.A.: Design of Comparative Experiments. Cambridge University Press, US (2008)
9. Kruskal, W.: Use of ranks in one-criterion variance analysis. J. Am. Stat. Assoc. **47**(260), 583–621 (1952)
10. Corder, G.W., Foreman, D.I.: Nonparametric Statistics for Non-Statisticians, pp. 99–105. Wiley, Hoboken (2009)
11. Kuhn, M.: Caret: Classification and Regression Training. R package version 6.0-41 (2015)

12. Vapnik, V., Golowich, S.E., Smola, A.: Support vector method for function approximation, regression estimation, and signal processing. Adv. Neural. Inf. Process. Syst. **9**, 281–287 (1997)
13. R Core Team. R: A language and environment for statistical computing. R Foundation for Statistical Computing, Vienna, Austria (2013).http://www.R-project.org/
14. Fernandez Martinez, R., Okariz, A., Ibarretxe, J., Iturrondobeitia, M., Guraya, T.: Use of decision tree models based on evolutionary algorithms for the morphological classification of reinforcing nano-particle aggregates. Comput. Mater. Sci. **92**, 102–113 (2014)
15. Fernandez Martinez, R., Martinez de Pison, F.J., Pernia, A.V., Lostado, R.: Predictive modelling in grape berry weight during maturation process: comparison of data mining, statistical and artificial intelligence techniques. Span. J. Agric. Res. **9**(4), 1156–1167 (2011)
16. Illera, M., Lostado, R., Fernandez Martinez, R., Mac Donald, B.J.: Characterization of electrolytic tinplate materials via combined finite element and regression models. J. Strain Anal. Eng. Des. **49**(6), 467–480 (2014)
17. Martinez de Pison, F.J., Lostado, R., Pernia, A., Fernandez Martinez, R.: Optimising tension levelling process by means of genetic algorithms and finite element method. Ironmaking Steelmaking **38**, 45–52 (2011)

A Hybrid Approach to Detecting the Best Solution in Nurse Scheduling Problem

Svetlana Simić[1], Dragan Simić[2(✉)], Dragana Milutinović[1], Jovanka Đorđević[3], and Svetislav Simić[2]

[1] Faculty of Medicine, University of Novi Sad, Hajduk Veljkova 1-9, 21000 Novi Sad, Serbia
drdragansimic@gmail.com

[2] Faculty of Technical Sciences, University of Novi Sad, Trg Dositeja Obradovića 6, 21000 Novi Sad, Serbia
dsimic@eunet.rs, sveta.simic.96@gmail.com

[3] Oncology Institute of Vojvodina, Put doktora Goldmana 4, 21208 Sremska Kamenica, Serbia
jovankad10@gmail.com

Abstract. Staff scheduling at hospitals is a widely-studied area in both, operation research and management science because of cost effectiveness that is required from hospitals. There is an interest for procedures on how to run a hospital more economically and efficiently. The goal of nurse scheduling is to minimize the cost of the staff and maximizing their preferences. This paper is focused on a new strategy based on hybrid model for detecting the best solution in nurse scheduling problem. The new proposed hybrid approach is obtained by combining case-based reasoning and general linear empirical model with arbitrary coefficients. The model is tested with original real world dataset obtained from the Oncology Institute of Vojvodina in Serbia.

Keywords: Nurse scheduling problem · Case-based reasoning · General linear empirical model

1 Introduction

Medical staff performance represents a significant determinant of public healthcare quality. There is a great pressure for cost reduction, which negatively influences work-life balance for a small number of employed physicians and nurses and often results in a decrease of demanded quality of services, since they often must take consecutive shifts or cannot take a day-off. Moreover, due to the challenging economic conditions, not only has ever greater number of physicians and nurses from public hospitals moved to live and work abroad, but a lot of them are also employed in private healthcare organizations to earn higher salaries [1].

This tendency has caused the critical issue in medical staff preferences, medical staff satisfaction is a fundamental part in providing the necessary care for patients. This problem can be divided in two parts: (1) physician scheduling problem, and on the other side, (2) nurse scheduling problem.

F.J. Martínez de Pisón et al. (Eds.): HAIS 2017, LNAI 10334, pp. 710–721, 2017.
DOI: 10.1007/978-3-319-59650-1_60

This physician scheduling problem (PSP) is more complex than the nurse scheduling problem (NSP), since residents still need an educational praxis to get licensed as physicians. Whereas many physicians generally have individual contracts with their hospital with specific and limited details, it is more challenging for the scheduling process to involve these intricate agreements and these physicians will not be scheduled with other hospital staff.

Therefore, traditional approaches to addressing the challenges of clinical staff organization and scheduling are not always effective in modern complex healthcare environment. Many staffing offices are chaotic, budgets are frequently over-run, and staffing levels too often fail to meet the demands. More state legislatures are mandating specific nurse staffing levels, and many nurses are dissatisfied with their work schedules. Optimal solutions derived from techniques with high computing times are usually less valuable than the ones based on a flexible algorithm or user intuitive application [2].

This paper is focused on new strategy based on hybrid approach to detecting the best solution in NSP. The new proposed hybrid approach is obtained by combining case-based reasoning (CBR) and general linear empirical model with arbitrary coefficients. The model is tested with original real world dataset obtained from the Oncology Institute of Vojvodina in Serbia. Also, this paper continuous the authors' previous research in nurse decision-making, scheduling and rostering healthcare organizations which are presented in [3–6].

The rest of the paper is organized in the following way: Sect. 2 provides an overview of the basic idea in NSP, related work with solution approaches based on: general methods, classical heuristics methods, and metaheuristics, and sub-section about case-based reasoning method. Section 3 presents the nurse scheduling problem proposed in this paper, based on hard/soft constraints, CBR representation of empirical data set, and the proposed algorithm for nurse scheduling problem. Preliminary experimental results are presented in Sect. 4. Section 5 provides conclusions and some points for future work.

2 Nurse Scheduling Problem and Related Work

The nurse scheduling problem (NSP) is a well-known NP-hard scheduling problem that aims to allocate the required workload to the available staff nurses at healthcare organizations to meet the operational requirements and a range of preferences. The NSP is a two-dimensional timetabling problem that deals with the assignment of nursing staff to shifts across a scheduling period subject to certain constraints [7].

In general, there are two basic types of scheduling used for the NSP: cyclic and non-cyclic scheduling. In cyclic scheduling, each nurse works in a pattern which is repeated in consecutive scheduling periods, whereas, in non-cyclic scheduling, a new schedule is generated for each scheduling period: weekly, fortnightly or monthly periods. Cyclic scheduling was first used in the early 1970s due to its low computational requirements and the possibility for manual solution [8].

2.1 Basic Idea in Nurse Scheduling Problem

Studies of nurse scheduling problems date back to the early 1960s. Despite decades of research into automated methods for nurse scheduling and some academic success, it may be noticed that there is no consistency in the knowledge that has been built up over the years and that many healthcare institutions still resort to manual practices. One of the possible reasons for this gap between the nurse scheduling theory and practice is that oftentimes academic community focuses on the development of new techniques rather than developing systems for healthcare institutions [9].

One of the most obvious areas in a hospital environment is the automation of appointment and resource scheduling. It is not always realized that nursing costs account for 50% of total hospital costs. It is even more rarely appreciated that the manner of nurses' deployment has a significant impact on a hospital's operating budget. Scheduling has a significant impact not only on costs but also on nurses' job satisfaction [10].

2.2 Related Work in Nurse Scheduling Problem

In the past decades, many approaches have been proposed to solve NSP as they are manifested in different models. The three commonly used general methods are: mathematical programming (MP), heuristics and artificial intelligence (AI) approaches. Many heuristics approaches were straightforward automation of manual practices, which have been widely studied and documented [11, 12].

For combinatorial problems, exact optimization usually requires large computational times to produce optimal solutions. In contrast, metaheuristic approaches can produce satisfactory results in reasonably short times. In the recent years, metaheuristics including: tabu search algorithm (TS), genetic algorithm (GA) and simulated annealing (SA), have been proven as very efficient in obtaining near-optimal solutions for a variety of hard combinatorial problems including the NSP [13].

Some TS approaches have been proposed to solve the NSP. In TS, hard constraints remained fulfilled, while solutions move in the following way: calculate the best possible move which is not tabu, perform the move and add characteristics of the move to the tabu list. The TS with strategic oscillation used to tackle the NSP in a large hospital is presented in [14]. The objective is to ensure enough nurses on duty, always, while considering individual preferences and requests for the days off.

Genetic algorithm (GA), which is stochastic meta-heuristics method, has also been used to solve the NSP. In GA, the basic idea is to find a genetic representation of the problem so that'characteristics' can be inherited. Starting with a population of randomly created solutions, better solutions are more likely to be selected for recombination into new solutions. In addition, new solutions may be formed by mutating or randomly changing the old ones [15].

2.3 Case-Based Reasoning

Case-Based Reasoning (CBR) is a technique that has its origins in knowledge-based systems. CBR systems learn from previous situations. The main element of a CBR system is the *CASE BASE*. It is a structure that stores problems, elements – *cases*, and their solutions. So, a case base can be visualized as a database that stores a collection of problems with some sort of relationship to solutions to every new problem, which gives the system the ability to generalize to solve any new problem.

The learning capabilities of CBR system rely on their own structures, which consist of four main phases: *retrieval*, *reuse*, *revision* and *retain*. Figure 1 shows a graphical representation of those four phases. The *retrieval* phase consists of finding the cases in the *CASE BASE* that most closely resemble the proposed problem. Once a series of cases have been extracted from the *CASE BASE*, they must be *reused* by the system. In the second phase, the selected cases are adapted to fit the current problem. After offering a solution to the problem, it is then *revised*, to check whether the proposed alternative is in fact a reliable solution to the problem. If the proposal is confirmed, it is *retained* by the system, modifying some knowledge containers and could eventually serve as a solution for problems in the future.

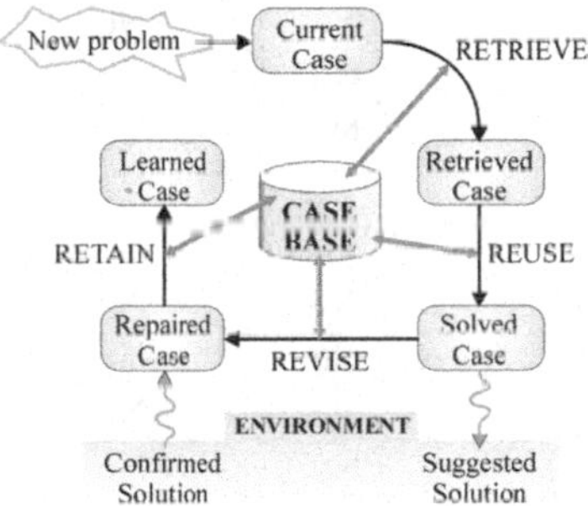

Fig. 1. Basic representation of the case-based reasoning cycle (Adapted from [16])

Case-Based Reasoning has been used to solve a variety of problems, and is used in financial predictions [17], health care sciences [18], and everywhere where images can play an important role [19].

3 Modeling the Nurse Scheduling Problem

This research is focused on cyclic scheduling on NSP in planning period in Intensive care unit at the Oncology Institute of Vojvodina (OIoV). Cyclic scheduling is used here, where each nurse follows a pattern repeated in consecutive scheduling periods.

3.1 Hard Constraints

Recently, duty rosters are generated manually by Head nurse for Intensive care unit, which enables the nurses to express their requests and preferences for working/or not working certain shifts, holidays and days off. Nurses in the Unit have different skills categories, meaning different qualifications, specialization training, experience and gender, presented in Table 1.

Table 1. Nurses' skill categories

Nurse-ID	Years of service - experience	Shift leader	Specialization training
N-01	11	Yes	Yes
N-02	6	No	No
N-03	10	Yes	Yes
N-04	31	No	No
N-05	8	Yes	Yes
N-06	15	Yes	Yes
N-07	13	Yes	Yes
N-08	13	No	No
N-09	11	Yes	Yes
N-10	10	Yes	No
N-11	16	Yes	No
N-12	11	Yes	No
N-13	12	No	No
N-14	4	No	Yes
N-15	20	Yes	Yes
N-16	17	Yes	No
N-17	1	No	No
N-18	1	No	Yes
N-19	1	No	No
N-20	1	No	No

Regular work days are 5 days per week, from Monday to Friday. Regular working hours are 7 h and 12 min. Full time nurses are defined by multiple (regular work days * regular working hours). When this number is rounded, it represents the total number of shifts allowed per month.

Nurses can work in three *On-duty* shifts: *Day* (D) (06:30–18:30), *Night* (N) (18:30–06:30) and *Morning* shift (X) (07:30–14:40). Day shift is defined by letter (D). There are also *Free* shifts which include: *Day-off* (O), *Sick days* (B), *Sick days on weekend* (C), *Maternity leave* (K), *Paid leave* (P), *Regular holiday* (O), *Annual leave on weekends* (V), *Annual leave* (Y).

Hard requests define a constraint that must be respected in the roster and *Soft requests* define the preferred option expressed by a nurse which is desirable, but can be violated in the roster if needed. Some typical values for a few of the constraints are given below:

- Min (max) nurses on shifts: In the OIoV, 3 nurses in *Day shifts*, 3 nurses in *Night shifts*;
- It is not desirable to work a *Night shift* followed by a *Day shift*;

- After 5 *Morning shifts*, 2 days off must be assigned;
- After a break of more than 7 days, (annual leave, sick leave) *Day shift* must be assigned;
- Maximum differences between *Day shifts* and *Night shifts* per nurse could be no greater than 5;
- At least one of the members of *Shift* must be *shift leader*, which is for every nurse defined in Table 1;
- Max (min) days: Full time nurses may not work more than pre-determined number of days.

The ideal and proposed work shift dynamic is: Day–Night–Off–Off–Off (DNOOO). Day-Night, meaning that two work shifts and three days off in five days is ideal shift dynamic. This is recommended by the Oncology Institute of Vojvodina management. Also, the DONOO dynamic is allowed, where there are two work shifts and three days off in five days, other combinations of two work shifts and three days off in five days are allowed as well. But, in the real word, when creating the nurse scheduling, it is impossible to have ideal work shift dynamic. For that reason, a more difficult shift dynamic is allowed, for example, three working days and two days off (DDNOO) (DNNOO). Other dynamics of three working days and two days off are allowed as well. After five Morning shifts (XXXXX) 2 days off must be assigned to create (XXXXXOO) dynamic.

3.2 Empirical Data Set – CBR Representation

For this experiment original real world data set from between 1 January and 15 January 2014, from Intensive care unit of OIoV is used.

The part of experimental data set is presented in Table 2. Where the columns are presented: *Case No.* – case number; *Nurse ID* = N 01; *Date* – starting date for the case (for Case No. = 1, Date = 01.01.2014); *Field 1* for date 01.01.2014 the *Value of shift* = D; *Field 2* for date 02.01.2014 the *Value of shift* = O; *Field 3* for date 03.01.2014 the *Value of shift* = O; *Field 4* for date 04.01.2014 the *Value of shift* = N; *Field 5 – Case Solution* for date 05.01.2014 the *Value of shift* = O). Then the rest of cases could be described, for example: Case No. = 3, Date = 03.01.2014); *Field 1* for date 03.01.2014 the *Value of shift* = O; *Field 2* for date 04.01.2014 the *Value of shift* = N; *Field 3* for date 05.01.2014 the *Value of shift* = O; *Field 4* for date 06.01.2014 the *Value of shift* = N; *Field 5 – Case Solution* for date 07.01.2014 the *Value of shift* = O. The end of short description looks like this: Case No. = 12, Date = 12.01.2014.; *Field 1* for date 12.01.2014 the *Value of shift* = O; *Field 2* for date 13.01.2014 the *Value of shift* = O; *Field 3* for date 14.01.2014 the *Value of shift* = O; *Field 4* for date 15.01.2014 the *Value of shift* = D; *Field 5 – Case Solution* for date 16.01.2014 the *Value of shift* = is empty and gray. There is no *Solution* for that case, and it will be calculated when the system calculates schedule for nurse N-01 for 16.01.2014. In CBR basic representation, *Case No.* = 12 presents *NEW CASE*, and the hybrid system will try to find best *Solution* for it. All cases (data set) stored in CASE BASE can be described in the same manner as for the previous nurse. All the cases in CASE BASE which have *Solution* will be used in *reused* and *revised* CBR phases for detecting the best *Solution* in nurse scheduling problem.

Table 2. Nurse-case duties is starting for calculation nurse schedule for 16th January

Case no.	Nurse-ID	Date	Field 1	Field 2	Field 3	Field 4	Field 5 solution
1	N-01	01.01.2014	D	O	O	N	O
2	N-01	02.01.2014	O	O	N	O	N
¦	¦	¦	¦	¦	¦	¦	¦
11	N-01	11.01.2014	D	O	O	O	D
12	N-01	12.01.2014	O	O	O	D	
13	N-02	01.01.2014	D	O	O	D	N
14	N-02	02.01.2014	O	O	D	N	O
¦	¦	¦	¦	¦	¦	¦	¦
23	N-02	11.01.2014	C	C	B	B	B
24	N-02	12.01.2014	C	B	B	B	
¦	¦	¦	¦	¦	¦	¦	¦
205	N-18	01.01.2014	O	O	D	O	O
206	N-18	02.01.2014	O	D	O	O	D
¦	¦	¦	¦	¦	¦	¦	¦
215	N-18	11.01.2014	N	N	O	O	O
216	N-18	12.01.2014	N	O	O	O	
¦	¦	¦	¦	¦	¦	¦	¦
228	N-20	01.01.2014	O	D	N	O	O
229	N-20	02.01.2014	D	N	O	O	D
¦	¦	¦	¦	¦	¦	¦	¦
239	N-20	11.01.2014	D	D	O	O	D
240	N-20	12.01.2014	D	O	O	D	

3.3 The Algorithm for Nurse Scheduling Problem

The basic steps of the proposed hybrid algorithm for nurse scheduling problem are summarized by the pseudo code shown in Algorithm 1. Our algorithm is inspirited by integration of CBR method, which is discussed in Subsect. 2.3, *CASE BASE* representation is shown in Subsect. 3.2. The proposed hybrid model is obtained by combining case-based reasoning and general linear empirical model with arbitrary coefficients. The general linear empirical model with arbitrary coefficient defined from Eqs. (1) to (3) is well known, and it is in detail presented and discussed in [20].

$$\mathrm{Va}(t,d) = \mathrm{S\_4}(t,d) + 0.5 * \mathrm{S\_3}(t,d) \tag{1}$$

$$\mathrm{Va}(t,n) = \mathrm{S\_4}(t,n) + 0.5 * \mathrm{S\_3}(t,n) \tag{2}$$

$$\mathrm{Va}(t,o) = \mathrm{S\_4}(t,o) + 0.5 * \mathrm{S\_3}(t,o) \tag{3}$$

Algorithm 1. *The algorithm for Nurse Scheduling Problem*

```
Begin
    Step 1:   --- Initialization.
              Constraints hard/soft;
              Nurse_number = 20;
              Nurse skills categories;
              Ideal shift dynamic = "DNOOO";
              Nurse-day duties = from 1st January to last day for prediction;
              Days = Time period;
    Step 2:   --- Calculation for time period.
                 for i=1:Days (all Time period) do

                    --- Calculation for Nurses.

                    for j=1: Nurse_number (all Nurses) do
                         --- Calculation for String_4
                         find String_4 for current nurse
                         find frequency for String_4 for current nurse
                         --- Calculation for String_3
                         find String_3 for current nurse
                         find frequency for String_3 for current nurse
                         --- Calculation weighted value
                         calculating weighted value "D" "N" "O" for cur. nurse
                         equation (1), equation (2) and equation (3)

                    end for j

                 --- End Calculation for Nurses.

    Step 3:   --- Loop over the time period.

                 Normalizing type of shift for nurses for current day
                 List – Day / Night Nurses as candidates for current day
                 Calculate nurse workload before current day
                 List – Day / Night most appropriate nurses according constraints
                 for current day
                 Nurse-day duties = Nurse-day duties +
                                     Day / Night shifts for current day

                 end for i

              --- End Calculation for time period.

    Step 4:   Post-processing the results and visualization.
End.
```

The empirical model with general linear empirical model with arbitrary coefficients is used in *Step 2*. In the proposed algorithm for *Nurse Scheduling Problem*.

4 Experimental Results

Equation (1) presents calculation of weighted value *Va(t,d) Day shift* occurrence *d* for nurse *t*, while *S_4(t,d)* presents frequency of *next letter* = *D* when it is calculated for nurse *t*. The same logic applies to *S_3(t,d)*. Also, Eq. (2) calculation of weighted value *Va(t,n) Night shift* occurrence *n* for nurse *t*, while *S_4(t,n)* presents frequency of *next letter* = *N* when it is calculated for nurse *t*. The same logic applies to *S_3(t,n)*. Equation (3) presents calculation of weighted value *Va(t,o) Day-off* shift occurrence *o* for nurse *t*, while *S_4(t,o)* presents frequency of *next letter* = *O* when it is calculated for nurse *t*. The same logic applies to *S_3(t,o)*. The values of *Va(t,d)*, *Va(t,n)* and *Va(t, o)* then must be normalized and as such represent probability for shift occurrence for a specific worker for the next day.

Table 3 presents calculation for the nurse candidates for the 16th of January based on the range from Eqs. (1) to (3). For every workday it is necessary to select three nurses for *Day shift*, and three nurses for *Night shift*.

Table 3. Nurse-case duties is starting the calculation for nurse schedule for 16th January, and Final Solution is given for 16th January

Nurse ID	Before revision						After revision		Final Solution
	Day shift	Night shift	Day-off	Shift leader	Num. day	Num. night	Day shift	Night shift	
N-01	**20.00**	**22.85**	57.14	**Yes**	4	2	**20.00**	–	**20.00 (L)**
N-02	0	0	100.00	No	3	1	–	–	
N-03	0	0	100.00	Yes	2	4	–	–	
N-04	0	0	100.00	No	0	0	–	–	
N-05	0	0	100.00	Yes	2	5	–	–	
N-06	0	0	100.00	Yes	0	0	–	–	
N-07	0	0	100.00	Yes	2	3	–	–	
N-08	**46.42**	14.28	39.28	No	4	3	**37.14**	**37.14**	
N-09	**66.66**	**26.66**	6.67	**Yes**	5	1	**0.00**	**66.66**	**66.66 (L)**
N-10	0	**44.44**	55.55	Yes	4	3	–	**44.44**	**44.44**
N-11	0	12.50	87.50	Yes	1	1	–	–	
N-12	0	0	100.00	Yes	2	0	–	–	
N-13	0	0	100.00	No	0	0	–	–	
N-14	**50.00**	16.67	33.33	No	3	4	**30.00**	**30.00**	
N-15	0	**36.84**	63.15	Yes	4	1	–	**36.84**	
N-16	0	0	100.00	Yes	1	1	–	–	
N-17	**60.86**	**17.39**	21.73	No	2	4	**48.69**	–	**48.69**
N-18	**78.26**	8.69	13.04	No	3	3	**78.26**	–	**78.26**
N-19	0	0	100.00	No	0	0	–	–	
N-20	9.67	**45.16**	45.16	No	6	1	–	**45.16**	**45.16**

The most appropriate nurses for *Day shift* and *Night shift* will be selected according to previous tables, Tables 1, 2 and 3. Looking only at Table 3 it could be concluded that *Before revision – Day shift candidate* will consist of the following nurses: N-18, N-09, N-17, N-14, N-08, and N-01; and that *Before revision – Night shift candidate* will consist of nurses: N-20, N-10, N-15, N-09, N-01, and N-17. But, it is interesting to see Table 3 where, in N-09, there is a great imbalance between *Day shift* – 5 and *Night shift* – 1. The system allows the greatest difference between *Day shifts* and *Night shifts* to be <= 2 in the same month. Therefore, N-09 cannot work *Day Shift*, because *shifts* type imbalance would be even greater. N-09 becomes *Night shift candidate*.

Also, *in revision – Day shift candidate*, after elimination N-01, will consist of the following nurses in the order: N-18, N-17, N-14, N-08, and N-01. But now, in the first three *Day shift candidate* does not satisfy the constraint that at least one member of *Shift* must be *shift leader*, this constraint is satisfied only for N-01. Finally, *Day shift* for 16th of January could be completed: N-18, N-17, and *shift leader* N-01.

Following the rules and constraints in CBR *revise* phase, N-09 is *Night shift candidate*, but on the other side first N-17 is defined for *Day shift*, and second N-08 has

Table 4. Calculated Final Solution Nurse-case duties schedule for 16th January, and the starting calculation for 17th January

Case no.	Nurse-ID	Date	Field 1	Field 2	Field 3	Field 4	Field 5 solution
1	N-01	01.01.2014	D	O	O	N	O
2	N-01	02.01.2014	O	O	N	O	N
¦	¦	¦	¦	¦	¦	¦	¦
11	N-01	11.01.2014	D	O	O	O	D
12	N-01	12.01.2014	O	O	O	D	**D**
241	N-01	13.01.2014	O	O	D	D	
13	N-02	01.01.2014	D	O	O	D	N
14	N-02	02.01.2014	O	O	D	N	O
¦	¦	¦	¦	¦	¦	¦	¦
23	N-02	11.01.2014	C	C	B	B	B
24	N-02	12.01.2014	C	B	B	B	**B**
242	N-02	13.01.2014	B	B	B	B	
¦	¦	¦	¦	¦	¦	¦	¦
205	N-18	01.01.2014	O	O	D	O	O
206	N-18	02.01.2014	O	D	O	O	D
¦	¦	¦	¦	¦	¦	¦	¦
215	N-18	11.01.2014	N	N	O	O	O
216	N-18	12.01.2014	N	O	O	O	**D**
258	N-18	13.01.2014	O	O	O	D	
¦	¦	¦	¦	¦	¦	¦	¦
229	N-20	02.01.2014	D	N	O	O	D
230	N-20	03.01.2014	N	O	O	D	O
¦	¦	¦	¦	¦	¦	¦	¦
239	N-20	11.01.2014	D	D	O	O	D
240	N-20	12.01.2014	D	O	O	D	**N**
260	N-20	13.01.2014	O	O	D	N	

extremely high percentage as *Night shift working candidate*, and now six *Night shift candidates* are: N-09, N-20, N-10, N-08, N-15 and N-14. Finally, *Night shift* for 16th of January could be completed: *shift leader* N-09, and the members are N-20, N-10. Now, the whole *shifts* for the 16th of January are completed.

In CBR *retained* phase, now is time to update some cases stored in *CASE BASE*, which are empty and are shown in gray in Table 2. It is necessary to fill the Field 5 *Solution* with appropriate *Shift* (*Day /Night /Morning*) or store some other *Free* shifts. For example, for case 12, the fields would be "OOODD" Also, in this CBR phase it is necessary to add twenty new cases in *CASE BASE*, for example: *case* 241 presents nurse N-01, for beginning data for 13.01.2014, for which the four fields would be "OODD" and the *Field 5 Solution* will be empty and gray, and presents new case for solving schedule for 17th January. The data store in CASE BASE after *retained* phase is presented in Table 4. The rest of the schedule for the whole period continues as previously described: algorithm, hard constraints, soft constraints and established rules.

5 Conclusion and Future Work

The aim of this paper is to propose the new hybrid strategy for detecting the best solution in nurse scheduling problem. The new proposed hybrid approach is obtained by combining case-based reasoning and general linear empirical model with arbitrary coefficients. The model is tested with original real world dataset obtained from the Oncology Institute of Vojvodina in Serbia.

The data set is represented in *CASE BASE* as a database structure where problems, elements – *cases*, and their solutions are storted. All the cases in *CASE BASE* which has *Solution* will be used in *reused* and *revised* CBR phases for detecting best *Solution* in nurse scheduling problem, usage hard/soft constraints, rules and general linear empirical model with arbitrary coefficients. In CBR *retained* phase, some cases stored in *CASE BASE* are updated, and the new cases are added.

Preliminary experimental results encourage further research because data set is stored in database and it is easy for manipulation. Our future research will focus on creating new hybrid model combined by intuitive thinking which will efficiently solve NSP. The new model will be tested with original real world dataset for longer periods, including the year 2016, obtained from the Oncology Institute of Vojvodina in Serbia.

References

1. Szabo, S., Ferencz, V., Pucihar, A.: Trust, innovation and prosperity. Qual. Innov. Prosperity **17**(2), 1–8 (2013)
2. Aickelin, U., White, P.: Building better nurse scheduling algorithms. Ann. Oper. Res. **128** (1), 159–177 (2004)
3. Simić, D., Simić, S., Banic-Horvat, S., Cvijanović, M., Gajić, B., Sakalaš, L.: Interdisciplinary approach to clinical decision-making. Curr. Topics Neurol. Psychiatry Relat. Disciplines **18**(1), 57–63 (2010)

4. Simić, D.: Nursing logistics activities in massive services. J. Med. Inform. Technol. **18**, 77–84 (2011)
5. Simić, D., Milutinović, D., Simić, S., Suknaja, V.: Hybrid patient classification system in nursing logistics activities. In: Corchado, E., Kurzyński, M., Woźniak, M. (eds.) HAIS 2011. LNCS, vol. 6679, pp. 421–428. Springer, Heidelberg (2011). doi:10.1007/978-3-642-21222-2_51
6. Simić, D., Simić, S., Milutinović, D., Đorđević, J.: Challenges for nurse rostering problem and opportunities in hospital logistics. J. Med. Inform. Technol. **23**, 195–202 (2014)
7. Burke, E., De Causmacker, P., Ausmacker, P., Berghe, G.V., Van Landeghem, H.: The state of the art of nurse rostering. J. Sched. **7**(6), 441–499 (2004)
8. Dowsland, K.A.: Nurse scheduling with tabu search and strategic oscillation. Eur. J. Oper. Res. **106**(2–3), 393–407 (1998)
9. Beddoe, G., Petrović, S., Li, J.: A hybrid metaheuristic case-based reasoning system for nurse rostering. J. Sched. **12**(2), 99–119 (2009)
10. Zelman, W.N., McCue, M.J., Glick, N.D.: Financial Management of Health Care Organizations: An Introduction to Fundamental Tools, Concepts and Applications. Wiley, Hoboken (2014)
11. Isken, M.W., Hancockm, W.M.: A heuristic approach to nurse scheduling in hospital units with non-stationary, urgent demand, and a fixed staff size. J. Soc. Health Syst. **2**(2), 24–40 (1991)
12. Warner, M., Keller, B.J., Martel, S.H.: Automated nurse scheduling. J. Soc. Health Syst. **2** (2), 66–80 (1990)
13. Cheang, B., Li, H., Rodrigues, B.: Nurse rostering problems - a bibliographic survey. Eur. J. Oper. Res. **151**(3), 447–460 (2003)
14. Millar, H., Kiragu, M.: Cyclic and non-cyclic scheduling of 12 h shift nurses by network programming. Eur. J. Oper. Res. **104**(3), 582–592 (1998)
15. Leksakul, K., Phetsawat, S.: Nurse scheduling using genetic algorithm. Math. Probl. Eng. (2014). http://dx.doi.org/10.1155/2014/246543. Article ID 246543
16. Aamodt, A., Plaza, E.: Case-based reasoning: foundational issues, methodological variations, and system approaches. AI Commun. **7**(1), 39–59 (1994)
17. Simić, D., Simić, S.: An approach to efficient business intelligent system for financial prediction. Soft. Comput. **11**(12), 1185–1192 (2007)
18. Corchado, J.M., Bajo, J., Abraham, A.: GERAm I: improving the delivery of health care. IEEE Intell. Syst. **3**(2), 19–25 (2008). Special Issue on Ambient Intelligence
19. Herrero, A., Corchado, E., Pellicer, M.A., Abraham, A.: MOVIHIDS: a mobile-visualization hybrid intrusion detection system. Neurocomputing **72**(13–15), 2775–2784 (2009)
20. Smyth, G.K.: Linear models and empirical Bayes methods for assessing differential expression in microarray experiments. Stat. Appl. Genet. Mol. Biol. **3**(1) (2004). Article 3. doi:10.2202/1544-6115.1027

Author Index

Printed in the United States
By Bookmasters